Traditional & Modern POLISH COOKING

Traditional & Modern POLISH COOKING

Hanna Szymanderska

Cover design: Radosław Pazdrijowski, Studio Gravite
Cover photo: Marcin Kiełbiewski;
    stylization: Marta Dzikowska-Hayes
Photos on pages: 45, 55, 61, 64, 69, 89, 93, 96, 109, 123, 129,
    135, 139, 143, 171, 177, 185, 193, 205, 209, 215, 219, 225,
    232, 237, 241, 255, 264, 271, 279, 281, 291, 299, 303, 309,
    323, 331, 339, 341, 345, 369, 374, 379, 401, 416, 418, 436,
    501, 512, 553, 565, 570, 593, 611, 653, 675, 680, 691,
    703, 711, 721, 734, 775, 813, 814, 817, 820, 822, 825, 833,
    834, 837, 840, 852, 854, 858, 860, 862, 864, 866, 870,
    873, 882, 884, 885, 887, 889, 891, 893, 896, 898, 899 –
    Magdalena Gugała-Woźniak
Photos on pages: 53, 66, 80, 84, 86, 101, 130, 145, 175, 196,
    229, 262, 288, 301, 319, 324, 357, 367, 376, 381, 383, 405,
    407, 409, 411, 420, 459, 461, 465, 467, 469, 479, 488, 497,
    561, 597, 636, 677, 688, 705, 708 – Roman Andrasik
Photos on pages: 28, 43, 81, 163, 457, 563, 615, 623, 741, 743, 755 –
    www.123rf.com
The author's photo on the dust jacket: Jarosław Sosiński
    (photo from Hanna Szymanderska's private collection)

Translation: Bogna Piotrowska, Katarzyna Zawadzka
Editorial elaboration: Barbara Gers
Proof-reading: Marzena Kowalska
Typography: Studio Gravite, Olsztyn

ISBN 978-83-7544-445-2

Distribution:
Wydawnictwo REA s.j.
Dział Handlowy
ul. Kolejowa 9/11, 01-217 Warszawa
Tel.: 22 631 94 23, 22 632 69 03, 22 632 68 82
Fax: 22 632 21 15
e-mail: handlowy@rea-sj.pl
www.rea-sj.pl

Editor's note

Hanna Szymanderska's book is a splendid compendium of information about Polish cooking, both in former times and today, both 'official' Polish cuisine and regional cuisine, food in central Poland and the food of the old Polish eastern border regions. The book contains a unique collection of 3000 easily accessible recipes that stir the imagination and provide inspiration for bold experimentation in the kitchen.

It is divided into twenty chapters on particular kinds of foods and drinks. These include flavoured butters, dips, soups, flour-based dishes, eggs and cheese, kashas and rice, potatoes, side dishes for soups and main dishes, sauces, fish, meat, poultry, game, mushrooms, vegetables, desserts, cold and hot drinks, cakes, liqueurs and preserves.

The book is written in colourful language and is very impressionistic. Each of the chapters has an introduction explaining the area of cooking that will be dealt with and giving information that is essential in the kitchen both for the beginner and for the experienced cook.

The chapters on liqueurs, mushrooms and game are a real rarity. The book also gives the terminology used in the past and in the present in Polish cuisine in the section entitled 'A Culinary ABC'. A careful reader will easily find the recipe that is of interest to him or her in the alphabetically arranged list of dishes.

The book can be considered a unique summary of the rich Polish culinary tradition.

All that remains is to wish you pleasant reading, and above all 'bon apetit'.

Contents

Chapter II
Soups hot and cold

Chapter III
Macaroni, noodles, dumplings

Chapter IV
Egg and cheese dishes

Chapter V
Kasha and rice

Chapter X
Meat

Marinades for meat   348

Cutlets – or everything from entrecôte to meatballs   349

Smoked meats   355

Pork   359

Pig's knuckles – a man's delight   371

Veal   378

Beef   400

Entrecôte   400

Boiled beef   403

Roast beef   406

Not only beefsteak   413

Zrazy   422

Beef Stroganov and goulash   426

Mutton and lamb   427

Rabbit   434

Offal   438

Chapter XI
Poultry

Chicken 458

Boiling fowl, capons, poulards 472

Goose 474

Chapter XIV
Vegetablesand fruit

Chapter XX
Fusion

A few words about Polish cooking

Every nation loves its own cuisine and prefers it to the cuisine of other nations. It considers it the best. All nations are right, since no nation can get by without its own cuisine.

(Edward Pomian Poṇerski, 1875–1964, a Pole who was one of the greatest authorities on French cuisine, and was a professor of the Institut Pasteur in Paris)

Is Polish cuisine worth preserving? Most definitely, it is. There are dishes that are well worth promoting.

But what do we mean by 'Polish cuisine'? Is it what it was centuries ago – buckwheat grits and pearl barley, sour milk, beans, peas, game and 'fatty meat with horseradish', as a Renaissance poet described it?

From the beginning, Polish cuisine was not based on orthodox nationalist assumptions. Thanks to its ability to adapt, Polish cuisine embraces Ukrainian borsch, Peking duck, steak tartare, fish à la grecque, Jewish-style carp, Viennese eggs, Brunswick brawn (head cheese), French puff pastry, Nelson beef collops, Lithuanian cold soup, Vilnius herring and Podolian dumplings.

Our culinary tastes stem from an intermingling of cultures – heartland Polish, Oriental, French, Italian, German and Jewish; they grew out of the coexistence for centuries of many nationalities within the framework of one state.

The most readily observable 'culinary fashions' are those introduced as a consequence of royal marriages: of Sigismund the Old with Bona Sforza, of Ladislaus IV and then John Casimir with Marie Louise de Gonzague-Nevers and of John III Sobieski with Marie Casimire de la Grange d'Arquien.

In the late 15th century overseas explorations brought a turning point in the mentality of Europeans and trade expanded massively.

16th-century Poland was a rich and culturally highly-developed country. It was this century that saw the origins of contemporary culinary traditions, although it also saw the beginning of a duality in Polish cuisine.

For a century after the arrival in Poland of Queen Bona in 1518, there was an ongoing dialogue between the advocates of traditional, Old Polish cooking and those who supported the new fashions. This was reflected in Polish literature, for example in the works of Słota, Rej, Potocki and Jeṇowski. Łukasz Gołębiowski wrote of the Old Polish period:

These dishes were of the whole country: borsch, barley soup, chicken broth, cabbage soup, pea soup, beer with cream, almond soup, sausage, meat cutlets, tripe, bigos, beef collops with buckwheat grits, black pudding, pierogi with cheese, pancakes, hretsushki (bliny with buckwheat grits), doughnuts, scrambled eggs, calf's foot jelly, smoked meats, hussar roast, saffron pike, carp in honey (in grey sauce)... Wereszczak sausage in onion sauce, young beetroot, half a roast goose, dumplings, ... knysze, pierogi, sour barley.

(Domy i dwory, 1830)

But the Old Polish dislike of innovation did not defend Polish cuisine against foreign specialties. In this period, they found their way above all into the royal kitchens and those of the aristocracy, but in the end they reached the gentry as well.

It is this mixture of Old Polish cuisine with the foreign influences which by various routes achieved primacy for a time in fashionable society before finally blending with the earlier traditions to produce what we today call 'traditional Polish cuisine'.

But it is worth knowing that in this cuisine, under the influence of Italian cuisine, the taste of some Old Polish dishes was made blander: thick sauces were replaced by lighter ones; and many vegetables and spices were added to the Old Polish menu.

Along with the Swiss, the Italians also laid the foundations of Polish confectionery.

Under Oriental influence, spices became widespread in Polish cuisine, giving a special taste to everyday fare.

The east left in Polish cuisine buckwheat, poppy seed, sorbets (frozen fruit juice), dried fruit and nuts, confitures or in other words fruit cooked in honey, nougat, makagigi (cake made of honey, poppy seed, nuts and almonds), halva.

Eastern ways of preparing meat were also retained in Polish cuisine: marinating, chopping; shashliks, beef tartare; cooking (mainly lamb) with dried fruit and pickled vegetables.

Christmas Eve almond soup, koutia and poppyseed twists are also leftovers from the Orient. And the general habit of eating 'peppery and saffrony' was not driven out by the more delicate flavours of French cuisine until the end of the 18th century.

Following the French, Polish cooking began to place more emphasis on varying the diet, on decorating serving dishes, on the delicate flavour of the dishes themselves; new techniques and methods of preparation and cooking were also introduced. The Polish diet began to include stuffings, pâtés, pies, broths and jellies (aspics).

New seasonings began to be used: truffles, capers, anchovies.

New terms also appeared: blanching, stuffing, baking, glazing, battering, larding, marinating.

The restaurant business, which began to develop from the 19th century, brought French cuisine into the homes of the aristocracy. It was restaurants that spread the fashion for French cuisine.

Jewish cooking also had a great influence on Polish cuisine, on the basis of 'constant dripping of water wears away the rock'. It fused into our cookery over the centuries – for after all, Poles and Jews coexisted peacefully in Poland from the times of Casimir the Great onwards – and left permanent traces in ways of cooking goose, herring and other fish.

Jewish dishes that survive include halka, goose pipes (stuffed goose necks), cabbage with sultanas and many fish dishes.

The partitioning of Poland had a major influence on Polish cuisine. The least influence can be seen in the Russian partition zone, where hatred of tsarist rule discouraged the adoption of Russian dishes; the cuisine of the Poznań region took over a great deal from German cooking: pig's hock, Eintopft dishes, cakes using yeast; and Cracow and Galician cookery is a mishmash of Hungarian cuisine (with Turkish and Balkan influences) and Austrian cuisine: pepper, aubergines, mamalyga or Hungarian goulash.

Late 19th century cuisine was not very different from what we know at the moment; the only possible differences are in the proportions of fruit and vegetables to meat.

Polish cuisine, like the national cuisines of all European countries, took shape over centuries when influences were mixed and increasingly refined regional cuisines based on local products took on a separate existence. One might say that 'high society' mixed with the provincial hoi-polloi. And it is a mixture of this kind that is typical of contemporary cooking everywhere, including Poland.

A culinary ABC

Al dente, a definition of a way of boiling something, literally 'to the tooth', or semi-hard. This term is mainly applied to ways of cooking pasta – which should not be over-boiled – as well as vegetables. Al dente boiling is assisted by adding a tablespoonful of butter or olive oil to the salted water.

Aspic is a very old way of presenting meat, poultry, fish and also fruit and vegetables which are cooled off in jelly and then placed on a dish and served cold.
In Old Polish cuisine, aspic enjoyed great popularity and meat and fish set in elaborate forms were to be found decorating all cold buffets.
The jelly for fruit and vegetables is made with fruit or vegetable juice and gelatine; for fish it is made from the water in which fish is simmered and for meat, and for the decoration of the dishes, stock – from calves' feet and bones, with a little beef and stew vegetables – is used to make the jelly. To make the aspic transparent, an egg white is beaten up with a little cold water, and then poured into the slightly cooled and strained stock; it is then brought to the boil and strained again through a fine sieve or muslin. Before leaving it to set again, a few drops of caramel and lemon juice should be added and it should be seasoned to taste. Coloured aspic is often used for decoration. The colouring is done as follows:
– green with spinach juice;
– red or pink with beet juice;
– yellow with saffron.

If brown aspic is required, clean onion skins should be added to the cooked broth. Boiled eggs, poultry, fish, pâtés, ham and tongue can be served set in aspic. Cubes of coloured aspic are used to decorate serving dishes with cold cooked and smoked meats. Covering a baked pâté in aspic not only gives it an attractive appearance, but also prevents its going off.

Au bleu – 'in blue' – is a way of cooking freshwater fish, mainly carp, trout and tench, or sometimes pike. The fish is gutted but the slimy liquid covering its body is left intact, and then simmered very slowly in salty water with added vinegar. The cooked blue fish is served whole, liberally sprinkled with melted butter, either hot or cold, with a spicy sauce. If the fish are to turn really blue, they must be fresh and not frozen.

Au gratin refers to a baked dish which is usually covered with white sauce and has melted butter poured over; it is then sprinkled with grated cheese or cheese mixed with breadcrumbs or finely chopped nuts.

Bain-marie is a utensil for keeping sauces, soups and vegetables warm. Its name comes from the French term *bain de Marie*, which means literally 'in Mary's bath'. The method consists in placing a vessel with some cooked dish (a sauce, a soup) in a pan with boiling water so that it stays hot but does not cook. Today this is called simply a hot bath, and we use it when a dish which is cooked cannot be served straight away.

We put the saucepan in which the sauce (or soup, or meat) has been cooked into a large pan containing hot water and cover it tightly. Dishes kept like this stay fresh. Vegetables like asparagus, green beans, cauliflower or potatoes should be carefully strained before placing in the bain-marie.

Batter. This is a thin, slightly salted dough used for frying cutlets, fish and poultry. It is made with flour mixed with water or milk, melted butter, egg or egg yolk and egg white beaten stiff. The ingredients should be carefully mixed with a spoon. The batter should be firm enough to stick to the meat etc. A piece of meat held on a fork is dipped into the batter and then placed in hot fat and fried slowly on both sides. Batter is best fried in deep fat.

Beating or mixing is the careful mixing of various products, for example, milk and eggs, cream with flour or egg yolk. Things are best beaten in a narrow, high pot with a special whisk, and it should be done as quickly as possible until a smooth liquid is obtained. This is the way to prepare all batters (for pancakes or noodles) and also the thickening for soups or sauces. The flour should be put first in the pot, and then the liquid (water, milk, wine, beer, cream) gradually added, until a smooth mixture is achieved. If all the liquid is added at once to the flour, lumps are formed which are later exceptionally difficult to get rid of. This process is usually done today in a mixer.

Blanching means brief immersion in boiling water before further cooking. Meat, vegetables and fruit can be blanched. It is sometimes done to take away an unpleasant odour, or bitterness, or an undesirable taste, and sometimes to facilitate removing the skin. For example, overly bitter fruit is blanched before making jam or preserves. The process involves throwing the product into boiling water, and then when the water comes back to the boil (after 2–4 minutes), straining it and immediately running it under cold water. At one time blanching was generally practised; it was thought that the products lost very little food value, while the taste of the dish was vastly improved. Today dieticians claim that in blanching 90% of sodium and calcium are lost, and blanching should therefore be restricted to absolutely essential cases,

for example, stuffed cabbage (gołąbki), or tomatoes in order to remove the skin.

Boiling. This is the most common form of cooking, and is carried out in varying quantities of water, vegetable stock, in water with wine and spices or in steam. Fish and dry pulse vegetables which have previously been soaked should be put into cold water. Meat, eggs for poaching, pasta and green vegetables should be put into boiling water. Asparagus and broccoli are usually steamed. Steaming is best done in a pan with a tightly closed lid, into which a special pan containing the product is placed, or in a pressure cooker. Thanks to the hermetic seal of the latter, a temperature of 120o is reached and the vegetables cook much faster and lose fewer vitamins.

Bouillon is a strong broth strained of fat, which is served hot in cups (with raw egg yolk), or cold. It is a very strong stock made from beef bones and meat, or from chicken, herbs and spices.

Bouquet garni is the French term for the mixture of herbs and spices that is added to broths and sauces during cooking. This aromatic bouquet (which is usually done up in muslin and removed after cooking) is made up of a few sprigs of parsley, 1–2 sprigs of fresh thyme, a bay leaf, and sometimes a peppercorn and allspice, a clove or a piece of cinnamon.

Braising is one of the forms of preparing meat, by simmering it in a covered pan in a strong gravy until it is tender. Braising should always be done in a thick-bottomed pan. Before braising, meat is usually lightly browned on all sides in very hot fat, or blanched, in order to improve the taste and aroma of the dish. Light frying prevents the meat shrinking too much during braising and improves the taste. It is usually lower-grade, tougher cuts of meat – requiring longer cooking at high temperature – that are braised. During braising, the meat should be sprinkled with stock, water or wine. Under the lid the water turns into steam, penetrates the meat, and makes it swell and release juices. As the liquid evaporates, it should be replenished, so that the meat does not stick to the bottom of the pan. It is also a good idea to turn the meat over two or three times during braising. Meat should be braised at a steady temperature of slow simmering, for it is only then that the water vapour acts evenly on the membranes that grow through the meat, causing them to swell and relax, so that the meat becomes tender and digestible.

Bryndza, or **brinzen**, is a soft ewes'-milk cheese with a strong piquant flavour, which is stored in salted water. It is produced in the Carpathian region of Poland, Slovakia, Hungary and Romania.

Bundz is a ewes'-milk preparation formed into large blocks. After a suitable period of drying, it can be eaten as it is, or salted and fermented into bryndza.

Cabbage patties are a kind of patty made from yeast pastry, with a cabbage stuffing. They are baked and served as an hors-d'oeuvre or with clear soups.

Candying means frying fruit in a very thick sugary syrup, so that after cooking each piece retains its shape. After carefully removing the cooked fruits from the syrup and patting them dry, they should be lightly sprinkled with caster sugar and again patted dry. A high level of sugar preserves the fruit. Candied fruits are an excellent decoration for gateaux and mazurka cakes, and can also be served with afternoon tea. Hard fruits are suitable for candying (pears, apricots, crab apples, cherries, plums), and also the skin of citrus fruits.

Caramel is burnt sugar which is added to dishes as a natural colouring agent. To prepare caramel, pour water into a saucepan and add sugar (100 grams of sugar to 2–3 tablespoons of water), and heat it until the sugar dissolves, thickens, begins to turn darker and then browns. At this point it can be added to sauces, soups or jellies, or a glass of water can be added and brought to the boil to make a thick syrup. This should be put in a jar, tightly sealed and kept in a cool place. It can then be added when needed to soups, sauces and aspics.

Carving is cutting up poultry and game or meat after cooking into even pieces without chopping the bones. With goose or turkey one should first remove the wings with a sharp knife, or if possible with poultry scissors, cutting through the thin ribs, and then cut the breast, carving slices crosswise from each side. Smaller birds are divided in half, and larger chickens into quarters. Large ducks, capons and pullets are carved like turkey.

Chipping or frying small pieces of vegetable (potatoes), meat, fish or pastry in very hot fat. The action on the dish of the very high temperature of the fat – it must be at c. 190° leads to a swift closing of the pores, and therefore to a trapping within the product of the vitamins, minerals and also the aroma, while at the same time preventing the fat penetrating the product. If the fat temperature is too low, the pores will not close and the product will be saturated with fat; if it is too high, the fat will begin to burn and the dish will stick to the pan. After chipping, the dish should be removed and surplus fat carefully removed; this is best done on a paper kitchen towel; it should only then be served. This method of cooking produces the best results with vegetables; thanks to the short period of frying, they conserve their most important nutritional values and also appearance, flavour, aroma and colour, while staying crisp and tasty.

Clarifying is the process used to remove thickening or impurities from liquids. In order to arrive at a clear liquid to make jellies or aspics etc. the boiled liquid should be poured out and chilled so that excess fat can be removed from the surface. Then the skimmed liquid should be brought quickly to the boil, and an egg white mixed with water (1 egg white mixed with 2–3 tablespoons of cold water to every litre of stock) should be added, stirred in and the liquid simmered. It should then be taken from the heat and left to cool until all the impurities have sunk to the bottom. Then we pour it through a colander lined with muslin or though a very fine sieve. The liquid that results gives a clear jelly. Clear broth, aspics and all jellies should be clarified.

Coquilles are small dishes in the shape of a shell, made from pottery or heat-resistant glass. They are usually used to bake and serve individual portions. Coquilles are used to bake chicken, fish, or egg dishes, after first being sprinkled with cheese or covered with melted butter and dusted with breadcrumbs.

Courtbouillon is a strong stock made from vegetables, spices and herbs, often with added white wine, which is usually used for cooking fish. The fish is just covered by the stock. Meat can also be stewed in a court bouillon, that is, it should be sprinkled with the stock, or with water or wine during cooking, so that it does not stick to the pan.

Croquettes are a kind of patty made from pancake batter. They are spread with a stuffing and then rolled up, egged and breadcrumbed and fried.

Another type of croquette is shaped like a ball or a roll, made from boiled potatoes, meat, fish, poultry, rice or beans, egged and breadcrumbed and fried in deep fat. Both kinds of croquette can be served as a hot hors-d'oeuvre, as an accompaniment of the main dish, or as a side dish with soup. They can also be served alone as a main dish with sauce or salad.

Curry is an Indian dish, usually made from lamb, poultry or fish and seasoned to be either hot or mild with a mixture of spices and herbs called curry powder. In curry dishes, the herbs and spices are fried first, and the meat or fish is added only later. The ingredients of curry powder vary, but the basis is always turmeric, mace, cinnamon, ginger, cardamom, cloves and pepper, mixed up in differing proportions. Some curry powders contain 20 or more spices and herbs.

Cutlets. The term 'cutlet' is used in Polish to refer both to meat which is filleted and beaten and to minced meat. The original French term, *côtelette*, comes from the word côte or side, and means a piece of flank meat, beaten flat, with the rib still attached, and it is usually coated in egg and breadcrumbs. Here, the favourite cutlets in Polish cuisine are pork cutlets, best served with potatoes and cabbage cooked with mushrooms.

Cutlets can be made from pork, veal, lamb, venison or wild boar (loin or saddle), but they can also be made from pork shoulder, ham or chump, or from leg or saddle of lamb. After beating lightly and sprinkling with salt and pepper and perhaps herbs, the cutlet should be coated in egg and breadcrumbs and fried in a fairly large quantity of very hot fat until it is golden on both sides.

Oval rissoles shaped from chopped or minced meat, often of various kinds like beef with pork or pork with veal, are also called cutlets in Polish. After the meat has been seasoned to taste and mixed with bread soaked in milk and a raw egg, they should be rolled in breadcrumbs and fried in hot fat.

The best-known type of cutlet made from poultry is *de volaille*, that is, a cutlet made from skinned chicken breast from which the breast bone has been removed, but part of the wing bone left intact. After lightly beating the breast meat, it should be formed into the shape of a large leaf which is broader by the bone and quite narrow on the opposite side. After the cutlet has been sprinkled with lemon juice and salted to taste with a pinch of herbs perhaps also added, a hard frozen piece of butter should be placed on it before it is rolled up (the end of the cutlet should be tightly closed, so that the butter cannot run out), covered in breadcrumbs and fried in very hot fat until it is golden in colour. If the *côtelette de volaille* is well-prepared, one must be careful when cutting the first bite, because if the knife is pushed in too sharply, it can lead to spraying melted butter everywhere. *Côtelette de volaille* is usually served with chips and vegetables Polish style (asparagus, Brussels sprouts, cauliflower, peas), which are boiled and then covered with melted butter and toasted breadcrumbs.

Decoration with flowers. Edible flowers can be used to make sure that our dinner plates are not boring, but colourful, healthy and tasty.

Raw vegetables and salads made of fresh fruit and vegetables are well known to us all as an exceptionally important and rich source of vegetables and mineral salts in our diet. It seems worth recalling old ways of making them more varied and exciting.

A 16th century recipe for a salad prepared for King Henry VIII of England mentions 50 ingredients in the form of leaves, seeds, marinated spices, blanched stems, buds and flowers. I think it is worth returning today to that old culinary art and add fresh and dried fruits, nuts, pumpkin and sunflower seeds, pine kernels, herbs and flowers to salads.

It is worth recalling that the leaves of plants with a strong smell blend in perfectly with the aroma-less lettuce or chicory, and that the flowers of many plants not only make a beautiful contribution in terms of colour, but also bring a delicately spicy flavour and aroma.

And so what edible flowers can be added to salad and which can be used to decorate dishes?

One of the most universally used herbs, which at the same time is an excellent salad plant is the marigold. Its lovely orange flowers give the salad a slightly spicy flavour and provide excellent colour effects.

The buds, leaves and flowers of the nasturtium sharpen the flavour of the salad; their appearance is excellent and they make an interesting decoration for dishes made with cold meats and hard-boiled eggs.

The following also provide a splendid and edible colour note to salads:
– the clusters of blue flowers of chicory,
– the coloured petals of pinks and carnations, but before serving you must remember to cut off the bitter white base of the petals,
– the dark red or pink flowers of the deadnettle,
– the colourful flowers of the pelargonium,
– little purple violets, which go usually with fruit salads,
– the pink and white petals of field daisies,
– the tiny starred flowers of borage and the related common stitchwort,
– the small blue, or sometimes pink, honeyed flowers of adderwort, with a mild, sweet flavour. These flowers can also be candied, added to deserts, and juice can also be squeezed from them to add to fruit salads,
– the coloured petals of all kinds of scented roses are also excellent for adding to lettuce, decorating serving dishes and all kinds of salads; one must however remember to cut off the bitter base of the petals,
– pansies of various colours, or the flowers of the althea and charlock add an excellent note of colour to serving dishes with cold meats, lettuce and salads; rosemary, with

its splendid scent of raspberry containing a hint of cloves, is good for adding to fruit salads and desserts.

I advise you to experiment and wish you success and good results.

Diablotins or croutons. These terms apply to two kinds of hot additions to clear soups: chicken broth, borsch or clear tomato soup:
– small cubes of French roll, buttered and sprinkled with grated strong cheese and cayenne pepper. These are placed in a greased tin and baked in a hot oven.
– bread sticks made of short pastry, brushed with egg white and baked until they are golden. The pastry should be spicy, and so one can also add, depending on taste, paprika, pepper, cayenne pepper or herbs, or one can sprinkle these on the pastry when it has been brushed with egg white.

Dressing is a salad sauce, typically one based on mayonnaise or a vinaigrette.

Egging and breadcrumbing means that a prepared piece of meat, fish, a croquette etc. is covered or dredged in turn with flour, beaten egg and then breadcrumbs. This should be done immediately before frying, in order to avoid the coating coming away from the flesh, a phenomenon which is caused by the quick evaporation of the juices given off by the meat. Various additional ingredients can be added to the beaten egg, for example grated cheese, chopped parsley or dried herbs. After the breadcrumbs have been applied they should be squeezed lightly by hand to make them stick, and then the breaded meat should be fried in very hot fat.

Another kind of coating, that is, batter, can be used for chicken or fish fillets and for cutlets.

Filet Mignon is a dish known worldwide. One portion consists of two tiny steaks of beef tenderloin. These are seethed without fat, either on a grill or in a frying pan, and are served with hard-frozen pats of butter flavoured with lemon, anchovy, chive or parsley.

Fillet is a term applied to an undercut of loin of beef, veal or pork, and also to chicken breast or saddle of wild boar, venison or hare. The shaped fillet, after being sprinkled with lemon juice, salt, pepper and if desired herbs to taste, is briefly sautéd in very hot fat. It is usually served with a sauce – hunter's sauce, or mushroom or tomato sauce; game fillets are usually served with rosehip or blackcurrant sauce. Fillets are usually served with chips, lettuce salad or delicate vegetables which are boiled or cooked in butter. Fish fillets are usually rolled in flour and fried, and served with grated horseradish or fried mushrooms.

Filleting consists in slitting a gutted fish along the back, removing the backbone and other bones and often removing the skin.
Filleting meat means cutting it across the grain, at a slight angle, after which it is lightly beaten and formed in the shape of an oval leaf.

Fines herbes is the French term for a combination of fresh herbs used to flavour sauces, meat, vegetables, omelettes, and also curd cheese and other cheeses. Depending on the dish, you can select the herbs according to your own taste and complement them with finely chopped onion, garlic or mushrooms. The usual components of fines herbes are finely chopped parsley, chives, dill, chervil, basil, lemon balm and thyme.

'Five minute' is the term applied to things which have been fried very quickly and are served in the frying pan.

Flambé – meaning 'in flames' – describes a process whereby a prepared dish is sprinkled with alcohol (brandy, rum, vodka), lighted and served in flames. Grilled or fried meat (steak), and also sweet omelettes and pancakes, are excellent served in this way.

Fricassee is a kind of very delicate goulash or stew made with white meat (veal, chicken, boiling fowl or lamb). The meat is cut into quite large pieces and simmered in stock (made from a small amount of soup vegetables and spices), thickened with a mixture of butter and flour, to which cre-am or raw egg yolks are added. Usually this sauce is lightly turned with lemon juice or wine vinegar, and chopped dill or cress is added. Fricassee is usually served with boiled rice.

Frying. An old kitchen proverb says: 'Fry quickly, boil slowly'. *Sauter* means to fry in hot fat, shaking the frying pan so that the dish does not stick to the pan; if a dish is described as sauté, it means fried (fish, meat, poultry), without egg and breadcrumbs, in hot fat.
Frying is done in fat alone without any added water. The fat should be heated on a hot point to a temperature of 180–200ºC. If the temperature is lower, the item to be fried will absorb fat, and become less tasty and less digestible. In hot fat, protein sets, but meat does not become more tender, and therefore only good cuts of meat are suitable for frying, for example, sirloin of beef, prime beef rib or prime flank, pork loin or ham. Meat, fish or poultry cut into strips is fried on a low flame, especially if it is egged and breaded, after the fat has first been heated very hot; this is because the breadcrumbs will brown quickly but the meat inside may remain raw. In order to fry something evenly on all sides (especially vegetables, potatoes and finely chopped meat), the frying pan should be shaken frequently. It is best to use a frying pan with a thick bottom. Meat can also be fried without fat, directly on a hot pan. There are special frying pans for this purpose, known as penny pans, with rounded dents on the bottom. Meat fried in this way is more digestible than meat fried in fat. The best fat for frying is lard. The frying time depends on the dish. The shortest frying time, two or three minutes on each side, is for rare steak. But nothing should be fried for too long (not longer than four to six minutes on each side), or the meat will become too dry. Some meats, after they have been quickly fried at a high temperature, can be finished off at a lower temperature, with added butter to improve the taste. If we are frying a larger number of portions of meat in a frying pan, the old fat should be removed with each fried portion and new fat put in.

Broiling means frying on a **grill**. The principle here is that the heat should be high, and therefore the meat, vegetables, fish or fruit are placed on the grill only when the charcoal is sufficiently hot (all the flames have gone out and the charcoal is glowing red); the grill should be very hot and lightly rubbed with fat.

Frying in a wok is a method of cooking that comes from the East. The wok is a useful invention, which is a cross between a saucepan and a frying pan. The usual way of cooking in a wok is quick frying at high temperature, while stirring all the time. In this way, all the ingredients, especially various kinds of vegetables, are not overcooked, and keep all their food value, and also their aroma and colour. The fat – usually vegetable oil – should be poured into the heated wok, usually 1 to 2 tablespoons, depending on the recipe. All the ingredients should be chopped into pieces of roughly equal size; and all the seasoning – herbs, sauces, spices etc. – should be prepared beforehand. The ingredients that require longest cooking should be put in first, and delicate ingredients at the very end. Meat cooked in a wok is exceptionally tender and juicy. A special wooden spatula is used for mixing ingredients in a wok.

Deep frying means using a quantity of fat that allows the products to float in it freely. Deep frying of small pieces of meat, fish, poultry, vegetables or potatoes must be done in very hot fat, at a temperature of up to 200°C. Lard, soya oil, or – best of all – boiled beef suet, should be used. As a result of the action of the very hot fat, the pores are quickly closed up in the products being deep fried, and by this means the vitamins, mineral salts, and also aroma are sealed inside. If the temperature of the fat is too low, the pores will not close and the product will become saturated with fat, which is not desirable. If the fat is too hot, it begins to burn and the products stick to the pan, which is even worse. In order to protect the products as much as possible from drying up, it is a good idea to egg and breadcrumb them before deep frying, or cover them in batter. The pan we use for deep frying should be only half-filled with fat, since the hot fat foams up after the products have been thrown in. Electric fryers or chip pans are excellent for deep frying. The products to be deep-fried should be thrown in handful by handful. After frying they should be drained of excess fat in a sieve or using

kitchen towel, and placed on a heated dish; only then should they be seasoned to taste with salt, pepper or herbs.

Frying fat for deep frying is usually appropriately prepared beef suet, lard or oil.

Galantine. This is an exceptionally elegant dish which takes a long time to prepare. It can be made from chicken, wild fowl, fish or meat, and is served as an hors-d'oeuvre. At one time, this name was applied to a delicate pâté made of tiny pieces of meat or poultry with spices, stuffed into a chicken skin from which all bones and flesh had been removed. Chefs in the past carefully sewed up the stuffed chicken, restoring its original shape, and then tied it in a cloth and boiled it; when it was cold they covered it with a chaud-froid sauce and decorated it with fruit or truffles. Chaud-froid sauce is a cold sauce which sets into a jelly; brown chaud-froid sauce is made from dark basic sauce made from strong veal stock; white chaud-froid sauce is made with a basic white sauce, cream and chicken or veal jelly.

Galantine is made today from chicken, wild fowl, fish, or meat cooked in vegetable stock, often with added white wine. Chicken for galantine must be carefully boned. Meat stuffing is placed on the flattened meat and then it is tightly rolled up, often wrapped in a linen cloth and tied. This is boiled and left to stand in the cooking juices for an hour, and then cooled under weights. It is then sliced crosswise and served with a spicy sauce, pickles or vegetable salad. It can also be covered with aspic after slicing.

Garnishing refers both to decorating serving dishes and to decorating the dish itself. Garnish is all the additions made to dishes from fish, meat and poultry. These can be exceptionally attractive and extravagant, or quite simple, consisting of a single one element (for example, boiled asparagus, broccoli or cauliflower), or several elements suitably arranged (for example, several kinds of vegetable, fried eggs, poached eggs, toast).

It is the garnish that often gives the name to the dish, for it indicates what has been used in the preparation. For example, in international cuisine, *à la Crecy* indicates a dish from white meat with the addition of carrots prepared in various ways; *à la Argenteuil* usually means a dish from poultry, veal or lamb which is always accompanied by asparagus (of which the best are grown in this town outside Paris); *à la florentine* means a dish with the addition of spinach, and so on.

Glazing means giving the dish a glossy surface. Meat served cold is glazed with strong stock mixed with gelatine. Pâtés are glazed to prevent them from going off, as the glaze protects them from action of the air. Cold meats, roasts, poultry, cutlets, hard-boiled eggs are also glazed, often only for decoration.

To prepare a glaze for meat and pâtés a stock should be rendered down, blended with gelatine so that the liquid is thick, and when it is cold, it should be evenly spread over the surface with a brush or feather to form a thin, shining layer.

Ingredients are the products that make up a dish, including seasoning.

Knel. This German word denotes a very delicate meat stuffing for dumplings cooked in clear chicken broth, for patties or for turkey. The dumplings for soup are sometimes called knelki.

Knel is usually made from veal (soft and white veal shoulder), chicken or game birds. Meat for knel should be very finely chopped and then pounded with a pestle or put in a mixer; it should then be sieved and salted. Cream should be beaten. The meat should be put in a bowl placed on ice, and beaten up with gradually added cream until the ingredients form an even, delicate paste. *Knelki* are an exceptionally delicious addition to clear broths or cream soups.

Larding. It is usually lean meat which is to be roasted that is larded – above all game, but also sirloin of beef, lamb, veal – and it very much improves the taste.

It is done by using a skewer to insert thin slices of bacon fat or streaky bacon, often with aromatic herbs or seasoning, into the meat. The slices of bacon prevent the meat from becoming too dry and make it turn a beautiful golden brown. If poultry is larded superficially its skin becomes

crisp and crunchy. The bacon fat saturates the larded game (and lean meat) with fat as it melts during roasting, and as a result the meat does not become too dry and browns well. The bacon fat is cut into thin even strips for larding, and is put into the surface of the meat in even rows using a skewer.

It is especially dark, lean meat that requires larding, in particular saddle and leg. Large joints of meat that are to be braised or roasted are larded. Lean beef, veal or lamb are larded with pieces of bacon fat about the thickness of the little finger. The meat is pierced with a sharp-pointed knife and the bacon fat is pushed inside. It is a good idea to put the slices of bacon fat in the freezer for a quarter of an hour beforehand, so that they harden, which makes larding easier. To make the taste sharper, the bacon fat can be marinated with grated and salted garlic, and sprinkled with paprika, pepper, marjoram or other herbs. Fillets of anchovy, ham, corned tongue, shallots, vegetables, plums or prunes can also be used for larding meat (to give it a special flavour or aroma). To change the flavour of mutton, it can be larded with cloves of garlic or with shallots. Small joints of meat are larded in a single row, while larger joints in several rows. When larding poultry, the strips of bacon fat should be inserted so that you can see both ends, just below the skin.

Another way of preventing lean meat from drying out is to bard it, or to roll the meat, poultry or game in very thin slices of bacon fat (bards). Meat cooked in this way does not dry out and is tender and juicy. Just before the roasting is finished, you can remove the slices of bacon fat so that the meat will brown nicely.

Marinade is a liquid prepared from water, white vinegar, wine or lemon juice with added spices (pepper, allspice, bay leaves, ginger, cloves) or herbs (juniper, thyme, rosemary, tarragon). Vegetables, especially onions and garlic, are often added to marinades. Meat, fish and poultry left for several days in a marinade becomes more tender, and acquires a better aroma and taste.

Mushrooms and vegetables can also be marinated in vinegar with the addition of seasoning.

Another kind of marinade is a liquid made from sour milk, skimmed milk, yoghurt, wine or white vinegar, which can be used to marinate meat, especially tough meat. Meat that is to be braised or roasted can be marinated in this way. In the acid marinade, the meat becomes more tender, and acquires taste and aroma, and afterwards it is much easier to roast or braise. To serve meat and poultry game-style, it is essential to marinade it. The right marinade can make beef, lamb, veal or poultry taste like game and gives it a special taste and aroma. Wine or vinegar should be boiled with a small amount of water to which spices and herbs have been added, often as well as onion, carrot and celeriac. Marinating is also an excellent way of keeping meat if you do not have a fridge. The meat is marinated for at least 12 hours and up to several days. If the meat is marinated over a longer period it should be regularly turned in order that it should marinate evenly. After removing it from the marinade it should be rinsed and dried, and while it is cooking, it should be regularly sprinkled with the strained marinade.

Pickling is another way of preserving meat by putting it into a solution of salt, saltpetre and sugar with the addition of seasoning like bay leaves, coriander, cloves, allspice, rosemary etc. for a period of a few days or up to two or three weeks. Pickling not only preserves meat but also gives it a special taste. Pickled meat is particularly suitable for boiling, and the cuts of meat most often pickled are ham, pork knuckle and tongue. One should remember that pickled meat is less digestible than fresh meat. The pieces of meat to be pickled should weigh not less than one kilo and the basis of the process is a thorough rubbing in of the prepared mixture of salt, saltpetre and seasoning. It is a good idea to heat the salt in a dry pan and to rub it in while warm. The quantity and variety of the ingredients rubbed into the meat depends on the quantity and kind of meat. This also determines the length of the pickling process which can last from five to twenty days. The rubbed meat should be placed tightly in a stone pan, covered with a plate, weighed down and left in a cool place; it should be turned over daily, so that it pickles evenly. After it is taken out it should be very carefully washed, or if it has been pickled for a long time, it should be soaked in cold water and boiled in water or spiced vegetable stock. Pickling scar-

let – *à l'ecarlate* – means pickling meat so that it takes on a bright red colour.

Mixing or blending of various products is done in a mixing bowl with a wooden spoon or spatula. Butter, cheese, egg yolk and sugar, ground almonds, flour etc. often have to be mixed together. If we are mixing butter with egg yolks, we first beat the butter until it is frothy, and then we add the egg yolks one at a time, beating constantly until the egg yolk blends completely with the butter, and only then do we add the next one. You should always beat in one direction, for otherwise the butter turns. If this happens, the turned mixture can only be improved by heating it slightly in a bain-marie, beating all the time while it is over the heat, until it again forms a smoothly blended mixture. Today, all this is usually done in a mixer.

Mousses. This is a kind of cold pâté prepared from various ingredients – fruit, fish, shellfish, game. A good mousse should have a lightly frothy consistency and should melt in the mouth. Fish mousses can be made from smoked, boiled or braised fish and also from tinned fish, of which the best are tinned tuna or salmon. The cooked fish should be mixed with cream, gelatine and butter, after which the mixture is put into a special mould, cooled and then, often after it has been decorated, jelly is poured over it. Beautifully decorated mousses are a great party piece; mousses made from left-over fish or meat make an excellent sandwich spread. The taste of a mousse depends on the seasoning. They can be seasoned with herbs, onion, garlic, horseradish or lemon. Quails' eggs, parsley, small shrimps or coloured strips of pepper are excellent for the decoration.

Oscypek, a ewes's-milk cheese which is salted and smoked, and shaped in decorative wooden moulds. It is a speciality of the Podhale (the Tatras) region of Poland.

Parsley root. Apart from the herb called parsley, with flat or curly leaves, the Poles grow root parsley as a vegetable. Its root, white or yellowish, has a flavour not unlike that of the parsnip.

Ragout is a kind of stew made with beef, mutton, pork or game. The taste of the ragout depends on the seasoning used (herbs, mushrooms, spices, vegetables). The meat is cut into small pieces, which are dredged with flour and fried in hot fat, and then put into a stew pan, seasoned, and covered with water, wine or broth and simmered in a covered pot. At the end, additional seasoning is added to taste and the ragout is thickened with cream or raw egg yolk. This is how dark ragout is made. For white ragout, the flour is replaced by potato starch, which when it is mixed in and cooked in the ragout, thickens the sauce.

Removing fat from chicken broth, meat stock or sauce is often necessary. Frequently when a sauce is left for a long time on the heat (this is the reason why a bain-marie is recommended) and some of the water in it evaporates, fat appears all over the surface. The slang term to describe this is that the sauce has 'blown up', and it does not look very appetising. The fat can be removed by pouring in a little cold water or wine and heating the sauce slowly, stirring it all the time, until the fat again blends smoothly into the liquid.

Roux is a thickener that is often used for soups, sauces or boiled vegetables. It is made with equal proportions of butter and flour. The flour is mixed with the melted butter, taking care that it does not brown, and then cold milk, cream or broth is added and stirred in carefully. It should be brought slowly to the boil, stirring all the time, and then added to soups, sauces or vegetables, and carefully stirred in.

Sieving or straining is a procedure applied to pâtés, sauces, vegetables, cream soups, and also jams and preserves, in order to make them smoother and more delicate, and sometimes more digestible, with a better taste. When we sieve meat, vegetables and fruit, we spread the juice in which they were cooked, until the whole pulp has passed through the sieve. In Old Polish cuisine, fine sauces and soups were sieved several times, the last time through a fine cloth; today, when we have mixers, this is not necessary.

Skimming scum means using a strainer-spoon to remove the scum that forms on the surface of certain items during cooking. In jams and preserves, the scum can be used to make cool drinks.

Soufflé. This can serve either as an excellent hors-d'oeuvre, or a main course, or else as a dessert.
Soufflés can be savoury – with added cheese, fish, poultry, meat, sausage, vegetables, mushrooms etc. – or sweet – made from fruit, nuts or almonds.
Savoury soufflés are made from a thick bechamel sauce, to which are added grated cheese, cooked meat (roast or fried), fish, poultry, vegetables either finely chopped or puréed (cauliflower, spinach, asparagus, beans or mushrooms). This hot sauce is the basis for the soufflé. The whole is bound with carefully folded in, stiffly beaten egg whites. Sweet soufflés are made from sieved boiled or baked fruit, or finely-chopped nuts (almonds), mixed with egg yolks blended with sugar and with stiffly beaten egg whites.
Making soufflés is not easy. The right proportions of ingredients are exceptionally important. The soufflé dish should be high and thickly greased. After the soufflé mixture has been poured into the dish it should be pushed away from the edge with a knife, so that it will rise. The oven should be preheated to the required temperature. While the soufflé is being baked the heat must not be turned down, and the oven door must not be opened or the dish moved. The dish should be placed fairly high on a grid, so that the soufflé cooks evenly. It should be baked for about 25 minutes, and served immediately on being taken out of the oven, since it collapses very quickly, which spoils its appearance.

Spices are plants, or parts of plants, with aromatic substances which are used to flavour food. These are usually plants brought in from exotic countries; they should be used sparingly and appropriately.

I. **Allspice**. The name reflects the variety of tastes in the small fruits of the pimento tree which grows mainly in Jamaica. The aroma is similar to that of cloves, cinnamon or mustard, but it is as hot as pepper. It is used as a spice in many different dishes, marinades, cooked meats or sausages.

2. **Bay leaves** have for centuries been associated with courage and virility and with the gods of the ancient world; they are dedicated to Apollo. Pythia, the priestess of the oracle at Delphi, put herself into a trance by chewing bay leaves, and wreaths of bay leaves were used to crown emperors and victors. Arab experts on cuisine (and not only on aphrodisiacs) claimed for centuries that the constant presence of bay leaves in a man's diet would ensure him success in all areas of life. Today bay leaves are everywhere added to stocks, soups, sauces and marinades.

3. **Cardamom** or **cardamon** belongs to the ginger family; it is the seeds of the cardamom plant that are used as a spice. We know from the writings of Dioscorides and Pliny that it was known to the ancient Greeks and Romans, who believed that it had medicinal powers acting on the stomach and heart, and also valued cardamom as an excellent spice with a stimulating effect. Onion and pea salad flavoured with cardamom, ginger and cinnamon was a highly rated aphrodisiac. In the middle ages, Christians were forbidden by a papal bull to use cardamom because of its excessively stimulating effects. Today, cardamom is an ingredient in many mixed spices and sauces. It can be used by itself in marinades for fish and vegetables, in sauces and soups or in meat dishes; the Arabs use it for example to flavour 'Bedouin coffee' which would 'bring a dead man back to life'.

4. **Cinnamon**. One of the oldest spices used by the peoples of Asia, this is the bark of the Ceylon cinnamon tree. In ancient times, it was thought to be a love potion, but was rarely used in cooking; it was usually used with apples, because it was thought that in conjunction with them it was particularly powerful. This is true to the present day, for it is difficult to omit it when making an apple charlotte or stewed apples. Its sweet spicy smell and taste also go well with dishes made with curd cheese or braised meat.

5. **Cloves** were known in ancient times; they were used mainly to freshen the breath and treat toothache. They only became fashionable as one of the spices used in European cuisine in the 9th century. They are today available whole or ground. Whole cloves are usually put into marinades and stewed fruit; ground cloves are used in stuffings, meat pâtés and sauces. Both should be used very sparingly because of the strong smell. They go very well with pepper, nutmeg, ginger, bay leaves and cardamom.

6. **Ginger**. This probably first reached Europe in about 340 BC thanks to Alexander the Great and it quickly became an ingredient of aphrodisiacs, since its stirring effects 'pleasantly fanned up the fires of passion'. This spice comes from the underground stems of a shrub that grows in southeastern Asia. Ginger can be bought dried, fresh or in syrup. It has a sweet and very sharp taste. It is added to dishes made from meat, game, poultry, to tripe, stuffings and salads.

7. **Nutmeg** and **mace**. These are two spices with a strong flavour and taste. Mace comes from the thick covering of the seed, while the nutmeg is the seed itself. It is used to spice sauces, tripe and cakes, mainly gingerbread. Grated nutmeg gives a pleasant lightly spicy flavour to boiled vegetables, peps up the bland taste of stewed fruit, and provides an interesting flavour for plums.

8. **Pepper**. The Greeks were the first Europeans to come into contact with pepper during Alexander the Great's expedition to India. They valued pepper highly and used it both as a spice and a medicine. The Romans got to know this 'heavenly grain' thanks to the Greeks, and it spread early to Northern Europe, where it became very popular throughout the Roman empire. Peppercorns are the fruit of the pepper plant. Black, green and white pepper all come from the same plant. The green peppercorn is an unripe fruit marinated in a salt solution, vinegar or alcohol; it is milder than the other kinds and has a strong aroma. Black peppercorns are the most pungent and are the ripest fruit dried in the open air. White peppercorns – which have the strongest aroma – are ripe fruit soaked

in water, stripped of their flesh and then dried. White pepper is used for delicate white meats and delicate vegetables.

There is yet another variety: pink pepper, but this does not come from the pepper plant, but is the fruit of a tree that grows in Peru. Pink pepper, like green pepper, is used for dishes that are to be mild in flavour but with a powerful aroma. A small pinch of pink pepper brings out the flavour well in fruit salads. Cayenne pepper is also not a true pepper, but comes from the dried pods of a plant which is a variety of capiscum. Cayenne pepper is the hottest of all the spices known today. It is not sprinkled onto dishes but carefully mixed into sauces. It is excellent in salads, shellfish or fish cocktails and in salads containing meat or fish.

9. **Saffron**. In ancient times it was believed that crocuses, from which saffron comes, were 'holy flowers'. Saffron itself was held to 'delight and stimulate, increasing or restoring energy'. According to the Greeks, dishes containing saffron made women incapable of thinking of anything but love. Saffron was therefore in great demand, and because it was exceedingly expensive people soon began to produce counterfeits. It is said that the Romans were the first to use marigold petals in place of saffron. It used to be said of Old Polish cuisine that it was 'peppery and saffrony', and this very expensive spice was used to flavour meat, tripe, sauces and to 'dye' Easter cakes. Usually three or four saffron stigmas are used, which are first soaked in hot water, milk or alcohol.

10. **Turmeric** comes from India, and was known to the ancient world as 'Indian saffron'. The colour and taste are similar to ginger; it has an intense flavour and a rather delicate smell. Today it is the main ingredient in curry powders, Worcester sauce and many mixed spices. It colours dishes yellow, and a pinch is enough.

Stuffing is the most common element used in preparing dishes. It can be the basis for preparing pâtés, pastes, meatballs, galantines and meat jellies, and also to stuff poultry, meat, fish, vegetables and mushrooms. The ingredients of stuffing can vary: finely chopped or minced poultry, meat, game, mushrooms, eggs and vegetables, which can be boiled, fried or raw, and are seasoned with herbs or spices, often with the addition of a filler in the form of soaked white bread, cooked rice, sauces, cream or raw eggs.

Soup vegetables, *włoszczyzna* in Polish. A selection of vegetables used for making vegetable, meat or fish stock. In Poland, it is traditionally sold in bunches of 3 to 5 carrots, 3–4 parsley roots, a piece of celeriac and leek, sometimes with a wedge of savoy cabbage added.

Tartlets are usually made from short pastry although also from choux pastry or raised dough, and filled with special salads, decorated and often covered with jelly. For dessert, they are filled with fruit or fruit mousses; when served as a hot hors-d'oeuvre or as a side dish to soup they are usually filled with a filling known as salpicon, usually made from cooked meat, vegetables, diced shellfish or mushrooms in a thick savoury sauce – cold mayonnaise or hot bechamel.

Tarts – these are popular today not only in French cuisine, and are made from short pastry (with a pinch of baking powder added). The pastry base for the tart is baked in a fluted tin, and baked fruit with jelly poured over or whipped cream are placed on the top. If we put savoury meat or vegetables on the tart base, the tarts can be served as a main dish or hors-d'oeuvre at dinner.

Tempering is running a hot dish under cold water. The following are tempered:
– blanched vegetables, to stop the cooking process;
– cooked macaroni or rice to rinse off the starch, and so that the strands of macaroni or grains of rice do not stick together;
– in order to reduce immediately the temperature, for example of hard-boiled eggs, so that it is easier to shell them, or of tomatoes (apricots, peaches) which have been blanched in order to make them easier to peel.

Terrine means in French a stoneware oven dish with a tightly fitted lid. It also means a kind of pâté, prepared and served in such a dish. This kind of pâté is baked without a pastry crust in a bain-marie in the oven. So that they do not dry up during baking, it is covered with very thin slices of bacon fat or streaky bacon (bards).

Thickening means adding cream mixed with egg yolks, cream mixed with flour or butter mixed with flour to a dish. A sauce or soup should be thickened just before it is poured into the soup tureen or sauce boat. When the thickening has been added, the sauce or soup should be quickly heated, stirring constantly, but not brought to boiling point, because the cream or egg yolk would turn if boiled, and the appearance and taste of the soup or sauce would be spoiled. Soup is lighter in colour and smoother in appearance after thickening.

Timbale is the French name for a deep ovenproof dish which is used for both cooking and serving. It also means a pie crust made from short or choux pastry for pâtés. In old cookery books pâtés baked in pastry crust are also called timbales.

Today the name timbale has come to mean dishes which after cooking are placed in moulds before being laid out on a dish. The most popular are timbales of rice. The boiled rice is placed in small moulds, pressed down firmly with a spoon, reheated and the small formed portions are placed on a serving dish. Dishes cooked – usually by steaming – in small moulds are also called timbales, for example herring timbales.

Tying with string. Corded string is best for tying rolls, rolled and stuffed roasts or game birds wrapped in bacon fat. Remember that first the string should be put in boiling water and then dried.

Vegetables. In the culinary art, not only taste is important, but also appearance. When we cook vegetables, we should pay attention to the way they are served. In the great cuisines of the world, the classic forms of cutting vegetables have special names: julienne, brunois, mirepoix:
– *julienne* means cutting vegetables into long thin strips or sticks, each 3–4 cm long and 1–2 mm thick,
– *brunoise* means dicing vegetables. This is how root vegetables are chopped for salads or clear soups. Both the julienne and brunoise method are used for chopping a single kind of vegetable, mixed vegetables, and also mushrooms, gherkins, ham, tongue or chicken breast. The chopped products are used as an aromatic addition to soups, sauces, stuffings and salads,
– *mirepoix* means chopping vegetables into large cubes. This method is also used for cutting up bacon fat, ham, streaky bacon, meat, poultry, game and fish that are to be used for goulash or quick-fried dishes.

CHAPTER I

THE COLD BUFFET

Flavoured butters

Flavoured butters, or in other words, butter mixed with various seasonings – savoury, aromatic, like for example parsley, lemon juice, mustard, sharp cheese, anchovy or capers – were until recently regarded as an excellent addition to meat dishes (steak, cutlets), or were put on toast or sandwiches. Today, they have 'won their independence' and are an important item in a cold buffet.

After the butter has been chilled and formed into balls, circles, cubes, stars or shavings, it is placed on decorative dishes or on lettuce leaves decorated with strips of cocktail gherkin or bell pepper. If this kind of butter is treated as a separate part of the buffet, it should be made in a variety of flavours.

It considerably improves the flavour of many hot dishes – cooked fish, shellfish, steak, cutlets, braised and roast meat, braised and roast chicken. The butter is then placed directly onto the dish just before it is served.

The general principle: When preparing flavoured butter, remember that the first thing to do is beat the butter with a wooden spoon or spatula until it is frothy, and then add carefully the chosen ingredients and seasoning. The butter should then be shaped into the required forms, refrigerated, and taken out of the freezer an hour before serving. The best known flavoured butter in the world is parsley butter, known as maître d'hôtel butter.

Maître d'hôtel

150 g butter, 1 tbsp lemon juice, 2 tbsps finely chopped parsley, salt, white pepper

Cream the butter, adding gradually the lemon juice. Towards the end add the chopped parsley, salt and pepper. Shape the butter into small balls, cubes or slices and refrigerate. Serve with beefsteaks, sautéd pork loin, sautéd kidneys, grilled entrecôte, lamb chops and lamb roast. You may also use it with canapés and toast with ham and cheese.

Serves 4 • preparation: 10–15 mins

Savoury butter

150 g butter, 150 g blue cheese, 1–3 cloves of garlic, 4 tbsps finely chopped herbs (basil, marjoram, dill and parsley), ¼ tsp honey, 1 tbsp lemon juice, salt, pepper

Cream the butter together with the crumbled cheese, salt, crushed garlic and pepper. Add gradually the honey, lemon juice and chopped herbs. Refrigerate. Use to garnish canapés or with beefsteaks, fish fillets and poultry.

Serves 4 • preparation: 10–15 mins

Herbal butter

Parsley butter

125 g butter, 1 tbsp cold water, 1 tbsp chopped parsley, 1 small onion, juice of ½ lemon, salt, pepper

Work the butter, water, very finely chopped onion and parsley into a smooth paste. Gradually add the lemon juice, salt and pepper. Refrigerate, then shape into balls. Use to garnish game cutlets or stewed and roast game cut into slices.

Serves 4 • preparation: 10–15 mins

Herbal butter with cheese

150 g butter, 1 Camembert, 1 tbsp lemon juice, salt, pepper, paprika, 3–4 spinach leaves, 1 small onion, 3–4 cloves of garlic, 1 tsp finely chopped basil leaves, a piece of dried pumpernickel

Blend the butter with the finely chopped onion, spinach, basil and lemon juice, add the crushed garlic, pepper, paprika and pieces of cheese. Work into a smooth paste. Transfer to a bowl, put into the fridge, sprinkle with the grated pumpernickel. Use to garnish canapés or shape into balls dredged with grated pumpernickel. You may thread such balls on skewers together with pieces of gherkin, pickled mushrooms and pepper.

serves 4 • Preparation: 10–15 mins

Herbal butter I

150 g butter, 1 tsp soya sauce, 1 tsp lemon juice, 1½ tbsps finely chopped herbs (mint, tarragon, savory and hyssop), salt, pepper

Cream the butter together with the soya sauce. Add the remaining ingredients, mix well, refrigerate. Serve with cooked meat and fish, and with grilled meat.

serves 4 • Preparation: 10–15 mins

Herbal butter II

150 g butter, 1 tsp mustard, 1 tbsp lemon juice, 1–2 cloves of garlic, 1 tsp each finely chopped chives, marjoram and savory, salt, a pinch of white pepper

Cream the butter, mustard and lemon juice. Add the herbs and crushed garlic, mix well. Refrigerate.

Preparation: 10–15 mins

Savoury herbal butter

150 g butter, 1 tsp each finely chopped tarragon, chives and onion, 3 anchovy fillets, 3 hard-boiled egg yolks, juice of ½ lemon, 1 tsp capers, a pinch of each salt, powdered ginger and grated nutmeg

Purée the fillets, add the condiments and mix with the softened butter. The mixture should be spicy and light green in colour. Serve with cooked meat, beefsteaks and fish.

serves 4 • Preparation: 10–15 mins

Basil butter

150 g butter, 2–3 tbsps finely chopped basil, 1 onion, 2–3 cloves of garlic, salt, pepper, 1 tsp lemon juice

Grate the onion finely, crush the garlic with salt and pepper. Cream the butter, adding gradually the onion, garlic, lemon juice and basil. Refrigerate.

serves 4 • Preparation: 10–15 mins

Tarragon butter I

150 g butter, 1 tsp each finely chopped tarragon, parsley and chives, ½ finely grated onion, salt, pepper

Cream the butter, adding gradually the lemon juice. Mix with the chopped herbs, add salt and pepper to taste. Use to garnish canapés, cutlets and fish.

serves 4 • Preparation: 10–15 mins

Tarragon butter II

125 g butter, 3 tbsps finely chopped tarragon, 1 tbsp lemon juice, salt, pepper

Cream the butter with the lemon juice. Mix with the chopped herbs, add salt and pepper to taste. Use to garnish canapés, cutlets and fish.

serves 4 • Preparation: 10–15 mins

Dill and lemon balm butter

150 g butter, 3 tbsps finely chopped dill, 1 tsp finely chopped lemon balm, salt, pepper, lemon juice

Cream the butter with the lemon juice, add salt and pepper. Mix with the chopped herbs.

serves 4 • Preparation: 10–15 mins

Lavender butter

150 g butter, ½ tsp each finely chopped lavender and sage leaves, 1 tsp finely chopped savory, 2 tsps finely chopped dill, 1 tsp lemon juice, salt, pepper

Cream the butter, mix with the finely chopped herbs. Add salt and pepper to taste. Serve with cooked or grilled fish.

serves 4 • Preparation: 10–15 mins

Thyme butter

100 g butter, 2 tsps finely chopped thyme leaves, 2 cloves of garlic crushed with salt, ½ tsp each lemon juice and soya sauce

Cream the butter, add the crushed garlic, lemon juice and soya sauce. Mix with the thyme and refrigerate.

serves 4 • Preparation: 10–15 mins

Rosemary butter

150 g butter, 3 tbsps grated Parmesan (or Cheddar), 1½ tsps finely chopped rosemary leaves, salt, pepper, ¼ tsp grated lemon rind

Cream the butter, add salt, pepper and lemon zest. Mix with the grated cheese and chopped rosemary. Serve with pasta or pork roast.

serves 4 • Preparation: 10–15 mins

Watercress butter

150 g butter, 2–3 tbsps chopped watercress, 1 tsp chopped lovage leaves, salt, pepper, lemon juice

Mix the chopped watercress and lovage with the softened butter. Add salt, pepper and lemon juice to taste.

serves 4 • Preparation: 10–15 mins

Green butter

150 g butter, 50 g bryndza cheese, 1 tsp each finely chopped chives, dill, parsley and celery leaves, salt

Cream the butter and bryndza, mix with the chopped herbs, add salt to taste. Serve with meat or use to garnish canapés.

serves 4 • Preparation: 10–15 mins

Fruit butter

Mountain cranberry butter

150 g butter, 150 g mountain cranberry jam

Cream the butter with the jam, refrigerate it. Serve with game, roast beef or beefsteaks.

serves 4 • Preparation: 10–15 mins

Redcurrant butter

100 g butter, 50 g redcurrant jelly, 1 tsp honey, a pinch of powdered ginger

Mix the jelly with the honey and ginger. Cream the butter, add the jelly and refrigerate. Serve with game.

serves 4 • Preparation: 10–15 mins

Orange butter

100 g butter, ¼ tsp grated orange rind, juice of 1 orange, salt, pepper

Cream the butter, mix with the orange juice and zest. Add salt and pepper to taste. Serve with game.

serves 4 • Preparation: 10–15 mins

Lemon butter

150 g butter, juice and grated rind of 1 lemon, 1 tsp brandy, salt, white pepper

Blend the butter with the brandy, lemon juice and zest. Add salt and pepper to taste, refrigerate. Serve with fried calf's feet, Wiener schnitzel or fried fish.

serves 4 • Preparation: 10 mins

Other kinds of flavoured butter

Anchovy butter I

125 g butter, ¼ tsp grated lemon rind, 60 g anchovy fillets

Chop the anchovies finely, then cream them together with the butter and lemon zest. Refrigerate.

serves 4 • Preparation: 10–15 mins

Anchovy butter II

150 g butter, 5 anchovy fillets or 1 tbsp anchovy paste

Cream the butter, mix it with the anchovy paste. Serve with grilled meat, boiled beef tongue, boiled beef, roast beef or beefsteaks.

serves 4 • Preparation: 10 mins

Garlic butter

150 g butter, 6–8 cloves of garlic, salt

Chop the garlic finely, mix it with salt and add to the softened butter. Refrigerate.

serves 4 • Preparation: 10 mins

Horseradish butter

150 g butter, 3 tbsps grated horseradish, 1 tbsp lemon juice, ½ tsp honey, salt, pepper

Mix the horseradish with the honey. Cream the butter together with the lemon juice. Blend with the horseradish, add salt and pepper to taste. Refrigerate. Serve with fried and cooked fish, smoked meats or hard-boiled eggs.

serves 4 • Preparation: 10 mins

Ginger butter

150 g butter, 1 tbsp lemon juice, ¼ tsp grated lemon rind, 1 tbsps finely chopped ginger, a pinch of caster sugar, salt

Cream the butter with the finely chopped ginger, lemon juice and zest. Add salt and sugar to taste. Serve with beef and roast poultry.

serves 4 • Preparation: 10 mins

Caper butter

150 g butter, ½ cup chopped capers, 1 tsp lemon juice, a pinch of caster sugar

Blend the chopped capers with the butter, lemon juice and sugar.

serves 4 • Preparation: 10–15 mins

Crab butter

150 g butter, 100 g drained tinned crabs, 1 tsp lemon juice, salt, pepper

Blend the butter with the crab meat and lemon juice, add salt and pepper to taste. Refrigerate.

serves 4 • Preparation: 10 mins

Prawn butter

150 g butter, 1 small tin prawns (100 g), 1 tsp lemon juice, a pinch of white pepper

Blend the butter with the prawns and lemon juice, season with pepper to taste. Refrigerate.

serves 4 • Preparation: 10 mins

Mustard butter

150 g butter, 1 tbsp mustard

Cream the butter, mix with the mustard. Serve with grilled entrecôte, pork chops, all kinds of broiled and fried meat.

serves 4 • Preparation: 10 mins

Nut butter

150 g butter, ½ cup ground nuts, 1 tbsp lemon juice, 1 tbsp brandy, salt, a pinch of each caster sugar and white pepper

Cream the butter, put in the nuts, brandy and lemon juice. Add salt, pepper and sugar to taste. Serve with fried and roast poultry or use to garnish canapés.

serves 4 • Preparation: 10 mins

Paprika butter

150 g butter, 1 grated onion, 1 tsp paprika, 1 tsp lemon juice, salt

Cream the butter together with the lemon juice, mix with the onion, paprika and salt.

serves 4 • Preparation: 10 mins

Tomato butter

150 g butter, 2 tbsps tomato paste, 2 tbsps finely grated onion, 2 tbsps grated cheese, pepper

Cream the butter together with the cheese, add the onion and tomato paste. Season with pepper to taste. Refrigerate.

serves 4 • Preparation: 10 mins

Milky agaric butter

150 g butter, 100–150 g milky agarics, 1 tbsps grated horseradish, 1 tsp hot mustard, salt

Drain the mushrooms, put them through a mincer, blend with the butter, horseradish and mustard. Add

salt to taste. Serve with boiled and broiled meat, cold dishes, canapés and toast.

serves 4 • Preparation: 10–15 mins

Ham butter

150 g butter, 100 g lean, finely chopped ham, 1 tsp lemon juice, 1 tsp vodka, 1 tbsp chopped parsley, salt, pepper

Cream the butter together with the vodka and lemon juice, combine with the remaining ingredients. Refrigerate.

serves 4 • Preparation: 10–15 mins

Sardine butter

150 g butter, 100 g tinned sardines, 1 small onion, 1 tart apple,1 tsp lemon juice, 1 tbsp dry white wine, nutmeg

Sauté the finely chopped onion in 1 tbsp of butter, sprinkle with the wine, then simmer until tender. Leave it to cool. Grate the apple finely, sprinkle with the lemon juice. Cream the butter with the apples, onion and sardines. Add the condiments. Serve with cold dishes, canapés and cutlets.

serves 4 • Preparation: 10–15 mins

Herring butter

150 g butter, 1 tsp lemon juice, 1 herring fillet, ½ tbsp mustard

Cream the butter with the lemon juice. Soak the fillet, then chop it very finely. Blend it with the mustard and with the butter. Refrigerate. Use to garnish canapés, serve with cold starters and with baked or boiled potatoes.

serves 4 • Preparation: 10–15 mins

Liver butter

150 g butter, 1 tsp lemon juice, 100 g chicken livers, 1 onion, 30 g butter, salt, pepper, a pinch of nutmeg

Chop the onion finely and cook it in butter, add the livers. Sauté for a while, then liquidize the mixture and sieve it. Add salt, pepper and nutmeg. Cream the butter with the lemon juice, then blend in the liver and onion mixture. Shape into balls and refrigerate.

serves 4 • Preparation: 10–15 mins

Home-made pork dripping

From the new continent the news is filtering through that lard and pork dripping – until recently banned by dieticians – are again being purchased and used for frying meat...

Professor Światosław Ziemlański, the head of the Department of Nutrition Physiology and Biochemistry in the Polish Institute of Food and Nutrition, advises us to use lard and dripping in sensible moderation, but admits that he has never put them on his list of "banned" fats:

'Lard and dripping contain quite a lot of saturated fats (30%–35%) and a relatively small amount of polyunsaturated acids (ca 6%) and 60% monounsaturated acids. This composition of lard means that it is the best and healthiest fat for frying, because it is not subject to polymerization, or in other words, the detrimental effects of high temperatures during frying.

'I have been singing the praises of lard and dripping for many years, but no one wanted to listen to me. But knowing the fondness of my fellow-countrymen for copying fashions from the West, I should think that when the fad for that cursed lard reaches these shores, then it will replace many much advertised fats that are really not suitable for frying. From the point of view of nutrition physiology and biochemistry this turnabout will be entirely justified.

'In science as in life, there are unfortunately fashions... One should eat a little of everything and think about the whole of one's diet, rather than just concentrating on one

foodstuff – animal fat... From time to time, we ought to eat bread and well-prepared dripping.'

For centuries dripping was used in Polish cuisine not only in the form of lard for frying but also – made from melted pork fat, bacon fat or cured or uncured streaky bacon – to eat cold on bread.

Perfect dripping, which will mean something different for each individual, can be made from bacon fat alone, or from bacon fat with cured streaky bacon; some people add onion, some people add garlic, some add marjoram, thyme, apples or plums. There are as many ways of making dripping as there are domestic kitchens.

Ursula's lard spread

300 g pork fat, 150 g lean smoked streaky bacon, 1 bulb of garlic, 1 tart apple, 1 tbsp marjoram, a pinch of salt

Put the pork fat, bacon and peeled and seeded apples through a mincer. Place in a pan and fry over low heat. Skin the garlic, dice it coarsely, add to the lard, stir. When the garlic has browned, add the marjoram and salt, stir again. Pour into an earthenware bowl and leave to set.

serves 4 • Preparation: 20–30 mins

Savoury lard spread

500 g pork fat, 150 g smoked streaky bacon, 150 g small champignons, 1 large onion, 1 tsp dried savory, salt, pepper

Chop the pork fat into small cubes, put in a hot pan, heat up, stir, then add the chopped bacon and fry over low heat. Wash and dry the mushrooms and onion, chop them finely. When the fat has been well rendered, add the mushrooms, onion and savory. Stir well and fry for a minute or two. Add a pinch of salt and pepper. Pour into an earthenware bowl and leave to set.

serves 4 • Preparation: 20–30 mins

Delicate lard spread

*500 g pork fat, 1 onion, 1 tart apple, 1 tbsp
finely chopped hazelnuts, 1 tbsp thyme, salt*

Chop the pork fat into fine cubes, place in a hot pan, heat up, stir. Add the finely chopped onion and apple. When the onion has browned, put in the hazelnuts, thyme and salt. Stir, then pour into an earthenware bowl.

serves 4 • Preparation: 20–30 mins

Christopher's lard spread

*500 g pork fat, 1 small onion, 5–6 stoned prunes,
½ tsp each dried tarragon and thyme, 1 tbsp
sunflower seeds, a pinch of each salt and pepper*

Rinse the prunes and soak them in water for an hour, then dry them and chop finely. Peel the onion and grate it. Chop the lard into small cubes, put in a hot pan, add the onion, prunes, herbs and coarsely chopped sunflower seeds. Stir and fry for a while. Add some salt and pepper. Pour into an earthenware bowl and leave to set.

serves 4 • Preparation: 20–30 mins

Helen's lard spread

*400 g smoked streaky bacon, 200 g pork fat,
3–4 cloves of galic, a pinch of dried tarragon*

Chop the pork fat and bacon finely. Put the pork fat into a hot pan. When it begins to melt, add the bacon and render. Add the finely chopped garlic and tarragon, stir, then pour into an earthenware bowl and leave to cool.

serves 4 • Preparation: 20–30 mins

Dips

The American dip has been catching on in Poland for many years; the word means a savoury sauce or cream. Sauces of this kind have long been familiar in Poland, but they were usually served with cold cooked meats and boiled vegetables. Today they are served in small bowls, usually at parties for the younger age group, and crackers, crisps, hard smoked sausage, cooked or raw vegetables (peppers, chicory, celery, fennel, artichokes etc.) are dipped into them, all chopped into small pieces for a single dipping.

The basis for the dip is usually cream cheese, cream, yogurt or mayonnaise, to which various seasonings such as herbs, fruit or pickles are added.

Simple mayonnaise dip

*½ cup mayonnaise, 3 tbsps cream, 1 tbsp
lemon juice, a pinch of each salt and sugar*

Whisk the cream with salt and sugar until the mixture has stiffened. Blend with the mayonnaise and lemon juice.

serves 4 • Preparation: 4–5 mins

Pineapple dip

*3 slices of tinned pineapple, 150 g smooth tofu,
½ cup pineapple juice, ½ cup single cream,
1 tbsp lemon juice, ¼ tsp grated lemon rind, a
pinch of each salt, cayenne and white pepper*

Blend all the ingredients, then refrigerate for some time.

serves 4 • Preparation: 4–5 mins

Avocado dip

*1 sizeable avocado, 200 g tofu, 2 tbsps lemon
juice, ½ cup single cream, 2–3 tbsps mayonnaise,
3 tbsps chopped almonds, ¼ tsp ground coriander,
salt, pepper, 2 tbsps chopped fresh coriander*

Peel the avocado, remove the stone, sprinkle with the lemon juice. Blend the avocado with the tofu, salt, pepper, ground coriander, cream and mayonnaise. Refrigerate the mixture, then add the chopped almonds and green coriander.

serves 4 • Preparation: 4–5 mins

Aubergine dip

½ cup thick mayonnaise, ½ cup single cream, a pinch of sugar, 1 aubergine, juice of 1 lemon, 1 hard-boiled egg, 500 g tinned ham, 1 tsp each soya sauce and very hot mustard, 2–3 cloves of garlic, 2 tbsps chopped chives

Bake the aubergine in the oven, then peel it, drain the excess juice on a sieve. Blend it with the garlic, lemon juice, mustard and soya sauce, combine with the finely chopped ham and egg. Fold in the cream and mayonnaise, sprinkle with the chives.

serves 4 • Preparation: 10–15 mins

Banana dip

2 bananas, 1 cup yogurt, ½ cup single cream, 1 tsp honey, 1 tbsp lemon juice, a pinch of each salt, curry powder and cayenne, 3 tbsps finely chopped parsley

Peel the bananas, blend them with the honey, lemon juice, salt, cayenne, curry powder and yogurt. Before serving, mix it with the finely chopped parsley.

serves 4 • Preparation: 4–5 mins

Camembert dip

1 mature Camembert cheese, 3–4 tbsps thick cream, 100 g dry white vermouth, 3–4 tbsps finely chopped chives, a pinch of each salt and pepper

Remove the hard skin from the cheese. Work the cheese, vermouth and cream into a smooth paste, add salt and pepper to taste, mix with the chives.

serves 4 • Preparation: 5–7 mins

Horseradish dip

1 cup yogurt, ½ cup kefir, 2–3 tbsps grated horseradish, 1 tsp mustard, 1 tbsp lemon juice, a pinch of each salt, pepper and sugar, 2 tbsps chopped herbs (lemon balm, mint, borage)

Blend the yogurt with the kefir, mustard, horseradish, lemon juice, sugar, salt and pepper. Mix with the finely chopped herbs.

serves 4 • Preparation: 3–4 mins

Pink horseradish dip

3 largish tomatoes, 1 large tart apple, 1 tbsp capers, 4–5 tbsps grated horseradish, salt, sugar, lemon juice, 2 cups yogurt, 2–3 tbsps sour cream

Blanch and skin the tomatoes, then liquidize and sieve them. Blend with the capers, horseradish, grated apple, lemon juice, cream and yogurt. Add salt and sugar to taste.

serves 4 • Preparation: 4–5 mins

Garlic dip with eggs

3 hard-boiled eggs, 10–12 cloves of garlic, 1 cup mayonnaise, 2 tbsps thick cream, juice of 1 lemon, ¼ tsp grated lemon rind, 50 g ham sausage, salt, pepper, a pinch of sugar, 1 tbsp chopped watercress

Chop the sausage finely. Process it with the egg yolks, crushed garlic with salt, mayonnaise, cream, lemon juice and zest, pepper and sugar until it has turned into a smooth paste. Mix with the finely chopped egg whites and watercress.

serves 4 • Preparation: 5–7 mins

Garlic dip

*1 cup curd cheese, 1 cup mayonnaise, salt,
½ tbsp honey, 3–4 cloves of garlic, 1 tbsp
chopped walnuts, 1 small red pepper*

Process all the ingredients into a smooth paste. Refrigerate.

serves 4 • Preparation: 3–4 mins

Egg dip

*3 hard-boiled eggs, 1 tbsp hot mustard, 3 tbsps
lemon juice, ½ tsp grated lemon rind, salt,
pepper, 1 cup olive oil, 1 tbsp capers, 1 tsp each
finely chopped lemon balm and parsley*

Blend the egg yolks with the mustard, half the capers, salt, pepper, lemon juice and zest. Whisking all the time, gradually pour in the oil. Add the remaining capers, chopped herbs and the finely chopped egg whites. Refrigerate.

serves 4 • Preparation: 5–7 mins

Caraway dip

*1 tbsp caraway seeds, 150 g full-fat curd
cheese, 3 tbsps finely grated cheese, ½ cup
single cream, ½ tsp paprika, salt, pepper*

Scald the caraway seeds, drain them, combine with the curd cheese. Process the mixture together with the cream, grated cheese, salt, pepper and paprika. Refrigerate.

serves 4 • Preparation: 5–7 mins

Cocktail dip

*1 cup yogurt, 1 cup sour cream, ½ cup ketchup,
3–4 tbsps redcurrant jelly, 3 tbsps lemon juice,*

*salt, pepper, ¼ tsp each paprika and curry
powder, 2–3 tbsps finely chopped parsley*

Blend the yogurt, cream and ketchup with the jelly, lemon juice, salt, pepper, paprika and curry powder. Mix in the chopped parsley. Serve with carrot and courgettes cut into thin strips.

serves 4 • Preparation: 4–5 mins

Carrot dip

*½ cup finely grated carrot, 1 tbsp lemon juice,
1 tsp honey, 1 cup mayonnaise, ½ cup single
cream, salt, pepper, 2–3 tbsps pine nuts*

Toast the pine kernels in a hot frying pan. Process half of them with the carrot, cream, honey, lemon juice, salt and pepper until the mixture has turned into a smooth paste. Mix with the mayonnaise and the remaining kernels, then refrigerate.

serves 4 • Preparation: 5–6 mins

Dill dip

*1 cup yogurt, ½ cup whipping cream, 100 g
cream cheese, ¼ tsp each white pepper,
nutmeg and grated lemon rind, 2 tbsps lemon
juice, 2 tbsps linseed, a bunch of dill*

Toast the linseed in a hot frying pan, then blend it with the yogurt, cream, cheese, salt, pepper, nutmeg, lemon zest and juice. Refrigerate. Before serving, mix in the chopped dill.

serves 4 • Preparation: 5–7 mins

Salmon dip

*200 g smoked salmon, 1 tsp vodka, ½ yellow bell
pepper, 2 beef tomatoes, 2 small tart apples, 1 small
onion, 1 tbsp capers, juice of 1 lemon, 1 cup yogurt,
½ cup kefir, 2–3 tbsps thick mayonnaise, salt*

Peel the onion and apples, grate them finely, sprinkle with some lemon juice. Blanch and skin the tomatoes, cut them in half, remove the seeds and dice the flesh. Wash

Carrot dip

the pepper and chop it finely. Cut half the salmon into fine cubes, sprinkle with the vodka. Process the remaining salmon with the capers, onion, apple, mayonnaise, yogurt and kefir. Put in the chopped salmon, tomatoes and paprika, mix well and refrigerate.

serves 4 • Preparation: 5–7 mins

Mint dip I

3 tbsps finely chopped mint, 2 tbsps finely chopped parsley, 1 tbsp grated lemon rind, 1 tbsp lemon juice, a pinch of sugar, 1½ tsps paprika, 1 tbsp soya sauce, 2 tbsps olive oil, 1 cup mayonnaise, 1 tbsp chopped mint

Process 3 tbsps of mint with the parsley, sugar, lemon rind and lemon juice, paprika, olive oil and soya sauce. Cover the bowl and refrigerate for one or two hours. Mix in the mayonnaise and chopped mint.

serves 4 • Preparation: 3–4 mins

Mint dip II

2 cups yogurt, 1 cup finely chopped mint, 1 tsp lemon juice, 1 tbsp chopped walnuts, 2 tbsps chopped chives, salt, a pinch of sugar

Process the yogurt with the mint, walnuts, salt, sugar and lemon juice. Refrigerate for one or two hours. Before serving, mix in chopped chives.

serves 4 • Preparation: 3–4 mins

Almond dip

50 g almonds, 1–2 cloves of garlic crushed with salt, ½ tsp cayenne pepper, 2 beef tomatoes, 3 tbsps red wine vinegar, 1 cup oil

Blanch the almonds, skin them, then toast in a hot frying pan. Scald the tomatoes and skin them. Process the tomatoes, garlic, almonds, vinegar and cayenne, adding gradually olive until the mixture has turned into a thick sauce. Pour into a sauce boat and refrigerate. Serve with fresh vegetables or crackers.

serves 4 • Preparation: 10 mins

Cucumber dip

1 large cucumber, 3–4 tbsps each chopped parsley and dill, 2–3 tbsps lemon juice, 1½ cups yogurt, ½ cup cream, salt, pepper, a pinch of sugar

Peel the cucumber, cut it lengthwise, remove the seeds. Chop it into fine cubes, sprinkle sparingly with salt and leave in a strainer for several minutes. Blend the yogurt with the cream, lemon juice, salt and sugar, refrigerate for a while, then combine with the cucumber, chopped dill and parsley.

serves 4 • Preparation: 8–10 mins

Nut dip

100 g unsalted peanuts, 1 large onion, 2–3 cloves of garlic, 2 tbsps soya sauce, 4 tbsps honey, 3 tbsps oil, 3 tbsps lemon juice, 100 g peanut butter, ½ tsp cayenne pepper, a piece of cinnamon bark, 3 bay leaves, ½ cup water, ¼ cup dry white wine

Blend the wine with the onion, garlic, half the nuts and cayenne into a smooth paste. Heat up the oil in a pan, put in the mixture and stirring all the time fry for 2–3 mins, then add the soya sauce, honey and lemon juice, bay leaves and cinnamon, pour in the boiled water and stirring all the time simmer for 3 mins. Take out the bay leaves and cinnamon, add the remaining nuts and peanut butter, simmer for a bit to make the sauce very thick. Allow it to cool, then refrigerate.

serves 4 • Preparation: 8–10 mins

Fruit dip

1 cup each yogurt and cream, ½ cup kefir, 2 tart apples, 1 pear, juice of 1 lemon, 1 sizeable onion, 3 tbsps chilli sauce, 1 tsp Tabasco, 1 tsp sugar, salt, pepper, 3 tbsps each chopped parsley, dill and chives, 2 tbsps chopped green olives

Peel the apples, pear and onion, grate them finely, sprinkle with lemon juice, then blend with the yogurt, cream and kefir, adding also salt, pepper, sugar, chilli and Tabasco. Mix in the chopped parsley, dill, chives and olives and refrigerate.

serves 4 • Preparation: 4–6 mins

Mushroom dip

100 g button mushrooms, 2 tbsps lemon juice, salt, pepper, 150 g cream cheese, 1 cup each yogurt and kefir, 3–4 tbsps finely chopped walnuts, 2–3 tbsps chopped watercress, 1 tbsp honey, ¼ tsp each grated lemon rind and cayenne pepper

Wash and dry the mushrooms, sprinkle them with lemon juice, salt and pepper, and leave aside for half an hour, then blend them with the cheese, yogurt, kefir, honey and cayenne until the mixture has turned into a smooth paste. Mix in the walnuts and watercress, then refrigerate. Best served with celery sticks.

serves 4 • Preparation: 30 mins

Savoury dip with raisins

100 g raisins, 2 tsps brandy, 1 tbsp honey, 1 tbsp lemon juice, 2 cups yogurt, 1½ tsps Worcestershire sauce, ¼ tsp marjoram, salt

Rinse the raisins, blanch and drain them. Put them in a bowl, sprinkle with brandy and cover. Process the yogurt with the lemon juice, honey, salt, marjoram and Worcestershire sauce. Chill a bit, combine with the raisins, mix thoroughly.

serves 4 • Preparation: 10–15 mins

Orange dip

2 large oranges, 1 cup mayonnaise, 3 tbsps thick cream, 2 tbsps hot mustard, salt, pepper, sugar

Peel the oranges, cut them into slices, remove the pips. Liquidize and sieve them. Mix with salt, pepper, sugar, mustard, mayonnaise and cream, cover and refrigerate. Put the peel from one orange into boiling water for 2–3 mins, then drain it. Remove the white skin, cut the peel into very thin strips. Chop very finely half of the peel, mix it with the sauce. Use the remaining orange strips to garnish the sauce.

serves 4 • Preparation: 8–10 mins

Orange and herb dip

grated rind and juice of 1 orange, 2 tbsps dry white wine, 1 tbsp boiled water, ½ cup olive oil, 2 tbsps each chopped mint, parsley and chives, salt, pepper

Blend the orange juice and rind with the wine, water, salt and pepper, adding gradually the oil in the process until the sauce has thickened. Mix in the chopped herbs, cover and leave for one or two hours on the bottom shelf of the fridge to 'mature'.

serves 4 • Preparation: 5–6 mins

Tomato dip I

½ cup mayonnaise, 2 tbsps thick cream, 3 tbsps ketchup, 5–6 drops of Tabasco, 1 tbsp sweet paprika, 2 beef tomatoes, salt, sugar to taste

Blanch and skin the tomatoes, cut them in half, remove the seeds and chop the flesh finely. Mix the mayonnaise with the paprika, salt, sugar and Tabasco, fold in the cream and ketchup, add the chopped tomatoes. Refrigerate.

serves 4 • Preparation: 5–6 mins

Tomato dip II

1 cup yogurt, 1 cup ketchup, 2 tbsps olive oil, a pinch of each salt, pepper, cayenne and sugar, 1 tbsp lemon juice, 4–5 tbsps finely chopped chives, 3 tbsps pickled green peppercorns

Blend the ketchup, olive and lemon juice, add salt, pepper, cayenne and sugar. Combine with the yogurt, chives and green pepper. Refrigerate.

serves 4 • Preparation: 5–6 mins

Radish dip

2 bunches small pink radishes, 1 bunch chives, 2 cups yogurt, ½ cup cream, salt

Process 1 bunch of radishes with salt, yogurt and cream, chill the mixture. Chop finely the remaining radishes and chives, combine with the sauce, mix thoroughly.

serves 4 • Preparation: 5–7 mins

Cheese and basil dip

*150 g feta cheese, 2 large tomatoes,
4 tbsps finely chopped basil, 1½ cups
yogurt, a pinch of white pepper, salt*

Blanch and skin the tomatoes, cut them into slices, remove the seeds. Process the feta and tomatoes with salt, pepper and 3 tbsps of basil. Pour in the yogurt and blend into a smooth paste. Chill for one or two hours. Before serving, mix in the remaining basil.

serves 4 • Preparation: 5–7 mins

Asparagus dip

*300 g green asparagus (fresh or tinned), 1 tbsp
butter, 1 tbsp lemon juice, salt, sugar, ½ cup
asparagus stock, 2–3 tbsps finely chopped
almonds, 1–2 cloves of garlic crushed with salt,
salt, pepper, paprika, 1 cup mayonnaise*

Boil some water with salt, butter, sugar and lemon juice. Put in the cleaned asparagus and cook for 15 mins, then take it out with a strainer, allow to cool, cut the tips off. Process the stems with the garlic, asparagus stock, pepper and paprika, then chill it. Chop the asparagus tops finely, add them to the sauce together with the almonds and mayonnaise. Mix thoroughly and refrigerate.

serves 4 • Preparation: 20–25 mins

Ham dip

*1 cup yogurt, ½ cup mayonnaise, 1 tbsp each lemon
juice and brandy, 200 g lean smoked ham, salt, pepper*

Put the ham through a mincer or chop it very finely. Mix the yogurt with the mayonnaise, lemon juice, brandy, salt and pepper. Combine the sauce with the ham, refrigerate.

serves 4 • Preparation: 5–7 mins

Herbal dip I

*1 cup yogurt, 100 g curd cheese, 1 tbsp thick cream,
1–2 cloves of garlic crushed with salt, ½ tsp celery-*
*flavoured salt, white pepper, 4 tbsps finely chopped
herbs (basil, savory, thyme, parsley, chives)*

Mix well the cheese with the cream, garlic, celery-flavoured salt and pepper until the mixture has turned into a smooth paste. Add the chopped herbs.

serves 4 • Preparation: 3–4 mins

Herbal dip II

*1 cup yogurt, ½ cup cream, 3 tbsps mayonnaise,
1 onion, 4 tbsps finely chopped herbs
(watercress, borage, chives, dill), salt, pepper*

Blend the cream with the mayonnaise, finely grated onion, salt and pepper. Chill well, then combine with the chopped herbs.

serves 4 • Preparation: 3–4 mins

Mousses

Mousse is a light, cold dish prepared from smoked, boiled or braised fish and also from tinned fish, from shellfish or from game, poultry, meat, smoked meats, or vegetables that have been grated into a smooth paste.

The main additional ingredient is cream or stiffly-beaten egg white, which gives the mousse a lightly frothy consistency, and the main binding agent is gelatine.

The main ingredient is mixed with cream, gelatine, butter etc., after which the mixture is put into a special mould, cooled and then, often after it has been decorated, jelly is poured over it. Finely decorated mousses are a great party piece, while mousses made from left-over fish or meat make an excellent bread spread.

In order to make the mousse the right shape, it should be placed in a mould into which slightly set jelly has been poured, and then left in the refrigerator to set.

A good mousse should have a lightly frothy consistency, and should melt in the mouth.

The taste of a mousse depends on the seasoning. They can be seasoned with herbs, onion, garlic, horseradish or lemon, but none of the ingredients should be allowed to disguise the delicate flavour of the main product.

Small shrimps, boiled quails' eggs, slices of lemon, olives, capers, sprigs of parsley or dill or coloured strips of pepper are excellent for the decoration of mousses set in small moulds.

Mousses should be prepared as follows:
1) the required amount of gelatine should be soaked in a light broth, water or white wine;
2) the main ingredient (fish, meat, smoked meat etc.) should be puréed with 2–3 tablespoons of cream, the gelatine and the additional ingredients given in the recipe; this mixture should be sieved, seasoned and slightly cooled;
3) the cream should be beaten stiff with a pinch of sugar added; and
4) the whipped cream should be gradually added to the setting purée. The first portion of added cream should be beaten in with a whisk, and the rest folded in gradually with a wooden spoon or spatula.

The prepared mixture can be placed in one large mould or in several smaller ones, covered with foil, and put in the fridge for 2–3 hours, or until it has completely set. Before serving, the mousse should be removed from the mould (dipping the mould for 3–4 seconds into hot water makes the task easier) in the following way: cover the mould with a plate and then upturn it so that the mousse comes out. Put the mousse on a serving dish and garnish it.

Cheese mousse

500 g curd cheese, 100 g finely grated sharp-tasting cheese, 1 cup yogurt, 1 large onion, 1 red bell pepper, 2 gherkins, 1 tsp green peppercorns, 30 g gelatine, ¼ cup light stock, salt, ¼ tsp cayenne pepper, a pinch of sugar, parsley, several strips of green, yellow and red bell pepper, several leaves of lettuce

Soak the gelatine in the stock, stir and leave aside. Blend the curd cheese with the yogurt, salt and cayenne into a smooth paste. Add the gelatine and mix well. Chop finely the seeded peppers, the peeled onion and the gherkins.

Add them to the cheese paste together with peppercorns and grated cheese. Rinse a mould with cold water, fold in the paste, put into the fridge for one or two hours until it has set. Line a serving dish with lettuce leaves, transfer the mousse onto them, garnish with pepper strips and parsley sprigs.

serves 4 • Preparation: 25–30 mins

Broccoli mousse

300 g broccoli, ½ tsp each salt, white pepper, grated nutmeg, dried thyme and dried basil, 1 cup cream, ¼ cup stock, 30 g gelatine, 1–2 tbsps water, salt, 1 tbsp butter, 2 cloves of garlic, 1 tbsp lemon juice

Boil some salted water with butter, lemon juice and garlic cloves, put in the broccoli and cook for 10 mins, then drain and allow it to cool. Soak the gelatine in water. Bring the stock to the boil, pour in the dissolved gelatine, stir well and allow to cool. Whip the cream until stiff. Process the broccoli with salt, pepper, nutmeg, thyme and basil, mix in the cool gelatine, then chill the mixture. Add gradually the cream, stir thoroughly. Pour the mixture into a mould, cover with foil and leave in the fridge until it has set (1–2 hours).

serves 4 • Preparation: 20–25 mins

Crab mousse with curd cheese

1 tin (100–150 g) crabs, 1 tbsp lemon juice, 200 g curd cheese, 4 tbsps cream, 1 tsp Worcestershire sauce, salt, pepper, 1 egg, 20 g gelatine, 2–3 tbsps white wine, ½ cup boiled water, several strips of red, yellow or green pepper, parsley sprigs

Soak the gelatine in wine or water. Take the crab meat out, sprinkle with lemon juice. Process the curd cheese with the raw egg yolk, cream, Worcestershire sauce, salt, pepper and crab meat, refrigerate the mixture for a while. Bring the water to the boil, add the soaked gelatine, stir well, allow it to cool. Blend half of the gelatine mixture with the paste, then refrigerate. Pour the remaining gelatine into a mould that has been rinsed with cold water, and leave it to set. Garnish the bottom of the mould with paprika strips and parsley sprigs. Beat the egg white until stiff, fold it gently into the crab and cheese paste. Transfer the mixture to the mould, cover it with foil and put into the fridge until it has set (1–2 hours). Line a serving dish with lettuce leaves, arrange the mousse on top.

serves 4 • Preparation: 20–25 mins

Salmon and crab mousse

100 g smoked salmon, 1 tin (100 g) crab meat, 1 tsp lemon juice, 1 cup cream, 20 g gelatine, 1 glass white wine, 3–4 tbsps water, salt, pepper

Whip the cream. Soak the gelatine in wine. Boil some water, pour over the gelatine, stir well. Process the drained crab meat with the chopped salmon and gelatine, chill the mixture. Add gradually the whipped cream, stirring all the time. Pour into small moulds and put in the fridge for an hour or two. Before serving, transfer to a serving dish and garnish.

serves 4 • Preparation: 15–20 mins

Salmon mousse

2 tins of salmon in brine, 1 cup single cream, 1 glass brandy, 1 cup chicken stock, 2 tbsps tomato paste, juice of ½ lemon, 1 tbsp gelatine, several cocktail gherkins, 2 each black and green olives, salt, pepper, a pinch of salt and grated lemon rind

Drain the salmon, add the brandy, tomato paste, lemon juice, salt and pepper and work it into a smooth paste. Whip the cream with a pinch of sugar, pepper and lemon zest, fold into the salmon paste. Bring the stock to the boil, dissolve the gelatine in it, stir well and allow to cool. Mix ¾ of the gelatine with the salmon paste. Pour several spoons of the remaining gelatine into a mould, taking care that it covers the whole bottom and walls. Put the mould into the fridge for one or two hours until the gelatine has set. Arrange sliced gherkins and olives in the mould, fold in the salmon paste, pour over the remaining gelatine, cover with foil and put into the fridge. Before transferring it onto a serving dish, for 3–4 seconds dip the mould into boiling water. Garnish with pepper strips or cherry tomatoes.

serves 4 • Preparation: 25–30 mins

Salmon and crab mousse

Tomato mousse

*300 g ripe beef tomatoes, 3 tbsps tomato ketchup,
2 tbsps tomato juice, 2 tbsps tomato paste,
a pinch of each salt, sugar and cayenne pepper,
¼ cup cream, 40 g gelatine, 1 cup stock, 1 cup
dry white wine, salt, pepper, sugar to taste*

Blanch and skin the tomatoes, steam them in a pan, then sieve. Mix them well with the ketchup, tomato juice and paste, add salt, sugar and cayenne. Soak the gelatine in wine. Bring the stock to the boil, pour in the gelatine, stir well. Process half the gelatine with the tomato mixture, chill it a bit. Rinse a mould with cold water, pour in the remaining gelatine and leave to set. Whip the cream and fold it gradually into the tomato mixture. Pour the mixture into the mould, cover with foil and put into the fridge for one or two hours to allow it to set. Transfer it to a serving dish and garnish before serving.

serves 4 • Preparation: 20–25 mins

Pike mousse

*1 kg pike, soup vegetables, 1 large onion, 1 bay
leaf, 8–10 peppercorns, 3–4 grains allspice, 1 clove,
1 glass dry white wine, ½ cup cream, 40 g powdered
gelatine, salt, pepper, 1–2 egg whites, 200 g small
tinned or frozen prawns, 1 lemon, parsley sprigs*

Clean the fish, wash it and divide into fillets. Rub the fillets with salt and leave in a cool place for an hour. Make a stock from the vegetables, onion, spices and fish trimmings. Cook it over low heat for 40 mins, then strain it. Put the fillets in a skillet, pour over the stock and simmer over low heat for 20 mins, then set aside to cool down. Soak half the gelatine in 2–3 tbsps of wine. Take out the fillets, remove the bones and skin. Liquidize the fillets together with the soaked gelatine and 2 tbsps of cream. Add salt and pepper to taste. Sieve the mixture, then put into the fridge to set a bit. Whip the remaining cream, then add it gradually to the fish mousse, stirring continuously. Transfer the mousse to small individual moulds and put into the fridge until the mousse has set. Soak the remaining gelatine in 3–4 tbsps of the cold fish stock. Bring the remaining stock to the boil, add the remaining wine and

simmer over low heat for 20 mins, or until 1 cup of stock has been left. Add the mixed egg whites to clarify the stock, mix thoroughly, then strain it and add the gelatine. Heat up (but do not allow it to boil), then leave to cool. Scrub the lemon, scald it with boiling water, dry and cut it into fine slices, remove the pips. Arrange the lemon slices on a serving dish, put the mousse from the individual moulds on top of them. Garnish with prawns, pour over the cool gelatine and return to the fridge until the mousse has set. Before serving, garnish with parsley sprigs.

serves 4 • Preparation: 1½ hrs

Tuna mousse

*2 tins tuna in brine, ½ cup milk, 3 tbsps capers,
3–4 cocktail gherkins, 1–2 tbsps chopped parsley,
1 cup whipping cream, 2 eggs, 1 lemon, 2 tbsps butter,
1 tbsp flour, 1 glass white wine, 20 g gelatine, salt,
pepper, parsley, red bell peppers for garnishing*

Melt the butter in a pan, add the flour and make a roux, dilute it with cold milk and, stirring continuously, simmer over low heat. Add the raw egg yolks, put in the tuna, stir well. Add the capers, 1–2 chopped gherkins and parsley. When the sauce has thickened, take off the heat and leave it to cool. Soak the gelatine in wine. Blend the sauce with the gelatine, add salt, pepper and lemon juice to taste, allow it to cool a bit. Whip the cream and add it gradually to the fish mousse, stirring all the time. Towards the end fold in the whipped egg whites. Transfer to a mould, cover with foil and put into the fridge to set. Decorate a serving dish with lettuce, arrange on top the mousse, garnish with gherkins, strips of red pepper and parsley sprigs.

serves 4 • Preparation: 30–35 mins

Smoked mackerel mousse

*500 g smoked mackerel, 1 glass dry white
wine, 2–3 cloves of garlic, 5 tbsps olive oil, 10 g
gelatine, ½ cup whipping cream, juice and grated
rind of 1 lemon, white pepper, salt, several thin
slices of lemon, several sprigs of parsley*

Soak the gelatine in 2 tbsps of wine. Put the fish in a pan, pour in the remaining wine, cover with boiled water.

Bring to the boil, then cook over low heat for 10 mins. Take off the heat and leave to cool. Take out the fish, remove the bones and skin, add garlic crushed with salt, pepper, lemon juice and zest. Process the mixture together with the soaked gelatine, then gradually add the oil. Refrigerate. Whip the cream and, stirring continuously, add it gradually to the mackerel paste. Transfer the mousse to a mould, cover with foil and put into the fridge. When the mousse has set, take it out of the mould and arrange on a serving dish lined with lettuce leaves. Garnish with parsley sprigs and lemon slices.

serves 4 • Preparation: 25–30 mins

Turkey liver mousse

600 g turkey livers, 2–3 cloves of garlic, 2 tbsps mustard, 5 egg whites, 1 tsp ground dried tarragon, ¼ tsp grated lemon rind, salt, pepper, 2 tbsps butter, 1 tbsp breadcrumbs and ground sunflower seeds

Peel the garlic and crush it with salt. Wash the livers, remove the membranes. Put the livers through a mincer, add the garlic and pepper, tarragon, lemon zest and mustard and work into a smooth paste. Fold in the whipped egg whites. Gently mix the whole. Grease small individual moulds with some butter, dust them with breadcrumbs mixed with ground sunflower seeds. Transfer the paste to the moulds, arrange the moulds in a baking tin filled with water, cover with aluminium foil and put into a hot oven (200°C). Bake for 15 mins, then remove the foil and allow the mousse to brown a bit. Before serving, garnish with parsley sprigs, lemon slices and strips of red, yellow and green peppers.

serves 4 • Preparation: 20–25 mins

Aspic

Today aspic is usually made with powdered gelatine or gelatine in leaves. You simply read the recipe on the packet and you have a ready-made dish. But it is worth knowing that the basis of all savoury dishes in aspic is really home-made stock. The most popular dish of this kind in Old Polish cuisine was calves' foot in aspic. In the reign of King Stanislaus Augustus in the late 18th century, ever more exotic savoury aspic dishes began to appear along with the fashion for French cuisine.

From the 19th century this name covered not only stock prepared from calves' feet or knuckles or from pigs' trotters, but also any kind of dish chilled in it. There were therefore aspics made from chicken liver, brains, tongue, fish, vegetables or even mushrooms, decorated with green herbs, slices of fruit and hard-boiled egg, gherkins, crayfish etc. They were often made in small decoratively fluted moulds and when taken out and placed on a serving dish formed an exceptionally colourful and tasty part of a cold buffet.

Home-made aspic is best prepared from calves' feet or pigs' trotters, from chicken cooked together with the feet, wings and neck, or from fish heads and bones.

A well-prepared calves' foot aspic requires no additional gelatine; stock made from chicken or fish usually needs gelatine added. A good aspic should be clear and not too hard when it is set. It can be coloured brown with caramel or onion skins boiled in the stock, or rose pink with beetroot juice, or green with spinach, or golden yellow with a few filaments of saffron or with carrot juice. You can improve its taste by adding wine: malaga or port is best, or dry white wine for a fish aspic.

Home-made aspic

800 g calves' feet, soup vegetables, 1 unpeeled onion with a clove stuck in it, 1–2 cloves of garlic, 2 bay leaves, 5–7 grains each allspice and pepper, grated rind of 1 lemon, 2–3 sprigs of each parsley, dill and thyme, salt, 1 egg white

Put the calves' feet into a pan, cover with 2 litres of hot water, add the washed and peeled vegetables, onion, spices, herbs, garlic and lemon rind. Bring to the boil, then cover and simmer over low heat for 3–4 hours. Remove the scum while it is cooking. Strain the stock, bring it again to the boil. Add the egg white mixed with 1 tbsp of cold water, put the liquid through a fine strainer, then allow it to cool and remove the fat on the surface. You may store the aspic in the fridge and use it whenever you need it.

Eggs in aspic

8 small hard-boiled eggs, 4 slices of tinned ham,
1 cup cooked green peas, 2 pieces of pickled red
pepper, 3–4 cocktail gherkins, 2–3 cobs of baby corn,
4 cups strong stock, 2 tbsps gelatine, salt, pepper,
1 tbsp lemon juice, 2 onions, 1 bay leaf, 2–3 grains
each pepper and allspice, 1 clove, a pinch of thyme

Soak the gelatine in 4–5 tbsps of cold stock. Bring the remaining stock to the boil, add the onion, spices and thyme, cover the pan and cook for 5–8 mins. Then strain it, add the lemon juice, pour the gelatine, stir well and take off the heat. Put the peas into a mould, pour over 1 cup of the aspic and leave till it has set a bit. Put on top the eggs and again pour over some gelatine, and when this has set, arrange decoratively pieces of ham and gherkins and repeat the whole process. Finally arrange on top pieces of pepper and corn cobs, pour the remaining gelatine and leave to set (preferably overnight). Turn the aspic out, put on a serving dish lined with lettuce leaves, garnish with parsley sprigs and lemon slices. Serve with some savoury sauce or with lemon juice.

serves 4–6 • Preparation: 15–20 mins

Eggs in aspic

Colourful wreath

*20 quail eggs, 20 cherry tomatoes, 1 tbsp
capers, 4 tbsps tinned sweetcorn, a bunch
of dill, 2 cups strong chicken stock, 2 tbsps
gelatine, salt, pepper, ½ cup soya sauce*

Hard-boil the quail eggs, cool them under cold water,
remove the shells. Put 10 eggs into a pan, pour over
the soya sauce and cook over low heat for 10 mins. Leave
aside to cool down. Soak the gelatine in 2 tbsps of boiled
cold water and leave it aside. Bring the stock to the boil,
pour in the gelatine. Stir and bring to the boil again, then
take off the heat. Pour 2–3 tbsps of the gelatine stock into
small bowls and leave to set. Arrange decoratively some
white and brown eggs and dill sprigs in each bowl, pour
over some gelatine stock. When the stock has set, put
some sweetcorn on top and cover with more gelatine
stock. When this has set, arrange cherry tomatoes and
capers, and pour over the remaining gelatine. Cover the
bowls with foil and put into the fridge. Then take the contents out of the bowls and put in a serving dish lined with
lettuce leaves. Garnish with parsley sprigs and lemon slices. Separately serve savoury horseradish or green sauce.

serves 4–6 • Preparation: 30–40 mins

Coloured fish in aspic

*2 cups fish stock, 1 tbsp gelatine (you will not need
it if you use enough fish heads and tails for the
stock), 1 tbsp lemon juice, flesh taken out of the fish
heads and tails, 4 hard-boiled quail eggs, ½ each
red and yellow bell peppers, 2 tbsps chopped dill*

Bring the stock with the lemon juice to the boil, mix in the
gelatine and leave to cool a bit, then add the dill. Shell
the eggs and cut them into quarters. Blanch the peppers in
boiling water for 3–4 mins, then strain them and cut in thin
strips. Take small bowls, pour in a bit of the stock, put in the
egg quarters and leave the aspic to set. Pour more stock,
arrange layers of the fish flesh and pepper, pour over the remaining stock and leave to set. Garnish with lemon slices.

serves 4 • Preparation: 20–30 mins

Vegetables in aspic

*200 g each kohlrabi, carrots, cauliflower,
asparagus and green peas, 100 g button
mushrooms, 2 tbsps butter, salt, sugar, juice
and grated rind of 1 lemon, 2 hard-boiled
eggs, 1 pickled red pepper, 3 cups chicken
or vegetable stock, 20–30 g gelatine*

Peel the carrot and kohlrabi, wash them and cut into
cubes, strips, etc. Wash the mushrooms and cut them
into quarters. Melt the butter in a pan, add the mushrooms, sauté them, add the kohlrabi and carrot. Sprinkle
with salt, pepper and lemon zest and stir. Pour in the hot
stock, bring to the boil, lower the heat, add the cleaned
asparagus cut into pieces, cauliflower florets and green
peas. Cover the pan and cook for 15 mins, then add the
lemon juice and sugar, salt and pepper to taste, and allow to cool. Drain the crisp vegetables on a sieve. Dissolve the gelatine in 2–3 tbsps of cold water, combine
it with the stock, stir well and leave to cool. Take small
bowls, pour several tablespoons of the stock into each
and allow it to set. Then arrange the vegetables, garnish
with hard-boiled egg slices and pepper strips, pour over
the remaining stock and leave to set. Serve with some
savoury sauce.

serves 4–6 • Preparation: 20–25 mins

Chicken in aspic

*chicken meat, vegetables, 2 cups
savoury stock, 2 tbsps gelatine*

Removed the bones and skin from the cooked chicken.
Clean 1 celery stick, half a pepper and 1 carrot, wash
them and cut into cubes. Soak the gelatine in 1 cup of cold
stock. Bring the remaining stock to the boil, pour in the
gelatine and bring to the boil, stirring continuously. Take
off the heat and allow to cool. Take small bowls, pour in
2–3 tbsps of stock into each. When the aspic has set, put
in layers of meat and vegetables. Pour over the remaining
stock and leave to set.

serves 4 • Preparation: 20–30 mins

Chicken in aspic

Spreads and pastes

Spreads and pastes are both for making canapés and sandwiches of various kinds and for decorative purposes. They can be prepared from a variety of products which go together in taste and colour.

They can also be served as an excellent addition to jacket potatoes, as filling in pancakes or as stuffing for vegetables (tomatoes, cucumbers, peppers, celery, chicory).

The chilled paste can be placed in a bowl and decorated with coloured peppers, cocktail gherkins, sweetcorn, tomatoes, pickled mushrooms, olives, capers, dill, and parsley. Its appearance should tickle the taste buds. At a party or other special occasion, pastes are best served with raw vegetables. 'Boats' made from chicory leaves or celery stalks filled with paste look beautiful. Tomatoes and cucumbers stuffed with paste are a high point in any cold buffet, as are stuffed peppers, which can be served in various ways. The tail of the pepper pod should be carefully cut off, the seeds removed, and the shell should be rinsed and dried, filled with paste, chilled well and then cut into slices with a sharp knife and placed on a serving dish lined with lettuce leaves. Halves of pepper in various colours can also be filled with paste.

Herbal spreads

Angelica and mint spread

1 cup angelica leaves, 1 cup young mint leaves, 1 tbsp lemon juice, ¼ tsp grated lemon rind, 2–3 tbsps thick mayonnaise, 2–3 tbsps finely chopped hazelnuts

Wash and dry the angelica and mint leaves, then process them with the nuts, lemon juice and zest. Add the mayonnaise, mix thoroughly and refrigerate before serving.

serves 4 • Preparation: 3–4 mins

Apple and dill spread

2 tart apples, juice and grated rind of 1 lemon, 3 tbsps freshly grated horseradish, 2 tsps chopped dill, 1 tbsp finely chopped young horseradish leaves, 1 tbsp mustard, 1 tbsp cream cheese, 6–7 tbsps thick cream, 1 tsp caster sugar, salt

Peel the apples, grate them finely, combine with the grated horseradish, lemon juice and zest. Add sugar, salt, mustard, cream cheese and cream. Mix thoroughly and refrigerate. Before serving, add chopped horseradish leaves and dill.

serves 4 • Preparation: 5–7 mins

Curd cheese paste with mustard seeds

250 g curd cheese, 2 tbsps butter, 3 tbsps thick cream, 1 tbsp ground mustard seeds, 3 tbsps chopped mustard leaves, 1 tsp lemon juice, a pinch of sugar, salt

Cream the butter with the lemon juice, mustard seeds and cream. Stirring all the time, gradually add the curd cheese. Add salt and a pinch of sugar to taste, mix in the chopped mustard leaves. Recommended in particular as bread spread and with boiled or baked potatoes.

serves 4 • Preparation: 8–10 mins

Green spread

1 cup young mustard sprigs, 1 clove of garlic, 1 small onion, 1 tbsp lemon juice, 1–2 tbsps olive oil, a pinch of each salt and sugar

Process the chopped onion and garlic with the remaining ingredients. Refrigerate before serving.

serves 4 • Preparation: 5–7 mins

Curd cheese spread with thyme and basil

200 g curd cheese, 2 tbsps yogurt, ½ tsp each lemon juice and soya sauce, a pinch of each salt, sugar and white pepper, 1 tsp each finely chopped thyme and basil leaves, ½ tsp finely chopped marjoram leaves

Blend the curd cheese with the yogurt, lemon juice and soya sauce, add salt, pepper and sugar to taste. Mix in the chopped herbs and refrigerate.

serves 4 • Preparation: 5–6 mins

Vegetable and fruit spreads

Aubergine spread

1 large aubergine, 2 tbsps yogurt, 2 tbsps olive oil, 2–3 crushed cloves of garlic, juice of 1 lemon, 1 tbsp chopped basil, salt, pepper

Rinse and dry the augerbine, cut it lengthwise in two, sprinkle with oil and bake in a preheated oven. Allow it to cool, then peel it and process together with the remaining oil, yogurt, garlic and lemon juice. Add salt and pepper to taste. Mix in the basil leaves and refrigerate.

serves 4 • Preparation: 20–25 mins

Peach spread

2 ripe peaches, 200 g curd cheese, 1 tsp paprika, 2 tsps curry powder, ½ cup cream, 1 glass port or sherry, ½ tsp each salt and white pepper

Blanch and skin the peaches, remove the stones. Process one peach with the cheese, cream and wine, add paprika, curry powder and pepper. Chop the other peach finely, add to the paste and refrigerate. Before serving, garnish with parsley sprigs.

serves 4 • Preparation: 5–7 mins

Devilled caviar

1 large garlic bulb, 1 large onion, 4–5 tbsps finely chopped parsley, 1 tin (70 g) of tomato paste, 2 tbsps olive oil, salt, pepper, a pinch of sugar

Chop the garlic finely, mix with salt, pepper, sugar and oil. Combine with the finely chopped onion and tomato paste. Add the chopped parsley and mix thoroughly.

serves 4 • Preparation: 5–7 mins

Mushroom caviar

50 g dried cep mushrooms, 5–6 cloves of garlic, salt, pepper, 2–4 tbsps mayonnaise, 1 hard-boiled egg, parsley

Rinse the mushrooms and leave them to soak overnight in a small amount of boiled water. Cook the mushrooms in the same water, reduce the stock, then process together the garlic crushed with salt. Add pepper and fold in the mayonnaise. Refrigerate. Garnish with parsley sprigs, sprinkle on top chopped hard-boiled egg.

serves 4 • Preparation: 30–40 mins

Pea spread with marjoram

1 cup split peas, 3 cups water, ¼ tsp each sugar and dried savory, salt, 1–2 cloves of garlic, 2 tbsps lemon juice, 2 tbsps linseed, 2 tbsps grated onion, 2 tbsps oil, ¼ tsp dried marjoram

Rinse the peas, cover with 3 cups of water and leave to soak overnight. Add sugar and savory and cook over very low heat. Add salt when the peas are ready. Reduce the stock a bit, then process the peas together with the garlic, lemon juice, marjoram and grated onion. Toast the linseed in a hot frying pan, grind it and add to the paste. Stir well, add salt and pepper to taste, then refrigerate. Use it as bread spread, sprinkled with chopped chives, parsley and soured cucumber.

serves 4 • Preparation: 30–40 mins

Spreads

Bean spread with celeriac

1 cup beans, 2–3 cups water, ¼ tsp each sugar and dried savory, salt, 3–4 tbsps finely grated celeriac, 1 tbsp grated onion, 2–3 tbsps mayonnaise, salt, pepper

Rinse the beans, cover with boiled water and leave overnight. Cook it over low heat, with sugar and savory. Add salt when the beans are tender. Reduce the stock, then process the beans, mix with the mayonnaise, onion and celeriac. Add salt and pepper to taste.

serves 4 • Preparation: 30–40 mins

Red bean spread

100 g red beans, 1 large onion, 3–4 tbsps chopped walnuts, salt, pepper, 2 tbsps each chopped coriander and parsley, 1 tbsp butter

Rinse the beans and soak them in water overnight. Cook them, reduce the stock, then process with the chopped onion, coriander, parsley, butter, salt and pepper. Mix in the chopped walnuts, garnish with parsley sprigs.

serves 4 • Preparation: 30–40 mins

String bean spread

250 g string beans (fresh or frozen), a pinch of each sugar and pepper, 1 tbsp lemon juice, salt, 1 large onion, ¼ small celeriac, 2 hard-boiled eggs, 2–3 tbsps olive oil, 2 tbsps chopped walnuts, salt

Bring water to the boil, add salt, sugar, pepper and lemon juice. Put in the string beans and cook until tender. Drain them, then process together with 2–3 tbsps of the stock. Fry the finely chopped onion in oil without browning it. Add the finely chopped celeriac and stir fry for a minute or two. Chop finely the hard-boiled eggs, combine with the bean paste, onion, celeriac and nuts. Stir thoroughly, add some salt to taste and refrigerate. Serve on lettuce leaves, garnished with slices of hard-boiled egg and halves of walnuts.

serves 4 • Preparation: 30–40 mins

Apple spread

2 tart apples, 1 tsp lemon juice, 1 large onion, ½ tsp salt, 300 g curd cheese, 2 tbsps cream, 1 tbsp chopped chives

Process the curd cheese with the cream, salt and finely chopped onion. Peel the apples, grate them finely, sprinkle with lemon juice. Fold into the cheese paste, refrigerate. Before serving, sprinkle with chopped chives.

serves 4 • Preparation: 5–7 mins

Apple spread with celery

2 tart apples, 3 celery sticks, 4 tbsps chopped walnuts, 2 tbsps lemon juice, 1 tbsp honey, salt, pepper, a pinch of cinnamon, 2 tbsps kefir

Peel the apples, grate them finely, sprinkle with lemon juice. Peel the celery stems. Chop finely 1 celery stick, combine with 2 tbsps of finely chopped walnuts. Process the remaining celery together with the apples, 2 tbsps of walnuts, honey, salt, pepper, cinnamon and kefir. Fold in the chopped celery and walnut mixtures, refrigerate.

serves 4 • Preparation: 10 mins

Carrot spread with celeriac

1 cup grated carrot, ¼ cup each finely grated celeriac and tart apple, 1 tbsp lemon juice, 2–3 tbsps finely chopped green pepper, 1 tbsp finely chopped cucumber, 1 tbsp thick mayonnaise, 25 g cream cheese, a pinch of each pepper and sugar, salt, 1 tsp ground linseed

Combine all the ingredients, mix them thoroughly and refrigerate.

serves 4–6 • Preparation: 10 mins

Pepper spread

1 each red and yellow pepper, 1 aubergine, 1 large onion, 1–2 tbsps oil, salt, pepper

Rinse the peppers and aubergine and bake in a hot oven for 40 mins. Peel and skin them when they get cool, remove the seeds from the peppers. Peel the onion and grate it finely. Process it together with the peppers and aubergine, adding gradually the oil. Add salt and pepper to taste, refrigerate.

serves 4–6 • Preparation: 5 mins

Mushroom spread with sesame seeds

*400 g button mushrooms, 2 tbsps olive oil,
3 tsps ground coriander, 2 bay leaves, 2–3 cloves
of garlic, 1 orange, 1 tsp grated lemon rind,
salt, pepper, 2 tbsps sesame seeds, 2 tbsps
chopped coriander leaves or parsley*

Rinse and dry the mushrooms, slice them. Heat up the oil in a pan, add the bay leaves, ground coriander and crushed garlic, stir. Put in the mushrooms and, stirring all the time, fry for 5–6 mins, then leave them to cool. Remove the bay leaves. Squeeze out the juice from the orange. Take off the orange peel, put it into boiling water for 2–3 mins, drain, and cut some of it into thin strips and chop (1 tsp) the rest finely. Toast the sesame seeds in a hot frying pan. Process the mushrooms with salt, pepper, lemon zest, 1 tsp of sesame seeds and orange juice. Mix in the remaining sesame seeds, the chopped orange rind and green coriander or parsley. Before serving, garnish with strips of orange peel.

serves 4–8 • Preparation: 15 mins

Mushroom spread with egg

*400 g mushrooms, 2 tbsps oil, 1 large
onion, 1 hard-boiled egg, salt, pepper, ¼ tsp
dried or fresh thyme, 1 tbsp butter*

Chop the onion and mushrooms finely, fry them in hot oil, reduce, then allow to cool. Process them together with the egg and butter, add salt, pepper and thyme, refrigerate.

serves 4–8 • Preparation: 10 mins

Watercress spread

*5 hard-boiled eggs, 1 small onion, 100 g butter,
1 tsp lemon juice, salt, white pepper, a pinch of
sugar, 4–5 tbsps finely chopped watercress*

Peel the onion and grate it finely. Cream the butter with salt, pepper, sugar and lemon juice, gradually adding the egg yolks. Mix in the finely chopped egg whites and watercress, season to taste, refrigerate. Serve in a bowl or pipe it into various shapes onto lettuce leaves.

serves 4–6 • Preparation: 15 mins

Herbal spread

*1 cup mayonnaise, 2 tbsps each finely chopped
onion, red bell pepper, parsley and dill, 1 tbsp
ground linseed, 1 tsp each finely chopped basil,
marjoram and chervil, salt, 1 tbsp lemon juice*

Combine all the ingredients, mix thoroughly, refrigerate.

serve 4–6 • Preparation: 10 mins

Curd cheese spreads

Cheese pastes for sandwiches should be moist, for they are then easy to spread: the more fat they contain, the easier they spread. The best way to make curd cheese spread is adding fresh cream to it. Remember that the cheese should be carefully crumbled and creamed, with no lumps. When ingredients containing a lot of water are added to cheese pastes (cucumbers, tomatoes, radishes), they should be sliced and then lightly drained on a strainer, and should be added at the last moment.

Piquant nut spread

*250 g curd cheese, 100 g thick mayonnaise,
100 g finely chopped walnuts, ½ each green
yellow and red pepper, 500 g raisins, 5–6 drops of
Tabasco, ¼ tsp cayenne pepper, salt, white pepper*

Blanch the raisins, drain them on a sieve. Whisk the curd cheese with salt, pepper, cayenne, Tabasco and mayonnaise, add the raisins, finely chopped peppers and walnuts. Transfer to a serving bowl, garnish with pepper strips and walnut halves.

serves 4–6 • Preparation: 10–15 mins

Beer spread

250 g cottage cheese, 4 tbsps butter, 1 onion,
¼ tsp cayenne pepper, 1 tsp caraway seeds, salt,
pepper, a pinch of sugar, ½ cup lager beer

Blend the cheese with the butter, beer, salt, pepper, cayenne and sugar. Mix in the finely chopped onion and caraway seeds, then refrigerate. Garnish before serving.

serves 4 • Preparation: 10 mins

Redcurrant spread

150 g curd cheese, ¼ cup single cream, 4 tbsps
redcurrant jelly, 2 tbsps grated horseradish,
2 tbsps orange juice, 1 tsp grated orange
rind, 1 tsp honey, salt, cayenne pepper

Blend the cheese with the horseradish and redcurrants, add the orange juice and zest, mix well. Add some salt and cayenne to taste.

serves 4 • Preparation: 5 mins

Celery paste

250 g curd cheese, 100 g Roquefort, 1 cup
yogurt, 2 celery sticks, 3–4 tbsps chopped
walnuts, 1 tbsps chopped chives, salt, pepper

Peel the celery, chop it finely. Blend the curd cheese with the Roquefort and yogurt into a smooth paste, mix with the celery, walnuts and chives, add salt and pepper to taste and refrigerate. Transfer to a serving bowl, garnish with walnut halves and strips of red pepper. You may also use the paste for filling celery sticks.

serves 4–6 • Preparation: 10 mins

Vitamin spread

250 g curd cheese, 5 tbsps double cream,
1 small onion, 1 red pepper, 1 pickled cucumber,
5 radishes, several drops of Tabasco, salt

Chop finely the radishes, peeled cucumber and cleaned pepper. Grate the onion, blend it with the cheese, cream, salt and Tabasco. Add the chopped vegetables, mix thoroughly and refrigerate.

serves 4 • Preparation: 10 mins

Linseed spread

200 g curd cheese, 2–3 tbsps yogurt, 2 tbsps
each finely chopped onion, red pepper
and celery, salt, 1 tsp ground linseed

Process the cheese with the yogurt, salt, linseed and grated onion. Combine with the pepper and celery, refrigerate.

serves 4 • Preparation: 10 mins

Watercress spread

200 g curd cheese, ½ cup each finely chopped walnuts,
watercress and finely grated carrot, salt, 2–4 tbsps cream

Process the cheese with the cream, carrot, salt and walnuts. Add the watercress and refrigerate.

serves 4–6 • Preparation: 10 mins

Apricot spread

200 g curd cheese, 2 tbsps cream, ½ cup chopped
walnuts, 150 g dried apricots, 1 tbsp lemon juice, 1 tbsp
dry white wine, caster sugar, salt, white pepper

Rinse the apricots, chop them finely, sprinkle with lemon juice and wine, then with sugar. Process the cheese with the walnuts and cream, add salt and pepper, combine with the apricots, mix well and refrigerate.

serves 4–8 • Preparation: 10 mins

Salmon spread

250 g curd cheese, ½ cup whipping cream,
a pinch of sugar, 150 g smoked salmon,
white pepper, salt, 1 tbsp chopped dill

Chop the salmon finely. Whip the cream with a pinch of sugar, blend with the cheese, salt and pepper. Add the salmon and mix thoroughly, then refrigerate. Sprinkle with dill before serving.

serves 4 • Preparation: 10 mins

Sardine spread

*250 g curd cheese, ½ cup whipping cream,
a pinch of each sugar, salt and pepper, 1 tbsp
ketchup, 1 small tin sardines, chives*

Process the cheese with the cream, salt, pepper, sugar and ketchup, put in the sardines together with the oil, blend them together. Transfer to a serving bowl, refrigerate, then garnish with chopped chives.

serves 4 • Preparation: 10 mins

Caraway spread

*250 g cottage cheese, 2 tbsps cream,
2 tsps ground caraway, 1 tsp caraway seeds,
1 onion, 1–2 cloves of garlic, ½ tsp paprika, salt,
a pinch of cayenne pepper, 1 tomato,
several sprigs of dill*

Grate the onion finely, crush the garlic with salt. Process the cheese, onion, garlic, cream, ground caraway, paprika, sugar and cayenne until it has turned into a smooth paste. Combine with the caraway seeds, garnish with tomato and dill.

serves 4 • Preparation: 10 mins

Herbal paste

*250 g curd cheese, ½ cup yogurt, 2 hard-boiled eggs,
1 tbsp olive oil, juice of 1 lemon, ¼ tsp grated lemon
rind, salt, ½ tsp each ground white pepper and sugar,
2 tbsps each chopped parsley and chives,
1 tbsp chopped tarragon, 1 tsp each
chopped basil and lemon balm, several
lemon balm leaves, 2 small tomatoes*

Blend the cheese with the yogurt. Process the egg yolks with the oil, lemon juice and zest, salt, pepper, sugar and cheese. Add the greens, mix thoroughly, chill a bit. Before serving, sprinkle with the finely chopped egg whites, garnish with lemon balm leaves and tomato quarters.

serves 4–6 • Preparation: 10 mins

Bryndza spreads

Bryndza is an ewe's milk cheese, stored in salt water, with a strong flavour. In Poland, it is produced in the Carpathian Mountains.

Bean spread

*200 g bryndza, 100 g cooked beans, ¼ tsp
cayenne pepper, 2 tbsps butter, 1 tbsp soya oil,
salt, 2–3 sprigs of parsley, 2 small tomatoes*

Process the beans with the oil, butter and bryndza, add salt and cayenne, refrigerate. Before serving, garnish with tomato quarters and parsley sprigs.

serves 4 • Preparation: 10 mins

'Awanturka' spread

*150 g bryndza, 50 g Roquefort, 50 g cottage cheese,
1 tin sardines, 1 tsp butter, paprika, caraway seeds,
1 soured cucumber, 2 tbsps chopped chives*

Blend the sardines, including oil, with the crumbled Roquefort and cottage cheese into a smooth paste. Add the butter and bryndza, mix in the finely chopped cucumber and chives.

serves 4 • Preparation: 10 mins

Onion spread

*150 g bryndza, 1 tbsp butter, 1 egg yolk, 1 onion,
5 tbsps cream, 1 tsp paprika, 2 tbsps each
chopped chives and red and yellow peppers*

Process the bryndza with the paprika, egg yolk, butter and cream, mix with the finely chopped onion, refrigerate. Before serving, sprinkle with chopped chives and peppers.

serves 4 • Preparation: 10 mins

Pastes from blue cheese and hard cheeses

Horseradish spread

200 g Roquefort, 1 tbsp yogurt, 3 tbsps thick mayonnaise, 5–6 drops of Tabasco, 1 tbsp grated horseradish, 1 small onion, 100 g fine salami slices, 2 tbsps chopped walnuts, 5–6 cocktail gherkins

Process the cheese with the mayonnaise, yogurt, grated onion, horseradish and Tabasco. Cut the salami slices into thin strips, chop the gherkins into fine cubes, and together with the chopped walnuts add them to the cheese spread. Mix thoroughly.

serves 4–6 • Preparation: 10 mins

Paste with capers

100 g Roquefort, 300 g curd cheese, 3 tbsps cream, 2 tbsps capers, 1–2 cloves of garlic, salt, pepper, 1 tbsp lemon juice, 2–3 tbsps chopped dill, 2 beef tomatoes

Blanch and skin the tomatoes, chop them finely, remove the seeds. Process the Roquefort with the curd cheese, cream, lemon juice, salt, pepper, garlic and capers. Add the tomatoes and dill, mix thoroughly, refrigerate. Garnish before serving.

serves 4 • Preparation: 10 mins

Walnut spread

250 g Roquefort, 4 tbsps cream, 2 tbsps chopped walnuts, 3 tbsps chopped chives, several walnut halves for garnishing

Blend the cheese and cream into a smooth paste, add the chopped walnuts and chives. Decorate with walnut halves, refrigerate. Serve on lettuce leaves.

serves 4 • Preparation: 10 mins

Camembert spread

250 g Camembert, 70 g butter, 1 tsp paprika, ½ tsp ground caraway seeds, 2–3 tbsps finely chopped parsley, 1 small onion, ¼ tsp white pepper

Blend the Camembert with the finely chopped onion, pepper, paprika and caraway. Refrigerate. Sprinkle with parsley before serving.

serves 4–6 • Preparation: 10 mins

Camembert spread with almonds

120 g Camembert, 100 g butter, salt, pepper, 3 tbsps finely chopped almonds, 1 tsp lemon juice

Remove the skin from the soft, mature cheese. Process the Camembert with the lemon juice, salt, pepper, butter and half the chopped almonds. Toast the remaining almonds until golden brown. Transfer the paste to a serving bowl, sprinkle with the toasted almonds.

serves 4 • Preparation: 10 mins

Walnut and cheese spread

200 g curd cheese, 75 g grated Cheddar, 2 tbsps thick cream, 1 tsp each mustard and ground caraway seeds, 4 tbsp grated wholemeal bread, 4 tbsps finely chopped walnuts, 3 tbsps butter, salt, pepper, lemon, parsley, 3–4 walnuts

Blend the curd cheese with the butter and cream. Add the chopped walnuts, grated Cheddar, bread, mustard, caraway, salt and pepper. Put into a serving bowl, cover and refrigerate. Before serving, decorate with walnut halves, lemon slices and parsley sprigs.

serves 4–6 • Preparation: 15 mins

Emmental spread with rosemary

250 g Emmental cheese, 200 g butter, a pinch of dried rosemary, 4 small pickled baby cobs, 10 pepper stuffed olives, 1 clove of garlic, 1 tsp each chopped dill, chives, parsley and green pepper, salt

ream the butter until foamy. Process it with the grated cheese, garlic crushed with salt and rosemary. Chop finely the corn cobs and olives. Add them to the paste together with the green pepper and chopped greens, mix thoroughly. Refrigerate for one or two hours.

serves 6–8 • Preparation: 15 mins

Egg spreads

Pink spread

4 hard-boiled eggs, 2 tbsps mayonnaise, 2 tbsps tomato paste, salt, pepper, sugar, 2 celery sticks

ix the mayonnaise with the tomato paste, salt, pepper and sugar. Peel the celery, chop it finely, combine with the chopped eggs and add to the sauce. Garnish with celery leaves.

serves 4 • Preparation: 10 mins

Ham spread

4 hard-boiled eggs, 100 g lean ham, 2 tbsps chopped parsley, 1 tsp hot mustard, 2–3 tbsps thick mayonnaise, salt, pepper

lend the egg yolks with the salt, pepper, mustard and mayonnaise into a smooth paste. Chop finely the egg whites and ham, combine with the chopped parsley and add to the sauce, mix thoroughly.

serves 4–6 • Preparation: 10 mins

Pepper spread

4 hard-boiled eggs, 3 tbsps mayonnaise, 1 tsp brandy, 2 tbsps butter, 2 tbsps marinated green peppercorns

rocess the egg yolks with the mayonnaise, butter, salt, half the green peppercorns and brandy. When the

paste is smooth, add the finely chopped egg whites and the remaining green peppercorns.

serves 4 • Preparation: 10 mins

Sardine spread

4 hard-boiled eggs, 1 tin sardines, 1 small onion, salt, pepper, 2–3 tbsps mayonnaise, 1 tbsps each chopped chives and chopped red and yellow bell peppers

rumble the sardines. Blend with the oil, egg yolks, mayonnaise, salt and pepper. When the paste is smooth, add the finely chopped egg whites, onion, chives and peppers. Refrigerate. Before serving, garnish with parsley sprigs and strips of red and yellow peppers.

serves 4–6 • Preparation: 10 mins

Green spread with tuna

4 hard-boiled eggs, 1 small tin tuna, 100 g spinach, 1 clove of garlic, 2 tbsps chopped parsley, salt, pepper, 1 tbsp lemon juice, 2–3 tbsps mayonnaise

inse the spinach. Blanch it in salted boiling water for one or two minutes, then sieve it. Blend it with lemon juice, garlic crushed with salt and tuna. Put in the finely chopped egg whites, mix well, refrigerate. Before serving, sprinkle with chopped parsley.

serves 4–6 • Preparation: 10 mins

Fish spreads

Anchovy spread

100 g anchovies or 2–3 tbsps anchovy paste, 2 hard-boiled eggs, 150 g butter, 3–4 cocktail gherkins, 1 tbsps capers, a pinch of each pepper and sugar, 1 tsp hot mustard, 1 tbsp lemon juice

hop finely the egg whites, capers, gherkins and parsley. Blend the egg yolks with the butter, mustard, lemon juice and anchovies. Combine with the chopped eggs, capers, gherkins and parsley, season to taste, mix thoroughly and refrigerate.

serves 4 • Preparation: 10 mins

Smoked trout spread

200 g smoked trout, 4 hard-boiled eggs, 1 tbsp butter, salt, pepper, 1 tbsp lemon juice, 1 tbsp Worcestershire sauce, 2 tbsps mayonnaise

Remove the skin and bones from the fish. Process the fish flesh with the egg yolks, butter, salt, pepper and lemon juice. Add the finely chopped egg whites, mayonnaise and Worcestershire sauce, mix thoroughly and refrigerate.

serves 4–6 • Preparation: 10 mins

Salmon spread

300 g smoked salmon, 3 beef tomatoes, 3 onions, 1 tbsp mayonnaise, a pinch of salt and pepper

Blanch and skin the tomatoes. Chop the peeled onion into cubes. Process the salmon, onion and tomatoes with the mayonnaise, salt and pepper. Refrigerate.

serves 4 • Preparation: 10 mins

Sprat spread

1 tin smoked sprats, 3 processed cheese cubes, 1 onion, 1 tbsp lemon juice, pepper, 2–3 tbsps finely chopped chives

Process the cheese with the sprats in oil, lemon juice and finely chopped onion, season with pepper. Combine with the chopped chives, refrigerate.

serves 4 • Preparation: 10 mins

Herring spread with apples

300 g herring fillets, 400 g tart apples, 125 g butter, a pinch of sugar, 2 tbsps chopped dill

Peel and core the apples. Put them through a mincer together with the herring, then process with the butter and sugar, season with cayenne pepper to taste. Chill the spread. Garnish with chopped dill before serving.

serves 6–8 • Preparation: 15 mins

Herring spread with bread

2 salted herrings, 2–3 onions, 2–3 slices of wheat bread without crust, ½ cup wine vinegar, 4–5 tbsps oil, 3 hard-boiled eggs, 2–3 cocktail gherkins, 3–4 pitted olives, several sprigs of parsley

Soak the herrings in water, then remove the skin and bones. Chop the flesh finely or put it through a mincer. Put the bread into a bowl, pour over the vinegar and leave aside for several minutes. Squeeze out the excess liquid from the bread. Process the bread with the finely chopped onion, herring, 2 hard-boiled eggs, salt, pepper and oil. Refrigerate, then put into a serving bowl and garnish with egg slices, gherkins and olives.

serves 4 • Preparation: 15 mins

Herring spread with coriander

5 salted herring fillets, 4 tbsps butter, 1 tart apple, 1 tsp lemon juice, ½ tsp ground coriander, 1 small onion, 1 hard-boiled egg, pepper, 1–2 tbsps mayonnaise

Soak the herring fillets for a while, then put them through a mincer or chop finely. Grate the peeled apple finely, sprinkle with lemon juice. Process the herring with the egg yolk, apple, coriander, finely chopped onion and pepper. Add the mayonnaise and finely chopped egg white, mix thoroughly. Refrigerate.

serves 4–6 • Preparation: 10 mins

Herring spread with bacon

300 g herring fillets, 200 g fatty smoked bacon, 2 large onions, salt, pepper, sugar, 2 tbsps chopped parsley

Chop finely all the ingredients or put them through a mincer, then process them. Chill the paste a bit and sprinkle with parsley before serving.

serves 8–10 • Preparation: 15 mins

Chicken spreads

Polish spread

250 g boiled or roast chicken, 2 hard-boiled eggs, 2 tbsps chopped chives, 2 tbsps each thick cream and thick mayonnaise, salt, pepper, a pinch of sugar, a pinch of grated lemon rind

Chop finely all the chicken and eggs or put them through a mincer, then process them, adding the chives, cream, mayonnaise, salt, pepper, sugar and lemon rind. Chill the paste a bit.

serves 4–6 • Preparation: 10 mins

Lithuanian spread

150 g boiled chicken, 1 tbsp butter, 1 tbsp lemon juice, 2 tbsps hot ketchup, 1 tsp green peppercorns, 3–4 tbsps mayonnaise, 2 hard-boiled eggs

Put the chicken and eggs through a mincer, then process them together with the ketchup, butter, lemon juice, salt, pepper and green peppercorns. Add the mayonnaise and mix thoroughly. Refrigerate.

serves 4 • Preparation: 15 mins

Smoked chicken spread

300 g smoked chicken, 150 g mushrooms, 1 large onion, salt, pepper, 2 tbsps butter, 2 tbsps cream

Chop finely the onion and mushrooms, fry them in butter, reduce the juices. Put the chicken and mushrooms through a mincer. Add salt, pepper and cream and blend into a smooth paste. Refrigerate. The paste should spread easily.

serves 4–6 • Preparation: 15 mins

Chicken liver spread with cheese

200 g chicken livers, 2 tbsps butter, 3 tbsps finely grated hard cheese, 2 tbsps thick cream, salt, pepper, 2 tbsps red wine, a pinch of dried basil

Fry the livers in butter, then sprinkle them with wine and basil and stew until tender. Put them through a mincer, add salt, pepper, cream and grated cheese and work into a smooth paste. Chill it a bit, then transfer to a serving bowl, sprinkle with finely chopped onion, garnish with strips of red pepper and parsley sprigs.

serves 4–6 • Preparation: 20 mins

Chicken liver spread, Jewish style

300 g chicken livers, 2 tbsps fat (preferably goose or chicken fat), 1 large onion, 2 hard-boiled eggs, 1–2 cloves of garlic, salt, pepper, 1 tbsp thick mayonnaise

Cut the livers, fry them lightly, take out with a strainer. Fry the finely chopped onion in the same fat, but do not let it get brown. Put the livers and onion through a mincer, combine with the finely chopped hard-boiled eggs, garlic crushed with salt, pepper and mayonnaise. Refrigerate, then garnish with strips of red pepper, parsley sprigs and lettuce leaves.

serves 4–6 • Preparation: 20 mins

Liver spread with mustard seeds

250 g chicken livers, 1 small onion, 3 tbsps brandy, 250 g butter, 2 tsps ground mustard seeds, 1 tsp salt, ¼ tsp each curry powder and nutmeg, a pinch of cayenne pepper, 1 tbsp finely chopped parsley

Rinse the livers, put them into a pan, cover with cold boiled water and cook for 12–15 mins under cover. Drain them, then process together with the finely chopped onion, butter, brandy and spices. Mix in the finely chopped parsley. Put into a serving bowl, cover with foil and leave in the fridge overnight. Serve well chilled.

serves 4 • Preparation: 20 mins

Other spreads

Sage spread

200 g veal liverwurst, ½ cup thick cream, 1 tbsp finely chopped sage leaves, 1 tbsp pistachio nuts, 4–6 pitted black olives, 1 hard-boiled egg, salt, pepper, several leaves of sage

Process the liverwurst with the egg, chopped sage and cream, add salt and pepper. Chop finely four olives and half the pistachios, mix with the paste, then refrigerate. Before serving, garnish with halves of the remaining olives and pistachios, and with sage leaves.

serves 4–6 • Preparation: 10 mins

Ham spread

200 g lean smoked ham, 1 tbsp hot mustard, 2 hard--boiled eggs, 3–4 tbsps thick cream or yogurt, salt, pepper

Put the ham and eggs through a mincer, then process them with the cream and mustard, add salt and pepper to taste.

serves 4–6 • Preparation: 5 mins

Delicious spread

150 g lean ham, 1 hard-boiled egg, 1 garlic-flavoured soft cheese, salt, pepper, 3–4 tbsps thick mayonnaise

Blend the egg yolk with the cheese and mayonnaise, add salt and pepper. Put in the finely chopped ham and egg white, mix thoroughly, then refrigerate.

serves 4 • Preparation: 10 mins

Savoury veal spread

200 g roast veal, 50 g grated tangy cheese, 1 marinated pepper, 1 tbsp green peppercorns, salt, pepper, cayenne pepper, 3–4 tbsps mayonnaise

Put the veal through a mincer, then blend it with the cheese and mayonnaise, add salt and pepper. Put in the finely chopped pepper and green peppercorns. Mix thoroughly and refrigerate.

serves 4–6 • Preparation: 10 mins

Smoked bacon spread

150 g smoked bacon, 1 large onion, 1 tbsp lard, 150 g cooked beans, 1 clove of garlic, 1 tbsp soya sauce, ¼ tsp each marjoram, green pepper and hot paprika, salt

Chop the bacon finely, fry it in lard. Add the finely chopped onion and sauté for a minute or two. Take off the heat and allow to cool. Process all the ingredients into a smooth paste. Refrigerate.

serves 6–8 • Preparation: 15 mins

Pâtés, terrines and meatloaves

Today, pâtés are made from everything: poultry, meat, game, fish, chicken livers, and also from mushrooms, vegetables and nuts.

There are two kinds of pâté: those baked in a pastry case and those without.

The best known pâté baked in pastry is the vol-au-vent, in which the case of choux pastry is baked separately from the filling, which is put in later and may be stewed chicken, or a vegetable, mushroom or fish ragout.

The galantine is an exceptionally tasty type of pâté but takes a very long time to make; it was once made exclusively from poultry but is now also made from meat and fish. The skin of a chicken, a goose neck, a fish skin or a thin slice of meat is filled with a pre-prepared stuffing and then sewn up with thread (often after first being wrapped in muslin or a linen tea towel), cooked in a strong vegetable stock, and then weighted down and cooled, and finally covered with jelly prepared from the stock with added gelatine.

Classic pâtés without a pastry case can be baked in the oven in an ordinary tin lined with greaseproof paper, or in a tin greased and dusted with breadcrumbs.

Although making pâtés is a longish process, it is not difficult and nothing can go wrong as long as the forcemeat is carefully prepared and the ingredients chosen with thought.

Whatever the kind of pâté, galantine or terrine, the ingredients of the stuffing should be thoroughly seasoned. It is therefore a good idea to place thick slices of the meat in a bowl or stoneware pot and sprinkle them with the seasoning given in the recipe, and also with salt, and possibly some vodka, brandy or wine, cover them and leave them overnight in the fridge before braising them. Remembering that the chicken liver is added to the pot only for the last 10–15 minutes.

To make the stuffing rise, bread or roll should be added, with the crusts removed; the slices of bread should be first soaked in milk, cream or broth.

The braised and cooled meat, bread and all the other ingredients given in the recipe should then be put two or three times through a mincer, using the pâté nozzle. If you want the pâté to be even smoother, process the minced meat and then sieve it.

It is a good idea to pour aspic over pâtés that have been baked in moulds. The delicate flavour of the aspic not only harmonizes with that of the pâté, but more importantly prevents it drying out.

And one more important piece of advice: a baked pâté, after cooling, should 'mature' for two or three days in the fridge, in order for its full taste and aroma to come out.

Pâtés can be served both hot and cold, and savoury sauces, pickles and marinades form an excellent accompaniment.

Nut pâté

1 cup each chopped walnuts, hazelnuts and peanuts, 1 cup crumbled dry brown bread, 2 onions, 3–4 cloves of garlic, 1 tart apple, 1 tsp lemon juice, 1 tsp finely chopped fresh sage (or ¼ tsp dried sage), 4–5 tbsps single cream, 2 eggs, salt, pepper, 3 tbsps butter

Chop finely the onion and garlic. Grate the apple, sprinkle with lemon juice. Melt 2 tbsps of butter in a pan, add the onion and garlic, sauté them, then put in the apple

and, stirring all the time, simmer for 2–3 mins. Allow the mixture to cool, combine it with the nuts, bread, cream and sage, mix thoroughly, add salt and pepper. Fold in the mixed eggs and work into a smooth paste. Grease a pâté mould with butter, fold in the paste and put into a preheated oven. Bake for 40 mins. Serve hot or cold.

serves 4–6 • Preparation: 15 mins • Baking: 40 mins

Mushroom and almond pâté

400 g mushrooms and 100 g button mushroom caps, 1 tbsp lemon juice, a pinch of cayenne pepper, 1 large onion, 3–4 cloves of garlic, 1 cup finely chopped almonds, 1 tsp dried thyme, 1 tbsp thick cream, 2 eggs, salt, pepper, 3 tbsps butter, 1 tbsp breadcrumbs, 1 tbsp almond flakes

Rinse and dry the mushrooms. Put the button mushrooms in a bowl, sprinkle with lemon juice and cayenne, cover and leave for 1–2 hours. Chop the remaining mushrooms together with the stalks. Chop finely the onion and garlic, fry them in butter (2 tbsps), add the chopped mushrooms and sauté for a minute or two over high heat, then lower the heat and fry until the liquid has evaporated. Take off the heat, allow it to cool, then put through a mincer. Blend the mushrooms with the cream and eggs, add almonds, thyme, salt and pepper. Grease a pâté mould with butter, dust with breadcrumbs, line the bottom with half the mushroom paste. Arrange the mushroom caps on top, cover with the remaining mushroom paste. Smooth out the surface, sprinkle it with almond flakes. Cover the mould with aluminium foil. Place it in an ovenproof dish filled with hot water and bake in a preheated oven for 40 mins, then remove the foil and bake for another 7–10 mins. When it cools down, put the pâté overnight in the fridge.

serves 4–6 • Preparation: 30 mins • Baking: 50 mins

Mushroom pâté

250 g mushrooms, 150 g pork, 50 g smoked bacon, 1 onion, 3 tbsps butter, 2 eggs, ½ cup single cream, 2 tbsps finely chopped parsley, salt, pepper, nutmeg, a pinch of each dried savory and basil, 300 g puff pastry

Sauté the finely chopped onion and mushrooms in butter, reduce the juices. Allow them to cool. Put the pork and bacon through a mincer twice, add the mushrooms and onion, cream, 1 whole egg and 1 egg white, parsley and spices. Work into a smooth paste. Rinse a pâté mould with cold water, line it with some of the pastry, put in the mixture, cover with the remaining pastry. Seal the edges, smear the mixed egg yolk on top. Cut out a circle in the middle of the pastry, insert a grease paper 'chimney', and put the mould in a preheated oven. Bake for 30–40 mins. Serve hot or cold.

serves 4–8 • Preparation: 40 mins • Baking: 40 mins

Dried mushroom pâté

150 g dried cep mushrooms, 2–3 onions, 3 bread rolls, 2 tbsps each chopped parsley and dill, 3 tbsps chopped hazelnuts, 100 g butter, 5 eggs, 1 cup thick cream, salt, pepper

Dried mushroom pâté

Rinse the mushrooms, cover them with water and leave overnight. Cook them the next day. Take the mushrooms out and soak the bread rolls (without crust) in the stock. Melt the butter in a pan, fry the finely chopped mushrooms and onion, add the squeezed out bread rolls. Stirring continuously, fry them together. Transfer the mixture to a large bowl, add some hazelnuts (2 tbsps), dill,

parsley, salt, pepper, raw egg yolks and cream. Work the mixture well, fold in the whipped egg whites and mix gently. Transfer to a pâté mould that has been greased with butter and dusted with hazelnuts, close the mould or cover it well with aluminium foil and put on top of a pot with boiling water. Put in the oven and bake for one hour. Serve hot or cold.

serves 4–8 • Preparation: 40 mins • Baking: 1 hr

Broccoli pâté

500 g broccoli, 1–2 cloves of garlic, 1 tbsp lemon juice, 1 tsp sugar, 2 tbsps walnuts, 400 g celeriac, 2 celery sticks, ½ cup cream, 4 egg whites, salt, pepper, nutmeg, 1 tsp soya sauce, 1 cup strong stock, 1 tbsp butter, 1 tbsp sifted breadcrumbs

Peel the celeriac, cut it in quarters and cook in the stock. Cook the broccoli in water with a pinch of salt and sugar and with lemon juice. Leave it to cool in the water. Process the celeriac with half the cream, salt, pepper and nutmeg, mix it with two whipped egg whites and with the finely chopped celery sticks. Process the broccoli separately, adding crushed garlic, soya sauce, pepper, the remaining cream and two whipped egg whites. Grease a pâté mould with butter and dust it with breadcrumbs. Put in alternating layers of the two mixtures. Cover the tin and place it in an oven-proof dish filled with water. Bake for one hour.

serves 4–6 • Preparation: 30 mins • Baking: 1 hr

Bean and apple pâté

100 g small dried white haricot beans, 1 tart apple, 1 tbsp sesame seeds, 2 tbsps chopped parsley, juice of ½ lemon, a pinch of grated lemon rind, salt, pepper

Rinse the beans and soak them overnight in water, then cook them, allow to cool, and drain. Toast the sesame seeds in a hot frying pan. Grate the peeled apple finely. Process all the ingredients. Put the mixture into a pâté mould, even out the surface, cover with foil and put in the fridge for the night. Serve cold.

serves 4 • Preparation: 45–50 mins

Cauliflower pâté

Carrot pâté

750 g new carrots, 4 tbsps butter, ½ cup chicken stock, 5 tbsps grated piquant cheese, 2 tsps honey, 2 tbsps chopped hazelnuts, salt, pepper, a pinch of ground coriander, 3 eggs, 2 tbsps chopped dill, 1 tbsp breadcrumbs

Peel the carrots and put them into boiling salted water. Cook for 10 mins, then drain. Melt 3 tbsps of butter in a pan, put in the chopped carrots, cover with the hot stock, add salt, honey and coriander, stir and simmer over low heat, then reduce the liquid. Process the mixture, allow it to cool, add the grated cheese and hazelnuts, salt and pepper to taste. Break in 2 whole eggs and 1 egg yolk. Work into a smooth paste, add the chopped dill and fold in the whipped egg white. Grease a pâté mould with butter and dust it with the breadcrumbs. Put in the mixture, cover the mould and put in a preheated oven. Bake for 25–30 mins. Serve hot, with bechamel or hollandaise sauce, or cold.

serves 4–6 • Preparation: 40 mins • Baking: 30 mins

Bell pepper pâté

2 large green bell peppers, 2 large onions, 2–3 cloves of garlic, 500 g beef tomatoes, 100 g mushrooms, 100 g finely chopped hazelnuts, 100 g breadcrumbs, 2 tbsps ground soya beans, salt, ¼ tsp each dried thyme, savory and tarragon, 1 egg, 2–3 tbsps single cream, 2–3 tbsps porridge oats

Rinse the peppers, bake them in the oven, then skin and remove the seeds. Chop them finely, combine with the finely chopped mushrooms, onion and garlic crushed with salt. Blanch and skin the tomatoes, then liquidize them together with the herbs, salt, cream and the raw egg yolk. Mix them with the peppers, onion and mushrooms. Add the hazelnuts, soya flour and breadcrumbs. Work into a smooth mixture, season to taste. Fold in the whipped egg white. Put into a greased earthenware baking mould, sprinkle with oats on top. Put in a preheated oven. Bake for 50 mins. Serve hot or cold with a savory sauce.

serves 4–6 • Preparation: 40 mins • Baking: 50 mins

Leek pâté

3 large leeks, 100 g mushrooms, 3–4 cloves of garlic, 100 g butter, 1 tbsp each celery seeds, dried basil and soup seasoning, 2 tbsps flour, 1 cup grated dry wholemeal bread, 1 cup each ground walnuts and hazelnuts, salt, pepper, 2 tbsps flour, 1 cup stock, 3–4 eggs

Wash the leeks thoroughly, cut them into fine slices. Rinse and dry the mushrooms, chop them finely together with the garlic. Melt the butter in a pan, put in the mushrooms, leeks and garlic, sauté them, stirring all the time. Add the celery seeds, basil and soup seasoning, and fry together until the vegetables have turned light brown. Reduce the juices, dust with flour and stir. Pour over the stock and stirring continuously cook until the sauce has thickened. Then put in the grated bread, nuts and spices, stir thoroughly and simmer for 2–3 mins. Take off the heat, allow it to cool a bit. Break in the eggs and mix thoroughly. Grease a pâté mould with butter and dust it with 1 tbsps of chopped nuts, put in the mixture, cover with aluminium foil and put in a preheated oven. Bake for one hour. Serve hot or cold.

serves 4–6 • Preparation: 40 mins • Baking: 1 hr

Spinach pâté, French style

1 kg spinach, ½ cup thick cream, 4–6 tbsps coarsely ground sunflower seeds, 100 g grated sharp cheese, 4 eggs, salt, pepper, nutmeg, 1 tbsp butter, 1 tbsp breadcrumbs, 1 cup stock, a pinch of sugar, 1 tbsp lemon juice

Bring the stock to the boil, add sugar and lemon juice. Put in the rinsed spinach and cook for 7 mins. Drain and strain the spinach, then process it together with the cream. Fold in the grated cheese, sunflower seeds, egg yolks and whipped egg whites. Grease a pâté mould with butter and dust it with breadcrumbs. Transfer the mixture to the mould and bake for 40 mins. Serve hot or cold.

serves 4–8 • Preparation: 15 mins • Baking: 40 mins

Cauliflower pâté

*1 large cauliflower, 2 tbsps lemon juice,
1 tbsp sugar, 2 bread rolls without crust,
½ cup single cream, 3–4 tbsps butter, 3 eggs,
salt, pepper, nutmeg, 1 tbsp breadcrumbs*

Cook the cauliflower in salted water with lemon juice and sugar, drain it, then process it together with the bread rolls that have been soaked in cream. Cream 3 tbsps of butter until foamy. Stirring continuously, add one egg yolk and 2–3 tbsps of cauliflower purée at a time. Whip the egg whites. Season the cauliflower with salt, pepper and nutmeg, fold in the whipped egg whites. Grease a pâté mould with butter and dust it with breadcrumbs. Put the mixture into the mould, seal it and place in a preheated oven. Bake for 30 mins. Serve hot, for example with tomato sauce.

serves 4–6 • Preparation: 40 mins • Baking: 30 mins

Spinach and cheese pâté

*1 kg spinach, 1 clove of garlic, salt, 1 tbsp lemon juice,
100 g feta cheese, 100 g curd cheese, 3–4 spring
onions, 3 tbsps olive oil, 1 bread roll, ½ cup single
cream, 3 eggs, 1 tbsp each chopped dill and
parsley, 100 g grated Parmesan, salt, pepper*

Boil some water with the garlic, 1 tsp oil and 1 tbsp lemon juice. Put in the rinsed spinach and cook for 5–6 mins, then drain it. Soak the bread roll in the cream. Fry the finely chopped spring onion in oil, but do not brown it. Squeeze out the bread roll. Process it together with the curd cheese, spinach and onion, fold in the finely grated feta, half of the Parmesan, chopped dill and parsley, add salt, pepper and eggs. Work into a smooth paste. Grease a pâté mould with oil, put in the mixture, even out the surface, sprinkle with the remaining Parmesan. Put in a preheated oven and bake for 45 mins. Serve hot or cold.

serves 4–8 • Preparation: 20 mins • Baking: 45 mins

Potato pâté, Kashub style

*500 g potatoes cooked in jackets, 200 g fresh herring,
1 bread roll without crust, ½ cup single cream,*
*100 g butter, 3 raw eggs, 2 hard-boiled eggs,
salt, pepper, breadcrumbs*

Soak the bread roll in cream for half an hour. Clean and wash the herrings, cut them into fillets. Peel the potatoes. Put one herring and the potatoes through a mincer. Beat the butter until foamy, adding one raw egg yolk and some bread roll and potato and herring mixture at a time. Work into a smooth paste, add salt, pepper and whipped egg whites, stir well. Grease a pâté mould with butter and dust it with breadcrumbs. Fold in half of the mixture, arrange on top strips of herring and egg slices, cover with the remaining mixture. Even out the surface, sprinkle with melted butter and put into a preheated oven. Bake for 30–40 mins. NB: The pâté increases in volume considerably, so remember to fill the tin only halfway. Serve hot or cold.

serves 4–6 • Preparation: 40 mins • Baking: 40 mins

Carp pâté

*1½ kg carp fillets, 2 tbsps lemon juice, salt, 200 g
chicken livers, 100 g stoned prunes, 3 tbsps
dry white wine, 200 g mushrooms, 1 bread
roll, ½ cup cream, 3–4 tbsps butter, 2 eggs,
salt, pepper, nutmeg, 1 tbsp breadcrumbs*

Rinse the prunes, blanch them, put into a bowl and sprinkle with wine. Cut the bread roll, put it in a bowl and pour over the cream, leave for half an hour. Wash the fillets, dry them, sprinkle with 1 tbsp of lemon juice, rub with salt and leave for half an hour. Chop the mushrooms, sprinkle them with lemon juice and pepper, and leave for half an hour. Rinse and dry the livers, sauté them in 1 tbsp of butter, allow to cool. Fry the fillets in butter, leave them to cool, then remove the bones. Put the fish, mushrooms, livers, prunes and bread roll through a mincer twice, add the spices, pour in 1 tbsp of melted butter, break in the eggs. Work the mixture into a smooth paste. Grease a pâté mould with butter and dust it with breadcrumbs. Fold in the paste, smooth out the surface, cover with aluminium foil. Put into a preheated oven and bake for 40 mins. Towards the end, remove the foil. When the pâté cools down, put it in the fridge and leave it there overnight.

serves 6–8 • Preparation: 30 mins • Baking: 40 mins

Potato pâté

1½ kg potatoes cooked in jackets, 250 g pork fat, 2 tbsps flour, 1–2 tbsps sour cream, 3 large onions, 50 g lean smoked streaky bacon cut into rashers, salt, pepper, 2 eggs, 1 tbsp lard, 1 tbsp breadcrumbs

Peel the potatoes, put them through a mincer, fold in the cream, add salt and pepper to taste. Cut the pork fat into fine cubes, render it in a hot frying pan, add the finely chopped onion and sauté for a minute or two. Add to the potatoes, mix well, break in the eggs, add flour and work into a smooth paste. Grease a pâté mould with fat and dust it with breadcrumbs. Transfer half of the paste, arrange the bacon rashers on top, cover with the remaining potato mixture, press, even out the surface. Put in a preheated oven and bake for 1½ hrs. Serve hot.

serves 4–6 • Preparation: 20 mins • Baking: 1½ hrs

Potato pâté

Bream pâté

1½ kg bream, soup vegetables, 3–4 grains each allspice and pepper, 1 bay leaf, 1–2 cloves, ¼ tsp grated lemon rind, 1 tbsp lemon juice, 1 onion, 500 g mushrooms, 1 bread roll, 1 cup mayonnaise, salt, pepper, nutmeg, 3 hard-boiled eggs, 3 raw egg yolks, 2 tbsps chopped parsley, 4 tbsps butter, 1–2 tbsps breadcrumbs

Clean, wash and dry the fish, sprinkle it with lemon juice and rub with salt sparingly. Make a stock from the vegetables, onion and spices, add lemon rind and lemon juice. Put in whole fish (take out the eyes) and cook over low heat for 40 mins. Leave in the stock to cool. Strain 1 cup of the stock and use it to soak the bread roll in. Fry the finely chopped onion in butter (2 tbsps), but do not brown it, add the diced mushrooms and sauté them for a minute or two, stirring all the time. Drain the cooked vegetables and fish on a strainer. Remove the bones and skin from the fish, sauté the fish meat in butter (1 tbsp). Put the squeezed bread roll, vegetables, parsley, fish, onion, mushrooms and hard-boiled egs twice through a mincer. Fold in the mayonnaise, add salt, pepper and nutmeg, break in the eggs and work the mixture into a smooth paste. Grease a pâté mould with butter and dust it with breadcrumbs. Transfer the mixture, smooth out the surface, sprinkle with breadcrumbs. Put in a preheated oven and bake for 30 mins. Serve hot or cold with a savoury sauce.

serves 6–8 • Preparation: 15 mins • Baking: 30 mins

Herring pâté

500 g salted herring, 1 cup milk, 200 g onion, 50 g dried mushrooms, ½ cup breadcrumbs, 400 g potatoes cooked in jackets, 3 tbsps oil, 1 tbsp butter, 2 eggs, 1 tbsp sour cream, salt, pepper, a pinch of each ground allspice, grated nutmeg, crushed marjoram and sugar

Rinse the mushrooms and soak them overnight in water, then cook them. Wash the herring, remove the skin and bones, pour over milk and leave for several hours, then dry them. Dice the onion finely and fry it in hot oil, but do not brown it. Add the herring and sauté for a minute or two. Put the mushrooms, peeled potatoes, herring and onion twice through a mincer, add breadcrumbs, cream, salt, pepper, sugar, allspice, marjoram and nutmeg, break in the eggs. Work the mixture into a smooth paste. Grease a pâté mould with butter and dust it with breadcrumbs. Transfer the mixture and put it into a preheated oven. Bake for 30 mins. Serve hot or cold with a savoury sauce.

serves 6–8 • Preparation: 20 mins • Baking: 30 mins

Veal liver pâté

500 g veal liver, 3 onions, 2 carrots, 150 g butter, 1–2 tbsps oil, 2 tbsps finely chopped parsley, 1 tsp salt, ½ tsp pepper, ¼ tsp grated nutmeg, 1 tbsps dry white wine

Dice the peeled carrots and onions coarsely. Melt 1½ tbsps of butter in a pan, put in the onion and carrots and sauté them for a minute or two over high heat. Sprinkle with the wine, cover the pan and simmer over low heat for 20 mins. Remove the membranes from the liver, cut the liver into cubes and fry in hot oil. Mince the vegetables, liver and parsley twice, using the pâté nozzle. Add salt and pepper to taste, fold in the remaining butter and put the mixture through a mincer again. Transfer it to a serving bowl and leave overnight in the fridge.

serves 6–8 • Preparation: 40 mins

Pork liver pâté, Lithuanian style

250 g pork liver, 1 tbsp lard, 3 tbsps butter, 1 egg, 1 large onion, 3 tbsps sharp cheese, 1 tbsp sharp cream, salt, pepper, 1–2 tbsps breadcrumbs

Rinse the liver, remove the membranes. Cut the liver into pieces, dice the onion. Fry them both in lard, sprinkle with water. Cover the pan and simmer for 15 mins, then leave it to cool. Put the mixture twice through a mincer. Beat the butter with the egg yolk, gradually combine it with the minced liver and grated cheese, add salt and pepper to taste. Fold in the cream and the whipped egg white. Grease a pâté mould with butter and dust it with breadcrumbs. Put in the mixture, press it down (to ¼ of the height of the mould), smooth out the surface. Put in a preheated oven and bake for 20–30 mins. Set aside to cool, then put into the fridge.

serves 4 • Preparation: 30 mins • Baking: 30 mins

Chicken liver pâté with thyme

600 g chicken livers, 300 g onion, 1 tbsp dried thyme, salt, pepper, 4 tbsps geese fat, 1 tbsp white wine

Fry the finely chopped onion in geese fat (1 tbsp), but do not brown it, sprinkle it with wine, cover the pan and simmer for 25 mins. Melt the remaining geese fat in a frying pan, put in the rinsed and dried livers and sauté it. Add thyme and take off the heat. Mince the warm onion and livers twice, using a pâté nozzle. Add salt and pepper and work into a smooth paste. Transfer to an earthenware mould, smooth out the surface and leave in the fridge overnight (it will keep for about ten days).

serves 4–6 • Preparation: 35 mins

Chicken liver and pork pâté

1 kg chicken livers, 350 g pork gorge (front of the neck), 300 g pork liver, 1 glass brandy, 2–3 eggs, 3–4 bay leaves, salt, pepper, ¼ tsp each ground ginger, nutmeg and cloves, 3 tbsps gelatine, ¼ cup stock, 1 small glass dry white wine, 100 g fine pork bards

Dissolve the gelatine in a mixture of stock and wine. Mince the rinsed and dried chicken livers, meat, pork liver and gorge three times, using the pâté nozzle. Add ginger, nutmeg, cloves, salt, pepper, brandy and the dissolved gelatine. Mix well, break in the eggs and work into a smooth paste. Line a pâté mould with some pork bards, put in the mixture, cover with the remaining bards. Sprinkle with crushed bay leaves on top, cover with aluminium foil and put in a preheated oven. Bake for one hour. Leave it in the oven to cool, then put it for to 3 days into the fridge. The pâté will keep in the fridge for up 1–2 weeks.

serves 8–10 • Preparation: 30 mins • Baking: 1 hr

Pheasant pâté

1 pheasant, 250 g pork gorge, 250 g boned veal, 300 g pork fat, ¾ cup dry white wine, 1 glass brandy, salt, pepper, a pinch of each nutmeg, ground cloves, ginger and juniper berries, ½ tsp dried sage, 3 thyme sprigs or 1 tsp dried thyme, 1 bay leaf, 50 g fine pork bards

Rinse the prepared tenderized pheasant, dry it, remove the skin, separate the meat from the bones, leave the breast meat aside. Mince twice (using the pâté nozzle) the remaining meat and giblets, together with the pork, veal and pork fat, add sage and crushed bay leaf. Put the mixture into a bowl, add salt, pepper, spices and herbs, pour in the wine and work into a smooth paste. Cut the pheasant breast into slices. Line a pâté mould with the pheasant skin and put in alternating layers of the meat mixture and breast slices. Cover with the remaining meat mixture, press lightly down, smooth out the surface. Prick with a toothpick, sprinkle with brandy. Arrange on top the pork bards. Seal the mould and put into a pan with boiling water. Bake in a preheated oven for one hour and a half. Allow it to cool a bit, weigh it down with a wooden board and leave aside for twelve hours, then pour over aspic made from vegetables and pheasant bones.

serves 8–10 • Preparation: 50 mins • Baking: 1½ hrs

Hare pâté, Silesian style

1 hare, 500 g smoked streaky bacon, 200 g pork liver, soup vegetables, 1 large onion, 5–6 grains each allspice and pepper, 1 bay leaf, 1–2 cloves, 1 cup stock, 1 bread roll, 100 g lard, 1 tbsp marjoram, ¼ tsp each ground ginger and thyme, salt, pepper, 1 crushed clove, 2 fine pork bards

Peel and dice the vegetables and onion. Draw and clean the hare, cut it into pieces, rinse (including the liver, lungs and heart) and dry. Heat up the lard in a large pan, put in the diced vegetables, sauté them for a minute or two, stirring all the time, add the offal and meat and fry for 3–4 mins. Add bay leaf, allspice, pepper and cloves, pour in the stock and simmer over low heat until the meat is very tender. Haft way through, add the smoked bacon and the fried pork liver slices and towards the end, put in the sliced bread roll. Leave the mixture to cool, then take out the allspice, pepper, cloves and the bay leaf. Bone the meat. Mince the meat and the remaining ingredients three times. Add marjoram, thyme, ginger, clove, salt and pepper, break in the eggs and work the whole into a smooth paste. Line a pâté mould with bards, put in the mixture, cover with

aluminium foil. Put in a preheated oven and bake for 90 mins. When the pâté is cool, put it into the fridge for one or two days. Serve with cranberry or redcurrant preserves.

serves 8–10 • Preparation: 30 mins • Baking: 1½ hrs

Veal pâté

200 g veal (loin or round), ½ cup dry crumbled bread (without crust), 800 g fresh cep mushrooms, 100 g shallots, 1 clove of galic, ½ tsp each dried basil, thyme, sage and caraway, 1 cup cream, 3 tbsps oil, 3 tbsps butter, 1 egg yolk, salt, ¼ tsp each ground white pepper, ginger and allspice, 25 g truffles, 1 cup strong stock, 1 tbsp gelatine

Cut the meat into cubes and put in a large earthenware dish. Fry half the finely chopped onions in 1 tbsp of butter, but do not brown it. Leave them to cool, then mix with the crumbled bread and add to the meat. Blend 3 tbsps of cream with ½ tsp of salt, white pepper, ginger and allspice, fold in the whipped egg white. Add the mixture to the meat. Cover the dish and leave overnight in the fridge. Rinse and dry the mushrooms and chop them finely. Heat up oil in a pan, put in the mushrooms, and, stirring continuously, sauté them for 5–6 mins. Melt 1 tbsp of butter in a frying pan, fry the remaining onion and finely chopped

Hare pâté, Silesian style

garlic, add to the mushrooms. Sprinkle with 3–4 tbsps of stock and simmer for a while. Allow it to cool, then process the mixture, sieve it, cover and leave overnight in the fridge. Put the meat and bread twice through a mincer, then process the mixture together with the mushrooms, cream, herbs and salt. Add the chopped truffles, stir well. Grease an earthenware mould with butter, put in the mixture. Cover with aluminium foil and place in a pan filled with hot water. Put into a preheated oven and bake for one hour. Dissolve the gelatine in 2 tbsps of cold stock. Bring the remaining stock to the boil, pour in the gelatine, bring again to the boil, then allow it to cool a bit. When the gelatine is almost set, pour it over the cool pâté. Put the pâté in the fridge for up to 24 hours.

serves 6–8 • Preparation: 1½ hrs • Baking: 1 hr

Springtime chicken pâté

500 g minced chicken meat, 100 g minced lean streaky bacon, 200 g chicken livers, 2 cups young nettle leaves, 1 onion, 1–2 cloves of garlic, 1 tsp thyme leaves, ½ cup sunflower seeds, salt, pepper, nutmeg, 1–2 tbsps breadcrumbs, 2 tbsps butter, 1 tbsp double cream, 2 eggs

Put the nettles into a strainer, scald with boiling water, then pour over cold water, drain and dry them. Dice the bacon into large cubes. Fry it in a hot frying pan, add the diced onion and liver, and sauté. Leave the mixture to cool. Mince the liver and bacon together with the nettles and sunflower seeds. Fold in the minced meat fried in

1 tbsp of butter. Add the cream, garlic crushed with salt, pepper and thyme, break in the eggs and work the whole into a smooth paste. Grease a pâté mould with butter and dust it with breadcrumbs. Put in the mixture and bake it in a preheated oven for 40–50 mins. Serve hot or cold with a herbal sauce.

serves 4–6 • Preparation: 30 mins • Baking: 50 mins

Home-made meatloaf

250 g raw streaky bacon, 250 g pork, 500 g veal, 250 g pork hearts, 500 g veal liver, 30 g dried mushrooms, 3 onions, 2–3 bay leaves, 6–8 grains each allspice and pepper, 1 tbsp lard, 2 tbsps butter, 1 tsp ground pepper, ½ tsp nutmeg, 1 tbsps honey, 3 eggs, 1 tsp lard, 1–2 tbsps breadcrumbs

Rinse the mushrooms and soak them overnight in water, then cook them. Heat up the lard in a large pan, put in the meat cut into large cubes (pork, veal, bacon and hearts), sauté for a minute or two, then add the mushrooms together with the stock. Add pepper, allspice, bay leaves and onion, cover the pan and simmer for one hour. Put in the liver cut into pieces and stew for another 15 mins. Allow it to cool, then mince two or three times. Add butter, pepper, nutmeg, honey and salt, break in the eggs and work into a smooth paste. Grease a pâté tin with butter and dust it with breadcrumbs. Put in the mixture, smooth out the surface. Put in a preheated oven and bake for 45–55 mins.

Serves 6–8 • preparation: 1½ hrs • baking: 55 mins

CHAPTER II

SOUPS HOT AND COLD

✳✳✳

In Old Polish cuisine, all kinds of soups played a major role. Łukasz Gołębiowski in his *Domy i dwory*, wrote:

Borsch, barley soup, chicken broth and cabbage soup – these are the true Polish soups. They are first rate made with beef or pork, bacon fat, sausage, boiling fowl, either clear or thickened. Poles have always liked soured dishes, which are appropriate for their country and said to be necessary for their health.

Vegetable stocks, bouillon and chicken broth

To cook bouillon or stock. Someone once said that 'soup is as old as the invention of the cooking pot'. For centuries, it was the most important item in the diet of people everywhere. Today it has rather unfairly lost this position.

To make good soup you must first prepare stock. There are hundreds of ways of making stock – vegetable or mushroom stock, fish stock, chicken or meat stock, bone stock. The taste of these basic stocks depends on what is added to them.

The taste of an ordinary vegetable stock is improved by adding a few cloves of garlic, 2–3 mushrooms, half a pepper, 1–2 tomatoes or a piece of courgette, as well as fresh or dried herbs, for example coriander, basil, rosemary, thyme or caraway.

Bouillon is the name generally given in Poland to a strong and usually skimmed stock made from meat, bones, chicken or fish with the addition of vegetables and spices.

Because it takes a long while to make stock, it is best to make a large amount. Stock can be kept in the fridge for 4–5 days, or it can be frozen in small containers or pasteurized in small jars and then kept for up to six months and used when required.

Meat stocks can be either light or dark. The best light stocks, which form the basis for many soups and sauces, are made by long boiling of saddle of veal or beef bones with added vegetables and spices. You must not forget that if you are making a clear bouillon, a raw egg white, together with a carefully washed and crushed eggshell, should be added after sieving, and then the stock should be again put through a fine sieve.

Vegetables, bones or meat for making stock should be simmered over a low heat in a large amount of water. Because stock is cooked for a long time, it is best to add salt at the end of the process. If too much water boils away, you can add boiled water or white wine at the end of the cooking process. After the stock has been cooked it can be strained through a fine sieve or a linen cloth and left to cool, after which the fat should be skimmed off.

Dark stocks are usually made from veal, beef, chicken or venison bones which have been baked in the oven or fried off in a frying pan and then chopped up.

Before baking any kind of veal or beef bones, or chicken ribs, main bones, necks, feet or wings, they should be lightly rubbed with olive oil, and then placed on a tin and put into a hot oven for about 30 minutes; after this they should be boiled with vegetables and spices.

A freshly cooked stock can be served as clear bouillon by itself in cups, or with meatballs, dumplings, noodles, rice or macaroni.

And when we have made the stock we can also make a wide variety of splendid soups.

Vegetable stock II

2 onions, 2 carrots, 4 celeriac sticks, 2 small leeks, 2 juicy tomatoes, 2 cloves of garlic, 2 bay leaves, ½ tsp peppercorns, 1 sprig each fresh rosemary, thyme and sage, several sprigs of parsley, salt, 2–3 tbsps olive oil, 8 cups water

Peel and rinse the vegetables, cut them into small cubes. Heat up the oil in a pan, add all the ingredients. Stir fry them over fairly high heat for 2–3 mins. Sprinkle with water and simmer over low heat for 15 mins. Pour in hot water, bring it to the boil and continue cooking over low heat for 20–30 mins. Add salt to taste. Strain the stock, press the vegetables gently to squeeze out all juices.

serves 4 • Preparation: 10 mins • Cooking: 50 mins

Vegetable stock I

2 onions, 3 carrots, 2 parsley roots, ½ celeriac, 1 small bulb of fennel, 1 leek, several grains each pepper and allspice, 1 bay leaf, 2 cloves, 1 sprig of fresh thyme, several sprigs of parsley, a piece of lemon rind, salt, pepper, 8 cups water

Peel the vegetables (apart from the onions). Rinse them and put into a pan. Add the lemon rind, spices and herbs. Cover with boiling water, bring to the boil, then simmer over low heat for 30–35 mins. Season with salt and ground pepper to taste. Strain the stock.

Meat bouillon. The meat from the bouillon will be very tasty, delicate and juicy if we allow it to cool in the stock (ca 30–40 minutes). A drop of brandy or lemon juice added to the meat while it is cooking will improve the flavour.

The most suitable meat for beef broth is the lower back near the tail; for the best broth you should use chicken giblets and seven different pieces of beef together with the tail. These should include back, a piece of sirloin, a steak and shin of beef, flank, a loin chop and entrecôte.

Beef broth should be cooked very slowly, for two or three hours, and veal broth should simmer for an hour and a half. Before veal is put into the stock pot, it should be scalded in boiling water.

While cooking broth, it is exceptionally important to remove the froth, and after it is ready to skim off the fat, since the fat contains a compound known as purine which is not very good for our health. It is easiest to skim off the fat after the broth has cooled.

Chicken stock. This will be sharper in taste and clearer if we dissolve a few bits of cheese in it; adding a pinch of saffron gives it a piquant flavour and a more intense colour. It also can be given a beautiful colour by adding singed pieces of unpeeled onion or else rinsed onion peel at the end of cooking.

Chicken broth can be given an interesting flavour by adding a small chilli pepper or grated lemon rind, a few leaves of sage or a handful of rosemary sprigs at the end of cooking.

serves 4 • Preparation: 10 mins • Cooking: 50 mins

Savoury chicken broth

legs, neck, wings and bones of 1 chicken, 200 g chopped veal bones, 3 carrots, 2–3 celeriac sticks, 1 fairly large leek, 2–3 cloves of garlic, 1 largish onion (unpeeled) studded with 4–5 cloves, 1 cored pepper, bouquet garni (1 bay leaf, 1–2 sprigs of fresh thyme, several sprigs of each parsley and dill, a piece of lemon rind, 1 small green pepperoni, ½ tsp caraway seeds, all wrapped in a piece of gauze), salt, pepper

Brown the veal bones in a frying pan. Put the bones and the chicken into a pan. Cover with 3 litres of water. Bring to the boil, then simmer over low heat for 15 mins. Remove the scum, add the vegetables and the bouquet garni and simmer for another 20 mins. Towards the end season with salt and pepper. Let it cool a bit, then strain the stock.

Fish stock. Fish heads and tails as well as all fish le-ft-overs form an excellent basis for fish stock. The taste is improved by adding coriander leaves or seeds, lemon rind, or a clove of garlic during cooking, or some dry white wine at the end. Fish broth is served with pieces of fish or vegetables cut in strips, or as a clear soup with meatballs or pasties, or as a cream soup with blended fish. Fish stock also forms an excellent basis for many soups, sauces and aspic.

serves 4 • Preparation: 20 mins • Cooking: 40–50 mins

Freshwater fish stock – basic recipe

several heads and other leftovers of carp or another freshwater fish, 2 large onions, 1–2 parsley roots, 1 carrot, ½ celeriac, 2–3 cloves of garlic, juice and grated rind from 1 lemon, 2–3 grains each allspice and pepper, several sprigs of each parsley, dill and coriander or ½ tsp coriander seeds, 1 glass dry white wine, 1 raw egg white

Wash the fish heads well, rub them with salt and leave for several minutes, take out the eyes. Boil 4–6 cups of water in a pan, add the peeled parsley roots, carrots and celeriac, garlic and onions, spices and lemon rind. Bring to the boil, then simmer for 15 mins. Add the greens, fish heads and lemon juice and continue cooking for another 15–20 mins. Remove the scum, clarify the stock with the egg white and strain. Pour in the wine and bring to the boil again. Use the stock for fish soups, aspic, sauces and mousses. You may keep it covered in the fridge for 2–3 days or freeze it in small containers and then store it for as long as six months.

serves 4 • Preparation: 20 mins • Cooking: 40–50 mins

An exceptionally nourishing and tasty broth

Take a fine piece of meat, remove the excess fat, add chopped up bones, a piece of beef liver. Wash them well. Place in boiling water. When the meat comes to the boil, skim off the froth. Then put in a pinch of salt and add a bunch of vegetables tied together, such as two or three carrots, four chopped leeks, celeriac leaves and a few sprigs of parsley and dill; add two cloves of garlic, half a white onion studded with cloves, and if you wish to have a dark broth, half of a baked onion, one shallot, a few grains of black pepper, a small piece of cinnamon, a bay leaf... Add to the broth chicken innards, feet, neck, liver. These all improve the flavour and strength of the broth. Simmer over a low but constant heat for at least six hours. When the broth is a golden colour, take it off the heat and when it has cooled a little, skim off the fat and strain the broth into another pot and season it according to taste.

Karolina Nakwaska, *Dwór wiejski* (pp. 18–19)

Broth, Old Polish style

500 g beef (entrecôte, roastbeef), 100 g chicken livers, ½ chicken, 2 carrots, 3 parsley roots, ½ celeriac, 1 singed onion, 1–2 cloves, several grains each pepper and allspice, a sprig of thyme, several sprigs of parsley, 2 dried cep mushrooms, salt, pepper, 2–3 tbsps chopped parsley

Rinse the mushrooms and soak them in a small amount of boiled water. Wash the beef and chicken, put them in a pan. Cover with 2 litres of water and bring to the boil. Remove the scum and simmer over low heat for 30 mins, occasionally skimming the froth. Peel and wash the vegetables. Add them to the stock together with the onion, spices, thyme, mushrooms and parsley sprigs. Simmer the stock for an hour, then strain it. Remove the membranes from the chicken livers, rinse the livers, cut them into cubes. Put into a pan, pour over the strained stock. Bring the livers to the boil, add the mushrooms cut into thin strips and pieces of cooked chicken. Season with salt and pepper. Serve with macaroni, semolina cubes or dropped noodles. Garnished with chopped parsley.

serves 4 • Preparation: 10 mins • Cooking: 1½ hrs

Freshwater fish stock – basic recipe

Royal broth

½ kg beef (roastbeef, entrecôte), ox tail, ¼ chicken, 150 g veal, 100 g minced beef, 1 raw egg white, 30 g chicken livers, 1 tbsp butter, 1–2 mushrooms, ¼ tsp ground pepper, soup vegetables, 1 onion larded with 1 clove, a wedge of savoy cabbage, 1 bunch of dill, 2 bay leaves, several grains each pepper and allspice, salt, grated lemon rind, 1 glass brandy

Boil 3 litres of water with bay leaf, allspice, peppercorns and onion. Wash the meat, scald the veal with boiling water (to make the broth clear). Brown the livers in melted butter, sprinkle with pepper. Put the ox tail, beef and fried liver into the stock. Bring the stock to the boil, then simmer for one hour. Add the chicken, veal, cleaned and washed vegetables, onion, mushrooms and dill. Simmer for another 40–50 mins, then strain the stock. Whip the egg white, mix with the minced beef and 2 tbsps of cold water. Add the meat to the hot stock and simmer for 30 mins. Put the stock through a fine strainer. Serve with macaroni and chicken meat cut into cubes.

serves 4 • Preparation: 10 mins • Cooking: 2½ hrs

Broth à la parisienne

400 g beef (top side, flank), 400 g beef thin flank, marrow bone, ox tail, chicken giblets, 2 small onions studded with 2–3 cloves, ¼ savoy cabbage, 1–2 celery sticks, a piece of celeriac, 2 leeks (only the white part), 1–3 carrots, a piece of turnip, 2–3 cloves of garlic, several sprigs of each parsley and dill, 1–2 sprigs of thyme, 1 bay leaf, salt, several slices of white bread, 1 tsp butter, 1–2 cloves of garlic

Bring 2½ litres of water to the boil, add thyme, bay leaf, the marrow bone wrapped in a piece of gauze (so as not to lose the marrow) and ox tail. Bring to the boil again, then simmer for 50 mins. Remove the scum, add the washed meat, parsley, dill, onion and peeled and washed carrots, turnip and celeriac. Simmer over low heat for another 60 mins. Add the celery, savoy cabbage, skinned garlic cloves, leek and chicken giblets. Simmer over low heat

for another hour. Strain the stock. Serve with garlic bread spread with the marrow.

serves 4 • Preparation: 10 mins • Cooking: 2½ hrs

Beef broth

750–1000 g beef (thick flank, entrecôte, roastbeef), 50 g chicken or veal liver, 1 onion, pepper, 1 tbsp butter, 2 carrots, 2 parsley roots, ½ celeriac, 1 kohlrabi, 2–3 radishes, 2–3 cauliflower florets, ½ fennel bulb, half a bunch of each parsley and dill, 1 peeled onion with 1 clove stuck in it, 1–2 bay leaves, 3–4 grains each allspice and pepper, salt, 1 tbsp lemon juice

Boil 3 litres of water with bay leaf, allspice, pepper, onions and clove. Sprinkle the meat with lemon juice, put into the boiling water. Bring to the boil, then simmer for one hour. Melt the butter in a frying pan, fry the chopped onion, but do not brown it, add the livers that have been washed, dried and chopped into fine pieces. Brown the liver well, sprinkle with pepper and add to the stock. Simmer the stock for another 15–20 mins. Add the peeled and rinsed vegetables and salt, then simmer for 30 mins. Strain the stock. Serve with macaroni or semolina cubes. Garnish with chopped parsley.

serves 4 • Preparation: 20–25 mins • Cooking: 2–2½ hrs

Borsch

In Lithuania from beet leaves, and in the Crown territories from the beetroot themselves. Czerniecki counts Crown borsch among milk dishes; there is also Lenten borsch with mushrooms and noodles. In some regions the common people make borsch from bread yeast, barberry, currants, raw gooseberries or cranberries which are crushed and diluted with water.

Łukasz Gołębiowski (*Domy i dwory*, vol. IV, p. 33)

'Our Polish borsch' is the title of a chapter in which Szymon Syreniusz writes: *Our borsch is known to all of us... It is useful as both a medicine and as a dish at table, and it is very tasty. As the root so the leaf... The infusion such as we make here is tasty – whether only simmered alone or with a capon or with ingredients such as eggs, cream or millet.*

From earliest times, a good borsch was the Poles' favourite soup and over the centuries earned itself the name of the national soup. It was first made from a plant called 'barshch' which grew as a weed in the meadows: *This plant is several feet high, and the thickness of its stems, the broadness of its leaves and the bunches of its dense flowers create the impression of a solid countryman ... but wherever barshch was growing it was greatly prized.* It was only much later that borsch began to be cooked from *red beet,... the vegetable of the poor.*

The oldest preserved recipe for borsch dates from the 16th century. According to Cezary Biernacki, borsch was and remains *the most ordinary, but in line with the added ingredients the most refined, of soups, a truly Polish soup, which is eaten with exceptional relish and even respect.* It was eaten readily because it sharpened the appetite and relieved the results of too much drink. It was served at the most exclusive tables and banquets, although as Koźmian states, *The English do not understand how Poles can enjoy borsch so much.*

According to Old Polish tradition there was a meatless borsch for Christmas Eve, and a thick borsch for New Year's Eve and Easter. The basis for both versions was a good soured beet juice, a crock of which at one time stood in every Polish home. It was often drunk straight as it was reviving and strengthening both for patients with a high temperature and those suffering from a hangover.

Christmas Eve borsch should be clear, bright red and sprinkled with oil and grated garlic; the best things to serve with it are noodles with mushrooms or choux pastry patties with fish, hard-boiled eggs or mushrooms.

Easter borsch is best made from smoked ham or white sausage stock, and can be served clear or thickened with cream in cups. It is also often served with hard-boiled eggs, ham cut into thin strips, or slices of white sausage.

Borsch is soured with lemon juice, red wine, or sieved redcurrants. Old cooks from the Podolia region had secret recipes for souring borsch with juicy cherries, which apart from doing the souring gave the borsch a beautiful dark red colour.

A good borsch should be sweet and sour and should have an intense red colour. To give it a fine colour, just before serving pour it through a sieve in which newly grated fresh beetroot has been placed.

Souring beetroot juice:

Take 1 kg of small young beets, a root of fresh horseradish, a teaspoonful of caraway seeds, one small carrot and one small parsnip, a piece of celeriac, three teaspoonsfuls of salt, a pinch of sugar and a slice of dry rye bread.

Peel, wash and dry the horseradish and vegetables, and cut them into slices. Put these in layers in a large jar, sprinkle with the salt, caraway and sugar; pour in 2–3 litres of lukewarm boiled water (so that the water covers the vegetables) and on the top place the slice of rye bread. Cover the jar with gauze and leave for five or six days in a warm place. Carefully remove the skin that has formed, pour the liquid through a fine sieve and put into bottles which should be tightly sealed. This can be kept in a cool place for several months. It is excellent for making borsch or for drinking, and is at its best after five or six days.

Easter borsch

500 g small beetroots, 2 cups sour beetroot juice, 4 cups strong bouillon, 200 g white sausage, 4 hard--boiled eggs, ½ tsp honey, ½ cup cream, 1 tbsp lemon juice, 1 clove of garlic, ½ tsp marjoram, salt, pepper

Peel the beetroots, rinse them and cut into thin slices. Pour over the bouillon, add the crushed garlic with salt and marjoram. Bring to the boil, then simmer for 20 mins. Put in the sausage and cook for another 20 mins. Take out the sausage, strain the stock, combine with the beetroot juice. Bring to the boil, add the honey, pepper and lemon juice. Fold in the cream and stir well. Serve with quarters of hard-boiled egg and slices of white sausage.

serves 4 • Preparation: 15 mins • Cooking: 50 mins

Christmas Eve borsch

Christmas Eve borsch

½ l sour beetroot juice, soup vegetables, pepper, salt, allspice, 1 bay leaf, 100 g dried mushrooms, 5–6 fresh beets, 1 glass dry red wine, 1–2 cloves of garlic, 1 tbsp lemon juice

Rinse the mushroom and soak them in water overnight, then cook them and drain. Make a stock of the beets, vegetables and spices. Strain it and mix with the mushroom stock. Add the beetroot juice – 3 measures of stock to 1 measure of juice. Heat up the soup, but keep it off the boil. Season with pepper, add salt and sugar to taste. Pour in the wine and shortly before serving add crushed garlic and lemon juice to taste. Pour through a sieve containing grated raw beetroots. Serve with dumplings stuffed with mushrooms.

serves 4 • Preparation: 20 mins • Cooking: 1 hr

Royal borsch

500 g game meat (hare, venison or wildboar), 500 g beetroots, soup vegetables, 1 onion, a piece of cinnamon, 1–2 cloves, 2–3 grains each allspice, juniper and pepper, a piece of lemon rind, 1 clove of garlic, 2–3 dried mushrooms, 4 cups boiled water, 3 cups sour beetroot juice, ½ cup thick sour cream, 1 raw egg yolk, ½ cup liquidized cherries, salt, pepper, sugar to taste

Scrub the beetroots thoroughly and bake them in the oven. Rinse the mushrooms and soak them in a small amount of water. Rinse the meat and put it in a pan. Add the spices and herbs, lemon rind, onion and mushrooms. Pour in water and bring to the boil. Remove the scum. Simmer the stock for an hour and a half, then strain it. Peel and grate the beetroots. Combine them with the game stock, add crushed garlic and salt. Bring to the boil, pour in the beetroot juice. Season with salt, pepper and sugar. Add the liquidized cherries, thin strips of mushrooms and meat cut into cubes (remove the bones). Add the cream mixed with the egg yolk.

serves 4 • Preparation: 15–20 mins • Cooking: 1½ hrs

Lithuanian borsch

*7–8 beetroots, 500 g wholemeal bread,
boiled water, soup vegetables, hare fillet,
250 g veal with bones, 2 beetroots, 3–4 grains
each allspice, pepper and juniper, 1 bay leaf,
3–4 dried cep mushrooms, salt, pepper, ¼ cup
natural cherry juice or 1 tbsp wine vinegar*

Make a sour beetroot juice in the following way: cut the bread into thin slices, peel the beetroots and slice them. In a stoneware jar arrange alternating layers of bread and beetroot, pour over lukewarm boiled water – enough to cover the beetroot. Put into a preheated oven for 2–3 hours. Take the jar out, stir the contents, cover with a piece of gauze and keep in a warm place for 2–4 days, then strain the juice. Peel and rinse the vegetables, wash the meat and mushrooms. Put the vegetables, meat, spices and mushrooms into a pan, pour over water. Bring it to the boil, then simmer over low heat for 1½ hours. Strain the stock. Peel and grate the beetroots, cover them with the stock and cook for several minutes, then strain the soup and combine it with the beetroot juice. Add some salt, pepper and cherry juice or vinegar. Serve with Lithuanian dumplings or with dumplings stuffed with mushrooms.

serves 4 • Preparation: 10 mins • Cooking: 2 hrs

Ukrainian borsch

*400 g garden beets, 100 g white haricot beans, soup
vegetables with savoy cabbage, 6 cups water, 2–3 large
potatoes, 1 small tin of tomato paste, 1 tbsp flour, 1 tbsp
butter, ½ cup cream, ½ cup sour beetroot juice, 1 clove
of garlic, salt, pepper, lemon juice and sugar to taste*

Rinse the beans and soak them overnight in cold water, then cook them. Add salt when the beans are ready. Make a stock from half the beets and vegetables (without the cabbage) and water. Strain the stock. Peel the potatoes and cut them in small cubes, cover with the hot stock and cook. Towards the end add the shredded cabbage. Grate coarsely the remaining beets and vegetables and cook them in a small amount of salted water. Make a roux from the butter and flour, blend it with several spoonfuls of the stock and, stirring all the time, simmer until the sauce has

thickened. Add the tomato paste and beetroot juice. Bring to the boil, add the beans, combine with the cooked vegetables and potatoes. Season to taste with pepper, sugar and lemon juice, add the crushed garlic and salt. You may also use bones to cook the stock.

serves 4 • Preparation: 30 mins • Cooking: 40–45 mins

Borsch with herring

*250 g beets, 1 salted herring, ½ cup milk, 50 g dried
cep mushrooms, 1 largish onion, 2 tbsps oil, salt,
pepper, 1 tbsp lemon juice, 1 cup white haricot beans*

Rinse the mushroom and soak them overnight in 5 cups of boiled water. Rinse the beans and also soak them overnight in water. Soak the herring in cold water, cut it into fillets. Remove the skin and bones, pour over the milk and leave for an hour. Scrub the beets and bake them in the oven (ca 25 mins). Cook the mushrooms, take them out and cut into thin strips. Rinse the herring, dry it and cut it into thin strips. Heat up one spoonful of oil in a frying pan and fry the chopped onion, but do not brown it. Peel the beets and grate them coarsely. Bring the mushroom stock to the boil, add the beets and onion and cook for 15 mins. Strain the soup, add the herring and mushrooms, season with lemon juice and pepper. Cook the beans, adding salt towards the end, drain them, mix with the remaining oil. Serve the borsch with the beans.

serves 4 • Preparation: 20 mins • Cooking: 40–45 mins

Clear borsch with prunes

*700 g beets, 100 g stoned prunes, 4 cups
boiled water, 2 cups beetroot and apple juice,
3 tbsps honey, a pinch of each ground cloves
and grated lemon rind, salt, pepper*

Scrub the beets and bake them in the oven. Rinse the prunes and soak them in two cups of boiled water, add the ground cloves and lemon rind and cook them together. Peel the baked beets and grate them coarsely. Pour over two cups of hot water and bring to the boil, then simmer for 10 mins. Strain the stock, season with salt and pepper, add the honey and the strained prune stock. Pour in the beetroot and apple juice. If necessary, add some pepper to taste. Serve with patties and diablotins.

serves 4 • Preparation: 30–35 mins • Cooking: 10–15 mins

Clear borsch

500 g beets, 250 g tart apples,
4 cups light chicken stock, 2–3 dried
cep mushrooms, 2 onions studded with
2–3 cloves, ¼ celeriac, 2–3 cloves of garlic,
1 bay leaf, 5–6 grains each allspice, juniper
and pepper, juice and grated rind from
½ lemon, salt, pepper and sugar to taste

Rinse the mushrooms and soak them in water, then cook them. Scrub the beets and bake them in the oven. Cook the stock with the onions, the peeled and grated celeriac, bay leaf, lemon rind, pepper, juniper and allspice. Peel the baked beets and grate them coarsely. Add them to the stock together with the grated apples and the mushroom stock. When the soup starts boiling, take the pot off the heat, add the crushed garlic and salt and leave for one or two hours. Then strain it, add salt, pepper and lemon juice to taste, and heat it up, but keep it off the boil. Serve hot with pasties, breadsticks or crackers.

serves 4 • Preparation: 10–15 mins • Cooking: 30–40 mins

Lvov borsch

5 cups beef stock, 600 g beets, 150 g crabapple
preserve, 2 lemons, 1 cup cream, salt,
pepper, sugar to taste, ½ tsp marjoram

Scrub the beets and bake them in the oven. Peel the lemon, slice it, remove the pips. Put the lemon slices, together with the crabapple preserve and marjoram, in a pan, cover with the hot stock and bring to the boil. Add the peeled and coarsely grated beets and simmer for about 15 mins. Rub the whole through a sieve, season to taste, add the cream. Serve with boiled potatoes with melted butter or cream.

serves 4 • Preparation: 10–15 mins • Cooking: 20–25 mins

Podlasie borsch

100 g dried cep mushrooms, 100 g stoned
prunes, 1–2 beets, 1 carrot, 1 onion, ½ small
cabbage, 2 tbsps tomato paste, salt, sugar,
lemon juice or wine vinegar, 2 tbsps oil

Rinse the mushroom and prunes and soak them separately overnight. The next day cook them till tender, strain them and leave the stock aside. Scrub the beets and bake them in the oven, then peel them and cut into strips. Shred the cabbage, put it into a pan, cover with the hot mushroom and prune stock. Simmer over low heat for several minutes. Peel the carrot and grate it coarsely. Peel the onion and cut it into small cubes. Heat the oil in a pan, fry the onion, but do not let it brown. Add the carrot and sauté it for a minute or two, stirring all the time. Add the mushroom cut into strips and tomato paste. Pour over 2–3 cups of boiled water and simmer for 10 mins. Add the prunes, combine with the cooked cabbage and beets, season to taste with salt, sugar and lemon juice. Stir thoroughly and simmer for a while longer.

serves 4 • Preparation: 30 mins • Cooking: 30 mins

Zhur or white borsch

Centuries ago, soup was made from grain which had been ground between stones. This is how zhur, also known as white borsch, that our ancestors liked so much, was made. Aleksander Brückner says that the Polish name *zhur* was derived from the German word *sauer* or sour. This is one of the oldest Polish soups, described as early as the 13th century, and for ages it was a national dish in Poland. This uncomplicated dish survived for centuries among the common people and in the cuisine of the ruling classes. Zhur was made on the basis of stock from meat, smoked meats, white sausage, the fore quarters of hare, herring or peas; it was thickened with milk or cream. Almost every region of Poland has its own typical way of making white borsch.

The basis for all of them is soured rye-flour juice which should be made a few days before, although it can also be kept for longer.

Soured rye-flour juice:

Take 100 grams of wholemeal rye flour, a crust of rye bread and 2 cloves of garlic. Pour over two glasses of lukewarm boiled water and leave in a warm place for four to five days until it acquires a pleasant sour smell and taste. If a skin of mould forms on the surface, it should be removed before the liquid is added to the soup. The longer the soured rye-flour juice stands, the sourer it will become; therefore if you do not use it at once, it is a good idea to pour it into bottles after four or five days, cork them tightly and keep in a cool place. But it is better still to make it fresh each time, since it tastes best after four to five days.

Lenten zhur

100 g fine rye flour, 100 g wholemeal rye flour, crust of wholemeal bread, 1–2 cloves of garlic, ½ celeriac, 2 parsley roots, 4–5 dried cep mushrooms, salt, 2 cloves of garlic, ½ cup sour cream

Make soured rye-flour juice in the following way: mix both kinds of flour well, pour it into a jar. Add the peeled garlic and bread crust. Cover with 4 cups of warm boiled water. Cover the jar with a piece of gauze and leave aside in a warm place for several days. Peel and rinse the celeriac and parsley roots, cut them into pieces and together with the rinsed mushrooms put them in a pan. Cover with 2 cups of hot water. Bring to the boil, then simmer until the mushrooms are tender. Strain the stock and cut the mushrooms into thin strips. Strain the flour juice, pour it into a pan, add the hot vegetable stock and strips of mushrooms. Simmer over low heat, occasionally stirring. Mix the cream with crushed garlic and salt, pour into the soup, and stir. Serve with boiled potatoes.

serves 4 • Preparation: 10 mins • Cooking: 30 mins

Old Polish zhur

1 l beef stock, 1 cup soured rye-flour juice, 1 cup juice from salted cucumbers, 1 cup cream, 1 tbsp flour, salt, pepper, marjoram, 1–2 cloves of garlic, 400 g white sausage

Bring the stock to the boil, put in the sausage and crushed garlic and simmer. Take out the sausage when ready. Add the cucumber and rye-flour juice to the stock, bring to the boil. Season with pepper and salt to taste. Add the cream mixed with the flour and marjoram. Put in slices of the cooked sausage and heat up. Serve with bread.

serves 4 • Cooking: 20–30 mins

Zhur with sausage

2 cups soured rye-flour juice, 300 g white sausage, 100 g smoked bacon, 1 onion, 2 dried cep mushrooms, 2 cloves of garlic, 1 tsp stock from soup cubes, 1 bay leaf, 2–3 grains allspice, 2 tsps marjoram, salt, pepper, 4 hard-boiled eggs, ½ cup thick cream

Rinse the mushrooms and soak them in water for 2–3 hours, then cook them. Boil 3 cups of water with bay leaf, allspice, onion and garlic. Add the mushrooms, mushroom stock and sausage. Simmer over low heat for 40 mins. Strain the stock, add the stock and bacon cut into cubes. Bring to the boil, pour in the rye-flour juice and put in the mushrooms cut into strips, the sausage cut into slices and marjoram. Bring to the boil again, take off the heat and mix with the cream. Serve with hard-boiled eggs cut into quarters.

serves 4 • Preparation: 10 mins • Cooking: 45 mins

Instant zhur

500 g bones, 250 g soup vegetables, 2 cups soured rye-flour juice, 1½ l water, 1 large onion, 200 g sausage, 5 eggs, ½ cup cream, 1–2 cloves of garlic, 1 tbsp grated horseradish, 1 tbsp lard, salt

Make stock from the bones and vegetables. Chop the sausage finely and fry it in lard, add the sliced onion.

Old Polish zhur

Strain the stock, bring to the boil, pour in the rye-flour juice. Add the sausage and onion and simmer over low heat for 5–7 mins. Mix the crushed garlic with salt and cream, add to the soup and stir. Season to taste with pepper and salt.

serves 4 • Preparation: 15 mins • Cooking: 5–7 mins

Podhale zhur

150 g mushrooms, 1 carrot, 1 parsley root, 500 g smoked bacon, 100 g ham, 100 g sausage, 100 g roast pork, 2 cups soured rye-flour juice, 1½ l water, 4 hard-boiled eggs

Cover the bacon with water and cook till tender, then take it out. Add the finely chopped mushrooms, carrot and parsley root to the stock, bring to the boil, then simmer for 30 mins. Pour in the rye-flour juice and again bring to the boil. Season with pepper and salt, add the cream, thin slices of bacon, roast pork, ham and sausage. Stir. Serve with hard-boiled eggs, with potatoes or bread.

Soured oat-meal juice:

Take 1 litre of boiled water and 1½ cups of oat meal (processed porridge oats). Put the flour into an earthenware jar, pour over 1 cup of warm (60°C) boiled water, stir well. Add the remaining water, cover with gauze and leave for four or five days in a warm place.

serves 4 • Preparation: 10–15 mins • Cooking: 30–40 mins

Cracow oats zhur

2 cups soured oat-meal juice, 1½ l potato stock, 1 cup cream, 1 tbsp flour, 150 g cottage cheese, salt, 2 tbsps chopped dill

Strain the freshly cooked potato stock, combine with the oat-meal juice, and bring to the boil. Mix the flour with the cream and pour into the soup. Bring the soup to the boil, add salt to taste. Before serving, put in the crumbled cheese and chopped dill. Serve with potatoes.

serves 4 • Preparation: 40 mins • Cooking: 10 mins

Przemyśl zhur with herring

2 cups soured oat-meal juice, 3 cups water, 1 salted herring, 4–5 dried cep mushrooms, ½ cup cream, salt, pepper

Soak the herring in water, then remove the skin and bones, cut the meat into thin strips. Rinse the mushrooms and soak them in boiled water for 2–3 hours, then cook them. Take the mushrooms out and cut them into strips. Add the oat-meal juice to the mushrooms stock, bring to the boil and season with pepper and salt to taste. Add the cream, stir well and heat up. Put in the herring and mushrooms and stir well. Serve with cooked peas or boiled potatoes.

serves 4 • Preparation: 15 mins • Cooking: 25–30 mins

Old Polish soups

The Old Polish term *polewka* or 'brew' was later replaced by the name *zupa* or 'soup' which came from the German.

Black brew or black soup is an excellent Old Polish soup which is unknown in other countries. It can be made from the blood of ducks, geese, hares or piglets, to which sieved dried fruit can be added.

The Horeszkos refused the girl to Soplica!
For they gave me, Jacek, black brew!

This is of course from the famous Polish epic poem *Pan Tadeusz* by the Romantic poet Adam Mickiewicz, for this was the Old Polish custom: in the homes of the gentry it was a delicate way of refusing a suitor the hand of a young lady that he was courting. This sweet and sour soup was the bane of bachelors seeking brides. Served to the young man seeking the hand of a young lady, it meant a refusal. It was unknown in other countries, but became famous in Poland not only because of its culinary qualities but because of the symbolic meaning that it acquired. From the 18th century, a great many recipes for this tasty soup appeared in cookery books.

Old Polish black soup

...It must be very carefully prepared. First, a little white vinegar should be boiled with salt, cooled, and then the blood of geese, ducks or piglets should be let into it as they are killed, and stirred constantly. Only the goose giblets are used in the soup, while the goose itself is roasted. The giblets should be boiled with several pounds of pork. The duck or piglet should be scalded and scorched over the fire to clean it and then placed in a pot to make broth. This is boiled, skimmed of scum and fat, and strained. Then soup vegetables are added with leeks, a few mushrooms, a whole onion, salt, some spices, allspice, pepper, a couple of bay leaves, and a piece of bacon fat together with the skin. When everything has boiled soft, the broth is put through a sieve, and the duck or piglet is removed and placed on a covered dish and left to cool quickly. These are used to make a dish with sauce, for which some of the clear broth should be kept aside. Then a tablespoon of flour is added to the blood and vinegar and mixed well, and added to the strained broth to taste. Then some good vinegar should be added together with a few lumps of sugar, and it should be heated, taking care that it does not turn. Dried pears and prunes, or in the summer fresh fruit (which give a very good flavour), should be boiled separately, and placed in the soup tureen together with noodles. The giblets should be served separately on a dish together with fruit and covered with the rest of the black soup.

Makary, *730 obiadów* (5th edition, 1903)

Black brew

soup vegetables, 1 large onion, 150 g pork fat, duck wings and giblets, juice from 2 lemons, 5 grains each juniper and allspice, 2–3 peppercorns, 1–2 cloves, 1 bay leaf, ¼ tsp grated lemon rind, 1 tbsp sugar, 1 tbsp flour, 100 g stoned prunes, 1–2 dried pears, 1 tbsp dark currants, 1 tbsp dry white wine, 1 tbsp butter, salt

Pour the lemon juice (or boiled wine vinegar) into a pan. Bleed a duck into it, add a pinch of salt and whisk vigor-ously so that the blood does not congeal. Cover the rinsed prunes and pears with boiled water and leave aside for half an hour. Rinse the currants, put them in a bowl and sprinkle with wine. Combine them with the prunes and pears and cook them. Stick the clove in the rinsed onion, peel and rinse the vegetables. Rinse the duck wings and giblets. Cut the pork fat into small cubes. Put all the ingredients into a large skillet, cover with boiling water, add the juniper, allspice, peppercorns, bay leaf and lemon zest. Bring to the boil and cook for 50 mins, then strain the soup. Mix the flour with sugar, add it to the blood and whisk again, adding one tablespoon of broth at a time. Combine with the prune and pear stock and the remaining broth and cook, whisking all the time. Cut the prunes, pears, flesh from the wings and giblets into strips. Add them to the soup together with the raisins. Serve hot, with noodles. Before serving, adjust the taste with lemon juice and salt.

serves 4 • Preparation: 30 mins • Cooking: 1 hr

Beer soups

This exceptionally popular Old Polish beer soup fell out of favour only at the beginning of the 20th century. There were very many varieties of meatless soups, mostly flavoured with sugar, cinnamon and sultanas and thickened with grated rye bread and usually served for breakfast (!) with croutons and lemon slices, or else with slightly dried up cottage cheese.

Sigismund the Old's beer soup

500 g wholemeal bread, 1 l lager beer, 2 cups water, 100 g butter, 100 g hazelnuts, 1–2 tbsps honey

Cut the bread (without crust) into cubes, put into a pan, cover with the beer and water. Bring to the boil, then simmer for 15 mins and put through a blender. Chop the hazelnuts finely, mix them with the butter and 1 tbsp of honey. Put into a pan placed on top of a pot with boiling water. Gradually pour in the beer mixture, whisking all the time. Add salt and, if required, more honey.

serves 4 • Preparation: 5 mins • Cooking: 15–20 mins

White beer soup

4 cups beer, 2 tbsps sugar, cinnamon, several cloves, ½ tsp grated lemon rind, juice from ½ lemon, 1 cup thick sour cream, 4 egg yolks, 1 tsp caster sugar, 250 g cottage cheese

Cook the beer with the sugar, cinnamon, cloves, lemon rind and lemon juice. Beat well the egg yolks with the caster sugar, and then with the cream. Pour in slowly into the soup, stirring all the time. Heat the soup up, but do not allow it to boil. Serve with cottage cheese.

serves 4 • Preparation: 10 mins • Cooking: 5–7 mins

The morning meal of our ancestor included their favourite soup made from beer, honey or sugar, eggs, saffron and cinnamon. Later a drop of wine used to be added to the soup, or instead of beer soup, some kind of wine soup was served.

Łukasz Gołębiowski, *Domy i dwory* (vol. IV, p. 103)

Beer soup I

4 cups lager beer, 3–4 slices of bread without crust, 2–3 cloves, a piece of cinnamon, 4 egg yolks, 4 tbsps sugar, 2 tbsps raisins, 1 tbsp butter, several slices of brown bread, 1 lemon

Bring 2 cups of beer with the crumbled bread, cinnamon and cloves to the boil, then simmer for a minute or two. Force through a strainer. Combine with the remaining beer, add the rinsed and dried raisins and butter, and bring the whole to the boil again. Whisk the egg yolks with sugar, add to the soup. Scrub the lemon, scald it with boiling water, dry it and cut into slices (remove the pips). Cut the brown bread into cubes and toast it in a hot frying pan. Serve the soup with the croutons and lemon slices.

serves 4 • Preparation: 10 mins • Cooking: 10 mins

Beer soup II

3 cups lager beer, ¾ cup boiled water, 2 egg yolks, 3 tbsps sugar, a piece of dry orange rind, 2–3 cloves, 1 cinammon stick, 2 pieces of dry brown bread, 1 cup thick cream, 200 g dried-up cottage cheese

Bring the water to the boil, add 1 tbsp of sugar, cinnamon, cloves and orange rind, put in the crumbled bread and simmer for 10 mins. Sieve it, mix with the beer and bring to the boil again. Add the cream and heat up a bit. Whisk the egg yolks and the remaining sugar, add the mixture to the soup and stir – keep it off the boil. Serve with cottage cheese cut into cubes.

serves 4 • Preparation: 10 mins • Cooking: 10 mins

Beer soup III

4 cups beer, 1 lemon, 1 tbsp olive oil, 1–2 tbsps honey

Bring the beer and honey to the boil, add the oil and sliced lemon (remember to remove the pips). Serve with croutons.

serves 4 • Preparation: 10 mins • Cooking: 10 mins

Beer soup IV

4 cups lager beer, 100 g wholemeal bread without crust, 1 tbsp butter, ½ tsp caraway seed, 2–3 tsps sugar, ½ cup boiled water, salt

Boil the beer with the caraway and crumbled bread, add a pinch of salt, sugar and butter. Cook for 5–7 mins, then force through a strainer. Dilute the soup with some boiled water, add more sugar if needed. Serve with brown bread toast.

serves 4 • Preparation: 10 mins • Cooking: 10 mins

Old Polish wine soup

For many centuries, this was the ladies' beloved breakfast soup. It was served hot, with a dash of sweet cream added, or else mixed with egg yolks whisked with sugar. Sometimes, clear wine soup was served without any extras.

4 cups dry red wine, 3 cups boiled water, 1 cup sugar, 2 lemons, 1 orange, 2–3 cloves, a piece of cinnamon

Peel the orange and lemons, cut them in thin slices, remove the pips. Mix the wine with water, add the sugar, cloves, cinnamon and fruit slices. Bring the whole to the boil, then cool it down. Strain, pour into a tureen and chill for two hours. Serve very cold, with sponge cakes or cookies.

serves 4 • Preparation: 5 mins • Cooking: 10 mins

Carnival soup

2 cups mead, 200 g each stoned prunes and dried pears, 150 g each dried apples, cherries and apricots, juice and grated rind from 1 lemon, ¼ tsp powdered cinnamon, 2–3 cloves, 2 egg yolks, ½ cup honey, 2 tbsps sugar

Rinse the prunes, pears and apples, cover with boiled water and leave overnight. Separately soak the rinsed cherries in water. The next day stone the cherries. Cook all the fruit, sieve them, mix with the honey, lemon juice and cinnamon. Boil I cup of water with the sugar, cloves and lemon rind, add the rinsed apricots and simmer for 20 mins. Combine the strained apricot stock with the puréed fruit, add the mead. Bring to the boil, put in the apricots cut into strips, thicken with the egg yolks. If the soup is too thick, add more wine or water. Serve with cookies.

serves 4 • Preparation: 40 mins • Cooking: 20–25 mins

Poppyseed soup

1 cup poppyseed, 2 cups milk, 3 cups water, 1 vanilla pod, 50 g raisins, 1 tbsp chopped candied orange peel, 2 egg yolks, 3–4 tbsps sugar

Rinse the poppyseed, cover with boiling milk and leave overnight in a warm place. Put the poppyseed through a mincer. Chop the vanilla finely. Beat it together with the poppyseed and 2 tbsps of sugar. Transfer the poppyseed to a pan, pour over hot water, add the orange peel and blanched raisins. Stir well and heat up over low heat. Blend the egg yolks with the remaining sugar, add to the soup and whisk thoroughly. Serve with ginger or almond biscuits.

serves 4 • Preparation: 20–30 mins • Cooking: 10 mins

Hawthorn soup

2 cups boiled water, 2 cups hawthorn wine, 4 tbsps honey-dew honey, 1 tbsp dried raspberries, 2 cloves, a small piece of cinnamon, ½ cup single cream

Pour the wine and water into a pan, add the cinnamon, cloves, dried raspberries and stir. Bring to the boil, then simmer over low heat. Take off the heat, season, add the honey and stir well. Strain the soup and add the cream. Serve with cookies or choix pastry balls.

serves 4 • Cooking: 10–15 mins

Knights' broth

soup vegetables, 500 g pork spare ribs or bones, 1 bay leaf, 1 clove, 3–4 grains each allspice and pepper, 300 g pork liver, ½ cup milk, 2 onions, 2 egg yolks, 2 tbsps butter, salt, pepper, ¼ tsp grated nutmeg, 2 tbsps dry white wine

Make a stock from the vegetables, bones and spices. Clean the liver of the membrane, cover with the milk and leave aside for an hour, then take it out and cut into slices. Slice the onions and fry them (but do not brown) in I tbsp of butter, put in the liver slices and fry them together. Add several spoonfuls of the stock and simmer over low heat. Strain the stock, remove the flesh from the bones. Put the meat, carrots, parsley root, celeriac, onion, half of the liver, and half the stock through a blender. Sieve the preparation, mix with the remaining stock, season with salt, pepper and nutmeg. Add the remaining liver cut in fine cubes, bring to the boil. Mix thoroughly the egg yolks with the wine and pour slowly into the soup, stirring all the time. Take off the heat. Serve with brown bread toast.

serves 4 • Preparation: 30 mins • Cooking: 1 hr

Spring broth

500 g new leaves of weeds (pigweed, nettles, goutweed, sorrel, sow-thistle, borage, horsefoot), ½ cup borage flowers, 2–3 potatoes, 1 large onion, 1 tbsp butter, salt, pepper, 1 cup cream, 4 cups chicken or vegetable stock, 1 tbsp lemon juice

Wash the leaves thoroughly, drain, then chop them finely. Peel the potatoes and cut them into cubes. Put the potatoes in a pan and cover with the stock. Bring it to the boil, add the chopped leaves and the finely diced onion fried in butter. Stir and simmer over low heat for 25 mins. Season to taste with salt, pepper and lemon juice, add the cream, stir and heat up. Garnish the soup plates with borage flowers.

serves 4 • Preparation: 10 mins • Cooking: 25 mins

Purée and cream soups

Cream of broccoli

500 g broccoli, 1 medium-sized onion, 1–2 crushed cloves of garlic, 1 tbsp butter, 4 cups chicken stock, ¼ tsp grated lemon rind, 1 bay leaf, salt, pepper, 3 tbsps lemon juice, ½ cup thick sour cream

Rinse the broccoli. Cut off the stalks, peel them and dice. Melt the butter in a pan, fry the chopped onion, but do not let it brown. Add the bay leaf and garlic and fry for a minute or two, stirring all the time. Put in the broccoli stalks, add the stock and bring to the boil. Simmer over low heat for 5 mins, take out the bay leaf and put in the broccoli florets. Cover the pan and simmer for another 10 mins. Season to taste. Take out part of the broccoli florets with a strainer. Leave the soup to cool down a bit, then put it through a blender and purée in a sieve. Add salt, pepper, lemon juice and zest. Heat the soup up, then take it off the heat. Mix in the cream, add the broccoli florets. Serve with white toast, choux pastry balls or quarters of hard-boiled eggs.

serves 4 • Preparation: 10 mins • Cooking: 20 mins

Cream of beets

5 cups chicken stock, 500 g garden beets, 1 large tart apple, 2 ripe pears, 1 glass dry red wine, 1 tsp finely chopped fresh ginger, 1 tsp potato flour, 1 cup thick sour cream, salt, if required 1 tbsp lemon juice and a pinch of sugar

Wash the beets, apple and pears, peel and grate them. Put them into a pan, add the chopped ginger, cover with the hot stock. Bring to the boil, then cover and simmer for two hours. Put the mixture through a blender, sieve it, then heat up. Mix the potato flour well with the wine, pour into the hot soup and, stirring all the time, heat the soup up until it has thickened. Add some salt to taste, if necessary also some lemon juice and sugar. Before serving, add some cream.

serves 4 • Preparation: 20–30 mins • Cooking: 10 mins

Old Polish lemony cream

3 cups dry white wine, 2 cups water, 3 tbsps breadcrumbs, a piece of cinnamon, 1 clove, grated rind from 1 lemon, 5 egg yolks, juice from 1½ lemons, 4 tbsps sugar, sponge biscuits

Boil the water with the breadcrumbs, cinnamon and clove, then sieve the mixture. Add the lemon zest and wine and heat up slowly. Beat the egg yolks with sugar into a fluffy paste, mix thoroughly with the lemon juice. Bring the stock to the boil. Stirring all the time, pour in the egg and lemon sauce. Take the pot off the heat at once. Serve with biscuits.

serves 4 • Preparation: 10 mins • Cooking: 10 mins

Cream of lemon

5 cups vegetable stock, 2 lemons, 2½ tbsps rice flour, 1½ tbsps butter, ½ cup single cream, 1 egg yolk, salt, 1 tbsp chopped lemon balm

Scrub the lemons, scald them with boiling water, grate the rind. Bring the stock to the boil, add the lemon zest and cook for 3–5 mins, then strain the liquid. Mix the butter with the rice flour, put into the hot stock and, stirring all the time, heat it up until the soup has thickened. Add the juice of one lemon and the cream mixed with the egg yolk. Stirring continuously, heat it up. Peel the other lemon, remove the white skin. Cut the lemon into cubes, remove the pips and put the lemon into the soup. Add some salt and, if necessary, a pinch of sugar. Serve hot, with croutons, or cold. Garnish with finely chopped lemon balm.

serves 4 • Preparation: 10 mins • Cooking: 10 mins

Cream of zucchini

8 small zicchini, 1 large onion, 3–4 cloves of garlic, 2 tbsps butter, 4 cups chicken or vegetable stock, 1 tbsp lemon juice, ¼ tsp grated lemon rind, 1 cup cream, 1 raw egg yolk, salt, pepper, 2 tbsps finely chopped parsley

Peel the onion and dice it into cubes. Rinse and dry the zuccini, grate coarsely. Melt the butter in a pan and fry the onion, but do not let it brown. Add the zuccini and finely chopped garlic, fry them quickly. Add the lemon zest, salt and pepper. Pour over the stock, bring it to the boil and then simmer uncovered for 10 mins. Leave it to cool a bit, then put it through a blender and sieve it. Add salt and pepper to taste and bring to the boil. Mix the cream well with the lemon juice and egg yolk, pour the mixture into the soup. Stir the soup, heat it up, but do not allow it to boil. Before serving, garnish with chopped parsley. Serve with choux pastry balls or croutons.

serves 4 • Preparation: 10 mins • Cooking: 15 mins

Old Polish cream of celeriac

1 large celeriac, 1 tsp lemon juice, 3–4 dried cep mushrooms, 4 cups stock, ½ cup thick cream, 1 egg yolk, ½ tsp dried lovage, ¼ tsp nutmeg, salt, pepper, 2 tbsps finely chopped celery leaves

Rinse the mushrooms and soak them overnight in a small amount of lukewarm water. Cook the mushrooms, then cut them into strips. Scrub the celeriac, peel and slice it. Sprinkle the slices with lemon juice, put into a pan, add the lovage. Cover with the stock and simmer for 30 mins. Then put it through a blender, sieve, combine with the mushroom stock. Bring to the boil, season with salt, pep-

per and nutmeg. Mix the cream with the egg yolk and pour slowly into the soup, stirring all the time. Add the mushroom strips. Garnish with the finely chopped celery leaves. Serve with white toast or choux pastry balls.

serves 4 • Preparation: 5–7 mins • Cooking: 30 mins

Cream of celeriac with ham

600 g celeriac (1 large root), 400 g potatoes, 150 g onion, 150 g well cured lean ham, 4 cups chicken stock, 2 tbsps lemon juice, 2 tbsps butter, 3 tbsps thick cream, 2 egg yolks, salt, pepper, 2 tbsps chopped celery leaves or parsley

Peel the celeriac, rinse it, grate coarsely, sprinkle with lemon juice. Peel the potatoes, wash them and cut into cubes. Peel the onions and chop them finely. Melt the butter in a pan, fry the onion, but do not let it brown. Add the celeriac and fry it quickly. Add the potatoes, stir well, pour over the hot stock and simmer for 30 mins. Leave it to cool a bit, then put it through a blender and sieve. Bring the puréed soup to the boil, add the ham cut into cubes, season to taste with salt and pepper. Mix the cream and egg yolks, pour the mixture slowly into the soup, stirring all the time. Keep the soup off the boil. Garnish with finely chopped greens.

serves 4 • Preparation: 10 mins • Cooking: 30 mins

Cream of celeriac with cheese

1 celeriac (300–400 g), juice from 1 lemon, 1 large onion, 1 large potato, 1 tart apple, 1 tbsp butter, ¼ tsp grated lemon rind, 150 g Roquefort, 4–5 cup chicken stock, ½ cup single cream, 2 egg yolks, ½ tsp grated nutmeg, 1 tbsp finely chopped celery leaves

Wash the celeriac, peel it and grate coarsely, then sprinkle sparsely with lemon juice. Peel the onion, chop it finely, fry in melted butter, but do not brown. Add the grated celeriac and fry for a minute or two, then put in the grated apple and the finely chopped peeled potato. Pour in the stock, bring to the boil, then simmer for 25 mins. Leave it to cool a bit, then put it through a blender and add the crumbled cheese. Pour into a pan, bring to the boil, season to taste with nutmeg, salt and lemon juice (if required, add a pinch of sugar). Mix the cream and the egg yolks and pour slowly into the soup, stirring all the time. Heat the soup up, but do not allow it to boil. Garnish with chopped celery leaves.

serves 4 • Preparation: 10 mins • Cooking: 25 mins

Cream of cauliflower

1 large cauliflower, 2 onions, 2 carrots, 1 parsley root, a bunch of parsley sprigs, 4 cups chicken stock, 1 cup milk, 1 tbsp butter, ½ cup single cream, ½ cup dry white wine, 1 egg yolk, salt, sugar, 1 tsp turmeric

Boil salted water with sugar, put in the cauliflower and cook it for 10–12 mins. Drain it, pour over cold water, divide into florets. Peel the onions, carrots and parsley root, chop them finely. Melt the butter in a pan, fry the onion (but do not brown it), add the carrots, parsley root and half the bunch of parsley, fry them quickly. Pour in the hot stock, add the cauliflower stalks and cook together for 40 mins. Put the vegetables through a blender and sieve them. Add the wine and cauliflower florets, simmer for 5–6 mins. Mix thoroughly the milk with the cream, egg yolk and turmeric, pour in the mixture into the hot soup. Stir it and keep it off the boil. Season to taste. Before serving, garnish with chopped parsley. Serve with croutons or choux pastry balls.

serves 4 • Preparation: 20 mins • Cooking: 40 mins

Cream of kohlrabi

2–3 young kohlrabi stalks with leaves, 1 cup cooked rice, 1 tbsp butter, 5 cups chicken stock, 1 cup single cream, 1 egg yolk, ½ cup tinned sweetcorn, 2 tbsps lean ham cut into thin strips, ¼ tsp each powdered ginger and grated nutmeg, salt, white pepper

Peel the kohlrabi stalks, cut them into cubes. Melt the butter in a pan, stir fry the kohlrabi, add the cooked rice, pour in the hot stock. Add half the kohlrabi leaves and cook for 30 mins. Leave the soup to cool a bit, then put it through a blender. Season with salt, pepper, ginger and nutmeg, stir and bring to the boil. Mix the cream with the egg yolk and the remaining finely chopped kohlrabi leaves.

Cream of cauliflower

Pour into the soup, add the drained sweetcorn and thin strips of ham. Heat up before serving.

serves 4 • Preparation: 5–7 mins • Cooking: 30 mins

Royal cream of fish

1 kg various fish (preferably a piece of each pikeperch, carp, salmon and pike), soup vegetables, 1 onion, 3 eggs, 100 g rice, 1 tbsp butter, 1 tsp lemon juice, ¼ tsp grated lemon rind, 1 tsp salt

Cook the rice with 1 tsp of butter. Rub the fish fillets with salt, fry them in butter, then cook them for a while. When the fish is cool, remove the bones. Make a stock from the vegetables and the lemon zest. Hard-boil the eggs. Put the fish meat, rice and eggs through a mincer. Pour the vegetable stock over the mixture and bring to the boil. Sieve it, then heat it up and season with salt and lemon juice. Serve with white bread toast or with fish balls.

serves 4 • Preparation: 40 mins • Cooking: 5–7 mins

Cream of fish with horseradish

1 kg small fish, 1–2 carp heads, soup vegetables, 1 onion, 1 piece of horseradish, 1 bay leaf, 3–4 grains each allspice and pepper, salt, ½ tsp dried basil, 1 tbsp butter, 1 tsp flour, ½ cup cream, 1 tbsp lemon juice

Clean the fish, rinse them and rub with salt. Make a stock from the vegetables, carp heads and spices. Put in the fish and cook for 30 mins. Strain the stock. Remove the fish bones. Sieve the fish meat and the vegetables, season with basil and stir. Make a roux from butter and flour, add some cream and pour into the soup. Stir the soup and heat it up, but do not allow it to boil. Serve with fish balls or brown bread toast.

serves 4 • Preparation: 20 mins • Cooking: 30 mins

Cream of mushrooms

500 g mushrooms, 1 large, finely chopped onion, 2–3 bay leaves, 1 tbsp each finely chopped fresh marjoram and tarragon, salt, pepper, ½ cup dry red wine, 1 tbsp lemon juice, 3–4 cups light stock, 2 tbsps butter, 3 tbsps chopped parsley

Melt the butter in a pan, fry the onion (but do not brown it), add the tarragon and marjoram and fry for a minute or two, stirring all the time. Put in the chopped mushrooms and fry over high heat for 4–5 mins, until they have browned and the sauce has evaporated. Add the crushed bay leaves, pour over the hot stock, cover the pan and simmer for 40 mins. Leave it to cool a bit, then put it through a blender. Pour in the wine, heat it up, add some salt, if required a pinch of sugar. Garnish with chopped parsley. Serve with choux pastry balls or white bread toast.

serves 4 • Preparation: 10 mins • Cooking: 40 mins

White cream of potatoes

400 g potato purée, 3 cups stock, 2 cups single cream, 2 egg yolks, 2–3 tbsps grated horseradish, 1 tsp flour, 2 tbsps butter, salt, pepper, 1 tbsp lemon juice

Melt the butter in a pan, add the flour to make a roux. Dilute it with a cup of stock and simmer, stirring all the time, until the sauce has thickened. Season with salt, a pinch of pepper and lemon juice. Mix the cream with the egg yolks and grated horseradish. Bring the remaining stock to the boil, add the purée, mix thoroughly. Pour in the sauce and bring the whole to the boil. Add the cream mixed with the egg yolks, stir well, heat up, but do not allow it to boil. Serve with white bread toast or choux pastry balls.

serves 4 • Preparation: 15 mins • Cooking: 10 mins

Golden cream

300 g potato purée, 1 cup carrot juice, 3 cups light chicken stock, 1 cup single cream, 1 tbsp butter, 1 tsp lemon juice, salt, a pinch of each pepper, grated nutmeg and sugar

Mix the butter with the lemon juice, sugar, nutmeg and pepper, add the cream and the carrot juice. Combine the stock with the potato purée, bring to the boil, pour in the carrot sauce. Mix thoroughly and heat up. Add some salt if required. Serve with white bread toast.

serves 4 • Preparation: 5 mins • Cooking: 5 mins

Cream of potatoes and sorrel

1½ l chicken stock, 250 g sorrel, 500 g potatoes,
tbsp butter, 1 cup thick cream, salt, pepper,
pinch of sugar, 4 hard-boiled eggs

Peel and rinse the potatoes, cut them into cubes. Put
in a pan, cover with the hot stock and cook. Wash
and drain the sorrel, chop it finely and fry in melted butter. Add the sorrel to the soup and simmer together for
7–8 mins. Put it through a blender and sieve. Season to
taste with salt, pepper, a pinch of sugar as required. Pour
in the cream, stir well and heat up. Serve with hard-boiled
eggs cut into quarters.

serves 4 • Preparation: 5–7 mins • Cooking: 20 mins

Cream of peas

400 g cleaned green peas, 3–4 spring onions,
tbsps butter, 1 tsp flour, 4 cups chicken or
vegetable stock, 1 cup cream, 1 tsp curry powder,
tsp lemon juice, a pinch of sugar, salt, pepper,
tbsp each chopped parsley and borage leaves

Rinse the onions and chop them finely. Melt the butter
in a pan, add the onions and fry for a minute or two,
stirring all the time. Sprinkle with curry powder, add 400 g
of peas, pour over 2 cups of hot stock and simmer for
20–25 mins. When it cools a bit, put through a blender,
then sieve. Bring the remaining stock to the boil in another
pan and cook the remaining peas. Combine with the pea
purée, add salt and pepper, lemon juice and a pinch of
sugar. Mix the cream well with the flour and pour into
the soup. Stirring all the time, heat the soup up until it has
thickened. Garnish with chopped greens.

serves 4 • Preparation: 10 mins • Cooking: 25 mins

Savoury cream of peas

400 g green peas, 2 carrots, 2 large onions, 2 celery
stems, 3–4 cloves of garlic, bouquet garni, 5 cups
chicken or vegetable stock, 100 g smoked bacon,
tbsps butter, 1 cup yogurt, pepper paste (1 red
pepper, 2 chilli pods, 2 cloves of garlic, a piece
of bread without crust, 4 tbsps olive oil, salt)

Bake the pepper in the oven, then skin it, remove the
seeds; chop the flesh finely, then blend it with crumbled
bread, chilli, peeled garlic and salt; gradually pour in the oil
in the process. Pour the mixture into a bowl and chill a bit.
Peel the onions, carrots and celery, chop them finely, put
into a pan, add the bouquet garni and peas, pour over the
hot stock and simmer over low heat for 35 mins. Take out
the bouquet garni and put the soup through a blender,
then sieve it. Heat it up to almost the boiling point, pour
into a tureen, mix with the yogurt and the paprika paste.
Serve with choux pastry balls or white bread toast.

serves 4 • Preparation: 30 mins • Cooking: 30 mins

Savoury cream of nuts and almonds

1 chicken breast fillet (ca 150 g), 1 onion, 1 carrot,
2 cloves of garlic, 2–3 peppercorns, 1 clove, 1–2 sprigs
of parsley, 1 sprig of thyme, 4 cups stock, ¼ cup
chopped walnuts, 3 tbsps almond flakes, 2 cloves
of garlic, 1 red onion, 1 tbsp butter, ½ cup cream,
1 raw egg yolk, ½ tsp ground pepper, salt

Peel the carrot, skin the garlic, wash the onion and stuck
in it 1 clove, rinse the fillet. Put all of them into a pan,
pour over the hot stock, add the peppercorns, parsley
and thyme and simmer for 40 mins. Take out the meat
when ready, strain the stock. Peel the red onion and two
cloves of garlic, chop them finely, then fry in butter without browning them. Add the nuts and almond flakes and
fry them together, stirring all the time. Combine with the
cooled stock, add some pepper and purée the mixture.
Bring the purée to the boil, add some salt if required. Mix
the cream with the egg yolk and pour into the soup. Heat
the soup up, but do not allow it to boil. Cut the chicken
meat into cubes and put them into the soup.

serves 4 • Preparation: 5 mins • Cooking: 40 mins

Cream of walnuts

250 g beef with bone, soup vegetables, 400 g shelled
walnuts, 3 egg yolks, 1 cup cream, salt, pepper,
a pinch of sugar, 1 tsp lemon juice

Make a broth from the meat and vegetables, strain it.
Grind the nuts or chop them very finely, then mix

with the cream and egg yolk. Pour into the broth and bring to the boil. Add salt, pepper, sugar and lemon juice to taste. Serve with white bread toast or crackers.

serves 4 • Preparation: 5 mins • Cooking: 1 hr

Cream of asparagus

*250 g veal bones, soup vegetables, 1 onion,
500 g asparagus, 2 cubes of sugar, 1 tbsp butter,
2 egg yolks, ½ cup cream, 1 tbsp chopped parsley, salt*

Make a stock from the bones, vegetables and onion. Separately cook the asparagus in a small amount of water with butter and sugar. Take out the asparagus with a strainer, cut off the tips and put them into a tureen. Put the asparagus stalks through a blender, then sieve the purée. Combine the processed asparagus, stock and water in which the asparagus was cooked. Bring to the boil, add salt, pour in the cream mixed with the egg yolks. Pour into the tureen. Garnish with chopped parsley.

serves 4 • Preparation: 5–7 mins • Cooking: 40 mins

Cream of asparagus with salmon

*1 tin asparagus (400 g), 4 cups chicken stock,
1 cup cream, 1 egg yolk, 1 slice of smoked salmon
(ca 100 g), 2 tbsps chopped dill, 1 tsp lemon
juice, salt, white pepper, a pinch of sugar*

Take out the asparagus, cut off the tips. Cook the asparagus stalks in the chicken stock, put them through a blender and sieve. Bring to the boil again and add the cream mixed with the egg yolks. Heat the soup up, but keep it off the boil. Season to taste with lemon juice, white pepper, sugar and salt, if required. Add the asparagus tips and the salmon cut into thin strips. Sprinkle with chopped dill.

serves 4 • Preparation: 10 mins • Cooking: 5 mins

Cream of salsify

*500 g salsify, 1 tbsp wine vinegar, 200 g potatoes,
200 g onion, 100 g roast turkey breast, 4 cups light
chicken stock, ½ cup cream, 2 egg yolks, salt,*
white pepper, 1 tbsp lemon juice, a pinch of sugar,
3 tbsps chopped dill*

Clean the salsify, putting the stalks immediately in water with vinegar (to prevent them getting dark). Peel the potatoes and onions, wash them and cut into slices. Dice the salsify. Bring the stock to the boil, add the potatoes, onion and salsify, again bring to the boil, then simmer for 30–35 mins. Put the vegetables through a blender, then sieve the purée. Heat up, add salt, pepper, lemon juice and some sugar to taste. Bring to the boil, add the turkey breast cut into cubes, pour in the cream mixed with the egg yolks. Stir and heat up, but do not allow it to boil. Serve with toast or choux pastry balls.

serves 4 • Preparation: 20 mins • Cooking: 35 mins

Cream of pears

*500 g pears, 2 tbsps lemon juice, 400 g dog rosehips,
3 tbsps honey, 1 tbsp finely chopped fresh ginger,
1 tbsp grated lemon rind, 1 cup dry white wine,
1 cup single cream, 1 egg yolk, 2 tbsps butter*

Top and tail the rosehips, cut them in half, remove the seeds, wash thoroughly. Put into a pan, add 1 cup of boiled water and leave for 2–3 hours. Then strain the berries, bring the water to the boil. Melt the butter in a pan, put in the rosehips and fry them for a minute or two. Pour in the boiling rose water and simmer covered over low heat until the berries are tender. Peel and core the pears, cut them into quarters, sprinkle with lemon juice. Boil 2 cups of water with the honey and lemon zest. Put in the pears and ginger, cover the pan and simmer over low heat. Combine with the rosehips, put through a blender, then sieve. Pour in the wine and bring to the boil. Mix the cream well with the egg yolk, add to the soup. Heat up the soup, but do not allow it to boil. Serve with choux pastry balls or white bread toast.

serves 4 • Preparation: 15 mins • Cooking: 15 mins

Green cream of lettuce

*2 heads crispy lettuce, 1 thick leek, 200 g new nettle
leaves, 100 g spinach, a bunch of parsley, 2 tbsps*

butter, 2 tbsps lemon juice, ½ tsp grated lemon rind, ½ tsp each salt and white pepper, 1½ l chicken stock

Wash the leek thoroughly, cut it into very thin slices. Wash and drain the nettle, spinach and parsley, chop them finely. In a large pan melt the butter, add the leek and fry it for a minute or two over high heat, add the nettle, spinach, parsley and shredded lettuce leaves, mix and fry to- gether for a bit. Sprinkle with lemon juice and zest and simmer for 10 mins, then pour in the hot stock. Bring to the boil, cover and simmer for another 5–6 mins. Leave to cool a bit, then put through a blender. Heat up the soup, add salt, pepper, some sugar and lemon juice if required. Serve with white bread toast or choux pastry balls.

serves 4 • Preparation: 25–30 mins • Cooking: 5–6 mins

Cream of endive with ginger

5 large endives, 3–4 large potatoes, 5 cups chicken stock, 2 tbsps finely chopped fresh ginger, ½ tsp each curry powder and ground caraway, juice of 1 lemon and 1 orange, ¼ tsp each grated lemon and orange rind, ¾ cup thick cream, salt, 2 tbsps finely chopped fresh lemon balm leaves

Peel and wash the potatoes. Rinse and drain the en- dives. Chop them finely together with the potatoes. Put into a pan, cover with the boiling stock. Add salt, ginger, lemon and orange zest. Bring to the boil, then simmer for 30–35 mins. Put through a blender, sieve, pour into a pan. Add the caraway, curry powder, lemon and orange juice and again bring to the boil. Pour in the cream, mix and heat up, but keep it off the boil. Garnish with chopped lemon balm leaves. Serve with patties or crackers.

serves 4 • Preparation: 10 mins • Cooking: 35 mins

Cream of pumpkin with sherry

1 kg pumpkin, 1 glass sherry, 1 cup cream, 4 cups chicken stock, 1 tbsp finely chopped fresh ginger, salt, pepper

Peel the squash, remove the seeds, cut the flesh into cubes. Bring the stock to the boil, add the squash

cubes, salt and ginger, simmer for 40 mins, stirring occa- sionally. Put the squash through a blender, mix the purée with the cream. Heat it up, add the sherry and season with pepper to taste.

serves 4 • Preparation: 5 mins • Cooking: 40 mins

Cream of vegetables with herbs

2 each small carrots, parsley roots and celery sticks, 1 red onion, 3–4 potatoes, 1 butter lettuce, 2–3 sprigs of each parsley and dill, 3–4 leaves of each basil and savory, 1 small sprig of thyme (or ¼ tsp dried thyme), 2 tbsps butter, 3 cups light chicken stock, salt, pepper, ½ cup cream, 1 tbsp lemon juice, 2 tbsps chopped chives, ½ red pepper, 50 g lean ham, 4–6 hard-boiled quail eggs

Peel the carrots and parsley roots and grate them coarse- ly. Peel the potatoes and cut them into cubes. Clean the celery sticks and dice them. Melt the butter in a pan, fry the finely chopped onion (but do not brown it), add the carrots, parsley roots, celery and potatoes. Sauté them, stirring all the time, pour over the hot stock and cook for 10–15 mins. Add the herbs and shredded lettuce and cook for another 15 mins. Put through a blender and sieve. Add the lemon juice, salt and pepper to taste. Bring to the boil, pour in the cream and mix well. Peel the eggs, cut them into quarters. Cut the ham and pepper into fine cubes and add them to the soup together with the quail eggs.

serves 4 • Preparation: 15 mins • Cooking: 25–30 mins

Cream of asparagus with dill

400 g green asparagus, 1 large onion, 1–2 potatoes, 3 cups light chicken stock, salt, pepper, 2–3 tbsps olive oil, ½ cup yogurt, 1 tbsp lemon juice, a pinch of sugar, 3 tbsps chopped dill

Peel and wash the potatoes, cut them into cubes. Peel the onion and chop it finely. Clean the asparagus and dice it. Heat up the oil in a pan, put in the onion and po- tatoes. Sauté them, stirring all the time. Add the aspara- gus, stir, cover the pan and simmer for 10 mins. Pour in the hot stock, bring to the boil, then simmer for another 20–25 mins. Add salt, pepper, lemon juice and sugar, leave to cool a bit, then put through a blender and sieve. Heat up and mix with yogurt and dill.

serves 4 • Preparation: 10 mins • Cooking: 35 mins

Cream of spinach

*150 g fresh spinach, some watercress, 1–2 potatoes,
1–2 onions, 1–2 cloves of garlic, 2 tbsps olive oil,
3 cups chicken stock, ½ cup cream, salt, pepper,
1 tsp lemon juice, ½ tsp chopped thyme leaves*

Peel the potatoes and onions, wash them and cut into cubes. Heat the oil in a pan, put in the potatoes and onion and sauté them, stirring all the time. Add the washed and drained spinach and watercress. Stir well, cover the pan and cook for 5–7 mins. Pour in the hot stock, bring to the boil, then simmer covered for 20–25 mins. Peel the garlic and chop it finely, mix it with salt and pepper. Leave the soup to cool a bit, then put it through a blender together with the garlic. Season to taste with lemon juice, heat up, pour in the cream. Before serving, garnish with chopped thyme.

serves 4 • Preparation: 5–7 mins • Cooking: 30–35 mins

Fish soups

There are many kinds of fish soup made from either one kind of fish – carp, eel, perch – or from a mixture of small fish, often with added tomato or red pepper purée. They are usually served with noodles, patties or fish balls.

Fish soup with crayfish

*1 kg small fish, 2–3 crayfish, soup vegetables, 2 onions,
2 frozen tomatoes or 1 tsp tomato concentrate,
2 bay leaves, several grains each allspice and
pepper, a pinch of nutmeg, 1 cup white wine*

Make a stock from the vegetables and spices, add the fish and cook for 25 mins, then strain the stock. Scrub and rinse the crayfish, put them into the boiling stock and cook for 10 mins. Take them out, remove the black bitter-tasting gut. Take out the white meat from the tail and claws, pound the shells. Sieve the vegetables, tomatoes and boned fish. Add the purée to the stock. Put in the meat from the claws and crushed shells, pour in the wine and cook over low heat for 15 mins. Put in the meat from the tails, season to taste. Serve with white bread croutons.

*serves 4 • Preparation:
15 mins • Cooking: 1 hr*

Carp
soup with raisins

*4–5 carp heads, 500 g carp fillets, soup vegetables,
1 large onion, 1–2 cloves, 3–4 grains each allspice
and pepper, 4–5 tbsps plum jam, 1 tbsp honey,
1 tsp lemon juice, 100 g raisins, 1 glass dry
white wine, salt, 1 cup cream, 1–2 egg yolks*

Rinse and dry the fillets, rub them with salt, wrap in foil and put in the fridge for 1–2 hours. Remove the eyes, wash the heads, rub with salt. Make a stock from the vegetables, onion and spices, put in the fish heads and bring to the boil. Simmer for 30–35 mins, then strain the stock. Put the fillets into a pan, pour over the hot stock and simmer for 15 mins. Take out the fish gently, remove the bones and cut the meat into pieces. Rinse the raisins, cover them with wine and leave to soak for a few minutes. Add the honey, lemon juice, plum jam and raisins to the stock, stir, bring to the boil. Pour in the cream mixed with the egg yolks, put in the fish pieces, heat up the soup, but do not allow it to boil. Serve with choux pastry balls or white bread croutons.

serves 4 • Preparation: 20 mins • Cooking: 1 hr

Spicy fish soup

2 salmon heads, 1 fillet of trout (150 g), 2 l water, 1 bay leaf, grated rind and juice from 1 lemon, 2–3 grains each pepper and allspice, 2 celery sticks, ½ bunch of parsley, 1 tsp dried mint, ½ tsp each dried rosemary and lemon balm, 1 large onion, 3 egg yolks, salt, pepper, 2 tbsps each chopped parsley and chives

Remove the eyes, wash the heads, rub them with salt and leave aside for several minutes. Rinse and dry the fillet, sprinkle with lemon juice, rub with salt and leave aside for half an hour. Boil the water with the onion, celery sticks, parsley, mint, rosemary, lemon balm, lemon rind, bay leaf, pepper and allspice. Simmer covered for 15 mins, put in the salmon heads. Bring to the boil, then simmer for 20 mins. Take out the heads and put in the trout, simmer for another 15 mins. Take out the fillet, leave it to cool, then remove the bones and cut the meat in cubes. Take out the flesh from the heads, put it through a blender together with the stock, then sieve it. Season with lemon juice, add a pinch of sugar if required. Mix some boiled water with the egg yolks, pour the mixture into the soup. Put in the trout pieces, heat up, add the chopped parsley and chives, stir and take off the heat. Serve with white bread croutons, diablotins or vegetable croquettes.

serves 4 • Preparation: 20 mins • Cooking: 50 mins

Fish broth

1 kg small fish (roach, perch, bream), salt, 1 tbsp lemon juice, 1 tbsp flour, ½ cup oil, 2 onions, 1 parsley root, peel from ½ orange, 1–2 cloves of garlic, salt, pepper

Clean the fish, wash and dry them, rub with salt, sprinkle with lemon juice, coat with flour and fry in very hot oil until golden brown. Leave 2–3 fishes aside. In a separate pan fry the finely chopped onion in oil, but do

not brown it. Boil 2 litres of water with the grated parsley root, orange peel, salt, pepper and finely chopped garlic. Add the fried onion and fish, bring to the boil, then simmer for 30 mins. Purée in a sieve. Remove the skin and bones from the remaining fish, cut the fish meat in cubes and add to the soup.

serves 4 • Preparation: 20 mins • Cooking: 40 mins

Eel soup (Kurpie region)

soup vegetables, 1 large onion, 3–4 lemon slices with rind (without pips), 1 tsp lemon juice, 1–2 cloves, 5–6 grains each pepper and allspice, 1 bay leaf, 1 eel (ca 1 kg), 4–5 prunes, 6–8 slices each dried apples and pears, 1 tsp honey, salt, pepper

Clean the eel, remove the skin and the backbone, cut the flesh into sizeable cubes. Sprinkle with salt sparingly and with lemon juice, leave aside for 15 mins. Rinse the fruit, cover with a small amount of boiled water and leave to soak for an hour. Peel the vegetables, rinse and chop them. Peel the onion and stud it with the cloves. Put the eel skin and trimmings into a pan, add the vegetables, onion, lemon slices, allspice, pepper and bay leaf. Cover with 5 cups of boiling water, bring to the boil, then simmer for 50 mins. Strain the stock, pour over the eel meat and simmer for 10 mins. Cook the soaked fruit, then cut into strips. Add the honey, lemon juice and fruit strips to the fruit stock, combine with the fish stock, stir and simmer for another 10 mins. Season with salt and pepper. Serve with white bread croutons or choux pastry balls.

serves 4 • Preparation: 20 mins • Cooking: 60 mins

Lithuanian fish soup

1 kg small fish (roach, perch, crucian carp), soup vegetables, 1 onion, 1 sizeable horseradish root, 1 large potato, 1 cup cream, 1 egg yolk, salt, pepper, 1 bay leaf, a pinch of dried basil, a piece of lemon rind, 1 slice of lemon (without pips), 2 tbsps chopped dill, 4–5 slices of brown bread, 1 tbsp butter

Peel and wash the vegetables, potato, onion and horseradish. Put in a pan, cover with 4 cups of water, add the basil and bay leaf and bring to the boil. Clean and wash the fish, rub them with salt, put into the boiling stock together with the lemon and lemon rind. Bring to the boil, then simmer for 40 mins. Strain the stock, bone the fish. Put the fish meat, vegetables, onion, potato and horseradish through a blender, then sieve and combine with the stock. Mix the cream and egg yolk. Bring the soup to the boil, turn down the heat and slowly pour in the cream and egg yolk mixture, stirring all the time. Heat up the soup, but do not allow it to boil. Season to taste. Cut the bread into cubes, put in a hot pan and toast it. Serve the soup with brown bread croutons.

serves 4 • Preparation: 25 mins • Cooking: 40 mins

Bream soup

1–1½ kg bream, ¼ tsp saffron, 2 bay leaves, 1 large lemon, ½ cup finely chopped nettle and sorrel leaves, 2 tbsps each chopped daisy leaves and spinach, 2–3 tbsps curd cheese, 1 cup yogurt, 1 tbsp butter, salt, pepper, 1 tsp lemon juice, 2 tbsps each chopped dill and chives

Clean the fish, wash and dry it, rub with salt, wrap in foil and put in the fridge for 1–2 hours. Scrub the lemon, scald it with boiling water, cut into slices, remove the pips. Boil 1½ litres of water with saffron and bay leaves, cook for 5 mins, then add the lemon slices and a pinch of salt. Cook for another 3–4 mins, put in the fish and simmer for 20–25 mins. Take out the fish, leave it to cool, then bone it and cut into pieces. Melt the butter in a pan, add the chopped greens, sprinkle with lemon juice and cook, then combine with the strained fish stock and cook for another 5 mins. Mix very thoroughly the yogurt and cheese, pour into the soup, stir well. Add the fish pieces, heat up the soup, but keep it off the boil. Before serving, sprinkle with dill and chives.

serves 4 • Preparation: 20 mins • Cooking: 30–35 mins

Milt soup

carp milt and roe, 2–3 carp heads, soup vegetables, 2 largish onions, 1 bay leaf, lemon rind, juice from ½ lemon, ½ tsp thyme, salt, 1 tbsp butter, 1 tsp flour, ½ cup single cream, 1 egg yolk

Make a stock from the vegetables, onion and carp heads, add the lemon rind and bay leaf. Strain the stock, add the thyme, lemon juice and the milt and roe from which the membrane has been removed. Simmer over low heat for 15 mins. Take out the milt and roe, cut into cubes. Make a roux from the butter and flour, add 2–3 tbsps of cold boiled water, pour into the fish stock and simmer until the soup has thickened. Mix the cream and egg yolk and pour into the soup. Stir, heat the soup up, but do not allow it to boil. Add the roe and milt, season to taste. Serve with white bread croutons.

serves 4 • Preparation: 15 mins • Cooking: 15 mins

Tench soup

750 g tench, soup vegetables, 2 onions, 250 g button mushrooms, 1½ tbsps butter, 2–3 tbsps chopped parsley, ½ cup cream, salt, pepper, 1 tsp lemon juice, a pinch of dried thyme

Make a stock from the vegetables and one onion. Clean the fish, rinse it and rub with salt, put into the stock and cook 25–30 mins. Wash and dry the mushrooms, cut them into strips, sprinkle with lemon juice and thyme. Chop finely the other onion, fry it in butter, but do not let it brown, add the mushrooms and sauté them, stirring all the time. Add 2–3 tbsps of the stock, cover and simmer over low heat for several minutes. Take out the fish, bone it, cut into cubes. Strain the stock, combine with the mushrooms and the fish, add salt and pepper. Bring to the boil, pour in the cream, stir well. Garnish with chopped parsley before serving. Serve with noodles or rice.

serves 4 • Preparation: 15 mins • Cooking: 1 hr

Piquant fish soup

500 g cod fillets, 2–3 dried cep mushrooms, 100 g champignons, 3 onions, 1–2 cloves of garlic, 1 red and green pepper, 2 tbsps butter, 1 tbsp flour, 2 bay leaves, 2–3 grains each pepper and allspice, ¼ tsp curry powder and grated lemon rind, 1 tsp soya sauce, 1 tbsp lemon juice, salt, pepper

Rinse the dried mushrooms, cover with one cup of boiled water and leave for one or two hours, then cook them. Sprinkle the fish with lemon juice and leave in a cold place for an hour. Fry the finely chopped onion in butter, but do not let it brown. Add the chopped champignons and fry over high heat for a while, stirring all the time. Sprinkle with flour, add pepper, curry powder, crushed garlic with salt, soya sauce and 2–4 tbsps of stock. Stir well and simmer covered. Boil 5 cups of water with one onion, lemon zest and spices. Put in the fillets, bring to the boil, then simmer for 15 mins. Take out the fish gently with a strainer, strain the stock. Wash and seed the peppers, cut them into strips. Cut the soaked dried mushrooms into strips. Put the peppers and mushrooms into the stock, bring to the boil, add the fish cut into cubes and the champignons. Stir and season to taste.

serves 4 • Preparation: 20 mins • Cooking: 25 mins

Mushroom soups

Christmas Eve mushroom soup

50 g dried cep mushrooms, soup vegetables, peppercorns, lemon juice, salt

Make a stock from the vegetables, add salt and pepper. Strain the stock (you may use the vegetables for vegetable or herring salad). Pour the stock over the rinsed mushrooms and cook them under cover. Strain the stock, adjust the taste with a bit of lemon juice and salt. Serve with all kinds of noodles. You may put the mushrooms cut into strips into the soup or use them for some stuffing.

serves 4 • Preparation: 10 mins • Cooking: 55–60 mins

Clear mushroom soup

15–16 caps dried cep mushrooms, salt, pepper, 6 cups boiled water

Rinse the mushroom, cover them with boiled water and leave overnight, then cook them until tender. Take them out, cut into thin strips, add to the mushroom stock. Add some salt and a liberal amount of pepper. Serve with noodles or patties.

serves 4 • Preparation: 20 mins • Cooking: 40 mins

Mushroom soup from the Kurp region

100 g dried cep mushrooms, 50 g each prunes, dried pears and apples, 2 carrots, 2 parsley roots, 1 small celeriac, 2–4 bay leaves, 5–6 grains each allspice and pepper, 2 tbsps oil, juice and grated rind from 1 lemon, 1–1½ tbsps honey, salt, pepper

Rinse the mushrooms, cover with hot water and leave aside for 15 mins. Peel and wash the vegetables, put into a pan, add the spices and rinsed fruit. Pour over 2–3 litres of hot water. Bring to the boil, then simmer for 30 mins. Add the mushrooms, grated lemon rind and half the lemon juice and cook for another 30 mins. Take off the heat, add the honey, the remaining lemon juice, salt and pepper, stir. Leave for several hours, then strain the stock. Put the fruit with the stock through a blender and sieve. Cut the mushrooms into strips, add to the soup, heat it up. Serve with noodles or toast.

serves 4 • Preparation: 30 mins • Cooking: 1 hr

Krupnik

Krupnik is a kind of soup made from vegetable and meat stock, thickened with kasha, usually barley, or rice.

Barley krupnik with peas

3–4 tbsps barley, 1 cup split peas, 3–4 carrots, 4–5 large potatoes, 2 large onions, 2–3 cloves of garlic, 1 tbsp lard, salt, pepper, 4 cups stock, 3 tbsps chopped parsley

Rinse the peas and soak them in water overnight, then drain them. Rinse the barley and drain it in a sieve. Peel the carrots and potatoes and dice them. Chop finely the onion and garlic. Heat up the lard in a pan, fry the onion and garlic (but do not let them brown), sprinkle with 2–3 tbsps of water. Stir, add the peas, pour in the stock and bring to the boil. Add the carrots and potatoes, bring to the boil again, then simmer for 10 mins. Put in the barley, stir and cook over low heat for one hour. Before serving, season with salt and pepper and sprinkle with chopped parsley.

serves 4 • Soaking: 12 hrs • Preparation: 20–25 mins • Cooking: 1½ hrs

Barley krupnik

100 g barley, 500 g potatoes, 100 g carrots, 5 cups strong beef stock, salt, pepper, 3 tbsps chopped parsley, ½ cup single cream

Rinse the barley, drain it in a sieve. Peel and wash the potatoes and carrots, dice them. Put the barley, potatoes and carrots into a pan, cover with the hot stock, bring to the boil, then simmer for 40 mins. Towards the end, add salt and pepper, pour in the cream and garnish with chopped parsley.

serves 4 • Preparation: 15 mins • Cooking: 40–45 mins

Peasants' krupnik

500 g ox tail, 300 g carrots, 300 g swede, 1 large leek, 2 onions, 4 tbsps butter, 1 tbsp flour, 5–6 tbsps barley, 3–4 bay leaves, several peppercorns, 2–3 grains allspice, ½ tsp dried thyme, ¼ tsp paprika, salt, 2 l water, 1 glass juniper vodka

Wash the ox tail and cut it into pieces. Melt 1 tbsp of butter in a pan, fry the ox tail until brown. Put the ox tail into a pan, cover with water, add pepper, bay leaves and thyme. Simmer for 40–45 mins. Peel the swede and carrots, cut them into thin strips. Wash the leek and slice it. Put the vegetables in a pan, add the rinsed barley, pour over the strained stock and cook for 20 mins. Fry the finely chopped onion in the remaining butter (but do not let it brown), sprinkle with flour, stir well. Add the onion to the soup, stirring all the time. Simmer for another 15–20 mins,

towards the end add salt, paprika and pepper to taste. Pour in the vodka and stir.

serves 4 • Preparation: 15 mins • Cooking: 1½ hrs

Rice krupnik

2 chicken legs, soup vegetables, 2 onions, 1 tbsp butter, ¼ cup rice, 2 egg yolks, juice and grated rind from 1 lemon, 1 tsp each chopped coriander, basil, dill and parsley, ½ tsp chopped thyme leaves, salt, pepper, paprika, a pinch of sugar if required

Put the washed chicken legs and the washed and peeled vegetables in a pan, pour in 6 cups of water and bring to the boil. Add the parsley, basil and thyme and simmer for an hour. Take the chicken out, strain the stock. Put the rinsed rice into a pan, cover with the stock and simmer for 10 mins. Bone the meat, cut it into cubes. Fry the finely chopped onion, but do not let it brown, add the meat and fry them together for a while. Add the chicken and onion to the soup, season with salt, pepper and paprika. Mix the egg yolks with the lemon zest and juice. Take the soup off the heat and, stirring all the time, pour in slowly the egg mixture. Garnish with chopped dill and corinader.

serves 4 • Preparation: 10 mins • Cooking: 55–70 mins

Red rice krupnik

4 lamb's knuckles, ½ cup rice, 1 kg tomatoes, 1 large onion, salt, pepper, grated nutmeg, 6 cups lager beer, 1 tbsp butter, 1 tbsp lemon juice, 2 tbsps finely chopped mint, a pinch of sugar if required

Put the rinsed knuckles into a pan, cover with the beer, bring to the boil, then simmer until the meat is tender. Take the meat out, leave it to cool, then bone it and cut into small pieces. Blanch and skin the tomatoes, cut them into cubes. Melt the butter in a pan, add the tomatoes and stew them over low heat, then sieve them. Add the finely chopped onion and the meat pieces, pour over the meat stock. Add salt, pepper and nutmeg, stir and cook for 10–15 mins. Add the rinsed rice and cook for another 20 mins. Season with lemon juice, if required add some more salt and a pinch of sugar. Sprinkle with chopped mint.

serves 4 • Preparation: 45 mins • Cooking: 35 mins

Green rice krupnik

*500 g young nettles, 3–4 spring onions, 2 tbsps
butter, 1 cup cooked rice, 1 tbsp lemon juice, ½ tsp
paprika, salt, 1 egg yolk, 2 tbsps chopped parsley*

Wash the nettles and onions, chop them and sauté
in butter. Sprinkle the rice with lemon juice, combine with the nettles. Cover with the stock and simmer for
5–6 mins. Mix the egg yolk with 2–3 tbsps of cold stock,
pour into the soup and stir well. Before serving, sprinkle
with chopped parsley.

serves 4 • Preparation: 10 mins • Cooking: 10–15 mins

Krupnik with prunes

*150 g stoned prunes, 100 g pearl barley,
2 tbsps butter, 2 tbsps honey, a pinch of salt,
2 cups water, 2 cups light chicken broth*

Rinse the prunes, cover them with lukewarm boiled
water and leave overnight, then cook them. Put half
of the prunes through a blender and sieve. Cut the other
half into thin strips. Pour the stock over the rinsed barley
and cook it for 20 mins. Add the prune purée, prune strips
and honey, stir and cook for another 30 mins. Take off the
heat, add the butter and stir.

serves 4 • Preparation: 20 mins • Cooking: 50 mins

Krupnik with mint

*½ cup pearl barley, 3 cups stock, 1 cup
yogurt, 1 tbsp butter, 1 large onion, 4 tbsps
finely chopped mint, salt, pepper*

Rinse the barley, pour over 1 cup of boiled water and
leave aside for 3–4 hours, then add it to the stock
and cook for 10–15 mins. Fry the finely chopped onion
in butter, but do not let it brown. Add the onion and the
chopped mint to the soup. Stir and cook over low heat for
another 15–20 mins. Add salt and pepper to taste. Mix the
yogurt with 2–3 tbsps of soup. Take the soup off the heat
and add the yogurt, then stir well.

serves 4 • Preparation: 10 mins • Cooking: 25–35 mins

Onion soups

Onion soup à la Przypkowski

There are many anecdotes about Tadeusz Przypkowski,
the founder of the Chapter of the Order of Pomian,
who in the grey days of the Polish People's Republic tried
to recall the heyday of Polish cuisine. I will quote one of
them. It was in 1964 that Professor Przypkowski wrote in
a letter to one of his friends:

*I have just come back from a meeting of the Voivod-
ship Committee of the Polish United Workers' Party in Kielce,
where I managed to push through the decision to introduce
regional recipes for use in the best local restaurants! The first
are to be Przypkowski's onion soup, Radziwiłł's collops and
Sobieski's blancmange! The Voivodship Committee has already
given orders to the Kielce bakeries for the production of brown
bread of the kind that the soup and collops require.*

He wrote elsewhere: *Przypkowski's onion soup (it is
under this name that it has become popular among the gourmands of Paris and has even been served in the best restaurant in Madrid) has been traditionally served for generations
in the Przypkowski family. While it has all the hallmarks of
Old Polish cuisine, it does not figure in any printed cookery
books.*

And here is the original recipe which I think is worth
making better known.

*6 large white onions, 6 pieces of brown bread, 3 tbsps
butter, 6 cups beef stock, grated nutmeg, powdered
ginger and cloves, curry powder, salt, pepper*

Heat up a frying pan well, brown the crumbled bread
in it. Melt the butter in another pan, fry the onion
sliced into fine rings, but do not let it brown. Put the bread
and onion in a pot, pour over the hot stock and simmer
for 40–50 mins. Rub through a sieve, add salt, season to
taste. Serve with hot savoury biscuits.

serves 4

Savoury biscuits for onion soup

*1½ cups flour, 125 g butter, 200 g yeast,
a pinch of sugar, ¼ cup lukewarm milk,
1 tsp ground caraway, salt, 1 egg*

Mix the yeast with sugar and milk and leave in a warm place for several minutes. Sift the flour, add the butter and chop it with the flour into a powdery mixture. Add some salt, caraway and yeast, work into a smooth dough. Sprinkle the working top with flour and roll the dough out. Cut out biscuits and arrange them on a greased baking sheet. Brush with some mixed egg on top. Bake in a preheated oven until golden brown.

Old Polish onion soup

*100 g brown bread without crust, 250 g onion,
2 tbsps butter, 3 egg yolks, ½ cup cream, salt*

Cut the bread into cubes, put in a pan, spread some butter on top of the cubes and put into a preheated oven. Keep in the oven until the bread dries and turns lightly brown. Dice the onion and cook it in the remaining butter. When the onion has become golden brown, add the bread, pour over boiled water (1½ l) and cook for 30–40 mins, then sieve. Bring to the boil and add the cream mixed with the egg yolks. Serve with white or brown bread croutons.

serves 4 • Preparation: 15 mins • Cooking: 40 mins

Onion soup with cheese

*300 g onion, 1–2 cloves of garlic, 3 cups beef stock,
2 tbsps butter, ½ tsp sugar, ¼ tsp dried thyme,
a pinch of each powdered nutmeg and cloves,
1 tsp flour, 3 tbsps grated Gruyère or Emmental
cheese, salt, pepper, 2 thick slices of white bread,
1 tbsp butter, 1–2 cloves of garlic, 1 tsp lemon juice*

Peel the onion, slice it finely. Melt the butter in a thick-bottomed pan, add the onion and fry it for 10 mins until golden brown. Sprinkle with sugar, stir. Cover the pan and simmer for 8–10 mins to brown the onion. Uncover, sprinkle with flour, stir. Add the garlic crushed with salt, thyme and cloves. Gradually pour in the cold stock. Turn up the heat and, stirring all the time, heat the soup up until it starts boiling. Then turn down the heat and simmer for 35–40 mins. Add salt and pepper to taste. Preheat the oven. Crush the chopped garlic with salt, lemon juice and butter. Spread the mixture on the bread slices, put the bread in the oven and bake it until golden brown. Pour the soup into individual ovenproof bowls, use half the grated cheese to sprinkle on top of each. Put one slice of bread in each bowl and sprinkle with the remaining cheese. Put into the oven for 5–6 mins (until the cheese starts melting).

serves 4 • Preparation: 25 mins • Cooking: 40 mins

Cabbage soups

Cabbage soup made from shredded white cabbage and or from sauerkraut had to be thick, served with cracklings or sausage.

Łukasz Gołębiowski, *Domy i dwory* (vol. IV, p. 33)

Spring cabbage soup

*1 young cabbage, 3 rhubarb sticks, 1 bunch of dill,
5–7 new potatoes, 2–3 spring onions, 1–2 new carrots,
2 tbsps butter, 100 g lean smoked bacon, 4 cups
chicken stock, 1 tsp flour, 1 tsp lemon juice, ¼ tsp
powdered caraway, salt, pepper, sugar to taste*

Rinse and dice the cabbage. Strip the stringy fibres from the rhubarb, cut it into thin slices. Peel and grate coarsely the carrots. Chop the spring onions. Melt 1 tbsp of butter in a pan, sauté the carrots, stirring frequently. Add the onion and cabbage and sauté for another 2–3 mins. Cover with the hot stock, bring to the boil, then simmer for 15–20 mins. Add the rhubarb and cumin, stir well. Cut the peeled potatoes into cubes. Melt the remaining butter in a frying pan, put in the bacon and potatoes, sprinkle with flour and fry them together, stirring all the time. Put the mixture into the soup, stir and cook for 10–15 mins.

Add salt, pepper, lemon juice and sugar to taste. Sprinkle generously with chopped dill.

serves 4 • Preparation: 30 mins • Cooking: 30–35 mins

Old Polish cabbage soup

*soup vegetables, 1 onion, 1 clove, 500 g pork ribs
(or bones), 1 small bay leaf, 1–2 grains allspice,
3–5 peppercorns, 7–8 juniper berries, 2 l water,
400 g sauerkraut, 20 g dried cep mushrooms,
3 tbsps plum jam, 1 tbsp lard, 1 tbsp flour,
salt, sugar, ¼ tsp ground juniper berries*

Rinse the mushroom, cover them with water and leave to soak overnight, then cook them. Rinse the ribs, peel and wash the vegetables and put all in a pan. Add the onion with a clove stuck into it, bay leaf, peppercorns, allspice and juniper berries. Cover with hot water and cook till tender. Strain the stock. Chop the cabbage, put into a pan, pour over the strained stock, add the mushrooms cut into thin strips and the mushroom stock. Cook for 30 mins, add the meat taken off the bones and cut into strips, the plum jam, juniper, and salt and sugar to taste. Stir and cook for several minutes longer. Thicken the soup with a roux made from the lard and flour. Serve with potatoes with cracklings.

serves 4 • Preparation: 10 mins • Cooking: 1 hr

Old Polish red cabbage soup

*1 red cabbage (ca 500 g), 100 g stoned prunes, 1 tbsp
honey, a pinch of ground cloves, 2 tbsps dry red wine,
2–3 potatoes, 1 onion, juice from 1 lemon, 1 tbsp butter,
1 tsp flour, 1½ l strong chicken stock, salt, pepper*

Rinse the prunes, cover them with I cup of stock and leave aside for 2–3 hours. Add the wine and cloves and cook. Leave to cool, then put through a blender together with the honey. Rinse the cabbage and dice it. Put it into a pan, pour over 4 cups of hot stock and cook over low heat for one hour. Season with lemon juice. Peel and wash the potatoes, cut them into cubes, cover with the remaining hot stock and cook for 15 mins. Fry the finely chopped onion in butter, but do not let it brown, sprinkle with flour, stir and add to the cabbage together with the plum jam and

cooked potatoes. Stir and heat up. Season to taste with pepper and lemon juice.

serves 4 • Preparation: 20 mins • Cooking: 55–75 mins

Cabbage soup, Ruthenian style

*500 g sauerkraut, 2 l light vegetable stock,
250 g smoked bacon, 1 bay leaf, 1 onion,
1 carrot, 1 parsley root, 2 tbsps tomato paste,
2 tbsps butter, 2–3 cloves of garlic, ½ cup cream,
salt, pepper, shop butter pastry, 1 egg*

Chop the sauerkraut, put into a pan together with the bacon, cover with the hot vegetables stock (2 cups). Add the bay leaf and ½ tbsp of tomato paste and cook under cover over low heat for 45–50 mins. Add the remaining stock and cook for another 30–40 mins. Peel the onion, carrot and parsley root, chop them finely and sauté in melted butter. Add the remaining tomato paste, season with pepper and pour into the soup. Stir the soup well, take it off the heat. Allow it to cool, then put it into the fridge for the night. The following day pour the soup into earthenware bowls, add some garlic crushed with salt into each of them. Seal each bowl with a layer of dough, brush with the mixed egg on top and put into a preheated oven for 30 mins.

serves 4 • Preparation: 10 mins • Cooking: 55–60 mins

Sauerkraut soup with mushrooms

*2 cups beef stock, 1 carrot, 1 parsley root,
1 medium-sized onion, 1 bay leaf, 7–9 peppercorns,
3–4 grains each allspice and juniper, ¼ tsp dried
lovage, 4–5 dried cep mushrooms, 1 cup boiled
water, 1 cup sauerkraut juice, 250 g sauerkraut,
1–2 cloves of garlic, salt, pepper and sugar to taste*

Rinse the mushrooms, cover them with boiled water and leave for 2–3 hours, then cook them. Wash the onion (without peeling it), peel the carrot and parsley root, put all into a pan, cover with the hot stock. Add the bay leaf, pepper, juniper, allspice and lovage. Bring to the boil, then cook over low heat for 30 mins. Strain the soup, combine with the mushroom stock, add the diced sauerkraut and the mushrooms cut into strips, and cook for 15 mins.

Pour in the sauerkraut juice and cook for another 5 min. Add crushed garlic with salt, stir, season to taste. Serve with sautéd potatoes or salted bread sticks.

serves 4 • Preparation: 10 mins • Cooking: 50 mins

Sauterkraut soup with caraway

2 cups sauerkraut juice, 150 g smoked bacon, 2 dried cep mushrooms, 1 large onion, 1 carrot, 8–10 peppercorns, 3–4 grains allspice, ¼ tsp caraway seeds, 1 bay leaf, 2 cups light stock, 2 tbsps chopped parsley

Rinse the mushrooms. Put them into a pan together with the bacon, onion, peeled carrot and spices. Pour in the stock, cover the pan and cook over low heat for 40 mins. Strain the soup, combine with the sauerkraut juice, bring to the boil, add some salt if required, season with pepper. Serve with croquettes, salted bread sticks or white bread toast. Sprinkle with chopped parsley before serving.

serves 4 • Preparation: 15 mins • Cooking: 40–45 mins

Potato soups

*Moderately seasoned but still hot
So nourishing
And so comforting
Potato soup, lovely potato soup*

– sang Wojciech Młynarski. As in Młynarski's song, so in real life, Polish potato soup has chopped crackling from bacon fat or smoked streaky bacon floating on the surface and some housewives add 2–3 dried mushrooms, or marjoram or caraway. Some make it golden with slices of carrot, and others make it green with chopped parsley. Some thicken it with cream and others serve it clear. This nourishing Old Polish soup with a French pedigree has as many flavours as there are households in Poland.

Old Polish potato soup with mushrooms

500 g potatoes, 20 g dried cep mushrooms, 1 medium-sized onion, 50 g each stoned prunes and raisins, 2 tbsps butter, 1 tsp flour, 1 glass white wine, salt

Rinse the prunes and cover them with 2 cups of boiled water. Rinse the mushrooms, cover them with 4 cups of boiled water and leave for 3–4 hours, then cook and strain the stock. Rinse and drain the raisins, pour over them the wine and leave aside for 15 mins. Peel the potatoes and cut them into cubes, cover with the mushroom stock and cook over low heat for 20 mins. Fry the finely chopped onion in butter, but do not let it brown, sprinkle with flour, then add some prune stock. Add the roux to the soup, put in the prunes cut into strips and raisins together with the wine. Bring to the boil.

serves 4 • Preparation: 20 mins • Cooking: 20–25 mins

Potato soup, Mazovian style

6 cups beef stock, 600 g potatoes, 1 large onion, a piece of celeriac, 1 carrot, 1 parsley root, 50 g pork fat, 50 g smoked bacon, 1 tsp flour, salt, pepper, 3 tbsps chopped parsley

Cut the pork fat and peeled onion into fine cubes, cut the peeled and washed carrot, celeriac and parsley root into thin strips. Render the pork fat in a frying pan, fry the onion (but do not let it brown), add the chopped vegetables and sauté over high heat for a minute or two. Turn the heat down and fry them for another 5–7 mins. Peel the potatoes, wash them and dice into cubes. Pour over the hot stock, bring to the boil, then cook over low heat for 20 mins. Add the sautéd vegetables, stir and cook for a while. Add salt and pepper. Fry the bacon cut into cubes in a hot frying pan, sprinkle with flour, add to the soup, stir and heat up. Before serving, sprinkle with chopped parsley.

serves 4 • Preparation: 15–20 mins • Cooking: 20–25 mins

Potato soup, Mazovian style

Green potato soup

*500 g potatoes, 1 large onion, 1 carrot,
1 parsley root, 3–4 cloves of garlic, salt, pepper,
¼ tsp ground caraway, 1 cup finely chopped
ground ivy leaves, 5 cups stock, 1 tbsp butter*

Chop the peeled onion into cubes, cut the peeled carrot and parsley root into thin strips or grate them coarsely. Melt the butter in a frying pan, fry the onion (but do not let it brown), add the carrot and parsley and sauté them. Peel and wash the potatoes, dice them in cubes, put them in a pan. Add the vegetables, pepper, caraway and 2 finely chopped cloves of garlic. Pour over the hot stock, bring to the boil, then cook over low heat for 20 mins. Add the chopped ground ivy leaves and the remaining garlic, stir and heat up. Add some salt and pepper to taste.

serves 4 • Preparation: 20 mins • Cooking: 20 mins

Ruthenian potato soup

*600 g potatoes, 300 g shoulder of pork, soup
vegetables, 2–3 grains each pepper and allspice,
1 bay leaf, 1½ l water, 2 large onions, 2 tart
apples, 1 tbsp lard, 1 tsp lemon juice, 2 tbsps
grated horseradish, 1 tsp green thyme
leaves or ½ tsp dried thyme, 1 tbsp chopped
parsley, salt, pepper, sugar to taste*

Put the peeled and washed vegetables and the meat into a pan, cover with hot water. Add pepper, bay leaf and allspice, and cook. Peel the apples and onions. Dice the onions, cut the apples in strips, sprinkle sparingly with lemon juice. Dice the peeled potatoes, put into a pan, cover with the strained stock, bring to the boil, then cook over low heat for 15 mins. Melt the lard in a frying pan, fry the onion (but do not let it brown), add the apples sprinkled with thyme and fry for a minute or two. Cut the cooked meat into cubes, add them to the soup together with the apple and onion mixture. Stir and cook for another 10 mins. Add the grated horseradish, some salt, pepper and sugar. Before serving, sprinkle with chopped parsley.

serves 4 • Preparation: 15–20 mins • Cooking: 30–35 mins

Potato soup from the Podhale region

*500 g potatoes, 300 g bryndza, 2 tbsps butter,
1 small lemon, salt, a pinch of each pepper and
sugar, 3 tbsps chopped parsley, 5 cups light chicken
or vegetable stock, ¼ tsp grated lemon rind*

Dice the peeled potatoes, put them in a pan, cover with the hot stock and cook for 20 mins. Peel the lemons, slice them finely, remove the pips. Blend the bryndza with the butter and grated lemon zest, put into the boiling soup and, stirring all the time, cook for 2–5 mins. Before serving put in the lemon slices and sprinkle with chopped parsley.

serves 4 • Preparation: 10–15 mins • Cooking: 20–25 mins

Tripe

Tripe was the favourite dish of Queen Jadwiga and King Ladislaus Jagiełło. It is a traditional Polish dish that has been known for centuries.

In Old Polish homes, tripe was served with ginger and a kind of haggis (the stomach stuffed with pearl barley, sliced and arranged around the tripe), with noodles made from oatmeal and meatballs. It was eaten with either white sauce or with saffron-flavoured yellow sauce.

But however it is cooked, tripe requires very careful cleaning and long cooking. Tripe is a rather heavy dish, but it is extremely tasty.

Traditional tripe

*1 kg beef tripe, 500 g beef with bone, soup vegetables,
1 onion, 1 bay leaf, 2–3 grains each allspice and pepper,
1 tbsp marjoram, 1 tsp each paprika, ginger and
nutmeg, 1 tbsp butter, 1 tsp flour, 6 tbsps grated cheese*

Clean and wash the tripe well. Put it in a pan, cover with hot water and cook for 5–10 mins, then drain and rinse. Pour in fresh water and cook again for several minutes. Repeat the process. Cover the tripe with hot water and cook until tender. Drain it. Make a stock from the meat, vegetables and onion, add allspice, pepper and bay leaf, then cook for a while. Strain the stock. Cut the vegetables and lean meat into strips. Cut the tripe into thin strips, mix with the meat and vegetables. Pour over the strained stock. Thicken with a roux from the butter and flour, bring to the boil. Season with marjoram, nutmeg, ginger and paprika. Serve with suet balls. Note: Cook the tripe one day earlier and season it with spices before serving.

serves 4 • Preparation: 1 hr • Cooking: 1 hr

Tripe à la niçoise

1 kg tripe, 2 tbsps butter, 1 tbsp flour,
150 g lean smoked bacon, 2 cups dry white wine,
2–3 tbsps tomato paste, 1 large onion, 2 cloves,
1–2 cloves of garlic, 1 bay leaf, 1 tsp dried thyme,
1 glass brandy, salt, pepper, 2–3 tbsps chopped parsley

Clean and wash the tripe, put in a pan, cover with boiling water and cook for 20 mins. Drain and return to the pan. Add the onion studded with cloves, garlic, bay leaf and thyme. Cover with cold water and cook for an hour and a half. Take out the tripe, drain it and cut into thin strips. Brown the finely diced bacon in a frying pan, add the butter, and fry for a minute or two, stirring all the time. Add the flour, dilute the roux with the white wine, combine with the tomato paste and, stirring continuously, cook until the sauce has thickened. Put in the cooked tripe and simmer for 30–40 mins. Towards the end, add salt and pepper to taste. Sprinkle with chopped parsley before serving.

serves 4–6 • Preparation: 20 mins • Cooking: 2 hr

Tripe à la piémontaise

700 g cooked veal tripe, 50 g bacon, 1 small savoy cabbage (ca 400 g), 2 leeks, 1 celery stick, 2 onions, 2 floury potatoes, 5–7 sage leaves, 1 bay leaf, 2 tbsps butter, 2 tbsps grated Parmesan, 6 cups beef stock, salt, pepper

Slice the cleaned and washed leeks and celery; cut the peeled potatoes into thick cubes; dice the onion and

bacon, chop the sage leaves. Cut the cooked tripe into thin strips. Melt the butter in a large pan, fry the bacon and celery, add the potatoes, leeks and onion and, stirring all the time, fry them lightly. Add the crushed bay leaf and sage. Pour in the hot stock, add the tripe, season with pepper and bring to the boil. Cover and cook over low heat for 50–60 mins. Shred the cabbage, add it to the tripe, stir (add some more stock if required) and simmer covered for another 50 mins. Before serving, add pepper and salt to taste, and mix in the Parmesan.

serves 4–6 • Preparation: 25–30 mins • Cooking: 2 hrs

Soups of all kinds

Soup is the overture, the preface, but it is something else as well. Its ingredients and flavour will give your guests some idea about what is to follow. Therefore put all the effort into the taste of the soup — just like a composer writing the overture to his new opera.

L. Ćwierciakiewiczowa

Mock turtle soup

In a saucepan, brown cubes of hazel grouse, partridge, pheasant, meat and veal in clarified butter, cover them with broth, add pork crackling and some vegetables, and make a strong stock which should be clarified and strained. Place it over heat and pour in arrowroot (which is the best potato flour) dissolved in cold water, add cayenne pepper, Madeira and brandy; slice boiled calf's head without gristle, salt and add an infusion of herbs made as follows: take 3 pinches of fresh marjoram, thyme, basil and parsley, 2 sliced shallots, 2 bay leaves and 1 mushroom, cover with ⅛ litre of boiling water and simmer under a tight lid.

(from the recipe of Tesler, chef to the counts Potocki)

Almond soup

250 g almonds, 2 tbsps almond flakes,
1 piece of cinnamon, 100 g sugar,
3 tbsps raisins, 1 l milk, ½ cup rice

Cook the rice. Rinse and blanch the raisins, then drain them. Blanch and skin the almonds, then chop and pound them, adding in the process a bit of water and lemon juice to enhance the flavour. Boil the milk with the cinnamon and sugar. Thin down the almond mixture with the milk, add the raisins and heat up, stirring all the time. Serve with rice sprinkled with almond flakes.

serves 4 • Preparation: 25–30 mins • Cooking: 5–6 mins

Walnut soup

1 l vegetable stock, ½ cup cream, 200 g chopped
walnuts, 2 egg yolks, salt, pepper, sugar

Blend the cream with the sugar, salt, pepper and egg yolks. Make a vegetable stock, add the chopped walnuts. Stirring all the time, gradually pour the cream mixture into the boiling strained stock – do not allow it to boil. Serve with white bread toast or choux pastry balls.

serves 4 • Preparation: 25–30 mins • Cooking: 5 mins

Old Polish caraway soup

soup vegetables, 1 onion, 1 clove, 1 bay leaf,
4 cups water, 300 g dry brown bread, 1 tbsp
caraway seeds, 2 egg yolks, 2 tbsps butter, salt

Chop the soup vegetables finely or grate them coarsely, stick the clove into the onion. Cut the bread into cubes and brown it in a frying pan. Put the vegetables, onion, caraway and bay leaf into a pan, cover with hot water, bring to the boil. Add the bread cubes and cook over low heat for 30 mins. Take the onion out, put the stock through a blender or sieve it. Add the butter and salt, pour in the egg yolks mixed with 1 tablespoon of water, heat up. Serve with white bread croutons.

serves 4 • Preparation: 10 mins • Cooking: 30 mins

Old Polish golden-brown soup

200 g veal with bone, soup vegetables,
2–3 dried cep mushrooms, 1 tbsp butter,
1 tsp flour, 2 tbsps ground caraway, salt

Peel and wash the vegetables and place them in a pan together with the meat and mushrooms. Cover with hot water, bring to the boil, then cook over low heat for 40–50 mins. Strain the stock. Make a roux from the butter and flour, dilute it with the stock. Process the cooked mushrooms and meat, mix with the stock, add the roux and bring to the boil. Serve with liver quenelles.

serves 4 • Preparation: 10 mins • Cooking: 50 mins

Hop soup

300 g new hop sprigs, 2–3 new hop leaves, 1 large
onion, 2 tbsps butter, 200 g green peas, salt, ¼ tsp
curry powder, 1 l chicken stock, 1 dry white bread roll

Cut the bread roll into cubes, brown them in butter (1 tbsp). Clean the hop sprigs, wash them and cut into pieces. Chop the onion finely and fry it, but do not let it brown. Bring the stock to the boil, add the onion, green peas and hop sprigs. Cook over low heat for 15 mins. Put the hop leaves into boiling water for a minute, drain them and chop finely. Add them to the soup together with the curry powder and a pinch of salt. Serve with croutons or choux pastry balls.

serves 4 • Preparation: 10 mins • Cooking: 15 mins

Soup with processed cheese

500 g new nettle leaves, 2–3 cubes of processed
cheese (e.g. Emmental), 1 cup milk, 1 egg yolk, salt,
pepper, ½ tsp curry powder, 1½ l chicken stock

Rinse and drain the nettle leaves, chop them finely. Bring the stock to the boil, add the curry powder and half the milk. Put in the chopped nettles and cook over low heat for 5 mins. Add the chopped pieces of cheese and, stirring continuously, cook until the cheese has melted. Season with salt and pepper. Pour in the egg yolk mixed with the remaining milk.

serves 4 • Preparation: 5–7 mins • Cooking: 10 mins

Shepherd's soup

1 cup chopped sorrel, 400 g onion, 2 tbsps chopped mint leaves, 2 tbsps oil, 1 egg, 200 g sheep's cheese, salt, pepper, 4–5 cups light stock or boiled water

Heat up the oil in a pan, fry the finely chopped onion (but do not let it brown), add the chopped sorrel and pour in the hot stock. Cook over low heat for 15 mins. Mix the grated cheese with salt, pepper, the egg and 2–3 tbsps of stock. Pour into the soup, stir well and heat up slowly for 5–6 mins. Sprinkle with chopped mint before serving.

serves 4 • Preparation: 5–6 mins • Cooking: 15 mins

Celeriac and apple soup

400 g celeriac, 400 g tart apples, 2 tbsps lemon juice, 4 tbsps butter, 4 cups chicken stock, ½ cup cream, 1 tsp potato flour, ¼ cup dry white wine, salt, a pinch of each white pepper, nutmeg and grated lemon rind, 2 tbsps finely chopped parsley

Peel and wash the celeriac and apples, grate them coarsely, sprinkle with lemon juice. Melt the butter in a pan, add the celeriac and apples and, stirring all the time, sauté them for several minutes. Pour in the hot stock and cook for 20 mins. Add salt, pepper, nutmeg and lemon zest, stir and bring to the boil. Mix the potato flour with wine, add the cream and pour the mixture into the soup, stirring all the time until the soup has thickened. Before serving, sprinkle with chopped parsley.

serves 4 • Preparation: 15 mins • Cooking: 20–25 mins

Bean soup with prunes

300 g beans, soup vegetables, 200 g stoned prunes, salt, a pinch of each pepper, nutmeg and sugar, 1 tbsp butter

Wash the beans and soak them overnight in water, then cook them in the same water. Make a stock from the vegetables and prunes, strain it. Cut the prunes into strips, add to the strained stock. Add salt, pepper, nutmeg and sugar. When the beans are ready, add some salt to them. Combine the beans with the stock, stir well and season to taste.

serves 4 • Preparation: 5 mins • Cooking: 1 hr

Dill soup

200 g veal with bone, soup vegetables, 2 bunches of dill, juice and grated rind from ½ lemon, salt, sugar, ½ cup cream

Make a stock from the meat and vegetables, strain it. Add the finely chopped dill to the strained stock, bring to the boil. Add salt, sugar and lemon juice, pour in the cream. Serve with rice or choux pastry balls.

serves 4 • Preparation: 5 mins • Cooking: 50–55 mins

Lemony soup

4 cups chicken stock, grated rind and juice from 1 lemon, 1 tsp honey, ½ tsp white pepper, 6–8 hard-boiled quail eggs, 4 thin lemon slices without pips

Bring the stock, together with the lemon rind, pepper and honey, to the boil. Add the lemon juice, mix well and add some salt. Serve with lemon slices and quail eggs.

serves 4 • Preparation: 25–30 mins • Cooking: 5–6 mins

Cucumber soup

2 cups chicken stock, 1 cup sour cucumber juice, 3 firm salted cucumbers, 100 g chicken ham, 2 tbsps chopped dill, 2–3 tbsps thick cream, 1 egg yolk, salt, pepper

Peel the cucumbers and chop them into small cubes. Chop finely the ham. Bring the stock to the boil, add the cucumber and cook for 10 mins. Add the cucumber juice and cook for another 3–4 mins. Put in the ham, add salt and pepper. Mix the cream with the raw egg yolk, pour into the soup. Stir well, heat up, but do not allow it to boil.

serves 4 • Preparation: 10 mins • Cooking: 15 mins

Red pepper soup

2 large red peppers, 1 large onion, 2–3 cloves of garlic, 3–4 juicy totatoes (fresh or tinned), 2 tbsps tomato paste, 2 tbsps olive oil, 1 tsp marjoram, salt, pepper, sugar, 150 g Mozzarella, 4 cups chicken stock

Blanch and skin the tomatoes, cut them into quarters. Halve and seed the peppers, wash and cut them into cubes. Cut the onion into thin slices. Heat up the oil in a pan, fry the onion without browning it, add the peppers and sauté them. Add the chopped garlic and tomato quarters. Pour in the hot stock, bring to the boil, then cook over low heat for 30–35 mins. Process the soup and sieve it. Season with salt and pepper to taste, add the mixture of tomato paste, Mozzarella and marjoram. Heat up, stirring all the time. Serve with white bread croutons.

serves 4 • Preparation: 15 mins • Cooking: 35 mins

Savoury pumpkin soup

1 kg pumpkin flesh, 2 leeks (only the white part), 1–2 cloves of garlic, 4 cups chicken stock, ½ cup yogurt, 1 tsp each ground caraway and ginger, salt, pepper, 2 tbsps olive oil, 2 tbsps chopped coriander

Wash the leeks well, cut them into thin slices; chop the garlic; cut the squash in cubes. Heat up the oil in a pan, put in the garlic and leek and sauté them. Add the ginger and caraway and, stirring all the time, fry for 1–2 mins. Add the squash, salt and pepper, stir well. Pour in the stock, bring to the boil, then cook over low heat for 30 mins. Leave the soup to cool a bit, then put it through a blender. Season to taste. Heat up and mix with the yogurt. Sprinkle with chopped coriander before serving.

serves 4 • Preparation: 15 mins • Cooking: 30 mins

Cold soups

Lithuanian cold borsch with beetroot leaves

It is cooked with soured beetroot juice and chopped beetroot leaves, with some cream. You should add to it crayfish tails, small pieces of cooked veal, capon or turkey, cucumbers cuts into fine cubes, hard-boiled eggs, but also pieces of asparagus, lettuce, chives and garlic. The soup is delicious, especially in hot weather.

Łukasz Go≥źbiowski, *Domy i dwory* (vol. IV, pp. 33–34)

Lithuanian cold borsch

5–6 young beetroot leaves, 2 young beets, ½ cup chopped fresh sorrel leaves, 3 tbsps chopped dill, 2 cucumbers, 3 cups veal stock, 2 cups cream, 200 g cooked veal or chicken breast, 4 hard-boiled eggs, 1 tin crayfish meat, salt, ice cubes

Wash the beets and leaves well, chop them finely, combine with the sorrel. Put into a pan and cover with the stock. Cook, then leave to cool. Add the cucumbers cut into cubes, the veal cut into pieces and chopped dill and salt. Combine with the cream and put into the fridge for 3–4 hours. Before serving, put in egg quarters, crayfish meat and ice cubes.

serves 4 • Preparation: 20 mins • Cooking: 20–25 mins

Belorussian cold borsch

500 g sorrel, 4 medium-sized cucumbers, 2 tbsps finely chopped chives, 1 tbsps grated horseradish, 4 tbsps chopped dill, 1 tbsp sugar, salt, 1 tbsp butter, 1 l kvass, 4 hard-boiled eggs

Clean the sorrel, wash and drain it, then chop it. Melt the butter in a small pan, add the sorrel, sugar and salt and simmer over low heat, then sieve it. Mix it well with the egg yolks and horseradish, and with the kvass. Peel the cucumbers and chop them into fine cubes, chop finely

Lithuanian cold borsch

the egg whites. Add both to the soup together with the dill and chives. Stir well and put into the fridge for 3 hours. Salt to taste.

serves 4 • Preparation: 10 mins • Cooking: 10 mins

Mazovian cold borsch

200 g fresh sorrel leaves, 1 beet, 2 cucumbers, a bunch of radishes, 3 tbsps each chopped dill and chives, a pinch of each sugar and pepper, salt, 4 cups sour milk, 4 hard-boiled eggs

Scrub the beet well. Bake it, then peel it and cut into strips. Rinse the sorrel, put it into a sieve and pour over first boiling and then cold water. Drain it and chop finely. Peel the cucumbers and chop them into fine cubes. Wash well the radishes together with the leaves; cut the radishes into cubes and chop half of the leaves finely. Mix the milk with salt, sugar and pepper, combine all the ingredients and mix thoroughly. Cover and put into the fridge for 2–3 hours. Before serving, add the cream and season to taste. Serve with hard-boiled eggs.

serves 4 • Preparation: 10–15 mins • Cooking: 20–25 mins

Cold fish soup

500 g small fish (roach, crucian carp), 250 g veal with bone, soup vegetables, 1 bay leaf, 3–4 grains each allspice and pepper, 2 onions, 2 cloves, a sprig of thyme, 4–5 sprigs of each dill and parsley, salt, grated rind from 1 lemon, ¼ tsp sugar, 2 tbsps lemon juice, 4 cups water, 200 g smoked eel, 2 cups thick cream, 4–6 tbsps chopped dill

Clean the fish, wash, drain and rub with salt, then leave it in a cool place for an hour. Put the peeled and rinsed vegetables and onion into a pan together with the spices, lemon zest and veal, cover with hot water and cook over low heat for 30 mins. Add the fish and cook for another hour, then strain and leave to cool. Put the boned fish meat, together with the strained stock, sugar and lemon juice, through a blender. Cut the veal into cubes. Skin the eel, remove the backbone and cut the flesh into cubes. Blend the soup with the cream, chill it, then add the veal,

eel and chopped dill. Add salt, sugar and lemon juice to taste.

serves 4 • Preparation: 1 hr • Cooking: 1 hr

Cold leek soup

125 g celery sticks, 200 g leek (only the white part), 250 g floury potatoes, 4 cups chicken or veal stock, salt, pepper, grated nutmeg, ½ cup single cream, 2–3 tbsps chopped chives

MARINATED SALMON: 200 g fresh salmon (without skin) cut into thin slices, 3 tbsps lemon juice, 4 tbsps olive oil, salt, freshly ground white pepper

Mix salt, pepper, oil and lemon rind. Spread the mixture on both sides of the salmon slices. Put the slices on a plate, cover with foil and place in the fridge for 40–60 mins. Clean the celery sticks, peel and rinse the potatoes, wash the leek. Chop them all finely, put into a pan, cover with the hot stock and cook over low heat for

Cold leek soup

30–40 mins. Add salt, pepper and nutmeg. Put the soup through a blender and sieve it, then leave to cool (stir occasionally). Add the cream, mix thoroughly and refrigerate for 4 hours. Before serving, dry gently the salmon slices, cut them into thin strips and add to the soup together with chopped chives.

serves 4 • Preparation: 15–20 mins • Cooking: 40 mins

Cold mint soup

3 cups yogurt, 1½ cups light stock, juice from 1 lemon, 1 large cucumber, 3–4 cloves of garlic, 4–5 tbsps finely chopped mint, salt, pepper

Mix thoroughly the finely chopped garlic with pepper and lemon juice, add the preparation to the stock mixed with the yogurt. Combine with the chopped mint and cucumber cut into fine cubes. Refrigerate for 2–3 hours. Serve with ice cubes.

serves 4 • Preparation: 10 mins

Cold tomato soup

1 kg ripe tomatoes, 1 tsp butter, ½ cup sherry, 1 tbsp Tabasco, salt, pepper, 2 cups yogurt, a bunch of chives

Rinse the tomatoes, dice them, put into a pan and stew over high heat. Add the butter, salt and pepper, cover and cook over low heat for 20 mins. Rub through a sieve, add the Tabasco, sherry and yogurt, stir well. Refrigerate for 3–4 hours. Before serving, sprinkle with chopped chives.

serves 4 • Preparation: 20–25 mins

Cold spring soup

3 cups sour milk, 250 g cucumbers, a large bunch of chives, 2–3 tbsps each chopped parsley, coriander and dill, salt, 1 tsp honey, 2–3 tbsps thick sour cream, 2 cups boiled cold water

Blend the milk with the cream, water, salt and honey, add the finely chopped herbs and cucumbers. Refrigerate for 3–4 hours.

serves 4 • Preparation: 10 mins

Cold fruit soups

Cherry soup

300 g sour cherries, 3 cups dry red wine, ½ cup sugar, 1 cup redcurrant juice, grated rind from 2 oranges, a piece of cinnamon, 3–4 cloves

Mix the wine with the sugar and orange zest, add cinnamon and cloves. Bring to the boil, then cover and cook over low heat for 10 mins. Take off the heat, allow to cool, then strain it. Rinse, dry and stone the cherries, process them with the wine and redcurrant juice. Refrigerate for 2–3 hours. Serve with sponge cakes or meringues.

serves 4 • Preparation: 15 mins

Spicy cherry soup

650 g stoned sour cherries, 1 cup boiled water, 1 cup dry white wine, 2 tbsps honey, ½ tsp powdered cinnamon, ¼ tsp each ground cloves, grated lemon rind and grated orange rind, 1 cup single cream, 1 tbsp icing sugar, 1 tsp lemon juice

Put 1 cup of cherries in the fridge. Place the remaining cherries in a pan, add the cloves, cinnamon and lemon and orange zest, cover with hot water and cook over low heat for 3–4 mins. Add the wine and simmer for another 4–5 mins. Take off the heat, allow to cool a bit, then process the cherries. Beat the cream with the icing sugar and lemon juice, blend it for one or two minutes with the soup. Refrigerate the soup for 3–4 hours. Before serving, garnish with the chilled cherries.

serves 4 • Preparation: 15 mins

Cherry and raspberry soup

500 g sour cherries, 250 g raspberries, grated rind and juice from 1 orange, 3 cloves, 3–4 tbsps honey, a pinch of salt, 1 cup yogurt, a handful of lemon balm leaves

Rinse and stone the cherries. Boil 4 cups of water with the cloves, salt, orange zest and orange juice. Put in the cherries and cook for 15 mins, then add the raspberries and cook for another 3–4 mins. Allow it to cool, then process the fruit together with the honey, sieve the mixture and blend with the yogurt. Refrigerate. Before serving, sprinkle with chopped lemon balm leaves.

serves 4 • Preparation: 20–25 mins

Lithuanian bilberry soup

4–6 cups bilberries, 200 g sugar, 1 cup
dry red wine, 2 cups cream

Put the bilberries through a blender and sieve them, then blend with the sugar and wine, mix in the cream and refrigerate for 3–4 hours. Serve with sponge cakes or white bread toast.

serves 4 • Preparation: 10 mins

Raspberry soup

6 cups raspberries, 1 cup dry white wine,
1–2 cloves, 200 g sugar, 4 cups cream

Boil the wine together with the sugar and cloves, strain the liquid and allow it to cool. Put 5 cups of raspberries through a blender and sieve them. Blend with the wine and cream and refrigerate for 1–2 hours. Before serving, put the remaining rapsberries into the soup. Serve with meringues or sponge cakes.

serves 4 • Preparation: 20 mins

Raspberry soup, Gypsy style

500 g fresh raspberries, 2 cups yogurt, ¼ cup
each lime blossom honey and milk

Process 500 g of raspberries with the yogurt, milk and honey. Refrigerate for 1–2 hours. Before serving, garnish the soup with the remaining fruit. Serve with choux pastry balls or sponge cakes.

serves 4 • Preparation: 5 mins

Grapefruit and raspberry soup

1 large pink grapefruit, 1 cup raspberries,
2 cups water, ¼ cup honey, 4–5 cloves,
1 tbsp sugar, a piece of cinnamon

Boil the water with the cinnamon, cloves and sugar. Cover the pan and simmer for 15 mins, then leave it to cool. Strain it, mix with the honey and refrigerate. Process the raspberries and the peeled grapefruit (from which the pips have been removed), sieve the mixture. Cover and put into the freezer for 10–15 mins. Take it out and mix thoroughly with the chilled honey syrup. Before serving, garnish with lemon balm leaves. Serve with meringues or choux pastry balls.

serves 4 • Preparation: 20–25 mins

Apricot and pear soup

125 g each dried pears, stoned dried apricots and
prunes, 3 cups boiled water, 1 cup dry white wine,
½ cup yogurt, 1 tbsp lemon juice, a piece of cinnamon,
¼ cup sugar, 2 red apples, a handful of raisins

Rinse the dried fruit, put into a pan, add the sugar and boiled water. Cover and leave overnight. Peel and core the apples, cut them into slices and add to the soaked fruit, put in the cinnamon. Bring the whole to the boil, then simmer for 30 mins. Rinse the raisins, blanch and drain them. Take out the cinnamon. Put the fruit through a blender, pour in the lemon juice, mix and refrigerate for 1–2 hours. Before serving, blend with the chilled yogurt.

serves 4 • Preparation: 30 mins • Cooking: 10–15 mins

Redcurrant soup

200 g redcurrants without stalks, 1 cup boiling
water, ¼ cup honey, a pinch of ground cloves,
1 cup yogurt, ½ cup cream, 3 tbsps almond
flakes, a sprig of lemon balm or mint

Rinse the currants, cover with boiling water, add the cloves and cook for 2–3 mins, then sieve and mix with the honey, yogurt and cream. Refrigerate. Toast the almond flakes in a hot frying pan, allow them to cool. Pour the chilled soup into bowls, sprinkle each portion with almond flakes and garnish with lemon balm or mint leaves.

serves 4 • Preparation: 10 mins

Gooseberry soup

400 g gooseberries, 150 g blackcurrants,
3 tbsps honey, ¼ tsp ground cloves, 1 cup thick
cream, 1 egg yolk, a pinch of salt, 2 cups water

Rinse and stalk the gooseberries and blackcurrants. Put them into a pan, cover with hot water. Add a pinch of salt and cook for 10 mins. Leave to cool a bit, then process together with the cloves and honey, and sieve. Mix the cream with the egg yolk, add to the soup and stir well, then refrigerate for 1–2 hours.

serves 4 • Preparation: 15–20 mins

Mixed fruit soup (garus)

2 tart apples, 2 juicy pears, 250 g purple plums,
3 cups water, 2 tbsps honey, a piece of cinnamon,
3–4 cloves, a pinch of salt, ½ cup cream,
1 tbsp sugar, a pinch of powdered cinnamon

Rinse and core the apples and pears, stone the plums. Put all fruit into a pan, add a pinch of salt, cinnamon bark and cloves. Cover with boiling water, bring to the boil, then cook over low heat for 20 mins. Take out the cinnamon and cloves. Put the soup through a blender and sieve it. Beat the cream with sugar and powdered cinnamon. Heat up the soup, mix with the cream. Serve hot or cold, with choux pastry balls or white bread toast.

serves 4 • Preparation: 25–30 mins

CHAPTER III

MACARONI, NOODLES, DUMPLINGS

Macaroni and noodles

Flour is obtained by grinding grain (wheat, oats, rye, barley or rice) and also sweetcorn, buckwheat and potatoes.

Wheat grain, from which the majority of flours are made, contains starch (above all gluten), fats, and vitamins from the B group. Because all these components are unevenly spread through the grain, the food value of the flour depends on the fineness of the milling.

Fine flour – the longest-lasting – is very white and is derived from grinding the very heart of the grain, the endosperm. Flour of this kind contains a great deal of starch, but far less protein, fewer minerals, and vitamins than flour which is ground from the whole grain. The most enzymes, vitamins, minerals, and high value fats and protein are found in the bran and germ of the grain. This is the reason why wholemeal flours have become so exceptionally popular recently. They have however one major drawback – they easily go off and quickly lose their food value. If therefore we want to bake using whole grain flour, it is best to make it at home in a grinder immediately before baking.

The qualities of flour that are retailed are determined by the ash that remains after burning 100 g of flour, and the type is defined by the number obtained by multiplying the percentage of ash by 1000. When baking, it is very important to choose the right type of flour.

The gluten content of the flour determines its suitability for baking. Gluten is elastic and it passes this property on to the dough. When liquid is added to the flour, the latter swells, and when it is being kneaded it takes the shape of fibres which blend together to give the dough its spongy structure. The higher the gluten content of the flour, the better the dough will rise and swell.

Wheat flour

(1) Fine flours are best for making macaroni and noodles of various kinds; they are also good for baking with yeast, both bread, rolls and savoury bread dishes or pastry for patties, and cakes of various kinds (sand cakes, fruit bakes, sweet rolls). These flours are quite a good source of thiamine, protein, nicotinic acid and iron; they also contain cellulose and zinc.

(2) Fine cake flour is used most frequently for making cakes. It makes a very soft and porous dough which rises easily. It is excellent for baking sponges and yeast cakes.

(3) Granular flour is best for short pastry and cakes. It makes a very springy dough and provides a hard structure for the cake, making it highly suitable for biscuits, savoury or sweet straws, cup cakes, shortcakes, Polish Easter cakes and also for choux pastry and French noodles. But it is entirely unsuitable for pierogi and pancakes.

(4) Graham flour is wholemeal wheat flour and an excellent source of nicotinic acid, iron, magnesium and a fairly good source of protein and zinc. The milling process does not destroy any of the nutritional value of the grain.

Rye flour is used mainly to bake bread and rusks; it is very often mixed with wheat flour because it does not contain enough gluten.

Barley flour was at one time the main ingredient in bread. Unfortunately, barley bread went stale very quickly. Today it is usually mixed with wheat flour in order to raise the gluten content. A small amount of barley flour added to wheat flour gives bread a special sweetish flavour. Wholemeal barley flour has a nutty flavour and is dark in colour. It can be used to bake biscuits or make pancakes.

Buckwheat flour is made from burnt buckwheat seed and has an intense sharp taste; it is often mixed with wheat flour if we want to give the dough an original flavour. It is often used in making bliny and pancakes.

Cornflour is gluten-free and is excellent for making many dishes (noodles, hominy, polenta), or desserts, cakes and biscuits as part of gluten-free diet. It is also used for thickening soups and sauces. But for making bread, wheat flour must be added.

Rice flour is a gluten-free flour which is made from both white and brown rice. It is very rich in starch and contains few B-group vitamins. It is generally used for thickening dishes and making cakes or biscuits.

Potato flour is yet another flour which is highly useful for a gluten-free diet. It is usually used for thickening dishes and for making blancmanges.

Soya flour does not contain gluten, but has a 50% protein content and is an excellent source of magnesium and isoflavones; it is also richer than other flours in thiamine and iron, and has a fairly good content of cellulose, nicotinic acid, calcium and zinc. This creamy flour produced from soya seed has a characteristic and sharply-defined flavour; it gives home baking moistness and a delicate nutty flavour. In a gluten-free diet, it can be used, together with potato flour, egg white and water, for making excellent pancakes. It is also a good basis for thickening soups and sauces. It can be added to bliny, pancakes and bread (in proportions of 1:3 with wheat flour). It is very rich in fats, but low-fat soya flour is also available. It should be stored in hermetically sealed jars in a cool and dry place.

Oatflour has a lightly nutty flavour and serves mainly to make baby foods and breakfast cereals, although it can also be used in bliny, pancakes and bread. When baking, you should mix it with wheat or rye flour.

***

A properly made pasta dough is smooth and shining. It should be kneaded for about 15 minutes in order to get as much air as possible into it. The appearance of air blisters in the dough means that you may stop kneading. The dough should then be covered with a cloth and left to 'rest' for thirty minutes, after which you should sprinkle a pastry board with flour and divide the dough into 3 or 4 parts, each of which should be rolled out and left for ten minutes or so to dry a little.

The dried piece of dough should be sprinkled with flour, rolled up and sliced with a sharp knife, or cut into narrow strips or squares. Macaroni for soup is best sliced into very narrow strips, but as an addition to a main dish it is best cut into rhomboids, squares, thick ribbons etc. The sliced pasta should be strewn onto a cloth that has been sprinkled with flour.

The best macaroni is made from 1 kg of flour with 6–8 eggs and a little water. A good pasta after cooking swells to four or even six times its original volume.

How can you calculate the right amount of pasta per person? Before cooking you should have:
50 g of dry pasta per portion when it is to be part of the main dish,
70 g per portion when it is to form the main dish with sauce,
and 15 g per portion when it is to be added to soup.

Pasta should be cooked in a large amount of salted water; if there is not enough water, the pasta will become mushy; fresh home-made pasta should be cooked for 2–3 minutes from the moment of coming to the boil, but it takes longer if it is made from rye flour. The cooking time of course depends on the size and thickness of the pasta. Pasta should be boiled 'almost covered' – it is best to put a wooden spoon between the pan and the lid, so that the pasta gets the required amount of air but does not get cool.

For the pasta not to stick during cooking, a teaspoon of butter or oil should be added to the water.

Rinsing the cooked pasta with cold water is intended to get rid of the starch; if this is not done, the pasta sticks together.

Dried home-made pasta which has not been cooked can be kept in a cool, dry place for about two to three months.

Macaroni

Macaroni dough – basic recipe

400 g flour, 4 eggs, salt, water if requered

Sift the flour onto a pastry board. Make a well in the centre and break in the eggs. Gradually mix in the flour, add salt. Make a stiff, smooth dough (add some flour if it is too soft, or some water if it is too dry). Divide the dough into five equal parts, knead each of them separately. Cover with a cloth and let it rest for 30 mins. Dust the board with flour and roll the dough out. Allow it to dry for 30–40 mins, then cut it finely with a sharp knife or a fluted pastry wheel, or else put it through a pasta machine.

serves 4 • Preparation: 10 mins • Cooking: 4–6 mins

Macaroni with herbs

400 g flour, 4 eggs, salt, 2 tbsps chopped basil, parsley or thyme

Mix the herbs with the eggs. Make a dough as in the basic recipe above. Cook in salted water with 1 teaspoon of oil.

serves 4 • Preparation: 10 mins • Drying: 30–40 mins • Cooking: 4–5 mins

Coloured macaroni

400 g flour, 3 eggs, 1 egg yolk

Make a dough as in the basic recipe above.

For green macaroni, add spinach juice or purée.
For red, add beet juice or tomato paste.
For yellow, add carrot juice or a pinch of saffron dissolved in water.

Cook in salted water with 1 teaspoon of oil.

serves 4 • Preparation: 10–15 mins • Drying: 30–40 mins • Cooking: 4–6 mins

Wholemeal macaroni

350 g wholemeal flour, 4 eggs, 1 tbsp olive oil, salt

Sift the flour onto a pastry board, add salt, mix it with the flour. Make a well in the flour, pour in the oil and break in the eggs. Knead a stiff dough that does not stick to your hands. Form it into a ball, cover with a cloth and let it rest for a bit. Roll the dough out thinly, then cut it, allow it to dry (30–40 mins). Cook shortly before serving in salted water with a teaspoon of oil.

serves 4 • Preparation: 10 mins • Cooking: 8–10 mins

Drop noodles

Batter noodles are made from flour and whole eggs, sometimes with a small amount of water added. The dough is fairly thin (although thicker than pancake batter), with the consistency of thick cream. After being dropped into boiling water, it should keep a shape much like macaroni. The amount of flour used in making these noodles depends on the number of eggs. The dough should be carefully mixed for a long time, so that as much air – which is an excellent raising agent – as possible can be worked in. The carefully mixed dough is dribbled in a thin trickle into boiling water or soup (chicken broth, tomato soup, dill soup) and cooked for two minutes. Batter noodles made with two eggs and 100 g of flour are enough for 4 to 6 persons. A small amount of boiled water or mineral water helps to make the noodles lighter and improves their taste. For the noodles to rise, you should sift the flour and

Drop noodles

then mix the dough for a long time with a spoon. The batter should be poured directly from the bowl in which it was made, and the trickle should be steady so that the noodles are of even size.

For flavoured noodles, you should add finely chopped herbs, chicken livers or ham towards the end of mixing the batter.

Drop noodles – basic recipe

2 eggs, 3–4 tbsps sifted flour, salt, a pinch of sugar

Blend the eggs with 1 tbsp of boiled water, salt and sugar. Gradually add the flour and work it thoroughly with a wooden spoon or spatula. Drop long noodles into boiling water, stock or milk, bring to the boil, stir well. Serve at once.

serves 4 • Preparation: 5 mins • Cooking: 2–5 mins

Fried drop noodles

*2 eggs, 3–4 tbsps sifted flour, 1 tbsp water,
1 tbsp rum, salt, oil for deep frying*

Blend the eggs with the water and salt. Gradually add the flour and rum, work thoroughly with a wooden spoon or spatula. Drop long noodles into hot oil, fry until golden brown. Take out with a strainer. Serve with soups.

serves 4 • Preparation: 5–7 mins • Frying: 20–25 mins

Hasty noodles

These Old Polish noodles, which are simple, healthy, cheap and highly digestible, and are an excellent addition to soups, but can also be served with spicy sauces, stewed vegetables or melted butter and sprinkled with herbs and grated cheese. The dough for hasty noodles must be so thick and hard that it could be grated or chopped with a meat cleaver. They are made by adding warm water to flour and mixing it in with a knife or a spatula. Hasty noodles are usually made to put into soup and are then cooked in the soup itself, which they also additionally

thicken. After the hasty noodles have been thrown in, the soup should be stirred carefully, so that the noodles do not stick together.

Hasty noodles – basic recipe

250 g wheat flour, ½ cup lukewarm water, salt

Sift the flour into a bowl. Gradually adding water and salt, knead a thick dough. Leave it to rest for a bit, then form small noodles with your thumb and index finger or by grating the dough coarsely. Cook in soup or in boiling water.

serves 4 • Preparation: 10–15 mins • Cooking: 5–7 mins

Wholemeal hasty noodles

200 g wholemeal flour, 1 egg, water, salt

Sift the flour into a bowl, break in the egg, add salt and gradually water. Knead a very thick dough, then let it rest. Grate the dough coarsely directly into boiling water or soup.

serves 4 • Preparation: 10 mins • Cooking: 10 mins

Buckwheat hasty noodles, Lithuanian style

*2 cups buckwheat flour, 1 tbsp wheat
flour, salt, boiling water*

Mix thoroughly the two kinds of flour with salt. Stirring all the time, pour in as much boiling water as the flour can absorb. With a wooden spoon work it into a thick dough until air bubbles appear on the surface. Let the dough to rest, then form small noodles with your thumb and forefinger, or grate the dough coarsely. Cook in milk.

serves 4 • Preparation: 15 mins • Cooking: 6–8 mins

Drop dumplings

Drop dumplings are made of sticky dough with a small quantity of eggs. The dough should be very thoroughly kneaded for a long time (it is best to use a blender), in order to get in as much air as possible, as this is the only raising agent in these noodles.

After the dough has been carefully kneaded, the dumplings should be scooped with a metal spoon into salted boiling water. Drop dumplings are used as an addition to soups, as part of a main dish, or as a main dish served with sauce, cheese, scrambled eggs, or butter with breadcrumbs. The dumplings should not be too large, because then they swell more, cook more quickly and do not absorb water. Dumplings for soup should be smaller than those for other dishes.

Drop into the boiling water only as many dumplings as cover the surface of the water and can float freely. They should be boiled not completely covered by the lid, as this improves the consistency of the dough and speeds up cooking. In order that they should not stick together after straining, it is a good idea to pour boiling water over them and serve them immediately.

Drop dumplings – basic recipe

400 g flour, 3 eggs, 1 tbsp melted butter,
salt, ½ cup lukewarm water

Blend the eggs with the water and add gradually to the sifted flour. Work into a smooth paste, add the melted butter and salt. Beat with a wooden spoon or in a blender until the dough is smooth. The longer you do it, the softer the noodles will be. Take a metal teaspoon and dip it in boiling water. With the spoon scoop a bit of the dough and drop into salted boiling water. Bring to the boil. Serve with soups, roast meat, vegetable stews or separately, sprinkled with melted butter and grated cheese or with cracklings.

serves 4 • Preparation: 15–20 mins • Cooking: 8–10 mins

French noodles

French noodles differ from simple drop noodles in that butter or other fat is added and more eggs are used. These ingredients raise the dough more and the noodles swell and are lighter. They are cooked for only a short time,

like drop noodles. They should be served immediately after cooking, for if they are kept they lose their lightness. They are served as an addition to clear soups, or with the main dish or as a dish in themselves.

First cream the butter, adding one egg yolk at a time until a smooth paste is formed. Then fold in the stiffly beaten egg whites and sifted flour. Mushroom or liver noodles are varieties of French noodles. Here, minced liver or mushrooms are added to the beaten butter and egg yolks; next the stiffly beaten egg whites are added, and finally the flour. The preparation is mixed gently, and then small noodles are scooped and dropped into the boiling water.

For so-called half-French noodles use less butter and fewer eggs and add a small amount of water (preferably mineral water because this increases the lightness of the dough). The best proportions are: 140 g of flour, 80 g of butter, 3 eggs, salt and half a glass of water.

French noodles – basic recipe

100 g butter, 5 eggs, 100–120 g
wheat flour, salt, dill, parsley

Cream the butter, adding one egg yolk at a time in the process. Whip the egg whites and fold them in. Add the flour and mix the preparation. With a teaspoon that has been dipped in boiling water form small noodles and drop them into salted boiling water. Cook for a while under cover, allowing for the noodles to expand. Take them out with a strainer. Excellent with clear soup, roast meat, Hungarian stew, ragout and Stroganov.

serves 4 • Preparation: 15 mins • Cooking: 5–6 mins

Delicious noodles

250 g flour, 250 g butter, 5 eggs, 150 g lean ham, 100 g
chopped hazelnuts, 100 g grated cheese, salt, pepper

Cream the butter, adding one egg yolk at a time in the process. Add gradually the finely chopped ham, ground hazelnuts, salt and pepper. Fold in the whisked egg whites, then the sifted flour and grated cheese. Mix thoroughly. With a teaspoon that has been dipped in boiling water form small noodles and drop them into salted boiling water. Cook until the noodles float to the surface.

Serve as a separate dish, sprinkled with melted butter, or with white meat roast.

serves 4 • Preparation: 15–20 mins • Cooking: 4–5 mins

Noodles made from scalded dough

Noodles made from scalded dough, that is choux pastry, are as light and fluffy as French noodles. The choux pastry can be made earlier, but the noodles should be cooked immediately before serving.

Noodles from scalded dough – basic recipe

100 g flour, 100 g butter, 1 egg yolk, 2 eggs, ½ cup water, salt

Bring the water and butter to the boil. Turn down the heat and pour in the sifted flour, stirring all the time to break down all lumps. Work the dough with a wooden spoon energetically until it has stopped sticking to the walls. Take off the heat, cool it a bit, then break in the eggs and the egg yolk, add salt and mix thoroughly. Cover and set aside in a cool place to allow it to rest and thicken. With a teaspoon drop small noodles into boiling salted water. Cover the pan and bring the water to the boil. When the noodles float to the surface, take them out with a strainer. Serve with clear soups or roast meat.

serves 4 • Preparation: 30–35 mins • Resting: 1 hr • Cooking: 4–5 mins

Podolian noodles

150 g buckwheat flour, 150 g cornflour, 100 g butter, 1 cup milk, 4 eggs, salt

Sift and mix well the two kinds of flour. Bring the milk to the boil. Stirring all the time, slowly pour in the flour, add the melted butter and salt. Beat the dough thoroughly with a wooden spoon until it has stopped sticking to the walls. Take off the heat and allow it to cool. Break in one

egg at a time and stir energetically. With a teaspoon form small noodles and drop them into boiling salted water. Stir well so that the noodles do not stick to the bottom. Bring to the boil. Strain and serve immediately with scratchings or melted butter, or as a side dish with the second course.

serves 4 • Preparation: 30 mins • Cooking: 8–10 mins

Volhynian noodles

200 g buckwheat flour, 300 g cottage cheese, 1 cup milk, 1 tbsp butter, salt, 3 eggs

Put the cheese through a mincer. Bring the milk and butter to the boil. Gradually pour in the flour, stirring vigorously to break down all lumps. Turn the heat down and work the dough until it no longer sticks to the walls. Take off the heat and allow it to cool. Stirring all the time, break one egg at a time and gradually add the cheese. Fold in the stiffly beaten egg whites. Stir lightly but thoroughly. With a teaspoon form small noodles and drop them into boiling salted water. Bring to the boil and cook for a bit. Strain the noodles and serve immediately, sprinkled with melted butter and sugar.

serves 4 • Preparation: 30–35 mins • Cooking: 5–6 mins

Baked buckwheat noodles

250 g buckwheat kasha, 2 cups stock, 300 g spinach, 1 large onion, 2–3 cloves of garlic, 2 tbsps oil, salt, pepper, nutmeg, 2 raw egg yolks, ½ tbsp butter, 1 cup thick cream, 3–4 tbsps grated cheese

Heat up a pan with a thick bottom, put in the rinsed and strained buckwheat and roast it. Pour in the boiling stock, bring to the boil, then cook over low heat until the liquid has been absorbed. Chop the rinsed and drained spinach finely. Heat up the oil in a frying pan. Fry the finely chopped onion and garlic (but do not let them brown), put in the spinach and, stirring continuously, sauté until the juice has evaporated. Allow the kasha and spinach to cool, then mix them together. Add salt, pepper and nutmeg, stir well. Break in the egg yolks and stir again, then leave the mixture aside for 30 mins. Grease an ovenproof dish with butter. With a metal spoon dipped in boiling water form largish noodles and drop them onto the dish. Pour over

Volhynian noodles

the cream, sprinkle with the cheese. Put into a preheated oven and bake for 20 mins.

serves 4 • Preparation: 40 mins • Cooking: 20 mins

Potato noodles and dumplings

There are many Polish names for varieties of potato noodles. To make potato dough you should use floury potatoes, and the dough itself should be made quickly, for if it is kneaded for a long time it becomes thin and the noodles are not tasty.

The noodles should be cut and boiled immediately after the dough has been made.

They are excellent fried up in lard or butter the next day.

You add various ingredients to the basic dough for potato noodles. These include ground walnuts or hazelnuts, cottage cheese, bryndza, grated cheese, chopped herbs, chopped herring or finely chopped cooked meats and sausage.

Noodles made from cooked potatoes should be brought back to the boil after being placed in boiling water, and then simmered in an open pan over low heat for 20 to 25 minutes. The noodles are ready when they float to the surface; they are shiny on the surface and soft and light inside.

Noodles and **dumplings** made from raw potatoes are best if some cooked potato (left over from the previous day) is added. If we want them to be light in colour and not dark and greyish, the raw potato should be grated into a bowl with water, and the grated potato should immediately be squeezed dry, formed into noodles and cooked. The cooked noodles should not be left standing in the water, for then the starch that they contain dissolves and the noodles lose their taste.

Traditional potato dumplings

1 kg raw potatoes, 300 g cooked potatoes, 1 large onion, 1 tbsp flour, salt, pepper

Put the cooked potatoes through a mincer. Grate the raw potatoes, squeeze out the excess juice and add the starch to the potatoes. Grate the onion finely. Mix the raw potatoes with the cooked potatoes and onion, add salt, pepper and flour. Work the mixture into a daugh. Form balls the size of walnuts, making a hole in the middle with your thumb. Drop the dumplings into a large amount of salted boiling water. Bring to the boil, then cook for 15 mins. Such dumplings are often stuffed: with cottage cheese or bryndza in the Tatra region, or with meat in Podlasie, but you may use any kind of stuffing. Here are several tips:

serves 4 • Preparation: 25–30 mins • Cooking: 15–20 mins

Meat stuffing for potato dumplings

500 g cooked meat, cooked carrot, a piece of celeriac and parsley root, 1 onion, 1 tbsp butter, 1 tbsp dried marjoram, salt, pepper, 1 egg or stock

Mince the meat and vegetables, mix them with the finely chopped browned onion. Add marjoram, pepper and salt, break in the egg or add 2–3 tbsps of stock. Work into a smooth mixture.

serves 4 • Preparation: 5 mins

Frankfurter stuffing for potato dumplings

250 g frankfurters, 250 g mushrooms, 250 g onion, 2 tbsps butter, 1 egg, salt, pepper

Scald the frankfurters with boiling water, skin them. Fry the diced onion and mushrooms in butter, reduce the juice, then together with the frankfurters put them through a mincer. Add chopped parsley, salt and pepper, break in the egg and work into a smooth mixture.

serves 4 • Preparation: 5 mins

Mushroom stuffing for potato dumplings

8–10 dried cep mushrooms, 2 hard-boiled eggs, 1 bread roll, 1 large onion, 2 tbsps butter, 2 tbsps finely chopped parsley, salt, pepper oak the mushrooms overnight in water. The following day cook them, then drain. Use the stock to soak the bread roll in. Fry the finely chopped onion in butter (1 tbsp). Put the mushrooms, squeezed out bread roll and hard-boiled eggs through a mincer, add the onion, parsley, salt and quite a bit of pepper. Mix thoroughly, fry in the remaining butter, then allow to cool.

serves 4 • Preparation: 20–25 mins

Potato dumplings

1 kg cooked potatoes, 2 eggs, 250–300 g wheat flour, 1–2 tbsps potato flour, salt

Put the potatoes through a mincer. Add the flour and salt, break in the eggs. Work into a smooth mixture. Sprinkle a pastry board with flour. Form the mixture into a ½ in. roll, flatten it lightly with a knife. Cut diagonally. Drop the dumplings into boiling salted water. Cook in a large amount of water. Serve with scratchings, melted butter or as a side dish with roast meat.

serves 4 • Preparation: 10 mins • Cooking: 15–20 mins

Savoury dumplings

1 kg cooked potatoes, 200 g grated cheese, 2 eggs, 250–300 g flour, salt, pepper

Put the potatoes through a mincer, mix with the flour and grated cheese, break in the eggs. Add salt and pepper and work into a smooth paste. Sprinkle a pastry board with flour. Form a roll, flatten it a bit with a knife, then cut diagonally. Drop the dumplings into a large amount of salted boiling water. Serve with scratchings, sprinkled with chopped parsley.

serves 4 • Preparation: 10 mins • Cooking: 15–20 mins

Farmer cheese dumplings

1 kg cooked potatoes, 500 g light curd cheese, 2 eggs, 1 cup flour, a pinch of salt, a pinch of cinnamon

Put the potatoes and cheese through a mincer. Put in the flour, add salt and cinnamon, break in the eggs. Work into a smooth mixture. Sprinkle a pastry board with flour. Form a roll from the mixture, flatten it a bit with a knife, then cut diagonally. Drop the dumplings into boiling salted

Traditional potato dumplings

water, preferably in several batches. Cook each batch for 3–5 mins, take the dumplings out with a strainer. Put into a warm serving dish, pour over melted butter mixed with browned breadcrumbs. Sprinkle with sugar.

serves 4 • Preparation: 10 mins

Highlander's farmer cheese dumplings

*1 kg cooked potatoes, 500 g curd cheese,
2 eggs, 1 cup flour, salt, 1 tsp pepper*

Put the potatoes and cheese through a mincer. Add salt and pepper, break in the eggs. Put in enough flour to make a fairly stiff mixture. Form small balls and drop them into salted boiling water. Cook for 10 mins. Before serving, pour over sour cream, melted butter or scratchings.

serves 4 • Preparation: 10 mins • Cooking: 10 mins

Łódź potato dumplings

1 kg potatoes, 250 g rye flour, salt

Put the peeled potatoes into a large pan, pour in enough water to cover them. Cook, then mash them (together with the water). Keep the pan over a low heat and, stirring all the time, add gradually the flour. Put the lid on and leave over low heat until the dough 'ripens'. When it no longer smells of raw flour, take a metal spoon dipped in boiling water and form largish dumplings. Arrange them in an ovenproof dish, pour over a fair amount of rendered bacon. Sprinkle with crumbled cottage cheese on top and put into a preheated oven. Bake for several minutes. Serve as a separate dish or as a side dish with meat or cooked cabbage.

serves 4 • Preparation: 20–25 mins • Cooking: 8–10 mins

Silesian potato dumplings

600 g potatoes cooked in jackets, 600 g raw potatoes, 3–4 tbsps wheat flour, salt

Peel the raw potatoes, grate them, squeeze out the excess juice. Peel the cooked potatoes and put them through a mincer. Mixed the two kinds of potatoes, add flour and salt and work into a fairly stiff dough. Sprinkle a

pastry board with flour. Form rolls from the dough. With your thumb and forefinger shape small noodles and drop them into salted boiling water. Cook for 10–12 mins. These dumplings are usually served with roast pork with cabbage, but they are just as tasty with other kinds of roast meat.

serves 4 • Preparation: 10–15 mins • Cooking: 10–12 mins

Rubbery potato noodles

1 kg potatoes cooked in jakcets, 250 g cooked beef, 250 g potato flour, 2 egg yolks, salt, ½ tsp pepper

Put the peeled potatoes and meat through a mincer, add salt and pepper to taste. Add the egg yolks and potato flour and work into a smooth mixture. Dust your hands with flour and form small noodles. Drop them into boiling salted water and cook for 5 mins. Before serving, pour over melted butter mixed with browned breadcrumbs.

serves 4 • Preparation: 5–7 mins • Cooking: 5–6 mins

Silesian potato dumplings

1 kg cooked potatoes, 250 g potato flour, 2–3 eggs, salt

Put the potatoes through a mincer. Mix them with the potato flour, break in the eggs, add some salt and work into a smooth paste. Dust your hands with flour and form small balls. Make a hole in each with your thumb. Drop into boiling salted water and cook for 15–20 mins. Serve with some sauce, with pork scratchings, or as a side dish with the second course.

serves 4 • Preparation: 10 mins • Cooking: 15–20 mins

Zakopane potato noodles

1 kg potatoes cooked in jackets, 200 g bryndza, 2 tbsps thick cream, 2 eggs, salt, 3–4 tbsps flour

Put the peeled potatoes and bryndza through a mincer. Put in the cream, break in the eggs, add salt and enough flour to make a fairly light dough. Sprinkle a pastry board with flour. Form the dough into rolls, flatten them with a knife, then cut diagonally. Drop the noodles into boiling salted water and cook for 10 mins. Before serving, pour over cream or melted butter mixed with browned breadcrumbs.

serves 4 • Preparation: 5–8 mins • Cooking: 10–12 mins

Lvov potato noodles

700 g potatoes cooked in jackets, 100 g poppyseed,
2 tbsps thick cream, 150–200 g wheat flour,
3 tbsps finely chopped almonds, 3 tbsps caster sugar,
3 eggs, ½ cup milk, salt

Rinse and drain the poppyseed, put it into a pan. Pour over the hot milk and cook over low heat for 30 mins, then drain it. Put the peeled potatoes and poppyseed through a mincer. Add the cream, sifted flour, eggs, sugar and almonds. Work into dough. Sprinkle a pastry board with flour. Form rolls from the dough and cut them diagonally. Drop the noodles into boiling salted water and cook for 10 mins. Take them out with a strainer. Arrange them in a warm serving dish, pour over melted butter and serve immediately.

serves 4 • Preparation: 40 mins • Cooking: 10 mins

Tartar noodles

400 g cooked potatoes, 800 g raw
potatoes, 150 g minced beef, 1 large onion,
salt, pepper, 1 tsp potato flour

Peel and grate the raw potatoes, squeeze out the excess juice. Put the cooked potatoes through a mincer and combine them with the raw potatoes. Add the finely grated onion, the meat, some salt and pepper and work into dough. With hands dusted with flour form small noodles and drop them into boiling salted water. Cook for 25–30 mins. Before serving, pour over pork scratchings.

serves 4 • Preparation: 10–15 mins • Cooking: 25–30 mins

Sunflower noodles

800 g floury potatoes cooked in jackets, 80 g sunflower
seeds, 50 g butter, 100 g wheat flour, 4 eggs, 2 tbsps
finely chopped parsley, 150 g chanterelles, salt, pepper

Chop the mushrooms finely and fry them in butter, add some pepper and cook over low heat for 10–15 mins. Toast 2 tbsps of sunflower seeds in a hot frying pan until golden-brown. Put the peeled potatoes and the remaining sunflower seeds through a mincer. Add the mushrooms, toasted sunflower seeds, some salt and pepper and stir thoroughly. Whisk the butter with the egg yolks and, beating all the time, gradually add the potato mixture. Towards the end fold in the egg whites and flour, and with a wooden spoon work the mixture into dough. Bring salted water to the boil. With a metal spoon form small noodles and cook them for 15 mins over medium heat. Before serving, pour over melted butter or some sauce.

serves 4 • Preparation: 40–45 mins • Cooking: 15–20 mins

Marjoram noodles

500 g potatoes cooked in jackets, 1 kg raw potatoes,
1 tsp dried marjoram, 1–2 tbsps wheat flour, salt

Put the cooked potatoes through a mincer. Grate the raw potatoes into a bowl full of water (to prevent them going dark), then drain them in a piece of linen. Combine the two kinds of potatoes, add the marjoram and salt and work into a light dough. If it is not thick enough, add some flour. With damp hands form elongated noodles. Cook them in hot water (do not boil) for 20 mins. Before serving, pour over melted butter or cracklings. Serve with salads.

serves 4 • Preparation: 20–25 mins • Cooking: 15–20 mins

Pan-fried noodles

800 g potatoes cooked in jackets, 50 g butter,
2 egg yolks, 1 tbsp flour, 1 tsp salt, grated nutmeg,
4 tbsps oil

Put the peeled potatoes through a mincer. Add the flour, melted butter, egg yolks, salt and nutmeg, and work into a smooth dough. With hands dusted with flour form a long roll, then cut it into noodles. Heat up a frying pan, gradually pour in the oil and fry the noodles in batches. Transfer the cooked noodles to a warm serving dish and keep them warm. Serve with lamb cutlets or roast lamb.

serves 4 • Preparation: 10 mins • Frying: 20 mins

Mushroom noodles

8 large potatoes, ½ cup milk, 500 g mushrooms,
2 tbsps each grated cheese and chopped
parsley, salt, 1 tbsp lard, 2 tbsps butter

Grate the peeled potatoes, squeeze out the excess juice. Pour over the boiling milk, mix thoroughly. Rinse the mushrooms, put them into salted boiling water and cook for 5 mins, then drain them and dice finely. Fry the mushrooms in hot lard, then add them to the potatoes. Put in the chopped parsley and add salt. Work into a smooth dough. With damp hands form small noodles. Drop the noodles into boiling salted water and cook until they float to the surface. Take them out with a strainer. Put into an ovenproof dish, sprinkle lavishly with melted butter and grated cheese and bake.

serves 4 • Preparation: 20–25 mins • Cooking: 10 mins

Knedle

This is a type of dumpling popular in many parts of Europe, including Silesia and Great Poland.

The length of time for which the knedle are cooked is very important. They should be placed in salted and very hot water (each knedel should be put in separately) and cooked for 10 to 25 minutes (depending on the kind) over a very low heat, so that they only simmer. The water should not be allowed to boil, as the knedle will then fall apart. If the water begins to boil, it should be cooled down by adding a few drops of cold water.

When sweet knedle are being cooked it is a good idea to add vanilla sugar, a piece of vanilla or a glass of rum to the water.

The cooked knedle should be removed with a strainer, carefully blotted and placed on warmed plates or a warmed dish, and immediately served. It is a good idea to boil one as a test at first, in order to check whether they do not fall apart while cooking. The reasons for them falling

apart can vary: too little egg, too little flour, or too much liquid. By this simple test we can soon discover whether the dough is satisfactory. If it is too thin, flour should be added, or if it is too hard, boiled water, milk or carbonated mineral water should be added. For knedle made with flour, coarse-ground flour is best, because it absorbs liquid more slowly but more effectively.

To form knedle from short pastry you should first dust your hands with flour; knedle made with soft dough (from breadcrumbs or flour) are formed with wet hands. You should remember that the knedle swell considerably in cooking, and that they should therefore be boiled in a large amount of salted water.

Knedle can be heated up by putting them for a moment in boiling water, or by slicing them and frying them in butter.

Highwayman's knedle

1½ kg potatoes, 2 tbsps butter, 2 eggs,
350 g semolina, salt, pepper, marjoram

Cook 500 g of potatoes. Grate the rest of them, squeeze out the excess juice. Put the cooked potatoes through a mincer. Add them to the grated potatoes. Pour in the melted butter and semolina, break in the eggs, add salt, pepper and marjoram. Work into a smooth dough. Form small balls from the dough. Drop them into boiling salted water.

serves 4 • Preparation: 10–15 mins • Cooking: 20 mins

Cinnamon knedle

1 kg cooked potatoes, ½ tbsp butter, 400 g flour,
3 eggs, ⅓ cup cream, salt, 1 tsp sugar, 1 tsp cinnamon

Put the potatoes through a ricer. Add the cream, eggs, melted butter, sugar and cinnamon, and work into a dough. Form small balls from the dough. Cook them in boiling salted water. Before serving, pour over melted butter mixed with browned breadcrumbs.

serves 4 • Preparation: 10 mins • Cooking: 10–15 mins

Stuffed knedle

DOUGH: 1 kg cooked potatoes,
1–1½ cups flour, 3 eggs, salt

Put the potatoes through a mincer. Break in the eggs, add salt and flour. Work into a smooth dough. Sprinkle a pastry board with flour. Make a fairly thick roll from the dough, then cut it into thick slices. Flatten out each slice, place some stuffing in the middle, and seal. Drop the knedle into boiling salted water. When they float to the surface, cook for another 10 mins over low heat. Serve with a sauce of your choice or with scratchings or melted butter.

serves 4 • Preparation: 5–7 mins • Cooking: 10 mins

Podolian stuffing for knedle

150 g pork fat, 2 large onions,
400 g cottage cheese, salt, pepper

Chop the fat finely, then render it in a frying pan. Add the finely chopped onion and fry it, but do not let it brown. Add salt and pepper, stir well and fry for a bit longer. When the mixture has cooled down, put in the cottage cheese that has been put through a mincer. Add salt and pepper to taste.

serves 4 • Preparation: 5–7 mins

Fish stuffing for knedle

600 g pollock fillets, 1 large onion,
1 bay leaf, 1–2 cloves, several grains each
pepper and allspice, salt, 1 tbsp lemon juice,
½ tsp grated lemon rind, 1½ cup light stock;

1 tbsp butter, 2 onions, 1 tbsp chopped dill, salt,
pepper, a pinch of cayenne pepper, 1 egg

Sprinkle the fillets with lemon juice and salt and leave for half an hour. Bring the stock with onion, spices and lemon zest to the boil. Put in the fillets and cook them over low heat for 20 mins. Leave them in the stock until they have cooled down. Take the fish out with the strainer, cut it finely. Fry the finely chopped onion in melted butter (but do not let it brown), add it to the fish. Add salt, pepper, cayenne, dill and the egg. Work into a smooth mixture (if the stuffing is not thick enough, add 1 or 1½ tbsps of breadcrumbs).

serves 4 • Preparation: 30 mins

Cabbage stuffing for knedle

1 small savoy cabbage, 2 onions, 3–4 dried
mushrooms, 2 hard-boiled eggs, salt,
1 tsp pepper, 1½ tbsps butter, ¼ cup milk

Rinse the mushrooms and soak them overnight in a small amount of boiled water. Cook the mushrooms, then chop them finely. Bring some salted water and the milk to the boil. Put in the cabbage quarters and cook them for 15 mins. Drain the cabbage, allow it to cool, then shred it finely. Fry the finely chopped onion in butter (but do not let it brown), put in the cabbage and mushrooms. Add a generous amount of pepper and fry, stirring all the time. When the mixture cools down, add the finely chopped egg and some salt and pepper to taste. Mix thoroughly.

serves 4 • Preparation: 25–30 mins

Silesian bread-roll knedle

8 dry bread rolls cut into thin slices,
1 large onion, 1½ cups milk, 3 tbsps finely
chopped parsley, 2–3 eggs, 1 tbsp buter,
½ tsp chopped fresh marjoram, salt, pepper

Put the bread into a bowl, pour over the warm milk and leave aside for an hour. Fry the finely chopped onion in butter (but do not let it brown), add the parsley, stir well, then take off the heat. When the onion has cooled, combine it with the bread, break in the eggs, add salt, pepper and marjoram. Work into a smooth mixture. Cook one knedel to check if the consistency is right. If it falls apart, add some breadcrumbs to the 'dough'. Cook over medium heat for 20 mins.

serves 4 • Preparation: 15–20 mins • Cooking: 20–25 mins

Yeasty knedle

500 g flour, 40 g yeast, 1 cup milk,
1 tsp sugar, 100 g butter, 2 eggs, salt

Crumble the yeast and mix it with sugar, 1 tsp of flour and warm milk. Leave in a warm place for several minutes. Sift half the flour into a bowl, pour in the yeast and melted butter (30 g). Work into a smooth dough. Cover with a cloth and leave in a warm place to rise. Break in the eggs, sift in the remaining flour and knead the dough until air bubbles begin to form and the dough is smooth and shiny. Leave again to rise. When the dough has risen, form small knedle. Arrange them on a pastry board dusted with flour and leave to rise. Fill a large pan ⅔ with water. Put on top a piece of gauze (take care that it does not touch the water). When the water begins to boil, put the knedle on the gauze, cover the pot with the bowl turned upside down and cook for 20 mins. Half way through, turn the knedle over.

serves 4 • Preparation: 1 hr • Cooking: 20–25 mins

Cheese knedle

4 stale bread rolls, ½ cup milk, 150 g Roquefort or some other blue cheese, 1–2 tbsp flour, 1½ tbsps butter, 2 eggs, 1 large onion, 1 tbsp chopped parsley, ½ tsp ground caraway seeds, salt, pepper

Cut the bread rolls into small cubes, put into a bowl, add the flour, salt, pepper, caraway and crumbled cheese. Fry the finely chopped onion in butter (but do not brown it), add it to the bread. Mix the milk with the eggs, pour into the bowl, stir the contents and leave for 10–15 mins. Work the mixture into a smooth 'dough'. Form small balls from it. Drop the balls into boiling salted water. Bring to the boil, then turn down the heat and cook for 15 mins.

serves 4 • Preparation: 10 mins • Cooking: 15–20 mins

Garlicky knedle

150 g semolina, 6–7 tbsps breadcrumbs, 500 g curd cheese, 3 eggs, 6 tbsps butter, 1–1 ½ tsps baking soda, salt, ¼ tsp grated nutmeg, 1–2 cloves of garlic, 2–3 tbsps finely chopped young garlic leaves

Put the cheese through a mincer. Cream the butter, break in one egg yolk at at time. Whisking all the time, add gradually the semolina, breadcrumbs, cheese and baking soda. Add the garlic crushed with salt and nutmeg. Whisk the egg whites, fold them in. Form small balls from the mixture. Drop them into boiling salted water and cook for 10–15 mins. Before serving, pour over some melted butter.

serves 4 • Preparation: 15–20 mins • Cooking: 10–15 mins

Apricot knedle

250 g curd cheese, 5 tbsps melted butter, 2 eggs, 100–150 g flour, apricots, sugar cubes (as many as apricots), butter, breadcrumbs and sugar for garnishing

Beat the butter with the cheese and eggs, add some salt. Put in enough flour to make a fairly soft dough. Make a large ball from the dough, cover it with a cloth and leave aside for half an hour. Stone the apricots. Put a sugar cube into each apricot. Sprinkle a pastry board with flour. Roll out the dough and cut out circles with a large glass. Wrap each apricot in one circle of dough, seal the edges very carefully. Drop into boiling water and cook for 10 mins. Before serving, sprinkle with sugar and pour over melted butter with browned breadcrumbs.

serves 4 • Preparation: 15–20 mins • Cooking: 10–12 mins

Strawberry knedle

500 g light curd cheese, 200 g butter, 4 tbsps sugar, 2 egg yolks, juice and grated rind of ½ lemon, 8 tbsps each wheat flour and semolina, 250 g strawberries, 3 tbsps finely chopped pistachios, a pinch of salt, 3 tbsps breadcrumbs

Put the cheese through a mincer. Beat 100 g of butter, 2 tbsps of sugar and egg yolks until foamy. Whisking all the time, gradually add the cheese, lemon juice and zest, flour and semolina. Work into a smooth mixture, then leave aside for half an hour. Add salt and the pistachios, mix thoroughly. With hands dusted with flour take pieces of the dough, flatten each, put a strawberry in the middle and seal carefully. Drop the knedle into boiling salted water and cook for 15 mins. Before serving, pour over melted butter with browned breadcrumbs and sprinkle some sugar.

serves 4 • Preparation: 20 mins • Cooking: 15 mins

Yeasty knedle with poppy seeds

500 g flour, 30 g yeast, 2 tsps sugar, ½ cup lukewarm milk, 2 eggs, grated rind of ½ lemon, 100 g butter, ½ tsp salt, 200 g plum jam, 2 tbsps rum, ¼ tsp cinnamon, 200 g minced poppy seeds, 100 g caster sugar, 200 g melted butter

Mix the yeast with the sugar and half the lukewarm milk, leave aside for several minutes. Sift the flour, break in the eggs, add some melted butter, lemon zest, yeast and the remaining milk, as well as a bit of salt. Knead the dough well, cover with a cloth and leave in a warm place to rise. Mix the plum jam with the rum and cinnamon. Take a bit of the dough and flatten it into a circle. Put some jam mixture in the middle, seal carefully, arrange on a pastry board and cover with a cloth. When the knedle have risen, drop them into boiling salted water and cook over low heat for 5–6 mins, then turn them round and cook for another 5–6 mins. Before serving, pour over melted butter and sprinkle sugar mixed with the poppy seed on top.

serves 4 • Preparation: 25–30 mins • Cooking: 7–8 mins

Plum knedle

1 kg cooked potatoes, 1½ cups flour, 3 eggs, salt, a pinch of nutmeg, 1 kg plums (if frozen, do not defreeze them), 3 tbsps sugar, ½ vanilla pod, 3 tbsps chopped walnuts

Put the potatoes through a mincer, add salt, nutmeg, eggs and flour. Knead into a smooth dough. Dust a pastry board with flour. Make a thick roll from the dough, cut it into thick slices. Mix thoroughly the sugar, chopped vanilla and walnuts. Rinse the plums and drain them. Stone them without separating the halves. Put inside each plum some sugar and walnut mixture. Flatten each piece of the dough, put a plum in the middle, seal the edges carefully. Drop the knedle into boiling salted water. Before serving, pour over some melted butter.

serves 4 • Preparation: 10 mins • Cooking: 10–15 mins

Pierogi, pancakes and croquettes

These dishes are as old as time and are known under very different names all over the world. Undoubtedly, the first pancakes were patties of ground flour and water that were baked on hot stones; their ancestors include both the Babylonian damper and the Jewish matzoh.

And it is not far from pancakes to pierogi.

The idea has taken hold that producing these dishes is a terribly time-consuming and unpleasant task. But just think what pleasure you can give your family with Russian pierogi, patties, a splendid koulebiac, or a wonderful pancake gateau – and you will immediately come to the conclusion that the effort is worth it. And apart from that, you can make a stock of both pierogi and pancakes. Pancakes can be kept in the fridge for several days, and ready-made pierogi can be frozen and cooked when needed. The stuffing for both can basically be made from anything that you have to hand – leftovers from roasts, smoked meats, braised meats or vegetables. Stuffing made from spinach with white cheese and nutmeg, for example, tastes quite different from goat's cheese with garlic stuffing, and different yet again from stuffing made from ham or bacon with grated cheese. Depending on the stuffing, pierogi and pancakes can be a simple daily dish, or grace the table at an elegant party.

In Poland, pierogi means a dish made from thinly rolled-out pastry cut into squares or circles and filled with various kinds of stuffing; boiled pierogi are served with melted butter, sour cream or dripping with crackling poured over them.

According to the old legend pierogi came to us from Russia. At one time pierogi were baked only for holidays, and every holiday had its pierogi which differed in shape as well as in the stuffing. There were *kurniki* – large pierogi for weddings, similar to cakes with many different kinds of stuffing which however always contained chicken; and *kny-*

sze or pierogi for wakes; and *koladki*, which were baked in January at the beginning of the New Year in memory of the pagan festival of Kolada; there were *hreczuszki* which were made from buckwheat flour; and also the sweet *sanieņki* and *socznie*, which were special pierogi baked usually for name days. Many of these Old Slavonic names have remained in Polish regional cuisine to the present day.

Pierogi can be boiled, baked or fried, like doughnuts, in deep fat. Everything depends on the pastry.

The simplest pastry for boiled pierogi is a mixture of flour and lukewarm boiled salted water. But there are as many ways of making the pastry as there are households in the country. Some housewives add eggs, others add olive oil, and yet others add melted butter, or a pinch of baking powder. Old Lithuanian housewives replace boiled water with juice from an onion, which gives an excellent taste.

One thing is certain – good pastry for pierogi must have the right consistency: it must be soft and elastic so that it is easy to form and sticks together. Well-made pastry should be wrapped in a damp cloth and left to rest.

After removing a portion of it to roll out, cover the rest of the pastry with a cloth so that it does not dry out.

There are many ways of forming pierogi. The pastry, when it has been divided into portions, can be:
- rolled out on pastry board and then, using a glass or a cutter, circles can be cut out, stuffed and stuck together;
- rolled into an elongated rectangle, along the long edge of which pats of stuffing are placed, and then this is covered with another rectangle of rolled out pastry and pierogi are cut out with a special cutter;
- a roll of pastry about 5 cm in diameter can be formed and 1 cm slices can be cut off, flattened in the hand to a thin cake and then stuffed and stuck together;
- the rolled pastry can be cut into rhomboids or squares, stuffed and stuck together at the top or as a ball.

When preparing pierogi you must remember that the stuffing should be neither too hard nor too runny: it is best if you can form it into small balls. The stuffing should not ooze out between the edges of the pastry, or it will cause the pierogi to fall apart while boiling.

The formed pierogi should be placed on a lightly-floured pastry board and covered with a cloth so that they do not dry out (for dried pastry will crack during cooking).

They should be cooked in a large, shallow pan with a large amount of salted boiling water, and should be thrown in gradually in handfuls; after each handful has been thrown in, stir the pot, so that they do not stick to the bottom, and boil until they come to the surface. The length of time for cooking depends on the thickness of the pastry, but is usually five minutes after the pierogi have come to the surface. They should not be boiled too hard, but simmered over a low heat, so that the delicate pastry does not dissolve. After straining them, you may quickly rinse them in cold water, so that they do not stick together, and arrange on a very hot serving dish. You should remove the cooked pierogi with a strainer spoon, arrange them on the hot dish and serve immediately. Depending on the stuffing, they should be served covered with melted bacon fat, onion fried in oil, melted butter, sour cream, or fresh cream with cinnamon or fruit juice.

Cooked pierogi can be heated up by throwing them into boiling salted water, frying them or putting them in the oven in an ovenproof dish covered with sauce, melted butter or cream and sprinkled with grated cheese.

Dough for boiled pierogi – basic recipes

Wheat flour dough

400 g wheat flour, 1–2 eggs, 2 tbsps melted butter, salt, boiled lukewarm water

Sift the flour onto a pastry board, make a hollow in the middle. Break in the eggs, pour in the melted butter, add some salt. Knead the dough, adding water, until it has become smooth and flexible. Wrap the dough in a clean cloth and leave for 30 mins to rest. Sprinkle the pastry board with flour, roll out the dough. Cut out circles. Put some stuffing on each circle and seal the edges carefully. Cook in batches in boiling salted water.

serves 4 • Preparation: 8–10 mins • Cooking: 20–30 mins

Lithuanian dough

400 g flour, 3–4 tbsps onion juice,
2 eggs, 2 egg yolks, salt

Sift the flour onto a pastry board, make a hollow in the middle. Break in the eggs, add the egg yolks, pour in the onion juice, add some salt. Knead the dough (do not add any water). Wrap the dough in a cloth and leave for 30 mins to rest. Sprinkle the pastry board with flour, roll out the dough. Cut out circles. Put some stuffing on each circle and seal the edges carefully. Cook in batches in boiling salted water.

serves 4 • Preparation: 10 mins

Buckwheat dough

400 g buckwheat flour, 80 g wheat
flour, salt, boiled water

Mix carefully both kinds of flour, toast it in a hot frying pan, but do not allow it to brown. Take off the heat, add some salt and gradually pour in hot water, stirring vigorously all the time so that the dough is not lumpy. When the dough cools down, take it out onto a pastry board sprinkled with flour. Form a roll from the dough, cut it into 1 cm thick slices. Flatten out each slice, put some stuffing in the centre, seal the edges carefully. Cook in batches in boiling salted water.

serves 4 • Preparation: 15–20 mins

Potato dough

1 kg cooked potatoes, 250–300 g flour,
1–2 eggs, salt, ¼ tsp baking soda

Put the potatoes through a mincer, add the sifted flour and baking soda. Break in the eggs, add some salt. Knead the dough. Transfer it onto a pastry board sprinkled with flour. Form a roll, cut it into slices. Flatten each slice

a bit, put some stuffing in the middle and seal the edges carefully. Cook in batches in boiling salted water.

Pierogi have come to Poland from Ruthenia. So to begin with, here's a recipe for what is known as **Russian pierogi** – 'those made of potatoes and browned onion with a bit of cottage cheese. At present the stuffing for pierogi is made almost exclusively from cottage cheese, which is a mistake, for cheese should be just an extra,' wrote the Polish film director Jerzy Passendorfer, who comes from Vilnius.

serves 4 • Preparation: 10–15 mins

Russian pierogi

DOUGH: 400 g flour, 1 egg, boiled water, salt

STUFFING: 800 g cooked potatoes, 200 g
cottage cheese, 2 large onions, 2 tbsps butter,
1 egg, salt, 1 tsp pepper or paprika

Brown the chopped onion in butter, allow to cool. Put the potatoes and cheese through a mincer, break in the egg, put in the onion, add salt and pepper and mix thoroughly. Sprinkle some flour on a pastry board. Make a roll from the dough. Cut it into 1 cm thick slices. Flatten each slice with your hands, put some stuffing in the middle, seal the edges carefully. Cook the pierogi in boiling salted water until they float to the surface. Before serving, pour over some melted butter or thick cream and sprinkle with coarsely ground pepper.

serves 4 • Preparation: 30–40 mins • Cooking: until they float to the surface

Stuffing for cooked pierogi

POTATO STUFFING

Lvov stuffing

*800 g cooked potatoes, 2 raw egg yolks,
2 tbsps thick cream, 4 tbsps chopped dill,
1 tbsp butter, salt, pepper, a pinch of nutmeg*

Put the potatoes through a mincer. Beat the egg yolks with butter and cream. Whisking all the time, gradually add the potato mash and dill, add some salt, season with nutmeg and pepper to taste. Sprinkle the cooked pierogi with melted butter.

serves 4 • Preparation: 5 mins

Kovno stuffing

*7–9 raw potatoes, 150 g smoked streaky bacon,
1 onion, salt, pepper, 1 tbsp butter, 1 egg*

Peel and rinse the potatoes, then grate them. Fry the chopped onion in butter (but do not let it brown), dice the bacon finely. Squeeze out the excess juice from the potatoes, put in the bacon and onion, break in the egg, add salt and pepper to taste. Mix thoroughly. Before serving, pour some melted butter, cream or pork scratchings over the cooked pierogi.

serves 4 • Preparation: 5–7 mins

CHEESE STUFFING

Old Polish stuffing

*200 g curd cheese, 1½ cups cooked rice,
1 largish onion, 1 tbsp butter, salt, pepper*

Brown the chopped onion in butter, then mix it thoroughly with the cheese. Combine with the rice, add

salt and pepper to taste, mix thoroughly. Before serving, pour some melted butter with browned breadcrumbs over the cooked pierogi.

serves 4 • Preparation: 5 mins

Monk's stuffing

600 g low-fat curd cheese, 2–3 eggs, salt

Put the cheese through a mincer, break in the eggs, add some salt and work into a smooth mixture. Before serving, pour some melted butter or cream over the cooked pierogi.

serves 4 • Preparation: 5 mins

Lithuanian stuffing

*600 g cream cheese, 1 egg, 3 tbsps chopped
tarragon, 1 tbsp butter, salt, pepper*

Whisk the butter with the eggs and cheese to form a smooth paste. Add the tarragon, salt and pepper to taste. Before serving, pour some lard with pork scratchings over the cooked pierogi.

serves 4 • Preparation: 5 mins

Lvov stuffing

*400 g grated cheese, 2 tbsps each chopped parsley,
ground walnuts and tomato paste, 1 tbsp butter,
salt, pepper, a pinch of each sugar and nutmeg*

Melt the butter in a frying pan, put in the walnuts and toast them a bit, add salt, pepper, sugar, nutmeg and tomato paste, mix thoroughly. When the mixture cools, add the parsley and grated cheese. Before serving, pour some melted butter over the cooked pierogi.

serves 4 • Preparation: 10–12 mins

Ruthenian stuffing

*200 g cottage cheese, 200 g cooked buckwheat
kasha, 1 onion, 1 tbsp butter, salt, pepper*

Fry the chopped onion in melted butter (but do not let it brown), mix it thoroughly with the cheese. Add the buckwheat, some salt and pepper to taste, mix thoroughly. Before serving, pour some melted butter or bacon scratchings over the cooked pierogi.

serves 4 • Preparation: 5–7 mins

Polish stuffing

200 g cottage cheese, 200 g smoked ham, 1 onion, 1 tbsp butter, 2 eggs, 1 tsp caraway, salt

Fry the chopped onion in butter (but do not let it brown), combine with the diced ham. Cream the cheese together with the egg yolks. Add the onion and ham mixture. Fold in the whisked egg whites, add caraway and some salt. Mix thoroughly. Before serving, pour melted butter, cream or scratchings over the cooked pierogi.

serves 4 • Preparation: 10 mins

MUSHROOM STUFFING

Kurp stuffing

100 g dried mushrooms, 1 cup chopped hazelnuts, 2–3 tbsps chopped parsley, 1 small onion, 1 tbsp butter, 1 egg, salt, ½ tsp pepper, ¼ tsp dried thyme

Rinse the mushroom and soak them overnight in a small amount of water. The following day cook them, drain and chop finely. Fry the finely chopped onion in butter (but do not let it brown), put in the mushrooms, add salt and pepper, and simmer over a low heat for a while. Dry roast the chopped nuts, then add them to the cool mushroom mixture. Put in the parsley and thyme, break in the egg. Work into a smooth paste. Add more salt and pepper if required. Before serving, pour over some pork scratchings or melted butter over the cooked pierogi.

serves 4 • Preparation: 30–35 mins

Little Poland stuffing

1 cup small beans (white, red, brown), 50 g dried mushrooms, 2 onions, 1–2 tbsps chopped walnuts, 1 tbsp butter, 1 tbsp soya sauce, a pinch of pepper, 1 egg

Rinse the beans and mushrooms, soak them overnight. Cook the beans the following day, adding some salt towards the end. Drain the beans and liquidize them or put them through a mincer. Cook the mushrooms, then dice them finely. Fry the finely chopped onion in butter, but do not let it brown. Combine the onion, mushrooms and beans, add soya sauce and walnuts, break in the egg. Add salt and pepper to taste. Mix thoroughly. Before serving, pour some bacon scratchings over the cooked pierogi.

serves 4 • Preparation: 30–40 mins

Vilnius stuffing

150 g dried mushrooms, 200 g smoked ham, 1–2 onions, 1 tbsp butter, salt, pepper, 1–2 tbsps breadcrumbs, 1 egg

Rinse the mushrooms, soak them in a small amount of water, then cook them. Take them out and, together with the ham, put them through a mincer. Fry the finely chopped onion in melted butter (but do not let it brown), add it to the mushrooms and ham. Add salt and pepper to taste, break in the egg, pour in the breadcrumbs. Work into a smooth paste. Before serving, pour some melted butter over the cooked pierogi.

serves 4 • Preparation: 30–40 mins

Lent stuffing

50 g dried mushrooms, 300 g carp (pike, bream or silver carp) fillets, 1 tbsp lemon juice, salt, 1 large onion, 2 tbsps oil, pepper, 1–2 tbsps breadcrumbs, 1 egg

Rinse the mushrooms and soak them overnight in water. Cook them, drain and dice finely. Rinse the fillets and dry them, rub with salt, sprinkle with lemon juice and leave aside for an hour. Heat up 1 tbsp of oil in a frying pan, put in the chopped onion, sauté it, then add the mushrooms. Add salt and pepper, stir well and simmer for several minutes. Fry the fish in oil in another pan, allow it to cool. Remove the bones and cut the flesh finely. Combine the fish with the mushrooms, leave the mixture to cool. Add more salt and pepper to taste, break in the egg, pour in the breadcrumbs and work into a smooth paste. Before serving, pour some butter with browned onion or some thick cream over the cooked pierogi.

serves 4 • Preparation: 30–40 mins

Mushroom and lentil stuffing

200 g lentils, 200 g mushrooms, 1 onion, 1 tbsp soya sauce, salt, pepper, a pinch of cayenne pepper, 1 egg, 1–2 tbsps breadcrumbs if required

Soak the lentils in water overnight, then drain them. Cover the lentils with boiled water and cook them, then reduce the liquid a bit. Leave the lentils to cool, then put through a mincer. Dice the onion and mushrooms finely, fry them in butter, add the mixture to the lentils. Add salt, pepper, cayenne and soya sauce, break in the egg and work into a smooth paste. Add some bread-crumbs if the paste is not thick enough. Before serving, pour some melted lard with scratchings over the cooked pirogi.

serves 4 • Preparation: 30–40 mins

OFFAL STUFFING

Jewish stuffing (kreplach)

300 g beef liver, 200 g onion, 100 g goose fat, 1 hard-boiled egg, salt, pepper

Rinse the liver, remove the membranes, then grill or fry it. Put the cool liver through a mincer. Chop the egg finely. Fry the finely chopped onion in goose fat. Mix it with the egg and liver, add salt and pepper to taste and work into a smooth paste. Fry the cooked pierogi in fat.

serves 4 • Preparation: 15–20 mins

Lvov stuffing

500 g veal tripe, 2 cups light stock, 1 tbsp lemon juice, 1 tbsp grated lemon rind, 3 tbsps chopped parsley, 1 tsp marjoram, salt, pepper, 1 egg

Wash the tripe thoroughly, then cook it in the stock until tender. Drain the cooked tripe, leave to cool, then chop finely. Put in the parsley and marjoram, add salt, pepper, lemon juice and zest. Break in the egg and mix thoroughly. Pour over some melted butter over the cooked pierogi or fry them in fat.

serves 4 • Preparation: 1 hr

Poznań stuffing

700 g veal lights, 2 cups stock, 1 bread roll soaked in milk, 1–2 onions, 2 tbsps butter, salt, pepper

Rinse the lights, cover with the stock and cook. Drain them, allow to cool, then put through a mincer. Brown the chopped onion in butter, mix it with the squeezed out bread roll and with the lights. Add salt and pepper to taste.

serves 4 • Preparation: 40–45 mins

VEGETABLE STUFFING

Ruthenian stuffing

500 g sauerkraut, 1 onion, salt, pepper, 1 tbsp oil

Chop the cabbage, put it into a pan. Sprinkle with 2–3 tbsps of hot water and simmer until tender, then reduce the liquid. Fry the chopped onion in hot oil (but do not let it brown), put in the cabbage, mix thoroughly and fry for a minute or two. Add salt and pepper to taste, then allow to cool. Before serving, pour some browned onion or bacon scratchings over the pierogi.

serves 4 • Preparation: 25–30 mins

Old Polish stuffing

400 g fresh cabbage, 150 g curd cheese, 1 large onion, 2 tbsps butter, salt, 1 tsp pepper, ½ tsp ground caraway

Put the cabbage into boiling salted water and cook for 5 mins, then drain, allow to cool and chop finely. Fry the finely chopped onion in butter (but do not let it brown), add the cabbage and, stirring all the time, fry for several minutes. Leave it to cool. Put the cheese through a mincer, add salt, pepper and caraway to taste, mix with the stewed cabbage. Before serving, pour some melted butter with browned breadcrumbs over the cooked pierogi.

serves 4 • Preparation: 20–25 mins

Little Poland stuffing

500 g sauerkraut, 50 g dried mushrooms,
100 g grated cheese, salt, pepper

Rinse the mushrooms and soak them overnight in water, then cook them and drain. Chop the cabbage, put it into a pan, pour in the hot mushroom stock. Cook for 30 mins, then reduce the liquid. Dice the mushrooms finely, add them to the cabbage. Leave the mixture to cool, put in the cheese, add salt and pepper to taste.

serves 4 • Preparation: 45–50 mins

Kuyavia stuffing

½ white cabbage (ca 400 g), 6–8 dried
mushrooms, 2 hard-boiled eggs, 3 tbsps
chopped walnuts, salt, pepper

Soak the mushrooms in water, then cook them. Shred the cabbage, sprinkle it with some salt and leave for several minutes, then squeeze out the excess juice. Add the cabbage to the mushrooms and cook them together for 15–20 mins. Leave the mixture to cool, then put it through a mincer. Add salt and pepper to taste, put in the chopped eggs and walnuts. Before serving, pour some melted butter or scratchings over the cooked pierogi.

serves 4 • Preparation: 30–35 mins

Carpathian stuffing

500 g white cabbage, 50 g pork fat, 2 onions,
300 g bryndza, 1 egg, salt, pepper

Shred the cabbage finely, put into a pan, sprinkle sparingly with water and simmer until tender, then reduce the liquid. Chop the fat finely and render it in a hot frying pan. Put in the cabbage and fry together for a minute or two. Add salt and pepper to taste. Leave it to cool, then chop finely together with the crumbled cheese. Break in the egg and mix thoroughly, adding more salt and pepper if required. Before serving, pour some melted butter or pork scratchings over the cooked pierogi.

serves 4 • Preparation: 35–40 mins

Kurp stuffing with lentils

1 cup lentils, 2 potatoes cooked in jackets,
2 largish onions, 2 tbsps oil, 1 hard-boiled egg,
1 raw egg, salt, pepper, 1 tsp dried marjoram

Rinse and drain the lentils, cover with lukewarm water and leave to soak overnight, then cook and drain. Fry the diced onion in oil, but do not let it brown. Chop the hard-boiled egg finely. Put the lentils and peeled potatoes through a mincer, mix in the onion and chopped egg. Add salt, pepper and marjoram, break in the egg and work into a smooth paste. Before serving, pour some melted butter or hot oil over the cooked pierogi.

serves 4 • Preparation: 40–45 mins

Lvov stuffing with horseradish

200 g grated horseradish, 1 tbsp lemon juice,
100 g butter, 150 g white bread, ¼ cup milk,
50 g raisins, salt, pepper, sugar to taste

Soak the bread in milk. Put the freshly grated horseradish into a sieve and pour some boiling water over. Drain it, then sprinkle with lemon juice and sugar. Rinse, blanch and drain the raisins. Beat the butter and egg yolk until fluffy. Whisking all the time, gradually add the squeezed out bread and horseradish. Add salt and pepper to taste, put in the raisins and mix thoroughly. Before serving, pour some melted butter over the cooked pierogi.

serves 4 • Preparation: 15–20 mins

Nettle stuffing

400 g young nettles, 2 hard-boiled eggs,
2 tbsps chopped chives, 1 tbsp butter, 1 large
onion, salt, pepper, 1 tsp lemon juice

Rinse the nettles, chop them finely. Fry the finely diced onion in butter (but do not let it brown), add it to the nettles and, stirring continuously, fry for a minute or two. Add lemon juice, salt and pepper to taste, reduce the liquid. Leave it to cool, then combine with the chopped egg and chives. Mix well and season to taste. Before serving, pour some melted butter or cream over the cooked pierogi.

serves 4 • Preparation: 10 mins

Spinach stuffing

1½ kg fresh spinach, 2 pieces of dry white
bread, ¼ cup milk, 2 tbsps butter, 1 tbsp
flour, 1 tbsp lemon juice, ¼ tsp grated lemon
rind, 7–8 cloves of garlic, salt, nutmeg

Rinse the spinach, blanch and drain it, then chop it finely. Soak the bread in milk, squeeze it out and mix with the spinach. Crush the chopped garlic with salt. Melt the butter in a pan, add the flour and make a white roux. Dilute it with milk, add the spinach, garlic, lemon juice and zest. Mix thoroughly and heat up until the mixture has thickened. Add salt, pepper and nutmeg to taste, leave to cool. Before serving, pour some melted butter with browned breadcrumbs over the cooked pierogi.

serves 4 • Preparation: 15–20 mins

FISH STUFFING

Kashub stuffing

400 g cod fillets, 1 cup vegetable stock,
100 g smoked streaky bacon, 1 large onion,
1 tbsp butter, 2 tbsps chopped parsley,
1–2 tbsps sifted breadcrumbs, 1 egg, salt, pepper

Cook the fillets in the stock, take them out with a strainer, leave to cool. Chop the bacon and onion finely, fry them in melted butter. Put the fish, onion and bacon through a mincer. Add the egg yolk, salt, pepper and parsley. Fold in the whisked egg white. Add the breadcrumbs and mix lightly but thoroughly. Before serving, pour some melted butter with browned breadcrumbs over the cooked pierogi.

serves 4 • Preparation: 15–20 mins

Warsaw stuffing

500 g fish (perch or silver carp) fillets, salt,
1 tbsp lemon juice, 1½ cups vegetable stock,
2 tbsps chopped walnuts, 2 large onions,
1 tbsp oil, 1 egg, 2 tbsps chopped parsley

Rub the fillets with salt, sprinkle with some lemon juice and leave for half an hour, then put them into a pan, cover with the hot stock and simmer over low heat for 15 mins. Take off the heat and allow to cool. Fry the finely chopped onion in oil, but do not let it brown. Chop the cooked fish, add the onion, walnuts, parsley, salt, pepper and the egg. Mix thoroughly. Before serving, pour some melted butter with browned breadcrumbs over the cooked pierogi.

serves 4 • Preparation: 15–20 mins

Pike and horseradish stuffing

500 g pike or pikeperch fillets, 1–2 onions, 2–3 tbsps
grated horseradish, 3 tbsps chopped hazelnuts,
1 hard-boiled egg, 1 raw egg yolk, ½ tsp honey,
1 tbsp lemon juice, salt, pepper, 1 tbsp butter

Rinse and dry the fillets, put them through a mincer, sprinkle with lemon juice. Mix in the honey and horseradish. Fry the diced onion in butter, chop the hard-boiled egg. Combine the fish with the hazelnuts, onion and egg, add salt and pepper to taste. Mix thoroughly with the egg yolk. Before serving, pour cream or melted butter over the cooked pierogi.

serves 4 • Preparation: 10–15 mins

MEAT STUFFING

Braniewo stuffing

500 g lean smoked bacon, 200 g cooked buckwheat kasha, 1–2 onions, 4 hard-boiled eggs, 2 raw eggs, 2 tbsps butter, salt, pepper

Dice finely the bacon and onion, fry them in melted butter. Sprinkle with 1 tbsp of water and simmer under cover. Chop the hard-boiled eggs, add them to the kasha, put in the bacon and onion mixture. Break in the eggs, add salt and pepper to taste and mix thoroughly. Before serving, pour melted butter, scratchings or cream over the cooked pierogi.

serves 4 • Preparation: 10 mins

Veal stuffing

300 g cooked veal, cooked soup vegetables (2 carrots, 1 parsley root, a piece of celeriac), ½ bread roll soaked in milk, 1 tbsp chopped parsley, salt, 1 tbsp butter

Put the squeezed out bread roll, vegetables and meat through a mincer, then fry the mixture in melted butter. Leave it to cool, add parsley and salt to taste. Before serving, pour some melted butter over the cooked pierogi. Serve with salads.

serves 4 • Preparation: 10–15 mins

Kovno stuffing

400 g lean smoked bacon, 50 g pork fat, 1 large onion, 4 hard-boiled eggs, 1 raw egg, 1–2 tbsps sifted breadcrumbs, ¼ tsp dried savory, 2 tbsps chopped parsley, salt, pepper

Chop the fat finely, render it in a frying pan. Add the diced onion and fry them together, stirring all the time. Put the bacon through a mincer, chop the hard-boiled eggs. Combine the bacon with the onion, hard-boiled eggs, savory and parsley. Break in the raw egg, add the breadcrumbs. Work into a smooth paste, add salt and pepper to

taste. Before serving, pour some fat with scratchings over the cooked pierogi. Serve with salads.

serves 4 • Preparation: 10–15 mins

Lithuanian stuffing

500 g cooked chicken, 1 cup cooked rice, 2 tbsps butter, 1 tbsp thick cream, salt, ½ tsp nutmeg

Chop the meat very finely or put it through a mincer. Fry it in butter, add the rice, cream and nutmeg. Add salt to taste. Before serving, pour some melted butter over the cooked pierogi, or else reheat them in the oven.

serves 4 • Preparation: 5–7 mins

Hunter's stuffing

400 g minced game meat (wild boar, venison or hare), 1 tbsp butter, ¼ cup cream, 1 tbsp each stock, red currant jelly and ketchup, 1 glass brandy, 2–3 tbsps chopped walnuts, 1 tsp lemon juice, ¼ tsp each ground cloves, pepper, ginger and honey, salt

Sprinkle the meat with lemon juice, then with the ginger, pepper and cloves mixed with honey and leave aside for an hour. Fry it in butter, stirring all the time. Allow it to cool, mix in the cream. Add the brandy, red currant jelly, ketchup and walnuts. Mix thoroughly, add salt to taste. Before serving, pour some melted butter over the cooked pierogi.

serves 4 • Preparation: 10–12 mins

Polish stuffing

400 g minced veal, 3 fillets of salted herring, ¼ cup milk, 1 large onion, 1 tbsp butter, 1 tsp pepper, salt

Pour the milk over the herring fillets and leave for half an hour, then take the fillets out, dry them and cut into fine cubes. Fry the chopped onion in butter (but do not let it brown), combine with the veal and herring. Add pepper and salt, mix thoroughly. Best cooked in a light stock. Before serving, pour some melted butter over the cooked pierogi.

serves 4 • Preparation: 5–7 mins

SWEET STUFFING

Pierogi with prunes

*400 g stoned prunes, ½ cup dry white wine,
2–3 tbsps chopped hazelnuts, a pinch of each
cinnamon and ground cloves, 1 tbsp honey*

Rinse the prunes and soak them in wine for 3–4 hours. Mix the nuts with the honey, cinnamon and cloves. Drain the prunes and stuff them with the hazelnut mixture. Sprinkle a pastry board with flour, roll out the dough (see pp. 152–153). Cut out small circles from the dough. Put some prunes in the middle of each circles, seal the edges carefully. Drop pierogi in batches into boiling salted water and cook for 4–6 mins. Before serving, pour some melted butter or cream over.

serves 4 • Preparation: 10–15 mins

Mazovian stuffing with poppy seed

*2 cups poppy seeds, 50 g raisins, 2 tbsps
finely chopped orange rind, 100 g chopped
walnuts, 3 tbsps honey, 1 tbsp brandy*

Rinse the poppy seeds, cover with boiling water and cook over low heat for 10 mins. Drain it, then put it twice through a mincer with a fine nozzle. Pour the brandy over the blanched raisins and leave for several minutes. Combine the poppy seed with the raisins, orange rind and walnuts, pour in the honey and mix thoroughly. Sprinkle a pastry board with some flour. Roll out the dough (see pp. 152–153) and cut out circles from it. Put some stuffing in the middle of each circles, seal the edges carefully. Drop pierogi into boiling salted water and cook until they float to the surface. Before serving, pour over some melted butter.

serves 4 • Preparation: 20 mins

Hazelnut stuffing

*400 g hazelnuts, 100 g hard bitter chocolate,
1 vanilla pod, 1–2 egg yolks, a pinch of salt*

Chop the vanilla and hazelnuts finely, grate the chocolate. Beat the egg yolks with the chocolate and a pinch of salt. Whisking all the time, gradually add the nuts and vanilla. When the pierogi are cooked, arrange them in an ovenproof dish, pour over melted butter, sprinkle with cherry liqueur and bake in the oven.

You can stuff pierogi with fresh fruit (plums, orange segments, bilberries, strawberries, apricots), fruit preserves (cherries, gooseberries, strawberries) or with frozen fruit. If you use frozen fruit, remember not to defreeze the fruit beforehand. Cooked pierogi are usually served with whipped cream, melted butter mixed with browned breadcrumbs or fruit juices.

serves 4 • Preparation: 10 mins

Kołduny

These are exceptionally juicy and aromatic dumplings, so small that they can be placed in one bite in the mouth, and crushed with the tongue against the palate, when they melt in the mouth giving a characteristic squeak. They should be stuffed loosely and lightly pricked with a fork, because the stuffing swells during cooking.

Kołduny dough – basic recipe

2 cups flour, 1 egg, boiled water, salt

Mix all the ingredients, knead the dough well, then roll it out thinly.

Lithuanian kołduny

*200 g boned leg of mutton, 200 g beef loin,
200 g mutton suet cleaned of membranes,
5–6 cloves of garlic, 1 tbsp dried marjoram, salt,
pepper, ¼ tsp sugar, 2–3 tbsps strong stock*

Chop the meat and suet finely, add the garlic crushed with salt, marjoram, pepper, sugar and stock and work into a smooth mixture. Make small pierogi from the rolled out dough. Drop them into a large pan of boiling salted water and cook over low heat for 5 mins. Serve with consommé or as a separate dish, with melted butter or cream poured over them.

serves 4 • Preparation: 15–20 mins • Cooking: 5 mins

Old Polish kołduny

300 g beef loin, 300 g marrow, 1 large onion, 1 tbsp butter, 1 tbsp dried marjoram, 1 tbsp pepper, salt

Extraxt the marrow from a marrow bone. Put the marrow and the meat through a mincer. Brown the chopped onion in butter, add it to the meat. Add marjoram, salt and pepper. Mix thoroughly. Roll out the dough thinly, cut out small circles from it. Put a rather small amount of the stuffing on each circle, seal the edges carefully. Drop into a large pan of boiling salted water. Serve as Lithuanian kołduny.

serves 4 • Preparation: 5–10 mins • Cooking: 5–6 mins

Polish kołduny

3 herring fillets, ½ cup milk, 100 g dried mushrooms, 2 onions, 2 tbsps butter, 2 tbsps chopped parsley, salt, pepper

Soak the mushrooms, then cook them. Pour the milk over the fillets and leave aside for 20 mins. Chop finely the cooked mushrooms and drained fillets. Fry the chopped onion in butter, add the mushrooms and, stirring all the time, sauté for a minute or two. Allow the mixture to cool, then add the herring, parsley, salt and pepper, break in the egg and work into a smooth paste. Make small pierogi and cook them in boiling salted water.

serves 4 • Preparation: 30–35 mins

Count Tyszkiewicz's kołduny

140 g dried mushrooms, 2 onions, 200 g smoked ham, 2 hard-boiled eggs, 1 raw egg, salt, pepper, 2 tbsps butter

Soak the mushrooms in water, then cook them. Fry the chopped onion in butter, add the diced mushrooms and fry them together, stirring all the time. Leave the mixture to cool, then add the chopped hard-boiled eggs and ham. Add salt and pepper to taste, break in the raw egg and mix thoroughly. Make small pierogi and cook them over low heat for 5 mins.

serves 4 • Preparation: 5 mins • Cooking: 30–35 mins

Ushka for red borsch

Dough for ushka – basic recipe

1½ cup flour, 1–2 tbsps olive oil, 1 egg, 1 egg yolk, salt, boiled water

Sift the flour onto a pastry board, make a hollow in the middle. Break in the egg, pour in the oil and add salt. Gradually adding water, knead the dough until smooth, then cover it with a cloth and leave to rest for several minutes.

Preparation: 10–15 mins

Stuffing from dried mushrooms

30 g cooked dried mushrooms, 1 large onion, 1–2 tbsps chopped walnuts, 1 egg, 1–1½ tbsps chopped parsley, salt, pepper, 1 tbsp oil

Prepare the dough as above and leave it to rest. Fry the chopped onion in oil (but do not let it brown), add the chopped mushrooms, parsley and walnuts. Add salt and rather a lot of pepper, break in the egg and work into a smooth paste. Sprinkle a pastry board with flour. Roll out the dough and cut small lozenges out of it. Put some stuffing in the middle of each lozenge. Fold the dough diagonally, seal the edges, then seal together the two outward corners. Cook in boiling salted water.

serves 4 • Preparation: 10–15 mins

Stuffing from fresh mushrooms

500 g fresh forest mushrooms, 1 large onion,
100 g goat's cheese, ½ cup single cream,
2 tbsps butter, 1 glass vodka, 2 tbsps chopped
parsley, salt, pepper, ½ tsp dried savory

Rinse the mushrooms, dry them on a piece of linen, then dice finely. Fry the chopped onion in butter (but do not let it brown), put in the mushrooms and fry for several minutes until the juice has evaporated. Take off the heat, pour over the vodka and set fire to it. When the flame is extinguished, heat again and add the cream. Add salt, pepper and savory. Mix thoroughly and stew for a bit, then leave to cool. Add parsley and the crumbled cheese. Stir well, add salt and pepper to taste. Roll out the pierogi dough and cut out small lozenges out of it. Put some stuffing in the middle of each lozenge, seal the edges. Cook in boiling salted water.

serves 4 • Preparation: 35–40 mins

Fried pierogi

Deep-fried pierogi, Polish style

STUFFING: 3 herring fillets, 500 g cooked
fish, 2 tbsps chopped parsley, 2 hard-boiled
eggs, 1 raw egg yolk, salt, pepper

YEAST DOUGH: 500 g flour, 30 g yeast,
½ cup milk, 2 eggs

Put the cooked fish and hard-boiled eggs through a mincer, add salt, pepper, the egg yolk and parsley. Rinse and dry the herring fillets, cut them into thin strips. When the dough has risen, roll it out and cut into squares. Put 2–3 herring strips and a bit of the stuffing on each square. Seal it, leaving a small hole at the top. Deep-fry the pierogi in batches until golden brown.

serves 4 • Preparation: 5–6 mins • Cooking: 6–8 mins

Fried pierogi

Baked pierogi, or patties

The best-known baked pierogi are called knysze and koulebiacs.

Koulebiacs are in fact very large pies shaped like a long loaf of bread. They are a specialty of Russian cousine, although the word *koulebiac* probably comes from the German word *kohlgeback*, meaning a pie filled with cabbage. The original Old Russian koulebiac was made only with yeast pastry and filled with many layers of stuffing made of buckwheat, cabbage, cooked fish, hard-boiled eggs and *vesiga*, or dried spinal marrow of the sturgeon. Each layer of stuffing was separated by a thin pancake. This dish was always part of the cuisine of the eastern Polish borderlands but has now spread to the whole of Poland.

When the dish entered international cuisine under the French version of the name, it became an exceptionally elegant dish, prepared with various kinds of pastry, usually choux pastry, and filled with exquisite stuffings made of poultry and fish (like salmon, perch and sole), mushrooms, rice or delicate cuts of meat or game.

Before serving it, you should cut the koulebiac in slices and sprinkle it generously with melted butter.

Small koulebiacs are also often made to avoid the problem of the pastry crumbling when it is cut.

Knysze at one time were 'small, round pierogi with a raised edge, with fried onion in the centre'. Today the name is applied to baked pierogi or patties, usually made with yeast pastry or also potato pastry, and filled with various kinds of stuffing. They can be served by themselves as a main dish or as a dessert if they are filled with a sweet stuffing.

Baked pierogi can be made from choux or puff pastry, short or potato flour pastry.

Dough for baked pierogi

Yeasty butter dough – basic recipe

3 cups flour, 150 g butter, 4 eggs, 1 cup milk, ½ sugar, ½ tsp salt, 50 g yeast

Mix the yeast with 1 tsp of sugar, add 2–3 tbsps of flour and lukewarm milk and leave in a warm place for 15–20 mins. Sift the warm flour into a bowl, add sugar and yeast and knead the dough. Break in the eggs and mix thoroughly. Pour in the melted butter, add some salt and work the dough for over ten minutes until it has become smooth and shiny. Cover with a cloth and leave in a warm place to rise.

serves 4 • Preparation: 25–30 mins

Shortcrust pastry – basic recipe

3 cups flour, 100 g each butter and lard, 3–4 tbsps sour cream, 1 tsp caster sugar, 1 egg yolk, 1 egg, salt

Sift the flour onto a pastry board, add the butter and lard and cut them in with a knife, until the mixture has become sandy. Add the cream and egg yolk, sugar and salt, break in the egg and knead quickly (too much kneading makes the dough lose its crispiness). Cover the dough in a cloth and put into the fridge for 2–3 hours. Sprinkle the pastry board with flour, roll out the dough. Cut circles or squares out of it. Put a bit of stuffing on each circle, seal the edges. Bake in a preheated oven (200–220°C) for 30 mins.

serves 4 • Preparation: 10–15 mins

Puff pastry (mille feuille) – basic recipe

Mille feuille pastry is an exceptionally time-consuming pastry to make. For those of you who would like to make it yourselves, I will give a few hints:

The basic ingredients of the pastry are flour and butter, in proportions of 1:1, with added ingredients of eggs or egg yolks, lemon juice or wine vinegar, which prevents the fat penetrating the pastry, or grated sour cottage cheese. First make an elastic pierogi dough, adding egg, lemon juice or white cheese. Roll the dough out on a dusted pastry board, smear it with butter generously, fold in half and roll out, again smear with butter and fold, repeating the whole sequence until the butter has been completely absorbed by the pastry. Remember to roll the dough with light but firm movements, always in one direction – away from yourself. The pastry should not be turned over.

Bake puff pastry in the oven preheated to 250°C for about 10 minutes, or until the pastry has risen, when you should turn down the temperature and continue baking for another 15–20 minutes.

Since ready-made puff pastry is generally available now, I recommend this in the following recipes.

Rough puff pastry with cheese – basic recipe

2½ cups flour, 200 g butter, 250 g cream cheese, ½ tsp salt, 1 tbsp lemon juice, ½ tsp grated lemon rind

Sift the flour onto a board, cut in the butter with a knife until the mixture has become sandy. Add salt, lemon juice, zest and the cheese. Knead well. Wrap the dough in a cloth and put into the fridge for 2–3 hours. Shape the pastry into a roll, cut it into medium-thick slices. Flatten each slice in your hands. Place some stuffing in the middle and seal the edges well. Put into a greased baking tin and bake in a preheated oven until golden brown.

serves 4 • Preparation: 20 mins

Potato dough – basic recipe

500 g cooked floury potatoes, ½ cup wheat flour, 2 tbsps potato flour, 1–2 eggs, 1 tbsp butter

Put the potatoes through a mincer, add the wheat and potato flour, pour in the melted butter, break in the eggs, add some salt and work into a fine dough. Dust a pastry board with flour. Shape the pastry into a roll, cut it into slices. Flatten each slice in your hands. Place some stuffing in the middle and seal the edges. Put the pierogi

on a greased baking tin. Bake in a preheated oven until golden brown.

serves 4 • Preparation: 15 mins

Bryndza patties

STUFFING: 300 g bryndza, 100 g grated smoked ewe's-milk cheese, 2–3 potatoes cooked in jackets, 1 egg, salt, pepper

DOUGH: 1 kg cooked potatoes, 1 raw egg yolk, 1 cup flour, 1 tbsp oil

STUFFING: Peel the potatoes. Put the potatoes and bryndza through a mincer. Add salt and pepper, put in the smoked cheese and egg. Work into a smooth paste. DOUGH: Put the potatoes through a mincer. Add the egg yolk and gradually the flour. Work into a smooth dough. Shape it into a roll, cut it into medium-thick slices. Flatten each slice in your hands, put some stuffing in the middle, seal the edges. Put the patties on a grease baking tin. Bake in a preheated oven until golden brown.

serves 4 • Preparation: 25–30 mins • Baking: 20–30 mins

Mushroom patties

STUFFING: 500 g fresh forest mushrooms, 2–3 large onions, 2–3 tbsps dry white wine, 2 tbsps butter, 2 tbsps grated cheese, salt, pepper, ½ tsp thyme

DOUGH: 500 g cooked floury potatoes, ½ cup wheat flour, 2 tbsps potato flour, 1–2 eggs, 1 tbsp butter

STUFFING: Rinse, dry and dice the mushrooms. Peel the onions and chop them finely. Melt the butter in a pan, fry the onion (but do not let it brown), add the mushrooms and fry for a minute or two. Sprinkle with the wine, add pepper, thyme and salt, stir well. Put the lid on and simmer for 30 mins. Reduce the liquid, leave the mixture to cool. Add the cheese and season to taste. DOUGH: Put the potatoes through a mincer, add the wheat and potato flour, pour in the melted butter, break in the eggs, add some salt. Work the mixture into a dough. Dust a pastry board with flour, shape the dough into a roll, cut it into slices. Flatten each slice with your hands, put some stuffing in the middle, seal the edges. Arrange the patties on a greased baking tin and bake in a preheated oven until golden brown.

serves 4 • Preparation: 1 hr

Fish patties

1 packet puff pastry (300 g), 1 tbsp flour, 1 egg

STUFFING: 600 g perch fillets, 1 tbsp lemon juice, 1 tbsp flour, 2 large onions, 1–2 tbsps oil, 2 hard-boiled eggs, salt, pepper

Rinse and dry the fillets, sprinkle them with lemon juice, some salt and pepper, coat with flour and fry in hot oil. Take out the fish. Fry the chopped onion in the same oil. Remove the bones from the fish, cut the flesh into fine cubes, add the chopped hard-boiled eggs and onion. Add salt and pepper to taste. Dust a pastry board with flour, roll out the defrozen dough, cut it into squares. Put some fish stuffing on each square, seal the edges. Arrange the patties on a greased baking tin, brush on top with the mixed egg. Bake in a preheated oven for 20–25 mins.

serves 4 • Preparation: 30–35 mins • Baking: 20–25 mins

Maltese patties

1 packet frozen puff pastry (300 g), 2 tins anchovy, 4–5 tbsps finely grated cheese, 1 tbsp butter

Defreeze the pastry a bit, roll it out, then cut into small squares. Put a piece of anchovy on each square, roll the pastry up. Coat each roll in grated cheese, then put on a greased baking tin. Bake in a preheated oven until golden brown. Serve with borsch or other clear soups.

serves 4 • Preparation: 10–15 mins • Baking: 20–25 mins

Old Polish patties

1 packet frozen puff pastry (300 g), 1 mixed egg

STUFFING: 150 g sorrel, 150 g smoked ham, 100 g bryndza, 1 small onion, 4 tbsps chopped hazelnuts, 1 tsp each chopped yarrow, radish and tarragon leaves, salt, pepper, 1 tbsp butter

Put the sorrel, yarrow and radish leaves in a sieve, pour over first boiling and then cold water, drain and dry well, then chop them finely. Cut the ham into thin strips. Fry the chopped onion in melted butter (but do not let it brown), add the chopped greens and fry for a minute or two, stirring all the time. Leave the mixture to cool. Stir in the bryndza, add the chopped tarragon, hazelnuts, salt and pepper and work into a smooth paste. Roll out the pastry, cut it into squares. Put some stuffing on each square, fold diagonally in half, seal the edges. Arrange the patties on a baking tin dusted with flour, brush them with the mixed egg. Bake in a preheated oven (200–220°C).

serves 4 • Preparation: 35–40 mins • Baking: 20–25 mins

Kołaczyki with bryndza

STUFFING: 400 g bryndza, 1 egg yolk, 1–2 tbsps single cream, 1 large onion, 1 tsp caraway, a pinch of pepper, 1 tbsp butter

DOUGH: 500 g flour, 50 g yeast, 1 tsp sugar, a pinch of salt, 2 cups boiled lukewarm water

STUFFING: Blanch the caraway seeds in a sieve, drain them. Fry the chopped onion in melted butter, but do not let it brown. Mix the bryndza with the cream and egg yolk. Mixing all the time, gradually add the onion and caraway. Season with pepper. Add salt if required (remember that bryndza is rather salty).
DOUGH: Mix the yeast with sugar and 2–3 tbsps of lukewarm water. Leave for 5–10 mins in a warm place. Sift half the flour into a bowl, pour in lukewarm water and yeast and mix well. Cover with a cloth and leave in a warm place to rise, then add salt and the remaining flour. Knead into a smooth, shiny dough. Cover and allow to rise again.

Make small patties from the risen dough. Make a hollow in each. Arrange the patties on a greased baking tin, put some stuffing into each hollow. Put the tin into a preheated oven (200°C) and bake for 40–45 mins.

serves 4 • Preparation: 40 mins • Baking: 40–45 mins

Yeast dough patties

Yeast dough – basic recipe

*500 g wheat flour, 2 eggs, 50 g butter, 1 cup milk,
½ tsp sugar, 1 tsp salt, 30 g yeast, 1 egg*

Mix the yeast with 1 tbsp of lukewarm milk, sugar and 1 tsp of flour, leave in a warm place. Sift the flour into a bowl, break in 2 eggs, add milk and knead the mixture. Add the yeast and knead for another 15 mins, until bubbles form in the dough (you may use a food processor). When the dough is smooth and shiny, pour in the melted butter and work the dough for several minutes longer. Cover with a cloth and leave in a warm place to rise. Take bits of the dough. Flatten each bit with your hands. Put some stuffing in the middle and seal well. Arrange the patties on a greased baking tin and leave to rise. Brush them with a mixed egg. Put into a preheated oven and bake until golden brown.

Preparation: 25–30 mins • Baking: 30–35 mins

Stiffing for yeast dough patties

Podolyan stuffing

400 g minced veal, 150 g mushrooms, 2 tbsps spicy mustard, 3 tbsps cream, 1 tbsp butter, 2 egg yolks, salt, pepper, ½ tsp each dried marjoram and thyme

Fry the finely diced mushrooms in butter, put in the meat and fry together for a minute or two, stirring all the time. Cover the pan and simmer for 5–6 mins. Allow the mixture to cool. Add salt, season with pepper, marjoram and thyme, add the mustard mixed with the egg yolks. Work into a smooth paste.

serves 4 • Preparation: 10–12 mins

Hunter's stuffing

300 g smoked sausage, 300 g fresh (champignon or forest) mushrooms, 2 large onions, 1 tsp ground juniper berries, 1 mixed egg, 1 tsp coarse-grained salt, 1 tbsp caraway

Fry the chopped onions in butter (but do not let it brown), add the diced mushrooms. Fry them together until the excess juice has evaporated. Add juniper, salt and pepper. Allow to cool. Put in the minced sausage and mix thoroughly. Arrange the stuffed patties in a grease baking tin. Brush them with the mixed egg and sprinkle with coarse-grained salt and caraway seeds. Bake until golden brown.

serves 4 • Preparation: 10–12 mins

Przemyśl stuffing

600 g cooked potatoes, 100 g buckwheat kasha, 3 tbsps lard, 1–2 onions, salt, pepper, 1 egg

Rinse the buckwheat, put it into boiling salted water and cook for 5–6 mins, then drain and allow to cool. Fry the chopped onion in lard, put in the buckwheat and, stirring continuously, fry for a minute or two. Put the potatoes through a mincer, combine them with the buckwheat and onion. Add salt and pepper to taste, break in the egg and work into a smooth paste.

serves 4 • Preparation: 10–15 mins

Warsaw stuffing

250 g lean bacon, 200 g cheese (Gouda, Edam), 50 g almond flakes, 2 tbsps butter, 1 egg yolk, salt, pepper

Grate the cheese finely. Put the bacon through a mincer. Beat the butter with the egg yolk, salt and pepper. Whisking all the time, gradually add the bacon and cheese. Put in the almond flakes and mix thoroughly.

serves 4 • Preparation: 8–10 mins

Baked patties and koulebiacs

Patties with cabbage

STUFFING: 500 g sauerkraut, 2 onions, 2 tbsps oil, 3 hard-boiled eggs, 1 tsp pepper, salt

DOUGH: 500 g wheat flour, 2 eggs, 1 tbsp butter, 1 cup milk, ½ tsp sugar, 1 tsp salt, 20 g yeast, 1 egg, 2 tbsps butter

Cook the cabbage in a small amount of water, then reduce the liquid. Drain the cabbage, allow it to cool and chop it finely. Brown the finely chopped onions in hot oil, put in the cabbage and fry for a bit. Season with pepper and simmer for a while. Take off the heat. Put the chopped hard-boiled eggs into the cool mixture. Add some salt. Mix the yeast with 1 tbsp of lukewarm milk, sugar and 1 tsp of flour, leave it in a warm place. Sift the flour into a bowl, break in the eggs, pour in the milk and knead for some 15 mins, when bubbles should appear (you may use a food processor). When the dough is smooth and shiny, pour in the melted butter and knead a bit longer. Cover with a cloth and leave in a warm place to rise. Make a roll from the dough and cut it into slices. Flatten each slice with your hands, put some stuffing in the middle, seal the edges. Put the patties in a greased baking tin and leave to rise. Brush the patties with some mixed egg on top and put into the hot oven for about half an hour. When they have turned golden brown, brush them with melted butter and bake for a bit longer.

serves 4 • Preparation: 1 hr • Baking: 30–35 mins

Koulebiac with spinach and hard-boiled eggs

STUFFING: 1 raw egg yolk, 1 kg spinach, 8–10 cloves of garlic, salt, pepper, a pinch of nutmeg, 1 tbsp lemon juice, a pinch of sugar, 2 tbsps butter, 1 tsp flour, 2 tbsps sour cream, 8 hard-boiled eggs

STUFFING: Rinse the spinach, put it in a sieve, pour over first boiling and then cold water, drain well, then chop finely. Melt the butter in a pan, put in the spinach and crushed garlic and, stirring all the time, fry for a minute or two. Mix the cream with the flour, sugar, lemon juice and nutmeg, pour the mixture into the spinach, stir well and heat up until the sauce has thickened.
DOUGH: Prepare the dough as in the basic recipe (see p. 167). When it has risen, roll it out, then transfer to a baking tin. Spread half the spinach on top, arrange the shelled hard-boiled eggs on the spinach, cover with the remaining spinach. Seal the edges of the pastry, cover with a cloth and leave to rise. Brush it on top with mixed egg and bake in a preheated oven (180°C) for 30–35 mins.

serves 4 • Preparation: 15–20 mins • Baking: 30–40 mins

Koulebiac with fish

STUFFING: 500 g pikeperch or pike fillets (or 3–4 salmon heads cooked in vegetable stock), 3 hard-boiled eggs, 1½ cups cooked rice, 2–3 tbsps chopped parsley, grated rind and juice of 1 lemon, 1–2 onions, 4 tbsps butter, salt, pepper, ½ cup dry white wine, ½ cup water

DOUGH: 500 g wheat flour, 30 g yeast, 100 g butter, 3 eggs, ½ cup milk, 1 tsp sugar, salt

STUFFING: Rub the fillets with salt, sprinkle them lightly with lemon juice and leave aside for several minutes. Melt 1 tbsp of butter in a pan, brown the chopped onion. Sprinkle the cooked rice with lemon juice, mix it with the onion, add the chopped parsley, lemon zest, some salt and pepper. Mix thoroughly, cover and leave aside for 30–40 mins. Melt 1½ tbsps of butter in a frying pan, put in the fillets, sprinkle them with wine. Cover the pan and simmer for 20 mins. Take the fish out, allow it to cool, remove the bones and skin. Cut the fish into small pieces (if you use salmon heads, take out the meat, remove the bones and cut the meat into pieces). Make a white roux from the remaining butter and flour, dilute it with boiled water, add several spoonfuls of the fish stock. Stirring all the time, heat it up until the sauce has thickened. Add some salt, pepper and lemon juice to taste. Put in the fish pieces, mix lightly and leave to cool.

DOUGH: Mix the yeast with 1 tbsp of flour, sugar and half the lukewarm milk. Leave it in a warm place for 15 mins. Sift the flour into a bowl, break in 1 whole egg and 2 egg yolks, pour in the melted butter and the remaining milk. Mix thoroughly, add the yeast and knead into a smooth, shiny dough. Cover with a cloth and leave to rise in a warm place (30–40 mins). Sprinkle a pastry board with flour, roll out the dough (to the tickness of 1 cm). Transfer the dough onto a piece of linen that has been sprinkled with flour. Spread the fish stuffing on the dough, sprinkle with the chopped hard-boiled eggs, cover with a layer of rice. Lift the sides of the dough so that they overlap, seal them together securely. Lift the koulebiac with the help of the cloth and slip it into a greased tin, so that the 'seam' is underneath. Leave it in a warm place to rise. With a sharp knife make several incisions in the dough to allow the steam to get out. Brush the koulebiac on top with mixed egg whites. Put into a preheated oven (180°C) and bake for 40–50 mins. Serve hot or cold.

serves 4 • Preparation: 1–1½ hrs • Baking: 40–50 mins

Koulebiac with cabbage and mushrooms

STUFFING: 500 g sauerkraut, 2 bay leaves, 2 cloves, 4–5 grains each pepper and allspice, grated rind of 1 lemon, 50 g dried mushrooms, 2 onions, 2 hard-boiled eggs, 2 tbsps chopped walnuts, salt, pepper, ¼ tsp ground juniper berries, 1 tbsp oil, 1 egg, 1 packet puff pastry (300 g)

Rinse the mushrooms, pour over 2 cups of water and leave to soak overnight, then cook them. Chop the cabbage, put it into a pan, pour over the strained mushroom stock. Add the bay leaves, pepper, allspice, cloves and lemon zest. Mix well, bring to the boil, then simmer over low heat for 30 mins. Brown the chopped onions in hot oil, put in the mushrooms cut into thin strips, add salt and pepper and fry for a bit, stirring all the time. Take the cabbage off the heat, remove the bay leaves and possibly pepper and allspice grains. Mix the mushrooms and onion with the cabbage, add juniper, pepper and salt to taste. Simmer a bit longer to reduce the juices. Leave to

cool, add the chopped walnuts and finely chopped hard-boiled eggs, mix thoroughly. Spread the stuffing on the rolled out dough. Seal the edges of the pastry. Brush on top with mixed egg. From the remaining bits of pastry, cut out various decorative patterns and stick them on top of the koulebiac. Prick small holes in the pastry to let the steam get out. Transfer the kulebiak into a baking tin dusted with flour. Put into a preheated oven (200°C) and bake for 30 mins. Serve hot or cold. If you prepare it earlier, wrap it up in grease paper and put into the fridge, then put it into a preheated oven for 10–15 mins before serving.

serves 4 • Preparation: 1 hr • Soaking: 12 hr • Baking: 30–40 mins

Koulebiac with millet, mushrooms and pikeperch

STUFFING: 1 cup millet groats, 2 cups vegetable stock, 2–3 grains each pepper and allspice, 1 bay leaf, 1 clove, 1 large onion, 800 g pikeperch fillets, 1 tbsp lemon juice, 2 tbsps each chopped parsley and dill, 2 tbsps butter, salt, pepper, ¼ tsp ground allspice, 4 hard-boiled eggs, 1 raw egg

DOUGH: 3 cups wheat flour, 200 g butter, 2 egg yolks, 1 egg, 1 glass rum, 1 tbsp lemon juice, ½ tsp grated lemon rind, salt

STUFFING: Bring the vegetable stock to the boil, add the onion and spices. Rinse the fish, dry it, sprinkle with lemon juice, salt and pepper. Put it into a pan, cover with the strained stock, bring to the boil, then simmer over low heat for 10 mins. Take the fish out carefully, leave it to cool, then cut it into pieces and remove the bones. Rinse and drain the millet, put it in a pan, pour over the strained stock and cook until the liquid has evaporated, then leave it to cool. Mix the chopped the hard-boiled eggs, dill and parsley with the millet. Add salt and pepper to taste, mix thoroughly.

DOUGH: Sift the flour onto a pastry board, add the butter. Cut the butter in with a knife, add the rum, lemon juice, salt, lemon zest, egg yolks and 1 whole egg. Knead a dough, cover it with a cloth and put into the fridge for an hour. Grease a baking tin with butter and dust it with flour. Put in half the rolled out dough. Spread half the millet on top, put in the fish pieces, cover with the remaining millet. Cover the whole with the remaining dough, seal the edges carefully. Brush with mixed egg on top. Put into a preheated oven and bake for one hour.

serves 4 • Preparation: 1 hr • Baking: 1 hr

Pancakes

Pancakes are good for everything – for a savoury bake, for a gateau, for croquettes, for patties; they can be served for breakfast, dinner or supper, for dessert or as a main dish.

Someone once said that, same as pierogi, 'pancakes are envelopes into which you can confidently place any filling'. Depending on the stuffing, they can be sweet or savoury; they can form an ordinary everyday meal or be a party piece at a grand reception. They were once traditionally cooked on 2 February for Candlemass and on Mardi Gras. The English like pancakes with ham and leeks; the Hungarians take pride in their *palascinta* filled with almond paste, and covered with chocolate and cognac; the French love their crupes Suzette with mandarin oranges and curaćao; the best American pancakes are filled with bananas and covered with rum.

Sweet pancakes are sprinkled generously with alcohol just before serving and then ignited and served flambé. Traditionally the most popular Polish pancakes were filled with cottage cheese mixed with orange peel or currants. All kinds of pancakes are popular today in Polish cuisine, both sweet and savoury.

Pancakes are a very simple dish that is easy to prepare, and they have yet another enormous advantage – large numbers of them can be fried and then kept covered in the fridge for several days.

Pancake batter should have the consistency of thick cream; if it is too thick, the pancakes will be thick and hard; if it is too thin, the pancakes will break and it will be impossible to turn them over in the pan. It is quite difficult to give the exact proportions of the ingredients, because everything depends on the size of the eggs and the dryness of the flour. So experience is very important in making pancakes.

After making the batter, you should fry one pancake: if it is too hard, add more water, and if it is too thin, add more flour.

The classic proportions for pancake batter are ¾ glass of sifted flour, two eggs, 1½ to 2 cups of liquid, a pinch of salt and often a pinch of grated nutmeg.

For savoury pancakes, you can use beer mixed with water; for sweet pancakes you can mix the water with cream or cream cheese (except that pancakes of this type should really not be rolled up, but only folded into four).

For really thin pancakes that are at the same time elastic, use whole eggs and carbonated mineral water; for thick and fluffy pancakes (known as biscuit pancakes) you should first add egg yolks with milk or milk and water, and then fold in the stiffly-beaten egg whites.

If you make biscuit pancakes, it is a good idea to divide the batter into two portions: fold in half of the beaten egg whites into the first portion and fry pancakes from it, and only then use the rest of the butter and egg whites to fry the the second batch of pancakes. The pancakes will then all be equally puffy.

To produce exceptionally fluffy pancakes, add a pinch (not more than ¼ of a teaspoon) of baking powder to the flour.

One thing must be remembered: there should be no lumps in pancake batter.

Therefore first sift the flour into the bowl, break in the eggs and then, whisking all the time, gradually add the liquid, following which cover the bowl and leave the batter to rest for at least an hour. Since the batter will get thicker, just before frying mix it up again thoroughly and if necessary dilute it with some water, yogurt, milk or beer.

In old cookery books you can find dozens of recipes for the pancake batter itself.

If the pancakes are to be really exceptional, the flour and liquid should be mixed only with the yolks of the eggs, and the whites beaten up and folded in separately. You must also add some fat to the batter: for sweet pancakes this is melted butter, and for savoury pancakes, olive oil or lard.

Pancakes

Colouring the pancake batter gives excellent results, both in taste and appearance; this can be done with juice from spinach, beetroot, tomatoes, with a pinch of saffron soaked in alcohol or with carrot juice.

For sweet pancakes served as dessert or as a main light supper dish, the batter can be flavoured with rum or liqueurs, including home-made fruit liqueurs.

Relatively thin-bottomed frying pans with an absolutely flat bottom are best for frying pancakes. Before frying the pancakes the pan should be heated well, salt sprinkled on it and then the heated salt poured off, the pan wiped with a clean cloth and smeared with bacon rind or brushed with some melted butter. Ladle some batter into the hot pan, spread it over the whole surface by a circling movement of the pan, and fry on a fairly low heat. When the batter browns lightly, turn the pancake onto the other side (by tossing or turning with a spatula), and then when fried slid it onto a plate. When all the pancakes are fried, they are stuffed with filling and folded in four, folded into an envelope or rolled up. They are then fried lightly again or baked in the oven; you may also coat them with egg and breadcrumbs and deep-fry them. Sweet or savoury gateaux can be made from the fried pancakes. Pancakes may also be cut into fine strips and used to garnish soup.

Pancake batter

Pancake batter – basic recipe I

1½ cups flour, 1 cup each milk and water, ½ tsp salt, 1 tbsp olive oil or melted butter, 3 eggs

Mix the milk with water and oil. Sift the flour into a tall bowl, break in the eggs and mix well, gradually adding the milk and water mixture and some salt. Cover the pan and leave for one or two hours. Before you start frying the pancakes, mix the batter again and add some liquid if necessary. Remember to mix it also each time you ladle it onto the frying pan.

serves 4 • Preparation: 10–12 mins

Pancake batter – basic recipe II

2 cups flour, 2 cups sour milk or yogurt, 2 eggs, salt, 1 tbsp olive oil or melted butter

Mix the milk with water and oil. Sift the flour into a tall bowl. Break in the eggs and stir vigorously, gradually adding the milk and salt. Cover the pan and leave it aside for an hour or two. Before you start frying the pancakes, mix the batter again and add some liquid if required. Remember to mix it also each time you ladle it onto the frying pan.

serves 4 • Preparation: 10–12 mins

Savoury pancake batter

1½ cups flour, 1½ cups lager beer, ¾ cup water, 3 eggs, ½ tsp salt, ¼ tsp each pepper and nutmeg, 1 tbsp oil

Beat the eggs with the beer, water and oil. Whisking all the time gradually add the sifted flour, salt, pepper and nutmeg. Beat slowly for 10 mins, then cover and leave aside for an hour or two. Before frying, mix vigorously again and add some more water if required.

serves 4 • Preparation: 10–12 mins

Beer pancake batter

1½ cups flour, 2½ cup lukewarm lager beer, 2 eggs, 1 tbsp olive oil, 1 tbsp brandy, salt, ¼ tsp each dried marjoram, thyme, sage, tarragon and pepper

Beat the eggs with the beer. Whisking all the time, gradually add the sifted flour, brandy, oil, herbs, salt and pepper. Beat slowly for 10 mins, then cover and leave aside for an hour or two. Before frying, mix vigorously and add some more beer if required.

You may cut pancakes into fine strips and use them to garnish soup or serve them as a side dish with the second course. You may also stuff them with meat, mushroom, vegetable or cheese filling and serve them with some savoury sauce.

serves 4 • Preparation: 10–12 mins

Sweet pancake batter

*1 cup flour, 1 cup milk, 2–3 tbsps carbonated water,
4 eggs, 1 tsp caster sugar, a pinch of salt, 1 tbsp butter*

Beat the egg yolks with sugar, salt and butter until fluffy. Whisking all the time, gradually add the milk and water, and then ¾ cup of sifted flour. Cover and leave to rest for 15 mins. Whisk the egg whites and fold them in together with the remaining sifted flour. Mix thoroughly and fry pancakes immediately.

serves 4 • Preparation: 15 mins • Resting: 15 mins

Hazelnut and honey pancakes

*¾ cup wholemeal flour, 1 cup buttermilk,
2 eggs, ½ tsp baking soda, 2 tbsps runny
honey, 3–4 tbsps ground hazelnuts, clarified
butter for frying, caster sugar for sprinkling*

Beat the eggs with the honey and buttermilk, add the sifted flour and baking powder and whisk for a minute or two longer, then leave the batter to rest. Add the hazelnuts and mix thoroughly. Before serving, sprinkle with caster sugar.

serves 4 • Preparation: 15 mins • Resting: 25 mins • Frying: 20–30 mins

Polish crêpe gateau

12–16 pancakes (see p. 188)

*FILLING: 600 g curd cheese, 3 eggs, 200 g caster
sugar, ½ vanilla pod, 50 g raisins, 2 tbsps vodka,
2 tbsps chopped walnuts, juice and grated rind of
1 lemon, 2 tbsps candied orange rind, ¾ cup cream*

Put the cheese through a mincer. Rinse the raisins, sprinkle them with the vodka and leave for one or two hours. Beat 2 egg yolks with the sugar and vanilla until fluffy. Add the raisins, orange rind and cheese and whisk until the mixture is smooth. Lightly fold in the whisked egg whites. Grease a cake tin with butter. Put in the crêpes, spreading some filling on top of each of them. Whip the cream with 2 tbsps of caster sugar and 1 egg yolk, add the lemon juice and zest. Pour the mixture over the crêpes. Put into a preheated oven and bake until golden brown.

serves 4 • Preparation: 1–1½ hrs • Baking: 10–12 mins

Green savoury pancakes

Pancakes are filled with the same kind of stuffing as pierogi. Stuffed pancakes are either fried or baked in bechamel sauce or sprinkled with cheese.

*250 g spinach, 1 cup milk, 2 eggs, 2 tbsps butter,
100–120 g flour, ½ tsp nutmeg, 1–2 cloves of garlic, salt*

Sift the flour into a pan, add the milk, salt and nutmeg, pour in the melted butter and work into a smooth paste. Cover the pan and leave aside for an hour or two. Rinse the spinach in a sieve, pour over boiling water, drain well. Chop the garlic and mix it with salt. Put the spinach, raw eggs and garlic through a blender. Add the purée to the batter, mix thoroughly, if required thin it down with a bit of carbonated water. Serve the pancakes as a hot side dish, with melted butter or cream.

serves 4 • Preparation: 10–15 mins • Frying: 30–35 mins

Croquettes

Two dishes are covered in culinary vocabulary by the term croquettes.

One are pancake rolls. The fried pancakes are spread with stuffing (see pierogi) and rolled up, then coated with egg and breadcrumbs, and fried brown in hot fat. These are usually served as a side dish with clear soups (chicken broth, borsch, tomato soup) and more rarely as a separate dish.

Another kind of croquettes are balls or rolls formed from stuffing, which are either egged and breadcrumbed or coated with flour and fried in deep fat, to be served with roast or fried meat (vegetable, potato, rice or mushroom croquettes), as additions to clear soups, or as a dish in themselves with various sauces (fish, meat, egg croquettes).

Both types of croquette can be served as a hot hors-d'oeuvre, as a part of the main course, or as a separate dish served with sauces or salads. They can be served either hot or cold.

Old Polish croquettes

20 pancakes (see p. 188)

500 g roast chicken, 150 g mushrooms, 2 tbsps butter, 2 tbsps chopped parsley, 2 eggs, 2 tbsps dry white wine, salt, pepper, ¼ tsp dried thyme, 1 tsp lemon juice, ¼ tsp grated lemon rind, breadcrumbs, fat for frying

Fry the diced mushrooms in butter, add the thyme, lemon juice and zest, salt, pepper and wine and simmer over low heat for 15 mins. Put in the finely chopped chicken and fry for a bit longer, stirring all the time. Take off the heat, allow it to cool, then mix in the raw egg yolks and parsley. Season to taste. Spread some filling on each pancake. Roll the pancakes up, dredge them in lightly beaten egg whites and in breadcrumbs, and fry.

serves 4 • Preparation: 30 mins • Frying: 10–12 mins

Tatra croquettes

20 crŷpes, 200 g bryndza, 2 tbsps yogurt, 2 eggs, 3–4 cooked potatoes, 4–5 spring onions, salt, pepper, breadcrumbs, fat for frying

Beat the bryndza with the raw egg yolks, salt and pepper. Mash the potatoes, mix them with the yogurt and chopped onions, then combine with the bryndza. Mix thoroughly. Spread some filling on each pancake. Roll the pancakes up, coat them in lightly beaten egg whites and breadcrumbs, and fry golden brown.

serves 4 • Preparation: 30 mins • Frying: 7–8 mins

Potato croquettes

1 kg potatoes, 1 tbsp butter, 2 eggs, 2 egg yolks, 3–4 tbsps flour, a pinch of nutmeg, salt, 2 tbsps breadcrumbs, 150 g lard

Peel the potatoes and cook them, then put them through a mincer. Mash them with the butter, eggs, nutmeg and salt. From the mixture shape small balls, dredge them with sifted breadcrumbs and fry in hot lard until golden brown. Serve with roast poultry and sirloin.

serves 4 • Preparation: 30 mins • Frying: 5–6 mins

Potato and walnut croquettes

500 g potatoes cooked in jackets, 1–1½ cups chopped walnuts, 1 egg, 1 egg yolk, 2–3 tbsps chopped parsley, salt, pepper

FOR DREDGING: 1 egg, breadcrumbs;

oil or clarified butter for frying

Peel the potatoes when still hot, put them through a mincer. Mash them together with the chopped walnuts and parsley, break in the egg, add the egg yolk, salt and pepper and work into a smooth mixture. With moist hands, form small balls, dredge them with the mixed egg and breadcrumbs. Fry until golden brown in hot oil or butter.

serves 4 • Preparation: 30 mins • Frying: 5–6 mins

Chicken croquettes

2 chicken breasts (500 g), 1 bread roll soaked in milk, 2 tbsps chopped walnuts, 2 eggs, ½ cup cream, 1 tbsp each chopped green basil and thyme leaves, juice and grated rind of 1 lemon, salt, pepper, a pinch of sugar, 2–3 tbsps flour, 1 tbsp sifted breadcrumbs, fat for frying

Squeeze out the breadroll to get rid of excess liquid. Put the meat and bread through a mincer. Add the walnuts, salt, pepper, sugar, lemon juice and zest, pour in the cream, break in the eggs. Add the herbs and work into a smooth mixture. If it is not thick enough, add some breadcrumbs. With moist hands, form small balls. Dredge them with flour and deep-fry them. Serve with rice or pasta, with tomato or pepper sauce.

serves 4 • Preparation: 15–20 mins • Frying: 10–12 mins

Vegetable croquettes

*cooked vegetables (2 carrots, 2 parsley roots,
½ celeriac), 4–5 potatoes cooked in jackets;*

*1 egg, 2 tbsps chopped parsley, 1 onion,
1 tbsp butter, salt, pepper;*

breadcrumbs, fat for frying

Fry the finely chopped onion in butter, but do not let it brown. Put the vegetables and onion through a mincer. Add salt, pepper and parsley, break in the egg, put in the breadcrumbs and work into a smooth mixture. Form small rolls from the mixture, dredge them with breadcrumbs and fry in hot fat until golden brown, then drain them on absorbent paper. Serve as hot hors-d'oeuvre, with borsch or fish soup.

serves 4 • Preparation: 10 mins • Frying: 10–12 mins

Krokiety drobiowe

Breadcrumb croquettes

*2 cups sifted breadcrumbs, 3–4 tbsps light
stock or dry white wine, 3 egg yolks, salt,
pepper, ½ tsp dried marjoram, 1 tbsp chopped
parsley; fat for deep frying (e.g. 250 g lard)*

Put the breadcrumbs in a pan, cover with the stock or wine and, stirring all the time, heat them up over low heat. When the breadcrumbs soak in the liquid, take off the heat, leave to cool, then whisk with the egg yolks, salt, pepper, marjoram and parsley. With moist hand, form small balls and deep-fry them until golden brown. Serve with roast meat.

serves 4 • Preparation: 10–15 mins • Frying: 5–6 mins

Egg croquettes

*8 hard-boiled eggs, 1 cup single cream, 2–3 tbsps
butter, 2 tbsps flour, 2–3 tbsps chopped chives, ½ cup
sifted breadcrumbs, 2 raw eggs, salt, pepper*

Make a roux from the butter and flour, add the cream and heat up until the sauce has thickened. Add salt and pepper to taste. Take off the heat, leave to cool, then add the chopped hard-boiled eggs and chives, break in 1 raw egg and pour in enough breadcrumbs to make the mixture thick. With moist hands form small balls, coat them in mixed egg and breadcrumbs. Deep-fry in hot fat until golden brown. Serve with roast meat, or with rice with tomato sauce.

serves 4 • Preparation: 25 mins • Frying: 5–6 mins

Cheese croquettes

*250 g grated cheese, 100 g flour, 80 g butter, 2 cups
milk, 2 egg yolks, salt, pepper, ¼ tsp each paprika,
savory, rosemary and mint, breadcrumbs, fat for frying*

Make a roux from the butter and flour, add some cold milk and, stirring all the time, heat it up over low heat. Add salt, pepper, paprika and herbs, mix well and take off the heat. Leave it to cool a bit. Put in the cheese and the egg yolks, mix thoroughly. When the mixture is cold, form small rolls, dredge them with breadcrumbs and fry in hot fat. Serve with clear or cream soups or for the second course with some sauce and salad.

serves 4 • Preparation: 20–25 mins • Frying: 5–6 mins

CHAPTER IV

EGG AND CHEESE DISHES

Egg dishes

Eggs provide excellent nourishment, both from the point of view of dietary requirements and from the gastronomic point of view.

(Edward Pożerski, *Nauka przyrządzania potraw*)

There are not many products that can compete with the egg from the point of view of nutritive value (two eggs are the equivalent of a pork cutlet). They are a major source of non-saturated fats and of carbohydrates, of phosphorus, iron, copper, calcium, manganese, zinc, arsenic, iodine, fluorine and vitamins A, D, B, B. These are all advantages.

There are however disadvantages: eggs contain cholesterol, avidin (a substance that inactivates biotin), and they also stimulate acid production, therefore it is best to combine them with alkaline-forming additions (for example, kasha and vegetables).

Despite the fact that eggs clearly have more advantages than disadvantages, the majority of doctors and dieticians recommend that (especially beyond the age of forty) consumption of eggs should be limited to two or three a week.

As a food product eggs are used universally; they are simply essential in the kitchen, and they bring out the flavour in many dishes. They are the basis for all baking and for desserts; beaten egg whites give them lightness and the consistency of velvet, while the yolks guarantee a marvellous taste and colour.

Eggs are a concentrate of almost all the elements necessary for life. They have a high protein content and many vitamins and minerals as well as easily digestible fats; and finally the taste of dishes prepared from them, from the simplest to the most complicated, makes eggs a foodstuff that is particularly valuable.

From eggs you can make a lot of dishes that constitute an unusual breakfast, hors-d'oeuvre, or main dish at dinner or supper.

So let us try to put eggs on the domestic menu as a full main course, an attractive hors-d'oeuvre, or an outstanding dessert.

But you should remember the following:

Use only fresh eggs. One bad egg will spoil any dish. An average fresh (one day old) egg will weigh about 50 grams (the longer it stands, the lighter it will become, and also less tasty). The best eggs are from young hens and should not be more than a week old.

To avoid unpleasant surprises when using eggs, you should first break them into a plate.

How can we check the freshness of eggs that we are going to boil?

Put one and a half teaspoons of salt into a jar, pour in a glass of water and put in the egg:
– the freshest eggs (up to four days old) will stay on the bottom of the jar;
– an egg between 8 and 10 days old will rise up a little and hang over the bottom;
– a bad egg will float to the surface of the water.

Eggs lose none of their splendid properties if they are kept for as long as two weeks in the fridge. They should be stored with the thickest end (which contains the air pocket) upwards.

Do not boil eggs immediately after taking them out of the fridge because they will crack while boiling.
When you put an egg in boiling water, remember that:
– after 2 minutes it is soft-boiled, with the white milky and the yolk runny;
– after 3 minutes, it is soft-boiled, with the white lightly set and the yolk soft;
– after 3 1/2 minutes, it is soft-boiled, with the white completely set and the yolk somewhat thickened;
– after 5 minutes, the white is set hard but the yolk is still soft;
– after 6 minutes, the white is set hard, and the yolk is firmly set;
– after 7 minutes and more, the egg is hard-boiled. Eggs should not however be boiled for more than 10 minutes, as they then become indigestible, and the white becomes rubbery while the yolk turns grey and crumbly.

Eggs taken out of the refrigerator quickly crack during boiling; they should be warmed before being placed in boiling water.

The colour of the shell has no bearing on the colour of the yolk (the darker this is, the higher the food value) but only provides evidence of the breed of the hen that laid it. Rhode Island Reds lay brown eggs, while Leghorns lay white ones.

NOTE! There may be millions of bacteria on eggshells, and therefore the egg should be washed or rinsed in boiling water before it is cracked.

If you wish to cut a hard-boiled egg in two, the knife should be immersed for a moment in boiling water, then the yolk will not stick to the knife.
Boiled eggs that are to be stuffed should be stuffed immediately, because a dark ring will form around the yolk if they are left standing. Stuffed eggs can be kept in the fridge for several hours. They should simply be covered with foil, so that they do not get dry. It is easiest to shell a boiled egg under running cold water.
The way in which eggs are served can completely change their taste, appearance and aroma. The simplicity of recipes for egg dishes makes it possible to prepare quickly a

full meal, and the time for preparation is not more than 30 minutes; moreover, omelettes and scrambled eggs offer enormous opportunities for demonstrating culinary imagination.

Egg salads

Egg and Spanish radish salad

6 hard-boiled eggs, 2 small Spanish radishes, 1 tbsp lemon juice, 1 small iceberg lettuce

DRESSING: 3–4 tbsps olive oil, 2 tbsps lemon juice, 1 tbsp mayonnaise, 1–2 cloves of garlic, salt, pepper, a pinch of sugar, 2–3 tbsps chopped watercress

Mix the finely chopped garlic with salt, pepper, sugar and mayonnaise, add the lemon juice and oil. Peel and rinse the radishes, grate them coarsely, sprinkle with lemon juice. Shred the rinsed and drained lettuce. Slice the shelled eggs. In a deep bowl arrange alternating layers of grated radish, egg slices and lettuce. Pour over the dressing, shake the bowl lightly to mix the ingredients. Garnish with watercress.

serves 4 • Preparation: 10 mins

Egg and asparagus salad

4 hard-boiled eggs, 12 asparagus tips, a handful of fresh dandelion leaves, 1 tbsp sesame seeds

DRESSING: 6 tbsps olive oil, 2 tbsps cream, 2 tbsps wine vinegar or lemon juice, 2 tbsps chopped parsley, salt, pepper, a pinch of sugar

Dry roast the sesame seeds. Rinse and drain the dandelion leaves, arrange them decoratively on a large serving plate. Put on top the asparagus tips and egg quarters. Mix the oil, cream and vinegar well, add salt, pepper and sugar. Put in the parsley and pour the dressing over the eggs. Garnish with parsley.

serves 4 • Preparation: 10 mins

Soft-boiled eggs

Soft-boiled eggs are healthiest and should be cooked as follows:

– **eggs à la Viennoise**: break the egg into a glass, put the glass in a saucepan containing boiling water for 3 minutes; when the white sets, add salt, pepper and butter, and mix;

– **soft-boiled eggs**, meaning that the white has set but the yolk is runny, should be boiled over a medium heat for 3 minutes after coming to the boil;

– **medium-hard boiled eggs** have the white set firm and the yolk beginning to set; they should be cooked for 4 to 5 minutes after coming to the boil, depending on the size of the egg.

Poached eggs are eggs that are soft-boiled (the white set, the yolk runny) without their shell. They should be boiled in water with vinegar added (2 teaspoons of 10% white vinegar to one litre of water). The best method for preparing poached eggs is to crack them one at a time onto a saucer or into a glass (taking care not to break the yolk), and then slid into simmering water with vinegar. They should be boiled for three minutes over a low heat, or the pan can be removed from the heat and the eggs left in it for four minutes, after which they are removed with a slotted spoon, arranged on a heated plate, with the whites evened out. They can be additionally fried in butter. Pached eggs are served with various sauces or baked on toast sprinkled with cheese.

Fédora eggs

8 eggs, 2 tbsps vinegar, 1½ tbsps butter, 1 tbsp flour, ½ cup milk, salt, pepper, 100 g mushrooms, 1 egg, breadcrumbs, 3 tbsps butter

Bring some water mixed with vinegar to the boil. Break in the eggs, cover the pan, take the pan off the heat and leave the eggs in hot water for 4 mins. Take out the eggs with a strainer spoon. Melt butter in a pan, add the flour and make a white roux. Add some milk and, stirring all the time, simmer till the sauce has thickened. Add the finely chopped mushrooms, stir and allow to cool. Dip the eggs one by one in the sauce, arrange them in a hot baking tin until they dry up. Then coat them with a mixture of raw egg and breadcrumbs and fry in butter until golden brown. Serve with potato purée and lettuce.

serves 4 • Preparation: 10 mins

Eggs in red wine sauce

8 eggs, 2 cups dry red wine, 1 large onion, 1 leek, 2–3 celery sticks, a sprig of thyme, 1–2 cloves of garlic, several grains each pepper and allspice, 1 bay leaf, ½ tsp salt, 3 tbsps butter, 1 tbsp flour

Fry (but do not brown) the finely chopped onion in butter (1½ tbsps), transfer it to a large pan. Add the diced leek, celery, thyme, pepper, allspice, bay leaf and garlic crushed with salt. Pour in 1 cup of water. Cover the pan and cook for 20 mins. Add the wine and cook under cover for another 5 mins. Break in the eggs into small saucers and one by one slip them into the boiling stock. Cover, take off the heat and leave for 3–4 mins. Take out the eggs with a strainer spoon. Remove the bay leaf, pepper and allspice grains. Put the stock through a blender, add the remaining butter mixed with flour. Stirring all the time, heat up the sauce. Put in the eggs and heat up again.

serves 4 • Preparation: 30 mins

Eggs in red wine

8 eggs, 2 tbsps vinegar, 8 bacon rashers, 8 slices of white bread, 2 cups dry red wine, 3 onions, 2–3 cloves of garlic, salt, pepper, cayenne pepper, a pinch of each thyme, tarragon and garlic salt, 3 tbsps butter, 1 tbsp flour

Melt 1 tbsp of butter in a frying pan, put in the bacon and brown it. Take the bacon out and put in the finely chopped onion, crushed garlic, thyme and tarragon. Add another tablespoon of butter and the flour, mix well, pour in the wine and cook over low heat, stirring all the time. Melt the remaining butter in a frying pan and brown the bread on both sides. Arrange the bread in an ovenproof dish, sprinkle with garlic salt. Put a rasher on each peace. Bring salted water with vinegar to the boil. Break in the eggs and cook them for three minutes. Take them out with a strainer spoon. Arrange the eggs on top of the rashers. Sprinkle the dish with salt and pepper and put into a preheated oven for 2–3 mins. Serve in the oven dish with the hot, thick sauce in a sauce boat. Serve with French fries or rice.

serves 4 • Preparation: 15 mins

Gourmet's eggs

8 eggs, ½ cup wine vinegar, 8 slices of white bread, 8 lettuce leaves, 200 g mushrooms, 350 g onion, 1 cup dry white wine, 3 tbsps butter, 3 tbsps cream, juice and grated rind of ½ lemon, salt, pepper, a pinch of sugar, 2 tbsps grated cheese

Fry (but do not brown) the finely chopped onion in 1 tbsp of melted butter, pour in the wine and simmer over low heat for 15 mins. Add salt and pepper, then put the sauce through a blender and sieve it. Fry the finely diced mushrooms in butter, add some salt, sugar and pepper to taste. Pour in the cream, add the onion purée, lemon juice and zest and grated cheese. Keep it over low heat for 10 mins, but do not allow it to boil. Bring water with vinegar to the boil. Carefully break in the eggs, cover the pan, take off the heat and leave for 3–4 mins. Take the eggs out with a strainer spoon. Use the remaining butter to brown the bread on both sides. Arrange the bread on lettuce leaves in a serving dish. Put one egg on top of each slice. Serve the sauce separately.

serves 4 • Preparation: 15–20 mins

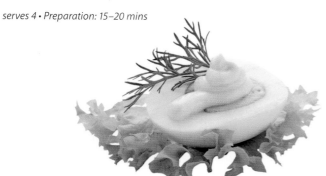

Hard-boiled eggs

Hard-boiled eggs are eaten by themselves, with salt or mustard, or they can be served with every kind of sauce or with olive oil. They can also be chopped and sprinkled over vegetables.

(Edward Poṇerski, *Nauka przyrządzania potraw*)

How to hard-boil an egg:
– the whole egg should be set firmly, therefore you must boil it for 7 to 8 minutes. Remember that if it is boiled too long it does not look appetizing and has an unpleasant smell.

Eggs in green sauce

8 hard-boiled eggs, 100 g grated sharp cheese, 2 tbsps butter, 2 tbsps flour, ½ cup stock, 1 cup single cream, 1 cup spinach, 1 tbsp each chopped parsley and dill, 1 tsp each chopped thyme and rosemary, ¼ tsp each ground ginger, pepper and celery salt, 1 tbsp lemon juice, a pinch of sugar, 1–2 pieces marinated red pepper, several sprigs of parsley, 1 tbsp anchovy paste

Melt the butter in a pan, add the flour and make a white roux. Dilute it with the stock, add the ginger, celery salt, pepper and lemon juice. Stirring all the time, simmer until the sauce has thickened. Add the cheese and stir until the sauce is smooth. Scald the spinach with boiling water. Put it through a blender and sieve it. Mix it with the cream and chopped greens. Pour the mixture into the sauce. Heat the sauce up (but keep it off the boil), put in the shelled eggs and heat up again. Serve with pasta or French fries. Such eggs can be also served cold. In that case, take the sauce off the heat and leave it to cool. Pour the sauce into a deep bowl, put in the egg halves (the cut side up). Put a bit of anchovy paste on top of each half. Garnish with pepper strips and parsley sprigs.

serves 4 • Preparation: 15 mins

Eggs in savoury sauce

8 hard-boiled eggs, 3 tbsps chopped walnuts, 3–4 cloves of garlic, ½ tsp each hot paprika, salt and ground ginger, 1 tbsp lemon juice,

a pinch of saffron, 1 glass dry white wine,
1 tbsp butter, 2 tbsps chopped dill

Mix the chopped walnuts with the garlic crushed with salt, ginger and paprika. Pour 1 tbsp of boiling water over the saffron. Melt the butter in a pan, put in the walnuts and fry them a bit, stirring all the time. Add the saffron, lemon juice and wine and simmer over low heat until the sauce has thickened. Grease an ovenproof dish with butter. Arrange egg halves in it, pour over the sauce, garnish with chopped dill. Put the dish in a preheated oven for several minutes. Serve with rice, salad or white bread.

serves 4 • Preparation: 10 mins

Eggs in yellow sauce

4 hard-boiled eggs, 4 tbsps orange marmalade,
3 tbsps sharp mustard, 3 tbsps dry red wine,
1 small onion, a piece of orange rind

Rinse the orange rind, cover with boiling water and cook for 3–4 mins, then drain it and cut it into thin strips. Chop the onion finely. Mix thoroughly the mustard with the marmalade and wine. Heat the mixture up over low heat. Add the orange rind and onion. Pour the sauce over the egg halves. Serve hot or cold.

serves 4 • Preparation: 10 mins

Hot sauces for hard-boiled eggs

Eggs in hot sauces are usually served with white bread or potatoes.

Mustard sauce

1 tbsp butter, 1 tbsp flour, 1 cup stock,
1 cup thick cream, 3 tbsps mustard, 1 tbsp
Worcestershire sauce, salt, pepper

Melt the butter in a pan, add the flour and make a white roux. Dilute it with the stock and, stirring all the time, simmer over low heat until the sauce has thickened. Add the mustard, Worcestershire sauce, salt, pepper and cream. Mix thoroughly and heat up, but do not allow it to boil.

serves 4 • Preparation: 5–7 mins

Herb sauce

1 tbsp butter, 1 tbsp flour, 1 cup stock, 1 cup thick cream,
3 tbsps each chopped basil, dill and chives,
1 tbsp lemon juice, ¼ tsp each grated lemon
rind and sugar, salt, white pepper

Make a white roux from the butter and flour, dilute it with the stock. Add salt, pepper and lemon zest. Stirring all the time, simmer over low heat until the sauce has thickened. Add the lemon juice, chopped herbs and cream. Mix thoroughly and heat up, but do not allow it to boil.

serves 4 • Preparation: 5–7 mins

Cheese sauce

1 tbsp butter, 1 tbsp flour, 1 cup stock, ¾ cup single cream,
200 g grated Emmental, 200 g lean ham, 1 tbsp lemon
juice, salt, pepper

Make a roux from the butter and flour, dilute it with the stock. Stirring all the time, heat it up. Add the cream, lemon juice, salt, pepper and cheese. Simmer until the sauce is thick and velvety. Add the diced ham and mix thoroughly.

serves 4 • Preparation: 5–7 mins

Cold sauces for hard-boiled eggs

Andalouse sauce

1 cup thick mayonnaise, 1 tbsp ketchup,
3 red peppers, salt

Chop the peppers finely and mix them with the mayonnaise, ketchup and a pinch of salt. Refrigerate.

serves 4 • Preparation: 5 mins

Polish sauce

*5 tbsps thick mayonnaise, 3 tbsps thick cream,
2 hard-boiled eggs, 1 tbsp freshly grated horseradish,
juice and grated rind of 1 lemon, a bunch of
chives, 2 tbsps chopped watercress, 1 clove of
garlic crushed with salt, a pinch of sugar*

Cut the shelled eggs in half, take out the yolks. Mix the yolks with the garlic, horseradish, sugar and mayonnaise into a smooth sauce. Add the cream, lemon juice and zest, horseradish, chopped chives, watercress and finely chopped egg whites. Cover and put into the fridge for a bit.

serves 4 • Preparation: 5–7 mins

Basil sauce

*1 cup finely chopped basil leaves, ½ cup
each grated Parmesan, butter and chopped pine
nuts, 8–10 cloves of garlic, 1 tsp salt, 2–3 tbsps
olive oil*

Beat the butter until foamy, gradually adding the garlic crushed with salt, basil, pine nuts, Parmesan and oil. When the sauce is smooth and velvety, put it into the fridge for a bit.

serves 4 • Preparation: 5–7 mins

Devilled sauce

*5 tbsps thick mayonnaise, 2 tbsps hot
ketchup, 1 tsp chilli sauce, 1 tbsp brandy,
1 tbsp lemon juice, ¼ tsp grated lemon rind,
salt, a pinch of each sugar and cayenne*

Whisk the mayonnaise with the brandy, lemon juice and zest. Mix in the ketchup, chilli sauce, salt, sugar and cayenne. Cover and chill a bit.

serves 4 • Preparation: 10 mins

Vitamin sauce

*5 tbsps thick mayonnaise, 2 tbsps yogurt,
2 tbsps each chopped dill, watercress and chives,
1 tsp pickled green peppercorns, 1 small finely chopped
green pepper, 1 tsp lemon juice, salt, pepper, sugar*

Mix thoroughly all the ingredients, refrigerate for a while.

serves 4 • Preparation: 5 mins

Walnut sauce

*½ cup mayonnaise, ½ cup finely chopped walnuts,
¼ cup dry white wine, 2–3 cloves of garlic, salt, a
pinch of each sugar and pepper, 1 tsp lemon juice*

Mix the finely chopped garlic with salt, pepper, sugar and lemon juice. Combine with the mayonnaise and wine. Add the walnuts, mix thoroughly. Pour into a glass jar, screw the top on and refrigerate for 1–2 hours.

serves 4 • Preparation: 5–7 mins

Russian sauce

*1 cup sour cream, 2 tbsps each yogurt and
thick mayonnaise, 1 each green, red and
yellow pepper, 4 tbsps chopped chives,
50 g black caviar, 5–6 drops of tabasco sauce,
1 tsp sweet paprika, 1 tsp horseradish mustard*

Rinse and core the peppers, cut them into small cubes. Mix half of the caviar with the mustard, tabsco, paprika, cream, yogurt and mayonnaise, add the chives and peppers. Chill a bit. Before serving, pour into a bowl and garnish with the remaining caviar.

serves 4 • Preparation: 10 mins

Cheese sauce

*200 g curd cheese, 100 g blue cheese,
juice of 1 lemon, 2 tbsps red lingonberry
preserve, salt, ½ cup light stock or water,
1 tbsp lingonberry preserve for
garnishing, several sprigs of dill*

Liquidize all the ingredients. Refrigerate for a while. Before serving, garnish with whortleberry preserve and dill sprigs.

serves 4 • Preparation: 5 mins

Baked eggs

Eggs, Warsaw style

8 eggs, water, ½ cup vinegar, 200 g mushrooms, 2 onions, ½ cup stock, ½ cup dry white wine, ½ cup thick cream, 3 tbsps butter, 1 tbsp flour, salt, pepper, cayenne, 100 g grated cheese

Fry (but do not brown) the finely chopped onion in butter (1½ tbsps), add the diced mushrooms and fry over high heat. Add salt and pepper, sprinkle with some wine and simmer over low heat. Melt the remaining butter in a pan, add the flour and make a white roux. Dilute it with the stock and remaining wine. Stirring all the time, simmer until the sauce has thickened. Add salt, pepper and cayenne to taste. Put in the mushrooms, stir well. Pour the sauce into an ovenproof dish. Boil some salted water with vinegar. Break in one by one the eggs (see p. 200), cover the pan, take off the heat and leave for 4 mins. Remove the eggs with a strainer spoon and put in the sauce. Sprinkle with the cheese, arrange knobs of butter on top. Put into a preheated oven for several minutes, until the cheese forms a golden crust on top. Serve with potatoes and salads.

serves 4 • Preparation: 15 mins

Eggs with tomatoes

6 hard-boiled eggs, 10 beef tomatoes, 1–2 cloves of garlic, 150 g grated cheese, 3 tbsps butter, 1 tbsp breadcrumbs, salt, pepper, 1 tsp dried thyme

Blanch and skin the tomatoes, cut them into thick slices. Slice the shelled eggs. Grease an ovenproof dish with butter, dust lightly with breadcrumbs and garlic crushed with salt. Put in alternating layers of tomatoes, sprinkled with salt, pepper and thyme, and egg slices sprinkled with cheese and knobs of butter. Finish off with a layer of tomatoes. Sprinkle on top with the remaining cheese, butter and breadcrumbs. Put into a preheated oven for 25–30 mins. Serve with potatoes or rice and with salads.

serves 4 • Preparation: 5–7 mins

Eggs stuffed with fish

6 hard-boiled eggs, 300 g cod fillets, 1 tbsp lemon juice, 1 tbsp chopped parsley, 2 tbsps butter, 1 tbsp flour, 1 cup single cream, ½ cup stock, salt, pepper, a pinch of sugar, several drops of Worcestershire sauce, 100 g grated cheese

Sprinkle the fillets with lemon juice, put in a pan, cover with lukewarm stock. Bring to the boil, then simmer over low heat for 15 mins. Take out the fish with a strainer. Reduce the stock a bit (leaving ¼ cup), strain and allow to cool. Chop the cooked fish, mix into a smooth paste together with the remaining lemon juice, salt and pepper. Shell the eggs and cut them lengthwise into halves. Take out the egg yolks and add them to the fish. Stuff the egg whites with the mixture. Make a roux from butter and flour, dilute it with the stock and, stirring all the time, cook until the sauce has thickened. Add salt, pepper, sugar, lemon juice, Worcestershire sauce and chopped parsley. Pour in the cream and mix thoroughly. Grease an ovenproof dish with butter, pour in the sauce. Put in the stuffed eggs, sprinkle them with the grated cheese. Put the dish into a preheated oven for 15 mins. Serve with French fries and salads.

serves 4 • Preparation: 20 mins

Eggs with mushrooms

6 hard-boiled eggs, 250 g mushrooms, 1 large onion, 100 g bacon, 100 g grated cheese, 2 tbsps chopped parsley, salt, pepper, 4–5 tbsps ketchup, 3 tbsps butter, 1 tbsp breadcrumbs

Fry the finely chopped onion in butter (but do not let it brown), add the diced mushrooms and sauté them. Add salt and pepper to taste. Leave the mixture to cool, then add the chopped parsley and finely diced bacon. Grease an

Eggs stuffed with fish

ovenproof dish with butter, dust it with breadcrumbs. Put in the mushrooms, arrange egg halves on them. Sprinkle with salt and pepper. Pour over the ketchup, sprinkle with the cheese, arrange knobs of butter on top. Put into a preheated oven for 20 mins.

serves 4 • Preparation: 5–6 mins

Eggs with Roquefort

6 hard-boiled eggs, 150 g Roquefort, 100 g grated hard cheese, 100 g butter, 1 tbsp flour, 1 cup milk, 1 cup cream, salt, pepper, 1 tbsp lemon juice, a pinch of sugar

Shell the eggs, cut them lengthwise into halves. Take out the egg yolks. Blend the Roquefort with the egg yolks and 2 tbsps of butter into a smooth paste, season with pepper. Stuff the egg whites with the mixture. Melt 2 tbsps of butter in a pan, add the flour and make a white roux. Dilute it with milk and, stirring all the time, simmer until the sauce has thickened. Add salt, sugar, pepper and lemon juice to taste. Pour in the cream, add half of the grated cheese and mix thoroughly. Heat the mixture up. Grease an ovenproof dish with butter. Put in the stuffed eggs, gently pour over the sauce. Sprinkle with the remaining grated cheese and put on top knobs of butter. Put into a preheated oven for 10–12 mins. Serve as a hot hors-d'oeuvre with white bread or as the main course with potatoes, rice or pasta.

serves 4 • Preparation: 8–10 mins

Stuffed eggs

Cut the hard-boiled eggs (either shelled or still in their shells) lengthwise with a sharp knife, remove the yolks and add them to the stuffing, and then fill the whites with this stuffing.

If you are preparing eggs in their shells (to be served hot), the white can also be chopped, and then the shells filled and either baked or lightly fried in butter under a lid.

They can be served hot with rolls or with potatoes and salad. Served cold, they are an exceptionally attractive dish on any table.

Stuffed eggs are best garnished with the following: baby sweetcorn cobs, stuffed olives, pickled shallots, small pepperoni, pickled green peppercorns, cherry tomatoes, slices of lemon or lime, crab, shrimps, anchovies, dill, parsley, and also cocktail cherries, slices of kiwi fruit or of peach.

Anchovy eggs

*4 hard-boiled eggs, 3 tbsps butter,
1 tsp soya sauce, ½ tsp each hot mustard,
cayenne and Worcestershire sauce,
1 tsp lemon juice, 1 tin anchovy,
1 tsp capers, 4 stoned black olives,
4 cocktail gherkins, 8 skinned almonds*

Shell the eggs, cut them lengthwise into halves, remove the yolks. Blend the yolks with butter, lemon juice, Worcestershire sauce, soya sauce, mustard and cayenne until the mixture is fluffy. Put 1 anchovy into each egg white, then pipe in some of the paste. Garnish with gherkin halves, olives, capers and almonds.

serves 4 • Preparation: 8–10 mins

Eggs with tuna

*8 hard-boiled eggs, 1 small tin of tuna,
salt, pepper, 1 tbsp mayonnaise*

*SAUCE: 200 g spinach, 5–6 tbsps thick mayonnaise,
2 cloves of garlic, 1 tsp lemon juice, salt, pepper,
a pinch of sugar, 2 tbsps chopped parsley*

Cut the shelled eggs lengthwise into halves, remove the yolks. Blend the yolks with the tuna, mayonnaise, salt and pepper into a smooth paste. Stuff the egg halves. Blanch the rinsed spinach for 2 mins, drain it, pour over cold water. Liquidize it together with the garlic crushed with salt. Add the mayonnaise, lemon juice and sugar. Mix in the chopped parsley. Pour the sauce into a fairly deep serving dish. Arrange the egg halves, cover with foil and refrigerate for 1–2 hours.

serves 4 • Preparation: 10 mins

Eggs with smoked trout

6 hard-boiled eggs, 50 g smoked trout,
1 tsp lemon juice, 1 tbsp thick ketchup,
salt, cayenne pepper, 2 tsps mustard,
1 sprig of parsley, lemon slices, 50 g lamb's lettuce,
3 hard-boiled quail eggs, 6 shrimps, 3 stoned olives

Shell the eggs, cut them lengthwise in two, remove the yolks. Blend three egg yolks and the mustard into a smooth paste, add some salt. Cream the remaining egg yolks with the trout, add salt, cayenne and ketchup. Put the pastes into two small piping bags with starred nozzles. Fill six egg white halves with one of them and six with the other. Rinse and drain the lamb's lettuce, arrange it in a circle on a large round serving dish. Put the lemon slices decoratively in the middle and surround them with the stuffed eggs. Garnish the trout eggs with shrimps and parsley, and the mustard eggs with halves of the quail eggs and olive slices.

serves 4 • Preparation: 15–20 mins

Eggs with caviar

4 hard-boiled eggs, 4 tbsps thick mayonnaise,
1 tsp brandy, a pinch of each salt, white
pepper and sweet paprika, 1 tbsp lemon juice,
2 tbsps caviar, several pickled spring onions,
several dill sprigs, ½ bunch of chives

Shell the eggs, cut them lengthwise into halves, remove the yolks. Cream the yolks with 1 tbsp of caviar, mayonnaise, salt, paper, paprika, lemon juice and brandy. Stuff the egg whites with the paste, garnish with the remaining caviar, spring onions, dill sprigs and chives.

serves 4 • Preparation: 8–10 mins

Eggs with salmon

4 hard-boiled eggs, 50 g smoked salmon, 4 tbsps thick mayonnaise, 1 tbsp advocaat, 1 tbsp chopped almonds, 1 tbsp lemon juice, salt, white pepper, cayenne pepper;

lettuce leaves, 3 tbsps capers and several endive leaves for garnishing

Cut the shelled eggs lengthwise in two, remove the yolks. Chop the salmon finely, cream it together with the egg yolks, mayonnaise, advocaat, lemon juice, salt, pepper, cayenne and chopped almonds. Refrigerate the paste for a while, then put it into a piping bag with a serrated nozzle and force it into the egg whites. Cut the endive leaves lengthwise into thin strips and stick them into the stuffing. Place some capers on top. Arrange the egg halves on a serving dish lined with lettuce leaves.

serves 4 • Preparation: 8–10 mins

Eggs, Polish style

6 hard-boiled eggs, 30 g dried mushrooms,
2 tbsps grated horseradish, 1 raw egg yolk,
2 tbsps finely chopped parsley, 1 tbsp oil,
3 tbsps butter, breadcrumbs, salt, pepper

Rinse the mushroom and soak them overnight in a small amount of water, then cook them. With a sharp knife cut the eggs (do not shell them) lengthwise into halves. Carefully take out the yolks and whites. Put the mushrooms and the eggs whites and yolks through a mincer or chop them very finely. Mix them with the butter, horseradish, parsley, salt, pepper and one raw egg yolk into a paste. Fill the egg shells with the mixture, sprinkle with breadcrumbs on top. Heat up the oil in a frying pan, put in the egg halves (with the stuffing down) and fry them. Serve hot or cold.

serves 4 • Preparation: 10–15 mins

Scrambled eggs

It takes no time to cook the dish, which is simply delicious if you use good quality eggs and butter. You can prepare scrambled eggs in two ways: either steamed or fried. The first method is simply excellent, but takes a bit longer.

(Edward Poŋerski, *Nauka przyrządzania potraw*)

Scrambled eggs are made from beaten eggs, sometimes with the addition of a small quantity of water, milk or cream. They are best fried in butter, and there are dozens of additions that enhance their flavour.

Scrambled eggs with walnuts

8 eggs, 1–2 tbsps champagne, 100 g finely chopped walnuts, 2 tbsps butter, salt, several lemon slices, several parsley sprigs

Beat the eggs lightly with the champagne and chopped walnuts. Melt the butter in a large frying pan. Pour in the eggs and fry them, stirring constantly. When the eggs set, add some salt. Put into a serving dish, garnish with lemon slices and parsley sprigs.

serves 4 • Preparation: 5–7 mins

Białowieża eggs

8 eggs, 250 g wild cep mushrooms, 2 tbsps beef stock, 1 small onion, 500 g pork fat, 2 tbsps milk, chopped parsley, salt, pepper

Skin, rinse and drain the mushrooms, dice them and stew in butter together with the finely chopped onion. Season with pepper. Beat the eggs lightly with the milk, add some salt. Render the diced pork fat in a frying pan, add the mushrooms. Pour in the eggs and fry until they set. Garnish with chopped parsley before serving.

serves 4 • Preparation: 5–7 mins

Kashub eggs

4 eggs, 4 tbsps single cream, 3 tbsps butter, 4 slices of wholemeal bread, salt, 3 tbsps chopped chives

Cut the bread into small cubes. Melt the butter in a large frying pan, brown the bread. Pour in the lightly beaten eggs and cream. Add some salt. Fry until the whites set. Sprinkle with chopped chives before serving.

serves 4 • Preparation: 5–7 mins

Kashub eggs with herring

8 eggs, 150 g herring fillets, ¼ cup milk, salt, pepper, paprika, 3 tbsps chopped chives, 2 tbsps butter

Pour half of the milk over the fillets and leave for half an hour, then take the fillets out, dry them and cut into thin strips. Beat lightly the eggs and milk, put in the herring and chives. Melt the butter in a large frying pan, pour in the eggs. Stirring all the time, cook over low heat. Season with pepper and paprika, add some salt if required.

serves 4 • Preparation: 5–7 mins

Scrambled eggs with garlic and vinegar

8 eggs, 2–3 cloves of garlic, 3 tbsps 6% wine vinegar, 3 tbsps butter, salt, pepper

Beat the eggs lightly with salt and pepper. Melt the butter in a frying pan, put in the finely chopped garlic and fry it golden brown. Pour in the eggs, stir well and cook over very low heat. When the eggs begin to set, add gradually the vinegar and continue frying, stirring all the time. Serve with lettuce or cucumber and onion salad.

serves 4 • Preparation: 5–7 mins

Old shepherd's eggs

8 eggs, 100 g pork fat, 50 g oscypek (smoked sheep cheese), 2–3 tbsps milk, 2–3 slices of wholemeal bread, salt, 2 tbsps chopped parsley

Beat the eggs lightly together with milk, salt and grated cheese. Render the finely diced pork fat in a hot frying pan, add the bread cut into cubes and brown it lightly. Pour in the eggs and, stirring continuously, fry them over low heat. Garnish with chopped parsley before serving.

serves 4 • Preparation: 5–7 mins

Scrambled eggs with chives

8 eggs, 3–4 tbsps chopped chives, 100 g tinned crab meat, salt, pepper, nutmeg, 3 tbsps sparkling water, 3 tbsps cream, 2 tbsps butter

Break the eggs into a pan, add salt, pepper, nutmeg and water and whisk thoroughly, gradually adding the cream, chives and, towards the end, the drained crab meat. Melt the butter in a large frying pan, pour in the egg mixture and fry quickly over medium heat. Stir well when the eggs begin to set.

serves 4 • Preparation: 5–7 mins

Scrambled eggs with cheese

4 eggs, 1 tbsp sparkling water, 1½ tbsps grated tangy cheese, 1 tsp hot mustard, 2 tbsps chopped parsley, 1 tbsp butter, salt, pepper

Beat the eggs and water well. Melt the butter in a frying pan. Pour in the eggs. When they begin to set, add the mustard and cheese and stir until the cheese melts. Add salt to taste, season with pepper. Mix in the chopped parsley. Serve with toasted white bread.

serves 4 • Preparation: 4–6 mins

Sunny side up eggs

This usually means eggs that are fried soft (the white is set but the yolk is runny). They are best fried in melted butter, preferably in a special frying pan with an indentation in the base, under a lid. Eggs can be fried with ham, bacon, vegetables or mushrooms in an ordinary frying pan, but the lid should always be on, so that a film of set white forms over the yolk.

Edward Poņerski, the Polish prince of French gastronomes, gave the following advice:

A fried egg is good if the white is set but not slippery and the yolk only slightly thickened, but nonetheless hot. In order for everything to work, you must be able to regulate the heat well, and it should be reasonably hot but not too strong... Put a large piece of butter in the pan, and wait until it has melted but not browned, then break two eggs, one after the other, gently into the butter, not holding them too high. The white will set immediately at the edges. Turn down the heat, or take the pan off the heat for a moment, take a knife and cut the set white, so that the runny white spreads and fills the gaps as it sets. Take care not to damage the yolk, because if it breaks or goes hard the dish will not be so good. When the whole white is set, add salt.

How can eggs best be fried?
(1) They should be fried in a special frying pan with a thick bottom.
(2) People on a diet can fry eggs in low-fat milk.
(3) Eggs will fry excellently with bacon, sausage or ham, but also with a slice of roast chicken, roast beef or pork or on cheese.
(4) Fried eggs go well with vegetables, and they can therefore be fried with slices of tomatoes, onions, pepper or on green peas or boiled potatoes.
(5) They also go well with mushrooms, both fried champignons and fresh wild mushrooms.
(6) They also do not go badly with fruit and herbs, for example with stewed apples or fresh herbs.
(7) They are also excellent fried with rice, pasta, meat or sauces and baked, as for example in the following recipe:

Eggs à la duchesse

4 eggs, 3 tbsps grated Emmental, 2 bacon rashers, 4 large mushrooms, 2 potatoes cooked in jackets, 4 tbsps single cream, salt, pepper, a pinch of nutmeg

Brown the rashers in a hot frying pan, take them out with a strainer. Fry the peeled and sliced potatoes in the same fat until golden brown, then transfer them to a plate. Melt the butter in the same pan and fry the diced mushrooms. Take four individual ovenproof dishes, grease them with some butter. Line each with potato slices, mushrooms and strips of bacon, sprinkle with some cheese. Cover with cream mixed with salt and nutmeg. Break one egg into each dish, sprinkle with the remaining cheese, salt and pepper. Arrange the dishes in a large ovenproof dish filled with water and put into a preheated oven for 10–12 mins. When the whites set, the eggs are ready.

serves 4 • Preparation: 10–12 mins

Flamenco eggs

8 eggs, 1 tbsp olive oil, ¾ cup cooked green peas, 6 cooked (or tinned) asparagus stalks, 6–10 pieces of pickled pepper, ¼ cup dry sherry, 2 tbsps chopped parsley, salt, pepper

SAUCE: 2 onions, 3–4 cloves of garlic, 300 g tomatoes, 1 red pepper, 3–4 tbsps stock, 2 tbsps olive oil, 100 g bacon, 1 bay leaf, salt, pepper, paprika

Prepare first the sauce: heat up the oil in a pan, fry the finely chopped onion and garlic (without browning them), put in the diced skinned and seeded tomatoes and pepper cut into strips. Sprinkle with some stock, add the bay leaf and simmer over low heat for 25 mins, stirring occasionally. Sieve the sauce (it should be quite thick), add salt, season with pepper and paprika, put in the bacon cut into thin strips. Grease an ovenproof dish with oil, pour in the sauce and spread it evenly on the bottom. With a spoon, make eight hollows in the purée. Gently break one egg into each hollow, taking care not to allow the white to spread outside. Arrange the green peas, asparagus pieces and pepper strips around each egg. Sprinkle with sherry, salt and pepper. Cover the dish with aluminium foil and put into a preheated oven for 20–25 mins. Garnish with chopped parsley. Serve with rice or bread.

serves 4 • Preparation: 30–35 mins

Oriental eggs

8 eggs, 500 g tomatoes, 2 medium-sized onions, 1 cup grated tangy sheep cheese, 3 tbsps butter, 3–4 tbsps chopped parsley, salt

Fry the onion cut into thin slices in butter (2 tbsps), but do not let it brown. Put in the diced skinned and seeded tomatoes and simmer over low heat for 10 mins. Add a bit of salt and the chopped parsley, mix thoroughly. Grease an ovenproof dish with butter, line it with the tomato and onion mixture. Gently break in the eggs, sprinkle them with the grated cheese and arrange knobs of butter on top. Put into a preheated oven for 10 mins, by which time the whites should set and the yolks remain runny.

serves 4 • Preparation: 10–15 mins

Eggs with peppers

4 eggs, 4 bacon rashers, 2 onions, 1–2 cloves of garlic, 1 carrot, 1 bunch of radishes, 1 each red and green pepper, 1 leek (only the white part), 100 g garlicky sausage, 1 tbsp each stoned green and black olives, 3 tbsps olive oil, ¼ cup stock, salt, pepper

Peel the carrot, onion and garlic. Core the peppers, rinse and dry them. Wash and dry the radishes and leek. Cut the peppers in strips, dice the radishes and carrot into fine slices, chop the garlic and onion finely. Heat up 1½ tbsps of oil in a pan, put in the carrot, leek, radishes and peppers and sauté them, stirring continuously. Pour in the stock and stew for a bit, then put in the diced sausage and simmer over low heat for 5–7 mins. Heat up the remaining oil in a pan, fry the onion and garlic (without browning them), put in the diced bacon and fry for a minute or two, stirring all the time. Add the mixture to the stewed vegetables, put some salt and pepper to taste. Grease an ovenproof dish with oil, line it with the vegetable mixture. Add the olives cut into slices. With a spoon make four hollows in the mixture. Break one egg into each hollow, sprinkle it with pepper sparingly. Put the dish into a preheated oven for 12 mins, by which time the whites whould set. Serve with rice or French fries.

serves 4 • Preparation: 15–20 mins

Eggs with beer and cheese

8 eggs, 8 beef tomatoes, 150 g grated cheese, 3 tbsps butter, ½ cup lager beer, salt, pepper

Blanch the tomatoes, skin them and cut into thick slices. Grease an ovenproof dish with butter, line it with the tomato slices. Sprinkle with salt and pepper. Gently break in the eggs. Pour 1 tbsp of beer over each egg, sprinkle with pepper, grated cheese and some butter flakes on top. Put the dish into a preheated oven for 15 mins. Serve with salads with white bread or potatoes.

serves 4 • Preparation: 5–7 mins

Eggs with tomatoes

8 eggs, 500 g tomatoes, 3 tbsps butter, 1 large onion, ½ cup cream, salt, pepper, 3 tbsps chopped chives, breadcrumbs

Blanch the tomatoes, skin and dice them. Melt 2 tbsps of butter in a pan, put in the finely chopped onion and fry it, but do not let it brown. Add the tomatoes and stew over low heat, then put the mixture through a blender and sieve it. Mix it with the cream, add salt and pepper. Grease an ovenproof dish with butter, sprinkle with breadcrumbs, pour in the tomato purée. With a spoon make eight hollows in the purée, break one egg into each. Put the dish into a preheated oven for 15 mins. Garnish with chopped chives before serving.

serves 4 • Preparation: 15–20 mins

Eggs à la russe

8 eggs, 1½ cups thick sour cream, ½ cup grated cheese, salt, 1 tsp butter

Pour the cream into an ovenproof dish. Gently break in the eggs. Sprinkle with the melted butter and with salt. Put into a preheated oven and bake for a while. When the whites set, sprinkle with the grated cheese and put back into the oven, until a golden brown crust forms. Serve immediately.

serves 4 • Preparation: 20 mins

Fried eggs, Old Polish style

4 eggs, 4 slices of wholemeal bread, 4 ham rashers, 2 tbsps cream, salt, pepper, parsley, 1 tbsp butter, 1 tsp olive oil

Heat up the oil in a frying pan, put in the bread and brown it on both sides. Grease an ovenproof dish with butter, arrange the bread on the bottom, cover it with the ham rashers, spread some cream on top. Put into a preheated oven. Melt some butter in a frying pan, break in the eggs and fry them. Sprinkle the eggs with salt and pepper. Arrange one egg on each slice of bread, garnish lavishly with chopped parsley.

serves 4 • Preparation: 15–20 mins

Eggs with spinach

1½ kg spinach, 8 eggs, 2 tbsps butter, 100 g grated cheese, 1 clove of garlic, salt, pepper, nutmeg, 2 tbsps grated Parmesan

Rinse the spinach and put it into boiling water for 5–7 mins, then drain it and chop finely. Melt 2 tbsps of butter in a frying pan, put in the crushed garlic, add the spinach, grated cheese, salt, pepper and nutmeg and fry for several minutes, stirring continuously. Transfer the spinach to four individual serving shells (or to one large ovenproof dish). With a spoon make two hollows in each. Break one egg into each hollow. Sprinkle it with salt, pepper and Parmesan. Put into a preheated oven for 8–10 mins, by which time the whites should set. Serve with white bread or pasta.

serves 4 • Preparation: 8–10 mins

Fried eggs with cheese

4 eggs, 4 thick cheese slices (Gouda or Cheddar), flour, salt, pepper, 203 tbsps butter

Dredge the cheese slices with flour. Melt the butter in a frying pan, put in the cheese and fry over low heat. When the cheese begins to melt, break one egg onto each slice and fry until the whites have set. Sprinkle with salt and pepper and serve immediately.

serves 4 • Preparation: 8–10 mins

Eggs in white bread

8 eggs, 1 French loaf, 1 cup thick cream, ½ cup stock, 1 tbsp flour, 1 tbsp butter, 3 tbsps chopped parsley, salt, pepper, a pinch of sugar, 2–3 drops Tabasco sauce, 1 tsp lemon juice

Cut the loaf into 8 thick slices, remove the inside. Brown the crusts in a frying pan. Melt the butter in a pan, add the flour and make a white roux. Dilute it with the stock, add salt, pepper, Tabasco, lemon juice and sugar, stir well and heat up until the sauce has thickened. Combine it with the cream and parsley. Grease an ovenproof dish with butter, pour in half of the sauce. Arrange the browned crusts. Break one egg into each crust, cover with the remaining sauce and put into a preheated oven for 10 mins.

serves 4 • Preparation: 10–12 mins

Omelettes

The history of the omelette goes back to Roman times. The French brought the art of omelette making to perfection and the Poles learnt about them in the times of Queen Marie, the wife of King John Sobieski, who adored omelettes. Omelettes are a universal dish: they can be served as a hot or cold hors-d'oeuvre, and can be a main dish at dinner or supper.

Omelettes can be divided into:

– natural omelettes, that is made with beaten whole eggs with salt and if desired a little water, milk or cream, and

– foamy omelettes which are fluffier, where the egg yolks are mixed with stiffly beaten whites and a little flour if desired.

The beaten eggs can be mixed with chopped fresh herbs, grated cheese, dried herbs or finely chopped vegetables. A classic omelette is fried on one side only, in a pan with a thick bottom. The egg mixture is poured into a pan containing hot fat; when the omelette is lightly fried underneath, while the upper side is still runny, the omelette should be slid onto a plate and turned over before returning it to the pan to be fried lightly for a moment. If we are serving an omelette with filling, it should be half-slid onto the plate, filled and then folded.

Omelettes are usually served very hot, immediately after frying, but they can also be served cold. If we are serving several omelettes, it is best to fry them in several pans.

A well-cooked omelette is fluffy, lightly browned on the bottom, well-fried at the edges and lightly set in the centre.

Natural omelettes are made without flour. The eggs are beaten with water and a pinch of salt, and fried over a low heat. They are usually served with boiled vegetables or with ham, sausages or cheese, with tomato salad, chicory salad or lettuce salad.

Foamy omelettes – with stiffly beaten egg whites and a little flour – are usually served sweet with fruit, jam, fruit syrup or whipped cream.

What do we need to know about cooking omelettes?

– For one omelette use one, or at most two, eggs. A larger number of eggs will make the omelette thick and less tasty.

– The eggs (which should always be at room temperature) should be lightly beaten with cold water (if they are beaten with milk, the omelette can become hard).

– Use one dessert spoon of cold water to one egg.

– Fry the omelette in butter or olive oil.

– Pour the egg mixture onto very hot oil and fry for 1 to 1½ minutes, after which we immediately transfer the omelette to a heated plate.

– Sweet omelettes can be served with slices of apple fried in butter with sultanas, spread with nut paste and sprinkled with chocolate curls, spread with marmalade and sprinkled with candied orange peel.

Sweet omelettes are made more refined if we sprinkle them with a little alcohol.

Omelettes offer enormous opportunities for composing a dish with various additions. Another variety of the omelette is called the mushroom, which is a foamy omelette made with a larger quantity of flour.

Herbal omelette

4 eggs, 4–5 spring onions, 1 tbsp each chopped mint leaves and parsley, salt, pepper, 2 tbsps butter

Chop the onions finely, combine them with the mint and parsley. Pour in the beaten eggs mixed with salt and pepper. Stir well. Melt the butter in a large frying pan, pour in the egg mixture and fry for 3–4 mins, then turn the omelette over and fry for another 2–3 mins.

serves 4 • Preparation: 5–7 mins

Omelette with vegetable stuffing

8 eggs, ¼ cup single cream, ¼ tsp cayenne pepper, 200 g smoked bacon, 1 cup finely sliced potatoes, 2 tbsps grated celery root, ½ cup finely diced green pepper, ¼ cup finely diced zucchini, 1 cup stewed tomatoes, 2–3 crushed cloves of garlic, 4 tbsps butter, salt, pepper

Herbal omelette

Dice the bacon and render it in a hot frying pan. Add 1 tbsp of butter and fry the onion (but do not let it brown), add the blanched tomatoes and fry for a bit, then put in the pepper, zucchini and celeriac. Stir well and sauté over high heat for 2–3 mins. Add the garlic crushed with salt and the tomato purée. Season with pepper to taste. Cover and simmer over low heat. Beat the eggs with the cream, add salt and cayenne. Fry the omelettes in four separate frying pans greased with butter. Stuff them with the vegetables and serve immediately.

serves 4 • Preparation: 8–10 mins

Omelette with mushrooms

6 eggs, 100 g mushrooms, 3 beef tomatoes, 3–4 cloves of garlic, 1 large onion, juice and grated rind of 1 lemon, 1 red pepper, 2 tbsps olive oil, parsley, salt, pepper

Blanch the tomatoes, skin them and cut into fine cubes. Wash and seed the pepper, cut it into strips. Dice the mushrooms, chop the onion finely. Heat up the oil in a frying pan, fry the onion (but do not let it brown), add the mushrooms and sauté them over high heat. Put in the pepper and, stirring continuously, fry for a minute or two. Put in the tomatoes, garlic crushed with salt, pepper, lemon juice and zest and simmer for 10 mins. Make omelettes from the eggs beaten with 2 tbsps of water. Stuff them with the vegetable mixture, garnish with chopped parsley.

serves 4 • Preparation: 20 mins

Omelette with leek (or spinach)

1 kg leek, 8 eggs, salt, pepper, 3 tbsps butter, ½ tsp sugar, 2 tbsps lemon juice

Cut off the green parts of the leek, wash the rest, cut lengthwise, then chop into fine slices. Melt 1½ tbsps of butter in a pan, put in the leek and, stirring continuously, fry for a bit. Add salt, sugar, lemon juice and pepper. Simmer for 20 mins, then take off the heat. Beat the eggs well with salt and pepper, fold them into the leek mixture, mix thoroughly. Melt the remaining butter in a large frying pan, pour in the egg mixture, put the lid on and fry for 10 mins. Turn the omelette over and fry for another

5–7 mins. Serve hot, cut into triangles, with some savoury sauce, or cold.

serves 4 • Preparation: 25–30 mins

Omelette with sausage

8 eggs, 4 spicy (paprika) sausages, 4 potatoes, 4–5 cloves of garlic, 4 tbsps oil, 2 tbsps tomato paste, 1 tsp chilli sauce, 2 tsps paprika, 2 tsps ground caraway, salt

Mix the tomato paste with 1 tbsp of boiled water, chilli sauce, paprika and caraway blended with the chopped garlic. Peel the potatoes, rinse them and dice into even cubes. Heat up the oil in a large frying pan, put in the potatoes and fry them golden brown. Add the tomato paste, stir well. Pour in enough boiling water to almost cover the potatoes and simmer over low heat for 30 mins. Put in the diced sausage, stir well and simmer for another 10 mins. Beat the eggs and, stirring continuously, pour them into the frying pan. Fry the mixture until the omelette is like thick cream. Add some salt and serve immediately with bread or rice and with salad.

serves 4 • Preparation: 35–40 mins

Omelette with feta cheese

150 g feta cheese, 6 eggs, 2 tbsps single cream, 1 tbsp finely chopped green olives, 4 tbsps butter, salt, pepper

Cut the feta into slices and fry it in butter in a large frying pan. Beat the eggs with the cream and salt, put in the chopped olives. Pour the mixture into the frying pan. Cover and fry for 4–5 mins over low heat. Remove the lid and fry for a bit longer. Sprinkle with pepper before serving.

serves 4 • Preparation: 6–8 mins

Omelette with ham

4 eggs, 100 g ham, 2 cloves of garlic, salt, pepper, 1 tbsp mineral water, 1 tbsp butter

Cut the ham into thin strips. Beat the egg yolks with salt and pepper. Whisk the egg whites, fold them into the egg yolks. Add the chopped garlic and ham. Mix thoroughly. Melt the butter in a large frying pan, pour in the mixture. Cover the pan and fry over low heat, then turn the omelette over and brown it lightly. Before serving, roll the omelette up.

serves 4 • Preparation: 6–8 mins

Vegetarian omelette

6 eggs, 2 cups soya sprouts, 100 g finely diced mushrooms, 1 tbsp each coarsely grated celery root, parsley root and finely diced onion, several bean pods (fresh cooked or tinned), 1 tbsp soya sauce, a pinch of salt, oil

Beat the eggs with salt and soya sauce, add the chopped soya sprouts, mushrooms, onion, parsley and celeriac. Mix thoroughly. Grease an ovenproof dish with oil, pour in the mixture, cover and put into a preheated oven for 15 mins. Remove the cover and bake for another 5–7 mins. Serve with tomato salad or lettuce.

serves 4 • Preparation: 20–25 mins

Various egg dishes

Once you have mastered the technique of cooking eggs, you can start preparing a large number of diverse dishes, and using your own inventiveness in this field.

(Edward Poṇerski, *Nauka przyrządzania potraw*)

Spinach bake

500 g fresh spinach, 1 large onion, 1 clove of garlic, 8 hard-boiled eggs, 4 tbsps butter, 1 tbsp flour, 1 cup grated cheese, ½ cup stock, 1 cup cream, salt, pepper, 1 tsp lemon juice, 2 cups cooked rice

Rinse the spinach, steam it for a while in a hot frying pan, reduce the juices. Leave it to cool, then put it though a blender. Melt 2 tbsps of butter in a pan, put in the finely chopped onion and, stirring all the time, fry it for 4–5 mins.

Add the garlic, salt and pepper, sprinkle with flour and, stirring continuously, gradually pour in the stock. Cook over low heat until the sauce thickens. Beat the cream with the spinach purée and half the cheese, pour into the sauce, stir thoroughly. Grease an ovenproof dish with butter, pour in half of the sauce, spread it evenly. Put in the rice. Arrange the shelled eggs on top. Pour over the remaining sauce, sprinkle with the remaining cheese, put knobs of butter on top. Put into a preheated oven for 15–20 mins. Serve with tomato salad and lettuce.

serves 4 • Preparation: 7–10 mins

Pumpkin bake

800 g pumpkin, 4 eggs, 2 onions, ¾ cup thick cream, 1 tbsp lemon juice, 2–3 grated cheese, 2 tbsps butter, salt, pepper, ¼ tsp grated lemon rind, 1 tbsp breadcrumbs, 3 tbsps chopped dill

Peel the pumpkin, remove the seeds. Rinse and dry the flesh, cut it into cubes. Melt 1 tbsp of butter in a pan, fry the finely chopped onion (but do not let it brown), add the pumpkin. Sprinkle with the lemon juice and simmer over low heat for 8–10 mins. Take off the heat, add salt, pepper and beaten eggs, stir thoroughly. Grease an ovenproof dish with butter, dust it with breadcrumbs, put in the pumpkin mixture. Beat the cream with sugar and lemon zest, pour over the pumpkin. Sprinkle with the cheese and put into a preheated oven for 15 mins. Before serving, garnish with chopped dill.

serves 4 • Preparation: 10–12 mins • Baking: 15 mins

Tarragon bake

8 hard-boiled eggs, 2 cups cooked rice, 2 leeks (only the white part), 1 tbsp butter, 2–3 tbsps strong stock, salt, pepper

SAUCE: 1 tbsp butter, 1 tbsp flour, 100 grated cheese, 2 tbsps chopped fresh tarragon, ¼ tsp dried tarragon, 1 bay leaf, ¼ tsp grated nutmeg, salt, pepper, ½ cup stock, 1 cup single cream

Wash the leeks thoroughly, cut them into thin slices. Melt the butter in a pan, put in the leek and fry for a minute or two, stirring all the time. Sprinkle with salt, pepper and some stock. Cover the pan and simmer for several minutes. Add the cooked rice, mix thoroughly, cover and keep warm. Make a roux from butter and flour, with dried tarragon and bay leaf. Dilute it with the stock, then simmer over low heat until the sauce has thickened. Add salt, season with pepper and nutmeg. Pour in the cream and heat up, then take off the heat, add the green tarragon and ⅔ of the cheese. Mix thoroughly. Put the rice into an ovenproof dish, arrange the shelled eggs on top. Pour over the sauce, sprinkle with the remaining cheese. Put into a preheated oven for several inutes. Garnish with parsley. Serve with salads.

serves 4 • Preparation: 20 mins

Warsaw bake

8 hard-boiled eggs, 200 g smoked bacon, 150 g grated cheese, 3 tbsps butter, 1 tbsp flour, 1 cup stock, 1½ cups single cream, 2–3 cloves of garlic, ¼ tsp each dried thyme, marjoram and basil, breadcrumbs, salt, pepper, 1 tsp lemon juice, a pinch of sugar, 3 tbsps chopped parsley, cooked pasta

Render the finely diced bacon in a frying pan. Take the bacon out with a strainer. Add 1 tbsp of butter to the fat, put in the flour and make a white roux. Dilute it with the stock and simmer, stirring all the time. Add the herbs, garlic crushed with salt, pepper, lemon juice and sugar, stir well. Beat the cream with half the cheese, pour into the sauce, stir again and heat up. Grease an ovenproof dish with butter, dust it with breadcrumbs. Pour in half the sauce, put in the pasta, spread the cracklings on top. Arrange the eggs on the pasta, pour over the remaining sauce. Sprinkle with the remaining cheese and breadcrumbs. Put into a preheated oven for 15 mins. Garnish with chopped parsley and serve immediately with lettuce or endives.

serves 4 • Preparation: 10–15 mins • Baking: 5–7 mins

Warsaw bake

Cauliflower bake

8 hard-boiled eggs, 1 onion, 150 g chicken breasts (or veal), 3 tbsps butter, 100 g grated cheese, ½ cup thick cream, 2 tbsps chopped parsley, 1 tbsp lemon juice, salt, pepper, 1 tbsp breadcrumbs, 1 large cauliflower

Fry the finely chopped onion in butter (1 tbsp), but do not let it brown. Add the minced meat and, stirring continuously, fry for a bit, then take off the heat. Cut the shelled eggs lengthwise, take out the yolks. Mix the yolks with salt, pepper and 1 tsp of cream, add the mixture to the meat. Stir thoroughly, season to taste. Stuff the egg whites with the mixture. Cook the cauliflower in salted water, then put it through a blender with 1 tbsp of butter and half the cheese. Mix the cream with the remaining cheese, add parsley, salt, pepper, a pinch of sugar and lemon juice. Grease an ovenproof dish with butter, dust it with breadcrumbs. Line the dish with the cauliflower purée. Arrange the stuffed eggs on top, pour over the cream. Sprinkle with the remaining breadcrumbs, put knobs of butter on top. Put into a preheated oven and bake for 20 mins. Serve with salads.

serves 4 • Preparation: 20–25 mins

Herbal bake

6 eggs, 2 tbsps dry white wine or light stock, 750 g French beans, 500 g new potatoes, 4 onions, 100 g butter, 1 tbsp each chopped basil, savory, tarragon, mint, dill and parsley, salt, pepper, 1 tbsp lemon juice, 1 tsp sugar

Boil salted water with sugar and lemon juice, put in the rinsed beans and cook them, then drain them and cut into small pieces. Melt some butter in a pan, put in the finely chopped onion, brown it lightly, add the beans and simmer for a while. Cut the peeled potatoes into thin slices, blanch them in boiling water for 3–4 mins, then drain them in a sieve. Grease an ovenproof dish with butter, line the bottom with the potato slices, sprinkle with salt and pepper. Cover the potatoes with the bean and onion mixture. Beat well the eggs with the chopped greens, salt, pepper

and wine (or stock). Pour over the beans. Put into a preheated oven and bake for 15–20 mins.

serves 4 • Preparation: 15 mins

Green bake

8 eggs, 3 tbsps each chopped chives, dill and parsley, 1 tsp chopped tarragon, 3 tbsps breadcrumbs, 2 tbsps butter, salt

SAUCE: 1½ cups cream, 3 tbsps chopped chives, salt, a pinch of each pepper and sugar, 1 tsp lemon juice

Grease a baking tin well with butter. Separate the egg yolks from the whites. Gently slip the yolks into the tin. Whisk the whites with salt, breadcrumbs and the chopped greens, fold carefully into the tin. Cover the tin with aluminium foil, place in a larger dish filled with water and put into a preheated oven. Bake for 30–40 mins. Very gently remove the bake from the tin and arrange it on a hot serving dish. Surround with cooked rice or mashed potatoes. Serve with a cold sauce, with lettuce or tomato salad.

serves 4 • Preparation: 35–45 mins

Egg bake, Parma style

8 eggs, 150 g Parmesan, 4 tbsps cream, 4 large beef tomatoes, 250 g smoked tongue, salt, pepper, ¼ tsp grated nutmeg, 3 tbsps butter, 3 tbsps chopped chives

Blanch and skin the tomatoes, cut them into thick slices. Cut the tongue into thin slices. Grease an ovenproof dish with butter, dust it with cheese. Line it with the tongue slices, cover with tomatoes. Gently break in the eggs, sprinkle them with salt, pepper and nutmeg, spread some cream on them. Sprinkle the remaining Parmesan on top and place knobs of butter. Put into a preheated oven and bake for 10–15 mins. Before serving, garnish with chopped chives. Serve with pasta, rice or white bread.

serves 4 • Preparation: 5–7 mins

Egg and cheese soufflé

*4 eggs, 1½ cups grated cheese, 1–2 tbsps flour,
¾ cup milk, ½ tsp soya sauce, ¼ tsp cayenne
pepper, salt, pepper, 3 tbsps butter*

Make a white roux from butter and flour, add the soya sauce, pepper and cayenne and cook until the sauce has thickened. Take off the heat, add the raw egg yolks and grated cheese, mix thoroughly. Whisk the egg whites stiff, fold them gently into the cheese batter. Grease well a tin, pour in the soufflé batter. Put into a medium-hot oven and bake for an hour. Serve with ketchup or with salads.

serves 4 • Preparation: 10–12 mins • Baking: 1 hour

Tomato soufflé

*3 eggs, 1 cup stewed puréed tomatoes, ½ cup stock,
1 cup grated cheese, 2 tbsps flour, 3 tbsps butter,
¼ tsp chilli powder, salt*

Melt some butter in a pan, add the flour and make a white roux. Dilute it with the stock and, stirring continuously, cook it over low heat until the sauce has thickened. Add the tomato purée, chilli and salt. Take off the heat, break in the raw egg yolks, put in the cheese and mix thoroughly. Fold in the whisked egg whites, mix thoroughly but gently. Pour the batter into a prepared tin and bake for one hour at medium-high temperature. Serve immediately.

serves 4 • Preparation: 10–15 mins

Eggs baked in wine

*8 eggs, 4 tbsps thick cream, 2 tbsps dry
red wine, salt, pepper, 1 tbsp butter*

Separate the egg yolks from the whites, putting each yolk in a separate vodka glass. Whisk the whites until stiff, sprinkle them with salt and pepper. Grease eight individual dishes with butter, put in the whisked whites. With a spoon make a hollow in the middle of each and slip in one raw egg yolk. Mix well the cream and wine. Cover each yolk

with the cream. Put the dishes into a preheated oven and bake for 10 mins. Serve immediately.

serves 4 • Preparation: 10 mins • Baking: 10 mins

Eggs in batter, Cieszyn style

*8 hard-boiled eggs, 2 raw eggs, ½ cup flour, ⅓ cup
milk, salt, 2–3 tbsps olive oil, 1 tbsp butter, parsley*

Separate the egg yolks from the whites. Whisk the whites stiff. Sift the flour into a bowl, add the yolks, milk, melted butter and some salt, work into a smooth batter. Fold in the whisked whites. The batter should be like thick cream. Cut the shelled hard-boiled eggs lengthwise. Dip each half in the batter and fry in hot oil until golden brown. Garnish with parsley before serving.

serves 4 • Preparation: 15–20 mins

Savoury fried eggs

*8 hard-boiled eggs, 1 tbsp anchovy paste, 2 finely
chopped anchovies, 2 hot green peppers, 1 tbsp olive
oil, 1 raw egg, 2 tbsps water, breadcrumbs, fat for frying*

Cut the shelled eggs lengthwise in half, take out the yolks. Bake the rinsed peppers in the oven, core them and put through a blender together with the egg yolks, anchovy paste and anchovies. Stuff the egg whites with the mixture. Put two halves together, coat each egg in eggs beaten with water and dredge with breadcrumbs. Fry in hot fat until golden brown.

serves 4 • Preparation: 15–20 mins

Breaded eggs

*4 hard-boiled eggs, 1 tbsp flour, 1 egg,
breadcrumbs, oil for frying*

Shell the eggs. Coat them in flour, lightly whisked egg and breadcrumbs. Press with your hands to make sure that the coating sticks well. Fry in hot oil until golden brown on all sides. Serve with fried potatoes, cold herbal sauce and salad.

serves 4 • Preparation: 5–7 mins

Egg cutlets

6 hard-boiled eggs, 1 raw egg, 3 potatoes cooked in jackets, 2 tbsps each chopped walnuts and dill, 1 tbsp chopped tarragon, 3 tbsps thick cream, 2–3 tbsps breadcrumbs, salt, pepper, 2 tbsps butter

Put the peeled potatoes through a mincer, add the chopped walnuts, dill, tarragon, cream, salt and pepper and mix thoroughly. Add the chopped eggs, break in the raw egg and work into a smooth paste. Wet your hands under cold water and form small cutlets. Coat each of them in breadcrumbs and fry in melted butter until golden brown. Serve with potatoes and cucumber or tomato salad.

serves 4 • Preparation: 20–25 mins

Egg cutlets with walnuts

5 eggs, 1 onion, 1–2 potatoes cooked in jackets, 1 bread roll soaked in milk, 1 tbsp chopped walnuts, 2 tbsps chopped parsley, 1 tsp flour, salt, pepper, 1 tbsp butter, 2–3 tbsps breadcrumbs, oil for frying

Fry the finely chopped onion in butter, but do not let it brown. Pour in the lightly beaten eggs and scramble. Leave them to cool. Put the peeled potatoes, squeezed out bread roll and scrambled eggs through a mincer. Add the flour, walnuts, parsley, salt and pepper and mix thoroughly. Wet your hands under cold water. Form small cutlets, coat them in breadcrumbs and fry in hot oil until golden brown.

serves 4 • Preparation: 20–25 mins

Egg bake

8 hard-boiled eggs, 4 largish onions, 1 cup dry white wine, 2 tbsps butter, 1 tbsp flour, 3 tbsps grated cheese, salt, pepper, cayenne, 1 tbsp breadcrumbs

Cut the peeled onions into fine half slices and fry them in butter (1 tbsp), without letting them brown. Sprinkle them with the flour, stir, pour in the wine and simmer over low heat for 30 mins. Grease an ovenproof dish with butter. Put in alternating layers of sliced egg and stewed onion, sprinkle each layer with salt and cayenne. Spread

the cheese mixed with breadcrumbs on top of the last layer and put in knobs of butter. Put into a preheated oven and bake for 15 mins. Serve with French fries, lettuce or tomato salad.

serves 4 • Preparation: 30–35 mins • Baking: 15 mins

Pickled eggs

12 small hard-boiled eggs, 1 large onion, 3 tbsps salt, 3–4 bay leaves, 1 tsp each peppercorns and mustard seeds, 4 cups water, 1 cup dry white wine

Boil the water with salt, bay leaves, mustard seeds and peppercorns. Cover the pan and simmer for 15 minutes. Add the wine, sliced onion and shelled eggs. Bring to the boil, then cook for another 3–4 minutes. Transfer to a large glass jar and leave to cool. Put on the lid and refrigerate for two or three days. Serve with mayonnaise, with cream and chive sauce or with ketchup.

serves 4 • Preparation: 20–30 mins

Eggs in white wine

10 hard-boiled eggs, 2 cups dry white wine, 3 tbsps salt, 1 cup wine vinegar, 3 red onions, 2–3 cloves of garlic, 4 chillis, 1 tsp mustard seeds, ½ tsp juniper berries

Boil the wine with salt, vinegar and spices. In a large glass jar arrange alternating layers of onion slices and shelled eggs. Pour over the hot marinade, leave to cool, then cover and refrigerate for two or three days. Serve with a savoury sauce.

serves 4 • Preparation: 10–15 mins

Lovers' breakfast

50 g smoked salmon, 4 eggs, 1 tbsp thick cream, 1 tsp butter, salt, pepper, 3 tbsps chopped watercress

Beat the cream with a pinch of salt and pepper. Grease two individual dishes with butter. Line them with thin strips of salmon. Gently break two eggs into each of them. Spread 1 tsp of cream on top of each. Place the dishes in a tin filled with lukewarm water and put into a preheated oven for 8–10 mins (or until the whites are set). Sprinkle with watercress before serving.

serves 4 • Preparation: 15–20 mins

Hot treat

4 slices of pumpernickel, 2 hard-boiled eggs, ¼ cup yogurt, 2 tbsps whipping cream, 2 cloves of garlic, 2–3 tbsps chopped parsley, 2 tbsps butter, 1 tbsp paprika, salt, pepper

Whisk the yogurt with the cream, salt, pepper, parsley and crushed galic. Chill the mixture a bit. Arrange the pumpernickel on a large serving dish. Spread the mixture on each piece, put an egg half (open side up) on top. Pour over melted butter mixed with paprika.

serves 4 • Preparation: 10–15 mins

Cheese dishes

In Poland, the tradition of eating hard cheese is relatively recent. Cheeses of this kind appeared at the beginning of the 19th century and were at that time a very expensive rarity. Known as Swiss cheeses, they were served, according to the French custom, at the end of dinner.

Cheeses can be eaten in various ways. They are excellent in sandwiches, for preparing pastes, for cocktail snacks, and they can be used to make hot hors-d'oeuvres and main dinner dishes, either vegetarian or meat dishes. They can also be used in baking both savoury and sweet dishes, and to prepare desserts. They give an original flavour to various dishes that are easy to prepare.

Cheeses are divided into soft cheeses, cheeses that mature through bacterial action and cheeses that mature through the action of moulds.

Soft cheeses: this group is made up mainly of cream and cottage cheeses, which are excellent for salads, pancakes, sweet or savoury bakes, and of ripened soft cheeses, like Brie or Camembert, which are delicate and mild white or cream cheeses with a soft, stretchy consistency; they are excellent as hors-d'oeuvres, and also fried in egg and breadcrumb coating.

Rennet cheeses, which mature through the action of bacteria, are divided into:
– very hard cheeses like Parmesan,
– hard cheeses like Cheddar or Gouda,
– semi-hard cheeses like Edam, Emmental or Gruyère.
The usefulness of cheeses in cooking depends on how they melt: for example Cheddar or Gruyère melt into a smooth mass, and are therefore excellent for preparing soups or sauces; Emmental melts into long threads, and is therefore usually used for fondue.

Grated cheese is an indispensable ingredient in almost any savoury bake and the best cheeses for this purpose are Edam, Gouda, Emmental and Gruyère.

Blue cheeses mature through the action of mould and include Roquefort, Gorgonzola or Stilton. Young cheeses of this kind have a mild and slightly acid taste; as they mature the taste becomes increasingly strong, as does the smell. All blue cheeses are suitable for hors-d'oeuvres, and are excellent for preparing strongly-flavoured pastes, sauces and salads.

Cheese salads

Savoury cheese salad

300 g various cheeses (Emmental, Gouda – the larger the variety, the better), 5 firm medium-sized tomatoes, 1 tin anchovy, 2 hard-boiled eggs, 1 tbsp capers, 2 tbsps chopped oregano leaves

DRESSING: 3–4 tbsps oil, 2 tbsps lemon juice, salt, pepper, a pinch of sugar, a pinch of cayenne, 2–3 lettuce leaves

Whisk thoroughly all the ingredients of the dressing, refrigerate it. Grate the cheeses coarsely or cut them into thin strips. Cut the anchovy in strips. Chop the egg whites. Blanch the tomatoes, skin and seed them, cut into small cubes. Mix the cheese with the anchovy, egg whites and tomatoes. Add the capers and some of the oregano (leave some for garnishing). Pour over the dressing, shake gently. Put the lettuce leaves on a serving plate, arrange the salad on top, sprinkle with the finely chopped egg yolks, garnish with oregano leaves. Serve immediately.

serves 4 • Preparation: 15 mins

Red salad

200 g cheese (Edam, Gouda), 100 g turkey ham, 1 small tin red beans, 1 red onion, 1 pickled red pepper

Dressing: 2 cloves of garlic crushed with salt, 4 tbsps mayonnaise, pepper, a pinch of sugar, ¼ tsp grated lemon rind, 1 tbsp lemon juice, 3 tbsps chopped chives, 1 tbsp marinated cherries, several sprigs of parsley

Whisk together all the dressing ingredients. Drain the beans in a sieve, pour over cold water and drain thoroughly again. Cut the cheese and turkey ham into thin strips, chop the onion finely, cut the pepper into cubes. Mix the ingredients, pour over the dressing, shake well. Garnish with marinated cherries and parsley sprigs.

serves 4 • Preparation: 10 mins

Fruit salad

150 g cheese (Emmental, Gouda), 150 g lean ham, 1 apple, 1 tbsp lemon juice, 2 tangerines, 2 tbsps raisins, 1 tbsp dry white wine, 3 tbsps mayonnaise, a pinch of each salt, cayenne and caster sugar, 3–4 lemon balm leaves

Cut the cheese and ham into thin strips. Cut the peeled apple into cubes, sprinkle with lemon juice. Blanch the raisins, drain them, then soak in wine. Divide the peeled tangerines into segments, cut half of them into cubes. Mix thoroughly the mayonnaise with the raisins, salt, cayenne and sugar. Combine all the salad ingredients, pour over the

dressing, shake well. Transfer the salad to a serving bowl and refrigerate. Before serving, garnish with tangerine segments and lemon balm leaves.

serves 4 • Preparation: 15 mins

Chinese cabbage salad

100 g walnuts, 150 Roquefort, 2 apples, 1 small Chinese cabbage, 3 tbsps chopped chives, 4–5 tbsps corn oil, 2 tbsps lemon juice, a pinch of pepper, salt to taste

Cut the peeled apples into strips, sprinkle with lemon juice. Add the shredded Chinese cabbage leaves, quarters of walnuts and the cheese cut into strips. Sprinkle with pepper, pour in the oil. Shake and mix gently. Add the chives, salt and more lemon juice to taste.

serves 4 • Preparation: 20 mins

Cheese and walnut salad

300 g cheese (Emmental, Tilsit, Edam), 1 large onion, 2 hard-boiled eggs, 2 tbsps chopped walnuts, 2–3 cherry tomatoes, 2–3 sprigs of dill

Dressing: 2 tbsps mayonnaise, 2 tbsps yogurt, 1 tbsp dried marjoram, 1 tbsp lemon juice, salt, a pinch of sugar

Mix thoroughly all the dressing ingredients, cover the bowl and refrigerate for a while. Grate the cheese coarsely or cut it into strips. Dice the onion and the eggs. Combine all the salad ingredients, pour over the dressing. Shake and mix gently, then put into the fridge for half an hour. Before serving, sprinkle with the chopped walnuts and garnish with tomato halves and dill sprigs.

serves 4 • Preparation: 15 mins

Frankfurter salad

100 g cheese (Gouda, Edam), 2 frankfurters, 4–5 spring onions, 3 tbsps chopped dill, 3 tbsps mayonnaise, salt, a pinch of each pepper and sugar, 1 tsp lemon juice, 2–3 radishes, 2–3 lettuce leaves

Mix the mayonnaise with the lemon juice, salt and pepper, refrigerate. Skin and slice the frankfurters. Cut the cheese into strips. Chop the onions together with the leaves. Mix all the salad ingredients, pour over the mayonnaise, stir thoroughly. Arrange the salad on lettuce leaves, sprinkle with dill, garnish with radishes. Serve immediately.

serves 4 • Preparation: 15 mins

Various cheese dishes

Cheese balls

200 g Roquefort (or some other blue cheese), 50 g each bryndza, cottage cheese and butter, a pinch of each caster sugar and cayenne, 1 cup chopped walnuts

Cream the bryndza with the butter, cottage cheese and blue cheese. Add half the chopped walnuts, sugar and cayenne. Wet your hand and shape small balls from the mixture. Coat each ball in the chopped walnuts. Arrange on a serving dish and refrigerate for one or two hours.

serves 4 • Preparation: 30 mins

Savoury cheese layer cake

12 thin tinned ham slices, 400 g whole-milk curd cheese, 1 hard-boiled egg, 2 beef tomatoes, ¼ each yellow and orange pepper, 1 tbsp each chopped lemon balm, mint, chives and dill, 1 tbsp sharp mustard, salt, pepper, a pinch of sugar

Blanch the tomatoes and peppers, skin them and chop finely (seed the tomatoes first). Chop finely the egg white. Cream the cheese with mustard, egg yolk, salt, pepper and a pinch of sugar. Add the egg white, tomatoes, peppers and greens. Mix thoroughly. In a rectangular mould arrange alternating layers of ham and the cheese mixture, finishing off with the ham. Press lightly, cover with foil and refrigerate for two or three hours.

serves 4 • Preparation: 30–35 mins

Cheese relish

250 g cheese, 5 eggs, 3 tbsps butter, ½ cup each milk and single cream, salt, pepper, 1 tsp herbs of Provence, 2 tbsps chopped walnuts

Grate the cheese. Blend the cream with the egg yolks, herbs, salt and pepper. Melt 2 tbsps of butter in a pan, add some flour and make a white roux. Dilute it with the milk and simmer until the sauce has thickened. Take off the heat, add the cheese and cream, mix thoroughly. Fold in the whisked egg whites. Grease an ovenproof dish with butter, dust it with the walnuts. Pour in the cheese mixture and put into a preheated oven. Bake for 40 mins. Serve with savoury salads.

serves 4 • Preparation: 20 mins

Hot relish

4 thin slices of wholemeal bread, 1 cup lager beer, 150 g grated cheese (Cheddar or Gruyère), 2 raw egg whites, a pinch of each salt and cayenne or chilli, 1 tbsp butter

Whisk the egg whites until stiff, mix them with the cheese, beer, salt and pepper. Grease an ovenproof dish with butter. Arrange the bread on the bottom, cover it with the mixture. Put into a preheated oven and bake for 10–15 mins.

serves 4 • Preparation: 10 mins

Savoury cheese cake

1 packet puff pastry (300 g), 250 g blue cheese (Roquefort, Danish blue), 1 cup each single cream and sour cream, 5 eggs, salt, pepper, 1 tbsp butter, 1 tbsp flour, 1 tsp lemon juice, a pinch of sugar

Melt the butter in a pan, add the flour and make a white roux. Add the single cream, salt, pepper, sugar and lemon juice to taste. Stirring all the time, simmer until the sauce has thickened, then take off the heat. Beat four egg yolks with the grated cheese and cream until the mixture is smooth. Pour in the prepared sauce. Fold in the stiff whisked egg whites. Roll out the pastry, divide it into two equal parts. Line a baking tin with one half, put in the cheese mixture, cover with the other half of the pastry. Brush on top with a mixed egg yolk. Put into a preheated oven (180–200OC) and bake for 35 mins. Serve hot with salads.

serves 4 • Preparation: 20 mins

Tatra cheese pie

DOUGH: 3–3½ cups flour, 250 g butter, ½ cup thick sour cream, 1 raw egg yolk, a pinch of salt, ½ tsp love-in-a-mist seeds

STUFFING: 250 g bryndza, 100 g bundz, 1 tbsp butter, 3 raw egg yolks, ¼ tsp dried savory, salt, pepper

DOUGH: Sift the flour onto a pastry board, add the butter and cut it in with a knife until the mixture is sandy. Add a pinch of salt, cream and egg yolk. Quickly work into a smooth dough. Divide into two halves. Add love-in-a-mist seeds to one part. Form the dough into two balls, wrap them up in foil and refrigerate for one or two hours.
STUFFING: Cream the butter and bryndza, add grated bundz and, stirring all the time, gradually add the egg yolks, salt, pepper and savory.
Roll out the dough into two fairly thick rectangles. Line two tin moulds with aluminium foil. Place the dough in them and bake it in a preheated oven until golden brown (10 mins). Transfer the love-in-a-mist rectangle onto a serving dish, spread the stuffing on it, cover with the other rectangle. Serve immediately. Delicious both hot and cold.

serves 4 • Preparation: 20–30 mins

Breaded salami cheese

400 g salami cheese, ½ tsp sweet paprika, 1 tbsp flour, 3–4 tbsps chopped walnuts, 1 raw egg, 2–3 tbsps lager beer, a pinch of salt, fat for frying

Remove the wax rind from the salami, cut the cheese into 8 even slices. Mix the breadcrumbs with the walnuts and the flour with the paprika. Beat the egg lightly

with a pinch of salt and the beer. Coat each slice of cheese in the flour, egg and breadcrumbs with walnuts. Fry in hot fat until golden brown on both sides. Serve as a hot relish, or with rice or potatoes and lettuce.

serves 4 • Preparation: 10 mins

Cheese schnitzels

500 g cheese (Tilsit, salami, Gouda), 2 eggs, 1 tbsp mineral water, 1 tbsp flour, 3–4 tbsps breadcrumbs, 2–3 tbsps olive oil, salt, cayenne pepper

Cut the cheese into thick (3 cm) slices. Sprinkle sparingly with salt and cayenne. Beat the eggs lightly with mineral water. Coat each slice in flour, eggs and breadcrumbs. Fry in hot oil until golden brown on both sides. The cheese inside should be half melted and the crust should be crispy. Serve with rice or potato purée and salads.

serves 4–6 • Preparation: 10 mins

Cheese rolls

400 g cheese (Gouda, Tilsit), 150 g thin rashers of smoked bacon, 2–3 tbsps finely chopped parsley, 1–2 tbsps oil

Cut the cheese into 12 equal, fairly thick sticks. Wrap up each stick in a rasher, secure it with a skewer. Heat up the oil in a frying pan and fry the rolls for 2–3 mins on all sides. Transfer them to a serving dish, sprinkle with chopped parsley. Serve immediately as a hot hors-d'oeuvre.

serves 4 • Preparation: 8–10 mins

Stuffed chicken schnitzels

2 chicken breasts, 1 tsp lemon juice, 4 lean ham rashers, 4 thick slices of cheese, 1 tbsp each flour, oil and butter, salt

Rinse and dry the breasts, divide them into four portions. Pound them lightly with a mallet and sprinkle with lemon juice and salt. Put a ham rasher and a cheese slice on each piece. Roll the meat up or fold in two, secure with a skewer. Coat in flour and fry in very hot oil on both sides until golden brown. Towards the end add the butter, cover the pan and simmer for a bit.

serves 4 • Preparation: 10–15 mins

Potato and cheese dumplings

750 g potatoes cooked in jackets, 200 g tangy cheese, 1–1½ cups wheat flour, 2–3 eggs, salt, pepper, 100 g smoked bacon, 1 tsp lard

Peel the potatoes, put them through a mincer. Grate the cheese finely, add it to the potatoes. Break in the eggs, add flour, salt and pepper and work into a smooth mixture. Divide it into two or three parts. Sprinkle the pastry board with flour, form a roll from each part of the pastry. Flatten it a bit and cut diagonally into dumplings. Cook the dumplings in batches in boiling salted water, take out with a strainer. Place them in a serving dish, pour over bacon scratchings. Serve with salads.

serves 4 • Preparation: 10–15 mins

Baked fennel

4 largish fennel bulbs, 3 tbsps butter, 3–4 tbsps Parmesan, salt, pepper, 1 tsp lemon juice, 1 tsp sugar

Remove the hard outer layer and stems from the fennel bulbs. Bring some water to the boil, add salt, sugar, lemon juice and butter. Put in the fennel and cook for 25 mins. Drain the bulbs and cut them into quarters. Grease an ovenproof dish with butter, arrange the fennel quarters, sprinkle with pepper and Parmesan liberally. Put on top knobs of butter and bake in a preheated oven for 25 mins. Before serving, garnish with chopped green fennel sprigs or dill. Serve hot as an hors-d'oeuvre or as a side dish with meat dishes.

serves 4 • Preparation: 25 mins

Home-made ricotta

1½ l full-cream milk, 1 cup natural yogurt

Mix the milk with the yogurt, bring to the boil, then simmer over low heat for 20 mins until the milk begins to coagulate. Put a double layer of gauze in a strainer, pour

Home-made ricotta

in the milk and leave until most of the whey has seeped through. Tie the gauze at the top and hang it up until the cheese has hardened and the whey drips off. It is excellent for fruit desserts and pasta served sweet.

serves 4 • Preparation: 20–25 mins

Mushrooms with cheese

12 mushrooms of equal size, 100 g grated cheese, 2 onions, 2–3 cloves of garlic, 4 tbsps chopped parsley, 1 tsp chopped thyme, 1 crumbled bay leaf, ½ tsp paprika, 1 tbsp lemon juice, salt, pepper, 3 tbsps butter

Rinse the mushrooms, remove the stalks. Put the caps for one minute in hot salted water. Drain them, run under cold water, dry them. Chop finely the mushroom stalks, onion and garlic. Melt 1 tbsp of butter in a frying pan, put in the onion, sprinkle it with the crumbled bay leaf and sauté it. Add the mushroom stalks, garlic and paprika, stir well and fry for another 4–5 mins. Take off the heat, add the thyme, lemon juice, parsley and half the grated cheese. Mix thoroughly, add salt and pepper to taste. Stuff the mushroom caps with the mixture. Arrange them in a greased ovenproof dish, sprinkle the remaining cheese on top, put in knobs of butter. Cover the dish with aluminium foil and put into a preheated oven. Bake for 30 mins, then remove the foil and bake for another 5–6 mins. The dish goes very well with cooked fennel bulbs and tomato salad.

serves 4 • Preparation: 10–15 mins • Baking: 30–35 mins

Green curd cheese pudding

500 g cottage cheese, 2–3 potatoes cooked in jackets, 100 g spinach, 2–3 cloves of garlic, 3 tbsps chopped parsley, 3–4 eggs, 2–3 tbsps sunflower seeds, 100 g butter, salt, pepper

Peel the potatoes, put them through a mincer. Crush the garlic with salt. Rinse the spinach and blanch it for 2–3 mins in salted boiling water, then strain it and put through a blender together with the potatoes, cheese and garlic. Cream the butter (leave 1 tbsp for later), adding one egg yolk and 1 tbsp of potato and cheese mixture

at a time. Add salt and pepper to taste and the finely chopped parsley. Fold in the stiffly whisked egg whites. Grease a mould with the remaining butter, sprinkle it with the chopped sunflower seeds. Put in the mixture. Seal the mould and put it into a pan with boiling water. Cook for 45–50 mins. When the pudding no longer sticks to the mould, take it out onto a serving dish. Serve with salads and sauces.

serves 4 • Preparation: 15 mins

Herbal cheese

250 g curd cheese or cream cheese, 2 tbsps finely chopped borage leaves, 1 tbsp chopped chives, salt, a pinch of sugar, several drops of lemon juice, 1 tbsp borage flowers

Cream the cheese with salt, sugar and lemon juice. Add the chives and borage leaves, mix thoroughly. Refrigerate before serving. Garnish with borage flowers.

serves 4 • Preparation: 3–5 mins

Home-made caraway cheese spread

250 g stale cottage cheese, 1 raw egg yolk, 2–3 tbsps butter, 1 tbsp caraway seeds, salt, a pinch of each pepper and cayenne

Crumble the cheese into a bowl, add a pinch of salt, cover and leave in a warm place for several days (the cheese will give off rather pungent smell). Melt the butter in a frying pan, put in the cheese and fry over low heat, stirring continuously until it has turned into a smooth paste. Take off the heat, add salt, pepper, cayenne, caraway and egg yolk. Mix thoroughly, then pour into a small bowl and leave to cool.

serves 4 • Preparation: 10–15 mins

Home-made mushroom cheese spread

250 g stale cottage cheese, 2–3 tbsps dry white wine, 100 g mushrooms, 1–2 cloves of garlic, ¼ tsp dried thyme, salt, pepper, 3 tbsps butter

Crumble the cheese into a bowl, sprinkle with salt, cover and leave for 4–5 days in a warm place. Rinse the mushrooms, drain them and dice the caps. Melt 1 tbsp of butter in a frying pan. Sauté the mushrooms, add pepper, thyme and garlic crushed with salt. Stir well, take off the heat. Pour in the wine, mix thoroughly. Melt the remaining butter in a pan, put in the cheese. Stirring all the time, fry until the cheese has turned into a smooth paste. Add the mushrooms and simmer over low heat, stirring all the time. Transfer to a serving bowl and leave to cool.

serves 4 • Preparation: 20–25 mins

Patties with raisins

500 g curd cheese, 3–4 tbsps flour, 3 eggs, 3 tbsps caster sugar, 3 tbsps raisins, 1 tbsp dry white wine, a pinch of salt, oil for frying

Put the cheese through a mincer. Rinse the raisins, sprinkle them with the wine. Beat the egg yolks with sugar until fluffy, then gradually add the cheese. Put in the raisins. Whisk the egg whites stiff, fold them into the cheese to-gether with the flour. Mix gently but thoroughly. Heat up the oil in a frying pan and with a spoon put small patties in. Fry them on both sides until golden brown. Serve with cream, sprinkled with caster sugar.

serves 4 • Preparation: 20 mins

Cheese in honey

400 g Edam cheese, 200 g honey, 1 tsp grated lemon rind, ½ tsp cinnamon, ¼ tsp ground cloves, 3–4 tbsps chopped walnuts

Cut the cheese into small cubes. Heat up the honey in a deep thick-bottom frying pan. Add the cloves, cinnamon and lemon zest. Stirring all the time, bring the mixture to the boil. Put in the cheese cubes immediately and heat up until the cheese has softened a bit. Take the cheese out and put it into individual serving bowls. Pour over the honey, sprinkle with the walnuts. A very original dessert in Old Polish style.

serves 4–6 • Preparation: 10–15 mins

CHAPTER V

KASHA
AND RICE

Honest Polish grits

There is kasha made from wheat, rye and barley as well as pearl barley, oatmeal, semolina, creamed wheat... They boil kasha for soup and as a main course, they boil it thick, grainy, with water, with milk, roasted with malmsey, sometimes with sultanas and plums, they eat it with butter, bacon fat, they bake it in the oven, they fry it.

(Łukasz Gołębiowski, *Domy i dwory*, vol. IV, pp. 41–42)

All over the world, dieticians recommend kasha as an ideal source of protein, mineral salts and vitamins. They recommend it for diabetics, in diets designed to reduce cholesterol levels, in digestive disorders and even in slimming diets. How wise our ancestors were when they ate a daily portion of kasha. Still in the 18th century kasha was one of the most popular dishes, and the greatest favourite was buckwheat, which was considered the healthiest of all. In ancient times, moreover, pearl barley was thought to be a food that gave strength and improved energy and potency.

All varieties of grain have an excellent influence on the human organism, and they all detoxify the system.

Kashas are highly calorific (339–360 Cal per 100 grams), they contain easily digestible, high-quality carbohydrates, protein, a minimal amount of fat, and a lot of vitamins of the B group (B^1, B^2 and PP); they also provide phosphorus, magnesium, iron and calcium. The contents of minerals and vitamins depends on the type of grain and the degree of processing. Kashas are a very good source of digestive fibre, which prevents the development of affluence-induced diseases, that is, for example, it reduces the blood cholesterol level, absorbs many toxic substances, making it possible to expel them, and counteracts many digestive problems.

Here is a breakdown of kashas according to the kind of grain and the degree of milling:

Barley kashas. The energy value of 100 g is 346 Cal; they contain carbohydrates = 75 g, of which fibre = 6 g, fat = 2 g, protein = 7 g, phosphorus = 206 mg, magnesium = 45 mg, calcium = 20 mg and iron = 1.6 mg. Barley kashas should not be stored for longer that 6 to 7 months.

Depending on the degree of milling, barley kashas are divided into the following:

1. Krupy or husked barley is the grain of barley with only the chaff removed. This barley kasha has the highest nutritive value, and is served as a side dish with meat, soups and in cutlets.
2. Hulled barley is a barley seed from which the outer layer has been removed in the process of polishing; the amount of fibre and other components has thereby been partly reduced. Hulled barley is excellent for barley soup, stuffed cabbage, and as a side dish with meat and sauces.
3. Cracked barley comes from breaking or splitting the barley seed. It is sub-divided into coarse, medium and fine. It is light grey in colour with a greenish or yellowish tinge.
4. Pearl barley is obtained by polishing cracked barley.
5. Roast pearl barley is obtained by roasting pearl barley.

7. Barley flakes.

Cracked and pearl barley can be cooked as a side dish to meats and sauces, and can be added to stuffed cabbage, cutlets and soups. Because in processing finer cracked barleys are deprived of their outer protective layer, the protein needs extra security to prevent it dissolving. We therefore need to add egg white to dry kasha (1 egg white to 300–500 g of kasha) and mix it with a wooden spoon until the lumps fall apart into separate grains; then we tip it onto a baking sheet and dry it in a hot oven. The dry kasha is then thrown into boiling water and cooked.

Buckwheat kashas. The energy value of 100 g is 359 Cal; they contain protein = 13 g, fat = 3 g, carbohydrates = 70 g, including fibre = 6 g, phosphorus = 459 mg, magnesium = 218 mg, calcium = 25 mg, iron = 2.8 mg.

Buckwheat is used to produced both roast and unroast kashas, and coarse and cracked kashas are also made, depending on whether the grain is whole or broken. Unroast buckwheat grits are the favourite, and the richest in protein and vitamins. It has been demonstrated that buckwheat works better than other foodstuffs in maintaining the proper level of glucose in the blood and counteracts diabetes.

Coarse roast buckwheat kasha is light or dark brown in colour, while cracked kasha is brownish-white; unroast kasha is greenish.

Unroast cracked buckwheat kasha is called Cracow kasha.

Coarse buckwheat grits, both roasted and unroasted, form an excellent addition to main dishes, pierogi, savoury flans and pies, bakes, koulebiacs; Cracow kasha is excellent for desserts, sweet bakes, and also as an addition to soup. It should be salted only after cooking, so that it does not darken in colour.

Millet kashas. 100 g contains: cabohydrates = 73 g, protein = 9.9 g, fibre = 3.2 g, potassium = 430 mg, phosphorus = 311 mg, magnesium = 162 mg, calcium = 20 mg, iron = 6.8 mg.

In comparison with other grains millet seeds are small, and after the chaff has been removed and the seeds polished the light yellow, round and very hard millet kasha is obtained.

It has a loose consistency and a rather pleasant taste. It is excellent in all kinds of milk soups and krupnik soups, and makes a good accompaniment to main dishes; it is best served with vegetables, and should be avoided with very spicy dishes.

Oat kashas. The energy value of 100 g is 387 Cal; they contain protein = 12 g, fat = 7 g, cabohydrates = 69 g, of which fibre = 7 g, phosphorus = 433 mg, magnesium = 129 mg, calcium = 54 mg, iron = 3.9 mg.

Oats are cracked to make porridge oats, but the main product is oat flakes which are used for milk soups, cutlets, dumplings and krupnik soups. In order to produce the flakes, the oat grains are first steamed and then rolled.

Wheat kashas. The energy value of 100 g is 345 Cal. The main wheat kasha – **manna** – is a small hard grain similar to semolina and is highly evenly granulated (0.75 mm). It is obtained by milling the husked grain. It is widely used in the kitchen in preparing desserts, milk soups, noodles, mousses and cakes.

Another kind of cracked wheat kasha is **bulgur** for which roughly husked ordinary bread wheat is used. Bulgur is sandy in colour and swells considerably during cooking.

Two kinds of kasha are produced from hard (durum) wheat: semolina and couscous. **Semolina** is a fine kasha made from hulled hard wheat and containing mainly parts of the wheatgerm; it is excellently suited to making energizing blancmanges. **Couscous** is ground and processed fine wheat kasha of an even granulation. The finest resembles pasta flour, and the coarsest resembles rice. It is a very useful and healthy product in the kitchen of an overworked housewife. It is cooked by pouring hot water or bouillon over it and leaving it for several minutes until it swells.

Kashas can be cooked to a dry or mushy consistency. The way of cooking depends on the kind of dish being made, and the degree of dryness or mushiness on the amount of water added to the raw kasha.

Coarse kasha – pearl barley, buckwheat and millet – is most often cooked to a dry consistency, while fine kasha – manna, Cracow kasha and corn kasha – is cooked until it is mushy.

Coarse kashas should be rinsed several times before cooking and drained well in a sieve.

Coarse kashas require a greater amount of liquid and cook more slowly than fine kashas. To cook coarse kashas to a dry consistency, you should allow 2 glasses of liquid to one glass of kasha; fine kashas require 1.5 glass of liquid to one glass of kasha. When cooking kashas to a mushy consistency we should allow more liquid.

It is best to use flat enamel pans with a thick bottom for cooking kasha; the capacity of the pan should be twice as large as the combined volume of the kasha and liquid. Kasha can be cooked in water, broth, mushroom stock, vegetable stock, milk or milk and water. We throw the kasha in boiling liquid, preferably with some fat added; we bring it back to the boil and then simmer under a lid over a very low heat. Yout can also put the pan into a hot oven or wrap in a blanket and leave for several hours.

If the kasha is to be a full meal for four people, you should take 2 cups of kasha; if it is to be a side dish for the main course, take 1½ cups; 3 to 4 tablespoons are enough for krupnik soup.

Dish	Kasha
Salads	millet, couscous, cracked barley, pearl barley
Soups, krupniks, milk soups	all barley kashas, millet, oat flakes
Served with soups	manna, Cracow kasha, millet, pearl barley, cracked barley, hulled barley
Cutlets	all kinds of kasha
Dumplings	manna, Cracow kasha, oat flakes
Meat and vegetable bakes	buckwheat grits, all types of barley kasha, couscous

Dish	Kasha
Sweet bakes	couscous, semolina, manna, Cracow kasha
Desserts	manna, Cracow kasha, semolina, couscous, pearl barley

Buckwheat

From buckwheat several kinds were made. Krakow kasha was mainly made in Radomsko, and was the most sought after; Anna Jagiellonka ordered it to be sent to her in Warsaw.

(Zygmunt Gloger, *Encyklopedia Staropolska*, vol. III)

This kasha, with its strongly individual taste and aroma, was most highly prized in Old Polish cuisine. It was an indispensable addition to popular dishes like collops, roasts and gravies. But it was also served with milk and sour milk, and also with bacon fat and crackling. Roast buckwheat grits were most popular because the flavour was stronger.

Toasted buckwheat

1½ cups roast buckwheat, 2 tbsps lard, 1 cup salted boiling water and 1 cup stock from dried mushrooms

Sift the buckwheat carefully. Heat up the lard in a pan, put in the buckwheat and, stirring continuously, toast it over low fire until the groats soak in the fat. Bring the water and mushroom stock to the boil, pour into the buckwheat and simmer over very low heat until all liquid has been absorbed. Cover the pan and put it into a hot oven for 40–45 mins.

serves 4 • Preparation: 5–7 mins

Buckwheat cutlets with mushrooms

1 cup buckwheat, 30 g dried mushrooms, 2 small onions, 2 eggs, ½ cup sunflower oil, salt, pepper, ¼ tsp dried thyme, ½ cup breadcrumbs

Rinse the mushrooms, cover them with 1 l of boiled water and leave overnight to soak. Cook them, then chop them finely. Heat up 1 tbsp of oil in a pan, put in the rinsed and drained buckwheat, stir well. Pour in the hot mushroom stock and cook the buckwheat to a dry consistency, then leave it to cool. Heat up 1 tbsp of oil in a frying pan, fry the finely chopped onion, but do not let it brown. Combine the buckwheat with the mushrooms and onion, add thyme, salt and pepper, break in the eggs and work into a smooth mixture. With moist hands shape medium-sized, fairly thick cutlets. Dredge each with breadcrumbs and fry in hot oil.

serves 4 • Preparation: 40 mins • Frying: 10 mins

Russian buckwheat

2 cups unroast buckwheat, 2 cups salted boiling water, 2–3 tbsps butter

Pour the buckwheat into a pan, cover with the boiling water and simmer over low heat until the liquid has been absorbed. Cover the pan and put into a hot oven for 40 mins. Moisten a pastry board with some cold water and, using a knife, spread the kasha evenly (ca 1 cm thick). Leave the board in a cool place overnight until the buckwheat has set. Cut the buckwheat into cubes and fry in melted butter. This kind of buckwheat goes very well with roast meat, especially served with mushroom sauce.

serves 4 • Preparation: 50 mins • Frying: 10–15 mins

Buckwheat with cheese

1½ cups buckwheat, 3 cups light stock, 2 tbsps olive oil, 2 onions, 300 g curd cheese, ½ cup cream, salt, pepper, 1 tbsp butter, 1 tsp breadcrumbs

Heat up the oil in a pan, put in the rinsed and drained buckwheat and, stirring all the time, fry it for a while. Pour in the hot stock, cover the pan and cook over fairly high heat for several minutes until all liquid has been absorbed. Wrap the pan in a blanket or put it into a hot oven. Put the cheese through a mincer. Fry the finely chopped onion in butter (but do not let it brown), put in the cheese, add salt and pepper. Mix the cheese with the buckwheat. Grease an ovenproof dish with butter and dust it with breadcrumbs. Put in the buckwheat and cheese mixture. Pour over the cream and place the dish in a preheated oven for 10–15 mins.

serves 4 • Preparation: 40 mins

Buckwheat cutlets with cheese

2 cups cooked buckwheat, 1 large onion, 1 tbsp butter, 100–150 g smoked meat trimmings, 2 tbsps dried smoked oscypek, 2 eggs, salt, pepper, breadcrumbs, fat for frying

Fry the finely chopped onion in butter, but do not let it brown. Add the chopped smoked meat and fry for a bit. Take off the heat and allow to cool, then add the grated oscypek. Put the cooked buckwheat through a mincer, combine it with the onion and meat mixture. Add salt and pepper, break in the eggs and work into a smooth mixture. With moist hands shape medium-sized cutlets. Dredge each with breadcrumbs and fry on both sides in hot oil. Serve with a savoury sauce and salads.

Buckwheat bake

serves 4

2 cups cooked buckwheat, 200–250 g roast veal or beef, ¼ cup soya sauce, 2 leeks (only the white part), 2 tbsps butter, 2 tbsps chopped sunflower or pumpkin seeds, 1 cup cream, 1 egg yolk, 2–3 tbsps grated cheese, 2 tbsps each chopped chives and dill

Preparation: 10–15 mins

Rinse and drain the leeks, slice them finely. Melt 1 tbsp of butter in a pan, put in the leeks and fry them, stirring all the time. Turn down the heat, add the chopped seeds and soya sauce and simmer over low heat for a while. Cut the meat into strips and combine with the buckwheat and leeks. Beat the cream with the egg yolk, salt, pepper, and the chopped chives and dill. Grease an ovenproof dish with butter. Put in the buckwheat, pour over the cream, sprinkle with the grated cheese. Put into a preheated oven and bake for 30 mins. Serve with salads or lettuce.

Cracow kasha

This delicate kasha is produced from milled buckwheat. It may be cooked both with salt and with sugar. *Radomsko and Cracow groats were particularly popular in Poland*, wrote Łukasz Gołąbiowski.

Roasted Cracow kasha

2 cups Cracow kasha, 1 raw egg,
3 cups water, salt, 100 g butter

Mix the kasha thoroughly with the lightly beaten egg. Spread it on a dry pastry board and leave to dry (the individual groats should not stick together; if they do, separate them with your fingers). Bring the salted water to the boil, add the butter, put in the dried kasha. Stir well, cover the pan and put into a preheated oven for 40–45 mins. Serve with chicken or veal caserole and with cep mushrooms in cream.

serves 4 • Preparation: 50–55 mins

Royal treat

This popular Old Polish pudding was allegedly invented at the Warsaw court of Anne Jagiellon.
1 cup Cracow groats, 1 raw egg, 2 cups milk, 3 tbsps butter, ½ vanilla pod, 4 raw eggs, 150 g sugar, ½ tsp grated lemon rind, 150 g raisins, 1 tbsp brandy, 3 tbsps caster sugar, 3–4 tbsps cherry preserve

Mix the kasha with one lightly beaten egg, spread it on a dry pastry board and leave to dry. Bring the milk, with butter and vanilla, to the boil. Put in the dried kasha into a pan, pour over the milk and cook over low heat for a bit. When the mixture thickens, cover the pan and put into a medium-hot oven for 40 mins, then allow it to cool. Rinse the raisins, pour over the brandy and leave aside for

Royal treat

several minutes. Whisk the egg yolks with the sugar and lemon zest, put in the kasha and raisins, mix well. Fold in the whisked egg whites. Grease a baking tin with butter, put in the mixture, place in a medium-hot oven and bake for 40 mins. Transfer onto a round serving dish, sprinkle with caster sugar, garnish with cherries. Serve hot or cold.

serves 4 • Preparation: 50 mins

Millet kasha

Millet kasha, made from cracked millet, was very popular in Old Polish cuisine, although its higher fat contents makes it go stale more quickly than is the case with other cereals. Cooked millet kasha is an excellent addition to meat stews. It may be prepared as a savoury or a sweet dish, with spices and with fruit.

Millet kasha with apricots and raisins

300 g millet kasha, 1 l milk, 1 tbsp butter, 1 tbsp honey, 100 g dried apricots, 50 g raisins, salt

Put the kasha into a sieve, pour over first boiling, then cold water, drain thoroughly. Bring the milk with butter, honey and a pinch of salt to the boil, put in the kasha, stir well. Add the scalded raisins and apricots cut into strips. Stir thoroughly, cover the pan and put into a preheated oven.

serves 4 • Preparation: 30–40 mins

Millet kasha with prunes and cheese

300 g millet groats, 250 g stoned prunes, 150 g curd cheese, 4 raw eggs, 3 tbsps honey, ½ tsp cinnamon, 3 tbsps butter, 3 cups milk, 1 tbsp breadcrumbs, salt

Put the kasha into a sieve, pour over first boiling, then cold water, drain well. Bring the milk with 1 tbsp of butter, salt and cinnamon to the boil. Put in the kasha, stir and cook over low heat. Cook the prunes in a small amount of boiled water, then sieve them. Cream 1 tbsp of butter with the honey, and, whisking all the time, add one egg yolk at a time. Whisk the egg whites. Combine the warm kasha with the prunes and honey mixture, fold in the egg whites. Grease an ovenproof dish with butter, dust it with breadcrumbs. Put in the kasha, spread on top the crumbled cheese. Put into a preheated oven for several minutes to make it really warm.

serves 4 • Preparation: 50–55 mins

Millet kasha with prunes

300 g millet kasha, 1 l milk, 2 tbsps butter, 2 tbsps sugar, 100 g stoned prunes, 50 g raisins, a pinch of saffron

Put the kasha into a sieve, pour over first boiling, then cold water, drain well. Rinse the prunes and blanch them for several minutes, then drain them and cut into strips. Blanch and drain the raisins. Bring the milk with saffron to the boil, add sugar and 1 tsp of butter. Put in the kasha, stir and cook it. Add the raisins and prunes, stir well. Grease an ovenproof dish with butter, put in the kasha, pour over the remaining melted butter. Put in a preheated oven for 15 mins.

serves 4 • Preparation: 50–55 mins

Millet kasha with cinnamon

400 g millet kasha, 1 l milk, ½ cup sugar, 1 tbsp cinnamon, 125 g butter, salt

Bring the milk with 1–2 tbsps of sugar to the boil. Rinse the kasha and put it into boiling salted water for 1–2 mins, then drain it and transfer to a pan. Cover with the hot milk and, stirring continuously, bring to the boil. Cover the pan and put it into a preheated oven (or else wrap it up in a blanket). When the kasha is ready, put it into a hot serving dish. Sprinkle with melted butter, sugar and cinnamon.

serves 4 • Preparation: 50 mins

Millet kasha with saffron

300 g millet kasha, 1 tbsp butter, 100 g pork fat, 100 g raisins, 1–1½ tbsps honey, several saffron stigmas, salt

Put the kasha into a sieve, pour over first boiling, then cold water, drain well. Bring water with butter to the boil, put in the saffron and kasha, stir well and cook. Blanch the raisins, then drain them. Mix the cooked kasha with the honey and raisins. Line an ovenproof dish with thin slices of pork fat, put in the kasha, cover with the remaining pork fat. Put the dish into a preheated oven and bake until the fat has turned golden brown.

serves 4 • Preparation: 50–55 mins

Millet pudding

300 g millet kasha, 1 cup milk, 4 tbsps butter,
5 eggs, 2 tbsps chopped dill, 1 tsp sugar,
salt, butter and breadcrumbs

Bring the milk and 2 cups of water to the boil, add some salt and 1 tbsp of butter, put in the kasha. Bring to the boil, then simmer over low heat until the liquid has been absorbed. Leave it to cool. Cream the remaining butter until foamy and, beating continuously, add one egg yolk at a time. Put in the kasha and dill. Whisk the egg whites and fold them into the mixture. Grease a mould with butter, dust it with breadcrumbs. Put in the millet mixture and seal the mould. Put the mould into a pot filled with boiling water and cook for about an hour. Serve with tomato, dill or cucumber sauce.

serves 4 • Preparation: 30 mins

Barley kasha

In the old days, before they learnt to make bread, people ate gruel from cracked barley, small spelt and wheat... Later they almost completely neglected this simple dish which they ate only on doctor's orders.

(Zygmunt Gloger, *Encyklopedia Staropolska*, vol. III)

Barley with mushrooms

300 g barley kasha, 2½ cups light stock, 3 tbsps
butter, 800 g cep mushrooms, 1 large onion,
½ cup cream, 1 raw egg, 2 tbsps grated cheese,
salt, pepper, 1 tbsp butter, 1 tbsp breadcrumbs

Rinse the barley, drain it in a sieve. Bring the stock to the boil, adding 1 tbsp of butter, salt and pepper. Put in the barley, stir well and simmer over low heat. Fry the finely chopped onion in butter (but do not let it brown), put in the mushrooms cut into strips. Sauté them, stirring all the time, add salt and pepper to taste, sprinkle with water. Put the lid on and simmer till they are tender. Grease an ovenproof dish with butter and dust it with breadcrumbs. Put in half of the kasha, spread the mushrooms on top, then cover with the remaining barley. Mix the cream with the egg, salt and pepper, pour over the kasha, sprinkle with the cheese. Put into a preheated oven for 15 mins.

serves 4 • Preparation: 50–55 mins

Pearl barley and cheese cutlets

250 g pearl barley, 3 cups stock, 200 g curd
cheese, 2 eggs, 2 tbsps each breadcrumbs and
ground sunflower seeds, 3 tbsps butter, salt,
pepper, a pinch of sugar, fat for frying

Mix the breadcrumbs with the sunflower seeds. Rinse the barley, then drain it. Bring the stock to the boil, put in the barley, add 1 tbsp of butter and cook over fairly high heat for several minutes. Mix in the remaining butter, cover the pan and put into a preheated oven for 25 mins. Take it out and leave to cool a bit, then put it through a mincer together with the cheese. Add salt, pepper and sugar to taste, break in the eggs and mix thoroughly. With moist hands shape small cutlets, dredge them with bread-crumb and sunflower mixture and fry in hot fat on both sides until golden brown.

serves 4 • Preparation: 40 mins

Maize kasha

Maize bake

300 g maize kasha, 250 g bryndza, 4 tbsps butter, salt

Bring 1 litre of salted water to the boil, put in the kasha, add 2 tbsps of butter and, stirring frequently, cook over low heat for 15 mins. Grease an ovenproof dish with butter. Put in alternating layers of kasha and crumbled bryndza, finishing off with the maize. Melt the remaining butter, pour over the kasha. Cover with aluminium foil and put into a preheated oven (190°C). Bake for 40 mins.

serves 4 • Preparation: 50–55 mins

Maize groats

300 g maize kasha, 2 tbsps butter, salt

Bring 1 litre of salted water to the boil, put in the kasha and, stirring occasionally, cook for 15 mins. Cover the pan and put it in a preheated oven or into a larger pot filled with boiling water. Bake or cook for 40 mins. Towards the end add the butter. Before serving, pour over some sweet juice. You may also serve it with the main course.

serves 4 • Preparation: 50–55 mins

Rice

Rice was first brought to Poland in the early 16th century, when it was originally used to cook a dish called *bijanka*, the pièce de résistance of Old Polish cuisine, which was served at the royal court only on special occasions. According to old cookery books, *bijanka* was a mixture made from rice flour, milk and almonds, 'steeped in rose water or some other scent'. Since the 19th century, rice has been used in Poland to prepare many delicacies, often variations on Italian or Oriental dishes.

Savoury rice salad

1 cup cooked long-grain rice, 3 pickled red peppers, 1 tin anchovy, 1 small tin tuna in oil, 5–6 olives, 2 small gherkins, 4–5 pickled onions, 6–8 pickled button mushrooms, lemon juice, 1 tsp grated lemon rind

Savoury rice salad

DRESSING: 2–3 tbsps oil, 3 tbsps ketchup,
1 tbsp lemon juice, salt, pepper, sugar

Mix the oil with the oil from the tuna and with the ketchup, add salt, pepper and sugar to taste. Sprinkle the rice with lemon juice, add the lemon zest, mix thoroughly and leave for 15 mins. Crumble the tuna with a fork, cut the anchovies into thin strips. Cut the peppers, gherkins, mushrooms and olives into strips. Combine all the ingredients, pour over the dressing, mix thoroughly. Refrigerate.

Note: You may heat this salad up in a saucepan and then serve it with kebabs.

serves 4 • Preparation: 15 mins

Green peas and ham salad

1½ cups cooked long-grain rice, 1 tin green peas,
200 g lean ham, 1 large red pepper, 3 tbsps chopped
walnuts, 3 tbsps raisins, 1 tbsp chopped fresh
marjoram leaves, 1 tbsp each chopped parsley and
dill, 3 tbsps lemon juice, 6 tbsps sunflower or olive
oil, pepper, a pinch of sugar, 2–3 small tomatoes

Sprinkle the rice with lemon juice and leave aside for 15 mins. Cut the pepper and ham into thin strips. Blanch and drain the raisins. Drain the peas. Combine all the ingredients, add salt, pepper and sugar to taste. Pour over the oil, mix thoroughly. Put into the fridge to chill. Before serving, garnish with tomato quarters and marjoram sprigs.

serves 4 • Preparation: 15 mins

Herring and rice salad

1 cup cooked rice, 1 tart apple, 1 tsp grated
lemon rind, 1 tbsp lemon juice, ½ cup milk,
1 herring, 1 salted cucumber, 1 pickled red pepper,
1 small onion, 2 tbsps chopped parsley

Dressing: 3 tbsps mayonnaise, 1 tbsp ketchup,
¼ tsp paprika, sugar, 1 tbsp lemon juice

Mix all the dressing ingredients, season to taste. Soak the herring in milk, then skin and bone it, and cut into small cubes. Chop finely the peeled onion and apple, cucumber and red pepper. Add lemon juice and zest to the rice, put in the remaining ingredients, mix thoroughly. Pour over the dressing, mix well again and leave in the fridge to chill. Sprinkle with parsley before serving.

serves 4 • Preparation: 15–20 mins

Chicken risotto

1 cup rice, 600 g cooked or roast chicken without
skin, 300 g fennel, 300 g tinned green peas, 3 tbsps
chopped dill, 2 tbsps oil, salt, pepper, ½ cup stock

Rinse and drain the rice. Cook it for 10–15 mins in 2 litres of salted boiling water. Pour in cold water, then drain the rice. Melt the oil in a thick-bottomed pan, put in the fennel cut into cubes and the chicken meat. Fry for a bit, stirring all the time, add salt and pepper to taste. Pour in the stock and simmer over low heat for 1–2 mins. Put in the rice and the drained peas, mix lightly, cover the pan and heat up over low heat for 7–10 mins. Before serving, sprinkle with chopped dill.

serves 4 • Preparation: 25–30 mins

Risotto with cep mushrooms

1 cup short-grain rice, 300 g fresh cep mushrooms,
1 large onion, 2 tbsps olive oil, 2 tbsps butter,
1 glass dry white wine, 1 tbsp tomato paste,
2 tbsps chopped parsley, 2–3 tbsps grated
Parmesan, 3 cups stock, salt, pepper

Rinse and drain the mushrooms, cut them into thin strips. Heat up the oil in a thick-bottomed pan, fry the finely chopped onion, add the mushrooms and parsley and sauté them, stirring frequently. Add the butter, put in the rinsed and drained rice. Stirring all the time, fry for 3–4 mins. Pour in the wine and 1 cup of stock, mix thoroughly. Cook over fairly low heat for 5–7 mins until the liquid has been absorbed. Pour in the remaining stock, add the tomato paste and simmer for another 15 mins, stirring occasionally. Before serving, sprinkle with Parmesan.

serves 4 • Preparation: 35–40 mins

Green risotto

1 cup short-grain rice, 3–4 cups vegetable or light meat stock, 500 g spinach, 1 large onion, 1–2 cloves of garlic, 1 tsp oregano, juice of 1 lemon, grated rind of ½ lemon, salt, pepper, 1 tbsp olive oil, 2 tbsps butter, 2 tbsps chopped walnuts

Rinse the spinach and simmer it in a covered pan in its own juices for 5–6 mins. Leave it to cool, then chop it. Heat up the oil in a pan, fry the finely chopped onion (without browning it) with crushed garlic and 1 tbsp of butter, put in the rinsed and drained rice. Stirring all the time, fry it for 4–5 mins. Pour in 1 cup of stock and cook until the liquid has been absorbed. Add the walnuts, spinach and oregano, pour in the remaining stock. Stir well, put the lid on and cook for 20 mins. Add the remaining butter, lemon juice and zest and simmer over low heat for 5–7 mins.

serves 4 • Preparation: 35–40 mins

Mushroom risotto

1 cup short-grain rice, 3 tbsps butter, 50 g mushrooms, 2 tbsps lemon juice, 1 tsp grated lemon rind, salt, pepper, 2–3 tbsps chopped parsley, 2–3 tbsps grated cheese, 3 cups stock

Melt 2 tbsps of butter in a thick-bottomed pan. Put in the rinsed, drained and chopped mushrooms and sauté them. Add the rinsed and drained rice and, stirring all the time, fry for 3–4 mins. Add salt, pepper, lemon zest and juice to taste. Pour in 1 cup of stock and cook until the rice has absorbed the liquid. Pour in the remaining stock, stir thoroughly. Put the lid on and cook over low heat for 20 mins. Before serving, mix in the remaining butter and the cheese, and sprinkle with parsley.

serves 4 • Preparation: 30–40 mins

Pilaf with smoked fish

1 cup long-grain rice, 3 cups milk, 400 g smoked fish (herring or mackerel), 4 tbsps butter, 100 g raisins, 100 g dried apricots, 50 g stoned prunes, 1 egg, 2 tbsps flour, a pinch of saffron, salt, 1 glass dry white wine

Pour the wine over the fruit and leave aside for 30–40 mins. Rinse and drain the rice, cook it in 2 litres of salted boiling water for 4–5 mins. Drain it, transfer to a thick-bottomed pan. Pour in the hot milk and cook over low heat until the rice has absorbed the liquid. Towards the end, add the saffron mixed in 1 tbsp of boiling water, stir thoroughly. Skin and bone the fish, cut it into small pieces and fry in 1 tbsp of melted butter. Melt 1 tbsp of butter in a small pan, put in the fruit together with the wine, cover the pan and simmer over low heat for 10 mins. Make a thin batter from the egg, 1 tbsp of water and flour. Melt 1 tbsp of butter in a thick-bottomed pan, pour in the batter, spread it evenly on the bottom. Put in the rice, pour over the remaining melted butter. Arrange the fish pieces and fruit on top. Cover the pan and cook over low heat for another 5–7 mins.

serves 4 • Preparation: 45 mins

Zucchini and rice bake

1½ cups cooked long-grain rice, 1 medium-sized zucchini, 1 cup single cream, 3 eggs, 200 g grated cheese, salt, pepper, a pinch of nutmeg, 2 tbsps butter, 1 cup stock, 1 tbsp lemon juice, 1 tsp grated lemon rind

Rinse the zucchini, peel it and cut into thick slices. Put it into a pan, pour over the hot stock and simmer over low heat for 10 mins. Take the zucchini slices out with a strainer, reduce the stock to half its amount. Mix the rice with the lemon juice and zest and with 1 tbsp of melted butter. Grease an ovenproof dish with butter, put in half the zucchini, spread the rice on top and cover with the remaining zucchini. Beat the eggs with the cream, add salt, pepper, nutmeg and cool zucchini stock. Pour the sauce over the bake, sprinkle the cheese on top, put in knobs of butter. Put into a preheated oven and bake for 30–35 mins.

serves 4 • Preparation: 40–45 mins

Prune bake

2 cups cooked rice, 5–6 dried mushrooms, 10–12 prunes, 3–4 tbsps chopped parsley, 2 tbsps lemon juice, 1 egg yolk, ½ cup cream, salt, pepper, 1 tbsp butter, 1 tbsp breadcrumbs inse the mushrooms and prunes, soak them separately in small amounts of water, then cook them and cut into thin strips. Reduce the prune stock to half its amount. Mix the rice with the lemon juice, mushrooms and prunes, add the chopped parsley. Beat the cream lightly with the egg yolk, add salt and pepper, pour in the prune or mushroom stock. Grease an ovenproof dish with butter. Put in the rice, pour over the cream. Put on top knobs of butter and sprinkle with breadcrumbs. Put in a preheated oven and bake for 20 mins.

serves 4 • Preparation: 30 mins

Lemony rice

1 cup long-grain rice, 3 tbsps lemon juice, grated rind of 1 lemon, 2 tbsps butter, 1 tsp ground pepper, salt

inse and drain the rice. Cook it in 2 litres of water for 10 mins, then drain it and pour over cold water. Mix the rice with pepper, lemon juice and zest, add salt to taste. Combine with the butter and put into an ovenproof dish. Cover the dish with aluminium foil and put in a preheated oven for 10–15 mins. Garnish with lemon slices. Serve with roast meat.

serves 4 • Preparation: 30–35 mins

Red rice

1 cup long-grain rice, 1 small onion, 1 clove of garlic, 1 tbsp chopped sage leaves, 4–5 beef tomatoes, 2 tbsps oil, 1 tbsp butter, 2 cups stock, salt

eat the oil in a thick-bottomed pan and brown lightly the chopped onion. Add the butter, crushed garlic and sage and, stirring all the time, fry for 2–3 mins. Put in the rinsed and drained rice and heat it up for 3–4 mins. Blanch and skin the tomatoes, cut them into cubes and add to the rice, pour in the stock, stir thoroughly. Put the lid on and simmer over low heat for 20 mins. Such rice goes perfectly with schnitzels, veal and chicken rolls and with roast chicken.

serves 4 • Preparation: 30–35 mins

Almond rice

1 cup long-grain rice, 2 cups stock, 1 tbsp butter, 150 g almond flakes, salt

inse and drain the rice, put it in a thick-bottomed pan, pour over the hot stock. Cover the pan and simmer over low heat for 20 mins. Toast the almond flakes in melted butter, add them to the rice. Add salt to taste. Put in a preheated oven for 5–7 mins. An excellent side dish with poultry and wild fowl.

serves 4 • Preparation: 25–30 mins

Orange rice

1 cup long-grain rice, 100 g butter, 2 oranges, 2 tbsps raisins, 1 tbsp sugar, 2 tbsps chopped almonds, ½ tsp curry powder, salt

inse the rice, cover it with cold water and leave aside for an hour, then drain it. Wash the oranges, blanch them, peel them finely. Put the peel into a small pan, pour in 2 cups of water and simmer over low heat for 10 mins. Drain the rind, then cut it into fine strips. Melt the butter in a thick-bottomed pan, put in the rice and, stirring all the time, fry it for 4–5 mins. Add the rinsed and drained raisins and salt to taste. Pour in 2 cups of boiling water. Stir thoroughly. Put the lid on and simmer over low heat for 20 mins. Cut one orange into fine cubes, remove the pips. Add the orange to the rice. Put in the almonds, orange rind and curry powder. Put into a preheated oven for 5–7 mins. Transfer to a warm serving dish, garnish with orange slices. This is a very fine addition to roast pork, poultry and veal. Without curry powder, it can make an excellent pudding served hot or cold.

serves 4 • Preparation: 40–45 mins

Rice with sage and hazelnuts

1 cup long-grain rice, 2 cups chicken stock, ½ cup chopped hazelnuts, 2 tbsps chopped sage leaves or 2 tsps dried sage, 3 tbsps butter, 2 tbsps chopped parsley, salt, pepper

Rinse and drain the rice, put it into a thick-bottomed pan. Add the sage, salt and pepper, pour in the stock, mix thoroughly. Put the lid on and cook over low heat for 20 mins. Melt the butter in a hot pan and toast the nuts for 2–3 mins. Add the nuts to the rice, mix the rice well, sprinkle it with parsley. Serve it with fried meat, fish and pultry.

serves 4 • Preparation: 25–30 mins

Sweet rice bake

2 cups cooked brown rice, 50 g raisins, 2 tbsps chopped almonds, 2 tbsps chopped nuts, 2 tart apples, 1 tbsp lemon juice, 2 eggs, 2 tbsps sugar, 4 tbsps butter, caster sugar

Peel the apples, grate them coarsely, sprinkle with lemon juice. Cream 2 tbsps of butter with sugar and, beating all the time, add one egg yolk at a time. Whisk the egg whites stiff. Mix the apples with the egg yolks, raisins, almonds and nuts. Add the mixture to the rice, fold in the egg whites. Grease an ovenproof dish with butter, put in the mixture, arrange knobs of butter on top. Put into a preheated oven and bake for 40 mins. Before serving, sprinkle with caster sugar.

serves 4 • Preparation: 50–55 min

CHAPTER VI

POTATO DISHES

✳ ✳ ✳

'Potatoes boiled with love taste better than sausage fried in anger,' says an old Polish proverb.

Potatoes appeared in Poland in the reign of Augustus II, on the royal estates where Saxon farmers, who brought them, had been settled. The Poles long despised them, claiming they were harmful to the health, and even the church taught this to the common people. When it was seen that in the Gdańsk area, among the Dutch and Germans settlers, potatoes cropped well, and were almost their only food, and kept them from hunger, and that they could be seasoned in many ways and many dishes made from them, potatoes were accepted by the neighbouring farmers, and then passed on to farther settlements, and became more and more widespread, so that at the end of the reign of Augustus III they were already well-known in Poland, Lithuania and Ruthenia, and today both the peasants and the gentry are nourished by them, and the higher classes do not despise them, and flour, vodka, wine and sugar are made from them

(Łukasz Gołębiowski, *Domy i dwory*, vol. IV, 1830)

In Poland they appeared for the first time in the 17th century. John III Sobieski sent them to his beloved queen Marie as a curiosity from the Imperial gardens in Vienna, but they got a mistrustful and cool reception at the royal palace at Wilanów outside Warsaw. 'Some special food hitherto unknown, strange, foreign, known as potatoes,' wrote Franciszek Morawski, the general and poet, in *My Grandfather's Court* (1783–1861). But before the end of the reign of Augustus III they began to be grown more generally, and by the reign of Stanislaus Augustus, they were being used for distilling vodka. They became really popular only after 1812, when they saved the population from starvation. And from that time on, Poland became a country of which the poet Włodzimierz Zagórski could write, 'Do you know the country where the potatoes grow ripe?'

It is difficult today to imagine a Polish menu without potatoes. For potatoes can be cooked in a variety of different ways. Connoisseurs steam them in their skins, and in this way all the taste and nourishment is retained.

Potatoes in the Parisian way

Grate peeled and boiled potatoes, mix them with fresh cream and two eggs, roll them in your hands into the shape of elongated potatoes, coat them with egg and breadcrumbs and fry in butter. Arrange them in a serving dish and garnish with parsley.

(*Praktyczny kucharz warszawski*, XXVII edition, 1926).

Purée. To make a good purée you need floury potatoes, hot milk and butter. Immediately after boiling and lightly drying them off you should put the potatoes through a ricer. Then cover them with hot milk, add butter and a pinch of grated nutmeg, place the pan with the potatoes over steam and mix firmly until you have a smooth, even, fluffy mass. Transfer the purée onto a warmed serving dish with a spoon that has been dipped in boiling water.
Rose purée has an interesting taste. Instead of milk, you pour warmed red wine into the grated potatoes. Green purée can be made by mixing the potatoes with sieved

cooked spinach; red by adding tomato paste and paprika; and golden by adding sieved cooked carrot.

French fries. French fries or chips should be fried in batches in very hot fat (oil or lard), and salted after being taken out of the chip pan. Remember that the fat must be heated up on its own to the required temperature; if it is not hot enough, the potatoes will absorb too much of it. Good results can be obtained by first throwing the sliced potatoes for two or three minute into boiling water. They should then be carefully dried on a tea towel and only then thrown into the hot fat. The secret of crisp chips lies in the careful drying of the potatoes before they are put in the hot fat.

Fried potatoes. These can be prepared using either raw or cooked potatoes. In the latter case, potatoes cooked in their jackets should be used. Raw sliced potatoes should be carefully dried on a tea towel. You then fry them under a lid over a low heat for twenty minutes, and then remove the lid and fry them for a few minutes over a higher heat. It is best to use clarified butter or oil for frying. Potatoes will brown very nicely and will have a crisp skin if you sprinkle them lightly with flour after slicing.

Baked potatoes. For baking you should choose large potatoes of uniform size. After washing them carefully, prick them with a fork (to prevent them bursting), wrap each in aluminium foil (with the shiny side inside), place on a baking sheet, and bake in a hot oven (220°C) for about an hour. Then remove the foil, cut them on the top in a cross and lightly squeeze so that they open; such potatoes can be served with herring, with flavoured butter or cream sauces, for example chive sauce.

You can also stuff baked potatoes. To stuff them, allow them to cool and then cut them in half, or slice off their tops, and carefully scoop out the inside, which should be finely chopped and added to the filling.

Boiled potatoes or potatoes cooked in their jackets are most suitable for noodles, bakes, salads, dumplings and potato cakes.

Potato pancakes will be white in colour if you add half a teaspoon of baking powder (to 1 kg of potatoes). You should however remember that baking powder accelerates the degeneration of B group vitamins, especially vitamin B².

Grated raw potatoes (for pancakes, dumplings and potato cake) should be placed in a linen bag and left for the juice to run out, after which the sediment (starch) should be added to them.

Potato salads

Potato salad with vegetables and herbs

5–6 potatoes cooked in jackets, 10 radishes, 3–4 beef tomatoes, 1 tbsp each chopped tarragon and lovage leaves, 2 tbsps each chopped dill and parsley, 1 tsp each chopped sage, mint and yarrow leaves

DRESSING: ½ cup each yogurt and mayonnaise, 1 tbsp lemon juice, salt, pepper, ½ tsp each ground paprika and caraway

Mix all the ingredients of the dressing and refrigerate. Blanch and skin the tomatoes, peel the potatoes, cut both into cubes. Chop the radish leaves finely, slice finely the radishes. Combine all the salad ingredients, pour over the dressing, mix thoroughly. This makes an excellent side dish with schnitzels, chicken cutlets and fried fish. The salad should be made shortly before serving.

serves 4–6 • Preparation: 20 mins

Potato salad with horseradish and hard-boiled eggs

500 g potatoes cooked in jackets, 3 hard-boiled eggs, 2 spring onions, 5–6 red radishes, 3 tbsps grated horseradish, 2 tbsps shredded horseradish, salt, pepper, ¾ cup yogurt, 2 tbsps olive oil, 1 tbsp lemon juice, a pinch of sugar, several parsley sprigs

Cut the peeled potatoes into cubes, sprinkle them with 1 tbsp of oil and with lemon juice, add pepper and salt, cover and leave aside for half an hour. Put the shredded horseradish into a sieve, pour over first boiling, then cold water, drain thoroughly. Slice the shelled eggs, chop the spring onions together with the leaves. Mix the yogurt with the remaining oil, grated horseradish, salt, pepper and sugar. In a salad bowl arrange alternating layers of potatoes, shredded horseradish and egg slices sprinkled with the chopped onion. Pour the dressing in, toss gently and refrigerate for 30 mins. Garnish with radish slices and parsley sprigs.

serves 4–6 • Preparation: 15 mins

Potato salad with peppers and herbs

4–5 potatoes cooked in jackets, 2 beef tomatoes, 1 each green and yellow pepper, 1 tbsp each chopped lovage, parsley, dill and chives, ½ tbsp each chopped sage and mint leaves, salt, pepper, 1 cup yogurt, 1–2 tbsps thick mayonnaise, 1 tsp lemon juice

Mix the mayonnaise with the yogurt, salt, pepper, sage and mint, chill it a bit. Blanch and skin the tomatoes and cut them into cubes. Core the peppers, rinse and dry them, cut them into strips. Cut the peeled potatoes into cubes, sprinkle them with lemon juice and a bit of pepper and salt. Combine them with the tomatoes, peppers and the chopped herbs. Pour the dressing over, toss gently and refrigerate for 30 mins.

serves 4 • Preparation: 15 mins

Potato salad with ham

4 large potatoes cooked in jackets, 100 g lean cooked ham, 2–3 beef tomatoes, a piece of each yellow, green and red pepper, 5–6 radishes, 2 cocktail gherkins, 4–5 spring onions, 2 tbsps lemon juice, pepper, 1 cup yogurt, 2 tbsps mayonnaise, 2 hard-boiled eggs, 2 tbsps chopped dill

Peel the potatoes, cut them into cubes, sprinkle with lemon juice, salt and pepper, then put into the fridge. Chop the onions finely. Peel the gherkins, skin the tomatoes, dice both. Cut the ham, radishes and peppers into strips. Combine all the above ingredient. Mix the yogurt with the mayonnaise. Pour the mixture over the potatoes. Toss gently but thoroughly, refrigerate for 30 mins. Before serving, sprinkle some dill on top and garnish with egg quarters.

serves 4–6 • Preparation: 40 mins

Potato side dishes

Potato purée with mint

800 g potatoes cooked in jackets, 2 egg yolks, 2 tbsps thick cream, 1 tbsp butter, 3–4 tbsps finely chopped mint leaves

Peel the potatoes, put them through a mincer. Pour in the melted butter, add the egg yolks and cream. Put the pan on top of a pot with boiling water and work the potatoes into a smooth paste. Add salt and mint and mix thoroughly. It is a perfect dish for lamb cutlets and roasts.

serves 4 • Preparation: 20 mins

Baked potatoes

16 new potatoes of equal size, 16 thin rashers, 250 g Gouda cheese, 2 onions, 1 tbsp caraway, 1 tsp freshly ground pepper, ¾ cup strong beef stock, 1 tbsp marinated green peppercorns, 2 tbsps butter, 1 tsp coarse salt

Put the peeled potatoes into boiling salted water for 5–7 mins. Separate the peeled onions into flakes. Wrap each potato in an onion flake and a rasher. Arrange them tightly in a greased ovenproof dish, sprinkle with ground pepper, green peppercorns and caraway. Pour in the stock. Cover the dish and put into a preheated oven for 10–15 mins. Take it out, remove the cover, put a thick piece of cheese on each potato, sprinkle the melted butter over. Return to the oven for another 10 mins.

serves 4 • Preparation: 40 mins • Baking: 50–55 mins

Savoury potatoes

1 kg potatoes cooked in jackets, 500 g fresh spinach, 1 onion, 3–4 cloves of garlic, 1 tbsp finely chopped ginger, 1 tsp each ground caraway, mustard seeds and turmeric seeds, ½ tsp each powdered fenugreek seeds and chilli pepper, 2 tbsps oil, salt

Rinse, drain and shred the spinach. Peel the potatoes and cut them into large cubes. Peel the onion and garlic and chop them finely. Heat up the oil in a large frying pan, sauté the onion, garlic and ginger, add the remaining spices and, stirring all the time, fry them for another 2–3 mins. Put in the potato cubes, mix thoroughly so that they are evenly dredged with spices. Put the spinach on top of the potatoes, cover the dish and simmer over low heat for several minutes. This is a dish that goes very well with fish and poultry.

serves 4–6 • Preparation: 15 mins

Onion potatoes

1 kg new potatoes of same size, 50 g butter, 1 cup onion juice, salt, pepper

Peel and rinse the potatoes, dry them, put in a pan, sprinkle with melted butter, and brown a bit. Add salt and pepper, pour in the onion juice. Cover the pan and put it into a hot oven for 30 mins, then remove the cover and bake for another 10–15 mins. Such potatoes go very well with pork and beef roasts.

serves 4 • Preparation: 50 mins

Herb potatoes

500 g potatoes, 1 cup chopped anise leaves, 1 fresh cucumber, salt, pepper, 50 g smoked fatty bacon

Cook the potatoes in their jackets. Peel them, cut into slices. Chop the bacon finely and render it in a large frying pan. Put in the potato slices and heat them up, add salt and pepper to taste. Take off the heat and add the chopped anise and cucumber. Serve hot with fried meat or fish.

serves 4–6 • Preparation: 30 mins

Baked potatoes

Dauphine potatoes

500 g potatoes cooked in jackets,
salt, pepper, oil for deep frying

DOUGH: 125 g flour, 80 g butter, 4 eggs,
a pinch of salt, 1 cup water

Bring the water with salt and butter to the boil. Take off the heat, pour in the flour and stir well. Put the pan again over low heat and stir all the time until the mixture no longer sticks to the walls. Take off the heat and, whisking all the time, break in one egg at a time. Put the peeled potatoes through a mincer, then fold them into the dough. Add salt and pepper to taste. Mix the dough thoroughly, then leave it to cool. Shape the dough into balls the size of walnuts and drop them into hot oil (hot but not smoking). When they are nicely golden and float to the top, take them out with a strainer and drain on absorbent paper. Serve immediately.

Note: To make this dish, you need very dry floury potatoes, therefore you are advised to cook them the day before. Remember that the fat should not be too hot, otherwise the potato balls will get burnt and will not puff up. You should not deep fry more than five to ten balls at a time. You may prepare the potato balls the day before, keep them covered in the fridge, and fry them shortly before serving.

serves 4 • Preparation: 40 mins • Frying: 10–15 mins

Stewed potatoes with prunes

1 kg potatoes, 250 g prunes, 2 onions, 2 tbsps butter,
1 tsp dried thyme, 2–3 cloves of garlic, 4 tbsps chopped
dill, 2–3 sprigs of fresh coriander (or parsley), 1 cup stock

Rinse the prunes and soak them in a small amount of water, then drain them and cut into strips. Chop the onion finely. Slice the peeled potatoes. Melt the butter in a flat pan, put in the potatoes and sauté them, then add the prunes and onion, mix carefully and fry them together for a bit longer. Sprinkle with salt, pepper and thyme, pour in the hot stock, put in the crushed garlic and the chopped greens. Cover the pan and simmer over low heat for 40 mins. Towards the end, remove the lid and

reduce the liquid a bit. An original side dish for all kinds of roast meat.

serves 4–6 • Preparation: 20 mins • Cooking: 40 mins

Potatoes in yogurt

1.3 kg potatoes, 3–4 tbsps oil, 1 tsp each caraway
seeds, ground coriander and cayenne pepper, ½ tsp
black mustard seeds, salt, 1 clove of garlic, 2 cups light
stock, ½ cup yogurt, 2 tbsps fresh coriander or parsley

Peel and rinse the potatoes, dice them into cubes, drain them in a sieve. Heat up the oil in a pan, add the caraway, mustard seeds and cayenne, cover the pan and fry until the mustard seeds stop popping. Remove the lid, put in the potatoes, mix well. Add the finely chopped garlic, pour in the stock and cook uncovered over fairly high heat for 20 mins. Pour in the yogurt mixed with the ground coriander, mix thoroughly and simmer over low heat for 5–7 mins. Before serving, sprinkle with chopped coriander. Serve as a separate dish or as a side dish with meat.

serves 4–6 • Preparation: 10 mins • Cooking: 50–55 mins

Stuffed potatoes

Potatoes with asparagus stuffing

*8 large potatoes cooked in jackets, 500 g (or 2 tins)
green asparagus, 100 g almond flakes, 1 clove
of garlic crushed with salt, 1 tsp lemon juice,
¼ tsp paprika, salt, pepper, 1 tbsp butter*

Cut the cooked potatoes lengthwise, carefully scoop out the inside, leaving only a thin layer lining the peel. Clean the asparagus and cook it in salted water. Drain it, cut off the tops and blend the rest together with the chopped almonds, half the potato pulp, butter, garlic and salt, pepper, paprika and lemon juice, working it into a smooth purée. Stuff the potato skins with the mixture, decorate each with the asparagus tops. Arrange the potatoes in a greased ovenproof dish, put into a preheated oven for 10 mins.

serves 4 • Preparation: 20 mins • Baking: 10 mins

Potatoes stuffed with liver, baked in foil

*8 rather large potatoes of equal size, 100 g pork
liver, 150 g minced pork, 1 large onion, 1–2 cloves
of garlic, 4 tbsps chopped chives, salt, pepper,
100 g grated cheese, 2 tbsps each oil and butter*

Scrub, rinse and dry the potatoes. Cut a slice off the top lengthwise. Scoop out most of the inside, leaving only a thin layer lining the peel. Fry (but do not brown) the chopped onion in 1 tbsp of oil, add the finely chopped potato pulp and liver, garlic and minced pork. Stirring all the time, fry the mixture for 4–5 mins. Add the chives, some salt and pepper to taste. Stuff the potatoes with the mixture. Prepare 8 pieces of aluminium foil, grease them with oil. Put one potato on each piece, sprinkle with some grated cheese, put on top a knob of butter. Wrap the foil tightly. Arrange the potatoes on a baking tin and put into a preheated oven (220°C). Bake for an hour. Serve with fresh salads.

serves 4 • Preparation: 20 mins • Baking: 1 hr

Potatoes stuffed with mushrooms

*8 large baked potatoes, 4 tbsps cream,
80 g grated cheese, 250 g finely chopped mushrooms,
2 tbsps butter, 2 tbsps chopped parsley, 2 eggs,
50 g finely diced ham, salt, pepper,
1–2 tbsps breadcrumbs*

Sauté the mushrooms in butter. Cut the potatoes lengthwise. Scoop out the inside, purée it with a fork, break in the eggs, blend with the cream and parsley into a smooth paste. Add the ham, mushrooms and grated cheese, mix thoroughly. Stuff the potatoes with the mixture, arrange them in a greased ovenproof dish, pour over melted butter, sprinkle with breadcrumbs. Put into a preheated oven for 15–20 mins.

serves 4 • Preparation: 15 mins • Baking: 15–20 mins

Potatoes stuffed with almonds

*8 large potatoes of equal size, 100 g chopped almonds,
3–4 cloves of garlic crushed with salt, juice of 1 lemon,
3 tbsps olive oil, 150 g finely diced mushrooms*

*SAUCE: 1 finely chopped onion, 2–3 cloves of garlic
crushed with salt, 1 tsp sweet paprika, ½ tsp cayenne
pepper or chilli, 1 tbsp wine vinegar or lemon juice,
100 g finely chopped almonds, 1 tsp each honey
and soya sauce, 1 tbsp oil, 2 cups light stock, salt*

Scrub the potatoes well, dry them, prick with a fork in several places. Arrange them on a baking sheet and put into a preheated oven for 50 mins. Mix the crushed garlic and salt with the lemon juice and almonds, adding gradually the oil. Cut the baked potatoes in half. Scoop out some of the inside. Add the potato pulp to the almond and garlic mixture, stir thoroughly. Add salt, pepper and diced mushrooms. Stuff the potatoes with the mixture. Arrange them in an ovenproof dish, put into a preheated oven and bake for 30 mins. Heat up oil in a pan, fry the finely chopped onion and garlic (but

Potatoes stuffed with cheese

do not let them brown), add paprika and cayenne, stir well and simmer over low heat for 2–3 mins. Add the honey, soya sauce, vinegar, stock and almonds. Mix thoroughly and simmer over low heat for 30 mins. If the sauce is too thin, add a teaspoon of potato flour mixed with 1 tbsp of water.

serves 4 • Preparation: 20 mins • Baking: 30 mins • Cooking: 30 mins

Potatoes stuffed with cheese

8 large potatoes cooked in jackets,
200 g low-fat curd cheese, 200 g Roquefort,
2 tbsps butter, 2–3 tbsps chopped chives,
1 tsp sweet paprika, salt, pepper, 1 tbsps coarse salt

Cut the potatoes lengthwise in half. Scoop out some of the inside and put it through a mincer together with the curd cheese and Roquefort. Add 1 tbsp of butter, salt, pepper and chives. Work the mixture into a fine paste. Fill the potato halves with the mixture and put each pair together. Grease a tin with butter. Arrange the potatoes on it, sprinkle them with paprika, salt and grated butter. Put into a preheated oven and bake for 15–20 mins. Serve hot or cold.

serves 4 • Preparation: 15 mins • Baking: 15–20 mins

Potatoes stuffed with spinach

8 large potatoes of same size, 2–3 cloves of
garlic, 200 g frozen spinach, 2 tbsps butter,
2 egg yolks, 2 tbsps each grated Parmesan and
Emmental cheese, salt, pepper, nutmeg

Peel the potatoes, cover them with lightly salted boiling water and boil them for 15 mins, then drain them and allow to cool. Cut off a slice from the top of each potato, scoop out the insides. Purée the pulp with a fork, then whisk it together with the egg yolks. Put in the spinach and mix thoroughly. Add salt and pepper to taste. Stuff the potatoes with the mixture, close each with the cut off top. Arrange them in an ovenproof dish greased with butter, sprinkle with grated cheese and put into a preheated oven. Bake for 10–15 mins (until the cheese gets nicely golden brown). Serve with salads.

serves 4 • Preparation: 10 mins • Baking: 10–15 mins

Potatoes stuffed with smoked bacon

8 large potatoes cooked in jackets, ½ cup finely
chopped love-in-a-mist leaves, 150 g processed
cheese, 100 g lean smoked bacon, 3–4 cloves
of garlic, 1 egg, 3 tbsps butter, salt, pepper

Cut the potatoes lengthwise, scoop out the inside carefully, leaving only a thin layer lining the peel. Dice the bacon finely. Chop finely the garlic, mix it with salt, pepper, butter, cheese and the potato pulp. Put in the love-in-a-mist leaves, break in the egg and work the mixture into a smooth paste. Fill the potato halves with the stuffing, arrange them in a greased ovenproof dish. Put into a preheated oven and bake for 20 mins. Serve with sauces or salads.

serves 4 • Preparation: 15 mins • Baking: 20 mins

Potatoes as main course

Peasant omelette

4 large potatoes cooked in jackets, ½ cup
chopped love-in-a-mist leaves, 1 largish onion,
100 g streaky bacon, 4 eggs, salt, pepper

Peel the onion and potatoes, cut them into thin slices. Heat up a large frying pan, render the bacon cut into cubes. Add the onion and sauté it, then put in the potatoes and fry them for another 4–5 mins. Mix the eggs with the chopped love-in-a-mist, salt and pepper, and pour the mixture into the frying pan. Cover and cook the omelette until the eggs have set.

serves 4 • Preparation: 15 mins

Potato blini

500 g powdered potato purée, 2 eggs, 2–3 tbsps flour, 70 g smoked ham or sausage, 1 tsp marjoram, salt, pepper, 2–3 tbsps butter

Cut the ham into fine cubes, mix with the eggs, marjoram, salt and pepper. Add the potato purée and flour and work into a not too thick batter. Fry the blini on a hot frying pan in melted butter. Serve with tomato or other salads, or else with cream sauce.

serves 4–5 • Preparation: 10 mins

Old Polish bake

8–12 cooked potatoes, 1–2 onions, 30 g dried mushrooms, 3–4 hard-boiled eggs, ¾ cup cream, salt, pepper, 2 tbsps butter, 2–3 tbsps breadcrumbs or chopped sunflower seeds

Rinse and drain the mushrooms. Soak them in a small amount of water, then cook. Drain them and chop finely. Reduce the mushroom stock a bit, add salt and pepper to taste, pour in the cream. Chop the peeled onion finely, slice the potatoes and eggs. Grease an ovenproof dish with butter and dust it with breadcrumbs or sunflower seeds. Put in alternating laters of potato slices, chopped onion, egg slices and mushrooms, finishing off with potatoes. Pour over the prepared mushroom sauce, sprinkle the remaining breadcrumbs or seeds on top. Put into a preheated oven for 20–25 mins. Serve with salads or salted cucumbers.

serves 4 • Preparation: 30 mins • Baking: 20–25 mins

Potato roll

8–10 potatoes, 1–1½ cup flour, 1 cup cream, 2 eggs, salt, pepper, 200 g pork fat, 100–200 g smoked meat trimmings, 2 large onions, 1 cup chopped parsley, salt, pepper, 2 tbsps butter

Chop the pork fat into small cubes, render it in a hot frying pan. Add the chopped onion and fry it, but do not let it brown. Put in the finely chopped smoked meat and, stirring all the time, fry for a minute or two. Add salt and pepper to taste. Take off the heat and add the chopped parsley. Put the cooked potatoes through a mincer, transfer them to a bowl. Break in the eggs, pour in the cream and, blending the mixture all the time, gradually add the sifted flour. Work into a smooth dough. Put the dough on a rolling board dusted with some flour, and roll it out to the thickness of 2 cm. Arrange the meat and onion mixture evenly on top and roll up the dough. Put the roll into a greased baking tin, sprinkle it with melted butter. Put into a preheated oven and bake until golden brown. Serve it hot, cut into thick slices, with salads, or cold, with a savoury sauce.

serves 4–6 • Preparation: 25 mins • Baking: 25–30 mins

Potato cake with mushrooms

1 kg potatoes, 100 g pork fat, 2 onions, 2 eggs, 2 tbsps flour, 1 tbsp semolina, salt, pepper, ½ tsp marjoram

Stuffing: 250 g cep mushrooms, 2 onions, 2 tbsps butter, salt, pepper, 2 tbsps thick cream

Wash and drain the mushrooms, cut them into thin strip and fry them in butter together with the finely chopped onion. Add salt and pepper to taste, cover the pan and simmer over low heat for 30 mins. Towards the end remove the lid and reduce the juices. Peel and wash the potatoes, grate them, squeeze out excess juice. Render the finely diced pork fat in a frying pan, add the finely chopped onions, mix well and fry for a bit. Put half of the potatoes into a well-greased baking tin, cover with the mushrooms and spread the remaining potatoes on top. Put into a preheated oven and bake for 20 mins. Take out, pour over the cream and bake for another 40 mins. Before serving, sprinkle with melted butter or pour over more cream (while baking the original cream will form a crumbly crust).

serves 4–6 • Preparation: 40 mins • Baking: 60 mins

Potato cake with cooked meat

1 kg potatoes cooked in jackets, 1 tbsp potato seasoning, 2 tbsps sour cream, 300–400 g boiled poultry, veal or beef meat, 2 onions, 2 eggs, 4 tbsps butter, salt, pepper, 2 tbsps breadcrumbs

Peel the potatoes and put them through a mincer, then blend them in a food processor together with one egg, cream, salt, pepper and potato seasoning. Put the cooked meat through a mincer. Chop the onion finely, fry it (without browning) in 1 tbsp of melted butter, allow it to cool, then mix with the meat. Add salt and pepper to taste and one raw egg yolk. Whisk the egg white stiff and fold it into the meat. Grease a large baking tin, sprinkle it with breadcrumbs and put in alternating layers of potato purée and meat mixture, finishing off with potatoes. Sprinkle with melted butter and put into a preheated oven for 30–40 mins. Serve hot with salads and lettuce, cream sauce or grated horseradish.

serves 4–6 • Preparation: 30 mins • Baking: 40 mins

Potato cake with roast goose

300–400 g roast goose trimmings, 1½ kg potatoes, 2–3 eggs, 1 large onion, 2 cups milk, ½ tsp pepper, salt, 1½ tsps marjoram, 1 tbsp butter, 1 tbsp breadcrumbs

Grate the peeled potatoes and onion, squeeze out excess juice (but do not press too hard). Mix the potatoes with the eggs, salt, pepper and marjoram, pour over the boiling milk and mix thoroughly using a wooden spoon. Cut the goose meat into thin strips. Grease a baking tin with butter and dust it sparingly with breadcrumbs. Put in alternating layers of potatoes and meat, finishing off with potatoes. Put into a preheated oven for one hour. Serve hot with cranberries or cream sauce, or cold with a savoury sauce.

serves 4–6 • Preparation: 25 mins • Baking: 1 hr

Potato bake with red wine

1 kg potatoes, 200 g smoked streaky bacon, 2 onions, 3 large tomatoes, 3–4 cloves of garlic, 1 cup dry red wine, ¼ cup stock, salt, pepper, ¼ tsp each dried tarragon and basil, a pinch of savory, 3 tbsps grated cheese, 1 tbsp butter

Cut the bacon into thin rashers and fry them lightly, then take the rashers out and fry the sliced onion in the fat. Chop the garlic finely and mix it with salt. Peel, rinse and slice the potatoes. Put the slices in a sieve, pour over boiling water, then drain the potatoes. Grease an ovenproof

Potato bake with red wine

dish. Put in alternating layers of potatoes, bacon, onion and sliced tomatoes, finishing off with a layer of potatoes. Sprinkle on top with garlic, pepper and herbs, pour over the wine and stock. Put into a preheated oven for 40 mins, then sprinkle the grated cheese on top and return to the oven for another 30 mins.

serves 4 • Preparation: 30 mins • Baking: 30 mins

Potato and curd cheese pudding

1 kg cooked potatoes, 500 g low-fat curd cheese, 1 tbsp cream, 4 raw egg whites, 3 tbsps each chopped chives and dill, salt, pepper, 3 tbsps butter, 2–3 tbsps chopped sunflower or pumpkin seeds

Put the cheese through a mincer, then blend it with the cream. Mince the potatoes, mix them thoroughly with 2 tbsps of melted butter, chives and dill. Fold in the cheese. Add salt and pepper to taste. Whisk the egg whites stiff and fold them into the mixture. Grease a baking tin with butter and sprinkle it with the chopped seeds. Put in the potato mixture, seal the tin and steam it for 40 mins. Serve hot with tomato salad or lettuce.

serves 4–6 • Preparation: 20–25 mins • Cooking: 40 mins

Herbal bake

1 kg potatoes, 2 onions, 2–3 cloves of garlic, 1 tbsp each chopped nettle leaves, sorrel leaves and marjoram, 1 tsp ground caraway, 2 eggs, 100 g grated cheese, 4 tbsps thick sour cream, salt, pepper, 1 tsp grated nutmeg, 1½ tbsps butter

Peel the potatoes, rinse them, then grate them and squeeze out excess juice. Chop the onion and garlic finely, sprinkle them with nutmeg. Mix well the potatoes with the onion, garlic and herbs, add salt and pepper to taste. Grease a baking tin with butter, transfer the potato mixture. Blend the eggs with the cream, add salt and caraway and pour over the potatoes. Arrange knobs of butter on top and put into a preheated oven. Bake for 50 mins. Take the tin out, sprinkle the cheese on top and return to the oven for another 15–20 mins. Serve with salads and sauces.

serves 4 • Preparation: 20 mins • Baking: 15–20 mins

Mushroom bake

200 g potatoes cooked in jackets, 400 g mushrooms (ceps, parasol mushrooms, oyster mushrooms), 4 hard-boiled eggs, 1 large onion, 1 cup thick sour cream, 1 egg yolk, 3 tbsps chopped parsley, 1 tbsp butter, 1 tbsp oil, salt, pepper

Heat up the oil in a pan and sauté the mushrooms cut into slices. Cover the pan and simmer over low heat, add salt and pepper to taste. Peel and slice the potatoes, eggs and onion. Grease an ovenproof dish with butter. Put in alternating layers of potatoes, eggs, mushrooms and onion, sprinkling each layer with pepper. Blend the cream and egg yolk, add salt and parsley. Pour the mixture over the potatoes. Put into a preheated oven for 30 mins. Serve with salted cucumbers or salads.

serves 4 • Preparation: 20 mins • Baking: 30 mins

Potato bake with tomatoes and ham

1 kg potatoes, 4 large beef tomatoes, 250 g ham, 250 g cottage cheese, 1 large onion, 1 cup stock, 1 tbsp butter, salt, pepper, ¼ tsp dried basil

Blanch and skin the tomatoes, cut into slices. Chop the onion finely, cut the ham into thin strips, crumble the cheese. Slice the peeled and rinsed potatoes, put them in a sieve, pour over boiling water and leave to drain. Grease an ovenproof dish with butter. Put in alternating layers of potatoes, ham, tomatoes, cheese and onion. Mix the stock with salt, pepper and basil and pour over the potatoes. Cover the dish with aluminium foil and put into a preheated oven for 35 mins. Remove the foil and return to the oven for another 30 mins. Serve with salads or with roast veal.

serves 4 • Preparation: 20 mins • Baking: 35 mins

Potato bake with onion and tomatoes

1 kg potatoes, 300 g tomatoes, 300 g onion, 100 g smoked bacon rashers, 3 tbsps butter, 3 tbsps chopped thyme leaves, salt, pepper

Blanch and skin the tomatoes, cut them into fairly thick slices. Slice the peeled and rinsed potatoes, put them in a sieve, pour over first boiling, then cold water. Do the same with the onion. Grease an ovenproof dish with butter. Put in alternating layers of potatoes sprinkled with salt and pepper, bacon rashers, onion and tomatoes. Sprinkle each layer liberally with the chopped thyme leaves and some melted butter. Cover the dish and put into a preheated oven for 40 mins. Remove the cover and return to the oven for another 10 mins.

serves 4 • Preparation: 15 mins • Baking: 50 mins

Potato bake with tuna

700 g potatoes, 250 g bread rolls cut into cubes, 1 tin tuna in oil, 1 cup dry white wine, 3 hard-boiled eggs, 3 tbsps chopped parsley, salt, pepper, ¼ tsp thyme, 1 tsp butter

Put the tuna in a bowl, crumble it with a fork. Add salt, pepper and thyme and blend with the wine. Put the bread cubes in a hot frying pan, add butter and fry them golden brown. Slice the peeled and rinsed potatoes and put them for 4 mins into boiling salted water, then drain them in a sieve. Pour half of the tuna sauce into an ovenproof dish, put in the potatoes and pour over the remaining sauce. Place the croutons on top.

Put the dish into a preheated oven for 50 mins. Before serving, sprinkle with finely chopped hard-boiled eggs and parsley.

serves 4 • Preparation: 25 mins • Baking: 50 mins

Potato layer cake

500 g potatoes baked in jackets the day before, 200 g sugar, 100 g finely chopped skinned almonds, 6–7 eggs, 2 tsps grated lemon rind, 1 tsp grated orange rind, ¼ tsp cinnamon, ¼ tsp ground cloves, 1 tbsp butter, plum jam

Peel the potatoes and put them through a mincer. Beat the sugar and egg yolks until foamy, adding gradually the lemon and orange zest, almonds, cinnamon and cloves, and then the potato purée a spoon at a time. Work the whole into a smooth mixture. Whisk the egg whites stiff and fold them in. Pour the potato dough into a greased baking tin and put into a medium-hot oven. Bake for 45–50 mins. Slice the cool cake horizontally into two or three layers and spread each layer generously with plum jam. You may also sprinkle the cake with some lemon juice.

serves 4 • Preparation: 30 mins • Baking: 45–50 mins

CHAPTER VII

GARNISHES

Soup garnishes

Forcemeat, a mixture of raw meat – chopped or minced veal, chicken, beef, pork and suet – and white bread, eggs and butter, seasoned with nutmeg, ginger and pepper. It serves to make small meat balls called pulpety or as stuffing for veal brisket, suckling pig, capon, poulard, kohlrabi or cabbage.

Łukasz Gołębiowski, *Domy i dwory*, vol. IV, p. 54

Meat or fish balls, or quenelles, served with soup became popular in Poland in the 19th century. They were made from suet, brains, crayfish, fish and various kinds of meat.

Suet balls

250 g beef kidney suet, 2–3 tbsps breadcrumbs, 2 tsps strong beef stock, 2 eggs, 2 tbsps chopped parsley, salt, pepper, nutmeg

Clean the suet of the membranes, cut it into fine cubes, then pound together with the stock, salt, pepper, nutmeg and eggs. Add the chopped parsley and sifted breadcrumbs. Mix thoroughly. With damp hands shape small balls. Drop them into boiling clear beef soup or boiling salted water. Serve with beef consommé or other clear soups.

serves 4 • Preparation: 20 mins • Cooking: 5–6 mins

Liver balls

150 g veal liver, 50 g kidney suet, 2–3 tbsps breadcrumbs, 1 tsp marjoram, salt, pepper, 1 egg

Put the suet and liver, from which the membranes have been removed, through a mincer. Break in the eggs, add the sifted breadcrumbs, marjoram, salt and pepper and work into a smooth paste. Shape small balls and cook them in boiling water. Serve with tripe or beef consommé.

serves 4 • Preparation: 15 mins • Cooking: 5–6 mins

Brains balls

500 g veal brains, 1 egg, 1 small onion, 1 tsp butter, 1–2 mushrooms, 2 tbsps breadcrumbs, ½ lemon, salt, 1 tbsp chopped parsley

Remove the membranes from the brains. Bring some water with lemon juice to the boil, put in the brains and cook for 5 mins. Stew the finely chopped onion and mushrooms in butter. Put the brains, onion and mushrooms into a bowl, break in the egg, add parsley, salt and sifted breadcrumbs, and work into a paste. Moisten your hands and shape small balls from the mixture. Drop the brains balls into salted boiling water. Serve with soup, for example lemon or dill soup.

serves 4 • Preparation: 15 mins • Cooking: 5–6 mins

Bone marrow balls

150 g beef bone marrow, 4–5 tbsps sifted breadcrumbs, 2 eggs, 1 grated medium-sized onion, 2–3 chopped cloves of garlic, salt, pepper, ¼ tsp nutmeg, 1 tbsp finely chopped parsley xtract the marrow by tapping the bone lightly. Whisk it together with the eggs to form a smooth paste. Add the breadcrumbs, onion, garlic, parsley and salt, season with pepper and nutmeg. Mix thoroughly. With moistened hands shape small balls. Drop the marrow balls into boiling water and simmer over low heat for 10 mins. Serve with consommé.

serves 4 • Preparation: 15 mins

Balls from roast veal trimmings

125 g roast veal, 1 tbsp thick cream, 1 tbsp butter, 2 tbsps sifted breadcrumbs, 1 small onion, salt, pepper

hop the veal and onion very finely. Pound them together with the remaining ingredients. Form the mixture into small balls and cook them in boiling water or consommé. Serve with consommé or red beet soup.

serves 4 • Preparation: 15 mins • Cooking: 5–6 mins

Savoury white bread croutons

1 cup oil, 1 tsp ground coriander seeds, 2–3 cloves of garlic crushed with salt, ¼ tsp pepper, white bread

ut the bread into thin slices, then into cubes. Heat up the oil in a pan, add the spices and garlic. Put in the bread, brown it golden brown, then take out with a strainer onto a kitchen towel to absorb the oil. You may prepare a larger quantity of croutons and preserve them in a metal tin, to be used when required.

serves 4 • Preparation: 10 mins

Brown bread croutons for white borsch or pea soup

brown bread, 1–2 tbsps butter, 1–2 tbsps milk, paprika

ut the bread into fairly fine cubes, arrange on a plate and sprinkle with milk. Melt the butter in a hot frying pan, put in the bread and, shaking the pan occasionally, dry up the bread cubes over low heat. Transfer to a heated bowl and sprinkle with paprika.

serves 4 • Preparation: 10 mins

Parmesan omelette cubes

2 eggs, 1 tsp butter, ½ cup milk, 30 g grated Parmesan, 1 tbsp chopped parsley, salt, a pinch of pepper

hisk the eggs with the milk, add the parsley, salt and pepper, put in the cheese. Grease an ovenproof dish with butter and heat it up. Pour the cheese mixture into the dish and put it into a preheated oven. When the mixture sets and rises, take it out, cut into cubes and allow to dry. Serve with clear soups.

serves 4 • Preparation: 15 mins

Semolina cubes

150 g semolina, 1 tsp butter, 2 cups light stock, salt

ring the stock to the boil, pour in the semolina. Stirring frequently, cook over low heat for 15 mins. Grease a large flat serving dish sparingly with butter. Put in the semolina, spread it out in an even layer and leave to cool. When it sets, cut it into small cubes. Serve with consommé or other clear soups, for example tomato soup.

serves 4 • Preparation: 35 mins

Chou pastry balls

40 g flour, 30 g butter, 1 egg, a pinch of salt

ring 3 tbsps of water with butter to the boil. Pour in the flour and whisk the mixture over low heat. Allow it to cool, break in the egg, add salt and stir it again with a spatula. Leave it in a cool place until the pastry has set. With a teaspoon or a piping bag with a small nozzle pipe small pastry balls onto a greased baking sheet, leaving enough space for swelling. Sprinkle with flour, put into a preheated oven and bake until golden brown. Chou pastry balls may also be deep fried in a large pan, remember however that you should put several balls at a time, so that they do not stick together when they expand, and then transfer them onto kitchen towel that will absorb excess fat. Serve with cream soups.

serves 4 • Preparation: 15 mins • Baking: 20 mins

Profiteroles

125 g flour, 125 g lard, 5 eggs, a pinch of salt

Bring to the boil ½ cup of water with lard, pour in the flour, add some salt. Mix over low heat until a smooth paste is obtained. Transfer the mixture to an earthenware bowl and continue stirring, blending in one egg at a time. Put the pastry into the fridge for one or two hours to allow it to set. Grease a baking sheet and dust it with flour. With a soup spoon or a piping bag pipe small portions of the pastry onto the baking sheet, spacing them out so they do not stick to each other when they swell. Put into a preheated oven. When the profileroles have risen and turned light golden, turn down the heat and leave them in the oven for 30 mins, allowing them to dry. Cut the profiteroles in half. Fill each half with some stuffing, sprinkle with grated cheese and bake shortly before serving.
Note: You may bake a larger quantity of profiteroles and keep them in a dry place for later use (without filling).

serves 4 • Preparation: 15 mins • Baking: 30 mins

Savoury shortcrust cookies

250 g butter, 3 cups flour, ½ cup milk, 40 g yeast, 2 tsps ground caraway, salt, a pinch of each pepper and savory, 1 egg

On a pastry board, mix the butter and flour with a knife to form a sandy mixture. Add the yeast mixed with the milk to the flour, combine with caraway, salt, savory and pepper. Work into a smooth dough. Leave in a cool place to rest. Roll out the dough and cut out small cookies from it. Arrange the cookies on a greased baking sheet, brush them with lightly whisked eggs. Put into a preheated oven and bake until golden brown. Serve with soups.

serves 4 • Preparation: 20 mins • Baking: 20 mins

Diablotins

½ French loaf, 2 tbsps butter, 2 egg yolks, 2 tbsps grated tangy cheese, ¼ tsp chilli, a pinch of salt

Cream the egg yolks with the butter, add salt, chilli and cheese. Cut the loaf into thin squares and spread each with the butter mixture. Arrange the squares on a greased baking sheet and put into a preheated oven for 5 mins. Serve with borsch, consommé and other clear soups.

serves 4 • Preparation: 5 mins • Baking: 5 mins

White cubes for cream soups

2–4 egg whites, salt, 1 tbsp wine vinegar or lemon juice

Bring salted water mixed with vinegar to the boil. Put in the egg whites and cook them. When they set, strain them, allow to cool and cut into cubes. Serve with cream soups or beef consommé.

serves 4 • Preparation: 5 mins • Cooking: 5 mins

Delicious snow balls for fruit soup

3–4 egg whites, 100–150 g caster sugar, a pinch of ground cloves or cinnamon

Whisk the egg whites, adding gradually the sifted sugar and spices. When the mixture is stiff and glassy, scoop bits of it with a hot teaspoon and drop into boiling water. Simmer for a while, then take out with a strainer.

serves 4 • Preparation: 5 mins • Cooking: 5 mins

Puréed vegetables

Red beet purée

5–6 baked beets, 5–6 boiled floury potatoes, 2 small red onions, 2 tbsps butter, 1 tsp caster sugar, 1 tbsp lemon juice, ½ cup thick sour cream, salt, pepper, 2–3 tbsps chopped dill

Sauté the finely chopped onions in butter. Peel the beet roots and potatoes, put them through a blender together with salt, pepper, sugar and cream. Add the lemon juice and onion, mix thoroughly. Transfer to a warm serving bowl and heat it up by steaming. Before serving, garnish with dill. Serve with fish and meat dishes.

serves 4 • Preparation: 15 mins • Heating: 10 mins

Aubergine purée with sesame seeds

2 aubergines, 2–3 cloves of garlic, 2 tbsps sesame seeds, ½ cup olive oil, ½ cup lemon juice, salt, 2 tbsps chopped parsley

Rinse and dry the aubergines, cut them lengthwise in half. Place them in an ovenproof dish, put into a pre-heated oven and bake until golden brown. Leave them to cool, then peel them, remove the seeds. Dry roast the sesame seeds. Crush the finely chopped garlic with salt, add 1 tsp of lemon juice. Liquidize the aubergines, garlic and sesame seeds, gradually adding the remaining lemon juice and the oil. Add some salt to taste and refrigerate for a while. Serve as an hors-d'oeuvre, garnished with chopped parsley.

serves 2 • Preparation: 30 mins • Chilling: 30 mins

Aubergine purée with coriander

4 medium-sized aubergines, 1 large red onion, 2–3 cloves of garlic, 1 tsp ground coriander, juice and grated rind of 1 lemon, 1½ tbsps olive oil, salt, a pinch of each salt and cayenne pepper or chilli, ¾ cup yogurt, 2 tbsps chopped parsley

Cut the aubergines lengthwise in half, sprinkle them with salt and leave aside for one hour. Then rinse them, dry, grease with oil, arrange on a baking sheet and put into a preheated oven. Bake them for 20 mins. Heat up oil in a pan, fry the finely chopped onion (but do not let it brown), add the chopped garlic, coriander and cayenne, and stirring all the time, fry for 2–3 mins. Put in the peeled and cubed aubergines, add the lemon zest. Stir well, put the lid on and cook for several minutes. Take off the heat, add lemon juice, salt, sugar and yogurt. Liquidize the mixture, then reduce it a bit. Heat it up, stirring lightly. Before serving, garnish with chopped parsley. Serve with white bread or as a side dish with roast meat.

serves 4 • Preparation: 35 mins

Broad bean purée

600 g young broad beans, 4–5 cloves of garlic, 2–3 spring onions, 2 tbsps chopped parsley, 4 tbsps olive oil, 1 tbsp lemon juice, salt

Rinse the beans, put in a pan, cover with boiling water and cook over low heat for 25 mins. Purée the beans in a bowl. Put the bowl on top of a pan with boiling water, add the lemon juice and crushed garlic. Stirring all the time, gradually pour in the oil. Transfer to a warm serving plate, garnish with parsley and finely chopped spring onions.

serves 4 • Cooking: 25 mins • Preparation: 5 mins

Brussels sprouts purée

800 g Brussels sprouts, 2–3 cloves of garlic, 2 tbsps butter, juice and grated rind of 1 lemon, ½ tsp each nutmeg and pepper, salt, ¼ tsp sugar, 2 tbsps dry white wine, ½ cup thick cream

Rinse and drain the Brussels sprouts, dice them finely, add the chopped garlic. Melt the butter in a double-bottomed pan, put in the sprouts and sauté them. Sprinkle with wine, cover the pan and simmer over low heat for 15 mins. Add salt, pepper, sugar, nutmeg, lemon juice and zest. Pour in the cream, stir thoroughly and cook uncovered for another 15–20 mins, stirring frequently. Serve with cutlets, medallions and fillets.

serves 4 • Preparation: 20 mins • Cooking: 15–20 mins

Brussels sprouts purée with almonds

800 g Brussels sprouts, 3–4 cloves of garlic, 3 tbsps butter, 2–3 tbsps chopped almonds, ¾ cup thick cream, ¼ tsp nutmeg, juice of 1 lemon, salt, pepper

Rinse and drain the Brussels sprouts, dice them finely. Melt the butter in a double-bottomed pan, put in the sprouts and chopped garlic and sauté them. Pour in the lemon juice, add salt, pepper and nutmeg, put in the cream. Stir well, then simmer over low heat for 30–40 mins, stirring frequently.

serves 4 • Preparation: 10 mins • Cooking: 40 mins

Spicy onion purée

*1 kg onion, 125 g butter, 1 tsp salt, a pinch of each
ground cardamom, cinnamon, cloves, ginger,
pepper and love-in-a-mist, 4–5 tbsps honey,
3 tbsps lemon juice, ½ tsp grated lemon rind*

Melt the butter in a pan, put in the chopped onion and
all spices. Stir well and fry for a bit, then put the lid on
and simmer over low heat for 30 mins, stirring occasionally.
Add the honey, lemon juice and zest. Liquidize the mixture.
Simmer it in an uncovered pan for 30 mins, stirring very
frequently. Serve as a side dish with fried meat.

serves 4 • Preparation: 35 mins • Frying: 30 mins

Sweet and sour zucchini and pumpkin purée

*500 g zucchini, 500 g pumpkin, 200 g onion,
60 g finely chopped fresh ginger, juice and
grated rind of 1½ lemons, 1 cup dry white wine,
3 cloves, 2 sprigs of fresh thyme, salt, pepper,
1 tbsp sugar, 1 tsp chopped thyme leaves*

Dice the peeled pumpkin, zucchini and onions, put
them in a pan, add the lemon zest and juice, ginger,
sugar, cloves, thyme sprigs, salt and pepper. Pour in the
wine and bring to the boil, then simmer over low heat
for 1½ hours, stirring frequently and adding some more
wine or water if required. Remove the cloves and thyme
sprigs, reduce the liquid lightly. Garnish with chopped
thyme leaves. Serve hot with roast poultry, white meat
or fried liver.

serves 4 • Preparation: 10 mins • Cooking: 1½ hrs

Pumpkin purée

*1 kg yellow pumpkin, 2 tbsps butter, 1 tbsp each
flour and tomato paste, ½ cup each stock and
cream, 1 tsp lemon juice, salt, ¼ tsp cayenne
pepper, a pinch of sugar and pepper, 1 tbsp
each chopped chives, dill, parsley and mint*

Peel the pumpkin, remove the seeds. Rinse the pulp,
drain and grate it. Melt the butter in a pan, put in the
pumpkin, sprinkle with the lemon juice, add salt. Stir well,
pour in the stock and simmer over low heat for 15 mins.
Liquidize the mixture and heat it up. Mix the cream with
the flour, tomato paste and cayenne, pour into the pumpkin purée. Heat up until the purée has thickened. Add the
greens, stir well, add salt, pepper and sugar to taste. Serve
as a hot hors-d'oeuvre or as a side dish with roast meat.

serves 4 • Preparation: 10 mins • Cooking: 20 mins

White bean purée

*400 g white beans, 80 g dark raisins
(sultanas), 100 g almond flakes, 2 tbsps olive
oil, 2 tbsps lemon juice, 1–2 tbsps dry white
wine, 2 tbsps chopped dill, salt, pepper*

Rinse the beans, cover with boiled water and leave aside
for several hours, then cook them, adding salt towards
the end. Reduce the liquid, then put the beans through
a blender. Put the raisins into a bowl, pour in the wine
and leave aside for 15 mins. Chop the almond flakes, add
them to the bean purée. Heat up the oil in a pan, put
in the beans, add the raisins together with wine, and the
lemon juice. Stir thoroughly and simmer over low heat
for 10 mins. Add salt and pepper to taste. Before serving,
garnish with dill. Serve as a hot hors-d'oeuvre or as a side
dish with roast white meat (veal, turkey, chicken).

serves 4 • Soaking: 6–8 hrs • Cooking: 50 mins

Red bean purée

*500 g red beans, 2 onions, ½ cup chopped walnuts,
a pinch of each coriander, dried thyme, marjoram,
rosemary, basil and curry powder, 1–2 tbsps lemon
juice, salt, pepper, 1 tbsp olive oil, 1 tbsp butter*

Soak the beans in water for several hours, then cook
them until tender, adding salt towards the end. Take
off the heat and drain them (preserve the stock). Fry the
finely chopped onion in oil, but do not let it brown. Put
the onion, walnuts and beans through a blender, adding the
herbs and spices, lemon juice, salt, pepper and 1–3 tbsps
of bean stock. Grease an ovenproof dish with butter, put
in the purée. Sprinkle it on top with some melted butter

and put into a preheated oven for several minutes. Serve as a hot hors-d'oeuvre or as a side dish with roast meat.

serves 4 • Soaking: 6–8 hrs • Preparation: 15 mins • Baking: 10 mins

Mashed green peas

600 g green peas (fresh or frozen), 3 tbsps butter, 50 g tinned ham, 3 tbsps thick cream, salt, a pinch of each white pepper and sugar, 2 tbsps chopped parsley

Melt the butter in a pan, put in the peas and parsley, add sugar, cover the pan and simmer over low heat for 30 mins. Chop the ham finely. Put the peas through a blender, then sieve them. Add the ham and cream, salt and pepper to taste. Heat up over low heat. Serve with roast poultry or veal.

serves 4 • Preparation: 40 mins

Apple purée

750 g tart apples, 3–4 potatoes cooked in jackets, 2 tbsps butter, 3 tbsps thick cream, salt, ¼ tsp pepper, a pinch of sugar

Peel and core the apples, dice them, put into a pan with melted butter (1 tbsp), cover and cook. Put the peeled potatoes through a mincer, then liquidize them together with the cream, apples, salt and pepper. Melt the remaining butter in a pan, put in the purée and, stirring all the time, heat up over low heat. Serve with fried liver, cutlets and roast venison.

serves 4 • Preparation: 20 mins

Mashed cabbage

1 white cabbage (1.3 kg), 2 onions, 1–2 bay leaves, 2 tbsps butter, 1 tbsp flour, salt, pepper, ¼ tsp nutmeg, 1 tbsp lemon juice, 1 cup cream

Rinse the cabbage, cut it into quarters, put into boiling salted water and cook for 10 mins. Drain, put into a pan, add the bay leaves and chopped onions, cover with fresh boiling water and cook until tender. Drain the cabbage, take out the bay leaves (reserve ¼ cup of the cabbage stock). Put the cabbage and onion through a mincer.

Melt the butter in a pan, add the flour and make a white roux. Dilute it with the cabbage stock, add salt, pepper and nutmeg. Stirring frequently, cook it until the sauce has thickened. Pour in the cream, add the cabbage purée, stir well and heat up. An excellent side dish with roast goose and venison.

serves 4 • Preparation: 30 mins

Red pepper purée

1 kg red peppers, 2 tbsps butter, 1 tbsp lemon juice, salt

Rinse the peppers, remove the seeds. Put the peppers into salted boiling water, add 1 tsp of butter and lemon juice and cook for 20 mins. Drain the peppers, put them through a blender, then sieve them. Melt the remaining butter in a pan, add the purée and fry for a minute or two. Add salt to taste. Serve with fish or roast meat.

serves 4 • Preparation: 30 mins

Nettle purée with peanuts

500 g young nettle leaves, 2 tbsps olive oil, 1 chopped onion, ½ cup peanuts, salt, 1 tbsp lemon juice

Put the nettles in a sieve, pour over first boiling, then cold water, chop the leaves finely. Grind the peanuts. Heat up the oil in a pan, fry the onion (but do not let it brown), add the peanuts and, stirring all the time, fry for one or two minutes. Put in the nettles and simmer for another 5–10 mins. Add salt and lemon juice to taste. Mix thoroughly. An excellent side dish with roast meat, fillets, veal and poultry schnitzels.

serves 4 • Preparation: 20 mins

Mashed turnip

1 kg turnip, 2 tart apples, 1 tbsp dried marjoram, salt, pepper, 3 tbsps butter, 2–3 tbsps thick cream

Peel and wash the turnip, cut it into thick cubes. Put into a pan, cover with 2 litres of boiling water, add some salt and cook for 30 mins. Reduce the liquid and liquidize the turnip together with the cream, adding salt, pepper and marjoram. Peel and core the apples, cut them into thin slices and fry in butter. Grease an ovenproof dish with butter, put in the turnip purée, cover with the apples and sprinkle with melted butter. Put into a preheated oven for 10 mins. Best served with roast lamb or pork.

serves 4 • Preparation: 35 mins • Baking: 10 mins

Mashed celeriac

*1 large celeriac (600 g), 3–4 largish
potatoes cooked in jackets, 2 tbsps cream,
1 hard-boiled egg, 2 tbsps butter, salt, pepper,
1 tbsp lemon juice, a pinch of sugar, 2 tbsps
chopped chives*

Scrub the celeriac and cook it in salted water. Peel the potatoes and celeriac, add the hard-boiled egg and put all through a blender. Add the lemon juice, salt, pepper and sugar to taste. Melt the butter in a pan, put in the purée, stir thoroughly. Put the pan on top of a pot with boiling water and, stirring all the time, warm it up. Before serving, garnish with chopped dill.

serves 4 • Cooking: 20 mins • Preparation: 10 mins

Oriental celeriac purée

*2 celeriac (800 g), 1 largish potato,
1 piece of fresh ginger roughly the size
of a walnut, 2 tbsps lemon juice, 4 tbsps
butter, ½ cup thick cream, salt, pepper,
1 cup stock*

Peel the celeriac and potato, rinse them, cut into thick cubes. Chop the ginger finely. Melt 2 tbsps of butter in a pan, add the ginger, stir well. Put in the celeriac and potato, sprinkle with lemon juice, add salt and pepper to taste. Pour in the stock, put the lid on and cook for 20 mins. Take the lid off, reduce the liquid, then put the mixture through a blender and add the cream. Melt the remaining butter in a pan, put in the purée, mix thoroughly and heat up. An excellent side dish with venison and roast meat ą la venison.

serves 4 • Preparation: 30 mins

Savoury lentil purée

*500 g brown lentils, 2 onions, 2–3 cloves of garlic,
½ tsp each ground mustard seeds and ground pepper,
1–2 bay leaves, 2–3 tbsps olive oil, 2–3 cups light stock*

Rinse the lentils, put them in a pan, cover with the hot stock. Bring to the boil, then cook for 20 mins. Add the bay leaves, garlic crushed with salt, mustard seeds and pepper. Stir thoroughly, put the lid on and cook for 20 mins. Take out the bay leaves, liquidize the lentils. Chop the onion finely and fry it in hot oil, but do not let it brown. Add the lentil purée, stir well and heat up. Serve as a hot hors-d'oeuvre or as a side dish with cutlets.

serves 4 • Preparation: 10 mins • Cooking: 40 mins

Fried and breaded side dishes

Breaded celeriac

*800 g celeriac, 2 eggs, flour, breadcrumbs,
salt, pepper, 1 tbsp lemon juice, 2 tbsps
chopped parsley, oil for frying*

Scrub the celeriac and put it into salted boiling water. Cook for 10–15 mins, strain, pour over cold water. Drain well, peel and cut into thick slices. Sprinkle with some lemon juice, salt and pepper. Coat each slice in flour, lightly beaten eggs and breadcrumbs, then fry in hot oil until golden brown on both sides. Garnish with chopped parsley. Serve with meat, fish and egg dishes.

serves 4 • Preparation: 25 mins • Frying: 5 mins

Fried celeriac

2 large celeriac roots, 2 tbsps lemon juice,
white pepper, salt, 1 cup olive oil

Scrub and peel the celeriac, rinse and cut into slices. Sprinkle with some lemon juice and pepper. Heat up the oil in a large frying pan, put in the slices and fry them on both sides. Take them out with a strainer, transfer onto a paper towel to get rid of excess fat. Sprinkle sparingly with salt. Serve with meat, poultry or fish dishes.

serves 4 • Preparation: 10 mins • Frying: 10 mins

Celeriac chips

1 kg celeriac, 2 tbsps lemon juice, ½ tsp each salt,
curry powder and paprika, oil for deep-frying

Scrub the celeriac thoroughly. Put into boiling salted water and cook for 4–6 mins, then drain, pour over cold water, peel and cut into even, fairly large sticks. Heat up the oil in a frying pan, gradually put in the celeriac and fry each batch until golden brown. Transfer the celeriac chips onto a paper towel to get rid of excess fat. Put the chips in a warm serving dish, pour over some sauce, mix thoroughly. Serve immediately.

serves 4 • Preparation: 10 mins • Frying: 5–7 mins

Walnut croquettes

500 g cooked potatoes, 1 medium-sized onion,
100 g shelled walnuts, 2 eggs, 1 tbsp chopped
parsley, salt, pepper, flour, breadcrumbs,
sunflower oil or butter for frying

Put the potatoes through a mincer, add the finely chopped walnuts. Fry the finely chopped onion in butter, but do not let it brown. Add the parsley, 1 tbsp of breadcrumbs, salt, pepper and 1 egg. Fold into the potato and walnut mixture. Work into a smooth paste, then shape into small patties. Coat each croquette in flour, lightly beaten egg and breadcrumbs, and fry on both sides in hot fat. Serve with cabbage with mushrooms or as a separate dish with mushroom sauce.

serves 4 • Preparation: 15 mins • Frying: 10 mins

Savoury quenelles

Various savoury quenelles provide an excellent addition to soups, meat dishes, vegetable dishes or as a separate dinner course.

Gourmet's pike quenelles

1 kg pike, salt, pepper, nutmeg, 100 g flour,
150 g butter, ½ cup milk, 4 eggs

Nantua sauce: 200 g butter, 2 raw egg yolks,
2 tbsps dry white wine, 1 tbsp lemon juice, 2 tbsp
crayfish butter, pepper, cayenne pepper

CHILLING: 30 mins

Clean the fish, rinse it and dry. Remove the skin, spine and bones. Put the meat through a processor, add salt, pepper and nutmeg. Sieve the mixture, fold in the whisked egg whites. Put into a bowl, cover with foil and place in the fridge. Melt half the butter in a pan, pour in the milk, bring to the boil. Turn the heat down and, mixing all the time, gradually add the flour. Stir until the batter comes away from the edges of the pan. Take off the heat and allow to cool. Beat the remaining butter until fluffy, add the egg yolks one by one. When the batter has cooled down, fold in the butter and egg preparation and the fish, stirring all the time to produce a smooth mixture. With a teaspoon form small noodles and drop them into salted boiling water. Cook over low heat for 15 mins. Serve with fish soup or nantua sauce.
NANTUA SAUCE: Melt the butter in a pan, take off the heat and allow to cool. In another pan beat lightly the egg yolks with the wine, put the pan on top of a pot of boiling water and, whisking all the time, gradually add the butter. Add salt, pepper and cayenne, lemon juice and towards the end the crayfish butter.

Fish quenelles

500 g cooked fish, 2–3 tbsps breadcrumbs and
chopped walnuts, 3 eggs, 2 tbsps finely chopped
parsley, 1 onion, 1 tbsp butter, salt, pepper,
¼ tsp each nutmeg and grated lemon rind

Fry the finely chopped onion in butter, but do not let it brown. Chop finely the fish, put it through a mincer. Add the onion, breadcrumbs, walnuts, parsley, salt, pepper and nutmeg. Break in the eggs and work into a smooth mixture. Leave for 15 mins to mature. With a teaspoon shape small balls and drop them into salted boiling water. Cook for 5–8 mins. Serve with fish soup or with salads, sprinkled with melted butter.

serves 4 • Preparation: 15 mins • Maturing: 15 mins • Cooking: 5–8 mins

Cod quenelles

800 g cod fillets, 1 cup cream, 2 eggs, 1½ tbsps corn flour, 2–3 tbsps wheat flour, salt, pepper, 1 tsp lemon juice, 1 tbsp finely chopped parsley

Sprinkle the fillets with some lemon juice, then put them through a blender together with half the cream and refrigerate. Mix the remaining cream with the corn flour, add the fish meat, salt and pepper. Break in the eggs, add the wheat flour and work into a smooth paste. Cover and put into the fridge for an hour or two. With a spoon shape small quenelles and drop them into salted boiling water. Cook until they float to the surface. Serve with fish soup or some sauce.

serves 4 • Preparation: 10 mins • Chilling: 2 hrs • Cooking: 5–8 mins

Meat quenelles

200 g veal and pork, 1 large onion, 2 eggs, pepper, 1 tsp herbal salt, 1 tbsp butter, 2–3 tbsps flour

Fry the finely chopped onion in butter, but do not let it brown. Put the meat through a mincer, add it to the onion. Add salt and pepper, break in the eggs. Work the mixture into a smooth paste. Make small balls from the mixture, coat each ball in flour and drop into salted boiling water. Cook for 15 mins. Serve with consommé and other clear soups, e.g. tomato soup.

serves 4 • Preparation: 10 mins • Cooking: 15 mins

Liver quenelles I

150 g veal or chicken liver, 1 tbsp butter, 3 tbsps flour, 2 eggs, 1 tbsp chopped parsley, salt, pepper

Cream the butter, adding gradually the finely chopped liver, egg yolks, salt and pepper. Whisk the egg whites stiff, add them to the liver mixture, sprinkle with some flour and mix thoroughly. With a teaspoon shape small quenelles and drop them into boiling salted water. Cook covered for 8–10 mins. They go very well with consommé and caraway soup.

serves 4 • Preparation: 15 mins • Cooking: 10 mins

Liver quenelles II

150 g liver, 1 large onion, 2 tbsps butter, 2 eggs, 3–4 tbsps sifted breadcrumbs, salt, pepper, 1 tsp dried marjoram, 2 tbsps flour

Fry the finely chopped onion in melted butter, but do not let it brown. Put the livers and onion through a mincer, add the egg yolks, salt, pepper and marjoram. Pour in gradually the breadcrumbs, work the mixture into a smooth paste, towards the end fold in the whisked egg whites. With damp hands form quenelles the size of walnuts. Dredge each with flour and drop into boiling salted water.

serves 4 • Preparation: 15 mins • Cooking: 10 mins

Breadcrumb quenelles

2 cups breadcrumbs, 3 egg yolks, ¼ tsp ground caraway, salt, pepper, 2 tbsps chopped parsley, 3–4 tbsps water

Pour the breadcrumbs into a pan, add warm water and heat up, stirring all the time. Take off the heat, add salt, pepper, parsley, caraway and egg yolks and work into a smooth paste. With your hands shape small balls. Drop them into boiling salted water or deep-fry them. Serve with roast pork.

serves 4 • Preparation: 15 mins • Cooking: 10 mins

Lvov dumplings

300 g breadcrumbs, ½ cup cream, 80 g grated cheese, 2 tbsps butter, 1 onion, 100 g ham, 2 tbsps flour, 2 eggs, salt, pepper, 100 g mushrooms

Dice the onion and mushrooms finely, fry them in butter. Cut the ham into thin strips. Pour the cream over the breadcrumbs, stir well. Combine the breadcrumbs with the cheese, ham, onion and mushrooms, put in the egg yolks, add salt and pepper to taste. Work into a smooth paste, fold in the whisked egg whites, sprinkle with flour and mix lightly but thoroughly. With a teaspoon shape small dumplings and drop them into boiling salted water. Cook for 5–7 mins, then take them out with a strainer. Pour melted butter over the dumplings. Serve with salads.

serves 4 • Preparation: 15 mins • Cooking: 5–7 mins

Saxon dumplings

500 g breadcrumbs, 1 cup milk, 50 g butter,
3 eggs, 1 bread roll, 100 g ham, 30 g flour

Sift the breadcrumbs, pour over the boiling milk, stir well and leave to cool. Cream 30 g butter and, whisking all the time, add one egg yolk at a time. Put in the breadcrumbs soaked in milk and mix thoroughly. Cut the bread roll into small cubes and put into a hot frying pan, sprinkle with melted butter and brown lightly. Cut the ham into fine cubes and, together with the croutons, add it to the breadcrumb mixture. Fold in the whisked egg whites. Mix lightly but thoroughly. Shape small noodles, dredge them with flour and drop into boiling salted water. When ready, take them out with a strainer and arrange on a warm serving dish. Sprinkle with pork fat scratchings.

serves 4 • Preparation: 30 mins • Cooking: 10 mins

Polenta dumplings

500 g maize kasha, 2 cups light stock,
3 eggs, 3 tbsps butter, salt

Mix the eggs well with the stock. Pour the kasha into a bowl and gradually add the stock and egg mixture, stirring all the time. Add salt and pepper, then 2 tbsps of melted butter, and stir well. Grease a baking sheet with butter and spread the mixture out in an even layer. Sprinkle with melted butter and put into a preheated oven for 5 mins. Prick the kasha with a fork in many place, return to the oven and bake until golden brown. Cut into small squares or lozenge shapes. Serve with sauces, goulash or as a side dish with roast meat.

serves 4 • Preparation: 15 mins • Baking: 10 mins

Oatmeal dumplings

100 g oatmeal, 1–2 tbsps flour, 2 tbsps butter,
1 egg, salt, 3–4 tbsps hot milk

Pour the milk over the oatmeal, stir well and leave to soak. Then add the flour, 1 egg mixed with 1 tbsp of water and melted butter. Work into a smooth batter. With a teaspoon shape small dumplings and drop them into boiling salted water. Serve with soup or milk.

serves 4 • Preparation: 30 mins • Cooking: 10 mins

Herbal oatmeal dumplings

3 cups oatmeal, 1 cup boiled water, 1 cup milk,
1 tbsp butter, 2 tbsps wheat flour, salt, ½ tsp
each dried savory, marjoram and pepper

Pour the lukewarm water over the oatmeal and leave to soak for half an hour. Bring the milk with butter to the boil, add some salt. Put in the oatmeal and simmer for a bit. Put in the herbs and pepper, break in the eggs and work into a smooth paste, adding flour if required. Season to taste. Shape small dumplings and drop them into boiling salted water. Stir gently to prevent them from sticking to the bottom. Towards the end pour in 1 cup of cold water. Strain the dumplings. Before serving, pour over melted butter, cream or pork fat scratchings.

Preparation: 40 mins • Cooking: 10 mins

Spinach dumplings

800 g fresh spinach, 150 g bryndza, 100 g low-fat
curd cheese, 2–3 tbsps stifted breadcrumbs, 2 eggs,
4 tbsps butter, 100 g grated Parmesan, salt, pepper

Rinse the spinach and put it into salted boiling water. Cook for 4–5 mins, then drain and chop finely. Put the spinach into a pan and steam it a bit over low heat. Beat well the curd cheese and bryndza, add salt, pepper and 1 tbsp of butter. Stirring all the time, add gradually the spinach, breadcrumbs, eggs and half the Parmesan. Mix thoroughly and put in the fridge for 30–40 mins. With a teaspoon shape small dumplings and drop them into boiling salted water. Cook for 5 mins, then take out with a strainer. Arrange the dumplings in a greased ovenproof dish, sprinkle with melted butter and the remaining Parmesan. Put into a preheated oven and bake for 20 mins. Serve with roast veal or poultry.

serves 4 • Preparation: 15 mins • Baking: 20 mins

Vegetable dumplings

cooked soup vegetables (2 carrots, 1 parsley root, ¼ celeriac), 2 tbsps bran, 2 tbsps oatmeal, 2 tbsps flour, 2 eggs, 1 tbsp butter or oil, 2 tbsps chopped parsley, salt, pepper

Put the vegetables through a processor. Cream the butter with the egg yolks. Beating all the time, gradually add the vegetables (8 tbsps), bran, oatmeal, parsley, salt and pepper. Stir well. Fold in the whisked egg whites, add the flour, mix lightly but thoroughly. With a teaspoon drop small dumplings into boiling salted water and cook until they float to the surface. Before serving, sprinkle with melted butter or sauce.

serves 4 • Preparation: 15 mins • Cooking: 10 mins

Bean dumplings

2 cups beans, 1 cup flour, 1 tsp dried savory, 2 eggs, ¼ cup single cream, 1–2 tbsps water, salt, pepper

Rinse the beans, cover them with boiled water and leave to soak overnight. Cook the beans, drain them, allow to cool. Put them through a mincer, add the savory, salt, pepper, cream, flour and, if required, water. Work into a smooth dough. Sprinkle a pastry board with flour and shape a roll from the dough. Cut it diagonally into dumplings. Drop them into boiling salted water and cook for 5–7 mins. Before serving, sprinkle with melted butter or pour over some cream.

serves 4 • Preparation: 1 hr • Cooking: 5–7 mins

Mushroom dumplings

70 g dried mushrooms, 2 eggs, 2–3 tbsps flour, 1 small onion, 2 tbsps finely chopped parsley, salt, pepper

Soak the mushrooms in water overnight. Cook them, strain, then put through a mincer. Fry the finely chopped onion in 1 tbsp of melted butter, but do not let it brown. Cream the remaining butter with the egg yolks. Whisking all the time, add gradually the cold onion, parsley, flour, salt and pepper. Fold in the whisked egg whites and some flour. Mix lightly but thoroughly. With a teaspoon shape small dumplings and drop them into boiling salted water. Cook for 10–12 mins. Serve with consommé, mushroom soup or as a separate dish, sprinkled with melted butter.

serves 4 • Preparation: 10 mins • Cooking: 10–12 mins

CHAPTER VIII

SAUCES

***

Mikołaj Rej in his "Żywot człowieka poczciwego" (Life of an Honest Man), complains of "various new titbits, which are called puffers, for the peasant puffs after eating them".

Puffer was one of the Old Polish names for sauces. Łukasz Gołębiowski confirms that in old Polish cuisine sauces had many names. There was "kontuz, the juice squeezed from meat pounded in a mortar, extract from ham, and albarys or fresh bouillon. ...In addition the culinary art invented also: condiment, or sauce for a roast or stew, salsa, or a sharp and bitter seasoning for meat or fish". Old Polish cuisine had a multitude of sauces, and the favourites included: yellow sauce with saffron, red sauce with cherry juice, black sauce with plum jam and grey sauce with stewed onion. In addition, there were almond, wine, mushroom, herbal, milk, bread or beer pouring sauces; there were white sauces made with sour milk and sugar, pepper, cinnamon, ginger, caper, olives, nutmeg, plums or cherries. ...Black and yellow sauces were made to go with fish, eel, turkey or sucking pig. Sometimes, these sauces were served separately as an hors- d'oeuvre.

(Ł. Gołębiowski, Domy i dwory, vol. IV, pp. 53–54.)

Nobody needs convincing of the enormous importance of sauces, both hot and cold, in the kitchen. And although dieticians often turn up their noses at them, claiming that they are not very healthy, the French rightly call them "the poetry of the kitchen". It is sauces that give many dishes their unforgettable flavour.

Sauces are an enormous separate chapter in gastronomic and culinary lore; it is sauces that determine the flavour and aroma of a given dish; they are not a dish in themselves but an accompaniment. They should therefore be very carefully chosen to go with a particular dish. The very tastiest and most complicated sauce will spoil the whole effect if it is served as an accompaniment to the wrong dish. But the very simplest dish can be made unbelievably attractive by a well-chosen sauce.

Cold sauces

Sauce à l'andalouse

1 cup thick mayonnaise, 1 tsp ketchup, 3 red peppers, salt

Dice the peppers finely, mix them with the mayonnaise, ketchup and salt. Chill a bit. Serve with smoked meat and hard-boiled eggs.

serves 4 • Preparation: 10 mins • Refrigerating: 30 mins

English sauce

1 lemon, 1 orange, 1 tsp cherry jelly, 1 glass white dessert wine, 1 tsp mustard, 2 tbsps finely chopped onion, a pinch of ginger, ½ tsp each sugar and paprika

ash the lemon and orange, grate their skin. Squeeze the juice from the fruit, add the grated rind, sugar, paprika, ginger, wine and jelly. Bring to the boil, then allow to cool. Mix the finely chopped onion with the mustard, add the mixture to the cool sauce. Refrigerate. Serve with roast meat.

serves 4 • Preparation: 15 mins • Refrigerating: 30 mins

Basil sauce I

1 cup finely chopped basil leaves, 3–4 cloves of garlic, 2 tbsps chopped walnuts, ½ cup salad oil, salt, pepper, 1 tsp lemon juice, 2 tbsps grated sharp cheese

lend the basil with the walnuts, garlic, salt, pepper and lemon juice, gradually adding the oil. Pour into a bowl, add the cheese and refrigerate. Serve with pâtés.

serves 4 • Preparation: 10 mins • Refrigerating: 30 mins

Basil sauce II

1 cup finely chopped basil leaves, ½ cup each grated Parmesan, butter and chopped pine nuts, 8–10 cloves of garlic, 1 tsp salt, 2–3 tsps olive oil

hisk the butter until foamy, adding gradually the garlic crushed with salt, basil, pine nuts, Parmesan and oil. Whisk until the sauce is thick, then refrigerate. Serve with hard-boiled eggs, smoked meat and tomatoes.

serves 4 • Preparation: 10 mins • Refrigerating: 30 mins

'Capri' sauce

2 tbsps each chopped lemon balm, basil, mint and tarragon leaves, 1 tsp chopped thyme leaves, 1 tbsp anchovy paste, 1 tsp sharp mustard, 3 tbsps dry white wine, 2 tbsps wine vinegar, ½ cup olive oil, 1 tbsp capers, 2 tbsps olives stuffed with peppers, 2 hard-boiled eggs, salt, pepper, 2 firm beef tomatoes

hell the eggs, take out the egg yolks. Cream the egg yolks with the mustard, salt and pepper. Blend it with the vinegar and wine, gradually pouring in the oil. Add

the chopped herbs, capers and olives and work into a thick smooth sauce. Blanch and skin the tomatoes, remove the seeds. Cut the flesh into fine cubes, chop the egg whites finely and add both to the sauce. Serve with hard-boiled eggs, smoked meat, cold meat and boiled fish.

serves 4 • Preparation: 15 mins

Onion sauce

¼ cup stock, 2 tbsps olive oil, 6–8 shallots, 2 tbsps mustard, juice of 1 lemon, a pinch of each sugar, salt and pepper

lean the shallots and grate them, then mix with the mustard. Stirring all the time, drip in the oil. When the oil has blended well with the mustard, pour gradually the lemon juice. Add salt, pepper, sugar and the stock. Mix well and refrigerate. Serve with cold roast meat or venison ham.

serves 4 • Preparation: 20 mins • Refrigerating: 30 mins

Horseradish sauce

4–5 tbsps freshly grated horseradish, 2 tbsps thick cream, 1 cup yogurt, 1 tsp lemon juice, ½ tsp honey, salt

ix well all the ingredients. Cover the bowl and leave in the fridge for 2–3 hours. Serve straight from the fridge with boiled and grilled meat, fish and vegetables.

serves 4 • Preparation: 5 mins • Refrigerating: 3 hrs

Horseradish and apple sauce

200 g horseradish, 100 g tart apples, ½ cup thick cream, 1 tsp lemon juice, 1 hard-boiled egg, salt, ½ tsp sugar

crub and wash the horseradish, grate it finely, then mix with the lemon juice. Add the grated apples and the finely chopped egg white. Blend the egg yolk with salt, sugar and the cream. Combine the two mixtures, chill the sauce. Serve with venison ham or cold meat roast.

serves 4 • Preparation: 20 mins

Horseradish with capers

4 tbsps grated horseradish, 1 tart apple, 1 tsp capers, 2–3 firm beef tomatoes, 1 cup yogurt, ½ cup thick cream, salt, ½ tsp honey, 1 tsp lemon juice

Blanch and skin the tomatoes, cut them into slices, remove the seeds. Blend the tomatoes with the yogurt, cream, salt, honey and horseradish. Peel and grate the apple, sprinkle it with the lemon juice. Add to the sauce together with the capers. Mix well and chill a bit. Serve with smoked meat, boiled or roast meat and hard-boiled eggs.

serves 4 • Preparation: 10 mins • Refrigerating: 30 mins

Horseradish sauce with apricots

1 large horseradish root, 2 tart apples, 3–4 dried apricots, 1½ tbsps chopped almonds, 1 glass dry white wine, 2 tbsps olive oil, 1 tbsp honey, 1 tbsp lemon juice, ¼ tsp grated lemon rind, salt

Scrub and wash the horseradish and grate it finely. Pour over boiling water, drain well, then mix with the lemon juice and rind, honey and olive. Blanch the apricots, cut them into fine strips. Peel and grate the apples, mix them with the wine, almonds and apricot strips. Add the mixture to the horseradish. Mix well, add salt to taste. Cover the bowl tightly and put into the fridge for 3–4 hours. Serve with boiled fish, veal roast or roast poultry.

serves 4 • Preparation: 20 mins • Refrigerating: 4 hrs

Horseradish sauce with mustard

3 tbsps grated horseradish, 2 tbsps stock, 3 tbsps cream, 3 tbsps dry white wine, 1 tbsp each redcurrant and cherry juice, 1 tbsp Dijon mustard, lemon juice

Pour 2 tbsps of boiling stock over the grated horseradish, mix well, then put through a blender together with the remaining ingredients. Refrigerate. Serve with venison cutlets, cold venison roasts or ham.

serves 4 • Preparation: 10 mins • Refrigerating: 1 hour

Green horseradish sauce

½ cup thick sour cream, 2 tbsps grated horseradish, salt, ½ tsp liquid honey, 3 tbsps chopped watercress, 3 tbsps chopped chives and onion

Mix thoroughly all the ingredients. Serve with fried or boiled fish.

serves 4 • Preparation: 5 mins

Cumberland sauce

100 g redcurrant jelly, juice of 1 orange, ½ tsp each grated lemon and orange rind, 2 tbsps grated horseradish, 1 glass white dessert wine, a pinch of each salt and sugar

Mix well the jelly with the horseradish and the lemon and orange zest. Add salt, sugar, wine and orange juice. Mix well and refrigerate. Serve with venison roast and cutlets.

serves 4 • Preparation: 5 mins • Refrigerating: 30 mins

Lemon juice

juice of 1 lemon, ½ tsp grated lemon rind, ½ cup finely chopped parsley, salt, ½ tsp white pepper, ½ tsp caster sugar, 3–4 tbsps olive oil

Blend all the ingredients, refrigerate the mixture. Serve with fish pâtés.

serves 4 • Preparation: 5 mins • Refrigerating: 30 mins

Garlic sauce I

8–10 cloves of garlic, 2 hard-boiled eggs, 1 tbsp mustard, 1 tbsp chopped coriander leaves, ½ cup olive oil, 2 tbsps lemon juice, salt, pepper

Chop the garlic finely, mix it well with salt, pepper and the egg yolk. Blend with the mustard and stirring all the time gradually add the oil. Towards the end, add the lemon juice and coriander. Chill a bit.

serves 4 • Preparation: 10 mins • Refrigerating: 30 mins

Garlic sauce II

*8–10 cloves of garlic, 2 eggs, 4 tbsps
sunflower oil, salt, a pinch of sugar*

Chop the garlic and cream it with salt and the egg yolks. Stirring all the time, add the oil, then sugar and lemon juice. Mix in the finely chopped egg whites. Refrigerate. Serve with boiled fish.

serves 4 • Preparation: 10 mins • Refrigerating: 30 mins

Devilled sauce

*5 tbsps thick mayonnaise, 2 tbsps hot
ketchup, 1 tsp chilli sauce, 1 tbsp brandy,
1 tbsp lemon juice, ¼ tsp grated lemon rind,
salt, a pinch of each sugar and cayenne*

Whisk the mayonnaise with the brandy, lemon juice and zest. Add the ketchup, chilli sauce, salt, sugar and cayenne. Cover the bowl and refrigerate.

serves 4 • Preparation: 5 mins • Refrigerating: 30 mins

Mustard sauce

*½ cup mayonnaise, 2–3 tbsps yogurt, 3 hard-
boiled eggs, 1 tsp ground mustard seeds,
3 tbsps chopped mustard plant leaves, 1 tbsp
lemon juice, ½ tsp caster sugar, salt*

Whisk the egg yolks with the lemon juice, mustard seeds, sugar and salt. Mix in the yogurt and mayonnaise. Add the chopped egg whites and mustard leaves. Refrigerate. Serve with chicory, iceberg lettuce and spinach.

serves 4 • Preparation: 10 mins • Refrigerating: 30 mins

Podhale sauce

*100 g dried grated oscypek or 50 g bryndza, ½ cup
chopped walnuts, 3–4 cloves of garlic, ½ cup oil,
salt, 1 tsp each chopped basil leaves and marjoram*

Mix the grated cheese with the garlic crushed with salt. Gradually add the oil and work into a smooth mixture. Add the chopped herbs and walnuts, mix thoroughly.

Refrigerate. An excellent savoury sauce to be served with cold meats, pasta and rice dishes.

serves 4 • Preparation: 10 mins • Refrigerating: 30 mins

Spanish sauce

*100 g lean ham, 2 tbsps butter, 2 cups strong beef
stock, 1 cup dry white wine, 1 small glass dry red
wine, 2 tbsps tomato paste, 1 carrot, 1 parsley
root, 1 onion, 1 tbsp chopped parsley, 1 tsp
chopped thyme, 1 small bay leaf, 4–5 mushrooms,
1 tbsp flour, a pinch of sugar, salt, pepper*

Peel the carrot, parsley root and onion, dice them finely and sauté in butter, then cover with the stock, put the lid on and simmer. Add the chopped mushrooms and ham, tomato paste, bay leaf, salt, sugar and pepper. Simmer over low heat for over an hour. Make a roux from the butter and flour, dilute it with the white wine, pour into the vegetables. Simmer for another 15 mins, then rub through a sieve. Add the red wine, thyme and parsley, and refrigerate. The sauce will keep in the fridge for several days. Serve with pâtés, cold meats and hard-boiled eggs.

serves 4 • Preparation: 30 mins • Refrigerating: 30 mins

Ginger sauce

*1 tbsp finely chopped fresh ginger, 1 tsp ginger
syrup, 1 cup redcurrant jelly, 2 tbsps brandy, 1 small
glass (30 g) dry ruby port, a pinch each ground
allspice and grated nutmeg, 2 tbsps lemon juice*

Whisk the brandy and wine with the allspice, nutmeg, ginger syrup and lemon juice. Blend with the redcurrant jelly and chopped ginger. Refrigerate. Serve with poultry pâté, venison and wild fowl.

serves 4 • Preparation: 5 mins • Refrigerating: 30 mins

Yogurt sauce

*1 cup yogurt, 1 small onion, 2 tbsps lemon juice,
½ tsp grated lemon rind, ¼ tsp ground mustard
seeds, salt, pepper, a pinch of sugar, 1 tbsp each
chopped mustard plant and coriander leaves*

Chop the onion. Put it through a blender together with the yogurt and the remaining ingredients. Serve with boiled vegetables and fish.

serves 4 • Preparation: 5 mins

Caper sauce

1 cup thick mayonnaise, 1 hard-boiled egg, 1 small onion, 1½ tbsps chopped capers, 1 tbsp lemon juice, 1 tbsp each chopped chives, chervil, parsley and tarragon

Blend the mayonnaise with the egg yolk, salt, pepper, lemon juice and the finely chopped onion. Mix in the chopped greens, capers and egg white. Chill a bit. Serve with frutti di mare, fish and meat.

serves 4 • Preparation: 5–7 mins • Refrigerating: 10 mins

Caviar sauce

2 hard-boiled eggs, 1 tsp caviar, 3–4 tbsps sunflower oil, juice and grated rind of 1 lemon, a pinch of sugar, 1 tsp finely chopped onion, salt, caster sugar to taste

Force the hard-boiled egg yolks through a sieve, gradually blend them with the oil. Dilute the sauce with the lemon juice. Add salt and sugar, mix in the onion, chopped egg whites and caviar. Refrigerate. Serve with boiled or fried fish.

serves 4 • Preparation: 10 mins • Refrigerating: 30 mins

Coriander sauce

½ cup chopped coriander leaves, 3–4 cloves of garlic, 3 tbsps chopped walnuts, 3 tbsps lemon juice, salt, pepper, 1 tsp honey, a pinch of powdered ginger, ½ cup stock

serves 4 • Preparation: 5 mins • Refrigerating: 30 mins

Blend well all the ingredients, then sieve the mixture, and refrigerate it. Serve with fish or meat.

Sauce maltaise

2 oranges, 1 lemon, ½ cup redcurant jelly, ½ cup port, 1–1½ tbsps honey, 3 tbsps hot mustard, salt, ¼ tsp powdered ginger

Scrub the oranges and lemon well, scald and dry the rind, then grate it. Peel the fruit, remove the pips. Liquidize and then sieve the fruit. Pour the juice into a pan, add the wine, ginger, grated lemon and orange zest, salt and honey, stir thoroughly. Bring to the boil, then remove from the heat and allow to cool. Whisk it with the jelly and mustard into a smooth paste. Cover the bowl tightly and refrigerate for 2–3 hours. Serve with roast veal and poultry, with smoked meat or cold roast.

serves 4 • Preparation: 15 mins • Refrigerating: 2 hrs

Poppyseed sauce

1 tbsp poppyseed, 6 tbsps honey, 1 cup olive oil, 6 tbsps pomegranate juice (or wine vinegar), 1 tsp ground mustard seed, ¼ tsp dried tarragon

Rinse the poppyseed, scald it with boiling water, drain well. Blend thoroughly all the ingredients. Chill a bit. An excellent sauce to be served with lettuce and vegetable salads.

serves 4 • Preparation: 10 mins • Refrigerating: 30 mins

Mint sauce

½ cup finely chopped mint leaves, 4–5 cloves of garlic, ½ glass dry white wine, 2 tbsps lemon juice, ½ tsp coriander, salt, pepper, 1 tsp honey, ¼ cup stock

Blend all the ingredients together. Cover the bowl and refrigerate. Serve with fried or roast lamb.

serves 4 • Preparation: 10 mins • Refrigerating: 30 mins

Cucumber sauce

*2 small cucumbers, 1 tsp each chopped mint leaves,
oregano and chives, 2–3 cloves of garlic, salt, pepper,
1½ cups yogurt, 1 tbsp lemon juice, 1 tsp olive oil*

Peel the cucumbers, cut them lengthwise. Remove the seeds and chop the flesh finely. Chop the garlic and mix it with salt, pepper, oil and lemon juice. Fold into the chopped cucumber, add the yogurt and mix well. Cover the sauce and refrigerate. Before serving, add the chopped greens and mix thoroughly. Serve with fish and roast meat.

serves 4 • Preparation: 10 mins • Refrigerating: 2 hrs

Oriental sauce

*1 small banana, 1 cup yogurt, 2 tbsps
shredded coconut, 1 tbsp lemon juice, ½ tsp
each powdered ginger and curry powder,
½ tsp white pepper, a pinch of salt*

Peel the banana and put it through a blender together with yogurt and 1 tbsp of shredded coconut. Add the lemon juice, ginger, pepper, curry powder and salt, and blend the whole again. Refrigerate. Before serving, mix in the remaining coconut. Serve with grilled vegetables.

serves 4 • Preparation: 10 mins • Refrigerating: 1 hr

Peanut sauce

*½ cup mayonnaise, ½ cup finely chopped peanuts,
¼ cup dry white wine, 2–3 cloves of garlic, salt, a
pinch of each sugar and pepper, 1 tsp lemon juice*

Blend the finely chopped garlic with salt, pepper, sugar and lemon juice. Mix with the mayonnaise and wine. Add the peanuts and mix well. Cover the bowl and refrigerate for 1–2 hours. Serve with smoked meat or hard-boiled eggs.

serves 4 • Preparation: 10 mins • Refrigerating: 1–2 hrs

Walnut sauce

*1 cup chopped walnuts, 3–5 cloves of garlic, 1 tsp
coriander powder, 1 cup stock, 2 tbsps lemon*

*juice, ½ tsp grated lemon rind, salt, pepper,
cayenne, 1 tbsp chopped coriander leaves*

Blend together all the ingredients. Chill the mixture a bit. Serve with boiled meat, fish and poultry.

serves 4 • Preparation: 10 mins • Refrigerating: 1–2 hrs

Hazelnut sauce

*½ cup shelled hazelnuts, 2 onions, 1 lemon, 3 cloves
of garlic, 1 tsp dried mint, a pinch of paprika,
2 cups fish stock, salt, pepper, a pinch of sugar*

Chop the garlic, grate the onion finely and mix them together with the mint, paprika, salt and pepper. Combine with the fish stock. Put in the lemon juice and finely chopped hazelnuts. Serve with baked fish.

serves 4 • Preparation: 15 mins

Nettle sauce

*1 cup thick mayonnaise, 1 hard-boiled egg, 1 cup young
nettle leaves, 1 tbsp lemon juice, ¼ tsp grated lemon
rind, 1 tsp honey, a pinch of each salt and pepper*

Put the nettle sprigs into a colander, pour over first boiling, then cold water, drain well and chop finely. Cream the egg yolk with the lemon juice and zest, honey, salt, pepper and mayonnaise. Add the finely chopped egg whites, stir well. Chill a bit. Serve with boiled vegetables: kohlrabi, cauliflower, salsify, hop sprigs.

serves 4 • Preparation: 10 mins • Refrigerating: 30 mins

Polish sauce

*3 hard-boiled eggs, juice of 1 lemon, grated rind of
½ lemon, ½ cup each thick sour cream and thick
mayonnaise, 1 tbsp grated horseradish, 4–5 tbsps finely
chopped chives, 1 tbsp finely grated onion, 1 tbsp finely
chopped watercress, salt, pepper, a pinch of sugar*

Blend the egg yolks with the lemon juice and zest, horseradish, grated onion and cream. Add the chives, parsley and finely chopped egg whites, then salt and sugar to taste, season with pepper. Mix well, cover and refrigerate for

Tomato sauce

3–4 hours. An excellent garnish for pâtés, smoked meat and hard-boiled eggs.

serves 4 • Preparation: 10 mins • Refrigerating: 4 hrs

Tomato sauce

400 g ripe tomatoes, 1 tbsp butter, 3–4 tbsps dry white wine, 1 green bell pepper, 1 large onion, 1 tsp dried oregano, ½ tsp pepper, salt, a pinch of sugar, 1 tbsp chopped basil

Wash the tomatoes, cut them into quarters. Melt the butter in a pan, add the tomatoes, sauté them, add salt, oregano, sugar and wine. Simmer over low heat for 30 mins, then sieve. Peel the onion, core the pepper, dice both and put them through a blender. Pour in the tomato purée and work the whole into a fine paste. Season to taste, add the chopped basil and refrigerate. Serve with fish and vegetable pâtés.

serves 4 • Preparation: 40 mins • Refrigerating: 1 hr

Ravigote

5 tbsps thick mayonnaise, ca ½ kg frozen spinach, 1–2 cloves of garlic, 1 tsp lemon juice, a pinch of caster sugar, salt, 1 tbsp Worcestershire sauce

Defreeze the spinach, drain it in a sieve, then blend with the crushed garlic, sugar and lemon juice. Fold in the mayonnaise, add the Worcestershire sauce. Chill a bit. Serve with boiled fish.

serves 4 • Preparation: 15 mins • Refrigerating: 1 hr

Rose hip sauce

1 cup rose hip jam, ½ glass dry red wine, 3 tbsps lemon juice, a pinch of cayenne, 2 tbsps coarsely chopped pistachios

Mix thoroughly the jam, wine, lemon juice and cayenne. Force the mixture through a sieve, add the chopped pistachios. Refrigerate. Serve with chicken and venison pâtés.

serves 4 • Preparation: 10 mins • Refrigerating: 30 mins

Anchovy sauce

1½ tbsps anchovy paste, 4–5 tbsps sunflower oil, 2 tbsps each black and green olives, 1 tsp capers, a pinch of caster sugar, 1 tsp lemon juice

Mix the anchovy paste with the oil, sugar and lemon juice. Stone the olives and cut them into thin strips, chop the capers. Add the olives and capers to the sauce, mix well. Refrigerate. Serve with boiled fish.

serves 4 • Preparation: 10 mins • Refrigerating: 30 mins

'Seven herbs' sauce

2 tbsps each finely chopped lovage, borage, watercress, chervil, chives, dill and tarragon, 2–3 cloves of garlic, 1 tsp mustard, 2 tbsps oil, 1 cup yogurt, ½ cup thick cream, salt, pepper, 1 tsp lemon juice, 3 hard-boiled eggs

Chop the garlic finely and crush it with salt. Blend with the lemon juice, chopped egg yolks, mustard and oil to make a smooth paste. Fold in the yogurt and cream. Chop the egg whites finely, add the herbs. Pour over the sauce, stir well. Cover the dish and refrigerate for 2–3 hours. Serve with boiled beef, smoked meat, cold meat and hard-boiled eggs.

serves 4 • Preparation: 15 mins • Refrigerating: 3 hrs

Sorrel sauce

100 g cottage cheese, 1 cup thick cream, juice and grated rind of 1 lemon, salt, pepper, ½ tsp honey, ½ cup finely chopped sorrel

Blend the cream with the lemon juice and zest, salt, pepper and honey. Mix in the chopped sorrel and refrigerate. Serve with boiled or fried fish and with veal.

serves 4 • Preparation: 5 mins • Refrigerating: 1 hr

Sauce tartare I

5 tbsps mayonnaise, 2 hard-boiled eggs, 3 cocktail gherkins, 3 marinated mushrooms, 1 tbsp grated horseradish, salt, sugar and pepper to taste, 1 tsp chopped parsley

Sieve the egg yolks, mix them with the mayonnaise, salt, pepper and sugar. Chop finely the gherkins, mushrooms and the egg whites. Fold them into the mayonnaise, add the parsley.

serves 4 • Preparation: 20 mins

Sauce tartare II

1 cup thick mayonnaise, 1 tbsp lemon juice, 1 tsp mustard, 1 onion, 4–5 cocktail gherkins, 1 tbsp capers, 1 tsp each chopped parsley, tarragon and chives

Mix the mayonnaise with the mustard, lemon juice and grated onion. Add the chopped gherkins, capers and greens. Leave for 1–2 hours to allow it to mature. Excellent with pâtés, smoked meat, cold roast and hard-boiled eggs.

serves 4 • Preparation: 10 mins • Refrigerating: 2 hrs

Sauce tartare III

2 hard-boiled eggs, 1 tsp mustard, 1 tbsp grated horseradish, 1 tsp chopped chives, a pinch of salt, lemon juice, 2 tbsps thick mayonnaise, 1 tbsp thick cream

Chop the eggs finely, mix them with the chives. Blend the mayonnaise with the mustard, cream, horserad-ish, lemon juice and sugar. Fold in the eggs. Add salt to taste, refrigerate. Serve with cold roast venison.

serves 4 • Preparation: 10 mins • Refrigerating: 30 mins

Sauce tartare IV

5–6 hard-boiled eggs, 1 tbsp mustard, 2–3 tbsps olive or sunflower oil, juice of 1 lemon, a pinch of sugar, salt, pepper, 1–2 cloves of garlic, 6–7 marinated button mushrooms, 1–2 marinated scallopini squash (pâtisson), 2–3 marinated onions, 2 tbsps chopped watercress

Sieve the egg yolks, add the mustard and gradually pour in the oil. Mix well, add the lemon juice and salt, pepper and sugar to taste. Finely chop the mushrooms, squash, onions and the egg whites, crush the garlic with a pinch of salt. Combine with the watercress and sauce. Stir well and refrigerate.

serves 4 • Preparation: 10 mins • Refrigerating: 30 mins

Tuna sauce

1 tin tuna in brine, 1 tbsp soya sauce, 1 tbsp vodka, ½ cup mayonnaise, 1 tsp green peppercorns, 1 tsp capers

Drain the tuna. Put it through a blender together with the green peppercorns, capers, soya sauce and vod-

...ka. Fold in the mayonnaise and refrigerate. Serve with fish and vegetable pâtés.

serves 4 • Preparation: 5 mins • Refrigerating: 1 hr

Turkish sauce

*1 cup chopped hazelnuts, 1½ cups yogurt,
½ cup olive oil, 2–3 slices of toasting bread
(without crust), 2–4 cloves of garlic, 1 tbsp each
chopped basil and oregano, salt, pepper*

Put all the ingredients through a blender and refrigerate. If the sauce is too thick, add some more oil or yogurt. Excellent with cold poultry dishes and with smoked poultry.

serves 4 • Preparation: 5 mins • Refrigerating: 1 hr

Vincent sauce

*½ cup mayonnaise, 1 tsp mustard, 2–3 tbsps cream,
½ cup finely chopped sorrel leaves, 1 grated onion,
2 finely chopped pickled cucumbers, 1 tbsp capers,
1 hard-boiled egg, 2 tbsps chopped chives, salt,
pepper, a pinch of sugar*

Blend the mayonnaise with the mustard, cream, egg yolk, sorrel, onion, salt, pepper and sugar to produce a smooth paste. Add the cucumbers, chopped egg white, chives and capers. Stir well, season to taste. Refrigerate. Serve with hard-boiled eggs, boiled vegetables, meat and fish, and with grilled meat.

serves 4 • Preparation: 10 mins • Refrigerating: 30 mins

Grape sauce

*300 g firm grapes, 3–4 tbsps chopped walnuts,
1 tbsp each chopped basil, tarragon and coriander,
1–2 cloves of garlic, 1 tbsp lemon juice, ¼ tsp grated
lemon rind, ¾ cup light stock, ½ tsp honey*

Squeeze the juice from the grapes. Put the juice and the remaining ingredients through a blender, then refrigerate. Excellent with grilled meat, roast meat and boiled poultry.

serves 4 • Preparation: 5 mins

Vitamin sauce

*5 tbsps thick mayonnaise, 2 tbsps yogurt,
2 tbsps each chopped dill, watercress and chives,
1 tsp marinated green pepper, 1 small finely chopped
green bell pepper, 1 tsp lemon juice, salt, pepper, sugar*

Mix together all the ingredients thoroughly, then refrigerate.

serves 4 • Preparation: 5 mins • Refrigerating: 30 mins

Green sauce

*2 bunches of parsley, 2 hard-boiled eggs,
2 tbsps capers, 6–8 stoned green olives,
3–4 slices of bread (without crust), ½ cup
each wine vinegar and olive oil, salt*

Soak the crumbled bread in the vinegar for 20 mins. Put it through a blender together with the chopped parsley, salt and oil. Add the finely chopped capers, olives and eggs. Chill a bit.

serves 4 • Preparation: 25 mins • Refrigerating: 1 hr

Herbal sauce

*1 tbsp each chopped parsley, chives, tarragon and
lemon balm, 1 tbsp finely chopped onion, salt, pepper,
a pinch of sugar, 1 tbsp lemon juice, 4 tbsps thick
mayonnaise, 1 tbsp yogurt, 1 hard-boiled egg*

Sprinkle the herbs with the lemon juice. Chop finely the egg whites and onion, add some salt, pepper and sugar. Blend the yogurt with the egg yolk and mayonnaise. Add the herbs, onion and egg white to the mixture. Refrigerate.

serves 4 • Preparation: 10 mins • Refrigerating: 1 hr

Cranberry and cream sauce

*100 g cranberries, 1 cup thick sour cream,
1 tbsp grated horseradish, grated rind
of 1 lemon, a pinch of sugar, salt*

Sieve the cranberries, mix them with the lemon zest and cream, add salt, sugar and grated horseradish. Put the sauce through a food processor. Refrigerate. Serve with cold venison.

serves 4 • Preparation: 5 mins • Refrigerating: 1 hr

Hot sauces

There is one important principle to observe when making hot sauces: if we make a base of butter and flour, then cold broth or milk or wine should be added to a hot base, or a cold base should be added to a hot liquid, and then carefully stirred in until the sauce has thickened, so that there are no lumps. Hot sauces can also be thickened with potato or corn flour mixed with a little cold water (or wine or beer), or with a raw egg yolk beaten into cream (or water or milk).

Another thing to remember when making sauces – almost all of them lose in taste when they are reheated, and therefore the sauce should be made immediately before serving, at the last moment, and only the necessary ingredients should be prepared beforehand.

A basic sauce can be made with light chicken or veal stock. The flavour of the sauce can be varied by adding lemon zest and lemon juice, herbs (parsley, chives, thyme, marjoram), capers, green peppercorns or white wine.

White sauce (roux) – basic recipe

2 tbsps butter, 1 tbsp flour, 2 cups stock, salt, white pepper, a pinch of sugar, ½ tsp lemon juice

Melt the butter in a pan, add the flour and make a white roux. Stirring all the time add the stock and simmer until the sauce has thickened. Add salt, pepper, sugar and lemon juice to taste.

serves 4 • Preparation: 5–7 mins

White cream sauce – basic recipe

3 tbsps butter, 1 tbsp flour, 1 cup chicken stock, ¼ cup whipping cream, 1 glass dry white wine, ¼ tsp grated lemon rind, salt, pepper

Melt 2 tbsps of butter in a pan, add the flour and make a white roux. Dilute it with the stock, add salt, pepper and lemon zest, and, stirring all the time, simmer until the sauce has thickened. Pour in the wine, heat up, then sieve the sauce. Bring to the boil, fold in the whipped cream. Add grated butter and whisk while heating it up over low heat.

serves 4 • Preparation: 10 mins

Bechamel sauce

This is a basic recipe for many light sauces for bakes, boiled vegetables and meat.

2 tbsps butter, 1 tbsp flour, salt, 1 tsp lemon juice, ¼ tsp grated nutmeg, a pinch of sugar, ½ cup milk, 1 cup single cream, 1 egg yolk

Make a roux from the butter and flour, dilute it with the cool boiled milk. Stirring all the time, simmer over low heat until the sauce has thickened. Add salt, nutmeg and lemon juice. Mix well. Beat the cream lightly with the egg yolk and add the mixture to the sauce. Heat the sauce up, but do not allow it to boil.

serves 4 • Preparation: 10 mins

Sauce hollandaise au supreme – basic recipe

The famous French chef, Edward Pożerski (Pojarski), a Pole by origin, called this butter sauce "the king of the sauces".

150 g butter, 4 egg yolks, 1 tbsp lemon juice, 2 tbsps boiled water, a pinch of salt

Put a saucepan with a long handle into a larger pot filled with boiling water. Pour in 2 tbsps of boiled water into the pan, break in 4 raw egg yolks and whisk them (holding the pan by the handle) until the egg yolks have thickened. Add butter – a teaspoon at a time – whisking the mixture all the time. Then put in the lemon juice and beat the mixture again until the sauce is as thick and white as cream. The hot sauce hollandaise should be as smooth as mayonnaise and it should smell of fresh butter. It is not difficult to prepare, the only hitch is that you must follow the recipe scrupulously and prepare the sauce immediately before serving. The important thing is to keep it off the boil all the time.

NOTE: If the sauce curdles, it can be re-emulsified by adding 1–2 tbsps of cold water and whisking it again. The sauce is usually served with vegetables, for example asparagus, artichokes, cauliflower, and also with white meat and fish. Depending on the dish it is to accompany, you may slightly alter its taste: for example, make it more piquant for fish dishes by adding a pinch of white pepper towards the end. For asparagus, add a pinch of sugar, and for caviar, mix in a bit of mace.

Sauce hollandaise serves as a basis for such famous sauces as béarnaise, charon, chantilly, mousseline, maltaise or delicious mustard sauce.

If we add ground mustard seed or mustard to sauce hollandaise, we obtain mustard sauce; if we mix it with whipped cream in a ratio of 1–1, we obtain a very delicate mousseline sauce, which is excellent both with asparagus and steamed fish.

If we blend sauce hollandaise with the juice and grated rind of an orange, we obtain a very original maltaise sauce, to go with white meat and poultry.

And if instead of adding water to a butter-based sauce we add finely chopped shallots and herbs (fresh tarragon and chervil) cooked in wine vinegar or dry white wine, we obtain béarnaise sauce. This is best with grilled meat, but is also excellent with eggs, fish and vegetables.

serves 4 • Preparation: 20 mins

Lenten sauce with cherries

Stone the cherries, blend them, cover with wine, put in some lemon peel and bring the whole to the boil. Strain the sauce through a colander, and heat again with sugar and ground cinnamon.

(W. Wielądko, *Kucharz doskonały*, vol. II, p. 191)

Velvet sauce

½ kg beef tomatoes, 1 red bell pepper, 1–2 cloves of garlic, ½ cup thick cream, 1 cup stock, 1 tsp paprika, ¼ tsp cayenne pepper, salt, 1 tsp lemon juice, ½ tsp sugar, 1 tbsp flour, 1 tbsp butter

Blanch, skin and dice the tomatoes. Peel the garlic and chop it finely. Simmer the tomatoes and bell pepper in a pan to soften them up, add ½ cup of stock, lemon juice, sugar, paprika, cayenne and garlic crushed with salt. Cover the pan and simmer over low heat for 20 mins, then sieve the mixture. Melt the butter in a pan, add the flour and make a roux. Dilute it with the remaining stock and, stirring all the time, simmer until it has thickened. Add the tomato and pepper purée, season with cayenne to taste. Fold in the cream, stir well. Heat the sauce up, but do not allow it to boil.

serves 4 • Preparation: 30 mins

Gooseberry sauce

250 g gooseberries, ½ cup thick sour cream, 1 tsp sugar, 1 tsp flour

Cook the gooseberries with sugar in a small amount of water, then sieve them. Mix the cream well with the flour, pour in the gooseberry purée and, stirring all the time, heat the sauce up. Serve with boiled venison.

serves 4 • Preparation: 30 mins

Peach sauce

1 kg ripe peaches, 2 red onions, 2–3 cloves of garlic, 2 tbsps sugar, ¼ cup each dry red wine, wine vinegar and orange juice, 2 tbsps lemon juice, 1½ tbsps butter, salt, pepper to taste

Melt the butter in a pan, fry the finely chopped onion, but do not let it brown. Add the garlic crushed with salt and sauté for a minute, stirring all the time. Add the stoned peaches, stir. Pour in the wine, orange and lemon juice and vinegar. Add sugar and pepper. Bring to the boil, cover the pan and simmer for 40 mins. Allow the mixture to cool, then put it through a blender and sieve it. Return to the pan, heat up and season to taste. Serve with pork roast or grilled spare ribs.

serves 4 • Preparation: 45 mins

Onion sauce

400 g onion, 1–2 cloves of garlic, 1 tsp soya sauce, 4 bay leaves, 1 tbsp chopped fresh oregano or 1 tsp dried oregano, 2 tbsps wholemeal flour, 2 tbsps oil, 2 cups stock, 1½ cups single cream, 2 tbsps dry white wine, salt, pepper

Heat up the oil in a pan, put in the finely chopped onion and fry it, but do not let it brown. Add the bay leaves and fry for a minute or two, stirring all the time. Put in the oregano, vegetable condiment, soya sauce and wine. Stir, cover the pan and simmer for 15 mins. Take out the bay leaves. Sprinkle the onion with flour, gradually add the stock, stirring all the time. Simmer until the sauce has thickened. Put it through a blender and sieve it, add salt and pepper to taste. Fold in the cream and heat up.

serves 4 • Preparation: 20 mins

Horseradish sauce

2 cups fish stock, ½ lemon, 3 tbsps grated horseradish, ½ cup thick sour cream, salt, ½ tsp sugar, 1 tbsp butter, 1 tsp flour

Make a roux from the butter and flour, dilute it with the stock, add the lemon juice, salt and sugar. Stirring all the time, heat it up until it has thickened. Fold in the cream mixed with the horseradish and heat up again, but do not let it boil. Serve with boiled and fried fish.

serves 4 • Preparation: 15 mins

Horseradish sauce with almonds

2 tbsps butter, 1½ tbsps flour, 1 cup stock, 1 cup cream, 1 cup freshly grated horseradish, 50 g almond flakes, salt, pepper, a pinch of sugar, 1 tbsp lemon juice

Melt the butter in a pan, add the flour and make a white roux. Dilute it with the cool stock and, stirring all the

time, simmer until the sauce has thickened. Add salt, pepper, sugar, almond flakes and cream. Heat up, fold in the horseradish and stir well. Serve with boiled meat, boiled vegetables (like cauliflower), boiled fish and hard-boiled eggs.

serves 4 • Preparation: 20 mins

Horseradish sauce with raisins

2 tbsps butter, 1½ tbsps flour, 2 cups milk, 4 tbsps thick cream, 2 egg yolks, 50 g raisins, 1½ cups freshly grated horseradish, 1 tbsp lemon juice, salt, sugar

Mix the freshly grated horseradish with the lemon juice. Blanch the raisins and drain them in a sieve. Melt the butter in a pan, add the flour and make a white roux. Dilute it with the milk and, stirring all the time, simmer until the sauce has thickened. Put in the raisins, salt and sugar. Beat the egg yolks with the cream and pour the mixture into the sauce. Stir well, heat up, add the horseradish and stir again. Serve with boiled pork or beef.

serves 4 • Preparation: 20 mins

Savoury bechamel sauce

2 tbsps butter, 1 tbsp wholemeal flour, 1½ cups milk, 1 small onion, 6–8 peppercorns, 1 bay leaf, 2–3 tbsps cream, 2 tbsps grated horseradish, ½ tsp ground mustard seeds, salt, pepper

Put the onion, bay leaf and peppercorns into the milk and slowly bring to the boil. Cover the pan, take it off the heat and leave for 15–20 mins. Melt the butter in a pan, add the flour, stir thoroughly. Thin the mixture down with the strained milk. Stirring all the time, simmer over low heat until the sauce has thickened. Add salt and pepper. Mix the ground mustard seeds with the cream, pour into the sauce and heat the sauce up, stirring all the time. Towards the end, fold in the horseradish. Serve with croquettes and steamed vegetables.

serves 4 • Preparation: 20 mins • Cooking: 10 mins

Lemon sauce

*1 cup stock, juice and grated rind of
1 lemon, ½ cup thick sour cream, 2 egg
yolks, 1 tsp flour, salt, a pinch of sugar*

Make a roux from the butter and flour, dilute it with the stock. Add the lemon zest and juice and, stirring all the time, simmer until the sauce has thickened. Add salt, sugar and a pinch of white pepper. Thicken the sauce with the lightly beaten egg yolks. Heat up, but do not let it boil.

serves 4 • Preparation: 15 mins

Garlic sauce

*100 g (2 tins) anchovies or 3 tbsps anchovy
paste, 5–7 cloves of garlic, 2 cups chopped
parsley, 120 g butter, pepper, ½ cup dry white
wine, 1½ cups light stock, 1 tbsp flour*

Melt the butter in a pan, add the finely chopped garlic and sauté it. Add the chopped fillets or anchovy paste, sprinkle with flour. Pour in the stock and simmer for a while over low heat, stirring all the time, until the sauce has thickened. Mix the parsley with the wine, pour into the sauce and heat it up.

serves 4 • Preparation: 10 mins

Piquant sauce

*100 g Tilsit cheese, 1 medium-large onion, 1 tbsp
ground mustard seeds, 1 tsp pepper, salt, 2 tbsps
butter, 2 tbsps flour, 1 cup stock, 2 cups single cream*

Melt the butter in a pan, add the flour and make a white roux. Dilute it with the stock and, stirring all the time, simmer until the sauce has thickened. Add the pepper, mustard seeds, finely grated onion and salt. Blend the grated cheese with the cream, pour the mixture into the sauce and simmer until the sauce is smooth.

serves 4 • Preparation: 20 mins

Hawthorn sauce

*2 cups dry white wine, 5 tbsps hawthorn jam, 1 tbsp
potato flour, juice of 1 lemon, ½ tsp sugar, salt*

Heat up the wine, add sugar, lemon juice and jam, stir well and bring to the boil. Mix the potato flour with 1 tbsp of water, pour into the sauce and, stirring all the time, bring the mixture to the boil and simmer until the sauce has thickened. Excellent with roast à la venison or with roast game.

serves 4 • Preparation: 10 mins

Pear sauce

*500 g pears, 1 tbsp lemon juice, 1 orange,
¼ cup sugar, ¼ cup 4% vinegar, ¼ cup dry
white wine, 1 tbsp finely chopped ginger,
½ tsp each ground cloves and cinnamon*

Scrub the orange, dry it and remove the peel with a sharp knife. Put the peel into boiling water for 2–3 mins, drain it, pour over cold water, drain again. Peel and core the pears, dice them, put into a pan, sprinkle with lemon juice. Add the finely chopped ginger and orange peel, pour in water, vinegar and orange juice. Bring to the boil and, stirring occasionally, simmer for a while, then add sugar, cloves and cinnamon, pour in the wine, and, stirring all the time, cook until the pears have turned into a thick sauce. Serve hot with white roast meat and poultry or cold with smoked meat, poultry and fish.

serves 4 • Preparation: 30 mins

Sauce hollandaise

*100 g butter, 2 lemons, ½ cup fish stock,
½ cup white wine, 4 egg yolks, salt*

Break in the yolks into a pan, beat them lightly. Add the fish stock, lemon juice, wine and salt. Put the pan on top of a pot with boiling water and whisk the eggs until the sauce begins to thicken. Gradually add knobs of butter and keep whisking until the sauce has turned white. Do not let it boil, or the yolks will curdle. Serve with boiled fish.

serves 4 • Preparation: 25 mins

Piquant sauce hollandaise (a simple recipe)

1 small onion, 1 clove of garlic, 3 tbsps butter, 2 eggs, juice of ½ lemon, 1 cup fish stock, salt, pepper, a pinch of sugar

Put the finely chopped garlic and onion, together with knobs of butter and 2 tbsps of warm stock into a food processor, blend all the ingredients (at low speed) to produce a smooth paste. Slowly add the remaining stock, lemon juice, salt, pepper, sugar and the eggs. Turn the speed up and mix the sauce a bit longer. Pour the sauce into a pan and, stirring all the time, heat it up. Serve hot with boiled fish.

serves 4 • Preparation: 10 mins

Curried apple sauce

500 g tart apples, 1 largish onion, 1 tbsp raisins, ½ tsp curry powder, 1 tbsp butter, ½ cup stock, 1 small glass dry white wine, salt, pepper

Fry the finely chopped onion in butter, but do not let it brown. Add the curry powder, stir. Put in the grated apples and the raisins which have soaked in wine, pour in the stock and simmer until the apples disintegrate. Put the sauce through a food processor, then sieve it. Add salt and pepper, heat up. An excellent sauce that goes well with all kinds of roast poultry. It can also be served cold.

serves 4 • Preparation: 25 mins

Apple sauce with cinnamon

1 kg tart apples, ½ cup dry white wine, ½ tsp sugar, 1 clove, ¼ tsp cinnamon, 1 tbsp butter, a pinch of each salt, sugar and pepper

serves 4 • Preparation: 20 mins

Peel and core the apples, cut them into quarters. Melt the butter in a pan, put in the apples and soften them. Add the clove, cinnamon and sugar, pour in the wine and

simmer for a while, then force through a sieve. Serve with roast geese or duck, roast wild duck or pheasant.

Juniper sauce

venison trimmings, 50 g raw streaky bacon, ½ cup stock, ½ cup dry white wine, 1 tbsp butter, 1 onion, 1 carrot, a piece of celeriac, 1 parsley root, grated rind and juice of 1 lemon, 1 tsp pounded juniper berries, 1 tsp flour, a pinch of sugar

Chop the venison trimmings and bacon, add the diced vegetables and sauté in butter. Pour in the stock and simmer over low heat. Add the juniper berries and lemon zest and juice. Simmer for one hour, allow to cool, then put the mixture through a blender and sieve it. Add a roux made from butter and flour, dilute it with the wine. Add some sugar and heat up. Serve with venison roast and pâté.

serves 4 • Preparation: 1 hr

Vegetable sauce

1 celeriac, 1 parsley root, 1 onion, 1 potato, 1 carrot, 2 tbsps chopped dill, 1 tbsp butter, 1 tsp flour, 1 lemon, 1 cup fish stock, ¼ cup dry white wine, salt, a pinch of each pepper and sugar

Peel and rinse the vegetables, dice them finely, put into a pan and cover with the fish stock. Put a lid on and simmer until the vegetables are tender. Make a roux from the butter and flour, dilute it with the wine. Add the lemon juice, salt, pepper and sugar to taste. Sieve the vegetables, mix them with the roux. Serve with fish cutlets or boiled fish.

serves 4 • Preparation: 30 mins

Caper sauce

1 cup fish stock, ½ cup dry white wine, 1 tbsp capers, 3 cocktail gherkins, 2 onions, 1 soaked herring, a pinch of each paprika, salt and sugar, 1 tbsp butter, 1 tsp flour, 1 tsp chopped dill

Fry the finely chopped onion in butter, but do not let it brown. Add the flour, thin the sauce down with the fish stock. Add the chopped herring and simmer for a while, then sieve it. Add the finely chopped gherkins, capers, paprika, sugar, salt if required. Mix the whole and heat up, but keep it off the boil. Add the chopped dill and serve with boiled fish.

serves 4 • Preparation: 15 mins

Caviar sauce

1 cup fish stock, zest and juice of ½ lemon, 1 tbsp butter, 1 tsp flour, 2 tbsps caviar

Make a roux from the butter and flour, dilute it with the fish stock. Add the lemon juice and zest and, stirring all the time, heat it up until the sauce has thickened. Add the caviar and stir well. Serve with boiled fish.

serves 4 • Preparation: 10 mins

Gherkin sauce

8–10 cocktail gherkins, 2–3 cloves of garlic, 2 tbsps chopped parsley, 1 tbsp butter, 1 tsp hot mustard, salt, pepper, a pinch of sugar, 1 tsp lemon juice, 1 egg yolk, 1 tbsp butter, 1 tbsp flour, 1 cup stock

Chop the gherkins and garlic finely. Melt 1 tbsp of butter in a frying pan, add the garlic and gherkins, sauté them. Add the parsley and salt, sprinkle slightly with water, cover the pan and simmer over low heat for 10 mins. Melt more butter in a pan, add the flour and make a white roux. Dilute it with the stock, add salt, pepper, lemon juice, a

pinch of sugar, mustard and cooked gherkins. Stirring all the time, simmer over low heat until the sauce has thickened. Take off the heat, thicken with the raw egg yolk and stir well.

serves 4 • Preparation: 15 mins

Mint sauce

½ cup finely chopped mint leaves, 500 g apples, 200 g green peas (tinned or frozen), 2 cups light stock, 1 tbsp butter, a pinch of sugar, salt, pepper, 1 tsp lemon juice

Peel the apples and slice them, then sprinkle with lemon juice. Melt the butter in a pan, put in the apple slices and sauté them, sprinkle sparingly with the stock, cover the pan and simmer over low heat for 15 mins. Add the peas, mint, salt and pepper, pour in the remaining stock and cook for another 5–7 mins. Allow the mixture to cool. Put it through a blender, heat it up and reduce the liquid a bit.

serves 4 • Preparation: 25 mins

Mustard sauce

1 cup fish stock, ½ cup dry white wine, 1 lemon, 2 egg yolks, 3 tbsps Dijon mustard, 1 tbsp butter, 1 tsp flour

Make a roux from the butter and flour, dilute it with the cool fish stock. Stirring all the time, simmer over low heat until the sauce has thickened. Mix together the juice, grated lemon rind and mustard, pour into the sauce. Add the wine blended with the egg yolks, add salt and sugar to

taste. Heat the sauce up, but do not allow it to boil. Serve with fish cutlets or boiled fish, or with venison cutlets.

serves 4 • Preparation: 10 mins

Sauce orléanaise

2 anchovies or 4 tbsps anchovy paste, 2 tbsps butter, 1 cup stock, 2–3 tbsps white wine, 2 cocktail gherkins, 1 tbsp capers, 1 carrot, zest and juice of 1 lemon, 1 tsp sugar, 1 tsp caramel, 1 tsp flour, 2 hard-boiled egg whites, salt, pepper, a pinch of nutmeg

Melt ½ tbsp of butter in a pan, put in the coarsely grated carrot and sauté it. Add the finely chopped cocktail gherkins, anchovies (or anchovy paste) and capers. Sprinkle with lemon juice and 2–3 tbsps of dry white wine. Simmer for 15 mins. Make a roux from the remaining butter and flour, dilute it with the stock. Add lemon zest, caramel, nutmeg, salt and sugar. Mix the whole and bring to the boil. Fold into the vegetable stew, add the chopped egg whites and ½ tsp butter. Heat the sauce up. Serve with venison cutlets and roast.

serves 4 • Preparation: 25 mins

Savoury sauce

2 tbsps butter, 1 cup stock, ½ cup dry red wine, zest and juice of 1 lemon, 1 carrot, 1 parsley root, a piece of celeriac, 2 tomatoes, 2 onions, 1 small bay leaf, 5–6 grains each allspice, juniper and pepper, ½ tsp tarragon, a pinch of cayenne (or chilli), 10 pickled button mushrooms, 1 tbsp capers, ½ tsp sugar, 1 tsp caramel, 1 tsp flour, salt

Grate coarsely the vegetables, cut the tomatoes and onion into quarters. Put them in a pan, pour in the stock, add the bay leaf, pepper, allspice, juniper, tarragon, lemon zest and juice and cayenne. Cover the pan and simmer for 40 mins, then sieve the vegetables. Make a roux from the butter and flour, dilute it with the wine. Add sugar, caramel, finely chopped mushrooms and capers. Pour the roux into the vegetables. Add salt and cayenne to taste. Heat it up. The sauce should not be too thick but fairly piquant. Serve with venison roast.

serves 4 • Preparation: 45 mins

Mushroom sauce I

200 g mushrooms, 1 large onion, 3 tbsps chopped parsley, ½ cup dry white wine, 1 cup stock, 4 tbsps butter, 1 tbsp flour, 1 tbsp lemon juice, salt, pepper, ¼ tsp sugar

Dice the mushrooms and onion finely. Melt 2 tbsps of butter in a pan, soften the onion, add the mushrooms and sauté them over high heat. Add salt and pepper, sprinkle with the lemon juice and wine and simmer for 10 mins. Melt the remaining butter in a frying pan, add the flour and make a white roux. Dilute it with the stock and cook for a bit, stirring all the time. Combine the roux with the mushrooms. Add salt, pepper, sugar and lemon juice to taste, mix in the chopped parsley. Heat up.

serves 4 • Preparation: 20 mins

Mushroom sauce II

250 g mushrooms, 2 onions, 2–3 cloves of garlic, 1 tbsp soya sauce, ½ tsp vegetable seasoning, 1 tbsp wholemeal flour, 100 g finely chopped walnuts, 2 cups stock, 1 cup single cream, salt, pepper, 2 tbsps oil, 1 tsp lemon juice

Cut half the mushrooms into slices. Chop the remaining mushrooms finely, put them into a bowl, sprinkle with lemon juice and pepper. Heat up the oil in a pan, fry the finely chopped onion, but do not let it brown. Add the mushroom slices and sauté them, stirring all the time. Add the chopped garlic, soya sauce and vegetable seasoning, sprinkle with flour, mix well. Gradually pour in the stock stirring all the time, until the sauce has thickened. Add the walnuts and put the whole through a blender. Heat the sauce up, add the finely chopped mushrooms, salt and pepper to taste. Pour in the cream and heat the sauce up.

serves 4 • Preparation: 20 mins

Parsley sauce

1 cup fish stock, 1 glass white wine, ½ lemon, salt, a pinch of sugar, 3 tbsps chopped parsley, 1 tbsp butter, 1 tsp flour, 2 egg yolks, 2–3 tbsps dry white wine or 2–3 tbsps thick sour cream

Make a roux from the butter and flour, dilute it with the fish stock. Add the lemon juice, salt and sugar. Stirring all the time, heat it up until the sauce has thickened. Add the parsley and pour in a lightly beaten mixture of wine or cream and egg yolks. Serve with fish cutlets.

serves 4 • Preparation: 10 mins

Orange sauce

1 orange, 1 lemon, 1 cup white dessert wine, 1 glass brandy, 1 tbsp honey, 1 tbsp raspberry jam

Scrub and scald the fruit, grate the rind and mix it with the honey. Add the wine and pour the mixture into a pan. Simmer over low heat for 10 mins. Put in the jam, lemon juice and orange juice. Cook for 5 mins. Towards the end pour in the brandy and stir well.

serves 4 • Preparation: 20 mins

Ruby sauce

500 g small red beets, 3–4 tart apples, 50 g raisins, 2 tbsps honey, 2 tbsps lemon juice, 1 tsp grated lemon rind, 2 cups stock, salt, pepper, ½ cup dry red wine, 5–7 radishes

Peel and wash the beets, then grate them together with the apples, put into a pan. Add the blanched raisins, honey, lemon juice and zest. Pour in the stock. Bring to the boil, then simmer over low heat for 40 mins. Allow it to cool a bit, then put through a blender or force through a sieve. Pour into a pan, add salt, pepper and some more honey if required. Reduce the juices, stirring the sauce all the time. Add the grated radishes and wine. Stir well and heat up. Serve with roast or fried poultry and veal.

serves 4 • Preparation: 50–55 mins

Watercress sauce

2 cups chopped watercress, 3 tbsps butter, 4 spring onions (without green parts), 2 tbsps dry white wine, 1 cup cream, salt, pepper

Melt the butter in a pan, put in the chopped onions and sauté them. Add the watercress and, stirring all

the time, fry for 2 mins. Sprinkle with the wine, bring to the boil. Take off the heat, add the cream, salt and pepper. Put the sauce through a blender and heat it up. Excellent with boiled fish.

serves 4 • Preparation: 5 mins

Anchovy sauce I

1 tbsp butter, ½ cup stock, 1 cup dry white wine, 3 anchovy fillets, 2 egg yolks, juice of ½ lemon, 1 large onion, ½ bay leaf, 1 tsp flour, salt, a pinch of sugar

Fry the finely chopped onion in butter, but do not let it brown. Add the crumbled bay leaf, sugar, chopped anchovies and lemon juice. Pour in the stock and simmer over low heat, stirring all the time. Thicken the sauce with a roux from butter and flour. Sieve the mixture, add the egg yolks lightly beaten with the wine. Stir well and heat up. Serve immediately with venison cutlets or roasts.

serves 4 • Preparation: 10–15 mins

Anchovy sauce II

100 g butter, 1½ tbsps anchovy paste, 2 tbsps lemon juice, 1 tbsp chopped capers, 1 tbsp chopped black olives, 2 cups stock, a pinch of pepper, 1 tsp potato flour

Melt the butter in a pan, add the anchovy paste and heat up, stirring all the time. Add some pepper, lemon juice, olives and capers. Pour in the hot stock and, stirring all the time, heat up. Thicken the sauce with the potato flour dissolved in 1 tbsp of cold water. Serve in a sauce boat with boiled fish, grilled vegetables or boiled white meat.

serves 4 • Preparation: 10–15 mins

Savoury celery sauce

1 celery stalk, 150 g onion, 1–2 cloves of garlic, 3–4 bay leaves, 1 tsp each finely chopped fresh thyme and rosemary (or dried herbs), 2 tbsps soya sauce, 2 tbsps breadcrumbs, 3–4 tbsps chopped walnuts, salt, pepper, 2 tbsps olive oil, 2–3 tbsps dry white wine, 2 cups stock, 1 cup single cream lean the onion and celery, dice them finely. Chop the garlic. Heat up the oil in a pan, fry the onion, but do not let it brown. Add the celery, stir well, sprinkle with wine. Cover and simmer for several minutes. Put in the bay leaves and garlic, take off the lid and cook for 1–2 mins. Add the herbs and soya sauce, breadcrumbs and nuts. Stirring all the time, slowly pour in the stock. Simmer over low heat, then remove the bay leaves. Put the sauce through a blender, add salt and pepper to taste. Pour in the cream, stir well and heat up.

serves 4 • Preparation: 10–15 mins

Cheese and nut sauce

100 g tofu (or grated cheese), 100 g finely chopped cashew nuts, 2 tbsps butter, 4 bay leaves, ½ tsp paprika, 1½ cups light stock, 1½ cup single cream, salt, pepper

Melt the butter in a pan, put in the bay leaves and heat up a bit. Add the nuts and paprika, stir well and pour in slowly the lukewarm stock, stirring all the time so that the sauce comes smooth. Cook over low heat until the sauce has thickened. Add salt, pepper and paprika to taste. Remove the bay leaves. Blend the tofu with the cream and pour into the sauce. Stirring all the time, heat the sauce up, but mind that it does not become 'too stringy'.

serves 4 • Preparation: 10–15 mins

Grey sauce I

1 large onion, ½ tsp gingercake spices, 3 tbsps almond flakes, 3 tbsps raisins, 1 tbsp flour, 1 tbsp butter, 1 cup light chicken stock, ½ cup red wine, 2 tbsps caramel, juice of 1 lemon, salt, pepper, ½ tsp ground cloves, a pinch of cinnamon

Peel the onion, chopped it finely and fry in melted butter, but do not let it brown. Sprinkle with flour, pour in the cool stock and, stirring occasionally, simmer until the sauce has thickened. Add the cloves and gingercake spices, caramel and lemon juice. Simmer for 20 mins. Rinse the raisins, pour over the wine and leave aside for 15 mins, then add them to the sauce. Add salt, pepper, cinnamon

and, if required, sugar to taste. Stir well and heat up for 5 mins. Serve with fish and boiled tongue.

serves 4 • Preparation: 25–30 mins

Grey sauce II

50 g almonds, 50 g raisins, 4 cloves, 4 grains allspice, 1 small bay leaf, 1 lemon, 30 g gingercake, 1 glass red wine, 1 tbsp honey, 1 tbsp butter, 1 tsp flour, 5 prunes, 2 cups fish stock

Blanch and drain the raisins, pour over the wine and leave aside for 15 mins. Stone and rinse the prunes. Scald the almonds, skin them and chop finely. Make a roux from the butter and flour, dilute it with the fish stock. Add the spices, gingercake, prunes and lemon juice. Cover the pan and simmer for 30 mins. Allow it to cool a bit, then put through a blender and sieve the sauce. Pour into a pan, add the raisins together with the wine, honey and chopped almonds. Stir well, heat up. Season to taste. Serve with boiled fish.

serves 4 • Preparation: 35–40 mins

Sorrel sauce

300 g sorrel, 1 tbsp butter, 1 tbsp flour, 1½ cups stock, ½ cup thick cream, 1 egg yolk, salt, pepper, sugar, 1 tbsp lemon juice

Clean and rinse the sorrel, drain it, chop and put into a pan. Sprinkle sparingly with the stock, cover the pan and simmer for 20 mins. Put the sorrel through a blender and sieve it. Melt the butter in a pan, add the flour and make a white roux. Dilute it with the remaining stock and, stirring all the time, simmer until the sauce has thickened. Put in the sorrel purée, add salt, sugar, lemon juice and pepper. Mix well. Beat lightly the cream and egg yolk, pour into the sauce. Stirring all the time heat the sauce up, but do not allow it to boil. Serve with croquettes or hard-boiled eggs, or with boiled white meat (veal, turkey, chicken).

serves 4 • Preparation: 25–30 mins

Asparagus sauce

400 g green asparagus (fresh or tinned), 1 clove of garlic, 100 g finely chopped cashew nuts (or almonds), salt, a pinch of each sugar, pepper, paprika and cayenne, 1 tbsp lemon juice, 1 tbsp butter, 2 cups light stock, 2–3 tbsps dry white wine, 1 tbsp butter

Bring the stock to the boil, adding sugar, pepper, paprika, butter and lemon juice. Put in the cleaned asparagus and cook for 12 mins. Allow to cool, then put through a blender and sieve it. Add the crushed garlic, nuts, cayenne and wine. Put it through the blender again, then heat the sauce up.

serves 4 • Preparation: 20–25 mins

Ham sauce

200 g ham (or ham trimmings), 2 tbsps butter, 1 cup stock, ½ cup white dessert wine, 1 tbsp grated lemon rind, ½ tsp pounded juniper berries (ca 10 grains), 1 tsp flour, a pinch of each sugar and pepper, salt

Dice the ham finely and simmer it in butter together with the lemon zest and juniper. Pour in some stock and cook for 30 mins, then put through a blender. Make a roux from the flour and butter, dilute it with the wine. Stirring all the time, simmer until the sauce has thickened. Fold in the ham mixture, add sugar, pepper and salt to taste. Mix well and bring to the boil. Serve with venison cutlets.

serves 4 • Preparation: 35–40 mins

Plum sauce

300 g purple plums, 2 tbsps butter, 1 tsp flour, ½ cup boiled water, 1 glass dry white wine, grated rind and juice of ½ lemon, ¼ tsp ground cloves, a pinch of salt, 1½ tbsps honey

Rinse the plums, stone them and soften in a pan. Sprinkle with water and stew over low heat for 15 mins, stirring occasionally. Melt the butter in a pan, add the flour and make a roux. Dilute it with the wine and, stirring all the time, simmer over low heat. When the roux has thickened, fold in the plum purée, add the lemon zest and juice, honey and

cloves. Stir well, heat up, but keep it off the boil. Serve with roast pork.

serves 4 • Preparation: 25–30 mins

Prune and horseradish sauce

150 g stoned prunes, 3 tbsps grated horseradish, 2 tbsps butter, 1 tbsp flour, 2 cups stock, juice and grated rind of ½ lemon, 1 tbsp sugar, salt, a pinch of pepper

Rinse the prunes and soak them for 1–2 hours in a small amount of water. Pour in 1 cup of stock, bring to the boil and cook for 40 mins. Liquidize the prunes, then sieve them. Melt the butter in a pan, add the flour and make a white roux. Dilute it with the remaining stock and, stirring all the time, simmer over low heat. When the sauce has thickened, fold in the plum purée, add sugar, salt, pepper, lemon zest and juice, and the grated horseradish. Mix thoroughly and heat up. Serve with pork roast.

serves 4 • Preparation: 40–45 mins

Plum jam sauce

½ cup plum jam, 1 small glass dry red wine, 1½ cups stock, 2 tbsps butter, 1 tbsp flour, a pinch of salt, ¼ tsp each ground cloves and cinnamon

Make a roux from the butter and flour, dilute it with the stock and, stirring all the time, simmer over low heat. When the sauce has thickened, add the jam, wine, cloves and cinnamon. Bring to the boil, then sieve it.

serves 4 • Preparation: 10 mins

Tuna sauce

1 tin tuna in brine, 250 g mushrooms, 100 g butter, 2 cloves of garlic, 1 tbsp tomato concentrate, 1 cup tomato juice, ½ cup stock, salt, pepper, a pinch of sugar, 1 tbsp lemon juice, 2 tbsps chopped parsley

Melt the butter in a pan, add the garlic cloves, sauté them, then take out. Put in the sliced mushrooms and stirring all the time fry for a minute or two. Sprinkle with some stock and simmer for 10–15 mins. Add the drained tuna, tomato concentrate and juice, salt, pepper, sugar and lemon juice. Stirring all the time, simmer for another 2–3 mins. Towards the end add the chopped parsley.

serves 4 • Preparation: 30 mins

Sauce vénitienne

5–6 mushrooms, 3–4 onions, 1 cup dry white wine, 1 cup fish stock, 2 tbsps olive oil, salt, pepper, 4 egg yolks

Stew the finely chopped onion and diced mushroom in oil. Add the wine and the fish stock, salt and pepper and simmer over low heat. Keep it off the boil while blending in the egg yolks one at a time. Heat the sauce up, whisking all the time until the sauce has thickened. Serve with boiled fish.

serves 4 • Preparation: 10–15 mins

Wine sauce

2 cups dry white wine, 5–6 new carrots, 2–3 onions, 2–3 cloves of garlic, 3 tbsps butter, 1 tbsp flour, ½ tsp dried thyme, 1 bay leaf, salt, pepper, ½ tsp honey, 1 tbsp lemon juice, ¼ tsp grated lemon rind

Peel and dice the carrots, onion and garlic. Melt 2 tbsps of butter in a pan, put in the diced vegetables and sauté them, stirring all the time. Add the thyme and bay leaf, sprinkle with flour and lemon zest, mix thoroughly. Pour in the wine and simmer over low heat for one hour. Liquidize the mixture in a food processor, then sieve it. Heat the sauce up, add salt, pepper, lemon juice, honey and 1 tbsp of butter. Mix well and heat up again. Serve with fish.

serves 4 • Preparation: 10 mins • Cooking: 1 hr

Hare liver sauce

hare liver, 1 tbsp butter, ¼ cup stock, 1 cup dry white wine, 1 small onion, 1 tsp flour, 1 tbsp chopped parsley, salt, pepper

Chop the raw liver finely. Fry the finely chopped onion in butter, but do not let it brown. Put in the chopped liver and parsley and sauté them. Cover the pan and simmer over low heat for 15 mins. Put through a blender and sieve the sauce. Make a roux from the flour and butter, dilute it with the wine. Add salt and pepper, fold in the liver mixture and heat up. Serve with roast hare.

serves 4 • Preparation: 25–30 mins

Green sauce

1 tbsp butter, 1 cup stock, 1 glass dry white wine, juice of 1 lemon, 1 egg yolk, 1 tsp each chopped tarragon, dill, chives, parsley and basil, a pinch of sugar, 1 tsp flour

Add 1 tbsp of stock to the chopped herbs and simmer them for a bit, taking care that they do not lose their colour, then take them off the heat. Make a roux from the butter and flour, dilute it with cold stock, add lemon juice and a pinch of sugar. Stirring all the time, simmer the sauce over low heat until it has thickened. Beat the egg yolk lightly with the wine, pour into the sauce and again, stirring all the time, heat it over low heat. Fold in the herbs, mix thoroughly, season to taste. Serve with roast wild fowl.

serves 4 • Preparation: 10 mins

Herbal sauce

2 tbsps chopped parsley, 1 tbsp each chopped thyme and marjoram, 2 spring onions with green parts, salt, pepper, 1 cup stock, ½ glass dry white wine, 1 tbsp butter, 1 tbsp flour, 1 tsp honey, juice and grated rind of 1 lemon, 1½ tbsps finely chopped tarragon

Put the lukewarm stock, onions, marjoram, parsley and pepper through a blender, then sieve them. Melt the butter in a pan, add the flour and, stirring all the time, slowly pour in the herbal stock and simmer until the sauce has thickened. Add salt, pepper, lemon juice and zest, honey and wine. Mix thoroughly, heat up, put in the chopped tarragon and mix well again. The hot sauce is an excellent addition to roast chicken and veal, and to grilled meat.

serves 4 • Preparation: 10–15 mins

Mock turtle sauce

2 tbsps butter, 1 cup stock, 100 g ham, ½ cup white dessert wine, 200 g tomatoes, 1 carrot, 1 parsley root, a piece of celeriac, 2–3 onions, ½ tsp each thyme, basil and sage, a pinch of chilli pepper, 1 tsp sugar, salt, lemon juice

Peel the vegetables and grate them coarsely. Dice the ham, cut the tomatoes and onions into quarters. Melt the butter in a pan, brown slightly the onion, add the grated vegetables and, stirring occasionally, sauté them. Put in the ham and tomatoes, pour in the stock, cover the pan and simmer over ow heat for an hour, then put through a blender and sieve the mixture. Add the herbs, lemon juice, salt and sugar, and cook or another 20 mins. Beat the flour with 1 tbsp of water and wine until smooth. Pour into the sauce, mix well and bring to the boil. Serve with hot venison ham or boiled tongue.

serves 4 • Preparation: 20 mins • Cooking: 55–60 mins

Cold sweet sauces

Aniseed sauce

1 cup milk, 2–3 tbsps sugar, a piece of vanilla,
2 egg yolks, 1 cup anisette (aniseed liqueur),
1 tsp potato flour, 2–3 tbsps single cream

Boil the milk with the vanilla and sugar, strain and bring to the boil again. Pour in the mixed potato flour and 1 tbsp water and, stirring all the time, heat it up, until the sauce has thickened. Beat lightly the egg yolks with the liqueur and cream and add to the sauce. Stir well, heat up, but keep off the boil. Serve with desserts and cookies.

serves 4 • Preparation: 5 mins

Peach sauce

2–3 peaches, 1 tbsp each lemon and orange juice, ¼ tsp each grated lemon and orange rind,1 glass dry white wine, 1 tbsp vodka, 3 tbsps honey, a pinch of ginger

Blanch and skin the peaches, remove the stones. Liquidize them together with the honey and wine, the juice and zest and with ginger. Mix with the vodka and chill a bit. An excellent addition to ice cream, desserts and fruit salads.

serves 4 • Preparation: 5–7 mins • Cooking: 30 mins

Apple sauce

500 g apples, 1 tsp lemon juice, 1 tbsp butter, 2–3 tbsps sugar, 2–3 tbsps dry white wine, ½ tsp cinnamon, ¼ tsp grated lemon rind, ½ cup whipping cream

Dice the peeled apples finely, sprinkle them with lemon juice. Melt the butter in a pan, put in the apples and soften them. Add the cinnamon, sugar and wine and simmer for 30 mins, then liquidize and leave to cool. Fold in the cream, chill a bit. Serve with pasta, kasha, pancakes and desserts.

serves 4 • Preparation: 30–35 mins • Refrigerating: 30 mins

Brandy sauce

2 eggs, 2 tbsps sugar, ¾ cup single cream, a piece of vanilla, 1 glass brandy

Boil the cream with the vanilla, strain it. Beat the egg yolks with sugar in a bowl. Rest the bowl on top of a pot of boiling water. Gradually add the cream, whisking all the time until the sauce has thickened. Take off the heat, pour in the brandy and mix thoroughly. Whisk the egg whites until stiff, fold into the cool sauce, chill a bit. Serve with ice cream and desserts.

serves 4 • Preparation: 25–30 mins • Refrigerating: 30 mins

Apricot sauce

1 tin apricots in syrup, 1 tbsp lemon juice, 1 tbsp honey, 3 tbsps almond flakes

Liquidize the apricots together with the syrup, honey and lemon juice. Add the almond flakes, mix well. Refrigerate for a while.

serves 4 • Preparation: 5 mins • Refrigerating: 30 mins

Fruit sauce

100 g each raspberries and blackberries, 2 tbsps lemon juice, 1 glass dry white wine, ½ cup single cream, 1 tsp caster sugar

Liquidize the raspberries and blackberries with the sugar, lemon juice and wine, then sieve the purée. Whip the cream with the caster sugar, fold into the fruit purée. Refrigerate for a while.

serves 4 • Preparation: 10 mins • Refrigerating: 30 mins

Punch sauce

juice and grated rind of 1 large orange, juice and grated rind of ½ lemon, 1 glass dry red wine, 2–3 tbsps very strong tea infusion, 1 glass rum, 2 egg yolks, 3 tbsps sugar, a pinch of cayenne

Mix the tea infusion with cayenne and lemon and orange zest and leave aside for 15 mins. Bring the wine to the boil. Beat the egg yolks with sugar until foamy. Rest the bowl on top of a pot of boiling water and whisk the sauce, gradually adding the hot wine. When the sauce has thickened, take off the heat and leave to cool, then combine it with the lemon and orange juice, the tea infusion and rum. Whisk well, chill a bit. Serve with ice cream, cream and pancakes.

serves 4 • Preparation: 30–35 mins • Refrigerating: 30 mins

Hot sweet sauces

Chocolate sauce

150 g hard bitter chocolate, 2 tsps instant coffee, ½ cup sugar, 1 cup water, 1 glass brandy, a pinch of powdered cardamom

Make a syrup from water and sugar, add the coffee and grated chocolate. Stirring all the time, cook over low heat until the chocolate melts. Add the cardamom and heat up for 2–3 mins. Take off the heat, pour in the brandy, mix thoroughly. Serve with desserts, ice cream and pancakes.

serves 4 • Preparation: 10 mins

Apricot sauce

300 g ripe apricots, 2 tbsps sugar, ¼ cup water, 1 tsp potato flour, 1 tbsp lemon juice, 1 tbsp honey, 2 tbsps brandy, a pinch of ground cloves

Boil the water with sugar, put in the stoned apricots and stew under cover for 20 mins. Liquidize the apricots, put in the cloves and lemon juice, then heat the purée up. Mix the potato flour with 1 tbsp of water, pour into the sauce. Stirring all the time, heat up the sauce until it has thickened. Take the hot thick sauce off the heat, pour in the brandy mixed with the honey, stir well. An excellent addition to desserts, pancakes and ice cream.

serves 4 • Preparation: 30 mins

Orange sauce

2 oranges, 1 tbsp lemon juice, 2 tbsps sugar, 1 glass orange liqueur

Squeeze the juice from the oranges. Wash the peel well and cook in boiling water for 2–3 mins. Strain and again cook it in fresh water for 10 mins. Strain, pour over cold water, remove the white pith. Cut the orange rind into thin strips. Boil the orange juice with the lemon juice, put in the orange rind strips and, stirring all the time, bring to the boil. Take off the heat, pour in the liqueur, mix thoroughly. Serve hot with pancakes and desserts.

serves 4 • Cooking: 15 mins • Preparation: 10 mins

Rose hip sauce

100 g cleaned fresh rose hips, juice and grated rind of ½ lemon, a piece of cinnamon, 1–2 cloves, 4 tbsps sugar, ¾ cup water, ½ cup dry white wine, 2–3 tbsps port, 2 tbsps blackcurrant jelly

Clean and rinse the hips, put them into a pan. Add the lemon juice and zest, cinnamon, cloves and sugar, cover with hot water. Bring to the boil, then simmer over low heat for 40 mins. Pour in the wine and cook for several minutes more. Allow to cool, remove the cinnamon and cloves, liquidize and sieve the sauce. Bring it to the boil, take off the heat. Combine the jelly with the port, pour into the sauce, mix thoroughly. Serve with desserts, pancakes and ice cream.

serves 4 • Preparation: 50–55 mins

Vanilla sauce

1 cup milk, 1 vanilla pod, 3 egg yolks,
3 tbsps sugar, 1 tbsp butter

Cook the milk with vanilla over low heat for 10 mins, then strain it. Beat the egg yolks with sugar until foamy in a bowl. Whisking it all the time, gradually add pieces of butter. Rest the bowl on top of a pot of boiling water and whisking all the time add gradually the hot milk. When the sauce has thickened, take it off the heat. Serve with chocolate and fruit desserts, pancakes and cookies.

serves 4 • Cooking: 10 mins • Preparation: 20–25 mins

Sour cherry sauce

400 g stoned sour cherries, 3 tbsps sugar,
a pinch of ground cloves, 150 g white
chocolate, ¾ cup whipping cream

Liquidize the cherries with the sugar and cloves, then sieve the purée. Grate the chocolate. Boil the cream in a saucepan. Rest it on top of a pot of boiling water and whisk the mixture, gradually adding the chocolate. When the chocolate has melted and the sauce thickened, fold in the cherry purée. Mix thoroughly and heat up over low heat. Serve with desserts, pancakes and cookies.

serves 4 • Preparation: 30–35 mins

Chocolate sauce

CHAPTER IX

FISH AND CRAYFISH

Freshwater fish

Fish have been eaten in Poland since the earliest times. During the period of the Piast dynasty 'the common people ate herring during Lent, while the richer people ate Polish fish of better kinds'. Salted herring were taken around the country in barrels, or on skewers. During the reign of Sigismund III, eels, herring, barbels, flounders, salmon, burbot, sturgeon, fry, sculpins and other fish were eaten during fasts.

In 1884 Łukasz Gołębiowski wrote:

Fish soup was cooked. Salmon and pike were usually served with yellow sauce, other fish with grey sauce. They were cooked Jewish-style, but also Hungarian, Czech, Dutch or Moravian style. Some were stewed whole, either with scales or scaled, or in large steaks; some were fried or braised without a drop of water, others were used for pâté or served cold in jelly, either fresh, or marinated, savoury or sweet, with honey, currants and figs, sprinkled with chopped egg and sauce, with vinegar and olive oil; some were stuffed and some were cooked plain, broken into pieces or made into fishcake cutlets of various shapes.

(*Domy i dwory*, vol. IV, p. 39)

In Old Polish homes fish were served in an amazing variety of ways, demonstrating the inventiveness of the cooks. They were given exotic colours – for example, trout and carp were coloured blue, scalded in boiling vinegar. They were covered with coloured sauces: yellow sauce obtained by use of the favourite Polish spice, saffron, or grey sauce (really brown) made with carmelized sugar, or white sauce with grated horseradish, or red sauce made with cherries or cranberries.

Wilhelm le Vasseur Beauplan, a French military engineer who in the 17th century constructed many fortifications in the east of Poland, was enchanted by one thing, even though he did not generally enthuse about Polish cuisine:

There is one thing in which the Poles are much superior to us: in everything concerning fish they are miraculously skilful. Apart from the fact that in this country there are very many fish, Poles cook them so well and give them such a choice flavour that even people who have gorged the most find their appetite roused. In this, they are superior to all nations, and this is not my opinion alone, a matter of my own taste, but it is the view of Frenchmen and other foreigners who have been received by them; they all think the same.

The Poles were aware of this, and the great Polish magnates claimed that they should employ a French pastry cook in the kitchen, but for fish, only a Pole would do. Polish cooks claimed that 'fish should only be cooked in wine, and fresh salmon must absolutely only be cooked in burgundy'. People were, it is true, shocked at such extravagance, saying that 'after all, the old Poles were stronger than today's Poles and had more fire in their bellies, even though they ate fish cooked in water', but even so, cooking fish in wine continued, since it was believed that it gave the fish a "choice flavour".

One could write endlessly about the advantages of fish. In terms of food value, fish are often superior to meat, for they are a source of high value and easily digested protein, and have many valuable mineral components – iron, calcium, phosphorus, copper, magnesium, potassium, iodine. They are also rich in vitamins from the B group, and vitamins A and D. Fish dishes are easily digestible and low-calorie, and dieticians count them (especially dishes made from saltwater fish) among the healthiest foodstuffs.

Salmon is the most prized of the freshwater fish. There are many varieties of salmon, and Atlantic and Pacific salmon are considered the best. They have a choice flavour and aroma, are ideal for baking, braising, and also for making extremely tasty stuffings (for example for koulebiac).

The **trout** is related to the salmon, and has white, juicy and very delicate meat. The tastiest are fish caught between May and July, weighing 250–350 g. They can be cooked in various ways. There is a dispute among gourmets about whether baked trout are best, or whether the honours go to "blue trout" cooked in white wine or water and vinegar. Trout is excellent for grilling, for frying as a whole fish, and also for braising and stuffing.

Common **whitefish** or **sea trout**, can be substituted for trout.

Other common freshwater fish include the following members of the carp family: **bream**, **barbel**, **roach**, **tench**, **silver carp** and **carp**. These are fatty and bony fish, white or light yellowy-pink in colour, succulent, delicate but unfortunately quite heavy. They are suitable for boiling, for making jellies, for frying, braising and stuffing.

Fish from the carp family often have a slightly muddy taste. In order to get rid of it you should either soak the fish for 3 to 4 hours in highly salted cold water, after which you should rinse them and dry them, or after filleting rub in salt and place them for 1 to 2 hours in the refrigerator. Before frying or boiling, it is worth lightly scoring the fish skin, as when it gets hot, it shrinks and causes the portion of fish to become misshapen. Fish of the carp family do not turn yellow during cooking if you add lots of onion and a few parsley roots to the water. You can give them a subtle flavour by boiling them in lager.

And now for two freshwater predators: the **perch** has meat that is similar in flavour and delicate white colour to the pikeperch. It tastes best when you fry small perch whole. It is a good idea to rub pikeperch and perch with salt (after cleaning them, when you must take care with the spiky dorsal fin), and leave them for 1 to 2 hours.

Pike has a highly prized, white, lean and delicate meat, but unfortunately it is very bony. Like the perch it is excellent both hot and cold. It can be boiled, braised, fried and baked, and is also an excellent ingredient for all kinds of stuffing. It is a good idea to rub pike with salt after cleaning and leave it for 1 to 2 hours. According to gourmands, the best way to serve it is Jewish style, that is, boiled in a stock made from soup vegetables and wine, a large quantity of onions and spices.

Pikeperch is a fine fish of the perch family, with delicate, fat white and very tasty flesh, which is excellent both hot and cold. Gourmands claim that the best way to cook it is as pike-perch Polish style – boiled in a light stock and before serving covered with melted butter and sprinkled with chopped hard-boiled egg and parsley. You can make cold pikeperch in jelly or mayonnaise, grill it, fry it or boil it.

What else should you remember?

– Steaming fish allows the delicate taste and aroma to be retained (which is especially important when cooking sole).
– Fish should be cooked in their own stock, and there should only be enough liquid to barely cover the fish. The stock should be prepared first from onion, celeriac, parsley root and spices (bay leaves, allspice, pepper and sometimes cloves), a slice of lemon (without pips), parsley, fresh thyme, and also the heads, bladders and bones of filleted fish. The taste of the stock can be improved by adding white wine. After cooking (30–35 minutes), the stock should be strained, cooled a little, and then poured over the fish and simmered over a low heat. The cooking time, depending on the size and variety of the fish, is from 15 to 25 minutes.
– Before cooking, the fish skin should be lightly scored, so that when it shrinks during the cooking process, it does not spoil the appearance of the fish.
– Fish should be fried in olive oil, cooking oil or melted butter. Before frying, you should carefully dry the fish with a paper towel.
– Small pieces of fish should be fried in deep fat.
– Fish are best baked in aluminium foil or greaseproof paper brushed with fat; they are then more delicate and

succulent. The vegetables, seasoning and stuffing used in the baking give the fish a particular taste and aroma.

– Fish rubbed with salt, lemon juice, herbs or spices should be left to steep in the fridge under cover. Hotter spices should be used rather for fatty fish (for example mackerel and carp).

– Frozen fish steaks should not be defrosted before frying, because they will fall apart.

– Fish served hot should be placed on well-heated dishes and plates.

And now a few words about the preparation of fish:

Tench, which have a double skin, should be scalded before cleaning by immersing them for 30 seconds (not longer) in boiling water. You should remember to cover the pan with a lid, and hold it down, because a tench that has been killed even a hour before can jump violently when immersed in boiling water.

Eel should not be scraped, but the skin pulled off. It is very difficult to kill a live eel, and so it should be 'put to sleep' as follows: put 1 l of vinegar into a container, add two dessert-spoons of salt, and when the salt dissolves, put the eel in, cover the pot and leave it for a few minutes. Then hang the eel on a hook, cut the skin around the head and, undercutting a little with a knife, pull the skin down to the tail.

Scales should not be scraped from **pike** as with other fish, but they should be shaved off with a sharp knife, cutting off the delicate top skin together with the scales, which in this way comes off in large patches, leaving the white skin underneath. If it is scraped in any other way, the skin will be black, and this should be scrubbed with a sharp brush steeped in salt until it turns white.

Carp, after washing, are cooked by gourmands together with the scales, because they claim that the most delicate taste of the fish is just underneath the scales. Minced carp is very delicate and tasty and is excellent for fish balls.

Pikeperch has a delicate white and fat flesh. It is more suitable for steaming or boiling (it tastes much worse fried), and is excellent served with hard-boiled egg, mushroom sauce, lemon or hollandaise sauce or cold with sharp-tasting sauces.

Catfish, which has no scales, should be scrubbed before cooking with a sharp brush steeped in salt, and an old catfish should be skinned entirely, since the skin is hard and does not taste good.

Trout does not need scaling either.

NOTE: When cooking fish, the salting and cooking time is often the total preparation time: while the salt is going through the fish, the stock can be prepared from vegetables and fish waste. Salting is a stage in preparing fish for cooking.

Carp, a truly Polish fish

Carp, Moscow style

Cut the gutted fish into three parts, put into a saucepan, pour in a bottle of good beer and a cup of vodka, put in a sizeable piece of butter mixed with flour, a bunch of parsley and spring onions, cloves, thyme, a bay leaf, basil, chopped onion. Add salt and pepper and cook over high heat. Take out the vegetables and serve the fish immediately.

(*Kucharz doskonały*, 1808)

Carp, Polish style

1 kg carp, 2 carrots, 2 parsley roots, celeriac, 3 leeks, 3 onions, 1 bottle lager beer, 1 cup vinegar, lemon, ½ tsp sugar, ½ tsp each ginger and thyme, 3–4 cloves, 4–5 grains each allspice and pepper, 2 tbsp capers, 1 cup white wine, rye bread crust, 1 tbsp butter, salt, sugar for caramel

Clean and wash the vegetables, dice them, cover with the beer and vinegar, add the spices, herbs and lemon zest and cook, then sieve. Cut the gutted and rinsed carp into sections, rub with salt and leave for an hour in a cool place. Put the fish into a skillet, pour in the puréed vegetable stock and cook for 20–25 mins. Add the wine, bread crust, the peeled and sliced lemon, butter and capers, cook for a while longer. Before transferring the fish to a serving plate, for colour add caramel to the sauce. Stir the sauce and pour it over the fish. Serve with boiled potatoes.

serves 4 • Macerating: 1 hr • Preparation: 35–40 mins

Boiled carp

ca 1.3 kg carp, 2 fish heads, 2 tbsps butter, 2 cups dry red wine, 3 large onions, 1–2 cloves of garlic, 200 g medium-sized mushrooms, 1 bay leaf, 1 sprig of fresh thyme, a bunch of parsley, salt, pepper, 1 tbsp lemon juice, ½ tsp honey, 1 tbsp fresh chopped thyme

Clean and wash the gutted fish, bone it, cut into thick strips, put into a bowl, sprinkle with lemon juice and salt, cover and put in the fridge for 1–2 hours. Put the fish heads and spine into a large pot, pour in a small amount of hot water, add the bay leaf, half the parsley, the thyme sprig, 1 onion, salt and pepper. Bring to the boil, then simmer for 30–40 mins. Strain the stock, then reduce it until less than a cup has been left. Melt the butter in a skillet, add the finely chopped onion and sauté it. Add the chopped mushrooms and fry over high heat for 2 mins. Reduce the juice, add the garlic crushed with salt, chopped thyme and the remaining chopped parsley. Pour in the wine and simmer under cover for 10 mins. Add the honey and fish stock, stir and bring to the boil. Put in the fish pieces, cover and cook over low heat for 40 mins.

serves 4 • Preparation: 30–35 mins • Cooking: 40 mins

Carp in beer I

carp (ca 1.5 kg), 200 g onion, 50 g raisins, 1 tsp honey, juice and grated peel of 1 lemon, ½ tsp ground cloves, salt, pepper, 2–3 tbsp olive oil, 1 cup beer

Wash and dry the gutted fish, rub it with salt, leave for an hour. Divide it into sections, sprinkle with pepper and ground cloves, leave again for an hour in a cool place. Blanch and drain the raisins. Heat up the oil in a skillet, brown finely cut onion, add the fish, pour in the beer. Cover with a lid and cook over low heat for 20 mins. Add the raisins and lemon juice mixed with the honey, sprinkle with lemon rind. Serve with boiled potatoes.

serves 4 • Preparation: 20 mins • Cooking: 20 mins

Carp in beer II

800 g carp fillets, 1 cup lager beer, 1 large onion, 5–6 grains each allspice and pepper, ½ tsp grated lemon rind, 1 tsp ground cloves, ½ tsp sugar, 60 g raisins, 1 tbsp chopped walnuts, 2 tbsp olive oil, salt

Rub the washed and dried fillets with salt and ground cloves, cover and put in the fridge for 1–2 hours, then cut them into portions. Rinse the raisins, blanch and drain them. Heat the oil in a skillet, fry the finely chopped onion (without browning it), add half the raisins, pepper and allspice. Pour in the beer, bring to the boil. Put in the fish portions, sprinkle with grated lemon rind. Cook over low heat for 15 mins. Add the remaining raisins, shake the skillet gently and simmer for another 5–6 mins. Serve hot or cold, sprinkled with chopped walnuts.

serves 4 • Preparation: 20 mins • Cooking: 20 mins

Carp in blue

1 carp (ca 1.3 kg), 1–2 carp heads, 2 cups vinegar, soup vegetables, 2 onions, 5–6 grains each allspice and pepper, 1 bay leaf, 3–4 cloves, a piece of ginger (the size of a walnut), 2–3 tbsps capers, 2 tbsps stoned green olives, dry rye bread crust, ½ tsp sugar, salt, pepper, 1 tbsp butter, lemon

Clean the gutted fish, cut the head, tail and fins off. Make a thick broth from the head, soup vegetables, onions and spices. Put the fish into a pan, pour in the hot vinegar, leave for several minutes. When it is cool, take the fish out and cut into sections, put into a skillet, cover with the strained stock, add the bread crust and cook over low heat for 15 mins. Carefully take out the fish. Season the sauce with salt, pepper and sugar, stir and sieve it. Return the sauce to the skillet, heat it up, add the capers, finely chopped ginger and olives cut into fine strips. Heat it up over low heat. Peel the lemon, cut it into thin slices, remove the pips. Put the fish and lemon slices into the sauce, heat up slowly for several minutes (but do not let it boil). Serve with boiled potatoes or bread roll.

serves 4 • Preparation: 35–45 mins • Cooking: 15 mins

Carp in grey sauce

1 carp, 1 lemon, 1 celeriac, 2 onions, 1 tsp sugar, 6 grains each allspice and pepper, ¼ tsp ground ginger,

2 cups beer, 50 g ginger cake, 1 tbsp butter, 1 tbsp plum jam, 50 g raisins, 30 g almonds, 30 g walnuts, salt

Clean and wash the fish, cut it along the belly, bleed it into a skillet into which you have put the juice from one lemon. Wash the fish, cut it into sections, rub with roasted salt and leave for an hour in a cool place. Make a stock from 2 cups of water, the soup vegetables, onion, spices, sugar, ginger and lemon zest, then sieve the cooked vegetables. Put the fish into the blood and lemon mixture, add the beer and the vegetable purée and cook for several minutes over low heat. Add the ginger cake, plum jam, chopped walnuts, almonds and blanched raisins (and a pinch of sugar if required). Shake the skillet gently. Heat up for 10–15 mins, but do not let it boil. Arrange the fish on a serving plate and pour hot sauce over it. Serve with boiled potatoes or bread roll.

serves 4 • Salting: 1 hr • Preparation: 40–45 mins • Cooking: 25–30 mins

Carp in black sauce

1.3 kg carp, soup vegetables, 2–3 onions, 4–5 grains each allspice and pepper, 1 bay leaf, ¼ tsp each ground ginger and marjoram, juice and fine rind of 1 lemon, 1 cup dark beer, 2–3 tbsps dry red wine, 1 tbsp honey, 3 tbsps chopped walnuts, 1 tbsp butter, 1 tsp flour, salt

Wash the fish, cut it along the belly, bleed it into a skillet into which you have put lemon juice. Clean the fish, wash and dry it, rub with roasted salt and leave for an hour. Cook the finely chopped onions, soup vegetables and spices in a small amount of water. Add the marjoram and finely chopped lemon zest to the cooking stock. Sieve the cooked vegetables. Put the fish pieces into a skillet, pour in the beeer, add the vegetable purée and the blood and lemon juice mixture. Bring quickly to the boil, then cook covered over low heat for 20 mins. Make a roux from the butter and flour, add the wine and simmer until the sauce has thickened, put in the honey and chopped walnuts. Pour the sauce into the fish, shake the skillet gently, simmer for a bit over low heat.

serves 4 • Salting: 1 hr • Preparation: 40–45 mins • Cooking: 25–30 mins

Carp à la Pomian

Edward Pożerski-Pomian (1875–1964) occupies an important place in the culinary history of France. He was a Pole, called 'the genius of taste' and 'king of chefs', who invented many dishes reverting to the tradition of Old Polish cuisine. His stuffed carp made the history of culinary art as 'carp à la Pomian'. The mushroom stuffing gives the fish a very special flavour. His recipe was later adapted for other fish dishes, such as 'carp fillets with mushrooms', 'baked carp in a mushroom ring', 'carp rings with mushrooms' or 'carp in bechamel'. Also the stuffing has been enriched with chopped parsley, chopped hard-boiled eggs, dried mushrooms and finely chopped onion.

1.5–1.7 kg carp, 50 g pork fat, 250 mushrooms, 1 medium-sized onion, 2–3 tbsp breadcrumbs, 2–3 tbsp single cream, 3 tbsp butter, 2 eggs, salt, pepper, ¼ tsp dried thyme, 1 glass dry red wine

Clean the gutted fish, but do not cut the head off, only remove the eyes and gills. Wash it thoroughly, dry, rub with salt inside and out, wrap in foil and leave for an hour in the fridge.

STUFFING: Chop the rinsed and dried mushrooms and the peeled onion finely. Render the finely cubed pork fat in a heated frying pan, add onion and mushrooms. Sauté them over high heat, then reduce the juice. Take off the heat, add salt, pepper and thyme, stir well, then leave to cool. Mix the cream with the breadcrumbs and leave to soak for several minutes. Beat the butter with the egg yolks. Stirring all the time, add the mixture to the breadcrumbs. Pour the whole into the mushrooms, add salt and pepper to taste. Fold in the whisked egg whites.

Score the skin of the fish in several places (so that the fish keeps its shape when the skin shrinks in the oven). Put the stuffing into the fish, close the belly with toothpicks. Place butter knobs on top. Grease an oven-proof dish with butter, put in the fish. Place it in a preheated oven and bake for 50–60 mins, basting it with melted butter from time to time and towards the end with red wine. Garnish with half slices of lemon (put green or black stoned olives in the eyeholes). Serve with baked or sautéd potatoes, sprinkled liberally with chopped parsley. Separately serve the roasting sauce (if required, thickened with a butter and flour roux).

Serves 4 • Salting: 1–2 hrs • Preparation: 30 mins • Baking: 50–60 mins

Carp stuffed with apples

*2 carps (ca 1.3 kg each), 1 kg tart apples,
3 tbsp grated horseradish, 1 tbsp lemon juice,
½ tsp grated lemon rind, 1 tbsp honey, salt,
3 tbsp butter, 1 lemon cut in fine slices*

Wash and dry the gutted fish, rub them inside and out with salt, cover and leave for 1–2 hours. Stuffing: Grate coarsely the peeled apples, sprinkle them with lemon juice, mix in the honey, horseradish and lemon zest. Stuff the fish, close the bellies with thread or toothpicks, put butter knobs on top. Grill or bake in a preheated oven, basting with melted butter. Garnish with lemon slices before serving.

serves 4 • Salting: 1–2 hrs • Preparation: 15–20 mins • Baking: 40–50 mins

Carp with flavoured stuffing

ca 1.5 kg carp, 6 thin rashers, 1 tsp ground pepper

Stuffing: 5–6 celery sticks, 1 large onion, 2–3 tbsps chopped parsley, 1 tsp fresh or ½ tsp dried thyme, ¾ cup breadcrumbs, 2 tbsps single cream, salt, 2 tbsps butter, a pinch of pepper and sugar, ½ tsp lemon juice

Wash and dry the gutted fish, rub with salt, leave for an hour in a cool place. Clean and wash the celery, cut it into thin slices. Chop the onion finely, fry it in 1½ tbsp of butter, but do not let it brown. Leave it to cool, then add the celery, breadcrumbs, parsley and thyme, season with salt and pepper, fold in the cream. Stuff the fish, seal the belly with toothpicks. Grease aluminium foil with butter, line it with rashers, sprinkle with pepper. Arrange the fish on the rashers, carefully wrap it up in the foil. Grill or bake it in a preheated oven for 40–50 mins.

serves 4 • Salting: 1–2 hrs • Preparation: 15–20 mins • Baking: 40–50 mins

Carp baked in vegetables

ca 1.3 kg carp, 2 carrots, 3 large onions, 6–8 potatoes, 2 parsley roots, ½ celeriac, salt, pepper, 3 tbsps butter, 1 tbsp chopped parsley, 2 tbsps grated cheese

Clean the fish, cut it into sections, rub with salt. Dice the peeled and washed vegetables finely. Slice the peeled potatoes, cover with boiling water, drain. Grease an ovenproof dish with butter, put in half the veg- etables and potatoes, sprinkle with salt and pepper. Put the fish pieces on top and cover them with the remaining vegetables and potatoes. Place butter knobs on top, sprinkle with parsley and grated cheese, cover with aluminium foil and put into a preheated oven for 60 mins. Serve hot.

serving 4 • Salting: 1 hr • Preparation: 15 mins • Baking: 50–60 mins

Fried carp

1 kg carp, flour, 1 egg, breadcrumbs, salt, sunflower oil, parsley

Clean and wash the gutted fish, cut it into sections (use the head, fins, tail and bladder to cook either fish soup or stock for sauces). Rub the fish with roasted salt and leave for an hour in a cool place. Dredge the fish pieces with flour, lightly beaten egg and breadcrumbs. Put them in a hot frying pan and fry on both sides until golden brown. Garnish with chopped parsley and serve with sautéd potatoes or white bread.

serves 4 • Preparation: 5 mins • Frying: 7–8 mins

Carp in melted butter

ca 1.30 kg carp, 1 large onion, 1 carrot, 1 parsley root, ¼ celeriac, ½ leek, salt, juice and grated rind of ½ lemon, 100–150 g butter, 2–3 tbsps chopped parsley, ½ lemon cut into slices

Clean and wash the gutted fish. Dry it, rub with salt and leave for 1–2 hours. Peel the vegetables, cover them with water, bring to the boil. Add the lemon zest, salt, the head and tail of the carp, and simmer for 30 mins. Strain the stock. Dice the carrot and parsley root. Cut the fish into sections, put into a skillet, pour over the boiling stock, add the lemon juice. Simmer for 15–20 mins, then take it out carefully, put in an ovenproof dish. Arrange the carrot and parsley slices around, pour over melted butter and put into a preheated oven for 4–5 mins. Before serving, sprinkle with greens and decorate with lemon slices.

serves 4 • Salting: 1–2 hrs • Preparation: 30 mins • Cooking: 15–20 mins

Baked carp

ca 1.3 kg carp, ½ tsp salt, 3–4 garlic cloves, parsley, 1 tbsp sunflower oil, 1 tbsp butter

Clean and wash the gutted fish (without head or tail), rub it with salt mixed with garlic, leave for an hour in a cool place. Grease an oven-proof dish with butter. Put a small bunch of parsley into the belly of the fish, close it with toothpicks or skewers. Sprinkle the fish with oil, put into in the dish, place slices of butter around. Put the dish into a preheated oven for 30 mins. Serve garnished with knobs of butter and chopped parsley, with boiled potatoes.

Salting: 1–2 hrs • Preparation: 15–20 mins • Baking: 30–35 mins

Carp rings with horseradish

1 carp, 1 egg, 1 white bread roll, 1 onion, salt, pepper, oil or butter for frying, 1 horseradish root

Clean and wash the gutted fish, bone it (use the bones, head, fins and tail to cook soup). Soak the bread roll in milk. Put the fish and the squeezed bread roll through a mincer. Add the finely chopped and fried onion, salt, pepper and egg to the fish. Work the mixture into a smooth paste and shape it into small rings. Fry them on both sides in hot fat. Garnish with coarsely grated horseradish before serving.

serves 4 • Preparation: 15–20 mins • Frying: 10–12 mins

Nobleman's carp

800 g carp fillets, 300 g apricots, ½ cup dry red wine, ¼ tsp each ground cinnamon, cloves,

Baked carp

ginger, sugar and grated lemon rind, lemon juice,
3 tbsps oil, 1 tbsps butter, 1 tbsp flour, salt

Wash and dry the fillets, rub them with salt, sprinkle lightly with lemon juice and put into the fridge for an hour. Blanch and skin the apricots, cut them in two, remove the stones. Put them through a blender together with the wine, remaining lemon juice and zest, cloves, ginger and sugar. Add sugar and salt to taste. Cut the fillets into portions, dredge with flour and fry in hot fat. Transfer them to a greased overproof dish, pour over the sauce and put into a preheated oven for 6–8 mins. Serve with pasta or rice and lettuce.

serves 4 • Macerating: 1–2 hrs • Preparation: 15 mins • Frying: 5–6 mins

Boiled carp with orange sauce

1.5 kg carp, soup vegetables, 2 onions, spices,
juice of ½ lemon, salt, a pinch of sugar

SAUCE: 3 oranges, 3 tbsps single cream,
1 tsp liquid honey, 50 g almonds

Make a stock from the vegetables, spices and fish leftovers. Clean and cut the gutted carp into sections, salt it and put into the fridge for 1–2 hours, then cover it with the strained vegetable stock and simmer for 20 mins. Prepare the sauce shortly before serving the dish: blanch and skin the almonds, chop them finely; squeeze the juice from the oranges; mix the juice with the almonds, cream and honey. Refrigerate and serve straight from the fridge. Use the fish stock to cook fish soup.

serves 4 • Salting: 1–2 hrs • Preparation: 20 mins • Cooking: 20 mins

Carp braised in beer

1 kg carp, 1 cup lager beer, 1 cup vinegar, 2 tbsps dried apples, ½ tsp grated lemon rind, 1 cup crumbled dry bread, 5–6 each cloves, allspice grains and peppercorns, 1 tsp basil, salt, 1 tbsp butter, pepper

Clean and wash the gutted fish, cut it into sections, salt it, sprinkle with pepper; pour over the vinegar and put in a cool place for 2 hours. Heat up the beer with butter and spices in a skillet. Carefully arrange the fish pieces in it, pour over the marinade and put the crumbled bread. Simmer for 35 mins under cover. Blanch the dried apples, chop them, add to the fish together with the lemon rind and a pinch of sugar. Simmer for another 10 mins. Serve hot or cold, covered with the sauce.

serves 4 • Macerating: 2 hrs • Preparation: 5 mins • Cooking: 40–45 mins

Braised carp in cream

ca 1.5 carp, salt, 1½ tbsps grated horseradish,
1 glass vodka, 1½ cups cream, 4–5 ground
cloves, 2 tbsps honey, salt, pepper, 2 tbsps
lemon juice and ½ tsp grated lemon rind

Clean, wash and dry the fish, rub it well with salt and leave for an hour. Mix the cream with the honey, salt, pepper, cloves, lemon juice and zest, vodka and horseradish. Put the fish into a skillet, pour over the sauce and cook covered over low heat for 40 mins. Serve with rice or pasta.

serves 4 • Salting: 1–2 hrs • Preparation: 5 mins • Cooking: 40 mins

Carp paprikache

1 kg carp fillets, 1 tbsp lemon juice,
100 g lard, 1 onion, 1 large green bell pepper,
1 tbsp dry white wine, 1 cup cream, 1 chilli
pepper, 2 tbsps flour, 1 tbsp paprika, salt

Rub the fillets well with salt, sprinkle with lemon juice and leave for an hour in the fridge. Grate or chop very finely the onion, clean the pepper, wash it and cut into strips. Cut the fish into strips. In a double bottom skillet heat the lard, add the onion and paprika and sauté them, stirring all the time. Sprinkle with water and continue cooking. Put in the fish, green pepper strips and crumbled chili pepper. Fry for a minute or two, stirring gently, sprinkle with wine and simmer under cover for 20 mins. Mix the cream with the flour, add to the fish, stir gently, heat up until the sauce has thickened (but do not let it boil). Serve with pasta or bread rolls.

serves 4 • Marinating: 1 hr • Preparation: 5–7 mins • Cooking: 20–25 mins

Carp in aspic

*1 kg carp, soup vegetables, 5 medium-sized
onions, several grains each pepper and allspice,
1 bay leaf, a pinch of sugar, 1 tsp grated lemon
rind, 1 tsp lemon juice, salt, 1 tsp gelatine*

Clean and wash the gutted fish, rub it with roasted salt and leave in a cool place for an hour. Make a stock from the vegetables, onions and spices, add the fish fins, tail, head and bladder (very rich in gelling agent). If you need more aspic, you should add some gelatine. Put the fish pieces in a skillet, cover with the drained fish stock and cook over low heat for 30 mins, then leave to cool. Gently take out the fish with a slotted spoon. Bone it and arrange on a serving dish. Decorate with the cooked diced vegetables (carrots, parsley root). Clarify the stock with egg whites, add a bit of sugar and lemon juice, season to taste with pepper. Pour the stock over the fish. Leave in the fridge until the stock has set.

serves 4 • Salting: 1 hr • Preparation: 20–30 mins • Cooking: 25–30 mins

Carp, Cracow style

*ca 1.5 kg carp, salt, 3 hard-boiled eggs,
2 raw eggs, 3 tbsps butter, ¼ tsp each pepper,
sugar and lemon juice, soup vegetables,
2–4 onions, several grains each of pepper
and allspice, 1 bay leaf, 1–2 cloves*

*SAUCE: 3 tbsps mayonnaise, 1 tbsp thick
cream, 1–2 finely chopped cocktail gherkins,
3–4 finely chopped pickled mushrooms,
a piece of pickled red bell pepper*

Scale the carp. With a very sharp knife remove the skin and rub it with roasted salt on both sides; wrap it up in foil and put into the fridge. Bone the fish meat. Put the peeled and diced vegetables, onions and spices into a skillet, cover with boiling water and cook over low heat for 30–40 mins. Put in the fish head, fins and spine, add salt and continue simmering for another 30 mins. Put the fish meat and hard-boiled eggs through a mincer. Cream the butter, and, stirring vigorously, add the raw egg yolks, salt, pepper, sugar, lemon juice and then the minced fish and eggs. Fold in the whisked egg whites and mix gently. Stuff the fish skin with the mixture. Wrap it in a piece of gauze, put into a skillet, pour over the fish stock, bring it to the boil and then simmer for 30 mins. Leave it to cool down, remove the gauze, cut the fish into slices. Reduce the stock well, add some gelatine if required. Pour a little of the stock into a serving dish and leave it to set. Arrange the fish slices on top, cover with some more stock and again leave to set. Mix the finely chopped mushrooms and gherkins with the mayonnaise and cream, add salt and pepper to taste. Refrigerate for a while. Before serving, pour the sauce over the aspic.

serves 4 • Salting: 5 mins • Preparation: 1 hr • Cooking: 25–30 mins

Carp pâté

*1.5 kg carp fillets, 2 tbsps lemon juice, salt,
200 g chicken livers, 100 g stoned prunes, 3 tbsps
dry white wine, 200 g mushrooms, 1 white bread
roll, ½ cup cream, 3–4 tbsps butter, 2 eggs,
salt, pepper, nutmeg, 1 tbsp breadcrumbs*

Rinse and blanch the prunes, drain them, put in a bowl, sprinkle with wine and leave aside. Cut the bread roll, put into another bowl, pour over the cream and leave for half an hour. Wash and dry the fillets, sprinkle them with 1 tsp of lemon juice, rub with salt, then leave for half an hour. Cut the mushrooms into slices, sprinkle with lemon juice and pepper, leave for half an hour. Wash and dry the chicken livers, sauté them in 1 tbsp of butter and leave to cool. Fry the fish in butter, allow to cool, then remove the bones. Put all the prepared ingredients through a mincer two or three times. Season to taste, add 1 tbsp of melted butter and 1 egg and work it into a smooth paste. Grease a baking tin with butter, dust it with breacrumbs. Fold in the paste, smooth out the surface. Cover with aluminium foil and put into a preheated oven. Bake for 40 mins, towards the end remove the foil. When the pâté has cooled down, leave it in the fridge overnight.

serves 4 • Salting: 30–40 mins • Preparation: 30 mins • Baking: 40–45 mins

Savoury silver carp rolls

Silver carp

Savoury silver carp rolls

4 fillets, 2 tbsps lemon juice, 2 tbsps grated horseradish, 4–5 spring onions with green parts, 2 thin slices of pork fat, 2 tbsps butter, 1 cup vegetable stock, 50 g smoked salmon, 1 tbsp flour, salt, pepper

Wash and dry the fillets, sprinkle them with lemon juice, rub with salt and pepper, cover and put into the fridge for 1–2 hours. Then take them out, put on a board. Spread some grated horseradish on each fillet, sprinkle with the finely chopped spring onions, cover with pork fat. Roll the fillets up and secure with a toothpick. Put the rolls in a skillet, pour in the vegetable stock. Cook over low heat for 20 mins. Take the rolls out with a slotted spoon, arrange on a hot serving dish and keep warm. Make a roux from the butter and flour, thin it with some cool fish stock, season to taste with salt and pepper. Stirring all the time, simmer it over low heat until the sauce has thickened. Pour it over the fish, sprinkle with the finely chopped salmon. Serve with French fries or boiled potatoes.

serves 4 • Marinating: 1–2 hrs • Preparation: 10–12 mins • Cooking: 20–25 mins

Silver carp with spinach

800 g fillets, 300 g spinach, 2–4 tbsps butter, 1 tbsps flour, 1 cup single cream, ¼ tsp each cayenne pepper and grated nutmeg, 1 tbsp lemon juice, 4 tbsps grated cheese, salt, pepper

Wash and dry the fillets, sprinkle them with lemon juice, salt and pepper, cover and put in the fridge for 1–2 hours. Clean and wash the spinach, put it into boiling salted water for 2–3 mins, then drain it. Make a roux from 2 tbsp of melted butter and flour, thin it with 3–4 tbsp of cold water, add salt, pepper, cayenne and nutmeg. Pour in the cream, stir and heat it up until the sauce has thickened. Grease an ovenproof dish with butter, put in portions of the fish, cover with the spinach, pour in the sauce. Sprin-

kle with grated cheese and put into a preheated oven for 20–30 mins.

serves 4 • Marinating: 1–2 hrs • Preparation: 10–15 mins • Baking: 20–30 mins

Pikeperch

Pikeperch, Polish style

ca 1.5 kg pikeperch, soup vegetables, 1 large onion studded with 1–2 cloves, 1 bay leaf, 5–6 grains each pepper and allspice, salt, pepper, a pinch of sugar, ½ tsp grated lemon rind, 3 cups boiled water, 2 cups dry white wine;

4 hard-boiled eggs, 3 tbsps butter, 2 tbsps finely chopped parsley, lemon, salt

Clean the gutted fish, wash and dry it, rub it outside and in with roasted salt, leave in a cool place for an hour. Make a stock from the vegetables, onion and spices, add sugar and lemon zest. Put the fish into a skillet, cover it with the wine and strained stock, cook for 25–30 mins. Leave the fish in the stock for half an hour to let the flavours mix. Melt the butter in a frying pan, add the chopped hard-boiled eggs and parsley, cook over low heat, shaking the pan from time to time so that the eggs do not burn. Heat the fish up, then take it out onto a serving dish, sprinkle with some lemon juice, surround with the hard-boiled eggs, garnish with lemon slices and parsley sprigs.

serves 4 • Salting: 1–2 hrs • Preparation: 30 mins • Baking: 25–30 mins

Pikeperch à la Capuchin

800 g pikeperch fillets, 100 g pork fat, 250 g button mushrooms, 1 large onion, 1½ cup thick cream, 1 tbsp flour, 1 tbsp butter, 3–4 tbsps oil, ¼ tsp curry powder, 1 tbsp lemon juice, salt, pepper

Clean, dry and bone the fillets, rub them with salt, cover and put into the fridge for an hour. Fry the chopped onion in butter, but do not let it brown, add the finely chopped mushrooms and cook for a while, stirring all the time. Season with salt, pepper and curry powder. Pour in the cream and lemon juice, stir and keep warm. Divide the fillets into portions, make small incisions and thread in small pieces of pork fat. Dredge the fish with flour and fry in hot oil until golden brown. Grease an oven proof dish with oil, arrange the fish in it, pour the sauce over. Put in a preheated oven for 5–6 mins.

serves 4 • Salting: 1 hr • Preparation: 10 mins • Baking: 5–6 mins

Kashub pikeperch

800 g pikeperch fillets, 1 tsp lemon juice, salt, 2 tbsps flour, 2 carrots, 1 parsley root, ¼ celeriac, 1 small leek (only the white part), 2 onions, ½ tsp ground allspice, 2 crumbled bay leaves, salt, pepper, a pinch of sugar, 1 tbsp dry white wine, 1 cup thick sour cream, 3 tbsps oil, 1 tbsp butter

Wash the fillets, cut them into portions, sprinkle with lemon juice, put in a cool place for an hour. Peel and wash the vegetables, cut them into thin strips. Heat the oil in a pan, fry the finely chopped onion in it, but do not let it brown. Put in the vegetable strips and stir fry them. Season with salt, pepper, allspice and bay leaves, sprinkle with the wine or water. Put a lid on and simmer for a while. Pour in the cream, stir well, season to taste. Dredge the fish pieces with flour and fry them in hot oil until golden brown. Arrange the fish in an oven-proof dish greased with butter, cover with the stewed vegetables and put into a preheated oven for 8–10 mins.

serves 4 • Marinating: 1–2 hrs • Preparation: 25–30 mins • Baking: 8–10 mins

Sandomierz pikeperch

1 medium-sized pikeperch, 4 large onions, 2–3 tbsps capers, 2–3 tbsps stoned olives, 4–6 marinated mushrooms, 2–3 tbsps butter, 2 cups cream, lemon, salt, pepper

Clean and wash the gutted fish, rub it with salt, cover and put into the fridge for an hour, then cut it into steaks. Grate the onions, squeeze out the juice. Put the fish into a skillet, pour in the onion juice, add some butter

knobs, cover and cook over low heat for 10 mins. Add the cream and simmer for another 10 mins. Transfer the fish onto a hot serving dish and keep it warm. Add the capers, olives cut into strips and lemon slices to the sauce, stir and heat up. Put in the chopped mushrooms. Pour the sauce over the fish. Serve with boiled potatoes sprinkled with chopped chives.

serves 4 • Salting: 1 hr • Preparation: 5 mins • Cooking: 20 mins

Spicy pikeperch, Lvov style

1 kg pikeperch, ½ cup grated horseradish, 2 large onions, 2 lemons, pepper, allspice, several cloves, 1 tbsp dried basil, salt, 2 tbsps butter

Pound together the pepper, allspice and cloves in a mortar. Clean and wash the fish, cut it into steaks, rub with salt and basil, and put in a cool place for an hour. Grease an ovenproof dish with butter. Arrange the pikeperch pieces in it, sprinkle with spices and grated horseradish, cover with slices of peeled lemon and onion, put knobs of butter on top. Cover with foil and put into a preheated oven for 40 mins. Serve with French fries and lettuce.

serves 4 • Marinating: 1 hr • Preparation: 10 mins • Baking: 40 mins

Pikeperch with vegetables

1 kg pikeperch, 1 tbsp butter, soup vegetables, onion, fish leftovers, salt

1 tbsp butter, 1 medium-sized onion, celeriac, kohlrabi, cauliflower, 2 tbsps chopped parsley, 1 tsp sugar, salt, 2 tbsps breadcrumbs, 1 cup thick cream, 1 tsp flour, 2 egg yolks

Make a stock from a small amount of water and the vegetables, onion, spices and fish leftovers. Clean and wash the fish, cut it into steaks, rub with salt and put in a cool place for an hour. Chop the carrots, kohlrabi and celeriac finely or grate them coarsely. Stir fry them together with the finely chopped onion in butter, add some fish stock. Towards the end add the breadcrumbs, salt and sugar and simmer for a while. Cook the cauliflower in lightly salted water with sugar and divide it into florets. Melt some butter in a frying pan, sprinkle the pikeperch with flour and fry it over low heat on both sides. Arrange the fish on a warm serving dish. Make a roux from the butter and flour, dilute it with the fish stock and cream, add the egg yolks and stir vigorously. Garnish the fish with cooked vegetables, pour over the sauce, sprinkle with parsley.

serves 4 • Preparation: 30–40 mins • Cooking: 20 mins • Frying: 8–10 mins

Pikeperch in savoury sauce

1 kg pikeperch, 2 parsley roots,
1 cup dry white wine, salt

SAUCE: 150 g tomatoes or 1 tbsp tomato concentrate,
½ cup Madeira, ½ lemon, 1 tbsp mustard, 1 tbsp butter,
1 tsp flour, ½ tsp sugar, 1 tbsp capers, 1 cocktail gherkin,
5 pickled mushrooms, 1 tbsp olives, 1 tsp caramel

Clean and wash the fish, salt it, put into a skillet, cover with water. Put in the diced parsley roots and white wine, simmer under cover. Make a roux from butter and flour, dilute it with the fish stock, add the Madeira, lemon juice and the sieved tomatoes. Stirring all the time, cook until the sauce has thickened. Add the mushrooms and gherkin cut into strips, capers, stoned and chopped olives, sugar, mustard and caramel, and, towards the end, the sieved fish stock. Arrange the fish on a serving dish, pour over the sauce. Serve with boiled potatoes.

serves 4 • Preparation: 20–25 mins • Cooking: 25–30 mins

Pikeperch à la Orly

1 kg pikeperch, 1 cup milk, 2 eggs, 1 tbsp melted butter,
3 tbsps flour, salt, pepper, fat for frying, chopped parsley

Clean and wash the gutted fish, cut it lengthwise into two, bone it. Rub with salt, then dry thoroughly with a cloth and cut into sections. Beat lightly the milk with two egg yolks, add salt and butter, fold in the whisked egg whites. Whisking all the time, add flour to produce a thick batter that sticks to the fish. Salt it. Sprinkle the fish pieces with pepper and coat them in batter. Deep fry them in oil. Transfer to a hot serving dish and keep warm. Serve with French fries and lettuce or with a spicy sauce. Garnish with parsley.

serves 4 • Salting: 1 hr • Preparation: 10 mins • Frying: 10–15 mins

Baked fillets of pikeperch

1 kg pikeperch, 1 cup dry white wine, 3–4 onions,
⅓ tsp dried thyme or several sprigs of fresh
thyme, pepper, 1 bay leaf, 2–3 grains allspice

Sauce: 1 tbsp butter, 1 tsp flour, 1 egg yolk, lemon juice

FORCEMEAT: 500 g fish, 1 tbsp butter,
1 medium-sized onion, 1 white bread roll,
5–6 mushrooms, 1 egg, 1 tbsp thick sour cream,
salt, pepper, a pinch of ground allspice

GARNISH: 2–3 cocktail gherkins,
2–3 mushrooms, 1 hard-boiled egg white

Fillet the cleaned and washed pikeperch. Rub the fillets with salt, sprinkle with pepper, leave in a cool place for an hour. Put slices of onion into a pan, arrange the fillets on top, add a bay leaf, thyme, pepper and allspice; pour in 1 measure of wine to 1 measure of water, cover and cook for 15 mins over low heat.

FORCEMEAT: Take out 2–3 pieces of fish, chop them finely, add the grated onion and simmer over low heat; add the bread roll that has soaked in water, the finely chopped mushrooms stewed in butter, 1 raw egg, salt, pepper and a pinch of allspice; stir thoroughly. Grease an ovenproof dish with butter, line it with the forcemeat, arrange the fillets in the middle. Sieve the fish stock and pour some of it over the fillets. Garnish the dish with the blanched and sliced mushrooms, the egg white and chopped gherkin. Cover with foil and put into a preheated oven and bake for about 15 mins. Make a roux from the butter and flour, dilute it with some fish stock, add juice from one lemon, then thicken with 1 egg yolk. Serve the sauce in a sauce boat.

serves 4–6 • Preparation: 20–25 mins • Cooking:
15 mins • Baking: 15–20 mins

Baked pikeperch

ca 1½ kg pikeperch or 800 g pikeperch fillets,
100 g butter, 2 tbsps breadcrumbs, 4–5 spring
onions with green parts, 1 bunch parsley,
salt, pepper, ½ cup dry white wine

Wash the fillets, rub them with salt and leave in a cool place for an hour. Slice the rinsed and dried mushrooms, chop the spring onions and parsley finely. Melt 2 tbsps of butter in a frying pan, sauté the mushrooms, reduce the juice. Sprinkle them sparingly with pepper and salt, add the onions, stir and fry for a minute or two. Grease an ovenproof dish with butter, dust it liberally with half of the breadcrumbs and parsley. Put in half of the stewed mushrooms and onion, arrange the fillets on top. Place knobs of butter on the fillets, cover with the remaining mushrooms, dust with breadcrumbs, add more butter and sprinkle with the wine. Put into a preheated oven for 1 hour.

serves 4–6 • Salting: 1 hr • Preparation: 10–15 mins • Baking: 50–60 mins

Pikeperch in piquant sauce

ca 1.5 kg pikeperch or 800 g pikeperch fillets, 4 large onions, 2 tbsps butter, 2 cups cream, 1 lemon, 2 tbsps capers, 2 tbsps green olives, 5–6 pickled saffron milk caps, salt, pepper, 4 tbsps finely chopped chives

Wash and dry the gutted fish, rub it with salt and leave in a cool place for an hour, then cut into steaks. Finely grate onions, squeeze out the juice. Grease a roasting tin with butter, put in the fish, pour over the onion juice. Cook over low heat for 15 mins, then add the cream and simmer for another 5–8 mins. Peel the lemon, slice it finely, remove the pips; cut the olives into strips. Add the olives, capers and lemon slices to the fish; simmer for a while. Arrange the fish on a serving dish, heat up the sauce, add the sliced mushrooms. Pour the sauce over the fish, sprinkle with the chives.

serves 4–6 • Salting: 5 mins • Preparation: 10 mins • Baking: 20–25 mins

Pikeperch à la Radziwiłł

1 pikeperch (2 kg), 2 onions, 1 carrot, 1 parsley root, ½ celeriac, 1 bay leaf, 1½ cups dry white wine, juice and grated rind of 1 lemon, 2 tbsps breadcrumbs, 3 tbsps flour, 100 g butter, 400 g mushrooms, 3 egg yolks, 1–2 tbsps white wine, 1 egg, 100 g crayfish meat or 1 tin small prawns, 1 French loaf, salt, pepper

Scale and gut the fish, cut off the head, tail and fins. Fillet it by making an incision along its spine, remove the skin. Sprinkle the fillets with lemon juice and leave in a cool place for half an hour. Clean and rinse the vegetables, put them into a pot, cover with 2 cups of boiling water. Cook for 30 mins over low heat, add the wine, then the fish head, tail, fins, spine and all big bones. Put in the bay leaf, salt, pepper and grated lemon rind and cook for another 20 mins. Strain in a large sieve or a piece fo gauze. Cut off 200 g of fish meat from the part near the tail and the sides and put it through a blender together with 2 tbsps of breadcrumbs, 1 tbsp of flour and 1 tbsp of butter. Break in 1 egg and work into a smooth paste (add more breadcrumbs if it is not thick enough). Shape small balls from the paste, dredge them with flour. Drop them gently into the boiling stock and when they float to the surface simmer for another 2–3 mins. Take the fish balls out with a slotted spoon. Bring the stock again to the boil. Slice the rinsed and dried mushrooms and fry them in 2 tbsps of butter. Cut the fillets into 8 even portions, put into the stock and simmer for 10–15 mins. Take them out gently with a slotted spoon, arrange on a hot serving dish and keep warm. Reduce the stock to 2 cups, strain it. Make a roux from the remaining butter and flour, dilute it with the fish stock, simmer over low heat, stirring all the time, until the sauce has thickened. Add the mushrooms, fish balls and crayfish meat (or prawns). Simmer over low heat, season with salt and pepper. Take off the heat and add the egg yolks mixed with 1 tbsp of white wine. Cut the loaf into 6 even slices and toast them in a frying pan. Put the cooked fillets on toast, pour the sauce over.

serves 6–8 • Salting: 30–40 mins • Preparation: 1 hr • Cooking: 15–20 mins

Pikeperch with crayfish meat

800 g pikeperch fillets, 20 crayfish, a bunch dill sprigs with seeds, 1 cup stock, 2 tbsps chopped dill, salt, white pepper, 2 egg yolks, 150 g butter, 5 tbsps breadcrumbs

Bring salted water with dill to the boil. Scrub and wash the live crayfish, then put them into the boiling water and leave to cool. Then take the crayfish out, pull out the black guts. Take out the meat from the tails and claws. Leave 8 shells aside and pound the remaining shells in a mortar. Melt some butter in a pan, put in the pounded shells and cook over low heat. Put the crayfish butter into a jar. Bring the stock with 1 tbsp of crayfish butter to the boil, season to taste. Blend 2 tbsps of crayfish butter with the egg yolks. Beating all the time, add the meat from the claws, 1 tbsp of chopped dill and sifted breadcrumbs. Add salt and pepper to taste. Stuff the 8 shells with the mixture. Rinse and dry the fillets, sprinkle them with salt. Grease an ovenproof dish with butter. Arrange the fillets in it, put the crayfish meat on top and place the stuffed shells around. Pour the stock over, sprinkle with dill, cover with foil and put into a preheated over (180°C) for 25 mins. Serve in the same ovenproof dish.

serves 4–6 • Preparation: 45–55 mins • Baking: 25–30 mins

Pikeperch, Lithuanian style

1 kg pikeperch, 250 g pork fat, 2 egg yolks, 2 tbsps grated horseradish, 2 tbsps chopped parsley, 1 tbsp lemon juice, salt, pepper, a pinch of sugar;

parsley sprigs, cherry tomatoes and lemon wedges for garnishing

Fillet the cleaned pikeperch, wash and dry it, sprinkle with lemon juice, salt and pepper and leave aside for half an hour. Cut the pork fat into very thin rashers. Mix the horseradish and sugar, parsley, lemon juice and egg yolks. Spread the mixture over the fish halves, put the two halves together, wrap in pork fat rashers, tie the whole with thread. Grill or bake them in a preheated oven. Take them out, remove the lard and garnish the fish with tomato quarters, lemon wedges and parsley sprigs.

serves 4 • Marinating: 30–40 mins • Preparation:
10 mins • Baking: 20–30 mins

Pikeperch, Lvov style

800 g pikeperch fillets, ½ cup grated horseradish, 2–3 onions, 2 lemons, 2–3 tbsps butter, 1 tbsp lemon juice, 1 tbsp dried basil, ¼ tsp each ground allspice and cloves, salt, pepper

Wash and dry the fillets, sprinkle them with lemon juice, rub with salt and basil, cover and put into the fridge for 1–2 hours. Scrub the lemons, scald them with boiling water, then slice them finely and remove the pips. Chop the onions. Grease an ovenproof dish with but-

ter, put in the fillets cut into portions, sprinkle with grated horseradish, onion and ground spices, cover with lemon slices and slivers of butter, sprinkle with pepper. Cover and put into a preheated oven for 30–35 mins. Remove the cover and bake for another 10 mins. Serve with French fries or sautéd potatoes and lettuce.

serves 4 • Marinating: 1–2 hrs • Preparation: 10 mins • Baking: 40–45 mins

Salmon

Marinated salmon

1 kg salmon, 2 cups dry white wine, 3 lemons, 3 onions, 2 carrots, ½ celeriac, 2 bay leaves, 5–6 grains each allspice and pepper, ¼ tsp each tarragon and rosemary, 3 tbsps olive or sunflower oil

Clean and wash the salmon, remove the skin and bones, cut into slices, sprinkle with salt. Cook the rest of the fish in a small amount of water together with the celeriac and carrots. Strain the stock. Dice the cooked vegetables, pour over the wine and lemon juice, add spices, sliced onions and herbs, pour in the strained stock. Cook until the onion is tender, then allow to cool. Fry quickly the salmon slices in oil, taking care they do not break up. Put the fried fish into a jar, pour in the cool marinade, cover with a clean piece of gauze and put in a cool place. Before serving, garnish with onion, parsley and marinated vegetables.

serves 4–6 • Preparation: 30–40 mins • Frying: 5–7 mins
• Cooking: 10 mins • Marinating: 2–3 days

Salmon in mayonnaise

500 g salmon, soup vegetables, 1 onion, 1 bay leaf, 3–4 grains each pepper and allspice, 2–3 cloves, salt, a pinch of sugar, ½ lemon, 2 tbsps thick mayonnaise, parsley

Clean and wash the fish, rub it with salt. Make a stock from the vegetables, onion, spices and fish leftovers.

Put the fish into a pan, pour over the drained stock and simmer. Gently take the fish out (use the stock to make a sauce or fish soup), remove the bones, cut the meat into portions. Arrange the cool fish on a serving dish, garnish with the mayonnaise, lemon slices and parsley.

serves 4 • Preparation: 10 mins • Cooking:
20–25 mins • Refrigerating: 1–2 hrs

Smoked salmon salad

150 g smoked salmon, 2 pickled cucumbers, 1 cup
pineapple cubes, 3 tbsps tinned sweetcorn, 1 cup
yogurt, 2 tbsps grated horseradish, several drops of
Worcestershire sauce, salt, pepper, 1 tbsp chopped dill

Blend the yogurt with the horseradish, Worcestershire sauce, salt and pepper, and put the mixture into the fridge. Cut the salmon and gherkins into cubes, add the sweetcorn and pineapple, pour over the cool sauce, shake gently. Before serving, sprinkle with chopped dill.

serves 4 • Preparation: 5–7 mins • Refrigerating: 30–40 mins

Gourmet's salmon

1 kg salmon fillets

MARINADE: ¾ cup lemon juice, 2 onions,
2 tbsps each olive oil and white wine vinegar,
1 tbsp each finely chopped ginger and green
coriander, ½ tsp finely chopped fresh chili
pepper, 1 tsp salt, freshly ground pepper

Skin and bone the fillets. With a very sharp knife cut them into very thin (several milimetres thick and 4–5 cm long) strips.
MARINADE: Cut the onion into thin half slices, mix the lemon juice with oil, vinegar, salt, pepper and chili, add ginger, onion and coriander. Put the salmon strips into a bowl, pour over the marinade, mix gently, cover with foil and put into the fridge for 5–6 hours. Serve on lettuce leaves, garnished with marinated onions, lemon slices and coriander or parsley sprigs.

serves 6–8 • Preparation: 20–25 mins • Marinating: 5–6 hrs

Salmon in butter

1 kg salmon, 1 lemon, 1 cup dry white wine,
1 onion, ¼ tsp basil, 1 bay leaf, 6 grains allspice

* 1 large onion, salt, 2 tbsps butter,
1 tbsp chopped parsley

Clean the salmon, cut it into steaks, rub with salt. Boil ½ cup of water with the wine, lemon juice, grated onion, spices and basil. Put the salmon into a skillet, pour in the marinade and cook for 30 mins over low heat. Take out the fish delicately, arrange it on a serving dish, sprinkle with parsley, baste with melted butter. Serve hot with French fries or cold with lemon. You may also use the fish stock as a sauce.

serves 4–6 • Preparation: 15–20 mins • Cooking: 25–30 mins

Braised salmon in wine

ca 1.5 kg salmon, 100 g butter, 1 cup Madeira or any red
wine, juice of ½ lemon, 3–4 bay leaves, salt, pepper

Clean the fish, wash and dry it, rub with salt and leave for an hour. Cut it into fairly thin steaks. Melt the butter in a double-bottomed pan, add the bay leaves, pour in wine and bring to the boil. Put in the salmon steaks, cover and simmer over low heat for ca 20 mins. Towards the end add the lemon juice, season with salt and pepper to taste, bring to the boil. Arrange the fish on a hot serving dish, reduce the sauce and pour it over the salmon.

serves 4–6 • Salting: 1–2 hrs • Preparation: 10 mins • Cooking: 20–25 mins

Salmon in sorrel sauce

4 salmon steaks (ca 700 g), 1 tsp lemon juice, 2 tbsps
butter, 2 tbsps olive oil, 4 spring onions or shallots,
2 tbsps dry white wine, ½ cup cream, 150 g fresh sorrel
leaves, salt, pepper, several mint or lemon balm leaves

Wash and dry the sorrel leaves, cut them. Melt the butter in a skillet, fry the finely chopped onion, but do not let it brown. Add the sorrel, sprinkle with the wine, stir and cook for a minute or two, stirring all the time. Add salt and pepper to taste. Wash and dry the salmon steaks, sprinkle them with lemon juice, salt and pepper. Put away for several mins, then fry in hot oil on both sides. Whip the cream lightly, fold it into the sorrel, stir and heat up. Arrange the salmon steaks on a hot serving dish, pour the sauce over, garnish with lemon balm or mint leaves.

serves 4–6 • Preparation: 15–20 mins • Frying: 7–8 mins

Sour-flavoured salmon

1kg salmon, 2 cups water, 1 cup juice of sour cabbage, 1 cup juice of soured cucumbers, 1 bay leaf, 2–3 grains allspice, 6–8 peppercorns, ½ tsp paprika, 1 tbsp chopped dill, 100 g butter, 2 tbsp chopped parsley, salt, 1 tbsp lemon juice

Bring the water with the cabbage and cucumber juice to the boil, put in the dill, bay leaf, allspice and pepper and leave aside for several hours. Clean and wash the fish, cut it into steaks, rub gently with salt, sprinkle with lemon juice and put into a skillet. Bring the water and spices to the boil, pour it over the fish and simmer for 20 mins. Take the fish gently out, arrange on a hot serving dish, baste with melted butter, sprinkle with parsley. Serve with boiled potatoes, cauliflower and/or fresh vegetable salad.

serves 4–6 • Preparation: 20–25 mins • Maturing: 5–6 hrs • Cooking: 20–25 mins

Salmon in onion sauce

1kg salmon steaks, 200 g onion, salt, pepper, grated rind and juice of ½ lemon, 1½ cups dry white wine, 4 tbsps butter, 1 tsp potato flour, several sprigs of dill

Rub the salmon steaks with salt, sprinkle with lemon juice and leave aside for 20–30 mins. Melt the butter in a frying pan, fry the chopped onion, but do not let it brown. Add some salt, pepper, lemon zest and juice. Stir well, pour in 1 cup of wine and cook covered for 15 mins. Arrange the salmon steaks in an ovenproof dish, sprinkle with melted butter and the remaining wine, cover and simmer for 15–20 mins. Liquidize and sieve the cooked onion, then heat it up, season with salt, pepper and lemon juice to taste, add a pinch of sugar if required. Mix the potato flour with 1 tbsp of cold boiled water, add to the onion sauce and heat up, stirring all the time, until the sauce has

Sour-flavoured salmon

thickened. Pour the sauce over the fish. Put the fish into a hot oven for several minutes. Before serving, garnish with dill sprigs. Serve with pasta or boiled potatoes.

serves 4–6 • Marinating: 30 mins • Preparation: 15 mins • Cooking: 15–20 mins

Salmon in lemon juice

4 salmon steaks, 2 tbsps lemon juice, 2 cups vegetable stock, 2 onions, salt, 3–4 peppercorns, 1 clove;

grated lemon rind and juice of 1 large lemon, 2 tbsps butter, 1 tsp flour, 2 egg yolks, salt, a pinch of sugar, ½ cup cream

Wash and dry the steaks, rub them with salt, sprinkle with lemon juice and leave for 15 mins. Peel one onion, stick one clove into it, put it into a skillet, pour in the hot vegetable stock, add peppercorns and salt. Bring to the boil, put in the fish steaks and simmer for 20 mins. Gently take out the fish, arrange the steaks on a hot serving dish. Reduce the stock to less than 1 cup, then strain it. Make a roux from the butter and flour, dilute it with the stock and, stirring all the time, simmer until it has thickened. Add the lemon zest and, and sugar to taste. Beat the egg yolks and cream lightly, add to the sauce, stir well, heat up and pour over the fish.

serves 4 • Marinating: 30 mins • Cooking: 20–25 mins

Salmon, country style

1 kg salmon, 2 carrots, ½ celeriac, 1 onion, 1 bay leaf, 4–5 grains each allspice and pepper, ¼ tsp rosemary, 2 tbsps butter, 1 tsp flour, lemon, ½ cup dry red wine, 1 tbsp redcurrant jelly

MARINADE: 1 lemon, ½ cup dry red wine, 2–3 cloves, a piece of ginger or ½ tsp powdered ginger, 2 bay leaves, several peppercorns

Prepare the marinade. Clean and wash the fish, put it into a large jar, pour over the cool marinade and leave for 24 hrs in a cool place. Take the fish out, salt it and leave for an hour. Peel, wash and dice the carrot and celeriac. Put the vegetables into a skillet together with the spices, ar-

range the salmon on top. Put in 1 tbsp of butter, cover and cook over low heat for 30 mins, basting with the marinade. Take the cooked fish onto a plate. Continue cooking the vegetables until tender, then sieve them. Make a roux from the butter and flour, dilute it with the lemon juice and wine, add the jelly and the vegetable purée, stir well. Put in the salmon and cook covered for several minutes. Take the fish out onto a serving dish and pour the sauce over.

serves 4–6 • Salting: 1 hr • Preparation: 20–30 mins • Cooking: 40–45 mins

Grilled or barbecued salmon

4 salmon steaks (ca 700 g), ½ cup thick cream, 2 onions, juice and grated rind of 1 lemon, 2–3 tbsps chopped parsley, salt

Mix the cream with salt and lemon zest. Wash and dry the steaks, rub with the cream, put them on a spit and grill them. Chop the onion finely, sprinkle with lemon juice, spread on top of the grilled steaks. Serve with French fries and tomato salad.

serves 4 • Preparation: 5–8 mins • Cooking: 10–15 mins

Baked salmon

4 salmon fillets, 1 tbsp lemon juice, 3–4 garlic cloves, 2 tbsps chopped parsley, 2 tbsps chopped walnuts, 2 large peaches, 4 thin slices of cheese, 2 tbsps butter, salt

Chop the garlic, mix it well with salt, chopped parsley and lemon juice. Wash and dry the fillets, rub them with the mixture, cover with foil and put into the fridge for an hour. Heat the oven to 200°C. Grease an ovenproof dish with ½ tbsp of butter, arrange the fillets in it, sprinkle with ½ tbsp of melted butter and put into the hot oven. Bake for 20 mins. Blanch and skin the peaches, stone them and cut into thick slices. Put peach slices on top of the fillets, then cover with cheese slices, sprinkle with walnuts and grated butter. Bake for another 10–15 mins.

serves 4 • Marinating: 1 hr • Preparation: 5–7 mins • Baking: 20 mins

Baked salmon with prawns

4 salmon fillets (ca 600–700 g), 1 tbsp lemon juice, salt, 2 tbsps butter, 150 g small prawns (frozen or tinned), 200 g tinned asparagus, ¾ cup cream, 2–3 tbsps light stock, 1 egg yolk, 3–4 tbsps grated Mozzarella cheese, salt, a pinch of each pepper and sugar, 1 tbsp lemon juice, 1 tbsp butter

Wash and dry the fillets, rub them with salt, sprinkle with lemon juice and leave aside for several minutes, then fry them in melted butter. Drain the asparagus, cut it into small pieces. Put the frozen prawns into slightly salted boiling water for 2 mins (or drain the tinned prawns). Beat the cream with the egg yolk, stock, lemon juice, salt, pepper, sugar and grated cheese. Mix it with the prawns and asparagus, then heat up. Grease an oven-proof dish with butter, arrange the fried fillets in it, pour over the sauce and put into a preheated oven for several minutes.

serves 4 • Preparation: 10 mins • Frying: 5–7 mins

Pasta with salmon in cheese sauce

300 g pasta (tagliatelle or quadrucci), meat from 3–4 cooked salmon heads, 3 tbsps butter, 1 tbsp flour, 1 cup fish stock, 1 cup mixed grated cheese, salt, pepper, 1 tbsp lemon juice, a pinch of sugar, 2–3 drops Worcestershire sauce, 1 cup cream

Make a roux from 2 tbsps of melted butter and flour, dilute it with the stock and, stirring all the time, cook until the sauce has thickened. Beat the cream with salt, pepper, sugar, lemon juice, Worcestershire sauce and grated cheese. Pour into the sauce and, stirring continuously, heat up, but do not let it boil. Put the salmon meat into the sauce. Cook the pasta in salted boiling water, drain it,

Baked salmon

put into a deep bowl, mix with the remaining butter, pour over the sauce.

serves 4 • Preparation: 10 mins • Cooking: 20–25 mins

Baked salmon, Geneva style

4 salmon steaks (ca 700 g), 1 tbsp lemon juice, soup vegetables, 1 onion with a clove stuck into it, 1 bay leaf, 3–4 grains each allspice and pepper, ½ tsp grated lemon rind, 2–3 sprigs of parsley, several sprigs of dill, 1–2 sprigs of thyme, 4–5 spring onions with green parts, 1 carrot, 1 parsley root, 1–2 celery sticks, 3 tbsps butter, 1 tsp potato flour, 1 cup dry red wine, a pinch of sugar, salt

Wash and dry the fish, rub it with salt, sprinkle with lemon juice, leave in the fridge for an hour. Make a stock from the soup vegetables, onion, spices and parsley, dill, thyme and lemon zest. Put in the fish and cook it over low heat for 15 mins. Leave it in the stock to cool. Clean and wash the carrots, parsley roots and celeriac, grate them coarsely, chop the spring onions finely. Melt the butter in a pan, put in the spring onions and grated vegetables, sauté them for a minute or two, then add 1 cup of fish stock, cover and simmer until the vegetables are tender. Season with salt, pepper and sugar to taste, then put through a blender and sieve the purée. Combine with the wine and heat up. Arrange the cooked fish in an ovenproof dish, pour over part of the sauce and put into a preheated oven for several minutes. Serve with pasta or rice, and with the remaining sauce in a sauce boat.

serves 4 • Preparation: 30–40 mins • Cooking: 15–20 mins

Pike

Pike à la flamande

Put the pike – whichever you prefer, either a whole fish or cut into steaks – into a skillet. Pour in half a cup of olive oil, half a bottle of sparkling wine, add salt, pepper, a mixture of parsley, onion, cloves and thyme, a bay leaf, some basil, lemon slices,

and 2 tbsps of stock. Simmer under cover over fairly high heat. When the fish is ready, arrange it on a serving dish. Strain the fish stock, add 1 tbsp of flour to thicken it, put in 1 tbsp of butter and a bit of parsley, bring it to the boil. Serve hot.

Kucharz doskonały, 1808

Pike, Old Polish style

1–1½ kg pike, 3 carrots, ½ celeriac, 3 onions, a large bunch of parsley, 3 bay leaves, 4 cloves, a piece of cinnamon, ¼ tsp mace, 2 cups white wine, 2 tbsps sunflower or olive oil, 2 tbsps each raisins, olives and capers, 2 lemons, 1 tsp sugar

* 1 tbsp butter, 1 tsp flour, salt

Clean and wash the fish, rub it with roasted salt and leave for an hour in a cool place. Put the fish leftovers (head, tail) into a pan, pour in 3 cups of water, add the vegetables, spices, onion and parsley, and cook them. Sieve the cooked vegetables. Cut the fish into steaks, arrange in a skillet, pour over the vegetable purée, add the wine, olive, the peeled and sliced lemons (without pips) and the remaining ingredients. Cook for 30–35 mins over low heat. Make a roux from the butter and flour, dilute it with 2 tbsps of water. Fold it into the sauce, shake the skillet lightly and cook a bit longer over low heat. Arrange the pike on a serving dish (you may put around fish balls or small fried fish), pour over the sauce, garnish with parsley sprigs. Serve with bread rolls or baked potatoes.

serves 4–6 • Preparation: 30–40 mins • Cooking: 30–35 mins

Pike with eggs

1 kg pike, 3 hard-boiled eggs, salt, pepper, 3 tbsps butter, 2 tbsps chopped parsley

Clean and wash the fish, rub it with salt and pepper, arrange in a greased ovenproof dish. Put into a preheated oven and bake for 30–45 mins at a low temperature. When the fish has browned, transfer it onto a serving dish, arrange boiled potatoes or French fries around, sprinkle with the chopped eggs, sprinkle with melted butter and a lot of parsley.

serves 4–6 • Preparation: 15–20 mins • Baking: 30–45 mins

Pike with eggs

Pike, Jewish style

1 kg pike, 2 onions, soup vegetables, 1 bay leaf, 1 clove, 4–5 grains each allspice and pepper, 3 onions

Stuffing: 250 g onion, a pinch of pepper, ½ tsp sugar, 2 tbsps breadcrumbs, 1 tbsp grated horseradish, egg white, pike meat, salt

Clean and wash the fish, rub it with salt and leave aside for an hour. Make a stock from the vegetables, onion, spices and fish leftovers, strain it. Cut the fish into portions, separate the flesh from the bones and skin, taking care not to damage the skin. Chop the flesh finely or put it through a mincer together with the onions. Add salt, pepper, sugar, horseradish, breadcrumbs and egg white, mix thoroughly. Fill the pieces of skin with the stuffing, arrange in a skillet, pour over the strained stock, add 3 sliced onions and simmer under cover for 60 mins. Leave to cool. Take the fish portions gently out, arrange them on a serving dish. Heat up the stock lightly, strain it, pour over the fish and leave in a cool place. By the time it gets cool, the sauce should set. The same dish can be made from other kinds of fish. Instead of the fish skin, you may use a piece of gauze to wrap up the stuffing like a large sausage, with the ends secured with a piece of thread. When it cools down, remove the gauze, cut the stuffing into slices and arrange them on a serving dish. With fish other than pike, you will probably have to add a bit of gelatine to the stock.

serves 4–6 • Preparation: 50–55 mins • Cooking: 60–70 mins • Setting: 1–2 hrs

Pike in grey sauce

1 pike, 3 cups sour beetroot juice, 100 g raisins, 1 bay leaf, allspice, pepper, 2 lemons, 1 beetroot, 1 kohlrabi, salt, a pinch of sugar, lemon, 1 tbsp butter, 1 tsp flour

Clean and wash the fish, cut it into portions, rub with salt and leave for an hour in a cool place. Cook the peeled and rinsed vegetables in the beetroot juice. Arrange the pike portions in a skillet, pour over the strained stock, add the peeled and sliced lemon and raisins. Cook for 40 mins over low heat. Make a roux from the butter and flour, dilute it with the fish stock, add sugar and salt

if required. Add it to the fish and shake the skillet gently. Serve with fish balls or with bread rolls.

serves 4–6

Pike with parsley

1 kg pike, 6 tbsps chopped parsley, 2 medium-large onions, 1 cup sunflower or olive oil, 2 lemons, salt, pepper

Clean and wash the fish, cut it into portions, rub with roasted salt and pepper and leave for an hour in a cool place. Heat the oil in a skillet, add the finely chopped onion and parsley, bring to the boil. Arrange the pike portions in the skillet, cover and simmer for 45 mins, shaking the pan gently from time to time. Towards the end, add lemon juice from two lemons. Serve hot or cold, garnished with lemon slices and sprinkled with chopped parsley.

serves 4 • Preparation: 10 mins • Cooking: 40–45 mins

Pike with sauerkraut

1 kg pike, 2 onions, soup vegetables, spices, 500 g sauerkraut, 1 tbsp oil, 2 tbsps breadcrumbs, 1 tbsp butter, salt

Clean and wash the fish, cut it into portions, rub with salt and leave for an hour. Make a stock from the onion, soup vegetables, spices and pike leftovers. Arrange the pike pieces in a skillet, pour over the strained stock and cook. Separately stew the sauerkraut in oil. Bone the cooked fish. Grease an ovenproof dish with butter, line it with some sauerkraut, arrange the fish portions on top, cover with the remaining cabbage, put in knobs of butter. Put into a preheated oven and bake for 30 mins. Take out, sprinkle with breadcrumbs and melted butter and return to the oven until it gets golden brown. Serve hot with potatoes.

serves 4–6

Pike in yellow sauce

1–1½ kg pike, 1 cup white wine, ½ cup vinegar, soup vegetables, 2 onions, 10 grains allspice,

*bay leaf, 1 lemon, 100 g raisins, 1 tbsp sugar,
½ tsp saffron, 1 tbsp butter, 1 tsp flour, salt*

Clean and rinse the fish, cut it into portions, rub with roasted salt and leave for an hour in a cool place. Make a stock from the fish leftovers, soup vegetables, onion and spices. Arrange the pike in a skillet, pour over the strained stock, add vinegar, raisins and peeled and sliced lemon. Simmer for 30 mins. Make a roux from the butter and flour, add sugar and saffron, thin down with the wine. Pour over the fish, shake the skillet gently and cook for a while over low heat. Arrange the pike pieces on a serving dish, garnish with the cooked diced vegetables, pour over the sauce. Serve with bread rolls or potatoes.

serves 4–6 • Preparation: 30 mins • Cooking: 30 mins

Prelates' pike

*1 kg pike, 3 onions, 2 carrots, 2 parsley roots,
1 celeriac, 4 tbsps butter, 1 glass white wine or
2 glasses rum, salt, pepper, a pinch of sugar*

Clean and wash the fish, cut it into portions, rub with salt and leave in a cool place for an hour. Peel and wash the vegetables, grate them coarsely or dice. Grease an ovenproof dish with butter, put alternating layers of vegetables, onion and pike. Sprinkle with salt, pepper and sugar, put on top knobs of butter, cover with aluminium foil and place in a preheated oven. Bake for 45 mins. When the vegetables are tender, add the wine or rum and cook for another 10–15 mins under cover. Serve with bread rolls or boiled potatoes basted with butter.

serves 4 • Preparation: 10 mins • Baking: 45–55 mins

Spit-grilled pike in cream

*1 kg pike, 1 celeriac, 1 parsley root, rind of ½ lemon,
salt, pepper, 1 tbsp butter, 1 tsp flour, 1 cup thick cream*

Clean and wash the pike, rub it with salt, leave for an hour in a cool place. Dry it with a piece of cloth, fill it with parsley, celeriac and lemon rind, all cut into strips. Brush with butter and grill on a spit or in a baking tin, often basting with cream. Make a roux from the butter and flour, add salt, a pinch of pepper and a pinch of sugar, dilute with

2 tbsps of water, adjust the taste with some lemon juice and add to the cream which dripped down from the fish. Arrange the pike on a serving dish, garnish with parsley sprigs, pour over the sauce.

Stuffed baked pike

*1 kg pike, 1 large onion, 2 tbsps chopped parsley,
3–4 large anchovies, 1 white bread roll, 2 eggs,
2 tbsps butter, ½ cup thick cream, salt, pepper*

Clean and wash the pike, skin it, but leave the head. Remove the bones. Put the fish meat, onion and bread roll, that was first soaked in water and squeezed out, through a mincer. Add the eggs, salt, pepper and chopped parsley, mix thoroughly. Fill the skin with the stuffing, sew it up. Prick the skin in several places to prevent it bursting in the hot oven. Grease an oven-proof dish with butter, arrange the pike in it. Prop it up with toothpicks or matches so it bakes with the back up. Put into a hot oven. Bake for 45 mins at a medium temperature, baste often with butter and cream. For carp cooked in this way, do not use cream for basting.

serves 4 • Preparation: 25–30 mins • Baking: 40–45 mins

Pike or pikeperch, Tartar style

*1 kg pike, 4 large onions, 1 tbsp butter,
2 cups thick sour cream, 1 tbsp capers, 1 tbsp
olives, 1 lemon, salt, a pinch of sugar*

Clean and wash the fish, rub it with roasted salt, cut into sections and leave for an hour in a cool place. Peel and grate the onions, squeeze out the juice. Heat up the juice in a pan with 1 tbsp of butter, put in the pike and simmer covered for 10 mins. Add the cream, capers, olives and peeled slices of lemon. Cook for another 40 mins over low heat. Put the fish on a serving dish, pour the sauce over. Serve with boiled potatoes.

serves 4 • Preparation: 5–7 mins • Cooking: 45–50 mins

Pike in horseradish sauce

*2 kg pike, soup vegetables, 1 large onion, 1 clove,
2 bay leaves, 5–6 grains each pepper and allspice,*

salt, 1 tsp vegetable seasoning or 1 soup cube,
2 cups water, 2 cups dry white wine, grated rind and
juice of ½ lemon, 2 tbsps butter, 1 tbsp flour, 1 cup
thick cream, 1 egg yolk, 1 cup grated horseradish,
1 tbsp lemon juice, white pepper, a pinch of sugar

Clean and wash the fish, rub it with salt, cover and leave in the fridge for 2–3 hours. Peel and wash the vegetables, dice them and put in a pan together with the onion with a clove stuck into it. Add pepper, allspice, bay leaves and lemon rind, cover with boiling water. Bring to the boil, add the vegetable seasoning or soup cube and continue cooking until no more than 1 cup of stock is left. Strain the stock, add the lemon juice and wine, bring to the boil again. Cut the fish into portions, arrange them in a skillet, pour over the boiling stock. Cover and cook over low heat for 20 mins. Make a roux from the butter and flour, dilute it with the fish stock and simmer, stirring all the time, until the sauce has thickened. Adjust the taste with salt, pepper, sugar and lemon juice, stir. Beat the cream and the egg yolk and horseradish, pour into the sauce. Stirring all the time, heat it up, but keep off the boil. Arrange the fish on a hot serving dish, pour over the hot sauce. Serve with small noodles and lettuce with hard-boiled eggs.

serves 4–6 • Preparation: 30–40 mins • Cooking: 20 mins

Pike, Polish style

1½ kg pike, 3 onions, 1 tbsp butter, 3 tbsps grated
horseradish, 1 bread roll soaked in milk, 50 g raisins,
1 tbsp dry white wine, 1 tbsp honey, 2 eggs, salt, pepper;

3 cups fish or vegetable stock, 4 grains each
pepper and allspice, 1 bay leaf, 1–2 cloves,
2 tbsps lemon juice, 1 tsp grated lemon rind,
2 onions, a pinch of sugar, 2 tbsps gelatine

Make a stock from 2 onions, pepper, allspice, bay leaf, cloves and lemon rind. Cook under cover for 20 mins over low heat. Chop finely 3 onions, fry them in butter without browning. Blanch the raisins. Clean and wash the pike. With a sharp knife remove the skin, bone the fish. Rub the skin with salt inside and out. Put half the fish meat, the onion and squeezed bread roll through a mincer. Cut the remaining fish meat into thin strips, sprinkle

lightly with salt and with lemon juice. Combine the minced fish with the horseradish, drained raisins and fish strips, add 1 raw egg yolk, honey, and salt and pepper to taste, and mix thoroughly. Wash and dry the skin, fill it tightly with the stuffing, wrap it in a piece gauze, tie the ends of the gauze. Put into a skillet, pour over the strained stock and cook covered over low heat for 1 hour. Take the fish out when it gets cooler. Put it on a board, cover with another board, weigh it down and leave till it is completely cool. Reduce the stock, adjust the taste with salt, pepper, sugar and lemon juice. Add the gelatine, clarify with egg whites and strain. Pour some of the stock into a flat serving dish and leave to set. Remove the gauze from the fish, cut it into slices. Arrange the slices in the serving dish and garnish them. Pour over the remaining stock and leave to set. Serve with lemon with a savoury sauce or horseradish.

serves 4–6 • Preparation: 40–50 mins • Cooking: 1 hr • Setting: 1–2 hrs

Pike, Kuyavian style

2 kg pike, coarse-grained salt, 2 l sour beetroot
juice, 1 leek (only the white part), 1 large onion,
1 carrot, 1 small celeriac, 1 large beetroot, 1 kohlrabi,
2 parsley roots, 3–4 peppercorns, 5–6 grains allspice,
2–3 bay leaves, grated rind of 1 lemon, 100 g raisins,
2 tbsps red wine, 1 lemon, 1 tbsp butter, 1 tsp flour

Clean, wash and dry the fish, rub it inside and out with salt, cover with foil and leave in the fridge overnight. Peel and wash the vegetables, grate them coarsely. Put into a pan, add pepper, allspice, bay leaves and lemon rind, cover with the beetroot juice and cook till tender, then sieve them. Rinse and dry the fish, cut it into portions, arrange in a skillet. Pour over the hot beetroot stock and cook under cover over low heat for 20–25 mins. Wash the raisins, pour over the wine and leave for a while. Wash and scald the lemon, cut it into slices, remove the pips. Mix the butter with flour. Take out the pike, arrange on a hot serving dish. Heat up the sauce, add the raisins and the butter and flour mixture. Heat up, stirring all the time, until the sauce has thickened. Add lemon slices and pour the sauce over the fish. Garnish with fish balls or boiled potato balls.

serves 6–8 • Preparation: 30–40 mins • Cooking: 20–25 mins

Pike, Mazurian style

*1 medium-sized pike, 500 g cabbage,
150 g fresh forest mushrooms (or champignons),
50 g lean streaky bacon, 2 onions,
1 tart apple, 1 tbsp tomato paste,
2 tbsps grated cheese, a pinch of sugar,
2–3 tbsps chopped parsley, 1 tbsp
flour, 1 tbsp oil, salt, pepper*

Clean the fish, cut off the head, tail and fins. Rub the flesh with salt, cover and put into the fridge for an hour. Make a stock from the head, tail and fins, strain it. Fry the finely chopped onion and mushrooms with the bacon cut into cubes. Shred the cabbage finely. Put the cabbage into a pan, add the sliced apple, fried onion and mushrooms, pour over the strained fish stock and cook over low heat. Season with salt and pepper, add tomato paste and sugar, stir. Cover and cook for several minutes more over low heat. Cut the fish into sections, dust with flour and fry quickly in very hot oil. Arrange in an ovenproof dish, cover with the stewed cabbage, sprinkle with grated cheese and put into a preheated oven for 10–15 mins. Before serving, sprinkle with chopped parsley.

serves 6–8 • Preparation: 30–40 mins • Cooking: 25–30 mins

Braised pike with mushrooms

*1 pike (1.2 kg), 500 g fresh boletus mushrooms,
2 onions, 60 g butter, 2 tbsps chopped parsley,
250 ml white wine, 1 tbsp flour, salt, pepper*

Clean the fish, rinse and halve it. Remove the bones. Cut the meat into cubes and salt it. Clean the mushrooms, rinse them, cut into cubes and fry in 2 tbsps of butter. Peel the onions, chop them and add to the mushrooms together with the parsley. Fry for 5 mins, then put in the fish, pour over the wine, season with salt and pepper and cook for 20 mins. Toast the flour with the remaining butter, add to the fish, cook for another 5 mins, stirring often. Arrange the fish on a serving dish, surround it with the mushrooms, pour over the sauce.

serves 4–6 • Preparation: 25–30 mins • Cooking: 25–30 mins

Trout

Trout, Dutch style

Clean and wash the fish, rub it with salt and leave for an hour. Put it in a skillet, pour in a bottle of white wine, add three small onions, bouquet garni, cloves, two cloves of garlic, a bay leaf, thyme, basil, a bit of butter mixed with flour. 15 minutes before serving put the fish into the oven, pour over the stock. When ready, take out the onions and bouquet garni. Arrange the trout on a serving dish, pour over the sauce and sprinkle with parsley.

Kucharz doskonały, 1808

Smoked trout in watercress sauce

2 smoked trouts, 1 cup thick sour cream, ½ cup thick mayonnaise, 1 cup watercress sprouts, ½ tsp grated horseradish, salt, white pepper, a pinch of sugar, 2 tbsps chopped watercress, 1 lemon, 2–3 leaves of lettuce

Blend the cream, mayonnaise and horseradish with the watercress, salt, peppet and sugar, refrigerate for a while. Wash and scald the lemon, dry it, cut into quarters. Skin the trout, remove the bones and the spine, divide into pieces. Line a serving dish with lettuce, arrange the trout portions on them, pour over the sauce. Garnish with lemon quarters and sprinkle with chopped watercress.

serves 4 • Preparation: 5–7 mins

Savoury trout

4 trouts, nettle leaves, new horseradish leaves, lovage sprigs, 2 tbsps chopped parsley, juice and grated rind of 1 lemon, salt, pepper, 2 tbsps butter

Clean the fish, wash and dry it, rub inside and out with salt and the lemon zest, sprinkle with some lemon juice. Coat each trout with nettle leaves, wrap up in a leaf of horseradish and then in foil, and put in the fridge for 2–3 hours. Combine one measure of each: lovage sprigs, nettle leaves and the freshest horseradish leaves with the chopped parsley. Take the fish out, remove the foil and nettle and horseradish leaves. Rub the trout with pepper, stuff with the mixture of green leaves. Grease an oven-proof dish with butter, arrange the trout in it and put into a preheated oven. Baste with the melted butter and bake for 20–30 mins.

serves 4 • Preparation: 10–15 mins • Baking: 20–30 mins

Trout with sage

4 trouts, 1 tsp dried sage, juice of 1 lemon, salt, pepper, butter for frying

Clean and wash the fish, rub with salt, sprinkle with lemon juice and pepper. Put a bit of sage into the belly of each of them. Fry in melted butter for 5 mins to each side. Garnish with chopped parsley and knobs of butter. Serve with boiled potatoes.

serves 4 • Preparation: 5 mins • Frying: 8–12 mins

Marinated trout

4 trout

* 1 cup vinegar, 1 cup dry white wine, ½ tsp each dried thyme and basil, 1 tbsp chopped parsley, 3 onions, several peppercorns, salt, 1 tbsp flour, * sunflower oil for frying

Clean and wash the fish, dry them, coat with flour and fry in hot oil for 5 mins to each side. Put the fish into a stoneware jar. Take the frying pan off the heat, pour in the vinegar and wine, add the sliced onion and all the spices. Cook covered for 10–15 mins over low heat. Place the trout in a jar, cover with the hot marinade and leave for several days in a cool place.

serves 4 • Preparation: 5–7 mins • Frying: 8–10 mins • Cooking: 15–20 mins

Trout, Cracow style

4 trout, 100 g sour cherry preserve, 50 g each cherry brandy, vermuth and vodka, juice and grated rind of 1 lemon, salt, pepper, a pinch of sugar and cayenne, 2–3 tbsps butter

Clean the fish, remove the eyes and gills, wash and dry them, rub with salt, pepper and the lemon zest.

Sprinkle lightly with lemon juice and leave for 1–2 hours. Fry in 2 tbsps of butter. Mix the brandy, vermouth and vodka with sugar, cayenne, pepper, lemon juice and cherries. Grease an ovenproof dish with butter, put in the trout, pour over the sauce and place in a hot oven for several minutes.

serves 4 • Frying: 1–12 mins • Baking: 6–7 mins

Trout fillets in gooseberry sauce

4 trout fillets, 1 tbsp lemon juice, salt, pepper, 2 tbsps flour, 1½ tbsps oil, 2 tbsps almond flakes

SAUCE: 400 g gooseberry, ¼ cup water, 2 tbsps butter, 1 tsp nutmeg, 2 tbsps sugar

Wash and dry the fillets, rub them with salt and pepper, sprinkle with lemon juice and leave in a cool place for an hour. Dredge the fillets with flour and fry in hot oil. Rinse the gooseberries, put them in a pan, add sugar and boiling water and simmer over low heat for 15 mins, stirring from time to time. Purée the gooseberries, mix with nutmeg and butter, heat up. Arrange the fillets in an ovenproof dish, pour over the sauce, sprinkle with almond flakes and put into a preheated oven. Serve with bread rolls as a hot snack or with potatoes and lettuce.

serves 4 • Preparation: 15–20 mins • Frying: 10–12 mins

Stuffed trout in cabbage leaves

4 large trout, 2 large onions, 4–6 cloves of garlic, ½ tsp ground coriander, ½ cup single cream, 2 eggs, 4 tbsps olive oil, 2 tbsps breadcrumbs, 8 cabbage leaves, salt, pepper

GARNISHING: 4 small tomatoes, several leaves of lettuce, 8 strips each yellow, red and green bell peppers, several sprigs of parsley

Wash the cabbage leaves, scald them with boiling water, then rinse with cold water and dry. Clean and wash the trout, remove the skin, taking care not to pierce it, rub it with salt. Remove the spine and bones, chop the meat finely. Combine the fish meat with coriander, salt, pepper, finely chopped onion, garlic, breadcrumbs, and

Stuffed trout in cabbage leaves

cream, break in the eggs and mix thoroughly. Fill the skins with the stuffing. Wrap each fish in a cabbage leaf and put into a large pan. Rest the pan on top of a pot with boiling water, cover and steam cook for 15 mins. Heat the oil in a large frying pan. Remove the cabbage leaves and transfer the fish onto the frying pan. Fry on both sides until golden brown. Arrange on a hot serving dish on lettuce leaves, garnish with tomato quarters and parsley sprigs. Serve hot or cold.

serves 4 • Preparation: 30–40 mins • Steaming: 15 mins • Frying: 4–5 mins

Trout in caraway sauce

4 trout, 2 onions, 1–2 cloves of garlic, 1 tbsp ground caraway seeds, ½ cup dry white wine, ½ cup boiled water or light fish stock, juice and grated rind of 1 lemon, ½ lemon in thin slices, 3 tbsps chopped parsley, 3 tbsps olive oil, 1 tbsp butter

Clean, wash and dry the fish, rub them with pepper and salt and fry in hot oil until golden brown. Chop the onions finely, fry them in butter but do not brown. Put in the chopped garlic and parsley, mix well, pour in the wine and water, bring to the boil. Add the caraway, cover and simmer for 10 mins. Put through a blender together with the lemon zest and juice, then sieve. Arrange the fried trout in an ovenproof dish, pour over the sauce and put into a preheated oven for several minutes. Before serving, garnish with lemon slices.

serves 4 • Preparation: 15–20 mins • Frying: 5–8 mins • Baking: 5–6 mins

Trout balls in walnut sauce

1 kg trout fillets, 1 cup breadcrumbs, 1 cup oil, 2–3 eggs, salt, pepper;

1–2 cloves of garlic, 2 tbsps vinegar, ½ cup dry white wine, 1 tsp honey, 3–4 tbsps chopped walnuts, ½ tsp pepper, 1 tbsp chopped parsley

Chop finely the fillets, squeeze them out to remove excess water, add 2–3 tbsps of breadcrumbs, salt and pepper, break in 2 eggs. Work into a smooth paste (add more breadcrumbs if the mixture is too soft). Moisten your hands and form small balls out of the paste. Coat each ball in breadcrumbs, lightly beaten raw egg and again in breadcrumbs. Fry in hot oil until golden brown. Mix the garlic crushed with salt with the vinegar, honey, wine, walnuts and 2–3 tbsps of breadcrumbs, add salt and pepper and bring to the boil. Put the fried balls into the sauce. Heat it for several minutes, then add chopped parsley, shake the pan, take it off the heat. Serve hot or cold.

serves 6–8 • Preparation: 14–20 mins • Frying: 10 mins

Tench

Tench fricassee

Clean the tench, put it into hot water to make it easier to remove the scales. Cut it into portions, fry in butter until golden brown. Add onion and grated nutmeg, cover with stock. Add crayfish meat, some cooked artichoke or green peas. Bring to the boil, pour in cream and heat up.

Kucharz doskonały, 1808

Tench ragout with horseradish, Lithuanian style

1 kg tench, ½ cup grated horseradish, ½ cup stock, 1 tbsp butter, 1 tbsp flour, 1 tbsp cream, 2–3 bay leaves, salt, pepper, sugar, 1–2 tbsps vinegar

Clean and wash the fish, remove the bones and spine, cut into small portions. Sprinkle with salt and pepper and leave aside for half an hour. Melt the butter in a pan, put in the fish, fry for a minute or two, then sprinkle with the crumbled bay leaves and with the stock and simmer for 10 mins. Blend the cream with salt, sugar, vinegar and flour. Sprinkle the cooked fish with the horseradish, pour over the cream and simmer for 15 mins.

serves 4–6 • Preparation: 15–20 mins • Cooking: 15– 20 mins

Tench and mushroom ragout in wine

1 kg tench, 20 g dried boletus mushrooms, 2 onions, 2 cups dry white wine, 4–6 grains allspice, 2–3 peppercorns, 1 bay leaf, 1 tbsp butter, 1 tsp flour, ½ lemon, 1 egg yolk, salt, pepper

Soak the mushrooms in water overnight, then cook them. Clean and wash the fish, rub it with salt and leave in a cool place for an hour. Fry the finely chopped onions in butter, but do not let them brown. Add the mushrooms cut into thin strips, allspice, pepper and bay leaf, pour over the wine, cover and simmer for 15 mins. Arrange the tench in a skillet, pour over the onion and mushroom stock and cook covered for 60 mins over low heat. Make a roux from the butter and flour, dilute it with 1 tbsp of water and lemon juice, add salt and pepper. When the sauce has thickened, add one egg yolk and, stirring all the time, heat up, but do not allow it to boil. Put the tench in a serving dish, garnish with the mushrooms, pour over the sauce. Serve with white bread toast.

serves 4 • Salting: 1 hr • Preparation: 15–20 mins • Cooking: 55–60 mins

Tench in red cabbage

1 kg tench, 1 red cabbage, 1 lemon, 1 large onion, 1 cup dry red wine, salt, 1 tsp sugar, 1 tbsp butter, 1 tsp flour

Shred the cabbage, scald it with boiling water, drain, sprinkle with lemon juice and salt it. Melt 1 tbsp of butter in a pan, add the finely chopped onion and 1 tsp of flour, stir, then dilute the mixture with the wine. Put the cabbage into the sauce, add the sugar, stir well, cover the pan and cook for 30 mins over low heat. Clean the tench, scald it with boiling water, cut into portions and salt it. Put into the cabbage pan, cover with a layer of cabbage and simmer for another 40 mins under cover. Arrange the fish in a serving dish and put the cabbage around.

serves 4–6 • Preparation: 35–40 mins • Cooking: 40 mins

Tench in cabbage

2 kg tench, salt, pepper, 1 tbsp flour, 2 eggs, 1 cup breadcrumbs, oil or clarified butter for frying;

soup vegetables, 2 large onions, 5–7 grains allspice, 1–2 bay leaves, 3–4 cloves, a small piece of cinnamon, juice and grated rind of ½ lemon, 1 tbsp honey, salt, pepper;

50 g dried mushrooms, 1 small (ca 1½ kg) white cabbage, 1 cup cream

Rinse the mushrooms and soak them in a small amount of water. Make a stock from the vegetables and onions, add cinnamon, cloves, lemon zest, bay leaves and allspice. Cook under cover for 40 mins, then remove the lid and simmer until 2 cups of stock are left. Shred the cabbage, salt it lightly and leave aside for several minutes, then squeeze it lightly and put into a pan. Pour over the strained stock, add the mushrooms cut into strips, bring to the boil, then simmer for 10 mins. Season to taste with salt, pepper, honey and lemon juice, stir thoroughly and simmer for several minutes longer. Reduce the juices, add the cream, mix well. Put the fish into a bowl, pour over boiling water. When the mucus turns white (the tench is covered with thick mucus), take the fish out, scale them and cut into portions. Dry, sprinkle with salt and pepper. Dredge lightly with flour, then coat in beaten up eggs and breadcrumbs. Fry in hot oil until golden brown. Grease an ovenproof dish with butter, line it with some cabbage, put on top the fish portions, cover with the remaining cabbage. Put into a preheated oven for several minutes. Serve with boiled potatoes.

serves 6–8 • Preparation: 1 hr • Baking: 10 mins

Tench in savoury sauce

1 kg tench, ½ celeriac, 2 carrots, 1 medium-sized onion, 1 tbsp butter, 2 lemons, 1 tbsp capers, 2 anchovies, 2 cloves of garlic, 1 bay leaf, 5 grains each pepper and allspice, a piece of dried rye bread, 1 tsp caramel, salt, butter

Clean and wash the fish, cut the bellies lengthwise, bleed into a skillet containing the juice from one lemon. Gut the tench, wash and cut into portions, sprinkle with salt. Put the fish portions into the skillet, add the finely chopped vegetables, onions, anchovies, capers, salt and spices, pour in the juice of 1 lemon. Cover the fish with water, put in the rye bread and butter. Bring to the boil and then simmer covered for 20–30 mins. Take the cooked fish out gently. Continue cooking until the vegetables are soft. Add the finely chopped garlic, caramel, a pinch of sugar if required, then sieve the sauce. Put the fish into the sauce, heat it up and serve immediately with kasha or scooped out potatoes.

serves 4 • Preparation: 10 mins • Cooking: 20–30 mins

Tench, Jewish style

*1 kg tench, 1 large onion, soup vegetables,
spices (allspice, pepper, bay leaf), salt*

*STUFFING: 3–4 onions, pepper, ½ tsp
sugar, 2 tbsps breadcrumbs, 1 egg white,
3 cloves of garlic, tench meat*

Make a stock from the vegetables, spices and fish trimmings. Clean and wash the tench, salt it and leave in a cool place for an hour. Gently remove the skin, taking care not to pierce it. Bone the fish meat, chop it and put through a mincer together with the finely chopped onion. Add the egg white, pepper, sugar and breadcrumbs, mix thoroughly. Fill the skin with the stuffing, sew the belly up with thread. Arrange the fish in a skillet, pour over the strained stock, add grated garlic and cook over low heat for 60 mins. Take the tench out gently and leave to cool. With a sharp knife cut it into thick slices. Arrange the slices on a serving dish, garnish with diced cooked vegetables, pour over the strained sauce and leave to set.

serves 4 • Preparation: 35–40 mins • Cooking: 55–60 mins

Tench in aspic

*1 kg tench, soup vegetables, 2 large onions,
4 cloves of garlic, 1 bay leaf, 4–6 grains each
allspice and pepper, salt, a pinch of sugar*

Make a stock from the soup vegetables, onions, spices and fish trimmings. Clean and wash the tench, salt them, put into a skillet, cover with the strained stock and simmer, adding the garlic towards the end. Take out the fish, remove the skin, spine and bones. Arrange the fish meat on a serving dish, garnish with diced cooked vegetables, pour over the stock and leave to cool. The stock made of tench always stays translucent, so it does not re-

quire clarifying. You do not have to add gelatine either since the tench skin contains enough gelling agent.

*serves 4–6 • Preparation: 15 mins • Cooking:
30–40 mins • Refrigerating: 1–2 hrs*

Small tench cooked in cream

*1 kg small tench, 1 cup thick sour cream, ½ lemon,
salt, a pinch of sugar, 1 tbsp chopped parsley or dill*

Clean, trim and wash the fish, salt them, put into a skillet. Pour over the cream and simmer over low heat for 20–30 mins, adding the lemon juice and a pinch of salt. Take out the fish and arrange them on a serving dish, pour over the sauce, sprinkle with parsley or dill. Serve hot with boiled potatoes sprinkled with melted butter.

serves 4–6 • Preparation: 10–15 mins • Cooking: 20–30 mins

Tench à la tripe

*1 kg tench, 2 large onions, 2 parsley roots,
½ large celeriac, 1 cup cream, 1 tbsp flour, 1 tbsp
butter, salt, pepper, 1 tbsp marjoram, ¼ tsp each
nutmeg and ginger, soup vegetables, spices*

Clean and trim the fish, wash, rub with salt and leave in a cool place for an hour. Remove the skin, spine and bones. Cut the meat into strips, put them into a skillet, add butter and simmer covered for 10 mins. Make a stock from the soup vegetables, spices and fish trimmings. Peel and rinse the celeriac, parsley roots and onion, cut them into thin strips, put into a pan and simmer in butter until tender. Transfer the cooked vegetables and the fish to a larger pan, add ginger, nutmeg, marjoram, salt and pepper, pour over the fish stock and simmer for 15 mins. Towards the end add the cream. Serve with bread rolls.

serves 4–6 • Preparation: 30–40 mins • Cooking: 15 mins

Bream

Bream in wine

1 kg bream, soup vegetables, spices, 2 onions, 1 cup dry white wine, 1 tbsp butter, 1 tsp flour, 1 tbsp capers, 1 lemon, 1 tbsp chopped parsley, a pinch of sugar, salt

Trim and wash the fish, rub it with salt. Make a stock from the fish trimmings, soup vegetables, onion and spices. Arrange the bream in a skillet, pour over 2 cups of the strained stock and the wine, and cook over low heat for 30 mins. Make a roux from the butter and flour, dilute it with the fish stock, add the capers, lemon juice, parsley and a pinch of sugar, stir thoroughly. Arrange the fish on a serving dish, pour over the sauce. Serve with bread rolls or boiled potatoes.

serves 4 • Preparation: 30–40 mins • Cooking: 30 mins

Bream, Jewish style

1 kg bream, 3–4 onions, pepper, salt, soup vegetables, spices, 1 tbsp breadcrumbs, 1 egg, 1 tbsp flour

Trim and wash the fish, remove the skin, spine and bones. Make a stock from the fish trimmings, soup vegetables, spices and 1 onion. Put the fish meat and 2 onions through a mincer, add salt, pepper, breadcrumbs and egg, mix thoroughly. Shape small balls from the mixture, dredge them with flour, then put into a skillet. Add the sliced onion, pour over the strained stock and cook for 30 mins. Take the balls out, arrange on a serving plate and pour over the sieved sauce.

serves 4–6 • Preparation: 15–20 mins • Cooking: 30 mins

Bream, French style

1 kg bream, 3 tbsps butter, 2 tbsps chopped parsley, salt

Trim and wash the fish, rub it with salt and leave in a cool place for an hour. Grease thickly aluminium foil or greaseproof paper with butter, wrap up the fish and put on the grill in a preheated oven. Bake for 30 mins in medium temperature. Take out the bream, arrange it on a serving dish, sprinkle liberally with parsley, garnish with lemon slices and butter.

serves 4 • Preparation: 15–20 mins • Baking: 30 mins

Crucian carp

Crucian carp, Lithuanian style

1 kg crucian carp, ¾ cup coarsely grated horseradish, 1 tbsp finely grated horseradish, ¼ cup fish or vegetable stock, 1 cup thick cream, 2 tbsps butter, 1 tbsp flour, 2–3 bay leaves, salt, pepper, sugar, 2 tbsps lemon juice

Clean, trim and wash the fish, dry it, rub with pepper and salt, sprinkle with lemon juice. Melt the butter in a skillet, put in the fish, sprinkle with the crushed bay leaves, coarsely grated horseradish and stock. Cover and cook over low heat for 20 mins. Mix the flour with salt, pepper, sugar, lemon juice and finely grated horseradish, pour the mixture over the fish, shake the skillet and simmer for another 8 mins.

serves 4 • Preparation: ca 30 mins • Cooking: 25–30 mins

Crucian carp in cream

1 kg crucian carp, 1 cup cream, soup vegetables, 1 onion, 1 bay leaf, 3–5 peppercorns, 3–4 grains allspice, salt, 1 tbsp butter, 1 tsp flour

Make a stock from the vegetables, spices and onion, then strain it. Clean trim and rinse the fish, arrange in a skillet, cover with the stock and cook for 10–15 mins. Make a roux from the butter and flour, dilute it with the fish stock and cream and, stirring all the time, heat it up. Put in the cooked fish and simmer for a while.

serves 4 • Preparation: 30 mins • Cooking: 15–20 mins

Crucian carp with onion

*1 kg crucian carp, 4 onions, 1 tsp sugar, a
pinch of pepper, 1 tbsp butter, 1 tsp flour,
1 tbsp chopped parsley, salt, ½ lemon*

Clean, trim and wash the fish, salt it, arrange in a skillet, sprinkle with the finely chopped onion, add sugar and pepper. Pour in enough water to cover the fish. Put the lid on and cook for 20 mins. Make a roux from the butter and flour, dilute it with 2 tbsps of water and the lemon juice. Arrange the fish on a serving dish. Combine the sauce with the onion, stir well, pour over the fish. Sprinkle the fish with parsley. Serve hot or cold with potatoes or white bread.

serves 4 • Preparation: 30 mins • Cooking: 20 mins

Crucian carp in sour beet juice

*1 kg crucian carp, 2 cups sour beet juice, 2 carrots,
1 beetroot, 1 medium-sized onion, 1 tsp caraway seeds,
1 tsp sugar, salt, pepper, 1 tsp butter, ½ cup thick sour
cream, 1 tsp flour, 1 bay leaf, 3–4 grains allspice*

Clean and trim the fish, cut off the heads and tails (which you may use for making a fish stock), wash and salt them, and leave in a cool place for an hour. Peel the beetroot and cook it whole. Pour the beet juice into a pan, add the sugar, spices, sliced onion, diced carrots and caraway, and cook under cover. Sieve the vegetables. Arrange the fish in a skillet, pour over the sieved stock and simmer covered for 30 mins. Make a roux from the butter and flour, dilute it with the cream and add to the fish. Shake the skillet gently to mix the ingredients. Arrange the fish on a serving dish, put the coarsely grated beetroot around and pour over the sauce. Serve hot with boiled potatoes.

serves 4 • Preparation: 30–40 mins • Cooking: 30 mins

Catfish

Catfish in cabbage

1 kg catfish, 1 tbsp flour, 1 tbsp butter

1 cabbage, soup vegetables, 2 onions;

*8–10 mushrooms, 2 tart apples, 2 tbsps
tomato paste, a pinch of paprika, ¼ tsp sugar,
2 tbsps grated cheese, 1 tbsp butter*

Clean and wash the fish, cut it into portions, rub with roasted salt and leave in a cool place for an hour. Make a stock from the fish trimmings and soup vegetables. Shred the cabbage, scald it with boiling water, put into a pan, cover with the strained stock and cook. Chop finely the onion and mushrooms and cook them in 1 tbsp of butter. When the cabbage is almost ready, add the onion and mushrooms, then the diced apples, tomato paste, paprika and sugar. Stir thoroughly and simmer for 10 mins. Dredge the fish portions with flour and fry them in butter. Grease an ovenproof dish with butter, put in the cabbage, arrange the catfish portions on top. Cover with the remaining cabbage, sprinkle with the grated cheese and put into a hot oven for 15–20 mins.

serves 4–6 • Preparation: 1 hr • Frying: 8–10 mins

Catfish steaks

*1 kg catfish, 2 tbsps butter, 2 onions, 1 lemon, 1 tsp
flour, 1 tbsp chopped parsley, 1 horseradish root*

Clean, trim and wash the catfish, cut it into steaks and salt it. Heat up the butter in a frying pan. Dredge the fish steaks with flour and fry them over low heat on both sides. Arrange them on a serving dish and keep warm. Soften the finely chopped onion in the same frying pan, add the parsley, add lemon juice and 1 tbsp of water or fish stock. Simmer for a while. Put some onion and parsley mixture on each steak, garnish with the coarsely grated horseradish. Serve with boiled potatoes or French fries.

serves 4–6 • Preparation: 10 mins • Frying: 8–10 mins

Eel

Eel in aspic

1 kg eel, soup vegetables, 2 onions, 1 bay leaf,
3–4 grains allspice, 5–6 peppercorns, 1 lemon,
salt, a pinch of sugar, 1 tbsp gelatine

Clean, wash and salt the eel, leave it in a cool place for an hour. Make a savoury stock from the spices, soup vegetables and the fish trimmings. Put the eel into a skillet, pour over the strained vegetable stock and cook for 30–40 mins. Dissolve one tablespoonful of gelatine in a cup of stock. Take out the eel, cut it into pieces, remove the bones. Arrange the pieces on a serving dish, garnish them with the cooked vegetables. Heat up the dissolved gelatine, add lemon juice and a pinch of sugar if required, stir well. Let the stock cool a bit, then pour it over the fish and leave to set.

serves 4–6 • Preparation: 15–20 mins • Cooking: 30–40 mins

Eel in parsley sauce

1 kg eel, 2 tbsps butter, 1 large onion, 2 tbsps
chopped parsley, ½ lemon, ½ cup fish stock,
½ cup dry white wine, 2 egg yolks, 1 tsp flour

Clean the eel, cut it into pieces, salt them. Heat up the butter in a frying pan, brown the eel on both sides. Take the fish out. Soften the chopped onion in the same frying pan, add the flour, dilute the sauce with the fish stock, stir well. Add lemon juice, wine and parsley, stir again and heat up. Return the eel to the pan and cook over low heat for a while. Before serving, add two egg yolks to the sauce and stir. Serve with rice or potatoes sprinkled with parsley or dill.

serves 4 • Preparation: 15 mins • Cooking: 10–15 mins

Braised eel

1 kg eel, soup vegetables, ½ lemon, 1 bay leaf,
4–5 grains each allspice and pepper, ½ cup thick sour
cream, 1 tbsp chopped dill, 1 tbsp butter, 1 tsp flour, salt

Wash the eel with a stiff brush dipped in salt, clean it, cut into pieces, rub with salt and leave in a cool place for 1–2 hours. Make a stock from the soup vegetables, onion and fish trimmings. Arrange the eel pieces in a skillet, pour over the strained stock, cover the pan and simmer for 30 mins. Make a roux from the butter and flour, dilute it with the cream, add lemon juice and dill. Pour the sauce over the eel, shake the skillet to mix the ingredients and cook for several minutes more. Serve with rice, kasha or French fries.

serves 4 • Salting: 1–2 hrs • Preparation: 30–40 mins • Cooking: 30–40 mins

Baked eel

1 kg eel, soup vegetables, spices, 1 onion, 1 cup dry
white wine, 1 tbsp butter, 1 tsp flour, ½ lemon, 2 egg
yolks, 250 g pasta, 2 tbsps grated cheese, 1 tbsp butter

Clean, trim and wash the fish, cut it into portions and salt them. Make a stock from the soup vegetables, onion, spices and fish trimmings. Put the eel into a skillet, pour over the strained fish stock, add the wine. Cover and simmer for 30 mins. Cook pasta in a slightly salted water. Make a roux from the butter and flour, dilute it with the cream and fish stock, add lemon juice. Pour the sauce over the eel and simmer for another 10–15 mins. Grease an ovenproof dish with butter, arrange the eel pieces in it and surround with the cooked pasta. Add the egg yolks to the sauce, stir and pour over the fish and pasta. Sprinkle with the grated cheese and dollops of butter. Put into a hot oven for several minutes. Serve hot.

serves 4 • Preparation: 30–40 mins • Cooking: 30 mins

Gourmet's eel casserole

1 kg eel, 1 carrot, 1 parsley root, ¼ celeriac, 1 leek,
1 onion, ½ cup dry white wine, 100 g mushrooms,
50 g almonds, 1 tbsp crayfish butter, 1 tbsp flour, 100 g
crayfish meat (or crab meat), 2 egg yolks, salt, pepper,
2 tbsps lemon juice, 2 tbsps chopped dill, 1 tbsp butter

Wash and trim the eel, skin it. Rub the meat with salt and leave in a cool place for an hour. Peel and rinse the vegetables, dice them, put into a pan, cover with 2 cups of hot water and cook. Put in the eel cut into portions and cook over low heat for 25 mins. Take out the fish carefully. Blanch and skin the almonds and chop them finely. Melt the crayfish butter in a small pan, add the flour, dilute with the wine and 1 cup of strained fish stock, add the finely chopped mushrooms and cook for 10 mins, stirring from time to time. Adjust the taste with salt and pepper, add the lemon juice, crayfish meat and dill, and at the end the egg yolks, stir thoroughly. When the sauce has thickened, take it off the heat. Grease an ovenproof dish with butter, line it with the eel meat, pour over the sauce, sprinkle with the chopped almonds and put into a hot oven for 20 mins.

serves 4–6 • Preparation: 20–25 mins • Cooking: 25–30 mins

Various freshwater fish

Fish, Greek style

750 g fish fillets (silver carp, carp), 1 large celeriac, 2 carrots, 2 parsley roots, 2 onions, 3 tbsps tomato paste, 3 tbsps sunflower oil, 6–7 peppercorns, 3–4 grains allspice, 1 bay leaf, salt, pepper, ¼ tsp sugar, ⅓ lemon

Sprinkle the fillets with lemon juice, salt them and leave in a cool place for an hour. Peel and rinse the vegetables, dice them or grate them coarsely. In a large skillet heat up the oil, put in the vegetables and onion, add salt, pepper, sugar and 2 tbsps of water. Put a lid on and stew until the vegetables are tender. Add the tomato paste and stir thoroughly. Fry the fillets in hot oil until golden brown on both sides. Put the vegetables on top of the fillets and simmer for a bit longer. Serve hot with rice or cold with white bread.

serves 4 • Preparation: 20–25 mins • Frying: 8–10 mins

Fish terrine in horseradish sauce

1–1.20 kg fish fillets (carp, silver carp, perch), soup vegetables, 1 bay leaf, 4–5 grains each allspice and pepper, 1 onion, salt, 1 bread roll, 2 tbsps butter,

2 large onions, 6 eggs, ½ cup thick sour cream, 2 tbsps chopped parsley, a pinch of sugar, salt, pepper

Make a stock from the soup vegetables, 1 onion and spices. Pour the strained stock over the fillets and cook for 20 mins. Put the cooked fish through a mincer together with the bread roll that has been soaked in milk and squeezed out, and 2 hard-boiled eggs. Break in 4 raw eggs, fold in ½ cup of cream, add parsley, salt, pepper and sugar and mix thoroughly. Put the mixture into a pie mould and steam for 90 mins. Serve with horseradish sauce.

serves 6–8 • Preparation: 45–50 mins • Cooking: 1½ hrs

Fish pâté in puff pastry

1 kg fish (carp, silver carp), 250 g mushrooms, 2 onions, 3 tbsps butter, ½ cup white wine, 1 cup fish stock, ½ lemon, 1 tbsp flour, 3 egg yolks, pepper, salt, ½ tsp each basil and thyme

Puff pastry: 200 g flour, 200 g butter, ½ lemon, or 300 g ready-made puff pastry

Make the dough (you may prepare it a day or two earlier and keep it in the fridge). Mix the flour with water and lemon juice until the dough is smooth and let it stand for an hour to make it more sprightly. Roll it out, divide into two pieces, spread some softened butter on top. Put one piece of dough on top of the other and roll them out together. Repeat the sequence of rolling out and folding several times, always moving the pin in the same direction and taking care that the sheet is of even thickness. Bake two rectangular sheets of pastry. Salt the fish, sprinkle it with lemon juice. Melt 1½ tbsps of butter in a skillet, put in the fish and braise slowly under cover until it is golden brown on both sides. In another pan cook the finely chopped onion and mushrooms in butter, add the wine and fish stock, and cook until the mixture has thickened. Add salt, pepper and lemon juice, mix in the egg yolks. Grease an ovenproof dish with butter, line it with one sheet of pastry, arrange on top pieces of boned fish, cover with the second sheet and put into a hot oven for several minutes. Serve hot. Instead of puff pastry, you can use dough made from 120 g flour, 80 g butter, 3 tbsps cream, 1 egg yolk and salt. Chop finely the butter together with the flour, cream and egg yolk, then wrap it up in a cloth and put into the fridge. Roll it out and bake it.

serves 6–8 • Preparation: 30–40 mins • Baking: 10–12 mins

Crayfish

" You praise all foreign fashions, but you do not know your own". Today a great deal is written about dishes prepared from mussels, shrimps, crabs and lobsters, while for centuries Polish cuisine has had its own particular gourmet dish which is in no way inferior in taste to frutti di mare. I mean **crayfish**. In the 18th and 19th centuries, they were extremely popular; they were served boiled, they were turned into soup, they were used to stuff pierogi, pike perch and sturgeon were garnished with crayfish tails, and crayfish sauces and butter were prepared. It is true that we have ever fewer clean rivers, lakes and streams, but crayfish are still the only shellfish that we can buy alive.

According to Old Polish tradition, crayfish are only good to eat in months that do not have an "r" in their Latin name – *maius*, *junius*, *iulius*, *augustus* – and so should be eaten from May to August. According to the greatest gourmands, the most succulent and aromatic crayfish come in June and July, when they change their shells. When buying crayfish it is very important to buy them fresh. Crayfish easily go bad and bad crayfish can lead to food poisoning. What should you do after buying crayfish?

(1) The live crayfish should be very carefully scrubbed with a brush and rinsed several times in fresh water. While scrubbing you should hold the crayfish with two fingers behind the shell and be careful of the claws.

(2) Boil salted water with dill in a large pan and throw the live crayfish into it one by one. Boil them for about 10–15 minutes until they turn from black to bright red. If they are cooked too long they become dry and tasteless.

(3) You can also cook crayfish in stock made from vegetables and spices, with added parsley or caraway.

(4) Leave the cooked crayfish in the stock to cool; then take them out and dry them.

(5) You can serve the boiled crayfish whole, arranged on a large dish and surrounded by paper napkins, and eat them in your fingers, pulling out the meat with special tongs.

(6) Before the preparation of any dish with crayfish, we should remove the bitter tasting gut attached to the end of the tail.

(7) The crayfish shells (if we are not going to use them for stuffing) together with the claws and tail should be dried and pounded in a mortar to make crayfish butter.

Crayfish butter I

shells and legs of 30 crayfish, 300 g butter

Pound the dry shells in a mortar. Melt the butter in a pan, add the shells and simmer over low heat, stirring all the time. Sieve the mixture, pour it into small jars, seal. Use for sauces and soups.

serves 6–8 • Preparation: 15–20 mins

Crayfish butter II

shells of 30 crayfish, 300 g butter, ½ tsp paprika, 1 cup of strained lobster stock

Pound the dried shells in a mortar, mix with the butter and paprika. Melt the mixture in a pan, add the hot stock and simmer for 10 mins. Take it off the heat, allow it to cool a bit, then skim the fat. Pour into small jars.

serves 6–8 • Preparation: 15–20 mins

Gourmet's crayfish snack

16 crayfish, soup vegetables, bouquet garni, a piece of lemon rind, 150 g butter, 1 glass brandy, 8–12 quail eggs, salt, a pinch of each pepper and caster sugar, 4–8 lettuce leaves, a bunch of dill

Prepare a stock from the vegetables and herbs, cover and simmer for 40 mins. Strain it and bring to the boil. Put in the thoroughly scrubbed crayfish and cook them for 15 mins. Take them out, remove the black intestine. Take out the flesh from the claws and tails. Hard-boil the quail eggs, cool and shell them. Dry the crayfish shells, then pound them in a mortar. Prepare crayfish butter and pour it into small jars. Mix 2 tbsps of crayfish butter with the meat from the claws, add salt, pepper, a pinch of sugar and the brandy, fold in the mayonnaise and refrigerate for a while. Line 4 cups with lettuce leaves, fill them with the mayonnaise. Garnish with the crayfish tails, halves of the quail eggs and sprigs of dill.

serves 4 • Preparation: 40–45 mins • Cooking: 15 mins

Crayfish bisque

250 g veal with bone, 15–20 crayfish, soup vegetables, bouquet garni, a piece of lemon rind, 4 cups water, 2 cups dry white wine, 2 pieces of dry white bread, 1 tbsp tomato paste, 2 tbsps butter, 2 egg yolks, salt, pepper, a pinch of sugar, 2 tbsps chopped dill

Prepare a stock from the meat, vegetables, and herbs. Cover and cook over low heat for 40 mins. Strain it and bring to the boil. Put in the crayfish and cook them for 10–15 mins. Then take the crayfish out with a straining spoon. Leave them to cool, then remove the black intestine and take the meat out from the tails and claws. Dry the shells and crush them in a mortar, mix with the butter and add to the stock. Cook for several minutes over fairly high heat. Strain the stock through a fine sieve (2 to 2½ cups of stock should be left). Bone the cooked veal, cut it into fine cubes. Pour the stock over the bread, add the meat and put the mixture through a blender and sieve it. Add the wine mixed with the tomato paste, stir and bring to the boil. Season with salt, pepper and sugar, thicken with the egg yolks mixed with 1 tbsp of boiled water. Put in the crayfish meat. Before serving, sprinkle with some dill.

serves 4–6 • Preparation: 45–50 mins • Cooking: 15 mins

Crayfish in cream, Polish style

30 crayfish, 10 sprigs of dill with seeds, salt, 2 tbsps butter, 1 cup thick cream, 1 tsp each chopped dill and chopped parsley, 1 tbsp breadcrumbs

Boil some water with dill and salt. Put in the well scrubbed crayfish and cook for 10–15 mins. Drain, remove the black intestine. Melt the butter in a skillet, put in whole crayfish, sprinkle with 3–4 tbsps of strained crayfish stock,

add salt, cover and simmer for 3–4 mins. Sprinkle with breadcrumbs, shake the pan lightly and, when the sauce has thickened, add the cream mixed with the dill and parsley.

serves 4–6 • Preparation: 15–20 mins • Cooking: 10–15 mins

Crayfish, Samogitia style

30 crayfish, 1 horseradish root, a sprig of fresh basil, 2 cups lager beer, 1 bay leaf, several peppercorns, salt, 1 tbsp butter, a bunch of dill

Boil some salted water with the peppercorns, bay leaf, basil and the peeled and washed horseradish. Cover the pan and simmer for 15 mins. Add the beer, bring to the boil and put in the well scrubbed crayfish. Cook for 10–15 mins, take off the heat and leave to cool. Take out the crayfish, drain them, brush with butter and arrange in a serving dish on lettuce leaves. Garnish with dill.

serves 4–6 • Preparation: 15–20 mins • Cooking: 15 mins

Crayfish in wine

30 crayfish, 10 sprigs of dill with seeds, 1 l dry white wine, ¼ tsp each cayenne pepper and dried thyme, a sprig of fresh thyme, salt, 1 tbsp butter

Boil the wine with the thyme and pepper. Bring some salted water with dill to the boil, put in the crayfish and cook for 3–4 mins. Take them out with a draining spoon, arrange in a skillet, pour over the wine and simmer for 10–12 mins, then leave to cool. Brush the crayfish with butter, arrange them in a pyramid on a serving plate. Use the wine to make a sauce with crayfish butter.

serves 4–6 • Preparation: 15–20 mins • Cooking: 3–4 mins • Stewing: 10–12 mins

Stuffed crayfish

30 large crayfish, salt, dill;

1 cup single cream, 1 cup semolina, 3 tbsps crayfish butter, 2 tbsps chopped dill, 3 eggs, 1–2 tsps breadcrumbs, 100 g butter

Cook the crayfish in salted water with dill. Drain them, remove the black intestine, take out the meat from the claws and tails, clean the shells. Leave aside the carapaces. Crush the claw and tail shells in a mortar and make crayfish butter. Cook thick semolina. Mix the crayfish butter with the egg yolks. Stirring all the time, add the semolina, then the chopped meat from the claws and tails, fold in the whisked egg whites. Fill the carapaces with the mixture. Arrange them in a skillet, pour over the cream, cover and simmer for 10 mins. Add the breadcrumbs, shake the skillet gently and heat up until the sauce has thickened.

serves 4–6 • Preparation: 15–20 mins • Cooking: 15 mins • Stewing: 10–15 mins

Crayfish ragout

30 crayfish, 10 sprigs of dill with seeds, salt, 300 g small boletus mushrooms, ½ cup light stock, 1 cup dry white wine, 150 g butter, 1 tbsp lemon juice, ¼ tsp grated lemon rind

Bring salted water and dill to the boil, put in the thoroughly scrubbed crayfish and cook for 10–15 mins, then leave to cool. Wash and dry the mushrooms, cut them into slices. Melt 1 tbsp of butter in a pan, cook the mushrooms, add salt and pepper, thyme and lemon zest, sprinkle with 2–3 tbsps of wine and simmer covered, stirring from time to time. Drain the crayfish, remove the black intestine, take out the meat from the claws and tail. Dry the shells and pound them in a mortar. Use them to make crayfish butter. Melt 3 tbsps of crayfish butter, add flour and make a roux, dilute it with the stock, stir thoroughly, heat up. When the sauce has thickened, add the mushroom and the crayfish meat. Adjust the taste with lemon juice, salt and pepper and simmer over low heat for 3–4 mins,

Crayfish, Samogitia style

stirring gently all the time. Sprinkle with dill before serving. Serve with bread rolls or boiled rice.

Note: Instead of boletus mushrooms, you may use cooked asparagus, cauliflower or green peas.

serves 4–6 • Preparation: 15–20 mins • Cooking: 10–15 mins • Stewing: 4–5 mins

Saltwater fish

Fish of the cod family are among the most popular in Poland. This means above all **cod** itself, but also **hake**, **walleye pollack**, **ling** and related varieties of deep sea fish. These are all lean and easily digestible fish, with white, crisp and delicate flesh, which easily falls apart during boiling or frying. For this reason, it is a good idea to sprinkle these fish generously with lemon juice and put them in the fridge for 1 to 2 hours before cooking. They then become firmer and will not disintegrate so readily; moreover, the lemon juice takes away their unpleasant smell.

There are a few other ways of taking away the strong smell of saltwater fish:

– for 1 to 2 hours, soak the fish in milk with added pepper, after which it should be dried;
– rub in herbs: marjoram, tarragon, basil or thyme, and leave for 30 to 60 minutes in a cool place;
– place around the fish grated vegetables (onion, celeriac, parsley root) or sliced onion, and leave for 1 to 2 hours in the fridge;
– cook them in savoury stocks with lemon juice and spices, or add sauerkraut or soured cucumber juice to the stock.

Fish from the cod family are excellent for baking, boiling, braising, stuffing and frying. But because they are apt to fall apart, it is better not to fry them sauté, but rather coated in flour, egg-and-breadcrumbs or batter.

Flat fish have delicate flesh from which very elegant dishes can be made. The **sole** is the king of flat fish, and there is also **halibut** which is the largest of them, **plaice**, **turbot**, **flounder**, and others.

They have white, delicate, aromatic, succulent, crisp and lean flesh (only halibut among them is moderately fatty). On one side, their skin is completely white, and on the other side, rough and dark. In order to remove this easily, you should immerse the fish for a moment in boiling water. These fish are excellent for making fish rolls. You only need to remember that the flesh from which the dark skin has been removed should be on the inside, since this will shrink most during boiling or frying.

Flatfish can be boiled in water, steamed, braised, grilled or baked. It is a good idea to sprinkle them with lemon juice and leave them in the fridge for 1 to 2 hours before cooking. It is best not to use too much seasoning for fish of this kind, or their delicate flavour will be lost.

Fish from the mackerel family are sea predators; their flesh is red, stronger tasting and fatter, with few bones, and it is firm and juicy. The family include **mackerel** itself, **horse mackerel** and **garfish**. They are excellent for grilling, braising, frying in batter or baking.

Cod

Cod is perhaps the most popular of sea fish. It seems worth recalling that there are several names for cod in regional Polish cookery books, and that dried salted cod is known as stockfish.

In the post-war period, mass fishing made this a cheap fish, and official propaganda suggested it as an alternative to meat, which was always in short supply. It is not therefore surprising that throughout the whole history of Communist Poland, cod was despised, and there was a rhyme: "eat cod, shit is worse"; this was all very unfair, as cod contains very few unsaturated fats and calories (100 g = 118 kcal), and eating low fat products of this kind leads to a fall of blood cholesterol levels, and reduces the risk of cancer and heart disease. This excellent fish, with a delicate flavour, and white, flaky, succulent flesh harmonizes very well with seasonings in all sorts of attractive ways. It can be baked with anchovy butter; it can be braised in an aromatic fish stock, and served hot or cold with various sauces; it can be fried or baked; it can be minced and made into fish balls, bakes, mousses and fish cakes. If the after-taste and smell of cod-liver oil is a problem, the fish should be sprinkled with lemon juice at least an hour before cooking, which will also make the meat firmer and tastier. Salting cod earlier also yields good results (as is the case with other saltwater fish), or covering it with slices of onion, or rubbing it with ground ginger.

Cod, Jewish style

800 g cod fillets, 500 g onion, 1 tsp dried tarragon, salt, pepper, sugar, 1 tbsp lemon juice, 3 tbsps butter

Rinse and dry the fillets, sprinkle them with lemon juice, tarragon, salt and pepper, and leave aside for an hour. Slice the peeled onion, cut the slices in half. Grease an ovenproof dish with butter, line it with half the onion, sprinkle with salt, pepper, tarragon and sugar. Arrange the cod cut into pieces on top of the onion, cover with the remaining onion, sprinkle with salt, pepper, tarragon and sugar. Pour over melted butter, cover and put into a preheated oven for 25–30 mins, then take off the lid and bake for another 5–7 mins. Serve with potatoes and red cabbage salad.

serves 4–6 • Preparation: 5 mins • Baking: 30–40 mins

Cod, Belarus style

800 g cod fillets, 5 large tart apples, 1 large onion, 1 cup thick cream, salt, pepper, 2 tbsps lemon juice, ¼ tsp grated lemon rind, 2 tbsps butter, 2 tbsps dry white wine, a pinch of sugar

Rinse and dry the fillets, sprinkle them with lemon juice, and leave aside for an hour or two. Now sprinkle them with salt and pepper, cut into portions. Peel the onion and chop it finely. Peel the apples and grate them finely, sprinkle with lemon juice, sugar and lemon zest, mix well. Grease an ovenproof dish with butter. Put in the onion, arrange the cod pieces, cover them with the apple, sprinkle with the wine and put into a preheated oven for 35 mins. Mix the cream with a pinch of salt, pepper and sugar, pour over the fish. Shake the dish lightly and keep in the warm oven for several minutes longer.

serves 4–6 • Preparation: 10 mins • Baking: 35–45 mins

Baked cod in mushroom sauce

600 g cod fillets, 500 g potatoes cooked in jackets, 1 large onion, 1 hard-boiled egg, 6–7 cooked dried cep mushrooms, 1½ cups cream, 3–4 tbsps grated cheese, salt, pepper, 1 tbsp flour, 1 tbsp butter, oil

Cut the fillets into thick strips, sprinkle them with salt and pepper, dredge with flour and fry in hot oil. Peel the potatoes, cut them into slices and sauté in oil. Dice the onion, cut the cooked mushrooms into fine strips, chop finely the hard-boiled egg. Grease an ovenproof dish with butter. Arrange the fish in the middle, surround it with the potatoes. Sprinkle with the onion, egg and mushrooms, then with pepper. Pour over the cream, sprinkle the grated cheese on top and put into a hot oven for 15 mins.

serves 4–6 • Preparation: 10 mins • Baking: 15–20 mins

Baked cod with tomatoes

800 g cod fillets, 4 large tomatoes, 2–3 cloves of garlic, 1 large onion, 2 tbsps lemon juice, salt, pepper, ¼ cup olive oil, 2–3 tbsps chopped parsley

Mix the finely chopped garlic with salt, pepper and 1 tbsp of lemon juice. Rub the fillets with the mixture and leave for an hour or two in the fridge. Blanch and skin the tomatoes, cut them into thick slices. Cut the onion into fine slices. Grease an ovenproof dish with oil, arrange the fillets, then the onion slices. Put on top the tomato slices. Sprinkle with the remaining lemon juice, oil, chopped parsley and salt. Put into a hot oven for 40 mins. Serve with rice or French fries and with lettuce.

serves 4–6 • Preparation: 3–4 mins • Baking: 40 mins

Baked cod fillets

600 g cod fillets, 1 lemon, 1 red bell pepper, 2 tbsps stoned green olives, 4 firm tomatoes, 2 tbsps tomato paste, 1 cup yogurt, salt, pepper, a pinch of sugar, 3 tbsps each chopped parsley and dill, 2 tbsps olive oil, 1 tbsp butter, 1 tbsp dry white wine

Scrub the lemon, scald it with boiling water, cut off the yellow rind, squeeze the juice out. Sprinkle the fillets with lemon juice and salt, leave for half an hour in a cool place. Blanch and skin the tomatoes, cut them into quarters. Wash the pepper, remove the seeds, cut it into strips. Cut the olives into quarters. Melt 1 tsp of butter in a pan, add the pepper, tomatoes and olives, sprinkle with wine and simmer for a while. Adjust the taste with salt and pepper. Heat the oil in a frying pan, fry the fillets cut into portions until golden brown. Mix the yogurt with the tomato paste, salt, sugar and chopped parsley and dill. Grease an ovenproof dish with butter, arrange the fish portions, cover with the cooked tomatoes and pepper, pour over the sauce and put into a hot oven.

serves 4 • Preparation: 15–20 mins • Baking: 10–15 mins

Cod in lemony sauce

750 g cod fillets (or other sea fish), 1 large onion, ½ lemon, 1 tbsp grated lemon rind, ½ tsp saffron, 1 tsp salt, 1 tsp pepper, ¼ tsp each ginger and mace (or nutmeg), 1 cup dry white wine, 1 tbsp butter, 1 tsp flour, 1 tbsp finely chopped parsley

Sprinkle the fillets with lemon juice, salt and pepper, leave for an hour in a cool place. Chop the onion finely and soften it in butter for several minutes. Heat butter or oil in a pan, fry the fish until light golden brown on both sides. Put the fish into a skillet, add the onion, pepper, ginger, nutmeg and saffron, pour in the wine and simmer covered for 30 mins. Make a roux from the butter and flour, dilute it with 2 tbsps of water, add the parsley, lemon zest and juice, stir well. Pour over the fish and shake the skillet gently. Arrange the fish on a serving dish and pour over the sauce. Serve with bread rolls.

serves 4 • Preparation: 5–7 mins • Cooking: 30–35 mins

Cod in savoury sauce

750 g fillets of cod (pollack or hake), soup vegetables, 2 large onions, 1 bay leaf, 4–5 grains each pepper and allspice, salt, a pinch of sugar

SAUCE: 1 cup sunflower oil, 4 tbsps tomato paste, 4–5 spring onions with green parts (or 1 largish onion), ½ tsp each ground pepper and allspice, 2 tbsps raisins, sugar to taste

Make a stock from the vegetables, onion and spices. Strain it, pour it over the fillets and cook over low heat for 15 mins. Chop finely the onion and soften it in hot oil, add the tomato paste, stir well, season with pepper and allspice, add the raisins and sugar to taste. Stir and heat up.

Cod in lemony sauce

Arrange the cooked fillets in a serving dish, pour over the sauce. Serve with French fries and lettuce.

serves 4 • Preparation: 30 mins • Cooking: 15–20 mins

Cod omelette

350 g cod cooked in vegetable stock, 5 eggs, 4 tbsps cold milk, 2–3 tbsps grated cheese, 2 tbsps flour, 1 tbsp butter, salt, a pinch of pepper

Bone the cooked cod, cut it into small portions. Break the eggs into a pan, add the cold milk and whisk with an egg whisk or a fork. Add the flour, salt, pepper and grated cheese, mix thoroughly. Melt ½ tbsp of butter each in two frying pans, put half the cod in each. Pour over the omelette batter. When the omelettes are cooked on top, slip them gently onto plates. Serve with lettuce.

serves 4 • Preparation: 5–7 mins • Frying: 6–8 mins

Cod with herbal cheese

4 thin cod fillets, salt, lemon juice, 2–3 finely chopped cloves of garlic, 2 tbsps finely chopped basil leaves, 1 tbsp chopped dill, 2 spring onions with green parts, 250 g cream cheese, 2–3 tbsps grated Parmesan, salt, pepper, 3 tbsps almond flakes, 2 tbsps butter

Rinse and dry the fillets, sprinkle with lemon juice, rub with salt and pepper and leave aside for half an hour. Chop the spring onions, put them through a blender together with the garlic, basil, dill, salt, pepper and Parmesan, fold in the cream cheese. Put a bit of the stuffing into the middle of each fillet, roll up, secure with a toothpick. Grease a shallow ovenproof dish with butter, arrange the rolls in it, pour over the melted butter, sprinkle with the almond flakes. Put into a hot oven for 20–25 mins.

serves 4 • Preparation: 10 mins • Baking: 20–25 mins

Cod fillets baked with vegetables

700 g cod fillets, 1 tbsp lemon juice, 1 tsp grated lemon rind, 4–5 large firm juicy tomatoes, 1 bulb fennel, 1 large leek (only the white part), 2–3 cloves of garlic, 1 bay leaf, 3–4 sprigs of thyme, ½ tsp Tabasco, 1 tsp turmeric, a pinch of powdered aniseed, salt, pepper, ½ cup dry white wine, 2 tbsps olive oil, 1 tbsp butter, ½ cup vegetable or fish stock, 2–3 tbsps chopped parsley

Sprinkle the fillets with lemon juice and zest, salt and pepper and leave for half an hour in a cool place. Scald and skin the tomatoes, cut them into cubes. Wash and dry the leek and fennel, cut them into thin slices. Chop the garlic finely. Heat 1 tbsp of oil in a pan, put in the leek and fennel, fry for a minute or two, stirring all the time. Put in the tomatoes and garlic and cook for another 2–3 mins. Add the turmeric, bay leaf and thyme, sprinkle with salt and pepper, pour in the stock and wine, stir well. Bring to the boil, cover the pan and simmer for 4–6 mins. Take out the bay leaf and thyme sprigs, reduce the liquid a bit. Heat the remaining oil in a frying pan, fry the fish fillets until golden brown. Grease an ovenproof dish with butter, arrange the fillets, pour over the sauce and put into a hot oven for several minutes. Before serving, sprinkle with chopped parsley. Serve with French fries, rice or pasta and with lettuce.

serves 4–6 • Preparation: 25–30 mins • Baking: 8–10 mins

Cod fillets baked with vegetables

Cod in green sauce

*700 g cod fillets, 1 cup chopped dill,
3 small onions, 2–3 cloves of garlic,
½ cup dry white wine, juice and grated
rind of 1 lemon, a pinch of saffron,
1 tbsp boiling water, 1 tbsp butter, salt,
pepper, 1 tbsp each chopped leaves of
coriander, tarragon, basil and mint,
1 tsp honey*

Sprinkle the fillets with salt, pepper and lemon juice. Melt the butter in a skillet, fry the finely chopped onion, but do not let it brown. Add the chopped garlic and simmer, stirring all the time. Put in the fillets, cover them with the wine. Sprinkle with the lemon zest, pour in the saffron mixed with water, sprinkle with lemon juice mixed with the honey. Cover the skillet and cook over low heat for 15 mins. Add the chopped greens, salt and pepper. Shake the skillet gently and simmer under cover for another 10–15 mins. Sprinkle with dill before serving.

serves 4 • Preparation: 5–7 mins • Cooking: 25–30 mins

Delicate cod stew

*800 g cod fillets, juice of ½ lemon, 3–4 tbsps
butter, 3 onions, 2 tbsps flour, 1 tsp sweet
paprika, ½ cup boiling water, 1 cup sour
cream, salt, a pinch of sugar*

Rinse and dry the fillets, rub them with salt, sprinkle with lemon juice and leave in the fridge. Melt 1 tbsp of butter in a frying pan, dredge the fillets with flour and fry them on both sides until golden brown. Remove them on a plate to cool, then cut them into cubes. Melt 3 tbsps of butter in a pan, fry the finely chopped onion, but do not let it brown. Sprinkle with paprika and fry for a minute or two, stirring all the time. Pour in the boiling water mixed with 1 tbsp of cream and cook over low heat, stirring all the time, until the sauce has thickened. Add the fish cubes and heat up slowly over low heat. Serve with boiled potatoes or rice.

serves 4 • Preparation: 15–20 mins • Frying: 8–10 mins

Halibut

Halibut in red wine

*800 g halibut fillets, 1 small onion, 200 g
mushrooms, 1 tbsp tomato paste, 1 cup dry red
wine, 3 tbsps thick cream, 1 tbsp butter, 2 tbsps
flour, ½ cup vegetable stock, ¼ tsp paprika,
1 tbsp lemon juice, 3 tbsps oil, salt, pepper*

Rinse and dry the fillets, sprinkle them with lemon juice, salt and pepper. Cover and leave in the fridge for an hour. Fry the finely chopped onion in 1 tbsp of oil, but do not let it brown. Add the diced mushrooms and, stirring all the time, fry for a short while over intense heat. Make a roux from the butter and 1 flat tbsp of flour. Dilute it with the cold stock and, stirring all the time, cook over low heat until it has thickened. Add the tomato paste, onion and mushrooms, adjust the taste with salt, pepper and paprika. Stir well and keep over low heat. Dry the fillets, dredge them with flour and fry in hot oil until golden brown. Arrange the fillets in an ovenproof dish. Combine the sauce with the wine and cream, stir thoroughly and pour over the fillets. Put into a preheated oven for 5–8 mins. Serve with rice or potatoes.

serves 4–5 • Preparation: 25–30 mins • Frying: 5–8 mins

Halibut in parsley sauce

*800 g halibut fillets, 1 large parsley root, 2–3 tbsps
chopped parsley, 6–8 stoned prunes, juice and grated
rind of 1 lemon, 2 tbsps flour, ½ cup milk, a pinch of
sugar, 1 tbsp oil, 1 tbsp butter, 1 cup cream, salt*

Dissolve 1 tsp of salt in the milk. Rinse and dry the fillets, put them in a bowl. Pour over the milk, cover and put into the fridge for one or two hours. Rinse the prunes and soak them in a small amount of boiled water. Peel the parsley root and cut it into thin strips. Take out the fillets, drain them, dredge with flour and fry in very hot oil. Transfer the fillets to a skillet, sprinkle with the water in which the prunes had soaked. Put on top the parsley strips and prunes cut into strips. Pour over the melted butter, cover and simmer for 5–7 mins. Blend the cream with

1 tbsp of flour, lemon juice and zest, sugar and salt if required. Pour over the fish, shake the skillet gently, sprinkle with parsley and simmer for another 5–6 mins. Serve with pasta or rice.

serves 6–8 • Preparation: 15 mins • Cooking: 10–15 mins

Sturgeon

It is said that once upon a time, sturgeon used to be caught in the Baltic. And at one time, it was also caught in the Vistula and Odra rivers – for it is a migrating fish that lives in the sea but for spawning returns to fresh water. But those days have passed. Sturgeon is imported from far away, at one time mainly from Russia, and has therefore become a luxury. Sturgeon, because it is so large – with the largest growing up to 4 metres long – is usually sold in pieces. It is an excellent fish for cooking on the spit or baking in the oven, and should be served like sirloin – at one time it was used to replace meat during Lent; it can also be used for making collops, for braising, marinating and smoking. It should be served hot with savoury sauces, for example with mustard or caper sauce. The choicest sturgeon – apart from the black caviar that comes from the fish – is served cold with a vinaigrette sauce.

Sturgeon in mushroom sauce

800 g sturgeon, juice and grated rind of 1 lemon, 1 cup light wine vinegar, 50 g dried cep mushrooms, 200 ml cream, 2 onions, 1 tsp flour, salt, pepper

Rinse the fish. Bring the vinegar, with lemon zest and juice, to the boil. Pour it over the fish and leave aside for 30 mins. Rinse the mushrooms and leave them to soak in 2 cups of boiled water for 1–2 hours, then cook them. Cut the cooked mushrooms into fine strips, strain the mushroom stock through a fine sieve. Remove the skin from the fish, cut the flesh into slices, sprinkle with pepper. Fry the peeled and chopped onion in melted butter, but do not let it brown. Put in the fish and simmer it for 10 mins, then add the mushrooms, pour in the stock and cook over low heat for 20 mins. Blend the cream with flour, add to

the fish. Shake the pan gently and heat up until the sauce has thickened (but keep off the boil). Serve with kasha.

serves 4–6 • Preparation: 10 mins • Cooking: 30–35 mins

Sturgeon with sauerkraut

800 g sturgeon, 700 g sauerkraut, 1 onion, juice of 1 lemon, 3 tbsps butter, 3–4 tbsps thick cream, 2 tbsps grated Parmesan, salt, pepper

Rinse and dry the fish, remove the skin. Divide the meat into portions, sprinkle with lemon juice and leave for half an hour in a cool place. Salt it, arrange the portions in an ovenproof dish, brush with half the butter and bake for 25 mins at 180°C. Scald the sauerkraut and chop it. Fry the finely chopped onion in butter, but do not let it brown. Put in the sauerkraut, mix well, cover and simmer for 40–45 mins. Add the cream, stir and heat up. Line an ovenproof dish with half the sauerkraut, arrange the fish portions on top and cover with the remaining sauerkraut. Sprinkle the Parmesan on top and place knobs of butter. Put into a preheated oven.

serves 4–6 • Cooking: 40–45 mins • Baking: 20–25 mins

Sturgeon in cream, Polish style

800 g sturgeon, 1 cup 3% wine vinegar, ½ cup vegetable stock, ½ cup dry white wine, 1 onion with a clove stuck into it, ¾ cup cream, 3 tbsps butter, 1 tsp flour, 2 tbsps chopped dill, salt, pepper

Clean the fish, rinse and dry it, put in a deep bowl and pour over the boiling hot vinegar. Leave aside for half an hour. Fry the peeled and finely chopped onion in 1 tbsp of melted butter, but do not let it brown. Pour in the hot vegetable stock and cook covered for 15 mins, then put it through a blender and sieve it. Take the fish out, dry it, divide into portions and sprinkle with salt. Fry them on both sides in butter. Remove the skin, transfer the pieces to a skillet, pour over the stock and wine and simmer for 15–20 mins. Blend the cream with the flour, dill, salt and pepper. Pour over the fish, shake the skillet gently and keep over low heat until the sauce has thickened – do not allow it to boil. Serve with baked potatoes or pasta.

serves 4–6 • Preparation: 15–20 mins • Cooking: 20–25 mins

Mackerel

This is a small fish, the size of a herring, which has tasty, though rather oily flesh. It can be prepared in many different ways: grilled, broiled, poached, stuffed and smoked.

Mackerel with soured cucumber

800 g mackerel fillets, 4–5 cloves of garlic,
2 tbsps lemon juice, 1–2 soured cucumbers,
¼ tsp powdered ginger, 2–3 tbsps chopped
parsley, 1 cup yogurt, 1 tbsp flour, 2–3 tbsps
oil, 1 tbsp butter, pepper, salt

Rinse and dry the fillets, sprinkle with lemon juice, cover and put into the fridge. Chop the garlic finely, mix it with salt and ginger. Rub the fillets with the mixture and return to the fridge for an hour. Dredge the fillets with flour and fry them in hot oil until golden brown. Grease an oven-proof dish with butter, put the fillets in, place slices of cucumber on each of them. Blend the yogurt with salt, pepper and parsley and pour over the fish. Put the fish into a preheated oven for 3–5 mins. Serve with French fries or baked potatoes.

serves 4–6 • Preparation: 10 mins • Baking: 5 mins

Mackerel in fruity sauce

800 g mackerel fillets, juice and grated
rind of 1 lemon, 1 tsp honey, 4 thin smoked
rashers, 1½ tbsps grated horseradish, 5 tbsps
redcurrant jelly, 2 tbsps oil, salt, pepper

Rinse and dry the fillets, sprinkle with lemon juice and leave in a cool place for half an hour, then salt them. Put together two fillets, wrap them up in rashers. Grease an ovenproof dish with oil, put the fillets in, sprinkle with the remaining oil. Put into a preheated oven for 15 mins. Mix well the redcurrant jelly with the horseradish, lemon juice and zest, honey, salt and pepper. Pour the sauce over the fish and bake it for another 15 mins.

serves 4–6 • Preparation: 10 mins • Baking: 30–35 mins

Pollack

Pollack in grapefruit sauce

750 g pollack fillets, ½ lemon, salt

* sunflower oil or butter for frying

* 1 tbsp butter, ½ cup thick cream, 1 grapefruit,
salt, pepper, a pinch of sugar, 1 tbsp
chopped parsley, 3 eggs, 1 tbsp flour

Sprinkle the fillets with lemon juice, salt them, dredge with flour and fry in hot oil until golden brown on both sides. Melt the butter in a pan, add the chopped hard-boiled eggs, heat up. Add the grapefruit juice, cream, salt, pepper and a pinch of sugar. Stir gently and heat up. Arrange the fish in a serving dish, pour over the sauce, sprinkle with parsley.

serves 4 • Preparation: 5 mins • Frying: 10 mins

Stewed pollack

750 g pollack fillets, 3 tbsps thin strips of horseradish,
3 large onions, 4–5 green peppercorns, 1 tsp marjoram,
salt, pepper, a pinch of sugar, 1 tbsp lemon juice,
1½ cups cream, 1 tbsp butter, 3 tbsps chopped dill

Rinse and dry the fillets, sprinkle with lemon juice, salt and pepper and leave aside for half an hour. Cut the fish into thick strips, sprinkle with the marjoram. Blend the cream with salt, sugar and pepper. Cut the onions into fine half slices. Grease a skillet with butter. Put layers of onion, fish and horseradish, pour over the cream, sprinkle with the green peppercorns. Cover the skillet and cook over low heat for 30 mins. Before serving, garnish with dill.

serves 4 • Preparation: 10 mins • Cooking: 30–35 mins

Pollack fillets with nuts

750 g pollack fillets, juice and grated rind of
½ lemon, 1 tsp powdered ginger, 1 tsp dried sage,
2–3 cloves of garlic, 2 tbsps flour, 3 tbsps oil, salt;

1 cup chopped sorrel, 1 chopped onion, 2 tbsps
butter, salt, pepper, ½ cup cream, 1 egg, 2 tbsps
chopped walnuts, 4 thin slices of lemon

Rub the fillets with salt mixed with garlic, sage, ginger, and lemon zest, sprinkle with lemon juice, cover and put into the fridge for an hour or two. Fry the onions in the melted butter, but do not let it brown. Put in the sorrel and cook together for a minute or two, then season with salt and pepper. Blend the cream with the raw egg and chopped walnuts, add to the sorrel and heat up, stirring all the time, and keep it warm. Heat the oil in a large frying pan. Dredge the fillets with flour and fry until golden brown on both sides. Arrange the fillets in an ovenproof dish, pour over the sorrel sauce and put into a preheated oven for 4–5 mins. Before serving, garnish with lemon slices.

serves 4 • Preparation: 20–25 mins • Baking: 4–5 mins

Pollack in cornelian cherry sauce

750 g pollack fillets, 1 cup dried cornelian cherries,
1 tbsp butter, 2 tsps sunflower oil, 1 lemon,
½ tsp each dried mint and savory, a pinch each
of chilli pepper and cinnamon, 3–4 cloves,
2 cloves of garlic, salt, pepper, sugar to taste

Sprinkle the fillets with lemon juice, salt, savory and mint, leave in a cool place for an hour. Rinse the cornelian cherries, pour over water and cook until tender. Purée them, mix with the finely chopped garlic, chilli, cinnamon, pounded cloves, salt, pepper, sugar, oil and 3 tbsps of water. Bring the mixture to the boil. Grease an ovenproof dish with butter, arrange the fillets, put in slices of butter and place in a preheated oven. Bake for 40 mins. Pour over the sauce before serving. Serve with bread rolls or French fries.

serves 4 • Preparation: 15–20 mins • Baking: 40 mins

Baked pollack fillets

750 g pollack fillets, 10 small potatoes, 1 onion,
pepper, ¼ tsp each thyme and basil, 1 lemon,
2 tbsps butter, 1 tbsp chopped parsley

Sprinkle the fillets with lemon juice, salt, pepper, basil and thyme, put in a cool place for an hour. Peel and slice the potatoes, scald them with boiling water, drain well. Grease an ovenprooof dish with butter, arrange the fish, sprinkle with the finely chopped onion, surround with the potato slices, put knobs of butter on top. Put into a preheated oven and bake for 45–50 mins. Sprinkle with chopped parsley before serving.

serves 4 • Preparation: 10 mins • Baking: 45–50 mins

Hake

Hake in green sauce

750 g hake fillets, 1 cup chopped dill, 1 tsp each
chopped coriander, tarragon, basil and mint leaves
(or ¼ tsp each dried herbs), 1 tsp sugar, 3 onions,
2–3 cloves of garlic, juice and grated rind of 1 lemon,
a pinch of saffron, 1 tsp butter, salt, pepper

Rinse and dry the fillets. Sprinkle them with lemon juice, salt and pepper. Cover and put into the fridge for an hour. Melt the butter in a skillet, fry the finely chopped onion and garlic, but do not let them brown. Put in the fillets, sprinkle them with lemon juice, pour over the wine, add the lemon zest, saffron, herbs and sugar. Cover and cook over low heat for 20 mins. Towards the end sprinkle with the chopped dill.

serves 4 • Preparation: 5–7 mins • Cooking: 20–25 mins

Hake ragout

500 g hake fillets, 4 medium-sized potatoes, 300 g
kohlrabi, 1 small cauliflower, 250 g daikon radish, 100 g
string beans, 250 g tomatoes, 2 onions, 3–4 cloves of
garlic, juice and grated rind of 1 lemon, salt, cayenne

pepper, a pinch of saffron, 1 tbsp boiling water, a pinch of monosodium glutamate, 4–5 tbsps oil, 1 cup stock

Pour boiling water over the saffron and leave for several minutes. Rinse and dry the fillets, cut them into strips. Put in a bowl, sprinkle with salt, monosodium glutamate, lemon zest and saffron. Leave for an hour in a cool place. Peel the onions, grate them and mix with the chopped garlic and cayenne pepper. Blanch and skin the tomatoes, cut them into quarters. Cut the peeled kohlrabi and radish into strips. Dice the string beans. Cut the potatoes into cubes. Divide the cauliflower into florets. Heat up 3–4 tbsps of oil in a skillet, put in the onion, garlic and pepper mixture. Fry for a minute or two, stirring all the time. Add the tomatoes and fry them stirring for 2–3 mins. Put in the potatoes, kohlrabi, string beans and radish and fry them for 2–3 mins. Pour in the stock, cover the pan and simmer for 10 mins. Heat up the remaining oil in a frying pan, put in the fish and, stirring all the time, fry it for several minutes. Transfer the fish into the skillet, stir, add the cauliflower. Pour over the oil in which the fish was fried and simmer for 15–20 mins. When the vegetables are tender, season to taste with lemon juice. Serve with rice or white bread.

serves 4–6 • Preparation: 20–25 mins • Cooking: 15–20 mins

Fillets in wine and nut sauce

750 g hake fillets (or halibut or cod), ½ cup skinned walnuts, 1 cup dry red wine, 1 lemon, 1 tbsp chopped parsley, 4 cloves of garlic, 3 cloves, 4–5 peppercorns, 1 medium-sized onion, salt, a pinch of sugar

Sprinkle the fillets with lemon juice, rub them with crushed garlic (2 cloves) mixed with salt and leave for 30 mins in a cool place. Chop finely the onion and parsley. Put them into a pan together with cloves and pepper. Pour over the wine, add 1 cup of water. Cover the pan and cook for 30 mins. Put in the fish and cook for another 30 mins. Then take out the fish, arrange it in a hot serving dish and keep warm. Add the remaining garlic and chopped nuts to the sauce. Heat up. Pour the hot sauce over the fish. Serve with white bread or French fries.

serves 4 • Preparation: 30–40 mins • Cooking: 30 mins

Hake with fruit

750 g hake fillets, 1 large onion, ½ cup skinned walnuts, 2 tbsps raisins, 2 tart apples, 50 g prunes, ½ tsp cinnamon, 4–5 cloves, ½ cup dry white wine, salt, pepper

* sunflower oil for frying

* ½ lemon, 1 tbsp butter, 1 tsp flour

Sprinkle the fillets with lemon juice and salt. Soak the prunes in water, cook them, then remove the stones. Dredge the fillets with flour and fry in hot oil. Transfer to a skillet, add the diced apples, onion, prunes, blanched raisins, cinnamon, cloves, salt and pepper. Cover the skillet and simmer for 20 mins. When the apples and prunes are cooked, add the chopped nuts. Add a pinch of sugar if required. Arrange the fish in a serving dish, pour over the sauce. Serve with white bread or French fries.

serves 4 • Preparation: 20 mins • Cooking: 20 mins

Hake fillets in bechamel

750 g hake fillets, 1 lemon, salt, pepper, 1 tbsp butter, 1 tsp flour, 1 cup milk, ½ cup thick sour cream, ¼ tsp sugar

* 2 tbsps oil for frying

* 2 tbsps chopped parsley, 2 tbsps grated cheese

Sprinkle the fillets with lemon juice, salt and pepper and leave for an hour in a cool place. Dredge the fillets with flour and fry them in hot oil. Transfer them to a skillet and keep warm. Make a roux from the butter and flour, dilute it with the boiled milk and cream. Stirring all the time, simmer over low heat until the sauce has thickened. Add salt, sugar, pepper, parsley and lemon juice, stir well. Pour the sauce over the fried fish. Sprinkle with the cheese and put into a preheated oven for 30 mins. Serve with white bread or French fries and with lettuce.

serves 4 • Preparation: 15 mins • Baking: 30 mins

Hake fillets in thyme batter

750 g hake fillets, 2 tbsps lemon juice, salt, pepper, a pinch of dried thyme, oil for frying

Batter: 100 g flour, 1 egg, 2–3 tbsps milk, 3 tsps dried thyme, salt

Rinse and dry the fillets. Rub them with salt, pepper and thyme, sprinkle with lemon juice. Cover and put into the fridge for an hour. Mix all the ingredients and make a batter as thick as thick cream (add a drop of boiled water if required). Coat the fillets with the batter and fry them in hot oil until golden brown.

serves 4 • Preparation: 10 mins • Frying: 8–10 mins

Flounder

Flounder fillets with kohlrabi

600 g flounder fillets, juice and grated rind of 1 lemon, 2 new kohlrabi with leaves, 1 small onion, 3 tbsps chopped parsley, ¼ cup dry white wine, ¼ cup cream, 3 tbsps butter, salt, pepper

Rinse and dry the fillets. Sprinkle them with lemon juice, a bit of lemon zest, salt and pepper, and leave for several minutes in a cool place. Mix 1 tbsp of butter with 1 tbsp of lemon juice and the remaining lemon zest, add 2 tbsps chopped parsley. Peel the kohlrabi and cut it into thin slices, chop the leaves finely. Chop the onion. Melt the remaining butter in a pan, fry the onion, but do not let it brown. Put in the kohlrabi and fry together for a minute or two. Add some salt and pepper, pour over the wine. Cover the pan and simmer for 5–6 mins. Spread some parsley butter on each fillet, roll it up, secure the end with a toothpick. Arrange the fish on top of the kohlrabi, sprinkle with the chopped kohlrabi leaves, pour over the cream and simmer under cover for 10–15 mins. Shake the pan gently from time to time. Towards the end, sprinkle with the remaining chopped parsley.

serves 4 • Preparation: 15–20 mins • Cooking: 15–20 mins

Hake fillets in thyme batter

Steam-cooked flounder fillets

700 g flounder fillets, 2 tbsps lemon juice,
salt, 2 tbsps chopped parsley, 1 cup water,
1 glass dry white wine, 5–6 sprigs oregano

Rinse and dry the fillets. Mix the lemon juice with salt, 1 tbsp of white wine and the chopped parsley. Spread the mixture on top of the fillets. Cover and leave aside for several minutes. Boil the water with oregano in the bottom pan, pour in the wine. Put in the perforated container, arrange the fillets in it. Cover and cook over low heat for 6–8 mins.

serves 4 • Preparation: 10 mins • Cooking: 6–8 mins

Flounder, Kashub style

4 flounders, 1 carrot, 1 parsley root, 1 onion,
juice of 1 lemon, 1 bay leaf, 4 grains allspice,
150 ml cream, 1 tbsp flour, 1 tbsp butter,
2 tbsps chopped dill, salt, pepper

Clean the fish, cut off the heads, tails and fins. Rinse, rub with salt and leave for 30 mins. Peel and wash the vegetables. Cover them with 1 l of water, add the spices, lemon juice and salt, and cook for 20 mins, then strain the stock. Put the fish into the strained stock and cook over low heat for 10 mins. Take out the fish and strain the stock again. Make a roux from the butter and flour, add 200 ml of stock and cook, stirring all the time, for 10 mins. Add the cream and dill, season the sauce to taste. Heat up the fish in the sauce and serve with boiled potatoes. Alternately, leave the fish in the broth, add the cream mixed with flour, salt, pepper and dill. Bring the whole to the boil. Pour it into a tureen and serve as soup.

serves 4 • Preparation: 30 mins • Cooking: 10 mins

Peppers stuffed with flounder

300 g fish fillets, 6 red peppers, 2 tbsps
chopped hazelnuts, 2 tbsps shredded coconut,
1 finely chopped celeriac, 1 tsp coriander,
¼ tsp ground caraway, 2 eggs, 1 tbsp lemon
juice, 1 tbsp potato flour, 2 tbsps oil, salt,
pepper

Rinse and dry the fillets. Sprinkle them with lemon juice, salt and pepper, cover and leave in a cool place for half an hour. Wash and core the peppers, cut them lengthwise in two. Chop the fillets, combine them with the celeriac, shredded coconut and hazelnuts, add a pinch of salt and some pepper, the caraway, coriander and potato flour. Break in the eggs and mix thoroughly. Fill the pepper halves with the mixture. Grease an oven-proof dish with oil. Arrange the peppers (open side up) in it, sprinkle with oil. Cover the dish with aluminium foil and put into a preheated oven for 10–25 mins. Towards the end remove the foil. Serve hot with rice or cold as an hors-d'oeuvre.

serves 4–6 • Preparation: 15 mins • Cooking: 20–25 mins

Sole

Sole, royal style

800 g sole fillets, 200 g mushrooms, 2 large oranges,
1 glass champagne, ½ cup whipping cream, juice and
grated rind of 1 lemon, 2 tbsps butter, salt, pepper

Rinse and dry the fillets. Sprinkle them with lemon juice, salt, pepper and lemon zest. Cover and put into the fridge for an hour. Wash and dry the mushrooms, cut them into strips and fry in butter. Reduce the juices, then transfer the mushrooms to a skillet. Arrange the fish on top, pour over the champagne mixed with the orange juice. Cover and simmer for 20 mins. Towards the end add the cream, shake the skillet gently, remove the lid and keep over low heat for another 5–7 mins. Serve with French fries or scooped potatoes.

serves 4–6 • Preparation: 5–7 mins • Cooking: 25–30 mins

Sole with oranges

800 g sole fillets, 2 small carrots, 2 leeks (only
the white part), ½ celeriac, 2 oranges, 2 tbsps
single cream, 1 glass (50 ml) orange liqueur,
1 tbsp lemon juice, 4 tbsps butter, salt, pepper

Rinse and dry the fillets. Sprinkle them with lemon juice and leave for half an hour. Peel and rinse the carrots and celeriac, cut them into thin strips. Wash the leeks and cut them into thin slices. Melt 1½ tbsps of butter in a skillet, put in the vegetables, sprinkle sparingly with water and simmer under cover for 10 mins. Peel one orange very thinly. Cut the peel into thin strips, put them into a sieve, blanch and drain them. Sprinkle the fillets with salt and pepper and fry them in 2 tbsps of butter (but do not brown them). Transfer them gently to an ovenproof dish. Melt the remaining butter in the pan, put in the orange peel and fry for a minute or two. Pour in the cream, liqueur and juice from the other orange, mix well. Pile the stewed vegetables around the fillets, pour over the sauce and put into a preheated oven for 3–4 mins. Before serving, garnish with orange quarters.

serves 4–6 • Preparation: 25–30 mins • Baking: 3–4 mins

Sole with mushrooms

750 g sole fillets, 10 mushrooms, 2 tbsps chopped parsley, 2 tbsps breadcrumbs, 2 tbsps butter, salt, pepper, 1 cup fish stock, lemon

Sprinkle the fillets with lemon juice and salt. Grease an ovenproof dish with butter. Arrange the fish, sprinkle it with the breadcrumbs, parsley and finely chopped mushrooms. Put on top dollops of butter, pour in the fish stock (or water) and put into a preheated oven. Bake for 40 mins. Serve with white bread.

serves 4 • Preparation: 5 mins • Baking: 40 mins

Dishes from various sea fish

Fish roulade

600 g fillets (haddock, silver carp), 1 bread roll soaked in milk, 2 tbsps grated horseradish, 3 tbsps chopped parsley, 1 small celeriac, juice of 1 lemon, 1 egg,

2 tbsps thick cream, salt, pepper, a pinch of each sugar and nutmeg, ¼ tsp grated lemon rind, 1 tsp butter, 2 cups vegetable stock, a few grains of each pepper and allspice, 1 onion, 1 clove, a pinch of sugar

Rinse and dry the fillets, sprinkle them with lemon juice and salt and leave for an hour in a cool place. Make a stock from the spices and onion, cook it for 20 mins. Peel and wash the celeriac, grate it finely, sprinkle with lemon juice. Add salt, nutmeg, grated lemon zest and cream. Squeeze the bread roll, put it through a mincer together with the fillets. Combine with the celeriac, horseradish and chopped parsley, break in the egg. Season with salt, pepper, nutmeg and sugar. Work into a smooth paste (add some breadcrumbs if it is not thick enough, or some cream if it is too thick). Take a damp cloth, baste it lightly with butter. Transfer the paste onto it, roll it up, tie with thread. Put into a skillet, pour over the strained vegetable stock. Cook over low heat for 40–50 mins. Leave it in the stock for several minutes, then remove the cloth. Cut the roulade diagonally into slices. Serve hot or cold with horseradish or sharp-tasting sauce.

serves 4–6 • Preparation: 30–40 mins • Cooking: 40–50 mins

Fish baked with cabbage

1 kg fish fillets (freshwater or sea fish), ½ small-sized cabbage, 2 cups rowan berries, 3 tbsps lard, salt

Wash the cabbage, shred it finely. Cut the fillets into small pieces. Rinse the rowan berries and dip them for a moment into boiling water, then drain them, rinse with cold water and dry. Grease a stoneware dish with lard liberally. Arrange layers of cabbage and fish, sprinkling each with salt. Put the rowan berries on top and more lard. Cover the dish, seal it with clay and put into hot ashes (in a bonfire). Bake for an hour. Alternately, arrange the layers of cabbage and fish in an ovenproof dish with a tight lid and bake in a preheated oven for 40–50 mins.

serves 4–6 • Preparation: 10 mins • Baking: 50 mins

Fish salad

500 g sea fish fillets, soup vegetables, 1 medium-sized onion, salt, 1 bay leaf, 3–4 grains each allspice and pepper, 1–2 cloves, 2 eggs, 6–8 mushrooms, pickled red pepper, 1 cocktail gherkin, ½ lemon, salt, a pinch of pepper, 4 tbsps mayonnaise, 1 tbsp chopped parsley

Make a stock from the vegetables, onion and spices. Strain it and pour over the fillets, cook for 20 mins. Take the fish out gently, cut into medium-sized cubes. Hard-boil the eggs and cut them into quarters. Cut the mushrooms into slices and scald them with boiling water. Cut the pepper and gherkin into strips. Put all the ingredients into a salad bowl, pour over the mayonnaise and toss gently. Garnish with lemon slices and chopped parsley. Put into the fridge for 30 mins. Serve cold with white bread.

serves 4–6 • Cooking: 25–30 mins • Preparation: 10 mins

Haddock stew

800 g haddock fillets, 100 g smoked streaky bacon, 150 g onion, 2 tbsps tomato paste, 1 tbsp oil, 1 tbsp butter, 1½ tbsps flour, salt, pepper, paprika, ¼ tsp grated lemon rind, ¼ tsp sugar, 1 tbsp lemon juice, 1½ cups vegetable or fish stock

Sprinkle the fillets with lemon juice, salt, pepper and paprika. Cover and leave in the fridge for an hour. Heat up the oil in a skillet. Fry the finely chopped onion, but do not let it brown. Add the bacon cut into strips and fry for a minute or two. Sprinkle with the flour, stir, pour in the stock, add the paprika and simmer for a while until the sauce has thickened. Add some sugar and the tomato paste. Cut the fillets into thick strips, dredge them with flour. Melt the butter in a frying pan and fry the fish until golden brown on all sides. Transfer the fish to the skillet, stir gently and simmer for a while. Serve with pasta, kasha or potatoes.

serves 4–6 • Preparation: 10–15 mins • Cooking: 8–10 min

Sea fish fricassee

800 g fish fillets, 2 large onions, 200 g mushrooms, 1 tbsp flour, 2 tbsps butter, 2 raw egg yolks, juice and grated rind of 1 lemon, salt, pepper, a pinch of sugar, 2–3 tbsps finely chopped parsley, 1 cup each stock and dry white wine

Rinse and dry the fillets. Sprinkle them sparingly with lemon juice, salt, pepper and grated lemon zest and leave for an hour in a cool place. Chop finely the onions and mushrooms. Melt the butter in a pan, fry the onion, but do not let it brown. Add the mushrooms and fry them together, stirring all the time. Sprinkle with the flour, mix well, pour over the stock and wine. Simmer, stirring all the time until the sauce has thickened. Put in the fish, cover the pan and simmer for 20–25 mins. Towards the end, adjust the taste with salt, pepper, sugar and lemon juice. Garnish with chopped parsley before serving.

serves 4–6 • Preparation: 10–15 mins • Cooking: 20–25 mins

Fish ragout with apples

800 g sea fish fillets, 1 tbsp lemon juice, 1 large onion, 2 tart apples, 2 tbsps chopped walnuts, 2 tbsps raisins, 50 g stoned prunes, 1 tbsp each butter and flour, ½ tsp each cinnamon and pepper, ¼ tsp powdered cloves, salt, ½ cup dry white wine, ½ tsp honey, 2–3 tbsps oil

Rinse and dry the fillets. Sprinkle them with lemon juice, salt and pepper and leave in a cool place for half an hour. Blanch and drain the raisins and prunes. Put them into a bowl, pour over 1 tbsp of boiled water and 3 tbsps of wine and leave for an hour. Cut the fillets into strips, dredge them with flour. Heat up the oil in a skillet, put in the fish strips and fry them until golden brown, add the butter. Peel the onion, chop it finely. Peel and core the apples, cut them into strips. Add the apples, onion, prunes and raisins to the fish. Sprinkle with cinnamon, cloves and water, pour in the remaining wine. Stir the whole gently, cover the skillet and simmer for 10–15 mins. Add the walnuts, season to taste, stir and simmer for another 5 mins. Serve with white bread or rice.

serves 4–6 • Preparation: 25–30 mins • Cooking: 15–20 mins

Fish roulade in aspic

750 g fish fillets (hake, pollack, cod), 1 tbsp lemon juice, 1 bread roll soaked in milk, 2 cups vegetable stock, 2 eggs, 2 onions, 1 bay leaf, several grains each pepper and allspice, 1 tsp gelatine

STUFFING: *2 large onions, 250 g mushrooms, 4–5 tbsps chopped parsley, 2 tbsps butter, salt, pepper*

GARNISHING: *½ lemon, 2 hard-boiled eggs, several sprigs of parsley*

Boil the vegetable stock, adding the onion, bay leaf, allspice and pepper. Towards the end add some lemon juice, salt, pepper and sugar to taste. Chop finely the onions and mushrooms, sauté them in butter. Put the fish fillets and the squeezed out bread roll through a mincer, break in the eggs, season with salt and pepper and work into a smooth paste. Transfer the paste onto a clean cloth and form it into a rectangle (ca 1½ cm thick). Sprinkle with the parsley, spread the onion and mushroom mixture. Lift up the linen and roll the paste, pressing it lightly with your fingers. Wrap up the roulade in the cloth, tie both ends. Put it into a skillet, pour over the stock and cook over very low heat (keeping it off the boil) for 40–50 mins. Leave it in the stock to cool down. Take the roulade out, remove the cloth. Cut it into slices. Strain the stock, bring it to the boil, add the dissolved gelatine and again bring it to the boil. Pour a bit of the stock into a large elongated serving dish and leave to set. Arrange the roulade slices on top, garnish them with slices of lemon and hard-boiled eggs and with parsley sprigs. Pour over the remaining stock and leave to set. Serve with savoury sauces.

serves 6–8 • Preparation: ca 1 hr • Cooking: 40–50 mins

Herring

During Lent, herring is eaten very frequently. It is prepared in various ways, with olive oil, vinegar and capers, or with vinegar and onion.

(Lucyna Ćwierczakiewiczowa, 1860)

In the Middle Ages herring belonged to cheap and common dishes. Later it was said that, had it been more expensive, it would have been one of the greatest delicacies the world knew. The main thing is that it has survived many centuries and changing fashions.

Fish cutlets

Take 4 herrings, soak them well and remove the bones, then chop the meat finely. Add 4 tbsps of sour cream, perhaps some breadcrumbs, 2 egg yolks, and also finely chopped onion and fresh butter. Mix everything well, shape into cutlets, coat with breadcrumbs and fry in butter.

(from *Przysmaczki polskiej kuchni*, 1850)

Herring salad with nuts

500 g herring, 2 tart apples, 4–5 potatoes cooked in jackets, 2 soured cucumbers, 1 medium-sized onion, 1 small cooked beetroot, 3 tbsps chopped walnuts or hazelnuts, 1 cup thick sour cream, 1 tbsp thick mayonnaise, a pinch of sugar, pepper, pickled bell peppers, parsley

Soak the herring in water, then remove the skin and bones. Cut the meat into small cubes. Peel the apples, potatoes, cucumbers and beetroot, dice them into small cubes. Chop the nuts and mix them with the cream and mayonnaise, add sugar and pepper, also lemon juice to taste. Combine all the ingredients in a bowl, toss gently. Garnish the salad with pieces of hard-boiled egg and pickled pepper and with parsley.

serves 6–8 • Preparation: 10–15 mins • Maturing: 1–2 hrs

Herring salad with red onion

2 herring fillets, 1 red onion, 1 peach, 1 tbsp chopped parsley, 1 tbsp lemon juice, 1½ tbsps grapeseed oil, a pinch of each pepper, salt and sugar, 3–4 thin lemon slices without pips

Rinse the fillets, dry them, cut into thick cubes. Sprinkle with lemon juice and pepper. Chop the onion, sprinkle it with 1 tsp of oil and a bit of salt. Blanch and skin the peach, remove the stone. Cut ¾ of the peach into fine strips, sprinkle with a pinch of sugar and lemon juice. Mix it with the chopped parsley. Combine all the ingredients, sprinkle with oil, toss gently and put into the fridge. Cut the remaining peach into fine slices. Garnish the salad with peach and lemon slices.

serves 4 • Preparation: 10 mins • Refrigerating: 1–2 hrs

Colourful herring salad

*500 g herring fillets, 1 tbsp coarsely ground pepper,
1 tart apple, 1 onion, 2 tbsps lemon juice, 1 large
firm soured cucumber, 3 potatoes cooked in
jackets, 2 cooked beetroots, 2 hard-boiled eggs*

*DRESSING: 3 tbsps thick cream, 2 tbsps thick
mayonnaise, a pinch of each salt and pepper,
1 tsp lemon juice, 1 tbsp green peppercorns*

Rinse and dry the fillets, cut them into thick cubes. Sprinkle with coarsely ground pepper and leave for an hour. Peel the potatoes, beetroots and cucumber, cut them into strips. Chop the onion and apples into thick cubes, sprinkle with lemon juice. Dice the egg whites and chop the egg yolks finely. Blend the cream with the mayonnaise, add lemon juice, salt, pepper and a pinch of sugar. In a salad bowl arrange alternating layers of the different ingredients, pour over the dressing, toss gently. Sprinkle with the egg yolk and green peppercorns, cover with foil and put into the fridge for an hour or two.

serves 4–6 • Preparation: 10 mins • Refrigerating: 1–2 hrs

Herring eggs

*500 g herring, juice of ½ lemon, 2 tbsps sunflower
oil, 6 eggs, 2 tbsps thick mayonnaise, 1 pickled
red bell pepper, 2 tbsps chopped parsley*

Soak and clean the herring. Halve them, sprinkle with lemon juice and oil, leave in a cool place for 30 mins. Cut the hard-boiled eggs into half. Wrap each egg half with a herring fillet, secure with a toothpick. Sprinkle a serving dish lavishly with chopped parsley, spread the mayonnaise on top and arrange the egg fillets. Garnish each fillet with a strip of pepper. Sprinkle the whole with chopped parsley.

serves 4–6 • Macerating: 30–40 mins • Preparation: 10 mins

Herring snails

*500 g herring, 150 g Gouda cheese, mayonnaise, a
bunch of chives, 3 tbsps sunflower oil, 1 red bell pepper*

Soak the herring, remove the skin and bones. Pour over the oil and leave for several hours in a cool place. Cut the cheese into ca 4 cm long strips. Take the herring out and cut it into thin strips. Wrap each cheese strip in herring, secure with a toothpick. Spread thick mayonnaise on a serving dish and arrange the herring and cheese snails on top. Sprinkle with the chopped chives, garnish with strips of red pepper.

serves 4–6 • Macerating: 5–6 hrs • Preparation: 10–15 mins

Herring in honey sauce

500 g salted herring, 3 cups milk

*SAUCE: 1 large onion, ½ cup olive oil, juice and
grated rind of ½ lemon, 4 tbsps honey, ¼ tsps each
ground allspice, cinnamon, cloves, cardamom and
pepper, 1 piece of dried gingerbread, a pinch of salt*

Wash the herring well, pour over the milk and soak for 24 hours. Cook the honey and spices over low heat in a covered pan. Peel the onion, scald it for 1–2 mins with boiling water, rinse with cold water and drain. Chop the onion finely, sprinkle with lemon juice, lemon zest and salt. Grate the dried gingerbread, mix with the oil, onion and honey. Take the herring out, remove the skin, spine and bones, rinse and dry, then cut into smaller pieces. Arrange in a serving dish, pour over the sauce. Cover with foil and put overnight into the fridge. Before serving, garnish with parsley sprigs.

serves 4–6 • Preparation: 25–30 mins • Refrigerating: 12 hrs

Ginger herring with nuts

*500 g salted herring, 3 cups milk, 1 cup sunflower
oil, 1 tsp chopped fresh ginger, 1 small cinnamon
stick, 4–5 cloves, 6–8 peppercorns, 1–2 grains
allspice, 250 g dried gingerbread, 250 g chopped
walnuts, 2 tbsps buckwheat honey, 2 tbsps
balsamic vinegar, ¼ tsp powdered ginger, several
sprigs of parsley, several walnut halves*

Wash the herring, pour over the milk and leave overnight. Rinse the herring, remove the skin, backbone and bones. Cut into sizeable pieces. Cook oil with ginger, cinnamon, cloves, pepper and allspice. Arrange the herring pieces in a glass jar, pour over the cooled oil and put into the fridge for 2–3 days. Prepare the paste: blend the honey with the vinegar, powdered ginger, grated gingerbread and chopped walnuts. Arrange the herring pieces on a serving dish, surround with the paste, cover with foil and put into the fridge for 2–3 hours. Before serving, garnish with parsley sprigs and walnut halves.

serves 4–6 • Preparation: 20–25 mins • Preparation of paste: 5 mins

Savoury herring in cream

300 g herring fillets, 2 cups milk, 5–6 cloves of garlic, 7–8 peppercorns, 1 tbsp white mustard seeds, 1 cup single cream, 2 onions, 1 tart apple, 2 tbsps lemon juice, ¼ tsp grated lemon rind, 1 flat tsp ground white pepper, ½ tsp mace or nutmeg, 3–4 thin lemon slices, several sprigs of parsley or dill, 2–3 thin strips of red pepper

Chop the peeled garlic. Boil the milk with the garlic, mustard seeds and peppercorns. Rinse and dry the fillets, arrange them in a glass jar, pour over the cool milk. Cover with foil and leave overnight. Take the fillets out, dry them and cut into pieces. Peel the onions and chop them finely, sprinkle with lemon juice, pepper and salt and leave for an hour. Peel the apple and grate it coarsely. Sprinkle with lemon juice and zest. Whip the cream with sugar, salt, pepper and nutmeg, fold in the onion and apples. Arrange the herring pieces on a serving dish, pour over the sauce. Garnish with lemon slices, red pepper strips and sprigs of dill.

serves 4 • Macerating: 1 hr • Preparation: 10 mins

Herring in cream

500 g herring, 1 tart apple, 2 onions, juice from ½ lemon, salt, a pinch of pepper, a pinch of sugar, 1 cup sour cream, 1 tbsp chopped parsley

Soak the herring in water for several hours. Take the skin off, remove the backbone and bones. Pour over the milk and leave for another hour. Peel the apple, grate it coarsely, sprinkle with lemon juice. Peel and slice the onions, scald the slices with boiling water. Dry the herring with a clean towel. Mix the cream with salt, pepper and

sugar. Arrange the herring in a serving dish, pile the onion and apple around. Pour over the cream, sprinkle with chopped parsley. Garnish with parsley sprigs.

serves 4 • Preparation: 10 mins • Maturing: 1–2 hrs

Royal herring

500 g herring fillets, 2 large onions, 1 lemon, 50 g almond flakes, 50 g raisins, ¼ cup dry white wine, ½ cup boiled water, salt, ½ tsp sugar, 1 clove, 1–2 grains each pepper and allspice

Boil the wine with the water, salt, sugar, clove, pepper and allspice. Simmer under cover for several minutes, then strain the liquid. Slice the onion, scald the slices with boiling water. Scrub the lemon thoroughly, scald it with boiling water, cut into cubes, remove the pips. Rinse the raisins, blanch and drain them. Rinse and dry the fillets, cut them into sizeable pieces. In a glass jar arrange alternating layers of herring and lemon, onion and raisins. Pour over the prepared marinade and leave in the fridge for two or three days.

serves 4–6 • Preparation: 30–35 mins • Marinating: 2–3 days

Herring, Lithuanian style

1 kg herring, 1 kg onion, 30 g dried mushrooms, 1 tin tomato paste, 1 cocktail gherkin, 2 smoked sprats, 1 tbsp sunflower oil, pepper, pickled bell pepper, parsley

Chop the onion finely, fry it in oil, but do not let it brown. Cook the mushrooms which had soaked in water overnight, then put them through a mincer together with the sprats and onions. Add the tomato paste, mix thoroughly, season with pepper to taste. Cut the herring, which had been soaked in water, skinned and boned, into small pieces, mix with the sauce and put into a glass jar. Put into the fridge for two or three days. Serve garnished with red pepper and parsley.

serves 6–8 • Preparation: 25–30 mins • Ripening: 2–3 days

Herring in vinaigrette

500 g herring, 1 onion, 1 tsp each pepper, marjoram and pounded juniper berries, ½ tsp nutmeg,

1 crumbled bay leaf, ½ cup sunflower or soya oil, 2 cloves of garlic, salt, juice of 1 lemon

SAUCE: Chop the garlic finely, mix it with salt, oil and lemon juice. Soak the herring in water, skin and bone it. Put it in a glass jar, alternating it with layers of sliced and blanched onion. Sprinkle each layer with spices and herbs. Pour over the sauce and leave in a cool place for two or three days. Serve garnished with onion, red pepper and parsley.

serves 4–6 • Preparation: 20 mins • Ripening: 2–5 days

Herring, Milanówek style

500 g herring fillets, 2 tbsps sugar, ½ cup oil, ¼ cup 6% vinegar, 3–4 tbsps tomato paste, 300 g onion, 2–3 grains allspice, 1 bay leaf, 15 g mustard seeds

Peel the onions and cut them into half slices. Heat the oil in a pan, fry the onion, but do not let it brown. Add the sugar and simmer for a while, stirring all the time. Pour in the vinegar, add the bay leaf, allspice and tomato paste, mix well and simmer for another 10–15 mins. Take off the heat, add the mustard seeds and leave to cool. Cut the herring into pieces. In a glass jar arrange alternating layers of the herring and the cool sauce. Close the jar and put into the fridge for 2–3 days. The herring will keep in the fridge for up to 2 weeks. Before serving, put it on lettuce leaves and garnish with parsley.

serves 4–6 • Preparation: 30–35 mins • Maturing: 2–3 days

Herring with prunes

500 g herring, 4–5 mushrooms, 2 pickled bell peppers, 4–5 prunes, 3 tbsps sunflower oil, 1 tbsp raisins, a pinch of pepper, 1 tbsp chopped parsley

Soak the herring in water, skin and bone it, cut into halves. Wash the mushrooms and cut them into strips. Soak the prunes, stone them and cut into strips. Rinse the raisins, blanch and drain them. Put the herring in a glass bowl, surround it with the mushrooms, the peppers cut into strips, prunes and raisins. Sprinkle with pepper sparingly. Pour over the sunflower oil and put overnight into the fridge. Serve cold as an hors-d'oeuvre or with boiled potatoes, garnished with chopped parsley.

serves 4–6 • Preparation: 15–20 mins • Ripening: 12–24 hrs

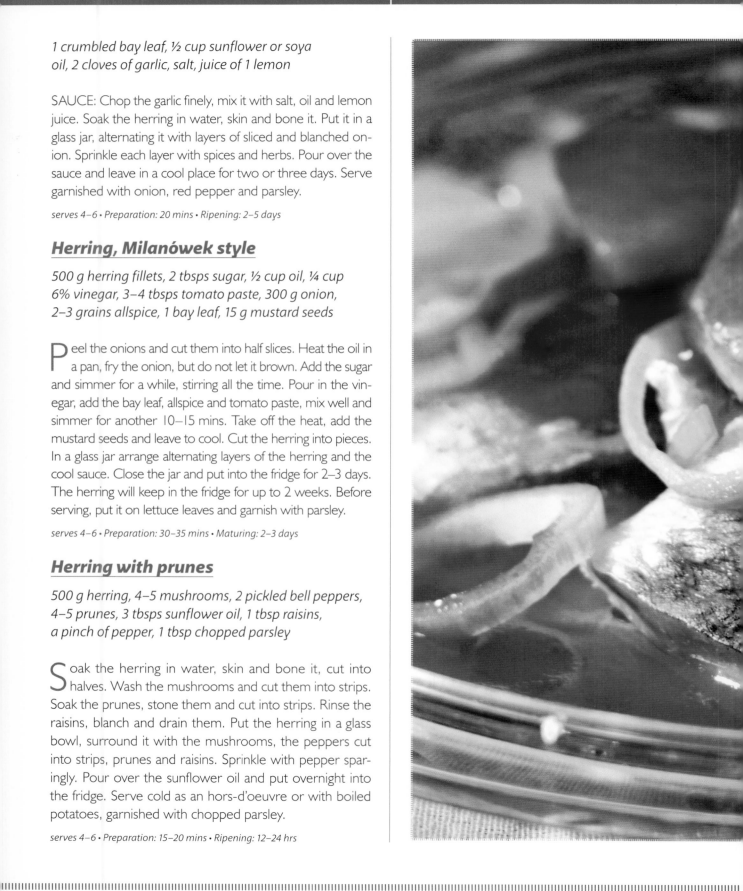

Herring, Milanówek style

Spicy herring

500 g salted herring fillets, 2 tsps caster sugar,
½ tsp each ground cinnamon, cloves and allspice,
¼ tsp ground pepper, 4–5 crumbled and ground
bay leaves, finely chopped fresh ginger root the
size of a walnut, 3–4 onions, 3–4 tbsps tomato
paste, 2–3 tbsps oil, salt, pepper, a pinch of sugar

Mix the sugar and all the spices. Rinse and dry the fillets, put them in a bowl. Sprinkle with the spices, cover with foil and put overnight into the fridge. Peel the onions, cut them into thin slices, and fry in oil, but do not brown. Add the tomato paste, a pinch of each salt, sugar and pepper, mix well and leave to cool. In a glass jar arrange alternating layers of herring and onion. You may keep spicy herring in the fridge for 3–4 days. Before serving, arrange the herring on lettuce leaves, cover with the onion and garnish with parsley sprigs.

serves 4 • Preparation: 15 mins • Maturing: 2–4 days

Herring in wine

500 g herring fillets, 3–4 red onions, 1 tbsp lemon juice

MARINADE: 1 cup dry red wine, ¼ cup 8% red wine
vinegar, ¾ cup sugar, 6–8 peppercorns, 4–5 cloves,
a piece of cinnamon, 1–2 grains allspice

Put all the ingredients of the marinade into a skillet, bring to the boil and cook over low heat for 10 mins, then leave to cool. Peel the onions, cut them into thin slices, sprinkle with lemon juice. Wash and dry the fillets, cut them diagonally into pieces. In a glass jar arrange alternating layers of the herring and onion. Pour over the marinade, cover and put into the fridge for at least three days. The herring will keep in the fridge for 2–3 weeks.

serves 4 • Preparation: 20–30 mins • Maturing: 3–4 days

Herring in white wine

500 g herring, 3 onions, 2–3 cloves, 1 cup dry
white wine, ½ cup raisins, 1 bay leaf, 3–4 grains
allspice, 3–4 grains pepper, parsley

Soak the herring in water, skin and cut it into small pieces. Boil 1 cup of water with the spices and a pinch of sugar, simmer it for a while under cover. Strain the marinade, leave it to cool, add the wine and bring to the boil again. Rinse the raisins and add them to the hot marinade. Cut the onions into slices, scald them with boiling water. In a glass jar put alternating layers of the herring and onion, pour over the cool marinade and leave in the fridge overnight. Serve the fish surrounded with onion as a cold hors-d'oeuvre, garnished with parsley sprigs.

serves 4 • Preparation: 25–35 mins • Maturing: 12–24 hrs

Herring in oil with mustard

500 g herring, 1 tbsp Dijon mustard,
3 bay leaves, 4 grains each pepper and allspice,
1 tbsp capers, 2 tbsps sunflower oil, lemon juice

Soak the herring in water, remove the skin and bone, cut in half. Spread some mustard on the inside of each fillet. Roll each fillet up, secure with a toothpick. Arrange the herring rolls in layers in a glass jar, alternating each layer with capers, pepper, allspice and bay leaves. Do not pack the rolls too tightly or they will not soak in the oil. Pour in the oil and leave in a cool place for several days. Before serving, sprinkle with lemon juice and garnish with parsley sprigs.

serves 4 • Preparation: 20–25 mins • Maturing: 4–5 days

Marinated herring with cream, beans and apple

500 g herring, 1 cup beans, 3 onions, ½ cup vinegar,
1 lemon, 6 grains each coriander, pepper and
allspice, 3 bay leaves, 1 tsp sugar, 1 glass dry white
wine, ½ cup thick sour cream, 2 tart apples

Rinse the beans, cover with 1 cup of boiled water and leave overnight to soak. Cook them in the same water with a pinch of salt. Bring 1 cup of water to the boil, put in 3 peeled and sliced onions and cook them. Strain the stock, add the spices, sugar, ½ cup of vinegar, a pinch of salt and juice of ½ of lemon. Cover the pan and simmer for 10 mins. When the marinade cools down, adjust the taste with more lemon juice and with wine.

Herring in oil with mustard

Take the herrings that had been soaked in water, skin and bone them, cut into halves and put in a glass jar. Pour over the marinade and leave in a cool place for 2–3 days. Before serving, arrange the herring on a serving dish, surround with the apples chopped into small cubes and with cooked bans. Pour over the cream and garnish with parsley sprigs.

serves 4–6 • Preparation: 1 hr • Maturing: 2–3 days

Herring tartare

3 herring fillets, 1 onion, 1 tbsp lemon juice, a pinch of each salt and caster sugar, 1 medium-sized firm soured cucumber, 4–5 pickled milk caps, 1 raw egg yolk, 2 tbsps olive oil, pepper

Peel the onion and chop it finely. Sprinkle with salt, caster sugar and lemon juice. Wash and dry the fillets, chop them into small cubes, sprinkle with pepper, add the egg yolk. Peel the cucumber and chop it finely together with the mushrooms. Combine all the ingredients, pour over the oil and put into the fridge for a short while.

serves 4 • Preparation: 10 mins • Refrigerating: 1 hr

Herring, Carpathian style

500 g herring fillets, 250 g bryndza, 1 cup cream, 3–4 cloves of garlic, 2–3 tbsps each tinned green peas and finely chopped red pepper (fresh or pickled), 2 tbsps chopped chives, salt, white pepper, a pinch of caster sugar, ½ tsp grated lemon rind, 3–4 thin lemon slices, several sprigs of parsley for garnishing

Chop the garlic finely, mix it with pepper, lemon zest and bryndza into a smooth paste. Whip the cream with a pinch of salt and sugar, fold into the bryndza. Cover and put in a cool place for a while. Wash and dry the fillets, cut them into small pieces, arrange on a serving dish. Mix the sauce with the chives, green peas and peppers, pour over the herring. Cover with foil and put into the fridge for an hour or two. Before serving, garnish with lemon slices and parsley sprigs.

serves 4–6 • Preparation: 20–25 mins • Maturing: 1–2 hrs

Herring, Hungarian style

500 g herring, ½ cup wine vinegar, 1 bay leaf, several grains each allspice and pepper, ¼ tsp sugar, 1 glass dry white wine, 1 tbsps tomato paste, 1 onion, 1 tsp paprika, 3 tbsps sunflower oil

Add ½ cup of water to the vinegar and boil together with the spices and a pinch of sugar, then leave to cool. Pour in the wine, add the tomato paste and oil, mix thoroughly. Peel and slice the onion, blanch it and drain well. Skin and bone the herring that had soaked in water. In a glass jar arrange alternating layers of the herring and the onion slices. Pour over the marinade and leave in a cool place for several hours (up to 4 days). Serve as a cold hors-d'oeuvre or with baked potatoes, garnished with slices of soured cucumber and parsley sprigs.

serves 4 • Preparation: 20–30 mins • Maturing: 1–4 days

Rolled herring

500 g herring, 1 cup vinegar or juice of 3 lemons, 3 large onions, 1 bay leaf, 6 grains allspice, 6 grains pepper, a pinch of sugar

Soak the herring in water, remove the skin and bones, divide into halves. Sieve the milt, mix it with 1 finely chopped onion and a pinch of pepper. Spread the onion and milt paste on each piece of herring, roll it up and secure with a toothpick. Boil the vinegar with 1 cup of water, add the spices, 2 onions cut into slices and a pinch of sugar. Arrange the herring in a glass jar, pour over the cool marinade and leave in a cool place for several days.

serves 4 • Preparation: 30–40 mins • Maturing: 3–4 days

Herring in marinade

500 g herring, 1 tbsp butter, 1 tbsp chopped parsley, 1 tbsps capers, 4 small onions, 1 bay leaf, 2 lemons or wine vinegar, 4 tbsps sunflower oil

Soak the herring in water, remove the skin and bones. Wrap in greaseproof paper basted with butter. Put into a preheated oven and bake at a low temperature for 15 mins, basting with butter. Leave the fish to cool in the oven. Take off the paper and cut the fish into smaller pieces. Arrange the herring pieces in a glass jar. Sieve the milt, add oil, lemon juice, chopped parsley, capers, bay leaf, a bit of chopped onion and, if required, some sugar and pepper. Mix thoroughly. Pour the marinade over the herring and leave overnight in a cool place. Serve as a cold hors-d'oeuvre.

serves 4 • Baking: 15 mins • Preparation: 30 mins • Maturing: 12–24 hrs

Marinated herring in mustard sauce

750 g herring, 2 large onions, 2 tbsps capers, 2 tbsps Dijon mustard, 2 tbsps sunflower oil, 2 bay leaves, 10 grains each allspice and pepper, 2 tart apples, 1 cup dry white wine, vinegar or lemon juice, a pinch of sugar

Soak the herring in water, remove the skin and bones, then soak it in milk and dry well. Peel the onions, cut them into slices. Blanch the slices in a sieve. Bake the apples, then sieve them together with the herring milt. Boil 1 part vinegar and 1 part water, add the spices and sugar. Mix the apple purée with the mustard, oil and wine, add the cool marinade and mix thoroughly. Arrange the herring in a glass jar. Sprinkle each layer with capers. Pour over the marinade and leave in a cool place for several days. Serve as a cold hors-d'oeuvre or with boiled potatoes. Garnish with chopped parsley.

serves 4–6 • Preparation: 30–35 mins • Maturing: 3–5 days

Rollmops

8 herrings, 8 small cocktail gherkins, 1 tbsp Dijon mustard, 1 tbsp capers, vinegar or juice of 3 lemons, 1 bay leaf, several grains each allspice and pepper, a pinch of sugar, 4 onions, pepper

Soak the herring in water, remove the skin and bones, cut into halves. Chop finely 2 onions, mix with pepper and mustard. Spread the onion and mustard mixture on the inside of each fillet, put half a gherkin on top. Roll up, secure with a toothpick. Bring 1 part vinegar and 1 part water to the boil. Add the seasoning, sliced onion and sugar, and simmer. Sieve the milt, blend it with the capers. Pour in the cool marinade and stir well. Arrange the rollmops

in a glass jar, pour over the marinade and leave in a cool place for several days.

serves 6–8 • Preparation: 25–35 mins • Maturing: 4–5 days

Herring stuffed with spinach

1 kg fresh fish (herring or sardines), 1 tbsp lemon juice, salt, pepper, 1 kg fresh spinach, 1 cup crumbled bread (without the crust), ½ cup milk, 2–3 cloves of garlic, 2–3 tbsps pine nuts, 3–4 tbsps chopped parsley, 3–4 tbsps breadcrumbs, 2–3 tbsps olive oil, salt, pepper

Clean and wash the fish, rub it with salt and pepper, sprinkle with lemon juice and leave aside for half an hour. Rinse the spinach, put it for 2–3 minutes into boiling salted water, then drain it, pour over cold water and chop finely. Soak the crumbled bread in milk for several minutes. Heat up 1–1½ tbsps of oil in a skillet, add the spinach and cook it for 5 mins, reduce the juices. Add the finely chopped garlic, parsley, pine nuts and squeezed out bread. Mix thoroughly, take off the heat. Season with salt and pepper. Stuff the fish with the cool mixture. Pack tightly in a greased flat ovenproof dish. Sprinkle with breadcrumbs and oil. Bake in a preheated oven for 20 mins.

serves 4–6 • Marinating: 30–40 mins • Preparation: 20–25 mins • Baking: 20–25 mins

Herring schnitzels

500 g fresh herring, 1 bread roll, 2 onions, 2 eggs, salt, pepper

* breadcrumbs for coating

* oil or butter for frying

Wash the fish, remove the skin and bones. Soak the bread roll in milk, then squeeze it out. Chop the onions finely and fry in oil or butter, but do not let them brown. Put the bread roll and herring through a mincer, mix with the onion, add salt and pepper. Shape small cutlets, coat each with breadcrumbs and fry until golden brown on both sides. Serve with parsley, caper or other sauce.

serves 4 • Preparation: 20–30 mins • Frying: 8–10 mins

CHAPTER X

MEAT

✳✳✳

There has never been a shortage of meat in Poland.

In poetry, prose and old cookery books, this conviction has always been expressed. And it is very visible in descriptions of all kinds of feasts, above all in descriptions of Polish Easter food.

The hare, good in itself, together with beef

wrote Tomasz Bielowski in his Myśliwiec in 1595, and in 1638 Stanisław Jeżowski went further, praising,

A top roast of fat beef can be good
And also roast goose, or capon in broth
And fresh beef steak, or veal,
Brawn with horseradish, tasty lamb with dill
Fat roast sucking pig... etc.

Ferdynand Chotomski (1797–1880), the soldier in Napoleon's army who was also a poet and humorist, praised Polish cuisine as follows:

Above fame and above laurels
I prefer your broth,
Tasty sirloin of beef
And roast veal.

For centuries, Polish cuisine was meat-based. The variety of meat dishes is enormous. From roasts, through rolls and stews to various kinds of cutlets, steaks, schnitzels and collops.

Once enormous game roasts took pride of place on Polish tables especially at Easter time: of wild boar, venison, elk, roast sucking pig or stuffed boar's head. Nowadays we usually prepare roasts from lamb, beef and sometimes veal in game style.

Today however, when dieticians are sounding the alarm, and calling for a change in our eating habits, we should not forget that meat is one of the main sources of protein and that a shortage of protein is as damaging as an excess.

And the cook should further know which meat is suitable for boiling and which should only be cooked as a roast... Roasts can be roast beef, hussar's roast, braised steak, roast veal with kidney, lamb with garlic or marjoram, roast kid, roast pork ... Mutton is only used in the better homes for the servants.

(Łukasz Gołębiowski, *Domy i dwory*, vol. IV, pp. 35–37)

The best meat for roasts is along the back, where it is tender, juicy, not too fat and without veins and gristle, and should be cut in a short joint (there are two exceptions to this rule: for rolled meat, we need a large, thin fillet of meat, and for hussar's roast, we need a long joint which is not too thick).

Lamb and beef should come from young animals, with white or light cream-coloured suet (dark yellow suet indicates that the meat is from old animals). Before roasting, it should be tenderized for several days in a marinade or with seasoning.

For a succulent roast you need a joint weighing at least 1–1½ kg without bones, because in roasting it will shrink as mush as to half its size; the extent of shrinking depends on the length of roasting and the temperature. Before roasting it is a good idea to blanch the meat, that is, throw it into boiling water for 2 to 3 minutes, or fry it lightly on all sides in very hot fat; this leads to the formation on the surface of a film of set protein, which prevents the juices escaping and the fat melting.

If the fat is at too low a temperature, it will soak into the meat, and the juices will run out; the roast will be indigestible, dry and will be less tasty.

After quickly frying off the meat, it should be placed in a roasting tin and roasted in a moderate oven (170°–180°) with or without a lid, and basted at first with water or wine and then with the gravy that forms, so that it will remain juicy and tasty.

If the meat is not blanched or fried off before roasting, we should rub it or cover it with fat, and put it in a hot oven (up to 230°C) to brown; after a few minutes we turn the temperature down to 180°.

If we roast without a lid, especially in a gas oven, it is a good idea to put a pan with water under the roast.

Slices of fatty bacon can be wrapped round meat roast on a spit (without fat). Lean beef, veal or lamb can be prevented from being dry if the bottom of the roasting tin is covered with fatty bacon, or if the roast is larded with bacon fat, or if the whole roast is wrapped in thin slices of it.

Bacon fat for larding should be cut in fingers or slices and chilled properly in the fridge.

Roasting in aluminium foil, or greaseproof paper brushed with fat, or in a roasting bag yields good results. Meat roast in this way shrinks much less, is easily digestible and more succulent and aromatic.

Roasting time depends above all on the size of the joint and the type of meat. Beef needs roasting longest, and veal the shortest time. In general, a joint that weighs more than a kilogram needs roasting for 70–90 minutes, or a shorter time on the spit. If the temperature is too high, the joint will dry out and will lose flavour; we should not therefore attempt to speed up the roasting process.

A joint is ready when on sticking in a skewer, a clear golden juice runs out, and the skewer itself goes into the meat without much difficulty. Meat should be left for a while in a warm oven after roasting. While it is resting the roast evenly absorbs the juice, and is therefore more moist.

A good roast needs to be properly prepared. Before roasting it should be quickly washed under running water, dried with a cloth, the tendons, bones and any excess fat should be removed (only a thin layer of 2–3 mm of fat should be left so that the juices will not boil away); it should be firmly squeezed in the hand or beaten with a wooden pestle, which makes it more tender. The taste of a roast is much improved by 'maturing' it in a marinade, or in vegetables and spices with oil or in sour milk, buttermilk or yogurt. Meat will quickly become tender if we wrap the joint in a linen cloth soaked with brandy. If we do not marinade or otherwise soak meat, especially beef and lamb, it is a good idea to sprinkle it with lemon juice and leave it for 2 to 3 hours in the fridge.

Seasoning, dressings and marinades are a very important part of many roasts, and greatly influence the taste, aroma and also the tenderness.

Marinades are a sharp, spicy dressing that conserves and tenderizes the meat, and also often sharpens the flavour or remove the typical smell (especially for mutton and lamb).

We should remember that the marinade should not be too acid and that we should not leave the meat in it for too long. Marinating not only influences the taste and tenderness of the meat, but also shortens the cooking time.

Rolls are an interesting and showy way of roasting. The basis of a roll is a large flat slice of meat covered in stuffing, which is then tightly rolled up, threaded round or wrapped in foil and roasted. Stuffing made with a large variety of ingredients, usually sharp in taste, gives rolls a choice flavour. They can be served hot or cold. Slices of roll, which after cutting reveal the colourful interior, make serving dishes much more attractive to look at.

Another kind of stuffed roast is hussar's roast, which is braised in its own gravy, and in the last phase of cooking stuffed with crumbled black bread or dried breadcrumbs with fat and grated onion. The stuffing is put into a series of deep incisions made across the grain of the meat.

Meat à la mode is an exceptionally tasty, tender and juicy form of roast. It is usually made with beef, although horsemeat or game can also be used. A variation on this theme is fricandeau, made from leg of veal. The joint is first tenderized for 48 hours in a vegetable and spice dressing made with oil, and is then barded either with strips of bacon fat (or streaky bacon), or with cloves of garlic, and is braised or roasted in a tightly closed roasting tin (together with the vegetables from the dressing). It is served hot with the sieved gravy from the roast, or cold with pickles, marinated mushrooms or savoury sauces.

Roast beef, which should be a joint from the hind quarters, first marinated in oil with vegetables, should be roasted for a short time in a hot oven. Roast beef should be rare, but not raw.

Marinades
for meat

Marinade for red meat (beef and mutton)

2 cups buttermilk, 1 large chopped onion, ½ tsp ground cloves, 1 crumbled bay leaf, ½ tsp each grated nutmeg, dried thyme and ground pepper

Mix all the ingredients well. Pour the mixture over the meat. Stand it in a cool place for 2–3 days, and turn the meat over from time to time so that it is thoroughly impregnated with the marinade.

Preparation: 5 mins

Marinade for meat à la game

2 cups lager beer, 2 finely chopped onions, juice and grated rind of 1 lemon, 3 crumbled bay leaves, a pinch of ground cloves, ½ tsp ground allspice, ½ tsp ground pepper

Mix all the ingredients, bring to the boil, then leave to cool. Pour the mixture over the meat. Stand it in a cool place for 2–3 days and turn the meat over from time to time so that it is thoroughly impregnated with the marinade.

Preparation: 5 mins

Marinade for all kinds of meat

1½ cups dry red wine, 3–4 tbsps oil, 1 finely chopped onions, ½ tsp dried thyme, 1 crumbled bay leaf, 8–10 coriander grains, 4–5 allspice grains, 2–3 garlic cloves, 3–4 peppercorns, ½ tsp salt

Mix the crushed garlic and salt with the remaining ingredients. Put the rinsed and dried meat in a stoneware dish. Pour the marinade on top, cover, weigh it down and stand in a cool place for 2–4 days. Turn the meat over from time to time so that it is thoroughly impregnated with the marinade.

Preparation: 2–3 mins

Wine marinade

1 cup dry white wine, ½ cup wine vinegar, 2–3 garlic cloves, a pinch of ground cloves, ½ cup diced celery, ½ cup chopped parsley, 1 chopped onion, 1 grated carrot, ½ tsp salt, ¼ tsp ground pepper

Mix the crushed garlic and salt with the remaining ingredients. Put the rinsed and dried meat in a stoneware dish. Pour the marinade on top and stand in a cool place for 1–2 days. Turn the meat over occasionally so that it is thoroughly impregnated with the marinade. Use for all kinds of meat and for poultry.

Preparation: 2–3 mins

Herbal marinade

2 cup dry white wine, 1 glass brandy, 2 tbsps oil, ¼ tsp ground juniper berries, ¼ tsp each dried rosemary, marjoram and thyme, 1–2 garlic cloves, 1 small diced leek, ¼ grated celeriac, 1 grated carrot, ½ tsp ground pepper

Mix thoroughly all the ingredients. Pour on top of the meat and stand in a cool place for 2–3 days. Turn the meat over quite often.

Preparation: 2 mins

Vegetable and oil dressing

1 large carrot, 1 large parsley root, 1 large onion, a piece of celeriac, ½ tsp sugar, 1 crumbled bay leaf, a pinch of ground cloves, 1 tbsp lemon juice, 3–4 tbsps oil, ¼ tsp each ground allspice and pepper

Grate the vegetables coarsely, combine with the finely chopped onion, oil, lemon juice, spices and sugar. Sprinkle the whole meat with the mixture, cover and stand in a cool place for 1–3 days.

Preparation: 5 mins

Cutlets – or everything from entrecôte to meatballs

'Cutlets', although the term itself is relatively new, constitute a bottomless pit in Polish cuisine. Hundreds of menus can be pulled out of it, and can be used endlessly. Three hundred years ago, cutlets did not really exist; roasts and braised meat were the main elements in meat cookery. But from the moment when smaller portions of meat began to be roasted or fried, a new name was given to them to describe the way they were cooked, and experts began to quarrel violently about differences between cutlets, schnitzels, fillets and collops.

In the category of 'cutlet' Polish cuisine therefore places: entrecôte and steaks, rump steak and schnitzel, loin chops and beef cutlets, and collops. One thing is certain – whatever name is used, cutlets must always be prepared from good cuts of meat, that is from the loin or saddle. If we have to make a cutlet from worse cuts, we must remember to tenderize the meat by marinating it, sprinkling it with vodka, lemon juice or vinegar, or rubbing it with special tenderizing salts. It is however better to make rissoles from meat of this kind, or braised cutlets (and while braising cover them with a small amount of wine, vodka or beer, because alcohol helps to make meat more tender).

The following meats are best for cutlets:

Lamb

– the hind quarters: the leg, with juicy and delicate meat, is excellent for frying, grilling or roasting, as steaks, collops or cutlets;
– saddle and shoulder: saddle is sold on the bone – for single or double chops; or boned, for fillets and medallions;

Leg and saddle of lamb, after the fat has been trimmed and the meat has been appropriately marinated, can be used instead of venison.

Veal

– shoulder and saddle: the meat is juicy and aromatic and is excellent for steaks and fillets;
– kidney joints, which are best for chops or escalopes (boned);
– the hind quarters (leg) or the noix of veal: I top leg, II the inner leg, III the fore part of the leg – these have lean, delicate, easily digestible and mildly flavoured meat which is excellent for schnitzels, collops and fillets; the shin has firm and aromatic meat which is good for grilling as steaks or fillets.

Pork

– loin and neck are sold both on the bone and boned, and they are excellent for frying, grilling or roasting as cutlets, fillets and collops;
– tenderloin is the finest cut of pork, suitable for escalopes and medallions;
– leg, or ham has delicate meat which is good for cutlets, steaks, collops, schnitzels, escalopes.

Beef

- sirloin, the most delicate part of the beef, is the equivalent of loin of pork. It is a juicy, long, boneless, piece of meat covered with a thin layer of fat that is attached to the backbone; it is divided into three parts: the head, the centre and the tail, or in other words the thin end. The centre part is excellent for steaks, chateaubriand steak and fillets, and the tail is right for tournedos, filet mignon and collops. The head is best for steak tartare, beef Stroganoff or ragout;
- entrecôte is the equivalent of middle saddle, and is excellent, juicy and delicate; it can be used for cutlets, steaks and collops;
- the leg is divided into: the outer part which is good for steaks and collops; the upper leg which is juicy and delicate and good for steaks and collops; and the rump, which is the best part for steaks;
- rib of beef, which is usually sold with a layer of fat, is tender and juicy and excellent for frying steaks or for roasting;
- shoulder is known in Polish as 'false sirloin': although it looks like sirloin, it is suitable rather for braising, mincing or for all kinds of stews and ragouts;
- shin provides very delicate meat for collops and cutlets.

Game

- saddle and leg are the best cuts for cutlets in both venison and wild boar. Meat from young animals does not have to be marinated, but older meat needs it, and rubbing the meat with aromatic oil allows it to stay juicy while being fried;
- game should be marinated in wine to which spices and herbs have been added: the best are thyme, marjoram and rosemary, and also juniper berries, garlic, sage, cloves, cinnamon and ginger;
- because all game is very lean, you can obtain good results when frying cutlets, fillets, chops or steaks by barding the meat with thin strips of raw or smoked bacon fat or streaky bacon. Before larding, it is a good idea to freeze the thin strips of bacon fat, as they then go in more easily.

Preparing meat for cutlets.
The meat should first be thoroughly but quickly rinsed under running water, and then dried with a cloth. You should cut off the fat, tendons and membrane with a sharp knife, taking care not to damage the flesh. This prevents the cut-

lets losing shape in cooking. The edge of the cutlets, where a ring of fat has been left, should be notched every 2 to 3 cm. Before frying, the meat should be carefully formed, that is cut into even, crosswise slices, lightly beaten with a pestle or the handle of a knife, or squeezed manually, making it into an oval, round or square shape. Pounding or squeezing meat that is to be fried is intended to make it tender and to even out the thickness.

Marinating. It is a good idea to marinate some kinds of meat (lamb, beef) before frying. A well-prepared marinade makes the meat tender and gives it a fine flavour. For the simplest forms of marinating meat, you can use aromatic oils, yogurt, buttermilk, sour milk or fruit juices (for example, pineapple juice).

Vinegar or wine marinades are more time-consuming; these are prepared using herbs, spices, often onion, garlic and vegetables. Marinating 'loosens' the tissue of the meat which, as a result, becomes more delicate and tender.

Meat should be left in the marinade under a lid in the fridge or a cool place, and should from time to time be turned over, so that it is thoroughly impregnated with the marinade. The time it is left in the marinade depends on how strong we want the taste to be. Frozen meat should not be marinated.

Frying. You should remember that all meat shrinks in cooking: when sautéed by about 20%, when egged and breadcrumbed by 10% and when battered by about 5%.

The fat temperature is very important when frying. The fat should be hot, but should not get brown or smoke. It is best to heat the fat to a temperature of about 170° to 180°C so that the meat will quickly and evenly brown but still remain juicy. If the temperature is too high, the fat will disintegrate and the meat stick to the pan; if it is too low, the juices will run out, the meat will absorb fat and will become indigestible and stringy. In both cases, the cutlets will not taste good.

There is an ongoing debate about whether you should salt meat before or after frying. Top-quality meat — and this is after all what cutlets are made from — should not lose its juices and become stringy after salting. But it is still better — especially in the case of beef steaks — to salt them immediately after frying. There are two stages in frying cutlets: first, you should fry both sides off lightly at a high temperature, for 1–3 minutes on each side; and then fry them properly for 2 to 4 minutes at a lower temperature, turning them over with a spatula, but remembering not to puncture the meat because this will lead to the juices running out. You should fry a large number of cutlets in batches, or in two frying pans, taking care that the fat temperature does not fall too low, and remembering to leave plenty of space between the frying cutlets, so that they fry and not stew.

The fat plays an exceptionally important role. It is best to use lard, olive oil, corn oil, rapeseed or coconut oil, and for sauté, clarified butter is best, because this retains not only the delicate aroma of butter, but also works well at high temperatures. The fat left in the pan can be used to prepare an excellent gravy. For this, you should pour 2–3 dessertspoons of broth, wine, boiled water or fresh cream into the hot pan, bring it to the boil, stirring all the time, and finally season to taste.

Note! In all the recipes where butter is used for frying, we are talking about clarified butter. Clarified butter is fresh butter heated to a temperature at which 'scum' forms on the surface. After this scum has been removed, the butter should be poured into a jar and kept in the fridge to use as required. Clarified butter is excellent for frying, because it withstands a much higher temperature than fresh butter and does not burn during frying.

Some kinds of cutlets, especially battered veal and chicken cutlets, should be deep-fried, that is fried in an amount of fat that allows the cutlets to float in it freely, so that a crisp crust forms around them. The fat temperature must be very high, and the cutlets should be fried in batches, so that they do not reduce the fat temperature too greatly. The pan in which this is done should not be more than half-full of fat, because the fat bubbles up during the process. The cutlets should be strained of excess fat after frying by placing them first on a strainer, then on kitchen towel, and they should then be kept on a dish in a hot oven.

Note that they should not be covered, or the crisp outer crust will go soft.

Stuffed cutlets have an excellent flavour. In order to stuff them, you should prepare a 'pocket'. Take a thick slice of meat, lightly beat it with the handle of the knife, put it on a board and with a sharp knife make a deep incision in the middle, but do not cut it right through. Fill the pocket with the prepared stuffing, stitch up the opening or close it with toothpicks, dredge the meat with flour or with eggs and breadcrumbs and fry it in hot fat.

All kinds of cutlets can be fried sauté, or floured, battered or egged and breadcrumbed. They should be breadcrumbed or battered immediately before frying.

Egging and breading. In culinary vocabulary, there are two basic breadcrumb preparations: ą l'anglaise, which means dipping the meat first in flour, then in egg beaten with water, salt and pepper, and finally coating it with breadcrumbs; and a la milanaise, which means covering the cutlet liberally with olive oil or melted butter and then coating it with breadcrumbs mixed with grated cheese. Meat should be coated immediately before frying (and the coating should be pressed firmly with the hand) to prevent the breadcrumbs absorbing the meat juices, because then the coating will stand off from the meat and the cutlet will be dry.

Egg and breadcrumbs. Usually meat is coated in flour, beaten egg and breadcrumbs. The egg can be beaten with boiled water, wine or beer, and also with carbonated mineral water. Recently a lot of ready-made egg-and-breadcrumb preparations have appeared on the market, but I would advise you to try to make your own. You can get good results from mixing the breadcrumbs with grated cheese, or by substituting chopped nuts, sesame seeds or sunflower seeds for the cheese; and adding finely chopped fresh or dried herbs or ground spices is an excellent way of improving the taste.

Battering. This is used mainly for cutlets made from white meat, that is, veal, turkey and chicken, and also pork. The batter is prepared from flour, eggs and liquid – water, bouillon, beer, wine or cream. To improve the taste, you can add spices to the batter – ground pepper, allspice, ginger, a pinch of cinnamon, finely chopped fresh herbs or a pinch of herbal mixture. Cutlets to be battered should first be dried, then floured and finally dipped in the batter. They are best fried in a large amount of fat, after which they should be dried off on a tea cloth. Meat fried in batter remains very juicy.

Grilling. This means basically frying without fat. The slices of meat for grilling should not be too thick, if you want them cooked evenly. Grilling over-thick slices of meat means that while the surface is nicely browned, the meat inside will remain raw. Before grilling, it is a good idea to rub the meat with olive oil or marinate it, and during cooking sprinkle it with the marinade and turn it regularly. It is best to use special tongs to turn the meat over on the grill; if we are doing the grilling in the oven, we should put a special tin under the grill for the fat to drip onto. Here are a few typical cooking times for a charcoal and electric grill:
beef steak, 2½ cm thick – 4 mins/3 mins on each side;
veal schnitzel, 1½ cm thick – 6 mins/4 mins on each side;
veal cutlet on the bone, 2 cm thick – 7 mins/5 mins on each side;
pork cutlet on the bone, 2½ cm thick – 7 mins/6 mins on each side;
lamb cutlet, 2½ cm thick – 5 mins/4 mins on each side.
What does the name cutlet include?

Cutlet is a polonized form of the French *côtelette*, which comes in turn from the word *côte* or rib. If therefore we were to be strict about it, a cutlet is a piece of meat (beaten flat) with the rib attached. It is often breaded.
But in Polish cuisine the name also covers dishes made from beaten meat, chopped and minced meat, fried meat, grilled meat and also dishes made from minced fish, potatoes, nuts and vegetables.

Beaten cutlets can be made from pork, veal, lamb, venison, wild boar (saddle or shoulder), and turkey, duck or chicken breast. After slicing, washing and drying the meat, it should be lightly pounded, sprinkled with salt, pepper and if desired herbs, egged and breadcrumbed and fried in hot fat on both sides until golden brown. It is best to fry it in very hot lard or clarified butter. After frying add a teaspoon of butter to the pan and leave it for a second over a low heat.

In Poland, the favourite beaten cutlet is the pork chop, usually served with potatoes and cabbage cooked with mushrooms.
In earlier times, when pork was not regarded as a superior meat and was only used to prepare sausages and smoked meats, veal or lamb cutlets en papillote were enormously popular in Poland, as were beaten cutlets made from poultry and game. Here is a recipe from the time when saddle of pork was regarded as a meat for the peasantry.

Veal cutlets en papillote

Veal cutlets are prepared from the saddle with the kidney. Cut off the thick side bone, slice the meat, pound it lightly, sprinkle with salt and pepper, and fry off in hot olive oil or melted butter. Separately sauté the chopped mushrooms, sprinkle them with bouillon, chopped parsley, salt and pepper. Cut a large heart out of greaseproof paper, brush it with olive oil, arrange a layer of mushroom stuffing, place the cutlet on top of this, cover it with the remaining stuffing, wrap it up tightly, and put in a hot oven for 10 minutes.

An interesting variant of beaten cutlets is côtelette de volaille, that is, chicken cutlet, or skinned chicken breast with the breast bone removed and with a part of the wing bone remaining. After lightly beating the meat you should form it into the shape of a large leaf, wider next to the bone and quite narrow at the opposite end. The meat should be lightly sprinkled with lemon juice and salt, and also with some herbs, and then a piece of hard frozen butter should be placed on it; it is then rolled up (the ends should be tightly sealed so that the butter cannot run out), egg and breadcrumbed and fried in hot fat until it is golden brown in colour. Remember that the first piece should be cut off with great care as a rough cut with a knife can cause the melted butter to spurt out. De volaille is usually served with French fries and vegetables Polish style – boiled asparagus, Brussels sprouts, cauliflower, green peas covered in breadcrumbs browned in butter. It can also be accompanied by sharp-tasting sauces, or with flavoured butter inside (parsley, herbal or anchovy butter).

Chopped and minced cutlets, or rissoles. In Polish cuisine, various types of rissoles are called cutlets: made from chopped or minced beef, pork, veal, chicken or mixed meats. The basic idea is to add white bread soaked in milk, lightly beaten raw eggs and seasoning to the meat, which is then carefully mixed, shaped into cutlets, and fried in very hot fat. The fried cutlets should be put in a pan and kept warm under a lid for ten minutes or so.

Fricadelles are elongated cutlets made from minced meat. They can be deep fried, fried in a frying pan, or braised in sauce.

Bryzol describes a piece of lightly pounded frying steak about 14 cm in diameter and ½ cm thick. It comes from the best part of beef sirloin, although occasionally from rump steak. For veal, pork, horsemeat or lamb bryzol, meat from the saddle is taken.

Escalope is the French word for fillet, meaning a flat slice of meat or fish. In Polish cuisine, the term is used to refer to small, round, lightly beaten cutlets, which are fried or baked, sautéd or egg and breadcrumbed, often served au gratin, or braised lightly in wine. According to the old rules, escalopes were prepared only from white meat, that is, veal, pork (saddle), turkey or chicken breast and sometimes from pork loin. The various names tell all about the method of preparation and cooking. There are therefore escalopes in wine, with orange, with herbs or mushrooms.

Fillets. This name also comes from the French. One of its meanings is sirloin (fillet steak), and the other designates a slice of meat removed from the bone, and also a boned piece of fish, or boned chicken or duck breast.

Fillets are usually prepared from sirloin of beef, or saddle of veal, pork, wild boar, venison or hare, and also from duck, turkey or chicken breast.

The meat should be cut against the grain, slightly crosswise, and then pounded lightly with a wet pestle, formed into the shape of an oval leaf and fried sauté in very hot fat, or grilled; before frying, it is often marinated in wine with herbs, or sprinkled with lemon juice and spices. Sauté fillets are usually served with sauces – hunter's sauce, or mushroom or tomato sauce, and game fillets with currant,

rosehip or juniper sauce. The fried fillets can also be quickly braised in the sauces with added vegetables or mushrooms, or they can be fried in egg and breadcrumbs.

They are usually served with French fries or potatoes baked with herbs, lettuce salad, or delicate vegetables that have been steamed or cooked in butter.

There is a very thin line between what we call fillets and what is called a cutlet or a steak. This can be seen clearly in the case of filet mignon which is the name given in international cuisine to a form of cutlet made up of two small rounds of beef steak (for one portion), usually cut from the thin end of beef sirloin (or loin of pork). These are cooked without fat, on the grill or in a special frying pan, and served with knobs of frozen flavoured butter on top and with French fries and vegetables cooked in butter (broccoli, asparagus, cauliflower).

Medallions are slices of lightly beaten meat which are formed into the shape of a round or oval medallion. Beef medallion means the same thing as steak, while chicken or veal medallions are the equivalent of escalopes.

Rozbratel comes from the German term *Rostbraten*, which means 'roast on the spit'. But in Polish cuisine it refers to beef or horsemeat cutlets.

Very different dishes go under this name. One thing is important: the beef must be from the upper front quarter of the animal, must come from young animals and must have been matured, so that after frying it retains its juiciness and tenderness.

The meat is cut into large (ca 200 g) and fairly thick (ca 2 cm) cutlets, so that after being thoroughly beaten out, each will cover a whole plate. A classic rozbratel, which was sometimes called a Galician cutlet, is fried in very hot fat and served garnished with fried onions, and usually with puréed or fried potatoes, vegetable salad or vegetables Polish style (boiled and covered with butter and browned breadcrumbs).

Rozbratel can also be prepared with anchovies, capers or stuffing; it can be braised in wine or cream. And here again, the distinction between cutlets and collops becomes blurred.

Rumsztyk, or rump steak is a name that comes from English and means a dish prepared from the best parts of beef or horsemeat – if possible from sirloin.

It should be a piece of meat cut against the grain and not too thin (ca 1½ cm) which is pounded lightly and then formed with a knife to give it a slightly elongated shape. Rump steaks from sirloin of beef, once known as 'square cutlets', should be fried quickly on both sides in very hot fat, so that the meat inside remains rare; however, if we make rump steaks from other joints of meat, after frying them off on both sides in hot fat, we should sprinkle them with some water, wine or light bouillon and braise them under cover until tender. Rump steaks are excellent when roasted on a spit after being first rubbed with olive oil or butter.

Rump steaks are usually served with a large quantity of browned fried onions, often with boiled vegetables or mushrooms, and boiled or puréed potatoes. All kinds of raw vegetable salads – lettuce, chicory – go well with rump steak. If we serve it au naturel, we pour its own juice over it; it can be garnished with fried eggs, slices of lemon or hard frozen pats of flavoured butter.

Steak. This name, once unknown in Old Polish cookery books, was made popular by the Americans. In English it means a piece of good-quality meat sliced off, and fried or roasted on the spit.

It was the Americans who invented the technique of roasting huge beef steaks on the bone, cut from the sirloin or rump. 'T-bone steak' is a name that comes from the shape of the bone in the middle of the steak, which is at least 4 cm thick and weighs 600 g. This is a portion for two people. In America the largest steak is sirloin steak, which is at least 6 cm thick and weighs 1.2 kg or more.

European steaks are much smaller; they are cut from shin of beef, which has very delicate meat. Two or three days before cooking, the should be rubbed with olive oil and kept in the fridge. It can also be cut from boned entrecôte from which the fat has been trimmed. One thing is important: that the meat for steaks should have hung, and should be cut in slices at least 2 cm thick. All the tendons should be cut from the washed and dried slice, and the fat edge should be notched every few centimetres, so that the steak does not become misshapen in cooking. Sirloin steaks should not be beaten, but thick steaks from other joints can

be lightly pounded or squeezed in the hand, formed and rubbed with olive oil; they can then be roasted on the spit or fried in very hot fat (for 1½ minutes on each side), after which the pan should be covered and left over a low heat for a while. Steaks should be cooked immediately before serving, and should be sprinkled with pepper and salt on one side after they have been fried. Despite what people think, beef is not the only meat from which steaks can be made: there can be veal steaks, pork steaks and lamb steaks as well as beef steaks.

Schnitzel is again a word that comes from German and means a flat slice of veal or pork which is lightly pounded, seasoned and usually coated with egg and breadcrumbs. The best known is the Wiener schnitzel, fried in lard. Its 'ancestors' are veal cutlets ą la milanaise, covered in egg and grated cheese and fried in butter.

A real schnitzel should be large, thin and fried almost like doughnuts, in a large amount of very hot fat; it is therefore a good idea to strain the ready schnitzel of excess fat on a paper towel.

Schnitzel is cut from the hind quarters of veal. After lightly but thoroughly beating the meat, you should sprinkle it with a little salt and lemon juice (which will make it more tender and juicy) and leave it for 20 to 30 minutes in the fridge, after which it can be formed into evenly sized cutlets. Each schnitzel should be first dredged with flour with a pinch of salt, then dipped in beaten egg and finally coated with breadcrumbs (remember to lightly press the breadcrumbs and to shake off the excess). Then you should immediately fry it on both sides in very hot lard. Schnitzels are best served with frozen butter knobs and slices of lemon.

Zrazy, or collops. This name first appeared in Polish cuisine over 200 years ago with the first edition of Wojciech Wielądko's *Kucharz doskonały*. Several decades later, Kazimierz Chłędowski wrote the following in his memoirs (*Galicja*, vol. I, 1843–1880): 'To my surprise I discovered that what we in Poland call rolled collops is in fact Italian by origin origin; I thought that this was an absolutely Old Polish dish like dumplings, while with some surprise I found the same things in an old provincial Italian kitchen'.

Collops are a universal dish; there are beaten, chopped and rolled collops. They can be made from various cuts of meat. The famous rolled collops a la Radziwiłł are made from veal (and are baked in rye bread after braising); beaten collops ą la Nelson, with mushrooms and onion, are made from beef; beaten collops ą la Napoleon are made from beef and braised in dry white wine with vegetables cut into thin sticks (carrots, parsnips, celeriac, kohlrabi, onion) etc. Beaten collops are usually made from beef, and generally from sirloin. Slices of meat should be thoroughly beaten with a pestle, sprinkled with flour, salt and pepper, fried and after frying covered with layers of vegetables, mushrooms, onion etc, and braised under a lid or baked in the oven; at the end, cream is often added. Chopped collops are a kind of rissole, served with sauces – usually mushroom, dill or caper sauce. They are best made of mixed beef and pork.

Rolled collops are slices of meat covered with stuffing and rolled up. The stuffing determines the taste, and there are very many stuffings known to Polish cuisine – made from meat, mushrooms, eggs, pork fat, soured cucumbers, onions etc. Meat stuffings can be made from beef, veal, pork, lamb or poultry.

Kasha is the traditional accompaniment of collops in Polish cuisine, usually buckwheat grits or pearl barley.

The array of dishes in the category known as goulashes or stews is also very large.

Fricassee means 'mess' in French. In Old Polish cuisine this was a dish made from various kinds of delicate, white meat (veal, chicken, pigeon) in a white sauce. Today it is usually made from veal braised with vegetables and then thickened with a roux made from butter and flour, or with cream or with egg yolks. Fricassee is also a dish made of pieces of fish in a cream sauce. It is usually served with rice or with pasta.

Potrawka in Polish means a delicate ragout made from white meat (chicken, boiling fowl, veal, lamb) or vegetables. Fairly large cubes of meat are cooked in a small amount of stock made from soup vegetables, thickened with a roux, or with cream and egg yolks. The sauce is usually soured with lemon juice, and seasoned with grated nutmeg and chopped dill, chives or cress. Mushrooms, asparagus, cauliflower and also crayfish tails or shrimps can also be added to the sauce.

Ragout is the French name for a dish made from beef, lamb, pork, game, poultry, fish and vegetables. The taste of ragout depends on the seasoning (herbs, spices, vegetables, mushrooms). The meat is cut into small pieces, which are sprinkled with flour, fried off in very hot fat and then braised with added water, bouillon or wine and seasoning. At the end of the braising process, the sauce is thickened with cream or with egg yolks, and seasoned to taste. This is how ragout brun, or dark ragout, is made.

Ragout blanc, or light ragout, is made by replacing the flour with floury potatoes. A typical example of light ragout is Irish stew.

Ragout is served with bread or potatoes and more elegantly with croustades, omelettes, truffles or mushrooms.

Vegetable ragout can be made from all kinds of fresh vegetables.

Smoked meats

For centuries, Polish cooking was famed for its excellent range of smoked meats, which were known far beyond the frontiers of the country.

Smoked meat products that are made from one piece of pickled meat include ham, gammon, bacon and smoked pork loin. Another group of products are made from smaller pieces of meat, appropriately prepared in a natural or artificial casing. Apart from sausages, these include liver sausage, brawns and pâtés.

Westphalian method of preparing hams

Let the meat lie fresh without salting for two days. Then to make it tender it should be pounded properly on the meaty side. To 30 pounds of meat you usually take 2 pounds of salt and an ounce of saltpetre. The salt should be dried on the stove or in a pan, and then ground fine, which gets out the moisture even more. Some of the ground salt is rubbed into the ham and the ham is left in a salt solution for four weeks, after which it is taken out and pressed, so that the juice runs out of it. When this happens, it should be salted again and should stay for another two days in the brine. Finally it is smoked, if possible in oak smoke.

Some advice which is worth remembering:
- rubbing ham with salt that has been dried out in a pan makes it easier for the salt to penetrate the meat, and so the ham is more tender;
- turning over the meat several times while it is being marinated helps it absorb the seasoning evenly;
- ham should be cooked over a low heat, so that the brine only simmers;
- after taking it off the boil, the ham should be hung in a linen bag in a cool and airy place, so that it becomes hard and firm;
- if ham is smoked, it should be cold-smoked slowly for several days.

Pork ham I

460 g salt, 20 grains each allspice and pepper, 20 juniper berries, 4 bay leaves, 3 cloves, 20 g sugar, 10 g saltpetre, 4 cloves of garlic, 15 g coriander

Bone the meat, rinse and dry it. Roast 300 g of salt with saltpetre in a frying pan and rub it into the meat. Put the meat into a rather small stoneware dish and cover with brine made from 1 l of water, 160 g of salt and spices. Stand it in a cool place for 15–20 days and turn the meat over every day.

Marinade prepared for ca 5 kg of meat

Pork ham II

460 g salt, 15 g saltpetre, 1 tsp each dried thyme, marjoram, basil and savory, 10 juniper berries, 10 grains each allspice and pepper, 2 bay leaves, 5–6 cloves of garlic, ¼ tsp sugar

Pound the herbs and spices in a mortar, mix them with 300 g of salt, saltpetre and sugar. Bone the meat, rinse and dry it. Rub it thoroughly with the mixture of salt and spices. Put the meat in a rather small stoneware dish. Pour over water boiled with the remaining salt. Cover with

a board, weigh it down. Leave the ham in brine for ca 20 days, turning it over every day.

Marinade prepared for ca 5 kg of meat

Pork ham III

5 g saltpetre, 5 g sugar, 1 clove of galic, 40 g salt for rubbing the ham

BRINE: 10 g saltpetre, 10 g sugar, 1 bay leaf, 2 cloves of garlic, 15 grains each allspice and pepper, 30 grains coriander, 2 onions, 400 g salt, 3 l water

Rinse and dry the meat, rub it with a mixture of saltpetre, salt, sugar and garlic. Place in a rather small stoneware dish. Pour over the cool marinade. Cover with a small board and weigh it down. Stand in a cool place for 2 weeks and turn the meat over every day. For smoked ham, you should first boil the marinated meat over low heat: ca 30 mins per 1 kg of meat. The meat is ready if it offers some resistance when pricked with a fork. Before boiling, you must take it out of the brine, and rinse and dry it. You can also dip it in batter and cook it in the oven.

Marinade prepared for ca 5 kg of meat

Wild boar ham

ca 5 kg meat, 460 g salt, 20 grains each allspice and pepper, 20 juniper berries, 4 bay leaves, 3 cloves, 20 g sugar, 10 g saltpetre, 4 cloves of garlic, 15 g coriander

Basically, wild boar ham is prepared similarly to ordinary pork ham. Since however wild boar meat is much tougher, it needs to be thoroughly pounded first and rubbed with 1 tsp of fine-grained sugar. For smoked ham, you proceed as with pork ham (see p. 460, I). You can either boil the cured ham or serve it raw.

Mutton ham

1 leg of mutton, 3–4 onions, 4–5 bay leaves, 150 g salt, 10 g saltpetre, 20 g sugar, 1 tsp each ground coriander, juniper and allspice, 6–8 pounded cloves

* soup vegetables, ½ cup dry white wine

Pork ham

Bone the leg, trim the fat. Rinse it and pound thoroughly. Dry the salt in a frying pan, add the saltpetre, sugar and spices. Rub the mixture into the meat. Put the meat in a rather small stoneware dish, place the bay leaves and sliced onion on top, sprinkle with the remaining salt and spices mixture if any is left. Cover with a small board, weigh it down. Leave for 24 hours until the meat releases juices, then stand it in a cool place for ca 20 days, turning the meat over every second day. Take the meat out, rinse and dry it. Make a court-bouillon from the soup vegetables and the wine. Put in the ham and cook it for 2 hours. Serve hot or cold. Instead of boiling it, you can also cure the meat and serve it raw. In this case, take it out of the brine, rub the spices off, rinse and dry the ham, then smoke it. Smoked ham keeps for a long time.

French sausage

Take 1 part of pork sirloin to one part of pork fat and dice them. Put in chicken stomachs, some onions called shallots. Chop the whole very finely, add spices and aromatic herbs and proceed as with other kinds of sausage.

Lithuanian sausage

3 kg shoulder of pork, 1 kg pork fat, 100 g salt, 1 glass pure alcohol, 15 g each pepper and allspice, ½ garlic bulb, 1½ tsps sugar

* pig's small intestines, well soaked

Remove the membrane and stringy bits from the meat. Chop the meat into small cubes, mix in the sugar and leave for 3–4 hours for the sugar to dissolve. Mix the finely chopped garlic with salt. Add it to the meat together with the pounded spices and alcohol. Work the mixture thoroughly (over an hour). Put in the finely chopped pork fat and knead for another 15–20 mins. Attach a special nozzle to the meat mincer and funnel the mixture into the intestine casing very tightly so that no air can get in. Tie off

the end with string. Cure for 2 days in cherry and juniper smoke. Store in a cool and airy place.

Pork salami

750 g boned loin of pork, 500 g pork fat, 4 tbsps salt, 10 g saltpetre, pepper, allspice, chilli pepper

* cow's or pig's intestines

Mince the meat and fat three times. Put into a bowl, add salt, saltpetre, pepper, allspice and chilli. Work the mixture thoroughly for over an hour. Cover and leave in a cool place overnight for the meat to blend in with the spices. Scrub the intestines and rub them with salt. Funnel the mixture into the intestine casing tightly, tie off the ends with string and leave overnight in a cool place. Pack the meat tighter the following day, retie the end and hang the salami in a cool airy place for 24 hours. Cold-smoke it for 3–4 days.

Well-cured salami

1750 g pork, 1750 g beef, 1750 g veal, 200 g pork fat, 1 garlic bulb, 13 g saltpetre, 200 g salt, 10 g pepper, 6 g each allspice and paprika, ½ cup pure alcohol or rum

* cow's and pig's intestines

Clean the meat, put it through a mincer twice, then transfer it to a stoneware bowl and work it thoroughly for 1 hour together with the alcohol and 2 cups of boiled water. Pound the spices in a mortar, chop the garlic finely, mix it with the salt, saltpetre and paprika. Cut the fat into fine cubes. Blend all the ingredients. Put the mixture into a linen bag, press it down with a wooden board (taking care that the juices do not run out) and leave in a cool place for 2–3 days. Scrub the intestines and rub them with salt. Funnel the mixture into the intestine casings, tie off the ends with string. Press them down and hang for several hours in an airy place. Smoke the salami for 2 weeks at medium temperature.

Pork brawn

Take pork sirloin and lean roast meat, clean them and chop as finely as possible. To 20 pounds of meat add 18 ounces of fine-grained salt and 12 ounces of coarsely ground pepper, and blend very thoroughly. Prepare beforehand a long large intestine, clean it and soak in salted lukewarm water with an addition of vinegar. Fill the intestine with the meat mixture the way you do when you make sausage. Tie off the ends and hang it quite high over glowing wood shavings with aromatic herbs, for example lavender and others. Smoke it for at least a week, 2 weeks at the most, then leave it hanging in a a cool pantry for three months.

Brawn (head cheese)

a pig's head, trotters and tongue, ¼ tsp marjoram, a pinch of nutmeg, a pinch of ground cloves, pepper, 2–3 tbsps salt

* 1 pig's gut

Cook the trotters and the chopped head, then leave to cool. Carefully remove all bones, cut the meat into thin slices. Cook the tongue separately and slice it. Put all the meat into a bowl, add the salt, ground spices and the finely chopped garlic. Pour in 1 cup of the stock, mix well and leave in a cool place for 2–4 hours for the meat to blend with the spices. Scrub and soak the stomach beforehand, rub it well with salt. Fill it with the meat mixture not too tightly (so that it does not burst). Strain the stock into a large pan, add some water if required. Put the brawn into the warm stock and simmer for 90 mins. When it gets cool, take it out, place on a wooden board, press down with another board and leave to set.

Pork

Pork from young animals is succulent and fatty, pale pink in colour, shining and moist. For roast pork you should select joints that have delicate meat – saddle, ham, shoulder, and even lean flank. Pork, unfortunately, quickly goes bad. It will stay fresh longer and be more tender if you cover it with freshly-cut nettles and wrap it in a linen tea towel. Pork becomes more tender, juicy and delicate if it is pickled, marinated or kept in a spice and olive oil dressing. Roast pork, especially saddle of pork, should be cooled before carving into portions, and then reheated in the oven.

Suckling pig à la Daube

A cleaned and salted suckling pig, larded with pepper and cloves, should be wrapped in a cloth and placed in a great cauldron, covered with bouillon with added white wine, pepper, cloves and bay leaves, and boiled. When it is ready, you lay it on a dish and cover it with another cloth. A suckling pig of this kind can be eaten either hot or cold.

(W. Wielądko, *Kucharz doskonały*, 1808)

Roast or stuffed suckling pig

At one time this was an essential element on the Easter table, but it is now an extreme rarity – but maybe you might try it? A very young animal used to be recommended for this dish, one that had only sucked its mother's milk. The piglet was stabbed in the shoulder, into the heart, and the blood was let into a saucepan containing vinegar, which was later used for black soup. The dead piglet was sluiced in boiling water and the hair was scraped off, and then it was shaved clean with a sharp knife. The cleaned piglet was singed over the fire, especially the ears, so that no hairs were sticking out. The piglet was then covered with cold water and left for an hour to cool. After soaking for an hour, the piglet was drawn, washed and rubbed hard and thoroughly with salt after which it was left in a cool place for two to three hours.
Suckling pig roasted on the spit is best, but it can also be roasted in the oven. For this, after stuffing it and sewing it up, it should be placed in a greased tin, with the belly down. The forelegs should be pulled up under the snout and skewered at the knees so that they do not stand out. The back legs should be similarly skewered. The suckling pig should then be placed in a hot oven and roasted for 2½ to 3 hours. While it is roasting, it should be basted frequently with melted butter or rubbed with a piece of pork fat held on a fork or stick, and also brushed with a feather soaked in beer. The sugar in the beer will make the suckling pig brown beautifully and the butter will make the crackling crisp. To find out whether the pig is ready, a skewer should be stuck in at the thickest point. If milky water comes out, the pig is still raw; if there is clear

fat, then it is ready. If the pig becomes too brown before it is ready, it should be covered with greased greaseproof paper basted with fat or with aluminium foil. The roast suckling pig should be placed whole on a serving dish, covered with melted butter and surrounded by cress. When carving, you should first remove the fore and hind legs together with the hams, and then cut the rest into even slices.

With a small suckling pig the real business is the stuffing which determines the flavour, you should decide on its composition beforehand.

White stuffing

is used to stuff lamb and suckling pig at Easter. Take the lights from the lamb that is to be stuffed, add to them calf lights and two pounds of fresh pork fat. Boil them in white bouillon until soft, strain them and chop finely. Take a pound of butter, melt it, break in ten eggs. Stirring constantly, add half a quarter of finely crumbled white bread, a quarter of small currants, some nutmeg, cinnamon, chopped lemon rind and some sugar. Mix everything thoroughly, then stuff the lamb or suckling pig. If you wish to have a yellow stuffing, you make it in a similar way, but add a little saffron.

(J. Szyttler, *Kucharz doskonały*, 1830)

STUFFING FOR SUCKLING PIG

Stuffing with raisins

suckling pig's liver and lights, 100 g pork fat, 1 bread roll, 1 cup milk, 1 tbsp butter, 3 eggs, 2 tbsps breadcrumbs, 150 g raisins, ½ tsp sugar, salt, pepper, nutmeg

Braise lightly the liver, lights and fat, leave to cool, then chop finely or put through a mincer together with the bread roll which has been soaked in milk. Blend the egg yolks with the butter in a bowl, add salt, nutmeg and pepper. Mix thoroughly with the forcemeat. Put in the rinsed raisins, sugar and breadcrumbs, fold in the whisked egg whites. Mix gently and use to stuff a piglet.

Preparation: 20 mins

Kasha stuffing

1 cup buckwheat kasha, 100 g pork fat, suckling pig's liver, kidneys and lights, 2 onions, 2 eggs, 1 tsp marjoram, ¼ cup strong stock, salt, pepper, nutmeg, 1 tbsp butter

Rinse, drain and cook the kasha. Chop finely the lightly braised offal and pork fat or else put them through a mincer. Fry the finely chopped onion, but do not let it brown. Add it to the meat, break in the eggs and mix thoroughly. Put in the kasha, season with salt, pepper, marjoram and nutmeg, pour in the stock and work the whole into a paste.

Preparation: 30 mins

Pâté stuffing

suckling pig's liver, kidneys and lights, 500 g veal, 2 carrots, 2 parsley roots, ½ celeriac, 2 onions, 2 bread rolls, 2 tbsps butter, salt, pepper, 2 tbsps chopped parsley, 100 g pork fat

Stew the peeled, rinsed and finely diced vegetables in butter together with the veal and offal (take the liver out after 20–30 mins) until tender. Boil the pork fat, then cut it into fine cubes. Put the vegetables, offal, liver and bread rolls that have soaked in milk through a mincer. Break in the eggs, add salt, pepper, parsley and the pork cubes. Pour in some stock and mix thoroughly.

Preparation: 40–50 mins

Liver stuffing

suckling pig's liver, 400 g veal liver, ½ cup breadcrumbs, 2 tbsps butter, ½ cup raisins, 1 tsp sugar, ½ tsp cinnamon, 3 eggs, salt, pepper

Braise the liver in butter, then chop it finely or put through a mincer. Add the breadcrumbs, eggs, blanched raisins, season with salt, pepper and cinnamon. Mix thoroughly.

Preparation: 20 mins

Mushroom stuffing

400 g veal, 100 g pork fat, suckling pig's liver, lights, kidneys and heart, 200 g mushrooms, 1 large onion, 1 bread roll, 3 eggs, 3 tbsps chopped parsley, 2 tbsps butter, salt, pepper, nutmeg

Stew the finely diced mushrooms and onion in butter. Put the raw or lightly braised meat and offal through a mincer together with the bread roll that has soaked in milk. Add the parsley, eggs and spices. Blend with the onion and mushrooms.

Preparation: 30 mins

Pork à la wild boar

2 kg boneless pork (ham, neck or shoulder), 2 onions, salt, ½ tsp ground juniper berries, 1 tbsp butter, 1 tbsp lard

MARINADE: ½ cup each wine vinegar and dry white wine, grated rind of 1 lemon, ½ tsp sugar, 10 grains each pepper and allspice, 20 juniper berries, 3–4 cloves, 1 bay leaf

SAUCE: 1 tbsp butter, 1 tbsp flour, 2–3 tbsps hawthorn, rosehip or plum jam, 1 cup stock, a pinch of each salt and pepper

Rinse and dry the meat, pound it well with your hand. Put into a stoneware dish, place onion slices on top. Pour over the hot marinade, cover with a small board, weigh it down. Stand in a cool place for 4–6 days, turning the meat over every day. Take the meat out, rinse it under running water and dry, rub it with salt, tie tightly with cotton thread. Brown it on all sides in hot lard, then transfer to a roasting tin. Melt the butter in a small frying pan, add the ground juniper, stir and pour over the meat. Put the meat into a preheated oven and cook for an hour and a half, basting frequently with the strained marinade and then with the pan drippings.
Sauce: Melt the butter in a pan, add the flour and make a white roux. Thin it with the stock and, stirring continuously, simmer until the sauce has thickened. Pour in the sieved roasting juices and hawthorn jam, add salt, pepper and, if required, lemon juice or sugar to taste, and stir well. Arrange the carved roast in an ovenproof dish, pour over the sauce and heat up, or else serve the sauce separately.

serves 6–8 • Marinating: 5–6 days • Preparation: 10 mins • Roasting: 90 mins

Pork roast with caraway

ca 1½ kg boneless pork (ham, shoulder or neck), 1½ tsps ground caraway, ½ tsp marjoram, 2 large onions, 1 tbsp lard, 1 cup stock, salt

Rinse the meat, pound it well with your hand, rub with salt, caraway and marjoram, tie tightly with thread. Brown it on all sides in hot lard, then transfer to a roasting tin. Sprinkle with the finely chopped onion and put into a preheated oven. Cook it for 90–100 mins, basting with the stock frequently. Cut the meat into slices, arrange them on a serving plate, pour over the roasting juices. Serve with potato dumplings and stewed cabbage.

serves 4–6 • Preparation: 10 mins • Roasting: 90 mins

Farmer's pork roast

1 kg boneless pork (neck or ham), 1 kg small potatoes, 5 spring onions, a bunch of parsley, ¼ tsp each dried thyme and sage, 1 crumbled bay leaf, 1 tsp lemon juice, 1 glass rum, ½ cup stock, 1 tbsp lard, salt, pepper

Rinse the meat, sprinkle it with lemon juice, rub with salt, pepper, some thyme and sage. Cover and set aside in a cool place for 1–2 hours. Tie it tightly with cotton thread and brown on all sides in hot lard. Transfer it to a roasting tin, sprinkle with rum, cover and put into a preheated oven for 25 mins. Rinse the peeled potatoes, cut them into quarters, blanch them with boiling water in a colander. Put them around the meat together with the spring onions. Sprinkle with the bay leaf, pepper, sage and thyme, put several parsley sprigs on top. Return to the oven and cook for another 50–60 mins, basting with the stock. Take out the meat, cut it into slices. Arrange the slices on a serving dish together with the baked potatoes and onions. Pour the sieved roasting juices over.

serves 4–6 • Marinating: 1–2 hrs • Preparation: 10 mins • Roasting: 90 mins

Pork in puff pastry

ca 2 kg boneless pork, 3 tbsps hot mustard,
1 tbsp dried tarragon, salt, pepper

BATTER: 400 g ready-made puff pastry, 1 egg yolk

Rinse the meat and pound it well with your hand. Mix the mustard with salt, pepper and tarragon. Rub the mixture into the meat. Wrap the meat in foil and put it into the fridge for 1–2 hours. Remove the foil. Roll out the pastry into a rectangle, place the meat in the middle and seal the edges very carefully. Transfer the meat onto a baking sheet slightly rinsed with water. Make an opening in the pastry and stick into it a rolled up piece of thick paper (to form a "chimney" through which the steam will get out). Brush the pastry with the lightly beaten egg yolk. Put into a preheated oven and bake for 2 hours at a low temperature. If the pastry gets brown too quickly, cover it with aluminium foil.

serves 6–8 • Marinating: 1–2 hrs • Preparation: 5 mins • Baking: 2 hrs

Stuffed pork roast

1½ kg boneless pork, salt, 2 tbsps lard, 2–3 tomatoes
(or 1 tbsps tomato paste), 1 medium-sized
carrot, 1 medium-sized parsley root, ¼ celeriac,
1 small bay leaf, 5 grains each pepper and
allspice, 1 tbsp flour, ½ cup thick sour cream

STUFFING: 50 g pork fat, 5–6 marinated herrings,
3–4 dried cep mushrooms, 1 tbsp capers, 1 large
onion, 1 tbsp butter, ½ bread roll, 1 egg, salt, pepper

Soak the mushrooms in water, then cook them. Soak the herrings for a bit, then skin and bone them. Soak the bread in milk, then squeeze it out. Put the mushrooms, herring, bread, capers and pork fat through a mincer (you may also add some meat trimmings). Break in the egg, add salt, pepper and the finely chopped and slightly softened onion, mix thoroughly. Pound a large, thin piece of meat with a mallet, sprinkle it with some salt. Spread the mixture on top, roll the meat up tightly, secure it with toothpicks or tie with thread. Brown the meat on all sides in hot fat. Add the peeled and coarsely grated vegetables, tomatoes

cut into quarters and spices. Pour in the mushrooms stock, cover, and simmer for over an hour. Mix the cream with the flour, pour into the roast and simmer for a while longer. Cut the meat into slices, arrange them on a serving dish, pour over the sieved cooking juices with the vegetables. Serve with bread or potato dumplings.

serves 6–8 • Preparation: 30–40 mins • Cooking: 60–70 mins

Pork roast stuffed with liver

1½ kg boneless pork (shoulder or ham), 1 tbsp lard,
1 tsp flour, 1 tbsp butter, 1 tbsp capers, 4–6 mushrooms,
1 cup stock, ½ cup white wine, salt, pepper

STUFFING: 150 g veal liver, 100 g pork fat,
1 medium-sized onion, 1 tbsp butter, 1 egg,
2 tbsps breadcrumbs, salt, pepper

Cut the peeled onion into slices, fry it, but do not let it brown. Put in the liver and braise it. Put the liver, onion and pork fat through a mincer, add the breadcrumbs, break in the egg, season with salt and pepper and mix thoroughly. Pound the meat into a large, thin sheet. Spread the filling on top. Roll up the meat tightly, tie it with thread. Brown the meat on all sides in hot lard, sprinkle it with some water and put into a preheated oven for 60 mins. Sauté the diced mushrooms in butter. Make a roux from the butter and flour, dilute it with the stock, put in the mushrooms and capers, add some roasting juices and wine. Cut the meat into slices, arrange them on a serving dish. Surround them with French fries or baked potatoes. Serve the sauce separately.

serves 6–8 • Preparation: 20 mins • Roasting: 1 hr

Pork stuffed with vegetables

1 kg boneless pork (preferably fairly thin
piece of ham or shoulder), 1 tbsp lemon juice,
2 garlic cloves crushed with salt, ½ tsp each
dried thyme, rosemary and sweet paprika;

250 g celery, ½ small pod of each red, green and
orange pepper (ca 150 g), 1 tbsp mustard, 3 tbsps oil,
1 cup stock, ½ cup thick sour cream, 1 tsp potato flour

Rinse and dry the meat, cut it lengthwise (but not all way through) and open it up. Pound it lightly, then shape it into a large rectangle. Sprinkle it with lemon juice, garlic and salt, rosemary, thyme and paprika. Cover with foil and put into the fridge for 2–3 hours. Dice the peeled and cleaned celery. Core the peppers and cut them into strips. Place the meat on a board, brush it with the mustard. Sprinkle the celery and peppers on top. Roll up the meat tightly, tie it with thread. Heat the oil in a roasting tin, brown the meat on all sides. Sprinkle it with some stock and put into a pre-heated oven. Cook it for an hour, basting with the stock. Cut the meat into slices, arrange them on a hot serving dish and return to the still hot oven. Pour the roasting juices into a pan, bring them to the boil. Thicken with the potato flour mixed with 1 tbsp of cold water. Pour in the cream, stir well and heat up. Serve the sauce in a sauce boat.

serves 4–6 • Marinating: 2–3 hrs • Preparation: 15 mins • Roasting: 1 hr

Pork roast with prunes

1½ kg boneless pork (ham or shoulder), 2–3 bay leaves, 20 juniper berries, 20 peppercorns, 300 g prunes, 1 cup dry white wine, 1 tbsp lemon juice, ¼ tsp grated lemon rind, 2 tbsps lard, 1 tbsp oil, ¼ tsp each ground cinnamon, juniper and sugar, 1 tsp each breadcrumbs and grated brown bread, salt

Rinse the meat, pound it well with your hand. Rub it with salt and juniper, sprinkle with lemon juice. Wrap in foil and put into the fridge for 2–3 hours. Soak the rinsed prunes in a small amount of water, then cook and stone them. Remove the foil from the meat. Brown the meat on all sides in hot oil. Transfer it to a roasting tin, add peppercorns, juniper berries, crumbled bay leaves, lemon zest and prunes. Pour over the melted lard and some prune stock. Cover and put into a preheated oven for over an hour, basting with the remaining prune stock from time to time. Take the meat out of the tin. Put the breadcrumbs and grated brown bread into the tin, pour in the wine, add sugar and cinnamon and bring to the boil, then sieve the sauce. Cut the meat into slices and arrange them in an ovenproof dish. Pour over half the sauce and heat up

in the hot oven for several minutes. Serve the remaining sauce separately.

serves 6–8 • Marinating: 2–3 hrs • Roasting: 60–80 mins

Stuffed loin of pork

1 kg boned loin of pork, 1 large onion, 1 tsp green peppercorns, 1 tsp chopped oregano leaves, ½ tsp green rosemary leaves, ½ tsp chopped thyme leaves, 1 tbsp each chopped coriander and parsley, 3 tbsps hot mustard, 2–3 tbsps olive oil, salt, 1 glass dry white wine, ½ tbsp lard

Pound the rinsed and dried meat with your hand, cut it lengthwise in half (but not all way through), rub with salt on all sides. Squash the green peppercorns and mix them with the mustard, olive oil and the chopped herbs. Put the mixture into the incision, close it with toothpicks or sew it up. Heat up the lard in a roasting tin. Put in the meat and brown it on all sides, then put into a preheated oven and cook, basting often with the wine and then with the pan drippings. Serve hot or cold.

serves 4–6 • Preparation: 5–8 mins • Roasting: 1 hr

Loin of pork, Tatra style

1 kg boned loin of pork, 100 g raisins, 2 large onions, 3 tbsps chopped walnuts, ½ tsp dried sage, 1 tbsp lard, 1 cup dry white wine, ½ cup stock, 1 tsp lemon juice, salt, pepper

Rinse the meat, scald it with boiling water and drain. Rub it with salt, pepper and sage, sprinkle with the lemon juice and leave in a cool place for an hour. Place the meat into a roasting tin greased with lard, spread the remaining lard on top. Put into a very hot oven for 10–12 mins. Rinse the raisins and soak them in the wine for 20–25 mins. Sprinkle the finely chopped onion on top of the meat, turn the temperature down and cook for another 10–15 mins, basting the meat with the stock. Sprinkle the meat with the chopped walnuts and wine, add the raisins and cook for 30–40 mins under cover, basting with the pan drippings frequently. Take the meat out of the tin and allow it to cool, then cut it into slices. Arrange the slices in an ovenproof dish and heat up in the hot oven. Reduce the sauce a bit, add salt and pepper to taste and serve in a sauce boat.

serves 4–6 • Marinating: 1 hr • Preparation: 5–6 mins • Roasting: 1 hr

Loin of pork, Podhale style

1 kg boned loin of pork, 150 g prunes, salt, 1 tsp each caraway and marjoram, 1½ tbsps lard

Rinse the meat, rub it with salt and marjoram and leave in a cool place for an hour. Soak the prunes, then drain them and mix with the caraway. With a sharp knife make a long incision in the meat and fill it with the prunes. Grease a piece of aluminium foil with lard and wrap the meat tightly in it. Place it in a roasting tin greased with lard and put into a preheated oven. Baste frequently with water. Towards the end, open the foil to allow the meat to brown nicely.

serves 4–6 • Salting: 1–2 hrs • Preparation: 5 mins • Roasting: 1 hr

Loin of pork with prunes

1½ kg loin of pork on the bone, 1 tsp marjoram, 3–4 cloves of garlic, 8–10 prunes, 1 glass red wine, salt, 1 tbsp lard, 2–3 cloves

Rinse the meat, rub it with salt, marjoram and crushed garlic and set aside in a cool place for 2–3 hours. Blanch and stone the prunes. Stick the cloves in between the bones. Grease a roasting tin well with lard. Place the meat in the tin, put the prunes around, add I tbsp of hot water. Put into a preheated oven and cook for 90 mins, basting frequently with the pan drippings. If the meat browns too quickly, cover it with aluminium foil. Towards the end pour over the wine. Serve hot, with the sieved roasting juices, or cold.

serves 6–8 • Marinating: 2–3 hrs • Roasting: 1⅓ hrs

Braised loin of pork in milk

ca 1½ kg boneless loin of pork, 1 l milk, 500 g small onions, salt, pepper, 1 tbsp lemon juice, 1 tbsp olive oil, 2 tbsps butter, 2 tbsps grated cheese

Brown the chopped onions lightly in I tbsp of butter. Sprinkle the rinsed and dried meat with the lemon juice, rub it with salt and pepper. Brown it on all sides in hot oil, then transfer to a roasting tin. Arrange the onion all around, pour over the hot milk, bring to the boil, then cover and simmer for 40–50 mins. Take the lid off, turn the meat over and cook for another 40 mins, until the sauce is reduced to ca 2 cups. Take the meat out, leave it to cool a bit, then cut diagonally into slices. Arrange the slices in a greased ovenproof dish. Season the thick sauce with salt and pepper to taste, sieve it, mix with the cheese, then pour it over the meat. Return the meat to the hot oven for several minutes. Serve with coleslaw or lamb's lettuce salad.

serves 6–8 • Preparation: 5 mins • Cooking: ca 90 mins • Baking: 5–7 mins

Roast pork with herbs

1 kg boneless loin of pork, 3 cloves of garlic, ½ tsp each dried sage and dried mint, salt, pepper, 1 tsp olive oil, 1 tbsp lard, ½ cup stock

Blend the finely chopped garlic with the herbs, salt, pepper and oil. Rub the mixture into the rinsed and dried meat, wrap the loin in foil and leave in a cool place for 2–3 hours. Brown the meat on all sides in hot lard, sprinkle it with water and put into a preheated oven. Cook it covered for an hour, occasionally basting with the roasting juices. Serve hot, with noodles or baked potatoes and the pan drippings, or cold.

serves 4–6 • Marinating: 2–3 hrs • Roasting: ca 1 hr

Loin of pork with apples and oranges

2 kg boneless loin of pork, 500 g tart apples, 2–3 oranges, 250 g prunes, ½ cup dry white wine, ½ tsp sugar, 1 tbsp butter, 1 tbsp fat

MARINADE: 1 cup wine vinegar, ¾ cup water, 3 tbsps olive oil, 1 glass vodka, 2 small onions, 5–7 cloves of garlic, 1 tsp each juniper berries and coriander grains, 1 tbsp peppercorns, 2 bay leaves, 1 tsp dried tarragon, 1 tbsp salt

Pound the coriander, bay leaves, pepper and juniper in a mortar. Bring I cup of water with the vinegar to the boil, put in the spices, sliced onion, garlic crushed with salt and tarragon. Simmer under cover for 10 mins, then take off the heat, add the oil and vodka and stir well. Put the rinsed, dried and lightly pounded meat into a stoneware dish, pour over the marinade, cover and weigh it down. Stand it for 4–5 days in a cool place, turning the meat over every day so that it is thoroughly impregnated with the marinade. Take the meat out, dry it and place in a greased roasting tin. Pour over the melted butter and put into a pre-heated oven for 10–12 mins. When the meat has browned nicely, turn down the heat and cook for 90–100 mins, basting often with the strained marinade. Rinse and drain the prunes, put into a pan, cover with ⅓ of the wine and cook over low heat. Cut the oranges into thick slices, remove the pips; pour over half of the remaining wine and cook. Cut the apples into quarters, sprinkle them with sugar, add the remaining wine and cook them. Arrange the sliced meat in an ovenproof dish, put the cooked fruit around it. Combine the reduced pan drippings with the wine from the fruit and heat up. Pour ⅓ of the sauce over the meat. Put the meat into the hot oven for a few minutes. Serve the remaining sauce in a sauce boat.

serves 6–8 • Preparation: 15 mins • Marinating:
4–5 days • Roasting: 2 hrs • Baking: 5–7 mins

Roast loin of pork with prune sauce

1 kg loin of pork off the bone, salt, pepper, 1 tbsp lard

SAUCE: 150 g prunes, 1 tbsp grated horseradish,
a pinch of each sugar and cinnamon, 1 tbsp
butter, 1 tsp flour, 1 glass white wine

Rinse the meat, rub it with salt and leave in a cool place for an hour, then put it into a preheated oven and cook for 90 mins, basting frequently with the pan drip-pings and with water. Soak the prunes overnight in a small amount of water, then cook and sieve them. Make a roux from the butter and flour, dillute it with the wine, add the puréed prunes, horseradish, sugar and cinnamon, and salt if required. Mix thoroughly and quickly heat up. Cut the meat into slices, pour over some pan drippings. Serve with potato noodles and with the sauce.

serves 4–6 • Salting: 1 hr • Roasting: 90 mins

Loin of pork, Old Polish style

ca 1 kg boneless loin of pork, 1 tsp lemon juice,
2 tsps marjoram, 100 g stoned prunes, 2 tbsps
honey, 2 large onions, 1 tbsp lard, 1 tbsp any
fat, ½ cup dry white wine, salt, pepper

Sprinkle the rinsed and dried meat with lemon juice, rub it with salt, pepper and half the marjoram, wrap in foil and leave for 3–4 hours in a cool place. Then brown the meat on all sides in hot lard, transfer it to a roasting tin, sprinkle with some wine and hot fat and put into a preheated oven for 20 mins. Soak the prunes in water for a while, then cook them briefly. Chop the peeled onions finely. Put the onion on top of the meat, place the prunes around, sprinkle with water in which they soaked and the remaining wine. Cover the tin and return the meat to the oven for another 40–50 mins. Take the meat out, leave it to cool a bit. Cut it into slices and arrange in an ovenproof dish. Add the remaining marjoram to the sauce, as well as the honey and pepper. Bring to the boil, then sieve it. Pour the sauce over the meat and put the dish into the hot oven for a few minutes. Serve with potato dumplings or baked potatoes.

serves 4–6 • Marinating: 3–4 hrs • Roasting: 1 hr • Baking: 4–5 mins

Pork tenderloin in orange sauce

500 g tenderloin of pork, ½ cup chicken stock, ½ cup
dry sherry, juice and grated rind of 1 orange, 1 tbsp
chopped sage leaves, 2 tbsps butter, salt, pepper,
1 tbsp lemon juice, 1 tbsp corn or potato flour, 1 small
orange and several sage leaves for garnishing

Sprinkle the rinsed and dried meat with lemon juice, rub it with salt and pepper and leave in a cool place for sev-eral minutes. Melt the butter in a skillet, brown the meat on all sides, pour in the sherry, chopped garlic and sage, and the orange zest. Bring to the boil, put the lid on and simmer for 20 mins, turning the meat over in the process. Take out the meat, transfer it to a hot serving dish and keep warm. Sieve the sauce and bring it to the boil. Mix the flour with the orange juice, pour into the sauce and, stirring all the time, heat up until the sauce has thickened. Season to taste. Cut the meat into diagonal slices, pour some of the sauce over, garnish with orange wedges and sage leaves. Serve the remaining sauce separately.

serves 4 • Preparation: 15 mins • Cooking: 20–25 mins

Pork tenderloin with apples

3–4 pork fillets, 3 large tart apples, 2 onions, 3 tbsps herbes de Provence, salt, pepper, 2 tbsps lemon juice, 1 tsp grated lemon rind, 3 tbsps olive oil, 1 tbsp butter

Sprinkle the rinsed and dried meat with 1 tbsp of lemon juice, rub it with salt, pepper and 2 tbsps of herbs and leave in a cool place for half an hour. Cut the peeled onion into thin slices. Heat 2 tbsps of oil in a pan, brown the meat on all sides, put in the onion and fry it, but do not let it brown. Take the meat off the heat but keep it warm. Cut the peeled apples into cubes. Heat 1 tbsp of oil in another pan, put in the apples, sprinkle them with the remaining herbs, add salt, pepper, lemon zest and the remaining lemon juice and, stirring all the time, cook for a while. Grease an ovenproof dish with butter, arrange the meat cut into diagonal slices in it. Put around the onion and apples and place in the hot oven for several minutes. Serve with scooped out potato balls, rice or noodles.

serves 4 • Macerating: 30–40 mins • Preparation: 20 mins • Baking: 10 mins

Streaky bacon with apricots

1–1½ lean raw streaky bacon, 100–150 g each dried apricots and prunes, 3 tart apples, 1 large onion, 3–4 cloves of garlic, 2 tsps sugar, 1 tsp marjoram, ½ glass dry white wine, 1 cup stock, 1 tbsp lard, salt, pepper

Blanch the rinsed prunes and apricots, drain them, put into a bowl, sprinkle with sugar, cover with the wine and leave aside for an hour. Mix the finely chopped garlic with salt, pepper and marjoram. Rub the mixture into the rinsed and dried bacon and leave it in a cool place. Roll up the bacon, tie it tightly with thread and brown on all sides in hot lard. Put it into a roasting tin, place thin slices of onion on top. Place in a preheated oven and sprinkle with the wine from the fruit. Cut the apricots and prunes into thin strips and the peeled apples into quarters. Add the fruit to the meat, cover the tin and cook for 90–100 mins, bast-

ing often with stock. Towards the end remove the cover. Serve hot or cold.

serves 6–8 • Macerating: 1–2 hrs • Preparation: 10 mins • Roasting: 90 mins

Pork roulade with meat and mushroom stuffing

ca 1 kg lean raw streaky bacon (a large thin piece), 1 tbsp lard, salt, pepper

STUFFING: 400 g minced pork, 200 g chanterelles, 1 small leek, 1 egg, 1 tsp salt, ½ tsp each pepper and rosemary

Rinse and dry the bacon, rub it with salt and pepper. Rinse the mushrooms and put them into lightly salted boiling water for 2–4 mins. Drain and dice them, combine with the finely chopped leek and the minced meat. Break in the egg, add salt, pepper and rosemary and work into a smooth paste. Spread the stuffing on the bacon. Roll it tightly, tie with thread, brush with the lard and put into a roasting bag. Place in a roasting tin and put into a preheated oven. Cook for 80–90 mins, from time to time sprinkling lightly with water. Serve hot, with potatoes and Brussels sprouts cooked with ginger, or cold, with a spicy sauce.

serves 6–8 • Preparation: 10 mins • Roasting: 80–90 mins

Pork roulade, Lithuanian style

ca 1½ boneless pork (shoulder or ham), 1 tbsp lard, 2–3 tomatoes or 1 tbsp tomato paste, 1 carrot, 1 parsley root, ½ celeriac, 1 bay leaf, ½ cup thick sour cream, 5 grains each allspice and pepper

STUFFING: 5–6 marinated herring, 4–5 dried cep mushrooms, 50 g pork fat, 1 tbsp capers, 1 large onion, 1 tbsp lard, ½ bread roll soaked in milk, 1 egg, salt, pepper

Soak the mushrooms overnight in water, then cook them. Skin and bone the soaked herring. Put the squeezed out bread roll, pork fat, mushrooms and herring (and some meat trimmings) through a mincer. Fry the onion in fat, but do not let it brown. Add the onion, capers, salt, pepper and egg to the mixture and work into a smooth paste. Rinse and dry the meat, cut it lengthwise,

Pork roulade with meat and mushroom stuffing

but not whole way through. Open it up and pound lightly with a mallet, then sprinkle with salt and pepper. Spread the stuffing evenly on top. Roll the meat up, tie tightly with thread. Dredge lightly with flour and brown on all sides in hot lard. Transfer it to a roasting tin, add the coarsely grated vegetables, tomato quarters, pepper, allspice and bay leaf. Sprinkle with the mushroom stock, cover and put into a preheated oven for 80–90 mins. Take the meat out. Sieve the sauce, fold in the cream mixed with flour, heat it up. Arrange the sliced meat on a hot serving platter and serve the sauce separately. It is best with bread dumplings, potato dumplings or potatoes.

serves 6–8 • Preparation: 20 mins • Roasting: 90 mins

Pork roulade with walnut and mushroom stuffing

ca 1½ kg boneless pork (ham or shoulder), 2 tbsps lemon juice, 1 tbsp lard, 2–3 tbsps dry white wine, salt, pepper

STUFFING: 50 g dried cep mushrooms, 2 tbsps chopped walnuts, 200 g minced veal, 3 tbsps butter, 3–4 egg yolks, ¼ tsp grated nutmeg, 1 small onion, ½ tbsp any fat

Cut the rinsed and dried meat lengthwise, but not whole way through. Open it up, pound lightly with a mallet and shape into a rectangle. Rub it with salt and pepper, sprinkle with lemon juice. Wrap in foil and leave in the fridge for 2–3 hours. Rinse the mushrooms and soak them in a small amount of water. Cook the mushrooms, chop them finely. Fry the finely chopped onion, but do not let it brown. Combine the mushrooms and onion with with the minced veal. Cream 3 tbsps of butter, adding one egg yolk at a time, season with salt, pepper and nutmeg to taste. Fold in the minced meat and walnuts. Take the pork out, spread it out. Arrange evenly the stuffing on top, roll the meat up, tie with thread. Brown it on all sides in lard, then transfer to a roasting tin, pour over the melted fat and wine and put into a preheated oven. Baste frequently first with the mushroom stock, then with the roasting juices.

Serve hot, with potatoes, lettuce or broccoli, or cold, with a savoury sauce.

serves 6–8 • Marinating: 2–3 hrs • Preparation: 15 mins • Roasting: 90 mins

Pork ragout with pears

500 g lean boneless pork (shoulder or ham), 1 large leek (only the white part), 500 g firm pears, 1 tbsp lemon juice, 1 large white onion, 1 tbsp sugar, 2–3 tbsps olive oil, ¼ tsp each ground caraway, cinnamon and black pepper, a pinch of cayenne pepper, 5–6 spring onions, 1 tbsp each chopped dill and parsley, ½ cup dry white wine, 1 cup boiled water

Cut the rinsed meat into fairly large cubes, chop the onion finely, wash thoroughly and slice the leek into rings. Peel and core the pears, cut them into half-slices and sprinkle with the lemon juice. Heat up 1½ to 2 tbsps of oil in a double-bottomed pan, fry the onion, but do not let it brown. Sprinkle with the caraway, cinnamon, black pepper and cayenne and, stirring all the time, fry for a bit longer. Put in the meat and brown it well, then add the water and simmer for an hour, occasionally sprinkling with the wine. Heat the remaining oil in another pan, put in the leek and fry it without browning, add the pears, sprinkle them with the wine, water and sugar, and cook for 20 mins, until the sugar becomes caramelized. Combine with the meat, stir and cook for another 30 mins, adding some wine and water if required. Add salt and pepper to taste. Chop finely the spring onions, mix them with the dill and parsley and sprinkle on top of the meat before serving. Serve with rice, kasha or noodles.

serves 4 • Preparation: 20–25 mins • Cooking: 90 mins

Pork and sorrel bake

700 g minced pork, 200 g sorrel, 1 cup breadcrumbs, 1 large finely grated onion, 2–3 cloves of garlic, 2 tbsps butter, 2 tbsps cream, salt, pepper

Mix the minced meat with the breadcrumbs, finely chopped garlic, grated onion and cream, add salt and pepper. Drain the rinsed sorrel. Grease an ovenproof dish liberally with butter. Put in alternating layers of meat and sorrel, finishing off with the meat. Sprinkle with melted butter on top, cover with aluminium foil, place in a tin

Pork ragout with pears

filled with water and put into a very hot oven. Cook for 40–45 mins. Serve hot or cold with spicy sauces.

serves 4–6 • Preparation: 5–7 mins • Baking: 40–45 mins

Roast spare ribs

1 kg spare ribs, 50 g stoned prunes and dried apricots, 1–2 tbsps raisins, 1–2 tbsps honey, 4–5 cloves of garlic, 3–4 tbsps soya sauce, ½ tsp ground pepper, ¼ tsp each ground ginger, cinnamon and aniseed, 1–2 tbsps oil, 1 cup dry white wine

Mix the finely chopped garlic with salt, pepper, cinnamon, ginger and aniseed, add 1 tbsp of honey, oil and soya sauce. Rub the mixture into the rinsed and dried spare ribs. Wrap the ribs in foil and put into the fridge for several hours. Put the prunes and apricots into a pan, cover with water and cook for a few minutes. Place the spare ribs on a greased baking sheet, put into a pre-heated oven, sprinkle sparingly with some fruit stock and bake for 25 mins. Turn over, spread with the prunes and apricots, sprinkle with the remaining stock and bake for another 25 mins. Arrange the spare ribs divided into portions on a hot serving dish. Sieve the sauce, pour it into a pan, add the remaining honey, wine and raisins, bring to the boil. Reduce the liquid, add salt and pepper to taste. Sprinkle the ribs with some sauce. Serve the remaining sauce separately.

serves 4 • Macerating: 4–6 hrs • Preparation: 15 mins • Roasting: 50–60 mins

Carpathian goulash with prunes

400 g boneless pork, 300 g boneless mutton, 300 g onions, 200 g stoned prunes, grated rind and juice of 1 small lemon, 1 cup stock, 1 cup dry white wine, 1 tbsp lard, 2 tbsps butter, 1 tbsp flour, salt, pepper, paprika, a pinch of grated nutmeg

Leave the rinsed prunes to soak in wine. Rinse and dry the meat and cut it into strips, sprinkle with salt, pepper, paprika and flour. Dice the onions into half slices. Heat the lard in a double-bottomed pan, brown the meat, add the butter and onion and fry for a minute or two, stirring frequently. Pour in the stock and lemon juice, add

the lemon zest, put the lid on and simmer for 30 mins. Put in the prunes together with the wine, stir well and cook for another 30 mins. Towards the end season with nutmeg, pepper and salt as required. Serve with rice or noodles.

serves 6–8 • Preparation: 10 mins • Cooking: 1 hr

Old Polish goulash with cep mushrooms

600 g lean pork, 50 g dried cep mushrooms, 200 g green peas (tinned or frozen), 2 cups stock, salt, pepper, 1½ tbsps flour

Rinse the mushrooms, cover them with 1 cup of stock and cook. Cut the rinsed and dried meat into strips, sprinkle with the flour and fry in very hot lard. Transfer the meat to a skillet, add the mushrooms cut into strips, salt and pepper. Pour in the remaining stock and the mushroom stock, put the lid on and cook for 30 mins. Add the peas, stir thoroughly, season with salt and pepper to taste and simmer for several minutes longer. Serve with kasha, pasta or potatoes.

serves 4–6 • Preparation: 20 mins • Cooking: 40 mins

Pork roulade with garlic and herbs

1 kg lean raw streaky bacon, 1 tsp salt, 6–7 cloves of garlic, pepper, ¼ tsp each marjoram, basil, savory, mint and sage, ½ tbsp lard

Mix the finely chopped garlic with salt, herbs and pepper. Rub the mixture into the rinsed and dried bacon. Roll the bacon tightly, tie it with thread, put into a bowl and leave overnight in a cool place. Brown it on all sides in hot lard, turn the heat down. Rinse the bowl with cold water. Pour the water into the bacon, put a lid on and simmer for 90 mins, occasionally adding a spoonful of water to prevent the bacon burning. Transfer the bacon to a serving platter, pour the cooking juices in and leave to set. Serve cold, cut into thin slices, with horseradish or green sauce.

serves 4–6 • Macerating: 12–24 hrs • Cooking: 90 mins

Pork ragout with prunes

250 g boneless shoulder of pork, 250 g boneless beef, 250 g onion, 250 g prunes and 250 g tart apples, 4 tbsps oil, 1 cup cider or apple juice, 1 cup stock, ½ cup sour cream, salt, pepper, sugar, 2–3 tbsps chopped lemon balm leaves

Rinse the prunes and soak them in a small amount of water. Rinse and dry the meat, cut it into cubes. Sprinkle with salt and pepper and brown in the hot oil, then transfer to a skillet. Fry the finely chopped onion in the same fat (do not let it brown) and add to the meat together with the prunes. Pour in the stock and cider (or juice), cover and put into a preheated oven for 50–60 mins. Cut the peeled and cored apples into thick cubes. Take the meat out of the oven, add the apples, lemon balm, salt, pepper and sugar and cook covered over low heat for 10–15 mins. Towards the end fold in the cream.

serves 4 • Preparation: 15–20 mins • Cooking: over 1 hr

Marinated pork fricassee

750 g lean shoulder of pork (off the bone), salt, pepper, 2 tbsps oil, ½ cup thick cream

MARINADE: 2 each carrots, parsley roots and onions, 4–5 cloves of garlic, 1–2 cloves, 5–6 peppercorns, 1 bay leaf, 1 tsp dried thyme, 3–4 finely chopped sage leaves

Peel the vegetables, dice them, put into a pan. Add the remaining ingredients of the marinade, pour in the wine and mix well. Rinse the meat, cut it into slices, put into the marinade. Cover and leave at the bottom shelf of the fridge for 4 days, turning the meat over every day. Take the meat out, dry it, cut into pieces. Cook the marinade, covered, over low heat for 10 mins, then put it through a blender and sieve it. Heat the oil in a pan, brown the meat, sprinkle it with salt and pepper, cover with the marinade and simmer, covered, for one hour. Fold in the cream and heat up. Serve with noodles or macaroni and with salads.

serves 4–6 • Marinating: 4 days • Preparation: 15 mins • Cooking: 1 hr

Pig's knuckles – a man's delight

This is the lower and exceptionally tasty part of the hind leg of pork, and for years has been the favourite dish of many men. It is an extremely popular dish in German cuisine, and has been a particular favourite in Poland in the cuisine of Silesia and the Poznań region.

Knuckle of pork can be cooked fresh, pickled or smoked. It can be boiled, braised or roast. There are a great many different views on how it ought to be cooked. Some people boil it with soup vegetables, others only with spices. Some claim that there is nothing to beat stuffed knuckle of pork stewed in beer with cloves.

The most popular accompaniments to boiled knuckle of pork are puréed peas and finely shredded horseradish. In the Poznań region, knuckle of pork is usually served with boiled red cabbage, and in Silesia with pea purée and stewed sauerkraut.

This fairly fatty, tasty and not very digestible dish goes excellently with a pint of cold beer or a glass of ice-cold clear vodka; I am not, of course, encouraging drinking, but this is in the interests of aiding the digestion.

Pig's knuckles pickled in brine

4 small knuckles, soup vegetables, 2–4 grains each allspice and pepper, 1 bay leaf, 1 onion, 1 clove

BRINE: 1 tsp each ground coriander, pepper and allspice, 2–3 bay leaves, 2–4 cloves, 2–3 cloves of garlic, 1 tbsp salt, 1 tsp saltpetre

Mix the finely chopped garlic with the salt, saltpetre and spices. Divide the mixture into two parts. Bone the rinsed knuckles, spread half of the mixture on the meat and rub it in. Arrange the meat tightly in a stoneware jar, cover with a wooden board, weigh it down and put into the fridge for 2 days. Boil 1½ to 2 cups of water with the remaining mixture, allow it to cool, then pour over the meat. Stand the meat in a cool place for 8–10 days, turning it over every second day so it is thoroughly impregnated with the brine. Now take the meat out of the brine, wash and dry it thoroughly. Roll up each knuckle, tie it with cotton thread and put into a large pan. Add the spices, onion and vegetables, cover with water and bring to the boil, then simmer over low heat until tender. Serve with puréed peas, with horseradish or mustard.

serves 4 • Marinating: 2+8–10 days • Preparation:
5–7 mins • Cooking: 60–70 mins

Pig's knuckles with ginger

2 large knuckles, soup vegetables, 30 g dried cep mushrooms, 1 glass brandy, 2 tbsps soya sauce, 1 tsp ground ginger, salt, pepper, 2 tbsps lemon juice

Clean and wash the knuckles, prick them with a fork, rub with the salt and pepper, sprinkle with the lemon juice. Arrange them tightly in a large pan, cover and leave overnight in the fridge. Rinse the mushrooms, cover them with water and leave to soak overnight. Put the knuckles into a large pan, cover with water, bring to the boil, then cook for 40 mins. Add the soup vegetables, pour in the mushrooms and simmer for an hour. Take out the knuckles, remove the bones. Cut the meat into portions, arrange them in a skillet. Sprinkle with the ginger and soya sauce. Cut the mushrooms into thin strips, add them to the meat. Strain the stock and pour some of it into the skillet. Simmer the meat over low heat for 20–30 mins, adding the brandy towards the end. Serve with rice and lettuce.

serves 4 • Macerating: 12–24 hrs • Cooking: 40 mins • Braising: 20–30 mins

Pig's knuckles in prune sauce

2 large knuckles, 1 cup dry red wine, 1 cup wine vinegar, salt, 2–3 bay leaves, ½ tsp pepper, 1–2 tsps juniper berries, 200 g prunes, 1½ tsps honey, ¼ tsp cinnamon, 1 tbsp butter

Clean and singe the knuckles, wash them, put into a pan. Cover with 4 cups of water and 1 cup of wine vinegar, add the spices and cook for 90 mins. Add some water to the rinsed prunes and cook them, then put through a blender and sieve. Take out the knuckles, remove the bones. Divide the meat into portions, place in an ovenproof dish. Brown the breadcrumbs lightly, add the

butter, honey, cinnamon, puréed prunes and wine, mix and heat up. Pour the sauce over the meat. Put the dish into a preheated oven for several minutes.

serves 4 • Cooking: 90 mins • Preparation: 10 mins • Baking: 10–15 mins

Pig's trotters

4 pig's trotters, 2 large onions, 5–6 cloves, 2 bay leaves, a bunch of parsley, 3–4 sprigs of thyme, ½ celery sticks, ¼ tsp each dried savory, basil and rosemary, 2 onions, 200 g mushrooms, 2 tbsps mustard, 3–4 tbsps breadcrumbs, 2 tbsps thick cream, 1 cup wine (Madeira), salt, pepper, cayenne pepper

Bring salted water to the boil, put in the onions studded with cloves, bay leaves, parsley, thyme sprigs, celery and dried herbs. Bring to the boil again, cover and simmer for 10 mins. Put in the cleaned and washed trotters and cook over low heat for ca 3 hours, then leave to cool. Take out the trotters, remove the bones, divide the meat into small portions. Spread some mustard on each portion, dredge it with breadcrumbs. Arrange in an ovenproof dish greased with butter, put into a preheated oven and bake for 15 mins. Fry the finely chopped onions in melted butter, but do not let it brown. Put in the diced mushrooms and sauté them. Turn down the heat, add salt, pepper, cayenne and wine, mix well. Fold in the cream and heat up for 2–3 mins (keeping the sauce off the boil). Before serving, pour the sauce over the meat.

serves 4 • Preparation: 10 mins • Cooking: 3 hrs
• Cooling: 2 hrs • Baking: 15 mins

Pork escalopes à l'orientale

800 g pork tenderloin, 3 tbsps soya sauce, 1 tbsp oil, 1½ tbsps lemon juice, 2 cloves of garlic, ¼ tsp each dried thyme and rosemary, ½ tsp honey, 1 tbsp lard, 4 tbsps single cream, 1 tsp potato flour, salt

Rinse the meat, cut it into slices (2–3 per person), press them down lightly and put into a bowl. Mix the crushed garlic with the honey, herbs, lemon juice and soya sauce, pour the mixture over the meat. Mix well, cover and leave in the fridge for an hour. Take the meat out, dry it and sauté in hot fat in a frying pan, then transfer it to a saucepan. Pour the remaining marinade into the frying pan, bring it to the boil, add the potato flour mixed with the cream and, stirring all the time, heat it up. Pour the sauce over the meat, cover the pan and simmer for a while. Serve with rice or French noodles.

serves 4–6 • Macerating: 1–2 hrs • Preparation: 10–15 mins

Pork fillets with lemon balm

600 g saddle of pork (off the bone), 250 g onion, 2 large tart apples, 1 cup cider, 2 tbsps apple jelly, 2 tbsps finely chopped lemon balm leaves, 2 tbsps cranberry jam, 2 tbsps oil, 1 tbsp butter, 1 tsp potato flour, salt, pepper

Cut the rinsed and dried meat into large slices, pound them lightly with a wet mallet. Shape them into fillets, sprinkle with salt and pepper. Brown on both sides in the hot oil, take out of the frying pan but keep them warm. Put some butter into the frying pan, sauté the onion cut into thin slices, but do not let it brown. Add the apples cut into slices and fry for a minute or two, then put in the fillets, sprinkle them with the wine and simmer for 4–5 mins. Combine the apple jelly with the cranberry jam, add them to the meat, stir gently and simmer for another 2–3 mins. Mix the potato flour with 2 tbsps of cold water, pour into the meat and heat up, stirring gently, until the sauce has thickened. Add salt and pepper to taste, put in the chopped lemon balm. Serve with baked potato purée or walnut and potato croquettes.

serves 4 • Preparation: 15–20 mins

Pork fillets with garlic, onion and rosemary

600 g loin of pork (off the bone), 2 onions, 1 tbsp lemon juice, 1 tsp grated lemon rind, 1 tbsp rosemary, 3–4 cloves of garlic, salt, pepper, 1 tbsp lard, 1 tbsp butter, 1 tbsp flour, 1 glass dry white wine

Cut the rinsed and dried meat into 4 fillets, pound them lightly with a mallet. Mix the crushed garlic with salt, pepper, rosemary, lemon juice and zest. Rub the fillets with the mixture, put them one on top of the other, cover and leave in the fridge for an hour. Melt the butter in a saucepan, fry the finely chopped onion, but do not let it brown.

Dredge the fillets with flour and fry them on both sides in the hot lard. Transfer them to the saucepan, sprinkle with the wine and simmer for a while.

serves 4 • Macerating: 1–2 hrs • Preparation: 15 mins

Pork chops, Italian style

700 g neck of pork (off the bone), 2–3 cloves of garlic, ½ tsp each ground pepper and fennel seeds, salt, 1 tbsp lemon juice, 1 tbsp flour, 1 glass dry white wine, 4 tbsps grated Parmesan, 3 tbsps oil, 2 tbsps butter, 1 cup stock, 3 tbsps tomato paste, sugar

Cut the rinsed and dried meat into 4 slices, pound them lightly with a mallet, sprinkle with lemon juice, pepper and fennel, spread some oil on top. Place the chops one on top of the other and leave aside for 20 mins. Dredge them with flour and fry on both sides in the hot oil. Arrange the meat in an ovenproof dish greased with butter, sprinkle with the wine, cover and put into a preheated oven. Put the finely chopped garlic into the frying pan, add the tomato paste, pour in the stock, add salt, sugar and pepper to taste and bring to the boil. Pour the sauce over the chops, sprinkle the cheese on top, put pats of butter and return to the oven for 10 mins. Serve with rice, macaroni or French fries.

serves 4 • Macerating: 20–30 mins • Preparation: 15 mins • Baking: 10 mins

Pork chops with cabbage

4 pork chops on the bone, 1 tbsp fresh chopped sage leaves, 1 small cabbage, ½ cup thick cream, 2 tbsps butter, ½ cup dry white wine, 3 tbsps grated cheese, salt, pepper, ¼ tsp dried sage, 1 tbsp lard

Pound the rinsed and dried chops with a mallet, sprinkle them with salt, pepper and dried sage. Rinse the cabbage and put it into boiling lightly salted water for 5–6 mins, then take it out and rinse under cold water. Shred the cabbage, put into a large pan, add salt and pepper, pour in the cream, stir thoroughly, cover and simmer over very low heat for 30 mins, stirring from time to time. Fry the chops on both sides in the hot lard, then take them out of the frying pan. Put in the fresh sage and wine into the same pan, bring to the boil, then pour the mixture into the cabbage.

Pork fillets, Chinese style

Grease an ovenproof dish with butter, line it with half the cabbage, put the chops on top and cover with the remaining cabbage. Sprinkle with the cheese, put in knobs of butter and place in a preheated oven. Bake for 40 mins.

serves 4 • Preparation: 40 mins • Baking: 40 mins

Pork fillets, Chinese style

600 g loin of pork (off the bone), 10–12 dried Chinese black mushrooms, 5–6 spring onions, 2 red peppers, 1 yellow pepper, 1 jar of pickled baby cobs, 3–4 cloves of garlic, ¼ cup soya sauce, 1 glass dry sherry, 2 egg whites, 1½ tbsps potato flour, pepper, sugar, salt, 2 tbsps oil, 2 tbsps sesame oil

Rinse the mushrooms, add several tablespoons of hot water to them and leave for half an hour to soak. Cut the rinsed and dried meat into thin slices, pound them lightly with the handle of a knife and shape into fillets. Mix the potato flour with salt and the lightly whisked egg whites. Rub the fillets with the mixture, put them on a plate and place in the fridge for half an hour. Chop the rinsed onions. Cut the rinsed and cored peppers into thin strips. Drain the mushrooms (keep the water), cut off the stalks and chop the caps into thin strips. Heat the oil in a large frying pan (or a wok), sauté the fillets, add the finely chopped garlic, peppers and mushrooms and fry for a minute or two, stirring all the time. Put in the onions and the drained corn cobs. Mix the mushroom water, soya sauce and sherry with sugar and pepper. Pour the mixture into the pan, bring to the boil, then simmer for 5 mins. Serve with macaroni or rice.

serves 4 • Macerating: 30 mins • Preparation: 10–15 mins

Spicy pork chops

600 g loin of pork (off the bone), 2 large onions, 3–5 cloves of garlic, ½ tsp each paprika, ground cardamom and coriander, ¼ tsp each ground caraway, ginger and mustard seeds, salt, 3 tbsps oil, ½ cup yogurt, 1 tbsp lemon juice

Cut the rinsed and dried meat into 4 chops, pound them lightly with a mallet. Grate the peeled onions. Finely chop the garlic and mix it with salt, lemon juice,

1 tbsp of oil and all the spices. Rub the chops with the mixture, put them one on top of the other, cover and leave in the fridge for 2–3 hours. Then fry them on both sides in the hot lard, sprinkle with the yogurt, put the lid on and simmer for 20 mins. Best served with rice.

serves 4 • Macerating: 2–3 hrs • Preparation: 25–30 mins

Pork fillets with apples

600 g boneless pork (loin or ham), 1 glass vodka, 4 tart apples, 1 tsp lemon juice, ¼ cup stock, ½ cup cream, salt, pepper, flour, 1 tsp lard, 2 tbsps butter

Peel and grate 2 apples, sprinkle them with the lemon juice and put through a blender together with the stock, salt, and pepper. Cut the rinsed and dried meat into 4 fillets, pound them lightly with a mallet and dredge with flour. Heat the lard in a frying pan, add 1 tbsp of butter and sauté the fillets for 4 mins to each side. Take off the heat, sprinkle with some vodka and arrange in an ovenproof dish greased with butter. Rinse and dry the remaining apples, halve and core them, make deep incisions in each half. Sauté the apple halves in the same frying pan. Combine the apple purée with the cream and the remaining vodka. Put the apple halves on top of the fillets, pour over the apple sauce, put in knobs of butter and place in a preheated oven. Bake for 20 mins. Serve with baked potatoes or French fries.

serves 4 • Preparation: 10–15 mins • Baking: 20 mins

Gdynia pork medallions with fruit

600 g loin of pork (off the bone), 4 peach halves (fresh or tinned), 100 g grated cheese, salt, pepper, 1 tbsp lemon juice, 1 tbsp each flour and lard, 2 tbsps butter

Cut the rinsed and dried meat into 4 chops, pound them lightly with a mallet and shape into oval medallions. Sprinkle with lemon juice, salt and pepper, dredge with flour and fry on both sides in the hot lard. Grease an ovenproof dish with butter, arrange the medallions in it, place one peach half on top of each, sprinkle with the cheese and put in pats of butter. Put into a preheated oven and bake until the cheese has melted. Garnish with a thick cold cranberry and horseradish sauce. Serve with French fries and lettuce.

serves 4 • Preparation: 10 mins • Baking: 15–20 mins

Grilled pork steaks

600–700 g neck of pork (off the bone)

MARINADE: ½ cup olive oil, ¼ cup each dry red wine and wine vinegar, 2 tbsps each soya sauce and Tabasco, 1 tbsp finely chopped fresh ginger (or 1 tbsp powdered ginger), 1 tbsp chopped thyme leaves

Mix all the marinade ingredients thoroughly. Cut the rinsed and dried meat diagonally into 4 slices, pound them lightly with a mallet. Spread the marinade on the meat slices, arrange them in a bowl, pour the remaining marinade over, cover and leave in the fridge for several hours. Grill the meat, basting it frequently with the marinade, or fry it in very hot fat.

serves 4 • Marinating: 5–7 hrs • Grilling: 20–30 mins

Pork medallions with herbs

600 g loin of pork (off the bone), salt, pepper, 2 tbsps olive oil, 1 tbsp butter, 2–3 cloves of garlic, 1 tbsp each chopped fresh marjoram, thyme and savory leaves, 3 tbsps chopped parsley, 1 tbsp lemon juice, ¼ cup dry white wine (or stock)

Cut the rinsed and dried meat into 4 portions, pound them lightly with a mallet, shape into oval medallions. Sprinkle with salt and pepper, rub sparingly with oil and leave aside for 10 mins, then fry in the hot oil. Take them out of the pan and keep warm. Put the chopped garlic and herbs into the pan, add the butter and, stirring all the time, fry for 1–2 mins, then pour in the wine and stir well. Put in the meat, cover the pan and simmer for 10 mins.

serves 4 • Preparation: 20–25 mins • Cooking: 10 mins

Gingery pork shashliks

500 loin of pork (off the bone), 2 small courgettes, 1 each red, yellow and green pepper, 2 onions

Pork medallions with herbs

MARINADE: 30 g fresh ginger, 3 tbsps dry white wine, 2 tbsps each soya sauce and oil, 1 tbsp tomato paste, ¼ tsp ground pepper, ½ tbsp Chinese seasoning

Peel the ginger and cut it into small cubes, mix with the tomato paste, wine, soya sauce and oil, add the pepper and Chinese seasoning. Cut the rinsed and dried meat, onion and courgettes into thin slices. Core the peppers and cut them into fairly large pieces. Put the meat and the vegetables into a large dish, pour the marinade over, cover and place in the fridge for 3–4 hours. Thread the meat, peppers, courgettes and onion onto 4 skewers and grill them, basting frequently with the marinade.

serves 4 • Marinating: 3–4 hrs • Preparation: 15 mins • Grilling: 15–20 mins

Savoury pork schnitzels

600 g neck of pork (off the bone), 50 g fatty streaky bacon, 1 tbsp hot mustard, 1 tbsp sweet paprika, 1 tbsp flour, 2 large onions, 1 tbsp lard, 1 tbsp butter

Cut the rinsed and dried meat into 4 slices, pound them lightly with the handle of a knife, spread mustard on top of each. Mix the flour with the paprika, coat the meat with the mixture. Heat up the lard in a frying pan and fry the meat on both sides until golden brown. Melt the butter in another frying pan, put in the bacon cut into small cubes and fry it, add the diced onion and cook a bit longer, stirring all the time. Cover the schnitzels with the bacon and onion mixture and keep over low heat for a while. Best served with potatoes fried in herbs, puréed vegetables or noodles.

serves 4 • Preparation: 10 mins • Frying: 10–12 mins

Chatelaine's zrazy

800 g lean boneless pork (ham), 100 g pork fat, 1 cup stock, 1 cup dry red wine, salt, pepper, 2 tbsps sharp mustard, 2 tbsps butter, 1 tbsp flour

STUFFING: ½ cup grated wholemeal bread, 2 large onions, 2 tbsps butter, 2 eggs, salt, pepper

STUFFING: Fry the finely chopped onion in butter, but do not let it brown, add salt, pepper, grated bread and eggs and mix thoroughly.
Cut the rinsed and dried meat into thin slices, pound them lightly with a mallet, sprinkle with salt. Spread some mustard on each of them, then some stuffing. Roll up tightly, secure the end with a toothpick or tie with thread. Dredge with flour, then fry in butter. Line a braising pan with thin slices of pork fat, put in the meat rolls, pour in the stock and simmer over low heat for 30 mins. Add the wine, stir and cook for several minutes longer, then reduce the sauce a bit. Serve with noodles and lettuce.

serves 4–6 • Preparation: 10–15 mins • Cooking: 35–40 mins

Rolled pork zrazy with sauerkraut

500 g boneless pork (loin or ham), 200 g sauerkraut, 1 onion, ½ tsp caraway seeds, 1 tbsp butter, 1 tsp tomato paste, ½ cup stock, 1 tsp paprika, salt, pepper, 2 tbsps oil, 2 tbsps flour, 2 tbsps grated cheese, 1 cup yogurt

Fry the finely chopped onion in melted butter, but do not let it brown. Put in the chopped sauerkraut, add the pepper and caraway. Mix well, sprinkle with some stock and simmer for several minutes, then leave to cool. Cut the rinsed and dried meat into 4 slices, pound them with a mallet, sprinkle with salt and paprika. Put some cabbage on top of each slice, roll it up, secure the end with a toothpick or tie with thread. Dredge the rolls with flour and fry in the hot oil until golden brown on all sides. Pour in the remaining stock mixed with the tomato paste, cover and simmer for 40 mins. Transfer the meat to an oven dish. Mix the yogurt with the cooking juices and 1 tsp of flour. Pour over the meat, sprinkle with the cheese, put knobs of butter on top and place in a preheated oven. Bake for 15 mins.

serves 4 • Preparation: 30 mins • Cooking: 40 mins • Baking: 15 mins

Pork fricadelles with cheese

500 g minced pork, 200 g grated cheese, 2–3 tbsps chopped parsley, 1 tsp grated nutmeg, salt, pepper, 2 eggs, 1–2 tbsps breadcrumbs, fat for frying

Combine the meat with the cheese, add the nutmeg, parsley, salt and pepper, break in 1 egg and work into a smooth mixture. Shape into oval patties, coat with mixed egg and breadcrumbs. Fry on both sides in hot fat until golden brown. Serve with French fries or potato purée and with lettuce.

serves 4 • Preparation: 15 mins • Frying: 10–15 mins

Pork fricadelles with herbs

600 g minced pork and veal, 1 small onion, 1 tbsp butter, 1 bread roll, ¼ cup dry white wine, 1 tsp hot mustard, 2 eggs, 4 tbsps finely chopped lovage leaves, 1 tbsp each finely chopped marjoram and rosemary leaves, salt, pepper, flour, oil for frying

Soak the bread roll in wine. Fry the finely chopped onion in butter, but do not let it brown. Combine the meat with the onion, bread roll and herbs, add the mustard, salt and pepper, break in the eggs and work into a smooth mixture. Shape into oval patties, coat with flour and deep fry in the hot oil. Serve with rice, with ketchup or tomato sauce.

serves 4 • Preparation: 15 mins • Frying: 10–15 mins

Pork steaks in cheese sauce

600 g loin of pork (off the bone), 2 tbsps butter, 1 glass dry white wine, 1 cup cream, 1 tsp each chopped marjoram, thyme and sage leaves, 120 g Camembert (without skin), 1 tbsp Dijon mustard, salt, pepper, several sprigs of parsley

Whisk the cream lightly. Cut the rinsed and dried meat into thin slices, pound them lightly with a mallet, sprinkle with pepper. Fry the meat in melted butter in a large frying pan, then transfer it to an ovenproof dish and keep warm. Pour the wine into the frying pan, stir well, scraping the bottom, put in the herbs and bring to the boil. Fold in the mustard and cream, add the cheese cut into pieces, season to taste and heat up until the cheese has melted. Pour over the meat. Before serving, garnish with parsley sprigs.

serves 4 • Preparation: 10 mins • Frying: 8–10 mins

Veal

'*The best season for veal is from May to September*,' advised Marta Norkowska 150 years ago in her famous manual, *Dwór wiejski*, and for a fricandeau she recommended meat from the saddle, thickly larded with bacon fat, fried and then braised with a bit of stock.

She advised that the '*roast should be served with the sieved pan drippings, potato purée or macaroni and spinach*'.

Veal is the meat from calves aged from two weeks to a few months, or even up to a year old. The tastiest meat comes from calves 6 to 8 weeks old; it is light pink in colour and shiny and has a slightly acid smell. Meat from calves that are too young is pale in colour, watery, soft and not too

Pork steaks in cheese sauce

tasty. For roasting, leg is best, but shoulder or saddle is also suitable.

Veal intended for roasting (a joint weighing no less than 1.5 to 2 kg) should be rinsed and then scalded in boiling water, which makes the outer fibre contract and prevents too much of the juices running out of the meat. The meat becomes more tender and delicate and gains a better flavour if we marinate it for 2 to 3 days in a wine or vinegar marinade, or soak it for 12 to 24 hours in sour milk, or sprinkle it with lemon juice, or cover it with paper-thin slices of fresh pineapple and leave it for 3 or 4 hours in the fridge.

Veal with anchovies

Cut the veal in pieces, cook it in salted water, then place it in a pan, cover with bouillon, put in a piece of butter and some grated nutmeg, and bring it to the boil. Rinse the anchovies, bone them, chop them finely, put in the pan and cook, add some lemon zest.

(Wojciech Wielądko, *Kucharz doskonały*, vol. I, p. 82)

Veal roast

2 kg leg of veal (off the bone), lemon juice,
2 cloves of garlic, salt, 2 tbsps butter

Rinse the meat, scald it with boiling water, then rub it with the garlic crushed with salt, sprinkle with the lemon juice and stand in a cool place for 2–3 hours. Grease a roasting tin with butter, put in the meat and place knobs on butter on top. Put into a very hot oven, baste frequently with butter to make the meat brown quickly. Turn the heat down and continue cooking, frequently basting with butter and water. Serve with French fries or boiled potatoes with the pan drippings, and with lettuce. It is also very tasty cold, accompanied by a piquant sauce.

serves 6–8 • Macerating: 2–3 hrs • Roasting: 90 mins

Marinated veal roast

2–3 kg leg of veal (off the bone), 150 g salt, 3 cloves of garlic, 10 g saltpetre, 1 tsp ground coriander

MARINADE: 2 tbsps salt, 1–2 bay leaves, 8–10 grains each allspice and pepper, 2–3 cloves

DOUGH: flour, a pinch of salt, fat for baking

Bring 1 cup of water to the boil, add the salt, pepper, allspice, cloves and bay leaves. Rub the rinsed and dried meat with the garlic crushed with salt and with saltpetre. Place in a stoneware dish, sprinkle with the coriander, pour over the cool marinade. Place a board on top, weigh it down. Stand in a cool place for 8–10 days, turning the meat over every day. Take the meat out, rinse and dry it. Knead a dough from the flour, salt and ½ cup of water. Roll it out to the thickness of 1 to 1½ cm. Wrap the meat up in the dough, seal the edges carefully. Place on a greased roasting tin and put into a preheated oven. Bake for 2 hours. Take it out of the oven, leave to cool, then remove the crust. Serve cold, cut into fine slices. Veal cooked in this way can also be cured in smoke or else prepared in aspic. In the latter case, place the meat slices in a large serving dish, pour over some stock made from vegetables and veal bones, then put into the fridge to set.

serves 8–10 • Marinating: 8–10 days • Preparation: 15 mins • Baking: 2 hrs

Veal roast à la venison

2 kg leg of veal (off the bone), 100 g pork fat,
1 cup thick sour cream, 1 tsp flour, 1 tsp ground juniper berries, 2 large onions, salt, 1 tbsp lard

MARINADE: 1½ cups 6% wine vinegar, 1 cup boiled water, ¼ tsp sugar, 6–8 cloves, 6–7 juniper berries, 10 grains each allspice and pepper, 1 bay leaf, juice and grated rind of 1 lemon

Rinse and dry the meat, rub it with the ground juniper, cover with the sliced onion. Place in a stoneware dish. Bring the water and vinegar to the boil, add the remaining marinade ingredients, cover and cook for 10 mins. Pour the hot marinade over the meat. Leave the meat in a cool place for 3–4 days, turning it over every day so that it gets evenly impregnated with the marinade. Cut the pork fat into thin strips, rub it with the remaining ground juniper. Take the meat out, rinse and dry it. Rub it with salt and lard with the pork fat bards. Put into a roasting tin, place

Marinated veal roast

the sliced onion around, pour the melted lard over. Place in a very hot oven (250°C) for 10–15 mins to let the meat brown. Turn the temperature down to 180°C and roast for 1½ hours, frequently basting with the drained marinade. Towards the end pour over the cream mixed with the flour. Cut the meat diagonally in slices, arrange them in an ovenproof dish and keep warm. Sieve the sauce. If you plan to serve the roast cold, do not add the cream.

serves 6–8 • Marinating: 3–4 days • Preparation: 5–6 mins • Roasting: 100 mins

Garlicky veal roast

2 kg leg of veal (off the bone), 8–10 cloves of garlic, ¼ tsp pepper, 1 tsp chilli pepper, salt, 2 tbsps butter

Crush the garlic, mix it with salt, pepper and chilli. Scald and dry the meat, rub it with the garlic mixture and leave in a cool place for 4–5 hours. Transfer it to a greased roasting tin, place knobs of butter on top and put into a preheated oven. Roast it for 90 mins, frequently basting with the butter and the juices from the dish in which the meat macerated. Serve hot, with baked potatoes and lettuce, or cold, with a savoury sauce.

serves 6–8 • Macerating: 4–5 hrs • Roasting: 90 mins

Veal roast with herbs

1½ kg boneless veal, 790 g small potatoes, 2 tbsps lard, 1 tbsp sunflower oil, salt, juice of ½ lemon, 4 cloves of garlic, ½ tsp each thyme, rosemary and mint, a pinch of salt, 2 tsps chopped dill

Mix the finely chopped garlic with the salt, pepper and herbs. Rub the scalded veal with the mixture, sprinkle with the lemon juice and leave in a cool place for 3–4 hours. Grease a roasting tin, arrange the meat in it, sprinkle it with the oil and put into a preheated oven for 45 mins, frequently basting with the pan drippings and water. Peel the potatoes, scald them with boiling water, drain well, sprinkle with some salt and thyme. Arrange them around the meat and cook for another 40 mins. Serve hot, with lettuce or cucumber salad.

serves 4–6 • Macerating: 3–4 hrs • Preparation: 10 mins • Roasting: 100 mins

Veal roast with mushrooms

1 kg boneless veal, 150 g mushrooms, 150 g pork fat, salt, pepper, juice of ½ lemon, 4–6 small onions, 1 tsp tarragon, ¼ tsp sage, 3 tbsps butter, ½ cup chicken or vegetable stock

Rub the scalded veal with salt and pepper, sprinkle with the tarragon and sage. Roll it up, wrap in thin slices of pork fat, tie tightly with thread and place in an ovenproof dish greased with butter. Surround with whole peeled onions and mushroom caps. Put into a preheated oven and roast for 90 mins, frequently basting with butter and stock. Cut diagonally into slices. Serve the meat, onions and mushrooms with boiled potatoes sprinkled with the pan drippings.

serves 4–6 • Preparation: 15–20 mins • Roasting: 80–90 mins

Spicy veal roast

1½ kg boneless veal, 4–5 cloves of garlic, ¼ tsp each ground cinnamon and cardamom, ½ tsp mace, salt, pepper, 1 tbsp lemon juice, 1 tsp honey, 2 tbsps olive oil, 1 tbsp butter, ½ cup dry white wine

Mix the finely chopped garlic with salt, pepper and half the spices (cinnamon, cardamom, mace). Rinse the meat, dry and squeeze it. Make incisions with the point of a knife, fill them with the garlicky mixture. Mix the remaining spices with the lemon juice, salt, pepper, honey and olive oil. Rub the mixture into the meat. Wrap it in foil and leave overnight in the fridge. Take the meat out of the foil, place in a roasting tin greased with butter and put into a preheated oven (240°C) for several minutes to brown it. Turn the temperature down and continue cooking, basting with the wine and then with the pan drippings.

serves 4–6 • Macerating: 12 hrs • Preparation: 15 mins • Roasting: 1½ to 2 hrs

Veal roast, Lithuanian style

2 kg leg of veal (off the bone), 1 carrot, 1 parsley root, 1 large onions, ½ celeriac, 3 tbsps hot mustard, 100 g pork fat, salt, 1 tbsp butter

Spicy veal roast

Grate the peeled and rinsed vegetables coarsely, mix them with the mustard. Rub the meat with the mixture, place it in a stoneware dish, put a board on top and weigh it down. Stand in a cool place for 3–4 days. Take the meat out, salt it, lard it with the pork fat and place in a roasting tin greased with butter. Put into a very hot oven for 10–15 mins, then turn the heat down and continue cooking for 90 mins, basting frequently with butter and with the meat juices from the marinade. If you want to serve it hot, towards the end pour 1 cup of cream mixed with 1 tsp of flour over the meat and sieve the sauce before serving.

serves 6–8 • Marinating: 3–4 days • Preparation:
5–6 mins • Roasting: 100 mins

Veal roast à l'anglaise

1½ kg boneless veal, 100 g smoked streaky bacon,
2 parsley roots, ½ celeriac, 2 large onions, 3 lemons,
salt, pepper, ½ tsp Worcestershire sauce, ½ tsp dried
sage, salt, pepper, 1 cup stock, 1 tbsp lard, 1 tbsp butter

Grate the peeled and rinsed parsley roots and celeriac coarsely, dice the onions finely. Scrub the lemons, scald them with boiling water. Grate the rind and squeeze out the juice of 2 lemons. Mix the juice and zest with the Worcestershire sauce and the vegetables and onion. Rinse the meat, dry it thoroughly, rub with the prepared mixture, wrap in foil and put into the fridge for 1–2 days. Cut the bacon into strips, sprinkle with the sage. Take the meat out of the foil, clean it of the vegetables, rub with salt and pepper and lard with the bacon bards. Shape it into an oval ball, tie tightly with thread. Brown it on all sides in the hot lard, then place in a roasting tin, surround with the marinated vegetables, pour the melted butter over and put into a preheated oven. Cook basting frequently with the stock. Take the meat out, cut it into slices and arrange in an ovenproof dish. Put the sauce through a blender, then sieve it and pour it over the meat. Garnish with lemon slices (without pips) and put into the hot oven for several minutes. Serve with baked potatoes or French fries, string beans, broccoli and potato salad.

serves 6–8 • Marinating: 1–2 days • Preparation: 10 mins
• Roasting: 100 mins • Baking: 5–7 mins

Veal roast studded with almonds

1½ leg of veal (off the bone), 100 g honey, juice of
1 lemon, salt, pepper, 50 g almonds, 2 tbsps butter

Squeeze out the rinsed and dried meat, rub it with salt and pepper, sprinkle with lemon juice and leave in the fridge for 2–3 hours. Blanch and skin the almonds. With the point of a knife make deep incisions in the meat, insert the almonds. Brush the meat with some melted butter, place in a roasting tin, pour the remaining butter over. Put into a very hot oven to brown the meat, then turn down the heat and continue cooking. Baste frequently first with the mixture of honey and lemon juice and then with the roasting juices.

serves 4–6 • Macerating: 2–3 hrs • Preparation:
5–7 mins • Roasting: 1½ to 2 hrs

Spit-roasted veal

1½ kg leg of veal (off the bone)

Marinade: 1 onion, 1 cup dry white wine,
3 tbsps olive oil, 4–5 cloves, 1 crumbled bay
leaf, ½ tsp dried thyme, 2 tbsps butter, ¼ tsp
each dried rosemary and sage, salt, pepper

Mix the finely diced onion with the wine, oil, cloves, bay leaf and thyme. Rinse and dry the meat, squeeze it out. Place in a stoneware dish, pour the marinade over, cover and leave in the fridge for 2 days, turning it over from time to time. Take the meat out, dry it, rub with salt, pepper, rosemary and sage, brush with some melted butter. Spear the meat on a spit and roast it, basting frequently with the marinade and melted butter.

serves 4–6 • Macerating: 2–3 days • Roasting: 100 mins

Roast veal à la Verdi

1½ kg leg of veal (off the bone), 200 g smoked
ham, juice and grated rind of ½ lemon, ½ tsp
dried tarragon, salt, pepper, 1 cup stock or dry
white wine, 1 tbsp lard, 1 tbsp butter, 5 bananas,
1 tbsp butter, 1 egg yolk, ½ cup cream, salt, a
pinch of each sugar and cayenne pepper

Sprinkle the ham cut into strips with the tarragon. Rinse and dry thoroughly the meat, sprinkle it with the lemon juice, rub with the lemon zest, salt and pepper and leave aside for 2–3 hours. Lard the meat with the ham bards, shape into an oval ball, tie tightly with cotton thread. Brown on all sides in the hot lard, then transfer to a roasting tin, baste with melted butter and roast in a hot oven for 60 mins, sprinkling frequently with the stock or wine. Slice the peeled bananas, sauté them in melted butter, then put through a blender. Add salt, cayenne, sugar, egg yolks and cream and blend into a smooth mixture. Take the meat out, remove the thread, cut the veal into slices. Arrange the slices in an ovenproof dish, surround with the banana purée and put into the hot oven for several minutes. Serve with rice or macaroni, with lettuce or chicory salad.

serves 6–8 • Macerating: 2–3 hrs • Preparation: 10 mins • Roasting: 1 hr • Baking: 15 mins

Lemony veal roast

1 kg loin of veal (off the bone), 1 large lemon, 2 tbsps fat, 3–4 tbsps breadcrumbs, 3 tbsps chopped parsley, 2 tbsps juice and grated rind of 1 lemon, ½ cup dry white wine, salt, pepper

Put the rinsed meat for 2 mins into boiling water, drain and dry it, rub with the lemon juice and zest and leave in the fridge for an hour. Rub it with salt, put into a greased roasting tin and place in a preheated oven for 40 mins, basting with the pan drippings and wine. Toast some breadcrumbs in a frying pan, add 2 tbsps of fat, take off the heat and leave to cool a bit. Pour in the juice from 1 lemon, put in the parsley, add salt and pepper and mix thoroughly. Take the meat out of the tin, make 2 cm deep incisions and insert the filling in them. Return to the roasting tin, sprinkle with the remaining breadcrumbs, pour over the pan drippings and cook in the oven for 15–20 mins. Serve with French fries and chicory salad.

serves 4–6 • Macerating: 1–2 hrs • Preparation: 10 mins • Roasting: 1 hr

Roast veal with tarragon

1 kg leg of veal (off the bone), 2 tbsps lemon juice, ½ tsp grated lemon rind, 1 tsp dried tarragon, ¼ tsp sugar,

2–3 tbsps dry white wine, 2 tbsps oil, 1 tbsp butter, 1 clove of garlic, a pinch of cayenne pepper, salt

Squeeze the rinsed and dried meat well. Mix the finely chopped garlic with the tarragon, lemon zest and juice, sugar, oil, wine and cayenne, and rub the mixture into the meat. Cover and leave in the fridge overnight. Salt the meat, put it into a roasting bag, sprinkle with the marinade and surround with knobs of butter. Close the bag, place on a roasting tin and put into a preheated oven. Cook for 40–50 mins. Serve hot or cold.

serves 4–6 • Macerating: 12 hrs • Roasting: 50 mins

Roast veal with dried mushrooms

1–1½ kg boneless veal, 30 g dried cep mushrooms, 2 onions, 50 g pork fat cut into thin rashers, ½ cup thick cream, 1 tsp dried tarragon, 1 tbsp lemon juice, 2 tbsps butter, salt, pepper

Put the rinsed meat into boiling water for 2–3 mins, drain and dry it, sprinkle with lemon juice, rub with pepper and tarragon and leave in the fridge overnight. Soak the rinsed mushrooms in water overnight, then cook them. Salt the meat, put into a roasting tin lined with pork fat rashers, sprinkle with the chopped onions, pour over the melted butter. Put into a very hot oven for 10–12 mins, then turn the temperature down and continue cooking for 30–40 mins, basting with the strained mushroom stock. Pour the juices out, sieve them, then return to the roasting tin. Add the mushrooms cut into thin strips and cook for another 10–15 mins, pouring over the cream towards the end. Serve with noodles, macaroni or rice.

serves 6–7 • Preparation: 10 mins • Macerating: 12 hrs • Roasting: 1 hr

Veal roulade à la mode

1 kg leg of veal (off the bone), 8 smoked streaky bacon rashers, 2 onions, 2 firm beef tomatoes, ¼ tsp each dried thyme, cinnamon and ground cloves, ½ tsp sugar, 1 glass brandy, 1 tsp lemon juice, ¼ tsp grated lemon rind, 2 tbsps oil, 2 tbsps butter, 2–3 tbsps dry white wine, ½ cup stock, salt, pepper, 1 tsp potato flour if required

Rinse and dry the meat, cut it lengthwise, but not whole way through. Pound it lightly with a mallet, shape into a rectangle, sprinkle with lemon juice, dust with salt and pepper. Mix the thyme, cloves, cinnamon, sugar, pepper and lemon zest with 1 tbsp of oil. Rub the mixture into the bacon rashers. Blanch and skin the tomatoes. Cut the tomatoes and the peeled onions into slices. Arrange the meat on a board, cover it with the bacon rashers, then the onion and tomatoes. Roll it up tightly, tie with thread and brown on all sides in the remaining hot oil. Transfer the meat to a roasting tin, put knobs of butter around, sprinkle with the wine and place in a preheated oven. Cook for 50–60 mins, basting frequently with the stock. Take the meat out, arrange it in an ovenproof dish and return to the hot oven. Pour the roasting juices into a pan, bring them to the boil, add salt and pepper to taste. Take off the heat, pour in the brandy, stir well. Serve in a sauce boat. You may thicken the sauce with 1 tsp of potato flour mixed with 1 tbsp of water.

serves 6–7 • Preparation: 30 mins • Roasting: 60 mins

Veal roulade stuffed with ham and eggs

1 kg boneless veal, 100 g pork fat, 50 g ham, 3 hard-boiled eggs, 1 raw egg, 1 tsp chopped basil leaves, 3–4 powdered dried cep mushrooms, 2 tbsps oil, 1 tbsp butter, 2–3 tbsps dry white wine, ½ cup stock, salt, pepper

Cut the rinsed and dried meat lengthwise, but not whole way through, shape it into a rectangle. Pound it lightly with a mallet, sprinkle with salt, pepper and mushrooms. Chop the ham and the hard-boiled eggs finely, combine with the basil, salt, pepper and the raw egg and mix thoroughly. Line the meat with thin pork fat rashers, sprinkle with salt, cover with the filling. Roll up tightly, wrap in the remaining pork fat rashers, tie with thread. Brown on all sides in hot oil, transfer to a roasting tin, pour over the melted butter. Put into a preheated oven for 50–60 mins, basting with the wine and stock. Serve hot or cold.

serves 4–6 • Preparation: 20–25 mins • Roasting: 60 mins

Veal roulade stuffed with eggs

1½ kg boneless veal, 2–3 powdered dried cep mushrooms, 50 g pork fat

* 50 g ham, 2 hard-boiled eggs, 1 raw egg, salt, pepper, 2 tbsps butter or lard

Pound the meat lightly to shape it into a rectangle. Rub it with salt, sprinkle with the mushroom powder, cover with thin pork fat rashers. Chop the ham and eggs finely, add some pepper, break in the egg, mix thoroughly, then spread the filling on top of the rashers. Roll the meat up tightly, tie with thread, place in a greased roasting tin, arrange knobs of butter around. Put into a preheated oven and cook slowly for 90 mins, basting frequently with the roasting juices. Serve hot or cold.

serves 6–8 • Preparation: 20 mins • Roasting: 90 mins

Veal roulade, Old Polish style

1 kg veal, 1 tsp lemon juice, 2 tbsps butter or lard, 1 tsp ground allspice, ½ cup orange juice, salt

STUFFING: 1 small onions, 1 tbsp butter or lard, ½ cup grated dry wholemeal bread, 1 tbsp breadcrumbs, 1 tbsp grated orange rind, 2 tbsps raisins, 1 tbsp dry white wine, ¼ tsp each dried tarragon, mint, basil and thyme, 1 egg

Rinse and dry the meat, cut it lengthwise, but not whole way through. Pound it lightly with a mallet to form a rectangle. Sprinkle with the lemon juice. Blanch the raisins and soak them in the wine. Fry the finely chopped onion in butter, but do not let it brown. Add the wholemeal bread and breadcrumbs and cook for a minute or two, stirring all the time. Take off the heat, put in the orange zest and herbs, add the raisins and salt to taste, break in the egg and mix thoroughly. Spread the filling on top of the meat. Roll the meat up, tie with thread, brush with some melted butter mixed with the allspice. Place in a roasting tin, pour over the remaining melted butter and put into a hot oven for 10–15 mins, then turn the temperature down and continue cooking, basting frequently with the orange juice and the pan drippings.

serves 6–7 • Preparation: 20–25 mins • Roasting: 60 mins

Gourmet's veal roulade

1 kg boneless veal, 2 tbsps oil, 1 carrot, 1 parsley root, ¼ celeriac, 1 cup stock, salt, pepper

STUFFING: 1 bread roll soaked in milk, 300 g minced veal, grated rind of 1 lemon, 3 tbsps chopped parsley, 50 g skinned and chopped almonds, 1 small onions, 1 egg, a pinch of each marjoram and grated nutmeg, salt, pepper

Rinse and dry the meat, cut it lengthwise half way through. Pound with a mallet and shape into a rectangle, sprinkle with salt and pepper. Squeeze the roll out, blend it with the minced veal, parsley and almonds, add salt, pepper, nutmeg, marjoram, grated onion and lemon zest, break in the egg and mix thoroughly. Spread the filling on the meat. Roll the meat tightly, tie with thread and brown on all sides in the hot oil, then transfer to a baking tin. Braise the coarsely grated vegetables in the pan and arrange them round the meat. Put the meat into a preheated oven and cook for 50–60 mins, basting with the stock. Take the meat out and sieve the sauce. Serve hot or cold.

serves 6–8 • Preparation: 20–25 mins • Roasting: 60 mins

Veal cooked in wine

1 kg leg of veal (off the bone), 1 onion, 1 carrot, several thyme sprigs, 1 celery stick, 1–2 bay leaves, 6–8 peppercorns, salt, 1½ cups dry white wine, 1 tin anchovies, 1 tbsp capers

Rinse the meat, pound it with your hand, form into an oval ball, tie with thread and scald with boiling water. Dice the peeled carrot, onion and celery. Put the meat into a pan, add the vegetables, thyme, some salt, the peppercorns and bay leaves, pour in the wine and enough cold water to cover the meat. Bring to the boil, cover and simmer for 1½ hours, then leave to cool.

AS A HOT DISH: Take the meat out, cut it into slices. Bring the stock to the boil and reduce it to 1½ cups, then sieve it. Grease an ovenproof dish with butter, arrange the meat slices in it. Put a piece of anchovy on each slice, sprinkle with capers and pour the sauce over. Put into a hot oven and heat up for several minutes. Serve with French fries or noodles.

AS A COLD DISH: Serve with a sauce made from 1 cup of mayonnaise, juice and grated rind of ½ lemon, a tin of tuna in oil and 1 tsp of sharp mustard. Put all the ingredients through a blender, then refrigerate. Cut the meat diagonally into slices. Arrange the slices on a serving dish, pour some sauce over. Garnish with anchovies and capers. Serve the remaining sauce separately.

serves 4–6 • Preparation: 1 hr • Cooking: 90 mins

Boiled marinated veal

2 kg leg of veal (off the bone), 2 cups milk, salt

MARINADE: 1 cup vinegar, 3–4 cloves, 6–8 grains each pepper and allspice, 3 onions, 3 carrots, 2 parsley roots, 1 leek, ½ celeriac, a pinch of sugar

Put the meat in a stoneware dish, pour the cold boiled milk over and leave in a cool place (the bottom shelf of the fridge) for 2 days. Take the meat out, dry it. Return to the dish and cover with the marinade made from the vinegar, 1 cup of boiled water and spices. Stand in a cool place for 3–4 days, then take the meat out, dry it and rub with salt. Grate coarsely the vegetables, put them in a large pan and cover with the marinade. Roll the meat tightly, tie with string, put into the pan and cook over low heat for up to 2 hours. Leave it in the marinade to cool. Serve cold, garnished with pickled saffron milk caps or cocktail gherkins, with sauce tartare or with green sauce (pp. 316–317 and 319).

serves 6–8 • Marinating: 2+3–4 days • Preparation: 10 mins • Cooking: 1½ to 2 hrs

Stuffed breast of veal

For stuffing you will need a flat piece of meat weighing about 1½ kg. With a sharp knife loosen the ribs and remove them, taking care not to cut through the meat. Make a pocket in the meat by cutting through the middle membrane. Fill the pocket loosely because the meat shrinks during roasting, while the stuffing swells and may burst through the seams.

1½ kg breast of veal, ¼ tsp ginger, salt, pepper, 1 tsp lemon juice, 1 tbsp butter, 6 thin raw lean bacon rashers

STUFFING: 1½ cups cooked rice, 1 large onion, 1–2 cloves of garlic, 2 tbsps raisins, 1 tbsp brandy, juice and grated rind of ½ lemon, 1 tbsp finely chopped basil leaves or ¼ tsp dried basil, ¼ tsp ginger, 4 tbsps butter, salt, a pinch of sugar, ¼ cup stock, 2 tbsps dry white wine

Rinse and dry the meat, remove the bones, make a pocket. Sprinkle the meat with the lemon juice, rub it with the ginger, salt and pepper and leave in a cool place for half an hour. Salt the rice sparingly, sprinkle it with the lemon juice. Rinse and drain the raisins, sprinkle them with the brandy. Brown the finely chopped onion and garlic in the melted butter, combine with the rice, add the basil, ginger, lemon zest, sugar and raisins. Mix thoroughly. Fill the pocket with the mixture, sew it up. Wrap the meat in the rashers, place in a roasting tin greased with butter and put into a very hot oven. Roast for 1½ hours, basting with the wine and stock and then with the pan drippings.

serves 4–6 • Preparation: 20–25 mins • Roasting: 90 mins

Braised breast of veal

1 breast of veal, 3 carrots, 3 parsley roots, 3 large onions, 1 celeriac, 4 tomatoes, salt, 1 cup white wine, 2 tbsps butter

* 100 g mushrooms, ½ tbsp soup seasoning

Dice the peeled and rinsed vegetables or grate them coarsely. Put into a pan together with the tomato quarters. Arrange the boned, rinsed and salted meat on top. Add 1 tbsp of butter and 1 cup of wine, cover and simmer until the meat is tender. Cook the sliced mushrooms in butter and soup seasoning. Take the meat out, cut into slices, surround with the cooked mushrooms and fried potatoes. Pour the sieved sauce over.

serves 4–6 • Preparation: 20–25 mins • Cooking: 60–70 mins

Breast of veal, Polish style

1 breast of veal (ca 1½ kg), salt, 1 tbsp lemon juice, ¼ tsp grated lemon rind, 3 tbsps olive oil, ¼ cup stock or dry white wine

STUFFING: 100 g veal or pork liver, 1 bread roll soaked in milk, 3 tbsps butter, 3 tbsps chopped parsley, salt, pepper, ¼ tsp grated nutmeg, 1 egg

Rinse and dry the boned meat, rub it with the salt and lemon zest, sprinkle with the lemon juice and leave in a cool place for an hour. Rinse and dry the liver, remove the membrane, chop it finely or put it through a micer. Cream the butter, then gradually add the liver, the squeezed out roll, salt, pepper and nutmeg. Fold in the stiffly whisked egg white with parsley. Mix thoroughly but gently. Fill the pocket with the forcemeat, sew it up. Heat the oil in a roasting tin, brown the meat on all sides, pour in the wine. Put into a preheated oven and roast, basting first with the wine or stock, and then with the roasting juices. Serve with puréed potatoes, cooked carrot or lettuce.

serves 5–7 • Preparation: 20–25 mins • Roasting: 90 mins

Breast of veal, Russian style

1 breast of veal (ca 1½ kg), salt, 1 tsp hot mustard, 2 tbsps lard, ½ cup stock or water

STUFFING: 300 g minced veal, 100 g pork fat, 100 g marinated beef tongue, ¼ cup single cream, salt, 1 tsp pepper

Rinse and dry the boned meat, rub it with salt, brush with the mustard and leave in a cool place for several minutes. Cut the cooked tongue into cubes, dice the pork fat or put it through a mincer. Mix the tongue, pork fat and the minced veal, add the pepper, salt and cream. Fill the pocket with the mixture, sew it up. Put the meat into a roasting tin, pour over the hot melted lard and place in a hot oven (250°C). Cook for 10–12 mins, then turn down the temperature and continue roasting for an hour, basting with the stock and then with the pan drippings. Serve with baked potatoes with rosemary and salted cucumbers.

serves 6–8 • Preparation: 20–25 mins • Roasting: 60–80 mins

Marinated breast of veal stuffed with tongues

1 breast of veal (ca 1½ kg)

* 1 kg veal or pork tonues, salt, pepper, 2 tbsps lard, 1 cup stock

MARINADE: 200 g dry wholemeal bread, 5 g saltpetre, 3–4 bay leaves, 10 grains each pepper and allspice, 10 cloves, 5–6 cloves of garlic, 1 tbsp sugar, 1 tsp salt, ½ cup 6% vinegar or 1 cup wine

Mix all the ingredients of the marinade, add 2 cups of water, bring to the boil, then allow it to cool and strain it. Put the rinsed tongues in a stoneware dish, pour over the marinade, place a board on top and weigh it down. Stand in a cool place for 5–6 days, turning the tongues over twice. Then take out the tongues, cook them in salted water and skin. Bone the meat, rub it with salt and pepper. Make a pocket, fill it with the tongues, sew it up. Place the meat in a greased roasting tin, put into a preheated oven and roast for 90 mins, basting frequently with the stock. Serve hot or cold, cut into thick slices.

serves 6–8 • Marinating: 5–6 days • Preparation: 10–15 mins • Roasting: 90 mins

Breast of veal stuffed with ham

1 breast of veal, 1 tsp salt, 1 tbsp butter

STUFFING: 100 g ham, 1 bread roll soaked in milk, 1 egg, 1 tbsp butter, 1 large onion, 100 g smoked tongue or smoked lean bacon, salt, pepper

Fry the finely chopped onion in butter, but do not let it brown. Put it through a mincer together with the squeezed out roll and the ham. Add the egg, salt, pepper and the tongue cut into cubes. Mix thoroughly. Rinse and dry the meat, bone it, make a pocket in it. Fill the pocket with the forcemeat, sew it up. Place the

meat in a greased roasting tin and put into a medium hot oven. Cook for 90 mins, basting frequently with the pan drippings.

serves 5–7 • Preparation: 20–25 mins • Roasting: 90 mins

Breast of veal stuffed with veal

1 breast of veal (ca 1½ kg), salt, 2 tbsps butter

STUFFING: 250 g veal, ½ cup single cream, 2 egg yolks, 2–3 tbsps breadcrumbs, salt, pepper, nutmeg

Rinse and dry the boned meat, sprinkle it with salt, make a pocket in it. Chop the veal finely or put it through a mincer. Mix it with the egg yolks and sifted breadcrumbs, add salt, pepper and nutmeg, fold in the whipped cream. Fill the pocket with the mixture, sew it up. Brush the meat with some butter and place it in a greased roasting tin. Put into a preheated oven and roast for 90 mins, basting frequently with melted butter and pan drippings.

serves 6–7 • Preparation: 20 mins • Roasting: 90 mins

Breast of veal stuffed with brains

1 breast of veal (ca 1½ kg), salt, 2 tbsps butter

STUFFING: 1 calf's brain or ½ ox brain, 3 tbsps breadcrumbs, 1 tbsp butter, 1 small onion, 1 egg yolk, 1 egg, 5–7 mushrooms, 1 tbsp chopped parsley, salt, pepper

Rinse and dry the boned meat, sprinkle it with salt, make a pocket in it. Sauté the chopped onion and mushrooms in butter. Blanch the brain in salted water, remove the membranes. Blend it with the egg yolks thoroughly, add the onion and mushroom mixture, the sifted breadcrumbs and parsley, fold in the whisked egg white. Fill the pocket with the stuffing, sew it up. Place the meat in a greased roasting tin, put knobs of butter around. Put into a preheated oven and roast for 90 mins, basting frequently with butter.

serves 6–7 • Preparation: 20 mins • Roasting: 90 mins

Gourmet's breast of veal

1 breast of veal (ca 1½ kg), 1 tbsp butter, 1 tbsp lemon juice, salt, 3 tbsps lard, ½ cup stock or dry white wine

STUFFING: 250 g calf's brains, 2 tbsps wine vinegar, 2–3 onions, 1 tbsp butter, 1 egg yolk, 1 egg, 3 tbsps chopped parsley, salt, pepper

Rinse and dry the meat, make a pocket in it. Cream the butter with the lemon juice and salt, rub the meat with the mixture. Soak the brains in water with the vinegar for several minutes, then remove the membranes and blood vessels. Fry the finely chopped onion in butter, but do not let it brown. Chop the brains and blend them with the egg yolks, add salt and pepper, fold in the stifly whisked egg white, onion and parsley. Fill the pocket with the stuffing, sew it up. Place the meat in a greased roasting tin, pour over the melted lard. Put into a preheated oven and roast, basting with the stock or wine and then with the roasting juices. Serve with noodles or dumplings and with salads.

serves 6–8

Breast of veal, Mazovian style

1 breast of veal (ca 1½ kg), 3–4 cloves of garlic, salt, pepper, ¼ tsp chili pepper, 1 tbsp olive oil, 2 tbsps lard

STUFFING: 4–5 potatoes, 1–2 onions, 2–3 tbsps potato flour, salt, pepper, 1 tsp chopped fresh marjoram leaves, 1 egg

Rinse and dry the boned meat, make a pocket in it. Crush the chopped garlic with the salt, pepper, chili and oil. Rub the meat with the mixture, wrap it in foil and leave in a cool place for an hour. Grate the peeled and rinsed potatoes, combine them with the finely chopped onion, marjoram, salt and pepper, add the potato flour, break in the egg and mix thoroughly. Fill the pocket with the mixture, sew it up. Heat up the lard in a skillet, put in the meat and brown it on both sides. Pour in ½ cup of boiling water (or stock), cover and simmer over low heat for one hour, adding more water if required. Serve with boiled potatoes, spinach purée and tomato salad.

serves 6–8 • Preparation: 20 mins • Cooking: 1 hr

Breast of veal stuffed with mushrooms

1 breast of veal (ca 1½ kg), 1 tbsp lemon juice, salt, pepper, marjoram, 2 tbsps butter, 4 large slices of smoked ham, 2 cups dry white wine, ½ cup cream, 1 egg yolk

STUFFING: 500 g small mushrooms, 2 large onions, 3–4 tbsps chopped parsley, 2 tbsps butter, ½ cup whipping cream, juice and grated rind of ½ lemon, salt, ½ tsp freshly ground pepper, ½ tsp grated nutmeg

Rinse and dry the boned meat, sprinkle it with the lemon juice, rub with salt and leave in a cool place for 2–3 hours. Chop the rinsed mushrooms finely, sprinkle them with the lemon juice and zest. Fry the chopped onion in butter, but do not let it brown. Add the mushrooms and fry them over high heat for a minute or two, then turn down the heat, pour in the cream and heat up, stirring all the time, to reduce the liquid and make it thicker. Take off the heat, add salt, pepper and nutmeg to taste, put in the parsley. Place the meat (the membranous side down) on a board, cover it with the ham slices, spread the filling on the ham. Roll the meat up and tie tightly with twine. Melt the butter in a skillet, put the meat in and brown it on all sides. Pour in the wine, cover the skillet and cook over low heat for an hour (turning the meat and basting it with the cooking juices from time to time). Take the tender meat out. Mix the cream with the egg yolk, pour into the skillet and heat up, stirring all the time, until the sauce has thickened. Pour the sauce into a sauce boat. Serve the meat hot, with baked potatoes or macaroni, and with spinach, or cold, with a savoury sauce.

serves 6–8 • Macerating: 2–3 hrs • Preparation: 20 mins • Cooking: 1 hr

Veal goulash, Gdańsk style

800 g boneless veal, 1 small carrot, 1 small onion, ½ small celeriac, 1 small lemon, 1 tbsp lard, 2 tbsps butter, 100 g cranberries

(or 3 tbsps low-sugar cranberry jam),
1 cup dry red wine, 1 cup stock, ½ tsp curry
powder, ¼ tsp each cinnamon, pepper
and nutmeg, salt, 1 tbsp flour

Cut the rinsed and dried meat into strips, brown them in the hot lard. Melt the butter in a skillet, sauté the vegetables cut into sticks, put in the browned meat and some stock and simmer for 40 mins. Add salt, pepper, curry and cinnamon, put in the peeled lemon cut into cubes (without pips) and the cranberries, pour in the wine and cook for a bit longer. Thicken with the flour mixed with 2–3 tbsps of stock, then heat up. Serve with maraconi, noodles or rice.

serves 4–6 • Preparation: 10 mins • Cooking: 40 mins

Veal goulash with ham

700 g leg of veal (off the bone), 100 g tinned ham,
1 large onion, 2–3 cloves of garlic, 2 chilli peppers,
2 celery sticks, 1 tbsp tomato concentrate, 100 g green
peas (cooked or tinned), 1½ cups stock, ¾ cup dry
white wine, 3 tbsps oil, 1 tbsp butter, 1 tbsp flour

Rinse and dry the meat, cut it into cubes, sprinkle with the flour. Heat up 1 tbsp of oil in a frying pan, add the butter, put in the meat and brown it lightly. Pour in the wine and simmer for 10 mins. Heat the remaining oil in a skillet, sauté the chopped onion, add the finely chopped garlic and the ham cut into cubes and, stirring all the time, fry for 2–3 mins. Peel and dice the celery, core the peppers and cut them into thin strips. Add both to the onion together with the meat. Pour in the stock, add the tomato concentrate, stir and bring to the boil. Add salt, cover and simmer for one hour. Put in the peas and cook until the meat is tender. Season with salt and pepper to taste, add a pinch of salt if required.

serves 6–8 • Preparation: 20 mins • Cooking: 1 hr

Veal ragout with orange

800 g boneless veal, 2 cloves of garlic,
1 small tomato, 1 orange, 1 cup stock,
2–3 tbsps single cream, 1 tbsp flour

Cut the rinsed and dried meat into cubes, sprinkle them with the garlic crushed with salt, cover and stand aside for an hour. Heat up the stock in a pan, put in the meat, bring to the boil, then simmer for 20 mins. Blanch and skin the tomato, remove the seeds, cut the flesh into cubes. Scrub the orange, with a sharp knife cut off the orange rind (without the bitter pith), pour over it some boiling water and cook for 2 mins, then drain, rinse under cold water, dry and cut into thin strips. Squeeze the orange. Add the tomatoes and orange rind to the meat and cook for a while. Mix the orange juice with the flour and cream, pour the mixture into the skillet and, stirring all the time, simmer until the sauce has thickened. Serve with noodles or rice.

serves 4–6 • Macerating: 1 hr • Preparation: 15 mins • Cooking: 30 mins

Veal ragout with celery

600 g boneless veal, 400 g celery, 1–2 cloves
of garlic, 2 tart apples, 2 tbsps olive oil, 1 tbsp
butter, 1 tbsp flour, ½ cup stock, ¼ cup dry white
wine, 1 cup thick cream, 1 tbsp each lemon
juice, curry powder and honey, salt, pepper

Cut the rinsed and dried meat into thin strips, sprinkle with salt and pepper. Peel the celery and cut into fairly thick slices. Chop the garlic finely. Heat the oil in a skillet, brown the meat slightly, add the garlic, celery and butter and sauté for 2–3 mins. Pour in the wine and stock, cover and cook for 10 mins. Cut the peeled and cored apples into sticks, sprinkle with the lemon juice and put into the meat together with the honey, curry powder, salt and pepper. Stir and simmer for 6–8 mins. Mix the cream with the flour, pour into the skillet and heat up until the sauce has thickened (keep off the boil). Serve with rice.

serves 4–6 • Preparation: 10 mins • Cooking: 30 mins

Veal ragout with vegetables

400 g boneless veal, 250 g each cauliflower, carrot,
green string beans and Chinese cabbage, 2–3 cups
stock, 1 tbsp grated Parmesan, grated rind of 1 lemon,
3–4 tbsps chopped parsley, salt, a pinch of each
pepper and thyme, 1 tbsp lemon juice, 1 tbsp oil

Rinse and dry the vegetables, divide the cauliflower into florets, dice the carrots, cabbage and string beans. Cut the rinsed and dried meat into cubes, sprinkle with salt, pepper, thyme and lemon juice, sauté in hot oil and transfer to a skillet. Cover with the stock, bring to the boil, then add the vegetables and cook for 30 mins, reducing the liquid towards the end. Mix the lemon zest with the parsley and Parmesan, sprinkle the mixture over the ragout. Serve with rice or white bread.

serves 6–8 • Preparation: 10 mins • Cooking: 30–35 mins

Veal ragout with mushrooms

500 g boneless veal, 150 g mushrooms, 2 onions, 1 leek (only the white part), 1 tbsp oil, 2 tbsps butter, 2 tbsps flour, ¾ cup dry white wine, ½ cup stock, 4–5 tbsps finely chopped parsley, ½ tsp dried thyme, 1 tsp pounded black pepper, a pinch of nutmeg, salt, 1 tbsp brandy, 2–3 tbsps cream

Cut the rinsed and dried meat into cubes. Slice the cleaned mushrooms and leek, dice the onion. Heat the oil in a skillet, put in the meat and brown it over high heat. Add the butter, onion and mushrooms and fry for a minute or two. Dust with the flour, stir, pour in the wine and cook for 4–5 mins, then put in half the parsley and the leek, add the thyme, nutmeg, pepper and salt, pour in the stock and simmer for 45 mins. Pour in the brandy and cream, stir well, heat up. Before serving, sprinkle with the remaining parsley.

serves 4–6 • Preparation: 10–15 mins • Cooking: 45 mins

Veal ragout with almonds

1 kg boneless veal, 1 tbsp lemon juice, 150 g almonds, 500 g onion, 4 tbsps butter, salt, pepper, ¼ tsp saffron, 1 tbsp boiling water, 1½ cups stock, 4 tbsps finely chopped parsley

Cut the rinsed and dried meat into strips, sprinkle with the lemon juice and pepper and leave aside for half an hour. Cut the peeled onion in half slices. Melt the butter in a skillet, fry the onion, but do not let it brown. Put in the meat and brown it, sprinkle it with salt and pepper. Add the saffron soaked in hot water, stir and cook for a while.

Pour in the stock, cover and simmer. Blanch and skin the almonds, cut them into strips, add to the meat. Stir and simmer for 30 mins. Towards the end, add the chopped parsley. Serve with white bread, rice or macaroni.

serves 6–8 • Macerating: 30–40 mins • Preparation: 10 mins • Cooking: 30–35 mins

Veal cutlets with Parmesan

600 g leg or loin of veal (off the bone), 1 tbsp lemon juice, 2 eggs, 2 tbsps flour, 100 g grated Parmesan, 3 tbsps butter, 1 small glass of dry white wine, salt, pepper, 2 tbsps chopped chives

Cut the cleaned meat into small cutlets, pound lightly with a mallet, sprinkle with the lemon juice, salt and pepper. Coat with flour, lightly beaten eggs and cheese and fry in melted butter. Transfer to a skillet, add the wine, sprinkle with half the chives and the remaining Parmesan, and simmer over low heat until the wine has evaporated. Before serving, sprinkle with the remaining chives.

serves 4 • Preparation: 25 mins

Spring scallops

800 g loin of veal (off the bone), 1 tbsp lemon juice, 1 tsp paprika, salt, 1 tbsp butter, 1 tbsp olive oil, 1 tbsp dry white wine, 1 kg small new potatoes, 200 g each young nettle leaves and spinach, 2–3 cloves of garlic, salt, pepper, a pinch of nutmeg, 1 cup single cream, 1 tbsp butter

Cut the rinsed meat into small cutlets (2–3 per person), flatten them lightly with a mallet, sprinkle with the lemon juice, paprika and oil and leave aside for half an hour. Rinse the spinach, put aside several large leaves and blanch the rest, drain and chop. Melt the butter in a skillet, put in the finely chopped garlic and spinach and sauté, add salt, pepper and nutmeg, pour in half the cream and simmer for a while. Wash and dry the potatoes, place them on a baking sheet and bake in a preheated oven. Fry the escalopes in a mixture of oil and butter, sprinkle them with the wine, cover and simmer for 10 mins. Take the potatoes out, make lengthwise incisions. Arrange them in a greased ovenproof dish, stuff with the spinach. Put the meat around the potatoes. Pour the remaining cream into the pan in which the meat was fried, stir, then pour over the meat. Place the dish in a hot oven for several minutes. Before serving, garnish with spinach leaves. Serve with tomato salad.

serves 4–6 • Macerating: 30–40 mins •
Preparation: 30 mins • Baking: 10 mins

Royal scallops

800 g loin of veal (off the bone), 2 eggs, 1 tbsp dry white wine, 1 tbsp mineral water, 3 tbsps grated cheese, 2 tbsps flour, 4 pineapple slices, 1 large firm tomato, 8 olives stuffed with almonds, salt, pepper, ¼ tsp each dried basil and thyme, 1 tbsp lemon juice, 2 tbsps olive oil, 1 tbsp butter

Cut the rinsed and dried meat into 8 portions, pound lightly with a mallet and shape into round scallops. Sprinkle with the lemon juice, salt, pepper, thyme and basil and leave aside for several minutes. Whisk the eggs with the wine and water, mix with the grated cheese. Coat the escalopes with flour and the egg and cheese mixture, fry in very hot oil 2 mins to each side. Transfer them to a greased ovenproof dish. Fry the tomato cut into 8 slices in the same frying pan. Place one tomato slice on each escalope, cover with half a pineapple slice, put one olive on top. Sprinkle with melted butter and put into a hot oven for several minutes. Serve with baked potatoes, French fries or potato purée, lettuce, string beans or boiled broccoli.

serves 6–8 • Preparation: 10 mins • Macerating:
20–30 mins • Baking: 10–15 mins

Veal scallops with mushrooms

800 g loin of veal (off the bone), 400 g fresh firm boletus mushrooms, 4 shallots (or spring onions without green parts), 1 tbsp each mustard, tomato purée and flour, 1 tsp potato flour, 3 tbsps oil, 2 tbsps butter, 2–3 tbsps finely chopped parsley, ¼ cup stock, ½ cup thick sour cream, salt, pepper, ¼ tsp dried thyme

Cut the rinsed and dried mushrooms into thin slices, dice the onion finely. Heat 2 tbsps of oil in a pan, fry the onion, but do not let it brown. Put in the mushrooms, add salt, pepper and thyme, stir, then fry for several minutes over low heat. Mix the potato flour with the stock, pour into the mushrooms and, stirring all the time, simmer until the sauce has thickened. Pour in the cream and keep warm. Cut the rinsed and dried meat into 8 portions, pound lightly with a mallet and shape into scallops. Sprinkle with salt and pepper, brush with the mustard mixed with the tomato purée, dust with flour. Heat the remaining oil in a frying pan, add the butter, put in the escalopes and fry them 3–4 mins to each side. Transfer them to a hot ovenproof dish, arrange the mushrooms around and put into a hot oven for 3–4 mins. Before serving, garnish with chopped parsley.

serves 6–8 • Preparation: 30–40 mins • Baking: 4–5 mins

Veal scallops, Italian style

800 g loin of veal (off the bone), 2 lemons, 1 tbsp capers, 3–4 tbsps finely chopped basil, ¼ cup light chicken stock, ¼ cup dry white wine, salt, pepper, 2 tbsps olive oil, 1 tsp butter

Cut the rinsed and dried meat into 8 portions, pound lightly with a mallet and form into scallops. Squeeze 1 lemon, grate the rind. Mix the juice and zest with the stock and wine. Cut ½ lemon into slices and squeeze the juice from the other half. Sprinkle the scallops with the juice, salt and pepper, then sauté them on both sides in very hot oil. Melt the butter in a skillet, put in the fried scallops, pour over the stock and simmer for 5–6 mins. Add the capers and half the basil, stir gently and simmer for a while. Arrange the scallops on a warm serving dish, sprinkle with the remaining basil, garnish with lemon slices. Serve with macaroni or rice, with boiled asparagus, broccoli or green peas.

serves 4–6 • Preparation: 20–25

Veal scallops in cream

800 g loin of pork (off the bone), 1 tbsp lemon juice, 1 tsp dried lovage, ½ tsp pepper, salt, ½ cup stock, ½ cup thick cream, 3 tbsps butter

Cut the rinsed and dried meat into 8 portions, pound lightly with a mallet or press down with your hand. Sprinkle with the lemon juice, a bit of pepper and lovage and leave aside for several minutes. Fry the scallops golden brown in the melted butter, transfer to a hot ovenproof dish and keep warm. Pour the stock into the frying pan, stir and bring it to the boil, add salt and the remaining pepper and lovage. Mix with the cream and heat up over low heat for 2–3 mins, then pour over the meat. Serve with noodles, macaroni or rice.

serves 4–6 • Preparation: 20–25 mins

Gypsy cutlets

600 g boneless veal, 100 g each lean ham and pork fat, 1 large onion, 1 each small carrot and parsley root, ¼ celeriac, ½ cup dry white wine, ½ cup stock, salt, pepper, 1 tbsp lard, 1 tbsp butter

Line a skillet with thin slices of pork fat (50 g), sprinkle with the finely chopped onion and grated vegetables, cover with the stock. Bring to the boil, then simmer for several minutes. Cut the rinsed and dried meat into cutlets, press them down with your hand. Cut 50 g of ham and the remaining pork fat into thin bards. Lard the cutlets with the bards, sprinkle with salt and brown on both sides in the hot lard, then put into the skillet. Pour in the wine and cook over low heat for several minutes. Cut the remaining ham into 4 slices and fry them in melted butter. Arrange the cutlets on a hot serving dish. Blend and sieve the cooking juices with the vegetables, add salt and pepper to taste. Place one ham slice on each cutlet, sprinkle sparingly with the sauce. Serve the remaining sauce separately.

serves 4 • Preparation: 20–25 mins

Veal cutlets with herbs

600 g boneless veal (loin), 3 cloves of garlic, ¼ tsp each dried sage, thyme, ginger, pepper and lemon zest, 1 tbsp each olive oil and lemon juice, salt, 2 tbsps flour, 3 tbsps melted butter, 2 tbsps dry white wine, 2–3 onions, 2–3 tbsps finely chopped parsley

Pound the finely chopped garlic with the sage, thyme, ginger, pepper and lemon zest, mix with the oil and lemon

juice. Cut the rinsed and dried meat into 4 portions, pound them lightly with the handle of a knife, rub with the herbal mixture. Place the cutlets one on top of the other, cover and put into the fridge for 1–2 hours. Salt them, dredge with flour and fry in melted butter. Transfer onto a warm serving platter. Brown the sliced onion in the frying pan, place it around the cutlets. Pour the wine into the frying pan, stir well, heat up, then pour over the meat. Put the cutlets into a hot oven for several minutes. Before serving, garnish with chopped parsley. Serve with French fries, lettuce and pepper salad.

serves 4 • Macerating: 1–3 hrs • Frying: 8–10 mins

Veal cutlets, Lithuanian style

600 g boneless veal (loin), 1 egg, 3–4 tbsps grated dry wholemeal bread, 2 tbsps flour, 4 tbsps clarified butter, ½ cup grated horseradish, 1 onion, juice and grated rind of 1 lemon, 1½ cups thick cream, salt

Cut the rinsed and dried meat into 4 portions, pound them lightly with a mallet. Sprinkle with salt, dredge with flour, coat with the mixed egg and grated bread. Press down to make the coating stick and fry in hot butter (2 tbsps) on both sides. Transfer to an ovenproof dish greased with butter. Melt the remaining butter in a pan, put in the finely chopped onion, fry for a minute or two, add the horseradish, 1 tbsp of grated bread, lemon zest and juice. Simmer for a while, adjust the taste with salt. Pour in the cream and stir. Pour the sauce over the cutlets, cover with aluminium foil and put into a hot oven for 10–15 mins.

serves 4

Veal cutlets à la milanaise

600 g boneless veal, 4 tbsps grated Parmesan, 4 tbsps sifted breadcrumbs, 2 eggs, 3 tbsps dry white wine, salt, pepper, 2 tbsps butter

SAUCE: 2 tbsps butter, 1 tbsp flour, 1 tbsp tomato concentrate, 50 g lean smoked ham, 4–5 mushrooms caps, salt, pepper, 1 cup stock, 2 tbsps chopped parsley

Melt 1 tbsp of butter in a frying pan, put in the finely chopped mushrooms and sauté them. Add the ham cut into strips and, stirring all the time, fry for a minute or two, season with salt and pepper. Make a roux from 1 tbsp of butter and the flour, dillute it with the stock and simmer, stirring continuously, until the sauce has thickened. Combine with the tomato concentrate and the mushroom and ham mixture, stir, adjust the taste and keep over low heat. Cut the rinsed and dried meat into four cutlets, pound them lightly with a mallet, sprinkle with salt and pepper. Coat them with the eggs mixed with the wine, then with Parmesan and again with the egg and wine mixture, and finally dredge them with breadcrumbs. Press the coating down with your hand to make it stick. Fry the cutlets in melted butter. Put cooked macaroni in the middle of a serving platter. Pour the sauce over the macaroni, arrange the cutlets around. Garnish with chopped parsley and serve immediately.

serves 4 • Preparation: 20 mins • Frying: 8–10 mins

Veal cutlets in tomato sauce

900 g loin of veal (on the bone), 2 tbsps olive oil, 2 tbsps butter, 2 tbsps flour, salt, pepper

SAUCE: ½ cup each Calvados, champagne, tomato purée and thick cream, 100 g butter, 2 egg yolks, 1 tbsp lemon juice, ½ tsp grated lemon rind, a pinch of each salt, pepper and sugar

Cut the rinsed and dried meat into cutlets. Slit the meat lightly by the bone, pound gently with a mallet. Sprinkle with salt and pepper, dredged with flour. Heat the oil in a frying pan, add the butter and fry the cutlets 4–5 mins to each side, then arrange them in an ovenproof dish. Put the remaining flour into the frying pan, brown it lightly, pour in the Calvados mixed with the tomato purée and bring to the boil, stirring all the time. Fold in the cream and keep warm. Melt the remaining butter in a pan. Whisk the egg yolks with salt, lemon juice and zest in another pan. Rest it on top of a pot of boiling water and, whisking all the time, gradually add the melted butter until the mixture is smooth. Adjust the taste with salt, pepper and sugar, take off the steam, pour in the champagne and the tomato sauce, stir well. Pour the hot sauce over the meat and put into a preheated oven for 2–3 mins. Serve with macaroni with butter and with chicory or lettuce.

serves 4 • Preparation: 10 mins • Frying: 8–10 mins • Baking: 5 mins

Veal medallions with sorrel

600 g loin of veal (off the bone), 200 g fresh sorrel, 3 tbsps butter, 1 tbsp lemon juice, 1 tsp honey, 1 tsp pepper, salt, 1 cup yogurt

Clean, rinse and drain the sorrel, chop it finely. Cut the rinsed and dried meat into 4 portions, pound lightly with a mallet to form round medallions. Fry in melted butter until golden brown on both sides, then arrange in an oven-proof dish, sprinkle with salt and pepper and sparingly with the lemon juice. Mix the pan fat with the yogurt, put in the sorrel and sauté, stirring all the time. Add the remaining lemon juice, honey and pepper, mix thoroughly. Cover the medallions with the sorrel and leave in a hot oven for 3–5 mins. Serve with macaroni, rice and puréed vegetables.

serves 4 • Preparation: 10 mins • Frying: 8–10 mins • Baking: 5 mins

Veal medallions, Spanish style

700 g leg of veal (off the bone), salt, 1 tsp lemon juice, 2 tbsps olive oil, 4 pieces of toasted bread, 1 tsp butter, 1 kg potatoes, ½ tsp each dried thyme and ground pepper, 1 tbsp flour, 3 tbsps olive oil, 500 g string beans

SAUCE: ¼ cup each wine vinegar and dry white wine, ½ tsp each grated lemon rind, sugar, salt and cayenne pepper, 2 spring onions (without green parts), 3 tbsps tomato purée, 2 egg yolks, 4 tbsps butter, 3 tbsps chopped parsley

Peel the potatoes, rinse and dry them, cut in eight. Heat the oil in a roasting tin in the oven. Mix the flour with the pepper and thyme, dredge the potatoes with the mixture, put them into the roasting tin and bake until golden brown. Put the finely chopped onions into a saucepan, cover with the vinegar and cook, stirring frequently, to reduce the vinegar by half. Put in the tomato purée, mix, heat up, then take off the heat. Pour in the wine, add the egg yolks, salt, pepper and lemon zest and whisk until the sauce has thickened. Rest the pan on top of a pot of boiling water and heat the sauce up. Whisking continuously, gradually add small pieces of butter. Cook the cleaned string beans in salted boiling water, drain them and cut into 4–5 cm pieces. Cut the meat into 4 portions, pound lightly with a mallet and shape into oval medallions. Sprinkle with lemon juice and salt, and fry in hot oil. Take the medallions out of the frying pan. Put in instead the cooked string beans and fry for a minute or two, stirring. Butter the toast and brown in a frying pan. Arrange the toast in the middle of a large serving platter, place one medallion on top of another. Pour over the sauce and pile the string beans on one side and the potatoes on the other. Serve the remaining sauce separately.

serves 4 • Preparation: 40–45 mins

Veal medallions with olives

700 g leg of veal (off the bone), salt, pepper, 2 tbsps stoned green olives, 3–4 tbsps chopped parsley, 2 tbsps olive oil, 300 g macaroni, 3 tbsps butter, 100 g grated Parmesan, 1 egg, ½ tsp grated nutmeg

SAUCE: 1 tbsp butter, 1 tsp flour, 1–2 cloves of garlic, 1 small tin tomato concentrate, 1 cup stock, ¼ cup dry white wine, salt, pepper, a pinch of sugar, ¼ tsp oregano

Make a roux from the melted butter and flour, dilute it with the stock and simmer stirring until the sauce has thickened. Put in the garlic crushed with salt, pepper and oregano, pour in the tomato paste mixed with the wine, heat up and adjust the taste with salt, pepper and sugar if required. Cook the macaroni al dente, drain it and chop into small pieces. Mix it with 2 tbsps of butter, the grated Parmesan, egg, nutmeg and parsley. Shape the mixture into small patties (as many as the pieces of meat) and fry in melted butter, then transfer to an ovenproof dish. Cut the meat into 2 cm thick slices, pound lightly with a mallet and shape into medallions. Sprinkle with salt and pepper and fry in oil until golden brown on both sides. Place the medallions on top of the macaroni patties, pour the thick sauce over and put into a preheated oven for several minutes. Before serving, garnish with the green olives.

serves 4 • Preparation: 30–40 mins • Baking: 10 mins

Castellan's veal steaks

600 g leg of veal (off the bone), 100 g lean smoked streaky bacon, 1 veal kidney, salt, pepper, 4 slices cheese, 2 tbsps lard, 1 tbsp butter

Rinse the kidney, cut it lengthwise, remove the tubules. Put the kidneys into a pan, cover with cold water and leave for 30–40 mins. Cut the rinsed and dried meat into 4 slices, pound them lightly with a mallet. Sprinkle with salt and pepper and fry in hot lard. Cut the bacon and drained kidney into 4 slices. Take out the steaks and arrange them in an ovenproof dish and fry the bacon and kidney in the same fat. Place a slice of bacon, kidney and cheese on each steak. Sprinkle with some melted butter and put into a preheated oven for 10 mins. Serve with rice and puréed vegetables or with French fries and lettuce or boiled vegetables.

serves 4 • Macerating: 30–40 mins • Frying: 8–10 mins • Baking: 10–12 mins

Neapolitan steaks

700 g boneless veal (leg), 1 large onion, 1–2 cloves of garlic, salt, pepper, 3 tbsps olive oil, 1 tbsp lemon juice, 1 tsp grated lemon rind, 4 tbsps chopped parsley

Crush the finely chopped garlic with salt, pepper, lemon zest and juice, mix in the grated onion and oil. Cut the rinsed and dried meat into 4 slices, pound lightly with a mallet. Spread some garlicky mixture on each slice, place on a plate, cover and put into the fridge for 2–3 hours. Fry or grill the meat. Before serving, sprinkle generously with parsley. Serve with rice or macaroni, with a tomato sauce.

serves 4 • Macerating: 2–3 hrs • Frying: 101–2 mins

Wiener schnitzels

600 g boneless veal, 2 eggs, 2 tbsps flour, ½ cup breadcrumbs, salt, pepper, 1 lemon, 3 tbsps lard, 2 tbsps butter

Rinse and dry the meat, cut it into 4 slices, press down firmly with your hand, sprinkle with salt and pepper. Mix the eggs with 1–2 tbsps of water. Dip the meat into flour, the beaten eggs and breadcrumbs, press lightly to make the coating stick. Fry in very hot lard until golden brown on both sides, then turn down the heat and continue cooking for another 2–3 mins. Arrange the meat on a warm serving dish, place thin slices of butter and lemon on each schnitzel, garnish with parsley sprigs.

serves 4 • Preparation: 5 mins • Frying: 12–15 mins

Swiss veal schnitzels

600 g leg of veal (off the bone), 8 thin ham rashers, 4 thick cheese slices (Gruyere or Emmental), flour, 1 egg, 1 tbsp white wine, sifted breadcrumbs, 1 tbsp lard, 2 tbsps butter, salt, pepper

Cut the rinsed and dried meat into 4 portions, pound them with a mallet into thin slices, sprinkle with salt and pepper. Cover half of each slice with a piece of ham, then cheese and another ham rasher. Fold in two, secure with a toothpick. Mix the egg with the wine. Dip the meat in flour, egg and breadcrumbs and fry in very hot lard for 2 mins to each sides. Turn down the heat, put in the butter and fry for several minutes longer. Serve with sautéed potatoes with herbs.

serves 4 • Preparation: 5 mins • Frying: 10–12 mins

Veal schnitzels with anchovy

600 g boneless veal, salt, pepper, 2 tbsps flour, 4 eggs, 1 tbsp lard, 3 tbsps butter, 4 slices of white bread, 1 tin anchovies, 8 capers

Cut the rinsed and dried meat into slices, pound lightly with a mallet, sprinkle with salt and pepper. Fry on both sides in very hot lard, then turn down the heat, add 1 tbsps of butter and continue frying for 2 mins to each side. Butter the bread and brown it on both sides in a frying pan or a toaster. Fry the eggs sunny side up in 1 tbsp of melted butter. Arrange the toast in a warm serving dish, place the schnitzels on them, cover each with an egg. Garnish each schnitzel with anchovies and two capers. Serve with puréed vegetables or with sautéd potatoes and lettuce.

serves 4 • Preparation: 10 mins • Frying: 8–10 mins

Veal schnitzels with liver and mushrooms

600 g leg of veal (off the bone), 100 g veal liver, ¼ cup milk, 200 g button mushrooms, 1 tbsp lemon juice, ¼ tsp ground coriander, 2 crushed cloves of garlic, salt, pepper, 3 tbsps butter, 2 tbsps dry white wine, 3 tbsps finely chopped parsley

Remove the membranes from the liver. Put the liver into a bowl, cover with the milk and leave aside for several minutes, then dry and cut into 4 slices. Slice the rinsed and dried mushrooms, sprinkle them with the lemon juice, coriander and garlic. Cut the rinsed and dried meat into 4 slices, pound lightly with a mallet. Melt 2 tbsps of butter in a frying pan and fry the schnitzels for 3 mins to each side. Sprinkle with salt and pepper and transfer to an ovenproof dish. Fry the liver in the same pan for 1 min to each side, then place it on top of the meat. Put the remaining butter into the pan and sauté the mushrooms. Continue cooking until the juices have been reduced, add salt and pepper. Put the mushrooms around the meat and place the dish in a hot oven for several minutes. Deglaze the pan with the wine, bring to the boil. Pour the gravy over the meat, sprinkle with chopped parsley. Serve with baked potatoes and savoury mayonnaise sauce.

serves 4 • Preparation: 10 mins • Frying: 10–12 mins • Baking: 3–4 mins

Veal zrazy, Old Polish style

700 g leg of veal (off the bone), 400 g tart apples, 2 tbsps dry white wine, juice and grated rind of ½ lemon, 1 tbsp lard, 3 tbsps butter, salt, pepper, sugar, 1 tbsp marjoram, 1 cup stock, 1 tbsp flour, 3 tbsps chopped parsley, ½ lemon

Peel and core the apples, cut them into quarters, sprinkle with lemon juice. Cut the rinsed and dried meat into thin slices, pound lightly with a mallet, sprinkle with salt and pepper, dust with flour and fry in very hot lard. Melt 1 tbsp of butter in a saucepan, put in the apple peelings, sprinkle with the lemon zest and half the marjoram. Place the meat on top, add the stock and cook over low heat. Melt 2 tbsps of butter in another pan, put in the apple quarters and soften them a bit, then sprinkle with sugar, the remaining marjoram and wine, stir gently and keep over very low heat. Arrange the meat on a warm serving dish, surround it with the apple quarters. Sieve the apple peelings, pour the sauce over the meat. Sprinkle with chopped parsley and garnish with lemon slices.

serves 4 • Preparation: 25–30 mins

Nobleman's zrazy

600 g leg of veal (off the bone), 4 thin smoked bacon rashers, 4 each apricots and prunes (without stones), ½ cup dry white wine, 1 tbsp hot mustard, salt, pepper, flour, 1 tbsp lard, 1 tbsp butter, 1 cup chicken broth, 1 thyme sprig, 1 bay leaf, 2–3 grains each allspice and pepper

Rinse the apricots and prunes, cover them with the wine and leave aside for an hour. Cut the rinsed and dried meat into 4 slices. Pound the slices flat with a mallet, brush with the mustard, sprinkle with salt and pepper. Place 1 rasher, 1 apricot and 1 prune on each slice, roll up the meat tightly, tie with thread or secture with toothpicks. Bring the stock to the boil, add the bay leaf, allspice, pepper and thyme, cover and simmer for 10 mins, then strain and mix with the wine in which the fruit had soaked. Dust the zrazy with flour. Heat the lard in a frying pan, add the butter and fry the meat rolls on all sides. Pour in the stock, cover the pan and simmer for 10–15 mins. Serve with noodles or kasha.

serves 4 • Soaking: 1 hr • Preparation: 15–20 mins

Zrazy stuffed with pork fat

700 g boneless veal, 100 g pork fat, 2 tbsps finely chopped sage leaves or 1 tsp dried sage, 2–3 cloves of garlic, salt, pepper, 2 tbsps olive oil, 2 tbsps butter, 1 cup dry white wine, ¼ cup stock, 1 carrot, 1 onion, 1 bay leaf, 1 thyme sprig, 2–3 parsley sprigs, 1 tbsp flour

Cut the rinsed and dried meat into slices. Pound the slices flat with a mallet. Put the pork fat through a mincer, blend it with salt, pepper, sage and the finely chopped garlic. Spread the mixture on each slice, roll it up, secure with a toothpick. Dredge with flour and brown in very hot oil. Transfer to a skillet, add the butter. Fry the finely chopped onion in the same pan, but do not let it brown, add the

finely diced carrot, sauté for a minute or two, then add to the meat. Sprinkle the zrazy with some stock, put in the bay leaf, thyme and parsley and simmer for a while, then pour in the wine, shake the skillet and cook for another 15–20 mins. Adjust the taste. Towards the end, take out the bay leaf, thyme and parsley and sieve the sauce. Serve with pasta.

serves 4 • Preparation: 15–20 mins • Braising: 15–20 mins

Swallows' nests

600 g veal, 200 g minced beef, 4 slices of lean ham, 4 hard-boiled eggs, salt, pepper, ¼ tsp grated lemon rind, 1 tbsp grated onion, 3 tbsps butter, 1 tbsp flour, ½ cup dry white wine or stock

Mix the minced beef with the onion, salt, pepper and lemon zest. Cut the rinsed and dried veal into 4 slices, pound them flat with a mallet, sprinkle with salt and pepper. Spread the beef on top, cover with the ham, place one shelled egg on each portion. Roll up the meat tightly, tie with thread, dust with flour and brown in butter. Transfer to a skillet, sprinkle with the wine or stock, cover and cook for 30 mins. Serve with French fries or rice and with salads.

serves 4 • Preparation: 15 mins • Braising: 30 mins

Veal fricadelles with rice

600 g boneless veal (shoulder), 1 large onion, 1 cup light stock, ½ cup rice, 2 tbsps tomato purée, 2 eggs, 1 tbsp potato flour, 2–3 cloves of garlic, salt, pepper, 1 tbsp chili pepper, ½ cup breadcrumbs, 3–4 tbsps lard

Put the rinsed meat into a pan, add the peeled onion, cover with the hot stock and cook till tender. Take out the meat and onion, allow to cool. Put the tomato purée and the rinsed rice into the stock and cook until the liquid has been absorbed, then leave to cool. Mix the finely chopped garlic with salt. Put the meat, onion and rice through a mincer, add the garlic, potato flour and pepper, break in the eggs and work into a smooth paste. Shape it into small patties, dredge with breadcrumbs and fry in very hot lard for 2 mins to each side. Turn down the heat and fry for a while longer. Serve with baked potatoes or puréed vegetables, with tomato, pepper or string bean salad.

serves 4 • Preparation: 40 mins • Frying: 6–8 mins

Veal fricadelles with walnuts

700 g boneless veal, ½ cup coarsely chopped walnuts, 1 large onion, 2 eggs, salt, pepper, 1 tbsp butter, 4 tbsps chopped parsley, 4 lemon slices

Put the meat through a mincer three times, mix it with the grated onion, break in the eggs, add salt and pepper and work into a smooth mixture. Divide it into 4 portions, place each on a wet wooden board, shape into a rectangle, sprinkle with the walnuts. Roll up, put in a greased roasting tin and bake until golden brown. Before serving, sprinkle with chopped parsley and garnish with lemon slices. Serve with baked potatoes or French fries, with lettuce or chicory salad.

serves 4 • Preparation: 15 mins • Baking: 10–12 mins

Veal croquettes with ham

300–350 g roast or cooked veal, 100–150 g smoked ham, 1 dry bread roll, ½ cup milk, 2 eggs, 1 onion, 1 tbsp butter, 1 tbsp tomato purée, salt, pepper, oil for deep frying, 3–4 tbsps breadcrumbs, several parsley sprigs

Fry the finely chopped onion in melted butter, but do not let it brown. Add the tomato purée, salt and pepper, stir and simmer for a while, then take off the heat and leave to cool. Soak the bread roll in milk, squeeze it out a bit, mix with the tomato sauce. Put in the minced meat and ham. break in 1 egg, mix thoroughly, season to taste. Shape small croquettes from the mixture. Dip them into the lightly beaten egg and breadcrumbs and fry in hot oil. Garnish with parsley sprigs. Serve with rice or macaroni with, for example, tomato sauce.

serves 4 • Preparation: 15 mins • Frying: 6–8 mins

Veal croquettes with liver

cooked veal and liver, 1 large onion, 1 tbsp butter, 1 tbsp flour, juice and grated rind of ½ lemon, 2 raw egg yolks, ½ tsp pepper, breadcrumbs or chopped walnuts for coating, fat for frying

Fry the finely chopped onion in butter, but do not let it brown. Sprinkle with the flour, stir well, take off the heat. Chop the meat and liver very finely, add the lemon juice and zest, pepper, onion and egg yolks, and work into a smooth paste. Add salt if required. Shape the mixture into small balls, coat them with breadcrumbs or chopped walnuts and fry until golden brown. Serve with rice and salad, or as a hot hors-d'oeuvre with pickled vegetables.

serves 4 • Preparation: 10–15 mins • Frying: 8–10 mins

Calf's ears sultane

Clean and singe the calves' ears thoroughly, boil them in water. Put them into hot stock, add several pork fat slices, parsley sprigs, onion, thyme, bay leaf, basil, cloves, salt and pepper and cook, then drain them, leave to cool and cut into smaller portions. Put into a skillet together with some ham, diced mushrooms, onion and some butter. Pour in a cup of champagne and stock, add parsley sprigs, onion and basil and simmer over low heat. Skim the fat, take out the parsley, dip the ham in mustard, heat up and serve hot.

(Wojciech Wielądko, *Kucharz doskonały*, 1808)

Veal à la salmon

1½ kg leg of veal (off the bone), salt

** 300–500 g veal bones,
soup vegetables, 2 bay leaves,
10 grains each allspice and pepper*

*MARINADE: 2 cups white wine
(or ½ cup 10% vinegar and 1 cup water),
¼ tsp sugar, 2 cloves, 1 large onion*

Prepare the marinade from all the ingredients. Rinse the meat, remove the membranes. Pound it with a mallet, place in a stoneware jar. Cover with the marinade and leave in a cool place for 1–2 days. Make a court-bouillon from the bones, vegetables and spices. Rinse and dry the meat, rub it with salt, roll up tightly and tie with twine. Put into a skillet, cover with the strained stock and marinade and cook over low heat for 3 hours, then leave in the stock for 24 hours. Take the meat out, cut it into thin slices. Serve cold with mayonnaise or sauce tartare.

serves 6–8 • Marinating: 1–2 days • Cooking: 3 hrs • Cooling: 24 hrs

Calf's feet in aspic

4 calves' feet, soup vegetables, 3 onions, 1 clove of garlic, 1 bay leaf, 5–6 grains each pepper and allspice, a pinch of sugar, salt, egg white, 2 lemons, parsley

Clean, singe and blanch the calves' feet. Put them into a large pan, add the peeled and rinsed soup vegetables, onion and spices, cover with water and cook over low heat for 3 hours. Take them out and leave to cool. Strain the stock (ca 1 l of court-bouillon should be left), add the juice from 2 lemons. Clarify the stock with the egg white, put it through a fine gauze or sieve. Bone the feet, cut the meat into thin strips. Put the meat strips into individual aspic moulds, cover with the cool stock and leave in a cool place to set. Unmould the aspic, arrange on a serving dish, garnish with lemon slices and parsley sprigs. Serve with horseradish, wine vinegar or lemon juice.

serves 6–8 • Preparation: 20 mins • Cooking: 2½ to 3 hrs • Cooling: 2–3 hrs • Refrigerating: 1–2 hrs

Beef

Beef, Irish style

Put a piece of beef in a pot, add two or three carrots, one parsley root, three or four small onions, a bunch of parsley, a clove of garlic, three cloves, a bay leaf, thyme, basil, cover with bouillon or water, add salt, pepper and simmer over a low heat. When the meat is half cooked, add two heads of cabbage prepared as follows: take two small heads of cabbage or one large one; take off the outer green leaves, boil the cabbage whole in water for half an hour, transfer to cold water, then strain well, pull outwards the leaves and put in between the leaves stuffing made from veal, mushrooms and artichokes, or from other meat; then divide them up into three of four leaves, make small rolls of cabbage, a little bigger than an egg; tie them up and cook them together with the meat.

When the meat is cooked, strain the stock, skim off the fat, arrange the meat on a dish, cut each cabbage in half and place around the meat. Make a sauce by sieving the bouillon, skim off the fat, heat and pour over the meat and cabbage.

(Wojciech Wielądko, *Kucharz doskonały*, 1808)

The meat from young beast is best, and it should be light red, lightly surrounded by white suet, delicate and shining. For roasting choose the upper part of the hind quarters, that is the sirloin, entrecôte and leg, and also the shin (for roulades).

For a roast to taste good and be tender and digestible, as well as having a pleasant aroma, the beef should be tenderized:
– in yogurt, buttermilk or sour milk for 12 hours to 3 days;
– in a wine or vinegar marinade for 2 to 5 days, and it should be turned over daily, so that it marinates evenly;
– in a dressing made of oil, vegetables and spices for 2 to 3 days.

Before placing the meat in the marinade or dressing, the excess fat should be trimmed off and the tendons removed; it should be washed quickly under running water, so that it will not lose its vitamins and minerals, and carefully dried. Sirloin and rump steak are roasted for shorter time and should be salted after cooking; other joints (leg and shin) should be salted before roasting. A roast that is to be cooked on a grill should be sprinkled with pepper and rubbed with olive oil or other fat (but not butter). Before roasting entrecôte it is advisable to tie it with thread, so that it does not get out of shape and is easy to carve into even slices when it is roasted. Beef is an excellent meat, both for elegant dishes – roast sirloin, steaks, tournedos, zrazy – and for more ordinary roasts, cutlets, rump steaks, goulashes, fricadelles.

Entrecôte

Entrecôte, also called a rib steak, is the name that comes from the cut of beef used – that is, between the ribs. It

Beef, Irish style

is a beef steak made from a piece of meat on the bone from the upper front quarter of the beast. In the middle of the steak there is meat, at the bottom the rib bone and marbled meat around the edge. The meat is cut along the rib into cutlets 2 to 3 cm thick. Marinating the meat before cooking gives good results. Entrecôte steaks should be fried for a short time in a very hot frying pan, not more than two at the same time, so that they brown nicely and do not lose too much of their juices. They are usually garnished with shredded horseradish, a slice of lemon and pieces of flavoured butter, or with sauce (for example béarnaise sauce).

Depending on the recipe, they can be served with French fries, runner beans, fried onions or mushrooms and always with horseradish, anchovy or chive-flavoured butter.

Marinated entrecôte

1 kg beef entrecôte, 2 onions, 1 cup dry red wine, 1 bay leaf, 1 tsp dried thyme, 3 tbsps olive oil, salt, pepper;

2 tbsps butter, 1 tsp lemon juice,
1 tbsp finely chopped parsley

Rinse the meat, remove the backbone. Cut the meat into slices along the rib, pound it lightly with a mallet. Mix the wine with 1 tbsp of oil, thyme and crumbled bay leaf. Put the meat into a pan, line it with onion slices, pour over the marinade, cover and leave overnight in a cool place. Take the meat out, dry it and brown on both sides in hot oil. Transfer to a skillet, cover with the marinade and cook over low heat for 30 mins, adding salt and pepper towards the end. Reduce the pan juices, sieve them and pour over the meat. Serve knobs of parsley butter separately.

serves 4 • Preparation: 15–20 mins • Marinating: 12 hrs • Braising: 30 mins

Grilled entrecôte

1 kg beef entrecôte, ¼ cup each soya sauce, brandy and lemon juice, 3–4 cloves of garlic, 3 tbsps chopped parsley, ½ tsp ground pepper, salt, 2 tbsps olive oil

Cut the rinsed and dried meat into 4 steaks, remove the backbone. Mix the soya sauce, brandy, lemon juice and pepper. Rub the mixture into the steaks, cover them and leave overnight in the fridge. Mix the finely chopped parsley with the oil. Take the meat out, rub it with the oil and grill, basting occasionally with the marinade. Salt it before serving.

serves 4

Entrecôte à la provençale

1 kg beef entrecôte, 4 tbsps olive oil, 1 glass dry white wine, 2 onions, 1 tsp tomato concentrate, salt, pepper

Remove the backbone, rinse and dry the meat, notch it along the edges every 2 cm. Heat 3 tbsps of oil in a large skillet, brown the meat on all sides, sprinkle with salt and pepper, cover and simmer over low heat for 30–40 mins (do not add any water). Heat the remaining oil in a pan, brown the onions cut into slices, sprinkle with salt and pepper. Pour in the wine mixed with the tomato concentrate, stir and cook for a while. When the meat is tender, cut it into slices along the ribs. Arrange the slices in an ovenproof dish, pour over the onion sauce and put into a preheated oven for 5–7 mins.

serves 4 • Preparation: 10 mins • Braising: 40 mins • Baking: 7 mins

Entrecôte, Italian style

1 kg beef entrecôte, 100 g beef marrow, 2 large onions, 3–4 firm beef tomatoes, 4 tbsps marinated shallots, 4 tbsps chopped parsley, salt, pepper, 4 tbsps oil, 2 tbsps butter

Remove the backbone, rinse and dry the meat, cut it into 4 portions, notch the fatty edges. Rub the meat with some oil. Chop the peeled onions finely, blanch and skin the tomatoes, cut them into cubes. Bring some salted water to the boil. Cut the marrow into 4 slices, place it in a sieve and dip into the boiling water for 3 mins, then drain. Fry the onion in 1 tbsp of hot oil, but do not let it brown. Put in the tomatoes, add salt and pepper and cook over low heat for 5 mins. Heat the remaining oil in a large frying pan and quickly fry the steaks for 3 mins to each side. Arrange the steaks in a hot ovenproof dish, sprinkle with salt and pepper, pour over the melted butter. Place a slice of marrow on each steak. Cover with the stewed tomatoes, arrange the shallots around, sprinkle with chopped parsley and put into a preheated oven. Serve with macaroni, scooped out potatoes, vegetable purée and lettuce or other kinds of salad.

serves 4 • Preparation: 20 mins • Baking: 4–6 mins

Boiled beef

Maria Ochorowicz-Monatowa wrote: *'Boiled beef is the most common dish, both in the poorest homes and at the most elegant tables. It is above all the favourite dish of all men, who consider it the basis for any good meal, and it is often served even at royal tables. Emperor Franz Joseph of Austria had a piece of boiled beef with a nice ring of fat every day for dinner.'*

Boiled beef is part of the classic culinary repertoire, and in fact comprises two dishes: broth, and a piece of meat served with various vegetables. When the recipe first developed is difficult to say. This is a dish from a simple and poor cuisine that eventually found its way onto elegant tables. It was prepared in hundreds of ways:

– with sauces: horseradish, dill, chive, mustard;

– baked, with béchamel, cheese or herb sauce;

– served with 'Dutch onions', 'Dutch cheese', 'with Swiss cheese Italian style', 'with fried mushrooms', 'with herring', 'with grated potatoes', 'royal style', 'bourgeois style', or 'country style'.

Each time it was served, boiled beef had a different taste The best meat for really fine boiled beef is best rib, for this is meat that stays juicy after cooking and is tender. It can be carved in nice, even, broad slices with a layer of delicate fat. 'Apart from this, a piece of meat from the middle rib is also good, or meat from the fore quarters,' was the advice given by Mme Monatowa.

Boiled beef should be carved into thin slices and garnished with boiled vegetables (from the broth), and also with runner beans, cauliflower, savoy cabbage cooked whole or Brussels sprouts, and is usually served with boiled potatoes, or puréed beans or potatoes. Cold sauces improve the flavour: these can be savoury mayonnaises or cream, herb, chive, horseradish or parsley sauce; hot sauces – horseradish, potato, mustard or dill – can also be served as an accompaniment

Almost anything goes with a good piece of boiled beef, including a light dry red wine.

Boiled beef, Lithuanian style

ca 1 kg beef (round), soup vegetables with a wedge of savoy cabbage, 1 large onion studded with 3 cloves, 4–5 grains each allspice and pepper, 4–5 juniper berries, a small piece of cinnamon, 1–2 bay leaves, 5–6 parsley sprigs, 150 g stoned prunes, ½ cup crumbled dry wholemeal bread, 1 tsp honey, ½ cup dry red wine, 2 tbsps butter, a pinch of each pepper and cinnamon

Rinse the prunes, cover them with water and leave aside for 2–3 hours. Rinse the meat, put it into a large pan, add 5 cups of boiling water, bring to the boil. Cover the pan and simmer for 30 mins. Put in the spices and herbs, the peeled and rinsed vegetables and onion, and continue cooking over low heat for 60–70 mins, adding salt towards the end. Cook the soaked prunes, then sieve them. Melt 1 tbsp of butter in a pan, add the honey and 4–5 tbsps of stock, stir well. Fold in the prune purée and bread. Stirring all the time, bring to the boil and simmer until the sauce has thickened. Add salt, pepper and cinnamon to taste. Take out the cooked meat, cut it across the grain into large slices, arrange in an ovenproof dish greased with butter. Pour the sauce over and put into a preheated oven for 15–20 mins.

serves 4–6 • Soaking: 2–3 hrs • Cooking: 90 mins • Baking: 15–20 mins

Beef à la mode

In Old Polish cuisine boiled beef was enormously popular in the 19th century, and at the very beginning of the 20th century it was an absolutely essential part of the Sunday dinner of the middle classes. In the second half of the 19th century, what were called English stoves, or in other words, stoves with hot points on the top and ovens, began to come into fashions – and at this stage, boiled beef began to give way to roasts in gravy.

In the early 20th century, beef à la mode became exceptionally popular, and that fashion has continued to the present day. This is a particular kind of roast beef (although it can also be made from game or horsemeat) which is exceptionally tender and succulent. For beef à la mode, you need meat from leg of beef. This can mean rump or shin, both are excellent for our purpose. For a succulent roast you need at least 1½ to 2 kg of meat, because during roasting it will shrink by more than 30%. In order to prevent it shrinking too much it is a good idea to blanch the meat before roasting, that is, to throw it into boiling water for two or three minutes, or to brown it off on all sides in very hot fat, so that a protective film develops on the surface of the meat to prevent the juices escaping. The fat must be very hot, because if it is at too low a temperature, the meat will absorb it, the juices will escape and the meat will be dry, less tasty and indigestible. Blanching or browning allows the meat to retain its succulence, tenderness, colour, taste and nutritional value. After it has been browned, the meat should be braised in a tightly closed pan over a low heat, and frequently sprinkled with water, wine or marinade, so that it remains succulent. If you rinse the lid in cold water, this also yields good results, since it allows the appropriate level of moisture to be retained inside the pan. The taste and aroma of the meat depend on its being properly prepared. After the meat has been washed and dried you should knead it in the hand, which makes it more tender, and then leave it for 3 to 5 days in a marinade or olive oil dressing with spices or herbs. If we do not have time for this and want to tenderize the meat quickly, we can sprinkle it with lemon juice, and wrap it in a linen cloth that has been soaked in vodka or brandy, and put it in the fridge for 2 to 3 hours. Meat cooked in this way should be larded with strips of pork fat or streaky bacon, pickled tongue or fat ham. It is advisable to rub the pork fat or bacon with a mixture of herbs and garlic or spices before it is used for larding and then leave it for 2 to 3 hours.

Beef à la mode

Take beef flank, lard it deeply with raw ham or bacon fat, put it in a pan, add six onions, three carrots, three parsley roots, a bay leaf, thyme, basil, pour in a bottle of wine and a bottle of white vinegar; add enough broth or water to leave the meat not entirely covered, add a little salt, cover the pan, seal it with pastry, and cook it on a tripod or over a medium heat (so that the meat does not cook too fast) for seven or eight hours; then open the pan, take out the meat, trim off the fat evenly. Place the meat on a serving dish, sieve the gravy in which it cooked and pour it over.

(Nauka dokładna sposobów warzenia... przez Tremona... do druku podana, Cracow 1839)

Larded beef à la mode

1½ kg boneless beef (thick flank), 100 g smoked streaky bacon, 80 g pickled ox tongue, salt, pepper, ¼ tsp each ground allspice, cloves, ginger, marjoram and cayenne (or chilli), 2 cloves of garlic, 1 carrot, 1 parsley root, a piece of celeriac, 1 onion, ½ lemon, ½ cup dry red wine, 1 slice of finely crumbled dry wholemeal bread, 1 tsp sugar, ½ cup stock, 1 tbsp fat for frying

Cut the bacon and tongue into strips, sprinkle them generously with a mixture of herbs and spices. Pound the meat with a mallet, rub it with the finely chopped garlic mixed with salt. Bard the meat with the bacon and tongue, sprinkle with the remaining spices. Brown it on all sides in the hot fat, put in the peeled and rinsed vegetables cut into slices. Add some stock, cover the pan and simmer for 90 mins, basting frequently with stock or water. When the meat is almost ready, add the bread and sugar, sprinkle with the lemon juice and wine and continue cooking for another 15–20 mins. Cut the meat into slices. Serve the sieved sauce separately. Serve with potatoes or bread dumplings.

serves 6–8 • Preparation: 15 mins • Braising: 90–120 mins

Spicy beef à la mode

ca 1½ kg boneless beef (round), 50–70 g pork fat, 1 cup stock, 1 cup dry red wine, 2 tbsps oil, a pinch of each ground allspice and cloves, 2 tbsps tomato paste, a pinch of sugar, salt, pepper, 1 tbsp potato flour if required

MARINADE: 1 parsley root, 1 carrot, a piece of celeriac, 2–3 cloves of garlic, 2 onions, 1 tsp each ground

Larded beef à la mode

allspice and pepper, ½ tsp each ground ginger and marjoram, ¼ tsp ground cloves, juice and grated rind of ½ lemon, 3–4 tbsps oil, ¼ tsp sugar

Knead the rinsed and dried meat in your hands. Grate the peeled and rinsed vegetables coarsely, chop the onions finely, crush the garlic with salt, mix them all. Add the lemon juice, zest, herbs and spices and mix thoroughly with the oil. Rub the meat with the mixture, put it into a stoneware bowl, spread the remaining mixture on top. Stand in a cool place for 2–3 days. Cut the pork fat into bards, rub them with salt, pepper, allspice and cloves and leave overnight in the fridge. Take the meat out, dry it, lard it and brown on all sides in very hot oil. Transfer it to a skillet, pile in the vegetables from the marinade, sprinkle with some stock. Cover the skillet and put into a preheated oven. Cook for 2 hours at a low temperature, basting frequently with stock and wine. Take out the meat from the skillet, put it in an ovenproof dish and return to the oven. Sieve the roast juices together with the vegetables, add the tomato purée, adjust the taste with salt, pepper, sugar and lemon juice. Heat the sauce up (it can be thickened with 1 tbsp of potato flour mixed with 2 tbsps of cold water). Cut the meat into slices. Pour some sauce over and serve the remainder in a sauce boat. It tastes best with noodles or bread dumplings, but can also be served with buckwheat or barley kasha, sautéd potatoes or French fries. It goes very well with steamed or braised vegetables, cabbage stewed in wine, salted cucumbers or coleslaw. Spicy beef à la mode can also be served cold, with pickled vegetables, saffron milk caps and gherkins, and with spicy yogurt or mayonnaise sauces.

serves 6–8 • Macerating: 2–3 days • Preparation: 10–15 mins • Roasting: 90–120 mins

Cold beef à la mode

1 kg beef (rump), 1 glass vodka (which is an excellent tenderizer), 1 tsp marjoram, 4–5 cloves, 5–6 grains allspice, 1 bay leaf, salt, fat for frying

MARINADE: 1 cup dry red wine, juice of ½ lemon (or 1 cup vinegar and 1 cup water instead of wine and lemon juice), 2 onions, 10 grains each allspice and pepper, 2 bay leaves

Make a marinade from all the ingredients. Knead the meat in your hands firmly, place it in a stoneware bowl, cover with the cold marinade. Stand in a cool place for 3–4 days, turning the meat over every day. Take the meat out, rinse and dry it, rub it with salt. Brown it on all sides in the hot fat, add the marjoram and spices, sprinkle with the vodka. Add 2–3 tbsps of water, cover the pan and simmer for 90 mins, basting frequently with cold water. Serve cold, cut into thin slices, with cocktail gherkins and pickled mushrooms or with a spicy cold sauce.

serves 6–8

Roast beef

Braised joint of beef, Old Polish style

1 kg beef (rump), 150 g pork fat, 7–8 cloves of garlic, 1 tsp marjoram, 2–3 sprigs of basil or 1 tsp dried basil, salt, pepper, 1 tsp flour

MARINADE: 1 cup wine vinegar, ½ cup dry red wine, 3–4 grains each pepper and allspice, 1–2 cloves, 1 onion, 2–3 garlic cloves, 1 tbsp dried tarragon, a pinch of sugar

Pound the meat with a mallet. Cut ⅓ of the pork fat into small cubes or put through a mincer. Blend it well with the crushed garlic, salt, marjoram and basil. Lard the meat with some of the mixture and rub with the remainder. Leave for 2–3 hours in a cool place. Prepare the marinade, bring it to the boil and pour over the meat, then leave aside to cool. Pour off the marinade, bring it to the boil and again cover the meat with it. Take the cool meat out, bard it with the remaining pork fat cut into thin slices. Brown it on all sides, add some marinade, cover the pan and simmer for 90 mins. Cut the meat into fine slices. Thicken the gravy with the flour, sieve it and serve in a sauce boat. Serve hot with buckwheat kasha or potatoes. If you plan to serve it cold, do not add flour to the gravy.

serves 4–6 • Marinating: 3–4 hrs • Preparation: 15 mins • Braising: 90 mins

Braised joint of beef, Old Polish style

Roast beef à la venison

*ca 1½ kg boneless beef (rump, sirloin), 1 large onion,
5–7 dried cep mushrooms, 1 cup thick sour cream,
1 tbsp lard, salt, pepper, 1 tbsp flour if required*

*MARINADE: 1 cup wine vinegar, 1 cup water, ½ tsp
grated lemon rind, 2 large onions, 2 bay leaves, 10 grains
each pepper and allspice, ¼ tsp each salt and sugar*

Cook the marinade. Rinse and dry the meat, knead it
firmly with your hands, place in a stoneware bowl,
pour the cool marinade over. Cover with a board, weigh
down and stand in a cool place for 4–5 days, turning the
meat over every day. Soak the mushrooms in water, then
cook them. Rinse and dry the meat, rub it with salt and
pepper and brown on all sides in the hot lard. Transfer it
to a roasting tin, pile the peeled and diced onion on top,
sprinkle with some strained marinade. Cover and put into
a preheated oven for an hour, then add the mushrooms
cut into strips and return to the oven for another 30 mins.
Baste frequently with the remaining marinade and then
with the mushroom stock. Towards the end pour over the
cream (or cream mixed with flour).

serves 6–8 • Marinating: 4–5 days • Preparation: 10 mins • Roasting: 90 mins

Hussar's roast beef

*ca 1 kg beef (sirloin), juice and grated
rind of ½ lemon, 1 cup dry white wine,
1 tbsp oil, 1 large onion, salt, pepper*

*STUFFING: 4 tbsps grated dry brown bread, 2 tbsps
fat, 2–3 onions, 2 egg yolks, salt, pepper*

Sprinkle the rinsed and dried meat with the lemon juice,
rub it with salt and zest and leave in a cool place for
an hour. Dry it a bit and brown on all sides in the hot
oil. Transfer to a skillet, sprinkle with the chopped onion
and water. Cover the skillet and place in a preheated oven
for 40 mins, basting frequently with wine and water. To
make the stuffing, chop the onion finely, fry it in fat, but do
not let it brown. Combine with the grated bread, add salt
and pepper, stir well and leave to cool, then mix with the
egg yolks. Take the meat out, notch it every 1½ cm and

fill every second notch with the stuffing. Sieve the gravy.
Return the meat to the skillet, pour the sieved gravy over
and put into the oven for another 20 mins, basting it with
the wine. It tastes best with potato croquettes or fried
dumplings, with the sauce served separately.

serves 4–6 • Macerating: 2 hrs • Preparation: 45 mins • Baking: 20 mins

Braised joint of beef with vegetables

*1 kg beef (rump), 2 parsley roots, 2 carrots,
1 celeriac, 1 kohlrabi, several cauliflower florets
or several asparagus stalks, 2 onions, 1 cup red
wine, 2–3 cloves, 4–5 grains each allspice and
pepper, 1 bay leaf, salt, fat for frying, 1 tsp butter*

Pound the rinsed and dried meat with a mallet, rub it
with salt and leave aside for 30 mins. Brown it on all
sides in the hot fat. Peel, rinse and dice the vegetables, line
a skillet with half of them. Place the meat on top, cover
with the remaining vegetables, add the butter and spices,
pour in the wine. Cover the skillet and simmer for 2 hours.
Take the meat out, sieve the vegetables with the gravy. Cut
the meat diagonally into slices, pour the sauce over. Serve
with baked potatoes.

serves 4–6 • Salting: 30 mins • Preparation: 15 mins • Braising: 90–120 mins

Roast beef with mint

*ca 1 kg fillet of beef, ¼ tsp dried mint, 2–3 cloves
of garlic, ¼ tsp cayenne pepper, 1 tsp lemon juice,
1 tbsp oil, 4 tbsps chopped fresh mint leaves, 1 tsp
chopped fresh tarragon leaves, 1 tbsp fat, ½ cup
dry white wine, a pinch of sugar, salt, pepper*

Mix the crushed garlic with the cayenne, dried mint,
1 tbsp of oil and lemon juice. Rub the rinsed and
dried meat with the mixture. Wrap it in foil and put in
the fridge for 3–4 hours. Place the meat in a greased ovenproof dish and put into a preheated oven for 30 mins,
basting it first with water and then with the roasting juices
and wine. Sprinkle it with the chopped herbs, add salt,
pepper and sugar to taste. Cover with foil and cook in the
oven for another 10 mins.

serves 4–6 • Macerating: 3–4 hrs • Roasting: 40 mins

Hussar's roast beef

Roast beef with rosemary

*ca 1 kg fillet of beef, 1 tbsp ground dried
rosemary, ½ tsp dried tarragon, 2–3 cloves
of garlic, juice and grated rind of 1 lemon,
50 g pork fat, 1 tbsp oil, salt, pepper*

Chop the garlic finely, mix it with the pepper, rosemary, tarragon and lemon zest. Rub the mixture into the pork fat, sprinkle with salt, place in a bowl and leave overnight in the fridge. Sprinkle the rinsed and dried meat with the lemon juice, rub in the remaining mixture. Wrap it in foil and leave in the fridge overnight. Cut the pork fat into strips, lard the meat with them. Brush the meat with oil, place it in a roasting bag. Seal the bag, place it in a roasting tin and put into a preheated oven for 30–35 mins. Salt the meat towards the end. Serve hot or cold, with a piquant sauce.

*serves 4–6 • Macerating: 12 hrs • Preparation:
15 mins • Roasting: 30–35 mins*

Fillet of beef in cabbage leaves

1 kg fillet of beef, salt, pepper, 1 tbsp Dijon mustard

** 500 g roast veal, 150 g mushrooms, 2 onions,
1 savoy cabbage, 2 tbsps chopped parsley, 1 egg,
salt, pepper, a pinch of salt, 50 g pork fat*

* fat for frying, 1 tbsp butter

Rub the fillet with salt, pepper and mustard and leave in a cool place for 3–4 hours. Cook the sliced mushrooms and onions in butter. Blanch the cabbage, separate 6–8 top leaves and put them aside. Add the rest of the cabbage to the mushrooms, cover the pan and simmer until tender. Put the roast veal, cabbage, mushrooms and onion through a mincer, add salt, pepper, sugar and parsley, break in the eggs and mix thoroughly. Brown the fillet on all sides in hot fat, allow it to cool, then cover with the stuffing, wrap in the cabbage leaves and slices of pork fat, tie up with thread. Place in a greased ovenproof dish and put in a preheated oven. Cook for 40 mins. Before serving, cut into slices and pour the pan drippings over.

serves 6–8 • Macerating: 3–4 hrs • Preparation: 40 mins • Roasting: 40 mins

Beef roulade with cheese

*ca 1 kg beef (rump), 100 g mild cheese, 1 onion,
3–4 cloves of garlic, 1 tbsp tomato purée,
1 cup dry red wine, 3–4 tbsps thick cream,
3–4 tbsps chopped parsley, ½ tbsp thyme,
½ cup strong stock, 2 tbsps oil, 1 tbsp flour, a
pinch of sugar, salt, pepper, cayenne pepper*

Rinse and dry the meat, cut it half way through lengthwise, pound with a mallet to form a rectangle of even thickness. Sprinkle with cayenne pepper. Combine the finely chopped onion with the garlic crushed with salt, thyme, parsley and 1 tsp of oil, mix thoroughly. Brush the meat with the tomato purée, line it with thin slices of cheese, spread the onion mixture on top. Roll the meat up tightly, tie with twine and brown on all sides in hot oil. Transfer to a skillet, sprinkle with some stock, cover and put into a preheated oven. Baste frequently with stock and wine and later with the pan juices. Towards the end, take the lid off and pour the cream mixed with flour over the meat. Cut the meat into slices, arrange them in a warm serving dish. Adjust the taste of the gravy with salt, pepper, thyme and sugar and serve it in a sauce boat.

serves 4–6 • Preparation: 15–20 mins • Braising: 1 hr

Fillet of beef à la Napoleon

1 kg fillet of beef

** 1 tbsp butter, 1 cup thick cream, 1 tsp thyme,
salt, pepper, ¼ tsp ground allspice, 1 tsp grated
lemon rind, 1 tbsp lemon juice, 3 onions, 2 carrots,
2 parsley roots, ½ celeriac, 1 tbsp capers*

Rub the rinsed meat with salt and leave in a cool place for 30 mins. Peel and rinse the vegetables, dice them or grate coarsely. Place the meat in a skillet or an ovenproof dish, pile the vegetables around, sprinkle with pepper, allspice, thyme and lemon zest, put slices of butter on top. Put into a preheated oven and cook for 30 mins. Add the capers and a pinch of sugar, sprinkle with the lemon juice, pour the cream over and return to the oven for another 20 mins. Before serving, cut the meat diagonally into slices

Beef roulade with cheese

and sieve the vegetables for a thick sauce to be served separately.

serves 4–6 • Salting: 30 mins • Preparation: 10 mins • Roasting: 30 mins • Baking: 20 mins

Fillet of beef in cream

750 g fillet of beef, 50 g pork fat, 100 g butter, 1 carrot, ½ celeriac, 1 parsley root, 1 small turnip, 4–5 grains each allspice and pepper, 1 bay leaf, ½ tsp grated lemon rind, 1–2 tbsps lemon juice, 1 tsp dried thyme, 1 tbsp flour, ½ cup thick cream, ¼ cup stock, 1 glass dry white wine

Lard the meat with thin strips of pork fat. Grate the peeled and rinsed vegetables coarsely, sprinkle them with the spices, herbs and lemon zest, mix thoroughly. Grease an ovenproof dish with butter, line it with the vegetables, place the meat on top. Sprinkle with lemon juice, pour melted butter over, cover and leave in the fridge for 1–2 days, turning the meat over twice. Take out of the fridge and bring it up to room temperature, then put into a preheated oven and cook for 40 mins, basting with the stock and wine. Take the meat out of the dish and keep it warm. Put the vegetables through a blender and sieve them. Adjust the taste with salt, pepper and lemon juice. Bring to the boil, pour in the cream mixed with the flour, stir well and heat up. Cut the meat diagonally into slices, arrange in a warm serving dish and pour some sauce over. Serve the remaining sauce separately.

serves 4 • Macerating: 1–2 days • Roasting: 40 mins

Fillet of beef larded with ham

ca 800 g fillet of beef, 50 g lean smoked ham, 50 g pork fat, 100 g mushrooms, ½ cup dry white wine, 1 tsp lemon juice, 1 tbsp fat, 1 carrot, 1 parsley root, 1 onion, 1 bay leaf, 3–4 grains each allspice and pepper, 1–2 cloves, ½ cup stock, salt, pepper

Sprinkle the rinsed and dried meat with the lemon juice, rub it with pepper and lard it with strips of ham and mushrooms. Cover it with bards of pork fat, tie with thread and place in a greased roasting tin. Pile around the finely diced vegetables and onions, add the spices and stock.

Cover and cook over high heat for 10 mins. Pour in the wine and put into a preheated oven for 30 mins, basting sparingly with the roasting juices. Take the meat out, sprinkle with salt and pepper. Cut it diagonally into slices (the meat should be pink inside) and serve with potato croquettes. Serve the sauce made from the sieved braising stock and vegetables separately.

serves 4–6 • Preparation: 20 mins • Braising: 30 mins

Fillet of beef in potato batter

1 kg boiled potatoes, 3 tbsps flour, 4 eggs

* 1 kg fillet of beef, juice of ½ lemon, 3 tbsps butter, 1 tbsp sunflower oil, salt, pepper, parsley

Rub the meat with the oil, sprinkle with the lemon juice and leave overnight in the fridge, then dry and salt it sparingly. Blend the minced potatoes with 2 tbsps of butter, salt, pepper and flour, break in 3 eggs and mix thoroughly. Roll the pastry out into a 1½ cm thick rectangle. Put the meat on it and roll it up in the pastry, seal the ends carefully. Brush it on top with lightly beaten egg. Put into a greased baking tin and place in a preheated oven. Bake for over an hour, basting frequently with melted butter. Cut it into thick slices, arrange them in a serving platter, garnish with parsley sprigs. Serve with béarnaise or bordelaise sauce. The meat should be pink inside. If the pastry browns to quickly, cover the tin with aluminium foil.

serves 4–6 • Macerating: 12 hrs • Preparation: 10 mins • Baking: 60–70 mins

Beef sirloin with herbs

ca 1 kg beef sirloin, 1 cup dry red wine, 4 tbsps oil, ¼ tsp dried thyme, 2 tsps each fresh basil, thyme, rosemary, coriander and lemon balm (1 tsp each dried herbs), 4–5 cloves of garlic, 2 tbsps herbal mustard, 1 tsp lemon juice, a pinch of sugar, salt, pepper

Mix the finely chopped herbs with the crushed garlic, salt, lemon juice, mustard and 1 tbsp of oil. Rinse and dry the meat, knead it firmly with your hand, rub with pepper and brown in hot oil. Transfer to a roasting tin, put into a preheated oven and cook for 30 mins, basting lightly with oil and water. Take the half-cooked meat out, allow it to cool. Rub it well with the herbal mixture, press firmly to make it stick. Return the meat to the roasting tin and put back into the oven for another 10–15 mins until it browns nicely. Cut it into slices and arrange on a warm serving platter. Mix the gravy with the wine, adjust the taste with thyme, salt, pepper and sugar, bring to the boil and pour over the meat.

serves 4–6 • Preparation: 40 mins • Roasting: 15 mins

Beef, Kashub style

ca 1 kg beef (rump, round), 15 cloves of garlic, 1 tbsp marjoram, 1 tbsp lemon juice, 100 g pork fat, 1 tbsp lard, ½ cup stock, ½ cup dry white wine, salt, pepper

Rinse and dry the meat, knead it with your hand. Mix the crushed garlic with the pepper and marjoram. Rub the pork fat and meat with the mixture. Sprinkle the meat with the lemon juice and wrap in foil. Leave the meat and pork fat overnight in the fridge. Lard the meat with thin strips of pork fat and brown on all sides in hot lard. Transfer to a roasting tin, sprinkle with salt, put into a preheated oven and cook, basting frequently with stock and wine and later with the pan juices. Serve hot or cold.

serves 4–6 • Macerating: 12 hrs • Preparation: 5 mins • Roasting: 1 hr

Burgher's beef

ca 1½ kg entrecôte, 2 tbsps oil, 1 cup stock, 2 large onions, 2 carrots, 1 bay leaf, 1½ tsps dried thyme, 3–4 cloves, 2 tbsps chopped parsley, 50 g streaky smoked bacon, 2 tbsps lemon juice, 2–3 tbsps dry white wine, salt, pepper, a pinch of sugar if required

Rinse the meat, remove the backbone and uncover the rib. Rub the meat with salt, pepper, half the thyme and lemon juice. Tie up with thread and brown on all sides in hot oil. Transfer to a skillet, put in the thin bacon rashers and the finely diced vegetables, add the cloves, bay leaf, remaining thyme and parsley. Cover the skillet and put it into a preheated oven. Cook for 70 mins, basting with stock. Take the meat out, cut it into portions, arrange in an ovenproof dish. Sieve the gravy and the vegetables, mix it with the wine, adjust the taste with salt, pepper and sugar if required. Pour some sauce over the meat and serve the rest in a sauce boat. Before serving, put the meat in the oven for 4–5 mins.

serves 6–8 • Preparation: 20 mins • Braising: 70 mins • Baking: 4–5 mins

Great Poland roulade

ca 1 kg beef (rump, round), 1 tsp lemon juice, 1 large finely chopped onion, 1 cup stock, 1 tbsp lard, 2 hard-boiled eggs, pepper

STUFFING: 150 g minced pork, 1 bread roll soaked in milk, 2 tbsps each chopped parsley, chives and dill, 2 tbsps thick cream, a pinch of sugar, salt, pepper

To make the stuffing, squeeze the roll out, blend it with the cream, salt, pepper, sugar, greens and the minced meat. Cut the rinsed and dried beef half way through lengthwise, pound it with a mallet to form a rectangle of even thickness. Sprinkle it with pepper and lemon juice, spread the stuffing evenly, put the eggs on top. Roll the meat up, tie with twine and brown on all sides in hot lard. Transfer to a skillet, sprinkle with 2–3 tbsps of boiling water, pile the onion on top. Cover the skillet and place in a preheated oven. Baste frequently with the stock and later with the pan juices. Towards the end, take the lid off. Serve hot, with some cream pour over it, with kasha or noodles, or cold, with pickles or piquant sauces.

serves 6–8 • Preparation: 20 mins • Braising: 1 hr

Not only beefsteak

According to an old dictionary 'beefsteak is a piece of best beef (from the rump or sirloin), fried without seasoning over a high heat.'

As we know, beef (or horse) sirloin is tender succulent and delicate; it is the best part of the beast and weighs from c. 700 to 2,500 g. Before preparing steak, you should remove the silvery membrane from the meat with a very sharp knife.

A classic steak is made from a thick slice of beef (3–3½ cm) cut from the central sirloin. It should be lightly beaten with the blunt side of a knife until it is 2–2½ cm thick, then sprinkled with freshly ground pepper, and fried on both sides in very hot fat; it should be salted after it is fried. A good steak should be succulent and slightly rare inside.

Worldwide, a four-point scale is used for frying steak:

1. Rare – fried for 1½ minutes on each side. The meat is well browned on the outside, but practically raw inside, and blood runs out when it is cut;
2. Medium rare (saignant) – fried for 3 minutes on each side. The meat inside is still pink and oozes pink juice;
3. Medium (à point) – fried for four minutes on each side; and
4. Well done (bien cuit) – fried for five minutes on each side; the meat is brown although it is still succulent.

Steak should be salted after cooking, arranged on a hot dish and covered with the gravy, which is made by deglazing the frying pan with a drop of Madeira, white wine or stock and reheating it over a low heat. Steak is usually served with chips, balled potatoes or rice, freshly shredded horseradish, well-chilled pats of flavoured butter or sauces. The best known varieties of steak are chateaubriand and tournedos.

Chateaubriand, château potatoes and sauce béarnaise

Chateaubriand is described in culinary dictionaries as a 'double steak'; this delightfully simple masterpiece of French cuisine is a steak about 6 cm thick cut from the widest part of beef sirloin and prepared as follows:

After rinsing, drying, slicing into portions and lightly beating, the meat should be rubbed with olive oil and left for 30 to 50 minutes in the fridge. Then it is fried in very hot fat until brown on the surface but juicy inside (about 5 minutes on each side). It is served with château potatoes, green peas, and béarnaise or Colbert sauce is always served separately in a sauce boat.

Château potatoes are made as follows: use a special scoop to form small balls from peeled and washed potatoes; these should be placed in a sieve and rinsed with boiling water or thrown into lightly salted boiling water for 2 to 3 minutes, after which they should be strained and cooked slowly in clarified butter. At the end a large amount of finely chopped parsley should be added.

For béarnaise sauce, you need 3 egg yolks, 150 g of butter, 2 spring onions, a small clove of garlic, 2 teaspoons of lemon juice, 2 teaspoons of dry white wine, a dessertspoon

each of fresh chopped tarragon and parsley, salt and pepper to taste.

The lemon juice should be brought to the boil in a saucepan with a drop of water, the wine, tarragon, parsley, finely chopped garlic and onion. It should be simmered for a few minutes with the lid on and then strained and cooled.

When the liquid is cooled, you should add the egg yolks and a pat of butter. Then rest the pan on top of a larger pan with boiling water and beat the liquid until the egg yolk begins to thicken.

At this point, take it off the heat and add the rest of the butter gradually, whisking all the time, until you have a smooth, even cream. Add salt and pepper to taste.

Instead of sauce, you may serve chateaubriand with frozen pats of flavoured butter – for example, parsley, horseradish or anchovy butter (see pp. 4, 8, 9). The plates should be well heated before this dish is served on them.

Tournedos are small round beefsteaks (each weighing 100–120 g) cut from the thinner part of sirloin. They can be fried in a frying pan (*tournedos sauté*) or grilled (*tournedos grillé*).

Today tournedos are part of world cuisine. They are fried in butter mixed with olive oil – quickly, so that they remain succulent, and pink inside; after frying, they are removed and kept warm, while the frying pan is deglazed with a small amount of Madeira or other wine to make the sauce. If we want a thicker sauce, we should mix a teaspoon of potato flour with a dessertspoon of water and add it to the sauce, after which a glass of brandy should be poured in and mixed.

Tournedos are usually served on toasted white bread placed on top of rice or finely creamed potatoes; as a rule they are accompanied by vegetables, fried mushrooms, poached eggs or sometimes apples. Almost any vegetables can be served with tournedos: aubergines, artichokes, asparagus, cauliflower, broccoli, runner beans, green peas, cooked in butter or cream. It is not therefore surprising that cookery books are full of recipes for tournedos and the name of the dish depends on what is served to accompany the steaks:

– **tournedos Masséna**, the favourite dish of Napoleon's Marshal André Masséna (1756–1817), who in 1807 commanded the French forces in Poland. The dish named after him consists of fried steaks served on fried artichoke hearts and garnished with cooked beef bone marrow and chopped parsley, obviously with Madeira sauce poured over;

– **tournedos à la Batty** are served on layers of toast filled with sieved goose liver with onion and sprinkled with finely chopped truffles;

– **tournedos Saint Germain** are placed on bread fried in butter, covered with fine potato purée, with green peas and with the cooking gravy mixed with white wine poured over;

– **tournedos Monaco**, either fried or grilled, are served on toast and garnished with a round slice of fried ham, fried calves' brains and button mushrooms, with the cooking gravy poured over;

– **tournedos Belle Hélene** was a dish invented as a result of the great popularity of Offenbach's operetta of the same name which was staged in Paris in 1865. At this time, the majority of Paris restaurants tried to include in their menu at least one highly exotic dish named after the heroine of the Trojan wars.

Tournedos Belle Hélene are grilled steaks served on toast and surrounded with hollowed artichokes filled with thick béarnaise sauce, served with apples, crisp potato straws and with cress or lettuce.

– **tournedos à la Countess Marica** are steaks placed on slices of artichoke and celeriac and baked in puff pastry; they are garnished with ham and pineapple and served with curry sauce.

There are of course many more varieties of tournedos and what you serve with them depends entirely on your taste and imagination. Only the small beef sirloin steaks are essential.

Garlic beefsteaks

700 g fillet of beef, 3 cloves of garlic, 2 bay leaves, salt, 1 tbsp olive oil, 1 tbsp butter

MARINADE: 2 cloves of garlic, 1 tsp ground pepper, 2 tbsps lemon juice, ½ tsp grated lemon rind, 2 tbsps olive oil

Mix the crushed garlic with the pepper, oil, lemon juice and zest. Cut the meat into 4 slices, pound them lightly with the handle of a knife or flatten with your hand. Spread the meat slices with the mixture, put one on top of the other, cover and leave in the fridge for 2–3 hours. Heat the oil in a frying pan, put in the peeled garlic cloves and

the bay leaves, sauté them briskly, then take them out. Put in the butter, let it melt and fry the steaks for 3–4 mins to each side (the meat should remain pink inside).

serves 4 • Marinating: 2–3 hrs • Frying: 6–8 mins

Ginger beefsteaks

700 g fillet of beef, 1 tbsp freshly chopped ginger, 2–3 cloves of garlic, 1 tsp ground black pepper, ¼ cup dry white wine, 2–3 tsps oyster sauce, 2 tbsps oil, 1 tbsp butter, 1 tbsp potato flour

Cut the meat into 4 slices, flatten them with your hand, dredge with potato flour. Heat the oil in a large frying pan, put in the ginger, pepper and the finely chopped garlic, sauté them briskly, stirring all the time. Fry the steaks over high heat for 1½ to 2 mins to each side. Turn the heat down, brush the steaks with the oyster sauce, turn them over, brush the other side with the sauce, sprinkle with the wine, cover and cook for another 2–3 mins over very low heat. Put the steaks on warm plates, pour the gravy over.

serves 4 • Preparation: 10–12 mins • Frying: 3–4 mins

Beefsteaks with green peppercorns

700 g fillet of beef, 3 tbsp pickled green peppercorns, 1 tsp coarsely ground black pepper, 1 glass brandy, ½ cup whipping cream, 2 tbsps each olive oil and butter, salt

Cut the meat into 4 slices, flatten them with your hand, dredge with the ground pepper. Heat the oil in a frying pan, sauté the steaks on both sides, salt them. Melt the butter in the same pan, add the brandy and stir. Fold in the cream and green peppercorns and bring to the boil. Serve at once, with French fries and lettuce.

serves 4 • Preparation: 10–12 mins

Beefsteaks with peppers and sweetcorn

700 g fillet of beef, salt, pepper, 3 tbsps melted butter, 80 g fatty streaky bacon, 1 tin sweetcorns, 1 each red and green pepper, 2 tbsps each oil

Hunter's beef medallions

and ketchup, 3 tbsps honey, ½ cup dry white
wine, salt, pepper, 3–4 tbsps chopped parsley

Core the peppers, rinse and dry them, cut into thin rings. Strain the sweetcorn. Cut the rinsed and dried meat into 4 slices, flatten them with your hand, sprinkle generously with pepper. Mix the honey with the ketchup and wine. Heat the oil in a pan, fry the finely chopped bacon, add the peppers and sauté them for 1–2 mins, stirring all the time. Put in the sweetcorn, add salt and pepper, pour in the wine and simmer for 3–4 mins, then keep warm. Melt the butter in a frying pan, fry the steaks, salt them. Arrange them in a warm serving dish, pour over the sauce, garnish with the chopped parsley.

serves 4 • Preparation: 15–20 mins

Hunter's beef medallions

*700 g fillet of beef (or venison), 1 tbsp lemon
juice, ¼ tsp ground juniper berries, salt, pepper,
1 tbsp olive oil, 30 g dried cep mushrooms, 200 g
button mushrooms, ¼ cup bouillon, ¼ cup dry
white wine, ½ cup cream, salt, 3 tbsps butter*

Rinse the dried mushrooms, cover with hot water and leave to soak for 2–3 hours, then cook and cut into strips. Cut the rinsed and dried meat into 4 portions, pound lightly with a mallet and shape into round medallions. Mix the lemon juice with the oil, salt, pepper and juniper. Rub the meat with the mixture, put into a bowl, cover and leave in a cool place for 2–3 hours. Melt 1½ tbsps of butter, sauté the medallions on both sides. Sprinkle with the remaining marinade and wine, cover and cook over low heat for a while. Rinse and dry the button mushrooms, slice them and sauté in butter. Add the mushroom strips, sprinkle with pepper and fry for a minute or two, stirring all the time. Put the mushrooms into the meat. Pour the bouillon and mushroom stock into the frying pan, bring to the boil, deglaze the pan. Reduce the liquid, add the sauce to the meat, fold in the cream and stir gently. Serve with scooped potatoes or rice.

serves 4 • Marinating: 2–3 hrs • Preparation: 15–20 mins

Beef cutlets in savoury sauce

*600 g boneless beef (fillet, round, entrecôte),
1 tin anchovies, 1½ tbsps anchovy paste, 2 tbsps
beef bone marrow, 2 onions, 1 tbsp grated
lemon rind, 2 tbsps chopped parsley, 1 tbsp
pickled green peppercorns, 2 tbsps butter, 3 tbsps
thick cream, 1 cup stock, a pinch of salt*

Cut the rinsed and dried meat into 4 fairly thick slices, slit each slice lengthwise. Chop the anchovies finely, blend them with the bone marrow. Stuff the cutlets with the mixture, secure with a toothpick. Brown them on all sides in melted butter. Transfer to a skillet, sprinkle with stock and cook over low heat. Put the finely chopped onion into the pan, sauté it briskly, add the lemon zest, anchovy paste, pepper and parsley, pour in the remaining stock and simmer for several minutes. Put the sauce through a blender and sieve it, heat it up and fold in the cream. Pour over the cutlets and cook together for a minute or two.

serves 4 • Preparation: 15 mins • Braising: 15–20 mins

Beef cutlets, Galician style

*800 g boneless beef (middle rib, chuck),
2 large onions, 3 tbsps butter, salt, pepper*

Cut the rinsed and dried meat into 4 slices, pound them lightly with a mallet. Sauté them in butter for 3 mins to each side, sprinkle with salt and pepper. Put in the sliced onion and fry until it has turned golden brown. Pour over some melted butter before serving.

serves 4 • Preparation: 10–12 mins

Beef cutlets, Hamburg style

800 g boneless beef, 4 eggs, 4 tbsps butter, salt, pepper

Cut the rinsed and dried meat into 4 slices, pound them with a mallet. Fry them on both sides in melted butter, transfer to a warm serving dish, sprinkle with salt and pepper. Fry 4 eggs sunny side up, arrange them on top of the meat, pour over some melted butter.

serves 4 • Preparation: 15–20 mins

Rump steaks with tarragon

Beef cutlets, Vienna style

800 g boneless beef, 2 eggs, 2 tbsps mineral water, 3 tbsps sifted breadcrumbs, salt, pepper, 2 onions, 4 tbsps butter

Cut the rinsed and dried meat into 4 slices, pound them with a mallet. Sprinkle with salt and pepper, dip into the eggs lightly beaten with mineral water, dredge with breadcrumbs. Fry in 2 tbsps of melted butter for 3–4 mins to each side, then keep them warm. Melt the remaining butter in another frying pan and brown the sliced onion nicely. Arrange the meat in a serving dish, surround with the onion, pour over melted butter.

serves 4 • Preparation: 15–20 mins

Rump steaks with tarragon

600 g beef, 1 large onion, 2 tbsps chopped tarragon leaves, salt, pepper, 3 tbsps butter, 1 tbsp lemon juice, ¼ tsp grated lemon rind, ½ cup stock

Cut the rinsed and dried meat into 4 slices, pound them lightly with a mallet. Sprinkle with pepper and sauté on both sides in melted butter. Salt the meat, transfer it to a skillet, sprinkle with some broth and simmer. Fry the onion in the same pan, but do not let it brown. Add it to the meat, pour in the remaining stock and cook over low heat for 10 mins. Put in the tarragon and lemon zest, sprinkle with lemon juice and stir gently.

serves 4 • Preparation: 10 mins • Braising: 10–15 mins

Rump steaks with horseradish

600 g boneless beef (sirloin, rump), 2 large onions, 4 tbsps butter, salt, pepper, 2 tbsps dry white wine or stock, 4 tbsps grated horseradish

Cut the rinsed and dried meat into 4 slices, pound them lightly with a mallet, sprinkle with pepper. Slice the peeled onion. Melt 2 tbsps of butter in a frying pan, brown the onion nicely, stirring all the time. Melt the remaining butter in another pan, sauté the steaks on both sides, turn down the heat and fry them for another 3 mins on each side. Salt them, arrange in a warm serving dish, surround with the browned onion. Deglaze the pan in which the meat was fried with the wine. Bring to the boil, then pour over the meat. Garnish with shredded horseradish. Serve with puréed, sautéd or baked potatoes and salads.

serves 4 • Preparation: 5 mins • Frying: 6–8 mins

Flemish rump steaks

600 g sirloin, salt, 2 tbsps flour, 1½ tbsps lard;

1 cup dry white wine, 1 carrot, 1 parsley root, ¼ small celeriac, 1 large onion, 2 bay leaves,

several grains each pepper and allspice, 1 tsp sugar, 1 tsp grated lemon rind, 3 tbsps oil

Grate the peeled and rinsed vegetables finely, mix them with sugar and lemon zest, press firmly to squeeze out the juice. Add the crumbled bay leaves, peppercorns and allspice, mix in the oil. Cut the rinsed and dried meat into 4 slices, pound them lightly with a mallet and shape the steaks. Line a deep dish with some vegetables, place the steaks on top, cover with the remaining vegetables. Cover the dish and leave overnight in the fridge. Take out the meat. Transfer the vegetables

Rump steaks with horseradish

to a skillet, pour in the wine and cook over low heat for 15 mins. Remove the bay leaves, pepper and allspice. Put the vegetables through a blender, sieve them and season to taste. Dredge the meat with flour and fry in hot lard for 3–4 mins to each side. Serve with puréed potatoes, rice or French fries, with the sauce in a sauce boat.

serves 4 • Marinating: 12 hrs • Preparation: 20–25 mins • Frying: 6–8 mins

Pepper steaks (steaks au poivre)

700 g sirloin or rump (off the bone), 2 tbsps coarsely ground black pepper, 1 tbsp olive oil, 1 tbsp butter, 1 large onion, salt, 1 glass brandy

Cut the rinsed and dried meat into slices. Pound them lightly with a mallet, rub with pepper and oil, grill or fry them. Fry the finely chopped onion in melted butter, but do not let it brown. Arrange the steaks in a serving dish, surround with the onion, pour over the brandy and flame it. Best served with French fries and lettuce.

serves 4 • Preparation: 5 mins • Frying: 6–10 mins

Steaks with honey

700 g rump (off the bone), 2 tbsps olive oil, 2 tbsps liquid honey, 3 tbsps green peppercorns, ¾ cup single cream, salt, pepper, 100 g butter

Mix the honey with salt, pepper and oil. Cut the rinsed and dried meat into 4 slices, flatten them with your hand. Brush the meat generously with the honey and put into the fridge for an hour. Melt the butter in a large frying pan, fry the steaks on both sides, pour in the cream, add the peppercorns and simmer for a while, turning the meat over to allow it to absorb the cooking juices.

serves 4 • Macerating: 1 hr • Preparation: 15 mins

Steaks marinated in wine

600 g fillet of beef (middle part), 1 cup dry vermouth, 3–4 cloves of garlic, 2–3 tbsps olive oil, 1 tsp dried basil, 3 tbsps chopped parsley, salt, pepper, 4 eggs, 1 large onion, 4 tbsps butter

Cut the rinsed and dried meat into 4 slices. Beat them lightly with the handle of a knife, brush with oil, sprinkle with the finely chopped garlic, pepper and basil. Put into a bowl, pour the wine over and leave overnight in the fridge. Cut the peeled onion into fine half slices, brown them lightly in butter. Fry or grill the meat, basting it with the marinade. Fry the eggs sunny side up. Arrange the meat in a serving dish, place one egg on each steak. Surround with the onion and sprinkle with parsley.

serves 4 • Marinating: 12 hrs • Preparation: 5–7 mins • Grilling: 6–8 mins

Gypsy steaks

700 g sirloin (off the bone), 2 large onions, 1 tbsps stoned green olives, ½ tsp Tabasco, salt, pepper, 3 tbsps olive oil, 2 tbsps butter, ½ cup dry white wine, ½ cup strong stock, ½ cup whipping cream, 1 tsp flour, 1 tsp lemon juice

Heat 1 tbsp of oil in a frying pan, add 1 tbsp of butter. Put in the finely chopped onion and sauté it, stirring all the time. Pour in the wine, cover and simmer until the onion is tender, then put it through a blender. Melt 1 tbsp of butter in a saucepan, add the flour and make a roux. Dilute it with the stock and simmer until the sauce has thickened, then add the lemon juice, salt, pepper and Tabasco. Combine the sauce with the onion and cream, rest the saucepan on top of a pot of boiling water and whisk vigorously until the sauce is smooth. Put in the finely chopped olives and stir. Cut the rinsed and dried meat into 4 slices, beat them lightly with the handle of a knife. Sprinkle with pepper and fry on both sides in hot oil, salt the steaks. Before serving, pour the sauce over the meat. Serve with baked potatoes with herbs (put peeled potatoes of equal size in a sieve, blanch and drain them, dredge with flour mixed with dried rosemary, savory and mint; put on a greased baking sheet and bake).

serves 4 • Preparation: 30–40 mins • Frying: 8–10 mins

Oriental steaks

700 g boneless beef (sirloin or fillet), 1 large onion, 2–3 cloves of garlic, 1 grated nutmeg, salt, pepper, 1 tbsp lemon juice, 1 tbsp dry white wine, 1 tbsp olive oil

Blend the grated onion and the finely chopped garlic, add the nutmeg, pepper, lemon juice, wine and olive. Cut the rinsed and dried meat into 4 slices, pound them lightly with a mallet. Rub them with the mixture and put in the fridge for 2–3 hours, then grill them. Serve with rice, lettuce or soya sprouts.

serves 4 • Marinating: 2–3 hrs • Grilling: 10–12 mins

Italian steaks

600 g fillet of beef, 2 tbsps oil, 2 tbsps soya sauce, 2–3 cloves of garlic, ½ tsp dried basil, ¼ tsp sugar, ½ tsp pepper, 1 cup dry red wine, 4 tbsps chopped dill, 2 tbsps clarified butter

Mix the finely chopped garlic with pepper, basil, soya sauce and oil. Cut the rinsed and dried meat into 4 slices, flatten them firmly with your hand. Rub them with the mixture, put in a bowl, cover and leave in the fridge for 1–2 hours. Melt the butter in a deep frying pan, fry the steaks for 3–4 mins to each side. Arrange the meat in a hot serving dish and keep warm. Add the wine to the bowl in which the meat macerated, stir well and pour into the frying pan. Bring to the boil, reduce the liquid, put in the dill and stir. Pour the sauce over the meat. Serve with macaroni, rice or puréed potatoes and with salads.

serves 4 • Macerating: 1–2 hrs • Preparation: 10–12 mins

Scandinavian fricadelles

500 g boneless beef, 2 large potatoes cooked in jackets, 1 medium-sized baked beetroot, 1 large onion, 2 eggs, ½ tsp each ground caraway and chilli, 2 tbsps lard, 1 tbsp butter, several parsley sprigs, 4 cloves of garlic, 4 tbsps butter, 1 tbsp lemon juice, salt

Cream 4 tbsps of butter with the lemon juice, add the finely chopped garlic mixed with salt. Shape the mixture into small balls, place them on foil and put into the freezer for one or two hours. Rinse and dry the meat, peel the potatoes and beetroot. Put the meat, potatoes and beetroot twice through a mincer. Add the finely chopped onion, caraway, chilli and salt, break in the eggs and mix thoroughly. Shape the mixture into small patties. Fry the

patties in hot lard, then transfer them to a skillet, add 1 tbsp of butter and keep over low heat for a while. Arrange the fricadelles in a warm serving dish, pile puréed vegetables around, garnish with parsley sprigs. Place a ball of garlic butter on top of each fricadelle.

serves 4 • Preparation: 30 mins

Shish kebab with herbs

600 g thick flank of beef, 150 g pork fat, 1 tsp each ground mustard seeds and coriander, ½ tsp ground caraway, 2–3 cloves of garlic, 2 tbsps lemon juice, 1 tbsp honey, 2 tbsps oil, salt, pepper, 3–4 sprigs of lemon balm, 1 large tart apple, 1 tsp lemon juice

Mix the finely chopped garlic with salt, caraway, mustard seeds, coriander, pepper, honey, lemon juice and oil. Rinse and dry the meat, knead it with your hands, cut into medium-sized cubes. Put them into a bowl, pour over the dressing, mix, cover and leave in the fridge for several hours. Rinse and dry the lemon balm sprigs. Cut the apple in half, core it, cut into thick slices, sprinkle with lemon juice. Cut the pork fat into even cubes. Thread the meat and pork fat on skewers, alternating them with apple slices and lemon balm leaves. Grill the kebabs, basting them with the remaining marinade.

serves 4 • Marinating: 4–6 hrs • Preparation: 10–15 mins • Grilling: 10–15 mins

Zrazy

These were the pride of Old Polish cuisine, although as Kazimierz Chłędowski wrote, "*in my culinary observations, I was surprised by the Italian origins of rolled zrazy; I thought that this was an absolutely Old Polish dish like dumplings, while with some surprise I found the same things in old provincial Italian cuisine*".
There are many varieties of zrazy in Polish cuisine, like beaten, rolled, stuffed zrazy, but they are always served in a sauce, either their own gravy, or mushroom or on-

ion sauce; they are usually accompanied by kasha, mainly buckwheat.

The stuffing determines the taste of rolled zrazy, and there are very many kinds of stuffing in Polish cuisine, made of meat, mushrooms, eggs, bacon fat, soured cucumbers, onions.

Polish rolled zrazy

700 g beef (thick flank, topside), salt, pepper, 2 tbsps lard, 1 large onion, 2 celery sticks, 5–6 peppercorns, 2–3 grains allspice, 1 bay leaf, 1½ cups stock

Cut the rinsed and dried meat into fairly thin slices. Pound them lightly with a mallet, sprinkle with salt and pepper. Spread them with the stuffing (see below), roll up, tie with thread. Brown them in hot lard, then transfer to a skillet. Put in the grated onion and diced celery, add the peppercorns, allspice and bay leaf. Cover with the hot stock, put the lid on and simmer for 50 mins. Before serving, sieve the sauce and remove the thread.

serves 4–6 • Preparation: 10 mins • Braising: 45–50 mins

STUFFING FOR ZRAZY

Horseradish stuffing

5–6 g tbsps freshly grated horseradish, 1 tsp lemon juice, 2 tbsps butter, ¼ cup breadcrumbs, 2 egg yolks

Put the grated horseradish into a sieve, blanch and drain it. Sprinkle it with lemon juice and sauté in melted butter. Take off the heat, mix in the breadcrumbs and egg yolks, add salt and work into a smooth paste.

Preparation: 2–3 mins

Onion stuffing

3 onions, 2 tbsps butter, 2 tbsps cream, 2 egg yolks, 1 tsp lemon juice, salt, pepper, 1–3 tbsps breadcrumbs

Fry the finely chopped onions in melted butter without browning. Take off the heat, mix in the breadcrumbs,

cream and egg yolks, add salt and pepper and work into a smooth paste.

Preparation: 10 mins

Mushroom stuffing

50 g dried cep mushrooms, 1 large onion, 2 tbsps butter, 1 hard-boiled egg, 1 raw egg, 1–2 tbsps breadcrumbs, 2–3 tbsps chopped parsley, salt, pepper

Soak the mushrooms in water, then cook them and chop finely. Fry the finely chopped onion in butter, but do not let it brown. Put in the mushrooms, add salt and pepper and cook for a while. Take off the heat, put in the chopped hard-boiled egg, parsley and breadcrumbs, break in the egg and mix thoroughly. Wrap rolled pieces of stuffed meat in thin slices of smoked streaky bacon, brown them and only then braise in mushroom stock. Towards the end, add some cream.

Preparation: 40–50 mins

Cabbage stuffing

300 g sauerkraut, 1 tbsp butter, 1 tbsp dry white wine, ¼ tsp ground caraway, 150 g smoked streaky bacon, 1 large onion, salt, pepper

Melt the butter in a skillet, put in the finely chopped sauerkraut, add the caraway and wine and simmer. Dice the bacon, brown it in a hot frying pan, add the finely chopped onion and sauté it without browning. Mix the cabbage with the bacon and onion, adjust the taste with salt and pepper, reduce the juices if necessary. Leave the mixture to cool, then spread it on pieces of meat.

Preparation: 40–50 mins

Royal rolled zrazy

700 g beef (topside, round), salt, pepper, 1 large onion, 6–8 dried cep mushrooms, 2 slices of dry wholemeal bread, 2 tbsps lard

STUFFING: 150 g onion, 2 tbsps butter, 1 cup grated dry wholemeal bread, 1 egg, salt, pepper

Rinse the mushrooms, soak them overnight in a small amount of water, then cook them and cut into strips. Cut the rinsed and dried meat into slices (across the grain). Pound them lightly with a mallet, sprinkle with pepper. Sauté the finely chopped onion in butter, add salt, pepper and grated bread, mix thoroughly. Spread the meat slices with the stuffing, roll them up, secure with a toothpick or tie with thread. Brown them on all sides in hot lard, transfer to a skillet. Brown lightly the finely sliced onion in the same frying pan, put in the mushroom strips, then add the mixture to the zrazy. Grate the bread slices, sprinkle the breadcrumbs on top of the zrazy. Pour in the mushroom stock, cover the skillet and simmer over low heat.

serves 4–6 •Soaking: 12 hrs • Preparation: 15–20 mins • Cooking: 50 mins

Old Polish zrazy

700 g beef (topside), 150 g pork fat, 3 tbsps hot mustard, 2–3 firm soured cucumbers, salt, pepper, 1½ cups stock, 1–2 juniper berries, a pinch of savory, ½ cup thick cream, 1 raw egg yolk, 2 tbsps flour, 2 tbsps lard, 2 tbsps dry grated wholemeal bread

Cut the pork fat into thin sticks. Quarter the peeled cucumbers lengthwise. Cut the rinsed and dried meat into slices, pound them lightly with a mallet. Sprinkle with salt and pepper, brush with mustard. On each slice place 2–3 pork fat sticks and 1–2 pieces of cucumber. Roll the meat up, tie with thread, dredge with flour and brown on all sides in hot lard. Transfer to a skillet, add the juniper and savory, sprinkle with the grated bread. Pour in the stock, cover and simmer for 50 mins. Before serving, sieve the sauce, adjust its taste with salt and pepper, fold in the cream.

serves 4–6 • Preparation: 10 mins • Cooking: 50 mins

Zrazy stuffed with ham

700 g boneless beef (middle rib, chuck), 1 tbsp lemon juice, salt, pepper, 2–3 tbsps flour, 2 tbsps lard, 1 cup stock, ½ cup dry red wine

STUFFING: 100 g ham, ½ cup cooked rice, 2 onions, 2 tbsps chopped walnuts, 2 eggs, 1 tsp finely

chopped fresh ginger or ½ tsp powdered ginger, ¼ tsp grated nutmeg, 1 tbsp butter, salt, pepper

Cut the rinsed and dried meat into portions. Pound them lightly with a mallet, sprinkle with lemon juice. Fry the finely chopped onion in butter, but do not let it brown. Add the ginger and sauté it, stirring all the time. Dice the ham, mix with the rice and onion, add the walnuts and nutmeg, break in the eggs. Mix thoroughly, adjust the taste with salt and pepper. Spread the meat slices with the mixture, roll them up, secure with a toothpick. Dredge them with flour and brown on all sides in hot lard. Transfer them to a skillet, cover with the hot stock, put the lid on and simmer for 40–50 mins. Towards the end, pour in the wine, shake the skillet gently and heat up. Serve with kasha and savoury salads.

serves 4–6 • Preparation: 10–15 mins • Cooking: 50 mins

Zrazy with potato and ham filling

700 g boneless beef, ¾ kg potatoes, 100 g lean bacon or ham, 2 onions, 2 carrots, 2 parsley roots, a piece of celeriac, 2 bay leaves, several grains of pepper and allspice, 2 cups stock, 1 cup sour cream, 1 tbsp flour, salt, 1 tsp pepper, 4 tbsps clarified butter

Dice the peeled and rinsed vegetables and onions. Melt 2 tbsps of butter in a large skillet, sauté the onion, then add the remaining vegetables, bay leaf, pepper and allspice. Pour in the hot stock, bring to the boil, cover and simmer for 10 mins. Cut the peeled and rinsed potatoes into small cubes, blanch and drain them, sprinkle with ground pepper. Combine the potatoes with the finely diced ham. Cut the rinsed and dried meat into portions. Pound them with a mallet, sprinkle some pepper and salt on top. Put some stuffing on each slice of meat. Roll the meat up, tie with thread, dredge with flour and brown on all sides in melted butter. Put into the skillet, cover and cook for 50 mins. Take the tender meat out, remove the thread. Sieve the sauce, adjust the taste with salt and pepper, pour in the cream. Return the meat to the skillet and cook for another 10 mins. Serve with dumplings, noodles or kasha.

serves 4–6 • Preparation: 30 mins • Cooking: 1 hr

POUNDED ZRAZY

Pounded Kurp zrazy

700 g beef (topside), salt, pepper, 2 tbsps lard, 1 large onion, 2–3 celery sticks, 5–6 peppercorns, 2–3 grains allspice, 1 bay leaf, 1½ cups stock, 1 tbsp flour

Cut the rinsed and dried meat into thin slices. Pound them lightly with a mallet, sprinkle with salt amd pepper, dredge with flour. Sauté them on both sides in hot lard, then transfer to a skillet. Put in the grated onion and diced celery, add peppercorns, allspice and bay leaf. Cover with the hot stock, put the lid on and simmer for 50 mins. Sieve the sauce before serving.

serves 4–6 • Preparation: 10 mins • Cooking: 50 mins

Zrazy à la Napoleon

700 g beef (round, topside), 50 g pork fat, salt, pepper, 1 tbsp flour, 4 tbsps butter, 2 carrots, 2 parsley roots, 1 kohlrabi, ½ celeriac, 1 large onion, 1 cup dry white wine, 1 lemon

DOUGH: flour, water

Cut the rinsed and dried meat into portions, shape them into small oval slices. Sprinkle with salt and pepper, dredge with flour and sauté briskly in 1½ tbsps of butter. Cut the peeled and rinsed vegetables into strips. Scrub the lemon, blanch it, cut into thin slices, remove the pips. Line a skillet with thin slices of pork fat. Put in alternating layers of vegetables (place knobs of butter on top), meat and lemon slices, finishing off with the vegetables. Pour the wine over. Knead the flour and water into rather tough pastry. Cover the skillet, seal it with the pastry. Place it in a large pan with boiling water and cook for 2½ hours over low heat (add more water to the bottom pan if necessary). You can also cook the zrazy in the oven for one to 1 to 1½ hours.

serves 4–6 • Preparation: 15 mins • Steam cooking: 2½ hrs, or Oven cooking: 60–90 mins

Pounded zrazy with vegetables

700 g boneless beef (middle rib, chuck), 2 leeks (only the white part), 2 carrots, ½ celeriac, 2–3 cloves of garlic,

2 tbsps soya sauce, 2 tbsps flour, 2 tbsps lard, 2 tbsps butter, 1 cup beef stock, 1 cup dry red wine, salt, pepper

Dice the peeled and rinsed vegetables. Cut the rinsed and dried meat into 4 slices. Pound them with a mallet, sprinkle with pepper, dredge with flour and fry in hot lard for 3 mins to each side. Melt the butter in a skillet, put in the meat, sprinkle with salt. Put the vegetables into the frying pan and sauté them briskly, then transfer to the skillet. Pour in the stock and cook for 40–50 mins. Towards the end, add the finely chopped garlic and the wine, adjust the taste with salt and pepper and cook for a while longer. Serve with pasta, kasha or French fries and with salads.

serves 4–6 • Preparation: 20 mins • Cooking: 50 mins

Hungarian zrazy

600 g sirloin, 2 large onions, 2 green peppers, 3–4 tbsps chopped parsley, 1 cup stock, 1 glass Tokay wine, ½ cup thick sour cream, 1 tbsp flour, 1 tbsp lemon juice, 1 tbsp paprika, salt, pepper, 1–2 tbsps lard

Cut the peeled onion into slices. Core the peppers and cut them into rings. Cut the rinsed and dried meat into slices. Pound them lightly with a mallet, fry on both sides in hot lard. Take out onto a plate, sprinkle with salt, pepper and paprika. In the remaining lard, first fry briskly the onion and then sauté the peppers. Line a skillet with the onion, put the meat on top, cover with the peppers. Pour in the stock, put the lid on and simmer for 20 mins. Add the wine and lemon juice, shake the skillet gently and cook for another 15 mins. Mix the cream with the flour and parsley, pour into the skillet. Stir gently and heat up until the sauce has thickened. Adjust the taste. Serve with noodles or rice.

serves 4 • Preparation: 15–20 mins • Cooking: 30–35 mins

Zrazy with leek

700 g boneless beef (middle rib, chuck), 2 tbsps flour, salt, pepper, 2 tbsps lard, 2 tbsps lemon juice, 1 cup stock, ½ cup thick cream, 4 leeks, 2–3 cloves of garlic, 2 tbsps butter, 1 tbsps tomato paste, 1 tsp chilli pepper, ½ tsp grated lemon rind, ¼ tsp sugar, salt, ¼ cup dry white wine, 3 tbsps chopped parsley

Cut the rinsed and dried meat into 4 slices. Pound them with a mallet, sprinkle with pepper, dredge with flour and fry in hot lard. Transfer to a skillet, add some salt, cover with the stock, put a lid on and simmer for 30 mins. Wash the leeks thoroughly, cut them into fine slices. Chop the peeled garlic finely. Melt some butter in a pan, put in the leek, sauté it, then add the garlic, chilli, lemon zest, sugar and salt. Pour in the wine mixed with the tomato paste. Stir well and add to the meat, then cook for another 30 mins. Towards the end, adjust the taste with lemon juice, salt and sugar, garnish with chopped parsley.

serves 4 • Preparation: 15 mins • Cooking: 1 hr

Zrazy with anchovies

700 g boneless beef, 2 tbsps flour, salt, pepper, 3 tbsps clarified butter, ½ cup each stock and dry red wine, 4 anchovy fillets (or 4 tbsps anchovy paste), 1 cup thick cream

Cut the rinsed and dried meat into 4 slices. Pound them lightly with a mallet, sprinkle with pepper, dredge with flour and sauté in butter. Transfer them to a skillet, cover with the stock and cook for several minutes. Mix the finely chopped anchovies (or anchovy paste) with the wine. Pour into the meat, stir and cook for 40 mins. Towards the end, fold in the cream, shake the skillet and continue cooking for a bit longer. Serve with kasha, noodles or sautéd potatoes.

serves 4 • Preparation: 10 mins • Cooking: 50 mins

Beef Stroganov and goulash

Today this delicately savoury dish has many varieties. Some cook it with sautéd mushrooms or else with soured cucumber cut into thin strips. Sometimes its flavour is more piquant thanks to the addition of some mustard or finely chopped chilli peppers.

Beef Stroganov

600 g fillet of beef, 2 large onions, 2 tbsps tomato concentrate, 2 tbsps lard, 2 tbsps butter, 1 tbsp flour, ½ cup stock or dry white wine, 1 cup thick sour cream, salt, pepper, 1 tsp paprika, a pinch of sugar, 1 tsp lemon juice, 2 tbsps chopped parsley

Rinse and dry the meat, cut it into fine strips, sprinkle with pepper and flour. Cut the onions into thin half slices. Heat the lard in a frying pan, put in the meat and sauté it briskly, stirring all the time. Transfer it to a skillet, sprinkle with some stock. Melt the butter in the same pan, sauté the onion, add the tomato concentrate, 2–3 tbsps of stock, salt, pepper, lemon juice and sugar to taste. Combine the onion with the meat, stir well and cook over low heat for 5–6 mins. Pour in the cream mixed with the remaining flour, stir and heat up. Garnish with chopped parsley before serving.

serves 4 • Preparation: 20–30 mins

Mazurian goulash with soured cucumbers

600 g beef, soup vegetables with savoy cabbage, 3–4 grains each allspice and pepper, 1 bay leaf, 1 clove, 1 onion, 600 g potatoes, 200 g soured cucumbers, 100 g onion, 2 tbsps lard, ½ cup cream, 1 tbsp flour, salt, pepper

Put the peeled vegetables and rinsed meat into a pan, add the spices and onion, cover with hot water, bring to the boil and simmer for 40 mins. Leave aside to cool, then take out the meat and vegetables. Strain the stock and reduce it to 1½ cups. Cut the meat into cubes. Chop the onions finely. Peel the potatoes and cucumbers and cut them into cubes. Heat the lard in a thick-bottomed skillet, put in the meat and onion and sauté them, stirring all the time. Blanch the potatoes in salted boiling water for 2–3 mins, drain them, run under cold water and drain again. Add them to the meat and sauté for a minute or two, then pour in the stock, add salt and pepper and simmer for 20 mins. Put in the cucumber and the finely chopped vegetables, stir and cook for a bit longer. Adjust the taste with salt and pepper. Mix the cream with the flour, pour into the goulash, stir and heat up. Serve with kasha or bread.

serves 4–6 • Preparation: 1 hr • Cooking: 25–30 mins

Beef goulash with leek

500 g beef (topside), 8 leeks (only the white part), 4–5 dried cep mushrooms, 3–4 cloves of garlic, 5–6 spring onions, salt, pepper, 2 tbsps lemon juice, ½ tsp dried thyme, a pinch of nutmeg, 1 bay leaf, 3 tbsps olive oil, 1 tbsp butter, ½ cup stock, 2 tbsps dry white wine, 1 tbsp flour

Cut the rinsed and dried meat into fine strips, put into a bowl, sprinkle with lemon juice and crumbled bay leaf. Mix the finely chopped garlic with salt, pepper, thyme, nutmeg and white wine. Pour the mixture into the meat, mix well, cover and leave overnight in the fridge. Soak the rinsed mushrooms overnight in a small amount of warm stock, then cook them. Take the meat out, dry it, dredge with flour and brown it well in 2 tbsps of very hot oil in a skillet. Turn the heat down, add the diced spring onions and the mushrooms cut into strips. Pour in the mushroom stock and marinade, stir, cover the skillet and simmer for 30–40 mins. Wash the leeks thoroughly, cut them into fairly thick slices. Heat the remaining oil in a pan, put in the leek, add the butter, cover and cook for a while. Add salt to taste and combine with the meat. Stir and cook together for another 10–15 mins. Serve with noodles, dumplings and rice.

serves 4–6 • Marinating: 12 hrs • Preparation: 1 hr

Beef goulash with asparagus

600 g boneless beef (topside, round), 300 g asparagus, 3 tbsps peanut oil, ¼ cup stock, salt, 2 tbsps cornflour or potato flour, 2 tbsps dry white wine, 2 tsps soya sauce

Cut the rinsed and dried meat into fine strips. Put them into a bowl, pour over the cornflour mixed with the wine and soya sauce, mix well and leave aside for half an hour. Clean the asparagus stalks, cut them into pieces. Heat 1½ tbsps of oil in a skillet, sauté the asparagus, pour in the stock, add salt, cover and cook for 8–10 mins. Heat the remaining oil in a frying pan, put in the meat and brown it lightly, stirring all the time. Add the meat to the asparagus,

mix thoroughly and cook together for a minute or two. Serve with rice, French fries or boiled new potatoes.

serves 4–6 • Preparation: 30–40 mins

Beef ragout with green asparagus

500 g fillet of beef, 400 g green asparagus, 2 large onions, 3–4 firm beef tomatoes, 1 tsp redcurrant jelly, 1 tsp hot mustard, 2–3 tbsps butter, ½ cup stock, 1 cup cream, salt, pepper, 2–3 tbsps chopped parsley

Blanch and skin the tomatoes, cut them into cubes. Dice the peeled onions finely. Clean the asparagus stalks, put them into boiling salted water and cook for 10 mins, then drain and cut into pieces. Melt 1½ tbsps of butter in a skillet, fry the onion, but do not let it brown. Sprinkle with salt and pepper, add the tomatoes and some stock, cover and cook for 10 mins. Add the mustard, jelly and cream, stir well and heat up slowly. Cut the rinsed and dried meat into fine strips. Melt the remaining butter in a frying pan, sauté the meat for 6 mins, stirring all the time. Sprinkle with salt and pepper and, together with the asparagus, add to the tomato and onion sauce. Simmer over low heat for a while. Before serving, garnish with chopped parsley.

serves 4–6 • Preparation: 25–35 mins

Mutton and lamb

Experienced cooks say that 'good mutton is dark red with white fat'. The most delicate meat is from lambs fed only on milk, and from ewes and tups not more than a year old.

Lamb, according to dieticians, is an easily digestible meat. It is light pink in colour, and does not have much fat, tendon or membrane.

Mutton is dark red and has a strong, characteristic smell, and a great deal of membrane and tendon, and a layer of fat or suet. This meat needs very careful preparation. Before roasting, the excess fat should be removed, leaving only a thin layer, which prevents the meat drying out too much. The membrane and tendons should also be removed. To tenderize the meat, it should be firmly kneaded in the hand, or beaten with a wooden mallet and then marinated or put in a dressing.

Mutton is best marinated in an acid marinade, which give it a gamey taste: in sour milk for 1–2 days, in an oil and spice or herb dressing for 1–3 days, or in a marinade of wine and vinegar for 2 to 4 days. The saddle or leg is best for roasting.

Roast mutton, Italian style

Take the best joint of mutton, remove the outer membrane and soak the meat, and lard it with endive and salt it. Make hard pastry from rye flour and roll it to a thickness of half an inch, spread it thickly with butter, place on it onions sliced in rounds, a bay leaf and a few cloves; place the joint in the pastry prepared in this way and wrap it up. Brush the pastry with fat, and put it in a hot oven for three hours. Before serving, unwrap the roast from the pastry, carve it, surround it with fried rye bread croutons shaped like wine corks, and pour sauce over it. It should be garnished with salsify fried in the gravy from the meat.

(Jan Szyttler, *Kucharz doskonały*, 1830).

Stuffed milk lamb

Next to the sucking pig, this was once the favourite dish on the Easter table.

1 baby lamb, salt, 1 tbsp butter

STUFFING: lamb offal, 200 g pork fat, 50 g mushrooms, 1 large onion, ½ cup breadcrumbs, 4 eggs, 1 tbsp butter, 2 tbsps chopped parsley, salt, pepper, nutmeg, a pinch of ground allspice

Rinse the dressed lamb, rub it with salt and leave in a cool place for 4–5 hours. Cook the lights and heart in a small amount of water. Chop the raw liver very finely. Cook the finely chopped mushrooms and onion in butter. Put the lights, heart and pork fat through a mincer, mix thoroughly with the egg yolks. Put in the liver, mushrooms, onion and breadcrumbs, mix again. Add the parsley, salt, pepper, nut-

meg and allspice, fold in the stiffly beaten egg whites. Stuff the lamb with the mixture, sew up the openings. Place the lamb in a greased roasting tin with slices of butter on top. Put into a preheated oven and cook for 10–15 mins over very high heat. Turn the temperature down and continue cooking for 90 mins, basting frequently with fat. Arrange the cooked lamb in a serving dish lined with cress.

serves 6–8 • Refrigerating: 4–5 hrs • Preparation: 30 mins • Roasting: 90–120 mins

Gamey lamb

1½ kg leg of lamb (off the bone), 1 tsp each ground juniper berries and marjoram, ¼ tsp dried rue, 2 large onions, 100 g pork fat, 1½ tbsps lard, salt, optional 1 cup thick sour cream

MARINADE: 1 cup dry red wine, juice and grated rind of 1 lemon, 1 bay leaf, 2–3 cloves, ¼ tsp each ground ginger and sugar, 5–6 grains each allspice and pepper

Prepare the marinade. Remove the membrane from the meat. Rinse and dry the meat, knead it with your hands. Rub it with the juniper, marjoram and rue. Put into an stoneware bowl, arrange the onion slices on top. Pour over the marinade, cover with a weighed down board, and leave in a cool place for 3–4 days. Turn the meat over every day. Take it out of the marinade, dry it, rub with salt, lard with thin pork fat strips. Arrange it in a roasting tin, pour the hot melted lard over and place in a preheated oven. Cook it over very high heat for 10 mins, then turn the temperature down and continue cooking, basting frequently with the strained marinade and later with the pan drippings. If you want to serve the lamb as second course, cut it into slices, put them in a warm serving dish; sieve the gravy, fold in the cream mixed with flour, bring to the boil and serve in a sauce boat.

serves 4–6 • Marinating: 3–4 days • Preparation: 5–7 mins • Roasting: 90 mins

Roast lamb with almonds

1½ kg leg of lamb (off the bone), 150 g almond flakes, 2 tbsps raisins, ½ glass dry white wine, 1 tsp salt, 1 green bell pepper

MARINADE: 2 finely chopped onions, 6–8 cloves
of garlic, 1 tbsp ground caraway, 2 tbsps ground
coriander, 2 green chilli peppers, 1½ cups yogurt

Remove excess fat from the meat. Crush the finely
chopped garlic with the onion, coriander and caraway.
Rinse and dry the meat, knead it well with your hands,
rub with half of the mixture, place in a stoneware bowl.
Blend the remaining mixture with the yogurt and the finely
chopped cored chilli peppers. Pour the marinade over the
meat. Cover the bowl and put into the fridge for 2–3 days.
Turn the meat over several times. Take the meat out, rub it
with salt, wrap carefully in aluminium foil, place in a roasting
tin and put into a preheated oven for 60–80 mins. Rinse
and drain the raisins, cover with the wine and leave aside
for half an hour. Dry toast the almond flakes. Remove the
cooked meat from the foil, sprinkle it with the raisins and
almond flakes and return to a warm oven for 10–15 mins.
Cut the meat into slices and garnish with strips of green
bell pepper before serving.

serves 4–6 • Marinating: 2–3 days • Preparation: 10 mins • Roasting: 90 mins

Leg of mutton à la venison

ca 3 kg leg of mutton (off the bone), 100 g pork fat,
1 cup thick cream, 1 tsp flour, salt, 1 tbsp lard

MARINADE: 1 cup vinegar, 2 cups lager beer,
2 onions, 2 tbsps juniper berries, 10 grains each
pepper and allspice, 1 bay leaf, ½ nutmeg

Cook the marinade and leave to cool. Remove excess
fat from the meat. Pound the meat with a mallet,
place in a stoneware bowl, cover with the cool marinade.
Put a small plate on top, weigh it down. Stand the meat in a
cool place for 4–6 days (up to 10 days). Take the meat out,
rinse and dry it, rub it with salt and leave in a cool place for
2–3 hours. Lard it with strips of pork fat, place in a greased
roasting tin and put into a preheated oven. Cook for 2 to
2½ hours, basting frequently with the strained marinade. If
you want to serve it hot, towards the end, pour over 1 cup
of thick cream mixed with 1 tsp of flour.

serves 8–10 • Marinating: 5–8 days • Salting: 2–3 hrs • Roasting: 2–2½ hrs

Leg of mutton, Gypsy style

1½ kg leg of mutton (off the bone), 2–3 cloves of garlic,
3 tbsps olive oil, 1 tbsps lemon juice, 3 tbsps hot mustard,
1 tsp tomato purée, ½ cup hot ketchup, 2–3 onions, 150 g
pork fat, 100 g lean ham, 150 g cocktail gherkins, 2 tbsps
each chopped parsley and chives, 2 tbsps lard, 1 tbsp flour,
½ cup stock, salt, pepper, paprika, sugar, 1 tbsp butter

Remove membranes and excess fat from the meat. Rinse
and dry the meat, knead it well with your hands. Crush the
chopped garlic with salt, paprika, pepper and a pinch of sugar.
Rub half of the mixture into the pork lard. Mix the remaining
garlic with the lemon juice, tomato purée, mustard and oil and
rub it into the meat. Place the meat in a bowl and cover it, wrap
the pork fat in foil and leave both in the fridge overnight. Cut
the pork fat into thin strips and lard the meat. Heat up the lard
in a roasting tin, brown the meat on all sides. Put in the finely
diced onion, sprinkle with some stock, cover and cook over low
heat for over an hour. Melt the butter in a saucepan, put in the
finely diced ham, add the flour and stir. Dilute with 2–3 tbsps of
cold stock and heat up until the sauce has thickened. Add the
ketchup, finely chopped gherkins, parsley and chives. Adjust the
taste with salt, pepper and sugar. Pour the sauce over the meat,
cook for a while longer and serve immediately.

serves 6–8 • Marinating: 12 hrs • Preparation: 15 mins • Braising: 70–75 mins

Hunter's leg of mutton

ca 3 kg leg of mutton (off the bone), 1 cup vinegar,
1 tbsp pounded juniper berries, 6–8 cloves of
garlic, 50 g pork fat, salt, pepper, fat for roasting

Remove excess fat from the meat. Pound the meat
with a mallet well, rub it with the garlic crushed
with juniper berries. Wrap in a cloth soaked in vinegar,
put into a stoneware jar and stand in a cool place for
4–5 days. Rub the meat with salt, lard it with the pork
fat strips and place in a greased roasting tin. Put into a
preheated oven and cook for 2 hours, basting frequently
with fat and water (or else spit-roast it). Serve hot, with
French fries or potato croquettes, or cold, with a savoury
sauce.

*serves 8–10 • Marinating: 4–5 days • Preparation:
15 mins • Roasting: 2–2 ½ hrs*

Baker's leg of mutton

1½ kg leg of mutton (off the bone), 2 tbsps lard or butter, 2 large onions, 1½ kg potatoes, 1–2 cloves of garlic, 1 tbsp lemon juice, ¼ tsp grated lemon rind, 1 tbsp dried thyme, 1 bay leaf, 3 tbsps chopped parsley, 1 cup stock, 1 tbsp lard, salt, pepper

Remove membranes and excess fat from the mutton. Rinse and dry the meat, knead it well with your hands. Rub with the lemon zest, pepper and crushed garlic, sprinkle with the lemon juice and place in a bowl. Cover and leave overnight in the fridge. Rub the meat with salt and brown it on all sides in hot lard. Transfer to a roasting tin and put into a preheated oven for 10–15 mins. Slice the peeled potatoes and onion. Grease an ovenproof dish well (melt the remaining fat), line it with half the potatoes and onions, sprinkle with salt, pepper, thyme and parsley, put in the bay leaf. Place the meat on top, pour over half of the melted fat. Cover with the remaining potatoes and onion, sprinkle again with pepper, salt, thyme and parsley. Pour over the remaining fat and hot stock. Put into a preheated oven and cook for 80 mins.

serves 4–6 • Marinating: 12 hrs • Preparation: 25 mins • Cooking: 90 mins

Leg of mutton with herbs

ca 3 kg leg of mutton (off the bone), 4–5 cloves of garlic, 1 tsp each thyme, rosemary, savory, basil and sage, ½ cup dry white wine, salt, 2 tbsps butter or lard

Remove excess fat from the leg. Rinse and dry the meat, pound it with a mallet, rub with a mixture of herbs, salt and crushed garlic, then stand it in a cool place for 3–4 hours. Place the meat in a greased roasting tin, put slices of butter on top, sprinkle with some wine and put into a preheated oven. Cook for 2 hours, basting frequently with the roasting juices. Serve hot, with baked potatoes with rosemary, or cold, with a savoury sauce.

serves 8–10 • Macerating: 3–4 hrs • Roasting: 2–2½ hrs

Leg of mutton with basil

ca 1½ kg leg of mutton (off the bone), 50 g pork fat, 2 tbsps dried basil, 5–6 cloves of garlic, 1 tbsp lemon juice, ½ tsp grated lemon rind, a pinch of sugar, 2 tbsps butter, 1 cup dry white wine or light stock, 1 tbsp oil, salt

Remove membranes, tendons and excess fat from the leg. Rinse and dry the meat, knead it well with your hands. Cut the pork fat into strips. Crush the finely chopped garlic with the basil and rub the pork fat with half of the mixture. Combine the other half with the lemon juice and zest, oil and a pinch of sugar, and rub the mixture into the meat. Put the meat and pork fat in separate bowls, cover them and leave overnight in the fridge. Take the meat out, lard it with the pork fat, rub with salt, put into a greased roasting tin and pour the melted over. Put the meat into a very hot oven for 10–15 mins. When it browns nicely, turn the heat down and cook for 70 mins, basting frequently with wine (or stock) and then with the roasting juices.

serves 4–6 • Macerating: 12 hrs • Preparation: 5 mins • Roasting: 90 mins

Leg of mutton in foil

ca 1½ kg leg of mutton (off the bone), 4–5 cloves of garlic, 1 tsp dried rosemary, ¼ tsp ground juniper berries, 1 tbsp lemon juice, 3 tbsps oil, ½ tsp each ground allspice and pepper, 1 tsp salt

Remove excess fat from the leg. Rinse and dry the meat, knead it with your hands, stud with 2–3 cloves of garlic and sprinkle with lemon juice. Crush the spices and herbs with the remaining garlic, salt and oil and rub the mixture into the meat. Put the meat into a bowl, cover and leave overnight in the fridge. Transfer it to a roasting bag or wrap it in aluminium foil, place in a roasting tin and put into a preheated oven. Cook it for 90 mins. Serve hot or cold.

serves 4–6 • Macerating: 12 hrs • Roasting: 90 mins

Leg of mutton, Poznań style

1½ kg leg of mutton (off the bone), 150 g smoked streaky bacon, 4–5 cloves of garlic, ¼ tsp each rosemary and sage, 1 tbsp lemon juice, ½ cup dry white wine, 1 tbsp lard, 1 tbsp any fat, salt, pepper

Remove membranes and excess fat from the leg. Rinse and dry the meat, knead it with your hands, then rub it with a mixture of the finely chopped garlic, pepper, sage, rosemary and lemon juice. Wrap in foil and leave overnight in the fridge. Salt the meat the following day, bard it with fine bacon rashers and tie with thread. Place it in a roasting tin greased with lard, pour over the melted fat and put into a very hot oven for 10–15 mins, then turn down the heat and cook for 70 mins, basting with wine and the roasting juices. Serve hot or cold with a piquant sauce.

serves 4–6 • Macerating: 12 hrs • Preparation: 5 mins • Roasting: 70 mins

Stuffed leg of mutton

1 kg lean leg of mutton (off the bone), 150 g smoked streaky bacon, 1 dried bread roll soaked in milk, 1 large onion, 100 g mushrooms, 2–3 tbsps chopped parsley, 2–3 cloves of garlic, 1 egg, 3 tbsps butter, 1 tsp lemon juice, 1 tsp honey, 3 tbsps olive oil, ½ cup dry white wine

Rinse and dry the meat, knead it well with your hands, cut in half but not whole way through. Pound it lightly with a mallet, shape into a rectangle. Sprinkle with lemon juice and pepper, rub with garlic salt, wrap in foil and put into the fridge for 3–4 hours. Put the squeezed out roll and the bacon through a mincer. Fry the finely chopped onion in 1 tbsp of butter, but do not let it brown. Put in the diced mushrooms and sauté them for a minute or two, then reduce the liquid and leave to cool. Cream the remaining butter with the honey, add salt and pepper, and, stirring all the time, put in the raw egg yolk, the bread and bacon mixture, the onion with the mushrooms and parsley. Fold in the stiffly whisked egg white. Spread the stuffing evenly on the meat. Roll the meat up, tie with twine and brown on all sides in hot oil. Transfer to a skillet, sprinkle sparingly with water, cover and cook, basting frequently with wine. Serve hot or cold.

serves 4–6 • Macerating: 3–4 hrs • Preparation: 30–35 mins • Braising: 1 hr

Mutton roulade with ham

1 kg leg of mutton (off the bone), 3 cloves of garlic, 1 tbsp lemon juice, 150 g ham, 1 bread roll soaked in milk, 50 g white beef suet, 1 onion, 2 tbsps chopped parsley, 1 tsp flour, 1 tbsp lard, 1 tbsp any fat, ½ cup 12% cream, 1 egg, salt, pepper

Remove excess fat from the leg. Rinse and dry the meat, cut it in half, but not whole way through. Pound lightly with a mallet, shape into a rectangle. Sprinkle with lemon juice, rub with a mixture of crushed garlic, salt and pepper. Cover and leave in a cool place for an hour.
STUFFING: Put the suet (without membranes), ham and the squeezed out roll through a mincer. Fry the finely chopped onion in hot fat, but do not let it brown. Combine the mince with the onion and parsley, add salt and pepper, break in the egg and mix thoroughly.
Spread the stuffing evenly on the meat. Roll the meat tightly, tie it with twine. Dredge it lightly with flour and brown on all sides in hot lard. Transfer it to a skillet, pour over the remaining melted fat. Sprinkle with water, cover and put into a preheated oven. Cook for 90 mins, basting with the roasting juices and with the cream. Serve hot, with macaroni or potato croquettes.

serves 4–6 • Macerating: 1–2 hrs • Preparation: 30–40 mins • Braising: 90 mins

Stuffed brisket of mutton

1 brisket of mutton, 2 cups soured milk, 203 cloves of garlic, 1 tbsp butter, salt, pepper, 1 tbsp thick sour cream

STUFFING: 200 g lamb or veal liver, ½ cup rice, 2 onions, 2 tbsps butter, 1 egg, 2–3 tbsps stock, ¼ tsp dried basil, 1 tbsp chopped parsley

Soak the rinsed brisket for 3–4 hours in soured milk, then dry it, make a long deep incision along the ribs. Rub the meat with garlic, salt and pepper. Braise the chopped liver and onion in butter, then put it through a mincer. Add the cooked rice, 2 tbsps of stock, salt, pepper, basil and parsley, break in the egg and mix thoroughly. Fill the incision with the stuffing and sew it up. Brush the meat liberally with the cream, arrange it in a greased roasting tin, put slices of butter on top. Put it into a preheated oven and cook for 90 mins, basting frequently with melted butter. Cut the meat into thick slices. Serve with potatoes and salads, with the gravy in a sauce boat.

serves 4–6 • Soaking: 3–4 hrs • Preparation: 20–25 mins • Roasting: 90 mins

Mutton cutlets with sorrel

800 g leg of mutton (off the bone), 1 tbsp lemon juice, 500 g sorrel, 5–6 spring onions, 3–4 cloves of garlic, 100 g butter, 1 tbsp flour, 1 glass dry white wine, 1 cup stock, ½ cup single cream, salt, pepper, nutmeg, a pinch of sugar

Remove excess fat from the leg. Rinse and dry the meat, knead it well. Cut into thin slices, rub with the crushed garlic and salt, sprinkle with lemon juice. Leave aside for 30–40 mins, then dredge the cutlets with flour. Melt 3 tbsps of butter in a frying pan and fry the cutlets on both sides, then transfer them to a skillet. Sauté the diced onions in the same frying pan, put in the meat, sprinkle with wine and cook for 15 mins. Pour in the stock and simmer under cover until the meat is tender. Melt the remaining butter in the skillet, put in the chopped sorrel and sauté it, stirring all the time. Add salt, pepper, nutmeg and sugar to taste, cover and simmer for 10 mins. Pour in the cream, stir and reduce the liquid a bit. Arrange the cutlets in a warm serving dish, pile the sorrel around. Adjust the taste of the gravy and serve it in a sauce boat. Serve with rice, French fries or noodles.

serves 4–6 • Macerating: 30–40 mins • Preparation: 30 mins

Mutton cutlets with apples

800 g boneless mutton (leg or saddle), ¼ tsp each ground pepper, lemon zest and ginger, 2 tbsps lemon juice, 1 tbsp olive oil, a pinch of sugar, salt, 500 g tart apples, 1 tbsp chopped thyme leaves, 1 tsp honey, ¼ cup dry white wine, 1 tbsp lard, 1 tbsp butter

Remove membranes and excess fat from the meat. Rinse and dry the meat, knead it well, cut into cutlets. Pound the cutlets lightly with a mallet, rub in a mixture of pepper, salt, lemon zest, ginger, lemon juice and oil. Cover and leave in the fridge for 1–2 hours. Peel and core the apples, cut them into slices and sauté in melted butter. Add the thyme, honey and wine, stir and simmer under cover for several minutes. Heat the lard in a deep frying pan and fry the cutlets on both sides. Sprinkle them with the dressing mixed with 1 tbsp of water, pile the apples around. Cover and simmer for 20–25 mins. Serve with rice or French fries and with lettuce.

serves 4–6 • Macerating: 1–2 hrs • Preparation: 30–35 mins

Lamb chops with olives

1 kg saddle of lamb (on the bone), 3 lemons, 4 firm beef tomatoes, 16 stoned green olives, a piece of cinnamon, salt, pepper, 2 tbsps olive oil, 2 tbsps butter, ¼ cup stock

Scrub the lemons, scald them with boiling water. Grate the rind and squeeze out the juice. Cut the rinsed and dried meat into 8 cutlets, place them in a deep bowl, sprinkle with the lemon zest, pour the lemon juice over. Cover the bowl and put it into the fridge for 2–3 hours. Fry the chops on both sides in very hot oil. Transfer them to an ovenproof dish greased with butter. Sprinkle with salt and pepper. Cut the tomatoes into thick slices and sauté them in the same frying pan. Add salt, pepper and crumbled cinnamon, sprinkle with some stock and simmer for 4–8 mins. Pile the tomatoes on top of the chop, cover the dish and put it into a preheated oven for 10–15 mins. Take the cover off, garnish with lemon slices and olives. Serve with rice.

serves 4 • Macerating: 2–3 hrs • Preparation: 30–35 mins

Lamb cutlets in puff pastry

600 g leg of lamb (off the bone), 2 kiwi fruit, 120 g packet of Camembert, salt, pepper, 1 tbsp lemon juice, 3 tbsps butter, 400 g packet of puff pastry

Rinse and dry the meat, cut it into 4 portions. Pound the cutlets lightly with a mallet, sprinkle with salt, pepper and lemon juice and leave aside for half an hour, then fry them on both sides in 2 tbsps of butter. Peel the kiwi fruit and cut it into fairly thick slices. Roll out the pastry, divide it into 4 squares. Place a cutlet on each square, put a quarter of the cheese on top and cover with 2 kiwi slices. Roll up and seal the pastry. Arrange the patties on a greased baking sheet, brush them with melted butter and put into a preheated oven (180–190°C). Bake for 15 mins. Serve with puréed vegetables, garnished with kiwi slices.

serves 4 • Macerating: 30–40 mins • Preparation: 30–40 mins

Mutton cutlets with mint

600 g boneless mutton (saddle or leg), 4 tsps anchovy paste or 2 anchovy fillets, 8 mint leaves, 1 large beef tomato, 4–5 cloves of garlic, pepper, salt, 2 tbsps oil, 1 tbsp butter

Remove excess fat from the meat. Rinse and dry the meat, cut it into 4 thick slices, pound lightly with a mallet. Crush the garlic with pepper. Blanch and skin the tomato, cut it into thick slices. Chop the fillets finely. Make a lengthwise incision in each cutlet, rub the pocket inside with the garlic and anchovies. Put in a slice of tomato and 2 mint leaves. Close the pocket with a toothpick, sprinkle the cutlets sparingly with pepper and, if required, salt. Fry on both sides in very hot oil, put in the butter and cook for a while longer. Serve with white beans or bean purée.

serves 4 • Preparation: 30–40 mins

Spicy lamb cutlets

800 g loin of lamb (off the bone), grated rind and juice of 1 lemon, 1 tbsp honey, 2–3 cloves of garlic, 1 tbsp finely grated onion, ½ tsp ground coriander, ¼ tsp each cayenne pepper and salt, 2 tbsps olive oil, 1 tbsp butter, several coriander or parsley sprigs, ½ lemon cut into thin slices

Mix thoroughly the finely chopped garlic with salt, cayenne, ground coriander, lemon zest and juice, oil and onion juice. Rinse and dry the meat (remove excess fat), cut it into slices. Pound them lightly with a mallet, rub with the spicy mixture, cover and put into the fridge for 2–3 hours. Fry the cutlets in melted butter or grill them, basting frequently with the dressing. Garnish with coriander sprigs and lemon slices. Serve with rice and puréed vegetables.

serves 4–6 • Macerating: 2–3 hrs • Preparation: 15–20 mins

Marinated lamb fillets

700 g fillets of lamb (leg)

LEMONY MARINADE: juice and grated rind of 2 lemons, ½ cup olive oil, 1–2 finely chopped cloves of garlic, 1 cup finely chopped basil leaves, a pinch of each pepper and sugar

Prepare the marinade by mixing all the ingredients, brush the fillets with it. Put the fillets one on top of another, pour the remaining marinade over. Cover and leave in the fridge for 3–4 hours. Grill the fillets, basting frequently with the marinade.

serves 4 • Marinating: 3–4 hrs • Grilling: 10–15 mins

Spicy lamb fricadelles

600 g boneless lamb meat, 1 large onion, 2–3 tbsps finely chopped parsley, ½ tsp dried thyme, ¼ tsp each ground caraway, coriander and chili, a pinch of each ground cloves, cinnamon, ginger, nutmeg, cardamom and pepper, 1 egg, salt, 1 tbsp oil

Put the meat through a mincer three times. Mix it with the finely grated onion, add the parsley and the spices and work into a smooth paste. Break in the egg, mix thoroughly and shape into small patties. Arrange the fricadelles on a greased baking tin and put into a preheated oven. Serve with rice or puréed potatoes and with tomato salad.

serves 4 • Preparation: 10 mins • Roasting: 15–20 mins

Mutton shashliks with herbs

1 kg leg of lamb (off the bone), 2 onions, 2 cloves of garlic, 5 lemon balm sprigs

MARINADE: ½ cup wine vinegar, 1 tsp each ground caraway, coriander and turmeric, 1 tbsp honey, 2 crumbled bay leaves, 1 tsp pepper, 2–3 tbsps water, 2 tbsps lemon juice

Put all the spices into a pan, add the water, cover and bring to the boil. Pour in the vinegar and simmer for several minutes. Add the honey and lemon juice, stir and leave to cool. Rinse and dry the meat, cut it into even large cubes. Cut the peeled onion into thick slices. Rub a stoneware jar with crushed garlic and put in alternating layers of meat and onion with lemon balm sprigs. Salt it sparingly, pour over the cool marinade. Cover and leave in the fridge overnight. Thread the meat cubes on skewers, alternating with onion slices. Grill or spit-roast the shashliks, basting them with the marinade.

serves 4–6 • Marinating: 12 hrs • Grilling: 15–20 mins

Mutton goulash with sauerkraut

*700 g boneless mutton, 500 g sauerkraut,
150 g onion, 3 tbsps lard, 1½ tbsps flour,
1 tbsp tomato paste, 1½ cups stock, ½ tsp each
paprika, dried marjoram and sugar, salt*

Rinse and dry the meat, cut it into cubes, sprinkle with salt and dredge with some flour. Heat 1½ tbsps of lard in a thick-bottomed skillet, put in the meat and, stirring all the time, brown it briskly. Pour in ½ cup of stock, cover and simmer for 40 mins. Chop the sauerkraut, put it into a pan, pour in 1 cup of stock and bring to the boil. Put the sauerkraut into the skillet, add the paprika, marjoram and sugar, stir well and cook for half an hour. Heat the remaining lard in a frying pan and sauté the finely chopped onion. Sprinkle with flour, dilute with 2–3 tbsps of cold stock, then pour into the goulash. Stir well and cook for a while longer.

serves 6–8 • Preparation: 1 hr

Lamb goulash with leek

*700 g lean lamb meat, 500 g leek, 2–3 cloves of
garlic, 3 tbsps tomato purée, 2 tbsps lemon juice,
1 tsp dried tarragon, ½ tsp each chilli and pepper,
¼ tsp sugar, salt, 2 tbsps oil, 2 tbsps butter,
1 cup each stock and dry white wine,
3–4 tbsps chopped dill*

Rinse and dry the meat, cut it into cubes. Put it into a bowl, sprinkle with lemon juice, pepper and chilli, cover and leave in the fridge for an hour. Wash the leeks thoroughly, cut them into broad strips. Heat the oil in a thick-bottom skillet, put in the meat and, stirring all the time, brown it briskly for 6–8 mins. Turn the heat down, add the butter and leeks and sauté them. Add the tarragon and some salt, pour in the hot stock, cover and simmer for an hour. When the meat is tender, pour in the wine mixed with the sugar and tomato purée, put in the crushed garlic, stir and cook for a while longer. Garnish with chopped dill before serving.

serves 4–6 • Marinating: 1–2 hrs • Preparation: 1 hr

Rabbit

The rabbit is often not appreciated enough, which is a pity because it has excellent meat with high food value. Rabbit meat is lean (4–8% fat), white, delicate and highly digestible, which is very important.

Braised rabbit with prunes

Rinse the rabbit, remove the membranes, divide it into portions, rub with thyme, cover with grated vegetables and finely chopped onion, wrap up the whole in a cloth soaked in vinegar and leave for 8 to 12 hours. Rinse the prunes and soak them in cool boiled water, and leave them – like the rabbit – for about 12 hours. Remove the stones from the soaked prunes. Clean the vegetables from the meat, and put them aside for later. Dredge the pieces of meat with flour and brown them on all sides in hot lard and margarine, then put them, together with the fat, in a saucepan, sprinkle with paprika and pepper, salt, and add the stoned prunes and the vegetables. Braise in the oven, from time to time basting with stock. When the meat is tender, it should be removed and put in a warm place, while the sauce is thickened with a small amount of flour and water. Bring the sauce to the boil and season to taste. The dish should be served hot, with pats of butter, with bread noodles or Silesian noodles.

(Elżbieta Łabońska, *Śląska kucharka doskonała*, 1990)

Rabbit in vegetables

*1 rabbit (ca 1½ kg), 60 g olive oil, 4 large onions,
2 aubergines, 2 courgettes, 750 g tomatoes,
3 peppers, 150 g dry white wine, 2–3 cloves of
garlic, 1 tbsp tomato concentrate, 8–10 stoned
black olives, salt, pepper, a pinch of sugar*

Rinse and dry the rabbit, joint it. Peel and dice the aubergines, courgettes and tomatoes. Core the peppers, cut them into strips. Heat 2 tbsps of oil in a skillet and brown the meat on all sides, then take it out. Add the remaining oil to the skillet and sauté the vegetables. Pour in the wine, add the garlic and tomato concentrate, salt and pepper. Put the meat in, cover and simmer for one hour.

Transfer the meat onto a serving dish, pile the vegetables around. Garnish with olives and serve with rice, macaroni or boiled potatoes.

serves 4–6 • Preparation: 10 mins • Braising: 1 hr

Rabbit with mushrooms and olives

1 rabbit, 1 tbsp lemon juice, 2 tbsps butter, ½ cup stock, ½ cup dry white wine, 2 onions, 200 g mushrooms, 2 tbsps tomato purée, 3–4 cloves of garlic, ½ tsp each marjoram, rosemary and thyme, 12–15 stoned green olives, salt, pepper, 1 tbsp chopped parsley

Sprinkle the jointed rabbit with lemon juice, rub it with salt and pepper and brown briskly on all sides. Transfer it to a skillet, put in the onions cut into fine slices, pour in the stock and simmer under cover. Sprinkle the diced mushrooms with the herbs and sauté them in butter. Add the tomato purée and olives, pour in the wine. Combine the mushrooms with the rabbit meat, cover and cook for 20 mins. Garnish with chopped parsley and serve with rice.

serves 4–6 • Preparation: 10–15 mins • Braising: 1 hr

Roast rabbit

1 rabbit, 2 tbsps lemon juice (or wine vinegar), 2 tbsps oil, 1–2 bay leaves, 2–3 grains each pepper and allspice, 4–6 juniper berries, 1 onion, 150 g smoked streaky bacon, salt, 2 tbsps butter, 1 glass dry white wine

Pound the spices in a mortar, mix them with the lemon juice and oil. Rub the rinsed and dried rabbit with the mixture, put it into a stoneware bowl, cover with slices of onion and stand for 24 hours in a cool place. Remove the onion, dry the meat. Lard the rabbit with strips of bacon and the onion. Arrange it in a greased roasting tin, place slices of butter on top. Put into a preheated oven and cook it, basting with the wine and with the pan juices. Divide the rabbit into portions and keep warm. Sieve the roasting juices. Serve with French fries and beetroot and horseradish relish.

serves 4–6 • Macerating: 24 hrs • Preparation: 10–15 mins • Roasting: 1 hr

Rabbit in cream

800 g jointed rabbit, juice of 1 lemon, 1 tsp grated lemon rind, 4 cloves of garlic, salt, pepper, 2 tbsps butter, 1 tsp flour, 1 cup thick sour cream, ½ cup stock, 2 tbsps chopped parsley

Sprinkle the rinsed and dried meat with lemon juice, rub it with a mixture of finely chopped garlic, salt and lemon zest and leave in a cool place for an hour. Melt the butter in a skillet and brown the rabbit, sprinkle it with some stock, cover and cook, adding pepper towards the end. Mix the cream with the flour, pour into the meat and simmer for a while. Garnish with chopped parsley. Serve with macaroni and rice.

serves 4 • Macerating: 1–2 hrs • Preparation: 5 mins • Cooking: 40–45 mins

Rabbit in wine

800 g jointed rabbit, 1 tbsp lemon juice, 100 g smoked lean bacon, 100 g mushrooms, 1 onion, 1 bay leaf, 2–3 grains allspice, 1 cup dry red wine, 2 tbsps butter, salt, pepper, 1 tbsp chopped parsley

Sprinkle the rinsed and dried meat with lemon juice, rub it with salt. Brown in butter, then transfer to a skillet. Fry the finely chopped onion in the same butter, but do not let it brown. Add it to the meat together with the bacon cut into cubes and the sliced mushrooms, bay leaf and allspice. Simmer for a while, sprinkle sparingly with water, pour in the wine and cook until the meat is tender. Make a roux from the butter and flour, dilute it with 3 tbsps of stock, pour into the meat. Shake the skillet gently and cook a bit longer, adding pepper and parsley towards the end.

serves 4 • Preparation: 5 mins • Cooking: 40–45 mins

Rabbit stew with ham

800 g boned rabbit meat, 150 g ham, 20 g dried cep mushrooms, 2 tbsps butter, ½ cup stock, 3 tbsps cream, 1 tbsp flour, salt, pepper, ¼ tsp each dried marjoram and thyme, 2 tbsps grated cheese

MARINADE: 1 small carrot, 1 small onion, 1–2 bay leaves, 5–6 peppercorns, 2–3 cloves, 1 tbsp chopped

Rabbit goulash

parsley, ¼ tsp dried thyme, a pinch of sugar, 1 tbsp oil, 1½ cups dry white wine, 1 tbsp lemon juice

Knead the rinsed and dried meat well, place it in a stoneware bowl, cover with the peeled and diced carrot and onion. Mix the remaining ingredients of the marinade, pour the mixture over the meat. Cover and leave in the fridge for 2–3 days, turning the meat over every day. Soak the rinsed mushrooms in the stock, then cook them. Take the meat out, dry it. Cut the meat and ham into cubes. Melt the butter in a skillet, put in the meat and ham, cover with the stock and strained marinade. Put in the mushrooms cut into fine strips, add salt, pepper, marjoram and thyme, stir and simmer under cover for 30–40 mins. Mix the cream with flour, pour into the meat, stir and heat up until the sauce has thickened (keep it off the boil). Before serving, sprinkle with parsley and grated cheese. Serve with white bread (preferably in small individual bowls) or with rice and salads.

serves 4–6 • Marinating: 2–3 days • Preparation: 10 mins • Cooking: 40 mins

Rabbit goulash

1 kg jointed rabbit, 6–8 grains each allspice and pepper, 3–4 bay leaves, 2 onions, 2 tbsps butter, ½ cup cream, 1 tbsp flour, 100 g chopped walnuts, 1 tbsp raisins, 2 tsps paprika, salt, pepper, a pinch of sugar, ¼ tsp grated lemon rind, 2 tbsps lemon juice, 2 cups dry red wine

Put the meat in a large pan, add the allspice, pepper, lemon zest and bay leaves, cover with boiling salted water. Bring to the boil, then simmer for I hour and leave aside to cool. Melt the butter in a saucepan, fry the finely chopped onion, but do not let it brown. Put in the walnuts, sprinkle with paprika and some strained stock. Bone the meat, cut it into cubes and add to the onion. Pour in the wine, add the blanched raisins, stir and cook for a while. Mix the cream with flour, pour into the meat, stir and heat up until the sauce has thickened (keep it off the boil). Adjust the taste with lemon juice, salt and pepper. Serve with rice or macaroni.

serves 4–6 • Cooking: 1 hr • Cooling: 1–2 hrs • Preparation: 20–25 mins

Rabbit ragout

1 kg boned rabbit meat, 250 g ham, 30 g dried cep mushrooms, 2–3 tbsps butter, 1 cup stock, 3–4 tbsps cream, 1 tbsp flour, salt, pepper, ½ tsp each dried marjoram and thyme, 3–4 tbsps gratd cheese

MARINADE: 1 small carrot, 1 small onion, 1–2 bay leaves, 5–6 peppercorns, 2–3 cloves, 1 tbsp chopped parsley, ¼ tsp dried thyme, a pinch of sugar, 1 tbsp oil, 1½ cups dry white wine, 1 tbsp lemon juice

Knead the rinsed and dried meat well, place it in a stoneware bowl, cover with the peeled and diced carrot and onion. Mix the remaining ingredients of the marinade, pour the mixture over the meat. Cover and leave in the fridge for 2–3 days, turning the meat over every day. Soak the rinsed mushrooms in the stock, then cook them. Take the meat out, dry it. Cut the meat and ham into cubes. Melt the butter in a skillet, put in the meat and ham, cover with the stock and strained marinade. Put in the mushrooms cut into fine strips, add salt, pepper, marjoram and thyme, stir and simmer under cover for 30–40 mins (until now you may prepare everything in the morning). Before serving, heat up the ragout, pour in the cream mixed with flour, stir and heat up again until the sauce has thickened (keep it off the boil). Serve with white bread, preferably in small individual bowls, garnished with parsley and grated cheese.

serves 6–8 • Marinating: 2–3 days • Preparation: 10 mins • Cooking: 30–40 mins

Rabbit pâté

rabbit meat, 750 g pork gorge, 5–6 dried cep mushrooms, ½ celeriac, 1 medium-sized onion, 4 eggs, salt, pepper, 1 tsp nutmeg, ¼ tsp ground juniper berries, 100 g veal liver

MARINADE: 1 cup dry white wine (or vinegar), 5–6 grains each pepper and allspice, 5–6 juniper berries, 1 onion

1 tbsp butter, 2 tbsps breadcrumbs

Make the marinade from all the ingredients. Put the meat into a stoneware bowl, cover with the marinade. Leave in a cool place for 5–6 days, turning the meat over every day. Soak the mushrooms, then cook them. Rub the dried meat with the ground juniper, put it into a skillet. Put in the gorge, celeriac and onion, add the mushrooms together with the stock, pour over the strained marinade. Cover and cook for 90 mins, adding the liver after the first 70 mins. Stand aside to cool. Bone the meat. Put the meat and the remaining ingredients twice through a mincer. Break in the eggs, add salt, pepper and nutmeg and mix thoroughly. Grease a pâté mould with butter, dust it with breadcrumbs. Fill it with the meat mixture. Put into a preheated oven and bake for 40 mins at medium temperature or steam-cook it. Take out of the mould when the pâté has cooled down.

serves 4 • Marinating: 5–6 days • Stewing: 90 mins • Preparation: 20–25 mins • Baking: 40–45 mins

Offal

– Offal should be bought as fresh as possible.
– Brains, tongue and sweetbreads require pre-soaking. Brains are first soaked in cold water until all the blood is rinsed out, and then the blood vessels and membranes are removed. Lamb and calf brains are pale pink and have a delicate taste. Brains are served fried whole, diced or made into a mousse.
– Small tongues should be pre-cooked for ten minutes and larger ones for half an hour; after this, they should be immediately plunged into cold water, skinned and cooked in a vegetable stock. Fresh tongues should be soaked for an hour in slightly acidified water.
– Lungs or lights are usually braised; they have little food value and are usually served in thick sauce.
– Hearts have a high food value and there is little waste. The most delicate are lamb and calf hearts; pigs' hearts are larger and hard while the hardest of all are beef hearts. They all need long cooking or pre-boiling before roasting.
– Liver is a very good source of iron.
– Kidneys have a very strong taste. Lamb and calf kidneys can be fried; beef kidneys are baked in pies or are added to other dishes that require a long cooking time.

Veal offal

calf's liver, lights, heart and kidneys, 100 g pork fat, 2 onions, soup vegetables, 2 bay leaves, 5 grains each allspice and pepper, juice and grated rind of 1 lemon, ½ cup dry red wine, 1 tbsp butter, 1 tbsp flour, 2 tbsps cherry preserves, 2 cloves, 1 tsp caramel, ½ tsp caraway

Wash the offal thoroughly. Put into a pan together with the soup vegetables, spices and some salt, pour in the wine and cook till tender. Take the offal out, drain it, then cut into strips. Fry the diced pork fat with the finely chopped onions. Put in the offal, stir and fry together for a minute or two. Add the coarsely ground cloves, pour in some strained stock, sprinkle with lemon juice. Cover and cook over low heat. Make a roux from the butter and flour, dilute it with some stock. Add the caramel, lemon zest, cherry preserves and salt. Pour the sauce into the offal, stir and bring to the boil. Serve with white bread or macaroni and a savoury salad.

serves 4–6 • Cooking: 40–45 mins • Cooling: 1–2 hrs • Preparation: 10 mins

Pig's offal ragout

500 g each pig's lights and liver, 1 pig's heart, 3 onions, 2–3 cloves of garlic, 1 tbsp wine vinegar, salt, pepper, 1 bay leaf, ½ tsp each dried thyme and marjoram, 4 tbsps butter, 1 cup stock, 1 glass dry white wine, 2 tbsps flour, a pinch of sugar, 2 tbsps chopped parsley

Wash the offal thoroughly. Remove membranes and veins from the liver. Cut the offal into small pieces. Chop the peeled garlic and onions finely. Melt 2 tbsps of butter in a skillet, sauté the garlic and onion without browning them. Put in the offal and fry briskly for a minute or two. Pour in the stock, add the bay leaf, marjoram and thyme, cover and simmer for 30 mins.

Melt the remaining butter in a saucepan, add the flour to make a roux, dilute it with the wine and vinegar. Add salt and sugar to taste, pour into the skillet. Stir well and cook for another 15–20 mins. Before serving, garnish with chopped parsley.

serves 4–6 • Preparation: 15–20 mins • Cooking: 45–50 mins

Tongue

The tongue belongs to the superior edible internal part of an animal. It has the same protein and mineral content is as meat and its flesh is very tasty. Before cooking it, you must remember to trim it by removing the fat parts and gristle, and then soak it for several hours in cold, slightly acidic water.

Grilled ox tongue

Cook the tongue in salted water, then skin it and lard it with fine pork fat strips. Spear it on a spit and grill it, then serve it with rémoulade... or simple vinaigrette. Ox tongues can be smoked and then cooked with various spices, which is done in the following way. Take several ox tongues, remove the thick skin from them, put them into a bowl. Salt each of them generously, press them down. Cover the bowl and leave the tongues to stand in salt for six days. Take them out, hang them up in a curing chimney and smoke them. When they are well cured, they will keep for a long time. If you want to have them cooked, cover them with water, add ground cloves and allspice, then cook them. Drain them before serving.

(Wojciech Wielądko, *Kucharz doskonały*, 1808)

Polish oysters, or stuffed calves' tongues

3 tongues, soup vegetables, 1 onion, 1 clove, 1 bay leaf, 2–3 grains each allspice and pepper, salt

STUFFING: 5 pickled herrings, 1 tbsps butter, juice of ½ lemon, 2 eggs, 2 tbsps finely chopped parsley, pepper, ½ cup breadcrumbs, fat for frying; 1 lemon, 1 horseradish root

Wash the tongues thoroughly, cover them with cold water and leave to soak for several hours. Make a stock from the vegetables, onion and spices, put in the tongues and cook for 1½ hours. Skin and bone the herrings, rinse them, put through a mincer or chop very finely. Cream the butter, adding 1 egg yolk and 1 tbsp of herring at a time. Put in the lemon juice and parsley, add some pepper and mix thoroughly. Take the tender tongues out, leave them to cool, then skin them and slice diagonally. Coat the slices with the herring preparation, roll them up, secure with a toothpick. Dip them into lightly beaten egg whites and in breadcrumbs and fry in very hot hat. Arrange the oysters in a warm serving dish, garnish with lemon slices and horseradish shavings. Serve hot, with potatoes, or cold.

serves 4–5 • Soaking: 4–6 hrs • Boiling: 90 mins •
Preparation: 15–20 mins • Frying: 6–8 mins

Calves' tongues in caper sauce

4 tongues, 1 onion, ½ celeriac, 2 carrots, 1–2 cloves of garlic, 1 tbsp capers, 100 g raisins, 1 glass dry red wine, 1 tsp cornflour or potato flour

Wash the tongues thoroughly, cover them with cold water and leave overnight. Drain them, put into a pan, pour in enough water to cover them. Add the diced carrot, celeriac, onion and garlic and cook for an hour. Pour in the wine, add the raisins and continue cooking for another 30 mins. Take the tongues out, skin them, slice diagonally. Reduce the stock, then put it through a blender and sieve it. Thicken it with the cornflour mixed in 1 tbsp of water. Put in the tongue slices and capers, stir and heat up, but do not boil.

serves 4 • Soaking: 8–12 hrs • Boiling: 90 mins • Preparation: 20 mins

Ragout from calves' tongues

3 tongues (ca 900 g), 2 cups vegetable stock, 2–3 bay leaves, 1 clove, 1 large onion, 10–12 peppercorns, salt; 3 tbsps butter, 2 tbsps flour, ½ cup dry white wine, 1 tbsp lemon juice, 1 cup sour cream, 3 tbsps capers

Wash the tongues thoroughly, rub them with salt, put into a pan. Add the onion with the clove stuck into it, bay leaves and peppercorns, pour over the hot stock, cover and cook for an hour. Take the tongues out, run them under cold water and skin. Cut them into fairly thick strips. Melt the butter in a skillet, add the flour and make a roux. Dilute it with the wine and 2 cups of strained stock and, stirring all the time, simmer until the sauce has thickened. Adjust the taste with salt and lemon juice, add the cream, put in the tongue strips and capers. Heat up slowly for several minutes.

serves 4 • Boiling: 60–70 mins • Preparation: 20 mins

Breaded veal tongues

2–3 tongues, 2 onions, 3–4 cloves, 1 leek, a piece of celeriac, 1 bay leaf, 12–15 peppercorns, 1 egg, flour, breadcrumbs, oil for frying, salt

Wash the tongues thoroughly, cover them with cold water and leave aside for 3–4 hours, then drain them. Make a stock from the vegetables and spices, put in the tongues and cook them for 1½ hours. Take the tongues out, leave to cool, then skin them and slice diagonally. Salt the slices and dip them into flour, lightly beaten egg and breadcrumbs. Fry in very hot oil until golden brown on both sides. Serve with potatoes and salads.

serves 4 • Soaking: 3–4 hrs • Boiling: 90 mins • Preparation: 10–15 mins

Pig's tongue in lemon juice

2 tongues, soup vegetables, 1 bay leaf, 2–3 grains each pepper and allspice, salt

SAUCE: grated rind and juice of 1 lemon, 1 cup whipping cream, 1 egg yolk, salt, a pinch of sugar, 1 tbsp butter, 1 tbsp flour

Wash the tongues thoroughly, rub them with salt and leave in a cool place for an hour. Put them into a pan, cover with water. Put in the vegetables and spices and cook for an hour. Take the tongues out, allow them to cool, then skin them and slice diagonally. Make a roux from the butter and flour, dilute it with some strained stock and, stirring all the time, simmer until the sauce has thickened. Add the lemon zest and juice, adjust the taste with salt and

pepper. Towards the end, pour in the cream mixed with the egg yolk. Put the tongue slices into a pan, pour the sauce over and heat up.

serves 4 • Salting: 1–2 hrs • Boiling: 60–90 mins • Preparation: 10–15 mins

Pigs' tongues royale

800 g pigs' tongues, soup vegetables, 3–4 grains each allspice and pepper, 1 bay leaf, 1 clove, 1 onion, ½ tsp grated lemon rind, salt

SAUCE: 2 oranges, 2 lemons, 3 bananas, 2 tomatoes, 1 glass dry white wine, salt, pepper, sugar, 5 tbsps thick mayonnaise

Wash the tongues thoroughly, rub them with salt, put into a pan. Add the spices and the peeled and diced vegetables. Cover with boiling water and cook over low heat. Take the tongues out, dip them into cold water for a minute, then skin them and slice lengthwise. Peel the fruit, skin the tomatoes. Cut them into cubes (remove pips and seeds). Mix the mayonnaise with the wine, add salt, pepper and sugar and combine with the fruit and tomatoes. Arrange the tongue slices in a serving dish, pour the sauce over, and refrigerate for an hour. Before serving, garnish with parsley sprigs.

serves 4–8 • Salting: 1 hr •Boiling: 60–90 mins • Preparation: 10 mins • Refrigerating: 1–2 hrs

Tongues in tomato sauce

800 g pigs' or calves' tongues, soup vegetables, 2–3 grains each pepper and allspice, 1 bay leaf, 1 small onion, clove, salt, 1 large onion, 400 g tomatoes, salt, a pinch of sugar, ½ tsp chilli pepper, 3 tbsps chopped parsley, 1 tbsp butter

Wash the tongues thoroughly, place them in a pan, put in the peeled vegetables, onion with one clove stuck into it, add the spices and salt and cook over low heat for an hour, or until the tongues are tender. Take the tongues out, allow them to cool a bit, then skin them and slice lengthwise. Fry the finely chopped onion in butter, but do not let it brown, add the skinned and quartered tomatoes, cover and simmer for a while. Pour in 1 cup of stock, add salt, chilli and sugar, then sieve the sauce. Put the tongue slices into the sauce, heat up. Serve with noodles or macaroni, sprinkled with chopped parsley.

serves 4 • Boiling: 1–2 hrs • Cooling: 1–2 hrs • Preparation: 10–15 mins

Pickled ox tongue

1 ox tongue, 5 g saltpetre, 20 g salt, 1 tsp sugar, ¼ tsp each ground pepper and allspice, 1 tsp ground juniper berries

STOCK: soup vegetables, 1 large onion, salt

Mix the saltpetre with the salt, pepper, allspice and juniper. Rub the washed and dried tongue with the mixture, put it into a stoneware bowl, cover with a board, weigh it down. Stand in a cool place for 8–10 days, turning the tongue over every second day. Prepare the stock. Take the tongue out, rinse it, put into the strained stock and cook over low heat for 90 mins. Skin the cooked tongue and cut it diagonally into slices. Serve cold or hot, with horseradish sauce.

serves 4 • Pickling: 8–10 days • Boiling: 90 mins • Preparation: 5 mins

SAUCE FOR PICKLED TONGUE

Polish grey sauce

2 tbsps butter, 2 tbsps flour, ½ cup stock, 2 tbsps raisins, 2 tbsps chopped almonds, 1 glass dry red wine, lemon juice, a pinch of each ground allspice and cloves, a piece of ginger cake

Prepare the tongue as above. Slice it diagonally, arrange in an ovenproof dish and pour the grey or horseradish sauce over. Put into the oven for 10 mins. Serve with puréed potatoes and soured cucumbers.

Preparation: 5 mins • Baking: 8–10 mins

Horseradish sauce

2 tbsps butter, 2 tbsps flour, 1 cup stock, 3 tbsps grated horseradish, salt, sugar, 2 tbsps lemon juice, 3 tbsps cream, 1 egg

Prepare the tongue as above. Slice it diagonally, arrange in an ovenproof dish and pour the grey or horserad-

ish sauce over. Put into the oven for 10 mins. Serve with puréed potatoes and soured cucumbers.

Preparation: 5 mins • Baking: 8–10 mins

Tongue in batter

500 g cooked ox tongue, ½ cup milk, 2 eggs, 3 tbsps melted butter, ¾ cup flour

Make a thick batter (like that for pancakes) from the flour, eggs and milk. Cut the cooked tongue diagonally into slices. Dip the slices into the batter and fry in the melted butter. Serve immediately.

serves 4–6 • Preparation: 10 mins • Frying: 6–8 mins

Ox tongue, Russian style

1 ox tongue, 1 tbsp vinegar, soup vegetables, 2 large onions, 4–5 grains each allspice and pepper, 1–2 bay leaves, 2–3 cloves, salt, 2 tbsps butter, 2 tbsps flour, juice and grated rind of 1 lemon, 50 g blanched raisins, 2 tbsps dry white wine, a pinch of each pepper and sugar

Wash the tongue thoroughly, cover it with cold acidic water and leave aside for 3–4 hours, then drain and rub with salt. Make a stock from the vegetables and spices, put in the tongue, bring to the boil, then simmer for two and a half hours. Take the tender tongue out, rinse it with cold water, skin it. Reduce the stock and strain it. Pour the wine over the raisins. Make a roux from the butter and flour, dilute it with the cool stock and, stirring all the time, simmer until the sauce has thickened. Add the lemon juice and zest, adjust the taste with salt, pepper and sugar. Put in the raisins and stir. Cut the tongue into diagonal slices, arrange them in a pan, pour the sauce over and heat up.

serves 4–6 • Soaking: 3–4 hrs • Boiling: 2½ hrs • Preparation: 10–15 mins

Ox tongue in wine

1 ox tongue, 100 g pork fat, 2 onions, 2 carrots, 2 cups stock, 2 cups dry white wine, salt, pepper, 1 bay leaf, ½ tsp dried thyme, 2 tbsps chopped parsley, 1 tbsp lard

Wash the tongue thoroughly, cover it with cold water and leave aside for 3–4 hours, then take it out and dry. Rub the tongue with dry-roasted coarse-grained salt, cover and leave in the fridge for 24 hours. Rinse it, put into a pan, cover with boiling water and cook for 40 mins. Take it out, run under cold water, skin and fry on all sides in hot lard. Transfer it to a skillet, pile the diced pork fat and sliced onion and carrot around. Add the spices, pour in the wine and stock and simmer for 2 hours. Take the tongue out, slice it diagonally. Reduce the stock, put it through a blender and sieve it. Put the tongue slices into the sauce and heat up. Serve with macaroni or potatoes.

serves 4–6 • Soaking: 3–4 hrs • Salting: 24 hrs
• Boiling: 40 mins • Braising: 2 hrs

Baked ox tongue

1 ox tongue, soup vegetables, 3–4 grains each allspice and pepper, salt, 1 bay leaf, 2–3 cloves of garlic, 1 onion, 3 tbsps butter, 4–6 tomatoes, 3 tbsps chopped parsley, 1 tbsp breadcrumbs, salt, pepper

Wash the tongue thoroughly, cover it with water, put in the vegetables and spices and cook for 90 mins. Take the tongue out, skin it and slice diagonally. Grease an ovenproof dish with butter, line it with half the tongue slices, sprinkle with some parsley. Fry the finely chopped onion and garlic in butter, but do not let them brown. Pour some of the preparation over the tongue slices. Put in a layer of skinned and sliced tomatoes, sprinkle it with parsley, salt and pepper and cover with the remaining tongue slices. Blend the remaining onion and garlic with breadcrumbs and brush the tongues with the mixture and sprinkle with the remaining parsley. Strain the stock and use it to sprinkle the tongue sparingly. Put into a preheated oven and cook for 30 mins. Serve with macaroni and salads.

serves 4–6 • Boiling: 90 mins • Preparation: 10–15 mins • Baking: 30 mins

Heart

Heart, especially calf's heart, is considered to be an excellent dish. It is rich in vitamins and protein (15%) and can be cooked in many different ways. You may roast and braise it, grill and stuff it.

Calves' hearts, farmer's style

2 hearts, 2 tbsps butter, 200 g lean bacon, 800 g potatoes, 200 g shallots, 1 cup stock, 1 bay leaf, 1–2 thyme sprigs, several parsley sprigs, salt, pepper, 2 tbsps chopped parsley

Clean and rinse the hearts, remove membranes and blood vessels. Brown the hearts in melted butter, then transfer them to a skillet. Pour in ⅔ cup of hot stock and simmer for 20 mins. Brown the bacon cut into cubes in the same butter. Peel the potatoes, cut them into cubes, scald with boiling water and drain well. Mix them with the fried bacon and add to the tongues. Put in the shallots, add the thyme, bay leaf and parsley sprigs, season with salt and pepper, pour in the remaining stock and cook for 50 mins. Take out the hearts, cut them diagonally into slices. Reduce the stock, remove the thyme and bay leaf. Adjust the taste of the potatoes with salt and pepper. Transfer the potatoes and onions to a deep serving dish, arrange the sliced hearts on top, garnish with chopped parsley.

serves 4 • Preparation: 1 hr

Calves' hearts with carrots

2 hearts, 750 g carrots, 2 tbsps butter, 1 onion, salt, pepper, 1 cup stock

Clean and rinse the hearts, remove membranes and blood vessels. Cut the hearts into strips, slice the peeled onion. Fry the onion in butter, but do not let it brown, put in the hearts and sauté them, stirring all the time. Season with salt and pepper, pour in the stock, put in the carrots cut into thick sticks. Cover and cook for one hour. Serve with rice or macaroni.

serves 4 • Preparation: 10–12 mins • Braising: 1 hr

Braised beef hearts

800 g beef hearts, 300 g streaky bacon, 1 onion; 2 tbsps oil, 2 cups stock, 1–2 bay leaves, 1 carrot, 1 leek (only the white part), 1–2 celery sticks, 2 firm beef tomatoes, 1 tsp tomato purée, 1 tsp sweet paprika, a pinch of each sugar, pepper and cayenne, salt, ½ cup cream, 1 tsp potato flour, 1 tbsp water

Soak the hearts in cold water for 1–2 hours. Take them out, remove fat, membranes and blood vessels. Lard the hearts with fine strips of bacon. Heat the oil in a frying pan, fry the finely chopped onion, but do not let it brown, then brown the hearts on all sides. Transfer the hearts and onion to a skillet, add salt, pepper, cayenne and paprika, pour in the hot stock, cover and simmer for 50 mins. Put in the cleaned and diced carrot, celery and leek and cook for another 20 mins. Blanch the tomatoes, skin and quarter them, put into the skillet and cook for 10 mins. Mix the potato flour with water and add to the hearts. Stirring all the time, simmer until the sauce has thickened. Blend the tomato purée, sugar, salt and cream, pour into the skillet. Stir and heat up. Serve with noodles or macaroni.

serves 4–6 • Soaking: 1–2 hrs • Preparation: 20 mins • Braising: 90 mins

Beef hearts in tomato sauce

800 g beef hearts, soup vegetables, 2–3 peppercorns, 1 bay leaf, 2 tbsps butter, 2 tbsps flour, 2 tbsps tomato concentrate, ½ cup thick cream, salt, pepper, a pinch of sugar, 4 tbsps chopped parsley

Wash the hearts thoroughly, halve them lengthwise, remove membranes and blood vessels. Cover with cold water and leave aside for half an hour. Bring them to the boil, put in the peeled vegetables and spices, and cook for an hour. Drain the hearts, cut them into small sticks. Make a roux from the butter and flour, dilute it with the strained stock, add the tomato purée, salt, pepper and a pinch of sugar. Put in the hearts, stir and simmer for a while. Towards the end, fold in the cream and add the chopped parsley. Serve with rice or macaroni and with salads.

serves 4–6 • Soaking: ½–1 hr • Boiling: 1 hr • Cooking: 10–15 mins

Granny's ragout

800 g beef hearts, 2 large onions, 2–3 cloves of garlic, 2 carrots, 1 parsley root, ½ small celeriac, 1 tbsp lemon juice, 1 tbsp tomato purée, a pinch of sugar, ½ cup dry red wine, 2–3 cups stock, ½ cup cream, 1 tbsp flour, 1½ tbsps caraway, 1 bay leaf, salt, pepper, 2–3 tbsps chopped parsley, 1 tbsp oil, 2 tbsps butter

Halve the hearts lengthwise, remove membranes and blood vessels. Cover with cold water and leave aside for an hour. Dry the hearts, cut them into cubes. Peel the carrots, parsley root and celeriac, cut them into sticks, sprinkle with the lemon juice. Slice the peeled onion. Heat the oil in a skillet, put in the hearts and sauté them briskly. Turn down the heat, add the butter, put in the onion and soften it for 4–5 mins. Add the bay leaf and the vegetables, pour in the stock, cover and simmer for an hour. Now pour in the wine, add the garlic crushed with salt, pepper and caraway, stir and cook for a while longer. Fold in the cream and heat up. Before serving, sprinkle with parsley.

serves 4–6 • Soaking: 1 hr • Preparation: 10–15 mins • Cooking: 65–75 mins

Spanish goulash

750 g hearts, 1 cup milk, salt, pepper, 1 tbsp butter, 300 g tomatoes or 2 tbsps tomato concentrate, 300 g red peppers, ½ cup thick sour cream, 150 g sharp cheese, 1 tsp flour

Wash and halve the hearts, soak them in milk for an hour. Dry them, remove blood vessels. Cut the flesh into cubes, put into a skillet. Pour in 1 cup of water (or stock), add salt, pepper and 1 tbsp of butter, cover and cook for 1⅓ hours (adding more water if required). Blanch the tomatoes, skin and quarter them, add them to the hearts together with the diced red peppers. Blend the cream with the flour, mix in the cheese, pour the preparation into the skillet. Stir and continue cooking until the hearts are tender. Serve with rice and green peas.

serves 4–6 • Soaking: 2 hrs • Boiling: 90 mins • Preparation: 10–15 mins

Goulash from beef hearts

500 g beef hearts, 1 tbsp flour, 2 tbsps butter, 2–3 cloves of garlic, 1 large onion, 200 g tomatoes, 1 each large red, yellow and green pepper, 2 bay leaves, ¼ tsp thyme, salt, pepper

Wash the hearts, remove blood vessels. Boil the hearts quickly, then cut them into pieces. Sprinkle with salt and sauté in butter. Add the chopped onion and continue frying for a minute or two. Transfer to a skillet, cover with some stock. Put in the garlic crushed with salt, the diced peppers and the skinned and quartered tomatoes, add the crumbled bay leaf and thyme. Cover and simmer for 2 hours. Thicken the sauce with some flour.

serves 4–6 • Preparation: 10–15 mins • Cooking: 2 hrs

Liver

Liver is rich in high-quality protein, mineral salts (especially iron), vitamin A, almost all group B vitamins and some vitamin C. For cooking purposes, the most tender and savoury variety of liver is calf's liver, pig's liver and poultry livers, in particularly the livers from fattened geese. Before cooking the liver, you should remove membranes and thick blood vessels. Sometimes it is advisable to soak the liver in milk for a while to give it a nice bright pink colour. Liver should be salted after it has been fried, otherwise it will get tough.

Beef liver is best grilled.

There are several things to remember when cooking liver:

– fry it very briskly;
– salt it only before serving if you want it to remain juicy. The liver that has been salted before cooking and which has been fried too long, gets tough, dry, grey and unsavoury;
– soak it in milk and it will preserve a light red colour, which is important if you want your pâté to have a nice light colour;
– liver can be combined with kidneys when you make a goulash or ragout. It can be cooked in wine or with savoury spices.

Meatloaf from mutton liver

Cook the mutton liver and lights with various vegetables. Chop them all very finely, break in four eggs, add some breadcrumbs, salt, allspice and pepper. Put in one cup of melted mutton suet. If you like, you may also add a handful of raisins or one chopped onion fried in butter. Grease a skillet, line it with pancakes... put in the preparation and leave for an hour in a medium-hot oven.

(M. Marciszewska, *Doskonała kuchnia*)

Calf's liver in herbal sauce

600 g calf's liver, ½ cup milk, 2 onions, 2–3 cloves of garlic, 1 cup chopped herbs (basil, thyme, lemon balm, parsley) or 1 tsp each dried herbs, 4–5 tomatoes, 250 g mushrooms, 1 glass dry white wine, ½ cup stock, 2 tbsps flour, 1 tbsp lard, 2 tbsps butter, salt, pepper

Melt the lard in a skillet, fry the chopped onion, but do not let it brown. Put in the sliced mushrooms and sauté them briskly. Add the garlic crushed with salt, dust with flour, stir, pour in the wine, cover and simmer for a while. Blanch and skin the tomatoes, cut them into cubes and put them into the skillet together with the herbs. Add salt and pepper, pour in the stock, stir and cook for another 10–15 mins. Soak the liver in milk for half an hour, then dry it, remove membranes and blood vessels. Cut the liver diagonally into slices, sprinkle with pepper. Dredge with flour and fry in melted butter. Salt it sparingly, put into the sauce and heat up. Serve with rice, macaroni or noodles.

serves 4 • Soaking: 30–40 mins • Preparation: 25–30 mins • Frying: 5–7 mins

Calf's liver with sage

600 g calf's liver, ½ cup milk, 2 onions, 2–3 cloves of garlic, 2 tbsps chopped sage leaves, 1 tbsp olive oil, 2 tbsps butter, salt, pepper, ½ cup dry white wine, 1 tbsp flour, several mint leaves

Soak the liver in milk for 30–40 mins, then dry it, remove membranes and blood vessels. Cut the liver into thin strips, dust them with flour. Fry the finely chopped onion and garlic in hot oil, but do not let them brown. Put in the butter, the chopped sage and liver strips and sauté over medium heat, stirring all the time. Sprinkle with salt and pepper, pour in the wine, stir and heat up. Before serving, garnish with mint leaves. Serve with macaroni or rice.

serves 4 • Soaking: 30–40 mins • Preparation: 20–25 mins

Braised pork liver

600 g pig's liver, ½ cup milk, 1 glass dry white wine, 1 small onion, 1–2 cloves of garlic, 1 tbsp chopped mint leaves, 1 tsp chopped parsley, 4–5 peppercorns, a pinch of each caraway, cinnamon and cayenne, 3 tbsps oil, 1 cup stock, 2 tbsps breadcrumbs, 1 lemon cut into fine slices

Rinse the liver, put it into a bowl, cover with the milk and leave aside for an hour, then dry it, remove membranes and blood vessels. Cut the liver into slices, put into a skillet, add the peppercorns, pour in the wine and simmer for 15 mins. Heat the oil in a pan, fry the finely chopped onion and garlic, but do not let them brown. Add the caraway, cinnamon and cayenne, stir, pour in the stock. Put in the liver slices, dust them with breadcrumbs, stir and simmer for another 5–6 mins. Garnish with lemon slices before serving.

serves 4 • Soaking: 1 hr • Preparation: 20–25 mins

Calf's liver with bananas

3 bananas, 600 g calf's liver, 1 egg, 2 tbsps flour, 2 tbsps breadcrumbs, 1 small glass brandy, 2–3 tbsps butter or margarine

Cut the liver into 2 cm thick slices. Sprinkle them with brandy, dip into flour, lightly beaten egg and breadcrumbs. Fry in butter for 2–3 mins to each side. Melt the remaining butter in another pan and sauté the peeled bananas cut into fairly thick slices. Arrange the liver in a warm serving dish, put several banana slices on each piece. Pour over the butter. Serve with macaroni or rice.

serves 4 • Preparation: 15–20 mins

Calf's liver, Lvov style

600 g calf's liver, 50 g pork fat, 3 tbsps grated cheese, 3 tbsps chopped parsley, 1 large lemon, salt, 2 tbsps butter

Marinade: 1 glass dry white wine, 1 tbsps mustard, ¼ tsp tarragon, pepper, 1 tbsp grated lemon rind

Rinse the liver, remove membranes. Mix the wine with the mustard, tarragon, lemon zest and pepper. Put the liver and pork fat in a bowl, pour over the marinade, cover and leave overnight on the bottom shelf in the fridge. Dry the meat and pork. Cut the fat into thin strips and lard the

liver with them. Brown the liver on all sides in melted butter, sprinkle it with the marinade and simmer for several minutes. Scrub the lemon, scald it with boiling water, then cut into fine slices, remove the pips. Slice the liver diagonally. Grease an ovenproof dish with butter, line it with the liver slices, cover with the lemon slices. Sieve the pan juices and pour over the liver. Sprinkle with parsley and grated cheese and put into a hot oven for 10–15 mins. Serve with French fries or noodles and with lettuce.

serves 4 • Marinating: 12 hrs • Preparation: 10 mins • Baking: 10–15 mins

Calf's liver with cream

800 g calf's liver, 1 cup milk, 100 g pork fat, 1 onion, 1 tbsp butter, 1 tsp flour, 1 cup cream, salt

Rinse the liver, remove membranes. Soak the liver in milk, then dry it, lard it with fine strips of pork fat and brown in butter on both sides. Transfer to a skillet, put in the sliced onion, sprinkle with water, cover and cook over low heat for 15–20 mins (if you cook it too long, the liver will get tough). Take the liver out, slice it and return to the skillet. Fold in the cream mixed with flour.

serves 4–6 • Soaking: 30–40 mins • Preparation: 20–25 mins

Calf's liver, Vienna style

800 g calf's liver, 1 cup milk, salt, 1 tbsp flour, 1 egg, breadcrumbs, 2 tbsps butter

Rinse the liver, remove membranes. Dry the liver, cut it into slices, sprinkle with salt, drip into flour, lightly beaten egg and breadcrumbs. Fry in butter on both sides. Serve with potatoes and lettuce.

serves 4–6 • Soaking: 30–40 mins • Frying: 8–12 mins

Calf's liver strasbourgeoise

800 g calf's liver, 500 g onion, 100 g butter, 1 cup lager beer, ½ cup cream, salt, pepper, a pinch of tarragon, 2 tbsps chopped parsley, 1 cup milk

Rinse the liver, remove membranes. Soak it in milk for 1–1½ hours. Dry it, cut into small pieces and fry in half of the butter. In another pan fry the sliced onion in the remaining butter, add salt and pepper. Sprinkle the liver with pepper, tarragon and parsley, pour in ½ cup of beer. Mix the remaining beer with the cream and pour into the onion. Cook the liver and onion separately for a while, then combine them, add salt to taste. Serve immediately.

serves 4–6 • Soaking: 60–90 mins • Preparation: 15–20 mins

Calf's liver in green sauce

600 g calf's liver, 4 onions, 1 cup dry white wine, 3 tbsps olive oil, 2 tbsps butter, salt, pepper, 3–4 tbsps chopped parsley, 1 tbsp fresh coriander leaves

Rinse the liver, remove membranes. Cut the liver and onion into slices. Fry the onion in hot oil, but do not let it brown, put in the parsley, stir, add the wine and bring to the boil. Put in the liver and cook for 5–7 mins. Sprinkle with salt and pepper, add more butter and heat up. Serve with puréed potatoes and salads.

serves 4 • Preparation: 10–15 mins

Calf's liver in wine sauce

600 g calf's liver, ½ cup milk, 1 tbsp flour, 3 tbsps oil, 1 large onion, 100 g lean ham, 4 tbsps chopped parsley, 1 glass dry red wine, salt, pepper

Rinse the liver, remove membranes. Soak it in milk, then dry and slice diagonally. Dredge the liver with flour and fry in hot oil for 1–2 mins to each side. Transfer to a skillet, sprinkle with salt and pepper and keep warm. Fry the finely diced onion, but do not let it brown. Put in the ham cut into cubes and cook, stirring all the time. Pour in the wine and cook for another 2–3 mins. Add the parsley, stir and pour over the liver. Serve immediately, with macaroni or noodles.

serves 4 • Soaking: 30–40 mins • Preparation: 10–15 mins

Marinated veal liver

700 g calf's liver, 4 tbsps olive oil, 1 tbsp wine vinegar, juice of 1 lemon, 1 large onion, 4 tbsps chopped parsley, ¾ tsp ground coriander, a pinch of ground caraway, salt, pepper, oil for frying

Rinse the liver, remove membranes and blood vessels. Cut the liver into thin slices. Mix the olive oil, vinegar, pepper and half the lemon juice in a bowl, put in the liver, cover and leave in the fridge for 2–4 hours, turning it over from time to time. Slice the onion, sprinkle it with caraway and lemon juice. Take the liver slices out and fry them in oil, then salt them. Arrange them in a serving dish, pile the onion around. Serve with rice and tomato salad.

serves 4 • Marinating: 2–4 hrs • Preparation: 10–15 mins

Calf's liver, Jewish style

600 g calf's liver, 4 onions, ¼ tsp pepper, 1 tsp salt, 1 cup stock, 3 tbsps butter, 1 tsp grated lemon rind, 1 tbsp lemon juice, a pinch of sugar, flour

Rinse and dry the liver, remove membranes. Cut the liver diagonally into slices, dice the onion finely. Melt 1½ tbsps of butter in a skillet, fry the onion, but do not let it brown. Add salt, pepper, sugar, lemon zest and juice, cook for a while, then pour in the stock and continue cooking over low heat for several minutes. Sprinkle the liver with pepper, dredge it with flour and fry in melted butter for 1½ mins to each side. Salt it and arrange in a warm dish, pour the onion sauce over. Serve immediately, with rice or puréed potatoes and with soured cucumbers.

serves 4 • Preparation: 8–10 mins

Calf's liver with apples

600 g calf's liver, ½ cup milk, 2 onions, 2 tart apples, 3 tbsps butter, salt, 1 tsp pepper

Soak the liver in milk, then dry it and remove membranes. Cut it into diagonal slices. Chop the onions, grate the apples coarsely. Melt 1½ tbsps of butter in a skillet, fry the onion, but do not let it brown. Put in the apples, stir and sauté briskly. Sprinkle with salt and pepper. Melt the remaining butter in a frying pan and fry the liver for 1½ mins to each side, then sprinkle with salt and pepper and add to the onion and apples. Simmer for a minute or two together and serve immediately with rice or puréed potatoes.

serves 4 • Soaking: 30–40 mins • Preparation: 10–15 mins

Calf's liver with tomatoes

*600 g calf's liver, 200 g tomatoes, 1 tart apple,
2–3 onions, ½ cup thick cream, 2 tbsps butter,
salt, pepper, paprika, 2 tbsps chopped parsley*

Rinse the liver, dry it, remove membranes. Cut it diagonally into slices. Melt half of the butter in a frying pan, fry the sliced onions, but do not let them brown. Simmer the peeled and sliced tomatoes and apple in a skillet. Fry the liver slices in butter briskly, then transfer them to the skillet, add the onion and stir. Sprinkle with pepper and paprika, fold in the cream and cook for a while. Towards the end, adjust the taste with salt and put in the parsley.

serves 4 • Preparation: 15–20 mins

Braised liver in pomegranate sauce

*500 g lamb's or calf's liver, 2 tbsps pomegranate
juice (or wine vinegar or lemon juice), ¼ tsp
each thyme and rosemary, salt, pepper, 3 tbsps
olive oil, 1 tsp flour, 2 tbsps chopped parsley*

Remove membranes and blood vessels from the liver. Slice the liver, dust it with flour and fry in oil on both sides. Sprinkle with thyme, rosemary and pepper, add the pomegranate juice and simmer for 2–3 mins. Add salt and parsley. Serve with noodles, rice or white bread.

serves 4 • Preparation: 10 mins

Spit-roast veal liver

*800 g calf's liver, 150 g fine bacon rashers,
2 tbsps butter, 3 tbsps strong stock,
salt, pepper, several sage sprigs*

Rinse and dry the liver, remove membranes. Cut it into thin slices the size of the bacon rashers. Put 2–4 sage leaves on each rasher, cover with a liver slice. Roll up and thread on the spit. Sprinkle with melted butter and cook in the oven, basting with the stock. Sprinkle with salt and pepper before serving.

serves 4–6 • Preparation: 10–12 mins

Savoury pork liver

*500 g pig's liver, 1 cup milk, ¼ tsp each salt, pepper and
nutmeg, 1 tbsp hot mustard, a pinch of chilli, 2 egg yolks,
2 tbsps melted butter, 3 tbsps breadcrumbs, fat for frying*

Rinse the liver and soak it in milk, then remove membranes and blood vessels. Slice the liver. Make a dressing from the melted butter, mustard, egg yolks, salt, pepper, chilli and nutmeg, stir well. Dip the liver slices into the dressing and breadcrumbs, then fry them until nicely brown on both sides. Transfer them to a skillet, pour in the remaining dressing and simmer for 30 mins. Serve with rice and salads.

serves 4 • Soaking: 30–40 mins • Preparation: 5–7 mins • Cooking: 30 mins

Fried marinated liver

*600 g pig's liver, ½ cup soya sauce, 1 small glass
sherry, 3–4 cloves of garlic, 2 tbsps chopped
parsley, 2 tbsps butter or olive oil, ½ cup milk*

Rinse the liver and soak it in milk, then dry it, remove membranes. Cut it into slices. Mix the crushed garlic with the sherry and soya sauce, put in the liver slices and leave in a cool place for 2–3 hours, turning over from time to time. Take the liver out, dry it and fry on both sides in melted butter. Sprinkle with parsley before serving.

serves 4 • Soaking: 30–40 mins • Marinating: 2–3 hrs • Frying: 4–6 mins

Calf's liver baked with pasta

*600 g calf's liver, ½ cup milk, 2 tbsps flour, 3 tbsps
oil, ½ tsp ground pepper, ¼ tsp marjoram, 50 g
butter, 50 g grated Parmesan, 250 g macaroni, salt*

Rinse the liver, cover it with the milk and leave aside for half an hour. Dry it, remove membranes and blood vessels. Cut it diagonally into slices. Cook the pasta. Mix the drained hot pasta with the butter and cheese, put into an ovenproof dish and keep warm. Mix the flour with the pepper and marjoram, coat the liver slices with the preparation. Fry the liver in hot oil for 2–3 mins to each side, then arrange the slices on top of the pasta. Put into a preheated oven for a while. Serve with lettuce and, if you want, with tomato sauce with mushrooms.

serves 4 • Soaking: 30–40 mins • Preparation: 20 mins • Baking: 5–6 mins

Stuffed liver escalopes

500 g ox liver, 1 tbsp chopped parsley, ½ tsp each sage, oregano, thyme and basil, 2 tbsps oil, 4 tbsps grated Emmental cheese, 2 tart apples, 1 onion, 1 egg, salt, pepper, nutmeg, 1–2 cloves of garlic, 3 tbsps butter, ½ cup dry red wine, 1 tsp brandy

Mix the parsley and herbs with the oil, garlic crushed with salt, pepper, nutmeg, egg and cheese, work into a smooth paste. Cut the liver diagonally into slices, make a long incision in each slice. Spread the preparation inside the pockets, secure with toothpicks. Slice the peeled and cored apples and stew them in 1 tbsps of butter, then keep them warm. Fry the finely diced onion, but do not let it brown. Pour in the wine and simmer till the onion is tender, adding the brandy towards the end. Fry the liver escalopes in butter on both sides, then arrange them in an ovenproof dish. Pile the apples around, pour the onion sauce over. Put into a preheated oven for several minutes. Serve with rice or macaroni.

serves 4 • Preparation: 10–15 mins • Baking: 8–10 mins

Roast beef liver

800 g ox liver, 150 g pork fat, lemon juice, salt, pepper, 1 cup milk, 1 glass dry white wine, 1 cup cream, 1 tsp butter, salt, pepper

Rinse the liver, remove membranes. Soak the liver in milk, then drain and dry it. Sprinkle the pork fat with lemon juice, salt and pepper and leave in the fridge for an hour, then put it into the freezer for a while. Cut half of the pork fat into slices and half into fairly thick sticks. Use the latter to lard the liver. Bard the liver with the pork slices, put it into a roasting tin and place in a preheated oven. Cook for 35–40 mins, basting with the wine and pan juices. Mix the cream with flour, salt and pepper, pour over the liver and heat up.

serves 4–6 • Soaking: 1 hr • Marinating: 1 hr • Preparation: 5 mins • Roasting: 35–40 mins

Calf's liver shashliks

600 g calf's liver, 150 g pork fat, 2 large onions, salt, pepper, 2 tbsps chopped chives

Rinse the liver, remove membranes. Cut the liver and pork fat into small slices. Slice the onion. Thread alternately pieces of liver, pork fat and onion on skewers and grill them. Before serving, sprinkle with salt, pepper and chives. It is a good idea to leave the pork fat for a while in a dressing made from oil, thyme, tarragon and parsley.

serves 4 • Preparation: 10–15 mins

Brains

Brain is a white offal, very rich in proteins, phosphorus, iron, group B vitamins and vitamin C. The best are calf's and ox brains.

You should first wash the brains in cold running water, then remove the membranes and blood vessels; soak the brains in cold water and blanch them in water with vinegar (vinegar prevents it getting grey). You can cook the brains in many different ways, the most popular of which is calf's brains, Polish style:

blanch the cleaned brains in water with vinegar (no longer than 15 minutes), allow them to cool, then cut them into pieces and fry together with sautéd onion; towards the end, break in eggs, stir and cook over low heat until the eggs set. This and similar preparations can be used as stuffing for pancakes, omelettes, vegetables and mushrooms.

Ox brains in cold sauce

Blanch the ox brains in boiling water with vinegar, leave to cool, then cut them into pieces. Dip them into lightly beaten eggs and breadcrumbs and fry in butter until golden brown on both sides. Arrange the brains in a serving dish and pour the cold sauce over. The cold sauce is made in the following way: take a handful of chives and pound them in a mortar together with sugar. Put in twenty hard-boiled egg yolks, a quarter of vinegar and the same amount of olive oil. Mix everything thoroughly and use to pour over the brains. Serve with vegetables.

(Jan Szyttler, *Kucharz dobrze usposobiony*, 1830)

Calf's brains fried in butter

*ca 600 g calf's brains, 1 cup milk, salt, 1 tbsp
butter, 1 tbsp flour, 1 egg, breadcrumbs,
fat for frying, 1 tbsp chopped parsley*

Cover the rinsed brains with milk and leave on the bottom shelf of the fridge for 1–2 hours, then cook them in the same milk. Drain them, divide into portions, sprinkle with salt and coat in flour, lightly beaten egg and breadcrumbs. Fry them on both sides in butter or oil. Before serving, pour over melted butter and sprinkle with chopped parsley. Serve as a hot hors-d'oeuvre or as the main course with potatoes and salads.

serves 4 • Soaking: 1–2 hrs • Blanching: 15–20 mins • Preparation: 5–7 mins

Calf's brains, Vienna style

*800 g calf's brains, salt, pepper, 1 tbsp vinegar,
1 egg, flour, breadcrumbs, 2 tbsps butter,
2 tbsps chopped parsley, 4 lemon slices*

Blanch the cleaned brains in salted water with vinegar. Drain them and cut into 4 portions. Sprinkle with salt and pepper and dip into flour, lightly beaten egg and breadcrumbs. Fry in melted butter until golden brown on both sides. Serve with potatoes and spinach or salads. Garnish each portion with a lemon slices and chopped parsley.

serves 4 • Blanching: 15–20 mins • Preparation: 5–7 mins

Calf's brains, French style

*600–800 g calf's brains, 2 tbsps vinegar, 70 g butter,
3 tbsps capers, 4–5 parsley sprigs, ½ tsp dried thyme,
1 bay leaf, salt, 1 tbsp flour, pepper, lemon juice,
2–3 slices of dried white bread, 2 tbsps chopped parsley*

Cover the cleaned brains with cold water with vinegar and leave aside for 15 mins. Rinse them under running water, remove membranes. Bring to the boil some salted water with several drops of lemon juice, parsley sprigs, thyme and bay leaf. Put in the brains and cook them for 20 mins over low heat, keeping the water off the boil. Leave them to cool, then take them out, dry and cut into slices. Sprinkle with salt, pepper and flour and fry in but-

ter on both sides until golden brown. Cut the bread into small cubes and brown it in butter. Arrange the brain slices in a warm serving dish, garnish with capers, croutons and chopped parsley.

serves 4 • Soaking: 15 mins • Blanching: 20 mins • Frying: 8–10 mins

Miller's brains

*ca 700 g calf's brains, 2 tbsps vinegar, 20 g flour,
40 g butter, 1 bunch of parsley sprigs, thyme,
1 bay leaf, 2 tbsps lemon juice, salt, pepper*

Soak the brains in water with vinegar for 15 mins, then remove membranes and blood vessels. Bring water to the boil, put in the thyme, bay leaf, several drops of vinegar and half the parsley sprigs. Put the brains into the boiling water and cook for 15 mins, then leave to cool. Drain the brains, slice them, sprinkle with salt, pepper and flour and fry golden brown on both sides. Arrange in a warm serving dish, pour over the frying juices, sprinkle with lemon juice and garnish with chopped parsley.

serves 4 • Soaking: 15 mins • Blanching: 15–20 mins • Frying: 8–10 mins

Baked calf's brains with celeriac

*600 g calf's brains, 2 onions, 50 g pork
fat, 2 eggs, salt, pepper, 2 tbsps butter,
1 large celeriac, 2 tbsps breadcrumbs*

Scrub the celeriac, put it into boiling salted water and cook for 5 mins, then leave to cool. Cover the cleaned brains with cold water with vinegar and leave aside for 15 mins. Remove membranes and blood vessels, chop the brains. Render the finely chopped pork fat in a frying pan, put in the finely diced onion and fry it without browning. Add the brains and fry for a while longer, stirring all the time. Adjust the taste with salt and pepper and leave to cool. Break in 1 egg and mix thoroughly. Peel the celeriac, cut it into slices. Coat each slice in lightly beaten egg and breadcrumbs and arrange in a greased ovenproof dish. Place some brains preparation and a pat of butter on each slice and put the dish in a preheated oven for 8–10 mins.

serves 4 • Soaking: 15 mins • Preparation: 15–20 mins • Baking: 8–10 mins

Baked brains with cheese

1 ox brain or 2–3 calf's brains, salt, pepper, allspice, nutmeg, 5 eggs, 2 tbsps chopped dill, 1½ tbsps butter, 1 tsp breadcrumbs, 2 tbsps grated cheese, 1 tsp vinegar

Cook the cleaned brains in salted water with vinegar, then leave them to cool. Sieve the brains, add 1 tbsp of butter and work into a smooth paste, adding 1 egg yolk at a time, salt, nutmeg, pepper, ground allspice and dill. Fold in the stiffly whisked egg whites. Grease an ovenproof dish with butter, dust it with breadcrumbs and some grated cheese. Put in the preparation, sprinkle it with the remaining cheese, place slices of butter on top. Put into a preheated oven for 20 mins.

serves 4 • Blanching: 15–20 mins • Preparation: 10 mins • Baking: 20 mins

Ox brains in mushroom sauce

700 g ox brains, 2 tbsps vinegar, ½ tsp thyme, several parsley sprigs, 1 bay leaf, salt, pepper, 100 g mushrooms, 2 tbsps butter, 2 tbsps flour, 1 egg yolk, 2 tbsps lemon jui ce, ¼ tsp grated lemon rind

Cover the cleaned brains with water with vinegar and leave aside for 15 mins. Rinse them and remove membranes. Bring to the boil some water with thyme, bay leaf, salt, pepper and parsley sprigs. Put in the mushrooms and blanch them for 3–5 mins, then take them out with a strainer. Put in the brains and cook them over low heat for 15 mins. Slice the mushrooms and cook them in 2 cups of water. Make a roux from the butter and flour, dilute it with the strained stock, adjust the taste with salt and pepper and cook over low heat for 10 mins. Take off the heat, mix in the egg yolk, add lemon juice and zest, put in the mushrooms and stir well. Drain the brains, put them in a serving dish and pour the sauce over.

serves 4 • Soaking: 15 mins • Blanching: 15– 20 mins • Preparation: 10–15 mins

Potatoes stuffed with brains

1 kg large new potatoes, 2 calf's brains or 1 ox brain, 1 onion, 2 tbsps chopped parsley, 1 egg, ½ cup each stock and thick sour cream, 2 tbsps breadcrumbs, 3 tbsps butter, salt, pepper, paprika

Soak th brains in cold water with vinegar for 15 mins. Remove membranes and blood vessels. Rinse and dry the brains, chop them finely. Fry the finely chopped onion in melted butter, but do not let it brown. Add pepper and paprika, put in the brains and fry for a minute or two. Add salt to taste, the chopped parsley and egg, work into a smooth paste and fry for a while longer. Wash the potatoes thoroughly, cover them with boiling salted water and parboil them. Drain them, cut a slice off the top and carefully scoop out the inside to form cylinders with 2 cm thick walls. Fill the cylinders with the preparation. Arrange the potatoes in a greased ovenproof dish. Pour over the cream mixed with the stock, sprinkle with breadcrumbs and put into a preheated oven. Bake for half an hour. Serve with salads.

serves 4 • Soaking: 15 mins • Preparation: 20–25 mins • Baking: 25–30 mins

Mushrooms stuffed with brains

12 large mushrooms, 400 g claf's brains, 4 tbsps butter, 3 tbsps chopped parsley, salt, pepper, 1 egg, 2 tbsps breadcrumbs

Rinse the mushrooms. Remove the stalks and chop them finely. Arrange the caps (gills up) in a greased ovenproof dish and put into a preheated oven for 5–6 mins, then take the dish out. Cover the cleaned brains with cold water with vinegar and leave aside for 15 mins. Take out the brains, dry them and chop finely. Melt some butter in a frying pan and sauté the chopped stalks, put in the chopped brains and fry for a minute or two. Season with salt and pepper, take off the heat. Add the chopped parsley, break in the egg and mix thoroughly. Fill the mushroom caps with the stuffing, sprinkle them with breadcrumbs, put pats of butter on top. Put into a hot oven and bake for 20 mins. Serve with white bread as a hot hors-d'oeuvre.

serves 4–6 • Soaking: 15 mins • Preparation: 10–15 mins • Baking: 20–25 mins

Brain croquettes

600 g calf's brains, salt, lemon juice, 1 slice of onion, 1 bay leaf, allspice, 1 tbsp butter, 1 tbsp flour, 2 tbsps stock, 2 eggs, 1 tbsp chopped parsley, salt, pepper, breadcrumbs, 2 tbsps butter

Bring some water to the boil, add lemon juice, salt, onion, allspice and bay leaf. Put in the brains and cook them, then take out with a strainer and chop finely. Make a roux from 1 tbsp of butter and flour, dilute it with the stock, take off the heat. Put in 2 egg yolks and the chopped brains and work into a smooth paste, adding chopped parsley, salt and pepper towards the end. Roll the preparation into small cylinders, dip them in the stiffly whisked egg whites, dust with breadcrumbs and fry in butter.

serves 4 • Blanching: 15–20 mins • Preparation: 10–15 mins • Frying: 5–6 mins

Brain dumplings

800 g ox or calf's brains, 4 tbsps butter, a bunch of parsley sprigs, 1 small grated onion, 1 cup breadcrumbs, 2–3 tbsps single cream, 2 eggs, salt, pepper, nutmeg

Clean the brains, cover them with boiling water with vinegar and leave aside for 10 mins. Take the brains out, allow them to cool, then chop them finely and braise in 1 tbsp of butter for 15 mins. Mix in the grated onion and finely chopped parsley. Cream the remaining butter with the egg yolks. Whisking all the time, gradually add the brains, cream and breadcrumbs. Adjust the taste with salt, pepper and nutmeg. Fold in the stiffly beaten egg whites (add more breadcrumbs if the mixture is not thick enough). Leave the preparation in a cool place for half an hour, then shape small dumplings from it. Drop the dumplings into boiling salted water, cook over low heat, then strain them. Before serving, cover the dumplings with melted butter with browned breadcrumbs, mixed with spinach purée.

serves 4–6 • Soaking: 10–15 mins • Preparation: 15–20 mins • Cooking: 5–7 mins

Ox brain cutlets

800 g ox brains, salt, pepper, 1 tbsp flour, 1 egg, breadcrumbs, 2 tbsps butter, 1 small onion, lemon juice, 1 bay leaf, 3–5 grains allspice, 1 tbsp chopped parsley

Remove membranes from the brains. Bring water to the boil, add lemon juice, salt, bay leaf and allspice. Put in the brains and cook them for 10–15 mins, then take them out, dry and cut into thick slices. Coat the slices in

flour, lightly beaten egg and breadcrumbs and fry in melted butter. Serve with potato purée, garnished with chopped parsley, and with lettuce.

serves 4 • Blanching: 10–15 mins • Frying: 6–8 mins

Kidneys

Pig's kidneys are smooth, shaped like haricot beans, with no fat around them. Ox (and calf's) kidneys are multilobed and usually have no fat on them. The kidneys of calves are sometimes covered with a thin layer of fat.

Kidneys are rich in proteins, group B vitamins and in particular iron.

Shashliks of sheep's kidneys

4 sheep's kidneys, 2 onions, 500 g tomatoes, 2 tbsps butter, salt, pepper, 1 tsp ground barberries, 2 tbsps chopped parsley

Clean the kidneys, remove membranes and blood vessels. Soak the kidneys in cold water for half an hour, then drain and dry them, and cut lengthwise in half. Brush each half with melted butter, sprinkle with salt, pepper and barberries. Thread them on skewers, alternating with tomatoes. Grill them, basting with melted butter. Slice the onion, scald with boiling water, then drain and cool it. Arrange the shashliks on top of the lemon slices, garnish with chopped parsley. Serve with rice or sautéed potatoes.

serves 4 • Soaking: 30–40 mins • Preparation: 15–20 mins

Kidneys with apples in cream sauce

6–8 calfs' or pigs' kidneys, 1–2 tart apples, 1 large onion, 1 glass Calvados, ½ cup cream, 3 tbsps oil, 1 tbsp butter, salt, pepper, sugar, 1 tsp lemon juice, 2 tbsps chopped parsley

Rinse the kidneys, halve them lengthwise, remove renal tubules. Cover the kidneys with cold water and leave aside for an hour. Cut them into slices, put into boiling water for a minute, then drain them. Fry the finely chopped onion in oil, but do not let it brown. Put in the kidneys and fry them for a minute or two, pour in the Calvados and stir well. Slice the peeled and cored apples, sprinkle them with lemon juice and soften them in butter, then add to the kidneys and cook together. Pour in the cream mixed with salt, pepper and sugar and simmer over low heat for 5–7 mins. Sprinkle with chopped parsley before serving. Serve with potato purée and salads.

serves 4–6 • Soaking: 1–2 hrs • Preparation: 20–25 mins

Kidneys in wine sauce

800 g kidneys, 2 onions, 3–4 cloves of garlic, 1 tbsp mustard, 1 cup dry red wine, 1 tsp flour, 1 tbsp water, 1 tbsp oil, 1 tbsp butter, salt, pepper, 2 tbsps chopped parsley

Skin the kidneys, halve them, remove fat and renal tubules. Cover them with cold water and leave aside for an hour, then drain and slice them, fry in hot oil and transfer to a skillet. Fry the diced onion and chopped garlic in butter, add the mustard and wine, stir well. Put in the kidneys, season with salt and pepper and cook over low heat for 20 mins. Towards the end, mix the flour with water and pour into skillet, stir and heat up till the sauce has thickened. Garnish with chopped parsley before serving.

serves 4–6 • Soaking: 1–2 hrs • Preparation: 25–30 mins

Calf's kidneys in garlic sauce

800 g calf's kidneys, 2 cups chicken or vegetable stock, 2 bay leaves, 5–7 grains each allspice and pepper, 2 large onions, 1 garlic bulb, 1 glass dry red wine, 2 tbsps oil, 2 tbsps butter, 2 tbsps flour, salt, pepper, 1 tsp paprika, a pinch of sugar

Halve the kidneys lengthwise, remove renal tubules. Cover the kidneys with cold water and leave aside for 20–30 mins. Bring some water to the boil, put in the kidneys and blanch them for 2–3 mins, then drain them and run under cold water. Bring the stock to the boil, add the bay leaves, allspice and pepper. Put in the kidneys and cook them for 20–30 mins. Take the kidneys out, allow them to cool. Cut them into slices, dredge with flour and fry in melted butter, then transfer to a skillet. Reduce the

stock to 1 cup of stock, strain it. Fry the diced onion in oil until golden brown, add it to the kidneys, stir, pour in the strained stock and wine. Bring to the boil, cover and cook for another five mins. Add the garlic crushed with salt, salt, pepper and paprika, stir and simmer for a bit longer. Serve with rice or macaroni and with salads.

serves 4–6 • Soaking: 20–30 mins • Cooking: 25–35 mins • Preparation: 10–12 mins

Pig's kidneys, Chinese style

6 pigs' kidneys, salt, 5–6 spring onions, 1 tsp fresh chopped ginger, ½ tsp cayenne pepper, 1 tsp sugar, 2 tsps sesame oil, 2 tbsps each soya sauce and lemon juice, 1 tbsp peanut oil

Halve the rinsed kidneys lengthwise, remove renal tubules. Slice the meat finely and put into a bowl, cover with cold salted water and leave aside for an hour (change the water after half an hour). Drain the slices and blanch them in boiling water for 2 mins. Heat the peanut oil in a frying pan for half a minute, put in the ginger, cayenne and the diced spring onions and stir-fry them for 1–2 mins. Put in the kidneys, stir, pour in the lemon juice and soya sauce, add some sugar. Stirring all the time, fry very briskly for one minutes. Take off the heat, add the sesame oil and stir well. Serve hot, with rice, or cold, with white bread.

serves 4–6 • Soaking: 1–1½ hrs • Preparation: 8–10 mins

Calf's kidneys in wine sauce

800 g calf's kidneys, 2 onions, 3–4 cloves of garlic, 1 tbsp mustard, 1 cup dry red wine, 1 tsp flour, 1 tbsp oil, 1 tbsp butter, salt, pepper, 2 tbsps chopped parsley

Clean the kidneys, halve them, put into a bowl, cover with cold water and leave aside for 1–2 hours. Drain and dry them, cut into fine strips and fry in oil, then transfer to a skillet. Fry the diced onion and chopped garlic in butter, add the mustard and wine, stir and cook for a while. Sprinkle the kidneys with salt and pepper, put in the onion and wine sauce, cover and simmer for 25 mins. Towards the end, add the flour mixed with 2 tbsps of water, stir and heat up until the sauce has thickened. Before serving, garnish with chopped parsley.

serves 4–6 • Soaking: 1–2 hrs • Preparation: 5–6 mins • Braising: 25 mins

Calf's kidneys, hunter's style

*4 calf's kidneys, 1 tsp ground juniper berries, 100 g
butter, 1 glass gin, 1 cup stock, ½ tsp pepper, salt*

Skin the kidneys, remove fat. Make a lengthwise incision
in each, remove renal tubules. Cover the kidneys with
cold water and leave in a cool place for an hour, then drain
and dry them. Melt the butter in a skillet, add the juniper
berries and cook for a while, then put in the kidneys and
fry them for 5 mins on each side. Sprinkle with salt and
pepper, pour over the gin. Shake the skillet and fry briskly
for a minute or two. Pour in the stock, cover and simmer
for 15 mins. Serve with baked or fried potatoes, sprinkled
liberally with the pan juices, and with lettuce.

serves 4 • Soaking: 1 hr • Preparation: 25–30 mins

Kidneys with cep mushrooms

*600–700 g calf's or pig's kidneys, 300 g small cep
mushrooms (or button mushrooms), ½ cup Madeira,
1 cup stock, 2 tbsps butter, ¼ tsp nutmeg, ½ tsp
dried thyme, salt, pepper, 2 tbsps chopped parsley*

Skin the kidneys, remove fat and tubules. Halve them,
cover with cold water and leave aside for 1–2 hours.
Dry them cut into strips and fry in melted butter. Put in
the sliced mushrooms and stir-fry them briskly. Add salt,
pepper, nutmeg and thyme, stir and fry for a while longer.
Pour in the stock, cover and simmer for 30 mins. Pour in
the wine and continue cooking for a while. Garnish with
chopped parsley.

serves 4–6 • Soaking: 1–2 hrs • Preparation: 10 mins • Cooking: 30 mins

Ox kidneys in onion sauce

*500 g ox kidneys, 600 g potatoes, 3 large
onions, 3–4 salted cucumbers, 1 tbsp flour,
3 tbsps butter, 2 cups stock, 2 bay leaves,
salt, pepper, 3 tbsps chopped dill*

Rinse the kidneys, skin them, remove fat and tubules.
Halve them lengthwise, put into a skillet, cover with
cold water and bring to the boil. Strain them, cover again
with cold water and cook for one hour. Soften the finely
diced onions in butter, dust with flour, pour in the hot stock
and simmer for 15 mins. Cut the cooked kidneys into strips,
put into the onion sauce. Sprinkle with the crumbled bay
leaves and pepper, stir thoroughly. Slice the peeled potatoes, scald them with boiling water and add to the kidneys
together with the diced cucumbers. Cover and simmer for
30–40 mins. Add salt to taste, garnish with parsley.

*serves 4 • Cooking: 90 mins • Preparation:
20–25 mins • Braising: 30–40 mins*

Pig's kidneys in vermouth

*800 g pig's kidneys, 2 tbsps flour, 3 tbsps
butter, 2 onions, 2–3 cloves of garlic, 100 g
streaky bacon, 150 g button mushrooms, 1 cup
vermouth, 1 tbsp brandy, salt, pepper*

Skin the kidneys, halve them, remove fat, blood vessels
and tubules. Cover with cold water and leave in a cool
place for an hour. Chop the onions and garlic finely and fry
them in 2 tbsps of melted butter. Dry the kidneys, brown
them on both sides in 2 tbsps of butter. Add the sliced
mushrooms and diced becon. Dust sparingly with flour
and fry for a minute or two. Put in the onion and garlic
mixture, pour in the vermouth, adjust the taste with salt
and pepper. Bring to the boil, cover and simmer for half an
hour. Towards the end, pour in the brandy and mix well.
Serve with macaroni, rice or noodles.

serves 4 • Soaking: 1 hr • Preparation: 10–15 mins • Cooking: 30 mins

Pig's kidney stew

*600 g pig's kidneys, 50 g pork fat, 1 tbsp butter,
1 onion, 1 tbsp ground caraway, 1 tsp ground
pepper, salt, ½ cup light stock, 1 tbsp flour*

Skin the kidneys, remove fat. Make a lengthwise incision,
remove tubules. Cover with cold water and leave aside
for half an hour, then blanch, drain and slice them. Brown
the diced pork fat in a skillet, add the butter and the finely
chopped onion and sauté it, stirring all the time. Sprinkle
the kidneys with pepper, caraway and flour, put into the
skillet and fry briskly, then salt them, pour in the stock and
cook for a while. Serve with rice, pasta or kasha.

serves 4 • Soaking: 30–40 mins • Preparation: 25–30 mins

Kidney ragout

600 g calf's kidneys, milk, 400 g mushrooms, 2 onions, 1½ cups port, 1 cup cream, 2–4 cloves of garlic, salt, pepper, 2 tbsps oil, 3 tbsps butter, 3 tbsps chopped parsley

Put the cleaned kidneys in a bowl, cover with milk and put into the fridge for 3 days, draining them and covering with fresh milk every day. Take the kidneys out, dry them and cut into strips. Melt the butter in a skillet and fry the diced onion, but do not let it brown. Add the sliced mushrooms and sauté them briskly, then simmer over low heat. Heat the oil in a frying pan and briskly brown the kidney strips, stirring all the time. Combine them with the mushrooms, pour in the wine, add crushed garlic and pepper, and cook for a while. Pour in the cream and salt to taste. Garnish with chopped parsley. Serve with white bread, rice or macaroni.

serves 6–8 • Soaking: 3 days • Preparation: 8–10 mins • Cooking: 25–30 mins

Lights

Baked calf's lights

Line a skillet with pork fat slices, put in various vegetables and onions, cover with the lights cut into pieces. Sprinkle with salt and water and cook until tender. Take the pork fat, vegetables and lights out, dice them finely and return to the skillet. Put in one spoonful of butter, half a bread roll soaked in milk and squeezed out. Mix everything thoroughly for 10 minutes, adding one of six egg yolks at a time. Add some pepper, fold in the stiffly beaten egg whites, stir very gently. Grease a baking tin with butter, dust it with breadcrumbs. Fill it with the preparation and put into a medium-hot oven for 45 minutes. Make a piquant and bitter sauce. Arrange the lights in a serving dish, pour over the sauce and serve immediately.

(Alina Gniewkowska, *Współczesna kuchnia domowa*, 1927)

Sour lights

800 g calf's lights, soup vegetables, 1 onion, 3 bay leaves, 5–6 peppercorns, 4 tbsps wine vinegar,

2 tbsps butter, 1 tbsp flour, 1 small glass dry white wine, 1 tsp salt, ½ cup cream, 1 tsp lemon juice

Wash the lights thoroughly. Make a stock from the vegetables, onion and spices. Put in the lights, add the vinegar and cook over low heat for one hour. Drain the lights, put them on a chopping board, cover with another board, weigh down and leave aside overnight. Slice the lights. Make a roux from the butter and flour, dilute it with ½ cup of the stock and cook over low heat. Add lemon juice, salt, wine and pepper, stir well. Put in the lights and simmer for another 15 mins. Towards the end, fold in the cream. Serve with noodles or bread dumplings.

serves 4 • Cooking: 1–1½ hrs • Cooling: 12 hrs • Preparation: 15–20 mins

Calf's lights, Lithuanian style

calf's lights, 2 carrots, 2 onions, 3 hard-boiled eggs, 4–6 potatoes cooked in jackets, salt, pepper, 1 cup thick sour cream, 2 tbsps butter, 1 crumbled bay leaf, 1 tbsp wine vinegar, 2 tbsps chopped parsley or dill, ½ cup stock

Put the lights in water with vinegar and leave in a cool place for an hour, then cook them in salted water. Drain them, cut into strips. Melt the butter in a skillet. Line the skillet with the strips of light, put the diced onion and carrots on top, sprinkle with pepper, crumbled bay leaf and stock. Cover and simmer for 30 mins. Cut the peeled potatoes and eggs in large cubes, salt them and add to the lights. Stir gently, fold in the cream and cook for a while longer. Before serving, garnish with parsley or dill. Serve with soured cucumbers.

serves 4 • Soaking: 1–1½ hrs • Cooking: 50–55 mins • Preparation: 30 mins

Lights in cucumber sauce

calf's lights and heart, soup vegetables, 1 onion, 1 bay leaf, ¼ tsp thyme, 10 peppercorns, salt, 50 g butter, 1 tbsp flour, 2 cloves of garlic, 1 firm soured cucumber, 3–4 cocktail gherkins, juice of ½ lemon, ½ tsp sugar, 1 cup thick sour cream

Put the lights, heart and the peeled vegetables into a pan, add the bay leaf, peppercorns and thyme, cover with salted water and cook for an hour. Take the offal out, drain and cut it into thin strips. Make a roux from the butter and flour, add the garlic crushed with salt. Dilute with 1½ cups of strained stock and, stirring all the time, simmer for 10 mins. Add the finely chopped cucumber and gherkins and lemon juice, adjust the taste with salt. Put in the offal strips and simmer for another 15 mins. Towards the end fold in the cream.

serves 4 • Cooking: 30–35 mins • Cooling: 1 hr • Braising: 20–25 mins

Calf's lights bake

calf's lights and heart, 1 carrot, 1 small celeriac, 1 onion, 50 g pork fat, 50 g butter, 1 bread roll soaked in milk, 3 eggs, ½ tbsp salt, pepper, 1 glass dry white wine

Rinse the offal, blanch it for a short while, take out, allow to cool, then cut into pieces. Render the diced pork fat lightly, put in the lights and heart, grated carrot and celeriac, pour in the wine, cover and simmer for half an hour. Leave to cool, then put through a mincer together with the squeezed out roll. Fry the finely chopped onion in butter, but do not let it brown. Mix it with the offal preparation. Add salt and pepper and mix thoroughly, adding 1 egg yolk at a time. Towards the end, fold in the stiffly beaten egg whites. Grease a baking mould, pour in the preparation and put into a preheated oven for one hour. Serve with dill or lemon sauce.

serves 4 • Preparation: 40 mins • Baking: 55–60 mins

Stomach

Braised pig's stomach

1 kg pig's stomach, 1 tbsp caraway seeds, 6–8 cloves of garlic, ½ tsp ground pepper, ½ cup stock, 3 tbsps chopped mint leaves or 1 tbsp dried mint, 2 tbsps butter, 3–4 tbsps thick sour cream, salt, 1 cup soured milk

Scrub the stomach thoroughly, cover it with cold water and leave in a cool place for 2 hours, then take it out

and dry it. Cover it with the soured milk and stand aside for 3–4 hours. Take it out and dip it into boiling water for 3–4 mins. Drain it and run under cold water, dry it and cut into strips. Put into a skillet, sprinkle with salt and mint, pour in the stock, cover and simmer for one hour. Add the finely chopped garlic, caraway, pepper, butter and cream, stir and simmer for several minutes longer. Serve with beans and boiled potatoes.

serves 4 • Soaking: 2+3–4 hrs • Preparation: 5–6 mins • Braising: 60–70 mins

Pig's stomach in vegetables

1 pig's stomach, 1 cup beans, 1 cup peas, 1 onion, 2 carrots, 4 potatoes, 1 tbsp tarragon, salt, pepper, 1 tbsp flour, 1 cup cream, 2 cups whey or soured milk

Soak the beans and peas overnight. Scrub the stomach thoroughly, soak it first in cold water and then in soured milk. Dip it into boiling water for 3 mins, drain it, run under cold water and cut into strips. Put the peas, beans, stomach and diced carrots into a skillet, cover with the stock and cook. Peel and slice the potatoes, scald them with boiling water, then add to the skillet. Reduce the liquid, add the butter and tarragon and fold in the cream mixed with flour.

serves 4 • Soaking: 2 x 3–4 hrs • Preparation: 10 mins • Braising: 60–80 mins

CHAPTER XI

POULTRY

Chicken

Roast chicken has a long culinary history. It is true that most of the descriptions in Polish literature deal with cold stuffed roast chicken to be taken on a journey, but there is a lot more to it than that. Chicken is a universal raw material because of the great range of possibilities for preparing it. It is excellent roasted, stewed, braised or fried; it can be eaten hot or cold; it can be cooked with many seasonings or with none, sweet or sour, in very hot and spicy sauce or in a very delicate way. It is difficult to think of another product which offers the cook so many opportunities to show off his skills; and in addition, today chicken dishes are among the cheapest available and are also healthy.

Chicken meat contains a great deal of zinc, magnesium, potassium, protein and group B vitamins which increase the ability of the organism to take energy from food and reinforce the immune system. Chicken meat is delicate, easily digestible and has great food and nutritive value; chicken fat contains much less cholesterol than other animal fats. In Old Polish cuisine, chicken and boiling fowl were cooked with dates, chestnuts, currants, oranges, almonds, plums. It was served with various sauces: red sauce made with morello cherries, black sauce from plum jam or prunes, grey sauce made with onion, or yellow sauce made with saffron. In the reign of King Augustus III of the Saxon dynasty mace and nutmeg, ginger, cloves, pepper, saffron, pine kernels, almonds, pistachios, currants, honey, lemon and truffles were all used to season roast chicken, and it was usually served with rice.

At the turn of the 18th and 19th centuries, French cuisine was in fashion, and spices and fruits were used less, while there was an increase in the number of dishes in which stuffings were used. Stuffed chicken began therefore to be served – mainly using stuffing made from minced veal, beef suet, liver, fruits, breadcrumbs, butter and eggs, and seasoned with pepper, ginger, nutmeg, fresh parsley and herbs.

Henryk Rzewuski wrote at this time, 'Then let half a dozen chickens be stuffed with filling made from dill and parsley,' and chickens cooked in this way became the standard Sunday dinner for decades.

The stuffing should be placed loosely inside the chicken, without pressing it in, because during cooking it swells in volume. You should place the chicken first in a hot oven (220–250°), so that the skin browns well. After about 15 minutes, turn down the oven to about 180-190°, and frequently baste the roasting chicken with butter, wine or water, and later with the pan drippings. If the chicken browns too quickly, cover it with aluminium foil. The chicken is ready if clear (not pink) juice runs out when a skewer is put in.

According to contemporary gourmands, chicken tastes good combined with all kinds of fruit, especially oranges, pineapple, kiwi, limes, lemons and pomegranate.

A 9–12 week-old chicken, which is not too fat, should be used for roasting. You should rinse it quickly but thoroughly under running water, dry it, and then rub it with the seasoning specified in the recipe. Remember that for every 400 g of soft chicken meat, you need half a teaspoon of salt, which should be rubbed into the chicken both inside and outside.

It is best to roast chicken in foil or on the spit, because it will then remain succulent. You can put a bunch of marjoram, thyme, parsley or mint inside the chicken, and the meat will then take on a unique aroma. Chicken can be stuffed with oranges or limes (with their rinds first scrubbed and rinsed in boiling water) and the meat will then be full of flavour and not sour. While in the oven, the chicken needs frequent basting with the fat and the roasting gravy. It is a good idea to put a tin containing water at the bottom of a gas oven, which will prevent the meat from drying out too much. Leftovers of roast or stewed chicken can be used to make salads, jellies, bakes or risottos.

Chicken Polish style, with saffron

Roast a chicken on the spit, or roast it carved. Put a piece of butter in a saucepan, mix it with flour, pour stock over it, add salt; cover dried and grated saffron with some stock to soak. When the chicken is ready, place it on a serving dish, remove the wings and legs, boil the sauce with the soaked saffron, pour over the chicken and serve hot.

(W. Wielądko, *Kucharz doskonały*, vol. I, p. 150)

Chicken salad with rice

*250 g chicken (boiled or baked), 1 cup cooked rice,
2 onions, 1 cup green peas (tinned or fresh cooked),
1 cup yogurt, ½ cup cream, ½ tsp mustard,
juice of 1 lemon, salt, sugar, pepper,
1 hard-boiled egg, 2 small hard tomatoes,
1 tbsp green olives, parsley sprigs*

Combine the cooked rice with the finely chopped onion, season with a dash of pepper and sugar, mix well and set aside in the fridge. Mix well the yogurt with cream, mustard and salt. Dice the chicken, strain the green peas in a sieve. Add the chicken and green peas to the rice, pour the sauce over and mix well. Decorate with olives, egg quarters, wedges of tomatoes and sprigs of parsley.

serves 4–6 • Preparation: 5–7 mins • Refrigerating: 1–2 hrs

Chicken salad, Roman style

*100 g cooked chicken meat, 2 leaves iceberg lettuce,
1 small endive, 3 tbsps tinned corn, 1 hard fleshy
tomato, 1 red bell pepper, 2 small hot peppers*

*DRESSING: 2 tbsps olive oil, 1 tbsp wine vinegar,
2 tbsps finely grated onion, 1 tbsp chopped
tarragon leaves, 1 tsp chopped parsley*

Mix well the dressing ingredients, cover, set aside to cool. Scald and skin the tomato, cut it into cubes, cut the endive into strips. Seed the hot peppers and the red pepper, wash and dry, chop finely. Strain the corn, dice the chicken meat and tear the lettuce leaves into small pieces. In a salad bowl place all the ingredients, cover with the dressing, mix well, cover and refrigerate for 10–15 mins. Before serving, toss gently again and sprinkle with chives.

serves 4 • Preparation: 5–7 mins • Refrigerating: 10–15 mins

Chicken salad with rice

Chicken salad with marinated pumpkin

*200–300 g smoked chicken, 1 cup cooked
rice,1 cup tinned corn, 3 tbsps marinated pumpkin,
1 heart Chinese cabbage, 2–3 tangerines,
1 tbsp lemon juice, 1 tsp curry powder*

*DRESSING: 3 tbsps mayonnaise, 3 tbsps yogurt, salt,
pepper, sugar, sprigs of parsley, 2–3 cherry tomatoes*

Mix well all the ingredients of the dressing, chill slightly. Sprinkle the rice with curry, mix, cover and set aside in the fridge for 1 hour. Peel the tangerines and divide into wedges, cut the Chinese cabbage into thin strips, dice the chicken and pumpkin, strain the corn. Combine all the ingredients of the salad with the rice, pour the dressing over, mix well, cover and set aside in the fridge for 1 hour. Before serving mix well again and decorate with sprigs of parsley and quarters of tomatoes.

serves 4–6 • Macerating: 1 hr • Preparation: 5 mins • Refrigerating: 1 hr

Chicken in Malaga

*2 chicken breasts (ca 700 g), 2 garlic cloves, salt,
pepper, 1 tbsp lemon juice and a pinch of grated
lemon rind, 2 tbsps butter, 1 cup Malaga, juice
and grated rind of 1 orange, ¼ tsp each ground
ginger, cinnamon and nutmeg, a dash ground
cloves, 50 g raisins, 1 tbsp vodka, 2 tbsps almond
flakes, 1 tangerine, 2 tbsp gelatine, 1 egg white*

Wash and scald the raisins, strain and cover with the vodka. Set aside for 15 mins. Rub the washed and dried meat with garlic blended with salt, pepper, grated lemon rind and juice. Wrap in foil and set aside in the fridge for 1 hour. Then sauté in melted butter, dredge with half of the spices, sprinkle with water, cover and simmer over low heat for about 30 mins. Take the meat out when tender, set aside to cool. Degrease the pan juices, add the remaining spices and grated orange rind, pour in the wine and orange juice, mix well and season to taste with pepper. Cook over low heat for 5–6 mins, add the egg white mixed with 1 tbsp water, clarify and mix with the gelatine. Peel the tangerine, divide into sections. Cut the cold meat into even slices, sprinkle with raisins and almond flakes,

decorate with tangerine sections and cover with the setting aspic. Leave aside until set.

serves 4 • Macerating: 1 hr • Preparation: 50–55 mins • Refrigerating: 1–2 hrs

Chicken, Polish style

*2 young chickens, 1–2 bread rolls soaked in milk,
3 tbsps butter, salt, pepper, sugar, 3 tbsps chopped
parsley, 2 tbsps chopped dill, chicken livers, 2 eggs*

Rub the washed chickens with salt and set aside in a cool place for 2–3 hours. Prepare the stuffing: squeeze dry the rolls and mix in a bowl with the finely chopped liver together with 1 egg yolk and 1 tbsp butter until smooth consistency is obtained. Add salt, a dash of sugar and pepper, parsley and dill. Mix well. Beat the egg white stiff and stir it in gently. Stuff the chickens and sew them up. Arrange on a greased tin and dot with knobs of butter. Roast for about 1½ hours, frequently basting with melted butter. If the chickens brown too much, cover them with foil or greaseproof paper.

serves 4 • Salting: 2–3 hrs • Preparation: 30 mins • Roasting: 90 mins

Sunday chicken

*1 chicken (ca 1½ kg), 2 oranges, 4 apples,
10–12 dried apricots, 50 g raisins, 50 g chopped
walnuts, 5–6 garlic cloves, 2 tbsps honey, 1 tbsp
lemon juice, 1 tsp marjoram, ½ tsp ground ginger,
½ cup orange juice, ½ tsp grated orange rind, salt,
pepper, sugar, ground cloves, 4 tbsps butter*

Mix the chopped garlic with salt (½ tsp), pepper and ginger, 1 tbsp liquid honey and lemon juice. Rub the washed and dried chicken with the mixture, wrap in foil and set aside in the fridge for 2–3 hours. Wash and dry the raisins and apricots, peel and core the apples, cut them in quarters, divide the peeled and seeded oranges into sections. Cut the apricots into strips and combine with 1 tbsp honey, add 2 apples cut into quarters, and sections of 1 orange, stir in the grated orange rind and raisins. Mix well together and stuff the chicken with the mixture. Sew up and place in a buttered roasting pan. Surround with orange sections, sprinkle with melted butter, cover with foil and bake in a preheated oven (190–200°C). After ½ hour

Sunday chicken

reduce the temperature to 180°C. Sprinkle with lemon juice and continue to bake for 40–50 mins. Mix the remaining apples with sugar, marjoram and cloves, remove the foil and arrange around the chicken. Bake together for about 20 mins.

serves 4–6 • Marinating: 2–3 hrs • Preparation:
20–30 mins • Roasting: 90 mins

Chicken legs in lemon aspic

4 chicken legs, 2 lemons, 1 lime, 2 tbsp liquid honey,
1 glass bison vodka, 2–3 garlic cloves, 1 tbsp sugar,
½ tsp coriander seeds, a dash of powdered tumeric,
1 bay leaf, 2–3 grains allspice, 2–3 peppercorns, 2 tbsps
butter, salt, pepper, 2 cups chicken stock, 1 tbsp gelatine

Gently de-bone the chicken legs. Prepare a paste: mix the chopped garlic with salt, honey and bison vodka. Rub the chicken legs with the mixture, place them in a bowl, cover and set aside for 1–2 hours. Scrub the lemon and lime thoroughly. Grate the rind and squeeze juice out of 1 lemon. In a flat saucepan melt the butter with 2 tbsps lemon juice and zest, put in the chicken legs and sauté for a few mins on each side until golden brown. Cover and simmer for about 20 mins until really tender. Cut the remaining lemon into thin slices, remove the seeds. Squeeze the juice out of the lime. Bring to the boil the chicken stock with a bay leaf, allspice, peppercorns and coriander, cover and cook for about 15 mins. Remove from the heat, and strain when cold. Stir in sugar, tumeric, lime juice and the remaining lemon juice, add the slices of lemon and simmer over low heat for about 10 mins. The stock should be sweet and sour. Mix the hot stock with gelatine until completely dissolved. Cool slightly. Pour a few tablespoons of jelly which is beginning to set onto the bottom of a serving bowl. Add a few slices of lemon. When the jelly sets, arrange the chicken legs basted with the pan juices, then pour over the remaining auspic.

serves 4 • Marinating: 1–2 hrs • Preparation:
45–55 mins • Refrigerating: 1–2 hrs

Chicken à la partridge

1 chicken (1½ kg), 50 g pork fat, 2 tbsps crushed
juniper, salt, 1 tbsp butter, ¼ cup strong stock,
1 tbsp sifted breadcrumbs, sprigs of parsley

Rub the washed chicken with salt and juniper, set aside in a cool place for 2 days. Now lard with thin strips of pork fat. Line a saucepan with 2–3 strips of pork fat, add the chicken and brown it over high heat, then reduce the heat, add 1 tbsp butter and the stock. Simmer covered for about 1½ hours, sprinkling from time to time with breadcrumbs. Serve hot, topped with the sauce and decorated with sprigs of parsley.

serves 4–6 • Marinating: 1–2 days • Preparation: 10 mins • Baking: 90 mins

Roast chicken with lemon

1 large chicken (ca 1.7 kg), 2–3 chicken gizzards,
2–3 chicken hearts, 1 tbsp lemon juice, 1 tsp grated
lemon rind, salt, pepper, 1 lemon, 1–2 garlic cloves,
2 sprigs fresh thyme, 1 medium onion, 2 tbsps
olive oil, 2 tbsps butter, 1 glass dry white wine,
¾ cup chicken stock, 1 tsp chopped thyme

Mix well salt, pepper and lemon rind with the olive oil, and rub the washed and dried chicken inside and out with the mixture. Scrub and scald the lemon, prick it with a fork in several places, peel the garlic. Stuff the chicken with the lemon, garlic and thyme, sew up, tie the legs and wings together. Place the chicken in a buttered roasting pan, surround with the livers, hearts and onion lemon. Roast for about 20 mins in the oven, then turn the chicken around, sprinkle with melted butter and continue to roast. After 20 mins baste it with the chicken stock and continue to roast for further 40 mins. Take the chicken out, cut it into serving pieces (remove the lemon and thyme). Mix the sauce, livers, lemon and garlic in a food processor, strain through a sieve, season with salt, pepper and with lemon juice, if desired. Bring to the boil, add the chicken gizzards cut into strips, pour in the wine, heat, add the chopped thyme and mix well together. Arrange the chicken in an ovenproof dish, pour it over with some of the sauce, and keep for a moment in a hot oven to heat up. Serve the remaining sauce in a sauceboat. Serve the chicken with couscous or baked potatoes. Before serving, decorate with slices of lemon and sprigs of parsley.

serves 6–8 • Preparation: 40–45 mins • Roasting: 90 mins

Roast chicken with savory

1 chicken (ca 1.3 kg), 2–3 tbsps chopped savory, 1 tsp ground ginger, 1 tbsp lemon juice, salt, 2–3 tbsps butter, 2–3 tbsps white wine

Sprinkle the washed and dried chicken with lemon juice, rub inside and out with savory, wrap in foil and set aside in the fridge for the night. The following day rub the chicken with salt and ginger and place in a buttered roasting pan, sprinkle with melted butter and roast in a preheated oven, sprinkling with wine and water, and then with the pan juices.

serves 4 • Marinating: 12 hrs • Preparation: 5 mins • Roasting: 90 mins

Chicken stuffed with mushrooms

1 chicken, salt, ½ tsp ground allspice, 1 tsp lemon juice, 2 tbsps butter

STUFFING: 500 g wild mushrooms (bay boletes), 1 large onion, 1 tbsp butter, 2 eggs, 2 tbsps chopped parsley, salt, pepper, ½ cup breadcrumbs

Sprinkle the washed and dried chicken with lemon juice, rub with salt mixed with allspice. Set aside in a cool place for 1 hour. Cut the well-washed mushrooms and onion and stew together in butter for about 20 mins. Uncover towards the end of cooking and steam off the excess liquid, stirring all the time. Blend the butter with egg yolks and parsley and then mix well with the cold mushrooms and breadcrumbs. Season to taste with salt and pepper. Add the stiff beaten egg whites and mix gently. Stuff the chicken with the mixture, sew the cavity up and roast for about 1 hour, sprinkling from time to time with melted butter and cold water. Divide the roast chicken into serving pieces. Serve with rice or potatotes and tomato salad.

serves 4–6 • Marinating: 1 hr • Preparation: 30–35 mins • Roasting: 60–90 mins

Chicken stuffed with green peas

1 chicken, salt, 2 tbsps butter, 1 tbsp lemon juice

STUFFING: 150 g ground veal, 1 cup tinned peas, 1 tbsp single cream, 1 tbsp chopped dill, salt, pepper, 1 egg

Rub the washed chicken with salt and lemon juice. Put the green peas through a sieve and mix with dill and the ground veal. Add salt, pepper, 1 egg and 1 tbsp cream. Mix well. Stuff the chicken with the mixture, sew up and place on a greased roasting pan. Dab with knobs of butter and roast in a preheated oven, from time to time sprinkling with melted butter. Serve sprinkled with the pan juices with French fries and lettuce salad.

serves 4–6 • Marinating: 1 hr • Preparation: 20–25 mins • Roasting: 60–90 mins

Stewed chicken

1 chicken, 1 cup dry white wine, 1 tbsp ground coriander, ¼ tsp ground caraway seeds, ½ tsp hot paprika, 2 garlic cloves, 1 onion, 1 tbsp lemon juice, salt, 1 tbsp butter

Cut the washed and dried chicken into quarters, rub with garlic mixed with salt, sprinkle with lemon juice and brown in butter. Transfer to a saucepan, add coriander, caraway, parprika and the finely chopped onion, sprinkle with water and braise for a moment. Add the wine and simmer for about one hour. Serve with rice or noodles.

serves 4 • Preparation: 5–7 mins • Cooking: 1 hr

Chicken in cream

1 chicken, 100 g butter, 2 cups cream, nutmeg, salt, pepper, dried sage

Wash the chicken and cut it into serving pieces, rub with salt. Heat the butter in a roasting dish, add the sage. Sear the chicken on all sides and roast in the oven for about 40 mins. Turn it over frequently, so that it browns evenly. When ready, arrange on a serving platter and keep warm. Meanwhile combine the pan juices with the cream, add a dash of nutmeg and heat up lightly. When the cream thickens, pour it over the chicken portions and serve.

serves 4–6 · Preparation: 5–6 mins · Roasting: 45–50 mins

Chicken with vegetables

1 chicken, 2 red peppers, 2 onions, 200 g tomatoes, 300 g potatoes, 1 tbsp butter, ½ cup dry white wine, 1 tbsp chopped tarragon, 1 tsp each dried tarragon and basil, salt, pepper, 1 tsp lemon juice

Sprinkle the washed and dried chicken with lemon juice, rub with salt, pepper, basil and tarragon, and set aside in a cool place for 2–3 hours. Now cut into serving pieces and sear on all sides in butter. Transfer to a saucepan, sprinkle with water, add the wine and cook over low heat. Peel and cut the potatoes into thin slices and scald with boiling water over a sieve. Skin the tomatoes and cut them into quarters, chop the onion, cut the pepper into strips. Mix all the ingredients, dust with salt, sprinkle with pepper and other herbs, and add to the chicken. Cover and stew all together over low heat. Before serving, sprinkle with fresh tarragon.

serves 4–6 · Marinating: 2–3 hrs · Preparation: 20–25 mins · Cooking: 40–45 mins

Chicken fillets with onion

2 chicken breasts (ca 700 g), 4 onions, a piece of cinnamon bark, 1 tsp vegetable seasoning, 2 tbsps thyme, 3 tbsps cooking oil

Sprinkle the chicken breasts with salt and pepper and sear in 2 tbsps oil. Transfer to a saucepan greased with oil. Cut the onions into rings and sauté in the reserved oil in the same frying pan. Add to the chicken. Put in a cinnamon stick (optional), sprinkle with thyme and pour in ½ cup water with 1 tsp dried vegetable seasoning. Cover and simmer for about 40 mins. Serve with potatoes.

serves 4 · Preparation: 8–10 mins · Cooking: 35–40 mins

Chicken fillets in cognac sauce

2 chicken breasts (ca 700 g), 1 tbsp lemon juice, 150 g mushrooms, ¾ cup cognac (or brandy),

1 cup single cream, 2–3 tbsps water, 1 chicken stock cube, salt, pepper, nutmeg, 1 tbsp olive oil, 2 tbsps butter, 2 tbsps chopped parsley

Divide the chicken breast into 4 pieces, beat lightly with a mallet, sprinkle with lemon juice, rub with salt, pepper and nutmeg and leave aside in a cool place for ½ hour. Dissolve the chicken stock cube in 2–3 tbsps boiling water. Slice the washed and dried mushrooms and sauté them in 1 tbsp melted butter, adding salt and pepper. In a frying pan heat the olive oil, add the butter and fry the fillets, then transfer to a saucepan and add the mushrooms. Take the frying pan off the heat, add the stock, cream and cognac and mix well. Pour the sauce over the fillets and simmer together for a moment. Before serving, sprinkle with parsley. Serve with French fries, noodles or rice.

serves 4 · Marinating: 30–40 mins · Preparation: 5–6 mins · Stewing: 30 mins

Chicken de volaille

2 chicken breasts (ca 700 g), 100 g butter, salt, 1 tsp lemon juice, 1 tbsp chopped parsley, 2 tbsps breadcrumbs, 1 tsp flour

Beat the fillets lightly with a mallet to the shape of large leaves. Sprinkle lightly with lemon juice and salt. Cream 2 tbsps butter with chopped parsley and a pinch of salt. Chill. Place a knob of parsley butter on each fillet and roll it up. Coat with breadcrumbs mixed with flour and fry in melted butter on both sides until golden brown. Serve with green peas, asparagus, carrots, cauliflower and French fries.

serves 4 · Marinating: 30–40 mins · Preparation: 15–20 mins · Frying: 8–10 mins

Chicken rolls stuffed with leeks

2 chicken breasts (ca 700 g), 1 tbsp lemon juice, 3 tbsps soy sauce, white pepper, 1 tsp oil, ½ cup dry white wine, 2 tbsps oil, 1 tbsp flour

STUFFING: 2–3 leeks (white part only), 2–3 tbsps grated cheese, 3–4 tbsps cream, 1 egg, salt, pepper

Chicken de volaille

SAUCE: *1 cup cream, 1 egg yolk, 2 tbsps caviar paste, salt, white pepper*

Combine lemon juice with pepper, oil and soy sauce. Divide the meat into 4 parts and pound each fillet lightly with a mallet. Put the meat in a bowl, cover with the sauce and set aside in a cool place for 1 hour. Wash and drain the leeks and cut them into thin half-slices. In a saucepan melt the butter, add the leeks and fry and stir for 1 minute. Sprinkle with 1 tbsp wine and simmer covered for 10 mins. Remove from the heat. Blend the cream with the egg and grated cheese, add to the leeks, stir, season to taste with salt and pepper, and set aside to cool. Take the meat out of the marinade and dry. On each fillet spread a portion of the mixture, roll the meat up and tie with thread. Coat in flour and fry in hot oil. Transfer to a saucepan, add the wine and simmer covered for about 20 mins. Combine the cream with the egg yolk, caviar paste and pepper (season with salt, if desired). Arrange the rolls on a warm serving platter and keep warm. Bring to the boil the meat juices, steam off the excess liquid and mix with the cream. Heat, but do not boil. Serve the chicken rolls with noodles or French fries. Serve the sauce in a sauceboat.

serves 4 • Marinating: 1–2 hrs • Preparation: 20–25 mins • Stewing: 20–25 mins

Grilled chicken legs

4 chicken legs, 2 tbsps honey, 1 cup soy sauce, 1 tsp ground ginger, 1 crushed bay leaf, ¼ tsp cayenne pepper

Mix well the soy sauce with honey and seasoning. Place the washed and dried chicken legs in a bowl, cover with the sauce and set aside for a few hours, turning over from time to time. Remove from the marinade and grill.

serves 4 • Marinating: 4–8 hrs • Grilling: 20–25 mins

Chicken legs, devil style

4 chicken legs, 40 g butter, 100 g breadcrumbs, 2 tbsps hot mustard

SAUCE: *1 small onion, 20 g butter, 2 cups dry white wine, 2 tbsps wine vinegar, salt, pepper, 1 tsp lemon juice*

Rub the chicken legs with salt, sprinkle with lemon juice and pepper and coat with butter. Roast in a medium hot oven for about 25 mins.
PREPARE THE SAUCE: Sauté the finely chopped onion in butter, add the wine, vinegar, 1 tsp pepper, some salt, and cook uncovered over low heat for about 5 mins.
Take the chicken legs out, let them cool and coat with mustard and breadcrumbs. Place again in the oven and brown the breadcrumbs. Arrange the chicken legs on a warmed serving platter, combine the pan juices with the sauce, heat up and pour into a sauceboat. Serve with French fries and salad, or baked tomatoes.

serves 4 • Marinating: 30–40 mins • Preparation: 30 mins • Baking: 5–7 mins

Chicken legs, hunter's style

4 chicken legs, 1 tbsp lemon juice, a dash each ground juniper and ground pepper, salt, 1 large onion, 2 bay leaves, 3–4 cloves, 5–6 grains each allspice and pepper, 1 sprig fresh or ¼ tsp dried thyme, ½ tsp chopped fresh ginger, 1 cup dry white wine, 300 g chokeberries, 2 tbsps oil, 2 tbsps butter, salt

Sprinkle the washed and dried chicken legs with lemon juice, rub with salt, pepper and juniper, and set aside in a cool place for half an hour. Chop the onion. In a flat saucepan brown the chicken legs in hot oil. Add butter and onion and sauté for a moment over high heat. Add the wine, bay leaf, cloves, allspice, pepper, thyme and ginger, and simmer covered for about 30 mins. Remove the meat when almost tender. Put the sauce through a sieve, stir in the chokeberries, mix well, add the chicken legs and simmer together for about 15 mins.

serves 4 • Marinating: 30–40 mins • Preparation: 5–8 mins • Stewing: 40–45 mins

Chicken wings with vegetables

800 g chicken wings, 1–2 onions, 3–4 garlic cloves, 1 celery stalk, 1 red pepper, 3–4 firm tomatoes, 1 banana, 1 tsp lemon juice, 1 tsp oregano, ½ tsp pepper, ¼ tsp each cayenne pepper and sugar, salt, 4–5 tbsps olive oil, ¼ cup light stock

Chicken legs, hunter's style

Rub the wings with salt and set aside in a cool place for one hour. Wash and core the pepper, cut it into cubes, dice the blanched and skinned tomatoes. Slice the banana, sprinkle with lemon juice. Finely chop the celery stalk. In a flat saucepan sauté the finely chopped onion and garlic in hot oil. Add the tomatoes, pepper, banana and celery, sprinkle with oregano, cayenne pepper, season with salt and sugar. Add the stock, mix well, cover and simmer for about 10 mins. Grease an ovenproof dish with olive oil, put in the wings and bake them for about 30 mins in a preheated oven. Top the crispy wings with the stewed vegetables, cover and bake together for about 15 mins. Serve with rice, noodles, or white bread.

serves 4 • Salting: 1 hr • Preparation: 20–25 mins • Roasting: 45–50 mins

Grilled chicken wings

1 kg chicken wings, 1 tbsp lemon juice, salt, 2 tbsps oil

SAUCE: ½ cup hot ketchup, 5 tbsps soy sauce, 3 tbsps wine vinegar, 1 glass vodka, 3 tbsps honey

Cut off and discard the chicken wing tips. Combine salt with lemon juice and oil, rub the wings and set aside in the fridge for 1–2 hours. Prepare the sauce combining all the ingredients. Place the wings on the grill and roast until brown. Cover with the sauce and continue to roast. Turn over several times, each time coating the wings with the sauce.

serves 4–6 • Marinating: 1–2 hrs • Roasting: 30–35 mins

Chicken wings in walnut shell

800 g chicken wings, 4 tbsps mild mustard, 1 tbsp lemon juice, 1 cup each ground walnuts (or hazelnuts) and breadcrumbs, 1 tbsp flour, ½ tsp each ground pepper and oregano, salt, ½ cup oil

Rub the washed wings with salt and set aside in a cool place for one hour. Mix well the breadcrumbs, flour, nuts, pepper and oregano. Blend the mustard with lemon juice. Spread the mustard on the wings, cover with the nut mixture and fry in hot oil until golden. Serve with noodles, rice, or white bread and salads.

serves 4 • Marinating: 1–2 hrs • Preparation: 5–7 mins • Frying: 10–12 mins

Chicken legs in garlic sauce

4 chicken legs, 1 large bulb garlic, ½ tsp each dried thyme and rosemary, 2 tbsps butter, 1 tbsp oil, ½ cup dry white wine, ½ cup stock, 1 tbsp lemon juice, salt, pepper, 2 tbsps chopped parsley

Combine half of the herbs, salt, pepper, lemon juice and oil. Rub the chicken legs in the prepared marinade and set aside in a cool place for 1 hour. In a large flat saucepan melt the butter and sear the meat on both sides until golden. Add the chopped garlic and parsley. Sprinkle with the stock and simmer covered for about 30 mins. Add the wine, mix well and continue to simmer for 10–15 mins. Take the meat out when tender, blend the sauce with an electric mixer, put through a sieve and return to the saucepan. Add the remaining herbs, season the meat with salt and pepper, heat up. Serve with dumplings or rice. Separately serve lettuce or red cabbage salad.

serves 4 • Marinating: 1–2 hrs • Preparation: 10 mins • Baking: 40–45 mins

Chicken fricassee, Polish style

4 chicken legs, 1 small cauliflower (ca 200 g), 2 carrots, ¼ celeriac, 1 parsley root, 1–2 onions, 150 g mushrooms, 2 tbsps butter, 1 tbsp flour, juice and grated rind of ½ lemon, 1 egg yolk, 1 sprig fresh or ¼ tsp dried thyme, 3–4 sprigs parsley, 1 bay leaf, 1 clove, salt, white pepper

Rub the washed chicken legs with salt and grated lemon rind and set aside in a cool place for one hour. Place the peeled carrots, celeriac, parsley root and cauliflower into 3 cups of boiling water, add thyme, bay leaf and the clove-stuck onion, and bring to the boil. Cook over low heat for about 5 mins, add the chicken legs and parsley sprigs. Continue to cook for about 30–40 mins. Take the meat out, set aside to cool, and remove the bones and skin. Cut the meat into pieces. Julienne the carrots and celeriac, divide the cauliflower into florets. In a saucepan melt 1 tbsp butter, sauté the mushrooms cut into strips, add the meat and the vegetables. In a frying pan melt the butter, add the flour and make a roux. Dilute it with the strained chicken stock and simmer until the sauce thickens.

Chicken legs in garlic sauce

Season with salt, a dash of pepper, and lemon juice, stir in the egg yolk. Add to the meat and heat up.

serves 4–6 • Marinating: 1–2 hrs • Preparation: 45–50 mins • Baking: 10–15 mins

Chicken fricassee with gooseberries

4 chicken legs, 2 cups stock, 250 g gooseberries, salt, 1 tsp grated lemon rind, 1 tbsp honey, 2 tbsps butter, 1 tbsp flour, ½ cup single cream

In a saucepan place the washed chicken legs and cover with the hot stock. Cook for about 40 mins, take out, set aside to cool, then bone the meat out and cut into serving pieces. In a small saucepan melt the butter, add the gooseberries, grated lemon rind and honey, pour in the reserved stock and cook for about 20 mins. Put the soft goosberries through a sieve and add to the saucepan. Add the meat and simmer over low heat for about 15 mins. Towards the end season with salt, add the cream blended with flour and heat up until the sauce thickens (do not boil!).

serves 4 • Preparation: 45–50 mins • Baking: 10–15 mins

Chicken ragout with pumpkin

4 chicken legs, 750 g pumpkin, 1 large onion, juice and grated rind of ½ lemon, 1 tbsp flour, 2 tbsps butter, 2 bay leaves, ½ cups stock, salt, pepper, ½ tsp each dried sage and thyme, 3 tbsps cream

In a saucepan cover the chicken legs with the hot stock, cook for a few minutes, then remove, set aside to cool. Bone out the meat and cut it into cubes, dust ligthly with pepper. Peel, seed and dice the pumpkin, place it in a bowl and sprinkle with sage and flour. Mix well and set aside for a few minutes. In a saucepan heat the butter and sauté the finely chopped onion, adding salt, pepper, thyme and a bayleaf. Fry and stir for a moment or two. Stir in the pumpkin, sprinkle with some stock and simmer together for a few minutes. In a frying pan heat the oil and brown the meat. Transfer to a saucepan with the pumpkin, pour in the stock, add grated lemon rind, mix well and stew for about 30–40 mins. Towards the end season with lemon

juice, salt and pepper, if desired. Add the cream, mix together and heat up.

serves 6–8 • Macerating: 20–25 mins • Preparation: 10–15 mins • Stewing: 30–40 mins

Chicken ragout with raisins

800 g chicken fillets, 1 tsp flour, 100 g raisins, ½ cup orange juice, 2 tbsps lemon juice, 1 tbsp grated orange rind, ¼ tsp each grated lemon rind and nutmeg, 1 cup light stock, 1 tbsp oil, 2 tbsps butter, salt, pepper, 1 tbsp each chives and parsley

Pour the stock, orange and lemon juice into a saucepan, add nutmeg and cook over low heat for about 15 mins. Wipe dry the washed meat, cut it into cubes, sprinkle lightly with salt and pepper, dust with flour. In a frying pan heat the oil and fry the meat for a few minutes, then add the butter, mix well and continue to fry for a moment or two. Transfer to the saucepan containing the sauce, add the raisins scalded with boiling water, salt, pepper, grated lemon and orange rind. Blend together well and simmer for about 30 mins. Serve with rice or noodles, sprinkled with chopped greens.

serves 4–6 • Preparation: 15–20 mins • Stewing: 30 mins

Chicken livers with sour cherries

600 g chicken livers, ½ cup milk, 250 g pitted cherries (can be frozen), 2 red onions, 1–2 garlic cloves, 1 tbsp fresh or ½ tsp dried thyme, ¼ tsp ground cloves, 1 tsp sugar, 3 tbsps chopped chives, 2 tbsps butter, 1 tbsp oil, salt, pepper

Cover the livers with milk, set aside for half an hour, then drain and dry them. Fry the chopped onion in the hot oil, add the chopped garlic and mix well. In a frying pan melt the butter and fry the livers. Combine with the fried onion, sprinkle with salt, pepper and thyme, and keep over very low heat. In a frying pan sauté the sour cherries, and when tender, sprinkle them with sugar and cloves. Continue to fry for a few mins until the liquid is reduced. Arrange the livers with onion on a warmed serving platter, cover with the cherries, sprinkle with the chives. Serve with white bread or potato purée.

serves 4 • Soaking: 30 mins • Preparation: 5 mins • Frying: 8–10 mins

Chicken gizzards in aspic

500 g cleaned chicken (or turkey) gizzards, soup vegetables, 3–4 grains each pepper and allspice, ¼ tsp dried rosemary, salt, 1 bay leaf, 6–8 hard-boiled quail eggs, parsley sprigs, 3 tbsps tinned peas, ½ marinated red pepper, 1 tbsp gelatine

Bring to the boil the washed gizzards with soup vegetables, rosemary and spices. Cut when tender into thin sticks. Bring to the boil the strained stock. Cover the gelatine with 2–3 tbsps cold water and leave to swell. Add to the stock, heat up and strain through a fine sieve. Pour in 2–3 tbsps aspic to small bowls, set aside to cool. Then in each bowl place a portion of gizzards, egg halves, green peas, finely chopped red pepper and a sprig of parsley. Top with some aspic, leave aside to cool. Serve decorated with parsley and slices of lemon.

serves 4–6 • Cooking: 50–60 mins • Preparation: 10–15 mins • Cooling: 1–2 hrs

Hot snack of chicken gizzards

400 g chicken (or turkey) gizzards, 400 g oyster mushrooms, 1 bunch spring onions, 2–3 garlic cloves, 3 tbsps butter, 1½ cup chicken stock, ½ tsp each chicken seasoning and herbs of Provence, 1 tbsp mustard, 2 tbsps lemon juice, salt, pepper, sugar

Place the washed gizzards in a saucepan, cover with hot stock and cook for about 50–60 mins. Remove with a slotted spoon, set aside to cool and cut into thick strips. Transfer the meat to a bowl, sprinkle with powdered chicken seasoning, garlic minced with salt, and herbes de Provence. Mix well. Reduce the stock to about 1 cup, strain. Cut the mushrooms into strips, and finely chop the spring onions. In a saucepan melt half of the butter, add the chicken gizzards and sauté for a while, stirring all the time. Pour in the reserved stock and simmer together for a moment or two. In a frying pan melt the remaining butter, add

the mushrooms and fry for about 5–6 mins, then combine with the gizzards, add the spring onion, stir in the lemon juice blended with mustard, pepper and a dash of sugar. Heat up. Serve with white bread and lettuce.

serves 4–6 • Cooking: 50–60 mins • Preparation: 10–15 mins • Baking: 8–10 mins

Chicken hearts, French style

600 g chicken hearts, 1 bay leaf, a sprig of thyme or ½ tsp dried thyme, 50 g pork fat, 1 tbsp butter, 1 glass dry red wine, 1 onion, 1 tbsp ketchup, 1 tbsp mustard, ½ cup stock, salt, pepper, 2–3 tbsps chopped parsley, 1 tbsp flour

Render the diced pork fat in a frying pan, add the butter and finely chopped onion and fry for a minute or two, stirring all the time. Put in the hearts, continue frying, then add the thyme, crumbled bay leaf and the wine and simmer for several minutes. Season to taste, add the mustard, ketchup, parsley and the stock, stir well and heat up. Serve with barley kasha or noodles. Garnish with parsley before serving.

serves 4 • Preparation: 5–6 mins • Stewing: 12–15 mins

Risotto from giblets and leek

1 cup rice, 1 tbsp butter, salt, 1 tsp lemon juice, 300 g chicken gizzards and hearts, 1 large onion, 6 leeks (white parts only), salt, pepper, 2 tbsps butter, 1 tsp breadcrumbs

Cook the rice in a large amount of water, rinse it under cold water, drain well. Mix it with 1 tbsp of butter and the lemon juice. Rinse the leeks thoroughly, cook them in salted water, then drain them. Fry the gizzards, hearts and chopped onion in butter, add some leek stock and simmer. When the giblets are tender, put them through a mincer, adjust the taste with salt and pepper. Butter an ovenproof dish, line it with half the rice. Spread the giblet mixture on it and then the cooked leeks. Pour over some melted butter mixed with breadcrumbs, cover with the remaining rice and put slices of butter on top. Place in a preheated oven and bake for 30 mins. Serve with lettuce or tomato salad.

serves 4–6 • Preparation: 25–35 mins • Baking: 30 mins

Boiling fowl, capons, poulards

There are several hundred varieties of hens, and they are judged by their capacity for putting on weight. In 5 weeks, some a weight of 2 to 2½ kg. Older birds, weighing about 3 kg, are tougher and need long braising or stewing.

Capons are castrated young cocks which are bred especially for their meat. The average weight of a capon is from 3 to 4½ kg. Castration leads to a slowing down of the metabolism and the bird puts on a lot of weight; its meat is more delicate. Capons are excellent for roasting.

Poulards are castrated fattened hens. Today's young hens which are killed before they begin to lay may have more delicate meat but they have much less taste than poulards.

A boiling fowl needs to be boiled or roasted for about 1½ hours, while young hens need from 45 minutes to an hour. A large fowl can be divided into 10 to 12 portions: two wings, two portions from each leg, and the breast into 2 to 3 portions on each side.
Boiling fowl, capons and poulards can be stuffed like turkeys, as follows:

– if the bird is left whole on the bone, they are stuffed in their entirety and then sewn up; after roasting the thread is removed;

– if the bird is to be boned, then after washing and drying it should be cut along the backbone, and all the meat cut off the rib cage with a sharp knife, after soaking, together with the innards, leaving only the bones of the wings and lower legs. The meat should then be carefully washed and rubbed with salt, stuffed, and the cut along the backbone should be sewn up.

– if we want to stuff the chicken under the skin, it is not necessary to bone it, but just lift the skin from the breast,

place a thin layer of stuffing under it and then sew up the skin. In lifting the skin, one should be careful not to puncture it, for then the stuffing will come out or dry out.

Fillets of spring chicken à la doque

Carve out breasts from spring chickens and remove the skin from them, slit them with a sharp knife and place thinly-sliced tongue, gherkins and green beans in the slits; put them in a pan which has been well greased with fresh butter; on the surface grate lemon peel and squeeze in the lemon juice. Cover with buttered paper and put them covered onto a hot point or into the oven for a few minutes before serving. You can serve them with buttered toast and covered with sauce.

(Jan Szyttler, *Kucharz dobrze usposobiony*, Wilno 1830)

Hen stuffed with noodles

1 young hen (2–2½ kg), 1 tbsp each grated thyme and rosemary, 2–3 garlic cloves, salt, pepper, 1 tbsp lemon juice, 2 tbsps olive oil, ½ cup stock

STUFFING: 200 g noodles (e.g. tagliatelle), 150 g ham sausage, 150 g mushrooms, 1 large onion, 2–3 tbsps chopped parsley, 1 tbsp butter, 3–4 tbsps grated cheese (e.g. Edam), 1 egg, salt, pepper

Mix the chopped garlic with salt, pepper, thyme, rosemary, lemon juice and 1 tbsp oil. Rub the washed and dried hen with the mixture, wrap in foil and refrigerate for 2–3 hours.

PREPARE THE STUFFING: Wash, dry and finely chop the mushrooms. Sauté the chopped onion in melted butter, add the mushrooms and stir and fry over high heat for a moment or two. Remove from the heat, combine with the diced ham sausage, season to taste with salt and pepper. Cook tagliatelle al dente, strain and mix with the grated cheese, raw egg yolk and chopped parsley. Add the mushrooms, onion, ham sausage and the stiff beaten egg white. Mix well and season to taste. Stuff the hen, sew the cavity, tie the legs and the wings crossed over the breasts. Arrange in a roasting pan, sprinkle with oil and roast for about 1½ hours in a preheated oven (200°C), often basting with stock, then with the pan drippings. Cut the hen into portions, place in an ovenproof dish, surround with the stuffing and pour the sauce over it. Heat up in a preheated oven for 10–15 mins.

serves 6–8 • Marinating: 2–4 hrs • Preparation: 35–40 mins • Roasting: 90 mins

Stuffed hen, Jewish style

1 stewing hen, 1 kg potatoes, 3 onions, salt, pepper, 1 tbsp cream, 150 g butter

Rub the washed and dried hen with salt inside and out. Set aside to cool. Put the boiled potatoes through a mincer or mash. Mix with 1 tbsp butter and 1 tbsp cream. Glass the very finely chopped onion in 1 tbsp of butter, and add to the potatoes together with salt and pepper. Mix well and stuff the hen with the mixture. Sew the cavity. Place the hen on a buttered roasting pan and roast in a preheated oven for about 1½ hours, frequently basting with the pan drippings and sprinkling with water from time to time. If the hen browns too quickly, cover it with aluminium foil. Serve cut into portions and sprinkled with the pan juices blended with parsley butter.

serves 6–8 • Salting: 1–2 hrs • Preparation: 30–35 mins • Roasting: 90 mins

Stewing hen, hunter's style

1 stewing hen (1½ kg), 100 g smoked ham, 500 g tomatoes, 500 g (or more) potatoes, 2 hot peppers, salt, pepper, 3 lemons, 1 head garlic, 100 g dry white wine, 50 g butter, 50 g lard, 1 onion, allspice, 1 bay leaf, oregano, basil, 250 g green peas

Divide the hen into serving pieces, season with salt, pepper, some of the garlic and herbs. Place in a dish, sprinkle generously with lemon juice and set aside for 2 hours to marinate. In a saucepan melt the butter and lard, brown the hen on all sides and add the skinned tomatoes, finely chopped onion, herbs and wine, and about 1 cup water. Stew over low heat for about 40 mins. Add the finely chopped hot pepper, diced ham, sliced boiled potatoes and green peas. Cook together for about 10 mins.

serves 4–6 • Marinating: 2–3 hrs • Preparation: 10–15 mins • Stewing: 45–55 mins

Capon or poulard à la pheasant

1 capon or fowl, 2 tbsps crushed juniper berries, 100 g pork fat

STUFFING: 1 bread roll soaked in milk, 1 tbsp butter, 2 eggs, ½ tsp each ginger and crushed juniper, salt, 1 tbsp chopped parsley, 1 chicken liver

Rub the dressed and washed capon inside and out with juniper. Set aside in a cool place for 2–3 days. Then rub with salt and lard with the pork fat. Set aside in a cool place for another 2–3 hours.

PREPARE THE STUFFING: Squeeze the bread roll dry and blend it with butter and egg yolks to smooth consistency. Add the chopped liver, juniper, ginger, salt and the stiff beaten egg whites and parsley. Mix gently, stuff the capon and sew the cavity. Arrange in a greased roasting pan, dab with knobs of butter and roast in a hot oven for about 1½ hours, often sprinkling with butter. If the meat browns too quickly, cover it with foil or greaseproof paper.

serves 6–8 • Marinating: 2–3 days • Salting: 2–3 hrs • Preparation: 20–30 mins • Roasting: 90 mins

Stuffed capon or poulard

1 capon or fowl, 100 g pork fat, 300 g veal, 1 chicken liver, 1 onion, 1 tbsp butter, 1 bread roll soaked in milk, 2 spice-salted herrings, 3 eggs, grated lemon rind, ¼ tsp powdered ginger, salt, pepper, sugar, ground allspice

Rub the dressed and washed fowl with salt, leave aside in a cool place for 1–2 hours. Soak the skinned and boned herrings in water.

Prepare the stuffing: Stew the pork fat, veal and liver with onion over low heat for 20–30 mins. Add a dash of pepper and allspice, and 1 tsp butter. Keep covered. When cooked, leave aside to cool.

Put the meat through a mincer. Cut the herrings into fine pieces and blend them into a fine paste with the egg yolks, lemon rind, pepper, salt and ginger. Squeeze the bread roll dry and add it to the mixture. Stir in the minced meat and knead everything together into smooth consistency. At the end add the stiff beaten egg whites and mix gently. Stuff the capon and sew the cavity. Arrange the bird in a greased roasting pan, dab with knobs of butter and roast for about 1½ hours, often sprinkling with melted butter. Serve hot.

serves 6–8 • Salting: 1–2 hrs • Preparation: 40–45 mins • Roasting: 90 mins

Goose

In traditional Old Polish cuisine, goose had to be served at Martinmass (11 November) and then at New Year. This tasty (but high-calorie and indigestible) bird was supposed to bring prosperity to the home. The Polish and Lithuanian delicacy known as 'half-goose', that is smoked goose breast, was far-famed, as also were 'goose pipes', which was a dish taken over from Jewish cuisine and meant stuffed goose necks. Goose meat is tasty, dark, with a pleasant aroma, but is unfortunately fat and indigestible, with the highest calorie value of any poultry: 345 calories per 100 g. The birds most often on sale are a few months old; young geese, 10–12 weeks old when they weigh 3 to 4 kg, have the best flavour and are not so fat. Fully grown birds are very fat (more than 30% fat) and are very indigestible.

The classic accompaniment to goose dishes is sour cabbage or red cabbage boiled with apples or pears. Potato dumplings or a fine potato purée go very well with goose.

The most popular dish is probably roast goose stuffed with apples, since apple juice goes very well with the aroma of goose and at the same time absorbs excess fat. Marjoram, ground caraway or ginger rubbed into the bird before roasting bring out the flavour of goose.

Stuffings made from prunes, buckwheat grits, fresh or sour cabbage, mushrooms, potatoes or pasta are exceptionally popular with goose.

It is a good idea to remove the neck and wings before roasting. Goose giblets – that is the head, neck, feet, wings and liver – can be used to make soup, while the rest of the bird is roasted. Barley soup made with a goose stock is excellent.

A roast goose (roasting time is from 2 to 3 hours depending on the weight) should be basted with cold water and then put back in a very hot oven for a few minutes. This makes the skin crisp.

Goose, Polish style

1. *Soak a dressed goose in cold water for 2–3 hours, then rub it with salt, cut in half, cover with boiling water and cook slowly.*
2. *Peel and rinse soup vegetables, add them to the goose when its meat is tender, add salt and slowly reduce the liquid to 1½ litres.*
3. *Make a roux from some fat and flour, dilute it with the goose stock, add salt, nutmeg and marjoram to taste.*
4. *Carve the bird into portions, put them into the sauce, bring to the boil. Before serving, mix in raw egg yolks. Serve in a round dish, with pearl barley piled around.*

(Zofia Czerny, Książka kucharska, 1954)

Goose with apples

1 young goose (ca 3–4 kg), 1 tbsp salt, 1½ tsp ground caraway seeds, 1 kg apples (preferably Rennet), 6–7 cloves, 3–4 tbsps chopped walnuts, 1 tbsp honey, 1 tsp butter, ½ cup dry red wine (preferably home-made hawthornberry or rosehip wine)

Wash the dressed goose and put it into cold water for 3–4 hours. Remove, wipe dry and rub inside and out with salt mixed with caraway. Set aside for 2–3 hours. Wash and dry the apples, scoop out the cores and stuff the cavities with the walnuts mixed with honey. Lard each apple with 1–2 cloves. Stuff the goose with the apples and sew up the cavity. Place the bird in a buttered roasting pan and roast for about 3–3½ hours, basting it with the wine and pan drippings. Serve with baked apples and sauerkraut stewed with raisins and honey.

serves 8–10 • Soaking: 3–4 hrs • Salting: 2–3 hrs • Preparation: 10 mins • Roasting: 3–3½ hrs

Goose stuffed with veal

1 young goose (ca 4 kg), 1 tbsp salt, 2 tbsps crushed marjoram, 2–3 garlic cloves, ½ cup stock, 1 tbsp butter

STUFFING: 300 g veal, 150 g goose or veal livers, 1 bread roll soaked in milk, 1 large onion, salt, pepper, 1 tsp marjoram, 2 eggs

Dress and wash the goose, remove the excess of fat and reserve it for the stuffing. Cover the goose with cold water and set aside for 3–4 hours. Mince the finely chopped garlic with salt and marjoram. Remove the goose, wipe it dry and rub with the prepared salt. Set aside for 3–4 hours.

Prepare the stuffing: Put the veal, onion and liver through a mincer, add the bread roll (squeeze it dry first), finely chopped goose fat, salt, pepper and marjoram. Mix well, break in the eggs and knead uniform pulp. Stuff the goose, sew the cavity and place the bird in a buttered roasting pan. Roast in a preheated oven for about 3–4 hours, basting from time to time with the stock and pan drippings. Divide the tender goose into serving pieces, arrange on an oven-proof platter and heat up in a preheated oven.

Roast goose with herbs

1 young goose (ca 3 kg), 1 cup dry white wine, ½ cup stock, 1½ tsps crushed juniper berries, 1 tsp crumbled rosemary, ½ tsp sage, salt, pepper, 1 tsp butter

Rub the soaked and dried goose inside and out with salt mixed with herbs and pepper. Set aside in a cool place for 4–5 hours (preferably overnight). Spread butter over the goose and roast in a preheated oven for over 2 hours, often basting it with pan drippings and sprinkling with stock and wine. Serve hot with baked potatoes sprinkled with rosemary, and with red cabbage salad.

serves 6–8 • Soaking: 3–4 hrs • Macerating: 8–12 hrs • Preparation: 3–4 mins • Roasting: 2½–3 hrs

Roast goose with apples and leeks

1 young goose (3–4 kg), 6–8 large apples (Antonovka or Boiken), 300 g leeks, 1 cup raisins, salt, pepper, 1 tbsp marjoram, 1 tsp butter, 1 glass dry white wine

Soak the washed goose in cold water for 3–4 hours. Pat dry and rub inside and out with salt and marjoram, then set aside in a cool place for 2–3 hours. Scald the raisins with boiling water, drain. Cut the cleaned and washed leeks into slices, peel, core and quarter the apples. Combine the leeks, apples and raisins, sprinkle with salt and season with pepper. Stuff the goose, sew the cavity. Place the goose in a lightly buttered roasting pan, sprinkle it with 3–4 tbsps water and prick with a fork, so that the fat could drip. Roast for 2–3 hours, basting with water and wine, then with the pan drippings. Turn the goose over after 1 hour, breast down. Serve it divided into portions and surrounded with the stuffing. Best with mashed or scooped out potatoes. Remove excess fat from the gravy. Serve the degreased sauce in a sauceboat.

serves 8–10 • Soaking: 3–4 hrs • Salting: 2–3 hrs • Preparation: 15–20 mins • Roasting: 2½–3 hrs

Goose stuffed with kasha

1 young goose (ca 3 kg), 3–4 garlic cloves, 2 tbsps marjoram, 1 tbsp lemon juice, salt, pepper

STUFFING: 1½ cups buckwheat kasha, 200 g chicken livers, 2 large onions, 1 parsley root, 1 carrot, 4–5 dried mushrooms, 2–3 garlic cloves, 2 tbsps each chopped parsley and dill, salt, pepper, 2 tbsps butter, 2 eggs

Wipe dry the washed goose and cut off the neck and wing tips. Put the goose on the board and with a sharp knife cut along the length of the spine. Remove the bones in such a way that the meat is not separated from the skin. Mince the chopped garlic with salt, pepper, marjoram and lemon juice, rub the goose, wrap it in foil and set aside for 2–3 hours in the fridge. Wash the mushrooms and soak them in some cold boiled water. Put the bones, wings and neck bones (reserve the skin for the stuffing and rub it with salt) in a saucepan, cover with 4 cups cold water and bring to the boil, Add 1 onion, mushrooms, peeled carrot and parsley root, salt and pepper, and simmer over low heat for about 1 hour. Strain through a sieve. Cook the washed kasha in the stock, set aside to cool. Chop the livers, and cut the onion and mushrooms into small pieces. In a frying pan melt the butter, sauté the onion, add the livers and mushrooms and sauté together for a moment. Remove from the heat. Blend the kasha with the egg yolks, chopped parsley and dill. Beat the egg whites stiff and stir in. Stuff the goose with the mixture, sew the cavity and place the bird in a greased roasting pan. Roast for about 1 hour in a preheated (250°C) oven. Turn over after ½ hour, and, when nice and golden, turn the heat down (to 180°–200°C) and continue to roast for a further 1 hour, basting the goose with water and then with the pan drippings. Before serving, cut into thick slices and surround them with the stuffing.

serves 8–10 • Salting: 2–3 hrs • Preparation: 1–1½ hrs • Roasting: 2½–3½ hrs

Goose breasts with herbs

goose breasts (ca 1 kg), 1 tbsp crushed marjoram, 1 tbsp sage, ¼ tsp thyme, 2–3 garlic cloves, 1 glass vodka, sugar, 1 tbsp butter

Soak the goose breasts in ligthly salted water, wipe dry and rub with garlic minced with salt and herbs, and set aside in a cool place for 3–4 hours. Now place the meat in a buttered roasting pan and roast in a preheated oven for about 30 mins, sprinkling from time to time with water. Wash and core the apples. Blend the butter with sugar and marjoram and stuff the cavities. Arrange the apples around the goose and bake together for about 1 hour. Towards the end sprinkle with vodka, cover the pan and continue roasting till ready.

serves 4–6 • Soaking: 3–4 hrs • Macerating: 3–4 hrs • Roasting: 1½ hrs

Goose thighs in dark sauce

4 goose thighs, 2 parsley roots, 2 carrots, ½ celeriac, 1 onion, 1 cup stock, 1 slice stale wholemeal bread, a dash each ginger, nutmeg and crushed cloves, 1 tsp caramel, 1 tbsp plum jam, grated lemon rind, ½ tsp sugar, 1 tbsp lemon juice, 1 glass red wine, salt, 2 tbsps goose fat or butter

Rub the washed goose thighs with salt and set aside in a cool place for half an hour. Coarsely grate the peeled and washed vegetables. Sauté the goose thighs in goose fat till golden. In a saucepan, melt 1 tbsp goose fat, put in the vegetables and the meat on top. Pour in the stock and simmer covered. Add ginger, grated lemon rind, cloves, nutmeg and sugar. When the vegetables are tender, add the caramel, crumbled wholemeal bread, lemon juice, plum jam and wine and continue to simmer together for a few minutes. Remove the thighs and put the sauce through a sieve. Season to taste if desired. Put the thighs in and

heat up. Serve with rice or potato croquettes, covered with the sauce.

serves 4 • Salting: 30–40 mins • Preparation: 15–20 mins • Stewing: 1 hr

Stuffed goose neck

neck skin of 1 goose, 1 egg, 2 tbsps sifted breadcrumbs, goose giblets, 1 tsp marjoram, 2 garlic cloves, 2 tbsps chopped parsley, salt, pepper, sugar, 2 tbsps butter, 1 cup strong stock, 1 tbsp dry white wine

Rub the washed neck skin with salt. Mince the butter with 1 egg yolk, add chopped garlic and the finely chopped goose giblets. Gradually add salt, pepper, marjoram, parsley and a dash of sugar. Beat the egg white stiff and add together with breadcrumbs to the prepared pulp. Mix gently (add some more breadcrumbs if the stuffing is too loose). Stuff the neck and sew from both ends. Place in a small saucepan, pour in the stock and wine, and simmer covered for about 1 hour. Before serving, you can briskly sauté the neck in butter. Serve hot, sprinkled with the braising liquid as a sauce.

serves 4 • Salting: 1 hr • Preparation: 10 mins • Stewing: 55–60 mins

Goose neck, Polish style

1 goose neck, goose giblets, 1 cup barley kasha, 1 small onion, 1 tbsp butter (or goose fat), 3 cups chicken stock, salt, pepper, 1 tbsp marjoram

Remove the skin from the goose neck, rub it with salt and marjoram, and set aside for about 15 mins. Cook the neck and gizzard in the stock, remove when tender and set aside to cool. Cover the washed barley kasha with 2 cups of hot stock and set it aside to swell. Take the meat off the neck and cut it finely. Sauté the chopped onion in butter (or goose fat), add the chopped meat and finely cut the gizzard and liver. Sauté together for a few moments, then combine with the kasha, add salt, pepper and the remaining marjoram. Mix well and stuff the skin with the mixture, sew up both ends and place in a saucepan. Cover with the reserved stock (hot) and bring to the boil, then simmer covered over low heat. Serve hot with the braising liquid as a sauce, or cold, with spicy sauces.

serves 4 • Salting: 30–40 mins • Preparation: 45–50 mins • Stewing: 40–45 mins

Goose necks, Jewish style

4 goose necks, 750 g potatoes, 2 onions, 3 eggs, salt, pepper, 1 tbsp goose fat

Wash the skin of goose necks thoroughly and dry. Peel and grate the potatoes. Sauté the finely chopped onion in goose fat till golden. Squeeze the excess of water from the potatoes. Mix the potatoes with the onion, break in the eggs, add salt and pepper and knead uniform pulp. Stuff the necks and sew from both sides. Arrange in a saucepan, pour in some salted boiling water and simmer over low heat for about 20 mins. Carefully remove with a skimmer. In a roasting pan heat 1 tbsp goose fat, arrange the necks and roast in a preheated oven for about 1 hour, sprinkling with the liquid in which the necks were cooking and later with the braising liquid. Serve with salads.

serves 6–8 • Preparation: 30–35 mins • Roasting: 55–60 mins

Goose liver medallions

800 g goose livers, 1 kg tart apples (Rennet), 125 g butter, 1 glass dry red wine, ½ cup chicken stock, 4–6 (depending on the number of servings) slices of white bread, salt, pepper, a dash of each thyme and marjoram

Remove the membranes from the livers, fry the livers in butter, then sprinkle with salt and herbs. Put the peeled and quartered apples into a saucepan, pour in the wine and stock, and stew until tender (about 15–20 mins). Butter an ovenproof platter, arrange the toasted pieces of bread and place the liver portions on each. Surround with the stewed apples and put into a preheated oven for a few minutes.

serves 4–6 • Preparation: 30 mins • Baking: 10–12 mins

Turkey

Turkey meat is the lowest-calorie meat of all poultry. 100 g of turkey breast contains 107 kcal and 2.6 g of fat (chicken breast contains 170 kcal and 9.8 g of fat; and overall chicken meat contains 155 kcal and 8.6 g of fat). It has very little fat or cholesterol, and at the same time high amounts of magnesium and phosphorus, small amounts of B vitamins as well as vitamin PP, and white turkey meat contains a lot of zinc, vitamin B_6 and vitamin B_{12}; it also has iron and potassium. It is recommended to allergic people.

In Polish cuisine for centuries – probably since the mid-15th century – turkey has been considered an exclusive dish which at one time was served relatively rarely. The most festive way of serving it was as turkey stuffed with chestnuts or stuffed and larded with truffles. It was served with Madeira sauce and garnished with roast fieldfares.

Turkeys can be purchased whole (they can weigh from 3 to 13 kg) or in portions. Younger birds are best for roasting, while older ones should be stewed or made into soup.

Depending on their age and breed, hen and cock turkeys weigh respectively 3½ to 10 kg and 5 to 15 kg. Meat from young birds, 15 to 24 weeks old, is best for culinary purposes, as it is tender and succulent.

An average portion per person is 150 g without bones, or about 300 g with bones. Fresh turkey will be more tender and succulent if it stands for 1 to 2 days in the fridge. A frozen turkey should be well defrosted before cooking, and this should be done slowly, placing it first on the bottom shelf of the refrigerator, so that it does not lose too much juice. The preparation process is very important with turkeys for roasting; the most important thing is to remove the tendons from the legs, since in cooking these shrink and harden, making the whole leg hard, so that it cannot be divided into portions. To remove the tendons, use a sharp knife to cut the skin round the knee joint, roll the skin up, cut the tendons with a sharp fine knife and pull them out one by one with pincers. If we are going to stew the turkey or roast it whole, the body should be trussed (with twine or skewers) so that the wings and legs do not stand out and therefore become dry in cooking.

Before roasting, the turkey should be rubbed inside and outside with a mixture of salt, lemon juice and pepper. It is best to roast it in a tin or on the spit, basted with melted butter and sprinkled with water, bouillon or wine, and later with the pan drippings. If we place the turkey breast down and cover it with buttered greaseproof paper or with aluminium foil, the bird will not dry out when roasted in a tin. The greaseproof paper or aluminium foil should be removed about 50 minutes before the roast is done so that the bird can brown evenly. It is a good idea to place a tin of water on the lowest shelf of the oven. A well roasted turkey should be juicy inside and have a nicely browned skin. To achieve this, we must frequently baste it or brush it with butter during roasting.

A stuffed turkey should be roasted for on average half an hour longer than a turkey that is not stuffed. The stuffing can be placed in the abdomen or crop. To stuff the crop, you should break the skin membrane with you hand and place the stuffing inside loosely; remember that in the cooking process the stuffing swells to more than twice its volume.

A turkey, like other poultry, should be placed in a very hot oven (ca 250°) and when it is nicely browned the temperature should be turned down (to ca 170°–180°). When roasting a whole turkey a poultry roasting thermometer – which measures the temperature inside the roast – is useful. A turkey is ready when a thermometer stuck into the leg reads 85°.

We should be careful to keep the oven temperature correct, since if the meat is roasted at too high a temperature it will dry out and lose a lot of its flavour. A roast turkey should be carved and then reheated. The slices should be placed in a flat pan, covered with a small quantity of sauce and heated under a lid. Carving a turkey is a difficult art.

A roast turkey is carved differently when it is to be served cold and when it is to be served hot. The carving should be done quickly after the bird is taken out of the oven, before it cools.

First, the legs should be removed, cutting the skin and meat around the joint and breaking the bone, and then each leg should be divided into 2 or 3 portions; then the wings should be removed, making sure that there is a piece of meat attached to each of them. The breast should be sliced on each side of the breast bone in thin, slantwise slices. If the turkey has been stuffed in the crop, this should be carved in slices against the grain of the breast.

Finally, the whole back should be broken off the breast bone, together with the parson's nose, and cut into three pieces. Because turkey cools very quickly while being carved, it should be placed before serving in an ovenproof dish and returned to a hot oven, covered with aluminium foil so that the meat does not dry.

The small pieces of meat that are left over after the turkey has been carved are best used for preparing salads, risotto or jellies.

The number of dishes that you can make from turkey is impressive. Turkey meat has the enormous advantage of being highly varied, from the delicate white meat of the breast, which has a taste similar to that of veal, to the dark brown meat of the legs which is similar to game; the dark and fatty meat of the neck is similar to pork.

The most elegant dishes made from turkey use the meat from the breast, which can be fried, roasted or stewed. The breast can be roasted whole, or made into medallions, fillets, collops or cutlets and then served sauté or egged and breadcrumbed.

Stewed turkey meat is often used to make cold hors d'oeuvres, like jellies or meat in mayonnaise sauces. Every part of the turkey can be made use of in a variety of ways.

The inferior parts – the wings, neck and lower legs – make excellent stews or stocks. Minced turkey meat can be used for meatballs and rissoles. Turkey can be seasoned with either spices or herbs. The spices most frequently used with turkey are ginger, nutmeg, paprika, bay leaves, allspice, pepper (white pepper is best) or cloves; the best herbs are coriander, oregano, rosemary, marjoram and sage. To cook a turkey oriental style, garlic and soy sauce are very important, and turkey meat is also often combined with shellfish, vegetables or many varieties of fruit, currants, almonds, walnuts or shredded coconut.

Turkey dishes are usually served with potato purée, French fries, mashed potatoes, dauphine potatoes, macaroni or rice. One common accompaniment is Florentine rice – which is cooked with onion and spinach.

Good vegetables to serve with turkey are asparagus, cauliflower or green peas; fruit is an excellent accompa-

Stuffed roast turkey

niment: slices of pineapple, orange or grapefruit, apples, cherries, pears and also cranberries or bilberries.

Stuffed turkey. Turkey was the traditional Easter dish, at one time usually stuffed with chestnuts and truffles. Turkey can be stuffed with various stuffings. The whole body is stuffed, with the crop packed out. An exception is the Old Polish custom of using two different stuffings: the abdomen was stuffed with a spicy stuffing and the crop with sweet stuffing.

Stuffing for turkey. There are at least a few hundred different stuffings for turkey: the most common is minced veal with breadcrumbs, rice or cooked kasha, with added onion or fruits, cooking apples, prunes, currants, nuts or almonds.
Another kind is sweet white bread soaked in milk with added turkey liver, butter and eggs and additionally almonds, nuts, currants or dried apricots. This was the most popular Polish-style stuffing. In 19th-century Polish cuisine, sweet chestnuts were very popular as stuffing for turkey.

Mock chestnut stuffing

Take two tablespoonfuls of almonds and several skinned bitter almonds, pound them thoroughly, add some sugar and a dozen hard-boiled egg yolks. Blend the mixture well and shape into chestnut-size balls, then dip them in hot caramel...

(Jan Szyttler, *Kucharz dobrze usposobiony*, Wilno 1830)

Stuffed roast turkey

Lightly butter the dressed and salted turkey. Spoon the stuffing into the neck end of the turkey and sew up. Place the bird in a very hot oven and roast over high heat for the first 20 mins, often sprinkling with melted butter. When the turkey is nicely browned, reduce the heat and continue roasting for over 2 hours. If it browns too much, cover it with foil or greaseproof paper. Often sprinkle with butter. In the past the most elegant way of serving stuffed turkey was to lard it with truffles.

serves 10–12 • Preparation: 3–4 hrs • Roasting: 3–3½ hrs

STUFFING FOR TURKEY

Sweet chestnut stuffing

*500 g fresh French chestnuts, 2 tbsps butter,
1 tbsp breadcrumbs, 1 tsp sugar, 50 g almonds,
a dash of each nutmeg and ground allspice,
1 tbsp rum, 2 tbsps cream, 3 eggs*

Cook the chestnuts in ligthly salted water and remove skin. Put the nuts through a mincer, then blend in a bowl into smooth pulp with the egg yolks and butter. Add sugar, spices, cream and rum. Mix thoroughly. Finely chop the scalded and peeled almonds, stir in the egg whites beaten stiff and the sifted breadcrumbs. Mix gently. Spoon the stuffing into the turkey neck. Hold the skin up to let the stuffing reach beyond the collarbones. Sew the cavity.

Preparation: 40 mins

Whole chestnut stuffing

*500 g fresh chestnuts, 2 tbsps
butter, salt, nutmeg, sugar*

With a knife cut a cross on one side of each chestnut. Cover with cold water and bring to the boil several times. Peel off chestnut shells and inner dark skin. Place the whole chestnuts in a small saucepan, add the seasoning and butter, and simmer covered for about 30 mins. Stuff the neck cavity, and if there are some chestnuts left, stuff them in the body cavity. When the turkey is ready, remove the chestnuts and arrange them on a serving platter around the bird.

Preparation: 40 mins

Chestnut and meat stuffing

*250 g boneless pork neck, 250 g veal, 250 g pork
fat, 1 small bread roll, 1 egg, 250 g chestnuts,
1 tbsp butter, salt, pepper, nutmeg, 2 onions*

Glass the very finely chopped onion in butter. Cook the chestnuts, peel off the shells and inner dark skin. Put them through a mincer together with the pork fat and bread roll (soaked in milk and then squeezed dry). Add the seasoning, onion and egg and mix together thoroughly. Stuff the neck cavity with the mixture and sew.

Preparation: 40 mins

Ham stuffing

1 cup rice, 2 tbsps butter, 150 g ham, 2 eggs, ½ cup thick sour cream, 1 tbsp chopped parsley, salt, pepper

Cook the rice and mix it with butter and thin strips of ham. Add the eggs, cream, parsley, salt and pepper. Knead uniform pulp. Stuff the neck cavity and sew it.

Preparation: 25 mins

Crayfish stuffing

1 turkey liver, 10–15 crayfish tails and legs, 1 tbsp crayfish butter, 2 eggs, 1 bread roll soaked in milk, 100 g mushrooms, 1 tbsp chopped parsley, 1 tbsp butter, salt, pepper, ½ tsp sugar

Stew the liver in butter, chop finely and put through a sieve. Add the finely chopped crayfish tails and legs. Mince the crayfish butter with egg yolks, add the finely chopped mushrooms and the bread roll squeezed dry. Combine with the liver and crayfish tails, season with salt, pepper and sugar. Mix well. Beat the egg whites stiff and gently stir in together with chopped parsley. Mix again very gently. Stuff the neck cavity with the mixture.

Preparation: 20 mins

Liver stuffing

500 g veal liver, 2 tbsps breadcrumbs, 100 g pork fat, 2 eggs, 1 tbsp butter, ¼ tsp each ground ginger and nutmeg, sugar, salt, pepper

Put the liver through a mincer and mix it with the finely chopped pork fat. Blend the egg yolks with butter, add seasoning and breadcrumbs. Combine with the liver and pork fat, add the egg whites beaten stiff. Mix well and stuff the neck cavity with the mixture, sew up.

Preparation: 10 mins

Stuffing with raisins and almonds

2 bread rolls soaked in milk and squeezed dry, 2 tbsps butter, 2 eggs, 100 g raisins, 50 g almonds. 1 tbsp sugar, 1 tbsp chopped parsley, ¼ tsp mace, salt

Blend the butter with egg yolks, add the rolls and combine into smooth, uniform consistency. Add the scalded, peeled and finely chopped almonds, scalded raisins and seasoning, and knead smooth pulp. Add the stiff beaten egg whites and mix gently. Stuff the neck cavity and sew.

Preparation: 15 mins

Prune and nut stuffing

½ cup rice, ¼ cup walnut meats, turkey liver, or 100 g veal liver, 50 g raisins, 100 g prunes, ½ tsp cinnamon, ¼ tsp ground cloves, 1 tsp sugar, salt, 3 tbsps butter

Soak the prunes overnight, then cook and cut into thin strips. Finely chop the walnuts, scald the raisins. Cook the rice. Blend the finely chopped liver with butter into smooth pulp, combine with the rice, add the walnuts, prunes, raisins and seasoning. Mix well. Stuff the neck cavity and sew up.

Soaking: 12 hrs • Preparation: 30 mins

Walnut stuffing

500 g veal or chicken liver, 1 bread roll soaked in milk and squeezed dry, 1½ cups walnut meats, 2 tbsps butter, 1 egg, salt, ½ tsp sugar, ¼ tsp nutmeg

In a bowl mix the butter with egg and bread roll into smooth pulp, gradually adding the finely chopped or minced liver, chopped walnuts, salt, sugar and nutmeg. Stuff the neck cavity with the mixture and sew.

Preparation: 20 mins

Double stuffed turkey, Polish style I

1 turkey (turkey hen ca 4–5 kg), salt, grated lemon rind and lemon juice, 100 g butter

STUFFING FOR THE NECK CAVITY: 200 g turkey liver, 2 egg yolks, 100 g raisins, 2 tbsps rum,

2 eggs, 3 tbsps chopped walnuts, 1 tbsp chopped almonds, 1 tbsp breadcrumbs, ¼ tsp each pepper, minced cloves and grated nutmeg, salt

STUFFING FOR THE BODY CAVITY: 400 g roast veal, 100 g pork fat, 4 anchovies or 1 tbsp anchovy paste, 1 tbsp capers, 1 large onion, 2 bread rolls soaked in milk, 1 large onion, 3 eggs, 100 g butter, salt, pepper, nutmeg

SALTING: 1–2 hrs

Rub the washed and dry turkey with salt, grated lemon rind and lemon juice, and set aside in a cool place for 1 hour.
PREPARE THE STUFFING FOR THE NECK CAVITY: Finely chop the liver. Pour the rum over the washed raisins. Blend the butter with 2 egg yolks, gradually adding the liver, raisins, almonds and breadcrumbs. Season to taste with salt, pepper, cloves and nutmeg. Stir in the raisins and stiff beaten egg whites. Stuff the neck cavity with the mixture.
PREPARE THE STUFFING FOR THE BODY CAVITY: Glass the chopped onion in 1 tbsp melted butter, squeeze the bread rolls dry. Cut the veal and pork fat into pieces. Put all the ingredients through a mincer twice, add the capers, anchovy paste, pour in the melted butter, break in the eggs and add salt, pepper and a dash of nutmeg. Knead smooth pulp. Stuff the body cavity and sew up.
Place the turkey in a buttered roasting pan, sprinkle with melted butter and bake for about 3 hours in a preheated oven, sprinkling frequently with water and basting with the pan drippings. If the turkey gets too brown, cover it with aluminium foil. Now arrange the bird cut into serving pieces on an ovenproof warm serving platter, surrounding it with both kinds of stuffing cut into slices. Heat up in the oven. Heat up the pan drippings and serve in a sauceboat. Delicious with cowberry preserve.

serves 10–12 • Preparation: 35–40 mins • Roasting: 3–3½ hrs

Turkey hen with rice stuffing

1 turkey hen (ca 3 kg), 1 tbsp lemon juice, 1 tbsp dried tarragon, salt, 2 tbsps butter

STUFFING: 100 g turkey liver, 1½ cups cooked rice, ½ cup single cream, 1 tbsp lemon juice, 1 cup chopped walnuts, 100 g prunes, 50 g raisins, 1 glass dry white wine, ¼ tsp each ground cinnamon and ground cloves, salt, pepper, 2 tbsps butter

Sprinkle the washed and dry turkey hen with lemon juice and rub it inside and out with salt and tarragon. Wrap in foil and set aside in the fridge overnight.
PREPARE THE STUFFING: Cover the washed prunes and raisins with the wine and set aside for half an hour. Sprinkle the cooked rice with cloves and cinnamon, mix with the cream and set aside for 15–20 mins. Briefly sauté the washed and dried livers in butter (should be pink inside), cool and cut into strips. Drain the prunes and raisins reserving the wine. Cut the prunes in strips, combine with the livers and raisins, walnuts and rice. Mix well and season to taste with salt and pepper. Stuff the bird, sew the cavity and place in a buttered roasting pan. Sprinkle with melted butter and cook in a preheated oven, sprinkling frequently with water and the reserved wine, then basting with the pan drippings. Cook for about 3 hours.

serves 6–10 • Macerating: 12 hrs • Preparation: 30–40 mins • Roasting: 3 hrs

Turkey hen stuffed with olives

1 young turkey hen (ca 3 kg), 300 g fat streaky bacon cut into thin strips, 500 g pitted black olives, 1–2 red onions, 3–4 garlic cloves, 2 tbsps marjoram, salt, 1 tbsp lemon juice, 1 tbsp olive oil, 1 tbsp butter

Mix garlic minced with salt with lemon juice, olive and half of the marjoram. Rub the washed and dried turkey with the mixture inside and out, wrap in foil and stand aside for 1–2 hours in the fridge. Combine the olives with the chopped onion, stuff the bird and sew the cavity. Cover the turkey with strips of bacon and place in a buttered roasting pan. Roast in a preheated oven for over 2 hours, turning the bird over from time to time, sprinkling, if necessary, with water. Delicious with baked potatoes and salads, or with boiled broccoli.

serves 6–10 • Macerating:1–2 hrs • Preparation: 25–30 mins • Roasting: 2–3 hrs

Stuffed turkey breast

*500 g turkey breast, 1 tbsp lemon juice, 7–8 medium-
large firm tomatoes, 3 large leeks, 2 onions,
2 eggs, 2 bunches parsley, 2 bunches chives,
6 slices of toasting bread, 4–5 tbsps grated cheese
(Cheddar type), 1 cup stock, 1 cup white wine,
2 tbsps butter, salt, pepper, grated nutmeg*

Crumble the toasting bread into small pieces, sprinkle with 2 tbsps wine, chop the greens. Finely chop the onions. Mince the bread with the greens, onion, cheese and egg yolks to smooth pulp. Season to taste with salt, pepper and nutmeg, mix with egg whites beaten stiff. Rinse the meat and pat it dry. Sprinkle with lemon juice, rub with salt and cut a pocket for stuffing. Fill the pocket with ⅔ of the stuffing and close it with skewers. Place the meat in a roasting pan and sprinkle with melted butter. Cook it covered for 1½ hours (200°C). Clean and wash the leeks, cut them lengthwise and then into 4 cm pieces. Scald and skin the tomatoes, cut them in halves, remove the seeds, then cut into strips. After 45 mins of baking add the vegetables to the meat. Pour in the stock and the white wine. 20 mins before the end of cooking top the meat with the rest of the stuffing, uncover and continue cooking for another few minutes. Serve in the roasting pan.

serves 4 • Preparation: 15–20 mins • Roasting: 90 mins

Turkey roll with prunes

*1 kg turkey breast, 200 g prunes, 2 tbsps chopped
lemon balm leaves, 1 tsp mustard, 1 tsp lemon juice,
2 eggs, 1 tsp salt, ¼ tsp ground pepper, 2 onions,
1–2 garlic cloves, 3–4 tbsps breadcrumbs, 1 glass dry
white wine, ½ cup double cream, 3 tbsps butter*

Soak the prunes in some water and cut them into thin strips. Lightly beat the washed and dried meat with a pestle and form a rectangle. Sprinkle with lemon juice and salt. Mix the finely chopped onion and garlic with the prunes, lemon balm, salt, pepper, mustard, eggs and breadcrumbs. Form smooth, uniform pulp and spread it on the meat. Roll up tightly and tie with thread. Brown the roll on all sides in melted butter and transfer to a roasting pan. Sprinkle with melted butter and bake in a preheated oven,

frequently basting with wine, then with the pan juices. Towards the end add the cream.

serves 4–6 • Preparation: 15–20 mins • Roasting: 55–75 mins

Honey escalopes

*700 g turkey breast, 1 large onion, 1 garlic clove,
1 tbsp butter, 2 tbsps oil, ¼ cup honey, ¼ cup
dry white wine, 1 tbsp lemon juice, 2 tbsps soya
sauce, 1 tsp finely chopped fresh ginger, 3–4 drops
Tabasco sauce, 2 tbsps ketchup, salt, pepper*

Cut the washed and dried meat into small cutlets and pat them lightly with the end of a knife. Mash the garlic with salt and lemon juice, half of the chopped ginger, 1 tbsp honey, pepper and soy sauce. Place the meat in a bowl, cover with the sauce and set aside in the fridge for a few hours. Turn it over from time to time, so that it marinates evenly on all sides. In a small saucepan mix the wine with the remaining honey and ginger, bring to the boil, add ketchup and Tabasco sauce, and keep on very low heat. In a frying pan heat the oil, add butter and sauté the meat taken out from the marinade. Transfer it to a saucepan with the sauce, add the remaining marinade and simmer together for a while. Serve with French fries, rice or French noodles.

serves 4 • Macerating: 4–7 hrs • Preparation: 5–7 mins • Stewing: 10 mins

Turkey twists

*600 g turkey breast, 2 tbsps lemon juice, 1 tsp
garlic salt, ¼ tsp each curry powder, powdered
ginger and pepper, 2 eggs, 3 tbsps breadcrumbs,
3 tbsps chopped walnuts, oil for frying*

Cut the washed and dried meat into thin long rectangles, sprinkle with seasoning and lemon juice, arrange on a plate, cover and set aside in the fridge for 1 hour. When the meat absorbs the flavours, make a slit through the centre of each strip and put one end through the opening, thus making a loose knot. Whisk the eggs with 1 tbsp fizzy mineral water. Mix the breadcrumbs with nuts. Soak each twist in the beaten eggs, coat with breadcrumbs and fry in hot oil until golden. Serve with boiled potatoes, or French fries and salads.

serves 4 • Marinating: 1 hr • Preparation: 10 mins • Frying: 10 mins

Turkey fillets in wine

600 g turkey breast, 1–2 onions, 2 tbsps hot mustard, ½ cup dry white wine, salt, 2 tbsps grapeseed oil

Grate the onions finely, mix with the olive oil, wine and mustard into smooth pulp. Cut the washed and dried meat into slices of the same size, put into a bowl and cover with the prepared sauce. Set aside in the fridge for 1 hour. Line an ovenproof platter with a large piece of aluminium foil and arrange the meat slices on it, sprinkle with salt and pour the sauce over. Wrap tightly in the foil and bake in a preheated oven for about 40 mins. Serve with French fries or scooped out potato balls, and endive or Chinese cabbage salad.

serves 4 • Macerating: 1–2 hrs • Preparation: 5–7 mins • Roasting: 40 mins

Baked turkey fillets

600 g turkey breast, 1 tsp lemon juice, 1 tin sweetcorn, 1–2 green bell peppers, 3–4 tbsps grated cheese, salt, pepper, 3 tbsps butter, 1 tbsp flour, ¼ cup light stock, ¾ cup single cream, salt, pepper, sugar, 1 tbsp lemon juice, 2 tbsps chopped parsley

Cut the washed and dried meat into 4 slices, lightly pound with the end of a knife, dust with salt and pepper, sprinkle with lemon juice and leave for a few minutes. Roast the bell peppers in the oven just enough to skin them. Remove the cores and seeds, cut the flesh into strips. In a small saucepan melt 1½ tbsps butter, add the flour and make a white roux. Dilute it with the stock, add salt, pepper, sugar and lemon juice. Stir the sauce and heat until thickened, then add the cream and heat again. In a frying pan melt 1 tbsp butter and sauté the fillets. Butter an ovenproof dish, arrange the fillets and surround them with the strips of pepper, sprinkle on the corn, cover with the sauce and sprinkle with the grated cheese. Bake in a preheated oven for about 30 mins. Serve with French fries, rice or noodles with salad.

serves 4 • Macerating: 10–15 mins • Preparation: 10 mins • Baking: 30 mins

Turkey cutlets with almonds

600 g turkey breast, 100 g almond flakes, 2 eggs, 2 tbsps oil, 2 tbsps butter, salt, pepper, 1 tsp lemon juice

Cut the washed and dried meat into 4 slices, lightly pound them with a pestle, sprinkle with lemon juice and dust with salt and pepper. Cut the almond flakes into thin strips. Beat the eggs with 1 tbsp water. Coat the meat slices with eggs, then with almond flakes, press with your hand. In a frying pan heat the oil, arrange the cutlets and fry each side until golden. Transfer when ready to a different frying pan, add the butter and keep warm for a moment. Best with dauphine potatoes and stewed apples stuffed with cowberries.

serves 4 • Macerating: 10–15 mins • Preparation: 5 mins • Frying: 8–10 mins

Marinated turkey cutlets

500 g turkey breast, 3 tbsps chopped chives, 2 cups yogurt, juice and grated rind of 1 large orange, 2–3 garlic cloves, 1 tbsp curry powder, salt, pepper

Mince chopped garlic and cloves with salt, grated orange rind, curry and pepper, stir in orange juice and yogurt. Cut the turkey meat into 4 cutlets and spread half of the marinade over. Set aside in the fridge for 3–4 hours. Place the cutlets in a sieve and drain. Place the sieve over a saucepan with boiling water. Cook the meat for about 15 mins. Pour the remaining marinade into a small saucepan and heat. Arrange the cutlets on a warmed serving platter, sprinkle with chives and pour the sauce over.

serves 4 • Macerating: 3–5 hrs • Steaming: 15 mins

Turkey mini rolls in mustard sauce

about 800 g turkey breast, 750 g potatoes, 3 leeks, 2 cups stock, 1 cup double cream, 1 small jar marinated bell peppers, 2 tbsps oil, 1–2 tbsps mustard, 2 tsps potato flour, 2 tbsps grated cheese, salt, ground white pepper, parsley sprigs for decoration

Clean and wash the leeks. Cut 2 leeks into slices. In a saucepan bring to the boil some water and add the leeks for 2–3 mins. Drain, rinse with cold water and drain again. Peel, wash and slice the potatoes. Grease an ovenproof dish and arrange the strained leeks and slices of potatoes. Sprinkle with salt and white pepper, cover with the cream and spread the grated cheese over the surface. Bake in a preheated oven (200°C) for about 45 mins. Separate the leaves of the remaining leek and cook for 3 mins in salted boiling water. Rinse with cold water and drain. Drain the peppers in a sieve. Cut the meat into 8 thin slices, lightly beat it with a pestle, and rub with salt and pepper. Cover each piece of meat with bell pepper and leek leaves. Roll and close with toothpicks. In a frying pan heat the oil, sear the mini rolls over high heat, frequently turning them over, so that they brown nicely on all sides, then pour in the stock, reduce the heat and simmer covered for about 10–12 mins. Take the tender rolls out, keep them warm. Pour the cream blended with flour and mustard into the same frying pan, mix well and heat the sauce for 2–3 mins until thickened. Then add the mini rolls (remove toothpicks) and heat. Serve with the baked potatoes and leeks, and with lettuce salad.

serves 4–6 • Preparation: 20–30 mins • Stewing: 15–20 mins • Baking: 45 mins

Rolled turkey zrazy with bell peppers

600 g turkey breast, 300 g smoked streaky bacon cut into thin rashers, 1 tbsp lemon juice, salt, pepper, 1 tbsp oil, 1 tbsp butter

STUFFING: 200 g mushrooms, 1 green and 1 red bell peppers, 1 onion, 4–6 tbsps cooked rice, 1 tbsp chopped basil, 2–3 garlic cloves, 2–3 tbsps soya sauce, 2 tbsps oil

Finely chop the washed and dried mushrooms. Wash and core the bell peppers, dry them and cut into fine cubes. In a frying pan heat the oil and sauté the chopped onion, add the mushrooms. Stir and sauté together over high heat. Add the peppers, reduce the heat and fry for 1–2 mins. Remove from the heat, add garlic, rice, soy sauce, basil, salt and pepper and mix thoroughly together. Cut the washed and dried meat into 4 slices, lightly pound with a pestle, sprinkle with lemon juice, and season with salt and pepper. Place a portion of the stuffing on each slice of meat, roll up. Wrap each roll with a rasher, and

close with skewers. In a frying pan heat the oil, add the butter and fry the zrazy. Serve with rice and lettuce salad.

serves 4 • Preparation: 15 mins • Frying: 8–10 mins

Roast turkey legs with hunter's sauce

4 turkey legs, salt, pepper, 1 tbsp oil, 1 tbsp butter

HUNTER'S SAUCE: 2 cups strong stock, 1 tbsp butter, 1 tbsp flour, 100 g streaky bacon, 2 onions, a dash of thyme, ¼ tsp each chopped parsley and tarragon, 100 g mushrooms, 1 glass white wine, 1 tbsp tomato concentrate

Rinse the turkey legs with cold water and dry. Rub with salt and pepper. In a large frying pan heat the oil with 1 tbsp butter and brown the meat. Transfer it to a roasting pan and roast in a preheated (200°C) oven for about 30–40 mins, basting from time to time with the pan drippings. In a very hot deep frying pan, fry the bacon cut into thin strips. Take it out and keep warm. Glass the finely chopped onion in the remaining fat, add the sliced mushrooms and fry for a moment or two, stir. Add the butter, pour in the stock, reduce the heat, cover and continue to cook for a few minutes. Pass through a sieve, add the flour mixed with wine and simmer over low heat, stirring until the sauce thickens. Stir in the tomato concentrate, chopped herbs and season to taste with salt. Add the fried bacon, and for decoration pickled onions and a diced celery stalk. Arrange the turkey legs on an ovenproof platter lined with the strips of fried bacon, pour the sauce over and heat up in a preheated oven for 3–4 mins. Serve with potato pancakes.

serves 4 • Preparation: 20 mins • Roasting: 30–40 mins • Baking: 3–5 mins

Gdańsk turkey goulash with cranberries

800 g turkey breasts, 1 small carrot, 1 small onion, ½ small celeriac, 1 small lemon, 1 tbsp lard, 2 tbsps butter, 100 g cranberries (or 3 tbsps low-sugar cranberry jam), 1 cup dry red wine, 1 cup stock, ½ tsp curry powder, ¼ tsp each ground cinnamon, pepper and grated nutmeg, salt, 1 tbsp flour

Cut the rinsed and dried meat into strips, brown it in very hot lard. In a saucepan melt the butter and sauté the julienned vegetables, add the meat, pour in the stock and braise for about 40 mins. Dredge with salt, pepper, curry, cinnamon, add the peeled lemon cut into cubes (remove pits) and the wine. Stir and simmer together for a moment or two, then thicken with flour blended with 2–3 tbsps stock. Heat up. Serve with rice, noodles or macaroni.

serves 4 • Preparation: 5–7 mins • Stewing: 40 mins

Turkey fricassee

1 kg turkey legs, 2 carrots, 2 parsley roots, ¼ celeriac, 1–2 celery sticks, juice and grated rind of 1 lemon, 1 egg yolk, 1 tbsp butter, 1 tbsp flour, salt, sugar, 4 tbsps finely chopped parsley, ½ cup yogurt

Cook the meat and the vegetables. Take the meat out when tender and reduce the stock to 2 cups. Set aside to cool. In a saucepan melt the butter, add the flour and make a white roux. Combine it with the strained cold stock and simmer and stir until the sauce thickens. Stir in the lemon juice and grated lemon rind, salt and sugar, add the diced meat and heat over low heat. Mix the egg yolk thoroughly with yogurt and parsley, add to the meat, mix and heat lightly (do not bring to the boil).

serves 4–6 • Preparation: 10 mins • Cooking: 40–50 mins

Turkey fricassee with ham

800 g turkey legs (boned out), 150 g ham, 20 g dried mushrooms, 2 tbsps butter, ½ cup stock, 3 tbsps cream, 1 tbsp flour, salt, pepper, ¼ tsp each dried marjoram and thyme, 2 tbsps grated cheese

MARINADE: 1 small carrot, 1 small onion, 1–2 bay leaves, 5–6 peppercorns, 2–3 cloves, 1 tbsps chopped parsley, ¼ tsp dried thyme, sugar, 1 tbsp oil, 1½ cup dry white wine, 1 tbsp lemon juice

Pound the rinsed and dried meat well with your hand, coat with the sliced carrot and onion, and place in an earthenware pot. Blend the remaining ingredients of the marinade and pour over the meat. Cover and place in the fridge for 2–3 days. Turn the meat over every day, so that it marinates evenly on all sides. Soak the washed mushrooms in the stock and bring to the boil. Take the meat out of the marinade, dry and cut into cubes. Cut the ham into cubes uniform in size. In a saucepan melt the butter, add the meat and ham, mix well, add the strained stock and marinade, add the mushrooms cut into strips, salt, pepper, marjoram and thyme, and mix together. Simmer covered over low heat for about 30–40 mins. Blend the cream and flour well, add to the meat, mix and heat until the sauce thickens (do not boil). Best served with white bread in small serving shells, sprinkled with grated cheese, or with rice and salads.

serves 4–6 • Marinating: 2–3 days • Preparation: 30 mins • Baking: 30–40 mins

Stuffed turkey necks in mushroom sauce

4 turkey necks and 1 leg (boned out and skinned) – ca 300 g, 1 tsp lemon juice, 200 g turkey liver, 2 eggs, ¼ cup thick cream, 100 g pistachio nuts, 2 tbsps chopped parsley, 2 tbsps butter, salt, pepper, 2 tbsps vegetable seasoning, 2 peppercorns, 2 allspice berries, 1 bay leaf, 1 onion

SAUCE: 400 g oyster mushrooms, 1 onion, ½ cup double cream, 2–3 tbsps chopped parsley, 2 tbsps grated Parmesan, 2 tbsps butter, salt, pepper

Take the skin of the washed turkey necks. Rub the skin with salt and set aside for 15–20 mins. Then place the necks in a pot, cover with boiling water, add allspice, pepper, bayleaf, onion and dried vegetable stock, bring to the boil and simmer for about 1 hour. Strain (take the meat off the neck bones and use for jelly or goulash). Sprinkle the washed and dried turkey leg meat with lemon juice. Chop the pistachio nuts. Put the meat and liver through a mincer and mix into uniform pulp in a food processor, gradually adding the eggs and cream. Season to taste with salt and pepper, mix well with the chopped parsley and nuts. Stuff the neck skin with the mixture, tie both ends and put into a flat saucepan. Cover with the strained stock and cook over low heat for about 25 mins.

PREPARE THE SAUCE: Sauté the finely chopped mushrooms and onion in butter, sprinkle with 2–3 tbsps stock and simmer for a moment or two. Mix the cream with Parmesan and parsley, add to the mushrooms and stir and simmer gently for about 4–5 mins. Arrange the necks in an ovenproof dish, pour over the sauce and bake in a hot oven for 3–4 mins. Serve with French fries, boiled potatoes or rice and with tomato salad.

serves 4 • Preparation: 40 mins • Cooking: 25 mins • Baking: 4–5 mins

Mexican salad

100 g mushrooms, ¼ tsp each ground pepper and dried thyme, 1 tbsp lemon juice, 1 tin red beans, ½ cup chopped walnuts, ½ small green bell pepper, ½ small yellow bell pepper, 100 g turkey ham, 1 tbsp chopped parsley

DRESSING: 2 tbsps oil, 1 tbsp wine vinegar, salt, a dash of dried basil, hot paprika

Mix thoroughly all the ingredients of the dressing and set aside to cool. Slice the washed and dried mushrooms and sprinkle with lemon juice, thyme and pepper, mix well together and set aside for 15–20 mins. Drain the beans. Core the bell peppers and put them for 3–4 mins into lightly salted boiling water, then drain, and rinse in cold water. Skin the peppers and cut them into cubes, combine with the chopped walnuts, ham cut into strips, beans and mushrooms. Pour the sauce over, mix gently and set aside in a cool place. Before serving, sprinkle with chopped parsley.

serves 4 • Preparation: 5–7 mins • Cooling: 20–30 mins

Turkey salad with watermelon

150 g turkey ham, 300 g watermelon, 100 g cheese (Gouda, Edam), 1 tart apple, 1 tsp lemon juice, ½ tin sweetcorn, 1 large onion, 2 tbsps raisins, mint or lemon balm leaves

DRESSING: ½ cup yogurt, 2 tbsps thick mayonnaise, 1 tbsp liquid honey, 1 tbsp lemon juice, salt, white pepper

Mix well the ingredients of the dressing, cover and set aside in the fridge for 1 hour. Drain the corn, cut the cheese into thin sticks and ham into strips. Remove the seeds from the watermelon and cut the flesh into cubes, or scoop it with a melon baller. Julienne the peeled apple, sprinkle with lemon juice, cut the onion into cubes. Combine the ingredients of the salad, pour the dressing over, mix well and decorate with mint or lemon balm leaves.

serves 4 • Cooling: 1 hr • Preparation: 5–6 mins

Turkey salad with pine nuts

1 turkey breast (ca 600 g), 2 small garlic bulbs, 2 thyme sprigs, 2 rosemary sprigs, ½ cup white wine, ½ tsp grated lemon juice, 1 tbsp olive oil, 1 tbsp butter, 200 g mixed lettuce, 1 tbsp pine nuts, 2 tbsps olive oil, 1 tbsp vinegar, salt, pepper

Peel the garlic and steam cook for 10 mins. Put the turkey breast on a board, sprinkle all over with salt, pepper and grated lemon rind. In a small flat saucepan heat the olive oil, add the meat and brown on both sides. Add the butter, cooked garlic and herbs, sprinkle with the wine, cover and simmer over medium heat for about 45 mins. Take the meat off the heat, set aside to cool a little, and cut into thin strips. Remove the garlic and the herbs from the sauce and heat the sauce over high heat. Steam off the excess liquid. Mix salt and pepper with oil and vinegar. On plates arrange leaves of lettuce and warm meat. Sprinkle with vinaigrette mixed with 2 spoons of the sauce reserved after braising. Sprinkle lightly with roasted pine nuts. Serve immediately.

serves 4–6 • Preparation: 50 mins

Turkey salad with asparagus and fruit

200 g roast turkey breast, 300 g cooked (or tinned) asparagus, 1 banana, 1 apple, 1 smallish orange, 1 tbsp lemon juice, leaves of lemon balm or mint

DRESSING: 3 tbsps thick mayonnaise, 1 tsp honey, 1 tbsp lemon juice, 1 tbsp dry white wine, salt, white pepper, cayenne pepper

Mix well the ingredients of the dressing and set aside to cool. Peel the fruit, core the apple and cut it into sticks, sprinkle with lemon juice. Cut the banana into half-slices, sprinkle with lemon juice, cut the orange into cubes, remove the pits. Cut the meat into cubes, and asparagus into segments. Combine the ingredients of the salad, sprinkle with the dressing, cover and leave in the fridge for 1–1½ hours. Before serving, decorate with the leaves of lemon balm.

serves 4 • Preparation: 5–7 mins • Refrigerating: 1–2 hrs

Turkey salad with new potatoes

250 g new potatoes, unpeeled, 150 g roast turkey or turkey ham, 3 spring onions (white parts and green parts), 3–4 leaves of iceberg lettuce, or the heart of butter lettuce, 5–6 hard-boiled quail eggs, 1 cup redcurrants, ½ cup chopped walnuts

DRESSING: 3 tbsps grapeseed oil, juice and grated rind of ½ lemon, 1 tsp liquid honey, 1 tsp hot mustard, 1 tbsp dry white wine or water, salt, pepper

Mix well the ingredients of the dressing, set aside to cool. Cut the ham and lettuce into strips, potatoes into cubes, finely chop the onions and chives. Cut the eggs lengthwise in half. Combine the ingredients of the salad, pour the sauce over, sprinkle with the currants and toss gently.

serves 4 • Preparation: 10 mins

Turkey salad with new potatoes

Turkey galantine

600–700 g turkey breast, 1 tbsp lemon juice

STUFFING: 250 g turkey thighs (boned out), 1 bread roll soaked in milk and squeezed dry, 100 g mushrooms, 1 tbsp butter, 3–4 tbsps finely chopped parsley, dried thyme, salt, pepper, ground allspice and grated lemon rind, 1 tbsp thick cream, 1 egg, 2 cups stock, 2 tbsps deep-frozen spinach, 1 egg white, 1 tbsp gelatine

Make a lengthwise incision in the meat. Lightly pound the breast with a pestle into a nice even fillet, sprinkle with lemon juice, wrap in foil and put into the fridge. Cut the mushrooms into small cubes and sauté in butter. Sprinkle them with grated lemon rind and thyme, mix well and remove from the heat. Put the washed and dried turkey thighs and bread roll through a mincer, add the mushrooms, chopped parsley, cream, salt, pepper and nutmeg, break in the egg and knead the whole into smooth paste. Place the stuffing on the fillet and roll. Wrap with a piece of gauze or linen cloth and put into a flat saucepan, cover with hot stock and bring to the boil. Cover and cook over low heat for about 40 mins. Remove, place on a wooden board, cover with another board, weigh it down and set aside to cool. Dissolve the gelatine in 3–4 tbsps cold stock. Reduce the remaining stock to 1 cup. Add the spinach, bring to the boil, then pass through a sieve. Add the aspic and heat up, stirring all the time. Add the egg white mixed with 1 tbsp water, clarify the stock for aspic and strain through a fine sieve. Unwrap the cold galantine, arrange on a deep narrow serving platter and cover with the cold aspic. Leave aside until set. Before serving you can cut the galantine into slices.

serves 4–6 • Marinating: 1–2 hrs • Preparation: 20 mins • Cooking: 40–50 mins • Refrigerating: 1–2 hrs

Turkey roll with buckwheat grits

800–900 g turkey breast, salt, pepper, 1 tbsp juice and ¼ tsp grated lemon rind, 1 tsp crushed rosemary, 3 tbsps butter, 5–6 dried mushrooms, 2 cups buckwheat grits, 1 small onion, 1 tbsp butter, ½ tsp dried thyme, 1 tbsp lemon juice, 1 egg, salt, pepper

Cover the washed mushrooms with cold boiled water and set aside overnight. Cook the following day. Cut the washed and dried meat lengthwise, enough to open it up (do not cut all the way through). Put on a board and pound with a pestle to form a large rectangle. Rub with salt and pepper on both sides, sprinkle with lemon juice, grated lemon rind and rosemary and set aside for 1 hour. Sprinkle the cooked kasha with lemon juice, salt and pepper and mix well. Glass the chopped onion in butter, add the chopped and cooked mushrooms, sprinkle with thyme and stir and fry for a moment or two. Remove from the heat, set aside and when cool combine with the kasha. Break in the egg and form a smooth paste. Place the meat on the board, spread the stuffing on it and roll up. Tie the roll with thread and place in a buttered roasting pan. Sprinkle with melted butter and put into a preheated (220°C) oven. Roast for about 1 hour, basting with the reserved mushroom stock and pan drippings. Serve hot or cold.

serves 4–6 • Soaking: 12 hrs • Preparation: 20 mins • Roasting: 1 hr

Turkey liver mousse

600 g turkey livers, 2–3 garlic cloves, 2 tbsps mustard, 5 egg whites, 1 tsp dried tarragon, ¼ tsp grated lemon rind, salt, pepper, 2 tbsps butter, 1 tbsp breadcrumbs and ground sunflower seeds

Mince garlic with salt. Put the washed livers (remove the membrane) through a mincer and combine with the garlic, pepper, tarragon, grated lemon rind and mustard. Add the stiff beaten egg whites and mix gently together. Butter individual ovenproof serving shells. Sprinkle with breadcrumbs blended with sunflower seeds and fill with the pulp. Place the shells in a form filled with water, cover with foil and put into a preheated (200°C) oven. Bake for about 15 mins. Remove the foil and let brown lightly. Before serving decorate with parsley sprigs and slices of lemon or rings of colourful bell peppers.

serves 4 • Preparation: 10 mins • Baking: 15 mins

Hot snack of turkey livers with plum sauce

8 turkey livers, 16 hazelnuts, 16 thin strips smoked streaky bacon, ½ tsps ground ginger, ½ cup soy sauce

SAUCE: 4 tbsps plum jam, 2 tbsps soy sauce, 2 tbsps lemon juice. Mix together into uniform sauce

Cut the washed livers into half, lard each half with a nut, wrap in a bacon strip and fasten with a toothpick. Place the livers in an ovenproof dish, cover with the soy sauce blended with ginger and set aside in the fridge for 1–1½ hours. Then bake in a preheated oven for 15 mins. Before serving, decorate with parsley sprigs. Serve the sauce separately.

serves 4 • Preparation: 10 mins • Cooling: 1–2 hrs • Baking: 15 mins

Turkey gizzards stuffed with meat

1 kg goose or turkey gizzards, 500 g minced meat (pork, veal), 1 onion, salt, pepper, nutmeg, 1 tbsp breadcrumbs, 1 egg, 1 tbsp butter, 1 tbsp lard

Sauté the finely chopped onion in fat, combine with the minced meat, breadcrumbs and egg. Season to taste with salt, pepper and nutmeg and knead to a smooth consistency. Cook the cleaned gizzards in salted water and when half tender remove and fill with the prepared stuffing. Fasten the stuffed gizzards with toothpicks and sauté in lard, transfer to a saucepan, sprinkle with the gizzard stock and braise covered for about 30 mins, basting with water. Serve with rice, noodles or potatoes and salad.

serves 6–8 • Cooking: 40 mins • Preparation: 10 mins • Baking: 30 mins

Baked turkey liver with potatoes

400 g turkey liver, ½ cup milk, 3–4 large potatoes cooked in their skins, 1 large tart apple, 1 tbsp lemon juice, 1½ cups cream, 2 eggs, 4 tbsps chopped parsley, 1 tsp marjoram, 1 tsp vegetable seasoning, ¼ tsp nutmeg, salt, pepper, 3 tbsps butter

Cover the cleaned and washed livers with milk and set aside for half an hour. Remove, dry and cut into pieces. Fry the livers in melted butter (1 tbsp), sprinkle with salt and pepper. Cut the onion in half-slices, place in a sieve, scald, and drain. Peel the potatoes, cut them in slices and arrange on a flat serving platter sprinkling with 1 tbsp melted butter and dredging with marjoram. Peel and core the apple, cut it into slices and sprinkle with lemon juice. Blend the cream well with the eggs, vegetable seasoning, salt, pepper, nutmeg and chopped parsley. Butter an ovenproof dish, line it with the slices of apples, top with the livers, onion and potatoes, pour over the cream sauce and bake in a preheated oven for about 30 mins. Serve with spicy salads.

serves 4 • Soaking: 30 mins • Preparation: 20 mins • Baking: 30 mins

Duck

Duck does not admittedly have such good meat as turkey, nor such delicate meat as chickens or poulards, but gourmands consider that in the autumn this is the best of poultry.

Ducks from 8 to 10 weeks old, when they weigh 2 to 3 kg, have the best flavour. Their meat is dark and tender, although unfortunately indigestible. 100 g of duck meat contains 240 kcal. It is a good source of protein, phosphorus, iron, potassium and B group vitamins; but it has more fat than chicken and has a higher calorie count. Duck can be roasted, fried, stewed and braised. The choice of the right seasoning and accompaniments is very important, since they bring out the flavour and aroma of the duck meat. Jellied duck and duck galantine are excellent duck dishes.

The aroma of duck roast with apples or oranges is wonderful. Duck can also be roasted with peaches, pineapple, figs, cherries and many other fruits; it can be stuffed with macaroni or mushrooms; it can be served glazed with honey, or stewed, or cooked with mushrooms and pearl barley, or in caper, tomato or onion sauce. Because there is almost no meat on the wings, they should be cut off if the duck is to be roasted, and the cleaned duck should then be rubbed with salt.

Fat ducks should be well basted with water during roasting, so that after the water has evaporated the duck will roast in its own fat.

Boiled or fried potatoes and any kind of salad, with fresh, marinated or stewed apples, can be served with roast duck that has not been stuffed.

Older birds are best used for ragout or risotto, and duck's giblets can be stewed in parsley or dill sauce.

It is now ever easier to buy duck portions – breast, boned breast, skinned fillets, or in other words the best parts of the bird. We should not be put off by the higher price of these portions, since in contrast with a whole duck nothing is wasted.

Duck stewed in caper sauce

Stew a cleaned and salted duck in butter in a pan, covering it with stock. When it is tender and browned, carve it in the usual way. Make a dark roux with half a tablespoon of butter and half a tablespoon of flour, thin it with the duck gravy and stock. Add two tablespoons of soaked capers and some caramel to brown the sauce, squeeze in a little lemon juice and place the duck back in the sauce. Simmering it for a quarter of an hour. Serve surrounded with macaroni or noodles.

(Maria Ochorowicz-Monatowa, *Uniwersalna książka kucharska*)

Duck galantine

1 duck (1½ kg), salt, 1 tbsp lemon juice, 200 g veal, 150 g pork, 200 g chicken livers, 1 bread roll soaked in milk and squeezed dry, 2 eggs, salt, pepper, 1 tsp grated nutmeg, 6–8 cocktail gherkins, 4–6 hard-boiled quail eggs, ½ each red and yellow bell peppers

ASPIC: 1 chicken carcass, soup vegetables, 1 washed unpeeled onion larded with 1 clove, 1 bay leaf, a few peppercorns and allspice grains, grated rind of ½ lemon, 1–2 tbsps gelatine

Wash the duck and cut off the neck and ends of wings. Place the duck breast down, cut lengthwise and bone the bird out trying not to damage the skin. Rub the skin with salt, sprinkle with lemon juice and set aside in a cool place. Put the chicken carcass and the duck bones in a pot, add the peeled and washed vegetables, onion and seasoning, cover with 4 cups of water, bring to the boil, then cook over low heat for about 1 hour.

STUFFING: Put the bread roll, veal, pork and liver through a mincer, add salt, pepper, nutmeg and the egg yolks. Form smooth pulp and add the stiff beaten egg whites. Mix together gently but thoroughly. Put the duck on a board and spread it with the mixture. Top with the cocktail gherkins, strips of red and yellow bell peppers and quail eggs. Roll and tie with thread. Place the duck in a saucepan, cover with the strained stock and bring to the boil. Reduce the heat and simmer gently for about 2 hours. Leave in the stock to cool, then take the meat out and place on a board, cover with another board and weigh it down.

Strain and cool the stock. Dissolve the gelatine in 1 cup cold stock. Bring to the boil the remaining stock and reduce to 1½ cups. Pour in the gelatine, mix well and bring to the boil. Pour half of the aspic into a deep dish, leave aside to set. Arrange the duck roll on top (remove thread!), pour over the remaining aspic and set aside in the fridge for a few hours. Before serving, cut into slices and decorate.

serves 4–6 • Macerating: 60 mins • Preparation: 90 mins • Cooking: 2 hrs • Refrigerating: 1–2 hrs

Duck, Polish style with peaches

1 duck (ca 1½–2 kg), 1 tbsp lemon juice, 1 tbsp marjoram, 1 tsp salt, 2 onions, 500 g peaches, 1 glass rum, 1 tsp sugar, 1 tbsp potato flour, 1 glass dry white wine, ¼ tsp ground ginger, ¼ tsp cinnamon, 1 tbsp lard, 2 tbsps butter

Mix salt with marjoram and lemon juice and rub the washed and dried duck inside and out with the mixture. Wrap in foil and set aside in a cool place for 2–3 hours. Heat the lard in a roasting pan and sear the duck on all sides. Add the finely chopped onion and fry together over high heat for a few moments. Reduce the heat, sprinkle the duck with half of the rum, pour the wine over, cover and braise over low heat for about 1½ hours. Scald the peaches, peel and cut lengthwise in half, remove the stones. Place the peach halves in a flat saucepan, sprinkle with sugar and a little water and stew covered for 2–3 mins. Take the duck out when tender, and divide into serving pieces.

Arrange the meat in a buttered ovenproof dish, surround with peach halves. Sieve the duck juices and combine with the peach juices, cinnamon, ginger and the remaining rum. Bring to the boil, stir in the potato flour mixed with 1 tbsp water and heat up until the sauce thickens. Pour part of the sauce over the duck and bake in a preheated oven for a few minutes. Serve the remaining sauce in a sauceboat. Serve the duck with macaroni, French noodles or rice.

serves 4–6 • Marinating: 2–3 hrs • Preparation: 15 mins • Roasting: 90 mins • Baking: 5–7 mins

Duck salad with avocado

2 avocado pears, 300 g roast duck breast (remove the skin), 200 g mushrooms, 2 tbsps juice of ½ lemon, 1 garlic clove, thyme, 2 red onions, 6–7 leaves iceberg lettuce, 1 tbsp chopped thyme leaves

DRESSING: 4 tbsps thick mayonnaise, 2 tbsps soya sauce, 2 tbsps lemon juice, 1 tsp liquid honey, salt, pepper

Mix well all the ingredients of the dressing, set aside in the fridge. Mix 1 tbsp lemon juice with the garlic minced with salt and dried thyme. Slice the washed and dried mushrooms and mix with the dressing. Cover and set aside in the fridge for a few minutes. Cut the onion into half-slices, tear the washed and dried lettuce into pieces. Cut the avocado flesh into sticks and sprinkle with lemon juice. Cut the duck meat into strips. Combine the ingredients of the salad, pour the dressing over, mix well and sprinkle with thyme.

serves 4–6 • Macerating: 20–30 mins • Preparation: 10 mins

Duck breast salad with lamb's lettuce

150 g lamb's lettuce (corn salad), 400 g roast duck breast (remove the skin), 100 g farfallini, 6–8 cherry tomatoes, 6–8 hard-boiled quail eggs

DRESSING: 4–5 tbsps olive oil, 2 tbsps lemon juice (or wine vinegar), ½ tsp dried tarragon, salt, pepper, sugar

Mix well the ingredients of the dressing, set aside to cool slightly. Cook the farfallini in salted water, drain, set aside to cool. Cut the duck breast into thin strips, rinse the lamb's lettuce and drain. Combine the farfallini with the lamb's lettuce and meat, add 3–4 quail eggs cut into halves, 3–4 cherry tomatoes, pour the dressing over and toss gently. Decorate with the remaining halves of quail eggs and tomatoes.

serves 4–6 • Cooking: 10–12 mins • Preparation: 5–6 mins

Duck in wine aspic

duck breast (ca 700 g), 1 tbsp oil, 1 tsp each dried marjoram, dried mint and dried oregano, ¼ tsp ground cloves, salt, pepper, 1 tbsp lemon juice, 2 oranges, ½ cup green peas (fresh cooked or tinned), a few lemon slices

ASPIC: 1 cup dry red wine, 1 cup boiled water, 2 tbsps sugar, 1 tsp salt, 2–3 cloves, 1 tsp grated lemon rind and juice of 1 lemon, 3–4 tsps gelatine

Mix the herbs well with cloves, salt, pepper, lemon juice and oil. Rub the washed and dried duck breasts with the mixture, wrap in aluminium foil and set aside in the fridge for 2–3 hours. Put the meat into a warmed roasting pan, sprinkle with water, cover and braise for about 1 hour, basting from time to time with water. Take the meat out when tender, set aside to cool, bone out and cut into nice, regular slices.
ASPIC: Put the wine and water into a saucepan, add salt, sugar, cloves, lemon juice and zest, and bring to the boil. Reduce the heat, cover and simmer over low heat for 4–5 mins. Mix the gelatine with 3–4 tbsps cold water and, when dissolved, add to the wine, mix and heat, then put through a sieve. Pour in a thin layer of aspic on the bottom of a deep bowl and leave to set. In the middle arrange the green peas, then surround the green peas with orange sections and pour over the aspic. When set, arrange the portions of the duck, and add the remaining aspic. Cover with foil and put into the fridge. Then turn onto a round serving platter, decorate with slices of lemon and parsley sprigs.

serves 4–6 • Macerating: 2–3 hrs • Stewing: 1 hr • Preparation: 20–30 mins • Refrigerating: 1–2 hrs

Duck roll with hazelnuts

1 duck (ca 1½ kg), 1 tbsp lemon juice, salt, pepper, 200 g pork fat, 2 eggs, 2 tbsps marjoram, 4–6 garlic cloves, 2 tbsps chopped hazelnuts, 250 g prunes, 1 glass dry white wine, 2 tbsps grapeseed oil

Cut the washed duck and remove the bones trying not to damage the skin. Cut out the fat and part of the meat. Rub the duck skin inside and out with salt, pepper and lemon juice, wrap in foil and set aside for 1 hour. STUFFING: Put the prunes in a small bowl, cover with the wine and set aside for 1 hour. Pass the meat from the duck's legs, reserved fat, meat and pork fat through a mincer, add the garlic minced with salt and pepper, nuts and marjoram. Pour in the wine in which the prunes were soaking, break in the eggs and work into smooth pulp. Arrange the stuffing on the skin of the duck. Put the prunes in the middle, roll, tie with thread and wrap in aluminium foil. Bake in a preheated oven for about 1½ hours. Leave in the oven to cool. Remove the foil and brown the meat on all sides in melted butter. Cut into serving pieces when cold, arrange on a serving platter on lettuce leaves and decorate with parsley.

serves 4–6 • Macerating: 1–2 hrs • Preparation: 30 mins • Baking: 1½ hrs

Roast duck with savory

1 duck (about 2 kgs), salt, pepper, 1 tbsp lemon juice, ¼ tsp grated lemon rind, a dash of dried savory, 500 g green peas (fresh cooked or deep-frozen), 1 large onion, 4–5 sprigs fresh savory

Mix 1 tbsp butter with the lemon juice and zest, salt, pepper and savory. Rub the washed and dried duck with the mixture and set aside in a cool place for 1 hour. Place in a roasting pan. Put 2–3 savory sprigs inside the duck, sprinkle with melted butter and roast in a preheated oven, basting from time to time with the stock (½ cup) and with the pan drippings. In a saucepan melt the butter, sauté the finely chopped onion, mix with honey, add the peas and pour in the remaining stock. Stir in the chopped fresh savory and simmer over low heat for about 25 mins. Season with salt and pepper to taste. Cut the tender meat into serving pieces, arrange in an ovenproof dish, surround with the peas and put into a preheated oven. Serve the strained meat juices in a sauceboat. Serve with boiled or roast potatoes.

serves 4–6 • Macerating: 1–2 hrs • Preparation: 35–40 mins • Roasting: 90 mins

Duck in honey glaze

1 duck (ca 2 kg), 2 onions, 2 carrots, 2 celery stalks, 2 thyme sprigs, 2–3 tbsps honey, 1 cup dry red wine, 1 tbsp butter, 1 tbsp oil, 1½ tbsps lemon juice, salt, pepper

Peel and slice the onions, carrots and celery. Take the leaves out of 1 thyme sprig and chop. Mix well the lemon juice with oil, 1 tbsp honey, chopped thyme leaves, salt, pepper and 1 tbsp red wine. Rub the washed and thoroughly dried duck inside and out with the mixture, wrap in foil and set aside for 1 hour. Remove from the foil, tie the wings and legs and place the bird in a buttered roasting pan. Sprinkle with melted butter and bake in a very hot oven for about 15 mins. Turn over, brown and reduce the heat. Surround the meat with slices of vegetables, add a thyme sprig and continue to roast, rubbing the duck with melted butter, and from time to time basting it with the pan drippings. Remove the tender meat, cut it into serving portions and place in an ovenproof dish. Blend the pan drippings with an electric mixer, put through a sieve, pour in the wine and bring to the boil. Season to taste with salt and pepper and steam off the excess liquid.

serves 4–6 • Marinating: 1 hr • Preparation: 30 mins • Roasting: 1½–2 hrs

Stuffed duck, Lvov style

*1 duck (ca 2 kg), 1 tbsp lemon juice, salt, 100 g
smoked ham or sirloin, 6–8 small mushrooms,
2 tbsps butter, ¼ cup each white wine and water*

*STUFFING: 500 g minced veal, 1 small bread roll soaked
in milk, 200 g chopped hazelnuts, 3 tbsps chopped
parsley, salt, pepper, ¼ tsp ground ginger, sugar,
a dash of grated nutmeg, 2 eggs, 2 tbsps butter*

Cut off the wings and neck, remove the bones, wash,
dry and rub the meat with salt and lemon juice. Set
aside in a cool place for 1 hour.
PREPARE THE STUFFING: Mix the butter with bread
roll (squeezed dry), salt, pepper, ginger, nutmeg, sugar,
chopped hazelnuts and parsley. Combine with the veal,
break in the eggs and form uniform, smooth pulp.
Stuff the duck, sew the cavities and brown the bird in
melted butter. Put into a preheated oven, surround with
the mushrooms and ham cut into thin strips, sprinkle with
water and roast for about 2 hours, basting with water and
wine, then with the pan juices. Serve hot with French fries
or noodles, or cold, cut into thin slices.

serves 4–6 • Salting: 2 hrs • Preparation: 30–40 mins • Roasting: 2 hrs

Duck stuffed with macaroni and mushrooms

*2 young ducks, 500 g home made macaroni
(or thin spaghetti), 3 tbsps butter, 100 g dried
mushrooms, 50 g smoked ham, 2 eggs, salt,
¼ tsp each white pepper and ground cloves, 1 tsp
lemon juice, 1 cup double cream, 1 egg yolk*

Cover the washed mushrooms with lukewarm boiled
water, set aside for the night and cook the following
day. De-bone the dressed and washed ducks, rub with
salt, pepper and cloves, sprinkle with lemon juice, wrap in
foil and place in the fridge for 2–3 hours. Chop half of the
mushrooms very finely and sauté in 1 tbsp melted butter.
Cook the macaroni al dente, drain and mix with the diced
ham and 2 eggs, mushrooms, salt and pepper. Stuff the
ducks with the mixture and arrange in a buttered roasting
pan. Roast in a very hot oven for about 20–30 mins. When

the ducks turn brown, pour the mushroom stock over,
cover and braise until tender. Take the ducks out, cut them
into serving pieces, put back into the oven to keep warm.
Cut the remaining mushrooms into thin strips. Blend the
cream well with the raw egg yolk. Steam off the pan juices,
add the mushrooms, pour in the cream, mix well, season
to taste with salt and pepper, and heat up.

*serves 6–8 • Soaking: 12 hrs Marinating: 3 hrs •
Preparation: 40 mins • Roasting: 2 hrs*

Duck stuffed with mushrooms

*1 duck (ca 2 kg), 1 tbsp lemon juice, 1 tbsp
olive oil, salt, pepper, ¼ tsp grated nutmeg,
1 tbsp butter, ¼ cup light stock*

*STUFFING: 250 g mushrooms, 150 g grated cheese,
50 g smoked streaky bacon, duck liver and gizzard,
3 tbsps chopped parsley, 1 tbsp chopped fresh thyme,
3 tbsps minced sunflower seeds, 1 tbsp breadcrumbs,
2 tbsps butter, 1 egg, salt, pepper, grated nutmeg*

Rub the duck with a mixture of salt, pepper, dash of
nutmeg, lemon juice and olive oil and set aside in the
fridge for 1–2 hours.
PREPARE THE STUFFING: Put the duck gizzard for a few
minutes into lightly salted boiling water, drain, rinse with
cold water and cut into thin strips. Finely cut the washed
and dried mushrooms, then sauté them in melted butter.
Cut the bacon and duck liver into small cubes and together
with the gizzard add to the mushrooms. Mix well and fry
together for a moment. Remove from the heat, add parsley, thyme, sunflower seeds and cheese, season to taste
with salt, pepper and a dash of nutmeg, break in the egg
and form smooth pulp. If too liquid, add breadcrumbs.
Stuff the duck, sew the cavities and place in a roasting pan.
Sprinkle with melted butter and roast for over 1½ hours,
basting with the stock and later with the meat juices.

*serves 4–6 • Marinating: 1–2 hrs • Preparation:
20–25 mins • Baking: 90–120 mins*

Duck with walnut stuffing

*1 duck (ca 2 kg), 1 tsp grated marjoram, salt,
½ tsp nutmeg, 1 tsp butter, 8 tart apples,*

8 cloves, 1 tbsp lemon juice, 1–2 tbsp chopped walnuts, 1 tbsp butter, 1 tbsp honey

STUFFING: 100 g ground walnuts, 50 g raisins, 1 duck (or turkey) liver, 3 eggs, 2 tbsps butter, ¼ tsp grated nutmeg, 1½ tbsp breadcrumbs, ¼ tsp sugar, salt

Mince marjoram with salt, nutmeg and butter. Rub the washed and dried duck with the mixture, wrap in foil and put into the fridge for 2–3 hours.
PREPARE THE STUFFING: Scald and drain the raisins. Finely chop the washed and dried liver. Blend the butter with egg yolks until frothy, gradually adding the chopped liver, walnuts, nutmeg and sugar, then add the raisins, breadcrumbs and stiff beaten egg whites. Mix together gently but thoroughly. Stuff the duck with the mixture and sew the cavities. Place the bird in a buttered roasting pan, dab with knobs of butter and roast in a preheated oven, often basting with water, then with the pan drippings. Core the apples and sprinkle them with lemon juice. Mince the walnuts with butter and stuff the apple cavities with the mixture. Lard each apple with a clove. After 40 mins of roasting, arrange the apples around the duck and continue to roast for over 1 hour. If the duck turns too brown, cover it with aluminium foil or greaseproof paper. Divide the duck when ready into serving pieces, arrange on a serving platter and surround with the apples. Serve the pan drippings in a sauceboat.

serves 4–6 • Marinating: 2–3 hrs • Preparation: 40 mins • Roasting: 2 hrs

Duck roll

1 duck (ca 1½–2 kg), salt, 1 tbsp lemon juice, 100 g pork fat

STUFFING: 200 g veal, 200 g pork, duck giblets, 1 bread roll soaked in milk and squeezed dry, 100 g mushrooms, 1 tbsp marjoram, salt, pepper, 2 eggs

STOCK: 300 g veal bones (or 2 chicken carcasses), duck bones, soup vegetables, 1 onion, 1 bay leaf, 1–2 cloves, 5–6 peppercorns, 5–6 allspice berries, 2 tbsps wine vinegar

Cut the washed and dried duck along the breast bone, remove all bones trying not to damage the skin. Flatten the meat lightly with a rolling pin, rub with salt and lemon juice, wrap in foil and put into the fridge. Cook the bones with vegetables and spices to make a stock.
PREPARE THE STUFFING: Put the pork, veal, duck giblets and bread roll twice through a mincer. Sauté the sliced mushrooms in butter, add to the meat together with egg yolks, salt, pepper and marjoram, and form smooth, uniform pulp, mixing it with the stiff beaten egg whites. Stuff the duck, sew the cavities and coat the bird with strips of pork fat. Wrap in gauze or linen cloth, place in a saucepan and cover with the sieved stock. Cover and cook over low heat for about 2 hours. Serve hot or cold, with spicy sauces and jelly made of the stock in which the duck was cooking.

serves 4–6 • Marinating: 1–2 hrs • Preparation: 40–50 mins • Cooking: 2 hrs

Braised young duck

1 duck (ca 1½ kg), salt, pepper, 1 tbsp lemon juice, 1 carrot, 1 parsley root, 2 celery stalks or ½ celeriac, 3 onions, 4–5 sprigs parsley, 1½ tbsps butter, 1 tsp flour, 1 cup chicken stock, 10–12 marinated mushrooms

Peel the vegetables, wash and cut into pieces. Sprinkle the washed and dried duck with the lemon juice and ligthly rub with salt and pepper. Set aside in a cool place for 1 hour. In a big flat saucepan melt the butter and sear the duck on all sides, add the vegetables and the hot stock. Cover and simmer for about 1½ hours. Take the meat out when tender, cut into serving pieces and remove the bones. Put the meat juices through a sieve, season to taste with salt, pepper and a dash of sugar, heat up. Stir in the flour mixed with 1 tbsp water and cook until the sauce thickens. Add the marinated mushrooms and the meat, and heat up. Serve with pearl barley or noodles.

serves 4 • Marinating: 1–2 hrs • Preparation: 10 mins • Stewing: 90 mins

Roast duck with oranges

1 duck (ca 2 kg), 4 oranges, 3 tbsps butter, 1 tbsp olive oil, salt, pepper, ½ cup dry white wine, 1 glass cognac, 1 tbsp lemon juice

Rub the washed and dried duck with salt and pepper, sprinkle with lemon juice and set aside in a cool place for 1 hour. Scald the oranges and peel them with a sharp knife. Put the rind into a small saucepan, cover with boiling water and cook for about 10 mins. Cut the rind of 3 oranges into thin strips, place it in a small bowl, pour in the cognac and cover. Add the remaining rind to the duck. Oil a roasting pan and arrange the duck dabbed with knobs of butter. Roast in a very hot oven until golden brown, then reduce the heat and continue to roast sprinkling the duck with the wine and the juice of 3 oranges and then basting with the meat juices. Remove the duck when tender, cut into serving pieces and discard the strips of orange rind. Arrange the pieces of duck in an ovenproof dish, sprinkle with the orange rind soaked in brandy. Cut the remaining orange into slices (remove any pits) and cover the meat. Put the dish into a preheated oven for a few minutes, heat up. Put the meat juices through a sieve, heat up and serve in a sauceboat.

serves 4–6 • Marinating: 1–2 hrs • Preparation: 1–2 hrs • Roasting: 90 mins • Baking: 5–7 mins

Duck roast with oranges, Polish style

1 duck (ca 1½ kg), 150 g chicken livers, 50 g orange marmalade, 3 tbsps lemon juice, salt, pepper, 2 tbsps butter, 1 glass dry white wine, 4 tbsps chopped walnuts, 1 tsp grated orange rind, 2 tbsps cognac, 4 oranges, 4 egg yolks, ¼ tsp sugar

Finely chop the washed and dried livers and blend them with 1 tsp butter, finely chopped walnuts, marmalade and grated orange rind, cognac, salt and pepper. Rub the washed and dried duck with salt, pepper and lemon juice, spoon the stuffing into the body cavity and sew closed. Place in a buttered roasting pan, sprinkle with melted butter and roast in a very hot oven over high heat until brown. Reduce the heat, and continue to roast, sprinkling the bird with the wine and juice of 1 orange, then basting with the meat juices. Cut the peeled oranges into cubes and remove the pips. Divide the bird when tender into serving pieces, arrange in an ovenproof dish and put for a few minutes into the hot oven to heat up. Put the meat juices through a sieve, and pour into a small saucepan. Add the raw egg yolks. Place the saucepan in a pot with boiling water. Beat the sauce over steam with a wire whisk for about 10 mins,

or until thick. Season to taste with salt, pepper and sugar, combine with the orange cubes, heat up. Pour some of the sauce over the duck just before serving, serve the remaining sauce in a sauceboat.

serves 4 • Preparation: 30 mins • Roasting: 1 hr • Baking: 10 mins

Marinated duck breasts

900 g duck breasts, 2 red onions, 2 oranges, 2–3 garlic cloves, 1 tsp freshly chopped ginger, ¼ tsp Chinese seasoning 'Five Spices', ¼ tsp ground juniper berries, 1 glass dry red wine, salt, pepper, 2 tbsps butter, 2–3 drops sesame oil, 1 tsp potato flour or cornstarch

MARINADE: 1 glass cognac, ¼ tsp grated lemon rind, 1 tbsp balsamic vinegar

Place the washed and dried meat in a bowl. Blend the cognac with grated lemon rind and vinegar and sprinkle the meat with the mixture. Cover and set aside in a cool place for 40–60 mins.
SAUCE: In a saucepan melt 1 tsp butter, add the chopped onion and sauté for a moment or two, stir. Dredge with juniper and Chinese seasoning, add honey and ginger, stir in the juice of 1 orange and wine. Cook over medium heat, stirring all the time. Season to taste with salt and pepper, remove from the heat, cover. In a frying pan melt the butter and sauté the duck breasts for 7–8 mins each side. Divide the fried breasts into 4 serving pieces, make an incision in each piece. Put the meat back into the frying pan, sprinkle with sesame oil and heat up for a moment. Heat up the sauce, add the potato flour diluted with 1 tbsp cold water. Stir and heat until the sauce thickens. Arrange the pieces of meat on a warmed serving platter, top with the sauce, surround with French fries. Serve with stewed red cabbage.

serves 4 • Marinating: 1 hr • Preparation: 20–30 mins

Duck breasts in pear sauce

800 g duck breast (or 1 young duck), 2 tbsps lemon juice, ¼ tsp dried thyme, 800 g firm juicy pears, 1–2 onions, ¼ cup water or dry white wine, ¾ cup cream, 1tbsp chopped thyme leaves, 1 tbsp

Marinated duck breasts

chopped parsley, ½ cinnamon stick, 1 clove, 1 bay leaf, salt, pepper, 4 tbsps butter, 1 tsp sugar

Mix 1 tbsp lemon juice with 2 tbsps butter, salt and thyme, rub the washed and dried duck breasts with the mixture. Wash, peel and core the pears, sprinkle them with lemon juice (1 tbsp). Spread the pear peel on a large piece of aluminium foil, place the duck breasts on top, wrap up and put in a roasting pan. Bake in a preheated oven for about 50 mins, then unwrap and lightly brown the meat.
SAUCE: Cut half of the pears into small cubes. In a saucepan melt 1½ tbsps butter and glaze the finely chopped onions, add the pears, bay leaf, cinnamon, clove, salt and pepper, and sauté for a moment or two, stir. Sprinkle with water, add the wine and simmer for about 20 mins. Remove the bay leaf, cinnamon and clove, leave aside to cool, blend in an electric mixer, put through a sieve and add to the saucepan. Season to taste, bring to the boil, stir in the cream and heat for about 5–6 mins. Bring to the boil some water with sugar and 1 tsp butter, add the halves of the remaining pears and cook for 2–3 mins, then take them out and drain. Arrange the meat cut into slices on a warmed serving platter, surround with pear halves and pour over the sauce. Best served with French noodles or pasta.

serves 4 • Preparation: 10 mins • Roasting: 50 mins • Cooking: 50 mins

Duck breasts in hazelnut sauce

600 g duck breast (off the bone), 1 tbsp lemon juice, 200 g chopped hazelnuts, 1 large onion, 5–7 garlic cloves, ¼ cup soy sauce, 2 tbsps liquid honey, 4 bay leaves, ½ tsp tumeric, 1 tbsp freshly chopped ginger, ¼ tsp cayenne pepper, salt, 2 cups light stock or water

Cut the washed and dried meat into strips and sprinkle with lemon juice. Chop the onion and garlic finely and blend with hazelnuts, honey, soy sauce, cayenne pepper and tumeric, add ½ cup stock and mix into smooth cream with an electric mixer. Put it into a saucepan and cook over high heat for 2–3 mins. Add the meat, bay leaves and ginger, pour in the remaining stock or water, mix well, cover

and simmer over low heat for about 1 hour. Serve with rice or French fries and lettuce salad.

serves 4 • Preparation: 5–7 mins • Stewing: 55–60 mins

Duck ragout with courgettes

600 g duck breast, 1 tbsp lemon juice, ½ tsp liquid honey, ¼ tsp pepper, a dash of dried thyme, 1–2 young courgettes (about 300 g), ½ each red and green bell peppers, ¾ cup stock, 3 tbsps tomato concentrate, 1 tsp herbes de Provence, salt, pepper, 1 tbsp oil, 1 tbsp butter

Mix the lemon juice with honey, thyme and pepper, rub the meat with the mixture and set aside in a cool place for 30 mins, then cut into cubes or strips, fry in hot oil and transfer to a saucepan. Add the butter, a dash of salt, sprinkle with 2–3 tbsps water and simmer over low heat for about 40 mins. Cut the washed and cored peppers into strips. Wash the courgettes and cut them into thick cubes. Mix the stock with the tomato concentrate, salt, pepper and herbes de Provence and add the mixture to the meat. Stir in the peppers and courgettes and simmer together for about 15 mins. Serve with pasta or white bread.

serves 4 • Marinating: 30–40 mins • Preparation: 10 mins • Stewing: 50–55 mins

Duck fricassee

1 duck (ca 1½ kg), 4–5 cups stock, 3 garlic cloves, 3–4 large cooking apples, ½ cup cream, 1 tbsp flour, salt, sugar

Place the washed duck in a saucepan, add garlic and hot stock, and cook over low heat. Cut the peeled apples into quarters, place them in a small saucepan and cover with 1 cup duck stock. Cook over low heat. Take out the tender duck, set aside to cool and bone it out. Cut the meat into thick cubes. Reduce the stock so that about 2 cups are left. Put the stewed apples through a sieve, combine with the remaining stock, add the diced meat. Heat up over low heat, add the cream blended with flour and stirring all the time continue to heat until the sauce thickens (do not boil!).

serves 4 • Cooking: 1–1½ hrs • Preparation: 20–25 mins

Duck baked with sauerkraut

*600 g duck breast, 400 g sauerkraut,
500 g cooking apples, 1 tbsp lemon juice,
sugar, 250 g potatoes, 2 large onions,
4–5 garlic cloves, 1 tsp caraway seeds,
salt, 2 tbsps oil, 1 tbsp butter*

Dice the onions, mince garlic with salt, chop the sauerkraut. Sear the washed and dried meat on both sides in very hot oil until golden. Take it out, and to the frying pan add the butter, onion and garlic. Stir and fry for 1–2 mins. Add the sauerkraut, caraway seeds, mix well and simmer covered for about 15 mins. Peel, core and slice the apples, sprinkle them with lemon juice mixed with a dash of sugar. Place the peeled and sliced potatoes in a sieve and scald, then drain. In an ovenproof dish arrange layers of sauerkraut, potatoes, apples and slices of meat. Cover and bake in a preheated oven for about 1 hour.

serves 4 • Preparation: 25 mins • Baking: 55–60 mins

CHAPTER XII

GAME

Game

A roast... from elk, known as the 'magna bestia'... or from roebuck, red deer or wild boar.

(Łukasz Gołębiowski, *Domy i dwory*, vol. IV, p. 37)

Bogdan Dyakowski wrote, 'Love of hunting was universal among us. The knights and gentry hunted for the sheer pleasure of the chase; the lower orders hunted mainly for profit. The Tatra highlanders, known for their liking for overcoming obstacles in the chase, were in particular famed for their love of hunting, as were the inhabitants of the forests and especially the Kurps.' Hunting went on all year round, in various ways and for different game: 'In the spring with a flintlock, in the summer with hawks, in autumn with hounds and in winter with falcons.'

*When a naked man reaches the forest
St Hubert gives him a whole dinner of forest fare.*

St Hubert had nothing to do with hunting, but rather with fishing; however, hunters chose him as their patron saint. In the 12th century he was first represented as an archer who never missed his target. He always encouraged hunters to offer up the first animal that they caught to St Peter the Apostle instead of to the pagan goddess of hunting. Wincenty Pol in his hunting tales offers the following hunter's dinner:

The dinner will be good, but we have to start with vodka; everything will be thrice in honour of St Hubert. And so first, three hunter's vodkas: poplar vodka, oak vodka and juniper vodka, all three years old, beautifully cleared and the safest at this time. There are three seasonings for these vodkas: finely ground angelica, roughly ground pepper and fresh badger fat to enliven the intestines, especially good for old huntsmen. Whoever uses it as medicine, drinks it with juniper vodka, beginning from St Hubert's Day until Christmas Eve.

After the vodka come the hors-d'oeuvres. First, royal smoked meats – venison tongue and goats' tongues with horseradish, for the second hors-d'oeuvre marinated wild kid, and for the third hors-d'oeuvre a capercaillie cheese surrounded by white truffles. Tomorrow we will have capercaillie, which is a royal hors-d'oeuvre, but when it is not available, you may take any other forest fowl, hazelcock or black grouse to make the cheese, but it should always be surrounded with white truffles.

After the hors-d'oeuvres, we will have borsch of two kinds. A good old hare will be used for borsch, and I broke the thicker bones myself so that the bone marrow would come out... After the borsch there will be a piece of nicely fattened wild boar meat, served straight from the oven in a rosehip sauce...

Since there are to be three dishes at all stages, before this roast there will be head of wild boar and jellied trotters, and then three pâtés: the first of wild ducks in pumpkin, the second of small wild fowl roasted in cabbage leaves, and the third of fieldfares in beds of cress. Then there will be three roasts in turn: first, roast haunch of venison with mushrooms, then saddle of venison with fresh mushrooms, and finally woodcock served with a kind of marmalade made from wild bilberries and other fruits. This is the end. It is only necessary to add three natural drinks: raspberry cordial, wild cherry cordial and old mead from forest bees.

To finish it all, there will also be candied sloes, bilberries cooked in honey, hazelnuts... And that will suffice for St Hubert to give a whole dinner from the forest.

The season for game is in the autumn and early winter when the meat has most flavour, which is closely linked with the food eaten by game animals: wild herbs, shoots and bark of young trees, mushrooms and forest berries – they all contribute to the aroma.

There are three kinds of game animals:
– the first are small wild fowl, beginning with thrushes and then in descending order of size;
– the second group comprises larger fowl – corncrakes, snipe, grouse, pheasants – and rabbits and hares;
– the third group comprises wild boar and deer.

In bygone times, Polish hunters only regarded the third group as game worth hunting.

Wild fowl, according to a dictionary of hunting terms published in 1970, is a category covering 'birds recognized by law as game birds that can be hunted; at present these are: great bustard, capercaillie, black grouse, hazel grouse, pheasant, partridge, quail, heron, woodcock, ruff, snipe, wild duck, wild geese, pigeons, fieldfare and mistle thrush; all of these are small wild fowl with the exception of the great bustard and capercaillie, which count as large game'.

Game is more nourishing than other meat as it contains more protein. It is regarded as a great culinary treasure which is an excellent part of any menu, and in the past roasts were served from aurochs, bison, elk, deer, wild boar and wild fowl – 'wild goose, bustard, capercaillie, black grouse, partridges from Ruthenia the size of pigeons but shaped like grouse, wild duck, and small fowl, namely, hazel grouse, pheasant, partridge, quail, heron, woodcock, ruff, snipe, and all kinds of doves and thrushes, blackbirds and young starlings' (Łukasz Gołębiowski, *Domy i dwory*).

The art of cooking game dates in Poland to the 16th century, and the great feasts of the magnates had an un-doubted influence on its development. A very large number of varied dishes were developed.

Here is some practical advice.

The structure of game meat is different from that of animals farmed for meat. Their way of life means that their muscles are more developed, and they have high blood content and little fat. In game, fat mainly grows up around the kidneys, with little on the surface. It is generally rejected in the kitchen because of its strong smell. This is why it is essential to lard the meat deeply with pork fat or streaky bacon to prevent the meat being too dry. The saddle (loin) is the best and most delicate meat in game animals. It is relatively thick, beginning with the neck muscles and running on both sides down the backbone. The thick layer of membrane and tendons has to be removed and then a smooth and uniformly succulent piece of meat is left, which can be used for schnitzels, fillets or roasts. The leg can also be roasted and is succulent and full of flavour, but a leg joint for roasting should not weigh less than 2 kg.

The meat should be tenderized before cooking. Game meat matures slowly and the first stage of the process should take place before it is skinned or plucked. In frosty winter weather you can hang game for about 2 months; in summer this can last about 5 days. The meat should be hung in a cool and airy place. Hanging does not work so well for an animal which has been hit more than once with shot and whose innards are damaged. These game animals or birds should be drawn without skinning and bled, and then clean, white balls of paper should be placed inside before it is hung to tenderize. In this case, however, the animal should only be hung for a short period of time. When the meat is tender, the animal should be skinned and cut up into joints for various dishes. If the game is to be eaten immediately, the veins should be drawn out at once, together with all the tendons and membranes until only the clean meat is left. In general the fore quarters of the animal, which have less muscle and have a surface layer of tendons and membrane (the neck, shoulder and upper leg) are suitable for pâtés, mincing or stewing. In addition, all the offal – heart, kidneys, lungs and liver – is used for pâtés. The hind quarters – the saddle and leg – can be cooked in various ways: fried, braised or roasted.

Before cooking game, the meat should be put through one more stage of tenderizing: marinating or pickling. The leg is usually marinated in vinegar, wine, lemon juice; the saddle is usually placed in dry seasoning. Milk is enough for the meat of young animals. Wild boar hams are pickled, that is rubbed with salt and saltpetre. Marinating offers the right conditions for the meat to mature further.

After game birds have been hung, they should be dry plucked and drawn, without scalding them, burned off over a spirit flame and prepared like poultry.

Marinades, which use hot spices for conserving and tenderizing the meat, are sometimes used to make the taste sharper or to remove the unpleasant smell. You should however remember that the marinade should not be too acid (which is why I recommend wine, lemon juice or wine vinegar) and the meat should not be left in it too long, 7 days at the most, because in this way it loses much of it nutritional value.

It is enough to leave meat from young animals, after hanging, for 12 hours in fresh milk, sour milk or buttermilk.

You should remember that the meat should frequently be turned over in the marinade, so that the spices soak in evenly. You should prepare 2 to 2½ litres of marinade for 5 kg of meat.

Marinades for game

Marinade with wild thyme

1 cup wine vinegar, 2 cups red wine, 7–8 black peppercorns, 7–8 allspice berries, 2–4 bay leaves, ½ tbsp salt, ½ tsp wild thyme, ¼ tsp ginger, 2 tbsps soya sauce, 1 onion, 1 carrot, 1 parsley root, a piece of celeriac

Bring to the boil, set aside to cool. Add soya sauce or liquid soup seasoning, wild thyme and powdered gin-

ger. Place the meat in an earthenware pot, pour over the marinade. Keep in a cool place for 4–5 days.

Marinade with vegetables

1 lemon (peeled and cut into slices), ¼ cup water, 1 onion, 1 carrot, 1 parsley root, a piece of celeriac, 2 bay leaves, 10 allspice berries, 10 black peppercorns, 2 cloves, ½ cup white wine

Bring to the boil and strain. Place the meat in an earthenware pot and pour over the marinade. Keep in a cool place for 4–5 days, remembering to turn the meat over from time to time.

Marinade for wild boar meat I

1 lemon (peeled and cut into slices), 1 cup red wine, 1 onion, 1 parsley root, a piece of celeriac, 20 juniper berries, 10 peppercorns, 2 bay leaves, ¼ tsp rosemary, ¼ tsp spruce needles

Bring to the boil, strain and pour over the meat. Keep in a cool place for 4–5 days, remembering to turn the meat over from time to time.

Marinade for wild boar meat II

1 lemon (peeled and cut into slices), 1 cup light beer, 2 onions, 3 bay leaves, 10 allspice berries, 10 black peppercorns, 1 clove

Bring to the boil, strain and pour over the meat. Keep in a cool place for 4–5 days, remembering to turn the meat over from time to time.

Marinade for wild boar meat III

1 lemon (peeled and cut into slices), 1 cup red wine, 2–3 cloves, a piece of ginger, 4–5 black peppercorns, 2 bay leaves

Bring to the boil, strain, pour over the meat. Keep in a cool place for 4–5 days, remembering to turn the meat over from time to time.

Marinade for wild boar meat IV

*1 lemon (peeled and sliced), 1 cup light beer,
1 onion, a piece of ginger, 2–3 cloves, 5–8 juniper
berries, 5–8 black peppercorns, 4 garlic cloves*

Bring to the boil, strain, pour over the meat. Keep in a cool place for 4–5 days and remember to turn the meat over from time to time.

Marinade for spit-roast game

*1 cup dry white wine, 5 tbsps olive oil, 1 tsp salt,
1 tsp dried thyme, ½ tsp pepper, sugar, 1 lemon
(peeled and sliced), 1 tbsp chopped parsley*

Mix well all the ingredients. Place the meat in an earthenware bowl, pour over the marinade and leave in a cool place overnight. It is enough to sprinkle the young game with dry wine. Wine can be also injected straight into the meat, which shortens the time for the meat to tenderize.

DRY SEASONING FOR GAME

Dry seasoning for game I

*(for 1 kg meat) 2–3 sliced onions (the more onion
you use, the more subdued the gamey flavour
of the meat becomes), ¼ tsp thyme, ¼ tsp
marjoram or rosemary, 10 black peppercorns,
10 allspice berries, 1 crumbled bay leaf*

Rub the well-washed meat with the herbs and spices, sprinkle with lemon juice, or olive oil, cover with slices of onion and place in an earthenware pot. Sprinkle with pepper and allspice, cover with a plate and refrigerate for 2–4 days.

Dry seasoning for game II

(for 1 kg meat) 3 tbsps crushed juniper berries.

*In this case do not wash the meat and do not
remove the membrane, just wipe with a dry cloth
and rub thoroughly with crushed juniper berries*

Place the well-rubbed meat in an earthenware pot, weight the meat with a small plate, cover and set aside in a cool place for 2–4 days. Take it out, rinse and remove the membrane.

HARE

A good hare should weigh 3 to 4 kg before it is skinned. It can be kept 4–6 weeks in its skin, but a skinned hare should be used within 2 or 3 days.

The saddle or haunch of hare is used for roasting and cutlets. The fore quarters, ribs and offal are suitable for pâtés and stews.

When preparing a hare at home, remember the following:

- cut the skin around the foot joint on all four legs with a very sharp knife;
- cut off the fore legs at the first joint, and cut off the head at the first neck joint;
- cut the muscles on the hind legs, tie the fetlocks tightly with string and hang the hare on a strong hook;
- place a piece of wood between the hind legs;
- pull off the skin from where it has been cut, up the leg. At first, you can assist the process with a knife, cutting the membrane that joins the skin to the body;
- when the skin has been drawn from both legs, cut off the tail, hold the skin firmly in both hands and pull downwards hard, keeping the skin in your hands as it comes off;
- the skinned hare should be removed from the hook, and the hind legs cut off at the foot joint;
- place the hare on a pastry board covered with a layer of clean paper;
- cut open the belly up to the breastbone, draw out the innards and cut off the intestine at the anus. From the offal, take out the lungs, heart, liver, kidneys and place them in a dish;

- cut off the anus deeply, together with the surrounding area. Wrap the rejected offal and the anus area in paper and throw away. Then wash the hare thoroughly under running water. Rinse it until the blood runs out. Wash the stomach cavity very carefully, drain it of water and place the animal on paper to dry;
- with a sharp knife cut off the saddle and haunches, removing the membrane.

Hare in cream, Polish style

1 hare (or only saddle and thighs), 100 g pork fat, salt, 1 tbsp butter, 1 cup thick sour cream, 1 tsp flour

MARINADE: 1 lemon or ¼ cup red wine, ¼ cup water, 1 onion, 1 carrot, 1 parsley root, ¼ celeriac, 2 bay leaves, 5–7 juniper berries, 5–7 allspice berries, sugar

Cook the vegetables in the marinade and grate them coarsely. Place the washed hare in an earthenware pot, cover with the grated vegetables and sliced onion, pour in the cooled marinade and set aside in a cool place for 2–3 days. Remove the meat from the marinade, wipe it dry and rub with salt. Place it in a saucepan, dot with butter, cover and stew for 30 mins, sprinkling from time to time with the strained marinade. After 30 mins add the vegetables removed from the marinade, top with the remaining marinade and simmer. When the hare is ready, remove it and divide into serving portions. Place them in an ovenproof dish. Pour in the reserved meat juices through a strainer, and add the cream blended with flour. Pour the sauce over the hare and bake for a few minutes in a preheated oven.

serves 4–6 • Marinating: 2–3 days • Stewing: 1 hr • Baking: 10–15 mins

Hare in cream

saddle and thighs of hare, 2 cups buttermilk, 4 dried mushrooms, 5–7 juniper berries, 3–4 allspice berries, 3–4 black peppercorns, 1 onion, soup vegetables, ½ cup thick sour cream, 2 tbsps butter, 1 tsp flour

Place the washed hare in an earthenware pot, pour in 2 cups buttermilk, cover and set aside in a cool place for 2 days. Change buttermilk after one day, and turn the

hare. Now take the hare out and wipe it dry. Grate the vegetables or chop them finely. Mince the juniper berries, pepper and allspice berries in a mortar, and rub the hare with the spices. Place the meat in a saucepan, coat with the vegetables and onion, leave aside in a cool place overnight. Remove the vegetables, rub the meat with salt and place it in a roasting pan, coat with the butter and the mushrooms, cooked and cut into thin strips. Place the dish in a preheated oven to roast for about 45 mins. From time to time baste with the sauce and mushroom stock. Towards the end, top the hare with the cream blended with flour and continue to cook over low heat for another 15 mins.

serves 4–6 • Soaking: 2 days • Marinating: 12 hrs • Roasting: 1 hr

Hare in its own sauce

saddle and thighs of hare, 100 g pork fat, 60 g butter, salt, pepper, 1 tsp flour, ½ cup stock

Trim the hare, remove the membrane and wash the meat, rub it with salt, sprinkle with pepper and lard with pork fat. In a saucepan melt the butter, add the meat dusted with flour and roast for about 1 hour in a preheated oven, frequently basting the meat with the melted butter and stock. When the dish is ready, cut the saddle into thin, diagonal slices, surround with the meat from the thighs, then pour over the sauce.

serves 4–6 • Preparation: 5 mins • Roasting: 1 hr

Hare in vegetable sauce

saddle and thighs of hare, 1 carrot, 1 parsley root, a piece of celeriac, 1 onion, 2 medium-large tomatoes or 1 tbsp concentrate, 50 g pork fat, 2 tbsps butter, 1 tsp flour, ½ cup stock, 4–5 juniper berries, salt

Remove the membrane and wash the meat. Place it in an earthenware pot, cover with the marinade and set aside in a cool place for 1–2 days. Now remove the meat from the marinade, wipe it dry, lard with pork fat and rub with salt. In a saucepan melt 1 tbsp butter, put in the meat, sliced vegetables and juniper. Sauté together for a few minutes over high heat, then lower the heat, add the tomatoes and stock, cover and simmer, from time to time pouring in some strained marinade. Remove the cooked hare, divide into portions and arrange on a warm serving platter. Make a roux with the butter and flour, combine with the hare juices, mix and pass through a sieve. Pour the sauce over the meat and put the dish for a few minutes into a preheated oven.

serves 4–6 • Marinating: 1–2 days • Preparation: 10 mins • Stewing: 1 hr • Baking: 5–6 mins

Hare in black sauce

1 hare, salt, 1 carrot, 1 parsley root, 1 onion, ¼ celeriac, 1 tsp ground juniper, 1 cup red wine, ½ cup stock, 100 g smoked streaky bacon or ham, 1 carrot, ½ celeriac, 2 tbsps butter

Cut up the hare, wash, wipe dry and rub with salt. Set aside for 2–3 hours. Then brown it in butter, place in a saucepan and coat with the coarsely grated vegetables and the sliced onion. Season the hare with juniper, pour in the stock and simmer for about 1 hour, sprinkling it from time to time with red wine. Remove the meat, cut it into serving pieces. Mix the sauce in a food processor and put it through a sieve. Peel and wash the carrot and celeriac, cut into matchsticks and blanch in salted water. Cut the bacon into cubes. Put the portions of hare into a saucepan, add the blanched vegetables and the diced bacon and top this with the sauce. Simmer for about 20 mins.

serves 4–6 • Salting: 2–3 hrs • Preparation: 10–15 mins • Stewing: 70–80 mins

Saddle of hare, hunter's style

saddle of hare (ca 1.3 kg), juice of 2 lemons, 1 tsp grated lemon rind, 4–5 garlic cloves, 150 g pork fat, 1 bunch spring onions, 200 g grapes, 1 large carrot, 1 cup dry red wine, 3–4 tbsps cream, 1 glass brandy, 2 cloves, 1 tbsp dried thyme, ½ tsp pepper, 1 bay leaf, salt, 1 tsp honey, 1 tsp lard

Remove the membrane, wash and dry the meat. Place it in a bowl, sprinkle with grated lemon rind and lemon juice, cover and set aside in the fridge for 2–3 hours. Mince the finely chopped garlic with pepper, stir in the wine and brandy, pour over the meat, cover and refriger-

ate for a few hours, turning the meat from time to time to make sure it marinates all over. Remove the hare from the marinade, cut the pork fat into thin strips, wrap them around the meat and place the meat in a larded roasting pan. Roast for about 40 mins in a well-preheated oven, basting the meat first with the marinade, then with the meat juices. Chop the spring onions, cut the washed and peeled carrot into cubes, halve the grapes and remove the seeds. Put into a saucepan the strips of pork fat removed from the hare, add the onion, carrot, thyme, the crumbled bay leaf and ½ tsp lard, pour in the marinade and bring to the boil, then cook over low heat for a few minutes. Blend the sauce in a food processor, then put it through a sieve and add the honey. Heat and stir, pour in the cream, season with salt, combine with the meat juices. When tender, cut the saddle into thickish slices, place them in an ovenproof dish, top with the sauce and bake for 5–7 mins in a preheated oven.

serves 4–6 • Marinating: 6–8 hrs • Preparation: 10–15 mins • Roasting: 40–45 mins

Hare, hunter's style

1 thigh of hare, 100 g pork fat, ¼ tsp pepper, ¼ tsp paprika, 1 onion, ½ glass red wine, 1 tsp crumbled wholemeal bread, ½ cup stock, 1 lemon, 1 cup sour milk

Remove the membrane and wash the meat. Place it in an earthenware pot, top with sour milk and set aside in cool place for the night. Remove from the milk, dry, cut into slices. Cut the pork fat into thin strips. In a saucepan arrange layers of the pork fat, meat, and finely chopped onion. Sprinkle each layer with pepper, salt and paprika, and lemon juice. Cover and put in a preheated oven for about 45 mins. Sprinkle with water from time to time. Bring to the boil the stock with the crumbled bread, pass through a sieve and mix with wine. Top the hare with the sauce and continue to bake for another 20 mins.

serves 4 • Soaking: 12 hrs • Preparation: 5 mins • Roasting: 1 hr

Baked hare

1 hare, 8 garlic cloves, 1 tsp minced rosemary, grated lemon rind and juice of 1 lemon, salt, pepper, 3 tbsps chopped parsley, 3 tbsps butter, 2 tbsps grated cheese rim and wash the hare, rub it with salt and dot with butter. Roast it in a preheated oven, basting with the sauce. When ready, cut the meat into serving pieces and remove the bones. Butter an ovenproof dish and add the meat, sprinkling it with pepper, grated lemon rind, rosemary and finely chopped garlic. Pour over the meat juices and lemon juice. Dot the hare with butter, sprinkle with the grated cheese and parsley, and roast for about 30 mins in a preheated oven.

serves 4 • Roasting: 1 hr • Cooling: 30–40 mins • Preparation: 10–15 mins • Baking: 25–30 mins

Hare in herbs

1 hare, 300 g streaky bacon, 8 garlic cloves, a sprig of each sage and rosemary or ¼ tsp each dried herbs, 1 onion, 3 carrots, 3 tbsps chopped parsley, salt, 1 tbsp butter, 2 cups sour milk

SAUCE: juice and grated rind of 2 lemons, 1 glass sweet red wine, 1 tbsp butter, 1 tsp flour

lace the trimmed and washed hare in an earthenware pot, cover it with the sour milk and set aside in a cool place overnight. Rinse, dry and lard the meat with thin strips of bacon and half of the garlic, rub with salt. Place the meat in a roasting pan, coat it with the sliced onion and carrot, sprinkle with the chopped herbs and dot with butter. Roast the hare for about 1½ hours, frequently basting it with its own juices and some water. When ready, divide the meat into individual servings and remove the bones. PREPARE THE SAUCE: Make a roux with the butter and flour, dilute with the wine and lemon juice, add grated lemon rind and finely minced garlic.
Butter an ovenproof dish, arrange the meat and sprinkle it with parsley and the finely chopped garlic. Put the meat juices through a sieve and combine with the lemon sauce. Top the meat with the sauce and bake for about 20 mins in a preheated oven.

serves 4–6 • Soaking: 12 hrs • Preparation: 2–2½ hrs

Hare with sauerkraut

1 hare, 1 cup thick sour cream, 50 g pork fat, salt, pepper, 1½ kg sauerkraut, 250 g melted butter, salt, pepper

ard the washed and trimmed hare with pork fat, season with salt and pepper and roast in a preheated oven, from time to time sprinkling the meat with 2–3 tbsps melted butter and water. Towards the end, top the hare with the sour cream. Squeeze the excess juice from the sauerkraut, cut it finely and place in a saucepan, sprinkling it with melted butter. Add salt and a pinch of pepper. Cover and simmer for about 1 hour. Arrange the portions of the hare in an ovenproof dish, pour over the sauce and surround with sauerkraut. Bake for about 10 mins.

serves 4–6 • Preparation: 60–80 mins • Baking: 10–15 mins

Hare with gherkins

1 hare, 2 small onions, 100 g pork fat, salt, 2 cups red wine, 3 cloves, 2 bay leaves, 5 peppercorns, 1 tbsp butter, 1 tsp flour, ½ baguette, 2 hard-boiled eggs, 4 gherkins, 10 pickled onions

ring to the boil the wine with the spices. Divide the washed meat into portions, rub it with salt. In a saucepan sauté the diced pork fat and brown in it the finely chopped onion. Add the hare and fry together over high heat for a moment or two. Reduce the heat, pour in the wine, cover and simmer. When the meat is ready, remove it, arrange on a serving platter and keep warm. Thicken the sauce with a roux prepared from the butter and flour. Put it through a sieve. Serve the sauce in a sauceboat. Decorate the hare with quarters of hard-boiled eggs, slices of gherkins and with pickled onions. Surround with pieces of toast.

serves 6–8 • Preparation: 5–7 mins • Stewing: 1 hr

Hare with tomatoes

saddle and thighs of hare, 100 g pork fat, salt, pepper, 1 onion, 2–3 garlic cloves, 1 tsp chopped parsley, 2 bay leaves, 2 tbsps breadcrumbs, 1 cup red wine, juice of 1 lemon, 150 g tomatoes or 1½ tbsps tomato concentrate and ½ tsp sugar, 1 glass brandy, 1 tbsp butter

ash the meat and remove the membrane. Cut into slices and pound them with a mallet, then sprinkle with salt, pepper and lemon juice and set aside in a cool place for 1 hour. In a saucepan briskly fry the pork fat cut into thin strips, add the sliced onion and minced garlic, mix lightly and sauté. Add the meat and brown it on both sides. Pour in the red wine, add breadcrumbs and bay leaves. Cover and simmer for about 1 hour. Remove the meat when tender. Add the quartered tomatoes to the sauce, bring to the boil and sieve the sauce. Combine the sauce and the meat and simmer together for a moment. Add a glass of brandy and sprinkle with parsley.

serves 4–6 • Preparation: 10–15 mins • Macerating:
1–2 hrs • Stewing: 55–60 mins

Hare with butter

saddle and thighs of hare, 150 g butter,
1 tbsp thyme, lemon juice, salt, pepper

Rub the washed meat with salt and pepper, set aside for 1 hour. Mix the butter with lemon juice and thyme. Place the meat in a roasting pan, coat with butter and roast for about 1 hour in a preheated oven, basting the hare from time to time with melted butter.

serves 4–6 • Salting: 1–2 hours • Roasting: 55–60 mins

Saddle of hare in currant sauce

saddle of hare, 100 g pork fat, 1 tbsp butter,
1 cup milk, ½ cup red wine, ¼ tsp grated nutmeg,
a pinch of cinnamon, a pinch of pepper,
½ cup currant jelly, 1 tbsp grated horseradish,
1 tsp lemon juice, grated rind of ½ lemon,
a pinch of sugar

Remove the membrane from the meat. Place the meat in an earthenware pot, cover with the milk and set aside in a cool place overnight. Remove, dry, rub with salt and lard generously with the pork fat. Roast it in an oven, basting frequently with butter and a little water or wine. Bring to the boil the wine with nutmeg, cinnamon, pepper, sugar and lemon rind. Chill and mix with the currant jelly, horseradish, lemon juice and the meat juices. Heat lightly. Serve the sauce in a gravy boat. Cut the meat into slices.

serves 4 • Soaking: 12 hrs • Preparation: 10–12 mins • Roasting: 55–60 mins

Saddle of hare with liver

saddle and liver of hare, 100 g pork fat, 1 cup red wine,
1 cup stock, lemon juice, salt, pepper, 1 onion, 100 g butter

Sauté the finely chopped hare liver and onion in 1 tbsp butter, add the red wine, stock, lemon juice, salt and pepper. Bring to the boil. Add the saddle larded generously with the pork fat, cover. Simmer for about 1 hour. When the meat is tender, add the remaining butter and roast the hare in a preheated oven for about 20 mins until brown. Cut the meat into slices, pass the sauce through a sieve and serve in a sauceboat.

serves 4 • Preparation: 10 mins • Stewing:
55–60 mins • Roasting: 15–20 mins

Roast hare with caraway seeds

saddle and thighs of hare, 100 g pork fat, 1 tbsp ground
caraway seeds, ¼ tsp pepper, 1 onion, 100 g butter, salt

Remove the membrane and lard the meat generously with the pork fat. Rub it with the caraway seeds, pepper and salt. Set aside in a cool place for 2–3 hours. Dice the onion and sauté it in butter. Add the hare and put the pan into a preheated oven. Roast for about 1½ hours, basting the meat frequently with butter and water.

serves 4–6 • Macerating: 2–3 hrs • Preparation:
5 mins • Roasting: 70–90 mins

Fore part of hare in spicy sauce

fore part of hare, salt, pepper, 1 onion,
½ tsp thyme, 2–3 allspice berries, 2–3 black
peppercorns, 1 bay leaf, 1 tbsp breadcrumbs,
2 tbps anchovy paste, 1 tbsp capers, grated rind
of 1 lemon, ½ cup dry wine, 100 g butter

Trim, bone out and wash the meat, salt it, sprinkle with pepper and fry together with the diced onion in butter. Add the bay leaf, pepper, allspice berries, thyme and wine, cover and simmer until the meat becomes tender. Brown the breadcrumbs in the remaining butter and add to the meat together with grated lemon rind, anchovy paste and capers. Mix well and simmer together for further 20 mins or so.

serves 4 • Preparation: 20–25 mins • Stewing: 50–60 mins

Fore part of hare with cream

*fore part of hare with lungs, liver and heart,
1 onion, 1 carrot, 1 parsley root, ¼ celeriac,
100 g streaky bacon, 5 allspice berries,
5 black peppercorns, 1 bay leaf, 1 tbsp
flour, ½ cup thick sour cream, salt*

Place the trimmed and boned meat together with the giblets in an earthenware pot and cover with the cold marinade. Set aside in a cool place for 1–2 days. Remove from the marinade and place in a saucepan tightly coating the meat with the sliced vegetables and onion. Dredge with the spices and top with some of the sieved marinade and water. Cover and simmer until ready. Remove the meat and giblets from the saucepan and cut into small pieces. Cut the bacon into cubes, render it, add the giblets and the meat, mix well and fry together for a moment or two. Sieve the cooked vegetables and mix with the marinade and the cream blended with flour. Season to taste with salt. Add the hare with the bacon and simmer together for a moment or two.

*serves 4 • Preparation: 20–25 mins • Marinating:
1–2 days • Stewing: 50–60 mins*

Fore part of hare in fruit sauce

*fore part of hare and giblets, 1 carrot, 1 parsley root,
¼ celeriac, 5–6 black peppercorns, 5–6 allspice
berries, 1 bay leaf, 1 onion, 1 tsp thyme, 1 cup stock,
1 tsp caramel, 1 tbp plum jam, 1 tbsp cranberry juice,
1 tbsp red wine, juice and grated rind of ½ lemon,
50 g grated gingerbread, salt, 2 tbsps butter*

Trim and bone out the meat, cut the giblets, and brown together in butter. Add the sliced vegetables and onion, allspice berries, pepper, bay leaf and lemon juice, and simmer, often sprinkling with the stock. When the meat is ready, take it out. Add the caramel to the vegetables, as well as plum jam, lemon juice and lemon rind, the wine and the crumbled gingerbread. Simmer together for a moment, put through a sieve. Add the meat to the sieved sauce and simmer together for about 20 mins.

serves 4 • Preparation: 20–25 mins • Stewing: 60–70 mins

Jugged hare

*1 hare, 2–3 garlic cloves, 1 cup cooking oil,
1 onion, 1 tsp paprika, pepper, 3 cloves, 2 bay
leaves, salt, ¼ tsp cinnamon, ¼ tsp saffron*

Wash and divide the hare, rub with the chopped garlic, sprinkle with pepper, chopped cloves, cinnamon, paprika and the crumbled bay leaf (no salt!). Place the prepared meat in a roasting pan, top with the oil and set aside in a cool place for 1–3 days. Turn over every day. Put the pan with the marinated meat over low heat, add the sliced onion and saffron. Season to taste with salt and fry slowly over low heat. Then sprinkle lightly with water, cover and simmer for about an hour.

serves 4 • Marinating: 1–3 days • Preparation: 5 mins • Stewing: 60–70 mins

Hare steaks

*saddle and thighs of hare, 100 g butter,
250 g mushrooms, salt, pepper, 1 tbsp
chopped parsley, 1 cup milk*

Remove the bones and membrane and place the meat in a pot, topping it with milk. Set aside in a cool place overnight. Then dry, cut into slices, pound with a mallet, season with salt and pepper, and set aside for 1 hour. Sauté the sliced mushrooms in butter. Fry the fillets in butter, transfer to a saucepan, top with the mushrooms and the grated cheese, dot with butter and bake in a preheated oven. Arrange on a serving platter, sprinkle with chopped parsley.

*serves 4–6 • Soaking: 1 hr • Salting: 1 hr • Preparation:
10 mins • Roasting: 30–40 mins*

Rolled fillets of hare

*saddle and thighs of hare, 150 g ham, 1 tbsp capers,
1 lemon, salt, pepper, 2 tbsps butter, 3 tbsps stock*

Trim and bone out the hare, cut it into slices, pound lightly with a mallet, sprinkle with salt and pepper. Scald the lemon and cut it into thin slices. On each fillet place a slice of lemon, a thin slice of ham and a few capers. Roll up the fillets, tie each with a piece of thread and brown them in butter. Transfer the fried fillets to a saucepan, add

1 tbsp butter, sprinkle with some stock and stew until tender. From time to time, pour in some stock or water.

serves 4–6 • Preparation: 15–20 mins • Stewing: 30–40 mins

Fancy fillets of hare

1 hare, salt, 150 g butter, 250 beef marrow, 100 g raw leaf lard, 250 g beef tongue, 1 bread roll soaked in milk, 3 onions, 1 tbsp chopped parsley, 100 g mushrooms, ¼ tsp nutmeg, 2 eggs, 1 glass dry red wine, 100 g pork fat, hare bones, 2 carrots, 1 parsley root, ¼ celeriac, 1 small leek, 100 g lean ham, 1 tbsp flour, white bread for toast

Remove the bones and membrane. Cut the meat into 1½ cm thick slices. Lightly pound them with a mallet, season with salt and pepper. In a little water cook the beef tongue. Remove when tender, set aside to cool, then remove the skin and cut. Put through a mincer the hare meat scraps, cooked tongue, beef marrow, leaf lard, 2 onions, mushrooms fried in butter and the bread roll squeezed dry. Do it twice, then pass through a sieve. Add the finely chopped pork fat, chopped parsley, salt, pepper, nutmeg, eggs and ½ cup wine. Knead the pulp well and place it in a buttered round tin, cover tightly and steam for about 1½ hours. Meanwhile prepare the gravy: Fry in the butter the finely chopped hare bones, thinly sliced vegetables, 1 onion and ham, add the tongue stock, season with salt and pepper, stir in 1 tbsp chopped parsley. Cover and simmer together for about 30 mins, then sieve. Make a roux with the butter and flour, add to the sauce and keep over low heat, stirring all the time until the sauce thickens (do not boil!). Fry the fillets over high heat, transfer to a saucepan, sprinkle with 3 tbsps sauce and simmer for about 20 mins. Prepare pieces of toast. Warm a large round serving platter. Arrange the forcemeat in the middle and surround it with the fillets placed on pieces of toast. Pour some sauce over the stuffing and serve the remaining sauce in a sauceboat. Serve the fillets with lettuce salad with vinaigrette dressing.

serves 6–8 • Preparation: 2–2½ hrs • Stewing: 20–25 mins

Hare fillets with anchovies

hare saddle and thighs, salt, pepper, 100 g pork fat, 3 anchovies, ½ cup dry white wine, 4 tbsps sour cream, 1 tsp flour, 2 tbsps butter, 1 tbsp chopped parsley

Remove the membrane and bones and cut the meat into slices. Pound them with a mallet, season with salt and pepper. On each fillet place a very thin rasher of pork fat and a strip of anchovy. Roll the fillets up, wrap them with thread and brown on all sides. Place the fried fillets in a saucepan lined with thin strips of pork fat, add the wine, cover and simmer. When the fillets are tender, add the cream blended with flour and chopped parsley. Keep over low heat for a moment or two.

serves 4–6 • Preparation: 20–25 mins • Stewing: 40–45 mins

Hare fricassee

500 g roast hare meat, 3 tart apples, 1 tbsp butter, 1 tsp flour, ½ cup stock, salt, sugar

Cut the hare leftovers into cubes, peel and core the apples and stew them in little water. Make a roux with the butter and flour, dilute it with the stock. Add the meat and apples, mix gently, season with salt and sugar to taste and simmer for a moment or two.

serves 4 • Preparation: 4–5 mins • Stewing: 5–7 mins

Hare fricassee in prune sauce

fore part of hare, 100 g streaky bacon or pork fat, 1 onion, 120 g prunes, juice of ½ lemon, 1 tsp flour, 1 clove, 3 allspice berries, salt, ½ cup stock

Bone out the meat, remove the membrane. Lightly sprinkle the meat with salt and flour. Cut the bacon into thin rashers and render it, adding the chopped onion. Add the meat and brown it. Scald the prunes and add to the meat together with the spices, lemon juice and stock. Cover and simmer. When tender, arrange the meat on a serving platter. Sieve the sauce and pour over the meat.

serves 4–6 • Preparation: 10–15 mins • Stewing: 40–45 mins

Hare pâté

Hare pâté I

1 hare with giblets, 450 g fatty pork, 300 g pork fat, 2 garlic cloves, salt, pepper, 1 tsp thyme, 50 g brandy, 2 eggs

Remove the bones and membrane from the saddle and thighs and cut the meat into slices. Sprinkle with salt, thyme and the brandy, and set aside in a cool place for a few hours. Bone out the front part of the hare and remove the membrane. Pass through a mincer 2–3 times together with 200 g pork fat, pork and giblets. Season the pulp with salt, pepper and thyme, sprinkle with 1tsp brandy, add 2 eggs and mix thoroughly. Grease a pâté mould, rub it with garlic and line with thin strips of pork fat. Alternate layers of the prepared mixture and the meat, and top the whole with a layer of the pulp. Close the form tightly and put it into a bain-marie. Steam for over 3 hours. Set aside to cool, remove from the mould. Serve cold.

serves 8–10 • Macerating: 6–8 hrs • Preparation: 10–15 mins • Steaming: 3–3½ hrs

Hare pâté II

saddle and thighs of hare, 500 g fat pork, 350 g chaps, 1 hare liver, 500 g goose livers, 2 bread rolls, 2 onions, 2 carrots, 1 celeriac, salt, pepper, ½ cup stock, 3–4 eggs, allspice, 1 bay leaf, nutmeg, 50 g pork fat

Cut 100 g chaps into cubes, render it and sear the meat cut into slices. Add the vegetables and onion, bay leaf and allspice berries. Pour in the stock, cover and simmer for about 1 hour. Add the liver, the remaining chaps and the bread roll cut into slices. Continue to simmer for further 40 mins. Cool and put through a mincer 2–3 times. Add salt, pepper, allspice and nutmeg. Stir in the eggs and knead the whole into smooth pulp. Line a pâté mould with strips of pork fat, spread the pulp and smooth it with a knife. Bake in a preheated oven for 1 hour. Can be cooked in a bain-marie as well. Serve cold with Cumberland sauce.

serves 8–10 • Stewing: 90–100 mins • Preparation: 10–15 mins • Baking: 60 mins

Hare in shells

fore part of hare, 50 g butter, 50 g pork fat, 1 onion, 1 glass wine, ¼ tsp ground pepper, ¼ tsp ground juniper, 1 egg, ½ cup stock, 3–4 mushrooms

SAUCE: 100 g onion, 1 tbsp butter, 1 tsp flour, juice of ½ lemon, sugar, 1 cup stock, ½ cup cream, salt

RICE WITH TOMATOES: 1 cup rice, 200 g tomatoes, 50 g butter, 2 tbsps grated cheese, 1 tsp salt

In a saucepan melt the diced pork fat, add the hare meat and fry. Glass the sliced onion in butter, add to the hare, pour in the stock, cover and simmer. When the meat is tender, set it aside to cool, then remove the bones and put the meat through a mincer, adding the meat juices and onion. Mix well with the egg and wine. Season to taste with salt, pepper and juniper. Butter small moulds and fill them with the mixture, cover and bake in a preheated oven for about 40 mins. Stew the tomatoes in butter, sieve them, transfer to a saucepan and cover with 1 l boiled water, add butter and salt. Bring to the boil. Add the rice, bring to the boil and bake in a preheated oven. When cooked, transfer the rice into a bowl and mix well with the grated cheese. Butter an ovenproof dish, put in the rice, press it well and bake in a preheated oven for 5–10 mins. Prepare the white sauce: Cut the onion into tiny cubes and sauté it in butter, pour over the stock, cover and simmer until tender. Now add the cream blended with flour. Pass the sauce through a sieve, season with salt, sugar and lemon juice. Heat. In the middle of a warmed serving platter arrange the rice with tomatoes and surround it with the 'cakes' removed from the moulds. Pour over the white sauce.

serves 4 • Preparation: 1 hr • Baking: 40 mins

Stuffed hare

saddle and thighs of hare, 1 tbsp butter, 2 garlic cloves, 100 g pork fat

MARINADE: 1 cup wine vinegar, 1 onion

STUFFING: 200 g streaky bacon, hare liver, 1 tbsp breadcrumbs, 3 egg yolks, 2 tbsps double cream, salt, pepper

Remove the bones and membrane and wash the meat. Place it in a pot and coat with slices of onion. Pour over the vinegar and set aside in a cool place for 1–2 days. Remove from the marinade, dry and cut pockets for stuffing. Put the bacon and liver through a mincer, add salt and pepper and mix well with the egg yolks, cream and breadcrumbs. Line a saucepan with thin rashers of pork fat, put in the meat with the pockets (with the stuffing up), coat with the remaining pork fat and bake in a preheated oven, frequently sprinkling the hare with the strained marinade. Add the butter mixed with minced garlic to the meat juices.

serves 4–6 • Marinating: 1–2 days • Preparation: 15–20 mins • Roasting: 45–50 mins

Spicy hare salad

500 g roast hare, 6 small gherkins, 4 anchovies, 1 tbsp capers, 1 small tart apple, 3 tomatoes, 1 tbsp chopped parsley, salt, pepper, a pinch of sugar

DRESSING: 3 tbsps mayonnaise, 2 tbsps thick sour cream, 1 tsp mustard, 1 tbsp currant jelly, 1 tsp tarragon, juice of ½ lemon, 1 finely chopped onion

Prepare the dressing mixing well all the ingredients. Cut the meat, anchovies, gherkins, apple and tomatoes into cubes, add capers, salt, pepper and sugar, and gently stir in the dressing. Put the salad into a bowl, sprinkle with parsley. Refrigerate for one hour before serving.

serves 6–8 • Preparation: 8–10 mins • Refrigerating: 1–2 hrs

Hare in aspic

fore part of hare, 50 g pork fat, 50 g streaky bacon, 2 calf's feet, 250 g beef, soup vegetables, 1 onion, 10 allspice berries, 2 bay leaves, salt, pepper, 1 tsp lemon juice

Remove the bones, rub the meat with salt and dust with pepper. Line a roasting pan with thin rashers of pork fat and arrange the meat snugly, covering it with thin rashers of bacon. Roast in a preheated oven, basting the hare with water from time to time. When the meat is ready, remove it, set aside to cool and cut into slices. Cook some strong stock with beef, hare bones, calf's feet, soup vegetables and

spices. Arrange the slices of the hare meat in small bowls, decorate with vegetables and cover with the strained stock seasoned with lemon juice. Leave to set. Serve cold with spicy sauce, for example mustard sauce.

serves 6–8 • Roasting/Cooking: 50–60 mins • Cooling: 40–50 mins • Preparation: 5–8 mins

Hare giblet balls

lungs, heart, liver and kidney of hare, 1 bread roll soaked in milk, 1 onion, salt, pepper, ¼ tsp thyme, ¼ tsp marjoram, ¼ tsp grated lemon rind, 2 eggs, 100 g butter, 1 tsp breadcrumbs

Glass the finely chopped onion in butter. Remove the membrane and put the giblets together with the bread roll (squeezed dry) through a mincer, then mix with the herbs, eggs and onion. Knead the pulp until smooth and uniform in consistency, season with salt and pepper. Form small balls and put them into boiling salted water. Cook for about 20 mins. Brown the breadcrumbs in a frying pan, add the butter. Serve the meatballs sprinkled with butter and breadcrumbs.

serves 4 • Preparation: 10 min • Cooking: 20 mins

Hare roll

saddle and thigh of hare, 350 g pork fat, 2 onions, 3 garlic cloves, ¼ tsp each ground pepper, ground allspice and ground cloves, 1 bay leaf (crumbled), grated lemon rind, 1 cup stock, 150 g breadcrumbs, 3 eggs, ½ tsp marjoram, ¼ tsp ginger, salt

Cook thick pulp of stock, breadcrumbs, marjoram and ginger. Set aside to cool. Remove membrane from the meat and finely chop it together with 200 g pork fat. Add the finely chopped onion, minced garlic, and spices. Salt and mix with the stock pulp. Add the eggs and knead very thoroughly. Form a long roll. Place the meat roll in a long, deep baking dish lined with thin strips of pork fat and slices of onion. Bake in a preheated oven, sprinkling from time to time with melted butter and some water. Serve cold with spicy sauces.

serves 6–8 • Preparation: 30 mins • Baking: 45–50 mins • Cooling: 1–2 hrs

Hare sausage

fore of hare (ca 1 kg), 250 g pork fat, 3 egg whites, salt, pepper, ¼ tsp ground allspice, pork caul fat

Clean the gut thoroughly in salted water. Put the meat and pork fat through a mincer, add salt, pepper, allspice and stiff beaten egg whites. Knead the pulp until smooth. Stuff the mixture into the dried intestine and sew the ends. Smoke in cold smoke for about 1 hour. Then place the sausage in some boiling water and keep it in it for 10 mins (do not boil!). Remove, hang in a cool, airy place. Serve lightly sautéd.

serves 6–8 • Preparation: 10–15 mins • Smoking: 60–90 mins • Heating: 10 mins

Wild boar

A young wild boar of two to three years is tasty and is thought to be fine game, but you have to know how to prepare it. An old boar has hard meat and an unpleasant smell. The loin and hams or haunches, and the ribs, are the best parts. Head of wild boar is served at the best tables like pork. The parts that you wish to cook should be skinned and larded with thick slices of fresh bacon fat, and then rubbed on all sides with salt mixed with pepper, chopped onion, parsley, thyme and bay leaves; you can also add a little finely chopped sage to this mixture. Cover the wild boar meat with it and place it in a deep dish, and first pour over melted butter and then strong vinegar. And so leave it for several days, from 4 to 6 days depending on the season of the year, turning it every day onto a different side. When it is ready, put it on the spit and pour over the marinade. Wild boar is served with a spicy sauce or Tartar sauce. The loin needs roasting for an hour, the hams for an hour and a half.

This was the advice given to her readers almost a century and a half ago by Karolina Nakwaska in her very popular *Dwór wiejski.*

Almost all this advice holds good today. Wild boar meat, which is similar in taste to pork, differs from pork only in colour and in the characteristic smell. It can be cooked like pork or beef. Wild boar hams smoked for three days in cold smoke can be kept for a long time and are very tasty cold.

Meat from old animals, after hanging, should be marinated for several days, best in a marinade of wine with added lemon juice, juniper, spices and onion; before roasting, it should be larded thickly with pork fat.

The meat from young animals, after first hanging, can simply be soaked in milk.

Rosehip or currant sauce is best to serve with wild boar. Horseradish, mustard, tomato or cream caper sauces are also excellent.

Stuffed boar head: Pièce de résistance of the Easter feast

MARINADE: lemon juice,1 cup red wine, 1 medium-large onion, 1 carrot, 1 parsley root, ¼ celeriac, 4–5 juniper berries, 8–10 peppercorns, 8–10 allspice berries, 2 bay leaves, ¼ tsp rosemary, ¼ tsp fresh spruce needles

STUFFING: 500 g veal, 500 g fatty pork, 2 bread rolls, 4 eggs, salt, pepper, ½ tsp grated nutmeg, boar tongue, ½ pickled ox tongue, a few truffles (well, button mushrooms would do), 200 g pork fat, 1 glass brandy or spirit

Cut off the boar head together with the neck, scald, and remove the hairs. Wash thoroughly. Split the head open from the bottom, carefully remove all the bones (do not damage the meat or the skin). Remove the tusks, clean them and reserve. Prepare the marinade. Place the de-boned head of boar carefully in an earthenware pot, pour in the cold marinade and set aside in a cool place for 2–3 days.

PREPARE THE STUFFING: put the veal and pork through a mincer twice and blend thoroughly with the bread rolls soaked in milk and squeezed dry, and with the eggs. Add salt, pepper and nutmeg, mix well. Cook the boar tongue and cut into thin slices. Slice the pickled ox tongue. Mix the sliced tongues with the sliced truffles, stir in the minced meat, sprinkle the whole with the spirit or brandy, and set aside for 2 hours. Remove the boar head from the marinade, dry. Spread the stuffing alternating with layers of the tongues and truffles. Sew the head from the bottom, sew up the eye sockets and press the head into shape. Cover the incision at the back of the neck with the pork fat, put a small piece of wood into the snout. Cover the whole head with a piece of linen, cutting the openings for the ears which should be covered with separate pieces of linen. Carefully place the boar head in a large pot and cover with the stock consisting of 1 l water, 1 l dry white wine, 2 bunches of soup vegetables, 3 onions, 10 juniper berries, 10 allspice berries, 10 peppercorns, 2 bay leaves, ½ tbsp salt, ½ tsp rosemary. Cover the pot and simmer the head for 7 hours. Leave it in the stock to cool. Strain the stock and reserve for the aspic. Take off the linen and place the head on a serving platter. Remove the piece of wood from the boar's muzzle. Now replace the tusks. Make the aspic using the reserved stock and adding some gelatine. Pour it over the boar's head, but first remove the pork fat from the back. Now the only thing is to decorate the boar's head with a garland of watercress, and stud it with some little skewers with mushrooms and hard-boiled eggs. Before 'demolishing' this unusual decoration, cut it into thin slices and serve it with cold spicy sauces.

serves 10 • Marinating: 2–3 days • Preparation: 1–2 hrs • Cooking: 7–8 hrs

Wild boar in sour cherry sauce

2 kg wild boar roast, 500 g sour cherries, 1 cup dry red wine, 50 g almonds, 3 tbsps sugar, lemon rind, salt, 1tbsp butter, 1 tsp flour, ½ cup white wine, ½ cup wine vinegar, ½ cup water, 1 bay leaf, 4–5 black peppercorns, 4–5 allspice berries,1 clove, a small piece of cinnamon, salt

Cook the meat in the white wine and vinegar. Remove when tender. Stone the sour cherries and cover them with 1 cup red wine and 1 cup boar stock. Cook for ½ hour, then put through a sieve and steam off the excess liquid. Make a roux with the butter and flour, add the peeled and finely chopped almonds, finely chopped lemon rind, ground clove and sugar. Add the puréed cherries and stir and cook together until the sauce thickens. Cut the meat into slices and arrange them on an ovenproof serving platter, pour over the sauce and put into a preheated oven for a few minutes.

serves 6–8 • Cooking: 2 hrs • Baking: 10–15 mins

Roast wild boar, hunter's style

1 kg boar ham, 100 g pork fat, 2 tbsps lard, 1 tsp flour, 2 onions, ½ cup light beer, 2 tbsps mustard, 1 egg yolk, 1 tbsp lemon juice, salt, pepper, sugar

MARINADE: 1 cup wine vinegar, 1 carrot, 1 parsley root, 1 onion, 1 bay leaf, 5–7 allspice berries, 5–7 peppercorns

Bring to the boil the marinade ingredients and set aside to cool. Remove the membrane and wash the meat, then pound it lightly with your hand and place in an earthenware pot. Top with the marinade and keep in a cool place for 2–3 days, turning the meat over every day. Remove the meat from the marinade, dry it and lard densely with pork fat. Rub it with salt and brown all over in the heated lard. Transfer to a saucepan, sprinkle with lard and add the sliced onion. Pour in the beer, cover and simmer, sprinkling it frequently with the strained marinade. When the meat is tender, remove it and cut into slices, then return to the saucepan. Mix well the egg yolk with the mustard, lemon juice, lemon rind and a pinch of sugar, salt and pepper. Cover the meat with the sauce and keep for a few moments over low heat. Carefully transfer the slices of meat onto a serving platter. Serve with potato dumplings or French fries. Sieve the sauce and serve it in a sauceboat.

serves 6–8 • Marinating: 2–3 days • Preparation: 10 mins • Stewing: 70–90 mins

Roast wild boar in spicy sauce

2 kg boneless meat (preferably haunch), 2 large onions, soup vegetables, 10–15 prunes, grated rind of 1 lemon and 1 orange, juice of 1 lemon, 100 g butter, 1 cup stock, 10 pepper grains, 5 tomatoes, 1 tsp flour, salt, 2 cups red wine

Put the washed meat into a saucepan, add the wine and set aside in a cool place for 1–2 days. Now remove from the marinade, dry and rub with salt, sprinkle with pepper and sear all over in lard. Transfer it to a saucepan, add the finely cut vegetables, sliced onion, quartered tomatoes and pepper, pour in the wine, cover and simmer for about 1½ hours. Soak the prunes overnight in a little water. Bring to the boil and put through a sieve. Add the lemon juice, grated lemon and orange rind, mix well. Make a roux with the butter and flour, dilute with the stock, add the puréed prunes and the meat juices. Mix well and pass through a sieve. Steam off the excess liquid. Cut the meat into slices, arrange them in an ovenproof dish, pour over the sauce and put for a few minutes into a preheated oven.

serves 6–8 • Marinating: 1–2 days • Preparation: 10–15 mins • Stewing: 80–90 mins

Roast wild boar in rosehip sauce

2 kg boneless meat, 100 g pork fat, 1 tbsp butter, 3–4 tbsp rosehip preserve, salt, pepper, 1 glass semi-sweet wine, 1 tsp flour, ½ cup strong stock, 1 tbsp lard

MARINADE: 1 cup dry wine, 5–6 allspice berries, 5–6 pepper grains, 1 bay leaf, ¼ tsp powdered ginger, 6–8 juniper berries, grated rind of 1 lemon, 2 onions, 2–3 garlic cloves, 6–7 prunes

Bring to the boil the marinade ingredients. Wash the meat and place it in an earthenware pot, pour over the cold marinade and set aside in a cool place for 4–5 days. Turn over frequently. Then remove the meat from the marinade and rinse it, dry and rub with salt and pepper, coat with thin strips of pork fat and sear on all sides in lard. Transfer to a roasting pan, coat with all the ingredients of the marinade and roast in a preheated oven for about 2 hours, frequently basting the meat with the marinade. Cut the meat into diagonal slices, transfer to an ovenproof dish and keep warm. Make a roux with the butter and flour, dilute with the stock and mix with the meat juices, then put through a sieve. Add the rosehip preserve and 1 glass wine, mix together and pour over the meat. Put for a few minutes into a preheated oven.

serves 6–8 • Marinating: 1–2 days • Preparation: 10–15 mins • Stewing: 80–90 mins

Roast wild boar with almonds

2 kg boneless meat (hunch, shoulder), salt, pepper, 150 g pork fat, 100 g butter, ½ cup double sour cream, 1 slice wholemeal bread, ½ cup red wine, 50 g almonds, 2 crushed cloves, 2 cups milk

Wash the meat, cover with the milk and set aside in a cool place overnight. Remove from the marinade, pound with a mallet, press hard with your hand and lard densely with pork fat. Rub with salt and pepper. Put the meat on a greased baking tin, dot with knobs of butter and roast in a preheated oven for about 1 hour, frequently basting with butter and water. In a small saucepan melt 1 tbsp butter, add the crumbled bread, mix and thin out with 1 tbsp water. Add the crushed cloves and the cream. Remove the meat for a moment and cover it with the prepared mixture. Put it back into the oven and bake until brown. Sprinkle it with the peeled and finely chopped almonds, cover with the wine and continue to bake for another 10 mins.

serves 6–8 • Soaking: 12 hrs • Preparation: 5 mins • Roasting: 60–70 mins

Sirloin (Saddle) of wild boar in apricot sauce

1½ kg saddle, salt, 1 tbsp lard

MARINADE: 1 cup red wine, lemon juice, 2 cups water, 2 onions, 6–8 prunes, 1 bay leaf, 10 allspice berries, 10 black peppercorns, 20 juniper berries, a dash of powdered ginger

SAUCE: 1 tbsp apricot jam, ½ tsp sugar, 1 tsp flour

Bring to the boil the ingredients of the marinade. Rinse the meat and place it in an earthenware pot, cover with the hot marinade and set aside in a cool place for 1–2 days. Turn over every day. Then strain, reserving the marinade, and wipe dry. Rub the meat with salt and sear on all sides in hot lard. Transfer to a casserole, add the prunes (from the marinade) and onions, sprinkle with the strained marinade, cover and simmer for about 2 hours, frequently basting with the marinade. When the meat is tender, remove it from the sauce, place on an ovenproof platter, sprinkle with the melted butter and roast for a few minutes in a preheated oven. Make a roux with the butter and flour, dilute it with a little water, add the apricot jam, cinnamon and sugar, pour in the remaining marinade and bring to the boil, stirring all the time. Combine with the meat juices and pass through a sieve. Cut the meat diagonally into slices and cover with the sauce. Serve the remaining sauce in a sauceboat.

serves 6–8 • Marinating: 1–2 days • Preparation: 10–15 mins • Stewing: 100–120 mins

Saddle of wild boar in strawberry sauce

1½ kg saddle, 2 garlic cloves,100 g pork fat, salt, 1 carrot, 1 parsley root, ¼ celeriac, 1 onion, 6–8 juniper berries, 6–8 allspice berries, 6–8 black peppercorns, 10 prunes, 2 tbsps lard, 1 glass dry white wine, 1 cup strong stock, 2–3 tbsps strawberry preserve, ½ lemon, ½ orange, 1 tbsp butter, 1 tsp flour, 1 cup milk

Rinse the meat, cover with the milk and set aside in a cool place overnight. Remove from the marinade, wipe dry and pound with your hand. Lard the meat with the pork fat, rub with salt and minced garlic. Sear on all sides in the lard, transfer to a casserole, add the sliced vegetables, onion and spices. Sprinkle with the stock and the wine, cover and simmer for about 1½ hours. Soak the prunes in a little water, bring to the boil and add to the sauce. Make a roux with the butter and flour, dilute with the remaining wine, add the sliced lemon and orange, bring to the boil. Remove the meat when tender and cut into slices. Arrange the slices on an ovenproof platter. Mix the meat juices with the lemon and orange sauce, heat up and pass through a sieve. Add the strawberry preserve, mix well. Pour the sauce over the meat and bake for a few minutes in a preheated oven.

serves 4–6 • Soaking: 12 hrs • Preparation: 10–15 mins • Stewing: 1½ hrs • Baking: 10 mins

Wild boar haunch in sour cherry sauce

2 kg haunch, 100 g pork fat, 1 cup sour cherry juice, 1 tbsp crumbled wholemeal bread, ¼ tsp cinnamon, 1 crushed clove, salt, 1 tbsp butter

MARINADE: 1 cup wine vinegar, 1 carrot, 1 parsley root, ¼ celeriac, 1 onion, 5–7 juniper berries, 5–7 allspice berries, 1 bay leaf, grated rind of 1 lemon, 2 cloves

Bring to the boil the ingredients of the marinade, allow to cool. Rinse the meat, knead it well with your hand,

place in an earthenware pot and cover with the marinade. Set it aside in a cool place for 3–4 days. Remove the meat, rinse it, wipe dry, lard with the pork fat and rub with salt. In a saucepan melt the butter and sear the meat on all sides. Add the marinated vegetables, sprinkle with the marinade, cover and simmer for about 1½ hours. Remove the meat when tender, cut into slices and place on an ovenproof platter. Pass the meat juices through a sieve, add the crumbled bread, cherry juice, cinnamon and the clove, mix well. Cover the meat with the sauce, and bake for a few minutes in a preheated oven.

serves 6–8 • Marinating: 3–4 days • Preparation: 5 mins • Stewing: 1½ hrs • Baking: 10 mins

Wild boar haunch in herbs

1 haunch, 150 g pork fat, ½ tsp crushed juniper berries, ½ tsp crushed cloves, ¼ tsp crushed pepper, ¼ tsp crushed allspice berries, ¼ tsp each dried thyme, basil and tarragon, 1 crushed bay leaf

MARINADE: 2 carrots, 2 bay leaves, 4–5 cloves, grated rind of 1 lemon, 2 cups white wine, 1 cup weak wine vinegar, 2 cups water, 100 g butter

Bone out and wash the boar haunch, remove the membrane. Knead well the meat and lard it with the pork fat, rub generously with salt, spices and herbs, then tie up tightly with thread. Place the meat in a pot and keep it in a cool place for 3–4 days. Now bring to the boil the wine with water, vinegar, spices and the finely chopped vegetables, put in the meat, add the marinade, cover and simmer for about 4 hours, basting with some water, if necessary. Remove the meat when tender, place it in a greased roasting pan, top it with melted butter and roast in a preheated oven until brown. From time to time sprinkle it with the strained stock. Arrange the meat on a serving platter, pour the meat juices over and set aside to cool. Serve cold with spicy sauces. However, if you wish to serve the boar haunch hot, the stock with the vegetables in which the boar was cooking should be sieved, seasoned to taste with salt and, if desired, with sugar, and poured over the meat.

serves 4–6 • Marinating: 3–4 days • Cooking: 4 hrs • Roasting: 10–12 mins

Saddle of wild boar in pastry

saddle of boar, soup vegetables, 1 bay leaf,
5–6 black peppercorns, 5–6 allspice berries,
2–3 cloves, 1 tsp rosemary, 1 tsp thyme,
100 g pork fat, salt, ½ cup dry white wine

PASTRY: 250 g flour, 1 tsp butter, 1 egg yolk

SAUCE: 4 tbsps grated horseradish, 1 tbsp
redcurrant juice, 1 tbsp sour cherry juice,
1 tsp Dijon-type mustard, juice of 1 lemon, salt

Rub the tenderized saddle well with salt, bard with thin strips of pork fat and tie up tightly with thread. Place the meat in a saucepan, add the finely chopped vegetables, spices and herbs, pour in the wine, cover and simmer for about 90 mins, sprinkling from time to time with water, so that the meat does not burn. Set aside to cool. Knead the dough, adding ½ cup warm water to the flour, butter and 1 egg yolk. Roll out the dough 1 cm thick. Sieve the meat juices. Spread the sauce on the dough, then place the meat on it and roll the dough and seal the ends tightly. Transfer to a greased baking tin and bake for about 40 mins in a preheated oven. Serve hot or cold with horseradish sauce. Mix well all the ingredients of the sauce, and serve the sauce in a sauceboat.

serves 6–8 • Preparation: 15–20 mins • Stewing: 90 mins
• Cooling: 1–2 hrs • Baking: 40–45 mins

Roast wild boar in pastry

2 kg ham, salt, 1 tbsp lard, 4 tbsps cream

MARINADE: 2 cups water, 1 cup vinegar, 7–8 allspice berries, 7–8 black peppercorns, 2–3 bay leaves, ¼ tsp thyme, 1 carrot, 1 parsley root, ¼ celeriac, 1 onion

PASTRY: 200 g butter, 3 eggs, ½ tsp cinnamon,
1 tsp sugar, salt, 200 g stale bread

Bring to the boil all the ingredients of the marinade. Rinse the meat, flatten it with your hand, place in an earthenware pot and cover with the marinade. Set aside in a cool place for 2–3 days. Remove, rinse, wipe dry and

rub with salt, then sear on all sides in lard. Transfer to a casserole, add the vegetables from the marinade, sprinkle with the marinade, cover and simmer for about 1½ hours. Remove from the casserole and set aside to cool. In a bowl cream the butter with the eggs, gradually adding sugar, cinnamon, a pinch of salt and the grated stale bread. Pour in the wine and mix well to form a thick batter. Leave it for a moment to rest, then mix again. Immerse the meat in the dough and place it on a greased baking tin, transfer to a preheated oven, top with the remaining dough and cream, and bake for about 1 hour until the dough turns golden brown. Remove, cut into slices and arrange on a serving platter. In a sauceboat serve the gravy thinned out with the strained marinade.

serves 6–8 • Marinating: 2–3 days • Stewing: 90 mins •
Cooling: 1–2 hrs • Preparation: 20 mins • Baking: 1 hr

Wild boar spareribs in cherry sauce

1 kg spareribs, salt, juice of 1 lemon,
soup vegetables, 1 onion, grated rind of
½ lemon, 5 allspice berries, 10 juniper berries

SAUCE: 500 g cherries, a pinch of cinnamon,
1 tsp sugar, ½ cup red wine, 1 small glass brandy,
1 small bread roll

Cook the meat in some water with lemon juice, soup vegetables, onion, juniper berries, allspice, salt and lemon rind. Remove from the stock, bone out and divide into serving pieces. Keep warm. Pour a cup of stock blended with wine on the cherries, cinnamon and bread roll. Bring to the boil, pass through a sieve, season to taste with sugar and brandy. Before serving, pour the sauce over the spareribs.

serves 4 • Cooking: 50–60 mins • Preparation: 15–20 mins

Stewed wild boar spareribs

1 kg spareribs, salt, 4–5 allspice berries, 4–5 black peppercorns, 2 bay leaves, ¼ tsp thyme, juice of 1 lemon, 2 slices stale wholemeal bread, 20 g almonds, ½ cup thick sour cream, 1 cup red wine, 1 sprig tarragon, 1 tbsp butter

Grate and sift the bread, mix it with the cream and chopped tarragon leaves. Cook the spareribs in some salted water with lemon juice, herbs and spices. Remove when tender. Set aside to cool and bone out. Rub the meat with the sauce, sprinkle with the chopped almonds, brown in butter, then simmer for a moment, sprinkling the meat with the wine.

serves 4 • Cooking: 50–60 mins • Cooling: 1 hr • Preparation: 15–20 mins

Wild boar bacon with sauerkraut

*500 g sauerkraut, 500 g wild boar bacon,
¼ tsp powdered caraway seeds, ¼ tsp ground
pepper, 10 juniper berries, 2 tbsps lard,
1 tsp flour, salt, 2 cups stock, 1 onion*

Blanch the finely chopped onion in lard, add the chopped sauerkraut, juniper berries, caraway seeds and pepper, and mix well. Simmer together for a moment. Add the bacon rubbed with salt, pour in the stock and simmer over low heat. When the bacon is tender, remove it and divide into serving pieces. Blend the flour with 1 tbsp water, add to the cabbage to thicken it, and mix well. Put the bacon in, heat up. Serve with boiled potatoes.

serves 4 • Preparation: 10 mins • Stewing: 50–60 mins

Roast bacon of wild boar

*2 kg wild boar bacon, 200 g sugar, 250 g prunes,
1 cup dry red wine, salt, ¼ tsp cinnamon*

Wash the prunes and soak them in little water. Rub the bacon with salt and in a frying pan brown it on both sides. Transfer to a casserole, cover with the wine and water in which the prunes were soaking. Cover and simmer. After 45 mins add the prunes. Remove the bacon when tender and cut it into 6–8 pieces. Coat each piece with the cinnamon and quite generously with sugar. Arrange the pieces of meat snugly in a roasting pan and bake in a hot oven until the sugar melts and turns golden brown. On a serving platter arrange the caramelized pieces of bacon and surround them with the prunes.

*serves 6–8 • Preparation: 15 mins • Stewing:
50–60 mins • Roasting: 10–15 mins*

Wild boar brisket

*2 kg brisket, liver, heart and tongue of young boar,
100 g butter, 100 g pork fat, 100 g mushrooms,
1 cup red wine, 1 onion, 1 egg, 1 tsp flour, salt,
juice of 1 lemon, soup vegetables, 1 onion,
5 juniper berries, 5 black peppercorns, 5 allspice
berries, 2 bay leaves*

Bring to the boil water with the giblets, lemon juice, soup vegetables and spices. Sauté the mushrooms and onion in butter. Bone out the brisket, rub the meat with salt. Pass the giblets, pork fat and mushrooms through a sieve, add salt, pepper and the egg. Mix well. Stuff the brisket with the mixture, sew up and place on a greased roasting tin. Coat the meat with the vegetables taken from the stock, add the spices, cover with the wine and roast in a hot oven, sprinkling the meat with the melted butter and the strained stock. When the meat is ready, take it out and place on a warmed serving platter. Thicken the sauce with flour, pass through a sieve and serve it in a sauceboat.

Cooking: 1 hr • Preparation: 25–30 mins • Roasting: 50–60 mins

Wild boar chops with almonds

*500 g loin of boar, 2 eggs, 2 tbsps chopped parsley,
1 tbsp chopped almonds, 2 tbsps lard, 1 tbsp flour, salt,
pepper, 2 garlic cloves, ¼ tsp marjoram, 1 cup milk*

Bone out the meat and soak in milk overnight. Remove, wipe dry and cut into fillets. Pound with a mallet, rub with garlic minced with salt, sprinkle with pepper and marjoram. Put one on top of another and set aside in a cool place for 1 hour. Then coat in flour and fry in hot lard. Mix the eggs with chopped almonds and green parsley, season to taste with salt and pepper. Arrange the fried meat in an ovenproof platter and cover with the egg mixture. Bake in a preheated oven for about 10 mins.

serves 4 • Soaking: 12 hrs • Macerating: 1–2 hrs • Preparation: 15–20 mins

Wild boar fillets in orange sauce

*700 g boneless saddle, 1 tbsp lemon juice,
salt, pepper, 2 tbsps clarified butter*

SAUCE: 1 large orange, 1 tbsp lemon juice, 1 glass orange liquer, ½ cup beef stock or boar stock, 3 tbsps butter, 1 tsp potato flour

Squeeze out the juice of a well-scrubbed orange, and boil the peel in boiling water. Drain, separate the white albedo, and cut the peel into thin strips. In a small saucepan melt the butter, add the orange peel, sauté for a few minutes, then add the orange juice. Cover and heat up over low heat. Wash and dry the meat, cut it into 4 slices, lightly pound with a mallet, sprinkle with lemon juice and pepper. Fry in hot butter and transfer to a warmed serving platter. Season with salt and keep warm. Pour the stock into the frying pan and mix well. Transfer the sauce to the saucepan with the orange. Add the lemon juice, bring to the boil, add the potato flour mixed with 2 tbsps water and stirring all the time heat up until the sauce thickens. Season to taste with salt and pepper, pour in the liquer, mix well and pour over the fillets. Bake for 4–5 mins in a preheated oven.

serves 4 • Preparation: 10–15 mins • Baking: 4–5 mins

Baked wild boar steaks

500 g loin of boar, salt, pepper, 2 fresh peaches, or 4 stewed peach halves, 100 g grated cheese, 1 tbsp butter, 1 tsp lemon juice, 1 tsp flour, lard for frying, 1 tbsp chopped parsley, 1 cup milk

Remove the membrane, wash the meat and flatten it with your hand. Place the meat in a pot, cover with milk and set aside in a cool place overnight. Remove, wipe dry and cut into 4 serving pieces. Pound with a mallet, sprinkle with lemon juice, salt and pepper. Leave in a cool place for 1 hour. Then sprinkle with flour and fry in hot lard. Butter an ovenproof dish, arrange the steaks and top each steak with half of a peach. Sprinkle with the grated cheese and melted butter and put into a preheated oven. Bake for 15–20 mins. Separately serve Cumberland sauce.

serves 4 • Soaking: 12 hrs • Macerating: 1–2 hrs • Preparation: 20–25 mins

Rolled wild boar zrazy

500 g loin of boar, 100 g mushrooms, 100 g smoked streaky bacon, 1 onion, 1 tbsp chopped parsley, 1 tbsp butter, 1 tbsp grated cheese, salt,

pepper, 1 garlic clove, 1 egg, 2 tbsps breadcrumbs, 1 tbsp flour, 1 glass white wine, 1 cup milk

Remove the membrane, wash the meat and flatten it with your hand. Place the meat in a pot, cover with milk and leave in a cool place overnight. Remove, wipe dry and cut into 4 serving pieces. Pound with a mallet, sprinkle with salt and pepper, rub with the garlic and set aside in a cool place for 1 hour. Cut the bacon into fine cubes and sauté briskly. Add the finely cut mushrooms and onion, season with salt and pepper to taste and simmer for about 10 mins. Cool, then mix with parsley and the grated cheese. Spread the mixture on each fillet, roll up and tie with thread. Coat in the flour, egg and breadcrumbs and fry in hot fat. Transfer to a saucepan, add 1 tbsp water, sprinkle with wine, cover and simmer for about ½ hour over low heat.

serves 4–6 • Soaking: 12 hrs • Macerating: 1 hr • Preparation: 20 mins

Ham of young boar, served hot

ham of young boar, 50 g butter, 1 tbsp salt, 1 tsp saltpetre

MARINADE: 1 cup vinegar, 1 cup water, 3–4 bay leaves, 1 tsp tarragon, 1 tsp rosemary, 4–5 cloves, juice and grated rind of 1 lemon

SAUCE: 50 g butter, 1 tsp flour, 1 soaked herring, juice of 1 lemon, 1 glass wine, sugar, salt, pepper to taste

Trim and bone out the ham, wash it, wipe dry, rub with the saltpetre and salt and place in an earthenware pot. Cover with the cold marinade and set aside in a cool place for 1–2 days. Transfer the ham to a saucepan, pour in 1 cup marinade and cook for 2½–3 hours. Remove when tender, and place on a greased roasting tin, sprinkle with the melted butter and roast about 15 minutes in a preheated oven. Make a roux with the butter and flour, dilute with 1 cup strained stock, add lemon juice and the finely chopped herring, season to taste with salt, pepper and sugar. Pour in the white wine, mix well and heat up. Cut the ham into diagonal slices. Pass the sauce through a sieve and pour it over the meat before serving.

serves 6–8 • Marinating: 1–2 days • Cooking: 2½–3 hrs • Roasting: 15–20 mins

Roebuck

The meat of roebuck is like that of roedeer, only tends to have a sharper taste in the case of older animals.

Venison in bourguignonne sauce

1½ kg haunch, 150 g smoked streaky bacon, 1 glass brandy, salt, pepper, 1 tsp thyme, 2 tbsps chopped parsley, 2 cups dry white wine, 3 onions, 2 carrots, 2 garlic cloves, 1 tsp ground pepper, 250 g mushrooms, salt

Cut 100 g streaky bacon into thin rashers, transfer to a soup plate and sprinkle with the chopped parsley and ½ tsp thyme, cover with the brandy and set aside in a cool place for 2–3 hours. Wash the meat and remove any veins. Wipe dry and cut deep as many times as many rashers of the bacon you have. Insert the bacon into the incisions. Tie the meat with thread, coat with the grated carrot, diced onion and chopped garlic. Place in an eartenware pot and sprinkle with salt, thyme and pepper, cover with the wine and set aside in a cool place for 1–2 days. Then take the meat out and sear on all sides in melted butter. Transfer to a casserole, add the vegetables from the marinade, pour in the marinade, cover and simmer for about 1½ hours. Dice and render the remaining bacon, add the sliced mushrooms and fry together, stirring all the time. Take out the meat when tender and place in an ovenproof dish. Roast for a few minutes in a preheated oven. Pass the meat juices through a sieve and blend with the mushrooms. Cut the meat into slices and pour over the sauce.

serves 6–8 • Macerating: 2–3 hrs • Marinating: 1–2 days • Stewing: 90 mins • Baking: 10–15 mins

Venison haunch, hunter's style

1½ kg haunch, 150 g smoked sausage, 3 tbsps grated horseradish, 3 slices stale wholemeal bread, 150 g mushrooms, 1 tsp lemon juice, salt, pepper, ½ tsp ground juniper, 2 tbsps lard, 1 tsp flour

MARINADE: ½ cup wine vinegar, grated lemon rind, 4–5 allspice berries, 4–5 black peppercorns, 4–5 juniper berries, 1 clove

Combine all the ingredients of the marinade and bring to the boil. Set aside to cool. Wash the meat and remove any veins. Knead it well with your hand and place in an earthenware pot. Pour in the marinade and set aside in a cool place for 1–2 days. Now take the meat out, rinse and wipe dry. Sprinkle with lemon juice, salt, pepper and juniper, and set aside in a cool place for 2–3 hours. Then brown the meat on all sides in hot fat, transfer to a casserole, sprinkle with the marinade, dredge with the flour and simmer covered for about 1½ hours, frequently sprinkling the meat with the marinade. Towards the end of the cooking add the sliced mushrooms and the sliced sausage. Take out the meat when tender, cut into slices and arrange on a warm serving platter. Keep warm. Mix the grated bread with the remaining marinade and horseradish, combine with the meat juices, mix well and heat up. Pour over the meat.

serves 4–6 • Marinating: 1–2 days • Salting: 2–3 hrs • Stewing: 90 mins

Venison saddle with cream

2 kg saddle, 300 g pork fat, 15–20 juniper berries, 1 cup thick sour cream, 100 g butter, salt, pepper, 1 tsp flour, 2 cups milk

Wash the meat and remove any veins. Flatten it with your hand, put into a pot, cover with the milk and set aside in a cool place overnight. Now take the meat out, dry it and lard densely with pork fat. Sprinkle with lemon juice, rub with salt, pepper and juniper and set aside in a cool place for 2–3 hours. Line the bottom of a roasting pan with thin rashers of pork fat, place the meat on top and roast it in a preheated oven until the pork fat turns golden brown. Then sprinkle with melted butter and roast for about 1½ hours, frequently basting the meat with water. 15 mins before the end of roasting, add the cream blended with flour.

serves 6–8 • Soaking: 2 hrs • Salting: 2–3 hrs • Roasting: 1½ hrs

Venison saddle served cold

2 kg saddle, 150 g pork fat, 1 tbsp butter, salt

MARINADE: ½ cup red wine, juice and grated rind of 1 lemon, 2 cloves, ¼ tsp powdered ginger, 2 bay leaves, 6–8 black peppercorns, ½ tsp tarragon, sugar to taste

Combine all the ingredients of the marinade and bring to the boil. Wash the meat and remove any veins, press it hard with your hand and place in an earthenware pot. Cover with the marinade and set aside in a cool place for 5–6 days. Turn the meat very often. Now take the meat out, rinse, wipe dry and lard densely with pork fat, rub with salt, then grill or roast, sprinkling frequently with melted butter and marinade. Serve cold with bilberries or cold sauces.

serves 6–8 • Marinating: 5–6 days • Roasting: 1½–2 hrs • Cooling: 2–3 hrs

Leg of roebuck with garlic

2 kg leg, 2 onions, 6 garlic cloves, 150 g pork fat, salt, 1 tbsp olive oil, 1 tbsp lemon juice, ½ cup red wine, 1 cup thick sour cream, 1 tsp flour, 2 tbps butter

Wash the meat and remove any veins. Press hard with your hand, place in a pot, pour in the olive oil and lemon juice, cover densely with the slices of onion and sprinkle with 3 finely chopped garlic cloves. Set aside in a cool place for 1–2 days. Take the meat out, rub with the garlic minced with salt, lard with the pork fat and place in a greased roasting pan. Coat with the onion and garlic from the marinade and roast in a preheated oven for about 2 hours, frequently basting with melted butter and wine. Take out the meat when tender, pass the meat juices through a sieve. Place the meat in the sauce, cover with the cream blended with flour and bake for a few minutes.

serves 6–8 • Marinating: 1–2 days • Roasting: 2 hrs • Baking: 10–12 mins

Leg of roebuck in spicy sauce

2 kg leg, 150 g pork fat, 1 onion, soup vegetables, 10 juniper berries, 4 black peppercorns, 2 cloves, salt, ¼ tsp paprika, 1 tbsp lemon juice, 2 cups milk, ½ cup red wine, 50 g prunes, 50 g walnut meats, 1 slice stale wholemeal bread, 1 tbsp butter, 1 tsp flour

Wash the meat and remove any veins. Knead it well with your hand, place in a pot and cover with milk. Set aside in a cool place overnight. Take the meat out, dry and sprinkle with lemon juice. Rub it with salt and paprika, set aside in a cool place for 1–2 hours. Dice the pork fat and fry briskly in a saucepan. Sprinkle with water and simmer

for a moment or two. Sear the meat on all sides in the hot butter, transfer to a casserole, pour in the wine and simmer covered. Soak the prunes in little water, bring to the boil and together with the liquid add to the roast. Take out the meat when tender, pass the sauce through a sieve and add the chopped walnuts and grated bread. Put the meat back to the casserole and keep over low heat for a moment or two.

serves 4 • Marinating: 1–2 days • Preparation: 5–7 mins • Stewing: 1½–2 hrs

Roebuck stew

600 g boneless shoulder, 1 onion, ¼ tsp rosemary, ¼ tsp crushed juniper, ¼ tsp ground pepper, ¼ tsp ground allspice

SAUCE: 2 tbsps plum jam, 1 tart apple, 1 tsp sugar, 1 tbsp chopped almonds, ½ cup stock, 1 slice grated stale bread

MARINADE: ½ cup red wine, 2 cloves, ½ tsp powdered ginger, 1 bay leaf, juice and grated rind of 1 lemon, 4–5 peppercorns

Combine the ingredients of the marinade, bring to the boil and set aside to cool. Wash the meat and remove any veins. Place it in an earthenware pot, cover with the marinade and set aside in a cool place for 1–2 days. Cut the marinated meat into cubes, dust with the herbs and spices, place in a bowl and set aside in a cool place for 1 hour. Cut the pork fat into small cubes, melt in a saucepan, add the meat and the finely chopped onion, and fry together for a moment or two, then pour in the stock and simmer. When the meat is half tender, add the chopped almonds, grated apple and plum jam. Dust with the grated bread, mix and add the sugar. Pour in the strained marinade and continue to simmer for an additional half an hour.

serves 4 • Marinating: 1–2 days • Preparation: 7–8 mins • Macerating: 1 hr • Stewing: 35–40 mins

Roebuck fricassee with apples

600 g boneless shoulder, ½ cup white wine, 500 g tart apples, 2 tbsps raisins, ½ cup double cream, 1 tsp flour, salt, pepper, sugar, juice and grated rind of 1 lemon, 2 tbsps lard, 2 cups milk

Wash the meat and remove the membrane. Place in a pot, cover with the milk and set aside in a cool place overnight. Then take the meat out, dry and cut into small pieces. Sprinkle with lemon juice, dust with salt and pepper, and set aside in a cool place for 1 hour. Now brown the meat in hot fat, sprinkle with the wine and simmer covered. Peel, core and slice the apples, add to the meat together with the raisins and grated lemon rind. Mix and simmer together for about half an hour. Towards the end of cooking add a pinch of sugar, pour in the cream blended with flour, and keep over low heat for a moment or two.

serves 4–6 • Soaking: 12 hrs • Preparation: 10 mins
• Macerating: 1 hr • Stewing: 35–40 mins

Rolled venison zrazy

600 g saddle, 2 cups milk, 100 g prunes, 100 g grated cheese, 50 g smoked streaky bacon, salt, pepper, ¼ tsp rosemary, 1 tbsp lemon juice, ½ cup double cream, sugar, 1 tsp flour, 2 tbsps grated horseradish, 1 slice stale wholemeal bread, fat for frying

Wash the meat and remove any veins. Put into a pot, cover with the milk and set aside in a cool place overnight. Now wipe the meat dry, cut into slices and lightly pound with a mallet. Soak the prunes overnight, then bring to the boil and cut into strips. Sprinkle the meat with lemon juice, dust with salt, pepper and rosemary. Put the zrazy one on top of another and set aside in a cool place for one hour. Cut the bacon into fine cubes. On each slice of meat place strips of prunes and diced bacon, sprinkle with grated cheese, then roll up the meat slices and tie them up with thread. Dredge with flour and brown in hot fat. Transfer the meat to a saucepan, sprinkle with water and simmer covered. Towards the end add the horseradish, grated bread and the cream. Season to taste with lemon juice and a pinch of sugar. Mix gently and continue to simmer for another 15 mins.

serves 4 • Soaking: 12 hrs • Preparation: 10 mins •
Macerating: 1 hr • Stewing: 35–40 mins

Venison mini zrazy

500 g venison haunch, 50 g smoked pork fat, 50 g butter, salt, pepper, grated rind of 1 lemon, 1 tsp flour,

1 small glass of Madeira, 1 tsp Worcestershire sauce, 2 tbsps stock, 1 bread roll for toast, 1 cup milk

Wash the meat and remove any veins. Place in a pot, cover with the milk and set aside in a cool place overnight. Then take out and dry. Cut the meat into small zrazy, lightly pound with a mallet and lard with strips of pork fat. Dredge with salt, pepper and grated lemon rind. Set aside for 1 hour. Dust the zrazy with flour and brown on both sides in the melted butter. Transfer to a saucepan, sprinkle with water and simmer for a moment or two. Make a roux with the butter in which the meat was frying and the flour, add the stock, wine and Worcestershire sauce, bring to the boil and pour over the meat. Serve with pieces of toast and red cabbage stewed in wine.

serves 4 • Soaking: 12 hrs • Preparation: 10 mins
• Macerating: 1 hr • Stewing: 40 mins

Venison fillets with beetroots

600 g saddle, 100 g smoked pork fat, 100 g butter, salt, pepper, juice of 1 lemon, 1 glass white wine, 1 bread roll for toasting, 500 g beetroots, 1 tbsp butter, ½ tsp sugar, salt, juice of ½ lemon

Cook the beetroots, then grate and stew in melted butter. Add salt, sugar and lemon juice. Mix well and simmer for a few minutes. Wash the meat, remove the membrane and press the meat well with your hand. Cut into slices, lard with the pork fat, sprinkle with lemon juice, dust with salt and pepper. Fry on both sides in melted butter. Prepare pieces of toast. Butter an ovenproof platter and place the pieces of toast in the middle. Put the fillets on toast and sprinkle them with the butter in which they were frying. Surround the meat with the beetroots and put the platter into a preheated oven for a few minutes.

serves 4 • Macerating: 1 hr • Preparation: 30–40 mins • Baking: 10 mins

Venison medallions in elderberry sauce

700 g boneless saddle, 1 tbsp lemon juice, salt, pepper, ¼ glass Madeira, 1 tbsp brandy, ½ cup stock, 3 tbsps elderberry jam, 1 tsp honey, 2 tbsps juice of elderberries, 2 tbsps butter, 1 tsp potato flour

Wash and wipe dry the meat. Cut into 4 serving pieces, lightly pound with a mallet and shape into elongated leaves. Sprinkle with lemon juice and brandy, dust with pepper and set aside for an hour. Salt and sear on both sides in melted butter. Place the medallions on a buttered ovenproof platter and keep warm. To the frying pan add the stock, bring to the boil and add the elderberry juice blended with the honey and jam. Heat up over low heat, season to taste with salt and pepper, add the wine mixed with potato flour. Cook and stir over low heat until the sauce thickens. Pour the sauce over the meat and heat up. Serve with French fries or potato and walnut croquettes.

serves 4 • Macerating: 1–2 hrs • Preparation: 15 mins

Venison steaks with mushrooms

600 g haunch, 100 g lean streaky bacon, 250 g mushrooms, 1 tbsp capers, 2 tbsps tomato concentrate, 1 small onion, salt, pepper, 1 tsp lemon juice, sugar, 2 tbsps lard, 1 tbsp flour, 1 cup milk, 1 glass white wine

Wash the meat and remove any veins. Cover with milk and set aside for the night. Take the meat out, dry and cut into slices, pound lightly with a mallet, then lard with thin strips of bacon, sprinkle with lemon juice, season with salt and pepper, dust with flour and fry in hot fat. Transfer to a saucepan, sprinkle with the wine, cover and simmer over low heat. Slice the mushrooms and onion and sauté lightly together, then add to the meat together with capers. Mix the tomato concentrate with 2 tbsp water, add salt, pepper and a pinch of sugar, pour in the remaining wine, mix well and add to the steaks. Mix gently and simmer covered for an additional 15 minutes.

serves 4 • Soaking: 12 hrs • Preparation: 10 mins • Stewing: 15–20 mins

Minced venison fingers

600 g meat (scrappings), 150 g pork fat, 2 onions, 2 eggs, 2 garlic cloves, 1 tsp marjoram, salt, pepper, 1 tbsp butter, 1 cup oil

Finely chop the onions and sauté one in butter. Put the meat and pork fat through a mincer, add both onions, minced garlic, marjoram, salt, pepper and the eggs. Knead smooth pulp and shape small oblong rolls. In a deep frying pan heat the oil and fry the rolls on both sides until brown. Serve sprinkled with melted butter.

serves 4 • Preparation: 20 mins • Frying: 4–6 mins

Venison meatballs

600 g venison, 200 g fat raw streaky bacon, 1 bread roll soaked in milk, 1 egg, salt, pepper, 1 onion, ½ tsp thyme, 2 tbsps breadcrumbs, 1 cup strong stock, 1 lemon, ¼ tsp nutmeg, 1 tbsp capers, 1 tbsp butter, 1 tsp flour, fat for frying

Sauté the finely chopped onion in butter. Put the meat, bacon and the bread roll (squeeze out the milk first) through a mincer. Add the onion, salt, pepper, thyme, egg and grated lemon rind. Knead smooth paste, shape the meatballs and bread them. Fry on all sides in hot fat. In a saucepan bring to the boil the stock and add the lemon cut into slices (remove the pips) and nutmeg. Cover and bring to the boil. Make a roux with the butter and flour, dilute with the strained stock, add the capers and mix well. Put in the meatballs and simmer together for a moment or two.

serves 4–6 • Preparation: 15 mins • Stewing: 20 mins

Venison offal in wine sauce

offal (liver, heart, lungs, kidneys), 150 g butter, 6 eggs, 3 tbsps breadcrumbs, 1 tsp cinnamon, 1 tsp sugar, 1 tbsp raisins, grated rind of 1 lemon, 50 g pork fat, salt

SAUCE: 1 glass Malaga, 1 glass Madeira, 3–4 tbsps single cream, 1 tbsp sugar, 1 tsp butter, 1 tsp flour

Parboil the lungs, kidneys and heart in lightly salted water. Take out when tender, wipe dry and cut into small pieces. Clean the liver and put it through a mincer, then through a sieve, and sauté over low heat, stirring constantly. Gradually add the egg yolks, sugar, cinnamon, bread crumbs, lemon rind, raisins and salt. Mix well. Add the chopped lungs, heart and kidneys. Mix and set aside to cool. Now add the stiff beaten egg whites and mix gently. Transfer the giblet pulp into a baking tin, buttered and lined with breadcrumbs. Cover with thin strips of pork fat and bake for about 1 hour in a preheated oven. Make a roux with the butter and flour, dilute with the Malaga, add sugar and bring to the boil, stirring all the time. Pour in the Madeira and cream, heat up. Arrange the baked giblets on a warmed serving platter. Serve covered with the sauce.

serves 4 • Preparation: 70–90 mins • Baking: 1 hr

Roebuck pâté

*1 kg boneless venison, 300 g fat streaky bacon,
50 g pork fat, venison liver or 150 g chicken livers,
200 g mushrooms, 2 onions, ½ loaf white bread,
3 eggs, 3 tbsps thick sour cream, ½ tsp thyme,
¼ tsp ground juniper, ¼ tsp rosemary, salt, pepper,
allspice to taste, 1 tbsp lard, 1 glass dry red wine*

Cover the meat with the wine and set aside in a cool place for the night. Cut into pieces and sauté in lard together with the diced bacon. Transfer to a saucepan, sprinkle with the wine from the marinade and some water, dredge with thyme, juniper, rosemary and salt. Cover and simmer for about 1 hour. Add the mushrooms and the liver cut into small pieces, and the white bread cut into slices. Simmer together for about 30 mins. Allow to cool. Put 2–3 times through a mincer. Add salt, pepper, allspice, cream and eggs, and mix well. Line a baking mould with strips of pork fat and fill it with the pâté. Cover with aluminium foil and bake in a preheated oven for about 1 hour. Serve cold with spicy sauces.

serves 8–10 • Marinating: 12 hrs • Preparation: 1–2 hrs • Baking: 1 hr

Roedeer

The finest pieces of roedeer meat are saddle and noix of leg. Spareribs and brisket are used to make pâtés, ragout or fricassee. Roedeer offal is also very tasty. The meat of older animals should be aged longer, and then tenderized in a weak vinegar solution, or in white or red wine, with spices and herbs (thyme, marjoram, rosemary). The meat of young animals needs only to age for a short time and then be left to soak for 12 hours in milk or buttermilk, although this is usually not absolutely necessary.

Roedeer cutlets, Old Polish style

600 g boneless saddle or haunch, 2 tbsps olive oil, 1 tbsp lemon juice, 1 tsp grated lemon rind, ½ tsp ground cloves, salt, pepper, 2 tbsps butter, 2 large ripe pears, 1 tbsp lemon juice, 1 tbsp honey, 1 tsp ground pepper, 1 tsp ground cinnamon, 1 cup dry white wine, ½ cup beef stock

Wash and wipe dry the meat. Cut into 4 slices and pound lightly with a knife handle. Mix well the olive oil with ground cloves, lemon juice and grated lemon rind. Rub the cutlets with the mixture, place one on top of another, cover and refrigerate for 1–2 hours. Mix 4 tbsps wine with lemon juice and honey. Peel and core the pears, cut them into eights and place in a saucepan. Cover the pears with the sauce, sprinkle with cinnamon and simmer covered over low heat for about 15 mins. In a frying pan melt the butter and fry the cutlets (3–4 mins each side). When ready place them on a hot ovenproof platter and keep warm. Pour the stock and the remaining wine into the frying pan, add pepper and bring to the boil. Surround the cutlets with pear wedges. Add the pear stock to the saucepan with the sauce, mix and pour over the cutlets. Bake for about 3–4 mins in a preheated oven. Serve with potato croquettes, potato dumplings or rice, decorated with lingonberry preserve.

serves 4 • Macerating: 1–2 hrs • Preparation: 20–25 mins • Baking: 3–5 mins

Roedeer medallions

1 kg saddle, 200 g smoked streaky bacon, ¼ tsp marjoram, ¼ tsp ground juniper, 1 crushed bay leaf, 1 tbsp hot mustard, 2 tbsps butter, 250 g mushrooms, salt, pepper, 1 glass dry red wine, 1 tsp lemon juice, 1 tbsp chopped parsley

Wash and wipe dry the marinated saddle, rub it with salt, spices and herbs, and spread with the mustard. Set aside in the fridge for 2–3 hours. Now take the meat out and cut into thick slices. Pound lightly with a mallet and fry in butter on both sides. Separately sauté the mushrooms cut into slices. In a saucepan render the finely chopped bacon, add the medallions, surround with the mushrooms, sprinkle with the wine and lemon juice, cover and simmer for about 40 mins. Serve sprinkled generously with chopped parsley.

St Hubertus's roast

1½ kg haunch, 1 cup milk, 20 g dried mushrooms, 1 cup thick sour cream, 200 g ham, 150 g grated cheese, lemon juice, salt, pepper, 1 tsp rosemary, 1 tbsp lard, 2 tbsps butter, 1 tsp flour, 500 macaroni

Wash the meat and remove any veins. Cover with the milk and set aside in a cool place overnight. Now take the meat out, wipe dry, rub with salt, pepper and rosemary, sprinkle with lemon juice and set aside in a cool place for 2–3 hours. Bring to the boil the mushrooms which had been soaking overnight. Cut into strips. Sear the meat on all sides in very hot lard, transfer to a saucepan and add the mushrooms and the mushroom stock. Cover and simmer. Cook the macaroni in salted water. Take out the meat when tender and cut diagonally into slices. Add the cream blended with the flour and meat juices. Butter an ovenproof dish, place a layer of macaroni, then a layer of meat, pour over the sauce and cover with a layer of macaroni. Sprinkle with the chopped ham and grated cheese and top with melted butter. Bake in a preheated oven for about 20 mins. Serve with endive or lettuce salad.

serves 4–6 • Soaking: 12 hrs • Macerating: 2–3 hrs • Preparation: 10 mins • Stewing: 40–50 mins

Roedeer roast

1½ kg haunch, 200 g pork fat, 1 tbsp butter, 3 onions, salt, pepper, 1 tbsp lemon juice, 1 cup dry white wine, 3 tbsps hawthorne preserve, 1 tsp flour

Wash the meat and remove any veins. Knead well with your hand, sprinkle with lemon juice, rub with salt and pepper, densely lard with pork fat. Set aside in a cool place to cool. Sauté the finely chopped onion in butter. Place the meat in a roasting pan, add the sautéd onion and roast in a preheated oven. After 30 mins add the wine. Continue to roast for further 1½ hours, from time to time sprinkling the meat with the wine and water. Take out when tender, carve into slices and arrange on a hot serving platter. Keep warm. Add the hawthorne preserve

to the sauce, dredge with flour and pass through a sieve. Pour the sauce over the meat.

serves 6–8 • Macerating: 2–2½ hrs • Preparation: 5 mins • Roasting: 1½ hrs

Roedeer roast in wild sauce

1½ kg haunch, 200 g pork fat, 1 carrot, 1 parsley root, ¼ celeriac, 1 onion, 1 tbsp butter

SAUCE: 2 tbsps redcurrant jelly, 2 tbsps sour cherry juice, lemon juice, 1 tsp caramel, ¼ tsp crushed juniper, 1 crushed clove, ½ cup dry red wine, 1 tsp flour

Wash the meat and remove any veins. Pound it with a mallet, press hard with your hand, rub with salt and lard densely with pork fat. Cut the remaining pork fat into small cubes, melt in a saucepan, add the meat and the finely diced vegetables. Sprinkle with water or stock and simmer covered for about 1½ hours. When the meat is half tender, add all the ingredients of the sauce and continue to simmer. Take out the meat when cooked and carve into slices. Thicken the sauce with a roux made with the butter and flour, pass through a sieve. Pour the sauce over the meat.

serves 6–8 • Preparation: 10 mins • Stewing: 1½ hrs

Rolled venison roast

deer shoulder, 100 g pork fat, 50 g butter, ½ cup stock, 2 onions, salt, pepper, 1 carrot, 1 parsley root, 1 kohlrabi, ¼ celeriac, ½ tsp thyme

MARINADE: juice of 1 lemon, ½ cup dry red wine, 2 cloves, 3–4 peppercorns, 3–4 allspice berries, 3–4 juniper berries, ¼ tsp ginger

Combine the ingredients of the marinade and bring to the boil, set aside to cool. Remove the flat bone from the shoulder. Wash the meat and remove any veins, press with your hand and lightly pound into an even fillet. Sprinkle with thyme, salt and pepper. On the meat spread thin strips of the pork fat and 1 sliced onion. Roll the meat tightly and tie up with thread. Place in an earthenware pot and cover with the marinade. Set aside in a cool place for 2–3 days, and turn over frequently. Peel and wash the vegetables and the other onion, grate them or cut into fine cubes. Take the meat out, dry, rub with salt and brown in butter. Transfer to a saucepan, coat with the grated vegetables and cover with the strained marinade. Cover and simmer for over 1 hour, from time to time sprinkling with the stock or water, if necessary. Take out the meat when tender, untie and cut into thick slices. Arrange on a serving platter, keep warm. Pour over the sieved sauce.

serves 4–6 • Marinating: 2–3 days • Stewing: 70–90 mins

Roast venison in herbs

1½ kg haunch, 200 g pork fat, 1 cup milk, salt, pepper, 1 tbsp soya sauce, ¼ tsp juniper, ¼ tsp thyme, ¼ tsp tarragon, ¼ tsp savory, 2 garlic cloves, 1 tbsp butter

Wash the meat and remove the membrane. Cover the meat with the milk and set aside in a cool place overnight. Remove, wipe dry, press with your hand and lard densely with pork fat. Rub with the herbs and garlic minced with salt, sprinkle with soya sauce and set aside in a cool place for 2–3 hours. Place the meat in a buttered roasting pan, sprinkle with the melted butter and roast in a preheated oven for about 2 hours, frequently basting with water and the meat juices.

serves 6–8 • Soaking: 12 hrs • Macerating: 2–3 hrs • Roasting: 2 hrs

Venison, hunter's style

1 kg meat, salt, pepper, 2 tbsps sunflower oil, 1 tbsp butter, 1 tsp flour, 5 onions, 5 tomatoes, 2–3 garlic cloves, 1 cup dry red wine, 5 peppercorns, 2 bay leaves, 1 tbsp chopped parsley, 2 sprigs fresh, or 1 tbsp dried marjoram

In a saucepan place the finely chopped onions, garlic, tomatoes, marjoram, chopped parsley, peppercorns and bay leaves. Add the red wine, cover and simmer. Wash the meat and remove any veins. Cut into small cubes, dust with salt and pepper and brown on all sides in hot oil. Transfer the meat to the saucepan with the vegetables, sprinkle lightly with water, cover and simmer, adding, if necessary, a little water or wine. Make a roux with the butter and flour to thicken the sauce.

serves 4–6 • Preparation: 20–25 mins • Stewing: 45–55 mins

Venison shashliks

600 g saddle, 4–5 garlic cloves, salt, pepper, ¼ tsp tarragon, 1 tbsp lemon juice, 1 tbsp oil, 150 g pork fat, 2 onions, 2 tomatoes, 1 tbsp butter

Wash the meat and cut into small, thickish slices. Rub with the garlic minced with salt, dust with pepper and tarragon, sprinkle with lemon and oil. Place in a bowl and set aside in a cool place for 2 hours. Cut the pork fat, onion and tomatoes into thick slices. Slide onto spit alternately the meat, pork fat, onion and tomatoes. Sprinkle with melted butter and spit roast.

serves 4 • Macerating: 2 hrs • Preparation: 5–7 mins • Roasting: 15–20 mins

Venison fillets on toast

1 kg saddle, salt, pepper, 50 g pork fat, 1 tbsp olive oil, 1 tbsp butter, ½ loaf white bread for toast, 100 g pâté, 500 g green peas

MARINADE: ½ cup dry red wine, ½ tsp thyme, juice and grated rind of 1 lemon, 2–3 peppercorns, 2–3 allspice berries, 1 clove, 1 bay leaf, a pinch of sugar

Combine the ingredients of the marinade and bring to the boil, then set aside to cool. Cover the meat with the marinade and keep in a cool place for 2–3 days. Remove and cut into fillets of uniform size, lightly pound with a mallet, season with salt and pepper and coat with olive oil. Cut the pork fat into as many strips as many fillets you have, and brown lightly in a frying pan. Remove the pork fat strips, transfer to a saucepan and add the butter to the melted fat. Fry the fillets on both sides and transfer to the saucepan with the pork fat. Sprinkle lightly with the marinade and simmer over very low heat. Fry toast in the remaining fat. Pass the cooked peas through a sieve, form a nice mound and arrange on a serving platter. Spread the pâté on the toasted bread, place a fillet on top of each piece of toast and top with a strip of pork fat. Serve sprinkled with melted butter.

serves 4–6 • Marinating: 2–3 days • Preparation: 15–20 mins • Frying: 6–8 mins

Venison schnitzels with rosemary

600 g saddle, juice of ½ lemon, 100 g ham, 1 tbsp rosemary, salt, pepper, 1 tbsp butter, 1 tsp flour

RICE: 1 cup rice, 1 onion, 1 cup stock, 4–5 tomatoes, 2 tbsps butter, salt, a pinch of saffron

Wash the meat and remove any veins. Cut into fillets, pound with a mallet, sprinkle with lemon juice, dust with rosemary, salt and pepper and place one on top of another. Set aside for 1–2 hours to cool. Sauté the finely chopped onion in butter. In a separate saucepan sauté the sliced tomatoes, then pass them through a sieve and combine with the onion. Pour in the stock, add salt and saffron, mix well, add the washed and drained rice, bring to the boil, cover and simmer for about 40 mins. Dust the fillets lightly with flour, fry in butter (2–3 mins each side), then transfer to a saucepan and keep warm. Fry the slices of ham (as many slices as schnitzels). Arrange the cooked rice in the centre of a warmed serving platter and surround with the schnitzels. Decorate each schnitzel with a slice of ham, sprinkle with the butter in which they were frying. Serve with lettuce salad.

serves 4 • Macerating: 1–2 hrs • Cooking: 40 mins • Frying: 4–6 mins

Venison steaks with stuffed potatoes

600 g saddle, juice of ½ lemon, 2–3 tbsps oil, 4–5 garlic cloves, 3 tbsps butter, 3 tbsps chopped parsley, 8 large peeled potatoes, 250 g smoked streaky bacon, 2 onions, 2 tbsps grated cheese, salt, ground pepper, nutmeg, 1 tsp thyme

Wash the meat and remove any veins. Cut it into slices, pound lightly with a mallet. Mix well the oil and lemon juice with thyme and pepper (¼ tsp). Rub each cutlet with the garlic minced with salt, transfer to a bowl, cover with the prepared oil and refrigerate for 4–5 hours. Wrap each potato in aluminium foil and bake for 45 mins in a preheated oven. Fry the finely diced bacon with finely chopped onion, set aside to cool. Then stir in the chopped parsley (2 tbsps), salt, nutmeg and pepper. Scoop out some of the flesh from each of the half-baked potatoes, chop it finely and combine with the bacon. Stuff the hollowed out potatoes with the mixture. Arrange in a greased roasting tin, sprinkle with the grated cheese, top with 1 tbsp melted butter and bake in a preheated oven for 15–20 mins. Sauté the marinated meat in melted butter, 2–3 mins on each side. When the potatoes are ready, arrange them on a hot serving platter and surround with the steaks. Sprinkle with the fat from the frying pan and decorate with the balls made of the butter blended with the chopped parsley.

serves 4 • Macerating: 4–5 hrs • Preparation: 1 hr • Baking: 15–20 mins

Roedeer mini zrazy with juniper sauce

300 g haunch, 150 g pork fat, 1 bread roll soaked in milk, salt, pepper, 2 tbsps lard, breadcrumbs for coating, 1 egg

MARINADE: 1 carrot, 1 parsley root, ¼ celeriac, 1 onion, 1 cup wine vinegar, lemon juice, a dash of sugar, 3–4 allspice berries, 3–4 black peppercorns, 8–10 juniper berries

SAUCE: 100 g venison scrappings, 30 g smoked streaky bacon, 1 onion, vegetables from the marinade, 1 tbsp ground juniper, 1 tomato, 1 tbsp butter, 1 tsp flour, ½ cup stock, a dash of sugar

Marinate the meat for 2–3 days. Remove and put it through a mincer with the pork fat and the bread roll squeezed dry. Add the egg, salt and pepper, mix well. Shape mini zrazy, bread them and fry in lard. Transfer to a saucepan and keep warm.

PREPARE THE SAUCE: In a saucepan melt the diced bacon, add 1 tbsp butter, the finely chopped meat scrappings, onion and vegetables, and simmer covered, sprinkling from time to time with the strained marinade. Add the ground juniper, salt and pepper, and continue to cook for another 40 mins.

Thicken the sauce with a roux made with the butter and flour, put through a sieve and add to the meat. Simmer for a few minutes over low heat.

serves 4 • Marinating: 2–3 days • Preparation: 40–45 mins

Roedeer zrazy, hunter's style

*1 kg boneless neck of deer, 4–5 garlic cloves,
100 g pork fat, 2 large onions, 1 flat tsp ground
caraway seeds, salt, pepper, fat for frying,
¼ cup stock*

Cut the meat into pieces 2–3 cm thick. Pound with a mallet, rub with the garlic minced with salt. Place one piece of meat on top of another and set aside in a cool place for 2 hours. Dice the onions, sauté one in butter, leave the other raw. Briskly brown the cutlets, then arrange tightly in a saucepan sprinkling generously with the fried and raw onion and caraway, alternating pieces of meat with thin strips of pork fat. Top with a layer of strips of pork fat. Sprinkle with the stock, cover and simmer, from time to time sprinkling with some more stock.

serves 4–6 • Macerating: 2 hrs • Preparation: 10 mins • Stewing: 45–50 mins

Rolled roedeer zrazy

*600 g haunch, 1 small onion, 50 g dried mushrooms,
50 g ham, salt, pepper, 1 tbsp single cream, 1 tbsp
lemon juice, 1 tsp flour,1 tsp chopped parsley,
1 glass red wine, 2 tbsps butter, 1 cup milk*

Wash the meat and remove any veins. Press it hard with your hand, cover with the milk and leave in a cool place overnight. Soak the mushrooms overnight.
PREPARE THE FILLING: Parboil the mushrooms for a moment or two, then cut into strips. Sauté the finely chopped onion in butter, stir in the mushrooms, the finely chopped ham, parlsey, 1 tbsp cream, salt and pepper. Mix well, simmer together for a moment, then set aside to cool. Wipe dry the meat and cut into slices. Pound with a mallet, season with salt and pepper, spread the filling, roll the meat up and tie with thread. Sauté in hot fat until brown on all sides. Transfer to a saucepan, pour in the mushroom stock, add a dash of sugar and lemon juice. Simmer over low heat. Make a roux with the butter and flour, dilute with the wine and thicken the sauce.

*serves 4–6 • Soaking: 12 hrs • Preparation:
20–30 mins • Stewing: 45–50 mins*

Rolled roedeer zrazy with liver

*1 kg haunch, venison liver, 1 large onion, 50 g
pork fat, 2 anchovies, 1 cup thick sour cream,
1 lemon, 1 egg yolk, 1 cup stock, 2 tbsps
butter, salt, pepper, 1 tsp flour, 1 cup milk*

Soak the liver in milk. Cut the meat into cutlets, pound with a mallet, season with salt and pepper.
PREPARE THE STUFFING: Melt the finely chopped pork fat, add the diced onion and sauté together for a moment. Remove the liver from the milk and chop it finely. Combine with the onion, mix, fry together, add salt and pepper and set aside to cool. Spread the stuffing on each fillet, roll and tie with thread. Dust with flour and fry in hot fat. Transfer to a saucepan, add the stock and simmer. Blend the remaining butter with the chopped anchovies, add the egg yolk, lemon juice and cream. Mix well and pour into the meat. Simmer over low heat for about 15 mins.

serves 6–8 • Preparation: 20 mins • Stewing: 40–45 mins

Ragout of roedeer liver

*1 liver, ½ cup milk, 3 onions, ½ tsp marjoram, 250 g
mushrooms, 2 garlic cloves, 2 tomatoes, 1 small glass
white wine, salt, pepper, 100 g butter, 1 tsp flour*

Soak the liver in the milk overnight. Stew the tomatoes in little butter and water, put through a sieve. Sauté the finely chopped onion and sliced mushrooms in butter, add pepper and marjoram. Cut the liver in strips and coat in flour. Fry in some fat, add to the sauce and cover with the wine. Simmer together for about 10 mins. Towards the end add salt to taste.

serves 4 • Soaking: 12 hrs • Preparation: 5–7 mins • Stewing: 10–12 mins

Roedeer goulash

*1 kg neck of deer, 3 onions, 3 bell peppers, 2 corn
cobs, 3 carrots, 4–5 potatoes, 1 cauliflower, 3 tbsps
butter, salt, pepper, soup vegetables, 2 peppercorns,
2 allspice berries, 1 small bay leaf, lemon juice*

Bone out the meat, remove any veins. Cut the meat into cubes, sprinkle with lemon juice, season with salt and pepper. Make a strong stock from the bones, vegetables and spices. Dust the meat with the flour and brown in fat. Transfer to a saucepan together with the onion sautéd in the butter. Pour in some of the stock and simmer covered for about 20 mins. Cook the corn cobs in salted water, separate the kernels and add to the meat. Cut the pepper and carrot into strips, potatoes into cubes, add the cauliflower florets and sauté together in butter. Add a few tablespoons of the stock and simmer for 5–10 mins. Combine the sautéd vegetables with the meat, mix gently, add the remaining stock and, if desired, thicken with a roux made with the butter and flour. Season to taste with salt, pepper and a dash of sugar. Simmer until tender.

serves 6–8 • Cooking: 1 hr • Preparation: 10–15 mins • Stewing: 40–45 mins

Roedeer spareribs in grey sauce

1 kg spareribs, 1 celeriac, 2 carrots, 2 parsley roots, 1 leek, 1 onion, 1 lemon, 2 bay leaves, 5 juniper berries, 5 allspice berries, ½ tsp thyme, salt, 1 cup dry red wine, ½ tsp sugar, 1 tbsp plum jam, 50 g raisins, 50 g almonds, a piece of cinnamon bark, ¼ cup stock, 2 tbsps lard

Sprinkle the spareribs with salt and brown in fat. Coarsely grate the washed and peeled vegetables and place in saucepan together with the sliced onion and leek. Add the spices and grated lemon rind, put in the spareribs, pour in some stock, cover and simmer. Take the spareribs out when tender, sieve the sauce, add sugar, lemon juice and wine. Simmer for about 20 mins. Add the spareribs, scalded raisins and chopped almonds. Simmer together for a moment or two.

serves 4 • Preparation: 20–25 mins • Stewing: 35–40 mins

Roedeer lungs in lemon juice

lungs and heart, 50 g butter, 1 glass dry white wine, 1 onion, 1 bay leaf, allspice, 1 tbsp salt, 1 tbsp sugar, ½ tsp thyme, grated lemon rind, lemon juice, 1 tsp flour

Wash the lungs separated from the trachea and the heart cut in half. Place in a saucepan, cover with salted water, add the grated lemon rind, allspice and bayleaf. Cook for about 1½ hours. Remove, cool and cut into thin 'macaroni'. Make a roux with the butter and flour, add the finely chopped onion, thyme, salt and sugar, dilute it with the strained stock. Add the lungs, mix well and simmer for a few minutes. Pour in the wine and lemon juice, bring to the boil stirring all the time. Many hunters think there is nothing comparable to venison lungs.

If you prepare the dish immediately after the hunt, you should collect the blood and prepare czernina: add some of the blood blended with vinegar to the lungs seasoned with lemon juice, the cooked and sieved prunes, raisins and a glass of red wine.

serves 4 • Preparation: 20–25 mins • Cooking: 1½ hrs

Roedeer tongues

500 g tongues, ¼ celeriac, 2 parsley roots, 1 carrot, 1 small leek, 200 g pitted prunes, ½ cup white wine, ½ cup thick sour cream, 1 tbsp butter, 1 tsp flour, 1 tbsp lemon juice, salt, pepper

Place the washed tongues together with the vegetables in some salted water, bring to the boil and remove when tender, reserving the stock. Skin and cut into diagonal slices. Bring to the boil the prunes which had been soaking overnight in a little water, pass through a sieve. Make a roux with the butter and flour, dilute with the strained stock, combine with the prune purée and wine, mix and bring to the boil. Remove from the heat, stir in the cream. Arrange the slices of the tongues in a saucepan, season with salt and pepper, pour over the sauce and simmer for 10–15 mins.

serves 4 • Soaking: 12 hrs • Cooking: 1–1½ hrs • Preparation: 10–15 mins • Stewing: 10–15 mins

Pâté of venison offal

liver, heart, tongue and half of the lungs, 2 bread rolls soaked in milk, 2 eggs, 1 onion, 3 garlic cloves, 1 tsp marjoram, 250 g pork fat, salt, pepper, allspice and nutmeg, 1 cup milk

Soak the bread rolls in milk, fry 200 g diced pork fat with the onion. Cover the offal (without liver) with salted water and bring to the boil. Take out when tender, strain in a sieve and put twice through a mincer together with the raw liver, the fried pork fat and the bread roll squeezed dry. Add the minced garlic, salt, pepper, marjoram, allspice, nutmeg and eggs. Form a smooth paste. Line a pâté mould with thin strips of pork fat, fill in with the mixture, close tightly and steam for about 1 hour.

serves 6–8 • Cooking: 1 hr • Preparation: 20–25 mins • Baking: 1 hr

Venison pâté served hot

1½ kg leg, 200 g kasha (pearl barley), 50 g dried mushrooms, 100 g pork fat, 50 g butter, salt

MARINADE: ½ cup dry white wine, lemon juice, 3 tbsps olive oil, ¼ tsp ground allspice, ¼ tsp ground pepper, ¼ tsp ground juniper, 1 crushed bay leaf

Wash the meat and remove any veins. Cut it into thin fillets, rub with the spices and cover with the wine blended with olive oil and lemon juice. Set aside in the fridge for 4–5 hours. Scald the mushrooms, cut them into strips, sauté in butter, sprinkle with water and simmer covered. Cook the kasha until half tender. Take the meat out of the marinade and brown lightly in butter on both sides. Line an ovenproof dish with thin strips of pork fat. Blend the kasha with the mushrooms, pour in the reserved marinade, mix well and add salt and a dash of sugar. In a dish alternate layers of the kasha and of the meat. Top with a layer of thin strips of pork fat and cover the dish with aluminium foil. Bake in a preheated oven for about 1½ hours. Serve hot with pickles or gherkins.

serves 8–10 • Macerating: 4–5 hrs • Preparation: 40 mins • Baking: 1½ hrs

Pheasant

And fowl, apart from chicken, included wild goose, bustard, capercaillie, black grouse, partridges from Ruthenia the size of pigeons but shaped like grouse, wild duck, and small fowl,

namely, hazel grouse, pheasant, partridge, quail, heron, woodcock, ruff, snipe, and all kinds of doves and thrushes, blackbirds and young starlings..., as also the pheasants which adorned the tables of the rich.

(Łukasz Gołąbiowski, *Domy i dwory*, vol. IV, pp. 37–39)

Pheasant is the most decorative game bird at all winter hunts and parties.

In Polish written sources, pheasant is mentioned for the first time in 1284, but they were bred in Poland on a wider scale only from the end of the 18th century. The most widespread pheasant in Poland is *Phasianus colchinus*, the name of which is a reference to the legend that pheasants were brought to Greece from Colchis by Jason after the Argonauts' expedition in search of the Golden Fleece.

Pheasant meat is admittedly drier than that of partridges, but they are thought of as a very refined dish because they can be served very elegantly in their feathers. For this purpose, you should cut off the head, wings and tail. The wings and tail should be arranged naturally on a mesh tray and dried out in a low oven.

To tenderize the meat satisfactorily, the bird should be hung by its feet, head down, in a cool and airy place. When the pheasant is sufficiently tenderized, a drop of clear liquid will appear on the beak.

Roast pheasant

Cut off the head and tail with their beautiful feathers, pluck the rest, draw, clean and lard the breast with thinly sliced bacon fat, salt, cover with slices of bacon fat, wrap in greased paper, truss with thick thread, put on the spit and roast for an hour in a low oven, basting with the fat. When it is almost ready, take off the paper and bacon fat and allow the bird to brown nicely; then take it from the spit, carve it according to the accepted practice, place it on a serving dish so that it appears to be whole. Then take the unplucked head and bind the end of the neck with strips of paper on both sides, and place it adjacent to the roast body. Wrap the end of the tail in the same way and place it where it should be. Sprinkle the pheasant with butter and serve as quickly as possible.

(Makary, 1903)

Roast pheasant with sauce

1 pheasant, salt, pepper, 100 g pork fat, 1 tbsp mustard, 2 tbsps currant jelly, juice and grated rind of 1 orange, ½ cup red wine, 1 tbsp butter

Trim and wash the pheasant. Lard it with pork fat, rub with salt and pepper and place in a greased roasting pan. Roast in a hot oven, from time to time basting with melted butter and water. When tender, divide the meat into serving pieces, arrange on a hot serving platter, pour over the pan juices and keep warm.
SAUCE: Blend well the mustard and grated lemon rind, currant jelly and orange juice. Season with salt and pepper, mix well with the wine. Serve cold in a sauceboat.

serves 2–4 • Preparation: 20 mins • Roasting: 70–80 mins

Pheasant with lentils

1 pheasant, 150 g pork fat, 5 peppercorns, grated lemon rind, 250 g lentils, 2 cups stock, 1 tbsp flour, 1 onion, 1 tbsp butter

Rub the trimmed and washed pheasant with salt, coat with strips of pork fat and brown in a saucepan. Add the sliced onion, lemon rind and pepper, pour in 1 cup of stock and simmer covered. Cook the lentils in the remaining stock until half tender. Take the meat out when tender and cut into serving pieces. Thicken the sauce with a roux made with the butter and flour, pass through a sieve and combine with the lentils. Steam off the excess liquid. Add the pheasant and simmer together for a few moments.

serves 2–4 • Preparation: 20 mins • Roasting: 70–80 mins

Pheasant with apples

1 pheasant, 100 g pork fat, 4 tart apples, 1 cup thick sour cream, salt, 2 crushed cloves, ½ tsp curry powder, a dash of cinnamon and sugar, 1 tbsp butter

Rub the trimmed and washed pheasant with salt, curry powder and cloves. Set aside in a cool place for 2–3 hours, then cover with thin strips of pork fat and tie with thread. Roast in the oven, from time to time basting with melted butter and water. Peel and core the ap-

ples, stew them in the fat reserved from roasting. Add the cream, cinnamon and sugar. Put the apple purée through a sieve. Cut the meat into serving pieces, arrange in an ovenproof dish, cover with the sauce and surround with the stewed apples. Bake in a preheated oven for a few minutes.

serves 2–4 • Macerating: 2–3 hrs • Preparation: 10 mins • Roasting: 70–80 mins

Pheasant with cabbage

1 pheasant, 100 g pork fat, 3 pineapple slices (out of tin), 1 kg sauerkraut, 1 tbsp honey, 250 g smoked streaky bacon, 1 cup champagne

Lard the trimmed and washed pheasant with pork fat, rub with salt and roast in the oven, from time to time sprinkling with melted butter. Rinse the sauerkraut, squeeze out the excess liquid, and chop finely. In a saucepan melt the diced bacon, add the chopped sauerkraut, mix well and simmer for about half an hour. Add the diced pineaple and simmer together uncovered for a few minutes. Pour in the champagne, mix well and simmer until the sauerkraut is cooked. Towards the end of cooking add 1 tbsp honey, mix well. Cut the roast pheasant into serving pieces, arrange in a greased ovenproof dish, surround with the sauerkraut and bake for a few minutes in a preheated oven.

serves 4 • Roasting: 60–70 mins • Cooking: 60–70 mins • Baking: 10–15 mins

Pheasant with mushrooms

1 pheasant, 50 g pork fat, salt, pepper, 1 tbsp butter, 200 g mushrooms, 2 tbsps chopped parsley, ½ cup dry white wine

Dress and wash the pheasant, rub with salt and pepper, lard with the pork fat and set aside in a cool place for 2–3 hours. Now place the bird in a roasting pan, sprinkle with melted butter and roast in a preheated oven, from time to time basting with its own juices and with wine. Towards the end add the mushrooms cut into thin slices and mixed with parsley. Cut the tender pheasant into serving pieces.

serves 2–4 • Macerating: 2–3 hrs • Preparation: 5 mins • Roasting: 70–80 mins

Stuffed pheasant

1 pheasant, salt, pepper, 1 glass brandy,
1 glass red wine, 150 g pork fat

STUFFING: 200 g veal, 3 chicken livers,
1 tbsp breadcrumbs, salt, pepper, 2 eggs

Dress and pluck the tenderized pheasant, rub it with salt and set aside in a cool place for 2–3 hours.
PREPARE THE STUFFING: Put the veal through a mincer, finely chop the liver. In a bowl blend the eggs with the liver, add the minced veal, breadcrumbs, salt, pepper and nutmeg, and mix thoroughly.
Stuff the salted pheasant with the mixture, sew up and coat with thin strips of pork fat, tie with thread and place in a greased roasting tin. Roast in a medium hot oven for about 1 hour. After 10–15 mins of roasting sprinkle the meat with brandy. Towards the end, remove the strips of pork fat to crisp the skin. Take out the roasted pheasant, cut it into serving pieces and arrange on a hot serving platter. Keep warm. Strain the meat juices and add the wine. Simmer for a few minutes to reduce the liquid. Serve the sauce in a sauceboat.

serves 2–4 • Salting: 2–3 hours • Preparation: 20 mins • Roasting: 60–80 mins

Pheasant stuffed with venison

1 pheasant, 100 g pork fat, 150 g haunch of deer,
50 g walnut meats, 1 tbsp chopped parsley,
1 egg, 1 bread roll soaked in milk, 1 tbsp butter,
salt, pepper, sugar, nutmeg, ½ cup dry white wine

Rub the trimmed and washed pheasant with salt, set aside in a cool place. Squeeze the bread roll dry and put it through a mincer together with the deer. Add the chopped walnuts, salt, nutmeg, sugar, pepper and parsley. Mix well with the egg. Fill the pheasant with the stuffing, sew up and coat with strips of pork fat. Tie lightly with thread and place in a greased roasting pan. Sprinkle with melted butter and roast, from time to time basting with wine. Towards the end remove the strips of pork fat to crisp the skin. Cut the meat into four serving pieces, ar-

range on a warmed serving platter and surround with potatoes baked with rosemary. Sprinkle with the gravy.

serves 2–4 • Salting: 1 hr • Preparation: 20 mins • Roasting: 60–80 mins

Pheasant stuffed with mushrooms and capers

1 pheasant, 100 g pork fat, 200 g mushrooms,
1 large onion, 1 tbsp breadcrumbs, 1 tbsp capers,
100 g butter, 1 tbsp ketchup, salt, pepper, a
dash of sugar, 1 tbsp chopped parsley, 1 egg

Rub the trimmed and washed pheasant with salt and set aside in a cool place for 1–2 hours. Sauté the finely chopped mushrooms and onion in butter, add salt and pepper, set aside to cool. Add the capers, parsley, breadcrumbs, ketchup and a dash of sugar, stir in the egg. Stuff the pheasant with the mixture, sew up, coat with thin strips of pork fat and roast in a preheated oven, sprinkling frequently with melted butter. Towards the end of roasting remove the strips of pork fat, so that the meat browns nicely.

serves 2–4 • Salting: 1–2 hrs • Preparation: 10 mins • Roasting: 60–80 mins

Pheasant stuffed with ham

1 well tenderized pheasant, 100 g lean
ham, 50 g bacon, 1½ tbsps finely chopped
sage, salt, pepper, 1 tbsp lemon juice,
2–3 tbsps olive oil, ½ cup dry red wine

Rub the trimmed and washed pheasant with salt, pepper and lemon juice. Set aside in the fridge for 3–4 hours. Mix the finely chopped ham with sage and stuff the peasant with the mixture. Fasten with wood picks and coat with very thin strips of bacon. Place in a greased roasting tin and roast for about 40 mins, sprinkling lightly with the wine. Remove the strips of bacon and brown the meat. Mix the meat juices with the bacon and with the remaining wine. Serve the sauce in a sauceboat.

serves 4–6 • Macerating: 3–4 hrs • Preparation: 10 mins • Roasting: 50–60 mins

Pheasant baked with cheese

1 pheasant, heart and liver of pheasant, 150 g
butter, 1 large onion, 250 g mushrooms, 1 cup

double cream, 1 glass dry wine, 100 g grated sharp cheese, 1 tsp flour, 1 tbsp chopped parsley

Divide the dressed and washed pheasant into 4 serving pieces, rub with salt and sear in butter. Transfer to a saucepan, sprinkle with wine and simmer for 10–15 mins. Finely cut the liver and heart, cut the mushrooms in thin strips, finely chop the onion. Sauté together in butter, sprinkle with wine and simmer covered. Transfer the meat to a buttered ovenproof dish, sprinkle with the sauce in which the meat was cooking, coat with the wine-stewed additions. Pour over the cream blended with the flour, sprinkle with the grated cheese and bake in a preheated oven for about 40 mins. Before serving, sprinkle with chopped parsley.

serves 4–6 • Preparation: 15–20 mins • Baking: 40–45 mins

Steamed pheasant

1 pheasant, 100 g pork fat, salt, ¼ tsp thyme, ¼ tsp pepper, 1 bay leaf, 1 tsp lemon juice, ½ cup dessert wine

Rub the dressed and washed pheasant with salt, pepper, thyme and a crushed bay leaf, sprinkle with lemon juice and leave aside in a cool place for 1–2 hours. Line a pâté form with thin strips of pork fat, put in the pheasant covered with strips of pork fat, pour in the wine. Cover tightly. Steam for about 2 hours. Before serving pour the meat over with the sieved sauce.

serves 2–4 • Macerating: 1–2 hrs • Preparation: 5 mins • Cooking: 2 hrs

Pheasant dumplings

pheasant breasts, 150 g veal, 3 bread rolls soaked in milk, 100 g butter, ½ cup cream, 3 egg yolks, 1 tbsp finely chopped parsley, salt, pepper, nutmeg, 2 cups stock

Squeeze the rolls dry and blend with butter in a bowl. Put the veal and pheasant meat through a mincer and blend well with the bread rolls. Heat up the cream and together with the egg yolks gradually blend into the mixture, stirring all the time. Add salt, pepper, nutmeg and parsley. Form a smooth paste (if too thin, add a roll, if too crumbly, add more cream). Shape balls out of the mixture and cook

them in little stock. Remove gently. Serve with some sauce, or as a side dish with roast pheasant.

serves 4 • Preparation: 10–15 mins • Cooking: 10–12 mins

Pheasant pâté

1 pheasant, 250 g pork fat, 150 g goose livers (or veal liver), 150 g mushrooms, 1 bread roll soaked in milk, 2 eggs, 2 egg yolks, salt, pepper, allspice, nutmeg, 1 tbsp butter, ½ cup stock, 1 glass white wine

Wash the drawn peasant and divide into serving pieces. Place in a saucepan, cover with the stock and cook. Remove when tender, de-bone and fry for a moment together with strips of pork fat. Return to the saucepan, add the mushrooms sautéd in butter, sprinkle with the wine and simmer for about 20 mins. Put through a mincer the liver soaked in milk, the roll (squeeze it dry) and the mushrooms. Do it twice. Add salt, pepper, allspice, nutmeg and eggs. Form a smooth paste. Butter a pâté form and put the mixture in it. Close tightly. Steam for about 1 hour. Can be also baked in the oven.

serves 6–8 • Cooking: 1 hr • Preparation: 30–35 mins • Baking: 1 hr

Wood grouse and black grouse

Both birds have fairly tough meat, which takes a long time to age, therefore they should be hung, head down, by their feet in a cool and airy place and remain there for as long as 14 days. Only then they are plucked, seared and drawn, and their heads and wings are cut off. With young birds it is enough to soak them overnight in milk, while older ones should be left to marinate, with some juniper and ginger added, for two or three days. Rather than roasting them, you are advised to braise them under cover, because then they become more tender and juicy.

Roast wood grouse in cream

1 wood grouse, salt, 150 g pork fat, 100 g butter, 1 cup thick sour cream

MARINADE: 1 cup wine vinegar, grated lemon rind, 2 bay leaves, 5 juniper berries, 5 allspice berries, 5 peppercorns, ¼ tsp thyme, ¼ tsp ginger, a dash of sugar, 1 onion

Combine all the ingredients of the marinade and bring to the boil. Set aside to cool. Place the drawn and washed bird in an earthenware pot and cover with the marinade. Set aside in a cool place for 4–5 days, turning over frequently. Now take the meat out of the marinade, wipe dry and lard with pork fat. Place in a roasting pan, sprinkle with melted butter and roast in a preheated oven. Sprinkle with the marinade frequently. Towards the end add the onion from the marinade. Take the meat out when tender and cut into serving pieces. Sieve the sauce and mix with the cream blended with flour. Season with salt and a dash of sugar. Arrange the grouse in the roasting pan, pour over the sauce and bake for a few minutes in a preheated oven.

serves 4 • Marinating: 4–5 days • Preparation: 5–7 mins • Roasting: 60–80 mins

Wood grouse, Old Polish style

1 wood grouse, 200 g pork fat, salt, pepper, ½ tsp ground juniper, 150 g mushrooms, 1 onion, 2 tbsps butter, 100 g walnut meats, 200 g ham or lean smoked streaky bacon, 1 tbsp chopped parsley, 1 tbsp breadcrumbs, sugar, nutmeg, 1 egg

MARINADE: 1 cup dry white wine, juice and grated rind of 1 lemon, 1 onion, 4–5 allspice berries, 4–5 peppercorns, 4–5 juniper berries, 2 cloves, 1 bay leaf, ¼ tsp sugar, a dash of ginger

Combine the ingredients of the marinade and bring to the boil. Marinate the drawn and washed wood

grouse for 4–5 days, turning over every day. Now take the meat out, dry and rub with salt, pepper and juniper. Lard the legs and breasts with thin strips of pork fat. Set aside in a cool place for 2–3 hours.
PREPARE THE STUFFING: Sauté the finely chopped mushrooms and onion in 1 tbsp butter. Chop the bacon finely. Mix 1 tbsp butter with breadcrumbs and chopped walnuts, add the mushrooms, bacon and parsley, season with salt, pepper, sugar and ginger. Stir in the egg yolk. At the end add the stiff beaten egg whites. Mix gently. Stuff the bird with the mixture, sew up and cover with strips of pork fat. Tie up with thread, place in a roasting pan, sprinkle with melted butter. Roast in a preheated oven, frequently basting with the strained marinade.

serves 4 • Marinating: 4–5 days • Macerating: 2–3 hrs • Preparation: 20 mins • Roasting: 70–90 mins

Wood grouse in vegetables

1 wood grouse, salt, pepper, ½ tsp juniper, 100 g pork fat, juice and grated rind of 1 lemon, 1 carrot, 2 parsley roots, ½ celeriac, 1 onion, 100 g butter, 1 cup stock

Rub the drawn and washed wood grouse inside and out with juniper and lemon rind, sprinkle with lemon juice and cover with the coarsely grated vegetables and sliced onion. Set aside in a cool place for 1–2 days. Take out the meat, rub with salt, lard with pork fat and sear in butter on all sides. Line a saucepan with strips of pork fat, put in the bird and the vegetables from the marinade, sprinkle with some stock and simmer covered, frequently sprinkling with the remaining stock. Take the meat out when tender, cut into serving pieces. Sieve the sauce and serve it in a sauceboat.

serves 4 • Marinating: 2–3 days • Preparation: 5 mins • Stewing: 60–70 mins

Wood grouse with olives and capers

1 wood grouse, salt, pepper, ¼ tsp rosemary, 100 g pork fat, 1 tbsp butter, sugar

MARINADE: wine and spices

SAUCE: 100 g pitted olives, 2 tbsp capers, 100 g grated cheese, 1 tsp butter

Place the drawn and washed wood grouse in an earthenware pot, cover with the marinade and set aside in a cool place for 3–4 days, turning over every day. Now take the meat out of the marinade, wipe dry, rub with salt, pepper and rosemary, lard with pork fat and sear on all sides in butter. Transfer to a saucepan, pour in the marinade and simmer covered. Remove when tender, cut into serving pieces and arrange in a buttered ovenproof dish. Sieve the meat juices, add the olives cut into strips and capers, season with salt, lemon juice and sugar, and simmer together for a moment or two. Pour the sauce over the wood grouse, sprinkle with the grated cheese and melted butter and bake in a hot oven for about 15 mins. Serve with potatoes baked with rosemary.

serves 4 • Marinating: 4–5 days • Preparation: 10 mins • Stewing: 60–70 mins • Baking: 15–20 mins

Wood grouse in wine

1 wood grouse, salt, pepper, ½ tsp thyme, 2 garlic cloves, 50 g lean streaky bacon, 100 g butter, 1 tsp flour, 2 cups dry white wine, sugar

Cover the drawn and washed wood grouse with the wine and set aside in a cool place for the night. Remove, wipe dry, lard with bacon and rub with garlic minced with salt, thyme and pepper. Set aside in a cool place for a few hours. Then sear the meat in butter, pour in some wine and simmer covered. Take the meat out when tender and cut into serving pieces. Thicken the sauce with a roux made with butter and flour, season to taste with lemon juice and sugar, put through a sieve and pour over the bird. Bake for a few minutes in a preheated oven.

serves 4 • Marinating: 12 hrs • Macerating: 3–4 hrs • Stewing: 60–80 mins • Baking: 10–12 mins

Wood grouse in redcurrant sauce

1 wood grouse, salt, 100 g pork fat, ½ tsp juniper, 1 tbsp currant jelly, 1 tsp sugar, ½ cup double cream, 1 onion, 50 g butter

MARINADE: 1 cup dry red wine, juice and grated rind of 1 lemon, 1 onion, 1 carrot, 1 parsley root, ½ celeriac, 2 bay leaves, 1 clove, ¼ tsp ginger, sugar

Combine the ingredients of the marinade and bring to the boil. Leave to cool. Place the drawn and washed bird in an earthenware pot, cover with the marinade and set aside in a cool place for 4–5 days, turning over frequently. Take the meat out, rub with salt, pepper and juniper, lard with pork fat. In a saucepan melt the remaining pork fat cut into cubes and sauté the chopped onion. Add the meat, sear it on all sides, pour in the marinade together with the vegetables and simmer covered. From time to time baste with water. Take out when tender and cut into serving pieces. Sieve the sauce, reduce the excess liquids, add sugar and the currant jelly, and simmer together for a moment or two. Pour in the cream blended with flour. Place the meat in an ovenproof dish, pour the sauce over and bake for a few minutes in a preheated oven.

serves 4 • Marinating: 4–5 days • Preparation: 10 mins • Roasting: 70–80 mins • Baking: 10–15 mins

Wood grouse served hot or cold

1 wood grouse, 100 g pork fat, salt, pepper, 2 tbsps butter, 2 tbsps cream, 2 cups milk

SAUCE: 1 carrot, 2 onions, 3 garlic cloves, 2 bay leaves, ½ tsp pepper, 50 g lean ham, 2 tbsps tomato concentrate, 4–5 cloves, 1 cup dry red wine, salt, ½ tsp sugar, juice and grated rind of 1 lemon, 2 tbsps chopped parsley

Cover the young drawn and washed wood grouse with the milk and set aside in a cool place for 24 hours. Then take the meat out, wipe dry, lard with pork fat, rub with salt and pepper and place on a greased roasting tin. Sprinkle with melted butter and roast in the oven. From time to time baste it with the butter and cream (just butter, if it is to be served cold).
PREPARE THE SAUCE: Coarsely grate the vegetables and chop the onions. Stew them in butter and add the crushed spices, grated lemon rind and pour over the wine. Cover and simmer for a moment or two. Add the diced ham, tomato paste and lemon juice, season with salt and sugar. Cover and simmer together for about 1 hour. Put through a sieve, stir in the chopped parsley and leave aside to cool. Serve the roast grouse with the cold sauce.

serves 4 • Soaking: 24 hrs • Preparation: 5–8 mins • Roasting: 70–80 mins

Wood grouse schnitzels

wood grouse breasts, 1 tsp ground juniper, salt, pepper, grated rind and juice of ½ lemon, 1 garlic clove, ½ lemon with rind, 100 g butter, 1 tbsp chopped parsley

De-bone the bird and remove the skin, then pound the meat lightly with a mallet. Rub with the garlic mixed with salt, sprinkle with lemon juice and dust with pepper, juniper and lemon zest. Place one schnitzel on top of another and set aside in the fridge for 3–4 hours. Fry the schnitzels on both sides in clarified butter, transfer to a saucepan, add the butter in which they were frying and keep over low heat for a moment. Serve decorated with parsley butter and slices of lemon.

serves 4 • Macerating: 3–4 hrs • Preparation: 15 mins

Wood grouse terrine

wood grouse leftovers (scraps left after making schnitzels), 1 small bread roll soaked in milk, 1 tbsp cream, 1 tbsp red wine, juice of 1 lemon, ¼ tsp each salt, pepper, allspice and nutmeg, 1 crushed clove, a dash of ginger, 1 tbsp butter

Place the meat and skin in a bowl, sprinkle with the wine and lemon juice, dredge with the spices and set aside in the fridge for 3–4 hours. Squeeze the roll dry and put it together with the meat through a mincer, then through a sieve. Blend with the butter and cream into a smooth paste. Butter a pâté mould, fill it with the mixture, cover and steam for about 1 hour. Serve hot with schnitzels, or cold with some spicy sauce.

serves 4 • Macerating: 3–4 hrs • Preparation: 20 mins • Cooking: 1 hr

Roast black grouse

1 black grouse, 150 g pork fat, 2 cups sour milk, salt, pepper, 1 cup thick sour cream, 1 tsp juniper, 1 tbsp butter

Place the tenderized, trimmed and washed black grouse in an earthenware pot and cover with the sour milk. Set aside in a cool place for the night. Now take the meat out, immerse for moment in boiling water, rub with salt,

pepper and juniper, lard with pork fat and set aside for another 2–3 hours in a cool place.
PREPARE THE STUFFING: Put the pork fat, streaky bacon and anchovies through a mincer. Sauté the finely chopped mushrooms and onion in butter, set aside to cool and combine with the minced ingredients, stir in the parsley, salt, pepper, nutmeg and 1 egg yolk. Add the stiff beaten egg white, mix well.
Stuff the bird with the mixture, tie up and coat with thin strips of pork fat, brown in clarified butter, sprinkle with some stock, cover and simmer, basting with the stock frequently. Remove the strips of pork fat when the meat is ready. Put the pork fat through a sieve, thicken the sauce with a roux of butter and flour. Serve the sauce in a sauceboat. Place the bird in a buttered roasting pan and bake in a preheated oven for a few minutes to crisp the skin.

serves 4 • Soaking: 12 hrs • Salting: 2–3 hrs • Preparation: 20 mins • Stewing: 1 hr

Black grouse in apricot sauce

1 black grouse, 150 g pork fat, 2 onions, 100 g walnut meats, 150 dried apricots, sugar, 1 tbsp butter

MARINADE: 1 cup dry white wine, grated lemon rind, lemon juice, 2 cloves, 2–3 allspice berries, 2–3 peppercorns, 5–7 juniper berries, sugar, ginger

Combine the ingredients of the marinade and bring to the boil. Trim and wash the black grouse and cover with the marinade. Set aside for 4–5 days. Soak the apricots in a little water overnight. Take the meat out, wipe dry, rub with salt and lard with pork fat. Parboil the apricots in the water they were soaking. Finely chop the walnuts. Roast the bird, sprinkling it from time to time with clarified butter and marinade. After ½ hour add the sliced onion, and towards the end the apricots and walnuts. Take out the meat when tender, cut into serving pieces. Put the sauce through a sieve, season to taste with salt and, if desired, with a dash of sugar. Serve it in a sauceboat.

serves 4 • Marinating: 4–5 days • Soaking: 12 hrs • Preparation: 15 mins • Roasting: 60–70 mins

Black grouse in spicy sauce

*1 black grouse, salt, pepper, 100 g pork fat, 50 g
butter, 50 g mushrooms, 1 bunch spring onions,
4 garlic cloves, 2 tbsps chopped parsley, 1 large
onion, grated lemon rind, 1 glass white wine,
2 anchovies, 4 tbsps oil, 1 tbsp mustard, sugar*

Wash the tenderized and drawn bird, rub it with minced garlic, coat densely with the finely cut mushrooms, spring onions, parsley and onion. Mix salt, pepper, juice and rind of lemon with oil, rub the bird inside and sprinkle outside. Set aside in a cool place for 24 hours. Then take the meat out, remove the seasoning, coat with strips of pork fat, tie up with thread and spit roast, frequently basting with clarified butter. Finely chop the anchovies, mince with the marinated vegetables, add salt, pepper, a dash of sugar and mustard, sprinkle with water or wine. Stew and set aside to cool. Serve with the roast black grouse.

serves 4 • Marinating: 24 hrs • Preparation: 15 mins • Roasting: 60–70 mins

Partridge and hazel grouse

These are among the most delicate and tastiest of game birds. Young partridges can be served even the day following shooting. They are recognizable by their yellow feet and black beaks, and have a soft breast bone. Older partridges have steel-coloured or scaly feet and white beaks, and should be hung feathered for several days before cooking.

When plucked and drawn, the birds should be washed carefully but quickly; if they are soaked in water they lose flavour. They should be roasted in a hot oven for no longer than 30 to 40 minutes.

The taste of roast partridge is much improved by a bunch of dried sage leaves added to the tin (thrown away after roasting). You can also get a good effect by making cuts in the breasts of the roast birds and filling them with lemon butter (butter blended with a little salt and lemon juice).

Partridges cooked in this way should be covered with a dish and left in the warm for the butter to melt. The roast birds should be arranged on a serving dish on white bread toast and surrounded with slices of lemon and sprigs of parsley.

Partridge in the snow

Beat sixteen egg whites into stiff peaks and spread the white around the edge of a serving dish with a knife, so that the centre is empty. Take the heads of the partridges with the necks, uncooked and unplucked, and place them in the middle so that the heads and beaks stand out. Place the dish in a warm oven, with the egg white and heads, so that it dries out well, but taking care that it should not brown. Take the dish out of the oven and place the carved roast partridges in the centre, pouring over their gravy, and garnishing with mushrooms or truffles, and serve immediately.

(from Szyttler, 1830)

Lordly delicacy, or baked partridges

*4 partridges, 4 thin slices pork fat, ground
juniper (dash), 500 g carrots, 50 g raisins,
100 g grated horseradish, 3 tbsps butter, 1 cup
cream, 2 tbsps lemon juice and ¼ tsp grated
lemon rind, salt, pepper, ½ tsp sugar*

Sprinkle the trimmed and washed partridges with lemon juice, rub with salt, pepper and ground juniper. Wrap in foil and refrigerate for 1–2 hours. Wrap each partridge in a very thin strip of pork fat, arrange the birds in a buttered roasting pan, and roast in a preheated oven for about 30 mins. Add the sliced carrots, remove the pork fat and continue to roast until brown. From time to time sprinkle with melted butter. Take the partridges out, cut each lengthwise in half. Mix the carrots, pork fat and the pan juices with an electric mixer, stir in the horseradish, scalded raisins, salt, sugar, pepper, grated lemon rind and lemon juice and mix well with cream. Arrange the partridge halves in an ovenproof dish, pour the prepared sauce over and bake in a hot oven for 8–12 mins.

*serves 4–8 • Macerating: 1–2 hrs • Preparation: 10 mins
• Roasting: 30 mins • Baking: 8–12 mins*

Partridges for gourmets

*2 partridges, 100 g pork fat, 50 g mushrooms,
50 g goose livers, 1 glass red wine, 100 g
butter, salt, pepper, ½ loaf white bread*

Trim and wash the partridges, rub with salt, coat with thin strips of pork fat and roast in the oven. Set aside to cool, separate the breast meat, put the remaining meat through a mincer together with the pork fat. Add the drippings and wine and simmer for a moment or two. Butter an ovenproof dish and arrange layers of the mixture, partridge breasts and sliced mushrooms. Top with the goose livers. Season with salt and pepper and bake in a preheated oven for about 20 mins. Fry pieces of toast in butter. Place the hot toast on a warmed serving platter and surround with the roasted partridges.

*serves 4 • Roasting: 30–40 mins • Cooling: 1–2 hrs
• Preparation: 20 mins • Baking: 20 mins*

Partridges, hunter's style

*3 partridges, 150 g pork fat, salt, pepper, 2–3 sprigs
of fresh (or ½ tsp dried) sage, 1 tbsp butter, salt,
1 roll, 3 garlic cloves, 1 onion, ¼ tsp ground juniper,
1 small carrot, ¼ celeriac, lemon juice, 1 cup stock,
1 glass dry white wine, 1 tbsp butter, 1 tsp flour*

Rub the trimmed and washed partridges with salt, put a sprig of sage inside each bird, or rub with dried sage. Coat each bird with strips of pork fat and roast, basting with clarified butter. Sauté the finely chopped onion and grated vegetables in butter, add the stock, cover and simmer for about 40 mins. Put through a sieve. Make a roux with the butter and flour, dilute with the wine, combine with the puréed vegetables, add lemon juice, salt, pepper and juniper. Mix well and simmer for a moment or two. Make pieces of toast, rub well with garlic and place on a hot serving platter. Arrange the partridges on the pieces of toast. Serve the sauce in a sauceboat.

serves 3–6 • Preparation: 40–50 mins

Partridges with apples

*2–3 partridges, salt, pepper, 1 kg tart apples,
150 g pork fat, 1 tsp butter, 1 cup cream*

Rub the trimmed and washed partridges with salt and pepper, coat with strips of pork fat, tie up with thread and roast for 15 mins. Peel and core the apples, cut into thick slices and cover the partridges from all sides. Roast together for a moment or two. Take the meat out, remove the strips of pork fat. Put the pork fat through a sieve together with the apples and the meat juices. Transfer to a saucepan. Add the partridges carved in half, cover with the cream, and sprinkle with melted butter. Stew for about 30 mins.

serves 4–6 • reparation: 15 mins • Roasting: 15 mins • Stewing: 30 mins

Partridges with sweet peppers

*2 partridges, 50 g pork fat, 4–5 garlic cloves,
1 onion, 2 sweet red peppers, 1 carrot,
¼ tsp thyme, salt, sugar, 1 glass dry
white wine, 1 tbsp butter*

Divide the trimmed and washed partridges in halves, rub with salt and fry in butter until golden brown. Transfer to a saucepan. In the grease from the fried partridges sauté the sliced onion and the julienned peppers. Transfer to the saucepan with the partridges, add the coarsely grated carrot, garlic minced with salt and thyme. Pour over the wine and simmer for about 45 mins.

serves 2–4 • Preparation: 50–55 mins

Partridges in wine

*2 partridges, 100 g pork fat, 2 onions, 2 carrots,
1 parsley root, ½ cup stock, ½ cup dry white wine,
salt, pepper, 1 clove, 2–3 allspice berries, 1 bay leaf*

Trim and wash the partridges, rub with salt, coat with strips of pork fat, tie up with thread. Wash and coarsely grate the vegetables, cut the onions into rings and place in a saucepan. Put the partridges on top, add the spices, pour in the stock and simmer covered for half an hour. Take the partridges out, remove the pork fat, cut each bird in half. Put the pork fat and the vegetables through a sieve. Transfer the purée back into the saucepan, cover the partridges with the wine and simmer for another 10 mins.

serves 2–4 • Preparation: 50 mins

Partridges in cream

2 partridges, 100 g butter, 1 cup thick sour cream, 1 tsp flour, juice of ½ lemon, salt, sugar, 3–4 sprigs of sage

Rub the trimmed and washed partridges with salt, place the sprigs of sage inside each bird. Arrange the partridges in a buttered saucepan, sprinkle with the melted butter and roast in the oven, frequently basting with the meat juices. Remove the partridges when half roasted and cut in halves. Discard the sage. Make a roux with the remaining fat, add lemon juice, a dash of sugar, pour in the cream and mix. Put in the partridges and simmer for about 15 mins.

serves 2–4 • Preparation: 50 mins

Partridges with vegetables

2 partridges, 100 g pork fat, 1 carrot, ¼ celeriac, 1 onion, 100 g tomatoes, 200 g Savoy cabbage, salt, pepper, grated lemon rind, 1 tbsp lemon juice, 1 tsp sugar, ½ cup dry white wine, 50 g butter

Rub the trimmed and washed partridges with salt, set aside in a cool place for one hour. Coat with strips of pork fat, sprinkle with melted butter and roast, frequently basting with the pan juices. Sprinkle with water if necessary. Finely chop the cabbage, cut the carrot, celeriac and onion into slices. In a saucepan melt the butter, add the vegetables, salt, pepper, lemon rind, pour in the wine and simmer for about 20 mins. Add the peeled and quartered tomatoes, stir in the pork fat removed from the partridges and cut into cubes. Season to taste with salt, sugar and lemon juice. Mix gently. Arrange the halved partridges on a buttered ovenproof platter, surround with the stewed vegetables and bake in a preheated oven for a few minutes.

serves 2–4 • Salting: 1 hr • Preparation: 40–50 mins

Partridges in redcurrant sauce

2 partridges, salt, 1 tbsp lemon juice, ½ tsp thyme, 100 g butter, 200–250 g redcurrants, 2 tbsps sugar, 1 cup dry white wine, a piece of cinnamon stick, 2 cloves, grated rind of ½ lemon and orange, 1 tsp flour

Rub the trimmed and washed partridges with salt and thyme, sprinkle with lemon juice and set aside in a cool place for 2–3 hours. Divide into halves, brown in butter and transfer to a saucepan. Pour in some of the wine, cover and simmer, frequently basting with water, wine and the pan juices. Bring to the boil the remaining wine with sugar, cinnamon, cloves, grated lemon and orange rind and orange juice, add the currants. Make a roux with the butter and flour, mix with the currants. Put the sauce through a sieve and add to the meat. Simmer until the partridges are tender.

serves 2–4 • Macerating: 2–3 hrs • Preparation: 40 mins

Roast partridges

2 partridges, 100 g pork fat, 1 flat tbsp sage, salt, pepper, lemon juice, ½ cup stock, 1 tbsp breadcrumbs, 2 tbsps chopped parsley

Rub the trimmed and washed partridges with sage, salt and pepper, sprinkle with lemon juice and set aside in a cool place for 2–3 hours. Then lightly lard with some pork fat. Cut the remaining pork fat into thin strips, arrange in a roasting pan and put the partridges on top. Roast in a preheated oven until brown. Sprinkle with breadcrumbs, pour in the stock and simmer for about 30 mins. Remove when tender, cut into halves and arrange on a hot serving platter. Pour over the sieved meat juices and sprinkle generously with chopped parsley.

serves 2–4 • Macerating: 3–4 hrs • Preparation: 40–45 mins

Roast partridges with juniper

4 partridges, 200 g pork fat, 4 potatoes, salt, 4 cloves, 10 juniper berries, 5 peppercorns, lemon juice, 50 g butter

Crush the cloves, juniper and pepper together in a mortar. Rub the trimmed and washed partridges inside and out with salt and the crushed spices. Set aside in a cool place for 3–4 hours. Stuff each partridge with a peeled raw potato (potatoes preserve moisture and the meat does not dry out). Coat the meat with thin strips of pork fat, tie up with thread and arrange in a roasting pan. Sprinkle with lemon juice, cover the roasting pan and place in a hot oven.

Roast the partridges for about 40 mins, frequently basting with their own juices. When tender, uncover, sprinkle with melted butter, raise the heat and brown the birds.

serves 4–8 • Macerating: 3–4 hrs • Preparation: 40–50 mins

Stewed partridges

2 partridges, 50 g pork fat, 50 g ham, 1 onion, soup vegetables, rind of ½ lemon, juice of 1 lemon, 2 tbsps sugar, 2 bay leaves, 1 cup dry white wine, ½ tsp thyme, 1 tbsp mustard, ½ cup stock, salt, pepper, 1 tsp flour, 50 g butter

Rub the trimmed and washed partridges with salt, lard with thin strips of pork fat and sear on all sides in butter. Transfer to a saucepan, add the chopped onion and soup vegetables, ham, finely chopped lemon rind, thyme and bay leaves. Pour in the wine and simmer for about 45 mins. Take out the partridges and cut into halves. Make a roux with the butter and flour, add to the vegetables and put through a sieve. Add the mustard, sugar and wine, mix well and bring to the boil. Put in the partridges and simmer for another few minutes.

serves 2–4 • Preparation: 45–55 mins

Partridges stewed in orange sauce

2 partridges, 70 g ham, 50 g mushrooms, salt, pepper, grated lemon rind, 1 glass white wine, 1½ tsp sugar, finely chopped orange rind, 100 g butter, 1 carrot, 1 parsley root, ¼ celeriac

Grate the vegetables and cook in little salted water, put through a sieve and mix with 1 tbsp butter. Trim and wash the partridges, rub with salt and sear on all sides in butter. Transfer to a saucepan, add the sliced mushrooms and ham cut into strips. Sauté for a moment or two. Add the puréed vegetables and grated lemon rind, pour in the wine and simmer covered for about 30 mins. Mix sugar with the finely chopped orange rind and orange juice, add to the stock, mix lightly and simmer covered until the partridges are tender.

serves 2–4 • Preparation: 45–50 mins

Partridges stewed in sauerkraut

2 partridges, 100 g pork fat, 1 large onion, 500 g sauerkraut, 1 cup dry white wine, ½ cup stock, 1 tbsp lard, 1 tsp flour, salt, 1 tbsp butter

Squeeze the sauerkraut to remove the excess liquid and chop finely. In a saucepan sauté the finely chopped onion in lard, add the sauerkraut, cover with the stock and simmer for about 40 mins. Rub the trimmed and washed partridges with salt, lard with pork fat and sear in butter. Sprinkle with wine and roast in a preheated oven for a few minutes until golden brown. Pour the remaining wine into the sauerkraut, mix well, add the partridges divided into halves and simmer together until the meat is tender. Brown the flour in a dry frying pan, add to the sauerkraut to thicken it, mix well. Arrange the meat on a warmed serving platter and surround with the sauerkraut.

serves 2–4 • Preparation: 55–60 mins

Partridges stewed in red cabbage

2 partridges, 100 g pork fat, 50 g butter, 1 head red cabbage (ca 1 kg), 2 onions, 1 tsp flour, salt, juice of ½ lemon, ½ tsp sugar, 1 cup dry red wine, a piece of cinnamon, 1–2 cloves, nutmeg (dash)

Rub the trimmed and washed partridges with salt, lard with pork fat, sear in butter, cover and simmer, sprinkling from time to time with wine. Cover the shredded cabbage with salted boiling water, bring to the boil and drain. In a saucepan melt 1 tbsp butter, add the cabbage and finely chopped onions. Simmer for a moment, then pour in the remaining wine, add sugar, cinnamon, cloves, a dash of nutmeg and lemon juice. Stew for about 15 mins. Halve the partridges and add them to the cabbage, pour in the sauce in which they were stewing and stew together until the meat is tender.

serves 2–4 • Preparation: 40–45 mins

Stuffed partridges

2 partridges, 100 g butter, 100 g pork fat, partridge hearts, livers and gizzards, 3 tbsps sifted breadcrumbs, 3 tbsps chopped parsley, sugar and nutmeg, salt, pepper, 1 egg

Rub the trimmed and washed partridges with salt and pepper and set aside in a cool place. In a bowl blend the finely chopped giblets with the egg yolk and butter, add a dash of sugar and a dash of nutmeg, salt and breadcrumbs. Then fold in the stiff-beaten egg white. Stuff the partridges with the mixture, sew them up and wrap in thin strips of pork fat. Tie with thread. Roast in the oven, sprinkling from time to time with melted butter. Towards the end remove the pork fat to crisp the skin.

serves 2–4 • Salting: 2–3 hrs • Preparation: 10 mins • Roasting: 20–25 mins

Partridges stuffed with green peas

2 partridges, 100 g lean streaky bacon, 50 g mushrooms, 50 g green peas, 2 tbsps chopped parsley, 100 g grated cheese, salt, pepper, ¼ tsp rosemary, 1 glass white wine, 1 tbsp butter

Rub the trimmed and washed partridges with salt, pepper and rosemary and set aside in a cool place for 2–3 hours. Cut the mushrooms into small pieces and sauté in butter. Add salt and pepper, leave aside to cool. Mix with the green peas, parsley and cheese. Stuff the birds, wrapping each with strips of pork fat. Arrange in a buttered roasting tin, sprinkle with melted butter and roast in the oven. From time to time baste with the meat juices and sprinkle with wine.

serves 2–4 • Macerating: 2–3 hrs • Preparation: 15–20 mins • Roasting: 20–25 mins

Partridges stuffed with pork

2 partridges, 100 g pork fat, juice and grated rind of 1 lemon, 50 g ham, salt, 1 bread roll soaked in wine, 100 g pork, 50 g mushrooms, salt, pepper, 1 egg, 100 g butter

Rub the trimmed and washed partridges with salt, sprinkle with lemon juice, lard with ham and set aside in a cool place for 2–3 hours. Put the pork meat through a mincer and sauté briefly in butter together with part of the pork fat and the finely chopped mushrooms. Set aside

to cool. Squeeze the bread roll dry and mix with butter. Gradually add the pork with mushrooms and the egg yolk, stirring all the time. Add the grated lemon rind, salt, pepper and the egg white beaten stiff. Mix well. Stuff the partridges, sew up, wrap each in thin strips of pork fat and roast in the oven. Sprinkle with melted butter from time to time. Towards the end of roasting, remove the pork fat to crisp the skin.

serves 2–4 • Macerating: 2–3 hrs • Preparation: 15–20 mins • Roasting: 20–25 mins

Partridge pudding

2 partridges, 3 eggs, ½ cup stock, 1 glass dry white wine, grated lemon rind, 2 cloves, 4 peppercorns, 1 tbsp butter, salt, 100 g pork fat

Pound the cloves together with pepper in a mortar. Wrap the trimmed, washed and salted partridges in strips of pork fat and roast. Separate the breast meat from the roasted partridges. Put the remaining meat and pork fat through a mincer, sieve and transfer to a saucepan. Add the stock, wine, pepper and cloves. Cook until thick, stirring all the time. Put the partridge breasts through a mincer, then through a sieve, mix with the grated lemon rind and 3 egg yolks. Season to taste with pepper. Butter a pâté mould and fill it with the breast meat mixture. Mix the other meat pulp with the stiff beaten egg whites and put on top of the breast pulp. Cover the form and steam for about 40 mins.

serves 4 • Baking: 20 mins • Cooling: 1 hr • Preparation: 20 mins • Cooking: 40 mins

Partridge pâté

4 partridges, 1 kg chaps, 750 g veal liver, 2 onions, 150 g mushrooms, 1–2 cloves, 1 bay leaf, 4 allspice berries, 4 peppercorns, 1 glass red wine, salt, pepper, 3 eggs, 1 cup milk, 50 g pork fat, 1 tbsp butter

Remove the membrane and soak the liver in the milk. Place the trimmed and washed partridges tightly in a saucepan on strips of pork fat. Add the spices and mushrooms and the onion cut into rings. Pour in 2 tbsps wine and simmer covered. In another small saucepan stew the chaps and the liver removed from the milk. Put the de-boned meat, liver and chaps twice through a mincer and mix with the meat juices. Break in the eggs, add salt and the remaining wine and form smooth pulp. Fill a buttered pâté mould with the mixture and cover. Steam for about 1 hour. Take the pâté out when cool. Serve cold with spicy sauces or lingonberries.

serves 10–12 • Stewing: 30 mins • Cooling: 1–2 hrs
• Preparation: 15 mins • Cooking: 1 hr

Hazel grouse

Hazel grouse fillets à la Astrakhan

Carve out fillets from fresh hazel grouse, remove membranes. Pound the fillets lightly to flatten them, put them in a frying pan greased with butter, sprinkle with salt and pepper. Pour over some Madeira and cook over low heat, then leave aside to cool. Make lengthwise incisions in them, fill them in with caviar. Arrange them in a roasting tin, cover with aspic. Place vegetable aspic in the centre of a round platter, arrange the fillets around it, decorate with more aspic.

(Antoni Teslar, Kuchnia polsko-francuska, 1910)

Roast hazel grouse with caper sauce

2 hazelhens, 100 g pork fat, 2 tbsps butter, salt, pepper, 10 pitted olives, 1 tbsp capers, grated rind and juice of 1 lemon, 1 cup dry red wine, 1 tsp butter

Rub the trimmed and washed hazelhens with salt and pepper, sprinkle with lemon juice and set aside in a cool place for 1–2 hours. Lard the birds with pork fat and arrange in a buttered roasting pan. Sprinkle with melted butter and roast, basting with butter from time to time. Take out when tender. Reduce the pan juices, stir in the flour, add the olives cut into strips, capers, grated lemon rind and lemon juice, pour in the wine and bring to the boil, stirring constantly. Place the halved hazelhens in a roasting

pan again, cover with the sauce and bake in a preheated oven for a few minutes.

serves 2–4 • Macerating: 1–2 hrs

Hazel grouse stewed with vegetables

2 hazelhens, 100 g pork fat, 100 g ham, 2–3 carrots, 1 parsley root, ½ celeriac, 1 onion, 3 cloves, 4–5 juniper berries, 10 peppercorns, 1 bay leaf, 2 cups dry red wine

Rub the trimmed and washed hazelhens with salt, lard with strips of ham, wrap each in strips of pork fat. Line a saucepan with strips of pork fat, sliced onion and carrot and spices. Put in the hazelhens, top with the coarsely grated parsley root and celeriac, pour in the wine and simmer covered for one hour. Take the hazelhens out, put the sauce through a sieve. Divide the meat into serving pieces, add to the saucepan with the sauce. Heat up.

serves 4 • Preparation: 15–20 mins • Stewing: 1 hr

Hazel grouse stewed in cream

2 hazelhens, 100 g pork fat, ½ cup single cream, 2 tbsps breadcrumbs, ¼ tsp nutmeg, salt, 50 g butter

Divide the drawn and washed hazelhens into quarters, rub with salt, coat with the pork fat and fry in butter for about 10 mins. Pour the cream over, add nutmeg, sprinkle with breadcrumbs and simmer covered for about 40 mins. Take the meat out and sieve the sauce. Put the meat back to the sauce and heat up.

serves 4 • Preparation: 15–20 mins • Stewing: 40 mins

Wild duck

The tasties among wild duck are mallard and teal. Both should be barded with pork fat slices and roasted for half an hour. It is advisable to add several juniper berries to the roasting tin.

After young ducks have aged properly, you should pluck and draw them, wash them thoroughly, sprinkle generously with salt and leave aside for an hour. Old ducks will taste better if you marinate them overnight. While roasting wild duck, remember to baste them frequently with melted butter and marinade.

Roast wild duck with garlic

1 duck, salt, pepper, ¼ tsp caraway seeds, ¼ tsp marjoram, 1 onion, 3 garlic cloves, ½ cup dry white wine, 100 g pork fat, 100 g butter

In a saucepan cover the drawn duck with boiling water and cook for about 10 mins. Remove and set aside to cool. Lard the meat densely with pork fat, rub with salt, pepper, caraway seeds and marjoram (inside and out). Set aside in a cool place for 1–2 hours. In a saucepan sauté the finely chopped onion and garlic in butter, add the duck and sear on all sides for about 10 mins. Roast in a preheated oven, from time to time sprinkling with wine.

serves 2–4 • Cooking: 10 mins • Cooling: 40–50 mins • Macerating: 1–2 hrs • Roasting: 45–55 mins

Wild duck with apples and tomatoes

1 duck, salt, 100 g butter, 100 g pork fat, soup vegetables, 1 onion, 1 cup stock, 2 cloves, 5 peppercorns, 5 juniper berries, 1 bay leaf, 3 tomatoes, 2 tart apples, ½ cup dry white wine, sugar, 1 tsp flour

Cover the dressed and cleaned duck with boiling water and cook for about 10 mins. Remove, leave aside to cool. Lard the bird with pork fat, rub with salt and pepper and sear in butter on all sides, then transfer to a saucepan. Sauté the chopped onion and grated vegetables in the butter drippings left over from frying the duck. Add to the meat, put in the spices and pour in the stock. Cover and simmer. Cut the tomatoes and apples into quarters and add to the duck. Simmer for about 30 mins. Take the duck out when tender and cut into serving pieces. Make a roux with the butter and flour, dilute with the wine and add to the saucepan. Bring to the boil and put through a sieve. Season to taste with salt and a dash of sugar. Put in

the meat and simmer together for a moment. Serve with the sauce poured over.

serves 4 • Preparation: 20 mins • Stewing: 30–40 mins

Wild duck in caper sauce

1 duck, salt, pepper, 1 tsp lemon juice, grated lemon rind, 2 tbsps butter, 1 tsp flour, 2 tbsps capers, 2 tbsps finely diced cocktail gherkins, 100 g pork fat, 1 cup stock

Rub the dressed and washed duck with salt and pepper, lard with pork fat and brown in butter. Pour in the stock and simmer covered. Take the meat out when tender and cut into serving pieces. Make a roux with the butter and flour, thicken the sauce and season it with lemon juice and grated lemon rind. Bring to the boil, put through a sieve and add the capers and cocktail gherkins. Put in the meat and keep (uncovered) over low heat for a moment or two.

serves 4 • Preparation: 10 mins • Stewing: 50–55 mins

Wild duck in cherry sauce

1 duck, 100 g pork fat, salt, pepper, ¼ tsp thyme, 1 tbsp butter, 300 g sour cherries, 1 tbsp flour, ½ cup thick sour cream

MARINADE: ½ cup dry red wine, ½ cup boiled water, juice and grated rind of ½ lemon, ¼ tsp thyme, ¼ tsp sugar, 2–3 cloves, a piece of cinnamon, 1 small bay leaf, 2 allspice berries, 2 peppercorns, 1 small onion

Combine the ingredients of the marinade and bring to the boil, set aside to cool. Place the dressed and washed duck in an earthenware pot and cover with the marinade. Set aside in a cool place for 2–3 days. Roast the meat in the oven, frequently sprinkling with melted butter. After 10–15 minutes of roasting, pour in the marinade and add the pitted cherries. Take the duck out when tender and cut into serving pieces. Make a roux with the butter and flour, thicken the sauce, sieve it, stir in the cream and season to taste with sugar and salt, and a dash of pepper, if desired. Arrange the meat in an ovenproof dish, pour the sauce over and bake for a few minutes in a preheated oven.

serves 4 • Marinating: 2–3 days • Preparation: 5–8 mins • Roasting: 50–55 mins

Wild duck with macaroni

1 duck, 500 g macaroni, salt, pepper, lemon juice, 100 g butter, 50 g pork fat, 2 tbsps grated cheese, 2 tbsps chopped parsley

Rub the dressed, washed and scalded duck with salt and pepper, sprinkle with lemon juice, lard with pork fat and place in a greased roasting pan. Sprinkle with melted butter and roast for about 20 mins. Cook the macaroni in slightly salted water. Strain. Stir in pepper and 50 g butter. Place the duck cut into serving pieces in the middle of a buttered ovenproof dish, sprinkle with the gravy, surround with the macaroni sprinkled with melted butter and grated cheese. Bake in a preheated oven for about 15 mins. Before serving, sprinkle with parsley.

serves 4 • Preparation: 5–7 mins • Roasting: 50–55 mins

Wild duck with dried mushrooms

1 duck, 100 g pork fat, 6–8 dried mushrooms, grated lemon rind, 4–5 juniper berries, 4–5 allspice berries, 4–5 peppercorns, 1 bay leaf, 100 g butter, lemon juice, ½ cup dry white wine, salt, sugar

Soak the mushrooms overnight and cook in little water. Sprinkle the dressed and washed duck with lemon juice, rub with pepper and lard with the pork fat. Brown the meat in butter and transfer to a saucepan. Add the spices, lemon rind and the mushrooms cut into strips. Roast in a preheated oven, sprinkling from time to time with the mushroom stock and melted butter. Towards the end of roasting pour in the wine, steam off the sauce and season to taste with a dash of sugar.

serves 4 • Soaking: 12 hrs • Preparation: 5 mins • Roasting: 50–55 mins

Wild duck stuffed with raisins and almonds

1 duck, 100 g pork fat, 1 tbsp butter, ¼ tsp thyme, ¼ tsp marjoram, a dash of juniper (crushed), ½ cup thick cream, lemon juice

STUFFING: 2 onions, ½ tbsp butter, duck liver, 2 tbsps breadcrumbs, 50 g almonds, 50 g raisins, ½ tsp sugar, nutmeg, salt, pepper, 1 egg

Rub the dressed and washed duck inside and out with salt, thyme, marjoram and juniper, sprinkle with lemon juice and set aside in a cool place for 2–3 hours.
PREPARE THE STUFFING: Finely chop the liver, scald the almonds and raisins. Peel and chop the almonds. Sauté the finely chopped onion in butter, leave to cool and mix with the liver, breadcrumbs, almonds, raisins, egg and a dash of salt, pepper, nutmeg and sugar.
Stuff the duck, sew up and place in a greased roasting tin. Roast it in a preheated oven, frequently sprinkling with melted butter. Towards the end cover with the cream.

serves 4 • Macerating: 2–3 hrs • Preparation: 15–20 mins • Roasting: 50–55 mins

Wild duck in red cabbage

1 duck, salt, pepper, ½ tsp crushed juniper berries, 1 large onion, 1 head red cabbage, 1 cup dry red wine, 100 g butter, ¼ tbsp lemon juice, a piece of cinnamon, 1 clove

Rub the dressed and washed duck with salt, pepper and juniper, sprinkle with lemon juice and set aside in a cool place for 2–3 hours. Put the finely chopped cabbage into salted boiling water, bring to the boil and drain in a sieve. Add the finely chopped onion and mix well. Divide the duck into serving pieces, brown in butter and transfer to a saucepan. Sprinkle with wine, cover and simmer for a moment or two. Add the cabbage, clove and cinnamon. Pour in the wine and simmer until the duck is tender. Season to taste with sugar and salt.

serves 4 • Macerating: 2–3 hrs • Preparation: 1 hr

Coot

Coots are slightly smaller than ducks. They are quite common in Poland, where they come in March and leave in November. They live on lakes and ponds and rarely come ashore. Young coots are very tasty, but preparing them takes quite a lot of time: first, they are hanged, feathered, for several days; then their skin is removed together with the feathers (the fatty layer under the skin has an unpleasant taste, not unlike cod liver oil). Older birds are then left in buttermilk for 2–3 days, and younger ones can be cooked immediately. You can use any recipe for wild duck to prepare coot dishes.

Roast coot

2 coots, 200 g pork fat, 1 tbsp butter, 1 cup thick sour cream, 1 tbsp crumbled wholemeal bread, salt, pepper, ¼ tsp ground juniper, 2 cups sour milk, 1 tsp lemon juice

Place the dressed and washed coots in an earthenware pot, cover with the sour milk and set aside in a cool place for 24 hours. Then take the coots out, wipe dry, rub with salt, pepper and juniper and densely lard with pork fat. Place the coots in a roasting pan, sprinkle with melted butter and roast in a preheatead oven, basting from time to time with melted butter and the pan juices. Take out when tender and divide into serving pieces. Add the crumbled bread to the sauce, stir in the cream seasoned with salt and 1 tsp lemon juice. Put the meat in and heat up.

serves 4 • Soaking: 24 hrs • Preparation: 50–60 mins

Coot, Old Polish style

2 coots, 1 tbsp butter, 200 g smoked streaky bacon, 1 tbsp grated horseradish, 3 tbsps chopped walnuts, 1 egg, 1 tbsp cream, salt, pepper, lemon juice, sugar, 2 cups milk

Place the dressed and washed coots in an earthenware pot, cover with the milk and set aside in a cool place overnight. Remove, rinse, wipe dry, sprinkle with lemon juice, rub with salt and pepper and set aside for 1–2 hours in a cool place. Mix the chopped walnuts with horseradish, cream and egg. Add salt, pepper and a dash of sugar. Coat the coots with the prepared mixture, and wrap each in strips of smoked bacon. Tie up with thread and arrange in a buttered roasting pan. Sprinkle lightly with melted butter and roast, basting from time to time with the pan juices and water. Cut the roasted coots into serving pieces, arrange on a warmed serving platter and pour the sauce over.

serves 4 • Soaking: 12 hrs • Macerating: 1–2 hrs • Preparation: 70–80 mins

Coot in cranberry sauce

2 coots, 200 g pork fat, 50 g butter, 150 g cranberries, grated lemon rind, lemon juice, 1 tsp grated orange rind, ½ tsp sugar, 1 cup dry white wine, salt, ½ lemon

Cover the dressed and washed coots with the wine, leave in a cool place overnight. Take out, wipe dry, rub with salt, lard with pork fat and place in a buttered roasting pan. Roast sprinkling from time to time with the melted butter and the wine in which the meat marinated. Add half of the lemon cut into slices. Take the meat out when cooked and cut into serving pieces. Arrange on a warmed platter. Transfer the meat juices to a small saucepan, add the cranberries, lemon juice and grated lemon rind, orange rind and sugar. Simmer for a moment and put through a sieve. Pour over the meat and put the platter for a few minutes into the hot oven to heat.

serves 4 • Marinating: 12 hrs • Preparation: 60–70 mins

Coot with anchovies

2 coots, 100 g butter, 4 anchovy fillets, ½ tsp ground allspice, 1 cup thick sour cream, salt

MARINADE: 1 glass dry red wine, juice of ½ lemon, 2–3 peppercorns, 2–3 each allspice and juniper berries, 1 bay leaf, a pinch of sugar

Combine the marinade ingredients, bring to the boil. Place the dressed coots in an earthenware dish, cover with the cool marinade and leave in a cool place for 2–3 days, turning them over frequently. Take the birds out, dry them, rub with salt and allspice, lard with the anchovy fillets. Arrange in a buttered roasting tin and put into a preheated oven. Baste with melted butter, the strained marinade and, towards the end, with cream.

serves 4 • Marinating: 2–3 days • Preparation: 60–70 mins

Coot pâté

3 coots, 600 g pork, 50 g pork fat, 1 tbsp lard, 4 eggs, 5–6 peppercorns, 5–6 allspice berries, 1 bay leaf, ½ French loaf, salt, pepper, ¼ tsp nutmeg, 100 g chicken livers, 1 tsp breadcrumbs, ½ cup dry white wine

Brown the dressed and washed birds, giblets and pork cut into cubes, transfer to a skillet. Add the bay leaf, pepper, allspice and wine, cover and simmer until tender. Take the meat out, remove the bones. Put the sliced bread and lightly browned chicken livers into the skillet and cook for a while, then leave to cool. Put the meat, bread and livers through a mincer two or three times. Adjust the taste with pepper, salt, allspice and nutmeg. Break in the eggs and mix thoroughly. Grease a pâté tin, dust it with breadcrumbs, line with pork fat slices and fill with the pâté mixture. Bake in a preheated oven for about an hour.

serves 8–10 • Preparation: 2 hrs • Baking: 1 hr

Woodcock

Woodcock, snipe and jack snipe are all wading birds. Their habitat are marshes, wetlands and humid woodlands. Woodcock is a small bird, the size of a pigeon, so preparing a meal you should have one for each person. Its meat does not need to be marinated. Young roast woodcocks are often served on toast spread with pâté. Older birds are best stewed and used for making stuffing and pâtés. To cook them, you may also use any recipe for partridge or pheasant dishes.

Woodcock, Mazurian style

2–3 woodcocks, 50 g pork fat, 2 tbsps butter, 200 g mushrooms, 2 tbsps chopped walnuts, 2 tbsps cream, salt, pepper, 1 tsp marjoram, 1 tbsp chopped parsley, 1 tbsp lemon juice

Finely chop the giblets and mix with the finely chopped mushrooms, parsley, walnuts and cream. Season to taste with salt and pepper. Rub the dressed and washed woodcocks with salt and marjoram, sprinkle with lemon juice and stuff with the prepared mixture. Wrap in strips of pork fat and place in a roasting pan. Sprinkle with melted butter and roast in the oven. During the roasting baste with the meat juices and water.

serves 2–3 • Preparation: 1 hr

Woodcock, Polish style

2–3 woodcocks, 2 tbsp butter, 2 tbsp sour cherry preserve, 2 tbsps grated horseradish, 1 cup single cream, 1 tsp flour, lemon juice, salt, pepper

Rub the dressed and washed birds with salt and pepper, sprinkle with lemon juice and set aside in a cool place for the night. Then dust lightly with flour, brown in butter and put into a saucepan. Sprinkle with melted butter, cover and stew over low heat, adding some of the cream. Mix the cherry preserve with the horseradish and the remaining cream blended with flour. Pour over the woodcocks and simmer together for a moment or two.

serves 2–3 • Macerating: 12 hrs • Preparation: 1 hr

Woodcock, hunter's style

2–3 woodcocks, 50 g pork fat, 1 tbsp butter, 4 chicken livers, woodcock giblets, 2 tbsps raisins, 1 small onion, 1 tsp chopped parsley, 1 small glass brandy

Finely chop the giblets and chicken livers. Mix the finely chopped onion with the giblets, raisins and parsley. Add salt and some of the brandy. Rub the dressed and washed woodcocks with salt and stuff with the mixture. Wrap the birds in strips of pork fat and spit roast them, basting from time to time with melted butter and the remaining brandy.

serves 2–3 • Preparation: 1 hr

Stuffed woodcock

2–3 woodcocks, 100 g pork fat, 3 tbsps butter, woodcock giblets, 1 onion, 5–6 mushrooms, ¼ tsp ground juniper, ¼ tsp ground pepper, 1 tsp grated cheese, 2–3 tbsps breadcrumbs, salt

Remove the giblets. Rub the birds with salt. Sauté the finely cut mushrooms, onion and giblets in butter, add juniper, pepper and the grated cheese. Mix well and fry together for a moment. When cool, mix with 50 g finely chopped pork fat and breadcrumbs. Dress and wash the woodcocks, stuff with the mixture, sew up and set aside in the fridge (lower shelf) for 2–3 days. Then take the meat out, wrap in the strips of pork fat and roast in a preheated oven, sprinkling with melted butter and water.

serves 2–3 • Macerating: 2–3 days • Roasting: 40–50 mins

Woodcocks in lemon sauce

6–8 woodcocks (or fieldfares), 2 tbsps butter, 1 tsp flour, lemon juice, salt, pepper, 1 small onion, 1 cup stock

Dress and wash the tenderized fowl, then rub with salt. Sauté the chopped giblets (hearts and livers) and onion in butter, add the stock and cook for about 30 mins, then sieve. Make a roux with the butter and flour, stir in lemon juice and add salt, pepper and the strained sauce. Heat up. Coat the salted meat with butter and place in a saucepan. Roast for about 30 mins. Pour the sauce over and simmer together for a moment. Serve with toasted white bread.

serves 6–8 • Preparation: 40 mins • Roasting: 30–40 mins

Quail

Quail meat is very delicate and fatty. The birds must be plucked very carefully, so as not to damage the skin. Young quails are specially recommended for broiling, while older ones are good for stewing under cover. When they are not fatty enough, you should first bard them with fine slices of pork fat or bacon, otherwise you wrap them in vine leaves. They need no more than 20 minutes in the oven, and are best served with rice or macaroni. Sometimes it is also advisable to marinate them in dry white wine with spices for 2–3 days.

Roast quails

4 quails, 100 g pork fat, 1 tbsp butter, grape leaves, 1 cup dry white wine, 4 cloves, a piece of cinnamon, white bread for toasting, salt

Put the dressed and washed quails in an earthenware pot, cover with the wine and set aside in a cool place

for the night. Then take the birds out, wipe dry, rub with salt and wrap in thin strips of pork fat and grape leaves. Place in a saucepan dabbed with butter. Roast in a preheated oven for 20–25 mins, sprinkling with the reserved marinade. When the birds are ready, remove the grape leaves and pork fat. Put the pork fat and the meat juices through a sieve. Fry some bread and arrange the quails on toast on a warmed platter. Serve the sauce in a sauceboat.

serves 4 • Marinating: 12 hrs • Preparation: 30–40 mins

Roast quails with ham

4 quails, 100 g pork fat, 100 g butter, 100 g ham, ¼ celeriac, 300 g green peas, 1 head lettuce, 2 tbsps chopped parsley, ½ tsp sugar, salt

Rub the dressed and washed quails with salt, wrap in strips of pork fat and spit roast, basting with butter. In a small saucepan melt some butter and add the grated celeriac, green peas, chopped lettuce and parsley, pour in 2 cups salted water, bring to the boil, simmer and strain through a sieve. Season to taste with sugar, steam off to reduce the liquid. Butter an ovenproof platter, line it with thin strips of ham and the pork fat removed from the quails. Arrange the birds and pour the strained sauce over, dot with knobs of butter and bake in a preheated oven for 10–15 mins.

serves 4 • Preparation: 35–45 mins

Quails stuffed with liver

4 quails, 1 tbsp butter, 1 glass dry white wine, salt, pepper

STUFFING: 100 g turkey liver, 1 tbsp butter, 1 glass brandy, 125 g mushrooms, ½ roll soaked in milk, 1 onion, 1 bunch dill, ½ tsp thyme, a dash of each ground ginger, cloves and cinnamon, 2 egg yolks, salt, pepper

Rub the dressed and washed quails with salt and pepper inside and out, sprinkle with wine and set aside in a cool place for 2–3 hours.
PREPARE THE STUFFING: Sauté the chopped onion and mushrooms in butter, add the liver and simmer together

for 5 mins. Set aside to cool. Squeeze the roll dry and put it through a mincer together with the onion, liver and mushrooms. Stir in the egg yolks, salt, pepper, brandy, dill, thyme and the spices. Add the stiff beaten egg whites and mix well. Stuff the quails, sew up and wrap in grape leaves. Arrange on a greased roasting tin, sprinkle with melted butter and bake for 10 mins in a preheated oven. Remove the leaves, brown the quails and cover with the remaining wine. Serve the meat juices in a sauceboat.

serves 4 • Marinating: 2–3 hrs • Preparation: 1 hr

Quails in nests

8 quails, 300 g pork fat, 100 g butter, 500 g boneless veal, 2 bread rolls soaked in milk, 2 eggs, lemon juice and grated rind, 1 onion, 1 tbsp chopped parsley, 1 tbsp chopped walnuts, a dash of each sugar and nutmeg

Rub the dressed and washed quails with salt and wrap in strips of pork fat. Place the birds in a saucepan, cover with rings of onion and bake for 10 mins in a preheated oven, sprinkling with butter and lemon juice. Squeeze the roll dry and put it together with the veal through a mincer. Add the grated lemon rind, parsley, finely chopped walnuts, salt, sugar, pepper, nutmeg and eggs. Form smooth pulp and shape 8 flat oblong cakes. Arrange them on a buttered tin, put a quail on top of each and bake. Put the meat juices through a sieve together with the pork fat strips removed from the quails. Pour over the quails towards the end of baking.

serves 8 • Preparation: 1 hr

Quails baked with potatoes

4 quails, 200 g smoked streaky bacon, 1 tbsp butter, 600 g peeled potatoes, 150 g grated cheese, lemon juice, ½ cup cream, a dash of each savory and rosemary, 1 tbsp chopped parsley, salt, pepper

Sprinkle the dressed and washed quails with lemon juice, rub with salt, pepper, savory and rosemary, set aside in a cool place for 2–3 hours. Wrap the birds in strips of bacon and roast in the oven, basting with melted butter. Cut the potatoes in thick slices, cover with salted boiling water and cook for 10 mins, then strain. Butter an ovenproof dish and arrange a layer of potatoes, lightly dusted with pep-

per. Add the strips of bacon removed from the quails and the quail halves. Cover them with the remaining potatoes, sprinkle with pepper, pour over the cream blended with parsley, top with the grated cheese. Bake in a preheated oven for 10–15 mins.

serves 4 • Marinating: 2–3 hrs • Preparation: 1 hr

Marinated quails

4 quails, 150 g butter, 200 g pork fat, 500 g potatoes, 100 g grated cheese, ½ cup single cream, nutmeg, 1 leek, salt, pepper

MARINADE: 1 cup dry white wine, lemon juice, 5 cloves, a piece of cinnamon bark

Bring the marinade to the boil. Set aside to cool. Dress and wash the quails, cover them with the marinade and set aside in a cool place overnight. Then wipe dry, rub with salt and wrap in strips of pork fat. Tie with thread and roast in the oven, sprinkling with the strained marinade. Peel, wash and cut the potatoes into slices, scald and strain in a sieve. Cut the leek into thin rings. Butter an ovenproof dish and arrange layers of potatoes and leek, sprinkling each layer with salt, pepper and nutmeg. Cover the potatoes with the cream, sprinkle with the grated cheese, dot with knobs of butter. Bake in a preheated oven for about 1 hour. In an ovenproof dish arrange quail halves, pour the pan juices over. Serve with the baked potatoes and lettuce salad.

serves 4 • Marinating: 12 hrs • Preparation: 1 hr

Quails with carrots

4 quails, 200 g pork fat, 500 g carrots, ½ cup cream, lemon juice, 2 tbsps grated horseradish, rosemary, sugar, salt, pepper

Sprinkle the dressed and washed quails with lemon juice, rub with salt, pepper and rosemary, set aside in a cool place for 2–3 hours, then wrap in strips of pork fat and roast. When ready, remove the pork fat. Arrange the quails on a warmed serving platter. Transfer the drippings into a small saucepan, add the coarsely grated carrots, stew together and season with salt, sugar and lemon juice. Continue to simmer for about 10 mins. Add the horseradish, cream and mix well together. Butter an ovenproof dish. Arrange the quail halves, surround with the carrots and bake in the oven.

serves 4 • Marinating: 2–3 hrs • Preparation: 1 hr

Quails with oranges

4 quails, 100 g butter, 2 oranges, 100 g raisins,
1 glass dry white wine, 1 small glass rum, lemon
juice and grated rind, ¼ tsp thyme, salt

Sprinkle the dressed and washed quails with lemon juice, rub with salt and thyme, set aside in a cool place for 2–3 hours, then brown on all sides in butter. Take the quails out and cut each into half. Scald the oranges, peel them and divide into wedges. In a saucepan stew the oranges in the butter reserved from browning the quails, pour in the wine and continue to simmer for 10 mins, then sieve. Add the raisins, grated lemon rind, orange rind cut into strips and simmer for another 5 mins. Add the rum and mix well. Arrange the quail halves on a buttered ovenproof platter, pour the orange sauce over and bake for about 15 mins in a preheated oven.

serves 4 • Marinating: 2–3 hrs • Preparation: 45–55 mins

CHAPTER XIII

MUSHROOMS

✳✳✳

Of mushrooms, the rich knew only: ceps, rufous milkcaps, morels, champignons and truffles... The peasants ate and still do eat all kinds of wild mushrooms with many different names, and in all this variety they make mistakes and take poisonous ones for edible, often paying for it with their health or their lives.

(Łukasz Gołębiowski, *Domy i dwory*, vol. IV)

In many cultures, mushrooms are the subject of numerous legends and are an important element in magic rites; in ancient Rome, they were regarded as the food of the gods, and the Egyptians only served them to their pharaohs, since 'something that appears magically overnight' should not be eaten by ordinary mortals.

Mushrooms have little nutritional value. They are made up of more than 90% water, and contain very small amounts of calcium, and even smaller quantities of phosphorus, iron and group B vitamins. But they have enormous culinary value, whether fresh, dried, marinated or salted.

For centuries, mushrooms have been the pride of Polish cuisine, and many tasty Polish dish use them; their aroma gives many dishes their 'Polish flavour'. In Old Polish cuisine, they were prepared as an hors-d'oeuvre and as a main dish, and were added to soups, sauces and stuffings. One or two dried mushrooms could change the taste of broth, and two or three were added to pea soup, cabbage soup, barley soup or potato soup.

Today, as in earlier times, they are an essential accompaniment of roasts, poultry, game, some fish and cabbage. It is difficult to imagine the traditional Polish Christmas Eve supper without them: for this, fried dried mushrooms are prepared, along with mushroom cutlets, cabbage with

mushrooms, noodles for borsch, mushroom soup, fish soups with mushrooms, kasha baked with mushrooms, and of course tens of stuffings for pierogi or koulebiacs.

In the 18th century, the first cultivated mushrooms – champignons – appeared on the table of King Stanislaus Augustus, and these in time ensured themselves a place in Polish cuisine. Champignons are equal in taste to edible forest mushrooms and have the enormous advantage of being available fresh all year round. Today, oyster mushrooms are also cultivated, which have less flavour and aroma than champignons, but are excellent for frying. Oyster mushrooms, with their soft, succulent white flesh (only the cap is eaten) should be young; the older mushrooms tend to be tough.

Savoury mushroom salad

500 g caps of new field mushrooms (boletes), 2 small onions, ½ tsp caraway, 2 tbsps lemon juice, 3–4 tbsps oil, ½ tsp honey, salt, pepper, ½ tsp chopped tarragon leaves, 1 tbsp each chopped dill and chives

Bring salted water with caraway to the boil, put in the mushrooms, cook them for 10–12 mins. Take the mushrooms out, drain them, pour over cold water, drain them again. Cut the mushrooms into quarters, put them into a bowl and combine with the finely chopped onions. Mix the lemon juice with honey, tarragon, salt and pepper and gradually add the oil. Pour the dressing over the mushrooms, shake gently, cover the bowl and put in the fridge for 1–2 hours. Before serving, toss the salad again and garnish it with dill and chives.

serves 4 • Preparation: 15 mins • Refrigerating: 2–3 hrs

Saffron milk cap salad

*500 g new saffron milk caps, 1 onion, 2 tbsps butter,
1 tbsp hot mustard, 1 tbsp lemon juice, 1 tbsp oil, 2 hard-
boiled eggs, salt, pepper, 2 tbsps chopped parsley*

Rinse and dry the mushrooms. Melt the butter in a frying pan, put in the mushrooms and brown them lightly. Take them off the heat, allow to cool, then cut into strips and put into a bowl. Peel and chop the onion, sprinkle it with lemon juice, salt and pepper; cut the egg whites into small cubes. Add the onion and egg whites to the mushrooms. Blend the mustard with the oil and pour the preparation over the mushrooms. Cover the bowl and put into the fridge for 1–2 hours. Before serving, garnish with the chopped egg yolks and parsley.

serves 4 • Preparation: 15 mins • Refrigerating: 1–2 hrs

Herbal mushroom salad

*500 g caps of new bolete mushrooms, a bunch of parsley,
3–4 sprigs of savory, 1 tbsp coriander seeds, juice and
grated rind of 1 lemon, 1 cup oil, 1 cup water, ½ cup dry
white wine, salt, pepper, 1 tbsp chopped coriander leaves*

Add the oil, lemon juice and zest, parsley, savory and coriander to the water, bring to the boil, then cover the pan and cook over low heat for 20–25 mins. Strain the liquid, add the wine, put in the rinsed mushrooms, cover the pan and cook for 10–15 mins, then take off the lid and cook for another 10–15 mins to reduce the liquid. Leave to cool, then put into the fridge for 1–2 hours. Before serving, transfer to a serving bowl and garnish with chopped coriander.

serves 4 • Cooking: 45–55 mins • Refrigerating: 1–2 hrs

Mushroom and ham salad

*250 g new, firm ceps, 2 tbsps olive oil, 1 clove of garlic, 100 g
lean ham, 2 hard-boiled eggs, 3–4 firm beef tomatoes,
1 small onion, salt, pepper, 2 tbsps lemon juice, ¼ tsp grated
lemon rind, 2–3 tbsps olive oil, 2 tbsps chopped parsley*

Rinse and dry the mushrooms, cut them into thin strips. Heat up some oil in a frying pan, put in the garlic, fry it for a minute or two, then take it out. Put in the mush-

rooms, sauté them briskly, cover the pan and continue cooking for 10 mins, then take off the heat. Blanch and skin the tomatoes, slice them finely; cut the ham into thin strips; chop the onion finely and cut the egg whites into cubes. Combine all the ingredients in a bowl, add some salt, pepper and lemon zest, sprinkle with lemon juice and oil. Toss the salad lightly, cover the bowl and put into the fridge for 1–2 hours. Before serving, garnish with chopped parsley and chopped egg yolks.

serves 4 • Preparation: 15 mins • Refrigerating: 1–2 hrs

Stuffed champignons I

*8 large champignons, 2–3 young sprigs of borage,
1 tbsp finely chopped rosemary leaves, 2 tbsps
each chopped parsley and chives, 1 small onion,
1–2 cloves of garlic, 150 g lean ham, 2 eggs, 3 tbsps
butter, salt, pepper, ¼ tsp chilli pepper, 1 tbsp lemon
juice, 1 tbsp borage flowers, several borage leaves*

Rinse and dry the mushrooms. Chop finely the stalks, onion and garlic. Dice the ham and borage sprigs. Melt 1 tbsp of butter in a frying pan, brown the mushroom caps lightly. Take the caps out, arrange them on a plate and sprinkle with lemon juice. Put ½ tbsp of butter into the frying pan, fry the onion and garlic, but do not let them brown. Add the chopped stalks and fry them for a minute or two, stirring all the time. Towards the end, add the ham, borage sprigs and rosemary. Season with salt, pepper and chilli, pour in the lightly beaten eggs and, stirring continuously, fry for a while. Take off the heat, add the chopped greens and mix thoroughly. Stuff the mushroom caps with the preparation. Arrange the caps in a greased ovenproof dish, sprinkle with some melted butter and put into a pre-heated oven. Bake for some 10 mins. Before serving, garnish with borage flowers and leaves. This dish makes an excellent hot hors-d'oeuvre and can also be served as second course with rice or French fries and with tomato salad.

serves 4 • Preparation: 15 mins • Baking: 10–15 mins

Stuffed champignons II

*12 small white champignons, 100 g cottage cheese,
2 tbsps almond flakes, 1 celery stick, 1 small red apple,
1 tsp hot mustard, 2 tbsps olive oil, 1 tbsp lemon juice,
2–3 finely chopped tarragon leaves, salt, pepper*

Put the rinsed mushrooms into lightly salted boiling water for one minute, drain them, pour over cold water, drain them again and remove the stalks. Dice finely the mushroom stalks, celery stick and the cored apple. Chop the almond flakes and dry-roast them. Blend the cheese with the mustard, add salt and pepper, then combine with the mushroom stalks, apple, celery and almonds. Mix the oil with lemon juice and chopped tarragon, brush each mushroom cap with the mixture. Arrange the caps in a serving dish, fill them with the stuffing and put in the fridge. Serve the mushroom caps on lettuce leaves, garnished with strips of pepper and sprigs of parsley.

serves 4–6 • Preparation: 10–15 mins • Refrigerating: 1–2 hrs

Breaded parasol mushrooms

8 young parasol mushrooms (with open caps), 1 cup milk, 2–3 tbsps flour, 2 eggs, 3–4 tbsps breadcrumbs, salt, pepper, 4 tbsps butter

Discard the stalks, rinse the caps carefully. Soak the caps in milk for half an hour, then take them out, drain them, sprinkle with salt and pepper. Dredge each cap with flour, lightly beaten eggs and breadcrumbs. Fry in melted butter until golden brown on both sides. Turn the heat down and keep them hot for another 8–10 mins. Serve with boiled potatoes, garnished with chopped dill.

serves 4 • Soaking: 30–40 mins • Preparation: 15–20 mins

Oyster mushrooms in batter

1 kg oyster mushrooms, 3–4 tbsps flour, 1 egg, ½ cup lager beer, 1–2 tbsps cream, salt, pepper, fat for frying

Blend the egg with the beer and cream, gradually add the flour, salt and pepper until the mixture has the consistency of thick cream. Cover with a lid and leave aside for 30–50 mins. Rinse the mushroom caps and dry them. Dust each cup with flour, then dip it in the batter. Fry in very hot oil on both sides until golden brown. Dry the fried mushrooms on absorbent paper and serve with some savoury sauce as an hors-d'oeuvre or with potatoes and salads as the main course.

serves 4–6 • Preparation: 5–6 mins • Frying: 6–8 mins

Saffron milk caps, Podlasie style

1 kg fresh milk caps, 2 large onions, 3 tbsps butter, 1 cup grated dry wholemeal bread, salt

Rinse and dry the mushrooms. Peel the onion, chop it very finely or grate it. Mix the onion with the grated bread. Melt the butter in a large frying pan, put in the mushrooms. Sprinkle them with the bread and onion preparation and fry over fairly high heat. Sprinkle with salt. Reduce the juices and serve immediately.

serves 4–6 • Preparation: 15–20 mins

Chanterelle stew

1 kg chanterelles, 2–3 cloves of garlic, 1 tsp dried thyme, 2–3 tbsps olive oil, ½ cup stock, 2 tbsps lemon juice, 2 tbsps tomato paste, salt, pepper, a pinch of sugar

Wash the mushrooms thoroughly, dry them. Heat up the oil in a pan, put in the mushrooms and fry them for a minute or two over high heat, stirring all the time. Turn down the heat and cook them for another 10–15 mins. Mix the tomato paste with the garlic crushed with salt, add the stock, pepper, sugar and thyme. Pour the mixture over the mushrooms, bring to the boil, then simmer for 50 mins. Towards the end, add lemon juice and adjust the taste with salt, sugar and pepper. Serve as a hot hors- d'oeuvre or for the second course with tomatoes and salads, or else as a side dish with meat.

serves 4–6 • Preparation: 70–80 mins

Chanterelles in cheese sauce

1 kg chanterelles, 2 large onions, 150 g smoked streaky bacon, 1 tbsp lard, 1 tbsp butter, ¾ cup cream, ¼ cup light chicken stock, 150 g cheese, salt, pepper, a pinch of sugar, 1 tsp lemon juice, 2–3 tbsps chopped parsley

Clean and wash the mushrooms, drain and dry them (halve larger specimens). Heat up the lard in a pan, add the bacon cut into cubes and fry for a minute or two. Put in the chopped onion and brown it. Add the mushrooms and fry them briskly over high heat for 10 mins, stirring all the time. Pour in the stock, add pepper, put the lid on and simmer for another 30 mins. Melt the butter in a small pan, add the grated cheese and heat up for 2–3 mins. Pour in the cream and cook until the sauce has thickened. Add the sauce to the mushrooms, adjust the taste with salt, pepper and lemon juice, add the parsley. Serve as a hot hors-d'oeuvre or as a separate dish with potato purée and tomato salad.

serves 6–8 • Preparation: 50–55 mins

Chanterelles in tomato sauce

750 g chanterelles, 750 g firm beef tomatoes, 2 large onions, 3 tbsps butter, 2–3 tbsps thick sour cream, salt, ¼ tsp chilli pepper, 3 tbsps chopped parsley

Wash and dry the mushrooms, halve larger ones. Blanch and skin the tomatoes, slice them. Cut the peeled onions in half slices. Melt the butter in a pan, fry the onion, but do not let it brown. Put in the chanterelles and, stirring continuously, fry over high heat for a minute or two. Add the tomatoes, put the lid on and simmer for 40 mins (sprinkle with some water or stock if required). Towards the end, adjust the taste with salt and pepper and fold in the cream. Garnish with chopped parsley. Serve as a hot hors-d'oeuvre or as a separate dish with rice and salads.

serves 6–8 • Preparation: 50–55 mins

Honey mushrooms in savoury sauce

1 kg honey mushrooms, 1 large onion, 1 cup chicken stock, 3 tbsps butter, 1 tbsp flour, 1 tbsp hot mustard, salt, pepper, 2 tbsps lemon juice, ½ tsp grated lemon rind

Wash the mushrooms thoroughly, dry them well, cut larger ones into half. Put them in a thick-bottomed pan, sprinkle with 1 tbsp of lemon juice. Cover the pan and simmer until the mushrooms have produced juice, then sprinkle lightly with salt and pepper. Fry the finely chopped onion in melted butter, but do not let it brown. Dust it with flour and, stirring all the time, fry for a minute or two. Pour in the stock and simmer until the sauce has thickened. Add salt, pepper, mustard, lemon juice and zest, stir. Mix the sauce with the mushrooms. Stir thoroughly, then simmer for another 15 mins and adjust the taste. Serve with kasha or noodles and with salads.

serves 4 • Preparation: 40–45 mins

Firewood agarics in garlic sauce

1 kg large firewood agarics, 3–4 cloves of garlic, 4–5 tbsps oil, 1 glass vodka, 1 cup stock, 1 tsp potato flour, 1½ tsps sugar, salt, pepper, a pinch of cinnamon

Wash the mushrooms thoroughly, changing water several times, dry them and halve the larger ones. Mix the stock with the sugar, garlic crushed with salt, pepper, cinnamon and vodka. Heat up the oil in a pan, put in 1 clove of garlic and fry it for a minute or two, then take it out. Put in the mushrooms and sauté them briskly over high heat for 5 mins. Pour in the stock, bring to the boil, then simmer for 25 mins. Towards the end, add the potato flour mixed with 1 tbsp of cold water and heat up until the sauce has thickened. Serve with kasha, rice or as a hot hors-d'oeuvre.

serves 4 • Cleaning: 15–20 mins • Preparation: 40–45 mins

Baked cep mushrooms

1 kg young cep mushrooms, 100 g each butter and cheese (e.g. Gruyère), 1 bread roll, ½ cup milk, 1–2 tbsps chopped walnuts, 1 tbsp olive oil, 1 tsp hot mustard, 1–2 cloves of garlic, salt, pepper, a pinch of each nutmeg, grated lemon rind and caster sugar, 1 tsp lemon juice

Clean the mushrooms, cut off the stalks. Arrange the caps on a greased baking sheet and put into a pre-heated oven for 15–20 mins. Soak the breadroll in milk. Chop the mushroom stalks very finely and fry them in 1½ tbsps of melted butter. Chop the garlic, crush it with salt, mix thoroughly with the squeezed out roll. Stirring all the time, gradually add ca 2 tbsps of melted butter, pepper, nutmeg, lemon zest and juice, then combine with the fried mushroom stalks. Grease an ovenproof dish with butter, line it with half of the mushroom mixture. Arrange the baked mushrooms caps on top. Put a fine slice of butter into each cap and dust it with some grated cheese. Cover the caps with the remaining mushroom preparation. Sprinkle chopped walnuts mixed with the remaining cheese on top. Put into a preheated oven for 45 mins.

serves 4–6 • Preparation: 30 mins • Baking: 45 mins

Cep mushrooms in cream

1 kg young cep mushrooms, 2 large onions, 100 g butter, 1 tbsp dry white wine, 1 cup thick sour cream, 1 tsp flour, salt, pepper, 3 tbsps chopped dill

Clean and wash the mushrooms, dry them, cut into thin slices. Peel the onion and dice it into fine half slices. Melt the butter in a pan, fry the onion, but do not let it brown. Put in the mushrooms and fry for a minute or two, stirring continuously. Add pepper and salt, sprinkle with wine. Put the lid on and simmer for 40 mins, stirring occasionally to prevent the mushrooms from sticking to the bottom. Mix the cream with flour and pour into the mushrooms. Stir well and simmer for several minutes longer, but keep off the boil. Before serving, garnish with chopped dill.

serves 4–6 • Preparation: 50–55 mins

Stewed mushrooms

1 kg young forest mushrooms (boletes), 1 large onion, 250 g smoked streaky bacon, 1 tsp dried thyme, 2 tbsps lemon juice, salt, pepper, 1 tbsp butter, 1–2 tbsps chopped parsley, 1–2 tbsps white wine

Wash and dry the mushrooms, cut them into thin strips. Chop the onion finely. Fry the mushrooms and onion in butter, then transfer them to a skillet. When the mushrooms produce juice, cover with a lid and simmer for 45 mins, stirring from time to time. Put in the bacon cut into small cubes, add pepper, thyme and salt to taste. Sprinkle with wine, stir thoroughly and simmer for several minutes longer. Before serving, sprinkle with lemon juice and garnish with chopped parsley.

serves 4–6 • Preparation: 50–55 mins

Wild mushrooms in herbal sauce

700 g fresh forest mushrooms, 40 g dried mushrooms, 2 tsps brandy, ½ cup boiling water, ½ tsp salt, 100 g leek (only the white part), 2–3 cloves of garlic, 12–15 saffron filaments, 3 tbsps oil, 1 tsp olive oil, 1 tbsp chopped coriander leaves, ½ cup chopped parsley, salt, pepper, 1 cup yogurt

Pour boiling water mixed with brandy over the dried mushrooms and leave them aside for 1–2 hours. Wash the fresh mushrooms thoroughly, pour over first boiling and then cold water, then drain them well. Cut the mushrooms into strips; slice the cleaned and washed leek finely. Heat up the oil in a pan, put in the leek and, stirring all the time, fry for a minute or two. Put in the mushroom strips, stir well, then fry over high heat for 4–6 mins. Add the finely chopped garlic, thyme and the dried mushrooms cut into fine strips. Pour in the mushroom stock, cover the pan and cook for 10–15 mins. Season with salt, pepper, parsley and coriander. Stir well, then simmer for another 25 mins. Pour 1 tbsp of boiling water over the saffron filaments, add the olive oil and yogurt, mix well. Uncover the pan, turn the heat up and reduce the liquid. Pour in the yogurt mixture, stir thoroughly and heat up. Serve hot or cold.

serves 4 • Soaking: 1–2 hrs • Preparation: 50–55 mins

Stewed mushrooms with walnuts

700 g fresh forest mushrooms, 2–3 onions, 3–4 cloves of garlic, 1 cup chopped walnuts, 2–3 tbsps each olive oil and lemon juice, 1 tsp each chopped coriander, parsley and dill, salt, pepper, a pinch of saffron, 1 tbsp boiling water, ½ cup light stock

Clean and wash the mushrooms, put them into a pan, cover with water and cook for several minutes. Drain them in a colander, pour over cold water, drain again, then cut into slices. Heat up the oil in a pan, fry the finely chopped onions, but do not let them brown. Put in the mushrooms and, stirring continuously, cook over high heat. Sprinkle lightly with the stock, cover the pan and cook over low heat for 20 mins, stirring occasionally. Crush the finely chopped garlic with salt, pepper, walnuts, coriander and parsley, mix into pulp. Pour 1 tbsp of boiling water over the saffron, then add it to the mushrooms. Add the herbal pulp and, stirring all the time, cook for 7 mins. Before serving, garnish with chopped dill.

serves 4 • Preparation: 40–45 mins

Mushroom ragout with tomatoes

1 kg fresh mushrooms (boletes), 150 g smoked streaky bacon, 2 onions, 3 large, firm beef tomatoes, 1 tbsp butter, 2 tbsps flour, salt, pepper, 1 tsp lemon juice, a pinch of sugar, 3 tbsps stock, 3 tbsps chopped dill

Clean and wash the mushrooms, dry them. Chop the stalks finely, slice the caps. Blanch and skin the tomatoes, cut them into quarters. Cut the bacon into cubes, fry it in a pan, put in the sliced onions, the chopped mushroom stalks and 1 tsp of butter. Cook over very high heat, stirring all the time, then put in the tomatoes and mushroom slices, add salt, pepper, sugar and lemon juice. Stir thoroughly, turn the heat down and simmer for 25 mins. Make a roux from the remaining butter and the flour, dilute it with the cold stock and heat up until the sauce has thickened. Pour the sauce into the mushrooms and cook over low heat for another 10–15 mins. Serve with potato purée or rice, garnished with chopped dill.

serves 4–6 • Preparation: 45–50 mins

Mushroom paprikache

750 g fresh boletes, 1–2 large onions, 1 tbsp paprika, salt, pepper, 3 tbsps lard, 1 cup thick cream, 2 tbsps chopped dill

Wash and dry the mushrooms, cut them into strips; dice the onion finely. Heat up the lard in a thick-bottomed pan, fry the onion (without browning it), sprinkle with the paprika. Put in the mushrooms, add salt and pepper. Cover the pan and simmer for 40 mins, stirring occasionally. Fold in the cream, adjust the taste with pepper and paprika. Stir well and heat up. Serve with noodles, potatoes or bread, garnished with chopped dill.

serves 4 • Preparation: 50–55 mins

Champignon paprikache

450 g champignons, 8–10 spring onions, 3 cloves of garlic, 200 g roast turkey, 1 tbsp paprika, salt, ½ tsp ground thyme and basil, 1 tbsp oil, 2 tbsps butter, 2–3 tbsps white wine, 1 cup stock, 1 tbsp flour

Peel the garlic and chop it very finely. Wash the mushrooms and cut them into slices. Cut the turkey into strips. Dice the spring onions. Heat up the oil in a pan, fry the garlic (without browning it), put in the mushrooms and onions and cook for a while. Dust with flour, stir well, sprinkle with wine, add paprika, salt, thyme and basil. Pour in the stock, put in the meat, stir well and simmer for another 15 mins. Serve with white bread or potatoes.

serves 4 • Preparation: 20–25 mins

Oyster mushroom goulash

800 g oyster mushrooms, 2 large onions, 3 large beef tomatoes, 2–3 green peppers, 1 tbsp paprika, salt, ¼ cup stock, 3 tbsps oil, 3 tbsps cream, 2 tbsps chopped parsley

Wash and dry the mushrooms; wash and core the peppers. Cut the mushrooms and peppers into strips. Blanch and skin the tomatoes, quarter them. Chop the onions finely. Heat up the oil in a pan, put in the onions and mushrooms, fry for a while over high heat, stirring all the time, then put the lid on and simmer for 5–7 mins. Put in the tomatoes and peppers, add paprika and salt. Stir well, sprinkle with the stock and simmer under cover for 20 mins. Towards the end, fold in the cream and mix thoroughly. Before serving, garnish with chopped parsley.

serves 4–6 • Preparation: 45–50 mins

Savoury mushroom bake

1 kg small forest mushrooms, 3 tbsps olive oil, 1½ tbsps butter, 4–5 spring onions, 3–4 cloves of garlic, salt, pepper, 1 tbsp each chopped chervil, green tarragon and coriander, 2 tbsps chopped chives

Wash, dry and slice the mushrooms. Heat the oil in a pan, put in the mushrooms and fry them for a while over high heat, stirring all the time, then reduce the juices. Melt 1 tbsp of butter in a frying pan, put in the chopped onions and fry for a minute or two. Add the finely chopped garlic, salt, pepper, tarragon and chervil. Mix well, then take off the heat. Grease an ovenproof dish with the remaining butter, put in the mushrooms, cover with the onion mixture. Put into a preheated oven for 15–20 mins. Before serving, garnish with chopped coriander and chives.

serves 4 • Preparation: 40–45 mins

Mushroom brawn

1 small pig's stomach, 250 g young boletes, 1–2 cloves of garlic, 1 tsp caraway seeds, ½ bunch of dill, 2 large onions, 100 lean smoked streaky bacon, 5 hard-boiled eggs, 50 g button mushrooms (caps), 1 tbsp lemon juice, 1 tsp pepper, 1 clove of garlic crushed

with salt, 2 raw eggs, 1 tbsp lard, salt, pepper,
1 tbsp ground caraway, 2 cups strong stock

Scrub the stomach well, put it into a pan, cover with boiling water and cook for 1½ hours. Take it out, drain well and allow to cool. Wash and dry the caps of button mushrooms, put them into a bowl, pour over the lemon juice mixed with garlic and salt and leave for an hour. Bring salted water to the boil, add garlic, dill and caraway seeds. Put in the washed mushrooms and cook for 2 mins. Take off the heat and leave to cool in the stock, then take the mushrooms out. Chop the mushrooms and the shelled hard-boiled eggs, fry the finely diced onion in lard, but do not brown it; cut the bacon into cubes. Combine all these ingredients, season with salt and pepper, add the button mushrooms and caraway, break in the eggs and work into a smooth paste. Fill the stomach tight with the mixture, saw the edges. Put it into a pan, cover with the stock. Bring to the boil, then simmer for 25–30 mins. Leave it to cool a bit in the stock, then take it out. Put it on a wooden board, cover with another board, weigh it down and leave to cool (3–4 hours).

serves 6–8 • Preparation: 2 hrs • Cooling: 3–4 hrs

Mushroom cutlets

100 g dried mushrooms, 1 large onion, 3–4 slices of white bread, 2–3 tbsps single cream, 2 hard-boiled eggs, 3–4 tbsps butter, 1 cup chopped walnuts, 1 cup breadcrumbs, 2 raw eggs, salt, pepper

Rinse the mushrooms and soak them overnight in water, then cook them and drain (use the stock to cook mushroom soup or borsch). Soak the bread in the cream. Melt 1 tsp of butter in a pan, fry the chopped onion, but do not let it brown. Put the onion, mushrooms and bread through a mincer, add the chopped hard-boiled eggs, walnuts, salt, pepper and raw egg yolks, mix thoroughly. Fold in the whisked egg whites, sprinkle with the sifted breadcrumbs and work into a smooth paste. Form small cutlets, dredge them with breadcrumbs and fry in melted butter or in oil. Serve as a hot hors-d'oeuvre or with boiled potatoes.

serves 4 • Soaking: 12 hrs • Preparation: 25–30 mins

Mushrooms with horseradish

100 g dried cep caps, 1 carrot, 1 parsley root, 2 onions, 2–3 bay leaves, 3–4 peppercorns, juice and grated rind of ½ lemon, salt, 1 horseradish root

Rinse the mushrooms, cover them with boiled water and leave overnight to soak. Add 1 cup of boiling water to the grated carrot and parsley root, diced onions, bay leaves, peppercorns, lemon juice and zest. Bring to the boil, put the lid on and simmer for 20–30 mins. Strain the stock, add it to the mushrooms and cook them till tender. Add some salt and reduce the stock. Take the mushrooms out and put them into a serving bowl, allow them to cool a bit, then sprinkle lavishly with grated horseradish.

serves 4 • Soaking: 12 hrs • Preparation: 30 mins • Cooling: 1 hr

Pâté from dried ceps

150 g dried cep mushrooms, 2–3 onions, 3 bread rolls, 2 tbsps each chopped parsley and dill, 3 tbsps chopped hazelnuts, 100 g butter, 5 eggs, 1 cup thick sour cream, salt, pepper

Cover the rinsed mushrooms with boiled water and leave them overnight to soak. Cook them till tender, then take them out. Soak the bread rolls (without crust) in the mushroom stock. Melt the butter in a pan, fry the finely chopped mushrooms and onions, add the squeezed out bread rolls and, stirring all the time, cook briskly for a minute or two. Transfer to a large bowl, add 2 tbsps of chopped hazelnuts, dill, parsley, salt, pepper, raw egg yolks and cream, and work into a smooth paste. Fold in the whisked egg whites, mix lightly but thoroughly. Grease a terrine, dust it with the remaining hazelnuts and fill with the mixture. Seal the terrine tightly with a lid or aluminium foil. Put it into a pot of boiling water and cook for 1 hour. Serve hot or cold.

serves 6–8 • Soaking: 12 hrs • Preparation: 40–45 mins • Baking: 1 hr

Spicy mushroom pâté

100 g dried mushrooms (agaric and bolete), 1 cup breadcrumbs, 1–1½ cups single cream, 4 eggs, 4 onions, 2–3 cloves of garlic, grated rind of 1 lemon, ¼ tsp marjoram, ¼ tsp basil, ¼ tsp sage, ¼ tsp ground caraway, ¼ tsp ginger, ¼ tsp cloves, ¼ tsp nutmeg, salt, pepper, 1 tbsp lard, 1 tbsp butter, 2 tbsps finely chopped walnuts

Rinse the mushroom and soak them overnight in a small amount of boiled water, then cook them. Put the breadcrumbs into a bowl, cover with 1 cup of cream, mix well and leave aside for half an hour. Fry the finely diced onions in the lard. Chop the mushrooms very finely or put them through a mincer. Add the mushrooms and onions to the breadcrumb mixture, put in the spices and herbs, eggs and some salt and work into a smooth paste (add more cream if the mixture is too thick). Grease a pâté mould with butter, dust it with walnuts. Put in the mixture, press it down, smooth the surface. Put into a preheated oven and bake for 30–40 mins. Serve hot or cold.

serves 4–6 • Soaking: 12 hrs • Preparation: 40–45 mins • Baking: 40 mins

Spicy mushroom pâté

Fried dried mushrooms

several dried cep caps (2–3 per person), 2 cups milk, salt, pepper, 1 tbsp flour, 1 egg, 1 tbsp breadcrumbs, oil for frying

Rinse the mushrooms and soak them overnight in boiled milk. The following day add 1 cup of boiled water and cook the mushrooms. Drain the tender mushrooms, sprinkle them with salt and pepper, then dredge them with flour, lightly beaten egg and breadcrumbs. Fry them in oil on both sides until golden brown. Before serving, garnish with parsley sprigs. Serve as a hot hors-d'oeuvre.

serves 4 • Soaking: 12 hrs • Preparation: 40–45 mins

Cutlets from dried mushrooms

70 g dried mushrooms, 2 bread rolls, 2 onions, 1 tbsp chopped parsley

FOR COATING: 1 egg, flour, breadcrumbs

Rinse the mushrooms and soak them in water overnight, then cook them (use the stock for mushroom soup or for cabbage). Put the mushrooms and soaked bread rolls through a mincer. Fry the chopped onion in oil, but do not let it brown. Mix the mushrooms and bread with the onion, add salt, pepper, egg and parsley, work into a smooth paste. Form small cutlets from the paste. Coat them with flour, lightly beaten egg and breadcrumbs. Fry in oil on both sides until golden brown. Serve with mushroom or onion sauce.

serves 4 • Soaking: 12 hrs • Preparation: 45–55 mins

Stewed dried mushrooms

250 g dried mushrooms, 1 l milk, 1 onion, 1 tbsp chopped parsley, ½ cup cream, salt, pepper, 2 tbsps sunflower oil, 1 tsp flour

Rinse the mushrooms and leave them overnight to soak in cold boiled milk. Cook the mushrooms, then drain them and cut into strips. Make a roux from the flour, oil and finely chopped onion, dilute it with the cream. Put in the mushrooms and simmer over low heat, stirring often.

Adjust the taste with salt and pepper. Before serving, garnish with chopped parsley.

serves 6–8 • Soaking: 12 hrs • Preparation: 50–55 mins

Mushroom patties

300 g shop puff pastry (1 packet)

*FILLING: 300 g champignons, 1 large onion,
1 tbsp chopped parsley, 1 tbsp cream, 1 tbsp
sunflower oil or butter, salt, pepper*

Rinse and dry the mushrooms, chop them finely together with the onion, then cook them in oil. Make a roux from the flour and butter, dilute it with the cream. Put in the mushrooms and onion, add parsley, salt and pepper. Cook over low heat, stirring all the time, until the mixture has thickened. Roll out the pastry and make small patties filled with the mushroom stuffing. Arrange the patties on a greased baking sheet and put into a preheated oven for 30 mins.

serves 4 • Preparation: 40–45 mins

Kurp sausage from honey mushrooms

*1 kg caps of new honey mushrooms, 1 tbsp lard,
3–4 cloves of garlic, 2 onions, 4 eggs, salt, pepper,
200 g smoked pork fat, well soaked pork intestines*

Clean the mushrooms, put them into lightly salted boiling water. Cook them for 30 mins, drain and leave to cool, then put them through a mincer. Hard-boil 3 eggs, shell them and chop them finely. Brown the chopped onion in melted lard, add it to the mushrooms. Put in the chopped eggs and garlic crushed with salt. Break in one egg, add some pepper and work into a smooth paste. Season to taste. Fill the intestines with the stuffing, secure the ends with a piece of string. Put the sausage into a pan, cover with cold water with a bit of salt. Bring to the boil, then simmer for 10 mins. Before serving, sprinkle with pork scratchings.

serves 4 • Preparation: 1 hr

Champignon shashliks

*600 g button mushrooms, 2 onions,
150 g smoked streaky bacon, 2 tbsps olive oil,
1 tbsp lemon juice, ¼ tsp grated lemon rind,
1–2 cloves of garlic, salt, pepper, ¼ tsp dried thyme*

Blend the oil with the lemon juice and zest, garlic crushed with salt, pepper and thyme. Rinse and dry the mushrooms, put them into a bowl. Pour over the oil dressing, mix well and leave in the fridge for 1–2 hours. Peel and slice the onion; cut the bacon into small square pieces. Thread the mushrooms, onion slices and bacon on skewers and grill them. Serve with bread or rice.

serves 4 • Macerating: 1–3 hrs • Baking: 8–10 mins

Patties from forest mushrooms

*600 g mushrooms (agarics and boletes), 50 g
pork fat, 1 large onion, 2 tbsps chopped parsley,
4–5 tbsps flour, 4 eggs, ½ cup oil, salt, pepper*

Rinse and dry the mushrooms, chop them finely together with the peeled onion. Heat 2 tbsps of oil in a frying pan, put in the diced lard, mushrooms and onion and fry them for a minute or two over high heat. Turn the heat down, cover the pan and simmer for 10–15 mins. Leave to cool, then add the parsley, flour and the eggs and work into a smooth paste. Add some salt and pepper to taste. Heat up the remaining oil in a frying pan. Drop in tablespoonfuls of the mixture and fry on both sides.

serves 4 • Preparation: 40 mins

CHAPTER XIV

VEGETABLES
AND FRUIT

Vegetables

In the 17th century, Poles already knew parsley, sweet and sour cabbage, onion, garlic, red beets, turnip, carrot, parsnip, peas, sorrel and spinach...
Later they learnt to grow and cook beans, lentils, kale, maize, celeriac, leeks, broadbeans and also cauliflower, broccoli, artichokes, asparagus, pumpkins, radishes and lettuce...

(Łukasz Gołębiowski, *Domy i dwory*, 1830, vol. IV, p. 43)

On vegetables: Best are those vegetables that come directly from the garden. Those that have been stored over winter are good only for garnishing various roast meats. Carrots preserve their flavour from May to December and you should remember to choose those that are red and not very large. Kohlrabi is nice when it is very young, while kale should be eaten after a light frost. Cauliflowers taste best in July, August and September. Cabbage stays fresh from August to December. Asparagus is recommended from mid-April to mid-June. Artichokes are best in May and October. Potatoes taste fine all the year round, provided they do not sprout.

(*Praktyczny kucharz warszawski*, XXVII, 1926)

Celeriac, when it is white and soft, is used for salads with rémoulade, with salt, pepper, olive oil, vinegar and mustard... New radishes are usually served as an appetizer before the main meal... Boiled cauliflower is often garnished with white sauce...
Parsley is used for garnishing various dishes... Leeks are used only to cook broths.

(W. Wielądko, *Kucharz doskonały*, vol. II, pp. 114–118)

Asparagus

Asparagus was first grown in Europe in the late Middle Ages and since then this delicate, low-calorie vegetable rich in nutritive elements and vitamins has been regarded as a delicacy. Each vegetable has its season, and in the case of asparagus it lasts for a very short time – about two months. When you buy asparagus, choose shoots that are fresh, fleshy and have tightly closed, firm buds. Fresh asparagus 'squeaks' when you rub two stems against each other and then it may be kept in the fridge for a maximum of three days if wrapped in a damp cloth. If you store them longer, the shoots wilt and yellow, the buds lose their firmness and the vegetable does not taste nice.

Asparagus

This is a delicious vegetable, a true treasure in your kitchen, therefore take care to have it all the time in your garden and try to serve it as often as possible.

(Karolina Nakwaska, *Dwór wiejski*, 1858)

This delicious and much-loved vegetable appears in mid-April and disappears towards the end of July. You should choose shoots that are white and have white or purple tips. You clean them by scraping them carefully with a knife, holding the shoots by the tips and keeping the knife flat. As soon as you scrape a shoot, put it into cold water, and once all of them are cleaned, take them out and tie them into bunches of 15–20 shoots each. You must put them into a lot of boiling water with some salt and sugar added (for 60 shoots, you should use 1 tablespoon of sugar and 1 tablespoon of salt), and cook them for 15–20 minutes, depending on the variety of asparagus and the thickness of the shoots... Take the asparagus out and place on a kitchen towel, untie the bunches, and sprinkle the stems with some of the water in which they were cooked. Serve with melted butter and browned breadcrumbs, or hollandaise sauce... They will be just as tasty if you serve them cold, with vinegar and olive oil.

(Marta Norkowska, *Najnowsza kuchnia wytworna i gospodarska*, 1904)

Asparagus salad de Luxe

1 tin asparagus (300 g), 100 g smoked salmon, 6–8 hard-boiled quail eggs, 1–2 tinned pineapple slices, 2–3 leaves iceberg lettuce, 2 tbsps chopped parsley

DRESSING: 2 tbsps mayonnaise, 1 tbsp cream, 1 tbsp lemon juice, ½ tsp grated lemon rind, salt, pepper, sugar

Mix well the ingredients of the dressing. Chill. Drain the asparagus, cut into pieces, cut the quail eggs into halves, cut the pineapple into cubes, and the salmon into strips. Line a salad bowl with lettuce leaves, arrange the asparagus and pineapple, sprinkle lightly with the dressing. Top with half of the quail eggs covered with salmon strips, pour over the dressing and decorate the whole with the remaining eggs. Chill before serving and sprinkle with chopped parsley.

serves 4–6 • Preparation: 10 mins

Asparagus salad with grapefruit

1 tin asparagus (250 g), 1 pink grapefruit, 1 marinated bell pepper, 100 g roast turkey, 2 sprigs lemon balm

DRESSING: ½ cup yogurt, 1 tbsp thick mayonnaise, 1 tsp mustard, 1 tsp honey, salt, pepper

Mix well the ingredients of the dressing, cool. Peel the grapefruit and take apart into sections. Remove the seeds and membranes, cut the flesh into cubes. Reserve the juice in a bowl. Cut the drained asparagus into strips,

and turkey into matchsticks. Combine the salad ingredients, pour over the dressing and toss. Chill. Just before serving decorate with lemon balm leaves.

serves 4 • Preparation: 5–6 mins • Refrigerating: 30–40 mins

Hot snack of asparagus

8–12 thin asparagus, 200 g cottage cheese, 3 tbsps butter, 1 tbsp hot mustard, salt, pepper, 1 egg, parsley sprigs

Peel the asparagus and boil in salted water, drain, cut into pieces uniform in size. Beat the butter with egg yolk, gradually adding the mustard, cottage cheese, salt and pepper. Beat the egg white until stiff, gently stir in the cottage cheese mixture. Butter individual ovenproof serving shells, fill them with the cheese mixture, topping each shell with pieces of asparagus. Bake in a preheated oven for about 30 mins, serve as a hot snack. Decorate with parsley sprigs.

serves 4 • Preparation: 20 mins • Baking: 30 mins

Asparagus in avocado dressing

1 tin asparagus (300 g), 50 g chicken ham

DRESSING: 1 avocado, 1 tbsp lemon juice, ¾ cup yogurt, 1 tbsp chopped dill, ¼ tsp curry powder, salt, pinch of sugar, sprigs of dill for decoration

Peel the avocado, cut in half and remove the stone. Cut into cubes and sprinkle with lemon juice, then mix in a blender with the yogurt, curry, a dash of sugar, salt and dill into smooth pulp. Chill well. Drain the asparagus and cut into pieces, cut the ham into thin strips. In two small salad bowls arrange the asparagus and ham in layers and pour over the dressing, decorate with sprigs of dill.

serves 4 • Refrigerating: 1–2 hrs • Preparation: 10 mins

Asparagus in cheese sauce

700 g asparagus, salt, 1 tbsp lemon juice, 1 tsp sugar, 1 tsp butter, 4 eggs, 250 g cottage cheese, ¼ cup cream, salt, pepper

Boil salted water with sugar, lemon juice and butter. Put in the asparagus, peeled and tied into bunches. Cook for 15 mins, remove. Beat the eggs in a saucepan, add the cream, mix well and put the saucepan over steam. Whisk the sauce, gradually adding the cottage cheese and salt. Arrange the asparagus in a buttered ovenproof dish, pour the thick sauce over and bake for a few minutes in a preheated oven.

serves 4 • Preparation: 20–25 mins • Baking: 10 mins

Asparagus in hazelnut sauce

700 g asparagus, salt, 1 tbsp lemon juice, 1 tbsp sugar, 1 tsp butter

SAUCE: 3 egg yolks, 100 g butter, 1 tsp white pepper, ½ cup finely chopped hazelnuts

Bring to the boil salted water with sugar, butter and lemon juice. Put in the peeled asparagus and cook for 15 mins, drain. In a saucepan blend the butter with egg yolks. Put the saucepan in a bain-marie and beat the sauce with a wire whisk, add pepper, salt and toward the end the hazelnuts. Mix well. Butter an ovenproof dish and line it with the asparagus cut to pieces, pour over the sauce and bake for a few minutes in a well-heated oven. Makes a very elegant hot snack, or a side dish with white meat.

serves 4 • Preparation: 20–25 mins • Baking: 10 mins

Asparagus gateau

2 bunches fresh asparagus, 3 eggs yolks, 1 tbsp lemon juice, 125 g butter, 2 tbsps sugar, 2 whole eggs, ½ cup semi-dry white wine, 3–4 tbsps flour, salt, white pepper, ½ cup whipped cream, 6–8 small radishes

Cook the peeled asparagus in salted water, set aside 5–6 asparagus heads, cutting the rest into small pieces. Mix well with the egg yolks and lemon juice. Blend the butter and sugar until frothy, gradually adding 2 eggs well beaten with salt, pepper and flour until you obtain thickish dough. Butter a baking form and line it with the dough. Place the asparagus on top and bake in a preheated

oven for about 30–40 mins. Serve cold, decorated with whipped cream, radishes and asparagus heads.

serves 4–6 • Preparation: 20–25 mins • Baking: 30–40 mins

Aubergines

Aubergines, also known as eggplants, are related to peppers and tomatoes. They may be purple, green, white, greyish-green, shiny or matt. Depending on the variety, they are egg-shaped, pear-shaped, round or oval. They originated in India where they grow wild. The small varieties probably come from China and are still widely cultivated in the Far East. They were grown as early as the 5th century by the Chinese and the Arabs. The latter, when they invaded today's Spain, brought them to Europe. In the Middle Ages, they were cultivated in France and Italy.

In Poland, aubergines were known as early as the 15th century, but they were then regarded as an ornamental plant. They began to be used in cooking only in the early 19th century, when they were usually prepared according to French recipes.

Aubergines can be cooked in many different ways. They are excellent when coated in egg and breadcrumbs, or stewed with onion or garlic. They are also tasty when stuffed, and are highly recommended for various spreads seasoned with garlic and herbs. In salads, they go very well with tomatoes and peppers.

Aubergines

This vegetable, which is ripe by mid-July, is closely related to tomatoes. Like with tomatoes, its purple fruits are cooked in many different ways. They probably taste best when they are sliced, salted and fried in butter, or else cut lengthwise in half and stewed in butter. The inside can also be scooped out, and they can be stuffed with meat or rice. They can be used for preparing salads with onion, chives, salt, pepper, oil and vinegar.

(Marta Norkowska, *Najnowsza kuchnia wytworna i gospodarska*, 1904)

Aubergines stuffed with livers

4 aubergines, 250 g turkey livers, 100 g butter,
1 garlic clove, 2 tbsp chopped parsley, 1 glass brandy,
3–4 tbsps chopped sunflower seeds, salt, pepper

Cut the washed aubergines lengthwise in half, scoop out the flesh, remove the seeds. Sprinkle the aubergine halves with salt and leave for 30 mins. Then dry and coat them with the chopped sunflower seeds, sauté in melted butter for half a minute on each side, allow to cool. Fry the livers in butter, cool and blend with the brandy, salt, pepper and the remaining sunflower seeds into smooth pulp, mix with chopped parsley. Spoon the mixture into the aubergine halves, place in an ovenproof dish and put into a hot oven for 10–15 mins. Serve hot or cold.

serves 4–6 • Salting: 30–40 mins • Preparation: 25–30 mins

Aubergines for vegetarians

2 large aubergines, salt, 2 onions, 2 large,
fleshy tomatoes, 1 sweet red pepper, 3–4 garlic
cloves, 50 g grated cheese, 2 tbsps almond
flakes, 2 eggs, 1 tsp each dried basil

and thyme (or 1 tbsp each chopped fresh
leaves), 3 tbsps olive oil, 1 tsp lemon
juice, salt, pepper, sugar to taste

Wash the aubergines and trim off the stalk ends. Cut the aubergines lengthwise in half, sprinkle liberally with salt and set aside for 30 mins. Rinse, dry, scoop some of the flesh and chop it finely. Scald and skin the tomatoes, cut them into cubes. Chop the peppers finely, removing the seeds, mince garlic with salt. Sauté the chopped onion in hot oil (2 tbsps), add the cut vegetables and garlic and sauté for 3–4 mins. Add the herbs, salt, pepper and a pinch of sugar, stir and remove from the heat. Beat the eggs thoroughly and pour them into the cooled vegetables, add the grated cheese and almonds, stirring thoroughly. Stuff the aubergine halves with the mixture. Coat an ovenproof dish with olive oil, arrange the aubergines, sprinkle them with olive oil and bake for 30 mins in a preheated (200°C) oven.

serves 4 • Salting: 30–40 mins • Preparation: 35–40 mins

Aubergines stuffed with mushrooms

4 aubergines, 150 g mushrooms, 1 medium-
large onion, 2 garlic cloves, 2 tbsps chopped
walnuts, 1 tbsp chopped parsley, ½ tsp chopped
fresh thyme, 2 large firm fleshy tomatoes,
3 tbsps butter, 2 tbsps grated hard cheese

Put the aubergines into slightly salted boiling water, remove from the heat and set aside for 5–6 mins. Remove, cool off, and then cut lengthwise in half, scoop out the flesh and chop it finely. Sauté the chopped onion with 1½ tbsps of butter, add the sliced mushrooms and sauté for 1–2 mins over high heat. Lower the heat, stir in the aubergine flesh, crushed garlic, mix well and sauté for 3–4 mins. Take off the heat, combine with the chopped parsley and thyme, add a pinch of salt and some pepper, mix well. Scald and skin the tomatoes and cut them into thick slices. Place the aubergines in a buttered ovenproof dish, stuff them with the mixture, sprinkle with the walnuts, cover with the tomato slices and sprinkle with the grated cheese. Pour melted butter on top and put in a preheated oven for about 15 mins.

serves 4 • Preparation: 25–30 mins

Stewed aubergines

500 g aubergines, 500 g French beans, 4 small
onions, 2 chilli peppers, 3–4 garlic cloves, 1 tbsp
finely chopped ginger, 2 bay leaves, 1 cup
coconut flakes, 1 cup hot milk, 2 cups single
cream, ½ cup oil, 1 tsp sugar, 1 tsp salt

Soak the coconut flakes in hot milk for half an hour, then sieve them and mix with the cream. Rinse and dry the aubergines and French beans. Cut the aubergines into thin slices, and the beans into small pieces. Finely chop the fresh, pitted chilli peppers, the onions and garlic and blend into smooth pulp. In a flat pan heat the oil, add the onion paste and stir and fry for about 1 min. Add the ginger and broken bay leaves and fry for 2 mins, stirring all the time. Stir in the coconut cream, mix together and bring to the boil. Add the aubergines and beans, and simmer over low

Aubergines with yogurt

heat. Adjust the taste with salt and sugar. Serve hot with white bread or rice, or as a side dish.

serves 4–6 • Soaking: 30–40 mins • Preparation: 25–35 mins

Aubergines with yogurt

2 aubergines, 4–5 garlic cloves, 2 small onions, 1 tbsp fresh chopped ginger, ½ tsp powdered coriander, 1 tsp crushed chilli, 1 tsp powdered caraway seeds, ½ tsp sugar, 1 tbsp oil, 2 tbsps butter, 1 cup yogurt, salt, pepper, 2 tbsps chopped fresh coriander

Wash and dry the aubergines. Cut them into thickish slices, sprinkle with salt and let stand for half an hour. Rinse, dry and transfer to a baking tray. Put in a hot oven for 6–8 minutes. Cut into cubes when cool. Heat the oil in a frying pan, add the chopped onion, garlic and ginger and fry for a moment, stirring all the time. Add the butter, caraway, powdered coriander, chilli and pepper and continue to simmer for about 5 mins. Stir in the aubergine cubes, salt and sugar, mix well and simmer for about 5 mins. Remove from the heat, add the yogurt, mix, sprinkle with chopped green coriander. Serve with white bread or rice.

serves 4 • Salting: 30–40 mins • Preparation: 25–30 mins

Aubergines, Mediterranean style

4 aubergines, 6 spice-salted herring fillets (or anchovies), 10–12 pitted black olives, 4 garlic cloves, 2 tbsps capers, 5–6 slices white bread, 1 tsp butter, 3 tbsps single cream, 3–4 tbsps chopped parsley, 1 tbsp chopped fresh thyme, pepper, salt, sugar, ½ cup olive oil

Cut the washed aubergines lengthwise in half, scoop out half of the flesh. Salt slightly and let stand for half an hour. Cut the bread slices into small cubes, brown in a hot skillet in butter. Leave aside to cool and sprinkle with the cream. Chop finely the fillets, olives, skinned garlic, capers and the aubergine flesh, combine with the chopped parsley and thyme. Season with pepper, a dash of sugar and salt to taste, mix with the croutons. Coat a baking tin with olive oil and arrange the aubergine halves stuffed with the mixture. Sprinkle with olive oil and bake in a preheated oven for about 1 hour.

serves 4 • Salting: 25–30 mins • Preparation: 1 hr

Beans

This is a vegetable of which there are many varieties. Of those grown in Europe, the most popular are French (string) beans and haricot beans. The pods are straight or curved, flat or cylindrical, and the seeds they contain differ widely in size and colour (from cream white through various shades of purple to black). Both pods and seeds (fresh or dried) can be used in many different ways: in salads, soups, bakes, pâtés, goulashes and sweet cakes.

When you cook French beans, you should first top and tail them, remove the strings if there are any (new varieties are usually stringless) and then cook them whole or cut into smaller pieces. They should be boiled from 12 to 20 minutes, depending on the variety. It is a good idea to add a pinch of sugar, several drops of lemon juice and a teaspoon of butter to the water. Remember not to cook them too long, or they will lose their nice bright colour.

French beans

There are two kinds of French beans: a light yellow variety, and a thinner, green variety. Both are prepared in the same way. The yellow variety is cheaper and the green one is more expensive, but is available till late autumn. Remove the strings from the young beans on both sides and cook in salted water until tender. Serve as a separate dish or with meat, covered with melted butter mixed with browned breadcrumbs.

(Marja Ochorowicz-Monatowa, *Uniwersalna książka kucharska*, 1910)

White beans in salad

Vegetable salads are usually served cold here, a method which is not as healthy and tasty as when you serve them hot. You may check this yourselves – once will be enough to convince you. Vegetables, potatoes and beans in particular, when they grow cold, get harder, so they cannot be tasty. My advice is: put the beans cooked in salted water into a bowl, add potatoes, carrots, beets, red cabbage, and arrange them all nicely. Pour quite a lot of olive oil over them and a bit of vinegar. Add pepper, salt, mustard, chopped anchovies or herring.

(Karolina Nakwaska, *Dwór wiejski*, 1858)

Three colour bean salad

*½ cup small white beans, ½ cup black beans,
½ cup red beans, 100 g turkey ham, ½ sweet
green pepper, 2 tbsps chopped parsley, 2 tbsps
chopped chives, 1 tsp chopped fresh basil*

*DRESSING: 2 tbsps mayonnaise, 3 tbsps yogurt,
1 tsp lemon juice, a pinch of grated lemon rind,
¼ tsp curry powder, ¼ tsp sugar, ¼ tsp pepper, salt*

Wash the beans. Soak them each colour separately for several hours in boiled water. Cook them separately, adding salt towards the end, drain. Mix well the dressing ingredients. Chill. Scald the pepper, rinse with cold water, remove the skin, clean out the seeds and cut into small cubes. Cut the ham into small cubes too. Combine all the ingredients of the salad, pour over the dressing, toss lightly. Chill.

serves 4 • Soaking: 12 hrs • Preparation: 35–40 mins • Refrigerating: 1 hr

Bean salad with goat cheese

*500 g new green beans, 1 tbsp lemon juice
and 1 tsp grated lemon rind, salt, 1 tbsp butter,
1 garlic clove, 1 tsp sugar, 100 g goat cheese,
1 large onion, 2 tbsps chopped fresh basil*

*DRESSING: 2 tbsps oil, 1 tbsp lemon juice,
1 tsp honey, 1 tsp thick mayonnaise, 1 tbsp bean
stock, salt, pepper, 2–3 cherry tomatoes, 1 hard-
boiled egg, 2–3 basil leaves for decoration*

Trim the beans, wash and cut into pieces. Bring some salted water to the boil with the addition of butter, garlic, sugar, lemon juice and lemon rind. Add the beans, cook until tender, drain (reserve some of the stock), leave aside to cool, then mix with the chopped basil. Mix all the dressing ingredients and chill. Cut the cheese into cubes, chop the onion and combine with the beans. Pour the dressing over, mix well and chill slightly. Sprinkle with chopped hard-boiled egg and decorate with basil leaves and tomato quarters.

serves 4 • Preparation: 25–30 mins • Refrigerating: 1 hr

Green beans with mint

*500 g green beans, 1 tsp butter, ½ tsp sugar,
1 tbsp lemon juice and ¼ tsp grated lemon rind,
1 hard, fleshy tomato, 1 bunch spring onions,
2 tbsps chopped fresh mint, 3 tbsps chopped parsley*

*DRESSING: 3 tbsps olive oil, 2 tbsps wine vinegar or
lemon juice, 1 tsp hot mustard, 1 tsp honey, salt, pepper*

Mix well all the dressing ingredients and set aside in the fridge. Boil some salted water with butter, sugar, lemon juice and grated lemon rind. Put the washed and trimmed beans into boiling water, cook until tender, drain, rinse with cold water, drain again and cut into small pieces. Mix the beans with mint, chopped spring onions and parsley. Pour the dressing over and mix well, chill. Scald the tomato, skin and cut into quarters and decorate the salad before serving.

serves 4 • Preparation: 25–30 mins • Refrigerating: 1 hr

Yellow beans goulash with sausage

*500 g yellow runner beans, green, orange and red
sweet pepper (one each; about 500 g), 300 g pork
sausage, 1 large onion, 250 g tomatoes, 4 tbsps
cooking oil, salt, ¼ cup stock, ½ cup cream*

Trim and wash the beans, cut into pieces and blanch for 2–3 mins in slightly salted boiling water. Drain, rinse with cold water, drain again. Rinse the peppers, remove the seeds and membranes, cut into strips. Scald and skin the tomatoes, cut into cubes, finely chop the onion. In a saucepan heat the oil, sauté the onion, then add the beans and peppers, fry for a moment or two, stir. Put in the tomatoes, add salt and sprinkle with the stock. Simmer covered for 15 mins, then add the sliced sausage, mix well and simmer together for another 10–15 mins. Pour in the cream, mix well and add salt, if necessary.

serves 4–6 • Preparation: 35–40 mins

Hot snack of green beans

*800 g runner beans, 4–5 sprigs fresh savory,
salt, 1 tbsp butter, 1 tsp lemon juice, ½ tsp sugar,*

1 large onion, 3–5 garlic cloves, ½ sweet red pepper, 50 g mushrooms, 2–3 celery sticks, 1 tbsp fresh leaves of wild thyme, 2 tbsp olive oil, ¼ cup stock, salt, pepper, ½ cup sour cream

Boil some salted water with butter, sugar, lemon juice and savory. Add the beans and cook for about 15 mins, then drain and transfer to an ovenproof dish. Finely cut all the vegetables and mushrooms. Heat the olive oil in a saucepan, sauté the onion and garlic, add the pepper, celery sticks and mushrooms, and sauté for a moment or two, stir. Sprinkle with the stock, cover and simmer for about 10 mins. Season with salt and pepper, add the wild thyme leaves and cream, and heat stirring all the time. Place the dish in a preheated oven for 4–5 mins.

serves 4–8 • Preparation: 35–40 mins

Baked beans with mushrooms

250 g coloured beans, 2 onions, 500 g fresh wild bolete mushrooms, 60 g pork fat, salt, pepper, 1 tsp lemon juice, a pinch of each sugar, dried savory and thyme, ¾ cup cream, 3 tbsps grated cheese, 1 tbsp butter, 1 tbsp chopped walnuts, 1 tbsp breadcrumbs

Wash the beans and soak them overnight in cold boiled water. Drain, cover with fresh water and cook for about 1 hour, adding salt, savory and lemon juice towards the end. Drain. Clean the mushrooms and cut them into slices. Finely chop the onions. Cut the pork fat into cubes and melt in a frying pan. Add the onions, sauté until golden brown, add the mushrooms and fry together for 10–15 mins, stirring all the time. Season with salt, thyme and pepper and combine with the beans. Mix well and simmer together for about 4–5 mins. Season to taste and combine with the cream. Butter an ovenproof dish, sprinkle with breadcrumbs and walnuts. Put in the beans with mushrooms, sprinkle with the grated cheese and knobs of butter, and bake in a preheated oven until the cheese is melted. Serve with salads.

serves 4 • Soaking: 12 hrs • Cooking: 1 hr • Baking: 10 mins

Beans with prunes

400 g dry white beans, 100 g smoked streaky bacon, 2 onions, 100 g prunes, 1 tbsp flour, 1 tbsp honey, salt, pepper, sugar, marjoram, savory, lemon juice

Wash the beans and soak them overnight in cold boiled water. Drain, cover with fresh water and cook for about 1 hour. Towards the end add salt, savory and lemon juice. Drain. Rinse the prunes and place them in a saucepan with ½ cup boiled water. Leave aside for half an hour, then cut the prunes into strips and parboil briefly. Reserve the liquid. Add the honey, lemon juice and marjoram. Chop the bacon and fry it in a frying pan. Peel, rinse and chop the onions. Combine with the bacon, sprinkle with flour and sauté until brown. Add 2–3 tbsps of the liquid from the prunes. Combine with the beans and prunes, mix well and simmer together for about 15 mins. Season with salt, pepper, sugar and, if desired, with lemon juice.

serves 4–6 • Soaking: 12 hrs • Cooking: 1 hr • Stewing: 15–20 mins

Giant white beans, hunter's style

200 g giant white beans, a pinch of savory, salt, 1 tbsp butter, 6–8 dried mushrooms, 100 g smoked streaky bacon, 150 g thin sausage, 2–3 gherkins, 1 large onion, 1 small tin tomato concentrate, 3 tbsps cream, ½ tsp hot paprika, 2 tbsps chopped dill

Wash the beans and soak them overnight in cold boiled water. Drain, cover with fresh boiled water, add 1 tbsp butter and a pinch of savory, and cook until tender. Drain, leaving little liquid. Wash the mushrooms and soak them for half an hour in boiled water, then cook and drain, reserve the stock. Cut the mushrooms into thin strips. Peel the onion and chop it finely, dice the bacon and melt it in a frying pan. Add the onion and sauté until brown. Then add the sliced sausage. Fry for a moment or two, stir. Combine with the beans, add the gherkins, peeled and cut, and the mushrooms. Pour in the mushroom stock, mix well and simmer together for a while. Mix the cream and tomato concentrate, add to the beans, mix well and season with salt and paprika to taste. Serve with bread.

serves 4 • Soaking: 12 hrs • Cooking: 50–60 mins • Stewing: 15–20 mins

Giant white beans in fruit sauce

*250 g giant white beans, salt, 1 tbsp butter,
10–15 pitted prunes, 1 onion, 50 g ginger cake,
2 tbsps gooseberry preserve, 2 cups stock, juice
and grated rind of ½ lemon, ¼ tsp grated nutmeg,
¼ tsp grated cinnamon, 1 tsp honey, 1 tbsp butter*

Wash the beans and leave out to soak in boiled water for the night. Drain and cover with fresh boiled water, add 1 tbsp butter and cook. Towards the end add salt. Drain, leaving little liquid. Wash the prunes and leave them to soak for 30 mins in some boiled water. Then cook and drain them, reserving the liquid. Combine the liquid from the prunes with the stock. Cut the prunes into strips. Sauté the chopped onions in butter and combine with the prunes. Remove from the heat. Soak the ginger cake in the stock, then mix it in a food processor with lemon juice and grated lemon rind, honey, nutmeg, cinnamon and gooseberry preserve. Put through a sieve, add the onion and prunes, heat. Combine with the beans and bring to the boil.

serves 4 • Soaking: 12 hrs • Cooking: 50–60 mins

Beetroots

Beetroots

Bake two large beetroots in ashes or in the oven (cooked in water, beets lose their colour). Choose nice sweet beets, with dark leaves and thin stalks, dark red inside.

(Karolina Nakwaska, Dwór wiejski, 1858)

Beets are one of the most popular vegetables in Poland. Our ancestors long ago were well aware of their positive influence on man's immune system, therefore each household kept a large supply of soured beet juice all through the winter. Latest research has confirmed that beetroots have detoxifying properties and strengthen the immune system.

They are rich in calcium, potassium, mangesium, iron and phosphorus, as well as in vitamins C, A and B. Beet juice, moreover, cleans the organism of toxins.

A fine dark-red beetroot is tasty both raw and cooked. It can be prepared in many different ways. The spices that are most frequently used with beets are caraway, coriander, horseradish, mustard and pepper.

Sour beetroot juice

If you want to have a tasty sour beetroot juice for borsch, cabbage soup etc., do not sour all the beetroots at one time but prepare fresh juice every two or three weeks. Leave small beetroots whole and halve the larger ones, put them into a small barrel, cover with cold water and leave in a warm place, preferably next to the oven, for 4–5 days. At the end of this period, take the barrel to a cool place to slow down the process of souring and make the juice keep well. You can drink the juice 6 days later... If you want to have the juice earlier than that, cover the beets with warm water and put in a crust of wholemeal bread; in this case, the juice will be ready after three days but it will not keep long.

(Marja Śleżańska, Kucharz polski, 1932)

Ćwikła, or grated beets with horseradish

1 kg small beets, 1 tbsp caraway seeds, 5 tbsps fresh grated horseradish, juice of 1 lemon, 1 tbsp sugar, 1 glass dry red wine, salt

Bake the washed beets in a hot oven. Set aside to cool. Peel, cut into thin half-slices, thin sticks, or shred them coarsely. Place the caraway seeds on a seeve, scald with boiling water, drain. Mix the freshly grated horseradish with lemon juice. Place layers of the beets in a jar, each layer sprinkled with salt, sugar, caraway seeds and grated horseradish. Pour in the wine mixed with what is left of lemon juice, cover and leave for 3–4 days in a cool place for the flavours to blend. Serve with cold meats.

serves 4–6 • Preparation: 30–40 mins • Macerating: 3–4 days

Beet salad

500 g small red beets

*DRESSING: 6 tbsps pomegranate juice
or red wine vinegar, 1 tbsp honey, ½ tsp
ground fennel seeds, ¼ tsp owdered ginger,
4 spring onions, 1 tbsp chopped dill*

Wash the beets and bake them in the oven, or cook. Peel when cool and cut into thin matchsticks. Mix the honey with pomegranate juice, ginger, salt, fennel seeds and oil. Add the finely chopped spring onions, pour the mixture over the beets, cover and refrigerate for 3–4 hours. Mix well before serving, sprinkle with dill.

serves 4 • Baking: 30 mins • Preparation: 10 mins • Chilling: 3–4 hrs

Beet salad with spring onions

*500 g small red beets, 1 bunch spring
onions, 2 tbsps chopped dill*

*DRESSING: 5–6 tbsps olive oil, 3 tbsps pomegranate
or lemon juice, 1 tbsp honey, ½ tsp ground
fennel seeds, ¼ tsp powdered ginger*

Mix thoroughly all the dressing ingredients. Bake or cook the washed beets, peel them, cut into julienne, combine with the finely chopped onion springs, pour over the dressing, cover and refrigerate for 3–4 hours. Mix well before serving, sprinkle with dill. Delicious with roast or fried meats.

serves 4 • Baking: 30 mins • Preparation: 5–7 mins • Cooling: 3–4 hrs

Beet salad with garlic

*300 g small beets, 100 g stoned cherries (fresh or
frozen), 1 smallish red onion, 1–2 garlic cloves*

*DRESSING: grated juice and rind of ½ lemon,
2 tbsps grapeseed oil, ¼ tsp each dried thyme,
tarragon and caraway seeds, salt, pepper*

Mix all the dressing ingredients thoroughly, cover and place in the fridge. Bake the washed beets in the oven. Peel when cool, cut into julienne or grate coarsely. Cut the onions finely, chop the garlic. Combine with the beets and the cherries, cover with the dressing and mix well.

serves 4 • Baking: 30 mins • Preparation: 5–7 mins

Beet salad with walnuts

*500 g smallish beets, 4–5 tbsps chopped
walnuts, 3–4 garlic cloves, ½ tsp crushed
coriander seeds, 2 tbsps chopped parsley, 2 tbsps
chopped fresh coriander, 3 tbsps wine vinegar
or lemon juice, 1 tsp honey, salt, pepper*

Bake the scrubbed beets in the oven, peel and grate coarsely, mix with the chopped walnuts. Blend the finely chopped garlic with salt, pepper, honey, vinegar and powdered coriander. Pour the mixture over the beets, mix well, cover and chill. Before serving, sprinkle with chopped parsley and fresh coriander.

serves 4 • Baking: 30 mins • Preparation: 5 mins • Refrigerating: 4–5 hrs

Beet salad with apple and pineapple

*2 small red beets, 1 tart apple, 1 tbsp
lemon juice, 2 tinned pineapple rings,
2 tbsps raisins, 1 tbsp dry white wine*

*DRESSING: 2 tbsps mayonnaise, 2 tbsps double
cream, 1 tsp hot mustard, ¼ csp dried tarragon,
¼ csp crushed dried thyme, salt, pepper, a pinch
of sugar, 4–6 walnut halves, 3–4 sprigs dill*

Mix well the dressing ingredients, and chill. Wash and dry the raisins, put them into a small bowl and add the wine. Bake the washed beets in the oven, or cook them. Leave them to cool when tender, peel and cut into thin strips. Drain the pineapple rings and cut into dice, peel and julienne the apple, sprinkling it with lemon juice. Mix all the ingredients, pour the dressing over, mix and set aside to cool. Decorate with the walnut halves and dill sprigs. Delicious with fried fish.

serves 4 • Baking: 30 mins • Preparation: 10 mins • Cooling: 1–2 hrs

Beet and herring salad

6 herring fillets, 2–3 small red beets, cooked, 1 cooked potato, 2 red onions, 1 orange, 3 tbsps chopped chives

DRESSING: 2 tbsps lemon juice, ¼ tsp grated lemon and orange peel, 1 tsp hot mustard, salt, pepper, a pinch of sugar, 4–5 tbsps olive oil

Mix the dressing ingredients thoroughly, cover, set aside to cool. Wash and dry the herring fillets. Cut the herrings, beets and the potato into thick dice. Chop the onion finely and cut the orange into small cubes. Combine all the ingredients, pour the dressing over and toss gently. Sprinkle with chives before serving.

serves 4–6 • Preparation: 10 mins

Beets in orange juice

1½ kg small red beets, ½ glass orange juice, 1 tsp freshly grated orange peel, 3 tbsps lemon juice and ½ tsp grated lemon rind, 2 tbsps honey, 1 tbsp potato flour, 2 tbsps butter, 2 tbsps dry red wine, salt, pepper

Bake the washed beets in the oven. Peel, cut into thin matchsticks. Bring to the boil lemon and orange juice with honey, butter, salt, pepper and grated orange and lemon rind. Mix the potato flour well with the wine, add to the saucepan with the juice and heat, stirring all the time until the sauce thickens. Put in the beets, heat. Serve with your main course of roast veal or roast chicken.

serves 6–8 • Baking: 30 mins • Preparation: 5–7 mins

Beets, Queen Marysieńka style

1 kg small beets, 2 tbsps butter, 150 g pitted prunes, 30 g raisins, 2 tbsps honey, ½ glass dry red wine, salt, 1 tbsp lemon juice

Rinse the prunes and soak them in a little water, then put them through a sieve. Bake the washed beets in the oven, peel and julienne. Scald the raisins with boiling water. In a frying pan, melt the butter, add the beets and fry for a short while, sprinkle with salt. In a saucepan boil the wine with honey and lemon juice, add the puréed prunes, raisins and the beets, mix and simmer all together for a while. Add salt and lemon juice to taste. Serve with roast chicken and white meats.

serves 6–8 • Baking: 30 mins • Preparation: 10–15 mins

Fried beets

500 g small beets, 1 onion, 1 leek (white part), 2 tsps chopped dill, 1 tsp caraway seeds, ¼ tsp ground coriander, 4 tbsps oil, ½ cup stock, 2–3 tbsps double cream, salt, pepper

Peel and julienne the beets, cut the onion and leeks into half-rings. Heat the oil in a deep frying pan and add the beets. Sauté for a while over high heat, then turn the heat down and continue to fry, stirring occasionally, for about 20 mins. Add the onion and leek, salt and pepper, caraway seeds and coriander. Mix well and continue to fry for a moment, then add the hot stock. Cover and simmer for about 20 mins. Towards the end add the cream mixed with dill and heat up. Serve hot with white bread or rice.

serves 4–6 • Preparation: 45–50 mins

Beets as accompaniment to venison

1 kg small red beets, 2 tart apples, 1 tbsp fresh grated horseradish, juice and grated rind of ½ lemon, salt, 1 tsp sugar, 2 tbsps butter, ½ cup thick cream

Scrub the beets with a brush under running water, bake them in the oven. Melt the butter in a small saucepan, add the coarsely grated beets and apples, fry for a moment or two, stir. Add salt, lemon rind, sugar and horseradish, mix well and simmer 4–5 mins. Pour in the cream and lemon juice, mix and heat up. Delicious with game and roast meats.

serves 6–8 • Baking: 30 mins • Preparation: 10 mins

Beets as accompaniment to fish

1 kg small red beets, 50 g raisins, 2–3 tbsp semi-dry red wine, 1 large onion, 1 tbsp honey, 1 tsp lemon juice, 2 tbsps butter, salt

Scrub the beets with a brush under running water and bake them in the oven. Peel and grate. Cover the washed raisins with the wine and put aside for a few minutes. In a small saucepan melt the butter, and sauté the finely chopped onions. Add the grated beets, salt, honey, raisins with the wine and lemon juice. Mix well and simmer, stirring frequently.

serves 6–8 • Baking: 30 mins • Preparation: 10 mins

Detox beetroot drink

¾ cup beetroot juice, ¼ cup carrot juice, 1 garlic clove minced with salt, 1 tsp lemon juice, 1–2 ice cubes, 1 tsp chopped parsley

Combine the lemon juice with garlic, beetroot and carrot juice, pour this into a glass, add ice cubes and chopped parsley. Mix well.

1 serving • Preparation: 1–2 mins

Russian beetroot cocktail

½ cup beet juice, ¼ cup celeriac juice, ¼ cup natural yogurt, a pinch of salt and pepper, 1–2 ice cubes, 1 tsp chopped chives, 1 tsp chopped fresh mint leaves

Put all the ingredients through a blender, mix with the chopped greens.

serves 1–2 • Preparation: 1–2 mins

Broad beans

Broad bean purée

We do not often eat this vegetable, which however is good and provides a nice change in our diet, on condition that you know how to cook it... Take a quarter of dried green broad beans, cover them with cold water, add some green spinach juice, salt, pepper, butter and pork fat. Cook the whole lot

and when the beans are tender, pour off the water, take out the pork fat and sieve the beans. Make croutons from white bread and butter, take them out with a strainer to allow the fat to drip off. Put the sieved broad beans into the butter, add some chopped parsley and chives and cook, stirring all the time, for ten minutes. Transfer to a serving dish, surround with the warm croutons and serve immediately.

(Karolina Nakwska, *Dwór wiejski*, 1858)

Broad beans with mint

1 kg young broad beans, 1 bunch spring onion, 1 tbsp honey, 3 tbsps chopped fresh mint, 1 cup olive oil, salt, pepper, 1–1½ cups light stock

In a large saucepan heat the oil, sauté the chopped onion and add the broad beans, salt, pepper, mint and pour enough of the light stock to cover the beans. Add honey, mix well and cover. Cook gently for about 20 mins. Remove the lid and steam off the excess liquid. Serve the hot, soft beans with chilled yogurt.

serves 4–6 • Preparation: 30–40 mins

Broad beans with celery and lettuce

600 g peeled young broad beans, 3 tbsps milk, the heart of a large lettuce, 1 large onion, 2–3 celery stalks, 2 tbsps chopped savory leaves, 1 tbsp chopped parsley, 1 tbsp sugar, salt

In a saucepan melt the butter, add the washed and drained broad beans, lettuce cut into strips, finely chopped onion and celery cut into slices. Add chopped parsley and 1 tbsp savory, pour enough boiling water to cover the vegetables, add salt, sugar, stir and simmer over very low heat for about 1 hour, stirring from time to time. Uncover and steam off the excess liquid. Before serving, sprinkle with the remaining fresh savory.

serves 4 • Preparation: 1 hr

Broad beans with mushrooms

400 g peeled young broad beans, 400 g young slippery jack (or button) mushrooms, 1 large onion,

3 tbsps butter, 1½ cups stock, ½ cup sour cream, 1tbsp flour, 2–3 tbsps chopped parsley, salt, pepper

Cook the beans in slightly salted water, drain. Melt the butter in a saucepan, sauté the finely chopped onion, adding the mushrooms cut into strips. Fry for a moment or two, stir. Sprinkle slightly with the stock and stew for a few minutes. Add the beans, salt, pepper, pour in the remaining stock. Mix well and bring to the boil. Mix the cream thoroughly with flour and add to the broad beans. Stir, heat up and sprinkle with chopped parsley before serving.

serves 4 • Preparation: 1 hr

Broad beans, English style

1 kg peeled new broad beans, 2 young parsley roots with leaves, 1 sprig fresh thyme, 1 sprig sage, 1 bay leaf, 3 tbsps butter, 2 tbsps chopped parsley, salt, pepper, 1 tbsp dry white wine, 1 tbsp lemon juice, ¼ tsp grated lemon rind

Wash the broad beans and put them into boiling water. Cook for 4–5 mins, drain, rinse with cold water and remove the skin. Mince the butter with lemon juice and lemon rind, wine and salt. Warm an ovenproof dish. Boil some salted water. Wrap the bay leaf, sage and thyme in a piece of gauze and cook under cover for a few minutes. Add the beans, cook and drain. Place the beans in the warmed dish, toss well with the prepared butter, sprinkle with pepper and parsley. Serve as a hot snack or a side dish to accompany the main course.

serves 4 • Preparation: 30–40 mins

Broad beans cutlets

700 g peeled new broad beans, 3 tbsps very finely chopped oregano leaves, ½ cup finely chopped walnuts, 2–3 tbsps breadcrumbs, 1 tbsp potato flour, 2 eggs, salt, pepper, cooking oil

Cook the broad beans in salted water, leave aside to cool. Peel, mash them with a fork, mix with the potato flour, chopped walnuts and oregano leaves. Add the eggs, salt, pepper and enough breadcrumbs to make dense pulp. Wet your hands and form small cutlets. Fry them in hot oil on both sides until golden. Serve as a hot snack, or with rice and sauces as the main course.

serves 4 • Preparation: 1 hr

Broccoli

This vegetable, which originated in Italy, was introduced to France by Catherine d'Medici and brought to Poland probably by Queen Marie Louise and Marie Casimire (Sobieski). Its cultivation developed on a larger scale only recently, but its popularity has been steadily growing. And no wonder, for broccoli is an excellent source of vitamin C, as well as of folic acid, and moreover contains beta-carotene, potassium, cal- cium and selenium.

Broccoli is much more delicate than cauliflowers. Depending on the variety, it has green or purple flowers, or more rarely pink or yellow flowers. Its florets do not keep long, tend to wilt and lose colour, but they freeze very well and then preserve their natural colour and nutritive value.

Broccoli florets are much more fragile than the stalks and therefore should be cooked for a shorter period of time. When you prepare broccoli, first cut off the florets, then peel the stalks, cut them into smaller pieces and cook or fry them for 10–12 minutes. Only then you should add the florets and cook them together with the stalks for 5–7 minutes. The leaves of broccoli are also edible. Young leaves are added to salads or cooked in butter.

If you want to serve broccoli florets raw, you should first soak them in salted or acidic water for 10–15 minutes and then dry them thor- oughly.

Broccoli

The purple variety is better than cauliflower, because much more tender. What is more, broccoli is available from early spring when there is a shortage of fresh vegetables. Take two nice, firm, round broccoli flowers with stalks, remove the leaves that grow along the stalks, but do not divide the flowers into florets. Cook in boiling water uncovered, preferably on a sieve, which will make it easier to take the vegetable out. Add some salt, 1 teaspoon of butter and 1 teaspoon of vinegar. Prick the stalks with a fork to check them for tenderness. If they are tender, take the pan off the heat and leave the broccoli in hot water to prevent it from getting cold while you prepare a white sauce with egg yolks. Strain the broccoli, arrange nicely in a pyramid in a serving dish and pour the sauce over it. You can also pour some melted butter mixed with browned breadcrumbs over it.

(Karolina Nakwaska, *Dwór wiejski*, 1858)

Broccoli salad with plums

300 g broccoli, 100 g purple plums, 1 tart apple, 1 tsp lemon juice, 2 sweet peppers (red and yellow), 1½ tbsps chopped parsley, 1½ tbsps chopped basil, 1½ tbsps chopped dill

DRESSING: ½ cup yogurt, juice and rind of ½ lemon, 4–5 garlic cloves, 1–2 tbsps thick mayonnaise, salt, pepper, sugar

Mix the chopped garlic with salt and pepper, combine with the yogurt, mayonnaise and grated lemon rind, cover and leave to chill. Soak the broccoli in salted water, drain and dry. Divide into florets, dice the stems, sprinkle with lemon juice and mix with 2 tbsps dressing. Peel and julienne the apple, sprinkle with lemon juice. Rinse and dry the peppers, clean out the seeds and cut the flesh into cubes. Pit the plums, cutting half of them into strips, and another half in halves. Combine the plum strips with the apple, peppers, broccoli and chopped greens, top with the dressing, toss gently but thoroughly, decorate with the plum halves.

serves 4 • Preparation: 20 mins

Broccoli salad with red and yellow bell peppers

300 g broccoli, 2 smallish bell peppers (red and yellow), 1 tart apple, 1 hard-boiled egg, 1 tbsp chopped chives, 1 tbsp chopped dill

DRESSING: 3 tbsp thick mayonnaise, 1 tbsp lemon juice, salt, pepper, sugar and cayenne pepper

Mix the dressing ingredients thoroughly, cover and let stand to chill. Divide the broccoli into florets, arrange in a serving bowl and cover with lukewarm salted water for 15–20 mins. Drain and dry. Peel the apple, seed the peppers and cut them into matchsticks. Combine with the broccoli, toss with the dressing, sprinkle with the chopped egg, dill and chives.

serves 4 • Salting: 15–20 mins • Preparation: 10 mins

Broccoli salad, Roman style

500 g broccoli, salt, sugar, 1tbsp lemon juice, 1 tsp butter, 2 tbsps capers, 2 tbsps coarsely chopped walnuts

DRESSING: 3 tbsps salad oil, 2 tbsps lemon juice, salt, pepper, 1 tsp honey, 1 tsp water, 1 tbsp chopped dill, 1 tbsp chopped chives

Cook the broccoli for 10–12 mins in boiling salted water with lemon juice, sugar and butter. Drain and leave to cool. Divide into florets, and julienne the peeled stems. Mix well all the ingredients of the dressing. Pour it over the broccoli, toss, chill and sprinkle with capers and walnuts.

serves 4 • Preparation: 15–20 mins

Broccoli with olives

500 g broccoli, 1 glass dry white wine, 2–3 garlic cloves, juice and grated rind of ½ lemon, 1 sprig thyme, 1–2 bay leaves, 1–2 tbsps olive oil, 2 tbsps pitted black olives, salt, pepper, sugar

Divide the broccoli into florets, peel the stems and cut them into thick slices. In a flat saucepan bring to the boil the wine with thyme, bay leaves, garlic and grated lemon rind and cook together for about 10 mins. Remove the garlic, bay leaves and thyme, add salt, pepper and sugar. Put in the broccoli and bring to the boil, then simmer for about 15 mins. Remove the broccoli with a slotted spoon, reduce the stock to 2–3 tbsps, add the olive oil and mix well. Add the broccoli and the olives cut into thick slices. Cover and keep for a while over low heat. Serve as a hot snack, or with the main course.

serves 4 • Preparation: 30 mins

Broccoli à la spinach

700 g broccoli, 1 tbsp butter, 1 tbsp flour,
3–4 garlic cloves, salt, pepper, nutmeg,
1 cup cream, 1 tbsp lemon juice

Peel the stems. Put the broccoli into boiling salted water for 5–7 mins. Drain, rinse with cold water and put through a mincer. Melt the butter in a saucepan, add the flour and make a roux. Dilute it with the cream, add the broccoli, garlic, salt, pepper, lemon juice and a dash of nutmeg. Mix thoroughly and simmer for a moment or two. Makes a delicious accompaniment to veal cutlets and roast chicken.

serves 4 • Preparation: 15–20 mins

Broccoli in wine

700–800 g broccoli, 4–5 garlic cloves,
3–4 tbsps olive oil, 1 tsp salt, ½ tsp white
ground pepper, 1 glass dry white wine

Rinse and dry the broccoli, peel the stems and incise a cross on each, so they will cook more easily. In a flat saucepan heat the olive oil, add the chopped garlic, put in the broccoli and sauté for 1–2 mins. Sprinkle with salt and pepper, gradually pour in the wine. Cover and simmer for about 20 mins. Serve with delicate roast meats.

serves 4 • Preparation: 25 mins

Broccoli au gratin

1 kg broccoli, 250 g lean streaky bacon,
2 hard-boiled eggs, 250 g mushrooms,
3–4 tbsps grated cheese, 2 tbsp butter

SAUCE: 1 tbsp butter, 1 tbsp flour, 1 cup
stock, 2–3 tbsps tomato concentrate, salt,
pepper, sugar, 1 tsp lemon juice

Slice the rinsed and dried mushrooms. Fry them in 1 tbsp butter, add salt and pepper. Wash the broccoli, cut and peel the stems. Dice the stems and put into boiling water for 5–6 mins, remove with a slotted spoon and place in a bowl. Put the florets in boiling water for 3–4 mins. Drain.

Cut the bacon into strips, slice the hard-boiled eggs. In a small saucepan melt the butter, add the flour and make a roux. Add the stock and simmer, stirring all the time, until the sauce thickens. Add the tomato concentrate, season with salt, pepper, sugar and lemon juice to taste. Butter an ovenproof dish, line it with the broccoli stems and slices of the hard-boiled eggs, top with the strips of bacon and mushrooms. Cover with the florets, pour in the sauce, sprinkle with grated cheese and knobs of butter. Place the dish in a preheated oven and bake for about 20 mins. Serve as a hot snack with white bread, or with potatoes and salads.

serves 4–6 • Preparation: 20–25 mins • Baking: 20 mins

Broccoli, Gypsy style

500 g broccoli, 1 bay leaf, 1 sprig sage or ½ tsp
dried sage, 1 tbsp lemon juice, salt, 150 g onion,
200 g firm fleshy tomatoes, 200 g mushrooms,
3–4 garlic cloves, 2 tbsps sunflower oil, 2 tbsps
butter, 2 tbsps dry white wine, salt, pepper,
2 tbsps chopped parsley, 2 hard-boiled eggs

Scald and skin the tomatoes, cut in cubes. Slice the washed and dried mushrooms, chop the garlic. Peel and cut the onions, sauté them in hot oil, add the butter and mushrooms and fry for a moment or two, stir. Add the tomatoes, salt, sprinkle with the wine and simmer about 10 mins. Add the garlic and pepper, mix well and simmer all together for another 10 mins. Boil some salted water with a bay leaf, sage and lemon juice. Peel the broccoli stems, cut them off, put together with the broccoli florets into boiling water and cook for about 15 mins. Chop the eggs and mix with parsley. Drain the tender broccoli and arrange in a warm serving dish, pour over the mushroom sauce, sprinkle with the eggs and green parsley. Serve as a hot snack, or as the main dish with rice.

serves 4 • Preparation: 25–30 mins

Broccoli with chicken livers

500 g broccoli, 500 g chicken livers, 1½ tbsps
finely chopped ginger, 50 g mushrooms, 50 g
frozen (or tinned) shrimps, ½ bunch spring
onion, 2 tbsp cornflour (or potato flour), 2 tbsp
lard, 1 tbsp soya sauce, salt, pepper

Wash the broccoli and separate into florets. Cook for 3–4 mins in boiling water and drain. Coat the dressed, rinsed and dried livers with the cornflour and seal in 1 tbsp very hot lard. Remove from the heat, sprinkle with chopped ginger, chopped spring onion and salt and pepper. In a flat saucepan heat the remaining lard, fry the sliced mushrooms, add the broccoli and fry all together for 2–3 mins. Put the frozen shrimps into boiling water for 1 min, drain. Add the shrimps and livers into the saucepan with the broccoli. Mix what is left of cornflour with 3–4 tbsps cold boiled water and soya sauce. Add to the livers, toss gently but well, heat until the sauce thickens.

serves 4–6 • Preparation: 20 mins

Brussels sprouts

Brussels sprouts were first described in around 1750 as a cabbage variety which originated spontaneously in the vicinity of Brussels, and it was in Belgium that they were first cultivated on a large scale over a hundred years ago.

This is one of the tastiest and healthiest varieties of cabbage, a very good source of vitamin C, beta-carotene, folic acid, vitamin E and potassium. While early night frosts are fatal for other vegetables, Brussels sprouts are best when picked after the first frosts: they are then really 'ripe' and tasty, and their sugar content grows.

Brussels sprouts should be very green and compact, with no wilted yellow leaves. The smaller they are, the better their flavour. They should not be stored in the fridge longer than a day or two for otherwise they lose their nutritive value and flavour.

Brussels sprouts can be cooked in boiling water, sieved to make Brussels sprout soup, baked with sausage, nuts or cheese, or braised. Boiled Brussels sprouts are seasoned with nutmeg or garlic, and served with butter or cream sauce.

Brussels sprouts, Spanish style

Strain the Brussels sprouts after cooking them in salted water. Put them in a pan, add a knob of butter and a pinch of nutmeg, and keep them warm. Meanwhile, slit the shells of chestnuts (2–3 per person), put them in a baking tin and roast them in a very hot oven. Peel them and mix them with the Brussels sprouts. Serve with melted butter mixed with browned breadcrumbs.

(Maria Norkowska, *Najnowsza kuchnia wytworna i gospodarska*, 1904)

Brussels sprouts salad with saffron milk caps

250 g small Brussels sprouts, 2 tbsps lemon juice, 8–10 soured or pickled saffron milk caps, 2 red onions, 2 tart apples, 1 sweet red pepper

DRESSING: 4 tbsps mayonnaise, salt, pepper, sugar, 2 tbsps chopped parsley

Mix the mayonnaise with salt, pepper and sugar. Cut the washed and drained Brussels sprouts into strips. Peel and coarsely grate the apples, mix with the Brussels sprouts. Scald the pepper with boiling water, rinse with cold water and skin. Dice the pepper and onions, cut the saffron milk caps into strips. Combine all the ingredients and cover with the mayonnaise, mix well, chill. Before serving, sprinkle with chopped parsley.

Preparation: 10 mins • Chilling: 1–2 hours

Brussels sprouts salad with raisins and almonds

250 g Brussels sprouts, 1 tbsp lemon juice, 1 large white onion, 50 g raisins, 1 tbsp dry white wine, 50 g almond flakes, 2 tbsps chopped parsley, 2 tbsps chopped basil, 2 tbsps chopped dill

DRESSING: 2 tbsps mayonnaise, 1 tbsp ketchup, 2 tbsps olive oil, ½ tsp sugar, salt, cayenne pepper

Mix the dressing ingredients with the chopped dill. Chill. Finely chop the onion and combine with the dressing. Rinse the raisins and soak them in wine for a few minutes.

Wash, trim and dry the Brussels sprouts. Cut them into quarters, sprinkle with lemon juice, combine with the raisins, chopped parsley and basil, mix well with the dressing. In a hot frying pan dry roast the almond flakes. Sprinkle the salad before serving.

serves 4 • Preparation: 10 mins

Brussels sprouts cooked in milk

*600 g Brussels sprouts, 1 tbsp sugar, 1 cup milk,
1½ cups water, 1 tbsp salt*

Clean the Brussels sprouts, rinse and drain. Boil the milk with water, salt and sugar. Add the Brussels sprouts and cook uncovered for 15–20 min, drain. Serve with melted butter or butter with browned breadcrumbs.

serves 4 • Preparation: 20–25 mins

Brussels sprouts cooked with garlic butter

*600 g Brussels sprouts, 1 tbsp sugar, 1 tbsp butter,
1tbsp salt, 1 tbsp lemon juice, 100 g spinach,
50 g butter, 6–8 garlic cloves, 1 tbsp soya sauce,
1 tbsp lemon juice, sugar and pepper*

Squeeze out the juice of the spinach. Boil some salted water with the spinach juice, sugar, butter and lemon juice, add the Brussels sprouts and cook for 10–15 mins. Mince the garlic with a pinch of sugar, pepper and butter, lemon juice and soya sauce. Drain the sprouts, place them in an ovenproof dish, dot with the garlic butter and bake 5–6 mins in a preheated oven. Serve as a hot snack, or as an addition to egg dishes, fish or meat.

serves 4 • Preparation: 20 mins • Baking: 5–6 mins

Brussels sprouts stewed with hazelnuts

*600 g Brussels sprouts, ½ cup chopped hazelnuts,
2 onions, 1 tsp chopped fresh tarragon, 2 tbsps
lemon juice and ¼ tbsp lemon rind, 100 g
butter, salt, a pinch of pepper and sugar*

In a hot frying pan dry roast the chopped hazelnuts. Scald and drain the cleaned Brussels sprouts. Melt the butter in a saucepan, sauté the chopped onions, add the hazelnuts and the sprouts. Mix well and simmer for about 20–25 mins, add salt, pepper and sugar to taste. Remove from the heat, mix with the lemon juice and lemon rind. Serve as a side dish with roast meat, or pork and veal cutlets.

serves 4 • Preparation: 30 mins

Brussels sprouts fricassee

*500 g Brussels sprouts, 500 g potatoes, 150 g smoked
streaky bacon, 1 tbsp lard, 1 large onion, 2 cups strong
stock, salt, a pinch of pepper and minced garlic, ½ cup
thick cream, 1 tsp flour, 1 tbsp finely chopped basil,
1 tbsp finely chopped dill, 1 tbsp chopped parsley*

Cut the bacon into cubes. In a saucepan heat the lard, add the bacon and fry until golden brown. Add the stock, bring to the boil, add the peeled and diced potatoes and washed sprouts. Cook for about 20 mins, season with salt, pepper and minced garlic. Mix well and cook another 10–12 mins. Steam off the excess liquid. Mix the cream with flour and the chopped green herbs, add to the saucepan, mix well and heat until the sauce thickens.

serves 4–6 • Preparation: 35–40 mins

Cabbage

Cabbage, the doctor of the poor, has excellent detoxifying properties. 200 g of raw salad from cabbage, broccoli, Brussels sprouts, kohlrabi or kale, eaten regularly every day, works wonders for the whole system.

According to recent research, our system needs selenium (contained in the cabbage) to produce glutathione, which is an important enzyme. To explain this in simple terms, a portion of raw cabbage produces a stream of glutathione particles which bind toxins, making them more easily expelled from the organism. The result is a better complexion and more energy.

Bigos

For centuries, bigos has been regarded as a very practical invention of Polish cuisine. Gourmets say that is combines everything that is most Polish in character, a practical approach with a lot of imagination. Next to borsch and zrazy, it is *the Poles' most favourite dish.* According to Cezary Biernacki, it is made from *'soured cabbage with chopped beef, veal and pork meat, smoked sausage, venison, pork fat cut into strips or mushrooms. Bigos is usually simmered for a long time on coal, and when it is reheated it gains in flavour and taste.'*

In the past, it was served as a hot breakfast, especially to those who were about to go on a journey or a hunt. It was eaten also before the main meal as a hot hors-d'oeuvre, when it was preceded by a glass of Polish brandy or Gdańsk vodka, or for the evening meal. It was an absolute must during carnival, the season of dance balls and sledge rides.

Every family had its own special recipe for bigos. Zygmunt Gloger wrote:

Old housewives know well that bigos was always made from shredded sour cabbage or else from fresh cabbage, but then with the addition of sour beetroot juice. It was always cooked with pork fat, pork loin and sausage, and roast game meat, especially hare, was added at the end. Peppercorns were added while it was being cooked, and the dish was sprinkled with ground pepper when on the plates.

Lithuanian bigos

1 head white cabbage (about 1½ kg), 500 g tart apples, 1 tbsp lemon juice, 100 g onion, 250 g roast beef, 250 g fatty pork meat, 2 front parts of hare, 60 g lard, 120 g sausage, soup vegetables, 2 bay leaves, 2–3 allspice berries, 2–3 juniper berries, 8–10 peppercorns, salt, ground pepper

Peel and wash the vegetables, put them in a saucepan together with the pork and hare meat. Add the allspice, bay leaf, juniper, pepper and salt and cover the whole with boiling water. Bring to the boil, then cook for about 1 hour over medium heat. Remove the meat when tender and strain the stock through a sieve. Finely chop the cabbage, scald it and put in a saucepan, covering it with the stock. Bring to the boil, then cook for about 30–40 mins over low heat. Peel and julienne the apples, sprinkle with lemon juice and add to the cabbage. Mix well together and simmer for about 20 mins. Cut the hare, pork and beef into cubes. In a frying pan, melt the lard and sauté the finely chopped onion. Add the meat and fry for a moment or two over high heat, stir. Add the cabbage, mix well and simmer together for about 1 hour. Towards the end add the thinly sliced sausage, and season to taste with salt and pepper.

serves 8–10 • Preparation: 3 hrs

Home-made bigos

1½ kg sauerkraut, 1 small head white cabbage (about 1 kg), 350 g pork ribs, 200 g smoked streaky bacon, 350 g cold meats (pieces of ham, cured pork shoulder, smoked sirloin, pork roast, roast poultry, roast beef), 300 g sausage, 200 g pitted prunes, 2 tbsps honey, 150 g raisins, 2 cups strong stock, 1 bay leaf, 10 peppercorns, 4–5 juniper berries, 4–5 allspice berries, 1 large onion, 1–2 cloves, ½ tsp dried thyme, 100 g lard, 1 cup water, 1 cup Madeira, salt, pepper, paprika

Wash the prunes and soak in a little boiled water for 1–2 hours. Blanch them and cut into strips. Wash and finely chop the cabbage. Place it in a sieve, scald, drain and put into a saucepan. Add the ribs, bay leaf, juniper, a clove-stuck onion, thyme and a pinch of salt. Pour in some boiling water and cook over low heat. In another saucepan melt the lard, put in the chopped sauerkraut, pepper and allspice, pour over the hot stock and cook over low heat. Combine both types of cabbage, remove the onion and cooked ribs. Separate the meat from the bones, cut into cubes and add to the cabbage. Dice the cold meats and add to the cabbage together with the prunes. Pour in the liquid in which the prunes were soaking, mix well and simmer for 2–3 hours, stirring frequently. Toss in the scalded raisins, honey, the thinly sliced sausage, stir in the wine, and season to taste with salt, pepper and paprika. Continue to simmer for another 15 mins or so. Bigos is best several days later, after having been frozen 2–3 times and reheated.

serves 8–10 • Preparation: 3–4 hours

Old Polish bigos

1Ł kg sauerkraut, 250 g fatty pork, 250 g lean beef, 200 g fresh streaky bacon, 100 g smoked bacon, 300 g sausage, 50 g ham, 50 g dried mushrooms, 100 g lard, 2 onions, 2 cups beef stock, 1 cup dry red wine, salt, pepper, 1 tsp caraway seeds or marjoram.

Follow instructions for Home-made bigos above.

serves 8–10 • Preparation: 3–4 hrs

Hunter's bigos

1Ł sauerkraut, 50 g pitted prunes, 20 g dried mushrooms, 700 roast meats (leftovers of roast game, poultry or pork, beef, duck), 300 g cold meats (ham, cured pork shoulder, bacon, sausage), 2 onions, 2 cups beef stock, salt, pepper, 1 bay leaf, 10–12 juniper berries, 1 cup dry red wine.

For instructions for Home-made bigos above.

serves 8–10 • Preparation: 3–4 hours

Classical bigos

1 head white cabbage (about 1½ kg), 1 kg sauerkraut, 500 g lean boneless beef, 500 g fat pork, 350 g sausage, 150 g lard, 50 g dried mushrooms, 150 g pitted prunes, 1 onion, Ł cup Madeira wine, salt, pepper, 1 bay leaf, 5–6 peppercorns, 5–6 allspice berries.

Follow instructions see Home-made bigos above.

serves 8–10 • Preparation: 2–3 hours

Spicy vegetarian bigos

1 head red cabbage, 250 g white beans, 1 bunch spring onion, 2–3 garlic cloves, 1 tsp white mustard seeds, 1 tsp caraway seeds, 2 tbsps cooking oil, 1 glass sherry, 2 tbsps wine vinegar, salt, pepper, 1 tbsp white mustard leaves

Wash the beans and soak in preboiled water overnight. The following day cook until tender, drain, preserve the water. Finely chop the cabbage, cut the spring onions, chop the garlic. In a saucepan heat the oil, add the mustard seeds and caraway seeds, cover and fry until the mustard seeds stop popping. Uncover, add the garlic and spring onions, fry for a moment, add the cabbage, mix all very well and continue to fry together for a moment or two over low heat. Add salt, pepper, pour in the vinegar and sherry, add the beans and again mix well. Stir in ½ cup liquid in which the beans were cooking, cover and simmer for about 20 mins, stirring from time to time. Uncover, steam off the excess liquid. Before serving, sprinkle with chopped white mustard leaves.

serves 4 • Soaking: 12 hrs • Preparation: 1–1½ hrs

White cabbage

White cabbage, Spanish style

Shred two small cabbages or one large cabbage, scald with boiling water, squeeze out well. Put into a skillet, add a heaped tablespoon of butter, cover and cook over low heat. Chop 1 onion, 1 turnip, 2 carrots, 1 parsley root and 2 tomatoes, put them into another pan, add 2 bay leaves and some thyme, pour in one glass of Madeira and 2 cups of water and cook until the vegetables are tender, then sieve them and add the purée to the cabbage. Cover and simmer a bit longer. Serve the cabbage with boiled or fried sausage.

(Marta Norkowska, *Najnowsza kuchnia wytworna i gospodarska*, 1904)

Cabbage salad with olives

¼ head white cabbage (about 300 g), salt, 3 tbsps small white beans (tinned or fresh cooked), 3 tbsps pitted black olives, 1 tbsp capers, 2 tbsps chopped parsley, juice of 1 lemon, 2 tbsps olive oil

Wash and dry the cabbage, chop it and sprinkle with salt. Leave aside for a few minutes, then squeeze out the excess liquid. Cut the olives into strips, combine with the cabbage, capers and beans, sprinkle with lemon juice, pour over the olive oil, mix well and sprinkle with chopped parsley.

serves 4 • Preparation: 10–15 mins

Cabbage salad with redcurrants

¼ head white cabbage (about 300 g), 200 g redcurrants, 1 small red onion, 1–2 garlic cloves

DRESSING: 2 tbsps lemon juice, 3 tbsps grapeseed oil, salt, pepper, 1 tsp honey, 1 tbsp sparkling mineral water

Mix well the dressing ingredients, leave aside to cool. Wash and dry the currants, remove the stems. Wash, dry and finely shred the cabbage, then sprinkle with salt and leave aside for a few minutes. Squeeze out the excess liquid. Chop the onion and garlic. Combine all the ingredients, pour over the sauce, mix.

serves 4 • Preparation: 10–15 mins

Cabbage salad with carrots

1 kg white cabbage, 300 g carrots, 3–4 tbsps honey, 3–4 tbsps thick mayonnaise, 5 tbsps pomegranate juice, salt, ¼ tsp ground pepper, 1 tsp celery seeds

Finely chop the cabbage, sprinkle with salt and leave aside for half an hour. Peel, wash and coarsely grate the carrots. Mix well the honey with pomegranate juice, salt and pepper, celery seeds and mayonnaise. Squeeze out the excess liquid from the cabbage, combine the cabbage with the carrots, pour over the dressing. Mix well, cover and refrigerate overnight. Mix well again before serving.

serves 4 • Preparation: about 40 mins • Maceration: 12 hrs

Health cabbage salad

200 g sauerkraut, 2 tbsps raisins, 2 tinned peach halves, 1 apple, 1 tbsp lemon juice, 1 tbsp honey, 1½ tbsps grapeseed oil

Scald the washed raisins and drain in a sieve. Cut the peach halves into matchsticks, peel and coarsely grate the apple. Sprinkle the apple with lemon juice and mix

with the runny honey and raisins. Chop the sauerkraut, pour over the grapeseed oil and combine with the apple, peaches and raisins. Mix well.

serves 4 • Preparation: 10 mins

Cabbage baked with blue cheese

1 head white cabbage (about 1.2 kg), 250 g blue cheese (Roquefort, Canzona), 5–6 tbsps finely chopped chives, ½ cup cream, 4–5 tbsps chopped almonds, salt, pepper, 1 tbsp butter, 1 tbsp lemon juice

Bring to the boil water with lemon juice, put in the cabbage and cook it for about 15 mins. Remove on a strainer, rinse with cold water, drain, cut into eights, remove the hard stump. Blend the cheese with the cream to form a smooth paste, add the chives, salt and pepper. Mix well. Butter an ovenproof dish and line it with the cabbage pieces. In a frying pan, dry roast the chopped almonds and sprinkle over the cabbage. Pour over the sauce and bake for 30–40 mins in a preheated oven. Serve with potatoes.

serves 4–6 • Preparation: 15–20 mins • Baking: 40 mins

Cabbage, country style

1 large head white cabbage, 1 tbsp butter, 200 g sliced pork fat, 800 g beef, soup vegetables, salt, pepper, 5–6 tart apples, 2 tbsps lemon juice

Cook the meat and vegetables. When tender leave to cool, reserve the stock, and put the meat and vegetables through a mincer. Season with salt and pepper to taste. Wash, core and slice the apples, sprinkle with lemon juice. Wash the cabbage, cut it in half and place in salted boiling water to cook for 5–7 mins. Remove, rinse with cold water, drain and separate leaves. Butter a large saucepan, line it with cabbage leaves and then arrange layers of pork fat slices, salted and peppered, alternating with layers of the sliced apples, minced meat and cabbage leaves. Pour in the strained stock. Cover the saucepan and put it into a hot oven for 1½ hours until the stock is absorbed. Serve with boiled potatoes and bechamel or mushroom sauce.

serves 6–8 • Cooking: 1 hr • Baking: 1½ hr

Cabbage stewed with apples

*1 small head white cabbage (about 800 g), 200 g
tart apples, 150 g onion, 1½ tbsps lard, 2 tbsps
honey, 5–6 peppercorns, 1 crushed bay leaf, 1 tsp
caraway seeds, 1 tbsp lemon juice, ½ cup stock, salt*

Lightly salt the finely shredded cabbage and set aside
for 30 mins. Melt 1 tbsp lard in a saucepan, add the
cabbage (squeeze out the excess liquid), add the honey,
mix well and add the stock. Stew partly covered for about
30 mins. Add the coarsely grated apples, seasoning and
the finely chopped onion browned in lard. Mix the whole
and continue to stew for another 30 mins. Season to taste
with salt, pepper and lemon juice. Add some flour to
thicken, if necessary. Makes a delicious addition to pork
roasts.

serves 4–6 • Salting: 30 mins • Stewing: 1hr

Stuffed cabbage rolls (gołąbki) with mushrooms

*1 head white cabbage, 1 cup cooked
rice, 2 onions, 1 tbsp butter, 70 g dried
mushrooms, 1 tbsp chopped parsley, salt*

*SAUCE: 1 tbsp butter, 1 tsp flour, mushroom
flavour, ½ cup cream, pepper*

Soak the mushrooms overnight, cook them and drain.
Reserve the liquid. Chop the onions and sauté in butter. Finely chop the mushrooms. Mix the rice with the
mushrooms, onion, parsley, salt and pepper. Scald the
cabbage, separate the leaves. Place some mixture on
each leaf and roll up firmly. Put ½ tsp butter on the bottom of a saucepan, and two cabbage leaves. Arrange
the cabbage rolls snugly side by side and pour over the
mushroom stock. Cover and simmer for about 1 hour.
Make a roux with the butter and flour, dilute it with the
mushroom stock and cream. Pour in the sauce and keep
the saucepan for a moment over low heat. Serve with
potatoes or bread, covered with the sauce and sprinkled
with parsley.

serves 4–6 • Soaking: 12 hrs • Preparation: 30–35 mins • Stewing: 1 hr

Stuffed cabbage rolls from Eastern borderlands

*1 head white cabbage, 2–3 tbsps tomato paste,
1 cup stock, 1 bay leaf, a pinch of sugar and pepper,
1 tbsp butter*

*STUFFING: 1½ cups cooked buckwheat kasha,
1–2 onions, 200 g full-fat cottage cheese, 1 tsp dried
marjoram, salt, pepper, a pinch of sugar, 1 tbsp butter*

Blanch the cabbage, rinse with cold water, separate the
leaves and remove the hard veins. Brown the finely
chopped onion in melted butter, put the cottage cheese
through a mincer and mix with lemon, marjoram and the
kasha. Season with salt, pepper and a pinch of sugar. Place
the mixture on each leaf, roll up firmly. Butter a flat saucepan and line it with cabbage leaves. Arrange the rolls in the
saucepan and add a bay leaf. Pour over the stock, cover
and simmer. 30 mins later add the tomato paste thinned
out with 2–3 tbsps stock. Season to taste with salt, pepper
and sugar. Shake the saucepan and continue to simmer for
another 15 mins or so.

serves 4–6 • Preparation: 20 mins • Stewing: 50–60 mins

Bieszczady gołąbki

1 head white cabbage

*STUFFING: 1 kg boiled potatoes, 100 g smoked
streaky bacon, 2 large onions, 2–3 tbsps flour, 2 eggs,
1 tsp marjoram, salt, pepper, ½ tsp grated nutmeg,
100 g butter, 2 carrots, 1 cup mushroom stock, 1 cup
cream, 1 tbsp hot ketchup, a pinch od sugar*

Blanch the cabbage, rinse with cold water, separate the
leaves and remove the hard veins. Put the still warm
potatoes through a mincer. In a frying pan, melt 1½ tbsp butter and add the finely chopped bacon and onion. Stir and fry
together for a moment or two. Set aside to cool. Add to the
potatoes with salt, pepper, marjoram and grated nutmeg.
Break in the eggs and form smooth pulp. Place the mixture
on each leaf, roll up firmly. Melt 2–3 tbsps butter in an oven
pan, line it with cabbage leaves and arrange the gołąbki snugly,
coating them with the sliced carrots. Sprinkle with the remain-

ing butter, pour over the mushroom stock, cover and place in a preheated oven. Bake for about 50 mins, adding the cream mixed with ketchup towards the end of cooking.

serves 4–6 • Preparation: 20 mins • Baking: 50–60 mins

Square noodles with cabbage

*250 g flour, 3 eggs, 2 tbsps butter, salt,
pepper, 1 head cabbage, 1 onion*

Cook the finely shredded cabbage, drain. Brown the finely chopped onion in butter, add the cabbage, salt and pepper. Cover and simmer for about 15 mins. Make firm dough, roll it thinly and, when it dries a little, cut into small squares. Cook the noodles in salted water, drain and mix with butter. Butter an ovenproof dish and place layers of noodles in it, alternating with layers of cabbage. Put knobs of butter on top and bake in the oven. You can add some chopped cooked mushrooms to the cabbage, or chopped hard-boiled eggs.

serves 4 • Preparation: 40–50 mins • Baking: 10 mins

Christmas Eve sauerkraut with peas

*500 g sauerkraut, 3–4 dried mushrooms soaked
overnight, 1 cup peas, 1 medium-large onion,
salt, pepper, marjoram, 2 tbsps sunflower oil*

Soak the peas overnight, then cook them in the same water, adding marjoram, salt and pepper to taste. Cook and drain the mushrooms. Finely chop the sauerkraut, add the mushroom stock and mushrooms cut into strips and cook together. Finely chop the onion and sauté it in the sunflower oil, add to the sauerkraut. Combine the sauerkraut and the peas when soft, mix well and cook together for another few minutes.

Peas and sauerkraut

*250 g peas, 750 g sauerkraut, 1 large
onion, 1 tbsp caraway seeds, ½ tsp
paprika, 2–3 tbsps cooking oil, salt*

Soak the peas overnight, drain the following day, cover with cold boiled water and cook. Add the salt towards the end

of cooking. In a flat saucepan heat the oil. Add the chopped sauerkraut and caraway seeds, cover with boiling water. Bring to the boil and cook for about 40–50 mins. Sauté the chopped onion in hot oil, remove from the heat, sprinkle with paprika. Combine the drained peas with the sauerkraut and onion, stir and fry together for a moment or two. Season to taste.

serves 6–8 • Soaking: 12 hrs • Preparation: 1 hr

Lent sauerkraut with mushrooms

*1 kg sauerkraut, 50 g dried mushrooms,
salt, pepper, 2 tbsps sunflower oil*

Soak and cook the mushrooms. Chop the sauerkraut, add a little water and oil, and stew. When soft, add the finely cut mushrooms and the mushroom stock, salt and pepper to taste. You can add some roux. Serve with potato and walnut croquettes.

serves 4–6 • Soaking: 12 hrs • Preparation: 1 hr

Red cabbage

Red cabbage with wine

Shred the red cabbage, scald it with boiling water. Make a roux from butter or other fat mixed with flour, dilute it with some stock, pour in some wine and vinegar, add some sugar. Put in the cabbage, cover and, stirring frequently, cook over low heat until it is tender. You may also add some currants to it.

(Marja Śleżańska, *Kucharz polski*, 1932)

Red cabbage salad with dried fruit

*1 head red cabbage (about 500 g), 50 g raisins,
50 g dried figs, 50 g dried apricots, 50 g chopped
walnuts, 2 tbsps dry red wine, 1 tsp honey,
3 tbsps olive oil, 2 tbsps lemon juice or wine
vinegar, salt, pepper, a pinch of sugar*

Shred the cabbage, place in a sieve and scald, drain, sprinkle with salt and leave aside for 20 mins. Mix the wine well with honey. Scald the raisins and apricots, dry well. Cut the apricots and figs into strips. Put the raisins, figs and apricots into a bowl, pour over the wine, mix and set aside for 15 mins. Squeeze the cabbage to remove excess liquid and combine with the fruit, mix well and sprinkle with lemon juice, pepper, sugar and salt, if necessary. Pour over the oil, mix again. Sprinkle with walnuts, refrigerate.

serves 4–6 • Salting: 20–30 mins • Preparation: 5–7 mins • Refrigerating: 30–40 mins

Spicy red cabbage salad

400 g red cabbage, 2 tart apples, ½ celeriac, 3 tbsps grated horseradish, 1 tbsp lemon juice

DRESSING: 1 tbsp honey, 5 tbsps oil, 4 tbsps lemon juice, salt, pepper

Mix well the dressing ingredients, cover and set aside to cool. Wash and finely shred the cabbage, sprinkle with salt and leave aside for an hour. Squeeze out the excess liquid, pour over the dressing, cover and refrigerate for 1 hour. Peel and coarsely great the apples and celeriac, sprinkle with lemon juice and mix with the grated horseradish. Combine with the cabbage just before serving, mix well.

serves 4–6 • Refrigerating: 1 hr • Preparation: 5–7 mins

Red cabbage salad with red wine

1 head red cabbage, 2 tart apples, 1 glass dry red wine, 1 tbsp lemon juice, 2 tbsps sunflower oil, 1 tsp sugar, salt, ½ tsp caraway seeds

Wash and shred the cabbage. Place it in a sieve, scald and rinse with cold water, drain. Peel and coarsely grate the apples, mix with the cabbage, sprinkle with the wine and lemon juice. Add salt, sugar and caraway seeds, then the oil, and toss.

serves 4–6 • Preparation: 10 mins

Red cabbage salad with cream

1 head red cabbage, lemon juice

DRESSING: 1 cup thick sour cream, 1 hard-boiled egg, 1 tbsp each chopped parsley, chopped onion and chopped chives, 1 tart apple, sugar, pepper

Wash and finely shred the cabbage, place it in a saucepan and add salted boiling water. Cook for 5–7 mins, then drain in a sieve, sprinkle with lemon juice and combine with the coarsely grated apple. Mix the sieved egg yolk with the cream, add the chives, onion and parsley, salt, sugar and pepper. Mix well. Put the cabbage with the apple in a salad bowl, pour over the dressing, sprinkle with the chopped egg white.

serves 4 • Preparation: 15 mins

Red cabbage salad with apples and horseradish

1 small head red cabbage (about 500–600 g), 2 tart apples, 3 tbsps grated horseradish, 1 tbsp lemon juice, 2 tbsps chopped walnuts

DRESSING: 4–5 tbsps salad oil, 3 tbsps wine vinegar, 1 tbsp honey, 1 tsp hot mustard, salt, pepper

Wash the cabbage and shred it. Put it into lightly salted boiling water, bring to the boil, drain, rinse with cold water, drain well. Mix well the dressing ingredients, set aside in the fridge. Peel and coarsely grate the apples, mix with the horseradish and lemon juice. Combine with the cabbage and chopped walnuts. Pour over the dressing, mix well, cover and set aside in the fridge for an hour.

serves 4–6 • Preparation: 15 mins • Chilling: 1 hr

Red and white cabbage salad

1 small head red cabbage (about 300 g), ¼ head white cabbage (about 300 g), 2 large tart apples, 3–4 tbsps chopped walnuts, salt, pepper, 4–5 tbsps salad oil, 3–4 tbsps lemon juice, 1 tbsp honey

Shred the white and red cabbage and sprinkle with salt. Coarsely grate the apples, sprinkle with lemon juice. Mix honey with lemon juice, salt and pepper, combine with the oil. Squeeze excess liquid from the cabbage, combine the cabbage with apples, pour over the dressing, mix and cover. Refrigerate. Before serving, mix again, sprinkle with walnuts.

serves 6–8 • Preparation: 15–20 mins

Red temptation

½ small head red cabbage, 100 g red beans (tinned), 1 red onion, 4 small fleshy tomatoes, ½ sweet red pepper, ½ bunch red radishes, 1 tbsp chopped parsley

DRESSING: 1 tsp crushed white mustard seeds, 5–6 garlic cloves minced with salt, 1 tbsp chopped fresh oregano leaves, salt, pepper, 2 tbsps red wine vinegar, 4–5 tbsps olive oil

Finely shred the washed cabbage and put it for 1–2 mins into lightly salted boiling water. Drain, rinse with cold water, drain again. Place the cabbage in a salad bowl, sprinkle with salt. Scald and skin the tomatoes, cut into thick cubes, cut the pepper into strips, slice the radishes, and cut the onions into half-slices. Drain the beans in a sieve. Combine the salad ingredients and pour over the dressing. Mix gently but thoroughly, cover, set aside in the fridge for 1–2 hours. Sprinkle with parsley before serving.

serves 4 • Salting: 20 mins • Preparation: 10 mins • Refrigerating: 1–2 hrs

Red cabbage stewed in wine

1 head red cabbage, 1 cup red wine, 2 cups stock, grated rind of ½ orange, 1 tbsp orange juice, salt

Shred the washed cabbage, put it into a saucepan and pour in the red wine and the hot stock. Cook over high heat without cover until the liquid has evaporated. When the cabbage is tender and the liquid evaporated, add the orange rind and orange juice. Add salt to taste. Serve with game.

serves 4 • Preparation: 40–45 mins

Red cabbage stewed with ginger

1 head red cabbage (600–800 g), 1 bunch spring onion, 2–3 garlic cloves, a walnut-size piece of fresh ginger, 2 tbsps raisins, 2 tbsps honey, ½ tsp cayenne pepper, salt, pepper, ¾ cup dry red wine, 3–4 tbsps olive oil

Finely shred the cabbage, blend the finely chopped garlic with salt, cut the spring onions, finely chop the ginger. In a flat saucepan heat the olive oil, add the spring onions, garlic, ginger and cayenne pepper. Stir and fry for a moment or two. Add the cabbage, mix well. Scald the raisins, cover with the wine, then mix with the honey and add to the cabbage. Sprinkle with salt and pepper, cover partly and simmer for about 1½ hours, stirring from time to time. Serve with white meat or poultry.

serves 4–6 • Preparation: 2 hrs

Red cabbage stewed with prunes

1 head red cabbage (about 1 kg), 1 cup dry red wine, ½ cup water, 1 tbsp honey, 1 tbsp lemon juice, 3–4 cloves, 1 small onion, 2 tbsps raisins, 1 tart apple, 5–6 prunes, salt, 2 tbsps butter, 2 tbsps chopped walnuts, 1 tbsp flour (optional)

Finely shred the cabbage. Soak the raisins and prunes for a few minutes in 2–3 tbsps wine. In a saucepan melt the butter, add the cabbage and stir and fry for a moment or two. Add salt and honey, sprinkle with lemon juice and water, then add the onion larded with cloves. Sauté together for a moment. Add the wine, mix well, cover and simmer for about 15 mins. Peel and julienne the apple, cut the prunes into strips and together with the raisins add to the cabbage. Mix well and continue to simmer for another 15–20 mins. Remove the onion with cloves, gently steam off the excess liquid (you may thicken the dish with flour mixed with 2 tbsps water). Before serving, sprinkle with chopped walnuts.

serves 4 • Preparation: 50–60 mins

Stuffed red cabbage

1 head red cabbage, 1 tbsp wine vinegar, 1 tsp sugar, salt, 3–4 tart apples, 1 tbsp honey, 1 tbsp chopped fresh ginger or 1 tsp powdered ginger, ½ cup light stock, 2 tbsps cooking oil, 1 tbsp lemon juice, sugar

STUFFING: 200 g boiled veal, ½ cup cottage cheese, 3–4 tbsps chopped walnuts, 2 eggs, 1 tsp mustard, salt, pepper

Bring salted water with vinegar and sugar to the boil. Put in the cabbage, but first remove the stump. Cook for a few minutes, remove, rinse with cold water, drain and separate the leaves. Put the meat through a mincer. Cream the cottage cheese with the egg yolks, mustard, salt, pepper and walnuts. Form a uniform paste. Place some stuffing on each leaf, roll up firmly. Sauté the cabbage rolls in hot oil. Grate coarsely the apples, sprinkle with sugar and lemon juice, mix well. Line a flat saucepan with cabbage leaves, top them with the apples. Arrange the cabbage rolls on the apples, cover with 2–3 cabbage leaves and sprinkle with some stock. Cover and simmer. Towards the end of stewing add the honey mixed with ginger. Shake the saucepan lightly.

serves 4–6 • Preparation: 20 mins • Stewing: 45–55 mins

Gołąbki with kasha

1 head red cabbage, 2 tbsps wine vinegar

*STUFFING: 1 cup cooked pearl barley, 2 eggs,
½ cup cottage cheese, ½ cup chopped walnuts,
salt, pepper, 1 tsp hot mustard, 1 large tart apple,
1 tbsp chopped fresh ginger or 1 tsp powdered ginger,
1 tsp honey, 1 tbsp lemon juice, ½ cup vegetable stock*

Bring to the boil salted water with wine vinegar. Remove the stump from the cabbage, place the cabbage in boiling water and cook for about 5 mins until the leaves soften. Drain, rinse with cold water. Separate and dry the leaves. Prepare the filling. Mix the eggs well with salt, pepper and mustard. Mix the walnuts with cheese, combine with the kasha and eggs. Remove hard veins from the cabbage leaves. Take two leaves at a time, place some stuffing, roll up tightly. In a large flat saucepan heat the oil and arrange the gołąbki snugly side by side. Sprinkle with ginger and the hot vegetable stock, cover and simmer. Towards the end uncover, steam off the excess liquid and add honey and lemon juice. Mix gently shaking the saucepan.

serves 4–6 • Preparation: 20 mins • Stewing: 45–55 mins

Chinese cabbage

There are two vegetables generally available in Europe which are called Chinese cabbage. One is *pe-tsai* which resembles a large romaine lettuce with broad irregular serrated leaves, and the other is *pak-choi* (*bok choy*) which has long fleshy leaf stalks and smooth-edged leaves, not unlike spinach.

The first of them is excellent for stews and stir-fried dishes, for ragout, goulash, soups and pasta dishes. It is also excellent raw in various salads.

Chinese cabbage salad with peaches

*1 small head Chinese cabbage (about 300 g),
2 tinned peaches, 2 tbsps raisins, 1 tsp brandy*

*DRESSING: 3 tbsps mayonnaise, 1 tbsp cream,
1 tsp lemon juice, 1 tsp curry powder, salt, pepper*

Combine all the ingredients of the dressing, chill. Wash and dry the raisins, pour over the brandy, leave aside for a few minutes. Wash and dry the Chinese cabbage, cut into strips. Julienne the peaches, combine with the cabbage and raisins, pour over the dressing, cover with cling film and leave in the fridge for about 1–2 hours. Toss before serving.

serves 4 • Preparation: 10 mins • Chilling: 1–2 hrs

Chinese cabbage salad with smoked chicken

5–6 Chinese cabbage leaves, 100 g smoked chicken breast, ½ sweet red pepper, 2–3 baby gherkins, 1 tsp capers, 3–4 hard-boiled quail eggs

DRESSING: 2 tbsps mayonnaise, 1 tsp thick cream, juice of ½ lemon, salt, white pepper, sugar

Mix well the dressing ingredients. Wash and seed the pepper. Dice the chicken meat, slice the gherkins, cut the Chinese cabbage leaves into strips and quail eggs into quarters. Combine the salad ingredients, pour over the dressing, mix gently but thoroughly. Cover with cling foil. Refrigerate for 1–2 hours.

serves 4 • Preparation: 10 mins • Refrigerating: 1–2 hrs

Chinese cabbage with apple and walnut filling

1 head Chinese cabbage (about 1 kg),
2 tbsps cooking oil, 1 glass dry white wine
or water, 2 tbsps chopped parsley

STUFFING: 3–4 apples, 1 tbsp lemon juice, 1 tsp
honey, 100 g chopped hazelnuts, 2 bread rolls
soaked in milk, salt, pepper, 1 tsp marjoram, 1 egg

Parboil the cabbage leaves in boiling water, remove, rinse with cold water, dry. Peel and coarsely grate the apples, mix them with honey and lemon juice, combine with the bread rolls (squeezed out dry), walnuts and marjoram, season to taste with salt and pepper. Add the egg and form a uniform paste. Place some of the mixture on each leaf and roll up firmly. Grease a saucepan, line it with cabbage leaves and arrange the cabbage rolls snugly side by side. Cover with the remaining leaves, sprinkle with oil and wine, or water, cover and bake in a preheated oven for about 20 mins. Before serving sprinkle, with chopped parsley.

serves 4 • Preparation: 10–12 mins • Baking: 20 mins

Stuffed Chinese cabbage

1 large head Chinese cabbage (about 1 kg), 1 cup
chopped walnuts, 3 tart apples, 1 tbsp lemon juice,
1 tsp honey, 2 bread rolls soaked in milk, 2 eggs, 3 tbsps
finely chopped parsley, salt, pepper, 1 tsp marjoram

Squeeze the bread rolls dry and mix with the chopped walnuts and parsley. Grate the apples and sprinkle with lemon juice, mix with the honey and a pinch of marjoram, combine with the bread rolls and walnuts, add the egg yolks. Form smooth pulp. Bring to the boil salted water with 1 tsp butter and marjoram. Put in the cabbage and cook it for 3–4 mins. Drain, rinse with cold water. Beat the egg whites stiff, mix gently but thoroughly with the prepared stuffing. Cut off 2–3 large cabbage leaves. Place the filling between the cabbage leaves, tie with thread. Butter a flat saucepan,

line it with the large cabbage leaves cut into strips, arrange the stuffed cabbage and pour over the melted butter. Preheat an oven lightly and bake for about 15 mins. Then turn off the heat and leave the dish inside for about 10 mins.

serves 4 • Preparation: 15 mins • Baking: 20–25 mins

Delicate gołąbki, Chinese style

1 head Chinese cabbage (about 1 kg), 500 g
minced poultry meat, 100 g poultry hearts, 100 g
poultry livers, 50 g pork fat, 1 bunch spring onions,
1 tsp powdered ginger, 1 bread roll soaked in
milk, 2 eggs, ½ cup dry red wine, 1 cup stock,
½ cup thick cream, salt, pepper, 1 tbsp butter

Bring to the boil salted water with 1 tsp butter and ½ tsp powdered ginger. Put in the washed cabbage, parboil for a few minutes, drain, rinse with cold water. Cut out the stump, separate the leaves. Finely cut the pork fat, render in a hot frying pan, add the chopped spring onions, fry for a moment or two, then add the minced meat and continue to fry for 2–3 mins, stirring all the time. Pour in half of the wine, stir, steam off the excess liquid, remove from the heat. Finely chop the hearts and livers, combine with the roll (squeezed off dry) and the briskly sautéd meat, add salt, pepper, ginger and eggs, mix well. Stuff the cabbage leaves with the mixture and roll up firmly, holding the gołąbki together with toothpicks, or tie them up with thread. Generously butter a saucepan, line it with the remaining leaves and arrange the gołąbki snugly side by side. Pour over the hot stock and bake for 25–30 mins in a preheated oven. Towards the end of baking add the cream mixed with the remaining wine. Shake the saucepan.

serves 4–6 • Preparation: 20 mins • Baking: 30 mins

Chinese cabbage gołąbki

1 head Chinese cabbage (about 750 g), 500 g minced
chicken, 1 stale bread roll soaked in milk, 50 g pork
fat, 1 bunch spring onions, 1 tbsp finely chopped fresh
ginger, ½ cup dry white wine, 2–3 tbsps thick sour
cream, 1 egg, salt, pepper, 1 tbsp butter, 1 cup stock

Blanch the cabbage for 4–5 mins in lightly salted boiling water. Remove, set aside to cool. Remove the thick veins from the cabbage leaves. Cut the pork fat into small

Chinese cabbage salad with leeks

cubes and fry in a deep frying pan. Add the finely chopped spring onions and ginger, and continue to fry together for a while, stirring all the time. Pour in the wine, bring to the boil and then simmer. Towards the end steam off the excess liquid and set aside to cool. Combine the minced meat with the cream, onion, salt and pepper, add the egg and form smooth pulp. Place the mixture on each leaf, roll up and, if necessary, hold with toothpicks. Arrange the goɀł.bki side by side in a buttered saucepan, pour over the hot stock and bake in a preheated oven for about 40 mins.

serves 4 • Preparation: 20 mins • Baking: 50–60 mins

Chinese cabbage salad with leeks

1 small head Chinese cabbage (400–500 g), 2 leeks (white part only), 1 tart apple, 1 tbsp lemon juice

DRESSING: 2 tsps wine vinegar, 1 tsp honey, salt, ¼ tsp ground caraway seeds, ¼ tsp dried thyme, 4–5 tbsps salad oil

Mix the honey with salt, caraway seeds, thyme and wine vinegar, gradually drizzling in the oil. Chill the sauce. Peel and coarsely grate the apple. Sprinkle with lemon juice. Wash the leeks thoroughly and cut them into thin strips, do likewise with the Chinese cabbage. Combine the cabbage with the apple and leeks, pour over the dressing, mix well.

serves 4–6 • Preparation: 10–15 mins

Baked Chinese cabbage with sprouts

1 large head Chinese cabbage (about 800 g), 2 cups wheat sprouts, 50 g raisins, 50 g pitted prunes, 1 glass dry white wine, 3 eggs, 3 tbsps butter, salt,1 tsp finely chopped fresh ginger (or powdered ginger)

Scald the cabbage and separate the leaves. Scald the raisins and prunes, drain. Cut the prunes into strips, combine with the raisins and pour over the wine. Cream 2 tbsps butter until frothy, gradually adding the egg yolks, a pinch of ginger and salt. Combine with the wheat sprouts, raisins, prunes and stiff beaten egg whites. Butter an ovenproof dish and line it snugly with half of the cabbage leaves. Cover with the mixture prepared with the sprouts, cover with the remaining leaves (the cabbage leaves and the sprout mixture should reach to half the height of the dish, as they will grow in volume). Cover the dish and place it in a preheated oven for about 20 mins. Serve with sauces, e.g. bechamel sauce.

serves 4 • Preparation:15–20 mins • Baking: 20 mins

Stewed Chinese cabbage with apricots

1 head Chinese cabbage (about 800 g), 100 g dried apricots, 30 g raisins, 3 onions, juice of 1 lemon, 1 tsp finely chopped fresh ginger (or powdered ginger), 2–3 tbsps butter, 1 cup dry white wine, 1–3 bay leaves, 5–7 cloves, salt, pepper

Cut the washed apricots into strips, wash the raisins, drain. Finely chop 2 onions, lard the third one with cloves and bay leaves.Wash and dry the cabbage and cut it finely. In a saucepan melt the butter, sauté the onions, add the chopped ginger, raisins, apricots and cabbage. Stir and fry for a moment or two. Season with salt and pepper, pour in the wine and add the clove-stuck onion. Bring to the boil and simmer uncovered for about 30 mins, stirring from time to time. Discard the onion, steam off the excess liquid, adjust seasoning, add lemon juice and mix well together. Serve with rice, or as a side dish with white meat.

serves 4–6 • Preparation: 40 mins

Savoy cabbage

Stuffed savoy cabbage

Remove the outer leaves from the cabbage. Cut the cabbage into four quarters, blanch them, take out and drain well. Open out the leaves one by one and put in a stuffing made from chopped sheep's kidneys and suet, mixed with two eggs, seasoned with salt and pepper. Put a bit of stuffing in between the leaves. Secure the cabbage quarters with thread, put them into a skillet. Add several spoonfuls of butter and several spoonfuls of stock and cook over a low heat, taking care that the cabbage does not burn. When the cabbage is tender, brown one spoonful of flour with some butter and add the mixture to the sauce. Before serving, sprinkle with breadcrumbs.

(Praktyczny kucharz warszawski, 1926)

Savoy cabbage salad with pine nuts

1 small head savoy cabbage, 2 tbsps pine nuts

DRESSING: 4 tbsps olive oil, 2 tbsps lemon juice or wine vinegar, 1 tbsp honey, 2 tsp poppy seeds, ½ tsp cayenne pepper, ½ tsp celery seeds, or ¼ tsp celery salt, salt

Blanch the finely shredded cabbage for 1–2 mins in boiling water, drain, rinse with cold water, drain well again and combine with the pine nuts. Stir together the poppy seeds with honey, celery seeds, pepper, salt and lemon juice. Mix with the olive oil, pour over the salad, toss, cover and put in the fridge for 2–3 hours. Mix well before serving.

serves 4 • Preparation: 10 mins • Refrigerating: 2–3 hrs

Stewed savoy cabbage

1 head Savoy cabbage (about 1 kg), 2 tbsps cooking oil, 1 tbsp lard, 3 tbsps soya sauce, 1 tbsp sugar, ½ cup strong stock

Shred the washed cabbage. In a saucepan heat the oil with lard, add the cabbage and fry for 3–4 mins over high heat, stirring all the time. Pour in the soya sauce, sprinkle with sugar, mix well, add hot stock and simmer for about 15 mins. Makes an interesting side dish with cutlets and roasts.

serves 4 • Preparation: 20–25 mins

Savoy cabbage stewed with hazelnuts

1 head savoy cabbage (about 800 g), 200 g hazelnuts, juice of 1 lemon, ½ tsp grated lemon rind, 3 tbsps honey, salt, pepper, 3 tbsps butter, 2–3 tbsps dry white wine, ¼ cup boiled water or light stock

Shred the cabbage and sprinkle lightly with salt. Melt the butter with honey in a saucepan, add the cabbage (squeeze out the excess moisture) and sauté for a few minutes, stirring all the time. Sprinkle with lemon juice and water, add pepper and grated lemon rind, mix, cover and simmer for about half an hour. Chop the hazelnuts finely, add to the cabbage, sprinkle with the wine, cover and simmer for 10–15 mins. Season with salt and pepper, if desired.

serves 4 • Salting: 10 mins • Preparation: 20–25 mins

Savoy cabbage head stuffed with meat

1 head savoy cabbage (1–1.20 kg), salt, 1 tbsp wine vinegar, 1 tsp caraway seeds

STUFFING: 500 g mince meat, 100 g streaky bacon, 2 tbsps tomato paste, 1 cup cooked rice, 2 onions, 2–3 garlic cloves, 3–4 dried mushrooms, 3 tbsps chopped walnuts, 3 tbsps chopped parsley, 2 eggs, cayenne pepper, salt, pepper, 2 tbsps cooking oil, 1 cup strong stock

Soak the washed mushrooms in a little boiled water. Cook and finely cut. Cut the bacon into small cubes, chop the onion and garlic. In the frying pan heat 1 tbsp oil, add the onion, garlic and half of the bacon and fry for a moment or two, stir. Remove from the heat, set aside to cool. Mix the rice well with the walnuts, chopped parsley and tomato paste. Put the minced meat into a bowl, add the rice, half of the chopped mushrooms, fried onion and garlic. Season with salt, pepper and cayenne pepper, break in the eggs and form smooth, uniform paste. In a big saucepan bring to the boil salted water with vinegar and cara-

way seeds. Add the cabbage and cook for a few minutes, turning it over 2–3 times. Take out, rinse with cold water, drain in a sieve. Spread the cabbage leaves apart, careful not to separate them from the stump. Place the prepared stuffing between individual leaves, starting from the inside. Leave out large outer leaves without the stuffing. Wrap the cabbage head with thread. In a large saucepan heat the oil, fry the remaining bacon and add the stuffed cabbage head. Sprinkle with the remaining mushrooms, pour in the stock and the mushroom stock, cover and stew over low heat for about 60–80 mins.

serves 4 • Preparation: 25–30 mins • Stewing: 1½ hrs

Stewed savoy cabbage leaves

1 head savoy cabbage (about 1 kg), 50 g lean smoked bacon, 1 tsp lard, 1 small onion, 4–5 garlic cloves, 1 bay leaf, ½ tsp caraway seeds, ¼ cup dry white wine, ¼ cup light stock, salt, pepper, lemon juice

Cut the washed cabbage in four, remove the stump. Melt the lard in a saucepan and brown the diced bacon. Add the chopped onion and garlic, stir and fry for a moment. Add the cabbage quarters, bay leaf, salt, pepper and caraway seeds, pour in the hot stock and wine, bring to the boil, cover and simmer for about 20 mins. Uncover and steam off the excess liquid. Remove the bay leaf. Season to taste with lemon juice, salt and pepper, if desired. Serve with roast duck, pork or goose.

serves 4 • Preparation: 30–40 mins

Stuffed savoy cabbage

1 head savoy cabbage, 1 cup cooked soya beans, ½ cup cooked rice, 50 g raisins, 50 g peanuts, 1 egg, grated rind of 1 lemon, ¼ tsp cinnamon, ¼ tsp cardamom, 2 tbsps butter, salt

Wash the raisins and soak them in the wine for a few minutes. In a food processor mix the cooked soya beans with peanuts, combine with the rice and drained raisins, season with salt, cardamom, cinnamon and grated lemon rind, add the egg, mix well. Put the cabbage head (choose a loose one) into boiling water and cook for a few minutes. Carefully remove it, rinse with cold water, drain and delicately spread the leaves. Starting from the centre stuff the cabbage with the prepared mixture. Tie up with cotton thread. In a large saucepan melt the butter, put in the cabbage, sprinkle with the wine in which the raisins were soaking, cover and simmer for about 30 mins. Before serving, arrange the cabbage on a warmed dish, cut it into quarters. Serve sprinkled with melted butter or tomato sauce.

serves 4 • Preparation: 20 mins • Stewing: 30–35 mins

Carrot

T he ancient Greeks called it *philtron*, or love potion, and indeed it was once used for preparing such concoctions. Old Arab recipes recommended regular consumption of carrots stewed in milk as a very effective means of awakening passion and improving sexual prowess. In Elizabethan England in the 16th century it was still regarded as the fruit of the goddess Venus. Today, doctors and dieticians tell elderly people to drink carrot juice with milk in order to refresh and improve the functioning of the whole system.

The carrot is an easily digested low-calorie vegetable (30 Cal per 100 g), very rich in various nutritive elements, vitamins and minerals. It is not only tasty and filling, but has also many healing properties: it improves the functioning of the liver and has a beneficial effect in treating stomach ulcers and inflammation of the mucous membrane of the stomach and intestines.

Carrots improve eyesight and increase the red cell count. And finally something that smokers should keep in mind: Professor W. Dontewill of Hamburg has discovered that provitamin A, contained in carrots, blocks the action of benzpyrene, a carcinogen in cigarette smoke, and transforms it into substances which are not harmful to your health.

In the kitchen, you may use this vegetable in many different ways. You should only remember to add fat (olive oil, butter or cream) to hot carrot dishes, because carotene dissolves in fat and only then turns into vitamin A.

Small carrots can be cooked whole, while larger ones should be cut into slices or cubes. They must be cooked in a small amount of water (or wine, or light stock) with a bit of butter and sugar, for 10–15 minutes or else steamed for about 20 minutes. They should not be overcooked, but kept firm and crispy. You may alter the flavour of carrots by adding herbs and spices, such as mint, aniseed, fennel, coriander, ginger, allspice, cayenne or curry powder.

Steamed carrots

Peel and rinse the carrots, cook them in stock, then purée them. Take 5 egg yolks, a handful of flour, one tablespoon of butter, half a cup of finely chopped bitter almonds, and a cup of sugar. Mix everything thoroughly with the purée. Put into a baking tin greased with butter and place the tin in a large pan of boiling water. Cover and steam. Before serving, pour over the whole a sauce made from sweet cream, egg yolks and sugar, with some cherry or other red juice added.

(M. Marciszewska, *Doskonała kuchnia*)

Carrot salad in black mustard seed dressing

4 large carrots, 3 tbsps cooking oil, 2 tbsp black mustards seeds, 2 tbsps lemon juice, 1 tsp honey, salt

P eel and wash the carrots, grate them coarsely and mix with honey, sprinkle with lemon juice and salt. In a frying pan, heat the oil, put in the mustard seeds and cover tightly. Keep over low heat until the seeds stop popping. Remove from the heat, pour the oil over the carrots, mix well.

serves 4 • Preparation: 10 mins

Carrot salad with fennel bulbs

3 large carrots, 2 tart apples, 2 small fennel bulbs, salt, pepper, 3 tbsps lemon juice, 1 tsp honey, 3–4 tbsps olive oil, 3–4 tbsps sesame seeds

P eel, was and dry the carrots, apples and fennel bulbs. Grate coarsely and sprinkle with lemon juice, mix well. Blend the lemon juice with honey, salt and pepper, combine with the olive oil. Pour the dressing over the salad, mix well, cover and refrigerate. In a hot frying pan dry roast sesame seeds. Finely chop fennel leaves. Sprinkle the well-chilled salad with the sesame seeds and fennel leaves.

serves 4–6 • Preparation: 10–15 mins • Refrigerating: 1 hr

Carrot salad with mint

4 large carrots, 2–3 tbsps oil, salt, pepper, 1 tbsp lemon juice, 2 tbsps chopped fresh mint, 1–2 tbsps sesame seeds, 1 sprig mint

Coarsely grate the peeled and washed carrots, sprinkle with oil and lemon juice, salt and pepper, mix, cover and refrigerate for an hour. In a hot frying pan dry roast sesame seeds. Before serving, sprinkle the salad with the sesame seeds and decorate with mint leaves.

serves 4 • Preparation: 10–15 mins • Cooling: 1 hr

Stewed carrots with tarragon

1 kg carrots, 1½ tbsps chopped fresh (or 1½ tsp dried) tarragon leaves, 3 tbsps butter, 1 glass dry red wine, ½ cup single cream, 1 tsp flour, 1–2 garlic cloves, 1 tsp honey, salt

Slice the peeled and washed carrots. In a saucepan melt the butter, add the carrots and fry for a few minutes, stirring from time to time. Towards the end of frying add the honey, garlic minced with salt, and tarragon. Mix well, pour in the cream blended with flour, mix again and heat.

serves 4–6 • Preparation: 45–50 mins

Carrots stewed with onion

1 kg carrots, 250 g small onions (shallots or spring onions), 1 tbsp olive oil, 1 tbsp butter, 2–3 garlic cloves, 1½ tbsps chopped fresh (or 1 tsp dried) thyme

Carrot salad with fennel bulbs

leaves, 2 bay leaves, 1–2 tbsps chopped parsley,
2–3 tbsps dry white wine, 2–3 tbsps cream

Dice the peeled and washed carrots. In a flat saucepan with a thick bottom heat the oil, add the carrots and butter and stir and fry for a moment or two. Stir in the peeled onions and fry together for 5–6 mins, then add garlic minced with salt, bay leaves, and sprinkle with the wine. Mix well, cover and simmer for about 20 mins. Add the cream and thyme, mix again and continue to simmer for 10–12 mins.

serves 4–6 • Preparation: 45–50 mins

Young carrots in mint sauce

2 bunches young carrots, 2 tbsps sesame seeds,
3 tbsps finely chopped mint leaves, juice and grated
rind of 1 lemon, 2 tbsps olive oil, ½ cup stock, salt,
pepper, 4 tbsps young green peas, powdered nutmeg

Peel the carrots and cut them into quarters. In a frying pan, heat the oil, put in the sesame seeds and fry them golden brown. Add the carrots and continue to fry for a little while, stirring all the time. Then add salt, pepper, nutmeg, lemon juice and grated lemon rind, green peas and stock. Mix well and simmer for a few minutes over low heat. Just before serving sprinkle with mint.

serves 4–6 • Preparation: 20 mins

Oriental delicacy with carrot

1 kg carrots, 4–5 cardamom seeds, a walnut-
size piece of ginger, juice of 1 lemon, 1 cup
yogurt, 1 cup sweet cream, 100 g butter, salt,
pepper, 1 tsp honey, 2 tbsps almond flakes

Pound the cardamom seeds in a mortar. Cut the peeled and washed carrots into thin slices, finely chop the ginger. Melt the butter in a saucepan, add the carrots and fry for a few moments, stirring all the time. Add the cardamom and fry together for 3–4 mins, add ginger, salt, pepper and mix well. Butter an ovenproof serving platter, arrange the carrots. Mix well lemon juice with honey, yogurt and cream and pour over the carrots. Bake in a preheated oven for 30 mins. Just before serving, sprinkle with almond flakes.

Serve as a hot snack, or as a hot side dish with roast poultry and white meats.

serves 4 • Preparation: 10 mins • Baking: 30 mins

Baked carrots

500 g carrots, ¼ cup lemon juice, ¼ apple purée,
½ tsp powdered ginger, 1 tbsp butter, salt

Cut the peeled and washed carrots into slices, combine with ginger, apple purée and tomato juice, sprinkle with salt. Butter an ovenproof serving platter, arrange the carrots and bake for 40 mins in a preheated oven. Makes an interesting side dish with white meats, or a light meal with rice.

serves 4 • Preparation: 10 mins • Baking: 40 mins

Stuffed carrots

6 large carrots, 1 tbsp butter, salt

STUFFING: 100 g smoked ham, 2 tbsps cooked kasha,
1 small onion, 1 tbsp butter, 2 tbsps thick cream, salt

Sauté the chopped onion in melted butter, add the finely chopped ham and fry together for a moment. Add the kasha and cream, mix well and season to taste. Remove from the heat. Cut the peeled carrots lengthwise, remove the yellow cores. Place the carrots in salted boiling water, cook 6–7 mins, remove, rinse with cold water, dry. Stuff them with the prepared mixture, arrange in a buttered ovenproof dish, sprinkle with melted butter, bake for about 20 mins. Serve with toasted white bread, or with potato purée and cooked green peas.

serves 3 • Preparation: 10–12 mins • Baking: 20 mins

Carrots, Lithuanian style

6 large carrots, 1 tbsp butter, salt, 8–10 dried cepes,
2 onions, 2 tbsps butter, 1 tbsp flour, 2 tbsps thick
cream, 2 tbsps finely chopped parsley, salt, pepper

Soak the washed cepes overnight in a little cold water. Cook the following day and chop. Cut the washed carrots lengthwise in half, remove the root ends. Put the carrots into salted boiling water for 5–6 mins, drain, rinse with cold water, set aside to cool. Finely chop the onions and sauté them in butter, add the mushrooms, cook together for a few minutes, season with salt and pepper to taste. In a small saucepan melt 1 tbsp butter, add the flour, make a white roux and dilute it with the mushroom stock. Simmer stirring all the time until the sauce thickens. Add the cream and fried mushrooms with onion and heat over low heat, stirring all the time. The mixture should be thick. Remove from the heat, mix with chopped parsley. Stuff the carrot halves with the mixture, arrange on an ovenproof serving platter, and bake for about 20 mins, from time to time basting with melted butter.

serves 4 • Soaking: 12 hours • Preparation: 30 mins • Baking: 20 mins

Cauliflower

Once called Cyprus cabbage, the cauliflower was known already to the Romans. It was brought to Poland before the times of Queen Bona, but it began to be grown on a larger scale only in the late 16th and early 17th centuries. In the 19th century, it was usually served 'Polish style', with melted butter mixed with browned breadcrumbs, or else 'French style', meaning *au gratin*, or baked with bechamel sauce. When you prepare the cauliflower, you should first cut off the green leaves and all blemishes, then rinse it and soak in salted water for several minutes. Cauliflower should be cooked in an uncovered pan and it is a good idea to add some bread crust to the water, which reduces the strong smell of the vegetable.

Apart from the traditional white cauliflower, green cauliflowers are also available. These have much smaller, peaked florets and contain more proteins and minerals and less fibre than the white variety, which means that they are easier to digest. Green cauliflowers are prepared in the same way as the white ones, that is, they can be boiled, broiled or baked. Both can be also eaten raw by themselves or in salads.

Cauliflower au gratin

Cook the cauliflower in the ordinary way in a large amount of salted water. Make a thick white sauce from some cauliflower stock, add an egg yolk and cream, as well as several drops of lemon juice. Put the cooked cauliflower into a skillet, coat with the sauce, sprinkle with Parmesan and breadcrumbs, and then with some melted butter. Put into a hot oven and brown it nicely towards the end.

(Antoni Teslar, *Kuchnia polsko-francuska*, 1910)

Cauliflower green salad

1 green cauliflower, salt, 1 tsp butter, 1 tsp sugar, 1 tbsp lemon juice, 2 tbsps chopped parsley, 2 tbsps chopped chives, 3 tbsps salad oil, 1 tbsp mustard, 1 tsp honey, salt

Mix well the honey with mustard and salt, gradually adding the oil. Boil some salted water with sugar, butter and lemon juice, add the cauliflower and cook for 10 mins. Drain, cool and divide it into florets. Place them in a serving dish, cover with the dressing and set aside in the fridge. Before serving, mix with chopped parsley and chives.

serves 4 • Preparation: 10–12 mins • Refrigerating: 1 hr

Cauliflower salad

1 small cauliflower, 1 tsp butter, 1 tbsp lemon juice, 1 tsp sugar, salt, 1 cup chopped borage leaves, 2 tbsps borage flowers, 1 tbsp chopped parsley

DRESSING: ½ cup yogurt, 2–3 tbsps thick mayonnaise, 2–3 garlic cloves minced with salt, pepper, a pinch of sugar, and a pinch of grated nutmeg

Bring to the boil some salted water with butter, lemon juice and sugar. Wash the cauliflower and boil for about 20 mins. Drain, cool and divide into florets. Combine with the borage leaves. Mix well the dressing ingredients and chill. Pour the dressing over the cauliflower, mix and sprinkle with chopped parsley and borage flowers.

serves 4 • Preparation: 30 mins

Cauliflower in herbal dressing

1 cauliflower, juice of 1 lemon, 1 cup light
stock, 2 tbsps butter, 1 tbsp flour,
½ cup double cream, 2 tbsps chopped
borage leaves, 1 tbsp chopped parsley,
1 tbsp chopped fresh basil, 1 tsp chopped
fresh lemon balm leaves, 1 tsp chopped yarrow,
1 tsp chopped fresh dill, 1 tsp chopped chives,
2 tbsps borage flowers, salt, pepper, sugar

Cook the cauliflower in salted water with 1 tsp butter, a pinch of sugar and 1 tsp lemon juice. Disolve a stock cube in a cup of the stock in which the cauliflower was cooking. Melt the butter in a small saucepan, add the flour and make a roux. Dilute it with the cold stock, season to taste with salt, pepper, sugar and lemon juice and, stirring constantly, cook it over low heat until the sauce thickens. Mix the chopped herbs with the cream and pour into the sauce. Stir and heat (do not boil!). Place the cooked cauliflower in a ovenproof dish, pour over the sauce and put it in a preheated oven for a few minutes.

serves 4 • Preparation: 30–35 mins

Baked cauliflower with herbs

1 large cauliflower, 1 large onion,
2–3 tbsps butter, 4 eggs, 4–5 tbsps
chopped dill, 1 tbsp chopped
coriander leaves, 1 tbsp chopped fresh
mint, 1 tbsp chopped parsley, salt, pepper,
1 tbsp lemon juice, 1 tbsp sugar

Cook the cauliflower in salted water with sugar, lemon juice and 1 tsp butter. Remove, drain and rinse with cold water. Divide into florets. In a frying pan, melt 1 tbsp butter and sauté the finely chopped onion. Butter an ovenproof dish and arrange the cauliflower florets. Sprinkle them with the sautéd onion and chopped dill. Beat the eggs with a wire whisk, add salt, pepper and the chopped herbs, and pour over the cauliflower. Bake in a preheated oven for 15–20 mins.

serves 4 • Preparation: 35–40 mins

Cauliflower goulash

1 large cauliflower, 500 g tomatoes,
300–400 g poultry sausage, 2 onions,
2 sweet green peppers, 1 tbsp hot paprika,
1 tbsp sweet paprika, salt, ¼ cup stock,
1 cup cream, salt

In a saucepan heat the oil and add the finely chopped onion. Cover and simmer for a moment or two. Sprinkle with the paprika, mix well. Add the skinned and sliced tomatoes and sweet pepper cut into strips. Cover again and simmer for about 15 mins. Divide the cauliflower into florets and cook it in salted water. Drain. Cut the sausage first into thick slices, then into strips. Put it to the saucepan together with the cauliflower, season with salt, sprinkle with the stock, mix well, cover and simmer for 5–6 mins, then add the cream, mix well and heat up.

serves 6–8 • Preparation: 30–35 mins

Cauliflower curry

1 large cauliflower, 250 g potatoes cooked
in their skins, 1 large onion, 1–2 garlic cloves,
1 large fleshy tomato, 2 tbsps sunflower
seeds, juice of 1 lemon and ¼ tsp grated
lemon rind, salt, 4 tbsps cooking oil,
1 tsp black mustard seeds, 1 tsp turmeric,
½ tsp ground coriander seeds, ¼ tsp cayenne
pepper, herbal salt, 1 cup light stock

Divide the cauliflower into florets, place them in a sieve and scald. Peel, dice and blanch the potatoes. In a saucepan heat the oil and add mustard seeds. Cover. When they stop popping, add the finely chopped onion, garlic, turmeric, coriander and cayenne pepper, and fry together for 5 mins, stirring constantly. Add the cauliflower florets and continue to fry for another 5 mins. Stir in the potatotes and simmer the whole for another 10 mins. Then add the tomato, grated lemon rind, sprinkle with lemon juice, mix well and add salt to taste. Sprinkle with the sunflower seeds. Best served with rice.

serves 4 • Preparation: 30–35 mins

Celeriac and celery

Celeriac and celery have been known for centuries as the vegetable of youth. The Romans believed in the aphrodisiac powers of celery and stuffed suckling piglets with the stems. Madame de Pompadour is said to have used them to cook various soups for Louis XV, apparently to very good effect. The Chinese still make many celery dishes, including beef, which are said to work wonders for male prowess. I could quote many more examples, but even though the latest research does not confirm the wonderful properties of this vegetable, let us not debunk the old myths, for without them life would be dull.

There are two varieties of this vegetable, one grown for its root and the other grown for its stems.

Celeriac, or **root celery**. Its young bulbous roots appear towards the end of May and the fully grown vegetable is harvested in November. Good celery root should be firm and unblemished.

Celeriac salads, sauces and side dishes stimulate the appetite and fortify the system. The flavour of the vegetable enhances the taste of soups, bakes and vegetable dishes. Celeriac is rich in phosphorus and sodium chloride (common salt).

The roots can be stuffed and served cold or hot, baked with cheese and sauces. The roots that are to be stuffed should be scrubbed thoroughly and cooked whole, then peeled, scooped out and filled with the stuffing of your choice. Highly recommended are creamed celeriac soups and celeriac purée. Remember that the peeled celeriac tends to darken quickly, therefore if you do not intend to cook it immediately, you should put it into water with some vinegar or lemon juice added. Celery roots cut into slices, cubes or sticks can be steamed, boiled or fried.

Celery. Celery is harvested from June to November. Its edible parts are the leaves and stems. The latter are 40–70 cm long and 3–4 cm broad. The stalks are fleshy and juicy; the whiter they grow, the tastier and less bitter they are. Celery is richer in minerals that celeriac. It has a high content of calcium, phosphorus and iron. Fresh celery juice is regarded as a very refreshing drink which soothes the nerves and improves the mood. It is recommended in antirheumatic diets and is excellent for hangovers.

Always buy fresh, light-coloured celery stalks, smooth and unblemished, with small green leaves.

Crispy celery stalks are an important element of cold buffets, serving both as garnishing and as 'spoons' for various dips, or else as appe- tizers served on sticks (together with ham, cheese, pineapple chunks, olives, kiwi slices, prunes). Celery can be eaten raw or cooked (for only 8 to 10 minutes), by itself or in salads, soups, sauces and meat and fish dishes. It can be baked with meat, vegetables, eggs, mushrooms, pasta and potatoes, and then served with tomato, bechamel or cream sauce, sprinkled with grated cheese.

Marinated celeriac

Peel young celery roots, slice them and blanch in salted water. Transfer them to a bowl, cover with vinegar boiled with pepper, allspice and bay leaves. Cover the bowl and leave overnight. The next day put the celery slices into jars, put in some chopped dill and parsley. Bring the vinegar to the boil and pour it over the celeriac while still hot. Seal the jars.

(Marja Śleżańska, *Kucharz polski*, 1932)

Celery boats stuffed with cheese

4–5 celery stalks, 150 g Roquefort-type cheese, 150 g full-fat cottage cheese, 2 tbsps butter, 2 tbsps finely chopped parsley, 4 pitted black olives, 4 cocktail gherkins, salt, pepper, sugar, a few drops of lemon juice

Blend the butter with salt, pepper, sugar and lemon juice. Put the cottage cheese and Roquefort through a mincer and gradually add to the butter, stirring all the time. Blend the whole into smooth pulp and mix with chopped parsley. Trim, wash and dry the celery stalks and cut them diagonally into sections of the same size. Fill in the celery stalks with the mixture, decorate with the halves of olives and with cocktail gherkins.

serves 4 • Preparation: 10–15 mins

Green snack of celeriac

800 g celeriac, 2 tbsps vinegar, 1 tsp butter, salt, sugar

DRESSING: 4 tbsps finely chopped parsley, 4 tbsps finely chopped chives, 1 tbsp chopped green celery leaves, 1 medium-large onion, 2–3 garlic cloves, 1 hard-boiled egg, 2–3 cocktail gherkins, ¾ cup mayonnaise, 2 tbsps mustard, salt, pepper, sugar

Boil some salted water with vinegar, butter and a pinch of sugar. Put in the scrubbed and washed celery roots and cook for about 40–50 mins. Drain, rinse with cold water, peel and cut into thin half-slices, and sprinkle with lemon juice.
PREPARE THE DRESSING: Mix well the mayonnaise with lemon juice, salt, pepper, sugar and mustard. Finely chop the gherkins, egg, onion and stir into the dressing. Pour over the cooled celeriac, toss and refrigerate.

serves 4–6 • Preparation: 1 hr • Refrigerating: 1 hr

Stuffed celeriac

4 small celery roots, ½ cup milk, 4 hard-boiled eggs, 3 tbsps finely chopped chives, 3 tbsps finely chopped parsley, 1 tbsp thick mayonnaise, ½ cup ketchup, salt, pepper, sugar, 1 lemon, leaves of lettuce, ½ orange pepper, celeriac leaves for decoration

Scrub well the celery roots, place them in a saucepan and cover with salted boiling water. Add the hot milk, bring to the boil, cover and cook over low heat for about 40–45 mins. Drain, rinse with cold water, peel and cut off the tops. Carefully scoop out the flesh with a teaspoon, leaving shells with 1 cm thick walls. Sprinkle with lemon juice. Finely cut the celeriac flesh and eggs. Combine with the chopped parsley and chopped chives. Blend the ketchup with mayonnaise, add salt, pepper, a dash of sugar and ½ tsp grated lemon rind. Mix gently but thoroughly. Fill in the celeriac shells with the stuffing. Arrange on lettuce leaves and decorate with strips of yellow pepper and celeriac leaves.

serves 4 • Preparation: 1 hr

Baked celery stalks

800 g celery stalks, 1 kg beef marrow bones, salt, pepper, 3 tbsps butter, 1 tbsp flour, ¼ cup single cream, 1 cup dry white wine or stock, 1 tsp lemon juice, a pinch of salt, pepper and sugar, 2 tbsps grated cheese, 1 tbsp breadcrumbs

In a small saucepan melt 1½ tbsps butter, add the flour and make a roux. Dilute it with the wine and cook stirring until the sauce thickens. Season to taste with salt, pepper, sugar and lemon juice, mix with the cream. Take the sauce off the heat. Cut off the leaves of celery stalks and chop them finely. Add to the sauce and cut the stalks into halves. Put the marrow bones put into boiling water for 2–3 mins, then extract the marrow with a wooden spoon handle. Cut into pieces. Butter an ovenproof serving dish, line it with the celery stalks, sprinkle with salt and pepper and coat with slices of the marrow. Top with the sauce, sprinkle with the cheese blended with breadcrumbs and top with dabs of butter. Bake in a preheated (200°C) oven for 40–45 mins. Best served as a hot snack with fresh wholemeal or white bread.

serves 4–6 • Preparation: 10–15 mins • Baking: 40–45 mins

Celeriac in onion bechamel sauce

1 large celery root (600–700 g), 2 large onions, 3 tbsps butter, 1 tbsp flour, 1 cup stock, 1 cup single cream, 2 egg yolks, salt, pepper, 1 tbsp lemon juice, ¼ tsp grated lemon rind, a pinch of sugar, 2 tbsps chopped celeriac leaves, 2 tbsps chopped parsley, 3–4 tbsps grated sharp cheese

Place a well scrubbed celery root in some lightly salted boiling water and cook it for about 20–25 mins. Remove, drain and rinse with cold water. Peel and cut into slices. In a large deep frying pan melt 1 tbsp butter, add the finely chopped onion and fry over high heat for a moment or two. Add ½ cup stock and simmer for 15 mins. Mix together in a food processor and put through a sieve. In a saucepan melt 1 tbsp butter, add the flour and make a white roux. Dilute it with the cold stock and cook over low heat until the sauce thickens. Add the sieved onion, salt, pepper, lemon juice and lemon rind, mix thoroughly. Blend the egg yolks with the cream and the chopped greens, stir in the sauce and heat until thick (do not boil!). Butter an ovenproof dish and arrange the celeriac slices, pour over the sauce and sprinkle with the grated cheese. Bake in a preheated oven for about 25 mins. Serve it as a hot snack, or a side dish with the main course.

serves 4–6 • Preparation: 30 mins • Baking: 25 mins

Celeriac salad with peaches

1 large celeriac, 2 tbsps lemon juice, 2–3 large peaches (tinned, if preferred), 3 tbsps raisins, 1 tbsp rum, 2 tbsps mayonnaise, 2 tbsps yogurt, salt, celeriac leaves, ½ peach

Place a well-scrubbed celeriac for 3–4 mins in some lightly salted boiling water. Drain, rinse with cold water, peel and cut into julienne, sprinkle with lemon juice. Scald the raisins and pour over the rum. Cut the peaches (peeled and stoned) into thin strips and combine with the celeriac and raisins, pour over the yogurt mixed with mayonnaise and salt. Refrigerate. Before serving, toss and decorate with peach slices and celeriac leaves.

serves 4–6 • Preparation: 10 mins

Celery salad with marinated mushrooms

500 g celery stalks, ½ cup chopped marinated mushrooms, 2–4 hard fleshy tomatoes, 4 tbsps chopped tarragon leaves, 4 tbsps olive oil, 1 tbsp wine vinegar, salt, pepper, sugar to taste

Trim the celery stalks and put them for 2–3 mins into some boiling salted water. Drain, rinse with cold water, drain again, slice and combine with the chopped mushrooms and half of the chopped tarragon. Sprinkle with vinegar, pour over the oil and sprinkle with salt, pepper and sugar. Mix well and refrigerate. Arrange in a serving bowl, decorate with tomato quarters and sprinkle with the remaining tarragon.

serves 4 • Preparation: 10 mins

Celery salad with walnuts

1 large celery, ½ cup chopped walnuts, 2 firm gherkins, 1 tart apple, 1 hard-boiled egg, 3 tbsps

yogurt, 2 tbsps mayonnaise, salt, pepper, sugar, 2 tbsps finely chopped celery leaves or parsley

Wash and peel the celery stalk and cut it into thin slices. Peel and dice the apple, combine with the celery and walnuts. Blend the yogurt with mayonnaise, salt, pepper and sugar, pour it over the salad, toss and refrigerate. Before serving, sprinkle with chopped egg yolk and celery leaves, decorate with strips of egg white.

serves 4 • Preparation: 5–7 mins • Refrigerating: 30–40 mins

Celeriac salad with mushrooms

1 medium-sized celeriac, 1 large tart apple, 200 g purple plums, 200 g button mushrooms, ½ cup chopped walnuts, ½ cup green peas (tinned or freshly cooked), 2 tbsps raisins, 1 tbsp brandy, 3–4 tbsps mayonnaise, salt, pepper, sugar and cayenne pepper, juice of 1 lemon

FOR DECORATION: walnut halves, 1–2 plums and some celeriac leaves

Mix well the mayonnaise with salt, pepper, sugar and 1 tbsp lemon juice, set aside to cool. Wash and dry the mushrooms, cut into strips, sprinkle with lemon juice and cayenne pepper. Scald the raisins, put them in a bowl and soak in the brandy for 1 hour. Scrub well the celeriac root and cook for 15–20 mins in salted boiling water. Drain, rinse with cold water, peel, cut into thin matchsticks and sprinkle with lemon juice. Coarsely grate the peeled apple and sprinkle it with lemon juice. Cut the pitted plums into thin strips. Combine the drained green peas with the plums, mushrooms, raisins, celeriac and apple, add the walnuts and pour over the dressing. Toss and refrigerate. Before serving, decorate with the halves of walnuts, plums and celeriac leaves.

serves 6–8 • Macerating: 1 hour • Preparation: 20 mins • Refrigerating: 30–40 mins

Savoury celeriac salad with cheese

1 medium celeriac root, 1 tbsp lemon juice, 250 g Emmental or GruyŹre cheese, 1 smallish onion, 1 bunch spring onions, 2–3 garlic cloves

DRESSING: 2 tbsps lemon juice, 1 tsp hot mustard, 3 tbsps olive oil, 1 tbsp cream, 1 tbsp mayonnaise, salt, pepper

Mix well the dressing ingredients, cover and refrigerate. Place the well-scrubbed celeriac root in lightly salted boiling water and cook for 15 mins. Drain, rinse with cold water, peel and cut into matchsticks. Combine all the ingredients of the salad, top with the dressing, mix well, cover and refrigerate for 1 hour. Before serving, sprinkle with chopped spring onions.

serves 4 • Preparation: 20 mins • Refrigerating: 1 hr

Celeriac salad with ham

1 small celery root, 1 tbsp lemon juice, 1 large onion, 1 tsp olive oil and 1 tsp lemon juice, 100 g lean ham, 1 tsp chopped parsley, 1 tsp chopped fresh thyme, 1 tsp fresh tarragon, 2 tbsps chopped walnuts, 2 hard-boiled eggs, 1 small tomato, parsley sprigs for decoration

DRESSING: 2–3 tbsps mayonnaise, sugar, salt and pepper, 1 tsp Worcestershire sauce

Sprinkle the finely chopped onion with lemon juice and olive oil, mix well. Place the well scrubbed celeriac root in some lightly salted boiling water and cook for 5–7 mins, drain and rinse with cold water, then peel, cut into thin matchsticks and sprinkle with lemon juice. Dice the ham and egg whites and combine with the celeriac and onion. Mix the dressing ingredients and pour over the salad. Cover and refrigerate for 30–40 mins. Before serving, mix with the chopped herbs and walnuts, sprinkle with chopped egg yolks and decorate the top with tomato quarters and parsley sprigs.

serves 4 • Preparation: 15 mins • Refrigerating: 30–40 mins

Polish celeriac salad

1 celery root, 1 boiled or roasted chicken breast, 1 cooked cauliflower, 1 cup chopped walnuts, salt, pepper, 2 tbsps lemon juice, 4–5 tbsps mayonnaise, ½ sweet red pepper, sprigs of dill

Cook the well-scrubbed celeriac root for about 15 mins in some salted boiling water. Remove, rinse with cold water, peel and cut into thin matchsticks, sprinkle with lemon juice. Divide the cooked cauliflower into florets, dice the chicken. Combine all the ingredients with the walnuts, season to taste with salt and pepper, blend with the mayonnaise, refrigerate. Before serving, decorate with strips of pepper and sprigs of dill.

serves 6–8 • Preparation: 20–25 mins • Refrigerating: 30–40 mins

Vegetarian celeriac salad

1 large celery root, 2 tbsps lemon juice, 2 celery stalks, ½ cup pitted sour cherries, 1 cup diced pineapple (tinned or fresh), 200 g mild cheese, ½ cup chopped walnuts, 1 cup kefir, salt, sugar, sprigs of parsley

Trim and peel the celery stalks, cut them into thin slices, and cut the cheese into small sticks. Put the celery root into lightly salted boiling water and cook for 5–6 mins. Drain and rinse with cold water, then peel, grate and sprinkle with lemon juice. Combine all the ingredients of the salad. Mix the kefir with salt, sugar and chopped walnuts. Pour over the salad and mix well. Set aside in the fridge to cool. Before serving, decorate with cherries and sprigs of parsley.

serves 6–8 • Preparation: 15 mins • Refrigerating: 30–40 mins

Breaded celeriac patties

2 large celery roots, 2 tbsps lemon juice, salt, pepper, flour, 1 egg, breadcrumbs, oil for frying

Cook the well-scrubbed celery roots for 10 mins in salted boiling water. Drain, rinse with cold water, peel and cut into slices, and sprinkle with lemon juice. Mix the egg with 1 tbsp water, salt and pepper. Coat the celery slices with flour, egg and breadcrumbs, and fry in hot oil until golden brown. Serve with salads.

serves 4 • Preparation: 20–25 mins

Celeriac in beer batter

2 large celery roots (about 1 kg), ½ cup milk, 1 tsp vegetable seasoning, 2 tbsps lemon juice

BATTER: 1½ cup light beer, 3 eggs, 3 tbsps finely chopped parsley, 3 tbsps chopped chives, 1 tsp dry basil, salt, pepper, oil for frying

Bring to the boil some water with vegetable seasoning, pour in the milk, add the well-scrubbed celery roots and cook over low heat for about 30–35 mins. Drain, rinse with cold water, peel and cut into thick slices, then sprinkle with lemon juice. Sift the flour into a bowl, add the egg yolks and mix, gradually adding the beer. Mix the batter well and add salt, pepper and basil. Cover and set aside for 30 mins. Now add the chopped parsley, chives and the stiff beaten egg whites. Mix gently but thoroughly. Immerse the slices of celeriac in the batter and fry them in hot oil on both sides until golden. Drain the excess oil and serve immediately with spicy salads.

serves 4 • Preparation: 40–45 mins

Baked celeriac with turkey ham

2 large celery roots (about 800 g), 300 g turkey ham, 1 red sweet pepper, 100 g cheese, 1 raw egg, ½ cup double cream, 3 tbsps chopped parsley, 2 tbsps butter, salt, pepper, a dash of nutmeg, ¼ tsp grated lemon rind, 2 tbsp lemon juice

Bring to the boil some salted water with lemon rind and 1 tbsp lemon juice. Peel and dice the celeriac and sprinkle with lemon juice. Place the celeriac in boiling water and cook for about 20 mins. Drain. Cut the ham into cubes, grate the cheese. Mix well half of the cheese with the cream and egg, and in a food processor blend with the celeriac, salt, pepper and nutmeg. Stir in the ham (200 g). Trim and wash the pepper, scald it, rinse with cold water and cut into very small pieces. Butter an ovenproof dish, line it with half of the celeriac, sprinkle generously with the chopped sweet pepper and top with the remaining celeriac. Sprinkle with the ham and cheese and dot the whole with butter. Bake for about 30 mins in a hot oven. Before serving, sprinkle generously with parsley. Serve with lettuce salad, or mixed spicy salads.

serves 4–6 • Preparation: 30 mins • Baking: 30 mins

Baked celery with ham

3 bunches celery stalks, 300 g sliced lean ham, 2 tbsps butter, 1 tbsp flour, ½ cup single cream, 3 tbsps grated mild cheese, salt, pepper, 1 tbsp lemon juice, ¼ tsp grated lemon rind, a dash of sugar, 1–2 tbsps dry white wine

Trim and wash the celery, cut off the leaves. Cut the stalks into 10 cm long pieces and put them for 2–3 mins into salted boiling water. Drain, rinse with cold water, dry. Finely chop the celery leaves. In a small saucepan melt 1 tbsp butter, add the flour and make a roux. Dilute it with the wine (or stock), add salt, pepper, sugar, lemon rind and lemon juice, mix well and heat up until the sauce thickens. Pour in the cream, add the celery leaves, mix well and heat up. Wrap the celery stalks in slices of ham and arrange them snugly in a buttered ovenproof dish. Pour over the sauce, sprinkle with the grated cheese and dot with butter. Bake in a preheated oven for about 30–40 mins.

serves 4 • Preparation: 15 mins • Baking: 30–40 mins

Celeriac stuffed with cured pork shoulder

4 large celery roots, 1 tbsp lemon juice, 100 g cured pork shoulder or bacon, 3 tbsp chopped walnuts, 1 large onion, 1 tbsp tomato concentrate, 1 egg, salt, pepper, a pinch of sugar, 2 tbsps butter, ¼ cup stock, 4 slices cheese, 2 tbsps breadcrumbs

Put the well-washed celeriac roots in some salted boiling water and cook for about 15–20 mins. Drain, rinse with cold water, peel, cut off the tops and gently scoop part of the flesh. Sprinkle the insides with lemon juice. In a frying pan melt 1 tsp butter and sauté the finely chopped onion, add the tomato concentrate, sugar, salt and pepper, mix well and remove from the heat. Finely chop the celeriac flesh, cut the cured pork shoulder into small cubes. Combine the chopped celeriac flesh with the onion, walnuts, pork shoulder, 1 tbsp breadcrumbs and egg. Blend together well. Fill the hollowed celeriac with the stuffing. Butter a baking dish, sprinkle it with breadcrumbs, arrange the stuffed celery roots and sprinkle them with the stock. Top each celeriac with a slice of cheese, dot with butter and bake in a preheated oven for about 30 mins. Serve as a main course with potatoes or rice and mixed salads, or as a hot snack.

serves 4 • Preparation: 30 mins • Baking: 30 mins

Celeriac stuffed with minced chicken

4 large celery roots, juice and grated rind of 1 lemon, 4 tbsps butter

STUFFING: 300 g minced chicken meat, 1 small onion, 2 tbsps chopped dill, salt, pepper, ¼ tsp grated nutmeg, 1 egg

SAUCE: 1 tbsp flour, ¼ cup chicken stock, 1 cup cream, 1 tbsp lemon juice, salt, pepper, sugar, grated nutmeg and ground ginger, 1 tbsp tomato concentrate, 3 tbsps grated cheese, 2 tbsps chopped dill

Place the well-scrubbed celeriac in some salted boiling water and cook for about 15–20 mins. Drain and rinse with cold water, peel and cut off the tops. Gently scoop out some of the flesh, leaving 1½ cm thick shells. Sprinkle the insides with lemon juice. Dice the reserved celeriac pulp and sprinkle it with lemon juice, a little salt and pepper and grated nutmeg. Sauté the finely chopped onion in 1 tbsp melted butter and set aside to cool. Then combine with the minced meat, add 1 tbsp chopped dill, salt, pepper and grated nutmeg. Break in the egg and knead well to form uniform pulp. Stuff the celeriac shells with the mixture. In a small saucepan melt 1½ tbsp butter, add the flour and make a roux. Dilute it with the cold stock and, stirring all the time, cook over low heat until the sauce thickens. Add lemon juice, salt, pepper, ginger, nutmeg, sugar and tomato paste, blend together and heat up (do not boil!). Butter an ovenproof dish and line it with the chopped celeriac flesh. Place the stuffed celeriac roots on top, pour over the sauce, sprinkle with the grated cheese and dot with butter. Bake in a preheated oven for about 30 mins. Before serving, sprinkle with dill. Serve with rice and mixed salads.

serves 4 • Preparation: 30 mins • Baking: 30 mins

Baked celeriac, Polish style

2 large celery roots (about 900 g), 1 tbsp lemon juice, ¼ tsp dried oregano, 1 cup strong stock, 3 tbsps butter, 4 tbsps grated smoked cheese (ewe-milk oscypek type)

Wash and peel the celery roots, dry and cut them into slices. Sprinkle with lemon juice and arrange in a saucepan, sprinkle with oregano, pour over 1 cup boiling stock and cook for about 20 mins. Drain and arrange in a buttered ovenproof dish. Sprinkle with the grated cheese and melted butter. Bake for 15–20 mins in a preheated oven. Serve as a hot snack or as a side dish with white meats.

serves 4 • Preparation: 30 mins • Baking: 20 mins

Celeriac stewed in wine

2 large celery roots (about 1 kg), 2 tbsps lemon juice, ¼ tsp grated lemon rind, salt, 1 glass Madeira wine, ¼ cup stock, 1 tbsp butter, 1 tbsp flour, 1 tsp sugar

Place the well-scrubbed celery roots in some salted boiling water and cook for 5–6 mins. Drain, rinse with cold water, peel and scoop out the flesh with a melon baller. Sprinkle the celeriac balls with lemon juice and place in a saucepan. Sprinkle with grated lemon rind and sugar, pour over the hot stock and Madeira wine, cover and simmer for about 15 mins. Add salt to taste and, if desired, some more lemon juice. Blend the butter with flour into smooth paste, add to the celeriac and, stirring gently, heat up until the sauce thickens. The celeriac balls make an elegant side dish with roast white meats and poultry.

serves 4 • Preparation: 25–30 mins

Celeriac stewed with prunes

1 kg celery roots, 2 tbsps butter, 3 tbsps raisins, 3–4 prunes, 2 eggs, ½ cup dry white wine, 1 tbsp lemon juice, salt, 1 tsp sugar, 1 tsp honey, 2–3 tbsps single cream

Scald and drain the raisins. Wash the prunes, cover them with 2 tbsps water and 2 tbsps white wine, cook and purée. Scrub the celery roots, place in some lightly salted boiling water and cook for about 10 mins. Drain, rinse with cold water, peel, cut into half-slices and sprinkle with lemon juice. In a saucepan melt the butter, put in the celeriac, add salt, sugar, sprinkle with the wine and simmer for a few minutes. Mix the egg yolks with the cream and, if necessary, with 1 tsp flour. Add to the celeriac, mix well and heat up until the sauce thickens (do not boil!). Makes a delicious side dish with poultry and white meats.

serves 6–8 • Preparation: 40 mins

Celeriac in egg sauce

1 kg celery roots, 2 large onions, 1 tart apple, 4 tbsps chopped parsley, juice and grated rind of 1 lemon, 1 cup light chicken stock, 4 tbsps butter, salt, pepper, ½ tsp sugar, a pinch of nutmeg, 3 raw egg yolks, 1 tsp potato flour, 2–3 tbsps dry white wine

Dice the onion, cut the celeriac and apple into thick slices, sprinkle with lemon juice. Butter an ovenproof dish and arrange in it layers of the celeriac, onion and apple, sprinkling each layer with salt and pepper, grated lemon rind, chopped parsley and knobs of butter. Pour in the hot stock and the remaining lemon juice, cover and simmer for about 20 mins. In a saucepan beat the egg yolks with sugar, nutmeg and 2–3 tbsps celeriac stock. Mix the potato flour with the wine and add to the sauce. Shake the saucepan a few times and heat up. Makes a delicious side dish with boiled meats.

serves 6–8 • Preparation: 40 mins

Celery salad with cucumber

2 celery stalks, 1 large tart apple, 1 smallish fresh cucumber

DRESSING: 3–4 tbsps salad oil, 2 tbsps lemon juice, salt, pepper, 2 tbsps chopped parsley

Mix the dressing ingredients, refrigerate. Trim and wash the celery, cut into thin slices and sprinkle with salt. Peel and coarsely grate the apple and sprinkle with lemon juice. Peel and julienne the cucumber. Combine the ingredients, pour over the sauce and mix well. Before serving,

sprinkle with chopped parsley. Serve as a side dish with roast meats, fried fish, chops.

serves 4 • Preparation: 10 mins

Celery and tomato salad

1 celery stalk, 500 g firm, fleshy tomatoes, 200 g Emmental cheese, 3 tbsps wine vinegar, 1 cup yogurt, 1 tbsp thick mayonnaise, ½ tsp herbs of Provence, salt, pepper

Mix the yogurt with the herbs, mayonnaise, salt, pepper and wine vinegar, leave aside to cool. Scald and skin the tomatoes and cut them into thick cubes (remove seeds). Trim the celery stalk, cut into slices and cut the cheese into matchsticks. Combine all the ingredients, pour over the dressing and mix together well.

serves 6–8 • Preparation: 10 mins

Celery and onion salad

500 g celery, 200 g onion, 1 tart apple, 100 g walnuts, 1 cup mayonnaise, lemon juice, 4 hard-boiled eggs, parsley, dill, salt, pepper, sugar

Trim the celery stalks and put them into salted boiling water for 2–3 mins. Drain, rinse with cold water, drain again and cut into thin slices. Cut the onion and peeled apple into small cubes and sprinkle with lemon juice. Blend the mayonnaise with lemon juice, salt, sugar and pepper. In a hot frying pan dry roast the chopped walnuts. Combine all the ingredients, mix with the dressing, decorate the salad with quarters of eggs and sprinkle with dill and parsley.

serves 6–8 • Preparation: 10 mins

Celeriac and lingonberry salad

1 smallish celeriac (about 300 g), 2 tart apples, 3–4 tbsps lingonberry jam, 2 tbsps chopped walnuts, 3 tbsps lemon juice, 1 tsp honey, 3 tbsps salad oil

Coarsely grate the scrubbed and peeled celeriac and peeled apples, sprinkle with 2 tbsps lemon juice. Combine with the lingonberry jam. Mix the remaining lemon juice with honey, add a pinch of salt and pepper, pour over the salad, toss and refrigerate. Before serving, sprinkle with chopped walnuts.

serves 4–6 • Preparation: 10 mins

Celery, Polish style

2 large celery stalks with leaves, 1 tsp sugar, 2 tbsps lemon juice, salt, 3–4 tbsps butter, 2 tbsps breadcrumbs

Trim the celery stalks and cut them into small sections. Boil some salted water with the addition of sugar, lemon juice and 1 tsp butter. Put in the celery sections and cook for about 15–20 mins. Remove them with a slotted spoon and arrange on a warmed serving platter, sprinkle with melted butter with browned breadcrumbs.

serves 4 • Preparation: 20–25 mins

Celeriac with hazelnuts

2 celery roots (about 800 g), 100 g smoked lean streaky bacon, 2 tbsps oil, 1 cup stock, ¼ cup double cream, 1 tbsp ground hazelnuts, 1 tbsp lemon juice, 1 tbsp dried oregano, salt, a pinch of pepper and sugar

Scrub and peel the celery roots, cut them into thickish matchsticks, sprinkle with lemon juice. In a saucepan heat the cooking oil and fry the diced bacon. Add the slices of celeriac and fry over high heat for a moment or two, stirring constantly. Reduce the heat, add salt, pepper and sugar, sprinkle with the stock and oregano, mix well, cover and simmer for about 40 mins. Blend the cream and hazelnuts, and add to the celeriac towards the end of stewing. Mix well. Serve as a side dish with roast meats or chops.

serves 6–8 • Preparation: 50 mins

Chicory (endive)

The first mention of chicory and its uses in the kitchen comes from 1651, from a cookery book written by the head cook to Henry IV of France. It is grown under straw mats or dark foil, therefore it is white in colour. It gives salads a mildly bitter taste. It can be served both cold and hot.

For cooking, you should remove some of the outer leaves and hollow out a small cone at the base. Cook it whole in salted water with some butter, lemon juice and sugar added, for some 20 minutes.

In Poland, chicory has been known for a long time, and it has been cooked in many different ways.

Endive

Cook white chicory like lettuce, then chop it. Make croutons in a pan, then take them out and put the chopped endive in their place. Add some pepper and salt and a pinch of flour. When the juices evaporate, pour in some cream. Before serving, garnish the endive with croutons.

(Karolina Nakwaska, *Dwór wiejski*, 1858)

Endive salad with walnuts

3 endives, 6–7 prunes, ½ cup chopped walnuts, 2 tbsps chopped watercress

DRESSING: 3 tbsps salad oil, 1 tbsp juice and ¼ tsp grated lemon grind, salt, ¼ tsp sugar, a pinch of cayenne pepper

Mix well all the ingredients, chill slightly. Soak the washed prunes in lukewarm water, set aside for 30 mins. Remove the hard and bitter butt ends of the washed and dried endive, cut the endive into stripes and combine with the drained prunes cut into thin stripes, and with chopped walnuts. Pour the sauce over, mix well and sprinkle with watercress.

serves 4 • Soaking: 30–40 mins • Preparation: 5–7 mins

Endive salad with spinach

1–2 endive heads, 100 g young spinach leaves,
200 g thinly sliced carrots, 50 g coarsely grated
horseradish, a few leaves of iceberg lettuce

DRESSING: 2–3 tbsps olive oil, 2 tbsps lemon juice,
1 flat tbsp honey, salt, pepper

Mix thoroughly the dressing ingredients, cover, chill.
Wash and dry the lettuce, spinach and endives, cut
into stripes and combine with the carrots and horseradish.
Pour the dressing over, mix well and refrigerate.

serves 4 • Preparation: 5–7 mins • Refrigerating: 1 hour

Endive in mustard seed dressing

8 endive heads, 1 large onion, 2 tbsps butter,
1 cup stock, ½ cup dry white wine, ½ cup single
cream, 1 tbsp flour, 3 tbsps ground mustard seeds,
1 tsp honey, 1 tbsp lemon juice, salt, pepper,
2 tbsps chopped mustard leaves (or sprouts)

In a saucepan melt 1½ tbsps butter and sauté the finely
chopped onion. Add the washed endive heads and
pour over the wine mixed with the stock. Bring to the boil,
cover and cook over low heat for about 15 mins. Remove
the cooked endives with a slotted spoon, and place them
in an ovenproof dish coated with the remaining butter. In
a food processor blend the sauce with salt, pepper and
honey, put through a sieve and add the ground mustard
seeds. Bring to the boil. Blend the cream with flour and
add it to the sauce. Mix thoroughly with a wire whisk, and
heat until the mixture denses. Pour it over the endives
and put into a preheated oven for 5–6 mins. Sprinkle with
mustard leaves before serving. Serve with French noodles
and coddled eggs.

serves 4 • Preparation: 30 mins

Endive with oregano seeds

4 endive heads, 2–3 onions, ½ cup fenugreek
sprouts, 2 tbsps chopped walnuts, 1 tbsp lovage
seeds, 2 tbsps lemon juice, 2–3 tbsps olive oil,
1 tbsp boiled water, salt, white pepper

Combine the honey with water and lemon juice, add
salt, a pinch of pepper and olive oil, mix well, chill.
Cut the onion into thin rings, place in a sieve and scald,
then rinse with cold water. Drain. Remove the butt ends
and discard, cut the endives into thick stripes and combine
with the onion, fenugreek sprouts and walnuts, pour the
dressing over and mix well. Sprinkle with oregano seeds.

serves 4 • Preparation: 10 mins

Endive boats

4 firm endive heads, grated lemon rind and
juice of ½ lemon, 2 large hard, fleshy tomatoes,
2 tangerines, 1 tbsp stuffed green olives, salt,
pepper, 1 tsp honey, 3 tbsps grapeseed oil

Scald, skin and seed the tomatoes, then cut into cubes.
Peel the tangerines, divide into quarters, cut into cubes.
Slice the olives. Mix well the lemon juice and lemon rind with
oil, honey, salt and pepper. Combine the tomatoes, tangerines and olives with the dressing, cover and set aside in the
fridge. Wash and dry the endive, remove the butt ends, cut
lengthwise and sprinkle with lemon juice. Arrange the endive
halves on a serving platter and stuff with the chilled salad.

serves 4 • Preparation: 10–12 mins • Refrigerating: 30–40 mins

Endive baked in tomato sauce

1 kg firm white endive heads, 200 g hard cheese,
½ cup thick cream, 3 tbsps tomato concentrate,
salt, pepper, 3 garlic cloves, 4 tbsps butter, 1 cup
stock, ½ cup cold milk, salt, pepper, sugar,
1 tbsp lemon juice, 1 tsp grated lemon rind

Bring to the boil salted water with 1 tbsp butter, 1 tsp sugar, grated lemon rind and lemon juice. Trim the endive
heads, put them into boiling water and boil for 10 mins over
low heat. Remove with a slotted spoon, rinse with cold water,
drain thoroughly. Coarsely grate the cheese. Mince 2 garlic
cloves with salt, pepper, a pinch of sugar, mix with the cream
and tomato concentrate. In a saucepan melt 1 tbsp butter,
add the flour and make a roux. Dilute it with the milk, pour in
the stock in which the endives were cooking and cook stirring
all the time until the sauce thickens. Remove from the heat,
season to taste and combine with half of the grated cheese.

Rub an ovenproof dish with 1 garlic clove, then butter it well. Arrange the endives and pour over the bechamel sauce. Then cover the whole surface with the cream sauce, sprinkle with the remaining cheese and bake for about 25 mins. Serve immediately in the dish in which the endives were baking.

serves 4 • Preparation: 15–20 mins • Baking: 25 mins

Endive baked with ham

8 firm white endive heads, 1 tbsp juice and ½ tsp grated lemon rind, salt, 1 tsp sugar, 1 tsp butter, 8 thin slices lean ham, 3 tbsps grated sharp cheese, 2 tbsps chopped walnuts, 2 tbsps butter, 1½ cups cream, 1 egg yolk, salt, pepper, sugar, 1 tsp lemon juice

Bring to the boil salted water with lemon rind and lemon juice, butter and sugar. Trim the endive heads and cook them in boiling water for about 10 mins over low heat. Remove with a slotted spoon, rinse with cold water, drain thoroughly. Wrap each endive head in a ham slice. Mix the grated cheese with chopped walnuts. Blend the cream with egg yolk, salt, pepper, a dash of sugar and lemon juice. Butter an ovenproof dish, arrange the endive heads snugly, pour over the cream, sprinkle with the cheese and walnuts and dot with butter knobs. Cover and put into a preheated oven for about 30 mins. Serve with potatoes and tomato salad.

serves 4 • Preparation: 15–20 mins • Baking: 30 mins

Courgette (zucchini)

This is a variety of marrow (summer squash). Its seeds were brought to Europe from America by Columbus. It was first cultivated in Italy, where it was called *zucchino*, or small gourd (*zucca*).

Not only the fruit, but also the flowers can be eaten. Only male flowers are used in cooking. The fragile sepals are removed and fried in batter. They are then cooked with

Endive salad

onion and garlic, mixed with cheese and used as a spread or as a filling for pierogi. They can also be added to soups, and they can be stuffed with cottage cheese and baked.

The fruit of the plant, which is either green or yellow, can be cooked in various ways. If courgettes are young, it is not necessary to peel them. Larger courgettes can be scooped out and stuffed. Courgettes go well with many dishes, especially those made from tomatoes, garlic and herbs. You may use them to cook vegetarian caviare: For this purpose blanch a sliced courgette, purée it together with peeled tomatoes, lemon juice and oil, add some salt and pepper. Courgettes can be salted, marinated, and used in fresh salads. They can be used to cook what we call 'Polish pineapple': blanched slices of zucchini cooked in thick sugar syrup with some lemon juice added.

You should use only firm courgettes which are bright green, orange, yellow or striped (depending on the variety), and you should store them in the fridge no longer than three days.

For culinary purposes, the best courgettes are the young small fruits. Older courgettes have harder skin that needs peeling, rather spongy pulp and hard seeds inside, and generally they are not as tasty as young ones.

Courgette patties with cheese

Rinse the courgettes, grate them coarsely. Add eggs, finely chopped garlic and parsley, flour mixed with baking soda and grated cheese. Mix the preparation finely. Heat some oil in a frying pan. Drop the mixture into the oil in spoonfuls to form small patties, and fry on both sides until golden brown. Serve with tomato salad.

(Kuchnia polska, 1997)

Courgette salad

1 young firm courgette, 1 tbsp lemon juice, 1 cup watercress, 1 bunch spring onions, 2–3 tbsps chopped walnuts

DRESSING: 2–3 garlic cloves, 1 tsp mustard, 1 tbsp lemon juice, 3–4 tbsps salad oil, salt, pepper, a pinch of sugar

Mince the garlic with salt, combine with the remaining dressing ingredients and refrigerate for a while. Wash the courgette and cook it for 2–3 mins in slightly salted

boiling water. Drain, rinse with cold water and dry. Cut unpeeled into thin julienne strips, sprinkle with lemon juice. Wash and dry the spring onions, chop finely and combine with the courgette and watercress. Pour the dressing over, mix and set aside in the fridge. Before serving, sprinkle with chopped walnuts.

serves 4 • Preparation: 10 mins • Refrigerating: 30–40 mins

Stuffed courgettes

4 young courgettes, 300 g minced poultry meat, 1 cup cooked rice, 1 large red onion, 2 tbsps chopped fresh or 1 tsp dried oregano, ½ tsp caraway seeds, salt, pepper, 2 tbsps tomato concentrate, ½ cup stock, ½ cup double cream, 1 tbsp lemon juice, a pinch of sugar, 1 tbsp butter, 1 tbsp lard

Wash the courgettes, cut them lengthwise and place in a sieve. Pour over boiling, then cold water. Scoop out the flesh. Finely chop the onions and sauté them in lard. Add the minced meat, caraway seeds, salt, pepper and rice and fry together for a few minutes, stirring all the time. Remove from the heat, mix with oregano. Finely chop the scooped out courgette flesh and combine with the meat. Stuff the courgette halves with the mixture, place them in a buttered ovenproof dish, sprinkle with the stock and bake in a preheated oven for about 20 mins. Mix the tomato paste well with the cream, lemon juice, salt and sugar, pour over the courgettes and continue to bake for another few minutes.

serves 4 • Preparation: 10 mins • Baking: 25–30 mins

Courgettes with walnuts

4 young courgettes, 1 large onion, ¼ cup chopped walnuts, 2 tbsps butter, 2 tbsps breadcrumbs, 1 tbsp tomato paste, 1 tbsp chopped green sage, salt, pepper, 1 cup sour cream, 2 tbsps chopped parsley

Wash and dry the courgettes, cut them lengthwise and scoop out some of the flesh. Put the courgettes for a minute into slightly salted boiling water, drain, rinse with cold water, dry. Sauté the finely chopped onion in 1 tbsp melted butter, add the tomato paste and breadcrumbs, mix well, remove from the heat, add the chopped courgette flesh, sage, walnuts, salt and pepper. Break in the egg and mix well. Stuff the courgette halves with the mixture and place them in a buttered ovenproof dish. Bake for about 20 mins in a preheated oven, adding the cream towards the end. Continue to keep warm for another 5–10 mins. Sprinkle with chopped parsley before serving.

serves 4 • Preparation: 10 mins • Baking: 25–30 mins

Courgettes with herbs and almond stuffing

4 young courgettes, 1 large onion, finely chopped, 3 tbsps grated wholemeal bread, ½ cup chopped almonds, ½ cup chopped hazelnuts, 1 tsp vegetable seasoning, 3 tbsps chopped parsley, 1 tsp chopped fresh marjoram, 1 tsp chopped rosemary, salt, pepper, 2 tbsps olive oil, 2 tbsps butter, 1 tbsp dry white wine or water

Wash and dry the courgettes, cut them in halves lengthwise and scoop out some of the flesh. Blanch for 1 min in slightly salted boiling water, drain, rinse with cold water, dry. Finely chop the flesh. In a frying pan, heat the olive oil, sauté the onion, add the reserved courgette flesh, parsley, marjoram and rosemary and fry for a moment or two, stir. Remove from the heat, add the grated wholemeal bread, mix well, leave aside to cool. Combine with the almonds, hazelnuts, salt, pepper and wine, or water. Mix well. Stuff the courgettes halves, place them on a buttered dish, dot with butter on top and cover with aluminium foil. Bake for 30 mins in a preheated oven.

serves 4 • Preparation: 10 mins • Baking: 25–30 mins

Courgettes stuffed with apple and green peas paste

4 young courgettes, 1 large onion, 2 apples, 200 g chopped hazelnuts, 100 g green peas (deep frozen or tinned), 1 tbsp chopped mint leaves, juice and grated rind of 1 lemon, salt, pepper, a pinch of sugar, 3 tbsps butter, a few mint leaves

Cut the washed and dried courgettes lengthwise in half, scoop out some flesh. Put the courgettes for 1 min into slightly salted boiling water, drain, rinse with cold water, dry. Chop the flesh finely. Peel the apples and onion,

cut into cubes. In a small saucepan melt 1½ tbsps butter, sauté the onion, add the peas, mint and courgette flesh, mix well and simmer for 5–7 mins. Add the apple, lemon juice and lemon rind, cover and continue to simmer for another 10 mins. Remove from the heat, leave to cool, then mix together with the nuts. Season with salt and pepper and stuff the courgette halves with the mixture. Arrange in a buttered baking dish, dot with butter and bake for 25–30 mins. Before serving, decorate with mint leaves.

serves 4 • Preparation: 10 mins • Baking: 20–25 mins

Courgettes stuffed with Cheddar

4 young courgettes, 2 large onions, 2–3 garlic cloves, 400 g grated Cheddar cheese, 1 tbsp chopped thyme leaves, or 1 tsp dried thyme, salt, pepper, 3 tbsps butter

Cut the washed and dried courgettes lengthwise in half, scoop out some of the flesh. Blanch the courgettes for 1 min in slightly salted boiling water, drain, rinse with cold water, dry. Chop the flesh finely. Melt 1½ tbsps butter in a frying pan, sauté the finely chopped onion and garlic, add the courgette flesh and fry for a moment. Add thyme, season with salt and pepper, mix well, remove from the heat, leave aside to cool. Combine with the cheese and mix well. Stuff the courgette halves with the mixture and arrange in a buttered ovenproof dish. Top with melted butter and place the dish in a preheated oven for 20–25 mins. Serve with rice or potatoes and tomato sauce, or with tomato salad.

serves 4 • Preparation: 10 mins • Baking: 20–25 mins

Courgettes stuffed with mushrooms

4 young courgettes, 2–3 large, fleshy tomatoes, 1 tbsp butter, ¼ cup stock, 2 tbsps chopped parsley, ½ cup cream, 400 g mushrooms, 2 tbsps cooking oil, 1 onion, 1–2 garlic cloves, 2 eggs, 1 bread roll soaked in milk, salt, pepper, ½ tsp dried thyme

Cut the washed and dried courgettes lengthwise in half, scoop out some of the flesh. Place the courgettes for a minute in slightly salted boiling water. Drain, rinse with cold water and dry. Chop the onion and sauté it in oil. Add the finely chopped mushrooms and fry for a moment or two, stir. Season with garlic minced with salt, pepper and thyme

and remove from the heat. Leave aside to cool, then combine with the bread roll (squeezed dry), add the eggs and blend together to form the stuffing. Stuff the courgettes and arrange them in a buttered ovenproof dish. Sprinkle with the stock, cover and cook for a few minutes over low heat. Scald, skin and dice the tomatoes. Mix them with the cream, season with salt and pepper, pour over the courgettes and simmer together for a few minutes. Serve with rice.

serves 4 • Preparation: 15–20 mins • Stewing: 20–25 mins

Cucumber

Next to cabbage and beets, the cucumber is the most popular vegetable in Poland. It is one of the most healthy vegetables, being a rich source of vitamin C and minerals, such as calcium, iron and phosphorus. It has a duretic effect, and thus is recommended for slimmers. There is however one flaw about it: it is a 'loner' – when mixed with other vegetables (tomatoes, peppers, lettuce) it destroys the vitamin C contained in them.

Stewed cucumbers with boiled meat

Peel several cucumbers, halve them lengthwise, salt them and leave aside for half an hour. Melt one table-spoon of butter in a pan, brown one finely chopped onion in it, put in the cucumbers and cook until they are tender. Dust them with some flour, add some stock, bring to the boil. Serve them with boiled meat. You may cook soured cucumbers according to the same recipe.

(Praktyczny kucharz warszawski, 1926)

Cucumber mousse

1 large long cucumber, 2 tbsps light wine vinegar, ½ tsp salt, 150 g full-fat cottage cheese, 150 g ewe-milk cheese, 150 cream cheese, 1 bunch chives, 2 spring onions with green parts, 2–3 garlic cloves, ½ cup yogurt, ½ cup thick cream, juice of ½ lemon, 1 tbsp chopped fresh tarragon leaves, 1 tbsp salt, 1 tbsp powdered aspic, ¼ cup hot chicken stock, salt, pepper, sugar

Cucumber mousse

Cut the peeled cucumber into small cubes, sprinkle with vinegar and salt, mix well, cover and set aside for 1–2 hours, then squeeze out well to remove the excess liquid. Dissolve the powdered aspic in the hot stock, mix with the yogurt and cream, and beat with a wire whisk until the cream thickens. In a food processor mix the cottage cheese with ewe-milk cheese, cream cheese, tarragon, garlic minced with salt, pepper, a dash of sugar and lemon juice. Combine with the chopped onions and chives, cucumber and the beaten cream. Mix well, place in a salad bowl or in individual small bowls, cover with cling film and leave in the fridge for a few hours.

serves 4 • Salting: 1–2 hrs • Preparation: 30 mins • Refrigerating: 3–4 hrs

Spicy cucumber paste

1 large cucumber, 1 medium-large onion, 1–2 garlic cloves, 3 small hot peppers, a piece (about 5 cm long) preserved ginger, 1 tbsp olive oil, juice of 1 lemon, salt, sugar

Finely chop the peeled cucumber, onion, garlic, pepper and ginger and mix with salt, lemon juice and olive oil. Set aside in the fridge to cool. Decorate with parsley and serve as a snack.

serves 4 • Preparation: 10 mins • Refrigerating: 1 hr

Elegant cucumber salad with walnuts and orange

1 large long cucumber, 1 orange, 1 tbsp chopped walnuts, 1 tbsp sunflower oil, juice of ½ lemon, salt, a pinch of sugar

Peel and cut the cucumber into thick cubes. Arrange it in a salad bowl with the orange cut into quarters, sprinkle with lemon juice, salt and sugar. Season with oil, toss gently and sprinkle with walnuts.

serves 4 • Preparation: 5–6 mins

Cucumber salad with garlic

1 large, long cucumber, 2 garlic cloves, 1 tsp chopped dill, 1 tsp chopped mint or parsley, 1 tbsp lemon juice, 1 cup yogurt, ½ tsp salt, ½ tbsp sunflower oil

Peel the cucumber, cut it into thin slices, arrange in a bowl and sprinkle with salt. Mix the yogurt well with oil, minced garlic and dill. Drain and squeeze the excess liquid from the cucumber, arrange the slices in a salad bowl, pour over the yogurt, sprinkle with the greens and refrigerate for an hour. Serve with cold meats.

serves 4 • Preparation: 10 mins • Refrigerating: 1 hr

Mixed salad with cucumber

1 fresh cucumber, 2 tomatoes, 1 sweet pepper, 1 bunch radishes, 1 bunch spring onions, 1 small head lettuce, 1 tbsp chopped parsley

DRESSING: 2 garlic cloves, 4 tbsps sunflower oil, lemon juice, salt, sugar, pepper

Mince the garlic with salt, add lemon juice, oil, a dash of sugar and pepper. Skin the tomatoes and peel the cucumber, remove the seeds from the pepper, and cut everything into small cubes. Finely slice the radishes. Add the lettuce torn into ribbons, and the chopped onion and parsley. Pour the chilled dressing over the salad and toss gently.

serves 4 • Preparation: 5–7 mins

Cucumber salad

2 large long cucumbers, ½ cup chopped borage leaves and 2 tbsps borage flowers, salt

DRESSING: 1 cup yogurt, 1 tbsp salad oil, juice and grated rind of ½ lemon, a pinch of ground white mustard seeds, 1 tbsp finely chopped white mustard leaves

Mix well the yogurt with oil, lemon juice and grated lemon rind, a pinch of salt and ground mustard seeds, set aside to cool. Peel the cucumber and cut into thin slices, dust with salt and leave aside for a few minutes. Remove the excess liquid, combine the cucumber with the chopped borage leaves and pour the chilled dressing over. Mix well and sprinkle with white mustard leaves and borage flowers. Prepare just before serving.

serves 4 • Salting: 15 mins • Preparation: 5–6 mins

STUFFED CUCUMBERS

Cucumbers stuffed with salmon paste

2 large long cucumbers, salt, 1 tin salmon, 2 hard-boiled eggs, 2 spring onions (without chives), 2–3 cocktail gherkins, 2–3 black olives, 2–3 slices marinated pepper, 1 tsp mustard, 1 tsp lemon juice, 2 tbsps thick mayonnaise, pepper

Peel the cucumbers and cut them widthwise into halves. Gently scoop out the seeds and liberally sprinkle inside and out with salt. Leave aside for 10–15 mins, then rinse and dry the cucumber. Drain the salmon and mix thoroughly with the mustard, mayonnaise, lemon juice, pepper and egg yolks. Cut the egg whites, spring onions, pepper and olives and in a food processor blend with the dressing. Stuff the cucumbers, wrap each in aluminium foil and refrigerate for 2–3 hours. Cut into thick slices before serving.

serves 4–6 • Salting: 10–15 mins • Preparation: 10 mins • Refrigerating: 2–3 hrs

Cucumbers stuffed with smoked mackerel

2 large long cucumbers, 300 g smoked mackerel, 2 hard-boiled eggs, 3 tbsps chopped chives, salt, pepper, 1 tbsp thick mayonnaise, 1 tbsp cream

Skin and bone the mackerel. Blend the meat with the egg yolks, mayonnaise, cream, salt and pepper, then mix with the finely chopped egg whites and chives. Stuff the cucumbers the same way as described in the recipe for cucumbers stuffed with salmon paste.

serves 4–6 • Preparation: 10 mins • Refrigerating: 2–3 hrs

Cucumbers with ham paste

2 large long cucumbers, 150 g lean ham, 2 hard-boiled eggs, 1 tsp mustard, 1½ tbsps mayonnaise, salt, pepper, a pinch of sugar

In a food processor, blend the finely chopped ham with egg yolks, mustard, mayonnaise, salt and pepper.

Mix with the chopped egg whites. Stuff the cucumbers the same way as described in the recipe for cucumbers stuffed with salmon paste.

serves 4–6 • Salting: 10–15 mins • Preparation: 10 mins • Refrigerating: 2–3 hrs

Cucumbers with cottage cheese paste

2 large long cucumbers, 200 g full-fat cottage cheese, 3 tbsps thick cream, 1 hard-boiled egg yolk, 1 tbsp chopped fresh mint, 1 tbsp chopped fresh tarragon, 1 tbsp chives, salt, cayenne pepper

In a food processor, blend the cottage cheese with egg yolk, salt, cayenne pepper and cream. Mix with the chopped greens. Stuff the cucumbers the same way as described in the recipe for cucumbers stuffed with salmon paste (p. 874).

serves 4–6 • Salting: 10–15 mins • Preparation: 10 mins • Refrigerating: 2–3 hrs

Cucumbers with wholemeal bread paste

2 large long cucumbers, 4 slices wholemeal bread, ¼ cup lukewarm stock, 150 g mushrooms, 2 tbsps lemon juice, dried thyme, 1 hard-boiled egg, 2 hard fleshy tomatoes, 1 tbsp thick mayonnaise, 2 small onions, 1 tbsp olive oil, 3 tbsps chopped dill, 2 tbsps thick cream, salt, pepper

Sprinkle the finely cut mushrooms with lemon juice, a dash of thyme and pepper. Pour the olive oil over the chopped onion. Scald and skin the tomatoes and cut them into small cubes, removing the seeds and the excess of liquid. Mix with the mayonnaise. Pour the stock over the crumbled bread, leave aside for a few minutes, then squeeze out dry. Blend with the hard-boiled egg yolk, cream and dill, combine with the mushrooms, tomatoes and onion. Mix well together, season to taste. Stuff the cucumbers the same way as described in the recipe for cucumbers stuffed with salmon paste (p. 874). Sprinkle with chopped egg yolk.

serves 4–6 • Soaking: 15–20 mins • Preparation: 15 mins • Refrigerating: 2–3 hrs

Cucumbers stuffed with steak tartare

1 large long cucumber, 200 g ground beef sirloin, 1 small onion, 1 garlic clove, 1 tbsp vodka, 3–4 drops Tabasco sauce, 1 egg yolk, salt, pepper, 3–4 black and 3–4 green pitted olives, 3–4 sprigs parsley, 2–3 lettuce leaves

Wash and dry the cucumbers and cut them in thick slices uniform in size. Gently remove the seeds (leaving some flesh on one side). Sprinkle with salt inside, turn upside down to get rid of the excess liquid. Mix well the ground meat with the chopped onion, garlic minced with salt, vodka, Tabasco sauce, pepper and the egg yolk. Chill. Stuff the cucumber slices with thus prepared steak tartare and arrange on a serving platter lined with lettuce leaves. Decorate with slices of olives and green parsley leaves.

serves 4–6 • Preparation: 10 mins • Refrigerating: 1 hr

Cucumbers, Zamość style

4 large hard gherkins, 200 g roast sirloin, 2 tbsps hot mustard, 2 anchovy fillets, pepper, 1–2 tbsps stock, 2 hard-boiled eggs, 1 tbsp grated cheese

Peel the cucumbers and cut them lengthwise in half. Gently remove the seeds and spread mustard inside the scooped out cucumbers. Finely chop the meat and combine it with the chopped anchovy fillets, mix with the stock and pepper. Stuff the cucumbers, sprinkle with chopped eggs and grated cheese. Arrange on lettuce leaves and decorate with strips of marinated red pepper.

serves 4 • Preparation: 10 mins

Cucumbers, Sandomierz style

4 large thick cucumbers, ½ kg pike-perch or pike fillets, 1 small bread roll soaked in milk, 1 large onion, 1 tbsp butter, 1 whole egg and 1 egg yolk, 8 thin pork fat strips, 1 cup fish or chicken stock, 1 tbsp flour, 1 tbsp butter, 1 tbsp lemon juice, sugar, 1 glass vermouth, salt, pepper

Chop the onion and sauté it in butter. Skin and bone the fish and put it through a mincer together with the bread roll (squeeze out the excess milk). Mix with the egg and sautéd onion, season with salt and pepper, and form

a smooth paste. Peel the cucumbers, cut them lengthwise in half and carefully remove the seeds. Place the cucumber halves in boiling water for 1 min, remove, rinse with cold water, dry well and stuff with the prepared mixture. Cover each cucumber half with a strip of pork fat. Place the cucumbers in a saucepan, pour in the stock, cover and stew for about 30 mins. In a frying pan, melt the butter, add the flour and make a roux. Dilute it with the stock taken from the stewing cucumbers. Cook stirring all the time until the sauce thickens. Season with salt, pepper, a pinch of sugar and lemon juice. Mix the egg yolk well with the vermouth, pour into the sauce, mix well and heat. Place the soft cucumbers on a hot serving platter and pour them over with the sauce. Serve with boiled or puréed potatoes and salads.

serves 4 • Preparation: 10 mins • Stewing: 30 mins

Baked cucumbers

4 cucumbers, 300 g mushrooms, 1 cup cooked rice, 1 large onion, 100 g smoked bacon, 2 tbsp butter, 3–4 tbsps chopped parsley, 2 cups dry white wine, 1 lemon, ½ cup olive oil, 1 tbsp honey, 1 tbsp tomato paste, 1 tsp ground coriander seeds, salt, pepper

Fry the finely diced bacon in melted butter, add the finely chopped onion and continue to fry, stirring all the time. Add the sliced mushrooms and fry over high heat until the liquid has evaporated, season with salt and pepper, add the rice and ¼ cup wine, mix well and simmer together for a few moments. Remove from the heat, combine with chopped parsley. In a large flat saucepan bring to the boil the wine, lemon juice and grated lemon rind. Add ½ cup water, salt, pepper, coriander, honey and tomato concentrate and cook together over high heat for about 5 mins. Wash the cucumbers well and cut them lengthwise in half. Scoop out the seeds. Put the cucumber halves into a saucepan with the sauce and simmer for about 10 mins. Gently remove with a slotted spoon. Butter an ovenproof dish and pack the cucumber halves snugly side by side. Stuff them with the prepared mixture. Cook the sauce for a few minutes until it thickens. Pour over the cucumbers. Cover the dish with aluminium foil and bake in a hot oven for about 15–20 mins. Remove the foil towards the end of cooking.

serves 4 • Preparation: 40–45 mins

Cucumbers stewed with dill

*500 g fresh cucumbers, 1 large onion,
4 tbsps wine vinegar, 1 tbsp honey,
½ tsp salt, 1 tbsp flour, 1½ tbsps butter,
½ tsp fennel seeds, 2 cups stock,
3–4 tbsps chopped dill*

Cut the peeled cucumbers lengthwise in half, remove the seeds and cut the flesh into thick slices. Mix well the vinegar with 1 tbsp boiled water, honey and salt. Arrange the cucumbers in a serving bowl and pour over the dressing. Leave aside for an hour. Melt the butter in a saucepan and sauté the finely chopped onion. Add the fennel seeds and flour and stir and fry for a moment or two. Add the cold stock and simmer stirring all the time until the sauce thickens. Add the cucumbers (first squeeze them out lightly) and simmer uncovered over very low heat for about 15 mins. Just before serving sprinkle with dill.

serves 4 • Macerating: 1 hour • Preparation: 15–20 mins

Cucumber fricassee

*500 g cucumbers (preferably long ones),
1 small head lettuce, 100 g sorrel, 2 chicken legs,
2 cups vegetable stock, 1 tbsp butter, ½ cup
cream, 1 egg yolk, salt, pepper, sugar, 1 tbsp
lemon juice and ¼ tsp grated lemon rind*

Rub the washed chicken legs with salt and grated lemon rind. Place them in a saucepan and pour in hot stock. Cook until soft and leave in the stock to cool. Cut the peeled cucumbers lenghtwise in half and remove the seeds. Cut into slices. Wash and dry the lettuce and sorrel, cut into strips. In a saucepan melt the butter, add the cucumbers and when soft add the lettuce, sorrel and a pinch of sugar. Sauté gently for a few minutes, stirring all the time. Skin and bone the chicken legs, cut the meet into strips, add to the cucumbers. Steam off the chicken stock leaving just 1 cup, season it to taste with salt, pepper and lemon juice. Add to the cucumbers, mix well and simmer together for a few minutes. Mix the egg yolk with cream, add to the saucepan, mix and heat, but do not boil. Season to taste, if necessary. Serve with rice or white bread.

serves 4–6 • Preparation: 40–45 mins

Hops

Hops have been known in the brewing industry for almost 6000 years. They give beer its lucidity, foaminess and mildly bitter taste, and have soothing and sleep-inducing properties.

According to the latest research, hops are good for the digestion and appetite, they soothe the nerves, cure indigestion, lower the blood pressure, but they also decrease sexual drive (men beware!) and cause melancholy, therefore they should be avoided in depressive states.

The edible parts of hops are the shoots and flowers. Young hop leaves taste best in spring, from late April to mid-June, and should always be blanched first to remove the bitter taste. They go well with various soups, in particular vegetable soups. Hop purée can be served with meat and roast poultry. Both the leaves and flowers can be added to salads garnished with cream. The taste of hop salad is like that of asparagus and chicory.

Young hop shoots are juicy and rich in B group vitamins, minerals and essential oils. They are used for making soups, omelettes, salads with vinaigrette, lettuce, onion, eggs and ham. Steamed hop shoots are an excellent side dish with the second course, not inferior to asparagus.

To prepare hop shoots, you should first cut them to a length of not more than 60 cm, then clean them, tie them into bunches and boil in salted water with some butter, sugar and lemon juice added, or else steam them. Before serving, pour melted butter with browned breadcrumbs over them. Alternatively, serve them with hollandaise sauce, or bake them with bechamel sauce. You can also pickle young hop shoots and serve them with cold meats, salads and second courses.

Hops

In early April, when there is a shortage of vegetables, you can pick young hop shoots and serve them instead of asparagus, to which they are similar in taste. As with asparagus, cut them off when they have just appeared above ground, or else pick the youngest upper shoots with the leaves still in bud.

Tie them in bunches and blanch them in salted water for several minutes. Then you should drain them, arrange them in a serving dish, and pour over melted butter with browned breadcrumbs.

(Karolina Nakwaska, *Dwór wiejski*, 1858)

Hop and red onion salad

200 young hop shoots, 1–2 red onions, 50 g turkey ham, 2 hard-boiled eggs, 2 tbsps chopped chives, 1 tbsp lemon juice, 2–3 tbsps olive oil, salt, pepper, a pinch of sugar

Mix thoroughly the dressing ingredients, leave to cool. Peel the hop shoots, put into a sieve and pour boiling water through them, then cold water. Drain thoroughly, cut into pieces. Cut the turkey ham into strips, the onion into thin slices. Dice the egg whites. Combine the salad ingredients, pour over the dressing, mix gently but thoroughly, leave aside to cool. Before serving, sprinkle with chopped egg yolk and chives.

serves 4 • Preparation: 5–7 mins • Refrigerating: 1–2 hrs

Lettuce with hop shoots

1 crisp lettuce, 100 g young hop shoots, 1 bunch spring onions, 2 hard-boiled eggs, salt, pepper, sugar, 1 tbsp wine vinegar, 1 tbsps salad oil

Peel and rinse the hop shoots, rinse the spring onions and lettuce. Dry. Cut the hop shoots and spring onions, tear the lettuce leaves into small pieces. Combine all, season to taste with salt, pepper and a pinch of sugar. Sprinkle over the vinegar and oil, mix well and decorate with slices of the hard-boiled eggs.

serves 4–6 • Preparation: 5–7 mins

Buttered hop shoots

Peel 600–800 g young hop shoots, rinse, dry and tie into bunches. Cook them in a tall pot in boiling salted water with a pinch of sugar, lemon juice and 1 tsp of butter. Serve sprinkled with melted butter.

serves 4 • Preparation: 15–20 mins

Hop shoots in sesame sauce

500 g hop shoots, salt, 1 tsp sugar, 1 tsp butter, 2–3 tbsps sesame seeds, 2 tbsps soya sauce, 1 tsp honey

Peel the hop shoots and put them into boiling water with sugar, butter and lemon juice to cook for 15 mins. Remove, cut into pieces 4–5 cm long. Arrange in a serving dish. In a frying pan, dry roast the sesame seeds. In a small saucepan bring to the boil soya sauce with honey, add sesame seeds, mix well and pour over the hop shoots, set aside to cool.

serves 4 • Preparation: 20 mins

Hop shoots in herbal sauce

600 g young hop shoots, 1 bunch spring onions, 2 tbsps butter, 2 tbsps finely chopped parsley, 2 tbsps chopped chervil, juice and grated rind of 1 lemon, salt, pepper, ¼ tsp grated nutmeg, sugar, 1 cup double cream, 2 egg yolks

Peel the hop shoots, rinse, dry and cut into pieces 4–5 cm long. Bring to the boil some salted water with sugar, 1 tsp lemon juice and ½ tsp butter. Cook the hop shoots for about 10–15 mins. Remove with a slotted spoon. Sauté the finely cut spring onion in melted butter, sprinkling it with the hop stock (¼ cup), add salt, pepper, grated nutmeg, lemon rind and lemon juice. Simmer for a moment, then add the hop shoots and mix well. Mix thoroughly the cream with egg yolks, chopped parsley and chervil and add to the hops. Heat gently, don't let it boil. Serve as a hot snack or as a side dish with roast poultry or veal.

serves 4 • Preparation: 20–25 mins

Hot snack with hop shoots

800 g hop shoots, 4–5 hop leaves, 200 g lean streaky bacon, 4–5 garlic cloves, 5–6 large fleshy tomatoes (or tinned ones), 2 tbsps oil, salt, pepper, lemon juice, sugar, 2 cups light stock, 2 tbsps chopped parsley, ½ cup grated cheese

Blanch the peeled hop shoots and washed leaves in boiling water for 2–3 mins, drain and rinse with cold water. Fry the diced bacon and finely minced garlic in hot oil. Add the hop shoots cut into pieces and chopped hop leaves. Pour in the hot stock and simmer covered for about 20 mins. Scald and skin the tomatoes, cut them into thick cubes and add to the saucepan. Season with salt, pepper, lemon juice and a dash of sugar, if desired. Mix well and cook for a few minutes over low heat. Transfer to an ovenproof dish, sprinkle with the grated cheese and keep in a preheated oven until the cheese melts. Serve sprinkled with chopped parsley.

serves 4–6 • Preparation: 40–45 mins

Cottage cheese baked with hop

400 g hop shoots, 4–8 hop leaves, 200 g cottage cheese, 3 tbsps butter, 1 tbsp hot mustard, salt, pepper, 1 egg, parsley sprigs

Peel the hop shoots and cook them in salted water, drain, cut into pieces uniform in size. Blanch the hop leaves in boiling water for 2 mins, drain, rinse with cold water and dry. Cream the butter and egg yolk, gradually adding the mustard, cottage cheese, salt and pepper. Beat the egg white and mix gently with the cottage cheese pulp. Butter individual ovenproof serving shells and line them with the blanched hop leaves. Put in the cottage cheese pulp and a few pieces of hop shoots into each dish. Transfer to a preheated oven and bake for about 30 mins. Decorate with sprigs of parsley and serve as a hot snack.

serves 4 • Preparation: 20 mins • Baking: 30 mins

Horseradish

This is one of the oldest Polish condiments, known as early as the Jagiellon period and popular also as a medicinal plant. Grated horseradish mixed with wine was regarded as a remedy for headaches, common colds and indigestion.

It is particularly important in winter and early spring, as it is very rich in vitamin C (100 mgl in 100 g). It also contains provitamin A, group B vitamins, anti-bacterial substances, a lot of potassium, calcium and magnesium.

Sharp-tasting horseradish is used with meat and fish dishes, and also eggs, vegetables and cheese.

Long, fine grated strips of horseradish are used for garnishing roast and braised meat dishes (having grated horseradish, you should sprinkle it with lemon juice to prevent it getting dark). Horseradish gives a sharp flavour to potato salads, stuffed cabbage leaves, pickled mushrooms, cranberries and beets. It also adds flavour to bean salads, kashas, potatoes and stewed mushrooms. You can add it to almost all brassica vegetables, such as kohlrabi, turnip, cauliflower or cabbage. Cooking deprives it of its special taste, therefore horseradish should be added to your dishes towards the end, shortly before serving.

In sauces, horseradish goes well with cranberries, blackcurrants, apple mousses and redcurrant jelly.

Horseradish root and leaves are excellent preservers of foodstuffs when added to pickled and marinated vegetables. Young leaves are sometimes added to vegetable salads, or cooked the same way as spinach.

Horseradish

Grate the horseradish, put it into melted butter, stir well, add a bit of stock. Mix some cream with salt, sugar, a bit of flour, vinegar and lemon juice. Pour the preparation into the horseradish, bring to the boil and, before serving, mix in one or two egg yolks.

(Marja Śleżańska, *Kucharz polski*, 1932)

Vitamin salad with horseradish

1 kg tart apples, 100 g grated horseradish, 1 tbsp honey, juice of 1 lemon, ¼ tsp grated lemon rind, salt

Peel and coarsely grate the apples, sprinkle with lemon juice, mix with the grated horseradish, grated lemon rind, honey and a pinch of salt. Arrange in a serving dish, seal with foil and refrigerate. Serve with roast chicken or turkey, or game, boiled meat or cold meats.

serves 4–6 • Preparation: 10 mins • Refrigerating: 1–2 hrs

Horseradish mayonnaise

½ cup mayonnaise, 3 tbsps grated horseradish, 2 tbsps grated apple, 1 tbsp lemon juice, a pinch of sugar

Mix well all the ingredients, cover and chill. Serve with corned beef, cold ox tongue or boiled carp.

serves 4 • Preparation: 2–3 mins • Refrigerating: 1–2 hrs

Horseradish cream with ginger

1 cup freshly grated horseradish, 1 cup double cream, ½ tsp powdered ginger, salt, juice and grated rind of 1 lemon, ½ tsp honey, 2 hard-boiled eggs

Blend the egg yolks with the cream, grated lemon rind, ginger and honey. Mix the freshly grated horseradish with lemon juice and a pinch of salt. Finely chop the egg whites. Combine the horseradish with the cream and egg whites, mix well and chill. Grated apple and cream counter the sharp taste of the freshly grated horseradish.

serves 4–8 • Preparation: 5–6 mins • Refrigerating: 1 hr

Horseradish sauce with almonds

2 tbsps butter, 1½ tbsps flour, 1 cup stock, 1 cup cream, 1 cup freshly grated horseradish, 50 g almond flakes, salt, pepper, a pinch of sugar, 1 tbsp lemon juice

Melt the butter in a saucepan, add the flour and make a roux. Dilute it with the cold stock and, stirring all the time, cook until the sauce thickens. Add salt, pepper, sugar, almond flakes and the cream. Heat up over low heat, adding the horseradish to the hot sauce. Mix well. Serve with boiled meat, boiled vegetables (e.g. cauliflower), boiled fish or hard-boiled eggs.

serves 4 • Preparation: 10 mins

Horseradish paste

1 carrot, ¼ celeriac, 4 tbsps grated horseradish, 4 tbsps thick mayonnaise, salt, 1 tbsp lemon juice and ½ tsp grated lemon rind, sugar

Peel and finely grate the carrot and celeriac, combine with the horseradish and mayonnaise. Mix well, season with a dash of sugar, salt, lemon juice and lemon rind. Chill.

serves 4–6 • Preparation: 5 mins • Refrigerating: 1 hr

Horseradish with cowberries

5–6 tbsps freshly grated horseradish, 1 tbsp lemon juice, 5 tbsps cowberry jam, 2–3 tbsps dry red wine, salt, 1 tbsp honey

Mix well the grated horseradish with lemon juice, honey, salt, jam and wine. Cover, chill and serve with cold roast meats, cold cuts or hard-boiled eggs.

serves 4 • Preparation: 2–3 mins • Refrigerating: 1–2 hrs

Potato salad with horseradish

500 g potatoes cooked in their skins, 3 tbsps grated horseradish, 2 tbsps horseradish flakes, 3 hard-boiled eggs, 2 spring onions, 5–6 red radishes, salt, pepper, ¾ cup yogurt, 2 tbsps olive oil, 1 tbsp lemon juice, sugar, a few sprigs of parsley

Dice the potatoes, sprinkle slightly with 1 tbsp olive oil and lemon juice, season with salt and pepper, cover and set aside for ½ hour. Place the grated horseradish in a sieve and pour over first boiling, then cold water. Drain. Slice the hard-boiled eggs and chop the spring onions with the green parts. Mix the yogurt thoroughly with the remaining oil, horseradish, salt, pepper and a pinch of sugar. In a serving bowl arrange layers of potatoes, horseradish flakes and eggs sprinkled with the chopped spring onion. Pour over the sauce, mix gently. Chill. Decorate with slices of radishes and sprigs of parsley.

serves 4 • Macerating: 30–40 mins • Preparation: 10 mins • Refrigerating: 1 hr

Russian salad with horseradish

250 g cod fillets, 150 g horseradish, 1 cup stock, 300 g potatoes cooked in their skins, 2 dill pickled cucumbers, 2 tbsps chopped chives, 1 tbsp chopped parsley, 1 tbsp chopped dill, juice and grated rind of ½ lemon, 1 tbsp salad oil, salt, pepper, 3 tbsps mayonnaise

Horseradish mayonnaise

Rub the cod fillets with salt, sprinkle delicately with lemon juice and place them in a saucepan. Cover with the hot stock and cook over low heat. When ready, leave the fillets in the stock to cool. Peel and dice the potatoes, sprinkle with salt, pepper, grated lemon rind and oil. Mix gently. Remove the fillets from the stock and cut them into cubes. Peel and slice the pickled cucumbers. Peel and finely grate the horseradish and sprinkle it with lemon juice. Combine all the ingredients, pour the mayonnaise over and mix everything carefully. Chill. Before serving, sprinkle with chopped greens.

serves 6–8 • Preparation: 25–30 mins • Refrigerating: 1 hr

Smoked salmon and horseradish salad

150 g smoked salmon, 2 pickled cucumbers, 1 cup diced pineapple, 3 tbsps tinned corn, 1 cup yogurt, 2 tbsps freshly grated horseradish, a few drops of Worcestershire sauce, salt, pepper, 1 tbsp chopped dill

Mix the yogurt with horseradish, Worcestershire sauce, salt and pepper. Set aside to cool. Cut the salmon and peeled pickled cucumbers into cubes, combine with the corn and pineapple, add the sauce and mix. Sprinkle with chopped dill before serving.

serves 4 • Preparation: 5–7 mins

Ham rolls with horseradish

8 thin slices tinned ham, 4 tbsps grated horseradish, ¾ cup cream, 3 tbsps cream cheese, 1 tbsp liquid honey, 1 tsp lemon juice, salt, 2 tbsps fine horseradish flakes, lettuce leaves, 1 small sweet red pepper, parsley sprigs

Mix the horseradish well with the honey, lemon juice and cream cheese. Whip the cream with salt, combine with the cream cheese and horseradish, cover with aluminium foil and set aside to cool. Spread the mixture on ham slices, roll up and arrange on a serving platter lined with lettuce. Sprinkle with horseradish flakes and decorate with sprigs of parsley and strips of pepper.

serves 4 • Preparation: 30–35 mins

Stewed apples with horseradish

3 large tart apples, 3 large onions, 300 g freshly grated horseradish, 300 g sugar, 3 tbsps lemon juice, 1 tsp grated lemon rind, 1 tsp each ground cinnamon, crushed cloves and hot paprika, salt, 1 tbsp butter

Peel and coarsely grate the apples, sprinkle with lemon juice. Finely chop the onions and combine with the apples, add sugar and other ingredients, mix well, cover and set aside for 2–3 hours. Melt the butter in a saucepan, put in the apples with onion and simmer until the mixture thickens. Remove from the heat, cool and mix well with the grated horseradish. Add salt to taste and, if desired, lemon juice. Serve with boiled or fried meats.

serves 4–6 • Macerating: 2–3 hrs • Preparation: 20 mins

Carrot salad with raisins and horseradish

4 carrots, 1 horseradish root, 3 tbsps raisins, 2 tbsps dry white wine, juice and grated rind of 1 lemon, 1 tbsp honey, 3 tbsps olive oil, salt

Scald and drain the raisins, put them into a bowl and cover with the wine. Peel the carrots and horseradish, rinse and grate coarsely, sprinkle with lemon juice. Blend the honey with salt, grated lemon rind, the wine in which the rasins were soaking, and olive oil. Combine the carrots with the horseradish and raisins, pour the dressing over, stir and chill.

serves 4 • Preparation: 10 mins • Refrigerating: 1 hr

Stuffed horseradish leaves

8–12 horseradish leaves, 400 g minced chicken, 1 tart apple, 1 tsp grated horseradish, ½ tsp honey, 2–3 tbsps chopped walnuts, salt, pepper, 1 egg, 2 tbsps butter, ½ cup stock

In a saucepan melt 1 tbsp butter, add the coarsely grated apple, honey and chopped walnuts. Stir and fry. Remove from the heat, cool and mix well with the minced meat, salt, pepper, grated horseradish and egg. Knead thoroughly and add some breadcrumbs, or walnuts, if not dense enough. Blanch the horseradish leaves for 3–4 mins. Drain and rinse with cold water, remove hard veins. Place the filling on each leaf and roll up. Arrange the rolls snugly in a buttered baking dish. Sprinkle with the stock, cover and put into a preheated oven. Bake for 40 mins. Serve with white bread as a hot snack, or with rice and salads as the main course.

serves 4 • Preparation: 15 mins • Baking: 40 mins

Carp cooked in cream with horseradish

1 carp (about 1½ kg), salt, 1½ tbsps grated horseradish, 1 glass vodka, 1½ cups cream, 4–5 ground cloves, 2 tbsps honey, salt, pepper, 2 tbsps lemon juice, ½ tsp grated lemond rind

Dress the carp, rinse and dry, and rub well with salt. Set aside for 1 hour. Mix the cream well with honey, salt, pepper, cloves, lemon juice and lemon rind, vodka and horseradish. Place the fish in a saucepan, pour the sauce over and simmer covered for about 40 mins. Serve with rice or macaroni.

serves 4 • Salting: 1 hr • Stewing: 40–45 mins

Tench cooked in horseradish, Lithuanian style

1 kg tench, ½ cup grated horseradish, ½ cup stock, 1 tbsp butter, 1 tbsp flour, 1 cup cream, 2–3 bay leaves, salt, pepper, sugar, 1–2 tbsps wine vinegar

Dress and rinse the tench, cut into small pieces, sprinkle with salt and pepper, cover and set aside for 30 mins. In a saucepan melt the butter, add the fish and fry for a moment or two, then dredge with the crushed bay leaves, sprinkle with the stock and cook for about 10 mins. Mix the cream well with salt, sugar, wine vinegar and flour. Sprinkle the half cooked fillets with the horseradish, pour the sauce over and simmer for about 15 mins.

serves 4 • Preparation: 15–20 mins • Stewing: 25–30 mins

Pikeperch baked with horseradish

1 kg pikeperch, 1 glass dry white wine, ½ cup cream, salt, 2 tbsps butter, 2 hard-boiled eggs, 4 tbsps finely grated horseradish, 3 tbsps chopped dill

Clean, rinse and dry the fish. Rub it with salt and leave for half an hour. Then place on a buttered ovenproof platter, sprinkle with melted butter and bake in a preheated oven for 30–35 mins, frequently sprinkling with the wine. 5 minutes before the end of baking, pour the cream over. Before serving, sprinkle with the finely chopped eggs, horseradish flakes and chopped dill.

serves 4 • Salting: 30–40 mins • Baking: 30–35 mins

Kale

About kale

Kale is softer than green cabbage and cooks quicker. It is a healthy vegetable, but only for those with perfect stomachs. How to cook kale: Take some leaves, chop them finely. Add grated beets and some yellow carrot to make the kale sweeter. Put it all into a pan, add some pork stock and cook. Serve it with boiled smoked pork or ham or with roast chestnuts.

(M. Wielądko, *Kucharz doskonały*, vol. II, p. 118)

Kale is a member of the cabbage family. Due to its fine bright green colour and decorative curly leaves, it is used mostly for garnishing. It has been largely forgotten as a vegetable, and it is still used only in the area of Poznań. Kale is very rich in minerals and vitamins, and also in calcium, iron, phosphorus and potassium. The carotene (provitamin A) contained in kale is much more digestible than that in carrots. Kale is also a good source of vitamin A, B, PP and C, and has a small amount of vitamin E and K. It is recommended for children, and also for all those who care about their complexion, nails and hair. It tends to be bitter, but you can get rid of the unpleasant taste by blanching it before cooking.

Kale is never eaten raw. Having blanched and drained it, you usually cook it in butter, or add it to other vegetables, such as tomatoes, celeriac, carrots, parsley roots, onion, garlic, as well as apples. You can also cook vegetarian patties from kale, as well as 'bigos' with streaky bacon or sausage. Kale is also good for soup cooked with potatoes and onion and thickened with milk or cream.

Kale salad with cranberry juice

500 g kale leaves, 250 g cranberries, 4–5 garlic cloves, 3 tbsps salad oil, salt, pepper, sugar, 2 hard-boiled eggs

Using an electric mixer mix 150 g cranberries with the salad oil blended with salt, pepper and sugar. Refrigerate. Put the kale leaves (remove the hard stems first) for 1–2 mins into lightly salted boiling water. Drain, rinse with cold water, dry and cut into thin strips. Pour the sauce over, combine with what is left of cranberries, sprinkle with chopped eggs.

serves 4–6 • Preparation: 4–6 mins

Kale salad with cream

500 g kale, 1 large onion, 2 gherkins, 2 large tart apples, 2–3 hard, fleshy tomatoes, 2 hard-boiled eggs, ½ cup cream, 1 tbsp lemon juice, salt, pepper, sugar, 1 garlic clove, finely chopped

Wash the kale leaves, put them into salted boiling water and cook for about 10 mins. Remove, drain, rinse with cold water, drain again, remove the hard veins and cut the leaves into strips. Scald and skin the tomatoes. Dice the onion and the tomatoes. Peel the apples and gherkins, cut them into julienne strips. Mix the cream with lemon juice, salt, pepper and finely chopped garlic. Combine all the ingredients and pour over the dressing. Mix gently, set aside in the fridge. Before serving, sprinkle with chopped eggs.

serves 4–6 • Preparation: 15 mins • Refrigerating: 30–40 mins

Sautéd kale

1 kg kale, 1 small onion, 3–4 garlic cloves, 2 tbsps olive oil, ½ cup cream, salt, 1 tsp lemon juice, a pinch of pepper and sugar, 1 tbsp flour, ¼ cup stock

Rinse the kale thoroughly, put into lightly salted boiling water and cook for about 15 mins. Drain, remove the hard veins and finely chop the leaves. Melt the butter in a saucepan, sauté the finely chopped onion and fry for a moment or two, then add the finely chopped kale, sprinkle with the stock, cover and simmer for a few minutes. Season with salt, pepper, sugar and lemon juice, mix well and simmer for another few minutes. Mix the cream with flour and minced garlic and add it to the kale. Stir and heat. Serve as a side dish with fish, meat or eggs, or with omelettes.

serves 4–6 • Preparation: 25–30 mins

Kale bigos

1 kg kale, 1 large tart apple, 2 onions, 300 g pork sausage, 1 tsp caraway seeds, 1 tbsp lard, 1 tbsp butter, 1 tbsp flour, salt, pepper, sugar, 1 tbsp lemon juice, 1 cup stock

Remove the hard veins from the kale leaves. Put the leaves into boiling water and cook for a few minutes. Remove, rinse with cold water, drain, cut into thin strips. Place them in a saucepan and cover with the hot stock. Add caraway seeds, salt, pepper and sugar, and cook over low heat uncovered. In a frying pan, melt the lard and fry the chopped onion and sliced sausage. Then combine this with the kale and coarsely grated apple. Mix the whole and simmer together. Thicken with a roux made with the flour and butter, mix well. Season with lemon juice, salt and pepper, if desired.

serves 4–6 • Preparation: 30–35 mins

Kohlrabi

This vegetable is a member of the cabbage family. Its bright green or purple fleshy stalk swells like a turnip. It was probably first grown in Germany. Legend has it that it was brought to Europe by Attila, the king of the Huns, or else that it came from China along the 'silk route'. It was first described by a European botanist in the 16th century.

In Polish cuisine, it has been known since the 19th century. Rich in minerals and vitamins, young kohlrabi is very tasty both raw and cooked. Cooked kohlrabi is a good accompaniment to roast meat and cutlets. It can also be stuffed and served as a separate dish. New green kohlrabi leaves can be used in salads and in cooked dishes. Kohlrabi should be peeled very finely, since its outer layer is the tastiest.

Browned kohlrabi

Take several young, nice kohlrabis, scoop their insides out to form balls the size of pigeon eggs. Brown them in melted butter mixed with 1 tablespoon of sugar, then take them out. Add one tablespoon of flour to the butter and brown it nicely, stirring all the time. Pour in two cups of skimmed stock, adjust the taste with salt. Put in the kohlrabi eggs and cook for an hour, stirring frequently so that they do not burn, which happens to inexperienced cooks.

(Karolina Nakwaska, *Dwór wiejski*, 1858)

Kohlrabi salad with soya sprouts

2 young kohlrabies with leaves, 100 g soya sprouts, 1 head Chinese cabbage (about 100 g), 1 red pepper, 1 small fresh cucumber, 2 celery sticks, 4–5 dried apricots, 1 tbsp dry white wine, 1 tbsp chopped walnuts

DRESSING: 4–5 tbsps salad oil, 2 tbsps lemon juice and ¼ tsp grated lemon rind, ½ tsp chopped fresh ginger, salt, pepper, ½ tsp honey

Mix the dressing ingredients. Chill. Wash the apricots and soak them in wine. Peel and coarsely grate the kohlrabies. Peel the celery stalks and cut into thin slices, cut the peeled cucumber and the Chinese cabbage into strips. Remove the core, seeds and white flesh from the pepper and cut it into strips. Cut the apricots into thin strips, cut the soya sprouts. Mix all the ingredients and pour over the dressing. Before serving, sprinkle with chopped walnuts and chopped kohlrabi leaves.

serves 6–8 • Soaking: 30–40 mins • Preparation: 10 mins • Refrigerating: 1 hr

Kohlrabi salad with tart apple

4 young kohlrabies, 2 tart apples, 1 tbsp lemon juice, 1 small fresh cucumber, 3 tbsps chives

DRESSING: ½ cup yogurt, 2 tbsps tomato paste, 1 tbsp lemon juice, 1 tsp mustard, salt, pepper, sugar

Peel the kohlrabies and apples and grate them coarsely, or cut into julienne strips. Sprinkle with lemon juice. Peel and dice the cucumber, combine with the apple and kohlrabies. Pour the dressing over, toss and refrigerate. Sprinkle with the chives before serving.

serves 6–8 • preparation: 10 mins • Refrigerating: 1 hr

Kohlrabi salad with spinach

2 young kohlrabies with leaves, 100 g spinach leaves, 2 bunches radishes, 100 g feta cheese, 3 hard-boiled eggs, juice of 1 lemon

DRESSING: 3 tbsps thick cream, 3 tbsps mayonnaise, 1 tbsp brandy, 1–2 garlic cloves, salt, pepper, ¼ tsp powdered ginger

Mince the chopped garlic with salt, pepper and ginger, mix well with the brandy and mayonnaise, cover and refrigerate. Wash and dry the spinach, cut it into strips, arrange in a serving dish and sprinkle with lemon juice. Peel the kohlrabies and cut them into matchsticks, dice the cheese, cut 2 eggs into half-slices, slice the radishes, chop 1 egg. Pour over the dressing and mix carefully but thoroughly. Set aside in the fridge. Before serving, sprinkle with chopped egg and kohlrabi leaves.

serves 6–8 • Preparation: 10 mins • Refrigerating: 1 hr

Kohlrabi salad with raisins

4 young kohlrabies, 1 small head radiccio, 3 tbsps raisins, 2 tbsps dry white wine, or water, juice and grated rind of 1 lemon, 1 tsp honey, 2 tbsps chopped walnuts, 2 tbsps salad oil, salt, pepper

Wash the raisins. Peel and julienne the kohlrabies. In a saucepan heat 1 tbsp oil and sauté the kohlrabies for 2–3 mins. Add the raisins, lemon juice and grated lemon rind, salt and pepper. Mix well and simmer for about 10 mins. Remove from the heat, leave aside to cool, place in a serving dish and mix with the honey. Set aside in the fridge. Cut the radiccio into thin strips, sprinkle with oil. In a hot frying pan dry roast the walnuts. Combine the radiccio with the kohlrabies, mix well and sprinkle with walnuts.

serves 4–6 • Preparation: 15 mins • Refrigerating: 30 mins

Kohlrabi stewed with raisins

*4 large young kohrabies, 1 small crisp lettuce,
3 tbsps raisins, 2 tbsps dry white wine,
3 tbsps chopped walnuts, 1 tbsp honey, 2 tbsps
lemon juice, salt, pepper, 2 tbsps olive oil*

Place the washed raisins in a small bowl and sprinkle with the wine. Peel the kohlrabies and cut into julienne. In a saucepan heat the olive oil, add the kohlrabies and fry for a moment or two, stir. Then sprinkle with water and simmer for about 10 mins. Add the raisins with the wine, lemon juice, salt and pepper. Mix well and simmer together for a moment or two. Add the honey, walnuts and lettuce cut into strips. Mix the whole. Remove from the heat, season to taste with salt and pepper, if desired. Serve with white bread, or as a side dish with meat.

serves 4–6 • Preparation: 20 mins

Kohlrabies stuffed with crayfish

*8 young kohlrabies, 200 g crayfish tails,
2 egg yolks, 4 tbsps breadcrumbs, 1 tbsp
chopped dill, 3 tbsps butter, 100 ml cream,
1 cup stock, 1 tsp flour, salt, pepper, sugar*

Rinse the kohlrabies and peel them thinly. Cut off the top slice, scoop out the flesh, leaving 1 cm thick shells. Chop the crayfish tails and mix with the egg yolks, breadcrumbs, 2 tbsps butter, cream and dill. Season the stuffing with salt and pepper. Stuff the kohlrabies with the mixture, cover with the cut off caps and arrange in a buttered ovenproof dish. Add as much stock as is needed to reach half the height of the kohlrabies. Simmer for 5 mins without cover, then for 20 mins covered. Mix the cream well with flour and the remaining stock, salt, pepper and sugar. Add to the kohlrabies, heat up until the sauce thickens.

serves 4 • Preparation: 40 mins

Kohlrabies stuffed with mushrooms

*200 g mushrooms, 2 onions, 1½ tbsps butter, 2 cups
stock, 2 eggs, 3–4 tbsps breadcrumbs, 4–5 tbsps
thick cream, 1 tbsp flour, 3 tbsps chopped parsley*

Place the peeled kohlrabies in lightly salted boiling water and cook for about 10 mins. Drain, cut off the tops, scoop out the flesh and cut it finely. Finely chop the onions and mushrooms and fry them in butter, add the kohlrabi flesh, breadcrumbs, salt, pepper and eggs and form smooth pulp. Stuff the kohlrabies. Arrange them in a flat saucepan, carefully pour over the stock, cover and simmer for about 20 mins. Mix the cream well with flour, chopped parsley and salt, add to the kohlrabies, shake the saucepan and heat up.

serves 4 • Preparation: 40 mins

Kohlrabies stuffed with veal

*8 young kohlrabies, 4 peppercorns, salt, 1 tbsp lemon
juice, a pinch of sugar, 300 g minced veal, 3–4 garlic
cloves, 3–4 tbsps breadcrumbs, 1 large onion, 3–4 tbsps
chopped parsley, 1 egg, salt, pepper, 8 slices lean
smoked streaky bacon, ½ cup stock, 1 tbsp butter*

Bring salted water with pepper, sugar and lemon juice to the boil. Add the kohlrabies and cook them for about 10 mins. Remove, rinse with cold water, drain. Cut off the tops and carefully scoop out the flesh. Chop the reserved flesh. Sauté the chopped onion in oil, add the meat and minced garlic and fry for a moment or two, stir. Remove from the heat, leave aside to cool. Then combine with the breadcrumbs and parsley, add the egg, salt and pepper and form smooth, uniform pulp. Stuff the hollowed kohlrabies and cover them with the cut off caps, wrap in the slices of bacon, and arrange in a buttered ovenproof dish. Add the stock and bake in a preheated oven for 20–25 mins. Serve with French fries or rice and green salad.

serves 4 • Preparation: 40 mins

Kohlrabies, Polish style

*8 young kohlrabies, 100 g ham, 50 g smoked
streaky bacon, 1 onion, 5–6 tbsps chopped
walnuts, 1 egg, salt, pepper, nutmeg, 2 tbsps
butter, 3 tbsps cream, 1 tbsp flour, 2 cups stock*

Peel the kohlrabies, put them in boiling salted water and cook for about 10 mins. Remove, rinse with cold water, drain in a sieve. Cut off the tops, scoop out the flesh. Dice the reserved kohlrabi flesh, chop the young kohlrabi leaves and combine with the finely chopped ham and bacon and with the sautéd chopped onion. Add salt, pepper, a pinch of grated nutmeg and 2–3 tbsps chopped walnuts. Stir in the egg, mix well and fill the kohlrabies with the mixture. Arrange the kohlrabies in a buttered ovenproof dish, pour over the stock, cover and stew over low heat for about 15 mins. Mix the cream well with flour and the remaining walnuts, pour into the kohlrabies, shake the dish so that the sauce spreads evenly, and simmer together for about 5–6 mins. Serve as a hot snack, or with potatoes and salads as the main course.

serves 4 • Preparation: 40 mins

Kohlrabies, Italian style

8 young kohlrabies, 1 onion, 350 g minced poultry meat, 1 tbsp dried thyme, 2 eggs, 2 tbsps thick sour cream, 1 tbsp breadcrumbs, 2 tbsps butter, 1 tbsp flour, 1 cup single cream, a pinch of nutmeg, 3 tbsps Parmesan cheese, 1 tbsp olive oil

Peel the kohlrabies and put them for about 10 mins into boiling salted water. Remove, rinse with cold water, drain in a sieve. Cut off the tops, scoop out the flesh. Finely cut the flesh and young leaves. In a frying pan, heat the olive oil and sauté the finely chopped onion. Add the meat and continue to fry for a moment or two, stir. Add the kolhrabi flesh and leaves, salt, pepper and 1 tsp thyme, and continue to fry for another 4–5 mins. Remove from the heat, leave aside to cool. Stir in the thick cream, 1 egg, breadcrumbs and carefully form the stuffing mix. Stuff the kohlrabies. Melt the butter in a saucepan, add the flour and make a roux. Dilute it with the single cream and, stirring constantly, cook until the sauce thickens. Season to taste with salt, pepper, nutmeg, add the remaining thyme, beaten egg yolk and 1 tbsp Parmesan. Mix well. Butter an ovenproof serving dish, arrange the kohlrabies, pour over the sauce, sprinkle with the remaining cheese. Bake for about 20 mins in a preheated oven. Serve as a hot snack or with potatoes and salads.

serves 4 • Preparation: 40 mins

Leek

The leek came to Poland from Italy, probably in the 16th century, and at first it was used only for making stock. Today, it is valued as a rich source of minerals and vitamins and is now used in salads, fried in batter, baked and added to sauces. The leek owes its fine taste and flavour to its essential oils which contain suphur and have antibacterial properties.

When buying leeks, pick ones with dark-green, fleshy leaves. Before you cook them, remember to remove the outer wilted leaves and cut off the root base, then rinse them very carefully under running water to wash out the earth which collects in between the leaves (it is a good idea to cut them lengthwise in half and separate the leaves). For cooking and baking, use only the white and light green part, and leave the dark green leaves to make stock or sauces.

Braised leeks

(1) *Wash the leeks very thoroughly. Cut off the dark green leaves (to be used for soup).*
(2) *Cut the leeks into 2 cm slices, cover with boiling water, put the lid on and cook on a very high heat.*
(3) *Melt the butter, add flour and, stirring all the time, brown it lightly, then take off the heat.*
(4) *Dilute the roux with some stock or water and, stirring all the time, bring it to the boil. Combine it with the leeks, add salt, pepper and vinegar to taste and put into a serving bowl.*

(Zofia Czerny, *Książka kucharska*, 1954)

Leeks with nuts

1 large leek (white part only), 100 g coarsely chopped hazelnuts and walnuts, 2 tbsps almond flakes, 4 hard-boiled eggs, 4–5 tbsps thick mayonnaise, salt, pepper, sugar, 1 tbsp lemon juice, sprigs of parsley

In a heated frying pan dry roast the hazelnuts and walnuts. Wash and dry the leak, cut into thin half-slices, sprinkle with lemon juice, combine with the nuts and season with salt, pepper and a dash of sugar. Add 3 hard-boiled eggs cut into thick cubes. Pour over the mayonnaise, toss gently but thoroughly. Chill. Before serving, sprinkle with almond flakes and decorate with 1 egg cut into quarters and parsley sprigs.

serves 4 • Preparation: 5–7 mins • Refrigerating: 30–40 mins

Leek salad with cucumbers

2 leeks, 2 fresh cucumbers, ¼ tsp ground caraway seeds, ¼ tsp ground cloves, ¼ tsp pepper, ¼ tsp salt, ½ tsp honey, ½ cup yogurt

Peel and slice the cucumbers, lightly sprinkle them with salt and set aside for a few minutes. Wash the leeks thoroughly and cut into thin rings. Mix the juice of the cucumbers with honey and blend in a food processor with the yogurt, pepper and caraway seeds. Chill. Combine the cucumbers with the leeks, pour over the chilled dressing and sprinkle with ground cloves. Serve as a side dish with poultry or fish.

serves 4 • Salting: 10–15 mins • Preparation: 5–10 mins

Leek salad with lemon balm

3 leeks, 4–5 garlic cloves, juice and grated rind of 1 lemon, 1 tbsp honey, 3–4 tbsps oil, 3–4 tbsps dry white wine, 2 tbsps chopped fresh lemon balm, 1 sprig fresh lemon balm

Wash the leeks thoroughly (cut off the green ends), dry and cut into thickish slices. In a flat saucepan heat the oil, add the finely chopped garlic and honey, mix well and add the leek rings. Sprinkle with the wine, lemon juice and lemon rind, mix together, cover and simmer for about 30 mins. Uncover, season with salt and pepper and mix well. Place the leeks in individual ovenproof serving shells, reduce the sauce, pour it over the leeks and bake for a few minutes in a preheated oven. Just before serving, sprinkle with the finely chopped lemon balm and decorate each shell with fresh lemon balm leaves. Makes a delicious snack served hot or cold.

serves 4–6 • Preparation: 40 mins

Leek salad

2–3 leeks (white parts only), 150 g purple plums, 1 tart apple, 2–3 garlic cloves, juice and grated rind

of 1 lemon, 3–4 tbsps salad oil, 3 tbsps chopped parsley, 3 tbsps chopped chives, salt, pepper, sugar

Cut the thoroughly washed leeks into thin half-slices, mix with oil. Peel and julienne the apple, mix with lemon juice and grated lemon rind. Cut the stoned plums into thin strips, sprinkle with a dash of sugar. Combine the salad ingredients, add the chopped garlic and greens, season with salt and pepper, toss well.

serves 4–6 • Preparation: 10 mins

Stewed leeks

1 kg leeks (white parts only), 3–4 garlic cloves, 1 tbsp chopped fresh ginger, 1 tsp crushed chilli, 1 tbsp ground caraway seeds, 2 tbsps butter, 1 cup yogurt, 2 tbsps dry white wine, 2 tbsps double cream, 3–4 tbsps finely chopped chives, salt, pepper

Cut the thoroughly washed leeks into thick slices. In a well-heated saucepan dry roast the chilli and caraway seeds, add butter, ginger and finely chopped garlic cloves. Stir and fry. Add the leeks, sprinkle with the wine, mix well and simmer for 5–6 mins. Blend in the cream and continue to simmer for another 2–3 mins. Remove the leeks with a slotted spoon, arrange them on a warmed ovenproof serving platter and keep warm. Combine the pan juices with the yogurt, season with salt, pepper, mix well (take care not to let it boil, or the yogurt will curdle), add the chives, mix, pour over the leeks and put into a preheated oven for 3–4 mins. Delicious with fish or poultry.

serves 4–6 • Preparation: 15–20 mins

Leeks stewed in wine

1 kg leeks, 1 tbsp oil, 2 tbsps butter, 2 cups dry white wine, 1 bay leaf, sprigs of parsley, 2 sprigs fresh thyme, grated nutmeg, salt, pepper, 3 hard-boiled eggs

Trim, wash and dry the leeks and cut diagonally into thickish slices. Heat the oil in a saucepan, add the leeks and butter, mix well and sauté for a moment, then add salt, pepper, 1 bay leaf, chopped parsley and thyme, pour over the hot wine. Cover and simmer for about 15 mins, then uncover to steam off the liquid. Arrange the leeks on a warmed serving platter, sprinkle with 2 finely chopped eggs. Decorate with parsley sprigs and egg quarters.

serves 4–6 • Preparation: 15–20 mins

Leeks stewed with apples

1 kg leeks, 300 g tart apples, 2 tbsps butter, salt, pepper, 1 tsp honey, 1 tbsp lemon juice, ½ tsp crushed dried thyme, 1 glass dry white wine

Trim and wash the leeks (discard the dark green parts) and cut into thickish slices. Melt the butter in a saucepan and add the leeks. Stir and fry for a moment, then sprinkle with the wine, cover and simmer for about 15 mins. Peel and coarsely grate the apples, sprinkle them with lemon juice, add to the leeks together with the honey, salt, pepper and marjoram. Mix well and simmer together for about 15 mins. Served with fried eggs and rice, the dish makes a delicious vegetarian meal. Can also be served with roast meats.

serves 4–6 • Preparation: 30–35 mins

Leeks baked with cold meats

1 kg leeks (white parts only), 300g leftovers of cold cuts, 2 hard-boiled eggs, ½ cup grated Roquefort-type cheese, 1 cup cream, 1–3 garlic cloves, 2 tbsps butter, salt, white pepper, ¼ tsp nutmeg, 1 tbsp lemon juice, 2 tbsps breadcrumbs or chopped walnuts

Pass the cold meat leftovers through a mincer and mix with the chopped garlic. Cook the trimmed and washed leeks for 10 mins in lightly salted boiling water. Drain, rinse with cold water and cut into pieces. Blend the cream well with half of the cheese, stir in salt, pepper, nutmeg and lemon juice. Butter an ovenproof dish, sprinkle with breadcrumbs or walnuts, line with the leeks and sprinkle with the minced cold meats and chopped eggs. Pour over the cream, sprinkle with grated cheese and dot with butter. Bake for about 30 mins in an oven preheated to 160–180°C. Serve as a hot snack or a side dish with roast potatoes and salads.

serves 4–6 • Preparation: 10 mins • Baking: 30 mins

Leeks baked with nuts

2 cups finely crumbled fresh bread, ¾ cup chopped hazelnuts and walnuts, 1–2 finely minced garlic cloves, 3 tbsps butter, 2 egg yolks, 1 tbsp chopped green basil, 1 tbsp chopped fresh rosemary, 1 tbsp chopped fresh oregano (or 1 tsp each dried herbs), 100 g grated cheese, 2 large leeks, 3 tbsps butter, 1 cup milk, 1 tbsp flour, 2 tbsps chopped fresh sage, salt, pepper, ½ tsp honey, 1 tbsp lemon juice

In a bowl blend the crumbled bread with the herbs, nuts and finely chopped garlic. Separately cream the butter, gradually adding the egg yolks and the bread mixture. Mix well with half of the grated cheese. Line a baking tin with the mixture and bake for about 15 mins in a preheated oven until golden brown. Wash and finely chop the leeks. Put them into a saucepan with melted butter and stir and fry for a moment or two. Sprinkle with flour, mix, add the milk and cook, stirring all the time until the sauce thickens. Season with salt, pepper, honey and lemon juice and mix again. Place the leeks on the baked pastry, top with the remaining cheese and bake in a preheated oven for about 20 mins.

serves 4 • Preparation: 25–30 mins • Baking: 20 mins

Leeks with red lentils

4 leeks (white parts only – about 600 g), 200 g red lentils, 2 carrots, ½ celeriac, a walnut-size piece of preserved ginger, 2 tbsps ginger syrup, 6–7 prunes, 2 cups stock, 1 tbsp butter, 1 tbsp oil, salt, pepper, 1 bunch dill

Soak the prunes in cold boiled water for about 30 mins, remove, cut into thin strips. Wash and peel the carrots and celeriac, cut them into small cubes, and cut the washed leeks into thin slices. In a saucepan heat the oil, add the butter, put in the carrots and celeriac. Stir and fry for about 5 mins. Combine the sautéed vegetables with the lentils, chopped ginger and prunes, season to taste with salt, pepper and ginger syrup, stir and heat. Sprinkle with chopped dill. Best served with boiled potatoes.

serves 4–6 • Preparation: 25–30 mins

Leeks baked with herbs

1 kg leeks, 2 tbsps chopped fresh mint, 3 tbsps chopped dill, 2 tbsps chopped fresh coriander, 2 tbsps chopped parsley, salt, pepper, 3 tbsps olive oil, ½ cup hot stock, ½ cup dry white wine

Put the washed leeks into boiling water and cook for 3–4 mins, drain, cut into pieces. Grease an ovenproof dish with oil, arrange the leeks, sprinkle with the mixed greens, salt and pepper, and pour over the wine mixed with the stock. Cover and bake in a preheated oven for 40–45 mins.

serves 4 • Preparation: 5 mins • Baking: 45 mins

Lentils

This close relation of peas and beans is cooked in a similar way. Lentils have several varieties differing in colour: green, brown and blonde. Lentil sprouts, that look like small brown balls, are an excellent addition to salads and sandwiches.

Lentils

This is one of the oldest vegetable plants, very nourishing and healthy. The larger the grains, the better they are. If you soak them in water overnight, they will cook quickly. Pour out the water in which they have soaked, add fresh water and cook until the lentils are tender. Add salt, put in one tablespoon of butter fried with ½ tablespoon of flour, and add juice from one lemon to give them a slightly bitter taste.

(Marja Śleżańska, *Kucharz polski*, 1932)

Lentils and spring onion salad

400 g lentils, 1 bunch spring onions

DRESSING: 1 tbsp hot mustard, 1 tsp honey, 2–3 garlic cloves, ¼ tsp grated lemon rind, juice of 1 lemon, 3–4 tbsps oil

Rinse the lentils and soak overnight. Cook in the same water until tender, drain and set aside to cool. Finely chop the garlic and mix with salt, honey, mustard, lemon rind and lemon juice. Gradually drizzle in the oil. Combine the lentils with the finely chopped spring onions, pour over the dressing, mix well, cover and refrigerate for 2–3 hours. Serve chilled.

serves 4 • Soaking: 12 hrs • Cooking: 35–40 mins • Refrigerating: 2–3 hrs

Lentil salad in herbal dressing

400 g brown or green lentils, 3–4 garlic cloves, 2 onions, 4 tbsps olive oil, 2 tbsps lemon juice, salt, 1 tsp ground coriander seeds, ½ tsp ground caraway seeds, ¼ tsp pepper, ¼ tsp cayenne pepper, 1 tbsp chopped coriander leaves, 1 tbsp chopped parsley, 2 tbsps chopped fresh mint

Place the washed lentils in salted boiling water and cook for 10 mins. Drain, put back into the saucepan, add the peeled garlic and enough boiled water to cover the lentils. Cook covered for about 30 mins, making sure the water doesn't evaporate and lentils do not burn. In a frying pan, heat 2 tbsps olive oil and sauté the finely chopped onion. Add pepper, ground caraway seeds, coriander and cayenne pepper and sauté together for 2–3 mins, stirring constantly, add salt. Drain the cooked lentils, combine with the onion, add the lemon juice and the remaining olive oil, mix all together thoroughly, set aside to cool, then cover and refrigerate for 1–2 hours. Before serving, mix well with the chopped greens.

serves 4 • Preparation: 50 mins • Refrigerating: 1–2 hrs

Vegetarian risotto

1 cup long-grain rice, 150 g lentils, 3 onions, 3 tbsps oil, 1 tbsp ground caraway seeds, 2½ cup stock, salt, pepper, 4 large fleshy tomatoes, 100 g sharp grated cheese, ½ tsp ground caraway seeds

Soak the washed lentils in preboiled (but cool) water for 3–4 hours. Rinse and drain the rice. In a large saucepan heat the oil and add the chopped onion. Fry for a moment or two, stir. Add the ground caraway seeds, mix well, add the rice and the drained lentils. Stir and fry for 3–4 mins, pour in the hot stock, add salt and pepper. Mix well, cover and cook over low heat for about 30 mins until the rice has absorbed the whole stock. Wash and dry the tomatoes, cut them in half, arrange on a baking tin and sprinkle generously with the grated cheese and lightly with the ground caraway seeds. Bake in a hot oven, serve with rice.

serves 4 • Soaking: 3–4 hrs • Preparation: 50 mins

Hot lentil goulash

2 cups lentils, 1–2 carrots, 2 large onions, 2 tart apples, 1 tbsp lemon juice, 1 cup stock, salt, pepper, 1 tsp curry powder, 2 tbsps single cream

Soak the lentils overnight. Peel the onions and cut them finely, cut the carrots and apples into sticks or cubes, sprinkle with lemon juice. Drain the lentils. In a saucepan sauté the onion in hot oil, add the carrots and apples and fry for 2–3 mins, stirring constantly. Add the lentils and fry all together for 1–2 mins, then add the stock, salt and pepper. Mix the curry powder with the cream, pour into the saucepan, mix well, cover and simmer until the lentils become tender. Serve with rice or white bread.

serves 4 • Soaking: 12 hrs • Preparation: 50 mins

Baked lentils and eggs

100 g green or brown lentils, 500 g firm fleshy tomatoes, 1 large onion, 2–3 garlic cloves, 1 green pepper, 1 red sweet pepper, 4 eggs, 2–3 tbsps chopped parsley, 2 tbsps dry red wine, 2–3 tbsps chicken stock, 1 bay leaf, salt, pepper, ½ tsp dried savory, 3 tbsps olive oil

Place the lentils in a saucepan and cover with lots of hot water. Cook covered for about 40 mins. Drain when soft. Wash and dry the peppers, remove the cores and seeds, cut into thin strips. Scald, skin and slice the tomatoes, finely chop the onion and garlic. In a frying pan, heat 2 tbsps olive oil, add the onion and garlic, fry for a moment or two, then add the peppers and fry for about 5 mins over low heat, stirring constantly. Add the lentils, bay leaf and savory, sprinkle with the stock and mix well. Add the tomatoes and simmer for about 15 mins. Season with salt and pepper to taste, remove the bay leaf and lightly steam

off. The mixture should be thick. Spread it on an oiled ovenproof dish, smooth the surface and make in it 4 holes with a spoon. Break an egg into each hole, sprinkle with the wine. Cover the dish with foil and bake in a preheated oven for about 25 mins. Serve when the egg whites are set.

serves 4 • Preparation: 50 mins • Baking: 25 mins

Lettuce

As those who know better claim, lettuce does not like the knife, therefore having rinsed it, you should separate its leaves and, if these are too large, tear them into narrow strips by hand. You then put them into a salad bowl and pour the dressing of your choice over. Lettuce is best prepared at the last moment and you should not salt it, or the leaves will wilt.

More and more varieties of lettuce are available commercially, the most common being **butter lettuce**, which has a round head and is on sale all year round, **iceberg lettuce**, which is crisp and round and has a very large firm heart; **cos (romaine) lettuce** and the **curly endive**, which do not form heads and have long leaves with a slightly bitter taste.

All varieties of lettuce go well with other vegetables: new cucumbers, radishes, spring onions, watercress, tomatoes, chicory or leek, and also with hard-boiled eggs, tuna fish, prawns, olives and citrus fruit. The best herbs to use with lettuce are mint leaves, lemon balm and basil.

Dressing and eating salad

Salad is an Italian dish. You can make it not only from lettuce or endive but also from any green plant, on condition that you have good vinegar and salt. And since this dish has become known in Poland, some people ask how it is best to prepare lettuce. Therefore I will tell you how it should best be eaten:

To dress it, add salt Polish style, olive oil German style, vinegar Italian style, and eat it French style, that is, with your fingers as the French do, so that no one snatches bits from your plate. For the rule is: use a knife and spoon when eating from a plate, because dipping your fingers in the plate is bad manners.

(Advice for Poles, dating from 1650)

SALAD DRESSINGS

Traditional salad dressing

1 cup thick sour cream, juice of ½ lemon, salt, ½ tsp sugar, 1 tsp chopped chives, 1 egg

Mix well the cream with sugar, salt, chives and lemon juice. Serve the lettuce salad in a salad bowl, add the dressing and toss to mix. Decorate with hard-boiled eggs.

serves 4 • Preparation: 1–2 mins

Pink salad dressing

1 cup thick sour cream, 2 tbsps ketchup, salt, sugar, 1 tsp chopped parsley

Mix well all the ingredients, chill and then pour the dressing over the lettuce arranged in a serving bowl.

serves 4 • Preparation: 1–2 mins

Avocado salad dressing

1 large ripe avocado, juice and grated rind of ½ lemon, 1 glass brandy, 1 tsp honey, 2–3 tbsps mayonnaise, 2–3 tbsps yogurt, salt, pepper, a pinch of cayenne pepper

Mix the avocado flesh with the brandy, honey, lemon juice and grated lemon rind, cover and chill.

serves 4 • Preparation: 1–2 mins

Simplest salad dressing

4 tbsps salad oil, 2–3 garlic cloves, salt, a pinch of sugar, pepper, 2 tbsps lemon juice, ¼ tsp cold boiled water

Blend the finely chopped garlic with salt, pepper, sugar and water and mix well with the oil and lemon juice.

serves 4 • Preparation: 1–2 mins

Vinaigrette salad dressing

4 tbsps sunflower oil, 2 garlic cloves, salt, a pinch of sugar, a pinch of pepper, lemon juice

Mince very finely chopped garlic with salt, pepper and sugar, gradually adding the oil until emulsified. Then add lemon juice and mix well.

serves 4 • Preparation: 1–2 mins

Mayonnaise salad dressing

1 egg yolk, 1 tbsp mustard, 4 tbsps sunflower oil, salt, sugar and pepper to taste, juice of ½ lemon

Mince well the egg yolk with mustard, adding salt and sugar, then gradually drizzle in the oil, stirring all the time. Add lemon juice at the end.

serves 4 • Preparation: 1–2 mins

French salad dressing

4 tbsps sunflower oil, lemon juice, 1 tsp ground mustard seeds, juice of 2 tomatoes, 2 tbsps white wine, 1–2 garlic cloves, salt, sugar

Mince very finely chopped garlic with salt, a dash of sugar, mustard seeds and tomato juice (you can sieve fresh tomatoes). Add the remaining ingredients and mix thoroughly. This dressing can be kept in the fridge for a few days.

serves 4 • Preparation: 1–2 mins

Iceberg lettuce with watercress

½ head iceberg lettuce, 150 g watercress, 2 tart apples, 1 tsp lemon juice, 2–3 tbsps chopped walnuts

DRESSING: 3 tbsps salad oil, 2 tbsps lemon juice, 1 tsp honey, salt, pepper, 1 garlic clove, finely chopped

Mix well all the ingredients of the dressing, set aside to cool. Coarsely grate the apples, sprinkle with lemon juice and combine with the chopped watercress, walnuts and iceberg lettuce torn into strips. Top with the dressing and mix well.

serves 4 • Preparation: 5 mins

Spring lettuce salad

1 small head iceberg lettuce, 1 tbsp chopped
yarrow leaves, 1 tbsp chopped plantain
leaves, 1 tbsp chopped young dandelion
leaves, 3–4 young radishes with leaves

DRESSING: 2 tbsps lemon juice, 3 tbsps
olive oil, ½ tsp honey, salt, pepper

Combine all the ingredients of the dressing and chill
slightly. Wash and dry the lettuce and tear it to pieces,
then combine with the chopped leaves of yarrow, plantain,
dandelion and radish, and with sliced radishes. Pour over
the dressing, toss and serve immediately.

serves 4 • Preparation: 5 mins

Lettuce salad with herbs

1 head lettuce, 2 tbsps chopped fresh basil,
2 tbsps chopped fresh marjoram, 2 tbsps chopped
fresh sage, 2 tbsps chopped fresh tarragon

DRESSING: 3–4 garlic cloves, 3 tbsps cream, 1 tbsp
mayonnaise, 1 tsp honey, 1 tbsp lemon juice, salt, pepper

Mix the finely chopped garlic with salt, pepper, honey
and lemon juice. Mix well with the mayonnaise and
cream. Chill. Wash and dry the lettuce and tear it to pieces. Place the lettuce in a serving bowl, sprinkle with the
chopped greens and pour over the chilled dressing, toss.

serves 4 • Preparation: 5 mins

Curly endive salad with walnuts

1 head curly endive, 2–3 tbsps chopped walnuts,
3 tbsps chopped fresh marjoram leaves, 1 tbsp
chopped dill, 1 tbsp chopped chives

DRESSING: 2–3 garlic cloves, 2 tbsps mayonnaise,
1 tbsp lemon juice, ½ tbsp mustard, 1 tsp
honey, salt, pepper, 2 tbsps olive oil

Mince well the garlic with salt and pepper, add honey
and lemon juice, mix with the mayonnaise and cream.

Refrigerate. Wash and drain the endive, tear it into pieces,
and place in a serving bowl. Sprinkle with the chopped
greens, pour over the dressing and sprinkle with chopped
walnuts.

serves 4 • Preparation: 5 mins

Stewed lettuce salad

6 small heads lettuce, 125 g butter, 2 bunches spring
onions, sprigs of parsley, 1 sprig thyme, 1 bay leaf,
salt, pepper, 1 tbsp honey, 2–3 tbsps dry white wine

In a small saucepan melt half of the butter and sauté the
finely chopped spring onions. Add ½ tbsp honey and
salt, mix well and simmer together over very low heat. In a
flat saucepan melt the remaining butter with the remaining
honey. Put in the washed and dried heads of lettuce and
sauté over low heat, until the lettuce yellows. Dredge with
pepper, add the spring onions, herbs and bay leaf. Sprinkle with the wine, cover and simmer for about 10 mins.
Uncover and steam off the liquid. Serve with veal cutlets
or pork chops.

serves 4–6 • Preparation: 15 mins

Maize (corn)

Maize, or sweetcorn, is a cereal with white or yellow
grains that can be used in many dishes, including salads and bakes.

Sweetcorn cobs with butter

*The cobs must be young, before the grains turn yellow. Re-
move the outer leaves and white silks underneath. Rinse the
cobs, put them into a large skillet, cover with boiling salted
water. Add a bit of sugar and cook for a good half hour until
the grains are tender. Wrap the cobs in napkins to prevent
them from getting cold and serve with salt and butter.*

(Marja Śleżańska, *Kucharz polski*, 1932)

Sweetcorn, Mexican style

Put a tin of sweetcorn into a frying pan with melted butter and fry it briskly, stirring all the time, until the liquid has evaporated. Melt fresh butter in a separate pan, mix it with cayenne pepper and add to the sweetcorn. Put the corn into small bowls or plates and serve hot.

(Antoni Teslar, *Kuchnia polsko-francuska*, 1910)

Young corn on cobs with butter

10 corn cobs, salt, sugar, 1 tbsp lemon juice, 100 g butter

Bring to the boil plenty of water with salt, sugar, lemon juice and 1 tbsp butter. Trim the corn cobs and immerse in boiling water. Cook over high heat for about 10 mins. Drain, arrange on a hot serving platter. Serve butter separately.

serves 5 • Preparation: 15 mins

Corn salad with plums

300 g purple plums, 1 tin corn, 1 small red pepper, 1 small orange pepper, 2 hard fleshy tomatoes, 2 hard gherkins, 1 tbsp capers, juice and grated lemon rind, salt, pepper, a pinch of icing sugar, 1½ tbsps grapeseed oil, 1 tbsp chopped parsley, 1 tbsp watercress sprouts, 1 tbsp wheat sprouts

Clean out the seeds, wash, dry and cut the peppers into thin strips. Scald and skin the tomatoes and together with the peeled cucumbers cut into cubes. Rinse the plums and remove the stones. Cut the plums into strips. Drain the corn in a sieve. Combine the salad ingredients, sprinkle with salt, pepper, grated lemon rind and sugar. Sprinkle with lemon juice, pour over the oil, mix well, cover and leave in the fridge for an hour. Combine with the greens, mix well and chill.

serves 4–6 • Preparation: 10 mins • Refrigerating: 1–2 hrs

Corn salad

Corn with vegetables

5 corn cobs or 1 tin corn, 250 g green beans,
1 small sweet orange pepper, 1 small red
pepper, 2 large onions, 3–4 fleshy tomatoes,
½ cup stock, 3 tbsps cooking oil, salt, sugar,
1 tbsp lemon juice, 3 tbsps chopped parsley

Cook the corn cobs in salted water, grate corn from the cobs. Remove the seeds and membranes from the peppers. Wash the peppers and beans, cut the beans into diagonal pieces and peppers into strips. Scald and skin the tomatoes, cut into pieces. Chop the onions and sauté in hot oil, add the beans and peppers, fry for a moment or two together, stir. Pour in the stock, add the tomatoes, mix well together, cover and simmer for a few minutes. Add the cooked corn grains, lemon juice, salt and sugar to taste, mix well and heat. Just before serving, sprinkle with parsley. Serve as a hot snack with white bread, or as a main dish with rice or kasha.

serves 4 • Preparation: 40–45 mins

Corn salad

1 tin corn, 2–3 baby gherkins, 6–8 marinated
mushrooms, 1 tart apple, 1 tsp lemon
juice, 2 tbsps chopped dill

DRESSING: 2–3 tbsps mayonnaise, 1–2 tbsps
yogurt, 1 tbsp hot mustard, salt, a dash
of sugar and cayenne pepper

Combine all the dressing ingredients, leave in the fridge to chill. Coarsely grate the peeled apple and sprinkle with lemon juice, cut the gherkins and mushrooms into cubes, drain the corn. Combine all the ingredients, pour the dressing over, mix well and refrigerate. Just before serving sprinkle with dill.

serves 4 • Preparation: 10 mins • Refrigerating: 1 hr

Baked corn

2 tins corn, 3–4 fleshy tomatoes, 3 large onions,
100 g thin slices turkey ham, 5 tsps grated cheese,
3 tbsps butter, salt, pepper, 2 tbsps chopped dill

Peel and slice the onions. Scald them, then rinse with cold water, drain. Scald and skin the tomatoes, then cut into slices. Drain the corn in a sieve. Butter an ovenproof serving dish and arrange layers of the corn, onion, ham slices and tomatoes, sprinkling each layer with salt and pepper. Sprinkle the top with grated cheese and dots of butter and bake in a preheated oven for about 20 mins. Serve as a hot snack, or with potatoes as a main dish. Just before serving, sprinkle with chopped dill.

serves 4 • Preparation: 10 mins • Baking: 20 mins

Marrow (gourd, squash)

Marrow contains a fairly large amount of minerals and vitamins. Either raw or cooked, it is recommended to those who suffer from bad circulation and liver and kidney disorders. It also has a beneficial effect as regards digestion, while juice from fresh marrow is a sleep-inducing remedy. The best are small young marrows from which soups, purée and pickles are made. They can be braised, baked, fried and stuffed.

Depending on the variety, marrows differ in colour. The most popular are green marrows which have a thick skin and are sweetish and yellow inside.

Stuffed marrows, Odessa style

Marrows resemble large cucumbers, but they belong to the same family as the courgettes. First peel some ripe marrows, cut off the tops on one side and scoop out the pulp. Fill them with stuffing and fry in butter on all sides. Transfer them to a skillet or a roasting tin, add 4 tablespoons of puréed tomatoes and the butter used for frying... Cover and cook. The stuffing is made from chopped raw meat (as for minced cutlets) mixed with some chopped browned onion, seasoned with salt and pepper. To this preparation you add some uncooked rice and grated potatoes and finally some dill and parsley.

(M. Marciszewska, *Doskonała kuchnia*)

Marrow salad

1 small young marrow, 3 tbsps chopped watercress, 1 small onion, 1 tbsp lemon juice, 2–3 garlic cloves, 1 tbsp mustard, 3 tbsps salad oil, salt, pepper, ½ tsp honey

Peel the marrow and blanch in lightly salted boiling water for 2–3 mins. Drain in a sieve, rinse with cold water and dry. Cut it lengthwise in half, remove the seeds and cut the flesh into julienne. Sprinkle with lemon juice and combine with the finely chopped onion, chopped garlic and watercress. Mix the mustard with honey, salt, pepper and oil, pour the dressing over the salad, mix well, cover and refrigerate.

serves 4 • Preparation:10 mins • Refrigerating: 1–2 hrs

Marrow pancakes

1 marrow (about 700 g), 1 tsp lemon juice, 2 onions, 150 g cottage cheese, 4 eggs, 1 tbsp butter, ½ tsp ground caraway seeds, ½ tsp pepper, ¼ tsp ground fennel seeds, salt, cooking oil

Peel the marrow, cut it lengthwise in half, remove the seeds. Coarsely grate the flesh and sprinkle with lemon juice. Finely chop the onions and sauté in melted butter. Add the grated marrow and stir fry for a moment or two. Steam off the excess liquid, remove from the heat, leave aside to cool. Add the caraway seeds, salt, pepper, fennel seeds and crumbled cottage cheese. Mix well, add the eggs and mix again. In a frying pan, heat the oil. Form little cakes with a spoon and fry them on both sides for 2–3 mins until golden in colour.

serves 4–6 • Preparation: 25–30 mins

Stuffed marrows

4 young smallish marrows, 200 g minced pork, 200 g minced veal, 1 large onion, 1 bread roll soaked in milk, 1 tbsp olive oil, 2 tbsps butter, 1 egg, 3 tbsps chopped parsley, salt, pepper, paprika, ¼ cup stock, 1 cup thick sour cream, 1 tsp flour, 1 tsp lemon juice, a pinch of sugar

Finely chop the onion and sauté it in olive oil. Add 1 tbsp butter and the minced meat and fry for a moment or two, stir. Leave aside to cool. Squeeze the bread roll dry and combine with the meat, chopped parsley, salt, pepper and paprika. Add the egg and knead the stuffing. Wash the marrows, cut them lengthwise in half and seed. Blanch the marrow halves in lightly salted boiling water for 2–3 mins. Carefully remove them with a slotted spoon, rinse with cold water and wipe dry. Stuff the halves with the mixture. Butter a saucepan and arrange the marrows. Sprinkle with the stock, cover and simmer for about 20 mins. Mix the cream with flour, lemon juice, a pinch of sugar, salt and pepper. Pour into the saucepan, mix carefully and heat uncovered until the sauce thickens.

serves 4–6 • Preparation: 30–35 mins

Baked marrows

1 kg young marrows, 1 cup chopped walnuts, 2 tbsps finely chopped parsley, 3 eggs, 1 cup thick sour cream, 50 g soft ewe-milk cheese, 4 tbsps grated sharp cheese, salt, pepper, 2 tbsps butter

Wash the marrows and cut into slices. Place in salted boiling water and cook for about 20 mins. Drain in a sieve. Mix the ewe-milk cheese thoroughly with the cream, walnuts and lightly beaten eggs. Mash the well drained marrows with a fork and mix with the cream sauce and chopped parsley. Butter an ovenproof serving dish and line it with the marrow pulp, sprinkle with the grated cheese and dots of butter. Bake for about 15 mins in a preheated oven. Serve with salads or pickles.

serves 4–6 • Preparation: 30 mins • Baking: 15 mins

Marrow stuffed with vegetables

1 large young marrow (1½ –2 kg), 3–4 carrots, 2 parsley roots, 1 smallish celeriac, 2–3 onions, 1 tbsp lemon juice, 1 tsp grated lemon rind, 4–5 hard fleshy tomatoes, 4–5 garlic cloves, 150 g grated hard cheese, 2 tbsps breadcrumbs, salt, pepper, 1 tsp paprika, ½ tsp dried, or 1 tsp fresh, chopped basil, ½ tsp dried, or 1 tsp fresh, chopped tarragon, ½ tsp dried, or 1 tsp fresh, chopped marjoram,

3 tbsps chopped parsley, 2 tbsps cooking oil,
2 tbsps butter, 2–3 tbsps stock or water

Peel the marrow, cut it lengthwise in half and seed. Put the marrow halves into salted boiling water and cook for 5–6 mins. Remove, rinse with cold water, drain. Peel and grate the carrots, parsley roots and celeriac, sprinkle with lemon juice. Scald, skin and dice the tomatoes. Chop the onions and sauté in hot oil, adding garlic mixed with salt and grated vegetables. Sprinkle with grated lemon rind. Fry for a moment or two, stir, then sprinkle the whole with the stock and simmer for 5–6 mins. Add the tomatoes, pepper, paprika, mix well and simmer for 2–3 mins. Remove from the heat, mix with half of the grated cheese and herbs. Butter an ovenproof dish and arrange the marrow halves. Stuff them with the prepared mixture, sprinkle with the remaining grated cheese mixed with the breadcrumbs and with melted butter. Bake for 15–20 mins in a preheated oven. Sprinkle with chopped parsley before serving.

serves 6–8 • Preparation: 20 mins • Baking: 20 mins

Vegetable pâté with marrows

1 kg young marrows, 200 g spinach, 100 g
onion, 1–2 garlic cloves, 3 tbsps minced peanuts,
½ tbsp minced flaked oats, 2 eggs, ½ cup single
cream, 5–6 tbsps breadcrumbs, salt, pepper,
¼ tsp powdered ginger, 1 tbsp finely chopped
fresh mint, 2 tbsps cooking oil, 2 tbsps butter

Heat the cream slightly and pour into a bowl with breadcrumbs. Mix well and leave aside for a few minutes. Wash the marrows, dry them and cut lengthwise in half. Remove the seeds and slice the flesh. Finely chop the onions and fry in hot oil, add the marrow slices and continue to fry for a moment or two, then cover and simmer for about 15 mins. When tender, remove from the heat, put the whole in a bowl, and mash with a fork. In a small saucepan melt the butter, add the finely chopped spinach and minced garlic and fry for a moment or two, stir. Add salt, mix well and steam off the excess liquid. Set aside to cool. Combine the cold marrows with the bread roll (soaked in milk and squeezed dry), peanuts, flaked oats, mint, ginger, salt, pepper and the eggs, and form pulp.

Butter a pâté mould, put in half of the pulp, cover with the spinach, then top with the remaining mixture. Place in a bain-marie and bake for about 1½ hours in the oven. Leave aside to cool, then refrigerate overnight. Serve with walnut or almond sauce. You can serve it hot with buckwheat kasha or couscous.

serves 8–10 • Preparation: 25–30 mins • Baking: 1½ hrs

Nettle

This is a plant that has been described by herbalists throughout the centuries. Some peoples thought it to have magic properties. The Germanic tribes dedicated it to the god of thunder and lightning. The Slavs believed that it chased away evil spirits and therefore included it in Corpus Christi flower wreaths and burnt it during thunder storms to protect their homes from lightning; they also censed cows with nettle smoke, in case evil witches meant to deprive them of their milk on St John's night.

Unfortunately the nettle later fell into oblivion, and is only now regaining its lost ground. It has become a popular ingredient of the so-called May diet which cleans the blood, fortifies the system, lowers the blood sugar content and improves the metabolism. Of all green plants, the nettle is the richest source of iron and, besides vitamins and minerals, contains many compounds which so far have not been thoroughly analyzed, although it is known that they have therapeutic qualities, like increasing immunity to various infections.

The edible parts of the nettle plant are the topmost leaves and stalks, collected from March on, preferably before the plants start blooming (later they become too stringy). Nettle leaves and young stalks can be braised, fried in batter, added to soups and salads, and also soured, like cabbage. Whole nettles are excellent for preserving fish and meat when a fridge is not available. Old cookery books contain many recipes for nettle soups, recommended as a 'healthy, cleansing dish for the early spring'. These nettle soups have an amazingly delicate taste so the effort of collecting the tops of the stinging plant is not in vain.

Juice from fresh nettles is the most perfect and potent of medicines, and is also the cheapest. So remember about this plant and eat it often, especially when you are on a low salt content diet.

Ruthenian nettle soup

Clean and cook ¾ litre of young spinach, the same amount of nettles and several handfuls of sorrel. Melt one tablespoon of butter and fry some chopped onion in it. Put in the spinach, sorrel and nettles and cook until tender. Pour in some stock, sieve the soup. Add some cream, heat up and serve with poached eggs.

(Wincentyna Zawadzka, *Kucharka litewska*, 1938)

Nettle salad with garlic

500 g young nettle, 3–4 garlic cloves, young sorrel leaves (handful), 2 tbsps chopped parsley, 1 tbsp chopped dill, 1 tbsp coriander, 1 tbsp chives, salt, pepper, 1 tbsp honey, 2–3 tbsps wine vinegar

Wash the nettle and parboil for 2–3 mins in lightly salted boiling water. Drain, rinse with cold water, drain again. Cut the nettle and sorrel into strips, combine with the remaining greens. Mince garlic with salt, pepper and honey, mix with vinegar, pour over the salad, toss.

serves 4 • Preparation: 5–7 mins

Festive salad with nettle

300 g young nettle stalks, 1 large red onion, 1 orange, 2 slices wholemeal bread

DRESSING: ½ cup double cream, 2 tbsps grated Parmesan, salt, pepper, nutmeg, 1 tbsp lemon juice, ½ tsp honey, a few yarrow leaves

Wash the nettle, place in a sieve, scald, then rinse with cold water, drain. Scald and peel the orange. Remove the white albedo of the orange peel and cut the yellow part into thin strips. Put them into boiling water for 1–2 mins, drain, rinse with cold water, drain again. Blend the cream with honey, lemon juice, salt, pepper, nutmeg and Parmesan until smooth. Chill. Cut the bread into small cubes and toast in a hot frying pan. Cut the orange into thick cubes, remove the seeds, cut the onion into half- slices. Combine the onion and orange with the nettle leaves and croutons, pour over the dressing, mix well. Decorate with strips of orange peel and yarrow leaves.

serves 4 • Preparation: 10 mins

Spicy nettle

800 g young nettle (shoots and leaves), 3 onions, 3–4 garlic cloves, ¼ cup chopped walnuts, 1 tbsp chopped fresh coriander, 1 tbsp chopped parsley and dill, 2 tbsps butter, salt, pepper, 1 tsp lemon juice

Parboil the washed nettle for 2–3 mins in salted boiling water, drain, rinse with cold water, drain again. Chop finely and mix with the walnuts and greens. In a saucepan melt the butter, sauté the finely chopped onion, add the nettle and finely chopped garlic, salt and pepper, sprinkle with lemon juice and simmer for a moment over low heat. Mix well together. Serve with chops or roast meats.

serves 4 • Preparation: 10–15 mins

Lent-time pelmeni with nettle

300 g young nettle leaves, 1 small onion, 1 tbsp butter, 2 hard-boiled eggs, 1 tsp ground pepper, salt, 1 tsp sifted breadcrumbs (optional)

DOUGH: 2 cups flour, 1 egg, 1 tbsp melted butter, salt, lukewarm boiled water

Knead the dough. Place the nettles in a sieve, scald and chop finely. Sauté the finely chopped onion in butter, add the chopped nettles and stir and fry for a moment. Remove from the heat, combine with the finely chopped hard-boiled eggs, salt and pepper, and mix well together. Sprinkle a pastry board with flour and roll out the dough. Cut out small circles. Now take a circle, spoon in a little filling, fold the top edge of the circle over the filling, seal it to the bottom edge very tightly with your fingers, pinch the edges together. Put the pelmeni in lots of salted boiling water and cook. Serve sprinkled with sour cream or melted butter.

serves 4 • Preparation: 40–50 mins

Monks' omelette with nettle

150 g young nettle leaves, 1 small onion,
1 tsp each finely chopped dill, chives, yarrow
leaves and celery leaves, 3 eggs, 1–2 tbsps
single cream, salt, pepper, 1 tbsp butter

Place the washed nettle in a sieve, scald, then chop finely and combine with the remaining greens. In a frying pan, melt the butter and sauté the finely chopped onion, add the herbs and fry for a few moments, stirring all the time. Beat the eggs with cream, salt and pepper, pour into the frying pan, mix well and put into a preheated oven. Bake until set and ligthly brown.

serves 4 • Preparation: 10 mins

Onion

The onion is the mainstay of all kinds of cuisine, adding flavour to both simple dishes and to the most elaborate culinary creations. It is probably the earliest cultivated vegetable, for it was known already 6000 years ago. Originally, it seems to have come from Asia. The Babilonians, Egyptians and Arabs regarded it as an aphrodisiac long before the Europeans even learnt about its existence. The onion was introduced into Europe first by the Greeks who used to eat a lot of it, and not only because of its alleged aphrodisiac properties, but also because it was said to give men courage.

There are many varieties of onion. Some are strong-flavoured and some are mild-flavoured. They are round or oval in shape. Their peel can be white, yellow, brown or red. The different varieties have different contents of essential oils, water and sugar. The lower the water and sugar content, the stronger the taste. Of all vegetables, the yellow and red varieties are the richest source of quercetin (an antioxidant which destroys some carcinogenic substances).

The therapeutic properties and nutritive value of the onion are a result of its diversified chemical composition. Apart from cellulose, viscous substances and essential oils, onions contain many vitamins, above all provitamin A, group B vitamins, vitamin C, E and K.

There are several varieties of onion, differing in their colour, shape and size. You should always choose firm specimens with a very thin skin and avoid those that have started to sprout leaves, or have a thick and dry skin. Onions should be stored in a cool, dark and airy place, and the purple variety is best kept in the fridge.

The purple variety is best served raw, in salads or on sandwiches. Green onions are young, unripe onions collected while their leaves are still green. They go excellently with sauces, stuffings and savoury bakes.

Yellow onions include large round Spanish sweet onion. Fairly thick, slightly browned slices are ideal as an addition to second course dishes. Finely sliced yellow onion can also be added to all sorts of salads, while the Spanish variety is very easy to stuff.

Red and pink onions are elongated in shape and they have much less flavour than the other varieties. For this reason they are best eaten raw in salads and also used for garnishing (cooked red onion loses its colour). If you store them too long, they tends to go bitter.

White onions have a mild flavour and are excellent for pickling and for kebabs, although you should always first blanch them for 2–3 minutes and then rinse them with cold water.

Spring onions (scallions) are small bulbs full of flavour, sold in bunches with their stalks still intact. They are particularly recommended for garnishing pasta, soups, casseroles, beans and other vegetables. They go very well in salads, but can also be cooked or braised. Scallions glazed in butter are an excellent accompaniment to meat and fish dishes. Before you steam them, you should blanch them for a few minutes and immediately rinse them with cold water. Scallions have the same mineral and vitamin content as common onions.

If the onion is called the queen of the vegetables, then the shallot, the favourite of French cuisine, deserves the name of the aristocrat of the onions.

Shallots constitute a source of vitamin C and folic acid. They have a very special flavour and subtler taste than ordinary onions. The yellow variety is larger and keeps better, but the red variety is smaller and tastier.

Shallots are best eaten raw or pickled, and their leaves can be used instead of ordinary spring chives. They should be cooked very briskly, preferably in white wine. Chopped shallots can be added to any sauce and various meat and fish dishes. Whole onions can be glazed and added to stews, goulashes, ragouts, soups and stuffings. Remember that chopped shallots should never be browned, or they will turn bitter. To skin them, you should use a very sharp knife, therefore it is a good idea to scald the onions in boiling water first.

Glazed shallots

Blanch the onions in boiling water, drain and skin them, then fry them in butter. Take them out with a strainer and transfer to a pan in which you have first made brown caramel. Pour over some stock, add salt and sugar to taste, cover and cook until tender. Towards the end, the liquid should be as thick as honey and the colour should be dark brown.

(Antoni Teslar, *Kuchnia polsko-francuska*, 1910)

Spring onion salad

2 bunches spring onions, 2 tart apples, 2 hard-boiled eggs, 3 tbsps chopped dill, 1 tbsp lemon juice, 3–4 tbsps cream, salt, sugar

Peel and julienne the apples, sprinkle with lemon juice and combine with the finely chopped onion and boiled eggs cut into cubes. Add a dash of sugar, salt and dill to the cream, mix well and pour over the salad, toss gently and set aside to cool.

serves 4 • Preparation: 5–7 mins • Refrigerating: 1–2 hrs

Onion salad with ewe-milk cheese

2 large onions, 1 cup olive oil, juice of 1 lemon, 2 hard-boiled eggs, 10–12 pitted olives, 1 tbsp capers,1 tin anchovies, 100 g oscypek (smoked ewe cheese), 4 tbsps chopped dill, salt, pepper

Cut the peeled onion into thin half-slices, place in a jar and sprinkle with lemon juice, add the olive oil, cover tightly and refrigerate overnight. The following day arrange on a serv-

ing platter, add the capers and anchovies cut into small pieces, olives cut into strips and cheese cut into cubes. Sprinkle with pepper, mix well adding salt, if desired (caution: anchovies, cheese and capers are quite salty). Just before serving, sprinkle with dill and the chopped hard-boiled eggs.

serves 4 • Macerating: 12 hrs • Preparation: 5–6 mins

Onions, Roman style

600 g shallots, 3 tbsps butter, 50 g raisins, 2 tbsps mustard, salt, pepper, ¼ tsp honey, ½ cup cream

In a saucepan melt the butter and sauté the onions. Add the raisins scalded with boiling water. Fry together for a while, stirring all the time, then add salt and pepper. Blend the cream with honey and mustard, pour over the onions, mix well, and cook covered over low heat. Serve with fish, meat and kasha.

serves 4 • Preparation: 25–30 mins

Onion, Monaco style

500 g small white onions, 100 g raisins, ½ cup olive oil, 1 cup water, juice and fresh grated rind of 1 lemon, 3 tbsps finely chopped parsley, ½ tsp powdered savory, ½ tsp ground coriander, salt, pepper, 2 tbsps tomato concentrate, a pinch of sugar

In a saucepan bring to the boil water with oil, salt, pepper, coriander, savory, lemon juice and lemon rind, cover and cook over low heat for about 20 mins. Wash the raisins, peel the onions. Add the tomato concentrate, onions, parsley and raisins to the stock, bring to the boil and simmer for 30–40 mins. Season with a pinch of sugar, and salt and pepper, if desired. Reduce the sauce slightly. Leave to cool, then chill. Serve as a cold appetizer, or as a side dish with white meat and poultry.

serves 4 • Preparation: 1 hr • Refrigerating: 1–2 hrs

Onion, Marie Therese style

800 g small white onions, 100 g raisins, 3 tbsps mustard, 100 g butter, ½ cup cream, salt, pepper, sugar

Scald and drain the raisins. Peel and rinse the onions. In a shallow saucepan melt the butter, add the onions, sauté for a moment, then add the raisins, pour in the cream mixed with mustard. Mix gently, sprinkle with salt, sugar and pepper and simmer, stirring occasionally. When tender, season to taste. Serve as a side dish with roast and fried meats, fish or poultry.

serves 4–6 • Preparation: 25–30 mins

Onions stuffed with apples

8 large onions uniform in size, 3 tart apples, 1 tbsp lemon juice, 1 large carrot, 1–2 garlic cloves, salt, pepper, ½ tsp honey, 1 cup wine vinegar, 1 cup light stock

Finely grate the peeled apples and carrot, sprinkle with lemon juice, mix with honey, salt and pepper. Remove the skin from the onions and carefully scoop out the centres. Finely chop the removed flesh and combine with the apples. Fill the cavities with the mixture. Bring the stock with vinegar to the boil, place the onions in a flat saucepan and add the hot stock. Set aside for 1–2 hours, then take out the onions and arrange on a serving dish, sprinkling with finely chopped garlic. Serve as a side dish with roast meats, preferably lamb.

serves 4–8 • Preparation: 10 mins • Marinating: 1–2 hrs

Onions stuffed with beans

8 large onions uniform in size, 200 g cooked beans, 2 tbsps butter, 1 tbsp chopped fresh rosemary, salt, pepper

Skin the onions and parboil for 10 mins in boiling salted water. Remove with a slotted spoon, rinse with cold water and drain. Carefully remove the centres. Blend the cooked beans with the onion centres, salt, pepper and rosemary. Stuff the onions with the pulp and arrange in a buttered shallow baking pan. Put a knob of butter on each onion and bake for 15–20 mins. Serve as a hot snack or as a side dish with roasts.

serves 4–8 • Preparation: 20 mins • Baking: 20 mins

Stewed onion in tomato sauce

200 g red onions, 800 g shallots, 2 tbsps tomato paste, 2 tbsps honey, ½ cup dry white wine, salt, pepper, 2 tbsps olive oil

Peel, rinse and finely chop the onions. Sauté them in olive oil, add the wine, salt, pepper and honey, mix thoroughly. Stew covered over low heat for about 20 mins. Add the tomato paste and simmer for a while, stirring all the time. Serve with roast meats.

serves 6–8 • Preparation: 30–35 mins

Onion stewed in wine

1 kg onions, 1 tsp ground coriander, 1 tsp freshly chopped ginger, 1 tbsp chopped green thyme, a pinch of saffron, 1 tbsp boiling water, 2 tbsps honey, 3 tbsps olive oil, 2 tbsps wine vinegar, 3 tbsps dry white wine, salt, pepper

Sauté the finely chopped onion in very hot olive oil, add honey, ginger, coriander and thyme, mix well and fry for a while over high heat, then sprinkle with the wine, cover and simmer for about 50 mins, stirring occasionally. Cover the saffron with boiling water, add to the onion, mix and cook uncovered for a few minutes, then steam off the excess liquid. Season with salt, pepper and vinegar to taste. Serve with grilled meats.

serves 4–6 • Preparation: 1 hr

Baked onions

12 onions uniform in size (preferably white or red), 3 tbsps pine nuts, 3 tbsps raisins, 1 glass dry white wine, ½ cup olive oil, salt, 1 tsp pepper

Place the peeled onions in a sieve, then scald and drain them. Scald and drain the raisins, and soak them in wine for 30 mins. Coat a baking pan with oil, arrange the onions, sprinkle them with salt, lots of pepper and olive oil, and bake in a preheated oven for about 30 mins. Then sprinkle with the raisins and pine nuts, add the wine in which the raisins were soaking and bake for another 25–35 mins. Serve as a hot snack, or with roast meat.

serves 4–6 • Preparation: 70–75 mins • Baking: 30 mins

Onions baked with minced meat

8 onions, 200–250 g minced meat, 3 tbsps breadcrumbs, 1 egg, 2 tbsps butter, salt, pepper, 1 cup stock, 2 tbsps grated hard cheese

Peel and rinse the onions, and parboil 6–8 mins in boiling slightly salted water. Remove with a slotted spoon, rinse with cold water and carefully remove the centres. Chop the scooped out flesh, combine with the meat and fry for a moment in butter. Add 1 tbsp breadcrumbs, salt, pepper, 2–3 tbsps stock and the egg. Fill the onions with this mixture and place them in a buttered baking dish, sprinkle with the stock and grated cheese and bake in a preheated oven for about 30 mins.

serves 4–8 • Preparation: 15 mins • Baking: 30 mins

Onions with rice stuffing

4 large onions, ¼ cup apple juice, 1 dessert apple, 1 orange

STUFFING: 1 cup long-grain rice, 1 sweet yellow pepper, 1 tart apple, 4 garlic cloves, 1 tsp ground coriander, ½ tsp curry powder, ½ tsp freshly ground pepper, 3 tbsps cooking oil, 1 cup stock

Peel the onions and blanch 2–3 mins in boiling water. Drain, rinse with cold water, drain again. Carefully remove the centres, leaving the sides 2 cm thick. Chop the onion which was removed. Cut the pepper and apple into small cubes. In a saucepan heat the oil, sauté the chopped onion, add the yellow pepper, garlic and apple, and fry for a while stirring all the time. Add the rice, pour in the hot stock, mix and cook over medium heat until the stock is absorbed by the rice. Season with curry, pepper and salt. Stuff the onions with the mixture, place them in a saucepan and cover with the apple juice, sprinkle with pepper and coriander. Cover and simmer for 40–50 mins. Heat up the remaining rice. Put the rice in a serving dish and decorate with knobs of butter and orange wedges. Make a border with the stuffed onions.

serves 4 • Preparation: 70–75 mins

Onions stuffed with ham

4 large onions, 250 g lean ham, 1 cup cooked rice, 1 tsp lemon juice, 3 hard fleshy tomatoes, 2–3 tbsps chopped parsley, 3 tbsps butter, salt, pepper, a pinch of cayenne pepper

SAUCE: 200 g processed cheese, 3 tbsps milk, 1 cup thick sour cream, 1 tbsp freshly chopped green herbs (thyme, mint, lemon balm), ½ tsp paprika

Skin and blanch the onions in boiling salted water for 2–3 mins. Drain, rinse with cold water, drain again. Carefully remove part of the centres, leaving the sides 2–3 cm thick. Sprinkle the rice with lemon juice, mix and leave out for a few minutes. Chop the reserved onion flesh, cut the ham into small pieces. Scald, skin and seed the tomatoes, cut them into cubes. In a deep frying pan melt 2 tbsps butter, sauté the onion, add the ham, tomatoes and rice and fry stirring for 2–3 mins. Remove from the heat and let the mixture cool slightly. Season with salt, pepper, cayenne pepper and sugar, if desired. Stir in the chopped parsley. Fill the onions with the stuffing, place them in a buttered ovenproof dish and bake for 4–5 mins in a well-heated oven. Mince the processed cheese thoroughly with the milk and cream, heat until melted, add the herbs and paprika. Pour over the onions and bake for about 8 mins. Serve with potatoes or rice and salads.

serves 4 • Preparation: 20–25 mins

Onions, Greek style

8 large onions (about 1 kg), salt, juice of 1 lemon, 8–10 cloves, ½ cup breadcrumbs, 2–3 tbsps single cream, 1 tin sardines in oil, 100 g ewe-milk cheese, 100 g salami, 2 hard-boiled eggs, 50 g almonds, 4–5 tbsps chopped parsley, salt, pepper, 2 tbsps lemon juice, ¼ tsp grated lemon rind, 2–3 tbsps butter

Peel and rinse the onions, then stick 1 clove in each. Boil salted water with lemon juice, add the onions and cook over low heat for 10–12 mins. Carefully remove with a slotted spoon, remove the cloves and hollow out the centres with a sharp knife. Finely chop the flesh which was removed. Pour the cream and oil from the tin of sardines over the breadcrumbs, mix well. Grate the cheese, finely cut the salami and egg. Combine the chopped parsley with lemon juice and breadcrumbs, add the salami, egg, cheese, chopped onion, salt, pepper and lemon rind. Mix well and stuff the onions with the mixture. Scald the almonds, peel them and chop. Butter an ovenproof dish, arrange the onion, sprinkle with almonds and dot with butter. Bake in a preheated oven for about 35 mins.

serves 4–8 • Preparation: 20 mins • Baking: 35 mins

Onion au gratin

1 kg onions, 4–5 tbsps butter, 4 eggs, 100 g grated Parmesan cheese, 2 tbsps chopped fresh, or 1 tsp dried oregano, 5 tbsps chopped chives, salt, pepper, 1–2 tbsps breadcrumbs

Peel and slice the onions, place them in a sieve, pour boiling water and drain. Cream thoroughly 4 tbsps butter, gradually adding 1 egg yolk at a time, oregano, salt and pepper. Beat the egg whites stiff, combine with the creamed butter, Parmesan cheese and chives. Butter an ovenproof dish, sprinkle slightly with breadcrumbs and line with the onions. Pour in the egg mixture, sprinkle with more breadcrumbs and bake in a preheated oven for about 30 mins.

serves 4–6 • Preparation: 15 mins • Baking: 30 mins

Parsnip

This vegetable, once known as the medieval potato, used to be harvested after the early ground frosts when it was sweet and delicious, having a mild nutty flavour. It was very popular in the ancient times and the Middle Ages, but later in many countries it gave way to the potato. It looks like the root parsley and tastes like the celeriac or sweet potato, and has a fairly high calorific value (70 Cal per 100 g). The root is soft, white or yellow in colour, and has a special sweetish taste. Because of these qualities, it is often used for preparing appetizers.

It can be added to soups, baked, puréed (preferably with onion) or fried (in slices coated with egg and breadcrumbs). Using grated parsnips and onion mixed with salt, pepper and eggs you may fry small patties. The parsnip goes very well with carrots, with the addition of some

ginger. Baked parsnips have a fine savoury and sweetish flavour. Boiled parsnips are served with meat or as a hot hors-d'oeuvre, with melted butter and herbs.

Parsnip

Peel the parsnip and cook it whole in salted water until tender. Cut it into slices and cook in butter, serve with bread fried in butter. The parsnip tastes best when you cook it with lamb ribs or with pork, in which case you should take out the meat and thicken the juices with browned flour.

(Marta Norkowska, *Najnowsza kuchnia wytworna i gospodarska*, 1904)

Parsnip salad

400 g parsnip roots, 1 tsp lemon juice, ½ cup chopped walnuts or hazelnuts, ½ cup raisins, ½ cup chopped parsley

DRESSING: 4–5 tbsps olive oil, 2 tbsps lemon juice and ½ tsp grated lemon rind, 2 tbsps white wine, 1 tsp honey, salt, pepper

Mix well the dressing ingredients, set aside to cool. Wash and dry the raisins. In a hot frying pan, dry roast the chopped nuts. Clean, wash and dry the parsnip, then grate it coarsely, sprinkle with lemon juice and mix with chopped parsley and half of the raisins and nuts. Pour over the dressing, toss and sprinkle with the remaining raisins and nuts.

serves 4 • Preparation: 10 mins

Glazed parsnip

1 kg small parsnip roots, 3 tbsps butter, juice and grated rind of 1 large orange, 2 tbsps sugar, 2 tbsps lemon juice, 2 tbsps sesame seeds, 2 tbsps finely chopped lemon balm, salt, pepper

Peel the parsnip roots and parboil them for 2–3 mins in boiling salted water. Cut into pieces uniform in size, sauté in butter, sprinkle with sugar and continue to cook for a few minutes, stirring all the time. Then add the orange juice and grated orange rind, and simmer over very low heat until the liquid evaporates and parsnips are well covered with glaze. Sprinkle with lemon juice, salt and a dash of pepper, dry roasted sesame seeds and chopped lemon balm leaves. Makes an unusual addition to roast white meat or poultry.

serves 4 • Preparation: 15–20 mins

Breaded parsnip

500 g parsnip roots, ½ cup milk, 2–3 tbsps flour, 2 eggs, ½ cup breadcrumbs, salt, pepper, oil or lard for frying

Put the peeled and washed parsnip roots into boiling water with milk and cook for about 10 mins. Drain, cool and cut each root lengthwise into slices. Beat the eggs with salt and pepper. Coat each slice of parsnip in flour, then in the beaten eggs and breadcrumbs. Fry in hot fat. Serve as a hot snack or a side dish with chops.

serves 4 • Preparation: 15–20 mins

Piquant parsnip salad

700 g parsnip roots, 4–5 cocktail gherkins, 4–5 marinated mushrooms, 4 tbsps chopped parsley, 4 tbsps chopped dill, salt, pepper, 3–4 tbsps olive oil, juice of 1 lemon

Cook the peeled and washed parsnip roots in boiling water, drain, rinse with cold water, dry and cut into julienne strips. Finely chop the gherkins and mushrooms, combine with the parsnip, season with salt and pepper to taste and sprinkle with lemon juice and olive oil, then with dill and parsley. Mix well. Serve as an addition to roasts or chops.

serves 4 • Preparation: 20–25 mins

Patty pan squash
(scallopini squash, pattison)

The pattison or patty pan squash or scallopini squash, due to its shape sometimes called the flying saucer, is related to the cucumber, but contains five times as much vitamin C as well as a fair amount of minerals (magnesium, potassium, iron, calcium). Like all members of the marrow family it comes in many colours and shapes. It may be light green or cream coloured (bell-shaped), green or dark green (discus-shaped).

The **golden patisson** has orange skin and greenish pulp. It is best in summer, when it is still half-ripe and soft skinned. It can be then cooked whole, without peeling, in salted boiling water, or else stuffed and baked. The older it is, the thicker its skin becomes and it has then to be peeled before cooking.

The **light-coloured patisson** it at its best when it is ripe and has a slightly floury flesh. All parts of it are edible: the skin, pulp and seeds. It can be boiled, stuffed and baked.

Young patissons are excellent for salads (with vinaigrette), boiled in water and garnished with melted butter and breadcrumbs, or fried or baked. Very small green and yellow squashes can be braised whole, pickled and salted. Larger ones are sometimed scooped and filled with a meat, mushroom or vegetable stuffing, preferably savoury. Patissons are very good when cooked with tomatoes and garlic.

Patisson chips

Peel and core the patissons, cut them into strips like French fries. Sprinkle them with pepper and brown them finely in very hot oil. Take them out and sprinkle with salt. Serve very hot.

(Irena Gumowska, *Te wspaniałe dyniowate*, 1993)

Patty pan squash, Polish style

2 patty pan squashes (about 800–900 g), salt, sugar, 1 tbsp butter, 1 tbsp lemon juice, butter, breadcrumbs

Peel the squashes, cut lengthwise in half, remove the seeds and cut the flesh into thin matchsticks. Bring to the boil some salted water with butter, sugar and lemon juice. Put in the julienned squash and cook for about 10 mins. Remove with a slotted spoon, arrange on a warm serving dish and top with melted butter with browned breadcrumbs.

serves 4 • Preparation: 15–17 mins

Patty pan squashes stuffed with kasha

4 patty pan squashes, 2 cups buckwheat kasha, 300 g mushrooms, 1 large onion, 1 tsp dried thyme, salt, pepper, 3–4 tbsps butter, 1 cup stock

Wash the squashes and parboil for 3–4 mins. Drain, rinse with cold water, drain again. Sauté the finely chopped onion in 2 tbsps melted butter, add the chopped mushrooms and fry together over high heat for 3–4 mins. Add 1 tbsp butter and kasha and continue to cook together for a moment or two. Remove from the heat, season with salt, pepper and thyme to taste. Cut the dried squashes lengthwise in half and remove the seeds. Stuff the halves with the mixture. Arrange in a buttered saucepan, sprinkle with the hot stock, cover and simmer for about 20 mins. Serve with mushroom or tomato sauce.

serves 4 • Preparation: 8–10 mins • Stewing: 20 mins

Peas

A proverb, probably English, says: 'Eat peas with the kings and cherries with the beggars'. Peas have been known for centuries, they have been highly valued in England since the 16th century and were very popular at the court of Louis XIV of France. In the past, peas fetched very high prices. During the reign of Sigismund III Vasa, Poles grew the more expensive variety called sugar peas.

Today, thanks to various methods of tinning and freezing, peas are available all year round. Fresh peas are best from June to August. The pods should be smooth and bright green; if they are yellowing in colour and have blemishes, it means that they have not been stored properly or have been picked too late.

Very young pods can be cooked in butter with a bit of stock or wine added, but generally speaking they are shelled. You should remember that 1–2 kg of pods produces not more than 400 g of shelled green peas.

Stewed green peas

Of the many varieties, the best are sugar snap peas, especially those from very large pods called 'telephone receivers'. The younger they are, the better they taste. Rinse one litre of shelled peas (for 5–6 servings), barely cover them with water, add some salt and one tablespoon of butter, cover and cook for half an hour. Add sugar to taste, dust with flour and cook for another 10 minutes. Serve with meat or as a separate dish with toasted bread... Before serving, mix in some chopped dill to enrich the flavour. The peas should be thick and contain only a small amount of liquid.

(Marja Ochorowicz-Monatowa, *Uniwersalna książka kucharska*, 1910)

Green peas, sweet pepper and egg salad

1 tin green peas, 1 sweet red pepper, 2 hard-boiled eggs, 1 tart apple, 1 tsp lemon juice, 1–2 small marinated patty pan squashes, ½ onion, 2–3 tbsps chopped parsley, 2–3 tbsps thick mayonnaise, salt, pepper, sugar

Blanch the sweet pepper, rinse with cold water, peel, seed and dice. Dice the apple, onion, patty pan squash and egg whites, sprinkle with lemon juice and combine with the drained peas. Mix with the mayonnaise, season with salt, pepper and sugar to taste. Chill. Before serving, decorate with chopped egg yolks and green parsley.

serves 4 • Preparation: 10 mins • Refrigerating: 1 hr

Green peas, potato and chicken salad

1 tin green peas, 2–3 potatoes cooked in jackets, 300 g boiled or roast chicken, 2 gherkins, 2 tbsps mayonnaise, 1 tbsp yogurt, salt, pepper, sugar, 1 tbsp lemon juice, 3 tbsps chopped dill, 2–3 cherry tomatoes

Peel and dice the potatoes, sprinkle them with lemon juice, pepper and salt. Drain the peas, peel and dice the gherkins and dice the chicken meat. Combine all the ingredients, season to taste with salt, pepper and sugar and add the mayonnaise and yogurt. Set aside to cool. Sprinkle with chopped dill and decorate with tomato quarters before serving.

serves 6–8 • Preparation: 10 mins • Refrigerating: 1 hr

Green peas with walnuts

500 g shelled green peas, 2 tbsps butter, 100 g walnuts, 3 tbsps parsley, salt, ½ tsp honey

Put the green peas into lightly salted boiling water and cook for 5–6 mins. Drain. In a saucepan melt the butter, put in the chopped almonds (or walnuts), brown slightly. Add the peas, salt and honey, mix well and heat up. Add chopped parsley, mix well. Makes an elegant side dish with roast poultry or veal.

serves 4–6 • Preparation: 10 mins

Green peas with almonds

500 g fresh (or frozen) green peas, 2 cups light chicken stock, 50 g almond flakes, 50 g butter

Wash the peas and put in a saucepan, cover with the hot stock. Cook for 6–10 mins, drain reserving the stock for soup. In a hot frying pan dry roast the almond flakes, add butter and, when melted, add the peas. Mix well and season to taste, if necessary. Place in a warmed bowl. Makes a delicious addition to roast veal or veal cutlets and roast poultry.

serves 4 • Preparation: 10 mins

Green peas with savory

500 g fresh green peas, 3 sprigs savory, 2 tbsps double cream, 2 tbsps chopped fresh savory leaves, a pinch of salt

Place 3 sprigs of savory in a saucepan, pour in 2 cups of water, salt lightly, cover and boil for 10 mins, then remove the sprigs, steam off the excess liquid, put the

peas in and cook uncovered for about 10 mins. Add the chopped savory, slightly cool and mix in a food processor into smooth pulp. Mix with the cream, add salt, if necessary, heat up. Serve with white meat.

serves 4 • Preparation: 20–25 mins

Green peas with tarragon

500 g fresh peas, 1 bunch spring onions, 1–2 garlic cloves, 2 tbsps chopped fresh tarragon leaves, salt, pepper, ½ tsp honey, 3 tbsps butter, ¼ cup light chicken stock

Melt the butter in a saucepan and add the peas and the finely chopped spring onions. Fry for a moment or two, stir. Add the garlic minced with salt, pepper and honey, sprinkle with the stock, mix well and simmer covered for about 10 mins. Then add the chopped tarragon, mix well and gently steam off the excess liquid. Serve with roast veal or poultry.

serves 4 • Preparation: 15 mins

Green peas with mint

1 kg very young green peas in pods, 6–7 sprigs fresh mint, ½ tsp salt, 2 tbsps butter, 2 tbsps chopped fresh mint, 1 tsp lemon juice,1 tsp honey

Bring to the boil water with salt, honey, lemon juice and sprigs of mint. Cover and boil for about 10 mins, then remove the mint, add the peas and cook for about 10–12 mins. Remove with a slotted spoon and place in a warmed serving dish. Pour over the melted butter and sprinkle with chopped mint.

serves 4–6 • Preparation: 20 mins

Green peas with sage

600 g green peas, 50 g lean raw streaky bacon, 7–8 garlic cloves, 2 tbsps chopped sage, 2 tbsps olive oil, ½ cup stock, salt

In a flat saucepan heat the olive oil and fry the finely chopped bacon. Add the finely chopped garlic and fry for a moment or two, stir. Put in the peas and continue to fry for another 2–3 mins, stirring all the time. Pour in the stock, mix well, cover and simmer for about 15 mins. Uncover, steam off the excess liquid, add sage, a dash of salt and mix together. Serve with roast or fried meats.

serves 4 • Preparation: 20 mins

Peas, hunter's style

500 g shelled fresh (or frozen) young green peas, salt, 1 tsp sugar, 1 tsp grated lemon rind, 150 g smoked lean streaky bacon, 200 g mushrooms, 1 tsp lemon juice, 1½ tbsps chopped fresh mint, ¾ cup cream, salt, pepper, 1 tbsp butter

Bring to the boil some salted water with sugar and grated lemon rind, add the peas and cook for 5–6 mins. Drain. Wash, dry and slice the mushrooms, sprinkle them with lemon juice. Cut the bacon in thin strips and fry in the melted butter, add the mushrooms and fry together for a moment, sprinkling with salt and pepper. Add the peas and simmer for a few minutes together. Pour in the cream, mix well, sprinkle with chopped mint. Serve with rice, or mix with cooked rice and bake in the oven.

serves 4–6 • Preparation: 15–20 mins

Peas with sauerkraut

1 cup dry peas, 700 g sauerkraut, 1 cup light stock, 1–2 onions, 2 tbsps lard, 1 tbsp butter, 1 tsp flour, 1 tsp caraway seeds, a pinch of salt, sugar and pepper, paprika

Wash the peas and soak in boiled water overnight. The following day drain and cover with fresh water. Cook until nearly tender, then add the butter, salt, steam off the excess liquid and mix in a food processor. Chop the sauerkraut, put it into a saucepan and pour over the hot stock. Add the caraway seeds, mix well and bring to the boil. Cook over low heat for about 40 mins. Combine the sauerkraut with the peas and cook together for a few mins. Chop the onions finely and sauté in heated lard, stir in the flour, season with salt and pepper, mix with the sauerkraut and peas. Season with paprika to taste. Bring to the boil. Serve with bread, or as a side dish with e.g. pork knuckle.

serves 6–8 • Soaking: 12 hrs • Preparation: 1 hr

Peas with sauerkraut and mushrooms

1 cup dry peas, a pinch of savory, 400 g sauerkraut, 1 cup stock, 200 g lean streaky bacon (boneless), 6–8 dried mushrooms, 1 large onion, 1 tbsp butter, ½ tsp dried basil, ½ tsp dried thyme, 1 raw potato, salt, pepper

Wash the peas and soak in boiled water overnight. In a separate small saucepan soak the mushrooms. The following day drain the peas and cover with fresh water, add savory and cook until tender, seasoning with salt towards the end. Cook the mushrooms. Chop the sauerkraut, put into a saucepan and pour in the hot stock and mushroom stock. Add the bacon and bring the whole to the boil, then simmer for about 40 mins. Take out the tender bacon and dice it, and cut the mushrooms into thin strips. Chop the onion and fry in butter until light brown. Combine the sauerkraut with the peas, mushrooms, bacon and onion, add basil, thyme and pepper. Mix well and cook together for a few minutes. Peel a potato, grate it and add to saueracraut, mix well, bring to the boil and season with salt and pepper to taste, if necessary.

serves 6–8 • Soaking: 12 hrs • Preparation: 1 hr

Sieved peas with savory

1 cup dry peas, ½ tsp dried savory, 2 onions, 1 cup stock, salt, sugar, 2 tbsps olive oil, 2 tbsps lemon juice

Wash the peas and soak in boiled water. Drain the following day, put into a saucepan, add the chopped onion and savory and enough boiled water to cover the peas. Cook over low heat for about 1 hour. Drain and mix together in a food processor with the stock, salt and pepper. Transfer to a saucepan, put in a bain-marie and stirring all the time heat, gradually adding lemon juice and olive oil.

serves 4 • Soaking: 12 hrs

Peppers

Peppers are very rich in nutritive elements, containing five times more vitamin C than citrus fruit. They are related to both potatoes and tomatoes and have many varieties. Sweet peppers are used in salads, pickles and various hot dishes, and they can also be stuffed. Hot peppers, both whole and powdered, are used exclusively as a condiment.

Turkish pepper

The shiny pods of Turkish pepper, which come in different colours and shapes, constitute a popular vegetable in Italy and Hungary. However they are rarely grown in Poland because they are difficult to cultivate and need a warm temperature. In the warmer climates, pepper pods are used in various ways. The sweet varieties are eaten raw. Half green pods are picked and put into wine vinegar, then taken out several days later, sliced, mixed with capers and sardines, and eaten as an appetizer. Ripe pods are quartered and grilled, then, when still hot, skinned, and after they have cooled down, dressed with vinegar and oil and served as a salad or sprinkled with Parmesan cheese and baked.

In Poland, we mostly eat the piquant varieties which are used in preserving pickles, including gherkins and cucumbers.

(Marta Norkowska, *Najnowsza kuchnia wytworna i gospodarska*, 1904)

Pepper rings I

1 red, 1 yellow, 1 green pepper

STUFFING: 1 tin sardines, 100 g Roquefort-type cheese, 200 g cottage cheese, 2 tbsps chopped parsley, 1 small onion, chopped, salt, pepper, 1 tsp lemon juice, a pinch of sugar, 1 tbsp butter

Rinse and dry the peppers, cut off the bottoms with stems, remove the seeds and white membrane. Blend the butter with Roquefort, chopped onion and parsley, season with salt, pepper and lemon juice to taste. Mix well. Stuff the peppers with the mixture and set them aside in the fridge for

2–3 hours. Before serving, cut the peppers into thick slices, arrange on lettuce leaves and decorate with parsley sprigs.

serves 6–8 • Preparation: 10–15 mins • Refrigerating: 2–3 hrs

Pepper rings II

1 red, 1 yellow, 1 green pepper

STUFFING: 200 ewe-milk cheese, 4 tbsps thick cream, 1 onion, 100 g lean ham, 2 tbsps chopped parsley, 2 tbsps chives, 1 tbsp butter, salt, pepper, 1 tsp lemon juice

Finely chop the onion and ham. Mix the butter with lemon juice, salt, pepper, ham and onion. Blend the ewe-milk cheese with cream, combine with the ham paste and mix well. Stuff the peppers and refrigerate for 2–3 hours. Cut into thick slices before serving.

serves 6–8 • Preparation: 10–15 mins • Refrigerating: 2–3 hrs

French salad with peppers

1 each large red, yellow, green, orange and purple peppers, 4–5 firm, fleshy tomatoes, 4–5 hard-boiled eggs, 2 spice-salted herring fillets, 2 tbsps pitted olives

DRESSING: 3–4 garlic cloves, ½ cup olive oil, 3–4 tbsps lemon juice or wine vinegar, 1 tbsp chopped parsley, 1 tbsp chopped chives, salt, pepper, sugar

Mince garlic with salt and pepper, a pinch of sugar, lemon juice and olive oil, mix with parsley and chives, cover, leave to cool. Place the washed and dried peppers in a hot oven for a few minutes. Skin them, cut in half, remove the seeds and white membrane, and cut the flesh into thick strips. Scald, skin and slice the tomatoes, cut the herring fillets into thin strips and eggs into slices. Arrange the tomato slices on a round serving platter, sprinkle with olive oil. Then top the tomatoes with the colourful strips of pepper, pour over the dressing and on top arrange the egg slices decorated with olives and herring strips. Pour over the dressing and put in the fridge for 30–40 mins.

serves 6–8 • Preparation: 25–30 mins • Refrigerating: 30–40 mins

Pepper salad with tuna

1 each yellow, orange and green sweet peppers, 5 large fleshy tomatoes, 1 bunch spring onions, 1 small red onion, 1 tin tuna in oil, 2 hard-boiled eggs, 1 tbsp capers, 1 tsp marinated green pepper, 2 tbsps chopped fresh coriander, 2 tbsps lemon juice, 3 tbsps olive oil, salt, pepper, sugar

Wash and dry the peppers, remove the seeds and white membranes. Cut the peppers into strips, finely chop the spring onions and red onion. Scald and skin the tomatoes, cut them into cubes (remove the seeds and excess juice), combine with the peppers and onion. Separate the tuna with a fork, combine with the capers and marinated green pepper, mix with the sweet peppers and tomatoes, season with salt, pepper and a pinch of sugar, sprinkle with lemon juice and oil, mix and set aside to cool. Just before serving, sprinkle with chopped hard-boiled eggs and parsley.

serves 6–8 • Preparation: 15 mins • Refrigerating: 30–40 mins

Peppers stuffed with cheese

2 large red and 2 orange sweet peppers, 100 g Emmental cheese, 150 g Gruyère, 100 g cottage cheese, 2 potatoes cooked in their skins, 1 cup cream, 2 raw eggs, 2 tbsps pitted black olives, salt, pepper, grated nutmeg, 2 tbsps butter

Peel the potatoes and mix them in a food processor with the cottage cheese, cream, salt, pepper and grated nutmeg, gradually adding the egg yolks. Combine the mixture with 1 tbsp finely chopped olives, grated Emmental, GruyŹre and the stiff beaten egg whites. Cut a slice from the stem end of the peppers, remove the seeds and white membrane. Stuff the peppers with the mixture and arrange them on a buttered ovenproof serving platter, sprinkle with melted butter and bake in a preheated oven (200–220°C). Just before serving, decorate with the remaining olives. Serve as a hot snack, or as a side dish with cutlets.

serves 6–8 • Preparation: 15–20 mins • Baking: 30 mins

Peppers stuffed with tuna

8 small yellow peppers, 3 potatoes boiled in their skins, 1 tin tuna in brine, 3 hard-boiled eggs, 3–4 garlic cloves, 1 large onion, 1 bunch chives, salt, pepper, 3–4 tbsps sunflower oil

Cut the peppers in half lenghtwise, remove the seeds and white membranes, wash, dry and sprinkle with salt inside. Chop the onion, cut the eggs and potatoes into small cubes. Drain the tuna and combine with the potatoes, onion, eggs and garlic minced with salt. Season with salt and mix well with 1 tbsp oil. Fill in the pepper halves with the stuffing. Grease an ovenproof serving platter with oil, arrange the peppers snugly filled side up, lightly sprinkle with oil and bake for about 40 mins in a preheated oven. Just before serving, sprinkle with chopped chives.

serves 4–8 • Preparation: 10–15 mins • Baking: 30–40 mins

Peppers stuffed with ewe-milk cheese

4 red sweet peppers, 300 g ewe-milk cheese, 100 g cottage cheese, 1 tbsp chopped dill, 1 tbsp chopped chives, 2 eggs, salt, pepper, 1 cup thick cream, 2 tbsps chopped parsley, salt, pepper, a pinch of sugar, 2 tbsps butter

Mix the ewe-milk cheese with cottage cheese, egg yolk and the chopped greens, season to taste and combine with the stiff beaten egg whites. Cut a slice from the stem end of the peppers, remove the seeds. Stuff with the mixture and place on a buttered ovenproof serving platter. Bake for 10 mins in a preheated oven. Blend the cream with salt, pepper, sugar and chopped parsley, pour over the peppers and continue to bake for another 20–25 mins. Best served with potatoes and tomato salad.

serves 4 • Preparation: 10 mins • Baking: 35–40 mins

Peppers with herbal stuffing

4 large peppers, 2 large onions, 5–6 garlic cloves, 200 g mushrooms, 1 cup cooked rice, ¾ cup grated cheese, 1 tbsp chopped thyme leaves, 10–12 black mustard seeds, salt, pepper, 6–8 ripe, fleshy tomatoes, 2 tbsps oil, 2 tbsps butter

Wash and dry the peppers and place them in a hot oven for 10 mins. Remove, cut lengthwise, discard the seeds and white membranes. Scald and skin the tomatoes. In a frying pan, heat 1 tbsp oil and sauté 1 finely chopped onion and garlic, add the chopped mushrooms, stir and fry for a moment or two. Remove from the heat, mix with the rice, grated cheese, thyme and mustard seeds, salt and pepper. Stuff the pepper halves with the mixture. In a frying pan, heat the remaining oil and sauté the other onion cut into cubes. Cut the tomatoes into thick slices. Butter an ovenproof serving dish, line it with the tomatoes, sprinkle with the sautéed onion and on top arrange the stuffed peppers. Sprinkle with melted butter and bake for about 30–40 mins in a preheated oven. Serve with rice or French fries.

serves 4 • Preparation: 15–20 mins • Baking: 30–40 mins

Peppers baked with ham

2 green, 2 yellow and 2 red sweet peppers, 300 g ham cut into thin slices, 150 g processed cheese, 1 tsp dried oregano, ½ tsp dried thyme, 1 tsp salt, ¼ tsp ground pepper, 3 tbsps grapeseed oil, ½ cup light stock, 3 tbsps chopped chives

Wash and cut the peppers into long, wide strips. Remove the seeds and white membranes. Mix the oil with salt, pepper and herbs. Arrange the strips of pepper on an ovenproof serving platter, sprinkle with the oil and set aside for 2–3 hours, then remove from the marinade. Wrap 3–4 colour pepper strips with a slice of ham and arrange the rolls on a serving platter with the remaining oil. Bake in a preheated oven for about 30–35 mins, then sprinkle with the cheese and bake for another 10 mins or so, until the cheese has melted. Before serving sprinkle with chopped chives. Serve with baked potatoes or rice.

serves 4 • Macerating: 2–3 hrs • Preparation: 45–50 mins

Pumpkin

Pumpkin is a rich source of vitamin A and it also contains quite a lot of vitamin C and folic acid. Pumpkins have very hard skin varying in colour depending on the particular kind (from greyish blue to yellow and bright orange), and have yellow or orange pulp inside. The brighter the colour of the pulp, the higher the vitamin content.

Some varieties are grown mostly for their seeds which are rich in easily digestible fats, proteins and vitamins A, C and E (recommended for various stomach, bladder and prostate disorders). The seeds are best eaten raw or slightly toasted with salt or sugar. Ground seeds can be added to cakes and pastries and also to bread.

Other varieties of pumpkin are used mostly for cooking. Their pulp can be cooked or pickled; during the cooking process, it disintegrates into fibres which can be served instead of pasta with many dishes. Such pumpkins are best cooked whole for about 30 minutes, then taken out and cooled under running water. You then halve them lengthwise, remove the seeds and scoop the pulp out. You may serve them with various sauces or bake them with butter, garlic and cheese, or else with peppers, tomatoes, ham and garlic. Pumpkins can also be used for dessert: cook them with tart apples, shredded coconut, chopped walnuts, honey and butter, and serve hot or cold.

Gourd with breadcrumbs and butter

Gourd is a common vegetable... but if you cook it the right way it makes a tasty, delicate dish. It is moreover easily digestible and should be recommended to those who suffer from various stomach disorders... Cut a gourd in half, scoop out the seeds, cut off the thick outside skin. Blanch the gourd, dice it... and cook in salted water with a pinch of sugar added. Before serving, pour over it some melted butter mixed with browned breadcrumbs.

(Marja Śleżańska, *Kucharz doskonały*, 1932)

Pumpkin stewed with apricots

Pumpkin salad with herbs

300 g pumpkin flesh, 1 large tart apple, 1 tsp lemon juice, 2 tbsps chopped fresh basil, 2 tbsps chopped parsley, 2 tbsps chopped fresh mint, 50 g raisins, 2 tbsps dry white wine, ½ cup chopped walnuts

DRESSING: 3 tbsps mayonnaise, 2 tbsps yogurt, 1 tbsp lemon juice, ½ tsp grated lemon rind, salt, white pepper, a pinch of sugar, 3–4 lettuce leaves

Mix all ingredients of the dressing. Leave aside to cool. Peel and julienne the apple, sprinkle with lemon juice. Wash the raisins and soak them in wine. Cut the pumpkin flesh (washed and dried) into julienne, sprinkle with lemon juice. Combine the pumpkin with the apple, raisins, ¼ cup chopped walnuts and the chopped greens. Pour over the dressing, mix well, chill. Before serving, arrange the salad in a salad bowl on lettuce leaves, sprinkle with the remaining greens and walnuts.

serves 4 • Preparation: 10 mins • Refrigerating: 1 hr

Pumpkin stewed with apricots

700 g pumpkin flesh, 250 g dried apricots, 1 glass dry white wine, 2 onions, ¾ cup chopped walnuts, ¼ tsp ground cloves, ½ tsp cinnamon, salt, sugar, 2 tbsps butter, 1–2 tbsps chopped parsley

Dice the pumpkin, put into a saucepan and add some hot water. Cook covered for about 30 minutes over low heat. Drain, mix with the cloves and cinnamon. Wash the apricots, cover them with the wine, bring to the boil, remove with a slotted spoon, leave to cool, then cut into thin strips. In a saucepan melt the butter, sauté the finely chopped onion, add the pumpkin, the apricots and the apricot stock. Mix carefully and simmer together for a few minutes. Season to taste with salt and sugar, combine with the walnuts. Before serving, sprinkle with chopped parsley. Serve as a hot snack, or with roast veal.

serves 4–6 • Preparation: 40–45 mins

Pumpkin stewed in cream

500 g pumpkin flesh, 1 each yellow, red and green sweet peppers, 2 large onions,

2–3 tbsps water or stock, 2 tbsps butter, ¾ cup cream, 1–2 garlic cloves, 1 egg yolk, salt, pepper, sugar, grated nutmeg, 1 tsp lemon juice

Cut the pumpkin flesh into thick cubes, onion into half-slices and peppers (first remove seeds) into thin strips. In a saucepan melt the butter, sauté the onions, add the peppers and fry together for a moment. When the peppers soften, add the pumpkin, sprinkle with water, mix and stew over low heat. Season to taste with pepper, nutmeg and sugar. Blend the chopped garlic with salt and mix the cream with the egg yolk, garlic and lemon juice. Pour the mixture into the saucepan, mix well and heat (do not boil!). Season to taste. Serve with bread or rice.

serves 4–6 • Preparation: 40 mins

Radish

This vegetable originated probably in Asia and became established in the Mediterranean basin. It has been cultivated as a salad vegetable for centuries (in Egypt as early as 2780 BC). The Greeks made offerings of it to their gods (radishes made of gold were dedicated to Apollo in the temple of Delphi). The Egyptians painted radishes on the walls of tombs. The Romans threw them at tedious, unimaginative speakers.

Both small pink radishes and large black ones were known in the ancient world. Horace wrote that they activated the stomach of the fat. In the 12th century, St Hildegard claimed that they cleansed the brain and gave one clarity of thought. And there is something in what they said, because the radish is an exceptionally good source of minerals (sodium, potassium, calcium, iron, iodine, phosphorus, magnesium) and vitamins (C, B_1, B_2, B_3 and B_6) and provitamin A.

Thanks to their 'looks' and special flavour radishes have been popular ever since ancient times, and their high vitamin and mineral content make them very healthy vegetables.

Radishes of both kinds act as diuretics and are therefore recommended by dieticians and film stars as an excellent component of slimming diets. They have a beneficial effect on the functioning of the liver and kidneys, control the metabolism and, probably because of their high sulphur content, improve the condition of the skin and hair.

The radish is an annual. Its edible root comes in various shapes and sizes, but should always be unblemished, and the leaves must be fresh and not yellowed and wilting.

The best are of course fresh radishes, but you can also store them for several days in a plastic bag in the fridge, on condition that you first cut off the leaves. To 'refresh' them and make them firm and crispy, you can put them for 20–30 minutes into cold water with a bit of salt added.

There are many varieties of radish, differing in size, shape and colour, the most popular of which are the following:

winter radishes which are usually round in shape, rather sharp in taste, with a rough skin that is black or mauvish; their vitamin and mineral content is much higher than in the case of small pink or red radishes;

radishes available all year round are small, round, oval or elongated in shape, red or scarlet; some are rather sharp in taste, others are mild;

daikon, a Far Eastern vegetable, also known as Japanese or Satsuma radish, which has become popular in Europe only recently. Its root is milder tasting (apart from the very thin and long variety, which has a sharp taste) than the traditional radish and is served as a side dish with meat, and added to soups and sauces. It is a highly recommended ingredient of various salads and goes well with spring onions, red peppers and tomatoes. It can be dressed with cream, yogurt, soya sauce, rice vinegar or lemon juice. As a side dish to meat, you may mix it with some freshly chopped ginger and soya sauce. It can also be sliced and blanched and served garnished with toasted sesame seeds.

Crispy, low-calorie radishes, which have a nice sharp flavour, can be added to various dishes, above all salads. They mix well with diced carrots, celery and broccoli with a yogurt dressing, as well as with chives and hard-boiled eggs dressed with cream. As garnishing, red radishes can add a bit of colour to sandwiches and meat dishes. It is also worth remembering the following:

– finely sliced radishes can be added to roast beef if you do not have any dried mushrooms at hand;
– blanched radish leaves added to spinach cooked in butter enhance the taste of this dish;
– finely chopped new radish leaves can be added to various salads, including those with lettuce; they can also be served on their own, mixed with chives and spinach, with salt, pepper, sugar, lemon juice and olive oil.

Radish

Common red radishes can make a delicate, tasty vegetable. Peel them finely and boil whole, then stew in butter with an addition of a fair amount of sugar. Do not cover the pan to allow the bitter flavour to escape. Serve with toast or as garnishing to beef loin.

(Praktyczny kucharz warszawski, 1926)

Radishes, Polish style

2–3 bunches radishes, salt, 1 tsp butter, ½ tsp sugar, 1 tsp lemon juice, butter and breadcrumbs

Trim, wash and drain the radishes. Bring to the boil some salted water with sugar, butter and lemon juice. Put in the radishes and cook for 1–2 mins. Drain, arrange in a serving bowl, top with melted butter and browned breadcrumbs. Makes a delicious side dish with chops or roasts.

serves 4 • Preparation: 10 mins

Stewed radishes

2–3 bunches young radishes, 2 tbsps butter, 1 cup stock, salt, pepper, sugar, 2–3 tbsps cream, 1 egg yolk, 1 tsp lemon juice

Trim and wash the radishes and cut them into quarters. Sauté in melted butter, sprinkle with a pinch of sugar, salt and brown lightly. Add the stock and simmer for about 15 mins. Put the green radish leaves into boiling water for 3–4 mins, then drain, rinse with cold water, drain again, chop and sprinkle with lemon juice. Blend the cream with egg yolk, salt and pepper, mix with the chopped radish leaves, pour into the saucepan and mix with the stewed radishes. Heat but do not boil. Serve as a hot snack, or as a side dish with white meats.

serves 4 • Preparation: 20–25 mins

Radishes under bechamel sauce

2–3 bunches young radishes, 1–2 garlic cloves, 2 tbsps grated cheese, 1 tbsp chopped walnuts, 3 tbsps butter, 1 tbsp flour, ½ cup stock, ½ cup cream, salt, a pinch sugar and pepper

Wash and blanch the radish leaves, drain, chop and blend with garlic minced with salt. Cook the radishes in a little salted water. In a small saucepan melt I tbsp butter, add I tbsp flour and make a roux. Dilute it with the stock and cook until the sauce thickens. Season with salt, pepper, sugar and lemon juice, blend with the cream and heat. Butter an ovenproof dish, line it with the radish leaves, arrange the cooked radishes on top and pour in the sauce. Sprinkle with the grated cheese, chopped walnuts and dots of butter. Bake in a preheated oven. Serve with white bread as a hot snack or as a supper dish.

serves 4 • Preparation: 30 mins

Stuffed daikon

2 large daikons, 100 g roast chicken or turkey, 100 g cheese, 1 smallish red pepper, 1 pickled cucumber, 4 tbsps chopped chives, 2 tbsps chopped dill, 100 g butter, 1 tbsp double sour cream, 1 tsp lemon juice, a pinch of sugar, ½ tsp salt, ½ tsp pepper

Trim, wash and dry the daikon, cut off the tips and remove the flesh with a long sharp knife, leaving out Icm thick walls. Peel the cucumber and remove the seeds and membranes from the pepper. Cut the cucumber, daikon flesh, pepper and meat into small cubes, grate the cheese. Blend the butter with lemon juice, cream, salt, pepper and sugar until fluffy. Combine the creamed butter with the vegetables, greens, meat and cheese, season to taste and stuff the daikon shells with the mixture. Flatten the stuffing with a spoon, wrap each daikon with aluminium foil and refrigerate for 2–3 hours to let the flavours blend. Cut into

slices before serving. Serve with bread and butter, or as an element of cold buffet.

serves 6–8 • Preparation: 20–25 mins • Refrigerating: 2–3 hrs

Colourful daikon salad

½ small daikon (about 100 g), 1 large hard fleshy tomato, ½ smallish yellow pepper, ½ smallish green pepper, 2 tbsps chopped chives, 3–4 hard-boiled quail eggs

DRESSING: ½ cup yogurt, 1 tbsp mayonnaise, 1 tsp hot mustard, salt, pepper, a pinch of icing sugar

Mix well all the ingredients of the dressing. Chill. Peel the daikon and grate it coarsely. Scald, skin and dice the tomato. Cut the washed and dried pepper into thin strips. Combine all the ingredients of the salad, pour over the dressing and mix. Decorate the salad with the quail eggs cut into quarters and sprinkle with chopped chives.

serves 4 • Preparation: 5–6 mins

Salsify

This is a root vegetable of which there are two varieties. Both have a taste not unlike asparagus.

True salsify, also known as oyster plant, has been grown in Poland since the 16th century. Its thick roots, with their numerous rootlets, are dark grey, and the pulp is cream white and has a very strong, slightly bitter flavour. Its taste is a bit like that of oysters, hence its popular name.

The peeled roots quickly darken, therefore they should be immediately put into water with a little lemon juice or vinegar added, and then cooked in boiling water with some lemon juice and one tablespoon of flour.

Black salsify has a more delicate flavour. Its roots have black skin and are snow white inside. Both vegetables can be prepared in the same way and contain a lot of nutritive elements.

NOTE: When peeling and cleaning the roots, remember to wear rubber gloves and be careful because salsify juice leaves stains which are very difficult to wash off. The roots should first be scrubbed with a brush under running water, then scraped and put into water with vinegar or into milk to prevent them darkening. They can also be scrubbed and cooked first, and only later peeled.

Salsify, or winter asparagus

This is an excellent vegetable which came to Poland from France and grows well in our climate. It is very nutritious and tasty. You can buy it at the market all year round, only remember to choose quite black roots. Scrape the roots very carefully with a knife, the way you do with asparagus, then cut them into chunks, rinse in cold water. Cover them with generously salted boiling water and cook until tender. Soften a finely chopped onion in a fairly large amount of butter, add salt, pepper, a dash of nutmeg, juice from one whole lemon and chopped parsley. Put in the cooked salsify, heat up and serve.

(Marta Norkowska, *Najnowsza kuchnia wykwintna i gospodarska*, 1904)

Salsify fried in batter

800 g fresh salsify roots, salt,
2 tbsps lemon juice, 1 tsp flour,
½ cup flour, ½ cup single cream,
2 eggs, salt, pepper, ¼ tsp dried thyme,
nutmeg, 100 g clarified butter

Boil some salted water with lemon juice and flour. Peel the salsify roots and wash in cold water, then put them into boiling water and cook for about 15 mins. Remove with a slotted spoon, drain. Blend thoroughly the cream (or milk) with egg yolks, stir in the flour, salt, pepper, thyme and nutmeg. Set aside for a while to rest. Beat the egg whites until stiff, combine with the batter and mix gently but thoroughly. Immerse salsify in batter and fry in melted butter.

serves 4 • Preparation: 25–30 mins

Salsify salad

500 g cooked salsify, 200 g cheese, 2–3 gherkins,
3 celery sticks, 1 tbsp lemon juice, 6–8 prunes,
2 tbsps each chopped dill, parsley and chives

DRESSING: 3 tbsps thick mayonnaise, 2 tbsps yogurt,
salt, pepper, 1 tsp hot mustard, ½ tsp sugar

Mix thoroughly the dressing ingredients, chill the sauce. Blanch the rinsed prunes for 3–4 mins, drain them, run under cold water, drain again, then cut them into fine strips. Trim the celery stems, slice them finely, sprinkle with lemon juice. Cut the gherkins into cubes and cheese into fine sticks, dice the salsify. Combine all the salad ingredients with the chopped chives, fold in the dressing. Sprinkle with chopped dill and parsley.

serves 6–8 • Preparation: 5–7 mins

Black salsify salad

500 g cooked black salsify, 1 tbsp lemon juice,
100 g tinned ham or turkey ham, 10 hard-
boiled quail eggs, 2 marinated pears, 3 tbsps
chopped dill, 1 tbsp chopped walnuts

DRESSING: 4 tbsps mayonnaise, ½ tsp grated
lemon rind, 1 tbsp lemon juice, 1 tsp honey,
salt, a pinch of cayenne pepper

Blend the honey with the lemon juice, zest and cayenne, mix in the mayonnaise and finely chopped walnuts and chill a bit. Cut the salsify into 1 cm long pieces, sprinkle with some lemon juice. Quarter the shelled quail eggs, dice the ham and pears. Combine the salad ingredients, fold in the dressing. Sprinkle with chopped dill.

serves 4–6 • Preparation: 5–7 mins

Boiled salsify

1 kg salsify roots, salt, 1 tbsp butter, 1 tbsp sugar, ½ tsp
grated lemon rind, 1 tbsp lemon juice, 1 tbsp flour,
3 tbsps butter, 2 tbsps chopped walnuts, 2 tbsps vinegar

Trim, peel and wash the salsify roots and cover them with water with vinegar to prevent the roots from turning brown in the air. Bring some water to the boil, add salt, butter, sugar, flour, grated lemon rind and lemon juice. Place the drained roots in the boiling water and cook for about 20 mins. Drain and arrange on a warm serving dish. Heat a frying pan and brown the walnuts, add the butter, melt it and pour over the roots. Serve as a hot snack or as a side dish with white meat.

serves 4–6 • Preparation: 30 mins

Salsify in dill sauce

800 g salsify or black salsify roots, salt, 1 tbsp lemon juice, 1 tbsps butter, 1 tsp sugar

SAUCE: 2 tbsps butter, 1 tbsp flour, 1 cup chicken stock, salt, 1 tbsp lemon juice and 1 tsp grated lemon rind, sugar, white pepper, ½ cup double cream, 1 egg yolk, 4 tbsps chopped dill

In a saucepan melt the butter, add the flour and make a white roux. Dilute it with the cold chicken stock and cook stirring all the time until the sauce thickens. Season with lemon juice and grated lemon rind, salt, a pinch of sugar and white pepper. Scrub, peel and rinse the roots, then place in water with vinegar to prevent them from turning brown in the air. Bring some water with salt, butter, sugar and lemon juice to the boil. Put the roots into boiling water and cook for about 20 mins. Drain and arrange on a warm serving dish. Blend the cream with egg yolk and chopped dill, pour into the hot thick sauce, mix and heat, but do not boil. Top the salsify with the hot sauce and serve immediately as a hot snack or with the main course.

serves 4 • Preparation: 30–35 mins

Baked salsify

1 kg young firm salsify roots, 250–300 g boiled chicken, 2 hard, fleshy tomatoes, 100 g butter, salt, pepper

SAUCE: ½ cup chicken stock, ½ cup cream, 1 tbsp flour, juice and grated rind of 1 lemon, 1 tbsp sugar, 4 tbsps grated cheese, 2 tbsps chopped walnuts

Scrub, peel and wash the roots and place them in water with vinegar to prevent them from turning brown in the air. Bring to the boil some salted water with 1 tbsp butter, 1 tsp sugar, grated lemon rind and 1 tbsp lemon juice. Put the roots in and cook for about 20 mins, then drain and cut each root in half. Cut the cooked chicken meat into thin slices. Scald, skin and slice the tomatoes. In a saucepan melt 3 tbsps butter, add the flour and make a roux. Dilute it with the stock and cook over low heat until the sauce thickens. Add salt, pepper, sugar, grated lemon rind, stir in the cream and heat the whole. Butter an ovenproof dish and arrange layers of tomatoes, slices of chicken and salsify. Top with the sauce, sprinkle with the cheese mixed with walnuts, and with dots of butter. Bake for about 20–25 mins in a preheated oven. Serve as a hot snack or as a main dish with mashed potatoes.

serves 4–6 • Preparation: 30 mins • Baking: 20–25 mins

Sorrel

The most popular Polish dish made from this vegetable is sorrel soup with cream and hard-boiled eggs. However, owing to its slightly bitter taste not unlike lemon, sorrel is excellent as an addition to meat dishes and sauces. Just a few sorrel leaves can change the taste and give a unique flavour to a dish.

White sauce with sorrel goes well with poultry, fish balls and baked potatoes.

A handful of finely chopped fresh sorrel leaves can replace lemon juice or vinegar in salads. They can be added to spinach, lettuce, potato and vegetable soup, to lamb and beef, to fish, poultry and game. You may also garnish sandwiches with them.

Cooked and puréed sorrel leaves are added to soups and sauces, and go very well with roast veal and pork, and with fish and omelettes.

Sorrel

Take a colander of sorrel, add some lettuce, a bit of chervil, chives, parsley sprigs. Clean and rinse all these greens, put them into boiling salted water and cook for 15 minutes. Take them out and rinse them in cold water. Drain them, squeeze out the water with your hands. Chop them, put into a pan together with a large knob of fresh butter, ½ tablespoon of flour, a pinch of salt and pepper. Cook for another 15 minutes, then pour in the cream. Take off the heat. Break in four whole eggs, add some sugar, check the taste. Put into a serving bowl, surround with poached or hard-boiled eggs... or use as bedding for stuffed veal.

(Karolina Nakwaska, *Dwór wiejski*, 1858)

Sorrel spring salad

1 cup young sorrel leaves, 1 cup young spinach leaves, 1 bunch radishes with leaves

DRESSING: 2 tbsps olive oil, 1 tbsp lemon juice, ½ tsp honey, ½ tsp mustard, salt, pepper

Mix well the dressing ingredients, leave aside to cool. Wash thoroughly the sorrel, spinach and radishes, drain. Finely chop the radish leaves, slice the radishes, cut the sorrel and spinach leaves into strips. Combine all the ingredients together, pour over the dressing, toss.

serves 4 • Preparation: 5–10 mins

Sorrel snack

500 g sorrel, 2 tbsps butter, ½ cup double cream, 1 raw egg yolk, salt, sugar and nutmeg, 1 tbsp chopped walnuts

Place the washed sorrel in boiling water and cook for 1–2 mins. Drain, rinse with cold water, drain again, chop. In a saucepan melt the butter, add the sorrel and simmer for about 15 mins, season with salt, a pinch of sugar and nutmeg. Blend the cream and egg yolk and stir into the sorrel. Stir and heat for 2–3 mins. Makes a delicious side dish with roast veal.

serves 4 • Preparation: 20–25 mins

Vegetable mousse on sorrel leaves

200 g parsley roots, 200 g celeriac, 2 tbsps chopped chives, 4 tbsps butter, ¼ cup stock, ¾ cup single cream, 1 tbsp flour, 1 egg, salt, pepper, 1 tbsp lemon juice, sugar, 24–28 sorrel leaves

Wash and scald the sorrel leaves. Line individual ovenproof serving shells with the sorrel leaves. Cut the peeled and washed vegetables into small cubes. In a saucepan melt 2 tbsps butter and add the parsley root and celeriac. Cook and stir for a moment or two, sprinkle lightly with stock and lemon juice, cover and simmer. When cooked, blend in a food processor with sugar, salt and pepper into smooth pulp. Blend the cream and egg yolk thoroughly. In a small saucepan melt the remaining butter, add the flour and make a roux, then dilute it with the cold stock. Cook and stir until the sauce thickens. Stir in the cream, heat, but do not boil. Remove the thick sauce from the heat, combine with the puréed vegetables and stiff beaten egg whites, add chopped chives. Mix well. Fill the shells with the mixture, place in a pan filled with hot water and bake in a preheated oven for about 45–50 mins. Remove the mousse from the shells, serve as a hot snack, or a side dish with roast meats.

serves 4 • Preparation: 30 mins • Baking: 45–50 mins

Spinach

Spinach tastes good only in spring and autumn, because then its leaves are tender. In summer it grows too much and becomes bitter, therefore you should use beet leaves instead of it in that season.

(Karolina Nakwaska, *Dwór wiejski*, 1858)

Due to its nutritive values, spinach is one of the most beneficial vegetables. A cup of fresh spinach provides 70% of the recommended daily intake of beta-carotene, and 10% of the daily recommended intake of vitamin B2, calcium and magnesium. It is also an excellent source of vitamin B6, folic acid, iron and potassium. This means that spinach protects us against cancer and coronary thrombosis, and regulates the heart beat and blood pressure.

How to cook spinach: Of all the vegetables, spinach is the healthiest and there is no disease in which it should not be allowed. Spinach is best in spring, when it is good for fever and for changes of mood... It does not need any spices, for to make it work it is enough to cook it in water with some butter added, and to sprinkle it with grated nutmeg.

(W. Wielļdko, *Kucharz doskonały*, vol. II, p. 119)

Spinach rolls

30–40 large spinach leaves, 1 cup cooked rice, 1 onion, 3–4 garlic cloves, 2 tbsps chopped parsley, 1 tbsp chopped mint leaves, 2 tbsps toasted pine nuts (or sunflower seeds), 2 tbsps lemon juice, ½ tsp grated lemon rind, salt, pepper, 2 tbsps butter, ¼ glass dry white wine or light stock

Place the spinach leaves in a sieve, scald and dry. Sauté the finely chopped onion in 1 tbsp butter, add the chopped garlic and rice. Stir and fry for 2–3 mins, remove from the heat. When cool, sprinkle with 1 tbsp lemon juice, add the nuts, mint, parsley, salt, pepper, grated lemon rind and mix thoroughly. Butter an ovenproof dish and line it with 4–5 spinach leaves. Place some stuffing on each leaf, roll up and arrange snugly in one layer in the ovenproof dish. Sprinkle with melted butter, wine (or stock) and cover with the remaining spinach leaves. Sprinkle with 1 tbsp lemon juice. Cover the dish and bake in a preheated oven for 20–25 mins. Now take it out from the oven and set aside to cool, until the whole liquid is absorbed by the spinach. An hour before serving, place the spinach rolls in the fridge.

serves 4 • Preparation: 10–15 mins • Baking: 20–25 mins

Spinach salad

500 g young spinach, 200 g button mushrooms, 2 hard-boiled eggs, 6 rashers lean bacon, 4 tbsps chopped watercress, 1 tbsp honey, 1 tbsp wine vinegar, 1 tbsp dry red wine, 1 tbsp lemon juice, salt, pepper

Slice the washed and dried mushrooms, sprinkle them with lemon juice and season with pepper. Cover and set aside for a few minutes. In a frying pan, render the diced bacon, add the honey and heat it, stirring constantly. Pour in the vinegar, mix well and remove from the heat. Add the wine, salt and pepper, and blend together thoroughly. Wash and dry the spinach, combine with the mushrooms and fried bacon. Pour over the dressing, mix well and add quarters of eggs. Sprinkle with watercress.

serves 4 • Macerating: 25–30 mins • Preparation: 10 mins

Spinach salad with soya sprouts

200 g fresh spinach, 100 g soya sprouts, 4–5 button mushrooms, 1 garlic clove, juice and grated rind of ½ lemon, fresh thyme sprig, ¼ tsp ground pepper, 2 small carrots, 2 hard-boiled eggs.

DRESSING: 3 tbsps oil, 1 tbsp wine vinegar, 2 tbsps soya sauce, 1 tsp honey, salt, pepper, a pinch of cayenne pepper

Mix thoroughly the dressing ingredients and set aside in the fridge. Mix the chopped garlic with pepper and lemon rind. Cut the washed and dried mushrooms into thin slices, sprinkle with lemon juice, stir in the garlic and thyme leaves, cover and refrigerate. In two small saucepans bring to the boil some salted water. To one saucepan put the spinach leaves, to the other soya sprouts. Cook each for 1 min, drain, rinse with cold water, dry. Cut the peeled carrots into very thin slices, combine with the spinach, sprouts and mushrooms, top with the dressing and mix well. Before serving sprinkle with chopped hard-boiled eggs, or decorate with egg quarters.

serves 4 • Maceration: 30–40 mins • Preparation: 5–7 mins

Spinach, Russian style

500 g fresh spinach, 1 small onion, 1 tbsp olive oil, 2 tbsps chopped walnuts, 1 cup yogurt, 2–3 garlic cloves, 2 tbsps chopped fresh mint, salt, pepper

Put the washed spinach into boiling salted water for 4–5 mins, drain, chop coarsely. Sauté the peeled and finely chopped onion in the hot oil, add the spinach and fry for a moment or two, stir. Add the garlic minced with salt, chopped mint and pepper, and pour in the yogurt. Stir and heat. In a hot frying pan dry roast the chopped walnuts. Place the spinach in a warmed serving bowl, sprinkle with walnuts and serve immediately as a hot snack with white bread, or as a side dish with roast white meats.

serves 4 • Preparation: 10 mins

Spinach with peanuts

500 g fresh spinach, 2 tbsps olive oil, ½ cup finely chopped onion, ½ cup very finely chopped peanuts, salt

Place the washed spinach in a sieve, scald it, drain and chop. In a large frying pan heat the olive oil and sauté the onion, add the peanuts, stir and fry until golden. Add the spinach and continue to fry for another 5 mins, stirring constantly. Serve as a hot snack, or as a side dish with roasts and chops.

serves 4 • Preparation: 10 mins

Green potato pound cake

500 g potatoes boiled in their skins, 600 g fresh (or 1 packet frozen) spinach, 1 large onion, finely chopped, 4 tbsps butter, 2 raw eggs, salt, pepper, 1 tbsp lemon juice, 1 tbsp chopped walnuts

Put the washed spinach into salted boiling water, add lemon juice and cook for 5 mins, drain. Peel the potatoes and put them together with the spinach through a mincer. In a frying pan, melt 1 tbsp butter and sauté the onion. Thoroughly blend 2 tbsps butter with lemon juice, salt, pepper and raw eggs, gradually adding the potatoes with spinach and onion. Butter a baking dish, sprinkle it with the walnuts and spread the mixture. Sprinkle with melted butter. Bake for 40 mins in a medium-hot oven. Makes a delicious side dish with beefsteaks, roast pork and poultry.

serves 4 • Preparation: 10–15 mins • Baking: 40–45 mins

Baked spinach with ham and cheese

1 kg spinach, 100 g butter, 100 g lean ham, 100 g Emmental cheese, 50 g Parmesan cheese, salt, 1 cup single cream, 1 tbsp lemon juice

Put the thoroughly washed spinach into salted boiling water, add lemon juice and cook for 3–4 mins, drain, squeeze out the excess liquid, place on a board and chop finely. Place the chopped spinach in a lightly heated frying pan, add the cream and heat over high heat stirring constantly until the spinach absorbs the cream. Remove from the heat. Dice the ham and cheese. Butter an ovenproof dish and line it with the spinach. Top it with the ham and cheese and sprinkle with Parmesan and dots of butter. Bake in a preheated oven for about 15 mins.

serves 4 • Preparation: 10 mins • Baking: 15 mins

Baked spinach

1½ kg fresh spinach, 200–250 g roast chicken or roast meat leftovers, 4 eggs, 1 tbsp butter, 2 tbsps chopped pumpkin seeds, 1½ cups milk, 2 tbsps butter, 4–5 garlic cloves, 1 tbsp lemon juice, salt, pepper, ¼ tsp dried thyme, 3–4 thin strips pork fat

Place the washed spinach for 1 min in boiling water, drain, rinse with cold water and chop coarsely, then mix with the minced garlic, salt and lemon juice. Chop the meat, or put it through a mincer. Beat the eggs with milk, flour, salt, pepper and thyme. Butter an ovenproof dish, line it with the pumpkin seeds and spinach, top with the chopped meat and cover with the batter. Cover with strips of pork fat and bake for about 50 mins in a preheated oven.

serves 4 • Preparation: 10 mins • Baking: 50 mins

Tomatoes

Like potatoes, tomatoes too come from South America where they were grown by the Aztecs (who called them *tomatl*) long before the arrival of the Spaniards. In 1519, Ferdinand Cortez's expedition discovered tomato plantations and soon the plant was imported to Spain. Still in the mid-18th century the tomato, referred to as 'Peruvian apple', 'golden apple' or 'love apple', was regarded as an ornamental plant and its fruit was thought to be inedible or even poisonous. Its properties as a vegetable were discovered in the 18th century in Spain and later in the Kingdom of Naples, from where the tomato was exported to northern Italy and the south of France. In Poland it was first grown in the early 19th century. At first, it was used for soups and sauces, and then gradually began to be stewed, fried, baked and stuffed. Very quickly tomatoes became the most popular ingredient of various salads and started to be processed into concentrates, pastes, ketchups and juices.

Tomatoes for salads and as an addition to cooked dishes should first be skinned. To make the task easier, first dip them for a few minutes into boiling water and immediately run them under cold water. In many recipes, you are also told to remove the seeds and juice, which is particularly important in the case of fried tomatoes.

The most popular variety are round red tomatoes available all year round from hot houses (unfortunately, soil-grown tomatoes are becoming rare). Other varieties include cherry and grape tomatoes, elongated tomatoes, yellow and orange tomatoes. Cherry and grape tomatoes are usually used in salads and as garnishing, or else as appetizers, when they are filled with various pastes. Unripe green tomatoes go into Old Polish sweet preserves and are also pickled or marinated.

Tomatoes are a rich source of vitamin C and potassium, the latter regulating blood pressure and having a beneficial influence on the nerve system. As is known, psychic and physical stress cause loss of potassium, and consequently tiredness and weakness. It is therefore worth remembering about tomatoes in moments of stress. Two small tomatoes cover 25% of the prescribed daily intake of potassium. Every day about 1 litre of water is expelled through our skin which, when dehydrated, loses its elasticity and firmness. Tomatoes, which are 91% water, act as an ideal miosturizer.

The tomato is also rich in folic acid which is necessary for the production of the 'hormone of happiness'. The right amount of this acid gives us more energy, and improves our memory and our ability to concentrate.

Tomatoes au gratin

Scald some 15 tomatoes with boiling water, then skin them. Cut off their tops, scoop out the seeds with a teaspoon. Ar-range the tomatoes in a dish, put a piece of butter, some salt and pepper into each of them. Sprinkle them with grated Parmesan and breadcrumbs, pour melted butter over them. Put into a medium-hot oven and bake for 45 minutes, or until they are nicely browned on top.

(Marja Śleżańska, *Kucharz polski*, 1932)

Tomato cocktail

2 large ripe tomatoes, 1 sweet red pepper, 1 red onion, 1–2 garlic cloves, 4–5 basil leaves, 1 tbsp lemon juice, ¼ tsp grated lemon rind, 1 tsp Worcestershire sauce, 3–4 drops Tabasco sauce, salt, pepper, 5–6 crushed ice cubes

Cut the sweet pepper in half, remove the seeds, bake for a moment and skin. Cut the flesh. Scald, skin and dice the tomatoes. Peel the onion and garlic, chop and mix together in a food processor with the pepper, tomatoes, basil and sauces. Add lemon juice and lemon rind, salt, pepper and ice cubes.

serves 1 • Preparation: 10 mins

Tomato juice

2 large tomatoes (about 250 g), 2 dessert apples (about 250 g), 1 tsp lemon juice, 1 small daikon (about 200 g), 4–5 ice cubes, salt, dried basil, 1 tbsp finely chopped parsley

Scald and skin the tomatoes. Peel, core and dice the apples and sprinkle with lemon juice. Peel and dice the daikon. Put the tomatoes, apples and daikon through a juicer. Mix the juice with salt, a pinch of basil, chopped parsley and ice cubes.

serves 1 • Preparation: 5–7 mins

Tomato salad with herbs I

600 g small hard tomatoes, 1 tbsp chopped anise leaves, 1 tbsp chopped borage leaves, 1 tbsp chopped lemon balm, 1 tbsp chopped dill, 2 tbsps freshly grated horseradish, 1 tbsp lemon juice, salt, pepper, 1 tsp sugar, 1 cup yogurt

Combine the chopped herbs with horseradish, lemon juice, salt, pepper and sugar. Mix well with the yogurt, cover and refrigerate for 30 mins.
Scald the tomatoes, then rinse with cold water, skin and cut into quarters. Arrange in a salad bowl and pour over the dressing, toss gently.

serves 4 • Refrigerating: 30–40 mins • Preparation: 5–7 mins

Tomato salad with herbs II

500 g small hard tomatoes, 1 tbsp borage flowers

DRESSING: 1 cup yogurt, 1 tbsp thick mayonnaise, 2 tbsps grated horseradish, 1 tbsp finely chopped borage leaves, 1 tbsp finely chopped lemon balm, ½ tbsp chopped anise leaves, ½ tbsp chopped dill, salt, sugar and pepper to taste

Mix well the dressing ingredients and set aside in the fridge. Scald the tomatoes, rinse with cold water, skin them and cut into quarters. Arrange in a salad bowl, pour over the dressing, toss gently. Before serving decorate with borage flowers.

serves 4 • Preparation: 15 mins

Stuffed tomatoes

4–8 medium-large tomatoes, firm and fleshy

Slice off the tops of the tomatoes and reserve to make hats. Scoop out the pulp and seeds. Sprinkle inside with salt, turn upside down and let drain, then fill the tomatoes with the stuffing.

serves 4 • Salting: 20 mins

STUFFING FOR TOMATOES

Stuffing I

100 g ewe-milk cheese, 100 g cottage cheese, 1 onion, 1 small tin sprats in oil, salt, 1 tsp pepper, ¼ tsp sugar, 1 bunch dill

In a food processor blend the sprats with ewe-milk cheese, cottage cheese, salt, pepper and sugar into smooth pulp. Mix well with the finely chopped onion. Stuff the tomatoes with the mixture, arrange them on a serving dish, cover with foil and refrigerate for 1 hour. Before serving decorate with sprigs of dill.

Preparation: 5–10 mins • Refrigerating: 1 hr

Stuffing II

1 cup cream cheese, 3–4 garlic cloves, ½ cup chopped fresh basil, salt, ½ tsp herbs of Provence, 8 whole basil leaves

Mix thoroughly the cream cheese with garlic minced with salt, basil and herbs. Stuff the tomato shells, cover with foil and refrigerate for about 20 mins. Just before serving decorate with basil leaves.

Preparation: 5–10 mins • Refrigerating: 1 hr

Stuffing III

150 g cottage cheese, 150 g tinned ham, ½ small yellow pepper, 2–3 tbsps chopped chives, salt, pepper, dill sprigs

Scoop out the tomato flesh and put through a sieve. Chop the ham and pepper into small cubes, blend the cheese with salt, tomato flesh, pepper and chopped chives. Combine with the ham, mix well. Stuff the tomatoes with the mixture, cover with foil and set aside in the fridge. Arrange on lettuce leaves and before serving decorate with sprigs of dill.

Preparation: 5–10 mins • Refrigerating: 1 hr

Stuffing IV

1 cup tinned peas, 1 cup stewed gooseberries, 2 hard-boiled eggs, salt, 2–3 tbsps thick mayonnaise, 2–3 tbsps chopped parsley

Chop the eggs and combine them with the peas and gooseberries, add salt and mix with mayonnaise. Stuff the tomatoes with the mixture. Before serving sprinkle with chopped parsley.

Preparation: 5–10 mins • Refrigerating: 1 hr

Stuffing V

1 tin tuna, 2 hard-boiled eggs, 1 small onion, chopped, 2 tbsps chopped parsley, 1 tsp lemon juice, sugar, salt, pepper

Separate the egg yolks and mix with the tuna, chopped onion and parsley. Season to taste with salt, pepper, sugar and lemon juice. Stuff the tomatoes with the mixture, sprinkle with dill.

Preparation: 5–10 mins • Refrigerating: 1 hr

Stuffing VI

150 g smoked mackerel (or herring), 1 onion, 1 hard-boiled egg, 2 tbsps chopped capers, 1 tbsp chopped olives, 2 tbsps chopped dill, salt, pepper, 2 tbsps thick mayonnaise

Skin and bone the smoked fish, divide into pieces and combine with the chopped egg, capers and olives. Mix gently but thoroughly with the mayonnaise, season with salt and pepper to taste. Stuff the tomato shells, sprinkle with dill.

Preparation: 5–10 mins • Refrigerating: 1 hr

Stuffing VII

100 g ewe-milk cheese, 100 g cottage cheese, 1 large onion, 1 small tin tuna in oil, salt, 1 tsp pepper, ¼ tsp sugar, 1 bunch dill

In a food processor mix the tuna with ewe-milk cheese, cottage cheese, salt, pepper and sugar into smooth pulp, combine with the finely chopped onion. Stuff the tomatoes, arrange them on a serving dish, cover with foil and refrigerate for 1 hour. Decorate with sprigs of dill before serving.

Preparation: 5–10 mins • Refrigerating: 1 hr

Tomatoes with herbs

8 tomatoes, ½ cup breadcrumbs, ½ cup chopped walnuts, ½ cup finely chopped parsley, 1 tbsp chopped fresh basil, 2–3 garlic cloves, 3–4 pitted green olives, 1 tsp salt, 1 tsp pepper, 2–3 tbsps olive oil

Cut off the tomato tops, scoop out the flesh, sprinkle the insides with salt, turn upside down and let drain. Put the pulp through a sieve, mix it in a food processor with the olive oil, salt, pepper, minced garlic, breadcrumbs and walnuts. Add the finely chopped olives, pepper, parsley, basil and mix well together. Fill the tomatoes with the stuffing, arrange them on an oiled ovenproof serving dish and bake for about 20 mins in a preheated oven in the temperature of 220°C. Serve as a hot snack or as a side dish with roast meat.

serves 4 • Salting: 10 mins • Preparation: 5 mins • Baking: 20 mins

Baked stuffed tomatoes

4 large fleshy tomatoes, ½ cup fresh oregano leaves, ½ cup grated cheese, 2–3 garlic cloves, 2 tbsps butter, salt, pepper

Cut off the tomato tops and gently scoop out the flesh. Sprinkle the insides with salt, turn upside down and let drain. Finely chop the pulp, combine with the garlic minced with salt, 1 tbsp butter, grated cheese and chopped fresh oregano leaves. Season with salt and pepper to taste. Fill the tomatoes with the stuffing and arrange on a buttered ovenproof serving platter, sprinkle with melted butter. Bake for 10–15 mins in a preheated oven. Serve as a hot snack or as a side dish with fried cutlets.

serves 4 • Salting: 10 mins • Preparation: 5 mins • Baking: 15 mins

Tomatoes with mushrooms

8 tomatoes, 250 g mushrooms, 1 large onion, 2 tbsp butter, 2 tbsps chopped parsley, 1 cup cooked rice, 1 tsp lemon juice,1 egg, 1 tbsp breadcrumbs, 1 cup double cream, 1–2 tbsps grated cheese, salt, pepper, sugar, 1 tbsp soya sauce

Cut off the tomato tops and reserve as lids, scoop out the pulp and remove the seeds. Sprinkle the insides with salt, turn the tomatoes upside down and let drain. Sprinkle the rice with lemon juice, salt, pepper and sugar. Sauté the chopped onion in melted butter, add the finely chopped mushrooms and fry for a moment over high heat, then set aside to cool. Combine with the rice and chopped parsley, add the egg and form smooth paste. Fill the tomatoes with the stuffing. Lightly butter an ovenproof serving platter, sprinkle it with breadcrumbs, arrange the tomatoes and cover them with the reserved lids. Mix well the cream with soya sauce, pepper and grated cheese, pour over the tomatoes. Bake for 20–25 mins in a well preheated oven.

serves 4 • Salting: 10 mins • Preparation: 10 mins • Baking: 25 mins

Tomatoes, home style

8 tomatoes, 4 hard-boiled eggs, 3–4 small red onions, 3–4 garlic cloves, 3–4 tbsps chopped parsley, 2–3 tbsps breadcrumbs, salt, pepper, 3 tbsps butter

Cut off the tomato tops and scoop out the pulp. Sprinkle the insides with salt, turn upside down and let drain. Put the pulp through a sieve. Sauté the chopped onion in 1 tbsp butter, add minced garlic and parsley, stir and fry for a moment or two. Remove from the heat, combine with the breadcrumbs, tomato pulp and chopped eggs, mix well together, season with salt and pepper to taste. Fill the tomatoes with the stuffing and arrange them snugly in a buttered ovenproof serving dish. Replace the reserved caps, sprinkle with melted butter and bake for about 25 mins in a well preheated oven. Serve as a hot snack, or as a side dish with roasts.

serves 4 • Salting: 10 mins • Preparation: 10 mins • Baking: 25 mins

Tomatoes, Lithuanian style

8 tomatoes, salt, 2 tbsps grated cheese, 1 tbsp butter, ¼ cup stock, 1 cup double cream, 3 tbsps chopped parsley

STUFFING: 3 hard-boiled eggs, 2 salted herring fillets, 1 onion, ½ bread roll soaked in milk, 1 tbsp butter, 2 tbsps double cream, salt, pepper

Cut off the tops of the tomatoes and scoop out the pulp. Sprinkle the insides with salt, turn upside down and let drain. Finely chop the herring fillets. Melt the butter in a saucepan, sauté the chopped onion, add the herring and fry together for a moment or two. Remove from the heat, set aside to cool and combine with the bread roll (squeezed dry), cream and chopped eggs. Fill the tomatoes with the stuffing and arrange in a buttered ovenproof serving dish.

Sprinkle with the grated cheese, pour in the stock and bake for about 30 mins in a preheated oven. Towards the end of baking pour in the cream blended with chopped parsley.

serves 4 • Salting: 10 mins • Preparation: 10–15 mins • Baking: 30 mins

Tomatoes, peasant style

8 tomatoes, 8 slices hard cheese

STUFFING: ¾ cup cooked rice, 250 g cooked minced meat (poultry, veal, beef), 1 onion, 3 eggs, 1 tbsp breadcrumbs, salt, pepper, 2 tbsps butter

Cut off the tops of the tomatoes, scoop out the pulp. Sprinkle the insides with salt, turn upside down and let drain. Sauté the finely chopped onion in 1 tbsp butter, combine with the rice, minced meat, breadcrumbs, salt and pepper, mix well with the eggs. Fill the tomatoes with the stuffing, arrange in a buttered ovenproof serving dish. Cover each tomato with a slice of cheese, sprinkle with melted butter and bake for about 20–25 mins in a preheated oven. Serve with boiled potatoes and salads.

serves 4 • Salting: 10 mins • Preparation: 10 mins • Baking: 25 mins

Tomatoes stuffed with meat

8 tomatoes, salt, 200 g minced pork, 100 g smoked pork fat or streaky bacon, 1 small red pepper, 1 small onion, 2–3 garlic cloves, 1–2 tbsps breadcrumbs, 1 egg, 3 tbsps butter, salt, pepper, 1 tbsp tomato paste

Cut off the tops of the tomatoes and scoop out the pulp. Sprinkle the insides with salt, turn upside down and let drain. Finely chop the pork fat (or bacon), onion and sweet pepper (remove the seeds first). Melt 1 tbsp butter, add pork fat, onion and sweet pepper. Stir and fry for a moment, add the meat, salt and pepper, and continue to fry together for about 5 mins. Remove from the heat, set aside, add the breadcrumbs, garlic minced with salt, tomato paste and break in the egg. Mix well. Fill the tomatoes with the stuffing, cover with the reserved caps and arrange on a buttered ovenproof serving platter. Bake for about 30 mins in a preheated oven. Serve with French fries and spinach purée.

serves 4 • Salting: 10 mins • Preparation: 10–15 mins • Baking: 30 mins

Baked tomatoes

2 large fleshy tomatoes, 1½ tbsps butter, 1 tbsp liquid honey, 1 tbsp chopped fresh thyme, 1 tbsp chopped parsley, ¼ tbsp grated lemon rind, ½ tsp lemon juice, salt, pepper

Preheat the oven to the temperature of 180°C. Mix 1 tbsp butter with the honey, salt, pepper, lemon juice, lemon rind and chopped herbs. Wash and dry the tomatoes, cut them in half and place in a dish cut side up. Spread the mixture of honey and herbs on the tomatoes and arrange them in a buttered ovenproof dish. Bake for about 20 mins in a preheated oven. Serve as a hot snack.

serves 4 • Preparation: 5 mins • Baking: 20 mins

Tomatoes au gratin

2 large, hard, fleshy tomatoes, 50 g lean ham, 2 tbsps pitted black olives, 2 tbsps chopped parsley, 1 tbsp butter, 1 tbsps chopped walnuts, ½ cup cream, 2 tbsps thick mayonnaise, salt, pepper

Preheat the oven to 200°C. Wash and dry the tomatoes and cut them in half widthwise. Butter an ovenproof serving dish, sprinkle it with chopped walnuts and arrange the tomatoes cut side down. Bake for about 10 mins. Cut the ham into small cubes, slice the olives. Blend the cream with mayonnaise, olives, ham, parsley, salt and pepper, pour over the tomatoes and bake together for another 10–12 mins.

serves 4 • Preparation: 5 mins • Baking: 25 mins

Turnip

Turnips are cooked the same way as swedes. One particularly delicate variety can be peeled and cooked whole or cut into elongated pieces with a help of a special serrated knife. The turnip, boiled in water, is then simmered for some time in butter... It is served in a flat dish and surrounded with croutons.

(*Praktyczny kucharz warszawski*, 1926)

The turnip has been known in Poland for centuries. Traces of its cultivation have been discovered at Biskupin, an old settlement dating to 700–400 BC. It is very rich in vitamins and minerals, and therefore in the Polish lore it is associated with strength and good health. Until the 18th century it was one of the most important vegetables in the Poles' diet. Next to the parsnip, it was served with meat, and was also braised, stuffed, smoked and soured.

Turnip fried in sugar

Peel several young small turnips, cut them into even quarters, the shape of wedges. Put them into hot butter and fry on all sides. Sprinkle them with sugar and a pinch of salt on all sides and continue frying, until they have turned golden brown. Add some stock and a small glass of Malaga and cook briskly over high heat until the tunrip is tender. Serve with roast mutton or beef.

(Marta Norkowska, *Najnowsza kuchnia wytworna i gospodarska*, 1904)

Turnip salad with carrot

2 medium-large young turnips, 1 carrot, 3 tbsps chopped dill, ½ cup cream, 2 tbsps lemon juice, salt, ¼ tsp honey

Mix well salt with lemon juice, honey and cream, chill. Coarsely grate the peeled and washed turnips, sprinkle with lemon juice and a pinch of salt, cover and refrigerate for an hour, then top with the chilled dressing. Mix well together and sprinkle with dill. Best served with roast beef and roast pork.

serves 4 • Preparation: 10 mins

Turnips stewed in cream

500 g young turnips, 2 tbsp cooking oil, 2 large onions, 1 tbsp flour, ½ cup thick cream, salt

Sauté the finely chopped onion in oil, add the coarsely grated turnips (washed and peeled first, of course), mix, sprinkle with water, cover and simmer for about 30–35 mins. Blend the cream with flour, season with salt, pour over the turnips, stir and heat for a moment. Serve with roast or fried meats.

serves 4 • Preparation: 40 mins

Turnips fried with herbs

500 g young turnips, grated rind and juice of 1 lemon, 1–2 garlic cloves, salt, pepper, 2–3 tbsps olive oil, 2 cups chopped watercress, chives, dill, coriander, mint and white pepper leaves

Peel, wash and dry the turnips, then cut them into slices. Heat the oil in a flat saucepan, add the peeled garlic, brown it, then remove. Put into the reserved oil turnip slices, fry for a moment, sprinkle with lemon rind and salt. Stir gently and continue to fry for 5–6 mins. Sprinkle with chopped greens, lemon juice and pepper, stir, cover and simmer for a few minutes until ready. Delicious with fried or roast meats.

serves 4 • Preparation: 40 mins

Young turnips stuffed with meat

4 young turnips, 1 tbsp butter, ½ cup cream, 2–3 tbsps grated cheese, salt, 200 g boiled beef, 2 onions, ¼ cup stock, 1 tsp flour, 1 tbsp butter, 1 tbsp cream

Cook the washed turnips in salted water for about 20 mins. Remove, rinse with cold water, drain, scoop out the pulp leaving 1 cm thick shells. Finely chop the pulp. In a saucepan melt butter and sauté the finely chopped onion, add the finely diced meat and turnip pulp, salt, pepper and a pinch of sugar. Stir and fry for a moment or two. Then sprinkle with flour, pour in the stock and simmer, stirring all the time. Towards the end add the cream. Stuff the turnip shells with the mixture, arrange in a buttered ovenproof dish, sprinkle with the grated cheese and dot with butter. Bake in a preheated oven for 10–15 mins. Serve with potatoes or rice, and lettuce or tomato salad.

serves 4 • Preparation: 20–30 mins • Baking: 25–30 mins

Savoury fruit dishes

Doctors and dieticians are always sounding the alarm bell: we do not eat enough fruit. So let us eat more fruit, not only in cakes and desserts, but also served as a savoury dish.

Savoury fruit snack

4 juicy pears, 8 purple plums, ½ cup green and black grapes, ½ celeriac, juice and grated rind of 1 lemon, 4 tbsps thick mayonnaise, 2 tbsps yogurt, 1 tsp mustard, salt, pepper, icing sugar

Cut the washed and dried pears lengthwise in half, remove the cores and scoop out part of the flesh, leaving a thin shell. Sprinkle the insides with lemon juice. Chop the flesh and sprinkle it with lemon juice. Blanch the peeled celeriac in lightly salted water, remove, rinse with cold water, grate and sprinkle with the remaining lemon juice. Cut the plums into thin strips. Halve and seed half of the grapes. In a food processor blend the mayonnaise, yogurt, grated lemon rind, salt and sugar. Add the plums, grapes and the pear pulp to the sauce and mix well. Fill in the hollowed pears with the mixture and decorate them with the remaining grapes.

serves 4 • Preparation: 10–15 mins

Fruit salad

1 large orange, 1 grapefruit, 1 banana, 1 tbsp lemon juice, 1 cup pitted sour cherries, a few lettuce leaves, 2 tbsps chopped walnuts and some halves, 1 cup yogurt, 2 tbsps mayonnaise, 1 tsp liquid honey, cayenne pepper, 1 tsp finely chopped orange rind

Scald the citrus fruit, dry and peel, cut into cubes, remove seeds. Cut the banana into thick cubes, sprinkle with lemon juice and combine with the orange, grapefruit and cherries. Blend the yogurt with honey, mayonnaise, cayenne pepper and chopped walnuts, pour over the fruit, mix well and refrigerate. Line a salad bowl with lettuce leaves, put in the salad, sprinkle it with orange rind and decorate with walnut halves. Serve as a snack, or as a side dish with schnitzels or roast white meats.

serves 4 • Preparation: 5–7 mins • Refrigerating: 30–40 mins

Savoury pear salad

4 hard, juicy pears, 2 tbsps honey, 2 tbsps lemon juice, ½ tsp ground pepper, ½ tsp ground caraway seeds, 2–3 lettuce leaves

Peel and core the pears. Cut the pears into thin slices. Line a serving platter with lettuce leaves and arrange the slices of pears. Blend the honey with lemon juice, pepper and caraway seeds, sprinkle the fruit and serve.

serves 4 • Preparation: 4–6 mins

Pear salad

3 hard pears, 1 tbsp sugar, 150 g lean ham, ½ small celeriac, 1 tbsp lemon juice, ¼ tsp ground paprika, pinch of salt and sugar

DRESSING: 3 tbsps thick mayonnaise, 1 tbsp sour cream, 1 tsp lemon juice, ¼ tsp paprika, salt, sugar

Bring to the boil a little water with 1 tbsp sugar. Add the peeled and cored pears cut into eights and cook them for 5–6 mins, drain. Peel, wash and julienne the celeriac, sprinkle it with lemon juice. Cut the ham into cubes, combine with the celeriac and pears, sprinkle with chopped walnuts. Mix well the dressing ingredients and pour over the salad. Mix, cover and refrigerate for 2–3 hours. Before serving arrange the salad on lettuce leaves and decorate with parsley sprigs.

serves 4 • Preparation: 10 mins • Refrigerating: 2–3 hrs

Coloured salad

3 ripe fleshy pears, a pinch of cayenne pepper, 1 tbsp lemon juice, 2 firm fleshy tomatoes, 1 each small green, red and yellow bell peppers, 2–3 tbsps chopped parsley, 1 tbsp hot mustard, 1 cup yogurt, salt, pepper and sugar

Peel, core and julienne the pears, sprinkle with lemon juice, dust with cayenne pepper. Cut the peppers into thin strips. Scald and skin the tomatoes and dice them, removing the seeds. Mix the mustard thoroughly with salt, sugar and pepper, stir in the yogurt. Combine the salad ingredients, stir in the dressing, refrigerate. Before serving, sprinkle with chopped parsley.

serves 4 • Preparation: 10 mins • Refrigerating: 30–40 mins

Stuffed pears I

8 pears, 200 g Roquefort-type cheese, ½ cup chopped sunflower seeds, 2 tbsps butter, juice and grated rind of 1 small lemon, 3 tbsps cream, salt, pepper, strips of marinated red pepper, sprigs of parsley

Place the pears in a sieve, scald them, then rinse with cold water, peel and cut in half, remove the cores. Sprinkle the pear halves with lemon juice. Blend the crumbled cheese with butter, a pinch of salt, pepper and grated lemon rind into smooth paste. Stir in the cream and chopped sunflower seeds. Stuff the pear halves with the mixture, cover with foil and refrigerate for 1–2 hours. Before serving place the pears on lettuce leaves, decorate with strips of red pepper and sprigs of parsley.

serves 8 • Preparation: 10 mins • Refrigerating: 1–2 hrs

Pears stuffed with blue cheese and walnuts

4 pears (not too sweet), juice and grated rind of ½ lemon

STUFFING: 100 g blue cheese (Roquefort-type), 1 tsp butter, 3 tbsps cottage cheese, 1 tsp vodka, 3 tbsps chopped walnuts, salt, pepper, ¼ tsp herbs of Provence, 1 chicory head, 8 walnut halves, 8 lemon balm leaves

Cut the peeled pears in half, remove the cores, sprinkle with lemon juice. In a food processor blend the blue cheese with cottage cheese, butter, salt, pepper, herbs of Provence and grated lemon rind. Mix with the vodka and chopped walnuts. Arrange the pear halves on the chicory leaves, decorate with walnut halves and lemon balm leaves.

serves 4–8 • Preparation: 10 mins • Refrigerating: 1–2 hrs

Stuffed pears II

4 large, fleshy pears, 1 glass brandy, 2 tbsps lemon juice, 150 g Danish blue cheese, 3 tbsps double cream, 1–2 drops Tabasco sauce, 2 tbsps raisins, 3 tbsps chopped hazelnuts, salt, pepper, a pinch of sugar

Peel and core the pears and cut them lengthwise in half, sprinkle with lemon juice. Top the washed raisins with the brandy. Mix the cheese with cream, salt, pepper, Tabasco sauce and sugar into smooth, uniform pulp. Stir in the raisins and walnuts. Top the pear halves with the mixture and serve.

serves 4–8 • Preparation: 10 mins • Refrigerating: 30–40 mins

Stuffed pears III

4 large, fleshy pears, 1 glass brandy, 2 tbsps lemon juice, 2 tbsps finely chopped almonds, 5–8 chopped capers, 150 g Roquefort-type cheese, 2 tbsps butter, 1 tbsp double cream, salt, pepper, parsley sprigs, a few lettuce leaves, 8 olives stuffed with sweet red pepper

Peel the pears and cut them lengthwise in half, remove the cores. Sprinkle with lemon juice and the brandy, and set aside in a cool place. Mash the cheese with a fork, and blend with butter, cream, chopped capers, salt and pepper into smooth, uniform pulp. Line a serving platter with lettuce leaves, arrange the pear halves and sprinkle them with the finely chopped almonds. Mix the pear marinade with the cheese pulp. Top the pear halves with the mixture (preferably with a special syringe), decorate with olives and parsley sprigs.

serves 4 • Preparation: 10 mins • Refrigerating: 30–40 mins

Pears, Monte Carlo style

4 large, hard pears, 3 cups water, 1 tbsp sugar, 2 bay leaves, 2–3 allspice berries, 2–3 peppercorns, 1 clove, a pinch of ginger, 1 glass gin or brandy

STUFFING: 250 g minced pork, 2–3 garlic cloves, 1 tbsp breadcrumbs, 2 tbsps dry white wine, 2 tbsps lemon juice, 1 tsp grated lemon rind, 1 tbsp shredded Gouda cheese, ¼ tsp ground allspice,

1 tbsp raisins, 2 tbsps almond flakes, 2 tbsps butter, 2 tbsps grapeseed oil, salt, pepper

Bring to the boil 3 cups water with ½ tsp grated lemon rind and 2 tbsps lemon juice, sugar, bay leaves, allspice, pepper and ginger, cover and continue to cook for another 5–7 mins over low heat. Peel and core the pears, place in boiling water and cook over low heat for about 3–5 mins. Set aside to cool. Top the washed raisins with 1 tbsp wine, and mix the remaining wine with breadcrumbs. Blend the minced meat with lemon rind, ground allspice minced with salt, garlic and pepper, add the cheese, breadcrumbs and egg, and knead smooth pulp. Sprinkle your hands with water and form 8 balls. Arrange them on a plate, cover with foil and refrigerate for 1 hour. In a frying pan, heat the oil, add butter and fry the balls. Remove the pears from the marinade, drain and dry, and arrange on a serving platter. Stuff them with the hot fried balls and pour 2–3 tbsps marinade on the frying pan, add the gin, heat and stir. Pour over the pears and serve immediately.

serves 4 • Preparation: 1½ hrs

Pears in red wine

4 large, hard pears, 1 tsp lemon juice, 1 glass dry red wine, a pinch of sugar, 2 garlic cloves, 8–10 chicken livers, 1 onion, 2 tbsps butter, 1 tbsp breadcrumbs, 2 eggs, salt, pepper, ¼ tsp dried basil, ¼ tsp dried tarragon

Chop the washed and dried chicken livers. Sauté the finely chopped onion in 1 tbsp melted butter, add the chopped livers and stir and fry for a moment or two. Sprinkle with salt, pepper and herbs, remove from the heat, add 2 egg yolks, mix well. Heat this over low heat and then again remove from the heat. Beat the egg whites stiff and mix with the prepared mixture, stirring in the sifted breadcrumbs. Finely chop the garlic. Peel the pears, remove the cores and sprinkle with lemon juice. Rub the insides with the minced garlic and fill in with the stuffing. Butter an ovenproof dish and arrange the stuffed pears tightly. Add the wine and bake for about 30 mins in a preheated oven. Makes a delicious snack or main course.

serves 4 • Preparation: 10–12 mins • Baking: 30 mins

Pears baked with smoked cheese

4 large, hard pears, 100 g smoked cheese, 1 glass brandy, 1 tbsp butter, 2 tbsps finely chopped hazelnuts

Coarsely grate the cheese. Generously butter an oven-proof dish. Peel and core the pears, cut them lengthwise in half. Arrange the pear halves in the dish, sprinkle with the brandy and top with the grated cheese. Bake for about 10–12 mins in a preheated oven. Before serving sprinkle with hazelnuts. Serve as a hot snack.

serves 4 • Preparation: 5 mins • Baking: 10–12 mins

Pears baked with Camembert

4 large, hard pears, 2 tbsps lemon juice, 150–200 g Camembert, 2 tbsps butter, ½ tsp cayenne pepper,

Cut the peeled pears lengthwise in half, remove the cores and sprinkle with lemon juice. Butter 8 sheets of aluminium foil. Place a pear half on each sheet, sprinkle with cayenne pepper and fill in the cavity with a piece of cheese. Wrap tightly in foil and grill, or bake in the oven.

serves 4 • Preparation: 20–25 mins

Pear sauce

500 g pears, 1 tbsp lemon juice, 1 orange, ¼ cup sugar, ¼ cup 4% vinegar, ¼ cup dry white wine, 1 tbsp finely chopped fresh ginger, ½ tsp ground cloves, ½ tsp cinnamon

Wash thoroughly the orange, dry it and remove the skin with a sharp knife. Put the peel into boiling water for 2–3 mins, drain, rinse with cold water, drain again. Peel and core the pears. Finely cut the flesh and put into a saucepan, sprinkling with lemon juice. Add the chopped ginger, the finely cut orange peel, add some water, vinegar and orange juice. Bring to the boil and continue to cook over low heat until the pears are soft. Add sugar, cloves and cinnamon, and pour in the wine. Cook and stir until the pears turn into pulp and the sauce thickens. Serve hot with white roast meats and poultry, or cold with cold cuts, poultry and fish.

serves 4–6 • Preparation: 1½ hrs

Spicy pears

4 large, hard pears, juice and grated rind of 1 lemon, 1 cup dry red wine, 1 cup pomegranate juice, 1 cup honey, a piece of cinnamon bark, 2–3 cloves, 2–3 tbsps finely chopped almonds

Peel the pears and cut them lengthwise in half, remove the cores, sprinkle with lemon juice. Bring to the boil the wine with cinnamon, cloves, grated lemon rind, honey and pomegranate juice. Place the pears in the boiling liquid and cook for 4–5 mins. Remove the pears gently and place them on a serving platter. Continue to cook the sauce until thick, remove the cloves and cinnamon, set aside to cool, then pour over the pears. In a hot frying pan dry roast the almonds and sprinkle over the pears. Makes an interesting side dish with white meats, or a dessert.

serves 4 • Preparation: 10–12 mins

Most unusual apple salad

3–4 apples with red skin, 200 g anise stalks, 2 bananas, ¾ cup chopped walnuts, 2 tbsps lemon juice, 2 tbsps orange juice, 3–4 tbsps mayonnaise, 1 tbsp honey, lettuce leaves, sprigs of parsley

Mix well the mayonnaise with honey and orange juice, cool lightly. Wash, core and dice the apples, sprinkle them with lemon juice, cut the bananas into slices and also sprinkle with lemon juice. Wash and dry the anise stalks, and cut into slices. Combine all the ingredients, pour over the dressing, mix with the walnuts and refrigerate. Before serving, arrange the salad on lettuce leaves and decorate with parsley sprigs. Serve with white meats or roast chicken.

serves 4–6 • Preparation: 10 mins • Refrigerating: 1–2 hrs

Spicy apple mousse

1 kg tart apples, 2–3 finely chopped fresh sage, 2 tbsps butter, 1 tbsp honey, 1 tbsp green peppercorns, a pinch of salt and pepper, 1 small glass dry white wine

Peel and core the apples, cut into small cubes, put them into a sauce-pan, sprinkle with the wine, cover and simmer until completely puréed. Add the honey, butter and green pepper mashed with a fork. Mix well, remove from the heat, add salt and pepper and blend into smooth, uniform pulp. Add the chopped sage, mix well and heat. Makes a delicious side dish with roast chicken a la venison, but can also be served as an unusual, superb dessert.

serves 4–6 • Preparation: 25–30 mins

Stewed apples

3 large tart apples, 3 large onions, 300 g fresh grated horseradish, 300 g sugar, 3 tbsps lemon juice, 1 tsp grated lemon rind, 1 tsp cinnamon, 1 tsp ground cloves, 1 tsp hot paprika, salt, 1 tbsp butter

Peel and coarsely grate the apples, sprinkle with lemon juice. Finely chop the onions, combine with the apples, mix with sugar and all the spices, cover and set aside for 2–3 hours. In a saucepan melt butter, add the apples with onion and cook over low heat until the mixture thickens. Remove from the heat, cool and blend thoroughly with the grated horseradish. Add salt to taste and, if necessary, some lemon juice. Serve with boiled or fried meats.

serves 6–8 • Macerating: 2–3 hrs • Preparation: 15–20 mins

Apples stuffed with herring salad

4 large tart apples, 3 salted herring fillets, 2 small cooked carrots, 2 small potatoes boiled in their skins, 1 large onion, salt, pepper, a pinch of cinnamon, 2 tbsps lemon juice, 3 tbsps thick mayonnaise, ¼ tsp icing sugar

Briefly soak the herring fillets, dry them and cut into small cubes. Chop the onion, sprinkle with 1 tsp lemon juice. Cut the carrots and peeled potatoes into small cubes, combine the herring with the potatoes, carrots and onion, sprinkle with pepper and cinnamon, stir in the mayonnaise and set aside to cool. Cut the tops off the apples, carefully scoop out the flesh. Finely chop the removed flesh and sprinkle it with lemon juice. Add to the salad. Sprinkle the insides of the hollowed apples with lemon juice and lightly dust them with icing sugar. Stuff the apples with the salad, decorate with sprigs of dill, arrange on lettuce leaves.

serves 4 • Preparation: 10–15 mins

Apples with celery stuffing

4 large tart apples, 2 onions, 3–4 celery stalks, 100 g chopped walnuts, 100 g chopped hazelnuts, 50 g shredded cheese, 3–4 bay leaves, 1 tsp vegetable seasoning, 2 tbsps chopped fresh thyme, salt, pepper, 3 tbsps butter, 1 tbsp lemon juice, 2 tbsps light stock or white wine

Peel the onion and celery stalks and cut them finely. In a saucepan melt 1½ tbsps butter, add the onion, celery and bay leaves. Fry for a moment, then sprinkle with wine or stock and simmer for about 10 mins. Wash and dry the apples, cut them lengthwise in half, remove the cores and some of the flesh. Sprinkle the apple halves with lemon juice so that they do not darken in the air. Cut the removed flesh finely and add to the onion together with thyme and vegetable seasoning. Mix well and simmer together until the apples turn into pulp. Take off the heat, remove the bay leaves, cool and then add the nuts and cheese. Mix well and stuff the apple halves with the mixture. Place them in a buttered ovenproof dish, sprinkle with melted butter. Cover with foil and bake for about 30 mins in a preheated oven. Uncover and keep warm for another 2–3 mins.

serves 4 • Preparation: 15 mins • Baking: 30–35 mins

Summer dream

250 g ripe hard apricots, 250 g mushrooms, 1 large endive, ½ cup cream, ½ cup yogurt, 2 tbsps chopped chives, salt, white pepper, sugar, 1 tbsp lemon juice

Wash and dry the mushrooms, cut them into thin slices and sprinkle with lemon juice and pepper. Slice the washed apricots (remove the stones), cut the endive into thin strips. Blend the yogurt with cream, salt, pepper, chives and sugar. Combine the ingredients, pour over the dressing and toss.

serves 4–5 • Preparation: 10 mins

Spicy apricots

8 large hardish apricots, 8 thin rashers streaky bacon, 3 tbsps full-fat cottage cheese, 1 tbsp butter, 1–2 drops Tabasco sauce, cayenne pepper

Cut the washed and dried apricots lengthwise, but not right through. Remove the stones, break them and remove the seeds. Scald and skin them, chop. Blend the cheese with 1 tsp butter, Tabasco sauce and cayenne pepper, mix with the chopped apricot seeds. Stuff the fruit with the mixture and wrap each in a rasher of bacon, fasten with a toothpick and arrange in a buttered ovenproof dish. Bake for about 15 mins in a preheated oven.

serves 4 • Preparation: 20–25 mins

Apricots stuffed with smoked trout

12 apricots, 250 g smoked trout fillets, 2 spring onions, 1 large cucumber (about 250 g), 1 tbsp chopped dill, 1 tbsp olive oil, 1 tbsp lemon juice, salt, pepper

Peel the cucumber, cut lengthwise in half, remove the seeds and cut the flesh into small cubes, sprinkle with salt and set aside for a few minutes, then remove the excess liquid. Skin and bone out the trout, cut it finely, combine with the dill and chopped spring onion, add the olive oil and lemon juice, and season to taste with salt and pepper. Mix well. Cut the washed and dried apricots lengthwise in half, discard the stones and stuff with the mixture. Arrange on a plate, cover with foil and refrigerate for 30–40 mins. Before serving, arrange them on lettuce leaves and decorate with sprigs of dill.

serves 4–6 • Preparation: 10 mins • Refrigerating: 30–40 mins

Prunes stuffed with walnuts

12 prunes, ½ cup dry white wine, ¼ cup chopped walnuts, 2 tbsps grated cheese, a pinch of nutmeg, salt, pepper, 6 very fine rashers of streaky bacon, a few lettuce leaves for decoration

Place the washed prunes in a bowl, pour over the wine and set aside for 2–3 hours. Combine the walnuts with grated cheese, salt, pepper, nutmeg and 1 tbsp of the wine in which the prunes were soaking. Mix well and stuff the drained prunes with the mixture. Cut the rashers of bacon lengthwise in half, wrap each prune with a rasher and fasten with a toothpick. Place the stuffed prunes on a buttered ovenproof serving platter and bake for about 10–15 mins.

serves 4 • Soaking: 2–3 hrs • Preparation: 5 mins • Baking: 10–15 mins

Plums stuffed with processed cheese

20 nice, firm purple plums, 100 g processed cheese, 1 tbsp buttter, 1 tbsp cream, 3 tbsps finely chopped hazelnuts, salt, cayenne pepper, 2 tbsps chopped dill, 4–5 lettuce leaves

Blend the processed cheese with salt, pepper, butter and cream into smooth pulp. Stir in the hazelnuts. Cut the washed prunes lenghtwise in half and stuff them with the mixture. Arrange the prunes on a serving platter lined with lettuce leaves and sprinkle generously with dill. Serve as a cold snack, or as a side dish with roast meats.

serves 4 • Preparation: 5–6 mins

Prunes stuffed with turkey livers

20 prunes, 1 tbsp lemon juice, 20 thin rashers of streaky bacon, 3–4 turkey livers, salt, pepper, a pinch of dried marjoram, 1 garlic clove, 2 tbsps butter

Bring to the boil 2 cups lightly salted water with ½ tsp butter, lemon juice and lemon rind. Add the prunes and cook for 1–2 mins, drain and set aside to cool. Chop the livers and sauté them in butter, mix with garlic minced with salt, pepper and thyme. Stuff the prunes with the mixture. Wrap each with a rasher of bacon, fasten with a toothpick, sprinkle with melted butter and bake in a preheated oven for about 20 mins.

serves 4 • Preparation: 10–12 mins • Baking: 20 mins

CHAPTER XV

DESSERTS

✳✳✳

Fruit, various sweetmeats, not to mention wine,
Oranges, almonds, figs, marzipan,
Marrons and other things, Italian Parmesan,
A great deal of money is spent on them each year,
The very amount can give one a headache.

J. Jeṇowski, *Oekonomia...*, 1638

In poor households, for dessert you were given a lump of
cheese, large or small, poppyseed cake, fruit cheese, pretsels,
which you could safely keep for two or three years, golden
ginger biscuits... Later, when people got richer, cooked des-
serts appeared: arkas, creams, jellies, compotes, with which
cheeses of foreign provenance were served, as well as Toruń
ginger bread and fruit, including Hungarian plums, large
stoned prunes imported to Poland, raspberries, wild straw-
berries, garden strawberries, apples, pears, cherries, walnuts,
water melons... apricots, figs, pineapples. And when fresh fruit
was in short supply, there were also raisins, dried figs, Turkish
nuts, and dates.

Łukasz Go≥źbiowski, *Domy i dwory*, vol. IV, pp. 56–57

Old Polish desserts

Arkas

This was a cold dessert, a favourite dish of King John III (Sobieski).

4 cups milk, 1 cup single cream, 10 egg yolks,
1 cup sugar, grated rind and juice of 1 lemon,
½ cup cream, ½ cup sweet cherry juice

Whisk the egg yolks with the single cream, towards the end add lemon juice and zest. Bring the milk with sugar to the boil. Take off the heat. Whisking all the time to prevent it from curding, gradually add the egg and cream mixture. Pour the preparation into a muslin bag, tie the bag up and hang it to let excess liquid drip off. Transfer the arkas to a crystal-glass bowl. Garnish with fruit or pour over the cream mixed with the cherry juice.

serves 4 • Preparation: 1 hr

Coffee blancmange

3 tbsps finely ground coffee, 3 cups single cream, 1 egg,
4 egg yolks, 150 g sugar, 1 vanilla pod, 4 tbsps caster
sugar, sour cherry preserves, several sponge biscuits

Coffee blancmange

Put the coffee into a small pan, pour over ½ cup of boiling water, cover and heat up over low heat, then put through a thick sieve. Bring the cream with vanilla to the boil. Whisk the egg yolks and sugar until fluffy, add one whole egg. Stirring all the time, slowly pour in the cooled cream. Dip individual dessert bowls in water, then dust them inside with caster sugar and fill with the cream. Put the bowls into a pan filled with hot water (to ¼ height of the bowls). Seal the pan tightly and steamcook until the mixture has thickened. Leave aside for the blancmange to cool, then turn it out of the bowls onto a flat serving dish. Garnish with fruit preserves, preferably cherries, and sponge biscuits.

serves 4 • Preparation: 30–35 mins • Refrigerating: 1–2 hrs

Chocolate blancmange

2 cups single cream, 1 cup milk, 100 g hard bitter chocolate, 100 g sugar, 2 egg yolks, 1 heaped tsp vanilla sugar, 3 tbsp gelatine

Bring the milk with vanilla sugar to the boil, dissolve the gelatine in it. Whisk the sugar and egg yolks until fluffy. Bring the cream to the boil, then take it off the heat, put in the grated chocolate and stir thoroughly until it has dissolved. Add the milk, fold in the whisked eggs and simmer over low heat, stirring continuously. Put the thickened cream into glass cups and leave to cool, then refrigerate for 1–2 hours.

serves 4 • Preparation: 20–25 mins • Refrigerating: 1–2 hrs

Flamri (flamery)

1⅛ l milk, 1 cup sugar, 120 g potato or rice flour, 1 glass Maraschino, 6 egg whites

SAUCE: 2 cups single cream, 150 g sugar, 8 bitter almonds, 6 egg yolks, 1 tsp potato flour, 1 glass Maraschino

To make the sauce: Bring the cream with finely ground almonds to the boil. Slowly fold in the egg yolks beaten with the sugar and potato flour dissolved in 2 tbsps of cold milk. Whisking all the time, heat up the mixture, then allow it to cool, add Maraschino and refrigerate. Bring 1 l of milk with sugar to the boil. Mix the remaining milk with potato flour, pour the mixture into the boiled milk. Stirring all the time, heat up until it has thickened. Take off the heat and leave to cool a bit. Add Maraschino to the milk custard, fold in the whisked egg whites. Rinse a mould in very cold water. Pour in the mixture and leave in a cool place to set, then refrigerate it. Turn the flamri onto a serving serving dish and pour the sauce over.

serves 4 • Preparation: 30 mins • Refrigerating: 1–2 hrs

Floating islands, or Polish sweet soup

4 eggs, 1 l milk, 200 g caster sugar, 1 vanilla pod

Bring the milk with vanilla and half the sugar to the boil. Beat the egg yolks and the remaining sugar until fluffy. Whisk the egg whites to stiff peaks. Using a tablespoon, drop portions of the whisked egg whites into the boiling milk, cook for a while, then take out with a strainer. Heat the egg yolks gently, slowly pour in the milk, stirring continuously, until the cream has thickened (do not allow it to boil). Pour the custard into a large tureen, place the cooked egg whites on top. Serve either hot or chilled as dessert.

serves 4 •Preparation: 20–25 mins

Custard

Custard was well known in old Polish cuisine. It is made from milk, eggs and sugar, and flavoured with chocolate, coffee, cinnamon, or vanilla. It is always served chilled, in bowls or cups.

The first step is bringing the milk with the chosen flavour to the boil, and then straining it. In the meantime, you should beat whole eggs or egg yolks only, and then gradually pour the preparation into the hot milk. Remember to whisk the mixture all the time until it has thickened. While you are whisking it, you should add the flavouring.

Pour the thick mixture into small moulds or ramekins. Place the moulds in a tin or pan half-filled with water and steam-cook the custard for about half an hour. You may also put the moulds into a preheated oven for 15 minutes or so.

Almond-flavoured custard

½ l milk, 1 tbsp butter, 1 egg, 4 egg yolks,
100 g almonds, 4–5 tbsps sugar,
50 g almond flakes

Blanch and skin the almonds, dry and grind them. Put them into a bowl and blend with 2 tbsps of sugar and 1 tbsp of water. Bring the milk with butter to the boil, add the almonds, simmer over low heat for 5–7 mins, pass it through a fine sieve. Beat the egg and egg yolks with sugar. Whisking all the time, pour in the almond milk, mix thoroughly. Pour the preparation into ovenproof moulds, put into a preheated oven and bake for 15 mins. Take out, leave to cool, then put into the fridge for 1–2 hours. Before serving, sprinkle some almond flakes on top.

serves 4 • Preparation: 35–40 mins • Refrigerating: 1–2 hrs

Chocolate-flavoured custard

2 cups single cream, 1 egg,
4 egg yolks, ½ bar bitter chocolate,
3 tbsps sugar

Heat the cream and melt the chocolate in it. Beat the egg yolks with sugar. Break in the egg and whisk well. Fold in the cream, mix thoroughly. Pour the preparation into ovenproof moulds. Place the moulds in a shallow pan filled with hot water. Cover the pan and cook for 30 mins. Leave to cool, then put into the fridge for an hour. Serve with whipped cream.

serves 4 • Preparation: 35–40 mins • Refrigerating: 1–2 hrs

Mousse

Mousse is a dessert made from liquidized fruit mixed with whisked egg whites (with some gelatine added), which make the preparation light and soft. Apart from egg whites, you usually add some cream to it, which is also used for garnishing.

Wild strawberry mousse

500 g wild strawberries, 3 eggs, 150 g caster sugar,
1 tsp gelatine, 3 tbsps dry white wine,
½ cup whipping cream

Rinse and drain the wild strawberries. Leave 2 tbsps aside for garnishing. Sieve the remaining strawberries and put the purée into the fridge for an hour. Bring the wine to the boil, dissolve the gelatine in it, stir thoroughly. Beat the egg yolks with the sugar. Whisk the egg whites. Combine the strawberries with the egg yolks, gently fold in the egg whites and cool gelatine. Whisk the mixture until it has thickened. Whip the cream. Put the mousse into cups. Garnish each cup with some whipped cream and strawberries. Put into the fridge for two hours.

serves 4 • Preparation: 15–20 mins • Refrigerating: 2–3 hrs

Apple mousse

500 g tart apples, 3 egg whites, 3 tbsps sugar,
2 tsp gelatine, 2–3 tbsps dry white wine,
½ tsp ground cinnamon

Peel and core the apples, dice and steam them. Pour in the wine and cook over low heat, add sugar and cinnamon, and liquidize the mixture. Dissolve the gelatine in 2–3 tbsps of boiling water, mix thoroughly, then leave to cool. Whisk the egg whites, mix them with the gelatine and the apples. Put the preparation into individual serving bowls and refrigerate.

serves 4 • Preparation: 15–20 mins • Refrigerating: 1–2 hrs

Blackcurrant mousse

1½ cups cleaned blackcurrants, 300 g cream cheese, 1 tbsp honey, 1 tbsp caster sugar,
1 tbsp gelatine, 1–2 tbsps boiled water

Dissolve the gelatine in water. Blend 1 cup of blackcurrants with the honey and sugar, mix in the cheese and

Fruit jelly

gelatine. Put the preparation into individual serving cups and refrigerate. Before serving, garnish with the remaining blackcurrants.

serves 4 • Preparation: 5–7 mins • Refrigerating: 30–40 mins

Jelly

This is a cold dessert made of fresh fruit juice, to which sugar and gelatine are added. Fruit jellies are usually decorated with whipped cream. Jellies are also prepared from soured milk mixed with gelatine and beaten egg yolks with sugar. These are usually garnished with fresh fruit.

You may also make a dessert from various kinds of jelly set in layers in glass cups or bowls.

Fruit jelly

600 g fruit (raspberries, blackberries, grapes, peaches), 100 g sugar, 1 tbsp gelatine, 1 orange, 1 lemon, 1 glass brandy

Rinse all fruit, drain well. Blanch, skin and slice the peaches. Juice the orange and lemon. Make a syrup from the sugar and 1½ cups of water, skim the scum. Put in the fruit, bring to the boil and immediately take out the fruit with a strainer. Mix the syrup with the gelatine, add the lemon and orange juice. Take off the heat, leave to cool, then pour in the brandy and mix thoroughly. Pour half the jelly into a serving bowl, leave to cool. When it sets, spread the fruit on top and cover with the remaining jelly. Refrigerate for 1–2 hours. Before serving, decorate with whipped cream.

serves 4 • Preparation: 25–30 mins • Refrigerating: 1–2 hrs

Apricot jelly

500 g apricots, ½ cup sugar, juice and grated rind of ½ lemon, 1–2 cloves, 1 cup dry white wine, 1 tbsp gelatine, 4 tbsps whipped cream

Rinse, blanch and skin the apricots. Make a syrup from the sugar and 1 cup of water, add the lemon zest and cloves. Skim the scum, take out the cloves. Put in the apricots, add the lemon juice and cook over low heat until the apricots are glazed. Take them out and strain them dry, then cut them into quarters. Dissolve the gelatine in ½ cup of hot water. Add the wine to the syrup, bring to the boil. Pour in the gelatine, stir thoroughly. Take off the heat and allow to cool. When the jelly begins to set, put 2–3 tbsps of it into each individual serving bowl and leave to set. Put some apricots on top and cover with the remaining jelly. Refrigerate for 1–2 hours. Before serving, decorate with whipped cream.

serves 4 • Preparation: 20–30 mins • Refrigerating: 1–2 hrs

Pineapple jelly

1 tin pineapple chunks, 15 cherries in syrup, 2 cups dry white wine, grated rind and juice of ½ lemon, ½ cup sugar, 3–4 tsp gelatine, ½ cup boiled water

Soak the gelatine in water. Drain the pineapple chunks. Bring the water with sugar, lemon juice and zest to the boil. Pour in the dissolved gelatine, stir well, and allow to cool. Put some jelly into individual bowls (⅓ height). When it begins to set, arrange pineapple chunks on top, decorate with cherries, cover with the remaining jelly and refrigerate.

serves 4 • Preparation: 15 mins • Refrigering: 1–2 hrs

Soured milk jelly

2 cups soured milk, 1½ tbsp gelatine, 4 tbsps sugar, ½ cup chopped walnuts, ½ vanilla pod, ¼ cup boiled water, several walnut halves for decorating

Toast the chopped walnuts together with 2 tbsps of sugar in a frying pan, add the chopped vanilla pod. Pour boiling water over the gelatine, stir well, then allow to cool. Beat the soured milk with a whisker, add the remaining sugar. Whisking all the time, gradually fold in the cooled gelatine. Add the chopped walnuts and mix thoroughly. Pour the mixture into individual serving cups and refrigerate.

serves 4 • Preparation: 15 mins • Refrigerating: 1–2 hrs

Caramel jelly

4 tbsps sugar, 1½ cups milk, ½ cup single cream,
½ vanilla pod, 2 tsps gelatine, ½ cup water

Bring the milk with the vanilla and 2 tbsps of sugar to the boil. Dissolve the gelatine in ¼ cup of boiling water, stir thoroughly and leave to cool. Brown the remaining sugar in a frying pan, but do not let it burn. Pour in the remaining water and cook until the sugar has dissolved. Cool the caramel a bit, combine it with the cream, strained milk and gelatine. Mix thoroughly, pour into individual serving bowls and refrigerate. Before serving, decorate with fruit preserves.

serves 4 • Preparation: 15 mins • Refrigerating: 1–2 hrs

Kissel

Kissel is a dish similar to jelly, prepared from fruit juice, but with potato flour added instead of gelatine.

Rose hip kissel

200 g dried rose hips, ½ cup sugar, 2 tbsps lemon juice,
4 cups water, 1½ tbsps potato flour, 2 kiwi fruit

Rinse the rosehips, soak them in 3 cups of boiled water for half an hour. Cook them in the same water, sieve. Mix the potato flour with water. Bring the puréed rosehip with the sugar and lemon juice to the boil. Pour in the potato flour and, stirring all the time, heat up the mixture. Peel and slice the kiwi fruit. Arrange the slices in individual serving bowls, cover them with the kissel and leave to cool.

serves 4 • Soaking: 30–40 mins • Preparation:
10–15 mins • Refrigerating: 1–2 hrs

Cream

In Polish cuisine, cream is a kind of cold dessert made from milk or cream, egg yolks, whipped egg whites and gelatine, mixed with puréed fruit, often with some alcoholic beverage added. It is usually decorated with almonds, nuts or chocolate flakes, and served with sponge fingers or meringues.

Abbess's cream with cookies

8 egg yolks, 7 cups milk, 50 g bitter chocolate,
150 g almonds, 1 packet of sponge fingers

Beat the egg yolks with the milk in a pan. Put the pan on the cooker and, stirring all the time, heat for 10––15 mins, but keep it off the boil. Blanch and peel the almonds, and chop them very finely. Crumble the sponge fingers. Take the pan off the heat. Whisking all the time, gradually add the crumbled sponge, grated chocolate and almonds. Pour the mixture into individual ovenproof dishes and put into a preheated oven for several minutes.

serves 6–8 • Preparation: 30–40 mins

Cookies made from egg whites

8 egg whites, 400 g caster sugar, juice and
grated rind of 1 lemon, 1 cup flour

Whisk the egg whites and sugar to stiff peaks. Mix them gently with the flour, lemon juice and zest. Using a spoon, drop portions of the preparation onto a baking sheet. Put the cookies into a medium-hot oven and bake till golden brown.

Strawberry cream with rum

500 g ripe strawberries, 4 eggs, 4 tbsps
sugar, ½ cup whipping cream, 1 glass white
rum, 2 cups whipped cream, several lemon
balm leaves, 2 tbsps wild strawberries

Rinse and dry the strawberries, force them through a sieve. Beat the egg yolks with the sugar in a pan. Rest the pan on a pot of simmering water over a low heat and whisk until the mixture has thickened. Whisk the egg whites to stiff peaks, mix them gently with the whipped cream, strawberries, rum and the egg mixture. Put the cream into individual serving cups and decorate with wild strawberries and lemon balm leaves.

serves 4 • Preparation: 25–30 mins

Strawberry cream with orange juice

500 g strawberries, 1 cup sugar, ½ cup water, juice of 1 large orange and ½ lemon, ¼ tsp each grated lemon and orange rind, 1 tbsp gelatine, 1 cup whipping cream; for decorating, ½ cup wild strawberries, several green lemon balm and mint leaves

Make a thick syrup from the sugar, water, lemon and orange juice (cook it for 10 mins, stirring all the time). Add the zest, mix in the gelatine. Take off the heat and allow to cool. Liquidize the strawberries, then sieve them. Whip the cream. Combine the syrup with the strawberries and cream. Put the mixture into individual serving dishes and refrigerate for 1–2 hours. Before serving, decorate with wild strawberries and lemon balm or mint leaves.

serves 4 • Preparation: 25–30 mins • Refrigerating: 1–2 hrs

Prune cream

200 g stoned prunes, 2 tbsps honey, 1 tsp gelatine, 1 cup whipped cream, some walnut halves

Rinse the prunes, cover with boiled water and leave for 2–3 hours, then cook and drain them. Process the prunes with the honey. Dissolve the gelatine in the water in which the prunes have soaked, add the mixture to the puréed prunes. Pour the preparation into individual serving bowls and put into the fridge. Before serving, decorate with whipped cream and walnut halves.

serves 4 • Soaking: 2–3 hrs • Preparation: 20 mins • Refrigerating: 30–40 mins

Apricot cream

250 g fresh (or tinned) apricots, 2 tbsps honey, 25 g propolis, 2–3 tbsps whipped cream, 50 g almonds

Blanch and peel the almonds. Leave aside several of them for decorating, chop the remaining ones finely. Stone the apricots. Process the apricots together with the propolis and honey. Refrigerate for a while, then put into individual serving cups. Sprinkle with the chopped almonds, decorate with whipped cream and almonds.

serves 4 • Preparation: 10–12 mins

Orange cream

6 eggs, 300 g sugar, 2 oranges, ¼ tsp cinnamon, ½ cup water, 1 small glass of dry white wine

Make a light syrup from 250 g sugar and water, cook over a low heat, stirring all the time. Wash and scald the oranges. Squeeze out the juice, take off fine skin. Put the peel into the boiling syrup and cook for 2 mins, then drain it and cut into thin strips. Bring the wine and the remaining sugar to the boil, put in the orange peel and cook over low heat. Beat the egg yolks with the orange juice and cinnamon, then combine the mixture with the syrup, whisking all the time, and finally fold in the whisked egg whites. Put the preparation into individual serving bowls and decorate with orange strips.

serves 4–6 • Preparation: 30 mins

Orange and nut cream

200 g curd cheese, 2 oranges, 1 tangerine, juice and grated rind of ½ lemon, 3 tbsps honey, 1 tbsp each chopped pistachios, pine nuts and hazelnuts, 2 tbsps almond flakes, 4 lemon balm leaves

Wash the oranges thoroughly, scald them with boiling water and dry. Peel one orange very finely, chop the flesh well. Squeeze out the juice, mix it with the honey, lemon juice and zest, cheese, nuts and almonds. Peel the other orange, cut it into fine cubes, remove the pips. Add it to the cheese preparation. Mix thoroughly and refrigerate for a while. Put the cream into individual serving cups, decorate with lemon balm leaves and tangerine segments.

serves 4 • Preparation: 10–12 mins • Refrigerating: 30–40 mins

Nut cream

250 g finely chopped walnuts, 300 ml goat's milk, 3–4 tbsps honey, 4 egg yolks

Put the chopped walnuts into a pan, cover with the milk and, stirring occasionally, cook over low heat until the mixture has thickened. Rest the pan on top of a pot with simmering water. Add the honey and, whisking all the time, put in one egg yolk at a time. Whisk until the cream has thickened. The cream will keep in the fridge for one or two days. It can also be served with cold ham or other meats.

serves 4 • Preparation: 25–30 mins

Ginger cream

4 tbsps candied ginger, 1 cup single cream, 2 eggs, 3 tbsps sugar, 2 tbsps white rum, 3 tsps gelatine, a pinch of salt

Soak the gelatine in 2 tbsps of cold boiled water. Beat the egg yolks with sugar until white. Pour the cream into a pan and heat up over low heat. Add the rum, fold in the beaten egg yolks and, stirring all the time, heat up. Pour in the dissolved gelatine, mix thoroughly and take off the heat. Whisk the egg whites with some sugar and salt into stiff peaks. Chop the ginger finely. Mix gently the cream, ginger and egg whites and put the preparation into individual serving bowls. Cover the bowls and put into the fridge for 3–4 hours.

serves 4 • Preparation: 15–20 mins • Refrigerating: 3–4 hrs

Wine cream

2 eggs, 2 egg yolks, 2 cups semi-dry white wine, 6–8 tbsps sugar, juice and grated rind of 1 lemon, 1 tbsp potato flour, 2 tinned peach halves, some candied cherries, 1 kiwi fruit

Mix the potato flour with 2–3 tbsps of wine. Beat the egg yolks with the sugar, pour the mixture into a

pan. Add the eggs, lemon juice and zest. Rest the pan on top of a pot with simmering water and whisk, gradually adding the wine and then the wine and potato flour mixture. Whisk until the cream is smooth and velvety. Put into individual serving bowls and leave to cool. Decorate with peach pieces, cherries and kiwi slices.

serves 4 • Preparation: 10 mins

Fruit desserts

Dessert of wild strawberries

400 g wild strawberries, 2 cups dry white wine, 1 cup honey, juice of 1 lemon, 2–3 sprigs of mint

Rinse and dry the strawberries. Put half of them into individual serving bowls and sprinkle them with some lemon juice. Put the remaining strawberries through a blender together with the honey, wine and the remaining lemon juice. Cover the strawberries with the preparation and put into the fridge for 2–3 hours. Before serving, decorate with mint leaves.

serves 4 • Preparation: 5–6 mins • Refrigerating: 1–2 hrs

Spicy pears

4 large firm pears, juice and grated rind of 1 lemon, 1 cup dry red wine, 1 cup pomegranate juice, 1 cup honey, a piece of cinnamon bark, 2–3 cloves, 2–3 tbsps finely chopped almonds

Peel the pears, cut them lengthwise into half, remove the cores. Sprinkle with lemon juice. Bring the wine with the cinnamon, cloves, lemon zest, honey and pomegranate juice to the boil. Put in the pears and cook for 4–5 mins. Take them out carefully, arrange on a serving dish. Continue cooking the wine and juice mixture until it thickens. Take out the cloves and cinnamon. Leave the sauce the cool, then pour it over the pears. Toast the almonds in a hot frying pan and sprinkle the pears with them.

serves 4 • Preparation: 15 mins

Pears in white wine with pistachios

4 firm juicy pears, juice and grated rind of 1 lemon, 2 tbsps honey, 50 g chopped pistachios, ¾ cup white dessert wine

Peel the pears (do not cut the stalks off), sprinkle them with lemon juice. Combine the honey with the pistachios and lemon zest into a smooth mixture. Arrange the pears upright in an ovenproof dish, coat them with the pistachio paste. Pour in the wine. Cover the dish and put into a preheated oven. Bake for 40 mins. Pour the sauce from the dish into a small pan. Bring it to the boil, reduce the liquid and pour it over the pears. Serve immediately.

serves 4 • Preparation: 10 mins • Baking: 40 mins

Blackberry pears

2 large juicy pears, juice and grated rind of 1 lemon, 2 tbsps honey, 1 cup boiled water, 300 g blackberries, 200 g Mascarpone cheese, 1 tbsp fruit liqueur, several lemon balm leaves

Bring the water with the honey, lemon juice and zest to the boil. Put in the peeled, cored and halved pears. Bring to the boil, then take off the heat and leave to cool. Put the cheese, 250 g of blackberries and the liqueur through a blender. Take out the pears, drain them, arrange on dessert plates and fill with the mixture. Decorate with the remaining raspberries and lemon balm leaves and refrigerate for a while.

serves 4 • Preparation: 30–40 mins • Refrigerating: 30–40 mins

Pears in blackcurrant sauce

4 firm juicy pears, 400 g blackcurrants, 150 g sugar, ½ vanilla pod, ½ cup blackcurrant liqueur (Cassis), 1 tbsp lemon juice

Rinse the blackcurrants, drain and stock them. Leaving aside 2–3 tbsps, liquidize and sieve the blackcurrants. Bring 2 cups of water with sugar to the boil. Put in the liquidized currants and simmer over low heat for 10 mins. Peel and core the pears, sprinkle them with some lemon juice. Put the pears into the blackcurrant sauce and cook for 15 mins. Add 2 tbsps of the whole blackcurrants and simmer for another 2–3 mins. Pour in the liqueur, shake the pan, then take it off the heat. Put the pears into four individual serving bowls. Mix the sauce well and pour it over the pears. Put into the fridge for 1–2 hours.

serves 4 • Preparation: 20–25 mins • Refrigerating: 1–2 hrs

Apples in wine sauce

4 large apples, 100 g dried figs, 50 g almonds, 1 tbsp dry white wine, 1 cup honey, 1 tbsp butter, ¼ cup water, ¼ cup white wine

Blach and peel the almonds, chop them finely, then toast in a hot frying pan. Add the finely diced figs and 1 tbsp of wine. Wash, dry and core the apples. Fill them tightly with the almond and fig mixture. Arrange the apples in an ovenproof dish. Bring the water and wine to the boil, add the honey and butter and simmer to melt them, but do not allow to boil. Pour the hot sauce over the apples. Put the apples into a preheated oven and bake for 20 mins. Leave them to cool, then refrigerate for a while.

serves 4 • Preparation: 10 mins • Baking: 20 mins • Refrigerating: 3–4 hrs

Apples with chestnuts

16 hard apples, 1 kg chestnuts, 250 g sugar, 1 vanilla pod, 2½ cups whipping cream, ½ cup peach jam, 4 tinned peach halves

Roast the chestnuts in a preheated oven, peel them, cut finely. Bring the cream, together with the sugar and the chopped chestnuts, to the boil, then force the mixture through a sieve. Wash the apples, carefully remove the cores. Fill the apples with the peach jam. Pour the cream mixture into an ovenproof dish, put in the apples and bake in a preheated oven. Before serving, decorate with peach slices.

serves 8–16 • Preparation: 30 mins • Baking: 20 mins

Baked peaches

*4 large firm peaches, 2 egg yolks, 3 tbsps caster sugar,
2 tbsps each finely chopped almonds and hazelnuts,
1 tbsp lemon juice, a pinch of cinnamon, 1 tbsp butter*

Whisk the eggs whites to stiff peaks. Whisking all the time, gradually add the sugar and then carefully fold in the lemon juice, hazelnuts, almonds and cinnamon. Wash the peaches, blanch them in boiling water for a minute, then rinse under cold water and peel them. Halve the peaches lengthwise, remove the stones. Grease an ovenproof dish with butter. Arrange the peach halves, pipe some meringue mixture into each half. Put into a preheated oven (150–160°C) and bake for 15 mins.

serves 4 • Preparation: 10 mins • Baking: 15 mins

Apricots baked in cream

12 apricots, 1 cup single cream, 4 egg yolks, 3–4 tbsps sugar, ½ vanilla pod, 1–2 tbsps caster sugar, 1 tsp potato flour, ½ cup water, 2 tbsps dry white wine

Wash and dry the apricots, cut them in half, remove the stones. Bring water with sugar to the boil. Put in 4 apricots and cook them briskly over high heat for 5–7 mins, then simmer for another 10 mins. Leave to cool, then liquidize and sieve them. Chop the vanilla finely. Beat the egg yolks with the caster sugar. Whisking all the time, gradually add the liquidized apricots and vanilla. Mix the potato flour with the wine, fold in the cream and the egg yolks. Whisk until the cream thickens. Arrange the remaining apricot halves in an ovenproof dish, pour the cream over and put into a preheated oven (200°C). Bake for 15 mins. Serve hot or cold.

serves 4–8 • Preparation: 15 mins • Baking: 15 mins

Christmas prunes

400 g stoned prunes, 1 cup dry red wine, 3 tbsps sugar, 2–3 cloves, grated rind of ½ lemon, finely chopped rind of ½ orange, 100 g almond flakes, 1 cup whipped cream

Bring the wine, together with the cloves, sugar and lemon zest, to the boil. Put in the washed and well drained prunes in a bowl, cover with the boiling wine, then leave overnight to soak. Arrange the prunes in individual serving cups, sprinkle them with orange rind and toasted almond flakes. Decorate with the well chilled whipped cream.

serves 4 • Soaking: 12 hrs • Preparation: 5 mins

Stuffed prunes

20 prunes, 3 tbsps candied orange peel, 3 tbsps chopped walnuts, 1 glass brandy, 1 tsp honey, 1 cup whipping cream, 4 tbsps caster sugar, 1 tbsp chopped hazelnuts

Rinse the prunes, put them for 2–3 mins into boiling water. Drain them, rinse under cold water and dry. Mix the finely chopped orange rind with the honey, brandy and walnuts. Fill the prunes with the stuffing, arrange them on a round platter. Pour over the whipped cream, sprinkle on top with the chopped hazelnuts. Cover the plate and refrigerate for a while.

serves 4 • Preparation: 10 mins • Refrigerating: 30–40 mins

Stuffed oranges

2 medium-sized oranges, 2 apples, 2 tbsps lemon juice, 4 tbsps finely grated horseradish, salt, sugar, pepper

Wash the oranges thoroughly, scald, then dry them. Halve them, then carefully remove the flesh. Grate the peeled apples finely, sprinkle them with the lemon juice. Chop the orange flesh, remove the pips. Mix the orange cubes with the grated apples and horseradish. Adjust the taste with salt, sugar and pepper and refrigerate for a while. Fill the orange halves with the stuffing.

serves 4 • Preparation: 10 mins • Refrigerating: 30–40 mins

Various desserts

Brown bread dessert

*300 g stale brown rye bread, 1 tbsp butter,
2 tbsps sugar, 3 tart apples, 1 tsp cinnamon,
1 tbsp lemon juice, 3 tbsps honey, ½ cup whipped
cream, 1 tbsp whortleberry preserve*

Peel the apples, sprinkle them with the lemon juice, then grate finely. Put them into a pan, dust with the cinnamon, add some water if required. Simmer over low heat for 10 mins, then add the honey, stir well and allow the mixture to cool. Grate the bread. Melt the butter in a frying pan, put in the breadcrumbs and sugar and roast them, stirring all the time. Put the bread onto a plate and leave to cool. In individual serving bowls, arrange alternating layers of the breadcrumbs and the apple mixture, finishing off with a layer of bread. Decorate with whipped cream and whortleberry jam.

serves 4–6 • Preparation: 25–30 mins

Spring dessert

*500 g rhubarb, 2 tbsps honey, ½ cup water,
1 cup whipped cream, 1 tsp ground aniseed,
2 tbsps chopped walnuts, 1 tbsp dried figs
cut into strips, 1 tbsp blanched raisins*

Strip the stringy fibres from the rhubarb stalks, cut the stalks into small pieces. Bring the water and honey to the boil, put in the rhubarb and poach it over low heat, then leave it to cool. Put the rhubarb into individual serving bowls and refrigerate for a while. Decorate the rhubarb with the cream mixed with the aniseed, sprinkle on top with the walnuts, raisins and fig strips.

serves 4 • Preparation: 20–25 mins • Refrigerating: 30–40 mins

Melon dessert

*1 melon, juice of 1 lemon and 1 orange, ½ tsp
grated orange peel, ½ tsp powdered ginger,
1 tbsp raisins, 2–3 tbsps dry white wine, 1 tbsp
chopped hazelnuts, 2–3 tbsps boiled water*

Rinse the raisins, drain them, then soak in wine. Put the lemon and orange juice and honey into a pan, bring to the boil. Add the orange zest, ginger, raisins together with the wine and some water. Simmer over low heat for several minutes. Put in the nuts, mix well, then leave to cool. Peel the melon, remove the seeds. Cut the melon into cubes or scoop out small balls. Put the melon into a serving bowl, pour the sauce over and chill well.

serves 4 • Preparation: 15–20 mins • Refrigerating: 1–2 hrs

Hot fruit dessert

*2 apples, 2 pears, 2 apricots, 2 plums, 1 tsp powdered
ginger, ½ tsp cinnamon, 1 tsp grated orange rind, 1 tbsp
finely chopped candied orange peel, ¼ tsp ground
cloves, 3 tbsps honey, ⅔ cup dry red wine, 1 tbsp butter*

Wash the fruit, cut them in half, core or stone them. Grease an ovenproof dish with butter, put in a layer of fruit, sprinkle it with the mixed spices. Pour over the wine mixed with the honey. Put into a preheated oven and bake for 40 mins. Serve hot, decorated with whipped cream.

serves 4–6 • Preparation: 5–7 mins • Baking: 35–40 mins

Fruit salad

*1 cup boiled water, 3 tbsps honey, juice and grated rind
of 1 lemon, 15 cardamom seeds, 1 tbsp lemon juice for
sprinkling the fruit, 2 large peaches, 3 plums, 3 apples,
1 pear, a bunch of grapes, a sprig of lemon balm*

Bring the water, together with the honey, lemon juice and zest, to the boil. Cover the pan and simmer for 10 mins, then take off the heat and mix with the ground cardamom. Peel and core the apples and pear, cut them in half and then into thin slices, sprinkle them with lemon juice. Stone the peaches and plums and cut them into slices.

Apricot soufflé

Mix all the fruit in a bowl, pour over the prepared syrup. Cover the bowl and put it into the fridge for 2–3 hours. Before serving, put the salad into individual serving cups and decorate it with lemon balm leaves.

serves 4–6 • Preparation: 15 mins • Refrigerating: 2–3 hrs

Soufflés

Apple soufflé

4 eggs, 4 large tart apples, 3 tbsps butter, 2 tbsps flour, 1 cup milk, 8 tbsps caster sugar, 3 tbsps raisins, 1 small glass of brandy, ¼ tsp cinnamon, 1 tbsp lemon juice

Peel and core the apples, slice them, sprinkle with lemon juice and cinnamon. Put the apples in an ovenproof dish greased with butter. Beat the egg yolks with the caster sugar until foamy. Blanch the raisins, drain them, then soak in the brandy. Whisk the egg whites to stiff peaks. Melt 2 tbsps of butter in a pan, add the flour and make a white roux. Dilute it with the cold milk and, stirring all the time, cook over low heat until it has thickened. When the sauce gets cool, combine it with the beaten egg yolks, add the raisins and a pinch of cinnamon, fold in the egg whites. Mix gently but thoroughly. Pour the mixture over the apples. Put into a preheated oven and bake until golden brown. Serve immediately.

serves 4–6 • Preparation: 30–35 mins

Apricot soufflé

1 kg apricots, 4 eggs, 8–9 tbsps sugar, ½ cup milk, 1 glass apricot liqueur, 1 tbsp butter

Blanch the apricots, skin them, cut into halves, remove the stones. Arrange the appricot halves in a greased ovenproof dish. Beat the egg yolks with 6–7 tbsps of sugar until fluffy. Whisking all the time, gradually add the hot milk. Add the liqueur, stir well, then pour the mixture over the apricots. Whisk the egg whites and 2 tbsps of sugar to stiff peaks and spread on top of the apricots. Put the dish into a preheated oven and bake until golden brown. Serve immediately before it collapses. This souffle can also be served cold, in which case you do not have to worry whether it collapses or not.

serves 4–6 • Preparation: 30–35 mins

CHAPTER XVI

HOT AND COLD DRINKS

Hot and cold drinks

Hot drinks warm up the system, stimulate the circulation, provide calories and make one feel better.

A typical Polish hot drink was **krupnik,** made with honey and spices, and drunk with melted butter. It was popular in central Poland, but was also known in other regions under different names.

Today krupnik is drunk cold, in small glasses, as a liqueur, but other hot alcoholic drinks have caught on in Poland; in order to fulfil their purpose, they should never contain too much strong alcohol, which stupefies rather than warms. Hot alcoholic beverages are excellent for parties in carnival time, for hunting and winter sleigh rides.

Traditional Polish low-alcohol drinks which are drunk hot are **mulled beer** and **wine with spices**.

Originally, they were served with the meal, and only in the early 20th century began to be served rather with dessert. You have to be careful how you prepare them: remember that the liquid must be kept off the boil and should cook under a lid so that the alcohol does not evaporate.

In various periods, **grog** was very popular. This is traditionally the favourite drink of sailors, known in all the cold seas of the world. The basis for grog is rum, which is the most warming of all alcohols.

Punch is an old ritual beverage of Hindu priests. Brought to Europe by the British, it has five basic ingredients: arrack, rum or wine, sugar, lemon juice, spices and tea. In the 19th century it was usual to serve hot punch at the end of a meal, especially after supper, and it became ultra-fashionable throughout Europe – served hot on special occasions like Christmas Eve, New Year's Eve or New Year's Day. According to Maria Ochorowicz-Monatowa's *Uniwersalna książka kucharska*, punch was "the traditional drink for seeing out the Old Year and seeing in the New".

Vladimir honey drink

1 l water, 200 g honey, 5 g each cloves, ginger, cinnamon and bay leaves

Mix the honey with the water, bring to the boil, then cook over low heat for 20 mins. Add the spices, cover and simmer for another 5–6 mins. Leave to cool, then strain it through a gauze and heat up. Serve hot.

Preparation: 50 mins

Moscow honey drink

1 l water, 200 g honey, 150 g molasses, 1 g cinnamon, 1 g cloves, 1 g hops, 1 g nutmeg and allspice

Bring the water with the honey and molasses to the boil, add the spices and hops. Cover the pan and simmer for 5–6 mins. Leave aside for 30 mins, then strain the liquid. Drink hot or cold.

Preparation: 40–45 mins

Beer with spices

3–4 cups lager beer, 4 tbsps honey, 4 cloves, 4 cardamom seeds, ½ tsp nutmeg, juice and grated rind of ½ orange

Put the beer with the spices, orange juice and zest into a pan, cover on and heat up, then strain the liquid, add the honey and heat up again. Serve hot.

Preparation: 10 mins

Mulled beer

2 cups lager beer, 2 egg yolks, 4–5 tbsps sugar, 3–4 cloves, a small piece of cinnamon bark

Mix 1 cup of beer with the spices, bring to the boil. Heat up the remaining beer. Whisk the egg yolks and sugar until foamy in a pot. Put it over a very low heat and, whisking all the time, gradually pour in the spicy beer, then add the remaining beer. Serve hot.

Preparation: 15 mins

Mulled beer with cream

3 cups lager beer, 3 egg yolks, 3 tbsps sugar, ¾ cup whipping cream, 3 cloves, ½ vanilla pod, 2 cm piece of cinnamon bark

Whisk the egg yolks and sugar until foamy. Pour the beer into a pan, add the spices, cover and heat up, then remove the spices out. Whisking all the time, gradually combine the beer with the egg yolks. When the liquid has become foamy, pour in the cream, stir well and serve immediately.

Preparation: 15 mins

Mulled wine

1 bottle dry red wine, 1 l water, ½ cup lemon juice, 1 small glass of vodka, 20 cloves, 20–30 grains allspice

Combine all the ingredients, bring slowly to the boil. Strain the liquid. Serve hot in tall glasses.

Preparation: 10 mins

Old Polish mulled wine

1 bottle dry red wine, 2 egg yolks, 1–2 tbsps honey (preferably buckwheat), 1 tbsp sugar, 3–4 cloves, a pinch of cinnamon

Whisk the egg yolks and sugar until foamy in a bowl. Pour the wine into a pan, add the cloves and cinnamon, cover and heat up (but do not let it boil). Take off the heat, add the honey, remove the cloves. Rest the bowl with the egg and sugar mixture on top of a pot of boiling water and, whisking all the time, slowly pour in the wine. Pour into glasses and serve immediately.

Preparation: 20 mins

Sailor's grog

1 cup golden rum, 2 tbsps lemon juice, 4 tbsps sugar, 4–8 crushed cloves, 2–3 pieces of cinnamon bark, 4 cups boiling water

Combine all the ingredients, heat up, add the water and stir well. Strain the liquid and pour into warm glasses.

Preparation: 5 mins

Traditional grog

4 cups water, 1 cup brandy, juice of 2 lemons, 1 tsp grated lemon rind, ½ cup sugar, 3–5 cloves, a piece of cinnamon bark

Bring the water to the boil, put in the sugar, lemon zest, cinnamon and cloves. Cover and simmer over low heat for 30 mins. Strain the liquid, add the lemon juice and brandy, heat up, but do not let it boil. Serve very hot.

Preparation: 30–35 mins

Carnival grog

2 bottles red wine (Burgundy), ½ l gin, 1 cup sugar, 250 g dried apricots, 150 g raisins, 1 tbsp grated orange rind, 1 tsp ground cloves, 2–3 pieces of cinnamon bark, 3–4 crushed cardamom seeds, 150 g almond flakes

Pour 1 bottle of Burgundy wine into a pan, put in the spices and orange zest wrapped in a piece of gauze, add the rinsed and drained apricots and raisins. Cover and simmer over low heat for 30–40 mins. Take off the heat, remove the spices. Add the sugar, the remaining Burgundy and gin. Stir well, allow to cool and leave overnight in the fridge. The following day, heat the grog up, but keep it off the boil, stir from time to time. Set the grog alight for several seconds, extinguish the flame by covering the pan with a lid. Pour into a warm punch bowl, garnish with almond flakes. Serve hot.

Preparation: 40 mins • Refrigerating: 12 hrs • Heating: 5–6 mins

Punch I

5 cups strong tea infusion, 10–11 tbsps sugar, ½ cup each lemon juice and brandy, 1 cup golden rum, 1 lemon

Slice the lemon. Pour the tea infusion into a pan, bring to the boil. Take off the heat, add the lemon juice, brandy, rum and sugar, stir well and heat up. Serve in warm glasses, decorated with lemon slices.

Preparation: 5–6 mins

Punch II

6 tsps tea leaves, 2 cups boiling water, 150 g sugar, 4 cups dry white wine, ½ cup rum, rind of 1 lemon

Scrub the lemon, blanch it, take off the yellow rind with a sharp knife. Put the tea leaves in a glass pot, cover with the boiling water and leave to brew for 5–6 mins. Strain the tea, mix with the sugar and pour into a pan. Add the wine and lemon zest, heat up but do not let it boil. Pour in the rum, stir well and heat again, but keep off the boil. Take off the heat and immediately pour into individual glasses or a punch bowl.

NOTE: Before you pour the hot punch into glasses, put a spoon into each of them to prevent it breaking. If you want to serve the punch flambé, rest a spoon on the rim of a glass, put in it a sugar cube soaked in brandy or rum and set it alight.

Preparation: 5–6 mins

Carnival punch

6 tsps tea leaves, 4 cups boiling water, 2–3 cloves, a small piece of cinnamon bark, 3 cups dry red wine, 3 cups white rum, 250 g sugar, juice of 2 lemons, 1 orange

Put the tea leaves into a glass pot, add the cloves and cinnamon. Cover with the boiling water, place on a heated plate and let to brew for 5–6 mins, then strain strain the infusion. Put the tea infusion into a pan, add the wine, sugar and lemon juice. Stirring all the time, heat until the sugar has dissolved. Pour in the rum and heat up again. Peel the orange, cut it into thin slices, remove the pips. Put the slices into a punch bowl and pour in the hot punch.

Preparation: 10–12 mins

Pineapple punch

1 tin pineapple cubes, 4 tsps tea leaves, 2 cups boiling water, 100 g sugar, 1 glass sweet red wine, juice of 1 lemon, 4 cups dry red wine, ½ cup brandy

Put the tea leaves into a glass pot, cover with the boiling water and leave to brew for 5–6 mins, then strain the infusion and mix it with the sugar. Put the pineapple cubes into a pan, add the sweet wine and pineapple juice, tea infusion, lemon juice and red wine. Heat the punch up, but keep it off the boil. Add the brandy and take off the heat. Pour into a punch bowl or individual glasses.

Preparation: 10–12 mins

Bishop

This is a very refreshing iced drink, recommended both for hot summer days and for dancing parties. It is made from various kinds of white wine: from light table wine to choice French wine and champagne. All sorts of fresh fruit are added to it, depending on the season, such as wild strawberries, strawberries, apricots, peaches, pineapple and oranges, all cut into small cubes. To enhance its flavour and strength, a glass of brandy or Kirsch, or Maraschino or Abricotine or some other liqueur is added to it. An exception is bishop, made from champagne, to which no spirits are added, only fruit, such as pineapple, strawberries or peaches. Bishop is usually served in a crystal glass bowl or jug, ¾ filled with crushed ice. It is poured into glasses with a glass ladle.

(M. Ochorowicz-Monatowa, *Uniwersalna książka kucharska*)

Orange bishop

3 cups Rhine wine or champagne, 2 oranges, 1 lemon, 100 g sugar, 2 cloves, 2 cm piece of cinnamon bark

Scrub the oranges and lemon, scald them with boiling water, squeeze out the juice and grate the rind. Put into a punch bowl, add the cloves and cinnamon. Add the sugar to 200 ml of hot water and bring to the boil. Pour the hot syrup over the fruit and leave aside for 2 hours, then strain, combine with the wine and chill.

Preparation: 3–4 mins • Macerating: 2 hrs • Refrigerating: 2–3 hrs

Peach and apricot bishop

6 cups white wine or champagne, 2 cups mineral water, 2 peaches, 4 apricots, 2 oranges, juice of 1 lemon, 10 ice cubes (preferably pineapple flavoured)

Chill the mineral water and wine in the fridge. Rinse and dry the fruit. Scald the oranges with boiling water, peel them, cut into slices, remove the pips. Put the orange slices into a punch bowl, add half the sugar. Blanch and skin the peaches. Cut the peaches and apricots into fairly thick slices. Add them to the bowl and sprinkle with the remaining sugar. Cover the bowl and put into the fridge for 3 hours. Then take it out, pour in the lemon juice, wine and mineral water, add the ice cubes, mix well. Serve in tall glasses, putting some fruit at the bottom of each.

Preparation: 5–6 mins • Macerating: 3 hrs

Old Polish bishop

1 bottle dry red wine, 1 glass rum, 2–3 tbsps caster sugar, ½ cup strawberry juice, ½ cup mineral water, 200 g wild strawberries

Juice the strawberries. Mix the juice with the mineral water and make ice cubes from the preparation. Rinse and drain the wild strawberries, put them into a punch bowl, sprinkle with the sugar and rum and put into the fridge for 1 hour. Then take them out, put in the ice cubes, pour over the wine and serve immediately (in tall glasses).

Refrigerating: 3–4 hrs • Macerating: 1 hr

Polish bishop

100 g bilberries, 3 tbsps liquid honey, 2 tbsps lemon juice, 1 cup rum, 2 cups bilberry juice, 1 bottle champagne, ½ cup mineral water

Chill the champagne well. Combine the mineral water with ½ cup of bilberry juice and make ice cubes from the mixture. Rinse and drain the bilberries, put them into a punch bowl. Pour over the honey, sprinkle with the lemon juice and some rum. Cover the bowl and put into the fridge for 1 hour. Take it out, pour in the remaining bilberry juice and rum, mix carefully but thoroughly. Add the champagne and the ice cubes. Serve immediately.

Refrigerating: 3–4 hrs • Macerating: 1 hr • Preparation: 2–3 mins

Wholemeal bread drink

3 slices wholemeal bread, 2 cups water, ½ vanilla pod, ½ cup sugar, juice and grated rind of 1 lemon, 1 cup orange juice, 1 cup dry white wine, 1 tbsp liquid honey, ice cubes

Chill the wine. Cut the bread into cubes and brown them in a hot frying pan. Bring the water, with sugar, vanilla and lemon zest, to the boil, add the bread cubes. Take off the heat and leave aside for 2–3 hours, then put the preparation through a fine sieve and a piece of gauze. Combine the liquid with the lemon and orange juice, honey and wine. Serve in tall glasses with ice cubes.

Preparation: 2–3 hrs

Honey and wine drink

4 cups dry white wine, 1 cup liquid honey (preferably buckwheat or acacia), 3 cups water, 1 tbsp each lemon and orange juice, 4 egg yolks

Bring the water to the boil, combine it with the lemon and orange juice. Whisk the egg yolks with the honey, gradually adding hot water in the process. Combine the preparation with the wine and mix thoroughly. Serve immediately.

Preparation: 10–15 mins

Apricot cordial

100 g dried stoned apricots, ¼ cup boiled water, ½ tsp each powdered ginger and honey, ¼ tsp each ground cinnamon and allspice, ¼ csp each ground cloves and nutmeg, 1 cup ginger beer, 1 csp lemon juice

Rinse the apricots, put them in a pan together with the spices. Cover with hot water, bring to the boil, then simmer over low heat for 20 mins. Take off the heat, allow to cool, then put through a blender together with the honey and beer. Heat up, add lemon juice to taste.

Preparation: 40 mins

Ginger drink

*2 large pieces of candied ginger, juice
and grated rind of 1 lemon, ½ cup honey,
3–4 cups water, 1 glass white rum*

Bring the water with the honey, lemon zest and finely chopped ginger to the boil. Cover and simmer over low heat for 5 mins. Take off the heat, add the lemon juice and rum. Mix thoroughly, strain and leave to cool. Serve chilled.

Preparation: 10 mins • Refrigerating: 1–2 hrs

Nectar of quail eggs

*20 quail eggs, 1 tbsp sesame oil, 1 glass
vodka, 1 cup liquid honey*

Break the eggs into a food processor, add the oil and honey and blend until the mixture is foamy. Add the cold vodka, mix well and pour into chilled glasses. Serve immediately.

Preparation: 10 mins

Coffee and tea

Brandy tea (Glühwein)

*6 tsps black Ceylon tea leaves, 1 cup pomegranate
juice, 1 cup pure apple juice, 1 cup sugar, ½ tsp aniseed,
1 tsp ground cinnamon, 3–4 cloves, 100 g brandy,
30 g each almonds, hazelnuts and raisins, 1 l water*

Pour the apple and pomegranate juice into a pan, add the sugar, cinnamon, cloves and aniseed. Cover and simmer over low heat for 10–15 mins (but do not allow it to boil!). Make a very strong tea infusion, strain it. Pour the tea into the juice and simmer under cover for another 20 mins. Put the skinned and finely chopped almonds and blanched and drained raisins into a glass bowl, pour over the strained juice. Serve hot in tall glasses. This is an excellent invigorating drink.

It has to be admitted that here [in Poland] coffee has considerably contributed to the reduction of alcohol consumption. In the morning, it was drunk with cream, apart from Lent, when almond milk was added to it. After dinner, it was consumed black or with cream, depending on individual preferences, and any man who drank it after dinner did not feel like drinking for two hours and spent the time in the company of women... Coffee after dinner and when paying a visit was simply a must. The hostess's good name depended on the quality of her coffee.

(Łukasz Gołębiowski, *Domy i dwory*, vol. IV, pp. 126–127)

Preparation: 30–35 mins

Coffee Fantasia

*1 tbsp finely ground coffee, 1 cup boiling
water, 1 tbsp grated bitter chocolate, a pinch
of cinnamon, 2 tbsps whipped cream*

Pour the coffee into one warm glass and the chocolate and cinnamon into another. Add ½ cup of boiling water to each glass, stir well, then mix the two liquids and decorate with whipped cream.

Preparation: 10 mins

Coffee with honey and ginger

*6 tbsps finely ground coffee, ½ tsp powdered ginger,
8 tbsps honey, 2 cups boiled water, 1 cup whipped cream*

Put the ginger into a pan, pour in the water, bring to the boil, then simmer for 3 mins. Pour the liquid honey into a jug, add the coffee and pour the ginger water over. Mix thoroughly, then leave to cool. Serve with whipped cream.

Preparation: 20–25 mins

Coffee with spices

3 tbsps finely ground coffee, ¼ tsp each cinnamon and ground cloves, 3 tbsps caster sugar, 2 cups boiled water

Combine the coffee with the cloves, cinnamon and sugar in a pan. Pour the water over and heat up slowly, but do not let it boil. Take off the heat, stir well, cover with a lid for a while, then pour into warm cups.

Preparation: 15 mins

Cardamom coffee

3–4 tsps ground coffee, 2 tsps ground cardamom, 1½ cups water, 2 tbsps honey, 3 tbsps milk

Put the coffee and cardamom into a pan, pour the boiling water over. Cover and simmer over very low heat for 5–7 mins. Take off the heat, strain, then mix with the honey and milk.

Preparation: 10 mins

Aromatic coffee

COFFEE ICE CUBES: 3 tbsps finely ground coffee, 1½ cups boiling water, 1½ tbsp caster sugar

SPICY COFFEE: 4 tbsps ground Mocha type coffee, a piece of orange (3◊6 cm) rind, a piece of lemon (2◊2 cm) rind, 4–6 cloves, ¼ csp ground cardamom, 2 tbsps brown sugar

Combine the coffee with the sugar, pour the boiling water over and leave to brew, then strain the liquid through a fine sieve. Pour it into moulds and put into the freezer. Put the lemon and orange rind, coffee, cloves and cardamom into a pan, cover with boiling water and simmer over low heat for 2–3 mins, then filter the brew and mix it with the sugar. Put some coffee ice cubes into tall glasses, pour in the hot coffee, stir well. The difference in temperatures brings out the full flavour of coffee and spices.

Freezing: 3–4 hrs

Spicy coffee

2–3 tbsps coffee, 2 cloves, a piece of cinnamon, 1 tbsp finely chopped hazelnuts, 2 grains allspice, ½ cup boiling water, ¾ cup hot milk, 2–3 tbsps honey, 2 tbsps whipped cream

Put the coffee into a pan, pour boiling water over and simmer over low heat for 5 mins. Add the hot milk, stir well, then strain the liquid and return it to the pan. Add the cinnamon, cloves, allspice and honey, cover and simmer for another 15 mins (do not let it boil!). Strain the liquid again, pour into wide wine glasses, decorated with whipped cream and sprinkle on top with chopped hazelnuts.

NOTE: All spices used in this recipe, as well as honey and hazelnuts are regarded as aphrodisiacs.

Preparation: 20–25 mins • Preparation: 5–6 mins

Coffee with ice cream

2 cups strong coffee infusion, 1 glass rum, 4 tsps sugar, 250 ml coffee or vanilla flavoured ice cream, 1 cup whipping cream, ½ tsp caster sugar

Combine the freshly brewed coffee with the sugar and rum, stir well, leave to cool, then refrigerate for half an hour. Whip the chilled cream with the sugar to stiff peaks. Pour the chilled coffee into 4 tall glasses, cover with the whipped cream and put one scoop of ice cream on top.

Preparation: 30 mins

Coffee with egg yolk

2 cups freshly brewed coffee, 2 egg yolks, 2 tbsps sugar, 1 glass brandy

Whisk the egg yolks with sugar until foamy. Mix in the brandy. Stirring all the time, pour in the strained coffee brew. Serve immediately.

Preparation: 5–7 mins

Cossack coffee

½ cup dry red wine, ½ cup very strong coffee infusion, 25 g vodka, 2–3 tbsps sugar

Put all the ingredients into a pan and bring to the boil. Serve in warm teacups.

Preparation: 10 mins

Royal tea

3 tsps black tea leaves, ½ cup dry white wine, 4 cloves, a small piece of cinnamon, a pinch of saffron, ½ tsp grated lemon rind, several fine lemon slices, 3 cups water, 1 tbsp sugar

Prepare a strong tea infusion. Pour the wine into a pan, add the lemon zest, cloves, cinnamon and saffron. Cover and simmer for 10 mins, but do not let it boil. Combine the strained wine and tea infusion with the sugar, mix well, pour into an ovenproof jug and heat up. Serve immediately, with lemon slices.

Preparation: 15 mins

Kvass

This is an almost forgotten cold beverage which in the 19th century was served as a refreshment on hot summer days or at dancing parties. It was made in many households, just like fruit wines and meads. Producing kvass called for a lot of experience, but the result was worth the effort.

Home-made kvass

500 g rye bread, 40 g yeast, 1 cup sugar, 50 g raisins, 3–4 blackcurrant leaves, 5–10 fresh mint sprigs, 4 l spring water

Bring the water to the boil, pour it over the bread and leave aside for 4–5 hours, then strain the liquid two or three times through a gauze. Pour the liquid into a large bottle, add the yeast mixed with sugar, mint and blackcurrant leaves. Leave it for 12 hours in a warm place to ferment, then strain it again and pour into clean bottles. Put several raisins into each bottle. Seal the bottles and keep them in a cool place for at least three days.

Bread kvass

3 l spring water, 250 g wholemeal bread, 40 g yeast, grated rind of ½ lemon, ½ tsp chopped fresh ginger, 1 cup honey, 1 tbsp sugar, 1 tbsp raisins

Toast the bread cut into cubes in a hot frying pan. Bring the water to the boil, pour it over the bread, stir well and leave overnight in a warm place. Mix the yeast with the sugar and 2–3 tbsps of bread water and leave in a warm place. Strain the water, combine with the liquid honey, yeast, ginger and lemon zest. Stir thoroughly, cover with a piece of gauze and leave in a warm place for 24 hours. Rinse and blanch the raisins. Strain the kvass again, pour into bottles. Put several raisins into each bottle. Seal the bottles and store them in a cool place for a day or two.

Caraway kvass

3 l spring water, ½ cup caraway seeds, 1 cup sugar, 20 g yeast, 1 tbsp raisins

Put the caraway seeds into a pan, pour in the water and bring to the boil. Cover and simmer for 20 mins. Leave it to cool, then strain the liquid. Mix the yeast with 1 tbsp of sugar and 3–4 tbsps of the caraway water and leave it in a warm place for half an hour. Dissolve the remaining sugar in the caraway water, add the yeast. Cover the pan with a piece of gauze and leave to ferment in a warm place. When it starts to foam, pour the kvass into clean bottles. Put several raisins into each bottle. Seal the bottles tightly and leave in a cool place for a few days.

Peter's kvass

800 g dry wholemeal bread, 25 g yeast, 100 g honey, ½ cup sugar, 100 g freshly grated horseradish, 4 l spring water

Bring the water to the boil, put in the bread and leave for several hours, then strain the liquid several times through a piece of fine gauze. Pour into a large jar, add the yeast mixed with sugar, cover and leave to ferment in a warm place for 12 hours. Strain the liquid again, mix it with the honey and horseradish and pour into bottles. Seal the bottles and leave them in a cool place for at least three days.

Instant cranberry kvass

1 cup cranberries, 1½ cups honey,
1½ l spring water, 20 g yeast

Clean, rinse and drain the cranberries. Cover them with 2 cups of boiling water, stir well. When they start producing juice, rub them through a fine sieve. Add more boiled water and leave to cool. Put in the yeast and honey, stir thoroughly and leave in a cool place for 24 hours, then stir well again and pour into bottles. Chill before serving.

Cranberry kvass

1 kg cranberries, 400 g sugar, 10 g yeast, 5 cloves

Rinse the cranberries, mash and sieve them. Put the skins into a pan, add 4 l of hot water and cook for 5 mins. Leave to cool, then strain the liquid. Pour the liquid into a large jar, add the sieved cranberries, the yeast mixed with some sugar, and the remaining sugar. Stir thoroughly to allow the sugar to dissolve and leave aside for 12 hours. Strain the liquid through a piece of fine gauze. Pour it into bottles. Put one clove into each bottle. Seal the bottles and store them in a cool place for three days. Chill before serving. Use this recipe to prepare kvass from other kinds of fruit, for example gooseberries, strawberries or raspberries.

Honey kvass I

500 ml honey, 1 tbsp sugar, 10 g
yeast, 3 lemons, 30 g raisins

Scrub the lemons, scald them with boiling water, grate the rind and squeeze out the juice. Mix the yeast with 1 tbsp of sugar. Bring 4 l of water to the boil, dissolve the

honey, then leave to cool. Pour the honey water into a large jar, put in the yeast, lemon zest and juice. Stir well, cover and leave aside for 12 hours. Strain the liquid through a piece of fine gauze. Pour it into bottles. Put 2–3 raisins into each bottle. Seal the bottles and store them in a cool place for five days. Be careful opening the bottles, because the kvass is very bubbly. Chill well before serving.

Honey kvass II

2 l spring water, 400 g honey, 13 g yeast,
juice and grated rind of 2 lemons

Bring the water to the boil, dissolve the honey in it, then allow to cool. Add the yeast, lemon juice and zest, stir well and leave to ferment in a warm place for 12 hours. Strain the liquid through a piece of fine gauze. Pour it into bottles. Seal the bottles and store them in a cool place for 3–4 days. Chill well before serving.

Gdańsk ginger kvass

6 l spring water, 2–3 fresh or dried ginger, 1 kg
dry whoelmeal bread, 750 g sugar, 20 g yeast

Put the bread into a large earthenware jar, pour in 3 l of warm boiled water. Cover the jar with a piece of gauze and leave overnight. Chop the fresh ginger very finely, put it into an enamelled pan, pour in the remaining water. Cover and simmer over low heat for 1 or 1½ hours. Strain both liquids, pour them into a large pan, add the sugar and heat up, stirring all the time to dissolve the sugar. Leave it to cool to the temperature of 30°C, add the mixed yeast and pour into an earthenware jar. Cover with a piece of gauze and store in a warm place for 2–3 days. Strain the kvass and pour it into bottles. Seal the bottles and put them in a cool place.

Red beet kvass

1½ kg small beets, 1 cup sugar, 30 g
yeast, 150 g wholemeal bread, grated
rind and juice of 1 lemon, 3 l water

Peel the beets, chop them finely and put into a jar. Pour over the lukewarm boiled water, add the dried bread.

Cover the jar and leave it overnight in a warm place. Strain the liquid, add the yeast dissolved in some warm water, the sugar, lemon juice and zest. Leave it to ferment overnight in a warm place. Strain the liquid through a piece of fine gauze, pour into bottles. Seal the bottles and store them in a cool place for 3–4 days.

Shakes

Banana shake

2 bananas, 1 cup coconut milk, a pinch of cinnamon

Put the peeled bananas and coconut milk through a blender. Before serving, sprinkle with cinnamon. Home-made coconut milk: Cover 1½ tbsps of shredded coconut with 1 cup of hot milk, leave aside for half an hour, then strain the liquid).

Preparation: 3–5 mins

Peach shake

2 peaches, 1 cup yogurt, ¼ tsp cinnamon, 1 tbsp honey

Blanch and skin the peaches, remove the stones. Cut the peaches into smaller pieces and liquidize them together with the honey, yogurt and cinammon. Chill before serving.

Preparation: 3–5 mins • Refrigerating: 30–40 mins

Sweet cherry shake

100 g each stoned sweet cherries and wild strawberries, 1½ cups yogurt, 1 tbsp honey, 1 tbsp chopped walnuts

Put all the ingredients through a blender. Chill before serving.

Preparation: 3 mins • Refrigerating: 30–40 mins

Apple and apricot shake

½ cup apple juice, 5–6 dried (stoned) apricots, ½ cup yogurt, a pinch of nutmeg, 1 tsp honey

Wash the apricots, cover them with a small amount of water and cook until tender. Add the honey and put through a blender together with the apple juice. Mix with the yogurt and nutmeg.

Preparation: 20 mins

Orange smoothie

2 tbsps each finely chopped anise leaves, dill and parsley, ½ cup orange juice, 1 tbsp lemon juice, 4 tbsps single cream, 1 tsp honey, ½ tsp white pepper, a pinch of salt

Put all the ingredients through a blender. Chill before serving.

Preparation: 5 mins

Plum shake

400 g purple plums, 2 cups yogurt, 2 tbsps honey, a pinch of ground cloves

Rinse and stone the plums, then put them through a blender together with the honey, yogurt and cloves. Chill before serving.

Preparation: 5 mins

Vitamin smoothie

8–10 ripe tomatoes, 1 tart apple, 1 tbsp lemon juice, 2–3 celery sticks, 2 quail eggs, 1 tsp Worcestershire sauce, 1 tsp lemon juice, 3–4 drops Tabasco, salt, pepper, 1 cup cold still mineral water

Blanch and skin the tomatoes, remove the seeds; cut the apple, sprinkle with lemon juice; peel and dice the celery sticks. Put them all through a blender, adding the remaining ingredients. Chill before serving.

Preparation: 5–7 mins

Tomato smoothie

*2 large ripe tomatoes, 1 red pepper, 1 red onion,
1–2 cloves of garlic, 4–5 basil leaves, 1 tbsp lemon juice,
¼ tsp grated lemon rind, 1 tsp Worcestershire sauce,
3–4 drops Tabasco, salt, pepper, 5–6 crushed ice cubes*

Cut the pepper in half, remove the seeds, sear the halves over the flame, then skin them and chop the flesh; blanch and skin the tomatoes, cut them into cubes; peel the garlic and onion and dice them. Put them all through a blender together with the basil, Tabasco, Worcestershire sauce, lemon juice, zest, salt, pepper and ice cubes.

Preparation: 5–7 mins

Energizers

Fruit energizer

*1 cup grapefruit juice, 3–4 dried apricots, ½ cup
boiled water, 1 tbsp honey, a pinch of nutmeg*

Rinse the apricots, pour over some hot water, cover and cook for 20 mins, then take the lid off to reduce the liquid. Put the apricots through a blender together with the honey and grapefruit juice. Before serving, sprinkle some nutmeg on top.

Preparation: 25–30 mins

Grapefruit energizer

*1 cup fresh grapefruit juice, 1 tsp lime juice or
2 tsps lemon juice, 1 csp ground love-in-a-mist seeds,
1–2 ice cubes*

Put all the ingredients through a blender.

Preparation: 5–7 mins

Detox plum drink

*200 g plums, 200 g celery, ¼ tsp chopped
fresh ginger, 1 large peach, 1 cup still mineral
water, 2 tbsps honey, 5–6 ice cubes*

Put the stoned plums and peeled celery through a juicer. Blanch and skin the peach, take out the stone, cut the flesh into cubes and put it through a blender together with the juice, ginger, honey, water and ice.

Preparation: 10 mins

Orange drink

*2–3 oranges, 1 tsp honey, 5–6 stoned prunes,
1 tbsp yogurt, a pinch of cinnamon*

Blanch and drain the prunes, cover them with the yogurt and leave aside for a while. Scrub the oranges, dry them and grate the rind. Squeeze out the juice (ca ¾ cup). Blend the juice with the plums, yogurt, honey and orange zest. Sprinkle with cinnamon before serving.

Soaking: 20–30 mins • Preparation: 5 mins

CHAPTER XVII

CAKES AND PASTRIES

Fruit tarts or flans

The Poles' favourite pastry with fruit is undoubtedly charlotte or apple tart. The first to bake fruit tarts were most probably the ancient Greeks. Later on, their conquerors, the Romans, adopted many local culinary habits, and developed a liking for fruit cakes. Gradually, as the Roman legions over-ran new territories, the custom of baking fruit cakes spread throughout the empire. Everything in these cakes had a meaning. The round shape signified the spiritual side of man's nature, while the rectangular shape was meant to bring prosperity. The same was true of the choice of fruit, and thus:
– cherries and strawberries stood for love;
– peaches stood for health, happiness, prudence and love;
– berries protected against evil forces;
– apples were to guarantee health, peace and love;
– blackberries promised wealth and additionally acted as an aphrodisiac;
– raspberries brought happiness, love and protection; and
– nuts assured wealth.
The belief in the magic properties of fruit has not died out, therefore perhaps we, too, should remember the ancient customs.

Peach tart

1 cup flour, ½ tsp baking powder, ½ cup caster sugar, 100 g butter, 2 tbsps dry white wine, ½ tsp grated lemon rind, a pinch of salt, 1 kg peaches, 2 egg yolks, 1 cup thick cream, 2–3 tbsps almond flakes

Sift the flour, mix it with the baking powder and sifted sugar, add the lemon zest. Cut in the butter with a knife. Add some salt and the wine and knead the dough thoroughly. Wrap it in clingfilm and put in the fridge. Put the peaches into boiling water for 1–2 mins, rinse them under cold water, then peel and halve, remove the stones. Roll the dough out and line a round baking tin with it, prick it with a fork all over. Arrange the peach halves (the round side up) on top of the dough and bake in a preheated oven (200°C) for 15 mins. Whisk the cream with the egg yolks, pour the mixture over the peaches, sprinkle with the almond flakes on top and return to the oven for another 20 mins.

Baking: 35 mins

Strawberry tart

250–300 g wheat flour, 125 g butter, 1 tbsp lemon juice, ½ tsp grated lemon rind, 100 g caster sugar, 1 egg yolk, a pinch of salt, 500 g fresh, ripe strawberries, 1 glass rum, 1 cup whipping cream, 2 tbsps caster sugar, 2–3 tbsps dry white wine, 1 tbsp gelatine

Sift the flour onto a pastry board, put in the butter and cut it in with a knife until the mixture is sandy in consistency. Add the sifted sugar, egg yolk, lemon juice, zest and salt. Knead briskly, then shape the dough into a ball. Wrap it in clingfilm and put in the fridge for 2–3 hours. Clean, rinse and dry the strawberries, cut them lengthwise in half, put into a bowl and sprinkle with the rum. Cover the bowl and put it in the fridge for an hour. Roll out the dough, line a round baking tin with it, prick it with a fork. Bake in a preheated oven for 20–25 mins. Bring the wine to the

Strawberry tart

boil, put in the gelatine and stir thoroughly. Whip the cream with the sugar, fold into the gelatine and leave to cool in the fridge. Mix the cream with the strawberries and spread the preparation on top of the cool pastry.

Baking: 20–25 mins

Mountain cranberry tart

*less than 2 cups f flour, 150 g butter, ½ cup sugar,
1 tsp baking powder, 1 egg, 1 cup sugar,
300 g fresh mountain cranberries, butter
and breadcrumbs for the baking tin,
1 cup whipping cream, 2–3 tbsps caster sugar*

Whisk the butter with the egg yolk until foamy, gradually add the sugar and then the flour mixed with the baking powder. Knead the dough, fold in the whisked egg white. Grease a rectangular baking tin with butter and dust it with breadcrumbs. Put in the dough, even out the surface. Put the cranberries on top, sprinkle them with sugar. Bake in a preheated oven (175°C) for 45 mins. Leave to cool. Before serving, decorate with whipped cream with sugar.

Baking: 45 mins

Easy apple tart

*2–2½ cups flour, 250 g butter, 2 egg yolks,
1 tbsp thick sour cream, ½ tsp grated lemon
rind, 2 tbsps caster sugar, 3 tbsps finely chopped
walnuts, 750 g apples, 2 tbsps sugar, 1 tbsp lemon
juice, 3 tbsps raisins, 1 tbsp rum, 1 tsp cinnamon,
¼ tsp ground cloves, caster sugar for dusting*

Sift the flour onto a pastry board, add the butter, cream, caster sugar and lemon zest. Mix the ingredients with a knife until the mixture is sandy in consistency. Add the egg yolks and walnuts and knead quickly. Shape the dough into a ball, wrap it in clingfilm and put in the fridge for 1–2 hours. Peel, core and dice the apples. Rinse the raisins and sprinkle them with rum. Soften the apples in a pan, add the lemon juice and sugar, and stirring all the time, cook for several minutes. Take off the heat, add the cinnamon, cloves and raisins. Divide the dough into two parts. Roll out one half on a pastry board dusted with flour and line a baking tin with it. Prick the dough with a

fork all over. Bake in a preheated oven for 10 mins, then take it out. Spread the apples on top of the pastry, cover with the remaining rolled out dough, prick it with a fork. Return to the hot oven for another 20 mins, until the crust has turned golden brown. Dust the cool tart with sifted caster sugar.

Baking: 10+20 mins

Babas

Babas were baked in Poland as early as the 17th century. They were made from wheat flour mixed with saffron, which gave them not only a nice colour but also a slightly spicy flavour. Easter babas contained raisins and candied fruit, and were iced and decorated with hundreds and thousands. Originally, such cakes went by a variety of names, such as kouglof, ko≥acz, or baumkuchen, and their present name is attributed to King Stanislas Leszczyński, who was well known as a gourmand.

Warsaw babas

*2 kg flour, 4 cups milk, 60 egg yolks, 15 egg whites, 100 g yeast,
3 cups clarified butter, 600 g sugar, 200 g sweet almonds, 50 g
bitter almonds, 200 g raisins*
*Cover 800 g of the choicest flour with boiling milk and whisk
well. When the preparation has cooled down, add the whisked
egg yolks and the yeast, dissolved in lukewarm milk with a
pinch of sugar. When you have kneaded the dough well
enough, cover it and leave in a warm place to rise. When
the dough is well risen, knead it for two hours, gradually adding the remaining flour. After the first hour of kneading, add
the clarified butter, and half an hour later put in the sugar.
Towards the end, add the almonds and raisins. Put the dough
into moulds greased with lard, filling them to ¼ of their height.
When the dough has risen to the top, put the moulds into a
hot oven.*

(M. Marciszewska, *Kuchnia doskonała*)

Ukrainian babas

1½ l egg yolks, 1½ cup egg whites, 4–4½ kg flour, 1 l milk, 200 g yeast in 2 cups of milk, 2 tsps salt, 2¼ cups butter, 3–5 cups sugar, 40 g bitter almonds. Put the egg yolks into a butter churn and beat them for one hour. Scald 2¼ litres of flour with boiling milk, mix thoroughly, cover with a piece of muslin and leave aside for half an hour. Pour the yeast into the eggs. Mix the scalded flour, work it well into a smooth mixture. Pour the yeast and egg mixture into it through a sieve, knead vigorously, sprinkle some flour on top, cover and leave aside to rise. When the dough has risen, gradually add 2 tsps of salt and about 2 litres of flour (depending on how dry the flour is) and work the dough for half an hour. Pour in the clarified butter and knead again. Add 3½ cups of fine sugar, some bitter almonds and lemon zest. Knead until air bubbles appear in the dough, then cover it and leave to rise. Prepare paper moulds, place them in baking pans and fill them ⅓ with the dough. Put them close to the oven and when the dough has doubled in volume, put into a hot oven. Turn the ready babas out onto a pillow and leave them to cool down.

Lacy baba

5 cups egg yolks, 1½ cups flour, less then 1 cup clarified butter, 1 copious cup sugar, 1 cup milk, 100 g good yeast
Beat the egg yolks in a butter churn or whisk them in an earthenware bowl until they turn white. Put them through a sieve, add the sugar and yeast mixed with milk, and continue whisking them energetically. Pour in the butter, add the flour and beat continuously for an hour until air bubbles form in the dough, then put the dough aside to rise. Put a paper mould into a baking pan, grease it with clarified butter, dust with breadcrumbs. Fill the mould to ⅓ of its height. When the dough has risen, put the pan into a hot oven. This operation must be performed very gently and smoothly, for any rapid movement can cause the baba to go gummy inside and make it more like common bread. Be just as careful taking the baba out of the oven. Turn the baba out from the mould in a warm place, away from draughts.

Egg cakes, or kołacze

Mix 3 l of dry flour with ¾ l of lukewarm milk and 10 g of yeast, and leave the mixture in a warm place. When it has risen, break in 10 whole eggs and add 10 egg yolks whisked with 500 g of sugar. Add some salt and the remaining flour, ½ l of clarified butter and orange zest. Knead briskly until the dough no longer sticks to your hands. Towards the end, put in 250 g of cleaned sultanas and mix them with the dough. Leave the dough to rise in a warm place, then transfer it onto a pastry board dusted with flour. Shape the dough into round rolls or put it into small moulds greased with butter and dusted with flour. When they have risen again, brush them with a lightly beaten egg and put into a hot oven for ¾–1 hour.

(Marya Ochorowicz-Monatowa, *Uniwersalna książka kucharska*)

Saffron baba

2 cups egg yolks, 1 cup sugar, 1 cup milk, 50 g yeast, 1½ cups flour, 1 cup melted butter, 1 tsp salt, 1 glass spirit, a pinch of saffron, ½ vanilla pod, grated rind of 1 lemon

Soak the saffron in the spirit overnight. Put the egg yolks into a stoneware bowl, rest the bowl on top of a pan of simmering water. Add the sugar and whisk the egg yolks until they turn white. Mix ½ cup of flour with 1 tsp of sugar and crumbled yeast. Combine the flour, vanilla, salt and lemon zest with the egg yolks. Pour in the yeast mixture and knead for 60 mins, adding the saffron and spirit in the process. Cover with a cloth and leave to rise in a warm place. Add the clarified butter and work it in until the dough is shiny and elastic. Fill a greased mould to ⅓ of its height with the dough and leave in a warm place to rise, then bake in a preheated oven for an hour.

Note: Take special care when you put the baba into the oven and take it out, or it will collapse.

Baking: 60 mins

Raisin baba

500 g flour, 10 egg yolks, 100 g sugar, 100 g butter, 1 cup milk, 30 g bitter almonds, ½ vanilla pod, 120 g sultanas, 120 g seedless raisins, ½ tsp salt, 60 g yeast

Baking: 60 mins

Make a yeast dough from the above ingredients, then add the clarified butter and work it in until the dough is shiny and elastic. Put in the blanched (warm) raisins and

Common baba

knead for another 30 mins. Cover with a cloth and leave to rise. Fill greased moulds to ⅓ of their height with the dough and leave in a warm place to rise again, then bake in a preheated oven for an hour.

Common baba

500 g flour, 40 g yeast, 80 g butter, 80 g sugar, 4 egg yolks, 10 g bitter almonds, 1 cup milk, 1 tsp salt, grated rind of 1 lemon

Mix the yeast with 1 tsp of sugar and lukewarm milk, add ½ cup of flour and leave in a warm place until the mixture has foamed. Put the egg yolks into a stoneware bowl, rest the bowl on top of a pan of simmering water. Add the sugar and lemon zest and whisk thoroughly. When the egg yolks have turned white, add the skinned and chopped almonds and salt. Pour in the yeast mixture, add the remaining flour and knead for 60 mins. Add the warm clarified butter and work it in until the dough is shiny and elastic. Fill a greased mould to ½ of its height with the dough, cover with a cloth and leave to rise in a warm place. Bake in a preheated oven for 60 mins. If the top browns too quickly, cover the baba with greaseproof paper.

Baking: 60 mins

Whisked baba

250 g butter, 8 eggs, 8 egg yolks, 250 g sugar, grated rind of 1 lemon, 2 cups milk, 100 g yeast, 1¼ kg flour, 1 tsp salt

Mix the yeast with 1 cup of warm milk, 1 tsp of sugar and ½ cup of flour. Rest a bowl on top of a pan of simmering water and whisk the egg yolks with half the sugar. Cream the butter in a stoneware bowl until foamy, add the remaining sugar, then continue whisking while you add one egg yolk and one egg at a time. When you have used all the eggs, add salt and lemon zest, pour in the yeast and the remaining milk. Whisking all the time, gradually work in the flour. Keep whisking until the dough is shiny and elastic. Cover with a cloth and leave to rise. Fill a greased mould to ⅓ of its height with the dough and stand in a warm place to rise, then bake in a preheated oven for an hour.

Baking: 60 mins

White baba

1 kg flour, 2 cups milk, 60 g yeast, 160 g sugar, 200 g butter, 30 g bitter almonds, 8 egg whites, 1 tbsp salt

Sift half the flour into a bowl and warm it up a bit. Crumble the yeast into a cup of warm milk. Combine the mixture with the warm flour and stand aside in a warm place. When the dough has risen, work in the remaining flour, fold in the whisked egg whites, add some salt and the finely chopped almonds. Knead the dough thoroughly, adding more milk if required. Pour in the clarified butter and work it in until the dough is shiny and elastic. Cover with a cloth and leave to rise in a warm place. When the dough doubles in volume, fill a greased mould to ½ of its height with it and leave to rise again, then bake in a preheated oven for an hour.

Baking: 60 mins

Almond baba

250 g flour, 40 g yeast, 1 cup milk, 100 g butter, 100 g sugar, 100 g skinned almonds, ½ vanilla pod, 3 eggs

Mix the crumbled yeast with the warm milk and some flour, and leave in a warm place. Put the egg yolks and sugar in a bowl, rest it on top of a pan of simmering water and whisk until the mixture turns white. Combine the whisked egg yolks with the yeast, add the finely chopped almonds and vanilla and knead thoroughly, then work in the warm clarified butter for another 30 mins. Towards the end, fold in the whisked egg whites. Put the dough into greased moulds and leave to rise in a warm place, then bake in a preheated oven for an hour.

Baking: 60 mins

Cocoa baba

1 cup milk, 2 tbsps cocoa, 2 eggs, 250 g sugar, 250 g flour, 10 g breadcrumbs, baking powder

Mix the cocoa with 1 tbsp of milk, pour in the remaining milk, bring to the boil, then leave to cool. Break the eggs into a bowl, rest it on top of a pan of simmering water and whisk them with the sugar, then add the cool cocoa.

Put in the flour, sifted breadcrumbs and baking powder and knead thoroughly. Put the dough into greased moulds and bake in a preheated oven for 30 mins.

Baking: 60 mins

Spicy baba

10 eggs, 250 g sugar, 250 g flour, 1 tsp saffron, 1 glass spirit, ½ tsp each cinnamon, crushed cloves and nutmeg

Soak the saffron overnight in the spirit. Put the egg yolks into a bowl, rest it on top of a pan of simmering water, and whisk the yolks with the sugar, adding the powdered spices. Whisking all the time, gradually work in the flour. Add the saffron and, towards the end, fold in the whisked egg whites. Put the mixture into a grease mould and bake in a preheated oven for an hour. Brush the cool baba with some icing.

Baking: 60 mins

Bread baba

8 eggs, 250 g sugar, ½ dried wholemeal loaf (which should give 1 cup of fine breadcrumbs), 1 glass dry wine, grated rind of 1 lemon or orange, ½ tsp each cinnamon, crushed cloves and nutmeg

Sprinkle the breadcrumbs with the wine, mix thoroughly and leave in a warm place for an hour. Rest a bowl on top of a pan of simmering water and whisk the egg yolks and sugar in it. Add the spices and zest, mix well. Fold in the stiffly beaten egg whites and the breadcrumbs. Mix carefully but thoroughly. Put into a greased mould and bake at medium temperature for an hour.

Baking: 60 mins

Buckwheat baba

2 cups buckwheat flour (or ground and sifted buckwheat kasha), 2 cups cream, 60 g sugar, 6 eggs, grated rind of 1 lemon

Put the egg yolks, sugar and zest in a bowl, rest on top of a pot of simmering water and whisk thoroughly. Add the cream and gradually work in the sifted flour. Towards

baba

the end, fold in the stiffly whisked egg whites. Transfer the dough to a greased mould and bake in a preheated oven for an hour.

Baking: 60 mins

Sweet buns

1½ cups milk, 50 g yeast, 2½ kg flour, 15 eggs, 250 g sugar, lemon zest, 250 g butter, 1 tsp salt

Mix the yeast with ½ cup of warm milk. Put ½ kg of flour into a bowl, pour over the boiling milk, stir thoroughly, then leave to cool. Pour in the yeast mixture, stir, cover with a cloth and leave overnight in a warm place. Rest a bowl on top of a pan of simmering water and whisk the eggs and sugar in it. Combine the mixture with the dough, add salt and lemon zest. Knead the dough, gradually working in the remaining flour, for an hour. Pour in the warm clarified butter and work it in until the dough is shiny and elastic. Cover with a cloth and leave in a warm place for two hours. Form small buns from the dough and place them on a greased baking sheet, then leave them in a warm place to rise. Brush the buns with a lightly beaten egg and bake in a preheated oven for an hour. Towards the end, brush the buns with melted butter.

Baking: 60 mins

Mazureks

*Easter mazureks
come in all shapes,
but have one thing in common:
they're sweet, sweet, ever sweet...*

Mazureks came to Poland from Turkey and made an astonishing career here. These are thin, flat shortbread pies, resembling the Austrian linzertorte, topped with candied fruit spreads. For centuries, mazureks have been the pride of the Easter feast.

Many different recipes for mazureks have been invented, but the main principle has always remained the same: a lot of topping over a thin waffle or shortbread crust.

The flavour of the shortbread is enhanced by the addition of ground almonds, walnuts or hazelnuts, and of spices, such as cinnamon, cloves, ginger, nutmeg or vanilla, not to mention lemon and orange zest. Then it is enough to brush the pie with some icing, spread it with cooked apples, and decorate it on top with candied fruit, orange peel and angelica, or sprinkle it with colourful hundreds and thousands.

For more ambitious cooks, I would recommend going back to the old Polish tradition and decorating your mazureks with colourful views and figures, and thus produce cakes that *recall Roman stone mosaics... with the most fantastic patterns, most fetching and tasteful.*

(Zygmunt Gloger)

Coconut mazurek

DOUGH: 1 cup flour, 100 g caster sugar, 100 g butter, 3 tbsps finely chopped hazelnuts, ½ vanilla pod, ¼ tsp grated lemon rind, 2 egg yolks, a pinch of salt

TOPPING: 150 g coconut flakes, ¾ cup sugar, 1 cup single cream, 1 tsp lemon juice, 1–2 tbsps potato flour

DOUGH: Sift the flour and caster sugar onto a pastry board, add the butter and cut it in with a knife until the mixture has a sandy consistency. Add the egg yolks, chopped vanilla, zest and nuts and knead thoroughly. Wrap the dough in clingfilm and put in the fridge for several hours. Line a baking tin with the rolled out dough, prick it with a fork all over and bake in a preheated oven (180–190°C). TOPPING: Mix the coconut with the sugar, add the warm cream, mix thoroughly and leave aside for 30–45 mins. Whisk the egg whites with the lemon juice into stiff peaks, sift in the potato flour, add the coconut and mix gently using a spatula. Spread the mixture on the lightly browned crust and put into the oven for another 15–20 mins.

Baking: 15–20 mins

Poppyseed mazurek

1 cup poppy seeds, 125 g butter, 125 g caster sugar, 125–150 g flour, 2 tbsps thick cream, 2 eggs, ¼ tsp each cinnamon, nutmeg and ground cloves, 2 tbsps chopped walnuts, 1 tbsp sugar

Rinse the poppy seeds, blanch them in boiling water, drain thoroughly and leave to cool. Sift the flour onto a pastry board. Add the butter and cut it in with a knife until the mixture has a sandy consistency. Add 2 egg yolks and 1 egg white, the poppy seeds, cream, sifted caster sugar and spices. Knead thoroughly, then wrap the dough in clingfilm and put it in the fridge for several hours. Roll out the dough. Cut out rhomboids or circles out of it. Arrange them on a greased baking sheet, brush each with lightly beaten egg white, sprinkle with sugar and chopped nuts. Bake in a preheated oven for 30–35 mins.

Baking: 30–35 mins

Sultan's mazurek

6 eggs, 300 g flour, 300 g sugar (flour and sugar should weigh as much as the eggs used), 200 g each sultanas, almonds, figs, candied orange peel and, if required, small dark currants

Rest a bowl on top of a pan of simmering water. Whisk the egg yolks and sugar in it. When the mixture begins to thicken, take off the heat and, whisking all the time, gradually add the flour. Chop finely the skinned almonds, figs and orange peel, blanch the raisins, and add them all to the dough. Fold in the egg whites whisked into stiff peaks. Grease a baking tin with butter and dust it with flour, line it with the dough. Bake slowly in a preheated oven for 20–30 mins.

Baking: 20–30 mins

Royal mazurek

370 g butter, 370 g flour, 120 g sugar, 120 g almonds, 4 hard-boiled egg yolks, 1 raw egg yolk, a pinch of salt, grated rind of 1 lemon; fruit preserves for decoration

Cream the butter and sugar in a stoneware bowl, add the sieved egg yolks (cooked and raw). Whisking continuously, add the zest and finely chopped almonds. When the mixture is smooth, add some salt and the flour. Knead the dough thoroughly, then leave it in the fridge for an hour. On a pastry board dusted with flour, roll out ⅔ of the dough into a square and line a greased baking tin with it. From the remaining dough, make a pencil-thick roll and arrange it in a lattice pattern on top of the pastry. Brush with lightly beaten egg and bake in a preheated oven for 30 mins medium temperature. Take out of the oven and put some preserves, for example cherries, into each square.

Baking: 30 mins

Raspberry mazurek

500 g flour, 70 g butter, 250 g almonds, 120 g sugar, 4 hard-boiled egg yolks, 1 raw egg yolk; icing from 500 g of sugar; 500 g raspberry jam

Sift the flour onto a pastry board, add the butter and cut it in with a knife until the mixture is sandy in consistency. Put in the skinned and finely chopped almonds, the egg, the sieved hard-boiled egg yolks and sugar, and briskly knead them together. Put the dough in the fridge for an hour, then roll it out into three or four squares of equal size. Place the squares on greased baking sheets and bake slowly for 30 mins. Spread the jam on the squares, put one on top another. Brush the mazurek with pink icing and decorate with preserves.

Baking: 30 mins

Mazurek from melted butter

*120 g sugar, 120 g flour, 120 g butter, 2 eggs, 60 g almonds, 1 tsp cinnamon, chopped nuts and almonds for sprinkling, * 1 egg*

Blend the eggs and sugar until they turn white. Whisking all the time, gradually add first the melted butter, then the cinnamon and chopped almonds, and finally the flour. Leave the dough for an hour in a cool place, then spread it evenly on a greased baking sheet. Brush it on top with lightly beaten egg and sprinkle with chopped nuts and almonds. Bake for 30 mins in a medium hot oven.

Baking: 30 mins

Chocolate mazurek on shortcrust pastry

DOUGH: 250 g flour, 180 g butter, 100 g sugar, 2 egg yolks, a pinch of salt

FILLING: 4 eggs, 250 g sugar, 250 g chocolate, 120 g flour, 120 g ground almonds, 120 g raisins

Sift the flour onto a pastry board, add the butter and cut it in with a knife. Add the egg yolks, sugar and salt and quickly knead the dough, then leave it for an hour in the fridge. Spread the dough evenly in a greased baking sheet and bake it golden brown. Beat the eggs and sugar until white, add the melted chocolate and, whisking all the time, gradually pour in the flour. Put in the raisins and chopped almonds. Spread the filling on top of the pastry crust and return to the hot oven for 20 mins.

Baking: 20 mins

Layered marzipan mazurek

SHORTCRUST PASTRY: 125 g flour, 90 g butter, 2 egg yolks, grated rind of 1 lemon

MARZIPAN PASTE: 250 g almonds, 250 g caster sugar, 3 egg whites, juice of ½ lemon, 250 g apricot jam

ICING: 250 g caster sugar, juice of 1 lemon;

gooseberry preserve for decorating

BAKING: 2–3 mins

Knead the shortcrust dough, roll it out finely. Place on a greased baking sheet and bake until golden brown. When the crust has cooled down, spread the apricot jam on top. Prepare the marzipan paste, roll it out and spread on top of the jam. Trim the edges, use egg white to stick marzipan trimmings over the sides. Leave overnight to allow it to dry a bit, then put in a preheated oven for 2–3 mins. Take it out, spread a thin layer of jam on top and then some icing, and decorate with fruit preserves.

Baking: 5–7 mins

Orange mazurek

60 g flour, 60 g almonds, 60 g sugar, 60 g candied orange peel, 3 hard-boiled egg yolks, 1 raw egg yolk, 3 egg whites, ¼ vanilla pod; wafers

ICING: 120 g caster sugar, grated rind and juice of 1 orange

Sieve the hard-boiled egg yolks into a bowl, add the raw egg yolk, sugar and vanilla and blend into a smooth paste. Put in the finely chopped almonds and orange peel, fold in the egg whites whisked to stiff peaks and mix gently. Place a wafer on a greased baking sheet, spread some filling on top, cover with another wafer, and repeat the procedure until all mixture has been used. Put for 5–7 mins in a preheated oven to allow the filling to set. Prepare icing by blending the orange rind with 1 tbsp of caster sugar. Add the orange juice and the remaining caster sugar and work into a thick mixture. Spread the icing over the mazurek. Put the mazurek into a preheated oven for a short while.

Baking: 5–7 mins

Rose hip mazurek

3 eggs, 1 cup sugar, 2 tbsps rosehip preserve, 120 g almonds, 60 g breadcrumbs

Whisk the eggs with the sugar and rose hip, add the ground almonds and sifted breadcrumbs and mix thoroughly. Cover a baking sheet with a sheet of greased paper, spread the mixture on top and bake in a preheated oven for several minutes. Take out of the oven, remove the paper by moistening it lightly. Brush the mazurek with pink icing, make a lattice pattern on top with white icing. Decorate with gooseberry or redcurrant preserve.

Baking: 5–7 mins

Cream mazurek

250 g flour, ½ cup thick cream, 2 egg yolks, 120 g caster sugar, ¼ tsp salt

* 1 egg white, sugar, raisins, nuts, almonds

Sift the flour onto a pastry board, add the butter and cut it in with a knife until the mixture has a sandy consistency. Add salt, the egg yolks and cream, and quickly knead the dough, then leave it overnight in the fridge. Roll out it thinly, cut into squares. Place the squares on a greased baking sheet dusted with flour. Brush them with egg white, sprinkle generously with raisins, sugar and chopped nuts. Bake in a preheated oven for 30 mins. Cut the mazurek when it is still hot, otherwise it will crumble.

Baking: 30 mins

Podolian mazurek

*6 hard-boiled egg yolks, ½ cup clarified butter, 1 cup thick cream, 1 egg, 30 g yeast, a pinch of salt, grated rind of 1 orange, 500 g flour, 50 g sugar, 2 tbsps milk * 1 egg white, chopped almonds and nuts*

Mix the yeast with the warm milk. Sieve the egg yolks into a bowl, blend them with the butter, sugar and the raw egg, adding one teaspoon of cream at a time. Combine with the yeast and gradually add the flour. The consistency should be that of bread dough, therefore add more flour if it is too runny. Put in the orange zest and some salt. Knead the dough for over 30 mins, then leave it in a warm place to rise. Grease a baking sheet, spread a thin layer of the dough on it, brush it with melted butter and again leave it to rise. Brush the dough with lightly beaten egg white, sprinkle the chopped almonds and nuts on top. Bake in a preheated oven for 30 mins.

Baking: over 30 mins

Warsaw mazurek

*200 g butter, 200 g almonds, 200 g sugar, 200 g flour, 6 eggs, ¼ vanilla pod, ¼ tsp each ground cloves, cinnamon and nutmeg, grated rind of 1 lemon or orange * icing * fruit preserves for decorating*

Cream the butter until frothy, mix in the ground almonds and sugar. Whisking all the time, add one egg and some flour at a time. When the mixture is smooth, add the spices and orange zest. Knead thoroughly. Roll out the dough on a pastry board dusted with flour and give it the shape of your choice. Use the rolled trimmings and egg white to make a higher border. Place on a greased baking sheet and bake in a preheated oven at me- dium temperature for 30 mins. Leave the mazurek to cool, then decorate with icing, fruit preserves or hundreds and thousands.

Baking: 30 mins

Macaroon mazureks

5 egg yolks, 6 egg whites, 200 g sugar, 200 g skinned almonds, 5–10 bitter almonds

Beat the egg yolks and sugar until white, add the ground or finely chopped almonds and work into a smooth paste. Fold in the egg whites whisked to stiff peaks, mix carefully. Grease small baking sheets with butter, dust them with some sugar and pour in the mixture. Put into a warm oven to dry them. Take them out and allow to cool, then coat with icing.

Drying: 5–7 mins

Wholemeal bread mazureks

200 g skinned almonds, 15 egg yolks, 200 g sugar, 7 egg whites, 200 g finely sifted breadcrumbs from dried wholemeal bread, ½ tsp cinnamon, grated rind of 1 orange

Grind the almonds or chop them very finely. Put them into a bowl and, whisking all the time, add one egg yolk at a time and some sugar, cinnamon and orange zest. When the mixture is smooth, fold in the egg whites whisked to stiff peaks. Put in the breadcrumbs and mix gently but thoroughly. Pour the mixture into small greased baking tins dusted with sugar. Bake at low temperature in a preheated oven for 20 mins.

Baking: 20 mins

Spicy raisin mazurek

*100 g sultanas, 100 g small dark currants,
100 g almonds, 200 g sugar, 25 g potato flour,
3 eggs, ¼ tsp each grated lemon rind, ground
cloves, cinnamon and nutmeg * wafers*

Whisk the eggs with the spices and lemon zest. Blanch, skin and grind the almonds, blend them in a stoneware bowl with the sugar and raisins. Gradually add the potato flour and fold in the egg mixture. Place wafers on greased baking sheets, spread them with a thick layer of the raisin mixture. Bake in a preheated oven at medium-high temperature for 15–20 mins.

Baking: 15–20 mins

Gypsy mazureks

*3 cups raisins, 1 cup almonds, 2 eggs,
1 egg yolk, 1 cup sugar, ½ cup flour,
1 tbsps chopped candied orange peel*

* wafers

Whisk the egg yolks and sugar in a stoneware bowl, put in the flour and, whisking all the time, gradually add the chopped almonds, orange peel and raisins. Fold in the egg whites whisked into stiff peaks and mix gently. Place wafers on a well greased baking sheet, spread them with a thick layer of the mixture. Bake at low temperature in a preheated oven until golden brown.

Mazureks with fruit jelly

*300 g sugar, grated rind and juice of 1½ lemons
and 3 oranges, 200 g tart apples, ½ cup almonds,
50 g pistachios or hazelnuts, 2 tbsps candied orange peel*

* wafers

Pour the juice into a pan, add the sugar and, stirring all the time, make a thick syrup. Peel and core the apples, dice them finely, put into the syrup and cook over low heat, taking care that they do not disintegrate. Put in the finely chopped almonds, nuts and orange peel. Place wafers on a greased baking sheet, spread them with a thick layer of the apple mixture. Put into a preheated oven to dry.

Baking: 5–7 mins • Drying: 10 mins

Nougat

*100 g almonds, 100 g walnuts, 200 g sugar, 1 cup
honey, 7 egg whites, ½ vanilla pod * wafers*

Blanch and skin the almonds and nuts, chop them finely and dry in the oven. Make a thick caramel syrup from sugar and water. Bring the honey to the boil in a separate pan and immediately combine it with the syrup. Whisk the egg whites into stiff peaks in a bowl. Rest the bowl on top of a pan of simmering water and gradually pour in the caramel and honey preparation. Mix thoroughly so that the egg whites do not stick to the walls. When the mixture thickens and is reduced in volume by half, put in the nuts, almonds and the chopped vanilla, and mix well. Spread the warm mixture on one wafer, cover it with another wafer and so on, until you have 3–4 layers. Cut with a very sharp knife dipped in cold water.

Preparation: 20–30 mins

Easter paskha and cheesecakes

*Because paskha means Pesach,
which is Easter in Polish...*

Next to babas and mazureks, paskha is a traditional Easter treat. It makes for a delicious, but alas high-calorie, dessert. It is made of whole-milk curd cheese, butter, sugar and egg yolks, and it is rich in candied fruit, raisins and chocolate.

When ready, the paskha should be wrapped in a damp piece of linen, weighed down with a wooden board and placed at the bottom of the fridge to 'ripen'. You serve it straight from the fridge.

Polish paskha

*1 kg whole-milk curd cheese, 120 g butter,
8 egg yolks, 350 g caster sugar, 1 tbsp brandy,
50 g each raisins, shelled walnuts, hazelnuts
and almonds, 30 g each dried figs and dates,
2 tbsps finely chopped candied orange peel;
cherry preserve or candied fruit for decorating*

Put the cheese twice through a mincer. Blanch and drain the raisins, put them in a bowl and sprinkle with brandy. Chop the nuts and almonds, dice the dates and figs. Cream the butter until frothy. Whisking all the time, add 1 egg yolk and 1 tbsp of sugar at a time. When the mixture is smooth, gradually put in the cheese, nuts, almonds, figs and dates. Towards the end, mix in the raisins. Wrap the paskha in a cloth and leave overnight in the fridge. Before serving, transfer it to a serving bowl, decorate with candied fruit or kiwi slices and tangerine quarters.

Preparation: 30–40 mins • Refrigerating: 12 hrs

Raspberry paskha

*500 g whole-milk curd cheese, 250 g raspberry
preserve, 150 g butter, 200 g caster sugar,
4 egg yolks, 1 whole egg, 1 cup thick cream*

Put the cheese twice through a mincer. Add the raspberry preserve, mix thoroughly, then sieve the mixture. Cream the butter. Whisking all the time, add 1 egg yolk and 1 tbsp of sugar at a time, then the whole egg. Gradually mix in the cheese and raspberry mixture and the cream. Work into a smooth paste, wrap in a cloth. Place on a chopping board, weigh down with another board and leave overnight in the fridge. Cover with some fruit jelly and leave to set or else before serving, decorate with fruit preserves.

Preparation: 30–40 mins

Vanilla paskha

*500 g whole-milk curd cheese, 6 hard-boiled
egg yolks, 250 g butter, 300 g caster sugar,
1 vanilla pod, 3 tbsps finely chopped almonds,
tinned apricots or peaches for decorating*

Put the cheese and egg yolks twice through a mincer. Chop the vanilla finely. Cream the butter until frothy. Whisking all the time, gradually add the sugar and cheese, and towards the end the almonds and vanilla. Wrap the paskha in a cloth, put on a chopping board, weigh down with another board and leave in the fridge overnight. Before serving, decorate with fruit.

Preparation: 30–40 mins

Cheesecake I

*600 g whole-milk cottage cheese, 400 g sugar,
12 eggs, 250 g butter, 1 vanilla pod, grated
rind of 2 oranges (or lemons), 2 tbsps flour*

Put the cheese twice through a mincer. Cream the butter and sugar. Whisking all the time, add 1 tsp of cheese and 1 egg yolk at a time, a bit of chopped vanilla and orange zest. Fold in the five egg whites whisked into stiff peaks. Add the flour and mix gently. Put the mixture into a greased baking tin lined with greaseproof paper and bake in a preheated oven for 60 mins.

Baking: 60 mins

Cheesecake II

*1 kg whole-milk cottage cheese, 10 eggs,
600 g sugar, 125 g butter, 100 g raisins, 50 g each
chopped almonds and walnuts, 2 tbsps chopped
candied orange rind, 2 tbsps potato flour*

Put the cheese twice through a mincer. Cream the butter with the sugar and egg yolks. Whisking all the time, add 1 tsp of cheese at a time. Dredge the orange rind, raisins, almonds and walnuts with potato flour (to prevent them from sinking to the bottom). Whisk the egg whites into stiff peaks and, together with the condiments, gradually fold into the cheese mixture. Put the mixture into a greased baking tin lined with greaseproof paper (up to ⅔ of its height). Bake in a preheated oven for one hour.

Baking: 60 mins

Viennese cheesecake

500 g whole-milk cottage cheese, 5 eggs,
125 g butter, 3 cooked potatoes, 1 tbsp potato flour,
1 cup sugar, 1 tsp baking powder, 50 g raisins,
½ vanilla pod, 1 tbsp chopped candied orange rind

Put the cheese and potatoes twice through a mincer. Cream the butter and sugar. Whisking all the time, add 1 egg yolk and 1 tbsp of the cheese mixture at a time. Fold in the egg whites whisked into stiff peaks. Add the blanched raisins and orange rind which have been dredged with potato flour and baking powder. Mix thoroughly. Grease a baking tin with butter and dust it with breadcrumbs. Put in the cheese mixture and bake it in a preheated oven for 45–60 mins.

Baking: 45–60 mins

Cheesecake on shortcrust

1 kg whole-milk cottage cheese, 10 eggs,
350 g sugar, 60 g butter, 120 g raisins, ½ vanilla pod

DOUGH: 250 g flour, 120 g butter, 2 egg
yolks, grated rind of 1 lemon

Put the cheese twice through a mincer. In an stoneware bowl, blend the cheese with 3 whole eggs, sugar and vanilla. Whisking all the time, add 1 egg yolk at a time and towards the end pour in the melted butter. Fold in seven egg whites whisked into stiff peaks and add the raisins. Make a dough from all the ingredients. Roll the dough out thinly and line a greased baking tin with it, trim the edges, make fine rolls from the trimmings. Spread the cheese mixture on the dough, arrange the trimmings in a lattice pattern. Bake in a preheated oven for an hour.

Baking: 60 mins

Ginger and honey cakes

The Polish tradition of baking gingerbread goes back to the early Slavonic times, when cakes made with honey performed a ritual function. In those times, when sugar was still unknown, the only highly valued sweetener was the honey of wild bees, which the early Slavs mixed with crushed wheat grain. This delicacy served at pagan feasts was the forerunner of today's gingerbread.

Over the centuries the Poles brought this recipe to perfection and became masters in making gingerbread. It was baked in all Polish homes. Unlike today, when it is one of the many treats of the Christmas feast, gingerbread used to be served on various occasions, mainly as something to nibble on with vodka.

The recipe was rather simple. The dough was made from pure honey, spices (cardamom, cloves, cinnamon, pepper, nutmeg, aniseed), one part rye flour and one part wheat flour, spirit and potash (the latter serving as a leavening agent). The preparation of it, though not very complicated, was hard work, and was regarded as a true art. The ginger dough was very tough and thick; one needed a lot of stamina to make and knead it. It matured slowly and could be kept unbaked for months. The crux of the matter was the leaven, which got better with age, and the recipe for preparing it was a closely guarded secret, revealed only to brides to be as part of their dowry.

Freshly baked Polish gingerbread cakes were as hard as stone and needed many weeks to get softer, but then they became delicious – soft and savoury, simply melting in the mouth.

As was once said, there were four things that Poland could be truly proud of: Toruń gingerbread cakes, Gdańsk vodka, Cracow maidens, and Warsaw shoes. Gingerbread was baked in Toruń as early as the early 17th century, and the local bakers' guild kept their recipe a closely guarded secret. The Toruń bakers made savoury gingerbread cakes to be nibbled on with vodka, and very sweet ginger cakes with raisins to be served with dessert. Once called honey cake, it is now known as 'piernik', from the Polish word for a mixture of spices.

You can make gingerbread dough a month before-hand and keep it at the bottom of the fridge. To assure the success of the final product, you need the right amount of baking powder or potash in your dough: with too much leavening agent the dough will rise excessively and the cake will collapse; with too little of it, the cake will not rise nicely and will be very hard. When the cake is baking, do not open the oven, or the dough will subside. A good gingerbread cake should be soft, sweet and fairly spicy.

Of all confectioneries, gingerbread cake is the most healthy.

Old Polish gingerbread

500 g honey, 2 cups sugar, 250 g butter,
1 kg flour, 3 eggs, 3 flat tsps baking soda,
½ tsp salt, 2 packets of gingerbread spices,
2 tbsps chopped walnuts, 2 tbsps finely chopped
candied orange peel, 3–4 finely chopped figs,
*2 tbsps finely chopped almonds * plum jam*

Slowly bring the honey, butter and sugar to the boil, take off the heat and leave to cool a bit. Gradually combine the lukewarm mixture with the flour, eggs, soda dissolved in a small amount of boiled milk, and spices. Towards the end, add the orange peel and nuts and beat well the mixture. Wrap the dough in a cloth and put in a cool place to mature (up to several weeks). Divide the dough into two or three parts. Roll it out and put in greased baking tins. Bake in a moderate oven for 60 mins, then take out and allow to cool. Warm the plum jam, spread it on top of one gingerbread rectangle and cover with the other rectangle. Place on a bread board, cover with a piece of paper, and weigh down with another bread board. Keep in a cool place for several days.

Baking: 60 mins

Sultan's gingerbread

1 kg flour, 500 g sugar, 20 g baking soda, grated
rind of 2 lemons, 500 g honey, cinnamon, cloves,
cardamom (or 2 tsps mixed gingerbread spices), 5 eggs

Bring the honey with the spices to the boil over low heat. Whisk the eggs with the sugar until frothy. Sift the flour

onto a pastry board, make a well in the middle and pour in the warm honey. Work the honey in with a knife and when it is cool enough add the egg mixture, lemon zest and soda, and knead until the dough is smooth and shiny. Wrap it up in a cloth and leave in a cool place to mature. Divide the dough into parts and place each on a greased baking sheet. Bake in a moderate oven for an hour. Leave for a week to mature, then spread with a filling of your choice.

Baking: 60 mins

Filling for sultan's gingerbread

2 oranges, 250 g sugar, 100 g skinned
and chopped almonds, 100 g chopped figs,
100 g raisins, 100 g dates, 100 g walnuts,
100 g hazel nuts and candied lemon peel, ½ cup honey

Take the peel off the scrubbed oranges. Put it into boiling water and cook, changing water two or three times. Take the peel out and chop it finely. Bring ½ cup of water and the sugar to the boil, put in the orange peel and the oranges divided into segments (without pips and fibres). Cook until the syrup thickens, but take care not to burn the fruit. Bring the honey to the boil, put in the chopped fruit and nuts and, stirring continuously, cook until the mixture is thick. Combine with the orange syrup and continue cooking for a minute or two, stirring all the time. Use the mixture to fill the gingerbread.

Preparation: 40–50 mins

Gingerbread with poppy seed

1 cup honey, 150 g fine sugar, 500 g flour,
2 eggs, 10 g baking soda, 1 cup milk,
1 tbsp of grated lemon rind, 1 tsp cinnamon

Slowly, over low heat, bring the honey, sugar and 1 cup of water to the boil, then leave to cool. Gradually mix in the flour, then add the remaining sugar, cinnamon, lemon zest, egg yolks and the whisked egg whites. Add the sifted poppy seeds and soda, knead thoroughly. Wrap the dough in a cloth and leave in a cool place to mature. Spread the dough in a greased baking tin, brush it with a lightly beaten egg and bake in a moderate oven for an hour.

Baking: 60 mins

Rum gingerbread

½ cup honey, 100 g sugar, 3 eggs, 1 tbsp melted butter, 1 tsp gingerbread spices, 1 tsp grated lemon rind, ¼ tsp cinnamon, 5 g baking soda, 1 small glass of rum, 350 g flour, 2 tbsps chopped walnuts, 2 tbsps chopped candied orange peel

Blend the honey and sugar in a stoneware bowl. Gradually add the eggs, butter, spices, lemon zest, cinnamon, soda and the flour. Pour in the rum and continue beating. When the dough is smooth, put in the nuts and orange peel, mix thoroughly. Put the dough into a greased baking tin and bake in a moderate oven for 90 mins. While it is baking, do not touch the baking tin until the cake is well set and risen, otherwise it will collapse and lose its spongy quality.

Baking: 90 mins

Glazed gingerbread

800 g flour, 8 eggs, 500 g honey, 2 cups caster sugar, 200 g butter, 1 tbsp baking soda, 1½ tsps gingerbread spices, 2 tbsps chopped walnuts, 1 tbsp chopped almonds, 2 tbsps finely chopped candied orange peel

Cream the butter and sugar, adding one egg yolk at a time. Blending all the time, combine with the honey, spices and flour. Towards the end fold in the whisked egg whites, add the baking soda, nuts, almonds and orange peel. Mix thoroughly but gently. Put the mixture into small greased baking tins (filling them to ½ of their height). Bake in a moderate oven for an hour. Pour the glazing over the cool cake.

Baking: 60 mins

Glazing for gingerbread

250 g butter, 1 cup sugar, 4 tbsps cocoa, 1 glass brandy

Put the butter into a pan, add 2 tbsps of cold boiled water, sugar and cacoa. Stirring all the time, bring to the boil, then cook over low heat for 5 mins. Take off the heat and stirring continuously pour in the brandy. Pour the mixture over the gingerbread and leave in a cool place for the glazing to set.

Preparation: 10 mins

Monastic gingerbread cookies

4 eggs, 200 g flour, 200 g sugar, 30 g chopped almonds, ¼ tsp ground cardamom

Whisk the sugar and eggs until white. Work in the flour, add the almonds and cardamom. Blend the mixture thoroughly. Grease a baking sheet, dust it with some flour. With a piping bag, pipe oblong cakes onto the sheet. Bake in a moderate oven, taking care that the cookies do not turn yellow.

Note: If there is not enough room on the baking sheet, whisk the dough continuously before you put the second batch in the oven.

Baking: 60 mins

Lithuanian honey cake

3 eggs, 1 cup thick cream, 500 g flour, 200 g sugar, 300 g honey, 2 tbsps gingerbread spices, 1 tsp baking soda

Bring the honey slowly to the boil, then leave it to cool. Beat the egg yolks and sugar until the mixture is white, then add the cream and mix thoroughly. Whisking all the time, gradually add the honey, spices and soda mixed with the flour. Fold in the egg whites whisked into stiff peaks. Pour the dough into greased moulds and bake in a moderate oven for an hour.

Baking: 60 mins

Poppyseed strudels

Poppyseed cake or strudel is the second most important cake in Polish cuisine after gingerbread cake. Christmas poppyseed strudel differs from the ordinary poppyseed

Poppyseed strudels

cake in that the layers of poppy seed are thicker and those of the dough much thinner.

Poppyseed cakes are made from ordinary yeast dough or from sweetened yeast dough, with the latter taking much less time and effort. But the taste of the poppyseed cake is not in the dough, but in the filling.

Yeast dough

300 g flour, 150 g butter, 1 egg, 2 egg yolks,
½ cup boiled milk, 150 g caster sugar, 540 g yeast,
a pinch of salt

Cream the butter and sugar, add the eggs, the yeast dissolved in lukewarm milk and salt. Mix thoroughly, then gradually add the flour and knead until the dough is shiny and does not stick to your hands. Cover the dough with a cloth and leave to rise in a warm place (for 3 hours). Roll out the dough thinly on a pastry board dusted with some flour, brush it with egg whites and spread evenly a thick layer of poppyseed filling (p. 1039) on top. Roll up the dough fairly tightly, seal the ends securely. Place the strudel on a greased baking sheet and leave in a warm place to rise, then put into a preheated oven and bake for an hour. When the strudel is cool, you may ice it and sprinkle with chopped almonds or nuts, or else with chopped candied orange peel.

Baking: 60 mins

Cream and yeast dough

400 g flour, 2 eggs, grated rind of 1 lemon,
150 g butter, 2 tbsps thick cream, 50 g yeast,
100 g caster sugar, a pinch of salt

Mix the yeast with the cream. Sieve the flour onto a pastry board, add the butter and cut it in with a knife until the mixture is sandy. Add the sugar, eggs, yeast, lemon zest and salt and knead until the dough is shiny. Roll the dough out. Spread a thick layer of the filling on top and roll up securely. Place on a greased baking sheet and leave to rise in a warm place for an hour. Brush with melted butter on top and put into a preheated oven for an hour.

Baking: 60 mins

Rich poppy-seed filling

300 g poppy seeds, 1 l boiled milk, 100 g butter, ½ cup honey, 100 g each finely chopped almonds and walnuts, 50 g finely chopped hazel nuts, 2 tbsps finely chopped candied orange peel, 2–3 finely chopped figs, 4 tbsps raisins, 1 cup sugar, 3 eggs, 1 glass rum, 1 vanilla pod

Rinse the poppy seed, cover with the boiling milk and cook for 40 mins over very low heat. Drain it well and put through a mincer several times. Melt the butter and honey in a large pan, add the finely chopped vanilla, nuts, almonds, figs, orange peel and the blanched raisins. Stir well, add the poppy seed and, stirring all the time, simmer for 10–15 mins. Cream the egg yolks and sugar, whisk the egg whites into stiff peaks. When the poppy-seed mixture cools, fold in the egg yolks and the egg whites, add the brandy, mix carefully.

Cooking: 10–15 mins

Modest poppyseed filling

1 cup poppy seeds, 1 cup boiled milk, ½ cup honey,
3 tbsps chopped walnuts, 2 tbsps raisins, ¼ vanilla pod

Rinse the poppy seed, cover with the boiling milk and cook for 30 mins over very low heat. Drain it well and put through a mincer several times. Add the melted honey, blanched raisins, chopped vanilla and nuts and mix thoroughly.

Cooking: 30 mins

Koutia

No Polish Christmas Eve dinner could make do without koutia. Everybody had it: the poor peasant and the magnate, although the name 'koutia' was used generally only in Lithuania, Rus and Podlasie...

Its name gave rise to the name of Christmas Eve dinner in the eastern borderlands of Poland. Koutia is an eastern delicacy, eaten east of the Vistula. The name comes from the Greek word *kukkia*, and came to Poland through Ruthenia. According to the Polesie tradition, Mary ate koutia on the day Christ was born, and that is why this delicacy was a must at Christmas Eve dinner.

For the pagan Slavs, partaking of the feast of kasha with poppy seed and honey was a sign of peace. Originally only barley, the sacred cereal, was used for making koutia. Honey was added to as an expression of sweetness, and poppy seed as a symbol of rest and peace. Some of the koutia was thrown up towards the sky in order to prevent bad crops. Koutia was kept in a pot under holy pictures, where it stayed throughout Christmas to serve as food for the spirits of the dead.

Traditionally, koutia must contain three basic ingredients: cereals, poppy seed and honey. The rest depends on family tradition, local custom, the cook's inventiveness and the availability of other condiments.

Koutia I

1 cup wheat grain, 1 cup poppy seeds, 1 cup honey

Cook the wheat till tender, changing water several times in the process. Drain it well. Cook the poppy seed, drain it, then blend it in a stoneware bowl. Add the wheat and honey. Transfer to a serving bowl and refrigerate.

Preparation: 50 mins • Refrigerating: 12 hrs

Koutia II

1 cup poppy seeds, 1 cup wheat grains, ½ cup caster sugar, ½ cup honey, 200 g chopped walnuts, 100 g chopped almonds, 3 tbsps blanched raisins, 4–5 each chopped figs and dates, grated rind of 1 lemon, 1 cup milk, a pinch of salt

Soak the wheat overnight, then cook it, changing water several times in the process. Drain it well. Rinse the poppy seed, cover with the boiling milk and bring to the boil, then mince it finely several times. Combine the poppy seed with the wheat, put in the remaining ingredients, mix thoroughly and refrigerate. Serve in a bowl, decorated with shortcrust cookies. The more honey and fruit you use, the tastier the koutia.

Preparation: 50 mins • Refrigerating: 12 hrs

Shortcrust cookies and poppy seed

120 g flour, 120 g caster sugar, 1 egg, 1 tbsp cream, 1 tbsp lemon juice

Knead a dough from the above ingredients. Roll it out on a pastry board dusted with flour and cut into small quadrangles. Arrange them on a greased baking sheet and bake in a preheated oven until golden brown.

Preparation: 20–30 mins

Poppyseed treat

1 cup poppy seeds, 2 cups milk, 4 tbsps butter, ½ cup honey, 50 g each chopped almonds and walnuts, 4–5 finely chopped figs, 1 tbsp chopped candied orange peel, 2 tbsps raisins, 2 egg yolks, 3 tbsps sugar, 1 glass rum, ½ vanilla pod

Rinse the poppy seed, cover with the boiling milk and cook over low heat for 30 mins. Drain it well, then put through a mincer several times. Cream the butter with the sugar and egg yolks, add the walnuts, almonds, figs, chopped vanilla, orange peel and blanched raisins, pour in the honey and mix thoroughly. Combine with the poppy seed, add the rum and mix again. Transfer to a serving bowl and refrigerate. Before serving, decorate with shortcrust cookies.

Cooking: 30 mins

Cakes and gateaux

Traditional layered cake

SPONGE CAKE: 120 g butter, 120 g sugar, 120 g flour, 3 eggs, 1 tsp rum, 2 bars of chocolate

MACAROON: 120 g almonds, 120 g caster sugar, 3 egg whites

SHORTCRUST: 140 g flour, 140 g butter, 60 g almonds, 60 g sugar, 3 hard-boiled egg yolks
* rose hip preserve

ST LAYER: Cream the butter and sugar, gradually add the egg yolks, grated chocolate and rum. When the mixture is smooth, fold in the egg whites whisked to stiff peak. Pour in the flour and stir thoroughly but gently. Put the dough into a greased baking tin and bake for 45 mins.
2ND LAYER: Whisk the egg whites and sugar into stiff peaks. Add the ground almonds and mix thoroughly. Pour the mixture into a greased baking tin and bake in a moderate oven for 35 mins.
3RD LAYER: Sift the flour onto a pastry board, add the butter and cut it in with a knife until the mixture has a sandy consistency. Add the sieved egg yolks, caster sugar and ground almonds. Knead the dough, then put it into the fridge for a while. Stretch half the dough to fill a greased baking tin, brush it with lightly beaten egg. Make thin rolls from the remaining dough and arrange them in a lattice pattern on top. Put into a preheated oven and bake for 45 mins. Spread the first two layers with the rose hip preserve, cover with the shortcrust layer. Put some jelly or fruit preserves into each lattice cell.

Baking: 45 mins

Granny's almond cake

250 g almonds, 250 g sugar, 8 eggs, ¼ cup breadcrumbs

FILLING: 250 g walnuts, 250 g sugar, ½ cup single cream, ½ vanilla pod

Cream the sugar and egg yolks, add the ground almonds and whisk into a smooth paste. Fold in the whisked egg whites, add the breadcrumbs and mix gently. Pour the paste into three greased baking tins and bake for 40 mins in a preheated oven. Dry-roast the walnuts in a frying pan, then grind or chop them finely. Blend them in a stoneware bowl with the sugar, add the chopped vanilla

and cream and work into a thick paste. Cover the pastry rounds with the filling, put them one on top of another. Pour the white icing over the cake, decorate with cherry preserves.

Baking: 40 mins

Bread cake

250 g almonds, 250 g sugar, 10 eggs, ½ cup dried grated and sifted bread, a pinch of each cinnamon and ground cloves, grated rind of 1 lemon * jam or chocolate for filling

Chop the almonds coarsely. Cream the sugar and egg yolks, add the spices and lemon zest. Fold in the whisked egg whites, add the breadcrumbs and almonds and mix gently but thoroughly. Pour the mixture into a greased baking tin and bake in a moderate oven. On the following day, cut the cake into rounds, cover each layer with jam or chocolate and re-form the cake.

Baking: 40 mins

Graham's cake with walnuts

180 g butter, 250 g sugar, 15 eggs, 120 g dried grated wholemeal bread, 120 g shelled walnuts, 120 g chocolate, 200 g flour, ¼ tsp each ground cloves and cinnamon, grated rind of 1 orange or lemon

GLAZING: 250 g chocolate, 100 g sugar
* 60 g walnuts or hazelnuts for decorating

Cream the butter in a stoneware bowl, gradually add the sugar, egg yolks, melted or grated chocolate, ground nuts and spices, and the orange zest. Fold in the whisked egg whites, add the sifted breadcrumbs and mix gently. Transfer to a greased baking tin and bake in a moderate oven for at least 60 mins. When the cake is cool, pour over the glazing and sprinkle with toasted, chopped nuts.

Baking: 60 mins

Polish chocolate cake

12 eggs, 200 g caster sugar, 250 g chocolate,
250 g almonds (unskinned)

FILLING: 250 g ground almonds (skinned), 250 g sugar,
juice of 1 lemon, ¼ chopped vanilla pod

GLAZING: 250 g chocolate, 100 g sugar,
40 g butter, ½ cup single cream

Cream the egg yolks and sugar in a stoneware bowl, pour in the melted chocolate and, whisking all the time, gradually add the ground almonds (unpeeled), then fold in the whisked egg whites. Pour the dough into a greased baking tin and bake in a preheated oven for 50 minutes at moderate temperature. On the following day, make a thick syrup from the sugar and 1 cup of water, add the ground almonds and cook for a minute or two. Take off the heat and beat until the mixture turns white. Add the lemon juice and vanilla and whisk for several minutes longer. Cut the cake into two or three rounds, spread each round with the almond filling, then re-form the cake and cover it with the glazing.

Baking: 50 mins

Sachertorte

180 g chocolate, 180 g butter, 180 g sugar,
180 g flour, 8 eggs * 250 g apricot jam

GLAZING: 100 g chocolate, 100 g sugar,
½ cup single cream

Cream the butter in a stoneware bowl, pour in the warm chocolate and, whisking all the time, add some sugar and one egg yolk at a time. Fold in the egg whites whisked to stiff peaks, pour in the flour and mix gently. Pour the mixture into a greased baking tin and put into a preheated oven. Bake slowly for 45 mins. Take the cake out, spread warm apricot jam on top, and when it dries up, cover the whole with the chocolate glazing.

Baking: 45 mins

Fedora chocolate cake (unbaked)

1ST LAYER: 250 g butter, 500 g chocolate,
50 g caster sugar

2ND LAYER: 250 g almonds, 1 lemon, 250 g sugar,
½ chopped vanilla pod, wafers * chocolate
glazing (see Icing and glazing)

1ST LAYER: Cream the butter in a stoneware bowl, pour in the warm melted chocolate and sugar. Whisk for 60 mins until the mixture is smooth, then place into the bottom of the fridge.
2ND LAYER: Blanch and skin the almonds, dry them, then grind. In a stoneware bowl blend them with the sugar, add the vanilla and lemon juice, and work into a smooth paste. Spread the two fillings alternately on wafers. Leave to set, then pour the glazing over the cake.

Preparation: 45 mins

Chocolate 'comber' cake

12 egg yolks, 8 egg whites, 200 g sugar, 250 g almonds (unskinned), 140 g chocolate, 50 g candied orange peel, ½ tsp each cinnamon and ground cloves, grated rind of 1 lemon
* chocolate glazing (see Icing and glazing)
* 40 g almonds for 'larding' the cake

Cream the egg yolks with the sugar and spices, add the warm chocolate and finely chopped candied orange peel. Fold in the egg whites whisked into stiff peaks and unskinned ground almonds. Mix gently but thoroughly. Pour the mixture into a greased bowl-shaped baking dish and bake in a preheated oven for an hour. When the cake is cool, pour over the chocolate glazing and stick in almond slivers.

Baking: 60 mins

Chocolate cake

180 g sugar, 180 g butter, 200 g flour,
5 eggs, 1 glass rum

FILLING: 3 egg yolks, 200 g chocolate, 100 g sugar, ¼ cup single cream, 250 g apricot jam

* rum icing (see Icing and glazing)

Cream the butter in a stoneware bowl, gradually add some sugar and one egg yolk at a time. Fold in the egg whites whisked to stiff peaks, add flour and mix gently. Pour the mixture into two or three small baking tins and put into a preheated oven. Mix the egg yolks and cream, add the sugar and grated chocolate. Simmer over low heat, whisking all the time, until the cream has thickened. Spread the cream on the baked rounds. Put the rounds one on top of another and cover with the apricot jam on top. When the jam has set, pour some rum icing over the cake.

Baking: 50 mins

Buckwheat cake

150 g buckwheat kasha, 150 g sugar, 8 eggs, 1 tbsp spices (ground cloves, cinnamon, lemon zest, nutmeg), 30 g plum stones

FILLING: 3 egg whites, 60 g sugar, 1 tsp grated lemon rind, 1 glass rum

TOPPING: 3 egg whites, 90 g sugar

Grind the buckwheat. Crack the plum stones and chop the kernels finely. Cream the egg yolks and sugar in a stoneware bowl, put in the spices and, whisking all the time, gradually add the whisked egg whites (1 tbsp at a time), ground buckwheat and plum kernels. Transfer the mixture to a greased baking tin and bake in a preheated oven for 50 mins at moderate temperature. Cut the cooled cake into rounds. Blend the egg yolks and sugar, add the rum and lemon zest. Spread the preparation on one round, cover with the other round. Rest a bowl on top of a pan of simmering water and whisk the egg whites and sugar into stiff peaks. Spread the mixture on top and put the cake into a warm oven for a while.

Baking: 50 mins

Layered cake with fruit preserves

250 g sugar, 250 g butter, 500 g flour, 2 egg yolks, 180 g almonds, grated rind of 1 lemon

* rose hip or wild strawberry preserves

* rose or rum icing

Blanch the almonds, skin and chop them finely. Sift the flour onto a pastry board, add the butter and cut it in with a knife to obtain a sandy mixture. Add the sugar, almonds, egg yolks and lemon zest. Knead and roll the dough until it is smooth, then leave it for 1–2 hours in the fridge. Keep rolling the dough for some 10 mins, then fold it the way you fold puff pastry and again leave in the fridge. Divide the dough into four parts, put them into four buttered baking tins and bake them. Spread three rounds with the preserves, put them all one on top of the other. Cover the cake with a chopping board and weigh it down, before you pour icing over and sprinkle it with chopped hazel nuts.

Refrigerating: 1–2 hrs

Poppyseed cake

1 cup poppy seeds, 120 g almond flakes, 250 g sugar, 12 egg yolks, 6 egg whites, ¼ tsp each cinnamon, ground cloves, nutmeg and orange zest

Scald the poppy seeds with boiling water several times, then drain well. Put the egg yolks and sugar into a bowl, rest it on top of a pan of simmering water and whisk the mixture. Add the poppy seed and spices and work into a smooth preparation. Fold in the egg whites whisked into stiff peaks and ground almonds, mix gently. Transfer the mixture to a greased baking tin and bake for an hour in a moderate oven. You may glaze the cool cake with some chocolate or rum icing.

Baking: 60 mins

Shortcrust poppyseed cake

PASTRY: 100 g butter, 60 g caster sugar, 180 g flour, 1 egg yolk

POPPYSEED FILLING: 1 cup poppy seeds, 240 g sugar, 8 eggs, 1 chopped vanilla pod

Sift the flour onto a pastry board, add the butter and cut it in with a knife until the mixture is sandy in consistency. Add the sugar and egg yolk and knead well, then put in the fridge for a while. Scald the poppy seeds with boiling water several times, then drain well. Blend in a stoneware bowl together with the sugar, adding one egg at a time and some finely chopped vanilla. Line a baking tin with buttered paper, spread the pastry at the bottom. Prick it with a fork all over and put into a preheated oven for a few minutes, but do not let it brown. Take the shortcrust out and cover it with the poppyseed topping. Return to the oven and bake for 50 mins.

Baking: 50 mins

Shortcrust cake

PASTRY: 300 g flour, 20 g cocoa, 150 g butter, 150 g caster sugar, 150 g almonds, 4 egg yolks, 1 egg, 1 tsp cinnamon, grated rind of ½ lemon, 4 tbsps single cream, 1 tsp baking soda

FILLING: 250 g apricot jam, 100 g ground almonds, 150 g ground walnuts, 50 g raisins, 2 tbsps brandy, juice of ½ lemon

Sift the flour, caster sugar and baking soda onto a pastry board, add the cocoa, butter, lemon zest, ground almonds, cinnamon and cream and mix the ingredients with a knife until the mixture is sandy in consistency. Add the egg and egg yolks and knead until the dough is smooth and shiny. Shape it into a ball, wrap in a cloth and put in the fridge for several hours. Blanch the raisins, cover them with the brandy and leave aside for a few minutes. Mix the jam with the lemon juice, ground walnuts and almonds, add the raisins. Roll the dough out, line a baking tin with it, trim the edges. Prick it with a fork all over and put in a preheated oven for a while. Then take it out and cover with the filling. Roll out the pastry trimmings, cut them into thin strips. Arrange the strips on top of the jam in a lattice pattern. Brush the top with lightly beaten egg whites and return the cake to the oven for 40 mins.

Baking: 40 mins

Black walnut cake

250 g shelled walnuts, 250 g sugar, 1 tsp ground coffee, 200 g chocolate, 1 tbsp breadcrumbs, 8 eggs, ½ lemon

FILLING: 250 g butter, 250 g caster sugar, 300 g chocolate, 40 g ground skinned almonds, 1 egg yolk, ¼ vanilla pod

Blend the eggs and sugar, add some lemon juice and zest. Whisking all the time, gradually add the coffee, melted chocolate and finely chopped or ground walnuts. Fold in the egg whites whisked to stiff peaks and sifted breadcrumbs, mix gently. Pour the mixture into three buttered baking tins and bake for 30 mins in a medium-hot oven. Cream the butter and sugar in a stoneware bowl. Whisking continuously, add the egg yolk, melted chocolate, chopped vanilla and ground almonds. Put the mixture into the fridge for a while, then spread it on top of the three rounds and on the sides of the cake.

Baking: 30 mins

Hazelnut cake

250 g butter, 250 g flour, 180 g sugar, 180 g hazelnuts

FILLING: 1 cup single cream, 60 g sugar, ¼ vanilla pod
* chocolate icing
* cherry preserve for decorating

Sift the flour onto a pastry board, cut in the butter with a knife. Add the sugar and ground hazelnuts and briskly knead the dough. Put it in the fridge for 1–2 hours. Divide the dough into four parts and bake four rounds in buttered baking tins. Whip the cream, sugar and vanilla, spread the whipped cream on each round and form them into a cake. Pour some icing on top and decorate with chopped nuts and cherries.

Baking: 30 mins

Orange cake

250 g almonds, 250 g sugar, 12 egg yolks, 8 egg whites, 2 oranges, 60 g breadcrumbs

* fruit jam for filling
* 1 orange for decorating

Whisk the egg yolks and sugar in a stoneware bowl. Add the juice of 2 oranges and grated rind of 1 orange. Whisking all the time, gradually put in the ground almonds. Fold in the whisked egg whites and breadcrumbs. Pour the mixture into two buttered baking tins and bake for 45 mins at medium-high temperature. Spread one pastry round with jam, cover it with the other round. Pour the icing over and decorate with orange segments.

Baking: 45 mins

Icing and glazing

The whole knack of a successful icing is in its cooking and whisking. If you do not cook it long enough, the icing will never set and thicken. If you cook it too long, it will get hard as stone when you whisk it. Too much acid (vinegar or lemon juice) makes the icing gluey.

The best thing for making icing are sugar cubes. Pour some water over the cubes, wait till the sugar dissolves, then add a few drops of lemon juice, cover and cook for 30 minutes. Test the icing when translucent bubbles appear on its surface: dip a fork in it and blow – when threads of sugar form, the icing is ready; alternately, if the last drop dripping from the spatula is followed by a thread of sugar, you may take it off the heat. When cooking, remember to skim the froth from the surface and to scrape in with a knife the sugar crystals that form on the sides of the pan.

Take the icing off the heat, pour it into a stoneware bowl and whisk it briskly. If the sugar hardens too rapidly, pour in several drops of boiling water and continue whisking. After 15 minutes of vigorous whisking, the mixture should be smooth.

If the icing is intended for a piped inscription or decoration, it should be cold and the surface of the cake completely dry.

Colouring:
for **pink** icing add some thick cherry syrup while you whisk it
for **yellow** icing add a pinch of saffron soaked in vodka
for **green** icing add some juice from cooked spinach
for **bright green** icing add egg white in which coffee beans have soaked overnight

Milk icing

250 g sugar, ½ cup milk, 1 glass rum

Put the sugar into a pan, pour over the milk. When the sugar dissolves, cook over low heat, stirring all the time, until the syrup has thickened. Take off the heat and stir vigorously with a spatula. Before pouring it over the cake, thin it down with the rum and, stirring continuously, heat it up a bit. Pour the icing over the cake while it is still hot. You may also cover a cake with cold icing, but having done that, you have to put the cake into the hot oven for several minutes.

Baking: 60 mins

Uncooked icing I

1 cup caster sugar, 1 egg white, juice of ½ lemon

Whisk the egg whites to stiff peaks in a bowl. Rest the bowl in a larger dish filled with ice and mixing vigorously with a spatula gradually add the sugar. Continue mixing for an hour to give the icing a thick consistency. Add the lemon juice and mix thoroughly. Use to cover mazureks which should then be put in a cool place to let the icing dry up.

Preparation: 60 mins

Uncooked icing II

1½ sugar, ½ cup potato flour, 2 egg whites

Blend the sugar with the potato flour and whisked egg whites in a bowl placed in a larger dish filled with ice cubes for 60 mins. Spread the icing over the cake, then put the cake in a warm oven to allow the icing to dry.

Preparation: 60 mins

Uncooked icing III

2 cups sugar, 2 egg whites, 1 tsp gelatine

Blend the egg whites with the sugar in a bowl placed in a larger dish filled with ice cubes, add the gelatine and continue mixing for several minutes longer. Spread the icing over the cake, then put the cake in a warm oven to allow the icing to dry.

Note: If you do not mix the sugar long enough, the dry icing will not be shiny.

Preparation: 60 mins

Uncooked icing IV

250 g caster sugar, 1 lemon, 1 tbsp brandy

Blend the sugar with the lemon juice and brandy. Continue stirring for an hour, until the mixture is smooth and shiny. Pour it over the cake.

Preparation: 60 mins

Uncooked icing V

200 g caster sugar, 3 tbsps rum, 1 tbsp lemon juice, 1 tbsp melted butter

Blend the sugar with the rum. Stirring vigorously, add the lemon juice and melted butter. When the mixture is smooth and shiny, pour it over the cake.

Preparation: 60 mins

White icing

250 g sugar, 1 tbsp lemon juice

Make a syrup from the sugar, ½ cup of water and the lemon juice. Continue stirring the cooked syrup for 10–15 mins.

Mixing: 10–15 mins

Punch icing

250 g sugar, juice of ½ lemon, 1 tsp strong tea infusion, 1 tsp rum

Dissolve the sugar in ¼ cup of boiled water, then cook a syrup. When it thickens, add the lemon juice, rum and tea and continue stirring for 25–30 mins.

Mixing: 25–30 mins

Orange icing

250 g sugar cubes, 1 orange

Scrub the orange, scald it with boiling water and dry it. Rub the sugar cubes against the orange. Dissolve the cubes in ¼ cup of water, then cook a thick syrup, mixing all the time. Take off the heat and continue stirring, adding the orange juice in the process.

Preparation: 60 mins

Coffee icing

250 g sugar, 3 tsps coffee

Cover the coffee with ½ cup of boiling water. Leave it to cool, then strain it and dissolve the sugar in the liquid. Mixing all the time, make a coffee syrup (take care to not let it boil over, as the syrup gets very frothy). When it thickens to a thread, take it off the heat and mix until it is smooth and shiny.

Preparation: 60 mins

Biscuits

Cream biscuits

400 g flour, 200 g butter, 150 g caster sugar, 3 tbsps finely chopped hazelnuts, 1 tbsp granulated sugar, 1 egg, 2 tbsps cream

Cream the butter with the sugar and 1 tbsp of chopped nuts, towards the end add the cream. Add the flour and mix thoroughly, then put in the fridge for a while. Dust a pastry board with flour, roll the dough out. Cut out biscuits with a cutter, place them on a baking sheet dusted with flour. Brush with egg whites mixed with water and sprinkle with chopped nuts and crystal sugar. Bake in a preheated oven until golden brown.

Baking: 10–15 mins

Almond biscuits

300 g almonds, 250 g caster sugar, 25 g butter, 5 eggs, 75 g flour, 1 packet vanilla sugar, a pinch of salt

Blanch the almonds, skin and grind them. Beat the eggs and sugar thoroughly. Mix the flour with the almonds, vanilla sugar and salt, gradually add to the eggs, and with a wooden spatula work into a smooth paste. Pour in the melted butter and mix well. Drop teaspoonfuls of the mixture onto a greased baking sheet. Flatten each biscuit with a knife dipped in cold water. Bake in a preheated oven for 10–15 mins. In a well sealed tin, the biscuits will keep for a month.

Baking: 10–15 mins

Raisin biscuits

125 g flour, 75 g raisins, 125 g butter, 125 g caster sugar, 2 eggs, 1 tsp rum

Rinse and drain the raisins, put in a bowl and cover with the rum. Blend the butter and sugar into a smooth paste. Whisking all the time, add one egg at a time. Towards the end, put in the raisins and flour, and mix thoroughly. Drop teaspoonfuls of the mixture onto a buttered baking sheet, dusted with flour. Flatten each biscuit with a knife dipped in water. Bake in a preheated oven for 10–15 mins.

Baking: 10–15 mins

Coconut biscuits

3 egg whites, 250 g caster sugar, 250 g desiccated coconut, 1 tsp grated lemon rind, 1 tbsp lemon juice

Whisk the egg whites with the sugar and lemon zest to stiff peaks. Add the coconut and lemon juice, mix gently. Drop teaspoonfuls of the mixture onto the buttered baking sheet. Bake in a preheated oven until light golden.

Baking: several minutes

Vanilla biscuits

250 g sugar, 4 eggs, 1 vanilla pod, 350 g flour, 180 g butter

Cream the butter and sugar, adding one egg at a time. Chop and pound the vanilla pod very finely. Add the vanilla to the creamed eggs, pour in the flour and work into a smooth dough. Drop it in teaspoonfuls onto a buttered baking sheet dusted with flour. Flatten each biscuit with a knife dipped in water. Bake in a preheated oven for 10–15 mins, or until golden brown. Dust the warm biscuit with caster sugar.

Baking: 10–15 mins

Cinnamon biscuits

170 g flour, 120 g caster sugar, 50 g powdered cinnamon, 2 ground cloves, 250 g butter

Cream the butter until frothy, blend with the sugar, then the cinnamon and cloves. Combine with the flour and knead well. Put the dough in the fridge for a while. Then roll the dough out on a pastry board dusted with flour and cut out biscuit with a cutter. Arrange them on a baking sheet dusted with flour and bake in a preheated oven.

Baking: 10–15 mins

Ginger biscuits

250–300 g flour, 2 eggs, 2 egg yolks, 250 g caster sugar, 1 tbsp powdered ginger, ½ tsp grated lemon rind

Break the eggs into a bowl, add the egg yolks and sugar. Rest the bowl on top of a pan with cold water. Place over low heat and whisk the eggs until the water begins to boil. Then add the lemon zest and ginger and continue whisking for several minutes longer. Take the pan off the heat, leave the mixture to cool. Add the flour and mix thoroughly. Roll the dough out on a pastry board dusted with flour and cut out biscuits with a cutter. Arrange them on a greased baking sheet and bake in a preheated oven until golden brown.

Baking: 10–15 mins

Aniseed biscuits

200 g flour, 200 g sugar, 8 eggs, 1 tbsp ground aniseed, 2 tbsps granulated sugar

Break the eggs into a bowl, add the sugar. Place the pan on top of a pan of simmering water and whisk the eggs. Take off the heat and allow to cool, then put over low heat and whisk until the mixture turns white. Again take off the heat and allow to cool, then add the aniseed and whisk for several minutes longer over low heat. Take off the heat, gradually add the flour and work it into a smooth dough. Grease a baking tray with butter, line it with a thin layer of the dough and put into a hot oven. When the pastry is still warm, sprinkle it with granulated sugar and cut into small squares.

Baking: 10–15 mins

Spicy biscuits

250 g flour, 1 tsp baking soda, 100 g caster sugar, 100 g butter, 1 egg, 50 g finely chopped walnuts, ½ tsp cinnamon, ½ packet vanilla sugar, ¼ tsp ground cloves, a pinch of ginger and saffron

Sift the flour onto a pastry board, add the baking soda, spices and very finely chopped nuts. With a knife cut in the butter into the mixture. Add the sugar, egg and vanilla sugar and knead the dough well. Wrap it in clingfilm or a cloth and put in the fridge for 1–2 hours. Roll out the dough on a pastry board dusted with flour and cut out biscuits with a cutter. Arrange them on a greased baking sheet and bake in a preheated oven for 10–15 mins. Brush the cool biscuits with some icing.

Baking: 10–15 mins

Walnut biscuits

3 egg whites, a pinch of salt, 150 g caster sugar, 180 g finely chopped walnuts, 1 tsp cinnamon, ¼ tsp grated lemon rind

Whisk the egg whites with the sugar and salt into stiff peaks. Fold in the nuts, cinnamon and lemon zest. Drop teaspoonfuls of the mixture onto a buttered baking sheet and put into a hot oven for several minutes.

Baking: several minutes

Orange rings

100 g ground almonds, 100 g caster sugar, grated rind of 2 oranges, 1 tbsp orange juice, 2 egg yolks

Place a bowl on top of a pan with simmering water, put in the egg yolks and sugar, and whisk them, adding the orange zest and juice in the process. Heat the mixture up, then allow it to cool and fold in the almonds. Shape small rings from the mixture. Arrange them on a baking sheet and put into a hot oven and leave to dry at a low temperature.

Drying: several minutes

Pretzels

350 g flour, 2 eggs, 300 g caster sugar, 1 packet vanilla sugar, 2 tbsps poppy seeds, 1 tbsp butter

Place a bowl on top of a pan with simmering water. Break in the eggs, add the sugar and whisk vigorously, putting in the vanilla sugar towards the end. Leave the mixture to cool, then whisking all the time, gradually add the flour and work into a smooth paste. On a pastry board dusted with flour, shape the dough into thin rolls, twist the rolls into an 8 shape and place them on a greased baking sheet. Brush the pretzels with melted butter and sprinkle with poppy seed. Bake until golden brown.

Baking: 10–15 mins

Marzipan sweets

500 g almonds, 500 g caster sugar, juice of 1 small lemon

Blanch and skin the almonds. Dip them in cold water and then leave overnight in a warm oven to dry. Grind them finely, put into a stoneware bowl together with the sugar and beat with a pestle very thoroughly. One by one put in the egg whites and work into a thick mixture. Transfer the mixture to a pan and warm up over very low heat, then turn onto a pastry board, add the lemon juice and knead for a while. Dust the board with custer sugar and roll out the mixture. Cut it into various shapes, then leave to dry a bit. Place the sweets on a baking sheet and put in a hot oven for 1–2 mins to dry up and turn light golden.

Drying: 1–2 mins

Warsaw mint and honey biscuits

3 cups flour, ½ tsp ammonia, 1 cup honey,
1 tsp dried mint

Bring the honey slowly to the boil, then leave it to cool. Fold in the flour, add ¾ cup of water, ammonia and mint. Knead a smooth dough, wrap it in a cloth and leave to mature. Then shape the dough into balls the size of a walnut and place them on a greased baking sheet. Bake in a preheated oven for 40 mins at medium-high temperature.

Baking: 40 mins

Cracow honey biscuits

300 g flour, 150 g sugar, ½ cup honey,
2 eggs, 4 egg yolks, ½ tsp each cinnamon,
ground cloves and baking soda

Cream the eggs, egg yolks and sugar until the mixture is white and thick. Whisking all the time, gradually add the flour. Pour in the honey and towards the end add the cinnamon, cloves and soda. Work into a smooth dough, wrap it up in a cloth and leave in a cool place to mature. Roll the dough out on a pastry board dusted with flour and cut out biscuits with a cutter. Leave them aside for several hours, then place them on a greased baking sheet and bake in a preheated oven for 30 mins at medium-high temperature until they are golden brown.

Baking: 30 mins

Honey kisses

300 g flour, ½ cup honey, 1 egg, 100 g sugar, 1 tbsp
butter, ½ tsp baking soda, 1 tbsp gingerbread spices

* *1 egg for brushing*
* *40 g almonds for decorating*

Bring the honey to the boil. Sift the flour onto a pastry board, make a well in the middle. Pour the honey into the well and cut it in with a knife. Add the sugar, spices, soda, butter and egg and knead very thoroughly, otherwise the cookies will not rise. Roll out the dough. Cut out biscuits with a cutter. Place them on a greased baking sheet, brush with beaten egg and decorate with almond or walnut halves. Bake in a moderate oven for 15–20 mins (the cookies should treble in volume). When the biscuits are cool, put them in a glass jar and leave for at least a week to soften.

Baking: 15–20 mins

Christmas Eve biscuits

500 g flour, 100 g honey, 100 g butter, 100 g poppy
seeds, 100 g sugar, 4 egg yolks, a pinch of salt

Melt the honey. Blanch, then drain the poppy seed. Beat the egg yolks and the butter until frothy. Whisking all the time, gradually add the sugar and poppy seed, then the cool honey and the remaining ingredients. Knead into a smooth dough. Roll the dough out on a pastry board dusted with flour. Cut out medium sized circles or elongated rectangles. Place the biscuits on a baking sheet greased with butter, prick them lightly with a fork. Bake in a preheated oven until golden brown.

Baking: 15–20 mins

Pretzels with poppy seeds

250 g flour, 120 g butter, 60 g caster sugar,
grated rind of ½ lemon, 1 egg yolk
* *egg white for brushing*
* *poppy seeds for sprinkling*

Sift the flour onto a pastry board, cut in the butter with a knife. Add the sugar, lemon zest and egg yolk and first work the mixture with a knife and then knead it by hand. Put the dough into the fridge for 2–3 hours. On a dusted pastry board, make thin rolls from the dough, twist them into an 8 shape. Place the pretzels on a greased baking sheet, brush them with egg white, sprinkle with poppy seeds. Bake in a preheated oven until golden brown.

Baking: 15–20 mins

Viennese biscuits

250 g sugar, 250 g wheat flour, 4 eggs, grated rind of 1 lemon, 10 ground cloves, ½ tsp cinnamon

Cream the eggs and sugar. Whisking all the time, add the cinnamon, cloves and lemon zest. Put in the flour and mix thoroughly. On a dusted pastry board, make thin rolls from the dough. Arrange them on a buttered baking sheet, brush with egg white, sprinkle with sugar and cinnamon, and bake in a preheated oven until golden brown.

Baking: 15–20 mins

Cinnamon stars

250 g caster sugar, 250 g ground unskinned almonds, 1 tsp cinnamon, 1 packet vanilla sugar, 3 egg whites, 2 tbsps sugar

Whisk the egg whites into stiff peaks, towards the end gradually fold in the sugar, ground almonds, cinnamon and vanilla sugar. Mix gently but thoroughly. Dust a pastry board with crystal sugar. Roll out the mixture, cut out stars from it with a cutter. Place the stars on a greased baking sheet and bake in a preheated oven until golden brown.

Baking: 15–20 mins

Aniseed snaps

140 g sugar, 140 g flour, 2 eggs, 1 tsp aniseed

Blend the eggs with the sugar until the mixture is white and thick. Warm it up, then add the sifted flour and knead well. Put in the aniseed and knead for a while longer. Roll our the dough on a pastry board dusted with flour and cut out round biscuits. Arrange them on a greased baking sheet, brush with melted butter. Bake in a moderate oven.

The biscuits should grow a bit in volume and get golden brown.

Baking: 15–20 mins

Ginger snaps

120 g caster sugar, 120 g flour, 120 g butter, 2 egg yolks, grated rind of 1 lemon, 1 tsp powdered ginger

Sift the flour onto a pastry board, cut in the butter with a knife. Add the sugar, egg yolks, lemon zest and ginger and knead thoroughly. Put the dough in the fridge for an hour, then roll it out on the pastry board dusted with flour. Transfer it onto a greased baking sheet and leave aside for an hour, then bake in a preheated oven at medium-high temperature until lightly golden.

Baking: 15–20 mins

Cheese biscuits

250 g curd cheese, 250 g wheat flour, 2 eggs, 250 g butter, grated rind of 1 orange and ½ lemon, 3 tbsps caster sugar

Sift the flour onto a pastry board, cut in the butter with a knife. Add the cheese, eggs, sugar and zest. Mix with a knife, then knead well. Put in the fridge for an hour. Roll the dough out on the pastry board dusted with flour and cut out small biscuit. Place them on a greased baking sheet and bake in a preheated oven until light golden.

Note: For crackers, which will go well with clear soup, use salt, pepper, caraway and ginger instead of sugar and zest.

Baking: 15–20 mins

Nutty sweetmeat

1 cup honey, 120 g caster sugar, 250 g walnuts

Cook the honey and sugar over low heat until the mixture browns slightly. Put in the finely chopped walnuts and continue cooking for a while longer. Transfer the mixture unto a moistened pastry board, roll it out, then cut into small pieces and leave to cool.

Preparation: 30–40 mins

Shortcrust biscuits

Poppyseed sweetmeat

*1 cup honey, 1 cup blanched (and drained)
poppy seeds, 120 g sugar*

Cook the honey and sugar over low heat until the mixture browns slightly. Put in the poppy seed and continue cooking for a while longer. Transfer the mixture unto a moistened pastry board, roll it out, then cut into small pieces and leave to cool. You can combine the two recipes by mixing ½ cup of walnuts and ½ cup of poppy seeds.

Preparation: 30–40 mins

Shortcrust biscuits

*100 g flour, 70 g butter, 30 g finely chopped
almonds, 40 g sugar, 1 hard-boiled egg
yolk, ½ tsp grated lemon rind*

* egg white for brushing

* crystal sugar or chopped walnuts for sprinkling

Sift the flour onto a pastry board, cut in the butter and egg yolk with a knife. Add the almonds, sugar and lemon zest and knead well. Put the dough in the fridge for one hour, then roll out the dough and cut out biscuits with a cutter. Place them on a greased baking sheet, brush with egg white and sprinkle with sugar or nuts. Bake in a moderate oven until golden brown.

Baking: 15–20 mins

Doughnuts

The traditional Polish Shrovetide pastries are doughnuts and fried pastry twists (*faworki*).
Doughnuts are a Viennese invention, but different varieties of them are known all over the world. When iced and filled with jam, they resemble the 'rich cousins' of various fritters and pancakes.

In Poland, they are made from a light and well risen yeast dough, to which you add a small amount of pure spirit (1½ tsp for 1 kg of flour), vinegar or citric acid, thanks to which the albumen contained in flour and eggs will coagulate and prevent the doughnuts from absorbing too much fat. The quality of doughnut pastry depends on the quality of egg yolks and flour. The latter should be rich in gluten.

The filling for doughnuts should be kept at room temperature. Its consistency should be more or less the same as that of the dough. Thick filling will pierce the pastry if the latter is runny, while with a fluid filling it becomes difficult to shape doughnuts.

Doughnuts are dusted with vanilla caster sugar, or iced while they are still warm.

The following instructions should be observed to prevent doughnuts absorbing too much fat during frying:

– add some alcohol, vinegar or lemon juice to the dough;

– do not use too much sugar, which causes doughnuts to burn;

– fry doughnuts in a shallow pan under cover in a large amount of hot fat so that they can freely float in it; after you turn them upside down, remove the lid;

– use fat that decomposes at very high temperature, e.g. lard or oil;

– maintain the right temperature: at a low temperature doughnuts absorb too much fat, while at an excessively high temperature they burn; and

– when frying, from time to time put in 1–3 slices of raw potato which will prevent the doughnuts from burning.

Take the fried doughnuts out and immediately drain them on absorbent paper. Only then should you ice them or dust them with caster sugar.

The traditional Viennese filling for doughnuts is apricot jam, while Poles prefer rose-petal or cherry preserves.

It takes several hours to prepare and fry doughnuts, hence it does not make much sense to use less than ½ kg of flour when frying them. For your doughnuts to be a success, you should remember the following:

– the dough must have the right consistency; if it is too hard, it will not rise; if it is not hard enough, doughnuts will absorb too much fat and will not be tasty;

– seal the filling very carefully inside, for the jam that escapes from a doughnut will turn into caramel and 'pollute' the fat in which the doughnuts are fried; and

– remember to maintain the right temperature; to check it, drop in a bit of dough – if the temperature is right, it will rise up and turn golden brown.

Yeast dough is made from a large quantity of egg yolks and fat and a relatively small amount of sugar. With the filling and icing, the doughnuts will be sweet anyway.

With too much sugar in the dough, the doughnuts will quickly burn on the surface, while inside they will remain moist and raw.

The risen dough is rolled out or stretched on a pastry board dusted with flour.

There are several methods of shaping doughnuts:

– cut out circles with a cup or a pastry cutter, put some filling in the centre, fold in the edges and press them, and shape the dough into balls; place the doughnuts 'seam' down on the pastry board and leave to rise. Using this method, you'll be left with trimmings of dough which you may knead together, roll out and cut out again, but remember that this second batch will take longer to rise;

– cut out double the amount of small circles, place some filling on one, cover with another and seal them by pressing the edges together;

– put the risen dough onto a pastry board dusted with flour, shape it into a thick roll and cut off small slices; stretch and flatten each slice on your palm, put some filling in the centre and seal the edges; the third method allows you to use all the dough, without any trimmings left over, but you need practice to use it successfully;

– fry doughnuts without any filling and stuff them when they are ready; do not roll out the dough but stretch it out by hand, cut out small circles and fry them, and finally fill them with some jam using a piping bag.

Arrange the doughnuts on a pastry board, cover them with a cloth and leave to rise.

So as the fat used for frying doughnuts does not burn, pour a little water into a large pan with a thick bottom, and only then put in the lard. You need ½ cup of water for 1 kg of lard. Put the doughnuts in with the seam up, cover the pan with a lid and fry until the doughnuts are browned on one side. Turn them over and continue frying in an uncovered pan. Do not drop the doughnuts in, but place them gently in the fat so that only one half of each of them is dipped in the fat. When they have been done on both sides, take them out with a strainer and drain off the fat with absorbent paper. Only then may you ice them (and sprinkle with candied orange peel) or dust them with caster sugar. Iced doughnuts stay fresh longer.

If we want your doughnuts to have a lighter coloured ring through the middle, the dough should be lighter and better risen. They will then float in the fat, immersed to less than half their thickness.

Scalded doughnuts are more mellow and lighter, and they do not go stale so quickly. First, dip them for two or three minutes in boiling water and when they float to the surface take them out and drain them. Only then should you fry them in fat. With this method, you use much less fat and the doughnuts are well risen and light, on condition that they have risen enough before being immersed in boiling water.

Polish doughnuts

1½ cups flour, 30 g yeast, 6 egg yolks, ¼ cup sugar, 7 tbsps butter, 1 tbsp vodka, 1 cup lukewarm milk, ¾ tsp salt, 1 tbsp sugar, grated rind of 1 lemon; lard for frying, rose-petal preseve for filling, caster sugar mixed with vanilla

Cut the vanilla into smaller pieces, mix with caster sugar and leave for several days. Mix the yeast with 1 tbsp of sugar and ¼ cup of milk, cover and set aside in a warm place. Blend the egg yolks with the sugar, then combine with the remaining milk. Sift the warm flour and salt into a bowl, pour in the egg yolk mixture and the yeast, add the lemon zest and mix thoroughly. Pour in the vodka and knead well, until the dough is smooth and shiny. Cover with a cloth and leave to rise in a warm place. Rub some fat into your hands and take small portions of the dough. Flatten them in your hand, put some jam in the middle. Fold up, seal the edges and shape into balls. Place them seam down on a cloth dusted with flour, cover with another cloth and leave to rise. When they have risen, turn them over, cover again and leave aside for a bit longer. Heat up the lard in a skillet with a thick bottom. Check the temperature by

dropping in a piece of dough: if it browns quickly, the temperature is right. Place doughnuts in the fat in batches so that they float freely. Fry them uncovered until browned on one side. Then turn them over and fry them on the other side (frying them in an uncovered pan means that when you turn them over they float on the surface, which leaves a lighter coloured circle in the middle). When done, take them out and drain on absorbent paper, then sprinkle with caster sugar.

Frying: 5–7 mins

Warsaw doughnuts

LEAVEN: 60–70 g yeast, ½ cup milk, 1 tbsp flour, 1 tsp sugar

DOUGH: 500 g wheat flour, 7 egg yolks, 130 g sugar, 1 packet vanilla sugar (or ½ vanilla pod), 1 cup single cream, 130 g butter, salt, ½ cup grated rose hip, 50 g finely chopped almonds, lard for frying, caster sugar or icing

Mix the yeast with the sugar, flour and lukewarm milk and set aside in a warm place for half an hour. Put the egg yolks, sugar and vanilla sugar into a bowl. Rest the bowl on top of a pot of simmering water and whisk them until they turn into a smooth cream. Sift the flour into a bowl, pour in the egg yolks and lukewarm cream and mix thoroughly with a spatula. Add some salt and the yeast and knead for at least 15–20 mins. When the dough no longer sticks to your hands, gradually pour in cool melted butter and work it in for several minutes. Cover with a cloth and leave to rise in a warm place for 1–1½ hours. Mix the rose hip with the almonds. Shape doughnuts filled with the rose hip and almond mixture and fry them.

Frying: 5–7 mins

Lvov doughnuts

500 g flour, 100 g butter, 10 egg yolks, 50 g yeast, 3–4 tbsps honey (heather or buckwheat), ½ cup whipping cream, 200 g chocolate, ¼ cup orange liqueur, ¼–½ tsp salt, fat for frying

Mix the yeast with the cream and set aside in a warm place. Blend the butter with the egg yolks, gradually adding the honey and sifted flour with salt. Pour in the yeast and knead until the dough is smooth and shiny. Cover with a cloth and leave in a warm place for 30–40 mins, by which time it should double in volume. Knead it again and with moistened hands shape into small balls. Place the doughnuts on a pastry board dusted with flour, cover with a cloth and let them rise. Heat up the fat in a skillet with a thick bottom. Put in the doughnuts in batches to allow them to float freely. Put the lid on and fry for two or three minutes, then take the lid off, turn each doughnut over and fry again uncovered. Take the doughnuts out and drain on absorbent paper. Melt the chocolate in a pan, pour in the liqueur, stir well. Place warm doughnuts on a plate and cover them with the chocolate mixture.

Frying: 5–7 mins

Doughnuts with raisins

500 g flour, 50 g yeast, 100 g sugar, 1 cup whipping cream, ½ cup milk, 100 g butter, 150 g raisins, 1 packet vanilla sugar, salt, oil for frying, 1 cup caster sugar, 1 tbsp cinnamon

Crumble the yeast, mix it with I tsp of sugar and warm milk and set in a warm place. Sift the flour onto a pastry board, add salt, sugar and vanilla sugar. Put in 80 g of butter and cut it in with a knife. Pour in the cream and yeast, and knead until the dough is smooth and shiny. Cover with a cloth and leave in a warm place for half an hour. Rinse the raisins, blanch and drain them. Add them to the dough and knead again. Heat up the oil in a skillet. Dip a tablespoon in melted butter and use it to drop the dough into hot oil. Fry the doughnuts in batches. Drain them on absorbent paper, then sprinkle with caster sugar mixed with cinnamon.

Frying: 5–7 mins

Doughnuts with cherry filling

1 kg flour, 80 g yeast, 1 tsp sugar, 2 cups milk, ½ cup melted butter, 8 egg yolks, ½ cup sugar, salt, cherry preserves, caster sugar, fat for frying

Mix the yeast with I tbsp of milk and I tsp of sugar, then set it aside in a warm place. Whisk the egg yolks with sugar until frothy. Pour in the melted butter and, whisking all the time, gradually add the milk and sifted flour. Combine with the yeast, add some salt and knead until the dough is shiny and smooth. Cover with a cloth and leave to rise, then knead again and divide into portions. Roll out each portion and cut out cricles. Put some cherry preserve in the middle of one circle, cover with another and seal the edges carefully. Fry in batches.

Frying: 5–7 mins

Chris's doughnuts

3 cups flour, 2 tbsps sugar, 60 g butter, 2 eggs, 3 egg yolks, 1 cup milk, 50 g yeast, 1 tbsp spirit, salt, plum jam, caster sugar, lard for frying

Mix the crumbled yeast with I tsp of sugar, I tbsp of flour and ½ cup of milk, then set it aside to rise in a warm place. Rest a bowl on a pot of simmering water and whisk the eggs and egg yolks with sugar and a pinch of salt. Sift the flour into a bowl, add the remaining milk, yeast and whisked eggs. Work into a smooth mixture, add the spirit and melted butter and knead until bubbles appear and the dough is smooth and shiny. Leave in a warm place to rise. Shape doughnuts, fill them with jam and fry in hot lard.

Frying: 5–7 mins

Kurp apple doughnuts

10 small tart apples, 4 eggs, 100–120 g flour, ½ cup fruit preserve, 50 g finely chopped walnuts, 1 tbsp honey, fat for frying, caster sugar, 1 tsp cinnamon

Peel and core the apples. Mix the fruit preserve with the honey and walnuts. Fill the apples with the mixture. Blend the flour with the egg yolks, fold in the egg whites whisked into stiff peaks. Dip the apples in the batter to cover them all. Gently put the apples into the hot fat and fry on both sides. Drain on absorbent paper and sprinkle with caster sugar mixed with cinnamon.

Frying: 5–7 mins

Margaret's cheese doughnuts

1½ cups flour, 300 g semi-skimmed curd cheese, 3 tbsps sugar, ½ cup milk, 60 g butter, 30 g yeast, 2 eggs, 2 egg yolks, grated rind of 1 orange, 1 tbsp orange juice, salt, fat for frying, caster sugar

Mix the yeast with 1 tsp of sugar, 2–3 tbsps of flour and milk and set in a warm place. Mince the cheese twice. Cream the butter and sugar, whisking all the time gradually add the eggs and egg yolks, then the cheese. Put in the orange zest, sifted flour, yeast, orange juice and salt and knead until the dough is smooth and shiny. Cover with a cloth and leave to rise. Form small balls from the dough, place them on a pastry board dusted with flour, cover and again leave to rise. Fry them in batches in hot fat. Drain them on absorbent paper and sprinkle with caster sugar.

Frying: 5–7 mins

Agatha's quick doughnuts

1½ cups flour, 250 g curd cheese, 1 tsp baking soda, 3 eggs, 1 tsp sugar, salt, 1 tbsp lemon juice, ½ tsp grated lemon rind, caster sugar, fat for frying

Mince the cheese, mix it with the eggs, sugar, salt, lemon zest and juice. Add the sifted flour and baking soda and knead thoroughly. Shape small balls and fry them in hot fat. Drain the doughnuts on absorbent paper, sprinkle them with caster sugar.

Frying: 5–7 mins

Scalded doughnuts

3½ cups flour, 40 g yeast, 8 egg yolks, 2 eggs, 1½ tbsps sugar, 8 tbsps melted butter, 2 cups milk, grated rind of 1 lemon, 1 glass rum, ½ tsp salt, plum jam, lard for frying, caster sugar

Mix the yeast with 1 tsp of sugar and 2–3 tbsps of lukewarm milk. Cover and leave in a warm place. Bring the remaining milk to the boil, take off the heat and slowly pour in 1 cup of flour, mixing all the time to eliminate all lumps. Fold in the yeast, cover and leave in a warm place for an hour. Whisk the egg yolks and whole eggs, gradually add the sugar and continue whisking until the mixture is frothy. Combine it with the dough, add the lemon zest. Cover with a cloth and leave in a warm place. When the dough doubles in volume, turn it onto a pastry board, add some salt, rum and the remaining flour, and knead for 15–20 mins. Gradually pour in the cool melted butter and work it in until all of it has been absorbed. Cover and leave for a while in a warm place, then divide into portions. Roll out each portion and cut out circles. Put some jam in the middle of each circle and carefully seal the edges. Put the doughnuts on a cloth dusted with flour and leave them to rise, then fry them in hot lard.

Frying: 5–7 mins

Vilnius doughnuts

500 g flour, 50 g yeast, 4 egg yolks, 1 cup single cream, 1 cup sugar, 150 g butter, ½ vanilla pod, 10 g bitter almonds, 25 g spirit, 1 tbsp rum, salt, lard for frying

Sift the flour. Blanch and skin the almonds, chop them finely. Pour ½ cup of cream into a pan, add the chopped vanilla and warm up over low heat. Bring to the boil, take off the heat and, mixing all the time, slowly pour in 150 g of flour. Continue mixing until the dough is smooth, then set aside to cool. Mix the yeast with 1 tbsp of sugar and the remaining warm cream, combine it with the dough, pour in another 150 g of flour and knead until the dough is smooth. Cover with a cloth and leave in a warm place for an hour and a half. Whisk the egg yolks, salt and sugar in a bowl resting on top of a pot of simmering water. Combine them with the dough, add the remaining flour and knead well. Pour in the melted butter, add the chopped almonds, spirit and rum and continue kneading until the dough is smooth but not shiny. Shape it into a large ball, brush with melted butter so as it does not dry up. Cover and leave to rise. Shape small balls from the dough, place them on a pastry board dusted with flour, cover with a cloth and leave to rise. Turn them over and again wait until they have risen. Fry the doughnuts in batches in hot fat. Drain them on absorbent paper. While still warm, sprinkle them with caster sugar or dip in some icing.

Frying: 5–7 mins

Faworki, or fried pastry twists

This is another Shrovetide delicacy, the preparation of which does not take as much time as doughnuts. In old Polish cuisine, the name 'faworki' applied to all kinds of pastry fried in deep fat and made from various kinds of dough. Today's faworki are thin wafers similar to the Italian cenci. The dough should have a silky consistency and be easy to roll out. The important thing is to 'pump' the dough with as much air as possible, because it acts as an excellent raising agent. For this reason, the flour must be sifted through a fine sieve and the kneaded dough 'beaten' hard with a rolling-pin for a good fifteen minutes. Having done that, you should cover it with cloth and leave to rest in a cool place for an hour.

There is a simpler method of preparing faworki dough. First whisk egg yolks with sugar, butter, some cream and spirit, as well as the amount of flour that would make it easy to work the mixture well. Then transfer the mixture onto a pastry board, add the remaining flour and quickly knead the dough.

The dough always needs to rest for a good while before you roll it out, but once you roll it out and cut out the faworki, you must fry them immediately, for dried up dough more easily absorbs fat and makes the fried twists less tasty.

The best kind of fat for frying faworki is lard or clarified butter (with a dash of spirit or vodka or else several raw potato slices). You should fry them in boiling hot fat (over medium heat) until they are golden on both sides. Do not put in too many faworki at a time. The more egg yolks and the less fat and sugar, the more crispy the faworki.

The surface of faworki, provided the dough has been kneaded properly and long enough, should be covered in air-filled bubbles, which makes them light and crispy.

Faworki

Take 1 pound of flour, break in 4 whole eggs, add 2 ounces of fresh butter, 2 ounces of caster sugar, 1 cup of single or double cream and 1 glass of arrack. Knead the dough well, roll it out very thinly and cut into 3–inch wide strips. Make a slit through the centre of each strip and pull one end through the opening. Fry in hot lard. Before serving, dust with sugar mixed with vanilla.

(Marta Norkowska, *Najnowsza kuchnia wytworna i gospodarska*, 1904)

English fried cookies

Beat 6 egg yolks with sugar until white. Add enough flour to make batter that will easily drip from a spoon. Heat up one part lard and one part butter. Take a spoonful of batter and drip it into the lard, turning the spoon this way and that. When the cookies turn golden brown on one side, turn them over, then take out and sprinkle with sugar.

Egg white faworki

Whisk 4 egg whites into stiff peaks. Add enough flour to knead dough, and roll it out. Pour in the egg yolks whisked with sugar. Mix thoroughly, then roll out not too thinly. Make faworki and fry them in hot lard.

(*Praktyczny kucharz warszawski*, 1926)

Faworki I

1¼–1½ cups flour, 4 tbsps butter, salt, 3 tbsps caster sugar, 5 egg yolks, 3 tbsps thick sour cream, 1 tbsp spirit or rum, caster sugar with chopped vanilla, lard and 1 tbsp of spirit for frying

Sift the flour. Beat the sugar and butter until frothy. Whisking all the time, gradually add the egg yolks, cream and rum, sifting in enough flour to work the dough easily. Mix for some 5 mins, then turn the dough onto a pastry board. Sift in the remaining flour, add salt and knead well. Cover with a cloth. Pour 1 tbsp of pure alcohol into a skillet, put in the lard and melt it. Divide the dough into portions. Roll out each portion very thinly and cut into 8–10 cm long strips. Make a slit through the middle of each strip and pull one end through the opening. Fry in hot fat over medium heat until golden brown on both sides. Take out with a strainer and drain on absorbent paper. Put on a serving dish and sprinkle with caster sugar.

Frying: 5–7 mins

Faworki II

1¼–1½ cups flour, 5 egg yolks, 1 tbsp thick cream, 1 tbsp caster sugar, 1 tbsp lemon juice, lard for frying, caster sugar for sprinkling

Sift the flour onto a pastry board. Add the egg yolks, cream, caster sugar and lemon juice. Knead them together and work into a dough that would be as hard as for pierogi. Beat it with a rolling pin long enough for bubbles of air to form, then wrap it in a cloth and leave to rest for 1–2 hours. Divide it into portions. Roll out each portion very thinly. Cut into strips 2–3 cm wide and 8–10 cm long. Make a slit through the middle of each strip and pull one end through the opening. Fry in batches in very hot lard until golden brown on both sides (from time to time put a piece of raw potato to the fat). Take out with a strainer and drain on absorbent paper. Put on a serving plate and dust with caster sugar.

Frying: 5–7 mins

CHAPTER XVIII

HOME-MADE BRANDIES AND VODKA

✳ ✳ ✳

According to Oskar Kolberg, every Polish manor house used to have a well-stocked medicine cabinet which contained such cures as alcohol-based infusions from lilies-of-the-valley, spices, cinnamon, cloves, sweet flag, angelica, celeriac, and many others. They served to keep the body warm, prevented common colds and migraines, induced sleep, and cured bad moods and melancholy.

Our great grandmothers knew hundreds of closely guarded secret recipes, which they shared with no one, but their most closely guarded secret were their recipes for ginger cake (often passed down to their successors as part of a bride's dowry), and for vodkas, brandies and liqueurs, which were handed down to the next generations in their last will. Sometimes only one member of a family knew the recipe, and then disclosed the secret only on his or her death bed.

The use of exact proportions was an art all of its own, and one needed years of practice, of trial and error, to attain perfection. Even with a detailed recipe, a lot depended on numerous external factors, such as the amount of water in the fruit, the sugar content, the soil where the fruit had grown, the time of the year when the herbs were collected, or the kind of water used.

Perfection calls for patience and long years of practice. Home-made brandies are ready to be drunk after several months of maturing, but they are at their best if you allow them to rest in bottles for one to three years. Then the taste and aroma get really delicious.

Here are some hints that you should remember:
(1) Never use weak vodka to make a brandy. Use either pure alcohol or a mixture of one part 70% proof vodka and one part pure alcohol.
(2) The fruit must be ripe and unblemished, and the spices fresh and full of flavour, otherwise you will spoil the taste of the brew.
(3) Home-made brandy gets tastier the longer it is left to mature, but only after it has been filtered and bottled. Leaving the fruit, herbs, spices, lemon or orange zest, stones and pips for too long in alcohol is counterproductive, since the excessive acid which is then produced will have an adverse effect on the taste and aroma of the brew.
(4) Fruit and herbs should macerate in tightly sealed jars or bottles.
(5) Filtered and bottled brandy must be tightly sealed (preferably with sealing wax) and stored in a cool, dark place. Only then will it preserve its colour.
(6) On the whole, it is impossible to suggest exact proportions. The general principle is: fill the jar with fruit up to 3/4 of its height and then cover the fruit with alcohol.
(7) Having strained and filtered the brandy, you may add sugar to the fruit, leave it for 12–15 days and then strain the syrup and combine it with the brandy.

(8) Liqueurs are much stronger and sweeter than simple infusions. To make liqueur, you should cover the fruit with pure alcohol which you subsequently strain and slowly pour into hot (80°C) syrup, stirring all the time. Only in this way will you obtain a crystal-clear beverage. The whole operation must be performed very carefully, away from open fire.

(9) The syrup should not be too thick, or the brew will start crystallizing and lose its opacity. It can be made from sugar, but the best syrup is obtained from honey which you have to skim after boiling it.

(10) If you want your liqueur to be thicker, add some potato starch to the syrup. Remember, however, to use a very large pan, because adding potato starch will cause the syrup to foam more.

(11) Home-made liqueurs can be stored for years without losing their flavour. In fact some of them, especially those made from fruit, get better with age.

(12) My advice is to label each bottle of home-made brandy or liqueur with the date of production.

Home-made brandies and liqueurs should be served in very small glasses, and they should be sipped slowly and relished. It is said that they warm up those who are cold, cure various heart conditions, have a reinvigorating effect, and act as aphrodisiacs.

Brandies, especially those with no sugar added, are excellent aperitifs and can also be drunk with meals, while liqueurs are served exclusively with coffee and dessert.

Krupnik

Krupnik is one of the oldest Polish home-made vodkas. It is drunk both hot and cold. Every home 'medicine chest' should contain a bottle of this excellent brew.

Polish krupnik

1 cup honey, 1 cup boiled water, 2 cups spirit, 100 g vodka, ½ vanilla pod, ½ nutmeg, 5–6 cloves,

½ tsp finely chopped ginger, a piece of cinnamon bark, finely chopped rind of 1 orange

Bring the honey and water with cloves to the boil, remove the scum. Add the orange zest, cinnamon, vanilla and nutmeg, cover and simmer for 15 mins. Take off the heat and leave, covered, to cool, then bring to the boil again. Strain the liquid and, while still hot, gradually pour in the alcohol. Stir well. Serve immediately while still hot, or filter it, put into bottles, seal tightly and store for 2–3 months.

Kurp krupnik

2 cups spirit, 1 cup honey, 1 cup boiled water, ½ cup sugar, ½ vanilla pod, ½ nutmeg, 3–4 cloves, a piece of cinnamon bark, 1 tsp grated orange and lemon rind

Bring the water with the spices to the boil, cover and simmer for 10–15 mins. Put the sugar into a large skillet and make caramel. Add the honey, stir well. Pour in the strained spicy water, bring to the boil, then take off the heat. Slowly pour in the alcohol, stirring all the time. Cover well and leave overnight to cool. The following day filter the brew, pour into a large jar and set aside for 10 days. When the sediments settle, carefully pour the liquid into bottles. Cork the bottles tightly and store for 2–3 months.

Lithuanian krupnik

200 g honey, 100 g sugar, 1 tsp dried rose petals, a piece of cinnamon bark, a piece of ginger, 1 small nutmeg, 8 juniper berries, 6 cloves, 2 cups spirit, 1 cup spring water

Put the honey, sugar and spices into a skillet, cover with water, put the lid on and cook for 10 mins. Take off the heat, skim the foam. Pour in the alcohol and stir well. Pour the liquid into a large jar, seal it tightly and leave for 24 hours, then filter the krupnik through a piece of gauze, return to the jar, seal and put in a cool dark place for at least 10 days. Carefully pour it into bottles, seal them tightly and store. The longer you store it, the better it is. Serve hot or cold, preferable with coffee.

Honey krupnik

500 g honey (heather or buckwheat), 2 cups spirit, 100 g brandy, 1 cup boiled water, 1 tsp citric acid

Bring the water with honey to the boil, skim the scum. Take off the heat, add the citric acid and brandy. Stirring all the time, gradually pour in the alcohol. Cover tightly, heat up, then set aside to get cool. Pour into a large jar, cork tightly and leave in a dark place for six months. Pour the clear liquid gently into bottles. Cork and seal the bottles and store them for two years. The longer it matures, the better it is.

Liqueurs

The tradition of liqueurs and cordials goes back to the 4th century BC. Today's liqueurs originated in Italy, where in the Middle Ages they were known as *rosoglio*.

They are rather potent (45 to 55% proof), sweet, and full of flavour. The best of them are produced from brandy or at least with an addition of brandy. Liqueurs are generally divided into three groups:
(1) bitter herby and spicy liqueurs,
(2) fruit liqueurs, frequently produced from fruit infusions,
(3) emulsive liqueurs, for example from eggs.
There are also special liqueurs, such as Goldwasser, as well as coffee, cocoa and tea liqueurs.

Thick, very sweet and delicate liqueurs with a low alcohol content are referred to as creams, for example coffee or banana cream.

Cherry liqueur

Take a large jar of unpitted cherries and pour July honey over them, cover and leave in the sun for at least three months. Decant the syrup, bring it to the boil. Add 70% vodka – 3 cups syrup to 1 cup vodka – and leave to cool down, then pour into bottles, seal tightly and store in the cellar. It should mature for at least a year, for it gets better and stronger with age.

17th century recipe from Nieśwież

Apothecary's liqueur

6 g coriander seeds, 3 g juniper berries, 3 g caraway, 3 g love-in-a-mist seeds, 3 peppercorns, 6 apple pips, 1 clove, ½ g anise, 1 g dried mint, 1½ g dried marjoram, ½ g turmeric, ½ g saffron, 2 cups spirit, 1 cup vodka, 1 cup boiled water, 300 g sugar

Put the herbs and spices (with the exception of saffron) into a glass jar, pour over the vodka and spirit, seal tightly and put away for 2–3 weeks. Decant and filter the liquid. Make a syrup from the water and sugar, skim the scum. Pour in the filtered vodka, stir well, cover and allow to cool. Return to the jar, add saffron, seal and leave in a warm place for another 2–3 weeks. From time to time shake the jar. Filter again, bottle, cork and store for a year or two.

Angelica and lemon balm liqueur

200 g chopped new angelica stems, ½ l each vodka and spirit, a piece of cinnamon bark, 10 cloves, 1 cup fresh lemon balm leaves, ¼ tsp grated nutmeg, 2 cups sugar, 1 cup water

Mix the vodka with the spirit. Put the rinsed and dried sprigs into a large jar, pour over the alcohol mixture, cover and leave for two weeks. Add the rinsed and dried lemon balm leaves, nutmeg, cloves and cinnamon, shake the jar, cover and leave to macerate for 7–10 days. Make a syrup from the sugar and water, allow it to cool, then pour into the jar. Stir well and leave for another 2–3 weeks, shaking the jar from time to time. Decant the liquid, filter it through gauze. Pour into bottles, cork tightly and store for several months. The longer it matures, the better it is.

Angelica liqueur

100 g angelica root, 100 g ginger root, 100 g finely chopped orange peel, 2 cups spirit, 500 g sugar, 3 cups water

Put the finely chopped angelica, ginger and orange peel into a jar, pour over the alcohol, seal the jar and leave in a warm place for 3–4 days, shaking it from time to time. Decant the liquid, filter it through gauze. Make a syrup from the sugar and water, remove the froth. Take off the heat, gradually pour in the alcohol, stirring all the time. Cover and set aside to cool, then return to the jar and leave for another 8–10 days. When the liquid has clarified, pour it gently into bottles, cork them and leave for several months.

Benedictine

30 g sweet flag root, 20 g angelica root, 10 g each finely chopped lemon peel and ginger, 10 g each cardamom, cinnamon bark and dried mint, 5 g each cloves and nutmeg, 1 vanilla pod, a pinch of saffron, 1 l spirit, 1 l boiled water, 500 g honey, 1 tbsp sugar

Scrub thoroughly the roots, dry them, chop very finely, put into a glass jar. Add the remaining spices and herbs, pour in caramel made from the sugar and spirit. Seal the jar and set it aside for 4–5 days. Pour in 3 cups of water, cover, shake well, then filter through gauze. Bring 1 cup of water and the honey to the boil, skim the froth. Take off the heat and slowly pour into the filtered alcohol, mixing all the time. Return the liquid to the jar, cover and, when sediments settle, pour it into bottles. Cork the bottles and store them in a cool, dark place for at least 5–7 months.

Elderberry liqueur

1 kg ripe elderberries, 1 l spirit, 500 g sugar, 1 l boiled water, 6–10 cloves, a piece of cinnamon bark, grated rind of 1 lemon

Pour the rinsed and drained elderberries into a jar. Mix the alcohol with 1 cup of water and cover the berries with it. Seal well and leave aside for two weeks, shaking the jar every day. Bring 3 cups of water, with lemon zest, cloves and cinnamon, to the boil, cover and simmer for 10 mins. Add the sugar and make a thick syrup. Skim the froth, take off the heat. Decant the elderberry infusion and gradually pour it into the syrup, stirring all the time. Return to the jar, close tightly and leave for 2–3 days, then filter and bottle. Cork the bottles and leave them for 2–3 months.

Lemon liqueur

3 lemons, 1 l spirit, 1 kg sugar, 2 cups water, 1 vanilla pod

Scrub the lemons, scald them with boiling water, dry them and peel finely, then cut the rind into strips. Put the lemon strips into a jar together with vanilla, pour over half the alcohol and leave aside for 4–5 days. Cut the lemons in half, put them into another jar and cover with the remaining alcohol. Seal the jar tightly and set aside for 2–3 days. Make a thick syrup from the sugar and water, skim the froth. Take off the heat and, stirring all the time, gradually pour in the filtered alcohol. Return to the jar, seal and leave for two days. Filter again, then pour into bottles. Cork the bottles and store them for at least half a year.

Bilberry liqueur

200 g bilberries, 10 g each cloves and finely chopped orange peel, 20 g piece cinnamon bark, 1 l spirit, 1½ kg honey, 2 cups boiled water

Put the berries and spices into a jar, cover them with the alcohol. Seal, shake well and set aside for 2–3 weeks, shaking from time to time. Bring the water and honey to the boil, remove the froth. Take off the heat and slowly pour in the filtered alcohol. Return to the jar, seal tightly and leave for 2–3 weeks, then filter again, bottle, cork and place in a cool dark place for several months.

Juniper liqueur

50 g juniper berries, 1 tbsp juniper needles, 3 cups spirit, 600 g honey, 1 cup boiled water

Put the berries and needles into a jar, cover them with the alcohol and seal well. Set aside for 10–12 days, shaking the jar from time to time, then filter the infusion. Make a syrup from the honey and water, skim the froth. Take off the heat and, stirring all the time, slowly pour in the filtered infusion. Return to the jar and leave for another 2–3 days, then filter again. Bottle and cork the liqueur and store it for 3–4 months.

Blackberry liqueur

forest blackberries (1 l of juice), 400 g sugar, 5 g each cloves and cinnamon bark, 1 small vanilla pod, 2 cups spirit, 1½ cups brandy

Liquidize and sieve the raspberries. Make a syrup from the sugar and water, add the cloves, cinnamon, vanilla and liquidized raspberries, and simmer for 5 mins. Take off the heat and, stirring all the time, slowly pour in the alcohol. Pour the mixture into a jar, seal tightly and set aside for two weeks, shaking the jar every day. Filter the liquid, add the brandy, seal again and leave for a month. Pour into bottles, cork them and leave for 6–8 months.

Caraway liqueur

50 g caraway seeds, 1 l spirit, 1 l boiled water, 750 g sugar

Pound the caraway in a mortar. Put it into a jar, pour over the alcohol, seal tightly, shake vigorously and set aside for two weeks, shaking the jar every day. Make a syrup from the sugar and water, remove the froth. Take off the heat and slowly pour in the caraway infusion. Cover and heat up a bit, then take off the heat and allow to cool. Filter the infusion, then return it to the jar and leave for another 2–3 days. Filter again and pour into bottles.

Spicy liqueur

8–10 cloves, grated nutmeg, 1 small piece of cinnamon bark, 1 tbsp dried mint, 1 tbsp finely chopped ginger, 1 tbsp grated lemon rind, finely chopped peel of 1 orange, 1 l spirit, ½ cup honey, 1 cup sugar, 4 cups boiled water

Put the spices into a jar, cover them with the alcohol, seal the jar and set aside for 3–4 days, shaking it every day. Make caramel from ½ cup of sugar, dissolved in 1 cup of hot water. Allow it to cool a bit, then add to the jar. Seal it again tightly and leave for two days. Bring 3 cups of water with sugar and honey to the boil, remove the froth, then take off the heat. Pour in the filtered infusion, stir and return to the jar. Seal the jar and set aside for 2–3 days. Filter again, pour into bottles and leave for several months.

Lime flower liqueur

1 cup fresh lime-tree flowers, 2 cups spirit, 600 g sugar, 1 cup spring water

Put the freshly picked lime flowers into a jar, cover them with the alcohol. Seal the jar, shake it and leave aside for four days. Decant the infusion and filter it through gauze. Make a thick syrup from the sugar and water, skim the froth. Take off the heat and, stirring all the time, slowly pour in the infusion. Cover, allow to cool, then pour into bottles. Cork the bottles and leave them for several months.

Walnut liqueur

500 g green walnuts, 1 l spirit, 500 g sugar, 2 cups water, 3 bitter almonds, 10–12 cloves, a piece of cinnamon bark

Rinse and dry the nuts, cut them into thick slices. Put the nuts, cinnamon and cloves into a jar, cover with the alcohol mixed with 1 cup of water. Seal the jar and set it aside for 3–4 weeks, shaking it every day. Decant the liquid, filter it through cheesecloth. Make a thick syrup from the sugar and 1 cup of water, skim the froth. Take off the heat and, stirring all the time, slowly add the filtered infusion. Cover and leave to cool completely. Filter again, pour into bottles. Store in a dark, cool place for at least a year. The liqueur has a fine golden-brown colour and a slightly bitter taste.

Quince liqueur

4 kg ripe quinces, 3 kg sugar, 1 vanilla pod, 5 cups water, 1½ l brandy, ½ cup spirit

Rinse and dry the fruit. Put them into a large skillet, cover with water. Bring to the boil, then simmer for 40 mins. Strain the liquid, add the sugar and vanilla and make a thick syrup, skim the froth. Take off the heat and, stirring all the time, slowly pour in the mixed spirits. Cover the pan and leave to cool, then filter the liqueur. Pour it into bottles, cork them tightly. This is regarded as a lady's drink.

Blackcurrant liqueur

3 l blackcurrant juice, 2 kg sugar, 1 l boiled water, 10 g allspice, 1 packet brewer's yeast, 1 kg sugar, 3 cups spirit

Pour the juice into a large jar, add 2 kg of sugar, allspice, water and yeast. Leave to ferment for three weeks. Add 1 kg of sugar more and set aside for another 6 weeks, then pour in the spirit, cover tightly and leave in a dark place to clarify. Filter the liqueur and pour it into bottles. Cork the bottles and store them for 3–4 months.

Rose hip liqueur

500 g rose hips, rind of 1 orange, 1 small piece of cinnamon bark, 1 cup honey, 1 cup water, 1 l brandy, ½ cup spirit

Top and tail the rose hips, remove the seeds. Put them into a jar together with the chopped orange peel and cinnamon. Cover with the mixed spirits, seal well and leave in the sunshine for two weeks, shaking the jar every day. Decant the liquid. Make a syrup from the honey and water, remove the froth. Slowly pour in the filtered infusion, stir well, seal tightly and set aside for 2–3 days. Filter again, pour into bottles, cork well and store for several months.

Sweet flag liqueur

50 g sweet flag roots, 50 cloves, 500 g sugar, 3 cups water, 1 l spirit

Scrub the roots, chop them finely. Put them into a jar, add the cloves, cover with the alcohol. Seal the jar and set aside for 10 days, shaking it every day. Make a syrup from the sugar and water, remove the froth. Take off the heat and slowly pour in the filtered infusion. Stir well, cover and leave overnight. Filter again, bottle, cork and store in a dark cool place for 3–4 months.

Sloe liqueur

1 kg sloes picked after early frost, 5–6 cloves, a piece of cinnamon bark, ½ tsp grated nutmeg, 4 cups vodka, 1 cup spirit, 500 g sugar, 2 cups water

Rinse the sloe and put them into a hot oven for several minutes, then stone them. Put the pulp and 6–8 stones into a jar, add the spices. Cover with the mixed spirits, seal well and leave for 10–12 days, shaking the jar from time to time. Put the infusion through cheesecloth, squeeze it out well. Make a syrup from the sugar and water, remove the froth. Take off the heat. Stirring all the time, slowly pour in

the infusion. Stir well, return to the jar, cover and leave for 2–3 days, then filter and bottle the liqueur.

Herby liqueur

25 g coriander seeds, 2 g aniseed, 2 g dried peppermint, 2 g dried sage, 2 g saffron, 4 g angelica root, 4 kg sugar, 2 l boiled water, 5 cups spirit

Put the herbs into a jar, add 3 cups of spirit. Seal tightly, shake well and place in a dark, cool place for 10–12 days. Put saffron into a small jar, add 1 large glass of spirit, seal the jar. In a large skillet, make a syrup from the sugar and water, remove the froth. Take it off the heat. Filter the macerated herbs and saffron, mix the liquid with the remaining spirit and slowly pour into the syrup, stirring all the time. Cover and leave overnight. Filter again, bottle, cork and store for 4–5 months.

Home-made brandies and vodka

Old Polish tea vodka

1 l 90% spirit, ¾ l Hungarian wine, 1 large glass slivovitz, 50 g carob, 20 g black tea leaves, 100 g sugar, ½ l water

Bring the water, with the sugar and finely chopped carob, to the boil, put in the tea leaves and make a strong infusion. Pour the spirit into a glass jar, add the strained tea infusion, wine and slivovitz. Shake vigorously, seal tightly and leave for 3 months to mature.

Vodka from blackcurrant leaves

When blackcurrant shrubs sprout the first fine shoots in spring, cut some off, together with their leaves. Put them in a glass jar, press them down lightly. Pour in 45% proof vodka and leave for a week. Decant the liquid and pour more vodka over the shoots, enough to cover them. Seal the jar and leave it now for two weeks, shaking it from time to time. Decant the liquid, squeeze out the leaves well. Mix the two infusions. Add some lemon juice to the mixture and pour into bottles. Cork the bottles and store them for at least half a year.

Blackcurrant vodka (smorodinovka)

Stalk some very ripe blackcurrants, put them into a glass jar, cover with 1 part pure alcohol to 1 part vodka made from blackcurrant leaves. Cork the jar and set it for 6–8 months in a sunny place, then strain the infusion, pour it into a smaller jar and seal tightly. Add sugar to the fruit – ½ kg of sugar to 1 l of infusion. Seal the jar and set it aside for several days, shaking from time to time. When the sugar has dissolved completely, strain the syrup, add it to the small jar, mix thoroughly. Seal the jar and leave it for 3 days, then filter the vodka through a piece of cheesecloth. Pour it into bottles, seal tightly and leave for at least half a year. The longer you allow it to mature, the better it becomes.

Anisette

¼ cup aniseed, 1 cinnamon stick, grated rind of ½ lemon, 5 cloves, 2 l 45% vodka

Put aniseed, lemon zest, crumbled cinnamon bark and cloves into a jar, add the vodka. Seal the jar and keep it in a warm place for a month, shaking it occasionally. Strain the infusion, filter it through a cloth and pour into bottles. Leave it to mature for 2–3 months.

Peach brandy

500 g sugar per 1 kg peaches, 4 cups vodka, 1 cup spirit

Halve and stone the peaches. Put the halves into a jar, add the sugar, cover with a cloth and leave overnight. Crack 3–4 stones, take out the kernels and add them to the fruit. Pour in the mixed spirits, seal the jar and leave it in a sunny place for three weeks, shaking it often, then transfer it to a warm place for another two weeks. Strain the infusion, filter it, pour into bottles and store for at least half a year to mature. Seal the peach halves in small jars; they will come in useful as an excellent addition to salads and desserts.

Old Polish cornelian cherry brandy

Use very ripe fruit to make this vodka. Put the fruit into a glass jar to ¾ of its height, fill the jar with 70% proof vodka (1 part vodka to 1 part pure alcohol). Seal the jar and leave it for a year. Strain the infusion, filter it and pour into another jar. Sprinkle the fruit generously with sugar (the amount depends on individual preferences), seal the jar and leave for 2 or 3 weeks, shaking it every day, by which time the sugar should have dissolved. Force the fruit through a cloth, pour the syrup into the vodka jar, cork it and leave for 3–4 days, then filter and pour into bottles. Keep the bottles in a cool, dark place and forget about it, for the longer it matures, the better it is.

Cornelian cherry vodka

300 g cornelian cherries, 100 g dried bilberries, 100 g raisins, 6 cups vodka, 2 cups spirit, ½ cup honey

The cherries should be very ripe, picked in late August or early September. Crush the cherries, put them into a jar together with the bilberries and raisins. Pour in the spirit, vodka and honey, shake well, seal the jar and leave for 2–3 months, shaking occasionally. Strain the infusion, filter it and bottle. Seal the bottles tightly and store them for at least six months. The longer you keep it, the better it is.

Angelica brandy

Fresh angelica roots and stems are obviously the best, but you may also use dried ones. When you make the brandy from freshly cut roots and stems, it will have a mellow olive-green colour. Fresh roots should be harvested in May or early June and they should be first scrubbed and washed thoroughly, and then diced.

50 g diced angelica root and 100 g diced angelica stem, 1 tsp grated orange rind, 4–5 grains cardamom, 3 l 45% vodka

Put all the condiments into a jar, cover with the vodka. Seal the jar and leave it in a warm place for 8–10 days, then filter the infusion and bottle it. Leave to mature for several months. The longer it matures in bottles, the better it becomes.

Pear brandy

Choose aromatic, mellow fruit. Rinse and dry the pears, remove the stalks. Dice them with a stainless-steel knife (do not remove the cores and pips), put into a jar to ¾ its height, fill with 75% proof alcohol (pure spirit mixed with vodka). Seal tightly and keep at room temperature for 6–8 months. Strain the infusion. Add sugar to the fruit (300–350 g sugar to 1 kg fruit), seal the jar again and leave for 2–3 months, shaking it regularly until the sugar has dissolved. Strain the syrup, force the fruit through a cloth. Combine the syrup and fruit purée with the infusion. Pour into a jar and leave for 3–4 days, then filter and pour into bottles. Seal the bottles and leave them in a cool, dark place for at least a year.

Tea brandy

4 tbsps tea leaves, 2 tbsps honey, 1 vanilla pod, 2 cups spirit, 2 cups sweet Tokay, ½ cup brandy, 1 cup spring water

Bring the water mixed with the honey and finely chopped vanilla to the boil. Put in the tea leaves and make a strong tea infusion. Strain the liquid, pour it into a small jar, add the Tokay, brandy and spirit, mix well, then seal and set aside for at least 2–3 months, shaking from time to time. Filter it and pour into bottles. Leave to mature for at least 2 months.

Rowanberry vodka

150 g rowanberries harvested after early frost, 20 g stoned prunes, 20 g raisins, 200 g sugar, 5 cups vodka, 1 cup spirit, 2 cups boiled spring water

Put the berries into a jar, cover them with the vodka and spirit and set aside for four weeks. Strain the infusion, pour it into a jar. Add the sugar to the fruit and stand aside for 8–10 days, shaking frequently to dissolve the sugar, then strain the syrup and add it to the infusion. Mix the fruit with the water and leave for 2 days, then strain the liquid and add to the vodka. Mix well, seal and leave for 3–4 months. Filter through a cloth and pour into bottles.

Sweet flag vodka

Sweet flag roots are best harvested in May or early June. They must be cleaned and washed well, and then diced.

50 g fresh or 20 g dried sweet flag root, 1 tbsp grated orange rind, several grains of cardamom, 1 crushed cinnamon stick, 3 l 45% vodka, 100 g brandy

Put all the condiments into a jar, pour in the vodka, cover and leave in a warm place for 8–10 days, shaking every day. Strain the infusion, filter it, mix with the brandy and pour into bottles. Leave to mature for several months. Our great-grandmothers used to serve this vodka with honey and sweet flag preserve.

Podlasie brandy

5 stoned prunes, 3–4 cloves, ½ vanilla pod, 2 tbsps raisins, 3–4 black peppercorns, 1–2 grains allspice, 1 bay leaf, 1 cup sugar, 1–2 tbsps water, 3 cups vodka, 1 cup spirit

Put the pounded cloves, peppercorns and allspice into a jar, add the chopped vanilla pod, the crumbled bay leaf, the prunes cut into strips and raisins. Make a light-brown caramel from the sugar and 1–2 tbsps of water and pour it into the jar, together with the vodka and spirit. Seal the jar tightly and set aside for 3–4 days, shaking every day. Filter the brandy, bottle it and store in a dry, cool dark place for several months.

Raspberry vodka

4 l raspberries, 2 l spirit, 2 l boiled water, 2½ kg sugar

Put the ripe raspberries into a large jar. Pour in a thick syrup made from the sugar and water, add the spirit. Seal tightly and keep at room temperature. Do not move or shake the jar for two weeks, by which time the fruit should settle at the bottom, leaving crystal-clear vodka at the top. Pour the vodka off very carefully and bottle it (do not filter, or it will lose its aroma). Seal the bottles and store them in a dark, cool place for at least 8–10 months.

Barbara's vodka

2 kg fresh raspberries, 1 kg sugar, ½ l deep-brown rum, 1 l 45% vodka, 2 lemons, 10–15 apricot stones, 2 cups boiled water

Crush the apricots stones, take out the pulp, remove the skin. Make a syrup from the sugar and water, with the apricot kernels and lemon juice, bring it to the boil. Purée the raspberries in a pan, pour in the cool syrup, cover and leave overnight. Bring to the boil again, strain through a thick cloth. While still hot, mix it with rum and vodka. Bottle and cork it, and store in a dark place.

Apricot brandy

Fill a large jar to ¾ its height with apricots cut into quarters, crush several apricot stones and add the kernels to the fruit. Pour in 90% proof alcohol to cover the fruit, cork tightly and keep in a warm place for 8–9 months. Decant the infusion, pour into a jar. Sprinkle the fruit generously with sugar (400 g sugar to 1 kg apricots), cover and leave in a warm place for 2–3 weeks, shaking the jar every day. When the sugar has dissolved, decant the syrup and force the fruit through a cloth. Add the syrup and fruit pulp to the infusion, mix well and leave for 4–5 days, then filter, bottle and store for half a year.

Walnut vodka

6 fresh green (unripe) walnuts, 2 cups 40% vodka, 1 cup spirit, 2 cups spring water, 200 g sugar

Chop the walnuts (picked in early July) finely with a strainless knife, put them into a jar. Add the vodka and seal the jar tightly. Leave for 6 weeks, shaking the jar occasionally. Make a syrup from the sugar and water, bring it to the boil, then allow it to cool. Mix it with the strained vodka infusion and the spirit. Bottle and cork the vodka, and store it for at least 2 weeks. An excellent remedy for dyspepsia.

Quince brandy

Cut the quince into cubes, remove the seeds. Put alternating layers of quince and sugar (1 kg sugar to 1 kg quince) in a jar , cover with a cloth and leave in a sunny place for 3–4 days. Add 70% proof alcohol, cover and leave for 4 months. Decant the infusion, bottle it and store preferably for 3 years. This is an excellent aromatic drink.

Polish cherry brandy

2 l bitter cherries, 1½ l spirit, 400 g July honey, 2 l mead

Put the cherries (with the stones) into a jar, cover them with the spirit. Seal the jar and set it in a sunny place for 5–6 weeks, shaking every day. Decant the liquid, press the fruit through thick cheesecloth. Melt the honey in a large pan and the mead, and bring to the boil. Take off the heat and allow to cool a bit. Stirring all the time, slowly pour in the cherry infusion. Filter it, bottle and cork, and store in a dark, cool place for at least a year.

Spicy orange vodka

10 oranges, 2 lemons, 1 vanilla pod, 1 cinnamon stick, 15 cloves, 1½ kg sugar, 5 cups boiled water, 2 l spirit

Scrub the citrus fruit, scald them with boiling water. Grate the rind and dice the pulp, remove the pips. Put the zest and fruit into a jar. Add the chopped vanilla, cinnamon and cloves, pour in the spirit mixed with 2 cups of water. Seal the jar tightly and set in a warm place for 2–3 weeks, then decant the infusion, press the fruit through cheesecloth. Combine the juice with the infusion and filter. Make a thick syrup from the sugar and 3 cups of water, remove the froth. Take off the heat and immediately gently pour in the brandy, stirring all the time. Chill the vodka in cold water or on ice, bottle and cork it, and leave to mature for several months.

Vodka with stout

2 bottles (0.33 l each) stout, 250 g sugar, 1 vanilla pod, 1 cup spirit

Bring the stout, with the sugar and chopped vanilla, to the boil, allow it to cool, then add the spirit. Pour the mixture into a jar, seal and leave for 2–3 days, then filter, bottle and leave to stand for at least a year.

Wild stawberry brandy

Excellent, aromatic, beautiful in colour and delicious to taste. It is best prepared from fresh forest fruit. Put wild strawberries into a jar, cover with 70% proof alcohol (1 part spirit to 1 part vodka) and leave to stand in a sunny place for 24 hours, but not longer! If you leave it longer, the tiny seeds of the fruit will give it an unpleasant bitter taste. Decant the infusion, squeeze the fruit through cheesecloth. For each litre of the infusion make a thick syrup from 500 g of sugar and 1 cup of water; skim the froth, take off the heat. While still hot, carefully pour in the alcoholic infusion, add 1 tbsp of lemon juice, and cool quickly by putting the pan into cold water or on ice. Stir well. Pour into bottles, cork and leave to stand for at least half a year.

Buckthorn vodka

Buckthorn is excellent in vodka, you must only remember that the stains left by it are extremely stubborn. The best time to harvest the fruits is soon after the early frost when they are most tasty (earlier their taste tends to be bitter). They must be processed immediately because they quickly ferment. Buckthorn vodka has a fine ruby red colour and an interesting flavour.
2 kg buckthorn fruit, 2 kg sugar, 2½ l 75% alcohol

Put the fruit into a jar, add 1½ kg of sugar and alcohol, shake lightly and leave to stand for 3–4 months. Decant the infusion into another jar. Add the remaining sugar to the fruit and set aside in a warm place for 2–3 weeks, shaking the jar frequently. When sugar has dissolved, strain the syrup through cheesecloth, combine with the infusion and leave for 2–3 days. Filter, bottle, cork and store a dark, cool place for several months.

Auntie's slivovitz

3 kg ripe stoned purple plums, 15 plum stones, 2 cups July honey, 1 l spirit, 3 l vodka, 50 g raisins, 250 g sweet grapes, 250 g stoned prunes, 0.75 l brandy

Crush the stones, take out the kernels. Put them into a jar together with the halves plums, add the honey, cover with cheesecloth and leave in a sunny place for 3 weeks. Pour in the spirit and 1 l of vodka, seal tightly and set aside for 4 weeks. Add the raisins, grapes and 1 l of vodka, cork and leave in a warm place till Christmas. Put the prunes in another jar, add 1 l of vodka, seal well and and also leave till Christmas. Pour off the liquid from both jars, filter it and pour into a large jar. Add the brandy, cork and set aside for 3 weeks. Bottle and cork the slivovitz and store it for at least a year. Making this golden-brown vodka

is quite an effort, but it is by no means wasted because the taste of the slivovitz is incomparable.

Dry slivovitz

This is one of the best home-made vodkas, produced from a variety of plums, beginning from the early varieties and ending with September quetsche plums. Gradually, as the season goes on, put successive varieties of plums (with stones) into a large jar. Cover with 90% proof spirit, seal tightly and leave in a sunny place for 1–2 weeks. Take the jar into a warm place and stand it there for a year. Decant the liquid, filter it and bottle. Add sugar to the fruit and leave for 2–3 weeks, shaking the jar from time to time. Squeeze the fruit through a thick gauze, filter it and bottle. The fruit juice makes an excellent liqueur.

Uncle's sloe vodka

200 g sloes, 100 g stoned prunes, 80 g raisins, 6 cups vodka, ½ cup spirit

Rinse the sloes picked after the first autumn frost, dry them, prick with a needle and put into a jar. Add the raisins and prunes cut into strips, cover with the mixed spirits. Shake well and set aside for 6 weeks, shaking from time to time. Decant the infusion, squeeze out the juice from the berries. Add it to the infusion, return the vodka to the jar and leave for another 2 weeks, then filter and bottle it.

Cranberry vodka

This is a very refreshing alcoholic drink made from berries picked after a spell of frosty weather.
cranberries, sugar, water, spirit, almond flavour

Put the cranberries into a jar (to ¾ its height), fill it up with the spirit. Seal the jar tightly and set aside in a warm place for 2 weeks. Decant the infusion, press the fruit through a piece of gauze. Mix the juice with the infusion. For one litre of liquid make syrup from 3 cups of sugar and 2½ cups of water, remove the froth. Add the almond flavour to the syrup (several drops per 1 litre). Take off the heat, slowly pour in the vodka, stirring all the time. Cool it quickly by dipping the pan in cold water. Return to the, seal and leave to mature for several days, then carefully filter and bottle the vodka, and store for several months.

CHAPTER XIX

SWEET AND SAVOURY PRESERVES AND PICKLES

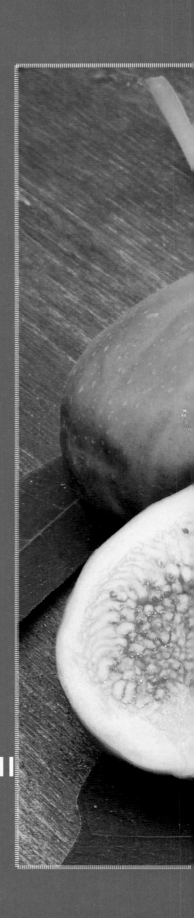

Fruit preserves

Confiture, or fruit cooked in thick syrup, is a speciality of old Polish cuisine. Such preserves were made from all kinds of fruit, but the greatest fame was enjoyed by confiture of rose petals and rose hip, wild strawberries, green gooseberries, pears and apricots. When they are prepared in the right way, the fruits remain whole, are glassy and suspended evenly in the thick syrup.

Wild strawberry preserve

500 g wild strawberries, 1 kg sugar,
1 cup water, 1 tsp brandy

Rinse and drain the strawberries, put them in a china bowl. Make a syrup from water and some sugar. Cover the strawberries with the hot syrup and leave overnight. Pour off the syrup into a pan, add 1 cup of sugar, bring to the boil. Allow it to cool a bit, then pour over the strawberries. Repeat the procedure on the third day, using the remaining sugar. On the fourth day, bring the poured off syrup to the boil, add the brandy and then the strawberries. Simmer for a while, shaking the pan from time to time. Put hot fruit into glass jars and seal well.

Blackcurrant preserve

1 kg cleaned blackcurrants, 1½ kg sugar

Put sugar in a pan, add enough water to be absorbed by the sugar and make a syrup. Put the blackcurants into the hot syrup and cook over low heat for 15–20 mins.

Pour it into a china bowl and allow to cool, then put into jars and seal well.

Mirabelle preserve

2½ kg mirabelles, 2½ kg sugar, juice of
2 lemons, grated rind of 1 lemon

Rinse and dry the plums, stone them. Put the plums in a pan, cover with the sugar and leave overnight. Bring the plums to the boil, then simmer for an hour, stirring frequently. Add the lemon juice and zest and, stirring frequently, cook for over an hour longer. Transfer the hot plums into jars, seal well.

Peach and apricot preserve

500 g peaches, 500 g apricots, 1 kg sugar, 100 g
orange liqueur, 2 tbsps dry white wine

Blanch the fruit, rinse under cold water, then drain, skin and stone. Crack several peach stones and chop the kernels finely. Dice half of the fruit, put in a pan, cover with the sugar and set aside for an hour, then sprinkle with the wine. Bring the diced fruit to the boil and, stirring all the time, cook over low heat until sugar has dissolved. Add the liqueur, chopped kernels and the remaining fruit cut into quarters and cook over low heat for another 20 mins, stirring gently. Put the thick jam into jars, seal well.

Pear preserve

1½ kg pears, 750 g sugar, juice of 1 lemon, 1 vanilla pod, a piece of ginger, 1 tbsp brandy, 1 cup water

Put the sugar in a pan, add 1 cup of water (or as much as the sugar can absorb) and make a syrup. Put in the chopped vanilla and simmer for several minutes, then take it out. Peel and core the pears, cut them into quarters and sprinkle with lemon juice. Put the pears into the hot syrup and simmer until the syrup has become translucent. Add the chopped ginger and brandy, stir gently and cook for a bit longer. Put into jars, seal well.

Old Polish preserve

750 g pears, 700 g lemons, 1 kg lime honey, 1 cup stoned bitter cherries, ½ cup cleaned redcurrants, ½ cup sultanas, ½ cup brandy

Pour the brandy over the cherries, cover and set aside for 2–3 hours. Blanch and drain the raisins. Peel the lemons, peel and core the pears. Cut them lengthwise into eight wedges. Remove the pips. Heat the honey in a pan, put in the pears, lemons, raisins and cherries together with brandy. Cook over low heat for 10–15 mins. Take off the heat, allow to cool a bit, add the redcurrants and shake the pan. Bring to the boil again, skim the froth, then cook over low heat for 40 mins, until the fruit is glassy. Put the hot preserve into jars, seal well.

Rose-petal preserve

500 g cabbage rose petals, 1 kg sugar, juice of 1½ lemons, ½ tsp grated lemon rind

Trim the white and yellowed tips of petals with scissors. Put the petals in a colander, pour over first boiling and then cold water, drain well. Spread the petals in a flat dish, sprinkle with lemon juice. Make a thick syrup from the sugar and 1 cup of water in a preserving pan, skim the froth. Put the petals into the boiling syrup, shake the pan to separate the petals. Take off the heat and leave aside overnight. Stirring with a wooden spatula to prevent the petals from sticking together, cook over low heat for 30 mins until the petals are translucent and the syrup is thick. Towards

the end, add the remaining juice and lemon zest, cook for a while longer, then take off the heat and stir continuously until the jam is cool. Put the cold preserve into clean jars and seal immediately.

Rose hip preserve

1 kg rose hips, 3 cups water, 1 kg sugar, 1 tbsp lemon juice

Top and tail the rosehips, remove seeds, rinse and drain well. Bring 3 cups of water to the boil, put in the rosehips and cook for 5 mins, then drain. Strain the reserved liquid through a piece of gauze, add 500 g of sugar and make a syrup. Put the rose hips into the boiling syrup, bring to the boil, take off the heat and leave aside overnight. Take out the fruit with a strainer. Bring the syrup to the boil, add the remaining sugar and lemon juice and cook for 10 mins, stirring occasionally. Put in the fruit and cook for another 15 mins, shaking the pan from time to time. Put into jars, seal well.

Green tomato jam

1 kg small green tomatoes, 1 kg sugar, 2 tbsps spirit, 1 tbsp finely chopped orange peel, juice and grated rind of 1 lemon

Rinse the tomatoes, cut them into quarters, remove the seeds. Put the tomatoes in a bowl, sprinkle them with the spirit and leave aside for 12 hours. Make a thick syrup from the sugar and 1 cup of water, skim the froth. Put in the tomatoes (and their juice) into the boiling syrup, shake the pan. Bring to the boil, then cook over low heat for 5 mins and set aside overnight. Cook the tomatoes until they are glassy, skim the froth. Towards the end, add the orange peel, lemon juice and zest, stir gently but thoroughly. Cool a bit, then put into clean jars and seal well.

Walnut preserve

1 kg green walnuts (preferably harvested in late June or early July), 1½ kg sugar, a piece of cinnamon bark, 2–3 cloves, 2 cups water

Rinse the walnuts, prick them with a toothpick, cover with cold water and soak for 3 days, changing water several times. Drain them, cover with hot water and cook over low heat until tender, then drain them again. Bring 2 cups of water to the boil in a large pan, put in the sugar, add the cinnamon and cloves. Cook until the sugar has dissolved, skim the froth and leave to cool. Cover the walnuts with the cool syrup and set aside for another 3 days. Take the nuts out, bring the syrup to the boil, skim the froth. Pour the syrup over the walnuts and leave for 12 hours. Cook the nuts thrice for 5 mins, each time allowing the jam to cool and removing the scum. Leave the jam to cool, then put it into clean jars and seal immediately. If you follow the procedure scrupulously, the jam should be deep black in colour.

Rowanberry preserve

1 kg rowanberries (harvested after early frost), 2 cups water, 1.20 kg sugar, 1 tbsp lemon juice, a small piece of cinnamon bark, 2 cups water

Rinse and drain the berries, remove the stems. Bring 2 cups of water to the boil, put in the berries and cook for 5–7 mins, then drain them. Bring 2 cups of water and 600 g of sugar to the boil, put the berries into the boiling syrup and cook for 10 mins, then set aside overnight. Pour off the syrup into a pan, add the cinnamon and remaining sugar and cook over low heat for 15 mins, stirring all the time. Take out the cinnamon, put in the rowanberries and lemon juice. Cook for 20–25 mins, shaking the pan from time to time. Put the hot preparation into jars and seal well.

Barberry preserve

500 g barberries (preferably stoneless variety), 1½ kg sugar, water, 1 glass brandy

Rinse and drain the berries. Put the sugar into a preserving pan, add as much water as the sugar can absorb, bring to the boil. Put the berries into the boiling syrup and cook over low heat for 15–20 mins, skim the froth. Pour in the brandy and cook for a minute or two. When the syrup has thicknened, take off the heat. Pour the jam into a china bowl, allow it to cool, then put into jars and seal well.

Crab-apple preserve

500 g crab apples, 1 kg sugar, water

Rinse the apples, put them into boiling water for several minutes, then drain. Make a syrup from 500 g of sugar and enough water to absorb it. Put the apples in a china bowl, cover with the warm (not hot) syrup and leave overnight. Pour off the syrup, combine it with 1 cup of sugar, bring to the boil and again pour over the apples. Repeat the procedure on the third day, using the remaining sugar. On the fourth day, pour off the syrup and cook it until it has thickened, put in the apples and cook together for a while, shaking the pan from time to time. Leave to cool, then put into jars and seal well.

Angelica preserve

1 kg fresh, tender angelica stems and leafy sprigs, juice and grated rind of 1 lemon, a pinch of salt, 5 l water, 1 kg sugar, ¾ cup water

Bring 5 l of water, with the juice, lemon zest and salt, to the boil. Cut the angelica stems into smaller pieces and put into the boiling water. Take off the heat and leave aside for 24 hours, then drain, rinse and dry them. Make a thick syrup from the sugar and ¾ cup of water, put in the angelica stems, bring to the boil. Take off the heat. Repeat this operation for several days, allowing 20–25 mins in all for cooking, until the syrup is thick and light green. On the last day, put the boiling hot preserve into clean jars, seal well. Turn the jars upside down, cover them with a blanket and leave to cool completely.

Candied sweet flag

500 g sweet flag roots, cleaned and diced, 1 kg sugar, 1 l boiled water

Put the sweet flag into boiling water and cook for 2–3 mins, then drain it. Repeat the operation two or three times, each time using fresh water. Drain the sweet flag, rinse it under cold water. Make a syrup from the sugar and water, pour it over the blanched sweet flag and leave aside overnight. Repeat the whole procedure for three days. On the forth day, cook it long enough for the sugar to crystallize, then allow it to cool. Arrange the sweet flag pieces on aluminium foil and put into a medium-hot oven to dry off.

Chocolate candies

500 g sweet flag roots, 2 cups sugar, 1 cup water, 2 tbsps lemon juice, 1 bar of dark chocolate

Make a thick syrup, add the lemon juice. Clean the sweet flag thoroughly, peel it and put into boiling water for several minutes, then rinse under cold water. Slice it and put into the boiling syrup. Stirring all the time, cook until sugar begins to crystallize, then take off the heat and leave to cool. Take out the sweet flag, drain it. Melt the chocolate in a small pan. Dip each piece of sweet flag in it, put on a sheet of aluminium foil and leave for the chocolate to set. These original, healthy and nice-tasting sweets with a sharp tang are recommended in particular for children and elderly people, as sweet flag is known to have a very beneficial effect on the digestive system.

Candied angelica

600 g young angelica stems, 3 cups sugar, 1 cup water, 1 tbsp lemon juice, 1–2 tbsps caster sugar

Strip the stringy fibres from the angelica stems, clean the stems and leafy sprigs, cut them into small pieces. Make a syrup from the water, sugar and lemon juice, put in the angelica. Bring to the boil, take off the heat and leave aside overnight. Repeat the operation for 3 days. On the fourth day, simmer over low heat until most of the water has evaporated. Take the angelica pieces out, lay them out on a baking sheet, dust with caster sugar and dry in a slow oven. Candied angelica is used in creams, cakes, tarts and pastries. Chewing angelica 'candies' helps to cure sore gums.

Jellies

Every good housewife's larder should contain some fruit jellies, which come in very handy when making sauces, decorating desserts, or stuffing cakes and pastries. The thing to remember is that they should not be too thick.

Quince jelly

2 kg quinces, sugar (70 g for 100 ml of quince juice)

Rinse the quinces, slice them, cover with 3 l of water and cook for 30 mins, then take off the heat and leave aside for 12 hours. Pour the cooked fruit into a fine strainer and let the juice run through without pressing the fruit pulp. Return the juice to the pan, add the right amount of sugar and cook for 20 mins; towards the end skim the froth. Pour a few drops of the juice onto a cold plate: if it solidifies quickly, the jelly is ready for potting. Pour jelly into clean jars, seal well and leave to cool.

Blackcurrant jelly

2 kg blackcurrants, sugar (80 g for 100 ml of juice)

Clean and rinse the blackcurants, top and tail them. Mash them with a fork and put into a pan. Add 300 ml of water and cook for 5 mins, then pour into a strainer to let the juice run through. Return the juice to the pan and bring to the boil. Add the right amount of sugar and simmer over low heat for 20 mins. To test whether it has begun to set, pour a few drops onto a cold plate: if it solidifies quickly, the jelly is ready for potting. Pour the hot jelly into sterilized jars and seal well. To make blackcurrant jelly from raw fruit, first juice the blackcurrants, then mix it with 1.2 kg of sugar for 1 litre of juice. Pour into a bowl and whisk until the sugar has dissolved. Skim the froth from the surface. Put the jelly into sterilized jars and seal well. Remember that jelly prepared in this way does not keep long. By the same method you can make jellies from redcurrants and whitecurrants.

Savoury blackberry jelly

1 kg blackberries, 1 cup boiled water, 1 glass dry white wine, ¼ tsp each cinnamon, nutmeg and ground cloves, juice of 2 lemons, ¼ tsp grated lemon rind, sugar

Rinse and drain the blackberries, put them in a pan, add the spices and lemon zest, pour in the water and wine and, stirring all the time, cook over low heat for 30 mins. When they cooled a bit, place them in a cloth and wring to extract the juice. Add 200 g of sugar to 1 cup of juice, squeeze in the lemon juice and, stirring continuously, cook for another 15 mins. Pot the hot jelly, turn the jars upside down, cover them with a blanket and leave to cool. This is an excellent addition to roast poultry and sauces.

Marinated fruit and vegetables

Marinated and pickled fruit and vegetables are not particularly healthy and have little nutritious value, but they are very tasty and useful as garnishing, or adding colour to a whole range of cold dishes. For a good marinade, you should dilute vinegar, preferably wine vinegar, with boiled water, and add to it salt, sugar or honey, and spices. The marinade is poured over blanched vegetables or fruit. You can marinade practically all stone fruits and berries, mushrooms and almost all vegetables.

In Poland, fruits are traditionally marinated in a honey marinade: for one kilo of fruit take 50 g of sugar, 50 g of honey, 1 cup of 7% wine vinegar, 1 cup of boiled water, 5–7 cloves, and 4–5 cardamom seeds.

A good idea is to add peppers to marinated fruit, which will then go very well with pâtés, cold roasts and smoked meats.

Marinated gooseberries

2 kg firm, ripe gooseberries, 1 cup wine vinegar, 2 cups boiled water, 400 g sugar, 5–6 cardamom seeds

Top and tail the gooseberries, rinse and dry them. Put into boiling water for a minute, then run under cold water and drain well. Bring the water with the sugar and cardamom to the boil, cover the pan and simmer for 7 mins, then add vinegar, bring to the boil again and leave to cool. Put the gooseberries into small jars, cover with the

cool marinade, seal and store in a cool place. Serve with roast meat, salads and hors-d'oeuvres.

Marinated gooseberries for sauce

500 g green gooseberries, 1 cup wine vinegar, 1 bay leaf, salt, a pinch of sugar, 1 tarragon sprig

Remove the pips from the gooseberries. Put the gooseberries for a minute in rather salty boiling water, then drain them. Arrange them tightly in a jar, cover with some lukewarm vinegar and leave overnight. Pour off the vinegar, drain the gooseberries in a strainer, then return them to the jar. Bring the remaining vinegar, with sugar, salt and bay leaf, to the boil, leave it to cool, then pour it over the fruit and put in the tarragon. Seal the jar and store in a cool place. Use for piquant sauces.

Cherries, French style

2–3 kg firm sweet cherries, 750 g sugar, 1 l wine vinegar, 2 tbsps honey, 2 cloves, 1–2 bay leaves, a small piece of cinnamon bark, 1 horseradish root, ½ tsp each coriander grains and mustard seeds, several cherry leaves

Bring the water, with the sugar, cloves, cinnamon and bay leaves, to the boil. Cover and simmer for 10 mins, towards the end add the honey and stir well. Rinse and dry the cherries, remove the stalks. Place the cherries into sterilized jars, put 1–2 cherry leaves, a piece of cleaned horseradish and several coriander and mustard grains into each jar. Pour over the hot vinegar. Seal the jars, turn them upside down, cover with a blanket and leave to cool. Serve the cherries with salads and all kinds of meat dishes, or use as garnishing for cold meats and cheeses.

Marinated pears I

2 kg pears (preferably bergamot), 1 kg sugar, 3 cups wine vinegar, 2 cups boiled water, juice of 1 lemon, a piece of cinnamon bark, 10 cloves

Rinse the pears, peel, halve and core them, put in a bowl and sprinkle with lemon juice. Bring the water, with the sugar, cloves and cinnamon, to the boil, pour in the vinegar, skim the froth. Put the pears into the boiling marinade, bring to the boil again, then slowly simmer for 30 mins until the fruit has become glassy. Take the pears out with a strainer and put them into warm sterilized jars. Reduce the syrup over a high heat, then pour it over the fruit. Seal the jars, turn them upside down, cover with a blanket and leave to cool, then store them in a cool place.

Marinated pears II

2 kg firm pears with stalks, 3 cups white wine vinegar, 500 g sugar, 1 fresh ginger root, 1 piece of cinnamon bark, 10 cloves, lemon rind

Scrub and blanch the lemon, peel it finely. Cut the rind into strips. Peel and slice the ginger. Bring 3 cups of water to the boil, add the vinegar, sugar, ginger, lemon rind, cinnamon and cloves. Cover and cook for 2–3 mins. Rinse the pears, peel them, halve and core them, but leave the stalks. Put the pears into the marinade, cover and simmer for 10 mins, then transfer them to sterilized jars. Cook the marinade for another 15 mins, reduce it a bit, then pour it hot over the pears so that the marinade covers the fruit completely. Seal the jars and store them in a cool place.

Pears in wine

1½ pears (preferably bergamot), 1½ kg sugar, ½ cup red wine, 3 cups boiled water, 2 walnut-size pieces of ginger, juice of 1 lemon

Rinse the pears, peel them, halve and core them. Put in a bowl and sprinkle with lemon juice. Soak the ginger in water for 2 hours, then drain and slice it. Make a syrup from the water and sugar, add the wine and ginger and bring to the boil. Put the pears into the boiling syrup, bring to the boil again, then simmer for 30 mins. Take the fruit out with a strainer and put into sterilized jars. Simmer the syrup for another 20–30 mins to reduce it and make it thicker. Pour the hot syrup over the pears. Seal the jars,

turn them upside down, cover with a blanket and leave to cool, then store them in a cool place.

Spicy pears

2 kg firm pears, 2 cups wine vinegar, ½ cup water, 500 g sugar, 80 g mustard seeds, 10 grains each allspice and pepper, a piece of cinnamon bark, 1 small horseradish root, ½ tsp grated lemon rind, 2 tbsps lemon juice

Rinse the pears, peel them, halve and core them. Put in a bowl and sprinkle with lemon juice. Bring the water, with the sugar, lemon zest and cinnamon, to the boil, add the vinegar. Pour the marinade over the pears and leave for 12 hours. Pour off the marinade into a pan, bring it again to the boil. Put in the pears and cook for 5–6 mins. Take the pears out and put them in sterilized jars. Put a piece of horseradish and several grains of mustard, allspice and pepper into each jar. Reduce the marinade a bit, take out the cinnamon. Pour the marinade over the pears. Seal the jars, turn them upside down, cover with a blanket and leave to cool.

Marinated apricots

1 kg apricots, 1 cup wine vinegar, ½ cup boiled water, 50 g sugar, 50 g honey, 5–6 cloves, a small piece of cinnamon bark, 2–3 cardamom seeds, 20 g salt

Blanch the rinsed apricots in boiling water for 2–3 mins, drain and stone them. Bring the water, with sugar, salt and spices, to the boil, cover the pan and simmer for 10 mins. Add the vinegar and honey and bring to the boil again. Put the apricot halves tightly in glass jars, pour over the strained marinade and seal the jars well.

Marinated plums

1 kg ripe purple plums, 1 cup wine vinegar, ½ cup boiled water, 50 g honey, 50 g sugar, 5 cardamom seeds, 5 cloves, a piece of cinnamon bark, 20 g salt

Bring the water, with sugar, salt and spices, to the boil, add the vinegar and honey and bring to the boil again. Put in the rinsed plums and cook for 2–3 mins, strain them and rinse under cold water. Put the plums (whole or halved) tightly in a jar, pour over the hot marinade. Seal the jar well, cover it with a blanket and leave to cool.

Plums marinated in red wine

2 kg ripe purple plums, 400 ml red wine, 400 ml 6% wine vinegar, 400–600 g sugar, ½ tsp salt, 3–5 cloves, a piece of cinnamon bark

Rinse and dry the plums, prick them with a pin. Bring the wine and vinegar, with the sugar and salt added, to the boil. Put the plums in a bowl and pour the marinade over. Cover and leave for 12 hours. Pour off the marinade into a pan. Bring it to the boil, then simmer for 8–10 mins, and again pour it over the plums and leave for 12 hours. On the third day, pour off the marinade, bring it to the boil, add the cloves and cinamon, put in the plums and cook for 2–3 mins. Skim froth, take off the heat. Take the plums out and put them in sterilized jars. Leave the marinade to cool, then cover the fruit with it completely. Seal the jars and store them in a dark, cool place.

Marinated bitter cherries

2½ kg large fine sour cherries, 1 cup wine vinegar, 1 cup honey, 1½ cups sugar, 1 tbsp lemon juice, ¼ tsp each powdered cinnamon and cloves

Rinse and drain the cherries. Squeeze some of them out to produce 1 cup of juice, put the rest in a bowl. Bring the juice, sugar and lemon juice, to the boil, add the vinegar, cinnamon, cloves and honey and bring to the boil again. Pour the marinade over the fruit, cover the bowl and leave aside for 24 hours. Pour the marinade off into a pan, bring it to the boil. Put the cherries into jars, pour over the lukewarm marinade. Seal the jars well and store in a cool place.

Pickled nasturtium buds as a substitute for capers

Pick nasturtium flower buds when they are soft and the size of capers, or use seeds enclosed in green bags. Put them in table salt for three hours, then transfer them to a jar. Add a handful of tarragon and a garlic clove, cover with vinegar. If

you do not find enough buds for the first time, you may always fill the jar gradually, provided you remember to leave them in salt for 12 hours before you actually marinate them. Pickled nasturtium buds are similar in taste to capers and can very well replace them in sauces, salads and aspics.

Aubergine, Armenian style

1 kg small aubergines, 250 g onion, 5–6 basil sprigs, ½ cup olive oil, 1 cup wine vinegar, 1 cup boiled water, 2–3 grains each pepper and allspice, 1 small bay leaf, 1 heaped tbsp salt, a pinch of sugar

Peel and slice the aubergines, sprinkle with salt and leave aside for 2–3 hours. Wipe the slices and sauté them in oil, then dry on absorbent paper. Cut the onion into fine slices. Bring the water with 20 g of salt to the boil, put in the spices and sugar and simmer for 10 mins, then add the vinegar and bring to the boil again. Arrange alternating layers of onion, basil leaves and aubergine in glass jars. Cover with the strained marinade, seal the jars and store in a cool place.

Garlic in wine

20 large garlic bulbs, 4 cups dry white wine, ¼ wine vinegar, 150 g sugar, 2 chilli peppers, 3 bay leaves, 2–3 tarragon sprigs, 1 tsp ground pepper, 1 heaped tbsp salt, olive oil

Bring the wine and vinegar to the boil, add the sugar, salt, tarragon, chilli, bay leaves and pepper. Put the skinned garlic cloves into the boiling marinade, take off the heat, cover and leave aside overnight. Bring the marinade with the garlic to the boil, continue cooking for 2–3 mins, then allow to cool. Put the garlic cloves in glass jars, cover them with the cool marinade. Put 1 tbsp of oil into each jar. Seal well and store in a cool place.

Pickled hop shoots

1 kg young hop shoots, 1 cup 6% wine vinegar, 1 cup boiled water, 2 tbsps salt, 1½ tbsps sugar, 2–3 bay leaves, 1 tsp coriander grains, 4–5 cloves of garlic, a walnut-size piece of fresh ginger, 4–5 grains each allspice and pepper

Rinse and clean the hop shoots, cut them into pieces and put into jars. Sprinkle with the finely chopped garlic and ginger. Bring the vinegar and water to the boil, add salt, sugar, bay leaf, allspice and pepper, cover and simmer for 5–7 mins. Pour the hot marinade over the hop shoots, seal the jars and pasteurize for 10 mins.

Pickled pumpkin

1 kg pumpkin (peeled and seeded), 1½ cups wine vinegar, ½ cup water, 500 g sugar, 1 tbsp powdered ginger, 4–5 cloves, 1 tsp grated orange rind, 2 tbsps orange juice, ½ tsp salt

Cut the pumpkin into cubes or scoop out the flesh with a baller. Bring the water, with ginger, cloves, salt, orange juice and zest, to the boil, cover and simmer for 10 mins. In another pan, bring the vinegar and sugar to the boil, put in the pumpkin cubes and simmer for 3–4 mins. Add the water with spices and cook for another 3–4 mins. Take the pumpkin cubes out with a strainer, put them into jars. Bring the marinade to the boil, reduce it a bit, then pour over the pumpkin. Seal the jars and pasteurize for 10 mins (unpasteurized pumpkin will get too sour).

Sweet pickled pumpkin

1 kg pumpkin (peeled and seeded), 2 cups 5% vinegar, 3–4 grains each allspice and pepper, 1 bay leaf, a piece of cinnamon bark, 3–4 cloves, 1 tbsp chopped fresh ginger, 2 cups sugar, ½ cup dry white wine, 1 tbsp white mustard seeds, salt

Bring the vinegar and sugar to the boil, add the spices, cover and simmer for 10 mins. Add the mustard seeds and salt and cook for another 5 mins. Cut the pumpkin into cubes or scoop out the flesh with a baller. Put in a bowl, cover with the hot marinade and leave overnight. Pour off the marinade, combine it with the wine and bring to the boil. Put the pumpkin into jars, pour over the cool

marinade, seal well. Pasteurize in a hot oven for several minutes.

Pickled wild succory buds

1 cup succory buds, salt, ½ cup 5% wine vinegar, ¼ cup water, 2 grains each pepper and allspice, 1 small bay leaf, a pinch of sugar, 1 chili pepper

Rinse and drain the succory buds, put them in a bowl, sprinkle with salt, mix well and leave for 12–15 hours, then rinse, drain and put them into small jars. Bring the vinegar and water to the boil, add the spices, cover and simmer for 10 mins. Cover the succory with the marinade, seal well and leave to stand for 10–14 days. Pour the liquid off. Prepare a new marinade, pour into the jars and seal well. Such succory buds can be successfully used instead of capers in salads, sauces, spreads and flavoured butter.

Spicy cucumbers

1 kg small firm cucumbers, 2 cups boiled water, 2 cups vinegar, 20 g salt

For one litre glass jar, take 2–3 grains each of allspice and pepper, ¼ tsp each of mustard seeds and coriander grains, 3–4 fresh basil leaves, 1 tsp each of dill seeds and dried tarragon, 2–3 spring onions, 1 small piece of horseradish, 4–5 strips of red pepper. Wash and dry the cucumbers, put them into jars, add the spices. Bring the salted water and vinegar to the boil, allow it to cool a bit, then pour over the cucumbers. Seal the jars and pasteurize them for 10–12 mins.

Pickled scallopini squash

1 kg small patissons, 1 thick horseradish root, 1–2 fennel sprigs with seeds, 1½ cups wine vinegar, ¾ cup boiled water, 2–3 grains each pepper and allspice, 1 bay leaf, 1 tbsp sugar, ½ tsp salt

Bring the water to the boil, add the salt, sugar and spices, cover and simmer for 10 mins. Add the vinegar and again bring to the boil. Wash the patissons thoroughly, scald them with boiling water, then rinse under cold water and dry. Put them into jars together with some strips of horseradish and dill sprigs. Cover with the cool marinade, seal well and pasteurize for 10 mins. Pickled patissons are excellent with all kinds of roast meat, cold meats and salads. They can also make a delicious hors-d'oeuvre when you stuff them with various spreads and cream cheese.

Tomatoes, Caucasian style

Bring water to the boil, add sugar and spices, cover and simmer for 7 mins. Pour in vinegar and again bring to the boil. Dice skinned garlic and cored peppers finely, combine with finely chopped greens, add a pinch of salt, mix well. Wash and dry the tomatoes, cut off their bases, remove seeds with a spoon. Stuff the tomatoes with the garlic paste, cover with the base. Put them tightly into jars, sprinkle with salt. Pour in the strained marinade, seal and store in a cool place. In 5 to 7 days the tomatoes will start getting yellow and turn spicy and piquant. They will keep longer if after 10 days you pasteurize them for 10 mins to prevent them getting too sour. This is an excellent addition to meat dishes.

Firewood agarics, Warsaw style

1 kg firewood agarics, 10 cloves of garlic, 1 tsp each ground pepper, juniper and allspice, 1½ cups wine vinegar, ½ cup boiled water, 1 bay leaf, 3–4 grains each pepper, allspice and juniper, ½ tsp sugar, salt

Wash the mushrooms thoroughly, scald them first and then rinse under cold water. Drain them well and put in an earthenware jar, sprinkling each layer generously with salt. Leave the jar in a cool place for 24 hours. Drain the mushrooms on a sieve, return to the jar, sprinkling each layer with finely chopped garlic and ground spices. Put a plate on top of the mushrooms, weigh it down and place the jar in a cool place for 2 weeks. Bring the water to the boil, add the pepper and allspice grains and juniper berries, some sugar and salt. Cover and simmer for 10 mins, then add the vinegar and bring to the boil again. Cover the mushrooms with the marinade and leave to cool. Transfer the mushrooms to small jars. Seal well and pasteurize for

30 mins. Store in a cool place. These mushrooms go very well with boiled fish and salads, especially potato salad.

Chanterelles in wine

1 kg chanterelles, ½ cup dry red wine, ½ cup 6% vinegar, ½ cup water, a piece of cinnamon bark, 5–6 cloves, 2 bay leaves, 4–6 grains each allspice and white mustard, 1½ tbsps sugar, 1 tbsp salt

Bring the water to the boil, add the spices, salt and sugar, cover and simmer for 5–7 mins. Pour in the wine and vinegar, bring to the boil again, then allow the marinade to cool. Wash the mushrooms thoroughly, scald them with boiling water, then put them into salted boiling water and cook for 20 mins. Drain them, rinse under cold water and drain again. Put them into jars, cover with the marinade. Seal and pasteurize for 10–12 mins.

Honey mushrooms with tarragon

1 kg honey mushrooms, 1 cup 6% vinegar, 1 cup boiled water, 1 large horseradish root, 3 tsps dried tarragon, 2 bay leaves, 5–8 grains each allspice, pepper and white mustard, 3 tsps hot paprika, 1 tbsp sugar, 1 tbsp salt

Clean the mushrooms, cut off the stems, wash the caps thoroughly, put into salted boiling water and cook for 5–6 mins, then drain, rinse under cold water and drain again. Bring the water to the boil, put in the spices, herbs, salt and sugar, cover and simmer for 20 mins. Pour in the vinegar and bring to the boil again. Put the mushrooms into sterilized jars, cover with the cool strained marinade. Seal and pasteurize for 10–15 mins.

Marinated saffron milk caps

1 kg saffron milk caps, 300 g onion, 10–12 grains allspice, 2–3 bay leaves, 6% vinegar, ¼ tsp sugar, 1 tsp salt

Wash the mushrooms thoroughly, drain them on a sieve, cut off the stems. In an enamelled pan, put alternating layers of mushrooms and onion slices. Sprinkle each layer with salt, sugar and crushed bay leaves, add some allspice. Cover the pan and cook over very low heat until the mushrooms produce juice, then take off the lid and simmer for 15–20 mins, stirring gently so that they do not stick to the bottom. Pour in enough vinegar to cover the mushrooms and simmer for another 15 mins. Put the hot mushrooms into sterilized jars, seal well, cover with a blanket and leave to cool. Store in a cool place.

Pickles

Pickles, a kind of vegetable salad, marinated in spicy vinegar, go very well with meat, salads and sauces, and are highly recommended as garnishing for a cold buffet. The wider the choice of vegetables, the more attractive the cold buffet looks.

Pickled mustard sprigs

500 g young mustard sprigs, 1 cup still mineral water, 1 cup dark spicy soya sauce

Cut the mustard sprigs into fairly large pieces, put them in an earthenware jar. Cover with a mixture of 1 part mineral water to 1 part soya sauce. Seal well and leave overnight or longer. If you first blanch the sprigs, they will lose some of their pungent taste. Use to garnish meat dishes or add to salads or bread spreads.

Country-style pickles

1 kg small ceps, 500 g green, yellow and red peppers, 500 g spring onions, 1 large garlic bulb, 1 tbsp lemon juice, 2 cups vinegar, 1 cup water, 2 bay leaves, 7–8 grains each allspice and pepper, 10 grains mustard, 2 tbsps sugar, salt

Blanch the mushroom caps, put them into salted boiling water and cook for 15–20 mins. Drain them, rinse under cold water and drain again. Peel the onion and garlic. Blanch the peppers, core them and cut into strips. Put alternating layers of mushrooms and vegetables in steri-

lized jars. Bring the water to the boil, put in the spices and lemon juice, cover and simmer for 10 mins, then add the salt, sugar and vinegar and simmer to reduce the marinade. Allow it to cool, strain and pour over the mushrooms. Seal the jars and pasteurize for 15 mins.

Stuffed aubergines

1 kg small aubergines, 1 cup chopped walnuts, 100 g garlic, 5–6 peppermint sprigs or 3–4 tsps dried mint, 1 cup wine vinegar, ¾ cup boiled water, 3–4 grains each allspice and pepper, 1–2 cloves, 1 tsp sugar, 2 tbsps salt

Rinse the aubergines, cut off their bases, scoop the seeds out. Put the aubergines into salted boiling water and cook for 3–4 mins. Rinse them under cold water, drain well by pressing firmly down. Mix the finely chopped garlic with the salt, mint and chopped walnuts. Stuff the aubergines with the mixture. Bring the water to the boil, add the spices and sugar, cover and simmer for 10 mins. Pour in the vinegar, bring to the boil, then allow the marinade to cool. Put the aubergines into an earthenware pot, cover with the marinade, put a lid on and leave in a cool place for 5–6 days. Transfer the aubergines to glass jars, bring the marinade to the boil and cover the aubergines with it. Seal and pasteurize for 10 mins. Stuffed aubergines make a delicious piquant hors-d'oeuvre and can also be served with meat.

Patisson salad

1 kg young small patissons, 500 g red onion, 500 g carrots, ½ tsp each coriander and white mustard grains, 5–7 peppercorns, 1 large horseradish root, 1 tbsp dill seeds, 2 cups wine vinegar, 1 cup boiled water, 1 tbsp sugar, 1 heaped tsp salt

Peel the carrots and onions, rinse and dry them. Slice the onions finely, cut the patissons into sticks. Put both in a bowl, sprinkle lavishly with salt, cover and leave overnight. Press to squeeze out excess juice. Put the vegetables tightly in a jar. Add some dill seeds and strips of horseradish to each jar. Bring the water to the boil, put in the coriander, mustard, pepper, sugar and salt (½ tsp), cover and simmer for 10 mins. Add the vinegar, bring to the boil again. Pour the hot marinade into the jars, seal well, cover with a blanket and leave to cool.

Green tomato salad I

4 kg green tomatoes, 12 onions, 1 cup salt, 4 cups 6% vinegar, 700 g sugar, 1 tsp each cloves, pepper and allspice, 4–6 bay leaves, a piece of cinnamon bark, a walnut-size piece of fresh ginger, 2 tsps mustard seeds, 1 cup boiled water

Cut the rinsed tomatoes and peeled onion into slices, put in a bowl, sprinkle with salt generously and leave overnight. Press to squeeze out excess juice, then drain in a strainer. Bring the water to the boil, add the spices and sugar, cover and simmer for 10 mins. Pour in the vinegar and cook for another 5–7 mins. Put the tomatoes and onion into the boiling marinade and simmer for 10 mins. Place the hot vegetables in jars, add mustard seed and (II) strips of blanched pepper. Continue cooking the marinade to reduce it, then cover the tomatoes with it. Seal well, cover with a blanket and leave to cool.

Green tomato salad II

4 kg green tomatoes, 6 onions, 2 red peppers, 1 cup salt, 4 cups wine vinegar, 500 g sugar, 1 cup boiled water, 1 tsp each cloves, allspice and pepper, 4–5 bay leaves, ¼ tsp each powdered ginger, cinnamon, coriander and tarragon, 2 tbsps mustard seeds

Cut the rinsed tomatoes and peeled onion into slices, put in a bowl, sprinkle with salt generously and leave overnight. Press to squeeze out excess juice, then drain in a strainer. Bring the water to the boil, add the spices and sugar, cover and simmer for 10 mins. Pour in the vinegar and cook for another 5–7 mins. Put the tomatoes and onion into the boiling marinade and simmer for 10 mins. Place the hot vegetables in jars, add mustard seed and (II) strips of blanched pepper. Continue cooking the marinade to reduce it, then cover the tomatoes with it. Seal well, cover with a blanket and leave to cool.

Silesian pickles

To make this salad, you will need large, overripe cucumbers with a yellowing peel. Halve them, remove the seeds with a spoon, and cut them lengthwise into fairly thick strips. Sprinkle with salt generously and leave overnight in a cool place.

1 kg large overripe cucumbers, 2 cups wine vinegar, 1 cup boiled water, 2–3 bay leaves, 5–7 grains each mustard, allspice and pepper, 1½ tbsps sugar, 50 g salt

Peel the cucumbers, halve them, remove the seeds. Cut the cucumbers into fairly thick strips, put in a bowl, sprinkle with salt. Cover and leave for 24 hours, then drain in a strainer and put into an earthenware jar. Bring the water with spices to the boil, add 1 cup of vinegar and bring to the boil again. Pour the marinade over the cucumbers, cover the bowl and leave for 2–3 days. Place the cucumbers in glass jars. Add the remaining vinegar and sugar to the marinade, bring to the boil. Cover the cucumbers with the marinade, seal the jars and pasteurize for 15 mins. This makes an excellent side dish with roast and smoked meat.

Cocktail gherkins

3 kg gherkins or small cucumbers, 6 cups boiled water, 4 cups 6% vinegar, several dill sprigs with seeds, 4–5 tarragon sprigs or 1½ tsp dried tarragon, 1 large horseradish root, 2–3 horseradish leaves, 1–2 chilli peppers or 1 tsp powdered chilli, 10 g white mustard seeds, 3–4 grains each pepper and juniper, 70–80 g sugar, 50 g salt

Bring the water and vinegar, with salt, pepper and juniper, to the boil. Wash the cucumbers thoroughly, place them in jars, put some dill, tarragon, strips of horseradish and horseradish leaves, several pieces of chilli and some mustard seeds into each jar. Cover with the cool marinade, seal and pasteurize for 10 mins.

Pickled turnip

12 young medium-sized turnips, 2 chilli peppers, 2 tsps finely chopped candied ginger, 3 tbsps salt

Scrub the turnips, rinse and dry them, cut into quarters. Put in a bowl, sprinkle with 2 tbsps of salt and leave at room temperature for 2 days. Take out the turnip, drain it well. Add the turnip juice to 2 cups of cool boiled salted water. Cut the turnip into slices, put into jars, sprinkling each layer with some ginger and chopped chilli pepper. Pour in the brine, seal the jars and store in a cool place. The turnip will be fit for consumption after 2–3 weeks, but should not be kept much longer than that.

Pickled radishes

1 kg small radishes, 200 g sugar, 1½ tbsps soya oil, 1 tbsp coarsely ground pepper, 15–20 green peppercorns, 2 cups wine vinegar, 1 cup boiled water

Bring the water and vinegar to the boil, add the oil, sugar, ground pepper and green peppercorns, cover and simmer for 10 mins. Wash and dry the radishes, prick them with a toothpick and put into the boiling marinade for 2–3 mins. Take them out with a strainer, put into jars, cover with the cool marinade. Seal and pasteurize for 25–30 mins. An excellent side dish with grilled meat.

Vegetables and mushrooms in brine

Salting, also known as souring, is the cheapest and most popular method of preserving vegetables, fruit and mushrooms for the winter. It basically consists in subjecting the foods to the process of fermentation brought about by the action of certain bacteria, which give such product a very special flavour.

Salted shredded vegetables, for example cabbage, should be pressed out and weighed down hard to produce enough juice to fill all the gaps and push out air bubbles. Vegetables and fruit that are processed whole, such as apples, plums and mushrooms, must be packed very tightly, preferably in earthenware jars, and covered completely with brine.

At first salted vegetables and fruit should be kept at room temperature (18°C), and later stored in a cooler place.

You can use all sorts of condiments in soured fruit and vegetables: small onions, garlic, peppers, horseradish, herbs and spices, as well as oak, cherry, blackcurrant, horseradish and vine leaves. Fir needles added to the brine will give soured mushrooms a special flavour. Spices not only enhance the taste of soured vegetables and fruit, but also, or above all, curb the development of yeast, bacteria and mould, the worst enemy of such products.

Soured vegetables and fruit are fit for consumption in 3–4 weeks. In the right conditions, they may be stored for 4–6 months. And if you transfer soured fruit or vegetables to glass jars and pasteurize them, they will keep for as long as a year.

Soured aubergines

1 kg small aubergines, 1 cup finely chopped celeriac, 2 whole celery sticks, ½ cup chopped dill, parsley and savory leaves, 2 garlic bulbs, 1 small chilli pepper, 5 cups water, 2½ tbsps salt

Rinse and dry the aubergines, make a lengthwise incision in each of them, scoop out the seeds. Scald the aubergines with boiling water, then rinse under cold water. Drain, put in a skillet, add 1 cup of cold salted boiled water and leave for 1–2 hours, then drain again. Put the celery sticks into 4 cups of water, bring to the boil, then simmer for 4–5 mins. Take the celery out, add some salt to the water and bring to the boil. Mix the chopped celery with the garlic crushed with salt, the greens and finely chopped chilli. Stuff the aubergines with the mixture, tie them with thread. Pack them tightly into a jar, add pieces of the blanched celeriac. Cover with the brine, put a small lid or plat on top and weigh it down. Keep for 4–5 days in warmth and then store in a cool place.

Sauerkraut

*2 kg white cabbage, 1 tsp each caraway
seeds, juniper berries, dill and mustard seeds,
1 small horseradish root, 30 g salt*

Shred the cabbage, sprinkle it sparingly with salt and
leave for 15–20 mins, then transfer to an earthenware
jar, sprinkling each layer with more salt, seeds and grated
horseradish. Press hard with your hands until juice is produced. Cover with clean gauze, place a small plate that fits
into the jar on top and weigh it down. Store in a cool place.
From time to time pour off excess juice and rinse the sides
of the jar and the plate.

Sour red cabbage, Silesian style

*2½ kg red cabbage, 500 g tart apples, 250 g onion,
½ tsp each sugar and caraway seeds, 50 g salt*

Shred the cabbage finely, cut the onion into thin slices,
grate coarsely the apples and the cabbage stump. Mix
all the ingredients with salt, sugar and caraway. Put into a
large sterilized earthenware jar. Press down hard, cover
with a plate that fits inside the jar, weigh it down and keep
at room temperature for 3–4 days. When the process of
rapid fermentation is over, pierce through the cabbage right
to the bottom of the jar in several places. Cover again and
store in a cool place. The cabbage should be ready within
10–15 days. If you want to store it long, transfer it to glass
jars and pasteurize for 10–15 mins.

Chinese cabbage in brine

*2–3 kg Chinese cabbage, 6 tbsps salt, 6–8 spring
onions, 3–4 chopped cloves of garlic, 1 tsp chopped
chilli pepper or ½ tsp cayenne pepper, 2 tbsps
finely chopped candied ginger*

Rinse and dry the cabbage, chop it coarsely, sprinkle with
4 tbsps of salt and leave for 15–20 mins, then rinse it
under cold water, drain and mix with the garlic, chopped
spring onions, ginger and chilli. Pack it tightly in a sterilized
earthenware jar. Bring 1½ cups of water with 2 tbsps of salt
to the boil, then allow it to cool. Cover the cabbage with
the brine, place a plate that fits inside the jar on top, weigh

it down. Store in a cool place. The cabbage will be ready
in 8–10 days. For storing it longer, you should transfer it to
small jars and pasteurize for 10–15 mins.

Soured cucumbers

*2 kg small firm cucumbers, 1½ tbsps dill seeds,
5–7 cloves of garlic, 1–2 bay leaves, several
leaves of each sage and savory, several leaves
of blackcurrant or cherry, 1 chilli pepper, several
peppercorns, 4 cups boiled water, 60 g salt*

Bring the salted water to the boil, add the bay leaves,
dill and peppercorns, cover and simmer for 5–7 mins,
then allow to cool. Wash the cucumbers and leave them in
cold water for an hour, then rinse them and dry. Put them
tightly in jars together with some garlic cloves, sage, savory,
blackcurrant leaves and pieces of chilli. Cover with a clean
cloth and leave at room temperature for 24–36 hours, then
seal the jars and store them in a cool place.

Peppers in brine

*3 kg green, red and yellow bell peppers,
2 l water, a large piece of horseradish root,
a handful of blackcurrant and cherry leaves,
3–4 cloves of garlic, 1–2 sprigs of dill with
seeds, 10–12 mustard seeds, 80 g salt*

Rinse the peppers, remove the seeds. Dip the peppers
for 2–3 mins in boiling salted water, then drain them,
rinse under cold water and drain again. Bring 2 l of water
with salt to the boil. Arrange alternating layers of blackcurrant and cherry leaves and of peppers in jars, add some
grated horseradish, garlic cloves, chopped dill and mustard
seeds. Cover with the cool brine, weigh down and store
in a cool place.

Plums in brine

*2 kg plums, ½ tsp powdered ginger, 8–9 cloves,
5–7 peppercorns, 2 tsps sugar, 3 tbsps lemon
juice, 4 cups boiled water, 20 g salt*

Bring the water with salt and sugar to the boil, allow it
cool, add the lemon juice. Pound the cloves and pep-

per in a mortar, mix them with the ginger. Rinse and dry the plums, remove the stones. Put the plums in layers in sterilized jars, sprinkling each layer with the spices. Pour over the brine, cover with a cloth and leave at room temperature for 3–4 days, then seal the jars and store them in a cool place. Serve with meat dishes and salads.

Saffron milk caps in brine

young, fresh saffron milk caps, salt, pepper, olive oil

Mix 4 parts salt with 1 part pepper. Wipe clean the mushrooms. Pour several spoonfuls of oil into jars. Put in the mushrooms, sprinkling each layer with the salt and pepper mixture. Place a saucer that fits inside the jar on top, weigh it down. After 2–3 days, seal the jars with wax paper and store in a cool place.

Saffron milk caps in olive oil

1 kg saffron milk caps, 2 cups olive oil, 100 g salt, pepper, marjoram, allspice

Clean the mushrooms, cut off the stalks. Bring 1 l of water with 3 tbsps of salt to the boil, put in the mushrooms and cook for 5 mins, then strain them and allow to cool. Place the mushrooms bottom down in a stoneware jar, sprinkle each layer with salt, marjoram and ground allspice. Press the mushrooms down, cover them with oil. Put a saucer that fits into the jar on top and weigh it down. Leave the mushrooms for several days until they produce juice, then transfer them to glass jars, seal well and store in a cool place. Makes an excellent hors-d'oeuvre and an addition to salads.

Salted saffron milk caps

2 kg young saffron milk caps, 1 bulb of garlic, 1 cup salt, 3–4 bay leaves, ½ tsp each allspice and rosemary leaves

Bring 2 l of water with 3 tbsps of salt to the boil, put in the cleaned mushrooms and cook for 5 mins, then strain the mushrooms, rinse under cold water and drain. Place them in layers in a stoneware pot, sprinkle each layer with garlic crushed with salt, rosemary, crushed bay leaves

and allspice. Put a saucer that fits into the pot on top and weigh it down. Store in a dark, cool place. Before using them, rinse the mushrooms thoroughly to remove salt. An excellent hors-d-oeuvre and an addition to salads.

Vine leaves in brine

4 cups water, 120 g salt, new vine leaves

Rinse the leaves, drain them, put into an earthenware pot, cover with cold water and leave for 4–5 hours, then take them out and drain well. Return the leaves to the pot, cover them with the cool brine. Put a saucer that fits inside the pot on top and weigh it down (the brine must cover the leaves completely). Stuff the leaves with meat.

Savoury relishes

Savoury gooseberry chutney

1 kg gooseberries, 2 cups sugar, 2 tbsps honey, ½ cup wine vinegar, 1 tsp each salt and caraway seeds, 1 tbsp chopped fresh ginger, 2–3 cloves of garlic, ¼ tsp each ground cloves, cinnamon, grated orange rind and pepper, 2–3 tbsps water

Bring the water with the caraway to the boil, cover and leave to cool down. Top and tail the gooseberries, rinse them and drain. Bring the vinegar and sugar to the boil, add the garlic crushed with salt and the spices, cover and simmer for 5 mins. Add the honey and strained caraway water, put in the gooseberries and cook for 30 mins, stirring all the time. Pour the mixture into small sterilized jars, seal well, cover with a blanket and leave to cool. An excellent addition to grilled fish, poultry and roast meat.

Rhubarb chutney

1 kg rhubarb, 2 large onions, 3–5 cloves of garlic, 1 tbsp mustard seeds, 2 tbsps chopped fresh ginger, 1½ cups sugar, 1 tbsp honey, 1 cup raisins, 1 tsp each ground allspice and coriander, ½ tsp cayenne pepper, a pinch of each ground cloves and cinnamon, 1 cup 5% wine vinegar

Strip the stringy fibres from the rhubarb stalks. Cut the rhubarb into thin slices, put in a pan together with the finely chopped onion and garlic, add the sugar, mustard seeds, ginger, raisins, allspice, coriander and cayenne. Stir well, cover and simmer over very low heat for 25–30 mins, stirring from time to time. Add the ground cloves and cinnamon, pour in the vinegar and honey, bring to the boil, then simmer again for 40 mins, stirring all the time. Pour the hot mixture into jars, seal well and pasteurize for 15 mins. Excellent with boiled poultry, meat and fish, and with cold meats.

Honey ketchup

4 kg ripe beef tomatoes, 1 large onion, 250 g honey, 1 cup wine (apple) vinegar, 2 pieces of cinnamon bark, 1½ tsps cloves, 1 tsp celery seeds, ¼ tsp cayenne pepper, 4 tsps salt

Bring the vinegar to the boil, add the cloves, cinnamon and celery seeds, cover and simmer for 15 mins, then leave to cool. Put the rinsed and quartered tomatoes in a pan and soften them, add the grated onion and cayenne and simmer for 20 mins. Sieve the tomato and onion mixture, reduce the liquid. Pour in the cool vinegar, add salt, and stirring all the time, simmer until the sauce has thickened. Add the honey and again simmer until thick. Pour into jars and pasteurize for 15 mins.

Spicy chutney

500 g purple plums, 10 stoned prunes, 1 large tart apple, 250 g raisins, ½ tsp each ground black pepper, ginger, cloves and cardamom, ¼ tsp cayenne pepper, 500 g honey, ½ cup wine vinegar

Rinse the prunes, soak them in boiled water, then cook them and cut into strips. Put the stoned plums in a pan, add the water in which prunes have cooked, and simmer for 20 mins. Add the prunes, grated apple, blanched raisins,

spices and the vinegar. Cook for 20 mins, stirring all the time, then add the honey and continue cooking until the sauce has thickened. Put the sauce into jars, seal well and pasteurize for 15 mins.

Pepper relish

1 kg red bell peppers, 1 lemon, 600 g sugar, ¼ cup dry white wine, 2–3 tbsps boiled water, ¼ tsp salt

Scrub the lemon, take off the yellow rind and chop it finely. Remove pips and put the flesh through a mincer together with cored peppers. Bring the wine with the water and sugar to the boil, put in the pepper and lemon mixture, add the lemon zest and salt. Stirring all the time, simmer for 40 mins until the sauce has thickened. Pour the hot sauce into small sterilized jars, seal well and pasteurize for 10 mins. Serve with hard-boiled eggs, cheeses, pâtés and smoked meat.

Country-style relish

2 kg ripe beef tomatoes, 4 large green bell peppers, 300 g onion, 250 g carrots, 1 lemon, 1 orange, ½ tsp each grated lemon and orange rind, 1 cup sugar, 1 cup dry white wine, 1 tsp salt

Core the peppers, cut them into strips. Peel the onions and carrots and dice them finely. Blanch the tomatoes, skin and quarter them. Soften the vegetables in a pan, add the wine and cook for 40 mins. Put the mixture, together with the orange and lemon flesh (remove the pips) through a blender, then sieve it. Add the sugar, salt, lemon and orange zest and, stirring frequently, cook for 30–40 mins. Put the hot sauce into jars, seal well and pasteurize for 15–20 mins.

Wild pear relish

1½ kg wild pears, juice and grated rind of 1 lemon, 1 cup sugar, 1 tsp powdered ginger, 1 cup dry white wine, salt

Peel the and core pears, soften them in a pan, then pour in the wine and continue cooking. Sieve them, add the lemon juice and zest, ginger, sugar and salt and, stirring all the time, simmer for 15 mins. Pour the hot sauce into jars, seal well and pasteurize for 10–15 mins. Serve with roast meat.

Savoury titbits

30 hard-boiled quail eggs, 1 onion, 3 cups vinegar, 7 cm long piece of cinnamon bark, 1 tbsp honey, 1 tsp herbes de Provence, 1 tsp cloves, ½ tsp coriander seeds, 2–3 peppercorns, 1 tsp finely chopped fresh ginger

Bring the vinegar, with the cinnamon, cloves, coriander and pepper, to the boil, add the ginger, honey and herbs, cover and simmer for 5–7 mins, then take off the heat. Cut the peeled onion into fine slices. Arrange alternating layers of quail eggs and onion in a jar, pour over the marinade, cover and put in the fridge for a week (it will keep in the fridge for over a half month). Use to garnish canapés and cold meat dishes, and for salads.

Home-made mustard

70 g ground white mustard seeds, 1 tsp ground turmeric, ¼ cup each white wine vinegar and olive oil, 1 tbsp crushed dried rosemary, 1 tbsp chopped green thyme leaves, 1 tsp each salt and white pepper, 1 tsp honey, 1 tsp cold boiled water

Mix the turmeric and mustard with the cold water and vinegar, leave aside for 15–20 mins. Add the pepper, salt and honey. Rest the pan on top of a pot of simmering water and whisk until the mixture has thickened. Leave the sauce to cool, then gradually add the oil, whisking all the time. Towards the end, add the tyme leaves. Put the mustard into a jar, seal well and leave for 8–10 days to mature.

Rhubarb paste

1 kg rhubarb, 1½ cups chopped onion, 1 cup raisins, 1½ cups sugar, 4–5 cloves of garlic, 2 tbsps finely chopped fresh ginger, 1 tbsp ground mustard seeds, 1 tsp each ground allspice and coriander, ½ tsp crumbled chili pepper, ¼ tsp each cinnamon and ground cloves, 2 tbsps honey, 2 tbsps dry white wine, 1½ cups wine vinegar, 1 tbsp salt

Strip stringy fibres from the rhubarb stalks, cut the rhubarb into cubes. Blanch and drain the raisins, put them in a bowl and sprinkle with wine. Soften the rhubarb and onion in a pan, add the raisins, finely chopped garlic, sugar, ginger, salt and the remaining spices. Simmer over low heat for 30 mins, stirring all the time, then put through a blender and sieve the mixture. Pour in the vinegar and simmer for another 30 mins. Towards the end, add the honey and reduce the liquid. Put the thick paste into jars, seal well and pasteurize for 10–15 mins.

Garlic in oil

300 g (10 bulbs) fresh garlic, 1 tbsp each love-in-a-mist seeds, black pepper, salt and garam masala, 3 tbsps fennel seeds, 1 tsp crumbled chilli pepper, sunflower oil

Skin the garlic cloves, put them in a jar, sprinkling each layer with spices and salt. Cover the garlic completely with sunflower oil, close the jar and leave in a warm place for 8–10 days, shaking it every day, then store in a cool place (preferably transferred to smaller jars) for up to several months. The longer it matures, the finer its taste. Use with salads and meat and vegetable dishes.

Cherries in redcurrant jelly

1 kg cherries, 500 g redcurrants, 1 cup sugar, ½ cup honey, 3–4 tbsps boiled water, a pinch of each cinnamon and ground cloves

Liquidize the redcurrants, then sieve them. Bring the water with sugar, cinnamon and cloves to the boil, add the redcurrant juice and honey, bring to the boil again. Stone the rinsed cherries, put into the boiling syrup and bring to the boil. Place in sterilized jars, seal well and pasteurize for 5–7 mins.

Spicy tomatoes

1–1⅛ kg small green tomatoes, 3 l water, 3 tbsps salt, 500 g sugar, 2 cups wine vinegar, 2 5-cm long pieces of cinnamon bark, 1 tbsp white peppercorns, 1 tsp whole cloves, 2 pieces of candied ginger, 2 tbsps ginger syrup

Clean, rinse and dry the tomatoes, prick each in several places. Bring the water and salt to the boil, put in the tomatoes and bring to the boil again, then take the tomatoes out with a strainer and drain them. Bring the vinegar to the boil, add the pepper, cinnamon and cloves, cover and simmer for 5 mins. Put in the sugar, chopped ginger and ginger syrup and continue cooking, stirring all the time. Place the tomatoes in jars, pour over the marinade, seal well. These tomatoes go very well with grilled meat and with salads.

Cucumbers with slivovitz

1 kg small firm cucumbers, 1 small horseradish root, some ice cubes, several dill sprigs, 15 peppercorns, 2 cups boiled water, 1 cup slivovitz, 30 g salt

Rinse the cucumbers, put them in a bowl, cover with water with ice cubes and leave for 2–3 hours, then drain, dry them and place in jars together with dill sprigs, horseradish strips and peppercorns. Bring the water with salt to the boil, then leave it to cool. Blend it with the slivovitz and pour over the cucumbers. Seal the jars and store in a cool place.

Sour cherry relish

2 kg large sour cherries, 500 g sugar, 200 g mild mustard, 50 g sharp mustard, 100 g freshly grated horseradish, 1 tbsp each white mustard seeds and coriander, 2½ cups boiled water

Rinse and dry the cherries. Bring the water with the sugar, coriander and mustard to the boil. Gradually put in the cherries and cook until the water again begins to boil (the cherries must not burn). Take them out with a strainer, put into sterilized jars. Continue cooking the syrup over low heat for 20 mins until it thickens, then add the horseradish and mustard seed and stir well. Pour the syrup over the cherries, seal the jars well, cover with a blanket and leave till cool. A very good addition to roast poultry and beef, also to be used in salads and for garnishing various dishes.

Cranberry relish

1 kg cranberries, 1 kg tart apples, 250 g chopped walnuts, 3 kg honey, ½ cup water

Clean and stalk the cranberries, cover them with ½ cup of boiled water and simmer until the fruit splits, then press through a fine sieve. Melt the honey in a large pan. When it begins to boil, put in the diced apples and cranberries. Simmer over low heat for 30 mins, stirring all the time. Add the chopped walnuts and, stirring continuously, simmer for another 30 mins. Pour the hot sauce into sterilized jars, seal well and pasteurize for 10 mins. Serve with white meat and roast poultry.

CHAPTER XX

FUSION

✳ ✳ ✳

Experts claim that the popularity of the most exotic cuisines – from Philippines, Burma, Senegal, also Armenia and Azerbaijan – is going to grow in the coming years. This applies also to Poland – although almost 50 years behind Western Europe in this field, Polish chefs are quickly making up for lost time.

Fusion, or international, cuisine is a combination of various culinary tastes and techniques. Its beginnings go back to 19th century America according to some, or Australia according to others. In any case, its rise has to do with the influx of arrivals from Japan, China or Indonesia who brought with them spices and condiments which influenced the cuisine of European settlers.

One thing is certain: fusion cuisine unites the West and the East, and combines elements of European, Asian and South American traditions as regards both the ingredients used and cooking techniques.

Poles have never been immune to foreign influences. As early as the 16th century, Queen Bona, the wife of the Polish king Sigismund the Old, introduced some vegetables which had previously been unknown in Poland. In the 18th century, under the rule of Stanislas Augustus, we became fascinated with anything coming from France, French cuisine included. Throughout the centuries we adopted Jewish, Greek, Armenian and Turkish influences. We even picked up something from the English kitchen, that most unexciting of culinary traditions – rare beefsteak.

Anchovies, capers, artichokes appeared on Polish tables centuries ago, and Polish cooks were well familiar with oil extracted from pumpkin seeds, walnuts and poppy-seeds, and vinegar produces from raspberries, basil, tarragon, dill, garlic, lemon and apples. It was only in the second half of the 20th century that these became practically unavailable.

Today this is no longer a problem. Supermarket shelves are crammed with condiments coming from all over the world. Back from holidays abroad, we fondly remember the tastes and flavours we experienced during our latest trip and we include them in our daily diet as part of traditional Polish dishes.

One thing should be remembered, however: when you experiment with exotic flavours, do not overdo it and treat what is basically Polish cuisine with due respect.

Oil

The answer to success in preparing sauces, salads and other dishes is the right choice of oil and vinegar.

The most popular and the most valued kind of oil is light **sunflower oil**. Its neutral flavour makes it suitable for dressings and for frying, stewing and roasting. Sometimes it is used instead of sesame or corn (or maize) oil.

Pumpkin (or **marrow-seed**) **oil** is very healthy, light and highly appreciated by connoisseurs. It is produced from finely ground, roasted seeds of a certain variety of pumpkin. Its colour varies from pale yellow through dark green to purple or dark brown. Some of its varieties lack any flavour, although usually pumpkin oil is thick and has a distinct nutty taste and aroma. It is used mainly in stews and roasts, often in combination with other kinds of oil.

Recent years have seen a dazzling career of **grape--seed oil**, not only in cookery, but also in cosmetology. Grape-seed oil is pressed from dried grape seeds which are a by-product of winemaking. It is pale greenish yellow in colour and has a slightly fruity taste. It is suitable for roasting, frying and stewing, and due to its light bitter-sweet taste and specific aroma it is often used in salad dressings and sauces. It is superior to other kinds of oil in that it preserves the natural flavour of all ingredients. When used for frying, it does not leave any smell or oily taste. It has a high smoke point of 251°C.

Poppy-seed oil was apparently first produced in the 17th century in Venice. It is now cold-pressed from blue poppy seeds and is getting increasingly popular in Europe. It is highly palatable, suitable for dressings, especially for potato and tomato salads, but also for cooking. It gives food a very specific poppy-seed flavour and is considered very healthy.

Walnut oil, produced exclusively by cold pressing, is an excellent dietary product due to its nice, nutty flavour and high iodine content. It is used in food preparation, especially in salad dressings, often mixed with other kinds of oil. Walnut oil extracted from roasted nuts is darker in colour.

Hazelnut oil (high priced) is often referred to as 'gourmet's oil' and considered one of the richest sources of vitamin E. Usually pressed from roasted hazelnuts (also called filberts), it has a dark-brown colour and a characteristic sweetish flavour. It should be stored in a dark place in a tightly closed bottle at room temperature. Hazelnut oil is used mostly for salad dressings, but also as a cooking oil. In combination with apple vinegar it makes an excellent dressing for lettuce. You may also add it to carrot juice and to various sweet dishes.

Groundnut (or **peanut**) **oil** has a very high smoke point, which makes it suitable for deep frying. It is light yellow to amber in colour and has a characteristic slightly nutty, delicate flavour. It has many uses in cooking: for frying and stewing meat, fish and vegetables, for salad dressings, sauces and marinades (meat marinated overnight in groundnut oil gets a special flavour). NB: when kept in the fridge, groundnut oil may lose its translucence, and even turn into jelly.

There are two more kinds of oil expressed from nuts. One of them is **macadamia oil** from the nuts of macadamia (also known as Queensland nuts) which grows in Australia. Macadamia oil is pale yellow, and it is used mainly in salad dressings, but also for stewing and frying. It is quite expensive.

The other is **almond oil**, cold pressed from dried kernels of sweet almond. Good almond oil is colourless and lacks any distinct flavour. Once a bottle is open, you should keep it in the fridge. It is advisable to buy it in small bottles and protect it from sunlight (that is why it is usually sold in dark bottles). Almond oil is used in salad dressings and also for stewing and roasting. Mixed with other kinds of vegetable oil it is added to fish and milk dishes as well as to salads and fresh fruit juices.

Corn (or **maize**) **oil** is a by-product of corn milling. It has almost no taste, a corn flavour and smooth, buttery consistency. Oil obtained from the germ of corn is pale, while that obtained from whole grains is darker in colour. Unrefined corn oil is darker, amber red in colour, while refined corn oil is darkish yellow, darker than other kinds of vegetable oil. Corn oil is highly recommended by dieticians. Too heavy for salad dressings, it is excellent for frying. Since it slightly foams at higher temperatures, it is not advisable for deep frying.

Wheat germ oil is extracted by cold pressing from the germ of wheat kernels. It is regarded as very healthy and highly recommended by dieticians. It is used mostly for dressings; its delicate taste adds a noble note to salads.

Soy-bean (or **soya-bean**) **oil** is obtained from soy-beans. Unrefined oil is pale amber in colour and has a characteristic flavour. Refined oil is pale yellow and translucent, and has a nice, almost neutral flavour. It is excellent for dressings and for cooking. It can be heated to 180°C, but fried, it loses its nutritive properties, therefore it is better to use it in salads.

Linseed (or **flax seed**) **oil** is obtained by cold pressing from seeds of the flax plant. It is highly recommended and has a peculiar savoury taste. It is greenish yellow in colour, and its solvent extracted variety ranges from greenish yellow to dark red. Once in Poland it was used in traditional Christmas Eve dishes. Today it is usually one of the ingredients of various salads.

Hemp oil is obtained by cold pressing from hemp seeds. Known in Polish-Lithuanian cuisine for centuries, it is particularly recommended as an ingredient of celeriac, sauerkraut and onion salads.

Rice bran oil, known all over the world, is extracted from the germ and inner husk of the rice plant and then refined. It is considered one of the healthiest kinds of oil, one that enhances the flavour of food products. It has a very high smoke point: 225°C. It is excellent both in salad dressings and for frying.

There is evidence that already 5000 years ago **red palm oil** was known and highly appreciated. It is obtained from the kernel of the African oil palm. It is a high quality product much sought after by cooks all over the world who use it for frying, in sauces and in mayonnaise. It can also be used as a natural colouring agent. Red palm oil has a high content of vitamin E and carotenes, which give it its rich red colour, and a natural source of what are called 'vitamins of youth'.

Avocado oil is obtained from the fleshy pulp surrounding the avocado pit. Refined cooking avocado oil has been introduced relatively recently. It should have no smell or flavour and be straw yellow in colour. It should be stored in tightly closed, dark containers. It tends to solidify, especially at low temperatures.

Coconut oil is produced from the kernel and meat of matured coconut, as one of the few kinds of oil which thicken and solidify at room temperature. Pure coconut oil, which has a consistency and colour of lard, can be bought in many supermarkets and shops with oriental condiments, usually in glass jars (not bottles). It should be stored in the fridge. NB: rancid coconut oil has a 'soapy' taste.

Sesame oil has a very nice flavour and characteristic taste, and can be anything from dark gold to red in colour. It is expensive, therefore used mainly together with other kinds of oil in salad dressings, soups and sauces, and with vegetables. It has a low smoke point, hence it is rarely used for frying or cooking in general. If used as a cooking oil, it is added towards the end of the process. Light sesame oil is pale yellow in colour and, like olive oil, can be used for cooking, including stir-frying of meat and vegetables on condition that you keep it off the smoke point.

Safflower (or **thistle**) **oil** is very valuable but expensive. It is obtained by cold pressing from the seeds of a thistle-like annual plant, sometimes referred to as bastard saffron. This pale yellow oil is particularly suitable for oil and mayonnaise dressings for salads and root vegetables (carrots, celeriac, parsnip). It can also be added to sauces and vegetable soups, but should not be used for stewing or frying. It relatively quickly goes rancid, therefore it is better to buy it in small bottles.

Flavoured oils are oils to which herbs and spices are added. The most popular of them is **chili oil** (or **hot oil**), made of vegetable oil infused with dried chili peppers. Chili oil is added to many Chinese dishes. In shops with Oriental condiments you can buy it in small bottles, which should be stored in the fridge if the oil is to preserve its flavour. It is used only as a condiment, never for cooking, sprinkled sparsely over a dish just before serving.

You can get all kinds of flavoured oil, but my advice is: prepare it yourself by mixing herbs and spices with olive, sunflower or grape-seed oil and then pouring the mixture into small bottles or jars. In this way you can produce lemon, pepper, garlic and dried tomato oils, all of them ideal with lettuce, goat's cheese, brie or camembert, toast and boiled or baked vegetables.

It is up to you, and to the thickness of your wallet, what kind of oil you choose: extra virgin olive oil, grape-seed oil, sunflower oil, soybean oil, corn oil, walnut oil, safflower oil or flavoured oil. It is however advisable to have at least two or three kinds at hand: basic vegetable oil of multiple uses – sunflower or soybean oil – a small bottle of sesame oil for oriental dishes and, for example, grape-seed oil for salads.

Vinegar

Vinegar has been used since ancient times, originally as a preserving agent, and then as a highly appreciated condiment, particularly its flavoured kinds. The most popular flavoured vinegar is wine vinegar which is infused with various fruit, herbs and spices, such as rosemary, tarragon, dill, garlic, chili, pepper, and violet seeds, and also with honey, nuts and shallots.

For your everyday use we recommend some good quality **wine vinegar** – white, red or rosé – and a small bottle of reddish brown, fairly mild **balsamic vinegar** (the real thing is produced in the vicinity of Modena). Balsamic vinegar is not too sour, it has a mild taste but very intense flavour, therefore it has to be used sparingly – one drop too much may kill the taste of the main ingredients. Apart from sprinkling berries, we use it mainly as a condiment for meat, in particular for carpaccio made from raw fillet of beef, deer or wild boar. If you add several drops of balsamic vinegar – instead of wine – to a pan in which you fried livers or duck, the sauce will gain an exquisite aroma and flavour. You may also use it in salad dressings, remember only that sprinkled on lettuce too early it causes discoloration. Any gourmet is bound to love vinaigrette of hazelnut oil with a dash of balsamic vinegar.

I suggest also **cider** (or **apple**) **vinegar** (or vinegar made from other fruit), which you can produce all year round at home, using the peel and cores of apples (or for example pears). In oriental dishes very mild cider vinegar with honey is an excellent substitute for very expensive rice vinegar. Cider vinegar is suitable for salad dressings, for bitter green vegetables, for fish, meat and fruit salads. It is also a fine addition to ginger and curry sauces. And it works wonders when you use it for cleaning the frying pan in which pork was fried. Among other fruit vinegars pale pink raspberry vinegar is good for salad dressings and, instead of lemon juice, for veal and chicken.

High quality **sherry vinegar** (*vinagre de Jerez*) goes well with many foods which it gives a deep, slightly tarty flavour. It is excellent for preparing vinaigrette with nut oil.

English **malt vinegar** has a sharp taste and is suitable for pickled and marinated vegetables, such as onion or garlic, and for chutneys.

In oriental cuisine vinegar is used to enhance the flavours. The most popular kind of vinegar is Japanese or Chinese **white rice vinegar**, pale yellow in colour, slightly sticky. It is mild in taste and is generally used for marinating vegetables, fish and frutti di mare, as well as for salad dressings and for noodles. It is most frequently added to sweet-and-sour dishes and to soups. Instead of white rice vinegar you may use ordinary white wine vinegar or fruit vinegar. I also recommend **Chinese red rice vinegar** – reddish orange in colour, translucent, slightly salty and slightly sour, and **black rice vinegar** – black or dark brown in colour and milder in taste. The former is used above all with frutti di mare, but also with grilled, fried and stewed dishes. The latter, milder than white rice vinegar, mixes well with sesame oil and is suitable for salads of frutti di mare.

There are also **Chinese sweet vinegar** – thick, pale brown in colour, similar to soy sauce, tasting of caramel and Chinese spices, which is suitable for pork as it neutralizes its high fat content; and **honey vinegar** with a fine, sweet aroma and a nice, slightly sour taste, which is used with sweet and sour poultry and meat in many Chinese provinces.

Capers

Capers are pickled or salted buds of the perennial shrub (*Capparis spinosa*) which grows in the Mediterranean basin. In summer caper buds appear gradually (when fresh they taste unpleasantly bitter). They are hand-picked and sorted according to size, and preserved in brine or vinegar. Salted capers are particularly tasty. Capers are categorized by their size as follows: the smallest called *non-pareilles*, most desirable, but also most expensive, followed by *surfines*, *capucines*, *capottes*, *fines*, and *mi-fines*. Capers make a delicious savoury, mildly bitter seasoning or garnish. They are used to season salads, mayonnaises and cold sauces, and are added to stews and roast meat (always towards the end of the cooking process). In cold dishes they combine well with olives and onion. Capers are used to garnish canapés and plates of cold meat, sliced hard-boiled eggs and curd cheese. According to the greatest 16th century surgeon, Ambroise Paré, 'capers sharpen your appetite and purge you'.

Artichokes

The Italians believed artichoke to have aphrodisiac properties and called them 'potatoes of love'. About unfaithful men they used to say that they had 'hearts of artichoke – one leaf for one lady'.

Al-kharshuf in Arabic, *artichaut* in French, *carciofo* in Italian, and *alcachofa* in Spanish, the artichoke (*Cynara scolymus* a. *cardunculus*) is related to the sunflower, chrysanthemum and chard. It belongs to the numerous family of the *Compositae* and is in fact a thistle. Its flowers form a large head with numerous triangular scales. The edible portion of the buds is the fleshy lower part of the bracts and the base, known as the heart. Artichoke flowers, purple in colour, form fine plumes. Artichokes are rich in vitamins and minerals, and are an excellent source of dietary fibre and vitamin C. They also contain a lot of calcium, phosphorus, iron, thiamine and niacin, and are low-calorie. They reduce the level of bad cholesterol, make us feel better and apparently increase 'our ability to experience pleasure'.

They are best boiled or steamed, served sprinkled with melted butter and pepper or with breadcrumbs toasted in butter. You should be warned of one thing however: if not cooked immediately, within 24 hours at the most, they start producing a poisonous greyish-green mould called *bremia*. In the recipes in this book only tinned artichoke hearts are recommended. Such hearts, preserved in oil, brine or vinaigrette, are an excellent addition to lettuce, vegetable salads, pasta and bakes.

Olives

Olives were grown already in ancient Egypt 5000 years ago and the plant was brought to Europe by the Greeks. In Greece it was dedicated to the goddess of wisdom Athena as a symbol of peace and fertility. For centuries olives have been used in sauces, stuffing and salads, eaten raw and preserved. **Green olives** and **black olives** come from the same plant; in fact they can be from green, through pink, red and purple to black, depending on when they have been harvested. All are added to cold appetizers and salads as well as to hot dishes: roast poultry, meat stews, stewed vegetables or Italian pizzas. Olives with red stuffing look particularly attractive when we slice them and use them to garnish various dishes. Olives stuffed with almonds or anchovies make an excellent appetizer, and the oil they contain helps the organism absorb alcohol.

Freshly picked olives are unpalatable due to their bitter taste and have to be first processed. To remove the bitter taste they need to be soaked in water (changed frequently) for a long time, then pickled for months in brine or in wine vinegar with olive oil, often with an addition of various herbs and spices (lemon zest, chili, rosemary, thyme, oregano or bay leaves). Green olives have lower oil content than ripe black ones, but they are less digestible.

A Spanish speciality are stuffed green olives, especially of the *manzanillo* variety, which are particularly fleshy and have relatively small pits. The traditional Spanish stuffing is called *anchoisale*, but producers stuff olive fruit today with almonds, capsicum, garlic, capers, lemon or orange paste, salmon or tuna paste, herbs, cheese...

Black and green (also stuffed) olives are added to many salads, but also to spaghetti, pizza, risotto, to lamb, partridge, rabbit and chicken. Large Italian olives, stuffed with beef, pork and chicken livers, coated in flour and fried in olive oil, are served instead of potatoes with lamb, brains or fried artichoke.

Pickled green pepper

The pepper plant was originally native to the south-western coast of India, today called the Malabar Coast, and once known as Malichabar – 'the land of pepper'.

Pepper is perhaps the best known and most popular condiment in the world and has played an important role in the history of culture. Pickled green pepper is a masterpiece of culinary art. Only in Malaysia, India, Sri Lanka and Indonesia it is added to dishes in its raw state. The rest of the world gets in small jars of pickle or dried in small packets. It has a very pungent taste. Unripe green peppercorns are pickled in brine, vinegar or spirit. Green peppercorns in brine have a very special taste and flavour. They are indispensable in preparing delicious beefsteaks in brandy and cream or salmon and avocado mousse.

Chestnuts

The sweet chestnut comes from Asia Minor and the Caucasus. As we learn from many ancient authors, it reached Greece still before Christ and very quickly spread to Italy, Spain and Gaul. The ancient Romans treated chestnuts as a vegetable – they mashed them, combined with cabbage and served with meat dishes.

In many parts of the world chestnuts are regarded as an aphrodisiac – especially served as chestnuts Mont Blanc, a sweet chestnut puree with brandy and whipped cream. Chestnuts can be prepared in all sorts of ways. Fresh chestnuts are roasted, cooked, stewed; they are used for stuffing turkeys, ducks, and chicken or for various desserts. You can buy them either fresh or tinned – preserved in brine or sugar (marrons glaces). You get them whole or as chestnut cream (crème de marrons), sweetened puree with vanilla. Both marrons glaces and crème de marrons are used for desserts, ice cream and cake fillings.

When you buy fresh chestnuts, choose fruit that are heavy and have unscarred shells. Fresh chestnuts can be stored in the fridge for up to three weeks. Never eaten raw, they are first roasted – slit the chestnut shells crosswise, put in a very hot oven (220°C), roast for 10–12 minutes, take out, leave to cool a little and shell them while they are still warm. Chestnuts that you add to various dishes are usually first cooked (for 20 minutes), then shelled. Whole kernels are added to soups, while to vegetable stews you add chopped chestnuts.

Water chestnuts

There are several water plants referred to by that name. The best known of them are **Chinese water chestnut** and **water caltrop**. The Chinese water chestnut (*Eleocharis dulcis*) is very popular in Chinese cuisine. It contains potassium, sodium, iron and vitamin C. The word 'chestnuts' refers to tubers on the plant's rhizomes from which stems and leaves grow up. Chinese water chestnuts have a shiny, dark brown shell covered with a paper-thin outer skin, and white sweetish, slightly crunchy meat. Chopped chestnuts are used in sauces and oriental soups, salads, meat and fish dishes, desserts and fruit salads, in fillings and stir-fry dishes. Chinese water chestnuts are available, whole or sliced, mostly in tins. Before you add them, drain them and rinse under running water. In an open tin they will keep in the fridge for 5–7 days, provided you change the water every day.

The water caltrop (*Trapa natans*) is native to Eurasia and was known in Europe as early as the Middle Ages. This is an annual aquatic plant with diamond-shaped floating leaves and feather-like submerged leaves. It has small flowers and its fruit are dark-brown nuts 2 to 2.5 cm in diameter with, depending on the variety, two or four barbs. Two-barbed fruit are grown in China, Japan and Korea. Water caltrops are added to many regional Chinese dishes.

Bamboo shoots

Bamboo shoots are recommended in particular to weight-watchers. They do not contain fat or cholesterol and are rich in thiamine (vitamin B$_1$), vitamin C and potassium. Young shoots of edible bamboo species are ivory white in colour and have slightly floury texture. They are conical in shape, slightly thicker at the base. Spring shoots are small, sweetish, soft, and ivory white in colour. They can be eaten as a vegetable or added to various dishes. Winter shoots are thicker and longer, cream yellow in colour, and have a more distinct flavour. In Asian cuisine they are both valued for their taste and crunchiness. Raw shoots are covered with a brownish skin which has to be removed before cooking. Fresh shoots will keep in the fridge for a couple of weeks.

In Europe bamboo shoots are usually sold in tins (in brine, with no herbs or spices), either whole or cut into smaller pieces or slices. Once you open a tin, transfer the shoots to a glass jar and keep in the fridge (frequently changing the water) for up to seven days. Also available are bamboo shoots in salt or in soy sauce (the latter makes them slightly brown, softer and springy). Because of their savoury taste, they are used mainly in soups and stews. Salted shoots are usually sold in plastic bags. Having opened such a bag, transfer the shoots to a glass jar with a tightly fitting lid and store them in the fridge – they will keep for a long time. Salted bamboo shoots have to be rinsed under running water before you use them.

Bamboo shoots are served as a vegetable dish or else as a sweetish addition to various dishes: oriental salads, stewed meat and stir-fried dishes.

Vine leaves in brine

No one knows whether stuffed vine leaves are a Greek or a Turkish invention. In the rest of Europe vine leaves in brine are available in special shops and most supermarkets.

Having opened a tin or jar of vine leaves, take the leaves out, rinse them under running water and dry them. Then you may stuff them with various fillings in the following way: put some filling in the middle of a leaf, turn the sides of the leaf up, and roll it up, beginning from the stem side. Place the rolls tightly in a heavy saucepan, cover with hot stock or water mixed with lemon juice and olive oil; press down with a heavy plate, put the lid on and cook over a low heat for 25–35 minutes. Such rolls can be made also from fresh, young vine leaves which must be first blanched in boiling salted water for 5–6 minutes, rinsed under cold water and dried on a paper towel.

Stuffed vine leaves are served as a hot starter or as part of the main course. It is also a good idea to cover them with a cup of olive oil and put into the fridge for 5–7 days, and then serve them as a cold starter, the way it is done in Greece.

Sun-dried tomatoes

Drying vegetables has been known for centuries in the whole Mediterranean region and preserving dried vegetables in oil makes them keep even longer. At the peak of summer halved fleshy ripe tomatoes are arranged on special nets and left to dry in the sun. They slowly lose moisture, get dark and wrinkly, and their flavour becomes more intense – in fact it is eventually so concentrated that you need only a small quantity to enrich the taste of a dish.

My advice is to buy soft dried tomatoes, deep red in colour, sometimes with a film of salt on them. Such tomatoes must be first soaked in water with vinegar for several minutes and dried on a paper towel. Sun-dried tomatoes go well with garlic, capers, chili, herbs (basil, rosemary, thyme, oregano). They are a must in the Mediterranean cuisine, added to sauces, pastes, pastas, bakes, salads, roast meat and poultry.

Sun-dried tomatoes are also available in oil, often flavoured with herbs and spices. They are then sold either in small glass jars or by weight. They enhance the taste of sauces, soups and stews, and can be added to vinaigrette dressings.

Ginger, fresh and preserved

In the depths of the stomach, kidneys and the lungs
ginger's burning flavour
satisfies one's appetite, excites the mind
and make love-making pleasant to the old.

(according to a medieval medical school from Salerno)

No wonder then that for centuries ginger has fired the imagination of master cooks and was used in various forms: fresh and dried, whole and powdered, pickled and candied. In medieval Poland it was an indispensable condiment for tripe, terrines and mulled wine. Ginger has an intense spicy, sweetish flavour and a sharp, burning, slightly bitter taste. This applies in particular to fresh ginger, and also to pickled or candied ginger. On the other hand powdered ginger has a somewhat different flavour and can hardly be a substitute for fresh roots. Pinkish pickled shredded ginger is often used in sushi.

A piece of ginger added to the milk in which rice is cooked turns a rather bland dish into a delicious pudding. Candied (or fresh) ginger adds flavour to cold soups of soured milk, yogurt or kefir. It is also a good idea to rub steaks or pork chops with a mixture of ginger, salt and pepper before you fry or grill them – the meat will taste better and be tender. The same applies to game, pork stews, poultry, mutton or roast bacon. Candied ginger is an excellent addition to punch, mulled wine and pears. It is also used for decorating fruit cakes and for ginger bread and ginger cookies. Possibilities are endless. You should only remember that it does not go well with herbs which must be added sparingly. The final warning is: don't overdo it, because too much ginger may spoil the dish. Ginger is best kept in a tightly closed jar in a dark place.

Oriental mushrooms

Some kinds of Asian mushrooms are available dried or in tins. Many of them can be replaced with locally growing champignons, saffron milk caps or blanched chanterelles. The most popular oriental mushrooms are:

Cloud ear fungus, also known as wood or tree ear, mu-er or mun from Chinese. Its black variety has wrinkly caps. Cloud ear mushrooms are usually sold dried (once you open a bag, transfer the mushrooms to a jar or tin with a tightly fitting lid) and need to be soaked in hot water for 20 minutes. In the process they grow in volume five times and recover their original appearance. You add them chopped into thin strips. They do not need prolonged stewing or frying. Due to their neutral taste, they go well with sharp-flavoured dishes, such as curries and savoury stews and fries seasoned with garlic, chili and soy paste.

Shiitake, sometimes called black forest mushrooms, are fleshy, juicy mushrooms popular in the East due to their medicinal properties: they lower cholesterol levels and thus prevent cardiac disorders, stimulate the immune system and contain lentinan, an anticancer agents, as well as antibacterial and anti-viral agents.

Shiitake grow on tree trunks. They look a bit like champignons, only they are larger and have more flavour; their caps are brown and their gills yellow. They are sold fresh or dried. Once the bag of dried mushrooms is open, to preserve their flavour its contents should be transferred to a jar or tin with a tightly fitting lid. Dried mushrooms need to be soaked in lukewarm water for at least 20 minutes (longer for larger specimens). Before you cook them, remember to cut off their stems which are too hard to digest.

Both fresh and dried shiitake have a distinct flavour which goes well with many meat, fish and vegetable dishes. As a separate dish they are cooked in well seasoned consommé. The water in which they have soaked can be used in soups and stews. The flavour of the mushrooms is improved when you add some oyster sauce to them.

Siang mushrooms, in Europe also known as Chinese mushrooms, recall European armillaria mushrooms. They have a strong flavour and are sold dried, which means you first have to soak them in water. They are used mostly with soups.

Pistachios

These are small nuts covered with a thin reddish yellow skin and whitish exterior shells which when ripe splits part way open – that is why in India they are also known as 'laughing nuts'.

Their flesh is light green, with a distinct flavour. Pistachios contain 54% fat (80% of which unsaturated), 23% protein and 15% carbohydrates. They are a rich source of iron. They are usually sold in shells, but you can also get them shelled and blanched. Always choose pistachios which are fresh and unblemished, bright green in colour. After you shell them, blanch them in boiling water so that they keep the colour and shed the skin. Then drain them, rinse under running cold water, and drain and dry them thoroughly.

Pistachios are used both for savoury and sweet dishes. Salted pistachios are excellent as a side dish, especially toasted in butter and served hot. They are also added to game, sauces, terrines and forcemeat. Unsalted pistachios are added to desserts and fruit salads, used for decorating cakes and cookies, but above for making ice cream which they give a characteristic flavour and nice colour.

Pine nuts

Pine nuts are one of the favourite ingredients in the cuisine of the Middle East and Mediterranean region. In Europe they come from the stone pine (*Pinus pinea*), which has been cultivated for its nuts for centuries from Lebanon to Spain. They have a sweetish taste and a refreshing,

slightly resinous flavour. Pine nuts are 1–2 mm long seeds that contain quite a lot of fat, mostly unsaturated, and are a source of vitamin B$_1$ and phosphorus, as well as protein and iron.

Always choose fresh pine nuts which have preserved their flavour. Store them in the fridge in a tightly closed jar (they will keep then for 2–3 months), because they tend to go rancid quickly.

Before you add them to the food, it is a good idea to roast them to get rid of their slightly turpentine smell. They taste best just toasted, but can also be added to fried or roasted dishes. They do a lot for sauces, salads, fillings, pastes and savoury fish and meat dishes, as well as for game and lamb, vegetables, various desserts and cakes. They are rather on the pricy side, therefore in many recipes you may use sunflower seeds instead of pine nuts.

Sesame seeds

Sesame seeds have nice, sweetish nutty taste, but no aroma. Their colour varies from cream-white (most popular) to charcoal-black. The cream-white seeds are small, flattish, shiny and not really hard. The brown ones are oval in shape and have a nutty flavour, while the black ones are sharper in taste. All of them gain in taste when you toast them slightly – then their nutty flavour is at its most intense.

Sesame seeds are sprinkled on top bread loaves and added to savoury and sweet dishes: Asian-style salads, salad dressings, rice, vegetables, meat stews, forcemeat, cheese pastes. They can also be used as coating for fried fish, veal medallions and chicken fillets. Black seeds are delicious as coating for stir-fried chicken and frutti di mare. Very popular Chinese starters are little balls of chopped shrimps with sesame seeds, served on toast. In Japan toasted sesame seeds or *gomasio* (sesame seeds with salt) are sprinkled on rice and other dishes and added to sauces. *Tahini*, oriental sesame paste (sometimes called 'sesame butter'), is added to sauces for noodles, rice and vegetables and spread on bread instead of ordinary butter.

Oriental noodles

Oriental noodles are made of flour, powdered soy beans, powdered sprouting mung beans or rice, mixed with water. Sometimes eggs are added for flavour. Some noodles need only to be soaked in water, others have to be boiled. Salads are made usually with deep-fried noodles. Dried noodles keep for a very long time. The most common oriental noodles known in Europe are:

Soy bean noodles (*fen*) are thin, cellophane-like transparent noodles. Before you cook them, soak them in hot or cold water for a few minutes, and, if you wish, cut them into smaller pieces. Soaked soy bean noodles are usually deep-fried or cooked in salted boiling water. Deep-fried noodles grow in volume and become crispy. Both boiled and deep-fried noodles are served with salads, meat, fish, vegetables and frutti di mare.

Rice noodles (*bee-sun*), also called 'long rice' or 'pink sticks', are made from powdered high-quality rice and water. They have more flavour than soy bean noodles, but they just as easily absorb the flavours of all other ingredients. They are protein-free, therefore recommended for coeliacs, diabetics and vegetarians. Rice noodles should be first soaked in water for 3–5 minutes, then drained and added to dishes towards the end of the cooking process: do not cook them too long. Soaked noodles can be also deep-fried (very briskly, for they tend to burn) or boiled in stock. Deep-fried noodles tend to grow in volume, therefore you are advised to do it in small portions (the way you fry potato chips). They are best served with fried dishes and with sauces.

Japanese soba noodles are like thin spaghetti, 30 cm in length. They are made from buckwheat flour or mixed buckwheat and wheat flour. They are basically beige in colour. For green noodles, green tea is added to the dough, and for pinkish noodles, the dough is mixed with beetroot juice. Soba noodles are cooked in salted boiling water till tender, then drained and rinsed in cold water. In Japan they are often served cold with soy bean paste or dip, frutti di mare or vegetables.

Savoury pastes and sauces

Cooks all over the world use hundreds of spicy mixtures in the form of powders, pastes or sauces. Pastes are a speciality of oriental cuisine, although they are also popular in the Mediterranean region.

Asian dishes are cooked in many different ways, but they share one common feature: they are cooked quickly, stir-fried in a little fat, and the variety of flavours is achieved by the addition of various pastes, sauces, herbs and spices.

Two basic kinds of paste are produced: fermented and unfermented. Unfermented pastes include above all those that are made from fresh products: herbs, vegetables, chilis or sesame seeds. These include nut paste, sesame paste, pesto and wasabi.

The best known fermented pastes are misso, natto, shrimp paste, black bean paste and tempeh.

Tahini is a nutty sesame paste, an ingredient of many traditional Jewish and Arab dishes. In Arabic cuisine it is often added to bread dough – 2 teaspoons of tahini instead of 1 egg – mixed with a little water. It can be used as a bread spread and a condiment for salads, broths, stews and salad dressings. It has an incomparable flavour which adds taste to various sauces, and to both savoury and sweet dishes. You can buy it in any supermarket (the darker variety, slightly bitter, is the best) or make it yourself.

Pesto – its full name *pesto alla genovese*, meaning Genoese pulp: in Italian *pesto* means 'to pound, to crush', and that is how you produce it – by pounding or crushing basil leaves, chopped garlic, pine nuts, salt, grated cheese and olive oil. In the original recipes the cheese to use is Sardo, parmesan or Pecorino. Pesto is one of the most popular pastes or spreads. It has many uses and gives a dish a peculiar Italian flavour. It can be used with pasta, grilled meat, as bread spread, for garnishing tomato soup, as a dip for crudités. There are different varieties of pesto – with other herbs instead of basil, with tomatoes, chilis, walnuts, almonds, pistachios, sunflower seeds, pumpkin seeds. Rocket instead of basil gives it extra piquancy, and a red pesto can be produced if instead of olive oil you add sun-dried tomatoes in oil. The important thing is to pound and crush the ingredients into a smooth paste.

Such sauce is also popular in Provence where it is called *pistou*. In supermarkets in Europe, apart from the traditional *pesto alla genovese*, you can get other pasta sauces: orange Calabrese sauce (*pesto alla callabrese*) made from red bell peppers, chili pepper, tomato concentrate, oregano and Ricotta and Pecorino cheeses; golden Sicilian sauce (*pesto alla siciliana*) made from tomatoes, nuts, Grana Padano and Ricotta cheeses, basil and pine nuts; and dark red *pesto rosso* made from sun-dried tomatoes, basil, oregano, thyme, marjoram, garlic and chilis.

Pesto sauces available in shops contain preservatives which make them last longer. Therefore we advise you to make your own pesto in a blender, or preferably in a mortar, because then it achieves its full flavour.

Anchovy paste

Anchovy paste has a distinctive fish aroma and flavour. In old Polish cuisine it enriched the taste of roast beef. It adds flavour to many dishes and a dash of it is enough. It is quite salty, therefore be careful when you salt a dish and do it only towards the end of cooking. Instead of anchovy paste you may use finely chopped anchovies.

Shrimp paste

Shrimp or prawn paste is a common ingredient of Southeast Asian dishes. It is made from brown or sand shrimps, which are first salted, cooked, dried and mixed. Depending on the region, its composition differs, as does the mode in which it is offered for sale: it is sold in hard rectangular blocks or in glass jars, when its colour is pinkish grey. In any form it has a pungent smell and flavour (not unlike that of a strong meat broth). It is added to almost all soups and sauces, and to many vegetable and rice dishes in Indonesia, Malaysia, China, Sri Lanka and Singapore. In the fridge it keeps for a long time, provided the jar is tightly closed. You add it sparingly to certain dishes, no more than the recipe instructs you to do.

Wasabi paste

Japanese wasabi paste is made from the root of the wasabi plant, called by some Japanese horseradish. It is burning hot, therefore sometimes described as *namida*, or 'tears', meaning that it makes your eyes water. In Europe wasabi is sold as a ready-to-use green paste in tubes or as white powder which has to be mixed with water – the 'safe' proportions are 1 tablespoon wasabi powder to 1 tablespoon water – then left aside for 10–15 minutes, which is enough for the mixture to turn a nice green colour. Wasabi paste is added to sauces served with various cold starters, to sushi and to fish dishes. With sushi, a thin layer of it is spread thinly between the fish and the rice or the paste is served separately.

Ajvar

Also known as Serbian or Balkan salad, ajvar is a flavourful, medium sharp relish made from aubergines, red bell peppers, oil and spices. It makes a delicious bread spread, but can also be added to many meat and vegetable dishes. It enhances the taste of boiled, stewed, fried, grilled or roasted dishes. One or two teaspoonfuls of ajvar can make a great difference. Its taste depends on the vegetables it has been made from. Ajvar mixed with cream or mayonnaise makes a delicious sauce for cold meats.

Sweet and savoury bean pastes

Yellow paste is made from fermented yellow soybeans, wheat flour, salt and water; it is sold in glass jars or tins, and can be sharp or sweet.

Red bean paste is made from sweetened beans and is often used in cake-making.

Pinto paste, popular in South America, is made from reddish brown pinto beans; in Mexico it is added to sauces, minced meat and tortillas.

Black bean paste comes in two varieties: savoury (in oriental cuisine), made from salted fermented beans, which is salty in taste and brown in colour; sweet, made from unfermented beans; in Mexico it is added to minced meat and to many sauces.

Tempeh is brown paste with a nutty taste; it is made from soybeans and sold usually in blocks or cubes.

Chili-based pastes

These are known in all parts of the world. In each region their composition may be different, but all contain two basic ingredients: chili peppers and oil. So there are chili pastes with ginger and garlic, for example **piri-piri sauce** used in Portuguese and African cooking, or Mexican salsas (like *salsa verde*, made from green japaleno peppers, onion, garlic and coriander, or *salsa arriera* from red serrano peppers, which is a delicious dip and can also be added to various sauces). A standard ingredient of North African cuisine is Arab **harissa**, made from red chilis, garlic, spices and oil – only for those 'who love fire burning in their throats'. In Tunisia, Algeria and Morocco it is served at virtually every meal: as an appetizer and bread spread, as a flavouring for couscous, scrambled eggs, meat and vegetable stews, roast meat and poultry. You can also get various Thai curry pastes and Indonesian sambal sauce, a chili based sauce available in various versions: with garlic, onion, candlenuts, tamarind concentrate, sweet lime, coconut milk, powdered aromatic ginger, ginger, tumeric, lemongrass, aromatic herbs and leaves. The most famous of them is **sambal oelek** (or **ulek**), a mixture of various cultivars of chili pepper, salt and oil, with a dash of brown sugar. This has to be used very sparingly – a tip of a teaspoon is usually enough.

Soy sauce

According to Shizuo Tsuji, the author of *Japanese Cooking: A Simple Art*, soy sauce used to be a secret ingredient of dishes prepared for banquets at the court of Louis XIV. This is probably the best known oriental condiment. It gives the dishes a brownish colour and inimitable flavour. Soy sauce was brought to Europe by Dutch merchants in the 17th century. Also known as *shōyu*, it has a very high content of protein, vitamins A, B, C and E, calcium, phosphorus and iron. Originally used in oriental cuisine, it is now very popular all over the world and used instead of Maggi sauce. The brand of soy sauce which is most sought after today is Kikkoman, which at room temperature may keep even for several years.

Soy sauce is a basis for many other sauces, such as **hoisin**, **Worcester** or oriental, honey-flavoured sauce for barbecued meat (e.g. chicken and shashlyks) called **char-siu**: first, brush the meat pieces with the sauce, leave aside for 30–40 minutes, then roast or grill. Those who suffer from high blood pressure should use soy sauce sparingly.

Soy sauce is added to consommé and other clear soups, to pumpkin, onion, vegetable, bean and barley soups instead of salt. It is also used for marinades. Its delicate taste goes well with sweet, sour or piquant flavours. It enhances the taste of some pulses, especially azuki beans and yellow soy beans – remember that with beans soy sauce should be added towards the end of the cooking process. Soy sauce enhances the taste of a variety of dishes, such as Chinese watercress soup, Hawaii banana salad, chicken and celery salad, eggs Indonesian style, Italian stewed red cabbage, savoury celeriac, fried French beans, stewed cod, beef fillets Japanese style, roast spare ribs, sweet and sour pork chops, duck, chicken with pineapple, pork stew with Chinese cabbage... The list is very long. Poultry brushed with soy sauce before roasting is not only tastier and flavourful, but also gets nicely golden brown.

Worcestershire sauce

Worcestershire or Worcester sauce is a delicious liquid condiment which is left to age in oak barrels. One tablespoon of Worcester is enough to enhance the taste of a dish. This aromatic, dark-brown sauce, not unlike Maggi sauce, has 20% sediment – therefore you must give it a good shake before you use it.

Worcester sauce has a distinctive, piquant flavour, slightly sweet and sour in taste. The exact recipe for this sauce is still a closely guarded secret. We only know that its ingredients include tamarind extract, peppers, garlic, molasses, ginger, malt vinegar and salt. To this list some also add nut and mushrooms sauce, sherry, brandy and... surprise, surprise... pork liver and anchovies. Worcester is added to stews, soups, forcemeat, steak tartare, drinks. It works wonders with spaghetti bolognaise, meat stews, bakes, sauces and pickles.

Hoisin sauce

Chinese Hoisin sauce is made from soy, garlic, chili peppers and spices, with some flour and sugar added. It is thick, reddish brown or dark brown in colour. It has a sweetish savoury taste and goes exceptionally well with vegetables and pork. It is used for marinades for meat, spare ribs, roast duck and roast chicken. It is often served as a dipping sauce for pieces of meat and vegetables.

Oyster sauce

Oyster sauce (*hor yo* or *hoyon*), known throughout the Far East, is a delicate liquid condiment made from cooked oysters blended with soy sauce, brine and potato or corn starch. This thick, brown sweet and salty concentrate has an almost neutral taste, but it enhances the taste of other ingredients. Added together with soy sauce, it gives any dish a fine exotic flavour, and it thickens sauces.

It is added to many meat dishes (especially stir-fried) and to salads, to vegetable dishes, poultry, crabs and lobster. It is also used in marinades: 1 tablespoon oyster sauce, 4 tablespoons soy sauce, 1 teaspoon sesame oil, ½ cup water. Oyster sauce should be kept in the fridge in a tightly closed glass jar.

Tabasco

This is something for those who like hot, spicy flavours, for it is one of the hottest sauces in any cuisine. Hand-picked tabasco peppers, crushed and salted, are left to age in oak barrels for three years, then combined with vinegar; the seeds and skins are removed, while the flesh with vinegar is left to mature for several months. Subsequently the liquid is strained and bottled. Originally Tabasco sauce did not contain any salt and was a speciality of Creole cuisine. Today it is popular all over the world.

Tabasco sauce (red or green) keeps for a very long time. A small bottle of it lasts for months, because one drop is usually enough to make a dish really hot. It is a good idea to add a drop of Tabasco to boiling water in which we cook vegetables or mussels.

Tabasco is used as a condiment in many soups, frutti di mare, stews and alcoholic drinks. A dash of it adds a special note to the taste of marinades, stews, poultry, salad dressing, omelette, beef steaks, potato chips, many sauces, red beans. As if that were not enough, Tabasco is added to vegetable juices and alcoholic drinks, and the famous bloody Mary simply cannot do without it.

Chili sauces

Chili sauces, popular in Far Eastern cuisine, are hot, savoury condiments made of grated chili peppers, garlic, vinegar, sugar and salt. Their simplest versions are similar to ketchup. Unlike Tabasco, they are fairly thick, but should also be used sparingly.

There are many varieties of chili sauce: with garlic, shallots, ginger, tomatoes. Some are very hot, some are savoury sweet and sour. Some are exclusively for poultry or for fried meat. They are added to braised and barbecued meat, to cold and hot sauces, to soups and to marinades for frutti di mare.

Star anise

Star anise, also called star aniseed or badiane, is the fruit of an evergreen shrub native to Southwest China. It is shaped as an eight-pointed star and each of the star's arms contains one seed. The star-shaped fruits are harvested just before ripening and then dried in the sun. Dried fruits are hard, reddish brown in colour.

Star anise was first imported to Europe in the 17th century by land, along the tea trail through Russia, hence it is sometimes called Siberian cardamom. Apart from Chinese and Vietnamese cuisine, it has never been as popular as ginger, but recipes in old cookery books prove that as early as the 17th century it was added as a seasoning to fruit preserves, juices and syrups.

Star anise has a very strong, spicy, burning flavour. In cooking both whole fruits and seeds are used, although the seeds' aroma is not as strong. Fruits are added to dishes whole or crushed in the mortar towards the end of the cooking process. Star anise is often accompanied by mandarin orange peel, cinnamon, Sichuan pepper, cloves and ginger.

Today star anise is added to stewed and roast fish, poultry and pork, frutti di mare and clear soups, and to vegetables, in particular leek and pumpkin. Sometimes instead of star anise you may use ordinary anise, fennel or cinnamon.

Garam masala

In Hindi *garam* means 'hot' and *masala* is 'mixture'. So garam masala is basically a blend of two or three ground spices (sometimes as many as fifteen). Blends of pepper and cloves are very hot, but there are many that are not so pungent, composed of cinnamon, cardamom and mace. **Green masala**, or a mixture of ginger, garlic, chili and coriander, is recommended with fish and chicken, while for vegetable and fruit salads your choice should be **chaat masala**, slightly sour in taste.

One of the most popular blends is hot, sour garam masala made from cinnamon, cumin, coriander, cardamom, cloves, black pepper, mace and bay leaves, which is often added to vegetarian dishes, in particular pulses, steamed vegetables and sauces. It is always added in small amounts, at different stages of the cooking process.

Curry

Contrary to what many may think, there is no place on earth where curry grows. This Indian invention is a blend of five to fifty different ground herbs and spices and there are many kinds of it, differing in composition, and consequently in colour and flavour. Mixing various herbs and spices is the quintessence of Indian cuisine and curried dishes are the quintessence of the Indian culinary art which is a result of thousands of years of experimenting with various gifts of nature.

Cardamom

Cardamom is one of the oldest spices and also the third most expensive one, after saffron and vanilla. It was highly appreciated in antiquity, became forgotten in the middle ages and again gained popularity during the crusades – it was then called *amon amomon*, meaning 'very piquant in taste' – but soon the pope forbade its use due to its alleged aphrodisiac qualities.

The Arabs prepare their strong coffee brew from ground cardamom seeds and coffee beans, and Arab women believe that by adding a few seeds to coffee they will win the heart of any man.

Cardamom is bought in seeds or powdered, however ground cardamom loses its intense aroma since the essential oils the seeds contain quickly evaporate. The whole flavour of cardamom is in its hard, small seeds which have to be crushed in a mortar or ground. If a whole pod is added to cooking food, it has to be taken out before you serve the dish.

It is said that cardamom is a spice that only a master cook can handle. It enhances the taste of both savoury and sweet dishes. A dash of it is enough to flavour soups and sauces, meat stews, rabbit or chicken, and fruit salads. It is an ingredient of some curry powders. It is added to fish and vegetable marinades, to cakes (ginger cakes first and foremost) and liqueurs.

Cumin

Cumin has been in use since ancient times. It has greyish-green seeds, not unlike caraway, and similar properties as caraway, though it is different in taste. Cumin has a hot, piquant, slightly bitter taste and heavy, sharp aroma.

The Iranian and Indian variety of cumin, called black cumin, has a sweetish flavour and is often confused with what is called blackseed, black caraway or Roman coriander. A spice related to cumin and caraway is ajwain, also known as ajowan or carom seeds. Whole cumin seeds or cumin powder are available in supermarkets and shops selling oriental spices.

To enhance the taste and flavour of cumin its seeds should be first toasted in a frying pan. They are used for fish, meat stews, root vegetables and pulses, marinades, pastes, curry, salads and cabbage. Combined with cinnamon, powdered cumin is added to mutton, poultry, beans, vegetables and minced meat. Powdered cumin should be added towards the end of the cooking process, while cumin seeds are best put in at the beginning.

Turmeric

Turmeric is a herbaceous perennial plant of the ginger family, native to India. In antiquity it was known as Indian saffron and later as Bourbon saffron, although it does not taste as saffron at all. It smells of pepper with a musky note, is bright orange in colour and has a sharp, spicy, slightly bitter flavour. It is used both for its flavour and for the golden orange colour it gives a dish. It is often combined with saffron. Powdered turmeric keeps its colour long, but fairly quickly loses its flavour – that is why it is advisable to buy it in small packets and transfer the content of a packet to a tightly closed jar. Remember to use it sparingly, or it will dominate all other flavours. You can add it to sauces, poultry, cream soups, omelette, beans, soy, pumpkin, lentils, vegetables, fish, mutton, potato and chicken salad. It is also used as a colouring agent in sauces, rice, pasta and pickled vegetables, and in yeast or sponge dough.

Sichuan pepper

Despite its name, the plant producing Sichuan pepper pods is related to neither black pepper, nor to chili peppers. It belongs to the family *Rutaceae*, just like lemons and oranges. Also known as aniseed pepper, fagara or Chinese or Japanese pepper, it is the source of one of the oldest Chinese spices. Until 300 years ago, when chili pep-

per took Asian cuisine by storm, its piquancy came above all from Sichuan pepper.

Sichuan pepper is the outer pod and seeds of this plant. The seeds, small, reddish brown in colour, have a unique aroma and flavour with slight lemony overtones. They are not as pungent as black or white pepper, but create a tingly numbness in the mouth. They remain hard as stone even after several hours of cooking, therefore it is advisable to add them powdered or wrapped in a piece of gauze.

For better effect you may first toast the seeds in a frying pan. Sichuan pepper is excellent with meat and poultry. In Chinese cuisine it is added to Sichuan duck or bell peppers with cucumber and onion. Sprinkling grilled chicken or eel with powdered Sichuan pepper neutralizes their fatty taste. Powdered Sichuan pepper is one of the ingredients of a traditional Chinese condiment called five-spice powder.

Five-spice powder

Five-spice powder, perhaps the most popular Chinese condiment, is a mixture of five spices. Its composition derives from ancient medical and culinary theories (5 has always been a magic number in China – there are 'five shapes', 'five elements', 'five tastes', 'five directions', etc). It is frequently added to meat which needs long cooking, and it is in such dishes that five-spice powder fully reveals its qualities. The best known of the five-spice recipes is Cantonese roast duck. The condiment is also used to flavour candied nuts and pickled vegetables. In the Far East it is a favourite when it comes to roast meat and poultry, fish, liver pâtés and marinades, in general, all piquant dishes.

Saffron

Saffron is called the king of spices, which 'gives joy and life, strengthens and restores energy'. It is the most expensive of the spices, therefore it is sold in very small quantities. It consists of dried stigmas of the saffron crocus, which take the form of either orange yellow powder or brownish filaments. The darker the filaments, the better the quality of saffron. A good way to store saffron is to mix 2 g saffron with 100 ml 70% vodka, to pour the mixture into a small bottle, cork it and keep away from light.

Saffron has a spicy, slightly bitter taste and bright orange colour. Even a tiny quantity of it is enough to enhance the taste of a dish and give it a warm golden colour. It is to saffron that *risotto milanese* and real *bouillabaisse* owe their flavour and colour.

Before adding saffron filaments to a dish, soak them in a tablespoon of boiling water, vodka or milk. Powdered saffron is added directly and the food has then to be stirred well to distribute the colour evenly. Saffron is often added to lemon or butter sauces served with fish and mussels, to rice, pasta, puddings and cake dough – usually to hot dishes and only rarely to cold dishes.

Saffron is the most expensive condiment, but you add only a dash to any dish not out of thriftiness, but because too much of it spoils the food, makes it bitter, smelling slightly of iodoform.

Soups

Caper soup with piquant meatballs

200 g **capers***, 3 tbsps butter, 1 tbsp flour, 3 cups chicken stock (or stock from cube), 1 cup dry white wine, 1 tbsp lemon juice, 1 cup cream, 1 egg yolk, a dash of each white pepper and salt (be careful because capers are salty)*

MEATBALLS: 250 g each minced beef and pork, 1 tbsp **anchovy paste***, 1 large onion, 1 bread roll soaked in milk, 2 tbsps grated cheese (Emmentaler), 1 egg, a dash of grated nutmeg, salt and pepper to taste*

MEATBALLS: Peel the onion, chop very finely or grate. Mix with the anchovy paste and grated cheese. Combine with the meat and bread roll. Season with nutmeg, salt and pepper, add the egg. Mix thoroughly, cover with clingfilm and refrigerate for 15 minutes.

In a large saucepan melt the butter, add flour and make a white roux. Pour in 1 cup warm chicken stock and cook over a low heat for 5–8 minutes. When it thickens, add lemon juice, capers and wine.

With moistened hands form the meat mixture into walnut-size balls. Bring the remaining stock to a boil in a separate saucepan. Put in the meatballs and cook over a low heat for 10–15 minutes. Combine with the caper soup, stir gently, adjust the seasoning. Simmer for 1–2 minutes. Mix the cream with the egg yolk and gently pour the mixture into the soup. Heat the soup up but keep off the boil.

Green asparagus soup with rice noodles

3 cups chicken stock (or stock from cube), 1½ cups dry white wine, fillet of chicken (300 g), 1 tsp lemon juice, ¾ cup water, 1–2 cloves garlic, 1–2 sprigs each dill, parsley and tarragon, 250 g green asparagus, 1 small leek, 60 g **cellophane rice noodles***, salt and pepper*

Rinse the chicken fillets, sprinkle with lemon juice, salt and pepper. Put into a saucepan, add the peeled garlic, dill, parsley and tarragon. Cover with water, put the lid on and bring to a boil, then turn down the heat and simmer for 15–20 minutes. Take the meat out, chop it finely and return to the skillet. Cut the rinsed asparagus into 3–4 cm long pieces, slice the carefully washed leek finely. Pour the chicken stock and wine into the saucepan, bring to a boil. Put in the asparagus and noodles, cover and simmer for 5–6 minutes. Add the chopped chicken and continue cooking for another 1–2 minutes. Add salt and pepper to taste. Before serving, sprinkle with chopped leek.

Mushroom soup with walnuts

250 g fresh **shiitake** *mushrooms, 250 g oyster mushrooms, 2 small onions, 1 tbsp olive oil, 3 tbsps chopped walnuts, 1 tbsp flour, 4 cups vegetable stock (or stock from cube), 2–3 tbsps* **sherry vinegar** *or dry sherry, nutmeg, salt and pepper to taste*

Finely dice the peeled onions, cut the cleaned mushrooms into strips. Heat the oil in a saucepan, put in the onions, cover and cook over a low heat for 4–5 minutes. Add the mushrooms and continue cooking for another 5 minutes. Put in the walnuts, sprinkle with flour and fry briskly, stirring all the time. Pour in the stock, stir well, quickly bring to a boil. Turn down the heat, cover and simmer for 20–25 minutes. Take off the heat, leave to cool a little. Liquidize the soup, return to the saucepan. Season with grated nutmeg and pepper, add salt if necessary. Pour in the sherry and slowly bring to a boil (spirit should evaporate but sherry flavour should remain).

Herbal soup

½ cup finely chopped parsley, 2 tbsps green mint leaves, 2 bay leaves, 1 tsp dried sage, ¼ tsp dried thyme, 5–6 cloves, 6 cups vegetable stock (or stock from cube), ¼ tsp freshly ground black pepper, 3–4 tbsps **soy sauce***, 400 g ripe tomatoes, 1 tbsp butter, 3 tbsps lemon juice, a pinch of sugar, salt, 2 cups cooked white beans, a dash of* **saffron***, 2 tbsps finely chopped parsley for garnishing*

Dice the tomatoes, put in a saucepan and sweat over a high heat. Add the butter, sugar, lemon juice, soy sauce and pepper. Cook over a low heat for 30 minutes. Bring the vegetable stock to a boil in another saucepan. Put in the bay leaves, cloves, dried herbs, ½ cup chopped parsley and mint leaves. Stir, bring to a boil, cover and simmer for 30 minutes. Liquidize and sieve the tomatoes. Combine with the strained stock and cooked beans. Put the saffron into a small hot frying pan, add 1–2 tablespoons hot stock, stir well. Combine with the soup, adjust the seasoning. Before serving, sprinkle with chopped parsley.

Fish soup with turmeric

750 g fish fillets (mixed cod, mackerel, sole), 2 carrots, ¼ celeriac, 1 large leek (white part only), 3–4 potatoes, 1 large onion, 1–2 cloves garlic, 2 tbsps butter, ½ cup cream, 1 lemon, 2 tbsps chopped dill, 3 tsps **turmeric***, 1 tsp fennel seeds, pepper, salt, 5 cups water*

Rinse the fish, cut into 4 cm long strips. Peel the onion and garlic. Dice the onion, finely chop the garlic. Wash the leek and slice finely. Peel, wash and dice the carrots and celeriac. Peel, rinse and dice the potatoes. Scrub the lemon, scald with boiling water. Grate 1 tsp lemon rind, juice the fruit. Melt the butter in a large saucepan, put in the onion and garlic, soften them, but do not brown. Add the carrots, celeriac, leek and

potatoes. Stirring all the time fry for 5 minutes. Add the lemon juice and zest, pour in 5 cups water. Cover and cook for ½ hour. Season with pepper and salt, take off the heat. Pour 1 cup strained stock into a saucepan, put in the fish strips. Bring to a boil, then simmer for 10 minutes. Put the vegetable stock through a blender, bring to a boil. Add the turmeric and cream. Stir well, put in the fish and slowly heat up. Before serving, sprinkle with fennel seeds and chopped dill. Serve with French sticks.

Bell pepper soup with shrimps

2 sweet red peppers, 1 each sweet yellow and green pepper, 2 leeks (white parts only), 300 g small shrimps (frozen or tinned, in brine), 2 tbsps finely chopped fresh **ginger***, 4 cups chicken stock, 1 cup cream, juice and grated rind of 1 lemon, 2 tbsps olive oil, 1 tbsp butter, salt, pepper, 3 tbsps chopped dill*

Wash the leeks thoroughly, slice finely. Rinse and dry the peppers, remove the stalks and seeds, cut the flesh into thin strips. Put half the pepper strips into a bowl, sprinkle with lemon juice. Heat the oil in a large saucepan, stir fry the remaining peppers, leek and ginger. Pour in the stock. Add salt, pepper and lemon zest. Cook for 15 minutes, then liquidize. Fry the reserved pepper strips in butter, add to the creamed soup. Bring to a boil. Put in the shrimps and cook for another 3–4 minutes. Pour in the cream, heat up. Adjust the seasoning, add lemon zest. Before serving, sprinkle with chopped dill.

Thai duck soup with water chestnuts

duck breasts (400 g meat), 1 tsp lemon juice, 1 duck or turkey liver, 8 cups water, 3 red onions, 2–3 cloves garlic, 2½ tsps ground coriander, ½ tsp each ground caraway and white pepper, 1 tbsp fish sauce, 1 tin (155 g) **water chestnuts***, 1 lemongrass sprig (c. 10 cm) or grated lime rind, 2 tbsps chopped fresh coriander*

Cut the rinsed and dried duck breasts in bite-size cubes, sprinkle with lemon juice and put in a saucepan. Add the liver and lemongrass (or grated lime rind). Cover with water, bring to a boil. Put the lid on and simmer for 1 hour. Strain the stock. Chop the peeled onions and garlic. Drain the water chestnuts, peel and slice them. Heat the oil in a frying pan and fry the onions and garlic for 2 minutes. Season with ground coriander, caraway and pepper and, stirring all the time, fry for another 2 minutes. Put in the duck meat, fry till the meat is nicely browned. Add the sliced water chestnuts and fish sauce, stir well. Bring the strained stock to a boil, skim excess fat from the surface. Put in the fried duck with onion, bring to a boil, then simmer for 10 minutes. Before serving, sprinkle with chopped coriander.

Zucchini soup with sherry

2–3 young, firm zucchini, 150 g finely grated Cheddar cheese, 50 g smoked bacon, 1 fairly large onion, 1 green bell pepper, 1½ cups light chicken stock (or stock from cube), 2 tbsps butter, 1½ tbsps flour, 1 cup milk, 1½ cups cream, 1 tbsp **Worcester sauce***, 1 small glass dry sherry, salt*

Rinse and dry the pepper, remove the stalk and seeds, cut the flesh into strips. Rinse the zucchini, grate coarsely. Peel and finely dice the onion. Cut the bacon into cubes. Heat a large, heavy saucepan, render the bacon. Take out the scratchings with a straining spoon. Fry the onion, but do not brown. Put in the zucchini and pepper, stir fry them. Pour in the hot stock, cover and cook over a low heat for 5 minutes. Make a roux from the butter and flour in a small pan. Thin it down with milk mixed with cream and Worcester sauce. Stirring all the time, simmer until the mixture thickens. Take off the heat, combine with the cheese. Add to the vegetables and heat up. Add salt to taste and sherry, stir well. Before serving, sprinkle some scratchings on top.

Oriental pumpkin soup

3 cups small cubes of pumpkin, 1 tbsp lemon juice, 200 g small frozen shrimps, 1 tbsp **anchovy paste***, 2 small onions, 1 large garlic head, ¼ tsp cayenne pepper, 6 cups chicken stock*

Sprinkle the pumpkin cubes with lemon juice and cayenne pepper, mix well, leave aside for 10 minutes. Peel and finely chop the onions. Chop the peeled garlic, cream

it with the anchovy paste. Put the frozen shrimps into boiling water for 1 minute, drain them, cut into pieces and combine with the anchovy and garlic paste and with the chopped onions. Put the mixture into a skillet, cover with the hot stock. Stir well and cook for 2–3 minutes. Add the pumpkin and simmer over a low heat for 10 minutes. Serve very hot.

Piquant cream of chestnuts

400 g fresh or tinned **chestnuts***, 4 cups chicken or vegetable stock (or stock from cube), 100 g wheat bread, a pinch of each salt, white pepper, ground nutmeg, ground allspice and sugar, 2 tbsps butter*

Roast the chestnuts (if fresh) in the oven and peel them, or drain them (if tinned). Put them into a saucepan, cover with the hot stock. Put the lid on and cook for 40 minutes. Take out 8 chestnuts, chop them finely and leave aside for the time being. Put the remaining chestnuts and the stock through a blender, add allspice, nutmeg, salt, sugar and pepper. Sieve the soup and return to the saucepan. Finely crumble the bread (without crust). Put into the soup and heat for 5 minutes. Add the butter, stir well, adjust the seasoning. Put in the reserved, chopped chestnuts.

Cream of chanterelles

400 g potatoes, 400 g fresh chanterelles, 1 large onion, 200 g tofu, 4 cups vegetable stock (or stock from cube), 3 tbsps butter, ½ cup **soy sauce***, 2 tbsps dry sherry or* **sherry vinegar***, freshly ground pepper, 3 tbsps chopped basil leaves*

Clean, rinse and dry the mushrooms, dice into fair-sized pieces. Melt 1 tablespoon butter in a heavy saucepan, fry the chanterelles, then take off the heat. Peel and dice the potatoes and onion. Melt the remaining butter in another saucepan, put in the onion, fry for 1 minute. Add the potatoes and stir fry for 3 minutes. Cover with the hot stock, bring to a boil, then cook over a low heat for 15 minutes. Rinse the tofu, cut into cubes, add to the soup. Continue cooking for 2–3 minutes, then put through a blender. Return to the saucepan and whisk vigorously till the soup is frothy. Bring to a boil, pour in the sherry (or sherry vinegar) and soy sauce. Season with pepper. Put in the fried mushrooms, stir and heat up. Before serving, sprinkle with chopped basil.

Piquant cream of carrots

*800 g carrots, 1 large onion, 1 wine apple, 1 tsp lemon juice, 4 cups light chicken stock, 1 cup thick natural yogurt, 2 tbsps finely chopped parsley, 2 tbsps butter, 3–5 drops **Tabasco**, salt, pepper*

Peel and rinse the carrots, onion and apple. Slice the carrots and onion. Core and slice the apple, sprinkle with lemon juice. Melt the butter in a saucepan, soften the onion. Add the apples and continue frying, stirring all the time. Put in the carrots, stir fry for another 3 minutes. Cover with the hot stock, put a lid on and cook over a low heat for 15 minutes until the carrots are soft. Leave to cool, then liquidize or sieve. Add the yogurt, mix, season to taste with salt, pepper and Tabasco. Before serving, sprinkle chopped parsley on top. Serve with toasted brown bread.

Cream of spinach

*600 g fresh spinach, 2–3 onions, 2 tbsps olive oil, 5 tbsps almond flakes, 1 tbsp ground **cumin**, 4–5 cups vegetable stock, salt and freshly ground black pepper to taste, ½ cup cream, ¼ tsp ground nutmeg*

Cut off the spinach stalks, wash, drain and dry the leaves. Finely chop the peeled onions and almond flakes. Heat the oil in a large, heavy saucepan, put in the onions, fry for 2–3 minutes. Add the almonds and cumin, stir fry for another 1–2 minutes. Put in the spinach leaves, stir thoroughly. Pour in the vegetable stock, cover and cook over a moderate heat for 10–15 minutes, stirring from time to time. Take off the heat, leave to cool a little, then liquidize. Return to the saucepan, season to taste. Before serving, combine with the cream and sprinkle nutmeg on top.

Cream of lentils

*400 g blonde lentils, 2–3 onions, 3–4 cloves garlic, 5–7 cups vegetable stock (lentils absorb a lot of liquid and you need to replenish it while cooking, otherwise the soup will be too thick), 3 tbsps olive or sunflower oil, 2 tsps **cumin** seeds, 1½ tsps crumbled dried chili, juice of 1 lemon, salt, pepper, 2 tbsps chopped parsley*

Rinse the lentils thoroughly under running water. Drain them on a sieve. Dice the peeled onions finely, crush the garlic. Toast the cumin seeds in a hot frying pan, then grind them. Heat the oil in a heavy saucepan, fry the onions, but do not brown. Add the garlic and stir fry for 2–3 minutes. Put in the lentils. Stir well until all seeds are coated with oil. Pour in some hot stock, bring to a boil. Add the ground cumin and chili. Cover and simmer until the lentils begin to disintegrate. Season with salt and freshly ground pepper, add lemon juice. Take off the heat, leave to cool a little, then liquidize. Heat up, adjust the seasoning, sprinkle chopped parsley on top. Serve with toast or choux pastry balls.

Cream of cauliflower and zucchini

*1 young zucchini, 1 small cauliflower, 1 large onion, ½–1 clove garlic, 1 tbsp finely chopped fresh **ginger**, 3 cups chicken stock (or stock from cube), 1½ cups thick cream, 1 tbsp butter, 1 tbsp **curry powder**, salt, pepper, 2 tbsps chopped dill*

Finely chop the peeled onion and garlic. Rinse the cauliflower, divide into florets. Put into a heavy saucepan, add the onion, garlic and ginger. Pour in 1 cup hot stock, bring to a boil, cover with a tightly fitting lid and cook for 25 minutes. Leave aside to cool, combine with the remaining stock and liquidize. Wash the zucchini, cut lengthwise and seed. Juliene the zucchini (unpeeled), combine with the curry powder. Melt the butter in a small pan, put in the zucchini, cover and cook over a low heat for 5 minutes. Heat up the cream of cauliflower, combine with the zucchini and cream. Season to taste with salt and pepper, stir and heat up, but keep off the boil. Before serving, sprinkle chopped dill on top.

Cream of pumpkin

*750 g pumpkin pulp, 2 onions, 1 tbsp butter, 1 cup cooked rice, 4–5 cups chicken stock, 2 tbsps dried shrimps, 2 tbsps lemon juice, 1 tsp **garam masala***

Soak the dried shrimps in 3–4 tablespoons stock for an hour. Cut 500 g pumpkin pulp in cubes. Melt the butter in a saucepan, soften the finely chopped peeled onions, but do not brown. Add the pumpkin cubes and continue frying for 5 minutes. Cover with the remaining stock, stir, bring to a boil, then cook for 20 minutes. Liquidize and sieve the soup, transfer to an oven-proof tureen. Add the rice and the remaining pumpkin cut into cubes. Salt and mix well. Combine the shrimps with lemon juice. Blend with garam masala, add to the soup. Cover the tureen and put in a preheated oven for 10–15 minutes.

Sweet chestnut soup

*250 g fresh or tinned **chestnuts**, 150 g bitter chocolate, 3 cups milk, 2 cups cream (18% or 22%), 2 egg yolks, 1 tbsp butter, rind of 1 orange, ½ cup water, 1 tbsp lemon juice mixed with 1 tbsp sugar, 2 tbsps sugar, ½ cup chopped hazelnuts, 2–3 cloves, 3–4 peppercorns, a pinch of salt*

Cook or roast the fresh chestnuts, skin them. Scrub the orange, scald it with boiling water. Take off the peel with a sharp knife, cut the peel into thin strips (4 tbsps). Bring the water with 1 tbsp lemon juice and 1 tbsp sugar to a boil. Put in the orange peel and cook for 15 minutes. Bring to a boil the milk with a pinch of salt, cloves and peppercorns. Continue cooking over a low heat for 4–8 minutes. Put the cooked, roasted or tinned chestnuts into a saucepan. Cover with the strained milk, cook for 15–20 minutes. Break the chocolate into pieces, put them in a small pan. Place the pan on top of a larger saucepan with boiling water. When the chocolate melts, add the butter, cream, chopped hazelnuts and orange peel. Whisk the mixture. Blend the egg yolks with 2 tablespoons sugar until foamy. Put the chestnuts through a blender, combine with the chocolate sauce, bring to a boil. Take off the heat and stirring vigorously gradually pour in the egg yolk and sugar mixture. Serve hot or cold, with toast, choux pastry balls or sponge fingers.

Gratins and bakes

Potatoes au gratin

*900 g potatoes boiled in jackets, 1 large red onion, 2–3 cloves garlic, 400 g tinned **artichokes**, c. 150 g mixed frozen vegetables, 125 g grated Gruyère, 125 g grated Emmental, 50 g crumbled blue-veined cheese (canzona or gorgonzola), 225 g tofu, 1 tbsp grated Parmesan, 2 tbsps fresh thyme leaves, 2 tbsps butter, salt, pepper, 1–2 thyme sprigs*

SAUCE: 1 tbsp butter, 1 tbsp flour, 2 cups milk, 1 cup cream, 1 tbsp lemon juice, a pinch of each sugar and white pepper

Slice the tofu. Drain the artichokes and cut them into pieces. Finely chop the peeled garlic and onion. Combine the cream with chopped thyme leaves and lemon juice. Peel and slice the potatoes.
SAUCE: Melt the butter in a small pan, put in the garlic and onion, fry but do not brown. Add the flour and cook, stirring all the time. Dilute with the milk and continue cooking until the roux thickens. Put in the frozen vegetables and artichokes, add half of each cheese. Pour in the cream, adjust the seasoning adding salt, pepper and sugar. Heat the sauce, stirring all the time.
Heat the oven to 200°C. Butter an oven-proof dish, line with half the potato slices. Put in the prepared sauce with vegetables on top, cover with the remaining potatoes. Sprinkle with a mixture of reserved cheeses and dot with butter. Place in the oven and bake for 30 minutes. Before serving, garnish with thyme sprigs.

Spinach au gratin with beef

*600 g minced beef, 400 g fresh spinach, 500 g potatoes, 1 large onion, 1–1½ tbsps olive oil, 1 tbsp ground **cumin**, 1 tsp crumbled fennel*

seeds, ½ tsp ground cinnamon, 1½ cups beef
stock, 1 flat tsp corn flour, 2 tbsps butter

Dice the peeled onion. Cut off the spinach stalks, wash,
drain and dry the leaves. Heat the oven to 200°C.
Heat the oil in a large, heavy frying pan, put in the onion
and meat, stir fry for 10 minutes. Add fennel, cumin and
cinnamon, continue frying for 1–2 minutes. Pour in the
hot stock, cover the pan and simmer for 10 minutes. Mix
the corn flour with 2–3 tablespoons cold water. Combine
the mixture with the meat and simmer, stirring all the
time, until the sauce thickens. Sweat the spinach leaves in
a large saucepan. Peel, rinse and slice the potatoes, parboil them in water for 2–3 minutes, then drain. Butter an
oven-proof dish. Line it with half the meat sauce, place a
layer of spinach and half the potatoes on top, cover with
the remaining meat sauce. Arrange on top the remaining
potato slices like fish scales. Sprinkle with melted butter.
Cover the dish with foil and place in the oven. Bake for
about an hour, or until the potatoes are done. Serve with
fresh vegetable salads.

Sauerkraut tart

DOUGH: 300 g wheat flour, 2 eggs, 125 g
butter, 2–3 tbsps sour cream, salt

FILLING: 600 g sauerkraut, ½ cup white dry wine,
3 cooking apples, 1 tbsp lemon juice, 1 tin **chestnuts**
(c. 400 g, c. 300 g when drained), 3 tbsps liquid honey,
1 egg yolk, 1 tbsp butter, 2 tbsps grated Emmental

Sift the flour onto the worktop. Add crumbled butter
straight from the fridge, cut it in with a sharp knife until the dough has a sandy consistency. Add salt, eggs and
cream and knead together. Wrap the dough in clingfilm and
refrigerate for 2–3 hours.
Rinse the sauerkraut, drain well. Chop and put into a
saucepan. Pour in the wine, bring to a boil, then stew
for 15 minutes. Peel and core the apples, cut them into
sticks. Put into a pan, sprinkle with lemon juice and 1 teaspoon wine, add sugar. Stir well and cook over a low heat.
Quarter the drained chestnuts. Heat the oven to 200°C.
Butter a large oven-proof dish. Put in alternating layers of
sauerkraut, apples and chestnuts, topping the whole with

sauerkraut. Roll out the dough. Cover the sauerkraut with
the dough, pierce it with a fork in several places. Brush
with mixed egg yolk, sprinkle with grated cheese. Put in
the oven and bake for 40 minutes (if the dough browns
too quickly, cover with foil).

Vegetables au gratin

4 small leeks (white parts only), 4 large broccoli
flowers, 1 small fennel, 2 tbsps butter, 1 tbsp flour,
2 cups milk or cream, 1 tbsp lemon juice, a pinch
of caster sugar, salt, a dash of white pepper,
2 tbsps **pesto**, 2 tbsps grated Cheddar cheese,
1 tbsp breadcrumbs, 1 tbsp almond flakes

Wash and dry the vegetables. Cut the leeks into
smaller pieces. Divide the broccoli into florets.
Slice the fennel fairly thickly. Blanch the vegetables in boiling water for 4–6 minutes, drain, rinse under cold water,
drain again.
SAUCE: Make a white roux from 1 tablespoon butter and
1 tablespoon flour. Simmer over a low heat, stirring all the
time and gradually adding milk or cream, until the sauce
thickens. Take off the heat. Combine with 1 tablespoon
grated cheese and pesto. Add salt, pepper, lemon juice
and sugar to taste.
Heat the oven to 180°C. Butter an oven-proof dish, line it
with the vegetables, cover with the sauce. Sprinkle breadcrumbs mixed with the remaining cheese and almond flakes
on top. Put in the oven for 10 minutes.

Buckwheat bake

1½ cups unroasted buckwheat groats, 1 egg white,
3 cups chicken stock (or stock from cube), 1 tbsp lard,
1 each red, yellow, orange and green bell pepper,
2–3 onions, 2 tbsps tomato concentrate, 2 egg yolks,
salt, pepper, a pinch of sugar, 2 tbsps **grape-seed
oil**, 3–4 tbsps grated cheese (Tilsit), 1 tbsp butter,
2 tbsps ground walnuts or breadcrumbs

Heat the oven to 150°C. Mix the buckwheat with the
egg white, spread on a baking tin and dry in the oven.
Bring the stock to a boil, add the lard. Pour in the buckwheat, stir and simmer over a low heat. When the groats

absorb the liquid, cover the pot, wrap in a blanket or put into the warm oven. Dice the peeled onions. Rinse and dry the peppers, remove the stalks and seeds. Cut the peppers into strips. Heat the oil in a saucepan, lightly brown the onions. Put in the pepper strips, stir and stew for a while. When the peppers soften, add salt, pepper, tomato concentrate and sugar (and 1–2 tablespoons water or stock if needed). Stir and simmer for 2–3 minutes, then take off the heat. Combine with the groats, adjust the seasoning. Butter an oven-proof dish, sprinkle with ground walnuts or breadcrumbs. Fill with the buckwheat, sprinkle grated cheese on top. Put in a preheated oven (180°C) and bake for 20 minutes. Serve with salads.

Baked corn grits with fruit

¾ cup corn grits, 2 cups milk, 1 tsp honey, 150 g prunes, 50 g raisins, 1 egg yolk, 1 cup cream, 1 tbsp lemon juice, 1 tsp grated lemon rind, 1 tsp vanilla sugar, 1 tbsp finely chopped candied orange rind, 1 tbsp almond flakes, 3 tbsps butter, salt

Blanch and drain the prunes and raisins. Quarter each prune. Mix half the milk with the grits. Bring the other half of milk, with salt and honey, to the boil. Combine with the grits. Stirring all the time, cook for 5 minutes. Add the prunes and raisins and continue cooking for another 2–3 minutes.
Use 1 tablespoon butter to grease an oven-proof dish. Put in the cooked grits, even out the surface. Mix the cream with egg yolk, vanilla sugar, lemon zest and candied orange peel, add lemon juice and almond flakes. Cover the grits with the mixture. Sprinkle melted butter on top and bake for 15 minutes at 180°C.

Baked corn grits with apples

1½ cups corn grits, 2 cups milk, 1 cup cream, 3 tbsps butter, 5 tbsps sugar, a pinch of salt, 500 g cooking apples, 2 tbsps lemon juice, 1 tsp ground cinnamon, 3 eggs, 2–3 tbsps finely chopped walnuts

Boil the milk with the cream, 1 tablespoon butter, 2 tablespoons sugar and a pinch of salt. Slowly pour in the grits, stirring all the time bring to a boil, then cook over a low heat. Break the eggs, separate the yolks from the whites. Peel the apples, grate them coarsely, sprinkle with 1 tablespoon lemon juice. Blend the egg yolks with the remaining sugar till foamy. Combine with the apples and cinnamon. Heat the oven to 180°C. Butter an oven-proof dish, sprinkle with chopped walnuts. Put in alternating layers of grits and apples, finishing off with grits. Whisk the egg whites with sugar into stiff peaks, add lemon juice towards the end. Spread the whisked whites on top of the grits. Put in the oven for 15–20 minutes.

Baked buckwheat grits with mushrooms

400 g buckwheat grits, 1 egg white, 30 g dried mushrooms, 3–4 cups boiled water, a sprig of thyme, 1 large onion, 3 tbsps butter, salt, freshly ground pepper, 1 tbsp breadcrumbs

Rinse the mushrooms, cover with boiled water. Leave aside for an hour, then add a thyme sprig and cook. Drain the mushrooms (reserve the liquid), allow to cool, then cut in thin strips. Mix the grits with the egg white, put in a warm oven to dry. Pour the dried grits in a heavy skillet, cover with 3 cups mushroom stock, add 1 tablespoon butter, stir, put a lid on and cook for 10–12 minutes. Chop the peeled onion finely, lightly brown in melted butter. Combine with the mushrooms, add salt and pepper, and continue frying for 5 minutes. Heat the oven to 170–180°C. Butter an oven-proof dish, sprinkle with breadcrumbs. Combine the grits with the mushrooms and onion, adjust the seasoning. Transfer the mixture to the oven-proof dish. Cover with foil and put in the oven for 20 minutes. Serve with boiled vegetables, tomato salads, with sunny side up eggs or egg patties.

Baked buckwheat grits with asparagus

1 kg white asparagus, salt, 1 tsp sugar, 3 tsps butter, 1 tbsp lemon juice, 250 g buckwheat grits, 2½ cups milk, 500 g apples, 2 eggs, 3 tbsps cream, 2 tbsps chopped dill, 1 tsp lemon juice, salt, pepper, sugar to taste

Boil salted water with sugar, butter and lemon juice in a tall saucepan. Peel the asparagus stalks, put in a saucepan with their tips up and cook for 10–12 minutes. Take them out and drain. Rinse and drain the grits, put in a pan, cover with hot milk and cook. Peel and core the apples, slice them, sprinkle with lemon juice. Cut the asparagus stalks into smaller pieces, combine with the apples, sprinkle with salt, pepper and sugar. Shake gently. Mix the cream with the egg yolks and whisked egg whites. Heat the oven to 170–180°C. Butter an oven-proof dish generously with butter. Put in half the grits, spread the asparagus with apples, cover with the remaining grits. Pour the cream sauce over, put in the oven. Bake for 30–40 minutes. Before serving, sprinkle generously with dill.

Pearl barley bake

1¼ cups pearl barley, 3 cups chicken stock (or stock from cube), 5 tbsps butter, 2 carrots, 1 parsley root, ½ celeriac, 1 large onion, 1 leek (white part only), 200 g button mushrooms, 1 tbsp tomato concentrate, 1 tsp sharp mustard, salt, pepper, ¼ tsp paprika, 3–4 tbsps grated cheese, 2 tbsps breadcrumbs

Rinse and drain the barley, put into 2 ¾ cups boiling chicken stock with 1 tablespoon butter. Bring to a boil, cover and continue cooking over a low heat. Peel the carrots, parsley root and celeriac, grate coarsely. Wash and slice the leek. Dice the peeled onion. Clean and slice the mushrooms. Melt 2 tablespoons butter in a saucepan, fry the onion, but do not brown. Add the remaining vegetables and stir fry, sprinkle with some stock and cook over a low heat. Melt 1 tablespoon butter in a pan, put in the mushroom slices and fry over a fairly high heat, stirring all the time. Combine the mushrooms with the vegetables. Mix the tomato concentrate with 2 tablespoons stock, mustard, salt, pepper, paprika and sugar. Combine with the vegetables, stir well and continue cooking for a while longer. Heat the oven to 180–190°C. Combine the vegetables with the cooked barley. Butter an oven-proof dish, sprinkle with breadcrumbs. Put in the barley mixture, with a knife even out the surface. Sprinkle with grated cheese and bake for 25–35 minutes. Serve with lettuce or vegetable salad.

Rice and fish bake

600 g hike fillets, 3 tbsps lemon juice, 1 tsp grated lemon rind, 3 cups cooked rice, 20 g button mushrooms, 1½ cups cooked or tinned green peas, 2 large fleshy tomatoes, 2 onions, 3–4 tbsps chopped chives, juice and grated rind of 1 lemon, 1 cup chicken stock (or stock from cube), 200 g mozzarella, 3 tbsps olive oil, 1 tbsp butter, 1 tbsp flour

Sprinkle the rinsed and dried fillets with 1 tablespoon lemon juice, salt and pepper, leave aside. Coat in flour and fry in 1 ½ tablespoons olive oil until golden brown. Mix the rice with the remaining lemon juice and with lemon zest. Slice the peeled onions and cleaned mushrooms, fry them in the remaining oil. Add salt and pepper. Combine the rice with the green peas and chives, cover with the hot stock and mix thoroughly. Blanch the tomatoes, skin and slice them, remove the seeds. Heat the oven to 170–180°C. Butter an oven-proof dish, line it with the rice mixture, put tomato slices on top, spread the onion and mushroom mixture, arrange fish fillets and cover with slices of mozzarella. Bake for 25 minutes. Before serving, you may sprinkle the top with chopped parsley. Serve with lettuce or endive salad.

Pasta, noodles and tarts

Pasta with capers

*500 g pasta (rotini), 150 g mozzarella, 2 tbsps **capers**, 5–6 cloves garlic, 3 tbsps **pine nuts**, 3 tbsps olive oil, 1½ tbsps lemon juice, 1 tsp freshly ground pepper, 2 tbsps finely chopped parsley, a handful of basil leaves*

Chop the garlic finely, grate the cheese. Cook the pasta in salted water, drain, transfer to a hot serving dish and keep warm. Heat the oil in a saucepan, pour in some oil and briskly fry the pine nuts, stirring all the time. Add the capers, lemon juice, grated cheese and parsley, stir thoroughly, take off the heat. Pour the sauce over the pasta, shake the dish well. Sprinkle with pepper and garnish with basil leaves.

Pasta with pumpkin and caper sauce

*400 g pasta (tagliatelle or rigatoni), 500 g pumpkin, 1 tbsp lemon juice, 3 tbsps **capers**, 1 small onion, 1–2 cloves garlic, 2 tbsps butter, salt, pepper, a pinch of each sugar, cayenne pepper and grated nutmeg, 1 cup cream, 1 tbsp finely chopped fresh oregano*

SAUCE: Peel the pumpkin, remove the seeds. Rinse the pulp, drain and cut in cubes. Finely chop the peeled onion and garlic. Melt the butter in a saucepan, soften the onion and garlic. Put in the pumpkin cubes, stir well, sprinkle with lemon juice and fry for 5 minutes. Add salt, pepper, sugar, cayenne and nutmeg, fold in the cream. Stir, cover and simmer for 10–12 minutes, stirring from time to time. Add the capers and oregano, mix well, heat up.
Cook the pasta in salted water, drain, transfer to a serving dish. Pour the sauce over, shake the dish and serve immediately.

Soy noodles with vegetables

*400 g **soy (cellophane) noodles**, 500 g tomatoes, 200 g French beans, 1 small zucchini, 1 red and 1 yellow bell peppers, 2 onions, 1–2 cloves garlic, 1 cup stock, 3 tbsps sunflower oil, 1 tsp **sesame oil**, 1 tsp chili powder, 2 tbsps chopped fresh basil leaves, salt*

Soak the noodles in 2 cups cold water for 30 minutes. Blanch and skin the tomatoes, cut into thick cubes. Crush the peeled garlic. Top and tail the beans, rinse them. Put for 5–6 minutes in boiling salted water, then drain, rinse under cold water and drain again. Chop the peeled onions. Rinse the peppers, remove the seeds. Cut into cubes. Wash the zucchini and cut into cubes. Heat 1 tablespoon sunflower oil in a large saucepan, put in the onions and soften. Put in the pepper cubes and when they brown nicely, add zucchini cubes. Mix well, turn down the heat, pour in the hot stock

and simmer for 10–12 minutes. Add the French beans cut into shorter pieces, tomatoes and garlic. Mix and continue cooking. Add the chopped basil, season with chili pepper and salt. In a large frying pan heat the remaining sunflower oil, put in the thoroughly drained noodles, sprinkle with the sesame oil. Stir fry quickly. Transfer the noodles to a large serving dish, arrange the vegetables around them.

Fried rice noodles with beef

*500 g **rice noodles**, 150 g fillet of beef, 5–6 cloves garlic, 1 small chili pepper, 1 tbsp finely chopped fresh ginger, 1 small onion, 2 tbsps **soy sauce**, 3 tbsps lard, 1 cup beef stock (or stock from cube), salt and pepper to taste*

Soak the noodles in warm water for 10–15 minutes, drain thoroughly. Chop the peeled onion finely. Cut the meat into thin strips. Cut the peeled garlic and cored pepper into fine sticks. Heat two tablespoons lard in a large saucepan, brown the meat for 1–2 minutes over a high heat. Add the pepper and garlic sticks, onion, 1 tablespoon soy sauce, ¼ cup stock, half the chopped ginger, salt and pepper. Mix well and simmer for 2–3 minutes. Heat the remaining lard in a large frying pan, put in the drained noodles and stirring all the time, fry for 30 seconds. Add the remaining ginger and soy sauce, continue frying for another minute. Pour in the remaining stock, stir, continue cooking. When the noodles absorb most of the liquid, transfer to a warm serving dish and arrange the meat around.

Rice noodles with coconut sauce

*300 g ribbon **rice noodles**, 2–3 cloves garlic, 2–3 shallots, 250 g French beans, 100 g cherry tomatoes, 3 tbsps peanut oil, ¾ cup coconut milk, 2 pieces **sun-dried tomatoes in oil**, 3 tbsps chopped unsalted peanuts, 2 fresh chili peppers or 1 tsp dried chili flakes, 3 tbsps chopped scallions (with green leaves), salt*

SAUCE: Chop the seeded chili peppers finely. Liquidize the sun-dried tomatoes, 1 tablespoon tomato oil, chili peppers, peanuts and coconut milk.
Put the noodles in a bowl, cover with slightly salted boiling water and leave for 8–10 minutes. Halve the rinsed cherry

tomatoes. Chop the peeled garlic and scallions finely. Top and tail the beans, rinse and dry them, cut into shorter pieces and put for 1 minute in slightly salted boiling water, then drain. Heat ½ tablespoon oil in a large wok, wash it over the sides, then pour it out. Put in the remaining oil, add the garlic and scallions, stir fry for 1 minute. Add the drained noodles and beans, stir and fry for 5 minutes. Put in the tomatoes, mix gently. Gradually pour in the coconut sauce, cooking and stirring all the time. Serve immediately.

Soy noodles with salmon

300 g **soy noodles**, 200 g salmon fillets, 3–4 scallions, 6 tbsps **grape-seed oil**, 1 cup dry white wine, 2 tbsps potato flour, 1 tbsp fresh chopped coriander, salt, freshly ground white pepper

Put the noodles in a bowl, cover with hot water and leave for 5–8 minutes, then drain. Rinse and dry the fillet, cut into thin strips. Sprinkle with salt and pepper, gently coat in potato flour. Wash and slice the scallions. Heat 1 tablespoon oil in a wok or a large, heavy frying pan, wash it over the sides, then pour out. Heat the remaining oil, put in the scallions and fish, stir fry over high heat for 10–20 seconds. Take out the onion and fish with a straining spoon, keep warm. Put the noodles cut into smaller strips into the wok. Fry for a minute, combine with the scallions and salmon. Sprinkle with coriander, pour in the wine and bring to a boil. Season with salt and pepper, take off the heat.

Chinese egg noodles with oyster sauce

300 g **Chinese egg noodles**, 500 g turkey thigh meat (off the bone), 1 large carrot, 4 tbsps **oyster sauce**, 2 eggs, 3 tbsps fizzy mineral water, 3 tbsps peanut oil, 2 tbsps chopped chives

Rinse and dry the meat, cut into bite-size pieces. Finely slice the peeled and washed carrot. Put the noodles into a large bowl, cover with salted boiling water and leave for 10 minutes. Heat ½ tablespoon oil in a large wok, wash it over the sides, then pour out. Put in the remaining oil, heat up. Put in the turkey meat and carrots, stir fry over a high heat for 5 minutes. Turn the heat down. Put in the well drained noodles and stir fry for 3–4 minutes. Mix the oyster sauce with eggs and mineral water. Pour the mixture into the wok, stirring all the time. Cook till the egg mixture sets. Before serving, sprinkle with chives.

Ligurian tart

DOUGH: 250–300 g flour, ½ tsp salt, 3–4 tbsps extra virgin olive oil, ½ cup ice-cold water

FILLING: 1 large tin (c. 500 g) **artichokes** in brine, 1 large onion, 150 g ricotta cheese, 3 tbsps grated Parmesan, 5 hard-boiled eggs, 3 tbsps olive oil, 3 tbsps chopped fresh marjoram leaves, 2 tbsps chopped parsley, 1 egg yolk, salt, freshly ground pepper, ¼ tsp ground nutmeg

Sift the flour into a bowl, mix with salt. Make a well in the centre. Gradually pouring in the oil, knead the dough until smooth and shiny. Shape into a ball, wrap in aluminium foil and refrigerate for 2–3 hours.
FILLING: Drain and slice the artichokes. Chop the shelled hard-boiled eggs. Soften and slightly brown the finely chopped peeled onion in 2 tablespoons oil, then transfer to a bowl. Combine the onion with the squeezed out ricotta, Parmesan, marjoram, parsley, artichokes and eggs. Add the raw egg yolk and mix gently. Season with salt, pepper and nutmeg. Cover and leave aside for 30–40 minutes for the flavours to intermingle.
Heat the oven to 190–200°C. Grease a round pizza tin with oil, sprinkle with flour. Divide the dough into two equal parts. Roll out one part thinly. Line the tin with it, so that its edges reach beyond the rim of the tin. Put the filling inn. Roll out the other part of the dough into a circle the diameter of the tin. Cover the filling, with moistened fingers seal the edges along the rim. Pierce the top with a fork in several places, brush gently with oil. Put into the oven and bake for 35–40 minutes until the crust is golden. Serve hot with tomato salad or cold.

Tart with a filling of Chinese cabbage

DOUGH: 1 cup flour, 100 g butter, 1 egg yolk, 1 tbsp thick sour cream, salt, ½ tsp grated lemon rind

FILLING: 500–700 g Chinese cabbage, 250 g tofu, 3 eggs, 4 tbsps **soy sauce**, 1–2 cloves garlic, 1 walnut-size piece of fresh ginger, 2 tbsps butter, 2 tbsps **sesame seeds**, 3 tbsps chopped coriander leaves, ¾ cup thick sour cream, salt, pepper, cayenne pepper

DOUGH: Sift the flour onto the worktop. With a sharp knife cut in the butter until the mixture is sandy. Add one egg yolk, cream, salt and lemon zest and knead well. Wrap in aluminium foil and put in the fridge for 2–3 hours.
FILLING: Toast the sesame seeds in a hot frying pan. Rinse and dry the cabbage, cut into thin strips. Finely chop the peeled garlic and ginger, combine with the cabbage. Melt the butter in a saucepan, put in the cabbage, cover and cook over a low heat for 10–12 minutes. Add salt, pepper, cayenne, coriander, sesame seeds and soy sauce. Mix well and continue stewing for another 2–3 minutes, then take off the heat. Heat the oven to 180–190°C.
SAUCE: Blend the tofu with cream, salt and pepper. Blending all the time add 1 egg at a time.
Combine the cabbage filling with the sauce. Butter a round baking tin, line it with the dough. Pierce the dough with a fork in several places. Put into the oven for 5–6 minutes. Take out when it is nicely golden brown. Put the filling into the baked case. Return to the oven (middle shelf) and bake for 40–50 minutes. Serve hot with tomato salad or lettuce.

Tart with tuna

DOUGH: 1 cup flour, 100 g butter, 1 egg yolk, salt, 1 tbsp butter

FILLING: 2 tins tuna fish in brine (360 g), 3 tbsps coarsely grated celeriac, 3 tbsps chopped onion, 3 tbsps butter, 2 tbsps flour, ½ cup each milk and vegetable stock, 2 eggs, 3 tbsps grated Gouda cheese, 3 tsps mild **curry powder**, chili pepper, salt pepper

DOUGH: Knead the ingredients, adding 1 tablespoon ice-cold water. Shape into a ball, wrap in aluminium foil and refrigerate for 20 minutes.
Butter a round baking tin, line it with the dough. Put in a preheated oven (200°C) and bake for 10 minutes.

FILLING: Briskly fry the onion and celeriac in butter to soften. Put in the drained, crumbled tuna, sprinkle with flour and 2 tsps curry powder. Fry for 1 minute. Pour in the stock and milk, stirring gently simmer for 10 minutes. Combine with the cheese, add chili, salt and pepper. Take off the heat and combine with 2 whisked eggs.
Transfer the filling to the baked tart case, sprinkle with the remaining curry powder. Bake at 180°C for 20 minutes. Serve hot with salads.

Tart with a sauerkraut filling

300 g frozen puff pastry, 3 tbsps butter, 300 g sauerkraut, 1 large onion, 1 tin crab meat (c. 150 g), 2 tbsps chopped **pistachios**, 1 tbsp **capers**, 1 tbsp lemon juice, ¼ tsp grated lemon rind, 2 eggs, 1 cup thick cream, 1 tsp potato flour, 1 tbsp boiled water, salt, freshly ground pepper, 2 tbsps chopped parsley, 6–8 sprigs parsley or chervil

Squeeze out excess liquid from the sauerkraut. Chop the sauerkraut finely. Peel and dice the onion. Melt 2 tablespoons butter in a frying pan, soften the onion. Add the sauerkraut and continue cooking. Season with pepper, add the capers, crab meat, chopped pistachios, lemon juice and zest. Mix thoroughly and simmer for 15 minutes. Adjust the seasoning. Heat the oven to 230–250°C. Mix the potato flour with 1 tablespoon cold boiled water. Whisk the eggs with the cream, combine with the potato flour and water. Butter a round baking tin, line with the defrosted dough. Place the cool filling in the unbaked case. Pour the cream sauce over. Put in the oven and bake for 30–40 minutes. Before serving, garnish with sprigs of parsley or chervil.

Tart with spinach and lentils

DOUGH: 150 g wholemeal wheat flour, 3 tbsps butter, ¾ flat tsps baking powder, 1 tbsp sunflower oil, 2–3 tbsps cold water, 1 tsp liquid honey or 1 tsp brown sugar

FILLING: 200 g blonde lentils, 200 g onion, 350 g fresh spinach, 1 tsp ground coriander seeds, 1 tsp ground **cumin**, 1 tbsp lemon juice, 1½ cups water, 1 tbsp soy or sunflower oil, salt, pepper, 2 tbsps **sesame seeds**

DOUGH: Sift the flour into a bowl. Add the baking powder, salt and chilled butter. Rub the butter in until the whole has a crumbly consistency. Mix the oil with honey and 1 tablespoon lukewarm water (or sugar dissolved in 2 tablespoons water). Pour the mixture into the dough and knead briskly (the dough should be moist; if it is too dry, add a little more water). Cover the bowl and chill the dough in the fridge.

FILLING: Finely chop the peeled onion. Rinse and drain the lentils. Cut the spinach stalks off, rinse the leaves and drain thoroughly. Heat the oil in a heavy saucepan, soften the onion. Add cumin and coriander, stir fry for 3–4 minutes. Put in the lentils, cover with boiling water, stir and bring to a boil. Cover and simmer for 12–15 minutes (or until the lentils are well cooked). Put the spinach into a smaller, heavy skillet, cover and sweat for 5–7 minutes. Take the lid off, reduce the liquid. Leave to cool, then chop and add the lemon juice. Combine with the cool lentils, mix thoroughly, adjust the seasoning.

Heat the oven to 200–220°C. Roll out the dough. Line a round baking tin with the dough, press hard down. Prick in several places with a fork and put in the oven for 5–6 minutes. Take out. Fill the half-baked case with the spinach and lentils mixture, cover with foil and put into the oven for 25 minutes. Toast sesame seeds in a frying pan. Sprinkle the top of the tart with them and return to the oven for another 5–7 minutes. Serve hot or cold.

Tart with cream cheese and feta

DOUGH: 400 g flour, 230 g butter, salt, 1 tsp dried herbs (herbes de Provence, herbes vénitiennes), 3–4 tbsps boiled ice-cold water

FILLING: 200 g feta, 200 g cream cheese, 4 eggs, 1 large red onion, 2–3 cloves garlic, 1 yellow bell pepper, 350 g fleshy tomatoes, 16–18 pitted **black olives**, 2 tbsps oil, 3 tbsps chopped dill or parsley, ½ tsp ground chili pepper, pepper, salt

DOUGH: Pour the flour with salt and herbs into a bowl. Chop the chilled butter, add it to the flour. Rub it with the flour until you get crumbly consistency. Sprinkle with 3 tablespoons cold water and knead briskly. Shape into a ball, wrap in foil and put in the fridge for 15 minutes. Then roll it out to 1 cm thickness. Line a round fluted baking mould with the dough. Cover with a piece of greaseproof paper, pour 300 g dried peas on top (this will prevent blistering). Heat the oven to 200°C. Put the mould in the oven and bake for 10 minutes by which time the case will be golden brown.

FILLING: Peel and finely chop the onion and garlic. Seed and rinse the pepper, cut into strips. Wash the tomatoes, slice or quarter. Cut the feta into cubes. Heat the oil in a saucepan, soften the onion and garlic. Add the pepper strips and simmer for 5 minutes. Transfer the contents to a bowl. Combine with the tomatoes, feta and sliced olives. Shake gently, season with salt and pepper.

Heat the oven to 190°C. Whisk the eggs with chili powder, cream cheese and dill (or parsley). Fill the baked case with the tomato mixture. Pour over the egg and cream cheese sauce. Put in the oven and bake for 40–45 minutes. Serve hot or cold.

Curd cheese and yogurt tart

400 g frozen puff pastry, 1 tbsp flour, 1 egg yolk, 1–2 tbsps **sesame seeds**

FILLING: 350 g full-cream curd cheese, 150 g grated Cheddar cheese, 300 g fresh spinach leaves, 3–4 scallions, 2–3 tbsps chopped basil leaves, 2–3 tbsps chopped chives, 1 cup thick natural yogurt, 2 eggs, ½ tsp each salt and freshly ground pepper

Rinse and drain the spinach leaves (having cut off their stalks). Blanch in salted boiling water for 3–4 minutes, then drain well. Blend the yogurt and eggs, gradually adding the curd cheese, Cheddar, spinach, salt, pepper and scallions. Combine with the chives and basil, adjust the seasoning.

Heat the oven to 200–220°C. Roll out the defrosted pastry on the worktop dusted with flour. Divide into two even rectangles. Whisk the eggs with 1 teaspoon water. Toast the sesame seeds. Line a baking tin with greaseproof paper. Place one rectangle inside, with the edges reaching beyond the rim. Put the filling in. Brush the edges with the egg mixture. Cover with the second rectangle. Tightly seal the edges of both rectangles. Make several incisions on top (to let steam out). Brush the top with egg. Put into the oven and bake 30–40 minutes. Serve hot or cold.

Oriental tart with smoked trout

DOUGH: 300 g flour, 200 g butter, 1 egg yolk, 1 tsp salt, 2–4 tbsps cold water, 1 tbsp lemon juice, ½ tsp grated lemon rind, aluminium foil, 1 cup dried beans

*FILLING: 250 g fillets of smoked trout, 1 tbsp **candied ginger**, 1 tbsp **ginger syrup**, 1 tsp drained marinated **green peppercorns**, 2 shallots or 1 small onion, 2 tbsps butter, 3 egg yolks, 2 tbsps milk, 1 cup thick sour cream, 1 tbsp each chopped parsley and chives, salt, pepper, a dash of sugar*

DOUGH: Sift the flour onto the worktop. Put the chilled butter on top and cut it in with a sharp knife to get a sandy consistency. Add the egg yolk, salt, lemon juice and zest, and cold water. Briskly knead. Shape the dough into a bowl, wrap in foil and refrigerate for 1–2 hours.
FILLING: Chop the candied ginger finely. Peel and chop the onions. Heat the oil in a frying pan, soften the onion for 10 minutes, but do not brown. Take off the heat, add the green peppercorns, ginger, crumbled fish fillets and ginger syrup. Shake energetically and leave aside for 15 minutes.
SAUCE: Whisk the egg yolks with milk, salt, pepper and sugar. Combine with the chives, parsley and cream.
Heat the oven to 200–220°C. Roll out the dough on the worktop dusted with flour. Line a round baking tin with it. Prick the dough with a fork in several places. Place a sheet of aluminium foil and weigh it down with beans. Put into the oven for 10 minutes, then remove the beans and foil and lightly brown the top of the case. Turn the temperature down to 180°C. Take the baking tin out, leave to cool, spread the filling evenly in the baked case. Pour the sauce over the filling and return the tart to the oven for 35–45 minutes. Allow it to cool a bit in the oven. Serve with lettuce, endive or rocket salad.

Koulibiak with carrots

*500 g frozen puff pastry, 1 egg yolk, 1 tbsp **sesame seeds**, 1 tsp butter, 1–2 tbsps flour*

*FILLING: 1–1.3 kg carrots, 2–3 tbsps oil, 1 tbsp lemon juice, 2 tbsps chopped fresh mint, 1–2 tbsps **sesame seeds**, 3–4 hard-boiled eggs, salt, pepper*

FILLING: Scrape the carrots. Cook them in lightly salted water, drain, peel and grate coarsely. Toast sesame seeds in a small frying pan. Shell and chop the hard-boiled eggs. Heat oil in a large frying pan, quickly fry the carrots. Take off the heat, combine with the eggs, mint and sesame seeds. Season with salt, pepper and lemon juice.
Heat the oven to 200–220°C. Roll out the defrosted pastry on the worktop dusted with flour. Spread with butter, place the filling on the pastry. Seal well the edges. Place the koulebiak the seal down in a greased baking tin. Brush on top with egg yolk, sprinkle with sesame seeds. Put in the oven and bake for over an hour.

Koulibiak with white and green filling

400 g frozen puff pastry, 300 g asparagus, 1 sizeable broccoli, salt, 1 tbsp sugar, 200 g grated Emmental cheese, juice and grated rind of 1 lemon, ¼ cup dry white wine, ½ cup cream, 2 egg yolks, 3 tbsps butter, 1 tbsp flour

FILLING: Peel the asparagus stalks. Peel and cut off broccoli stalks. Bring salted water, with sugar and a dash of lemon juice and butter, to a boil. Put in the broccoli stalks and cook for 5 minutes, then put in the asparagus and broccoli florets. Cook for 10 minutes, drain and leave to cool. Cut the asparagus into shorter pieces and broccoli stalks in cubes.
Make a white roux from butter and flour, dilute with the wine. Simmer over a low heat until the sauce thickens. Add salt, pepper, lemon juice and zest, and a dash of sugar. Pour in the whisked egg yolks and cream. Heat up, stirring all the time, then take off the heat.
Roll out the defrosted pastry on the worktop dusted with flour. Spread the filling on top, seal the edges. Place the koulebiak the seal down in a greased baking tin, pierce it with a fork in a few place. Brush with melted butter and bake in a preheated oven.

Koulibiak with fish and anchovy paste

DOUGH: 500 g wheat flour, 30 g yeast, 100 g butter, 3 eggs, ½ cup milk, 1 tsp sugar, salt, 1 egg yolk

FILLING: 700 g white carp fillets, 1 tbsp lemon juice, ¼ tsp grated lemon rind, salt, freshly ground pepper,

*2 large onions, 3 tbsps **anchovy paste** or 10 anchovy fillets, 3 tbsps chopped parsley, 3 tbsps butter*

DOUGH: Mix the yeast with 1 tablespoon flour, sugar and ¼ cup lukewarm milk. Leave in a warm place for 15–20 minutes. Sift the flour into a bowl, break in 1 whole egg, add 2 egg yolks. Pour in the melted butter and the remaining milk. Mix thoroughly, add the yeast and knead into smooth, shiny dough. Cover with a dish cloth and leave to rise in a warm place for 30–40 minutes.

FILLING: Rinse and dry the fillets, sprinkle with lemon juice and zest, pepper and salt. Wrap in clingfilm and refrigerate for 1–2 hours. Take out, cut into thin strips. Dice the peeled onion. Melt 1 ½ tablespoons butter in a heavy frying pan. Put in the onion and soften it. Take off the heat, add salt and pepper, combine with chopped parsley. Melt the remaining butter in another frying pan, briskly fry the fish strips. Chop the anchovies finely.

Roll out the dough, place the rectangle in a baking tin. Spread it with the cooked onion, arrange fish slices on top. Coat with anchovy paste or sprinkle with chopped anchovies. Cover with the remaining onion and parsley mixture. Seal the edges, cover with a dish towel and leave to rise. Then brush with egg yolk and bake in the oven (180°C) for 30–35 minutes.

Koulibiak with beef

DOUGH: 500 g wheat flour, 200 g chilled butter, 1 tsp baking powder, ½ tsp salt, a pinch of **saffron** soaked in ½ glass vodka, 1 tbsp lemon juice, ¼ tsp grated lemon rind, ½ cup ice-cold water, 1 egg

FILLING: 450 g minced beef, 2 young kohlrabi, 1 large potato, 2 tbsps chopped parsley, 2 tbsps butter, salt, pepper

DOUGH: Sift the flour and baking powder onto the worktop. Add coarsely grated butter, cut it in with a sharp knife to get sandy consistency. Add the saffron soaked in vodka and lemon juice and zest, salt and water, briskly knead the dough. Wrap in clingfilm and refrigerate for 2–3 hours.

FILLING: Cut the peeled kohlrabi in matchsticks. Coarsely grate the peeled and washed potato. Combine with the meat, kohlrabi and parsley. Season with salt and pepper.

Heat the oven to 200–220°C. Roll out the dough on the worktop dusted with flour. Spread with butter (1½ tablespoons), place the filling on top. Seal the edges. Place the koulebiak the seal down in a greased baking tin. Brush on top with egg yolk. Cut out a small round opening in the dough. Put into the oven, bake for 12–15 minutes. Then turn down the temperature to 180°C and continue baking for another 40 minutes.

Open tart with mussels

DOUGH: 300 g flour, 150 g chilled butter, 1 tbsp lemon juice, ½ tsp grated lemon rind, 4 tbsps thick cream, salt, a pinch of white pepper

FILLING: 300–400 g frozen shelled mussels, salt, 4 cloves garlic, 1 thyme sprig, 2 parsley sprigs, 1 bay leaf, 5–6 large, fleshy tomatoes, a pinch of each paprika and cayenne pepper, 2–3 tbsps grated Gruyère, 2–3 **slices sun-dried tomatoes** in oil, 3 tbsps butter, 1 tbsp flour

DOUGH: Sift the flour onto the worktop. Mix in pieces of chilled butter. Cut the butter in with a knife to get a sandy mixture. Add salt, pepper, lemon juice and zest, and cream. Briskly knead the dough. Wrap in foil and refrigerate for 2–3 hours.

FILLING: Bring water to a boil. Add salt, garlic, thyme and parsley sprigs. Cover and cook for 5 minutes. Drop in the frozen mussels and simmer over a low heat. Take off the heat and leave to cool.

Blanch and skin the tomatoes. Quarter them, sweat in a heavy skillet, then sieve. Cut and crush 2 peeled cloves of garlic. Take out the mussels with a straining spoon. Melt 2 tablespoons butter in a heavy skillet, put in the garlic and mussels. Stir fry for 5 minutes, add the tomatoes. Season with salt, pepper and cayenne, mix thoroughly and leave to cool. Drain the sun-dried tomatoes, cut into thin strips.

Heat the oven to 180–190°C. Roll out the dough on the worktop dusted with flour. Butter a round baking tin, dust with flour and line with the dough. Prick the dough with a fork and bake for 5–7 minutes. Take out, put the filling in the baked case, sprinkle with grated cheese and garnish on top with strips of sun-dried tomatoes. Return to the oven for 30–40 minutes. Before serving, garnish with parsley sprigs.

Cheese bake with tomato sauce

750 g ricotta or curd cheese, 100 g grated Parmesan, 3–4 eggs, ½ cup each chopped basil leaves and oregano, ½ tbsp each paprika and salt, ¼ tsp freshly ground black pepper, 1 tbsp olive oil, lettuce, basil and oregano leaves for garnishing

SAUCE: 100 g sun-dried tomatoes in oil, 2–3 cloves garlic, 3 tbsps pine nuts, ½ cup olive oil, salt, pepper

SAUCE: Crush the peeled garlic. Toast the pine nuts or sunflower seed in a hot frying pan. Blend the tomatoes with the pine nuts, garlic, salt, pepper and oil. Refrigerate. Heat the oven to 180–190°C. Brush a round baking tin with oil. Break the eggs, separate the yolks from the whites. Blend the ricotta (or curd cheese) with Parmesan and egg yolks, add salt, pepper and chopped herbs. Adjust the seasoning. Whisk the egg whites into stiff peaks, fold into the cheese mixture. Carefully transfer to the baking tin, even out the surface with a knife dipped in water. Put into the oven and bake for 30–35 minutes. Before serving, cut into wedges and garnish with basil and oregano leaves. Place each wedge on a lettuce leave. Serve hot or cold, with tomato sauce.

Three-layered savoury cake

1 round loaf, 100 g butter, 2 tbsps thick mayonnaise, 8–10 each cherry tomatoes and stoned black olives, 1 tsp capers for garnishing

MUSHROOM PASTE: 500 g button mushrooms, 2 hard-boiled eggs, 2 tbsps finely chopped hazelnuts, 1 tbsp lemon juice, 1 tbsp sunflower oil, 2–3 tbsps mayonnaise, salt, freshly ground pepper, ½ tsp finely chopped fresh thyme leaves

Clean, rinse and dry the mushrooms. Slice and fry in hot oil. Leave to cool, sprinkle with lemon juice. Mince the mushrooms and shelled eggs, blend with salt, pepper, thyme and mayonnaise. Transfer to a bowl, cover and refrigerate for 30–40 minutes.

ANCHOVY AND EGG YOLK PASTE: 100 g anchovy paste, 5 hard-boiled egg yolks, 1 tbsp slivovitz, 2 tbsps mayonnaise, pepper, a pinch of sugar

Blend the finely chopped egg yolks with the anchovy paste, slivovitz and mayonnaise. Season with pepper and sugar. Refrigerate.

OLIVES AND CALF'S TONGUE PASTE: cooked calf's tongue (300 g without skin), 100 g olives stuffed with peppers, 1 tbsp capers, ¼ cup dry white wine, 2 tbsps mayonnaise, salt, cayenne pepper, ½ tsp freshly ground black pepper, a pinch of caster sugar

Put the tongue, olives and capers through a mincer, combine with wine, salt, black pepper, cayenne, sugar and mayonnaise. Refrigerate.

Remove the crust from the loaf. Cut the bread into 6 fairly thin slices. Butter each slice on one side. Spread a thick layer of each of the pastes on two slices. Put one slice on top of the other in alternating layers. Press down gently but firmly. Coat the whole with the mixture of mayonnaise and the remaining mushroom paste. Refrigerate for a short while. Before serving, garnish with tomatoes, capers and olive halves.

Savoury tuna and cheese cake

1 round loaf, 2 tbsps butter, 8–10 each pitted black and green olives and cherry tomatoes, parsley sprigs

TUNA PASTE: 2 tins tuna fish in brine, 2–3 celery stalks, 10 green olives stuffed with peppers, 2 hard-boiled eggs, 1 tbsps finely chopped parsley, 4 cups thick mayonnaise, lemon juice, salt, pepper

Crumble the drained tuna with a fork. Blend with lemon juice, salt, pepper and mayonnaise. Remove the stringy fibres from the celery stalks. Chop very finely the celery stalks, olives and shelled eggs. Combine with the tuna paste and parsley.

CURD CHEESE AND APPLE PASTE: 200 g curd cheese, 2–3 tbsps cream, 1 tsp caster sugar, 3 tbsps finely chopped walnuts, 2 small sweet apples (green and red), juice and grated rind of 1 lemon, 1 tsp finely chopped mint leaves

Wash and core the apples, dice finely. Sprinkle with half the lemon juice and caster sugar, mix well. Put the curd cheese through a mincer. Combine with the chopped walnuts and gradually with the cream, remaining lemon juice and lemon zest. Add the chopped mint.
Remove the crust from the loaf. Cut the bread into 4 fairly thin slices. Butter each slice on one side. Spread a thick layer of each of the pastes on two slices. Put one slice on top of the other. Cover with a buttered slice of bread. Coat the whole on top and on the sides with the remaining tuna paste. Wrap in foil and refrigerate for 2–3 hours. Before serving, garnish with olive and tomato halves and with parsley sprigs.

Crêpe batter: 1½ cups flour, 3 tbsps melted butter, 2 eggs, 2–3 tbsps water, 2–3 tbsps cream, salt, a pinch of pepper

Beat the eggs with water and cream, add salt and pepper. Mix with the sifted flour. Leave the batter to rest, then mix well. The batter should be as thick as thick cream. Pour some batter into a very hot frying pan and fry fairly thick pancakes.

Oriental crêpe cake

12–16 crêpes, 2 tbsps butter, 3–4 scallions, 250 g each carrots and young **bamboo shoots** (tinned), 50 g dried **cloud ear mushrooms**, 2–3 cloves garlic, 1 fresh chili pepper, 3 tbsps each **soy sauce** and soy oil, 1 tbsp potato flour

Soak the rinsed mushrooms in boiling water, leave aside till cool. Drain and cut in thin strips. Finely slice the peeled carrots, drained bamboo shoots and scallions. Chop finely the chili pepper and garlic. Briskly fry in hot oil, add the vegetables and mushrooms, stir fry for 4–6 minutes. Mix the soy sauce with the potato flour. Pour the mixture into the vegetables, stir and heat up until the sauce is thick. Leave to cool. Butter an oven-proof dish. Put in the crêpes one on the top of another, spreading the filling on each layer. Coat with melted butter and bake in a preheated oven. Serve hot, with pickles or lettuce.

Exotic roulade

6 large crêpes

SAUCE: 1 cup cream, 2 tbsps chopped basil leaves, 1 tsp lemon juice, salt, pepper, a pinch of caster sugar

AVOCADO PASTE: 2 avocados, 2 tbsps lemon juice, 3 firm, fleshy tomatoes, 250 g tinned crab meat, a bunch of chives, 2 tbsps butter, salt, pepper, 2 tbsps garlic vinegar

AVOCADO PASTE: Mix the vinegar with salt and pepper. Blanch and skin the tomatoes, chop finely, combine with the drained crab meat. Cover with the vinegar. Halve the avocados, remove the stones, scoop out the flesh and chop it finely, then sprinkle with lemon juice. Combine with the crab meat, mix well. Cream the chopped chives with 1 tablespoon lemon juice and butter.
Arrange the crêpes in a rectangle on a piece of aluminium foil. Spread first the chive butter and then the avocado paste. Roll up, wrap in foil and refrigerate for 1–2 hours. Whisk the cream with salt, pepper, lemon juice and a pinch of caster sugar. Combine with finely chopped basil leaves and place in the fridge for a while. Take out the roulade, unwrap it, cut into slices. Arrange the slices on a bed of lettuce in a serving dish. Serve the sauce separately.

Kasha and rice dishes

Millet pilaf

200 g millet groats, 1½ cups boiling water or chicken stock, 2 young aubergines (c. 600 g), 1 large onion, 2–3 cloves garlic, 100 g dried apricots, 1 cup dry white wine, juice of ½ lemon, 2 tbsps **tahini** (sesame paste),

2 tbsps **soy sauce**, 1 tbsp ground coriander, 3–4 cloves, 2 tbsps chopped parsley, salt, pepper, oil for frying

Rinse the apricots, cut into thin strips, combine with the crushed cloves. Rinse the millet, drain and mix with coriander. Finely chop the peeled onion and garlic. Fry for 2–3 minutes in hot oil. Add the millets and continue frying for another 3–4 minutes, stirring all the time. Put in the apricots, cover with 1 ½ cups boiling water, stir well. Pour in the wine, bring to a boil, cover and simmer over a low heat for 20–30 minutes. Season with salt and pepper. Rinse the aubergines, slice, sprinkle with salt and leave aside for 20 minutes. Then rinse again, dry on a paper towel and fry in very hot oil until golden brown on both sides. Place the slices on a paper towel to remove excess fat. Then arrange in an oven-proof dish.

Mix the tahini paste with 3 tablespoons boiled water, lemon juice and soy sauce. Pour the mixture over the aubergines. Put in a preheated oven (180°C) and bake for 20–30 minutes. Shape small piles of millet, arrange in a warm serving dish. Put aubergine slices around, coat with the sauce and sprinkle with chopped parsley.

Cubes of crushed buckwheat

1 cup crushed buckwheat, 4 cups light chicken stock or boiled water, 1 tbsp butter, salt, 2 tbsps chopped dill or coriander

Bring 4 cups stock or water to a boil, put in butter. Pour in the buckwheat in a steady stream, stirring continuously. Once all of it has been added, keep cooking over a low heat and stirring until the grits form a smooth mixture. Mix the buckwheat with the chopped dill or coriander, add salt to taste. Rinse a large shallow dish with water. Pour the grits in, with a knife dipped in cold water even out the surface. Leave aside. When cool, cut into cubes. Buckwheat cubes can be served with clear or milk soups.

Semolina patties

1 cup semolina, 2 cups chicken stock (or stock from cube), 2 tbsps butter, 3 tbsps grated pungent cheese, 1 tbsp ground walnuts, 3 tbsps finely chopped parsley, 1 egg, salt, pepper, breadcrumbs, sunflower oil or **grape-seed oil** for frying

Bring the stock to a boil. Pour in the semolina in a steady stream, stirring continuously to prevent lumps. Cover and simmer or put in a preheated oven. Leave to cool, then transfer to a bowl, add the walnuts, grated cheese, salt, pepper and chopped parsley. Break in an egg and work into a smooth mixture. Shape the semolina into small patties. Coat each in breadcrumbs and fry on both sides in hot oil. Serve with salads.

Semolina drop scones

1½ cups semolina, 3 cups milk, 3 tbsps butter, 3 tbsps sugar, grated rind of 1 lemon, 4 eggs, a pinch of salt, oil or lard for frying, caster sugar or fruit syrup

Bring the milk and butter to a boil. Pour in the semolina in a steady stream, stirring continuously. Cover and simmer, stirring all the time to prevent it sticking to the bottom. When ready, leave to cool. Break the eggs, separate the yolks from the whites. Cream the egg yolks with the sugar, towards the end add salt and lemon zest. Whisk the egg whites into stiff peaks. Combine the semolina with the egg yolks, gently fold in the egg whites. Heat the fat in a large frying pan. With a spoon drop in small portions of the mixture and fry golden brown on both sides. Before serving, sprinkle with caster sugar or coat with fruit syrup.

Semolina cubes

100 g semolina, 1 tbsp butter, salt, 1–1¼ cups water

Bring the water, with butter and salt, to a boil. Pour in the semolina in a steady stream, stirring continuously. Once all of it has been added, keep cooking over a low heat for 15 minutes until it thickens. Rinse a large shallow dish with cold water. Pour the semolina in, with a knife dipped in cold water even out to 1 cm thickness. Leave aside. When cool and set, cut into cubes. Serve with clear soups.

Millet and carrot bake

300 g millet grits, 4 cups vegetable stock, 2–3 carrots, 1 tsp lemon juice, a dash of grated lemon rind, 1–2 onions, 100 g butter, salt, a pinch of sugar, 23 tbsps finely chopped parsley

eel and rinse the carrots, grate coarsely, sprinkle with lemon juice. Dice the peeled onions. Melt 2 tablespoons butter in a heavy frying pan, put in the onion and fry without browning. Add the carrots, stir and continue frying for a while longer. Sprinkle with salt, sugar and lemon zest, stir. Pour the grits into a sieve, rinse first with boiling, then with cold water. Drain thoroughly. Put into a heavy saucepan, cover with the vegetable stock. Add 1 tablespoon butter, stir and simmer until the mixture thickens. Combine with the cooked vegetables, mix well and season to taste. Transfer to an oven-proof dish and bake in a preheated oven for 30–40 minutes. Before serving, sprinkle with melted butter and chopped parsley.

Millet and pumpkin bake

300 g millet grits, 2 cups milk, 500 g pumpkin pulp (without skin or seeds), 5 tbsps butter, 2 tbsps sugar, a small piece of vanilla, 2 eggs, 50 g raisins, ½ cup chopped walnuts, salt, ¾ cup cream

lanch the millet, rinse under running water, drain thoroughly. Bring the milk and 1 tablespoon butter, vanilla and salt to a boil in a saucepan. Put in the millet, cover and simmer. Cut the pumpkin into cubes. Melt 1½ tablespoons butter in a deep frying pan, put in the pumpkin cubes and fry, stirring gently. Add the millet, stir carefully and continue cooking, then leave aside to cool. Heat the oven to 170–180°C. Soak the raisins in boiling water for 5 minutes, then drain. Cream 2 tablespoons butter with sugar and eggs. Combine the millets with the raisins and butter and egg mixture. Grease an oven-proof dish with the remaining butter, sprinkle with the chopped walnuts. Put in the millet and pumpkin mixture, even out the surface. Bake in a preheated oven for 20 minutes. Before serving, pour whipped cream over.

Saffron couscous

300 g couscous, ¾ cup chicken or vegetable stock, 1 tsp crumbled saffron filaments, ½ cup vodka

ut the couscous in a bowl. Soak the saffron in vodka for 5–6 minutes, then add to the boiling stock. Pour the hot stock over the couscous. Mix thoroughly with a

fork and leave aside for 20–30 minutes, stirring from time to time. This makes an excellent side dish, especially for poultry, baked vegetables or salads.

Couscous with bell pepper sauce

250 g couscous, 1½ cups light chicken stock, 2–3 tbsps grated Parmesan

SAUCE: 3 red bell peppers (c. 600 g), 100 g butter, 4 tbsps cream, 1 tsp **Tabasco**, 2 tbsps chopped fresh basil leaves or 1 tbsp dried basil, salt, pepper

AUCE: Rinse and dry the peppers. Grill or bake in a very hot oven, then skin and seed. Blend the flesh with 2–3 tablespoons stock. Melt the butter in a saucepan, add the pepper puree, Tabasco, basil and cream. Cover and simmer for 8–10 minutes, stirring occasionally. Add salt and pepper to taste.
Put the couscous in a bowl, cover with boiling stock to 1 cm above the couscous. Leave aside for 8–10 minutes. When the grits swell, stir with a fork. Pour the sauce over, sprinkle with Parmesan on top. Serve with lettuce.

Piquant rice

200 g long-grained rice, 8 **sun-dried tomatoes** in oil, 2 cups tomato juice, 1–2 cloves garlic, 1 chili pepper pod, 2 tbsps tomato paste, 1 tbsp olive oil, salt, freshly ground black pepper

inse and drain the rice. In a heavy saucepan bring the tomato juice to a boil. Pour in the rice, stir, cover and simmer for 15 minutes. Crush the peeled garlic. Drain the sun-dried tomatoes and cut into thin strips. Seed the chili pod and chop finely. Mix the tomato paste with oil, garlic, sun-dried tomatoes and chili. Add salt and pepper to taste. Pour the mixture into the rice, stir well. Cook for another 2–3 minutes, adjust the seasoning. Serve with white meat and poultry.

Herbal rice

1½ cups rice, 1 cup olive oil, 2 tbsps chopped lovage leaves, 1 tbsp each chopped mint, tarragon and parsley, salt, 1 tbsp butter

Parboil (10 minutes) the rice in a large amount of water, then drain. Heat the oil in a large frying pan, put in the rice and fry, stirring continuously. Combine the rice with the herbs, add salt. Put into a buttered oven-proof dish, cover and place in a preheated oven for 10–15 minutes.

Spicy rice

400 g long-grained rice, 1 large onion, 1 tsp cumin seeds, 6–8 cardamom pods, 7–8 cloves, 10–12 peppercorns, 2 pieces (5–6 cm each) cinnamon bark, 3 cups boiled water, 2 tbsps butter, salt

Rinse the rice, cover with cold water and leave aside for 30–40 minutes, then drain thoroughly. Finely chop the peeled onion. Break the cinnamon bark into smaller pieces, crush gently the cardamom pods. In a large, heavy saucepan melt the butter, put in the onion and fry, but do not brown. Add the cinnamon, cumin, cloves, peppercorns and cardamom. Stirring all the time keep frying for a while longer. Then pour in the rice, stir and fry over a fairly high heat for 2–3 minutes. Pour in the water and stirring continuously bring to a boil. Turn down the heat, cover the saucepan and simmer for 20 minutes. Take the lid off, turn off the heat and leave the rice for 8–10 minutes. Then transfer to a serving dish. Serve with vegetables, chicken stew, roast veal and lamb.

Ginger rice

1½ cups short-grained rice, 1–2 onions, 1½ tbsps diced fresh ginger, 4 tbsps butter, 3 cups water, 1 tsp salt, 1 tsp finely chopped fresh ginger

Cover the rice with cold boiled water and leave for 1–2 hours, then drain thoroughly. Put the peeled onions and diced ginger through a blender, juice them. Combine the juice with 3 cups hot water. Put the drained rice into a saucepan, cover with water with juice, stir and cook for 20 minutes, or until the rice absorbs the liquid. Melt the butter, combine with salt and finely chopped ginger. Combine with the rice. Stir, cover and simmer for 5–8 minutes. This is an excellent accompaniment to roast poultry, fish and vegetables.

Apricot rice

200 g basmati rice, 1 red onion, 1 tbsp olive oil, 2.5 cm piece of fresh ginger, 10 juniper berries, 1 tsp fresh or dried thyme, 10 dried apricots, 300 ml vegetable stock, parsley

Peel the ginger, grate or chop very finely. Rinse the apricots, cut into thick strips. Grind the juniper berries coarsely or pound in a mortar. Finely chop the peeled onion. In a large non-stick saucepan heat the oil. Put in the onion and fry over a low heat for 2–3 minutes. Add the ginger, juniper and thyme, stir fry for 15–20 seconds. Put in the rice and apricots, cover with the hot vegetable stock, stir and bring to a boil. Cover and simmer over a low heat for 15–20 minutes, or until the rice is ready. Serve immediately, sprinkled with chopped parsley. Such rice makes a delicious accompaniment to veal scallops, chicken or turkey fillets and roast poultry.

Coconut rice

500 g basmati rice, 1 red onion, 2 tbsps butter, 4 green cardamom pods, 1½ cups coconut milk (or 2 cups milk with 4 tbsps shredded coconut), salt

If you do not have tinned coconut milk, do the following: mix 4 tablespoons shredded coconut with 2 cups milk, stir well and leave for 30–40 minutes, then strain the milk, press out the liquid.
Crush the cardamom pods, finely chop the peeled onion. Rinse the rice, drain thoroughly. Melt the butter in a large, heavy saucepan, stir fry the onion to soften it. Add the cardamom, put in the rice and heat up, stirring all the time to coat all grains in butter. Cover with the coconut milk to 1 cm above the rice surface (add some boiled water if necessary). Add a dash of salt, stir and bring to a boil. Cover and simmer over a very low heat until the rice absorbs the liquid. Mix with a fork, cover and continue cooking for another 8–10 minutes.

Nutty rice

1 cup long-grained rice, ½ tsp powdered saffron, 2 tbsps walnut oil, a dash of each salt and cinnamon,

2 tbsps each coarsely chopped hazelnuts, unsalted peanuts, almond flakes and raisins, 1 tsp brandy

In a large, heavy saucepan heat 1 ½ tablespoons oil, put in the rinsed and drained rice and fry, stirring all the time until all grains are coated in oil. Pour in lukewarm boiled water with saffron, stir and bring to a boil. Add salt, cover and simmer over a low heat for 20 minutes. Rinse the raisins, sprinkle with the brandy and leave aside for 5–8 minutes. Heat the remaining oil in a frying pan and toast the chopped nuts and almond flakes.
Transfer the cooked rice to a serving plate, sprinkle with raisins and toasted nuts. Such rice goes well with roast chicken, poultry fillets, fish and roast leg of mutton.

Rice with sage and nuts

1 cup long-grained rice, 2 cups chicken stock, ½ cup chopped hazelnuts, 2 tbsps chopped fresh sage leaves or 2 tsps dried sage, 3 tbsps butter, 2 tbsps chopped parsley, salt, pepper

Put the rinsed and drained rice in a heavy saucepan, add sage, salt and pepper. Cover with the hot stock, stir. Put the lid on and simmer for 20 minutes. In a large frying pan melt the butter and toast the nuts for 2–3 minutes, stirring continuously. Combine with the cooked rice and sprinkle with chopped parsley. Serve with meat, poultry and fish.

Saffron rice with chicken livers

*250 g arborio rice, 500 g chicken livers, 1 large cooking apple, 1 small tin green peas, 1 large onion, 1 large red bell pepper, 1 tbsp chopped fresh thyme leaves, 6 cups chicken stock (or stock from cube), 100 g butter, 3 tbsps grated Parmesan, 1 g **saffron**, salt, white pepper, parsley sprigs*

Dice the peeled onion. Seed the bell pepper, cut into cubes. Rinse and dry the livers. Bring the stock to a boil. Soak the saffron in 3 tablespoons hot stock for 3–5 minutes. Pour the rice into a large saucepan, cover with the hot stock, put a lid on and cook for 15 minutes over a moderate heat. Add the saffron, stir well and continue cooking for another 3–4 minutes. Melt the butter in a large,

heavy frying pan. Put in the onion and pepper cubes, stir fry briskly. Take out with a straining spoon, put in the livers. When they brown evenly on all sides, push the livers to the edges of the frying pan and place in the middle the peeled and cored apple, cut into small wedges. Sprinkle the livers with pepper and salt and cook over a very low heat for another 1–2 minutes. Drain the rice well, transfer to a large saucepan. Combine with the pepper cubes, onion and drained green peas. Sprinkle with thyme and Parmesan, stir thoroughly and heat up. Put the hot rice in the middle of a large round serving dish, arrange the livers and apple around. Garnish with parsley sprigs.

Risotto with bell peppers

*1 cup long-grained rice, 750 g lean pork (off the bone), 1 tbsp lemon juice, 300 g fleshy tomatoes, 1 of each green, red, yellow and purple bell pepper, 2 cloves garlic, ½ tsp powdered **saffron**, ¼ cup olive oil, salt, freshly ground pepper, 1 tbsp chopped parsley, 3 cups light chicken stock or water, parsley sprigs*

Rinse and drain the rice thoroughly. Rinse and dry the meat, cut into cubes. Sprinkle with lemon juice and pepper, leave aside for 15 minutes. Wash the bell peppers, remove the stalks and seeds, dry and cut the flesh into fine strips. Blanch and skin the tomatoes, seed them, cut the flesh into cubes. Peel the garlic. In a large, heavy saucepan heat the oil, put in the garlic and brown it, then remove with a straining spoon. Put in the meat and briskly brown on all sides, stirring continuously. Take the meat out, arrange on a plate. Put the pepper strips and tomatoes into the saucepan, fry for several minutes over a low heat. Blend the fried garlic, chopped parsley and saffron. Combine the mixture with the meat. Return the meat to the saucepan, pour in 1 cup stock or water, cover and simmer for 15–20 minutes. Put in the rice and, stirring continuously, heat up for 2–3 minutes. Add the remaining hot stock or water, adjust the seasoning. Stir thoroughly, cover and put into a preheated oven (180°C) for 25–30 minutes. Before serving, garnish with parsley sprigs.

Pilaf with smoked fish

1 cup long-grain rice, 3 cups milk, 400 g smoked fish (herring or mackerel), 4 tbsps butter, 100 g raisins, 100 g dried apricots, 50 g stoned prunes, 1 egg, 2 tbsps flour, a pinch of **saffron***, salt, 1 glass dry white wine*

Cover the dried fruit with wine, leave aside for 30–40 minutes. Rinse and drain the rice, put into 2 litres salted boiling water. Cook for 4–5 minutes, then drain and transfer to a heavy saucepan. Cover with hot milk and cook over a low heat until the rice absorbs the milk. Towards the end add the saffron mixed with 1 tablespoon boiling water and stir.

Bone the fish, remove the skin. Divide the meat into bite-size pieces and briskly fry in 1 tablespoon melted butter. Put the fruit and wine into a small saucepan, add 1 tablespoon melted butter, cover and cook over a low heat for 10 minutes. Make batter from 1 egg, 1 tablespoon water and flour. In a heavy saucepan melt 1 tablespoon butter, pour in the batter and spread evenly on the bottom. Put in the rice, pour the remaining melted butter over. Surround with the fruit and fish, heat up over a low heat for 5–7 minutes.

Poultry

Chicken with pistachio stuffing

1 large chicken (c. 2 kg), salt, 1 tbsp lemon juice, 4 tbsps butter

STUFFING: 2 cups cooked rice, a pinch of **saffron***, 1 tsp vodka, 100 g shelled* **pistachios***, 2–3 tbsps each chopped chives, dill and parsley, 1 large onion, 2 cloves garlic, 50 g butter, 3–4 tbsps cream (36%), salt, pepper*

Bone the bird carefully, taking care not to damage the meat or skin (this is best done by making a long inci-sion along the spine, beginning at the neck). Rub with salt, pepper and lemon juice. Refrigerate.

STUFFING: Soak the pistachios in boiling water, drain and skin, chop coarsely. Finely chop the peeled onion, crush the peeled garlic. Soften the onion and garlic in melted butter. Leave to cool, then combine with the pistachios, rice and the other ingredients. Add the cream, season with pepper and salt, mix well.

Heat the oven to 190°C. Stuff the chicken, sew up the vent. Place in a roasting tin, dot with butter (2 tablespoons). Put in the oven and roast for an hour, occasionally bast-ing with melted butter and pan juices. Turn off the heat and leave the bird in the oven for another 20–25 minutes. Serve hot or cold.

Chicken in white sauce

400 g chicken breasts, 1 glass vodka, 1 tsp salt, 1 tsp **five-spice powder***, 200 g asparagus (fresh or tinned), ½ Savoy cabbage, 1 onion, 1 tbsp finely chopped fresh ginger, 1 cup chicken stock, 1 tbsp potato flour, ½ cup cream, 2 tbsps butter*

Rinse and dry the chicken breasts, sprinkle with vodka, salt and five-spice powder. Cover and leave aside for an hour. Put the cleaned asparagus stalks into boiling, lightly salted water for 3–4 minutes, drain, rinse under cold wa-ter and cut into small pieces. Cook the cabbage in boiling water for 4–5 minutes, drain, rinse under cold water and shred. Cut the chicken meat in strips. Chop the peeled onion finely. Heat the butter in a large saucepan, soften the onion. Add the ginger and briskly fry over a high heat. Put in the meat and stir fry for 3–5 minutes. Cover with the hot stock, bring to a boil. Put in the asparagus pieces and shredded cabbage, sprinkle with the remaining vodka. Simmer for 5 minutes. Mix the cream with the potato flour. Pour into the meat and stirring continuously heat up until the sauce thickens.

Chicken in coconut sauce

4 chicken thighs (boned), 1 large onion, 2 tbsps white or blue poppy seeds, 1 tbsp coriander seeds, 1 tsp **cumin***, ½ cup shredded coconut, 1 cup yogurt, 2–3 cloves garlic, 2 tsp* **ginger paste** *(or chopped fresh* ginger), 3–4 **green cardamom** seeds, ¼ tsp ground cloves, 2 chili peppers, ½ cup thick cream, 1 cup light chicken stock (or stock from cube), 2–3 tbsps oil, salt

Cover the poppy seeds with 1 cup warm boiled water, leave aside for 10–15 minutes. Finely chop peeled garlic. Seed the chili peppers. Blend the poppy seeds with the chilis, garlic, coriander, cumin, shredded coconut and chicken stock. Finely slice the peeled onion. Mix the cream with the ground cloves and a pinch of salt. In a large, deep frying pan heat the oil and soften the onion. Add the ginger paste or finely chopped ginger. Put in the rinsed and dried chicken thighs. Fry on both sides over a high heat for 4–5 minutes. Add the blended spices, stir, bring to a boil. Turn down the heat and simmer for 3–4 minutes. Pour in the yogurt, sprinkle with salt and stew for 5–7 minutes. Add the cream, stir and heat up. Serve with rice.

Piquant chicken with vegetables

1 chicken (c. 1½ kg), 1 young aubergine, 250 g French beans, 1 large onion, 4–5 cloves garlic, ½ tsp each ground ginger, **curry powder** and **turmeric**, ½ cup tomato concentrate, 1 cup chicken stock, ½ cup oil, salt, pepper, optional a dash of sugar

Joint the rinsed and dried bird. Fry golden brown in hot oil. Take out and keep warm. Soften the peeled and diced onion and chopped garlic in the same oil. Put in the aubergine cut into large cubes. Sprinkle with water and cook until the aubergine is tender. Top and tail the cleaned French beans, cut into short pieces, add to the aubergines together with spices. Stirring continuously, fry for 5 minutes. Mix the tomato concentrate with salt, pepper and chicken stock. Combine with the vegetables, stir. Line an oven-proof dish with the vegetables, arrange the chicken pieces on top. Put into a preheated oven for 30–40 minutes. Serve with rice.

Chicken à la égyptienne

1 chicken (c. 1.2 kg), 1 tbsp lemon juice, 2 tbsps liquid honey, 2 tbsps butter, 2 tbsps ground walnuts, 1 tbsp finely chopped **candied ginger**, salt, ¼ cup light stock, 1 tbsp **peanut oil**

Rinse and dry the bird, rub with salt and lemon juice, leave aside for half an hour. Heat the oven to 180–190°C. Melt the butter, combine with the honey. Rub the chicken with the mixture inside and out. Place the bird in a greased roasting tin and put in the oven. Baste often with stock. Combine the ginger and walnuts. 10 minutes before the chicken is due to be taken out, sprinkle the mixture on top of the bird, turn up the heat and brown it. Best served with rice.

Chicken in nutty sauce

4 chicken thighs, 1 tbsp lemon juice, salt, 1 tbsp oil, 2 tbsps water or white wine

SAUCE: 1 tbsp **curry powder**, 3 tbsps butter, ½ cup finely chopped walnuts (or ¼ cup peanut butter), 1 tsp **cumin**, 2 tsps brown sugar, 1 fresh chili pepper, 2 tbsps water, 1 tbsp oil, 1 green bell pepper, 1 tin (440 g) baby corn cobs, 3–4 scallions, 1–2 cloves garlic, ½ tsp grated fresh ginger, 1 cup bean shoots

Rinse and dry the thighs, rub with salt, sprinkle with lemon juice. Brown on both sides in hot oil, then sprinkle with water or wine, cover and stew for 30 minutes. Take off the heat and leave to cool.
SAUCE: Rinse and dry the bell and chili peppers, remove the stalks and seeds, cut into cubes. Dice the scallions (with chives), crush the peeled garlic, drain the corn cobs, rinse and drain the bean shoots. Skin and bone the chicken thighs, cut the meat in strips.
Heat the oil in a heavy frying pan (if you use a wok, remember to wash its sides with oil). Put in the peppers, corn cobs, scallions, garlic and ginger. Stir fry for 2 minutes over a high heat to soften the vegetables. Add the bean shoots, chicken meat and sauce. Stir and keep cooking for 2 minutes over a high heat. Take off the heat and serve immediately with rice.

Chicken in pesto sauce

600 g chicken fillets (4 pieces), juice and grated rind of ½ lemon, 1 ½ cups **pesto** sauce, ½ cup yogurt, ½ cup grated Parmesan, ½ cup chopped parsley, ½ tsp each freshly ground black pepper and salt, 4 cups vegetables

Piquant chicken with vegetables

Chicken in pesto sauce

(e.g. cauliflower and broccoli florets, French beans, asparagus, zucchini cubes, shredded Savoy cabbage)

SAUCE: Blend the pesto with the chopped parsley, yogurt, salt, pepper and Parmesan. If you feel like it, add some lemon juice. Cover and refrigerate for an hour. Heat the oven to 180°C. Make small incisions in the fillets. Sprinkle the meat with lemon juice and zest, leave aside for 10 minutes. Salt, arrange in a greased oven-proof dish. Put in the oven for 25 minutes. Steam cook the rinsed and dried vegetables or blanch them in boiling water. Drain and arrange around the meat. Put in the oven for 2–3 minutes, then take out and cover with the pesto sauce. Serve immediately with pasta or rice.

Chicken for weight watchers

600 g chicken fillets, 1 tsp salt, 1 tbsp lemon juice, 1 tbsp **soy sauce**, *3–4 tbsps sake, 1–2 tbsps* **wasabi paste**

Mix the soy sauce with the lemon juice and sake. Cut the rinsed and dried meat into thin slices, sprinkle with salt. Arrange the slices in a saucepan with a tightly fitting lid, sprinkling each layer with the prepared sauce. Cover the saucepan, place on top of a pot of boiling water. Turn the heat up and cook for 20 minutes. Transfer the meat to a warm serving dish and spread the wasabi paste on the slices. Serve as a hot snack or with rice and salad.

Stuffed chicken

1 large chicken, 1 bread roll, 50 ml cream, 150 g butter, 100 g dried apricots, 50 g raisins, 1 ½ tbsps pickled green peppercorns, 2 eggs, 1 tbsp semolina, ½ tsp each dried thyme, dried basil and ground nutmeg, 3–4 cloves garlic, 1 small onion, salt and freshly ground pepper, 4 bay leaves, 2 pieces cinnamon bark, 1–2 **star anise** *fruits, ½ cup chicken stock (or stock from cube)*

STUFFING: Soak the bread roll in cream. Rinse and dry the bird, cut off the wings, thighs and neck. With a knife carefully (taking care not to damage the skin) separate the skin from the meat. Sew up with twine the openings where the neck, wings and thighs were. Put the meat and the bread roll through a micer. Blanch the almond and raisins in boiling water, then drain. Peel the onions and garlic, chop very finely. Cut the apricots in strips. Melt the butter in a saucepan, soften the onion and garlic, add the apricot strips, green peppercorns and raisins. Take off the heat, mix with the semolina, salt, pepper and herbs. Combine with the minced meat and egg yolks. Whisk the egg whites into stiff peaks, fold in.

Fill the chicken skin fairly loosely with the stuffing (which grows in volume when roasted). Give the whole an elongated shape. Place on top pieces of cinnamon and bay leaves, secure them with thread. Heat the oven to 180°C.

Pour the chicken stock and half the melted butter in a roasting tin. Put in the stuffed chicken, coat it with the remaining melted butter. Cover and put in the hot oven for 15 minutes. Take out, sprinkle with 2 tablespoons hot water, add star anise fruits. Return to the oven for 40 minutes. If necessary, baste with water to make the skin go golden brown. Take out the roast, place the stuffed chicken on a bread board, cover with another board. When it gets cool, cut diagonally into slices. Such stuffed chicken goes well with chutney and savoury fruit sauces.

Marinated chicken fillets

4 chicken fillets (c. 600 g), 1 tbsp lemon juice, a bunch of coriander, 3 tbsps sunflower or **peanut oil**

MARINADE: *2 tbsps* **sesame oil**, *2 tbsps* **oyster sauce**, *2 tsps sugar, ½ tsp ground white pepper, 2 scallions (without leaves), 1 tsp finely chopped fresh ginger*

Chop the onions very finely. Blend with the ginger, sugar and pepper, with sesame oil and oyster sauce. Rinse and dry the meat. Cut each fillet lengthwise into two. Sprinkle with lemon juice. Put in a bowl, pour the marinade over, stir. Cover and leave aside for 30–40 minutes. Take half the coriander. Pick the leaves, throw out the stalks. Arrange coriander leaves on 4 pieces of meat, cover with the other four, secure with toothpicks along the edges. Heat the peanut oil in a frying pan. Fry the fillets golden brown on both sides. In a small saucepan heat up the marinade. Drain the fried fillets on a paper towel, arrange in an oven-proof dish. Pour the marinade over and put in a preheated oven for a short while to warm. Before serving, garnish with coriander sprigs.

Chicken breasts, Mediterranean style

4 chicken fillets, 2 tbsps lemon juice, 2 tbsps olive oil, 2 large onions, 4 cloves garlic, 150 g chorizo or chorizo-style sausage, 1 tin (410 g) skinned tomatoes, 1 tbsp chopped fresh thyme leaves, 150 g **olives stuffed with almonds**, *1 small glass dry white wine or light stock, 2 young zucchini, freshly ground black pepper, salt, 3 tbsps chopped parsley*

Rinse and dry the fillets, sprinkle with lemon juice, salt and pepper. Slice the peeled onions. Coarsely chop the peeled garlic. Slice the sausage. Rinse and dry the zucchini, cut into cubes. Heat the oil in a large saucepan. Briskly fry the fillets, 2 minutes to each side. Take the meat out. Fry the onion, garlic and sausage for 5 minutes in the same oil. Return the fillets to the saucepan. Add thyme, tinned tomatoes with juice and olives, stir well. Season with plenty of pepper, sprinkle with wine or stock, bring to a boil. Cover and simmer for 25 minutes, stirring from time to time. Add the zucchini and cook for 10–15 minutes longer. Before serving, sprinkle with chopped parsley. Serve with rice, potatoes or wholemeal bread. It gets better with each reheating.

Piquant chicken fillets

800 g chicken fillets, 1 tsp lemon juice, 1 tsp oil, freshly ground black pepper, ¼ cup **sesame seeds**, *½ tsp* **anise seeds**, *1 tsp ground ginger, ½ tsp cayenne pepper, 8–12 cloves garlic, 2 tbsps* **soy sauce**, *2 tbsps liquid honey, 2 tbsps* **balsamic vinegar**, *2 tbsps* **sesame oil**

Rinse and dry the fillets, divide them into 4 portions. Toast the sesame seeds in a frying pan. Mix with the anise seeds, cayenne, salt, black pepper, lemon juice and oil. Pound lightly the meat with a mallet. Rub each piece with the prepared mixture. Put in a bowl, cover and leave aside for 15 minutes.
SAUCE: Mix the soy sauce with the honey and balsamic vinegar. Leave aside for 15 minutes

Crush the peeled garlic. Heat the oil in a large frying pan. Fry the fillets, 3–4 minutes to each side. Transfer the meat to a hot serving dish and keep warm. Stir fry the garlic in the same oil, pour in the sauce. Stir well, then cook over a low heat. When the sauce thickens, pour it over the fillets. Serve immediately, with rice or rice noodles, steamed broccoli or French beans.

Oriental chicken shashlyks

800 g chicken thighs (boned), 1 tbsp **sesame oil**, *salt, pepper*

MARINADE: 1 large onion, 4–5 cloves garlic, 1 tsp freshly chopped ginger, 1 ½ tbsps chili sauce, 1 tsp **shrimp paste**, *3 tbsps each lemon juice and boiled water, 1 tbsp honey, 1 tsp sugar*

Skin the thighs. Rinse and dry the meat, cut into large even cubes. Mix all the ingredients of the marinade. Place the meat in a bowl, cover with the marinade, shake. Leave aside for 2–3 hours, shaking from time to time to make the meat marinate evenly. Skewer the meat, sprinkle with salt and pepper, brush with oil and grill in the oven, basting with the marinade from time to time. Serve with rice, with slices of pineapple and cucumber.

Chicken thighs with artichokes

8 chicken thighs (boned, c. 600–799 g), 3 tbsp flour, 1 tbsp dried thyme, salt, pepper, 3 tbsp sunflower oil, 1 tin (500 g) **artichokes** *in brine, 2 red bell peppers, 2–3 cloves garlic, 4–5 tbsps pitted* **black olives**, *¼ cup dry white wine, ¾ cup chicken stock, grated rind of 1 lemon, salt, pepper, fresh thyme sprigs and lemon wedges for garnishing*

Remove the stalks and seeds from the bell peppers. Rinse the peppers, cut into thin strips. Chop the peeled garlic, halve the olives, drain and quarter the artichokes. Heat the oven to 150°C. Rinse and dry the chicken thighs. Mix the flour with salt, pepper and dried thyme. Coat the thighs with the mixture. Heat the oil in a large, heavy frying pan. Fry the meat golden brown on both sides. Transfer to an oven-proof dish. Place in the

Chicken thighs with artichokes

preheated oven. Briskly fry the garlic in the same oil, add the peppers and artichokes, stir fry for 5 minutes. When the peppers soften, add the olives and wine. Turn up the heat and allow the wine to evaporate. Pour in the stock, add lemon zest and cook for a while over a high heat. Adjust the seasoning. Arrange the vegetables over the thighs, garnish with thyme sprigs and lemon wedges. Serve with pasta, rice or French fries.

Baked chicken thighs

*4 chicken thighs, 1–2 cloves garlic, 1 tbsp finely chopped fresh ginger, 1 tbsp **garam masala**, salt, pepper, a pinch of **turmeric**, 2 tbsps oil, ½ cup yogurt, ½ lemon*

Heat the oven to 180–190°C. Blend the peeled garlic with oil, yogurt and spices. Coat the rinsed and dried thighs with the mixture and arrange in an oven-proof dish. Put into the oven and cook, basting from time to time with the remaining yogurt mixture. Before serving, garnish with lemon wedges. Serve with rice or potato chips.

Chicken thighs in piri-piri sauce

*4 chicken thighs, 1 tbsp lemon juice, 2 onions, 5–6 firm, fleshy tomatoes, 2 carrots, 1 parsley or parsnip root, 1 each red and yellow bell pepper, 2 cm long piece cinnamon bark, salt, pepper, 2 cups light stock or water, 5–6 drops **piri-piri** or **Tabasco sauce**, 3–4 tbsps olive oil*

Rinse and dry the chicken thighs, rub with salt, pepper and lemon juice. Scrape and rinse the carrots and parsley (or parsnip) root, julienne them. Blanch, skin and quarter the tomatoes. Remove the stalks and seeds from the peppers. Rinse the flesh, cut into strips. Slice the peeled onions. Heat some oil in a large, heavy saucepan. Fry the chicken thighs golden brown. Add the onions, carrots, parsley (or parsnip) and cinnamon bark. Fry briskly together. Put in the tomatoes, add salt, pepper and piri-piri (or Tabasco) sauce. Pour in the hot stock (or water), cover and simmer for 20 minutes. Put in the pepper strips, stir and continue cooking for another 15 minutes. Towards the end slightly reduce the sauce. Serve with rice or couscous.

Piquant chicken goulash

*500 g chicken fillets, 1 tbsp lemon juice, ¼ tsp grated lemon rind, 1 tsp **walnut oil**, 1 each red and green bell pepper, 2 fresh chili peppers, 2 large onions, 10–12 cloves garlic, 1 cup chopped fresh basil leaves, ½ small lime, 2 tbsps olive oil, 2 tbsps **soy sauce**, salt to taste*

Mix the lemon juice and zest with the walnut oil. Cut the rinsed and dried meat into thin slices. Cover with the sauce, mix and leave aside.

Peel the onions and garlic. Dice the onions, finely chop the garlic. Scrub the lime, blanch and halve, then slice each half and cut the slices into strips. Remove the stalks and seeds from all peppers. Cut the flesh into strips. Heat the olive oil in a large, heavy frying pan or wok. Soften the onions and garlic. Put in the meat and stir fry over a high heat for 2–3 minutes. Add the pepper strips and keep cooking for another 4–5 minutes. Then put in the lime strips, basil and soy sauce. Stirring all the time continue cooking for 3–4 minutes. Add some salt if needed. Serve with rice or pasta.

Spanish chicken stew

*1 kg chicken thighs (boned), 1 tbsp lemon juice, salt, freshly ground pepper, 2 tbsps flour, ¼ cup **grape-seed oil**, 2 onions, 5–6 fleshy tomatoes, 1 each red and green bell pepper, 150 g green peas (fresh, tinned or frozen), 150 g button mushrooms, 1 cup pitted **green olives**, 1 tbsp pitted **black olives**, 1 tsp honey, 1 cup chicken stock, 1 tbsp chopped parsley*

Rinse and dry the meat, cut in cubes. Sprinkle with lemon juice, salt and pepper, leave aside for 15 minutes. Remove the stalks and seeds from the peppers. Rinse and dry the flesh, cut into strips. Chop the peeled onions. Blanch and skin the tomatoes, cut in cubes and seed them. Halve the olives and slice the cleaned mushrooms. Coat the chicken meat with half the flour. Heat the oil in a large saucepan. Put in the meat and brown, stirring all the time. Take out with a straining spoon, transfer to a plate. Fry the onions, peppers and tomatoes in the same oil for 1–2 minutes. Add salt, pepper and honey, stir, cover and simmer for 10 minutes. Combine with the fried meat, cover with the stock and stew over a low heat for 40 minutes. Add the olives, green peas and mushrooms, keep cooking for another 15 minutes. Make a roux from the remaining flour and water. Pour into the saucepan and simmer till the sauce thickens. Adjust the seasoning. Serve with rice or white bread.

Greek ragout

800 g chicken fillets, 200 g onion, 4 large, firm tomatoes, 1–1½ tbsps tomato concentrate, 50 g anchovy fillets (a small tin), 10 cloves pickled garlic, 2 tbsps **capers**, 100 g **pine nuts**, 2–3 tbsps olive oil, 2 tbsps honey, ½ tsp ground black pepper, ¼ tsps each ground cloves and coriander, salt, 1 tbsp each chopped parsley and coriander, ½ cup dry white wine, ½ cup light stock

Cut the rinsed and dried fillets into fairly thick strips. Dice the peeled onions. Heat the oil in a heavy saucepan. Soften the onions, put in the meat and brown on all sides. Sprinkle with ground pepper, coriander and cloves. Add the honey and stock, stir, cover and simmer for 15 minutes. Finely chop the anchovies and garlic, add to the meat, stir and keep cooking for another 15 minutes. Blanch and skin the tomatoes, cut in cubes and seed. Chop the flesh finely, put in a separate saucepan and sweat them. Combine with the tomato concentrate and wine, then simmer over a low heat for 5–8 minutes. Combine the tomatoes with the meat, stir and cook for another 10 minutes. Towards the end add the capers and toasted pine nuts, stir and cook for a while longer. Before serving, sprinkle with chopped parsley and coriander.

Hot chicken and mushroom snack

500 g roast or boiled chicken meat, 250 g button mushrooms, 2–3 cloves garlic, 1 cup cream, 1 egg, 3–4 tbsps grated cheese, salt, pepper, 1 tsp **curry powder**, a pinch of ground juniper berries, 2 tbsps butter, 2 tbsps chopped parsley

Rinse and drain the mushrooms, quarter and brown in butter. Cut the meat into small slices. Chop the peeled garlic, blend with salt, pepper and juniper. Mix the cream

with the egg, combine with the prepared garlic, curry powder, half the grated cheese and parsley. Heat the oven to 180–190°C. Grease individual oven-proof dishes with butter. Line them with chicken meat and mushrooms, pour the sauce over, sprinkle with grated cheese. Bake in the oven for 15 minutes. Serve with white bread and salads.

Poultry gizzards

500 g chicken (or turkey) gizzards, 1 small onion, 1 tsp chopped ginger, 3–4 **star anise seeds**, a piece of cinnamon bark, ½ tsp flavour enhancer (sodium glutamate), 1 small glass sherry, 1 tbsp **soy sauce**, 2 ½ chicken stock (or stock from cube)

Clean and wash the gizzards. Put into boiling, slightly salted water, cook for 3–4 minutes. Strain, rinse under cold water. Bring the stock to a boil, add the onion, ginger, star anise, cinnamon and soy sauce. Put in the gizzards, add the sherry. Bring to a boil, cover and simmer for one hour. Take off the heat, leave to cool. Before serving, cut the gizzards diagonally into slices as a cold snack. You can also use them for a kind of goulash, in which case you must strain the stock, reduce it and thicken with potato flour; then put the gizzards into the sauce and heat up; serve with rice, sprinkled with chopped scallions.

Chicken liver curry

600 g chicken livers, 2 tbsps flour, ½ tsp salt, ½ tsp freshly ground pepper, 3 scallions, 2–3 cloves garlic, 1 tbsp **curry powder**, 1 tbsp marinated **green peppercorns**, 1 tbsp **peanut paste** (or 1 ½ tbsps ground peanuts and ¼ cup stock), ¼ cup stock, ½ cup cream, 2 tbsps **peanut oil**, 1 tbsp butter, 2 tbsps chopped coriander

Finely chop the peeled garlic and scallions. Cut the rinsed and drained livers in fairly thick strips. Combine the flour with pepper and salt. Coat the livers in the mixture. Heat 3 tablespoons oil in a heavy frying pan. Fry the livers briskly for 3–4 minutes, then take out with a straining spoon. Pour out the oil. Heat the remaining oil, soften the scallions and garlic. Add the butter, curry powder, peanut paste and green peppercorns. Pour in the hot stock, stir and cook to

Piquant chicken wings

reduce the liquid. Add the cream, heat up. Put in the livers, stir. Before serving, sprinkle with chopped coriander. Serve with rice or soy noodles, or with rice.

Piquant chicken wings

1 kg chicken wings, 1 cup honey, 3 tbsps **soy sauce**, *1 tsp* **Tabasco sauce**, *½ tsp each ground ginger and garlic salt*

Mix the liquid honey with soy sauce, Tabasco, ginger and garlic salt. Arrange the washed and dried wings in a large, shallow saucepan, coat with the prepared sauce and leave aside for 2–3 hours, turning them over two or three times. Take the wings out of the marinade and roast in the oven or grill, sprinkling with the marinade from time to time. They are best served with roast potatoes with herbs.

Goose stuffed with pasta

1 young goose (c. 2.5 kg), salt, ½ tsp each ground caraway, allspice and pepper, 1 carrot, 1 parsley root, 1 leek, 2 cups light stock or water

STUFFING: 300 g tagliatelle, 2 egg yolks, ¼ tsp ground mace or nutmeg, ¼ tsp ground allspice, 2 tbsps cream, 2 tbsps melted butter

SAUCE: 1 tbsp flour, 2 tbsps each **capers** *and sliced* **green olives**, *3 tbsps butter*

Cover the bird with cold water, leave aside for 2–3 hours. Take out, dry and put on a board. Make an incision along the spine, take out the spine bones. Rub the bird with salt, caraway, allspice and pepper. Leave to rest in a cool place for 2–3 hours.
STUFFING: Cook the pasta in boiling water, drain. Transfer to a saucepan, pour in the melted butter, add 2 egg yolks, mace (or nutmeg), allspice and cream. Mix thoroughly. Stuff the goose with pasta, sew up the vent.
Peel and wash the vegetables, slice them. Line a roasting tin with the vegetables, place the bird on top. Put in a preheated oven and roast, basting first with a little stock, then with the pan juices. Turn the goose over frequently.

Transfer the bird to a hot serving dish and keep warm. Pour the roasting juices with vegetables into a saucepan, combine with the remaining stock mixed with flour, bring to a boil. Sieve the sauce, serve in a sauceboat.

Spit-roasted duck

1 young duck (c. 1 ½ – 2 kg), salt, 2–4 peaches in syrup, ½ lemon, 5–8 fresh mint or lemon balm leaves

MARINADE: 1 tbsp honey, 2 tbsps **sesame oil**, *2 tbsps* **soy sauce**, *1 tbsp finely chopped fresh ginger*

SAUCE FOR BASTING: 1 tbsp honey, 1 tbsp lemon juice, 1 tbsp soy sauce, 2–3 tbsps chicken stock (or stock from cube), 1 tsp ground ginger

Mix all ingredients of the marinade. Bring 2–3 litres of water to a boil in a large pan. Put in the rinsed bird, take off the heat and leave for 5–6 minutes. Take out, allow to cool, then dry and rub inside and out with salt. Leave aside for 15 minutes. Brush inside and outside with the marinade several times, leave in a cool place for an hour.
Mix the ingredients of the basting sauce. Heat the oven to 220–250°C. Truss the bird with twine. Put it on the spit and roast in the oven, basting with the prepared sauce. Half way through turn down the temperature to 180°C and continue cooking, basting with pan juices. When the bird is tender, turn off the heat and leave the duck in the oven for a while longer. Then take it out, joint it and arrange on a hot serving dish. Put sliced peaches and lemon around, garnish with mint or lemon balm leaves. Serve with rice.

Stuffed duck in honey sauce

1 duck (c. 2–2½ kg)

SAUCE: ½ cup rosemary or thyme honey, 7–8 tbsps **oyster sauce**

STUFFING: 3–4 scallions, 2–3 celery stalks, 6–8 cloves garlic, 2 fresh chili peppers, 4 bay

Duck breasts with cabbage and leeks

leaves, ¼ cup each chopped basil and coriander leaves, salt, freshly ground pepper

Rinse and dry the bird (remove excess fat if necessary). Heat the oven to 220–230°C.
STUFFING: Rinse and dry the scallions, cut into 3–4 cm pieces. Wash the celery, remove stringy fibres, slice the stalks. Seed the chilis, chop finely. Crush the peeled garlic, crumble the bay leaves. Put the vegetables in a bowl, combine with the chopped herbs, garlic, bay leaves, salt and pepper. Stuff the duck, sew up the vent. Mix the honey with the oyster sauce, heat lightly. Fill a roasting tin with 2 cups hot water. Place the bird on the gridiron resting on the roasting tin. Cover the duck with aluminium foil and cook for one hour. Turn down the temperature to 190–200°C. Empty the roasting tin into a saucepan, return to the oven. Take the foil off, with a knife delicately lift up the skin of the bird to allow excess fat to flow down. Brush the bird with the prepared honey and oyster sauce, continue cooking for 40–50 minutes, basting frequently with the sauce.
Joint the bird, arrange on a platter. Pour the sauce over. Serve with rice or with rice or soy noodles. It is just as good served cold.

Duck breasts with cabbage and leeks

4 duck breasts (boned, c. 800 g), 2 leeks (white parts only, c. 250 g), 1 Chinese chard, grated rind from 1 large orange, 5 tbsps **oyster sauce**, 1 tbsp **sesame seeds**, 1 tbsp **soy oil**

Wash the leeks thoroughly, slice finely. Cut the Chinese chard in 1 cm wide strips. Rinse and dry the duck breasts. Heat the soy oil in a wok, brush the sides with oil. Pour the oil out. Put the breasts in and brown 5 minutes to each side over a high heat. Take the meat out, place on a board. Cut with a sharp knife into thin slices. Coat with half the oyster sauce. Use the rendered duck fat to fry the leeks and orange zest briskly. Add the chard, stir fry to soften it. Put in the meat and keep frying for 2–3 minutes, stirring gently. Add the remaining oyster sauce, stir fry for another 1–2 minutes. Toast the sesame

seeds in a small frying pan, sprinkle over the duck. Serve with rice.

Duck à la Acapulco

1 duck (c. 2.5 kg), 2–3 cooking apples, 1 tbsp lemon juice, 1 large onion, 1 tsp **Tabasco sauce**, 2 tbsps butter, 1 cup semi-dry red wine, 1 tsp paprika, salt, pepper

Rinse and dry the bird, rub lightly with salt. Dice the peeled onion. Cut the peeled and cored apples in thick sticks, sprinkle with lemon juice. Combine with the onion. Stuff the duck with the mixture, sew up the vent. Heat the oven to 200°C. Brush the whole bird with butter, put in a roasting tin and place in the oven. Roast for one hour, sprinkling lightly with water and then basting with pan juices (after half an hour turn the bird over). Mix the wine with paprika and Tabasco. Pour over the bird and keep roasting for another 30 minutes. Take the duck out, joint it, arrange on a hot serving platter and surround with the stuffing. Quickly reduce the roasting juices and serve them separately in a sauceboat. Serve with rice or pasta or potato chips.

Duck breasts with peanuts

2 duck breasts, 4 tbsps green peas (fresh or frozen), 4 champignons, 4 tbsps peanuts (unsalted), 1 tsp **five-spice powder**, 1 coffee spoon **sesame oil**, 2 tbsps **soy sauce**, 1 tsp sugar, 3 tbsps **rice oil**, ¼ cup chicken or vegetable stock

Chop the peanuts, toast in a hot frying pan. Rinse and dry the duck breasts, make incisions on the skin side. Heat 1 ½ tablespoons oil in a frying pan, fry the breasts for 4–5 minutes to each side (the meat should be juicy). Allow to cool, then cut into thin slices. Wash and drain the mushrooms, cut into thick slices. Heat the remaining oil in the frying pan, put in the mushrooms, green peas and sliced duck breasts. Add five-spice powder, sugar, soy sauce and stock. Cook 3–5 minutes over a high heat to reduce the liquid. Put in the peanuts, stir and sprinkle with sesame oil. Serve with rice, pasta or potato chips.

Marinated duck breasts, Chinese style

2–3 duck breasts (c. 1 kg), 1 tbsp butter

MARINADE: 7 tbsps **soy sauce**, 4 tbsps honey, 1½ tbsps vinegar (6%), 1 tsp finely chopped fresh ginger, 1½ tsps **five-spice powder**

SAUCE: 2 tbsps **chili sauce**, 1 tbsp **soy sauce**, 1 tbsp chopped fresh ginger, 1 tbsp honey, 3–4 cloves garlic

Combine the marinade ingredients. Rinse and dry the duck breasts, put in a bowl, pour the marinade over. Cover the bowl with clingfilm and refrigerate for 2–3 hours, turning the meat over 2–3 times.
Take the breasts out, arrange in a greased roasting tin, sprinkle with the marinade and put in a preheated oven (200–220°C). Cook for 50 minutes, basting first with the marinade and then with pan juices.
Blend the finely chopped, peeled garlic with the ginger, soy sauce, honey and chili sauce. Combine with the pan juices and heat up. Serve the duck hot or cold, cut into fine slices.

Duck (or turkey) livers with cloud ear mushrooms

12 duck or turkey livers, 5–6 dried cloud ear mushrooms, 1 tbsp peanut oil, 1 tsp finely chopped fresh ginger, 3–4 cloves garlic, 2 cups chicken stock (or stock from cube), 1 tbsp sugar, ½ cup **rice wine** or **sherry**, 1 tbsp potato flour, 1 tsp salt, a pinch of sodium glutamate, 1 tsp **sesame oil**

Slice the livers, drop into boiling water and cook for 5 minutes. Take out and drain thoroughly. Finely chop the peeled garlic. Rinse the mushrooms, cover with boiling water and leave aside for 15 minutes. Then drain and cut into thin strips. Heat the peanut oil in a wok or a heavy frying pan, put in the ginger and garlic, stir fry briskly. Pour in the stock and wine. Add the spices, livers and mushrooms. Cook over a high heat for 4–5 minutes. Mix the potato flour with 2 tablespoons cold boiled water. Add to the livers and heat up, stirring all the time, until the sauce

thickens. Before serving, sprinkle with sesame oil. Serve with rice.

Turkey roulades

4 turkey breast fillets (c. 600 g), salt, freshly ground pepper, 1 cup **green pesto**, 1 tbsp breadcrumbs, 2 cups chicken stock, 1½ tbsps butter, 2 tbsps lemon juice, a pinch of sugar, 4–8 basil leaves

Mix the pesto with the breadcrumbs. Rinse and dry the fillets, pound gently with a mallet, sprinkle with salt and pepper. Spread each fillet with pesto sauce (leaving the edges free). Roll up tightly, beginning at the thinner end. Wrap each fillet in aluminium foil, seal well. Arrange the roulades in a heavy skillet, cover with hot chicken stock. Bring to a boil, then cook over a low heat for 25–30 minutes, turning over from time to time. Take the roulades out, remove the foil. Place them on a hot serving dish and keep warm. Reduce the liquid in the saucepan (to no more than 1–1 ½ cups). Take off the heat. Whisk, gradually adding pieces of butter. Add the lemon juice, salt and pepper to taste. Stir and heat up, keeping off the boil. Pour some of the sauce over the roulades, serve the rest in a sauceboat. Garnish the meat with basil leaves. Serve hot roulades with pasta, rice or potato chips, or cold, cut diagonally into slices.

Turkey stuffed with chestnuts and liver

1 young turkey hen (c. 3 kg), 1 kg fresh **chestnuts** (or 2–3 tins), 100 g pork fat, 1 turkey liver, 2 onions, 3 tbsps chopped parsley, 1 glass brandy, salt, pepper, 150 g butter, 3–4 thin slices of pork fat

Rinse the birds, rub it with salt, leave aside for an hour.

STUFFING: Roast the chestnuts in a hot oven, peel them. Finely dice the pork fat, liver and onions. Place in a bowl, sprinkle with brandy and pepper, mix well. Melt 2 tablespoons butter in a frying pan, put in the diced mixture, add the parsley. Fry for 10 minutes, stirring continuously. Take off the heat, combine with the chestnuts, season with salt and pepper to taste.
Stuff the turkey, sew up the vent. Tie slices of pork fat with thread. Place the bird in a roasting tin, coat with melted

Turkey roulades

butter. Put into a preheated oven and cook for about 2 hours, basting regularly with melted butter. Take out, remove the thread and pork fat slices, return to the oven and keep roasting until the skin is nicely brown. Baste with pan juices. Turn off the heat, leave the roasted bird in the oven for 20 minutes, then take out and carve. Put the turkey pieces in an oven-proof dish, surround with the stuffing and heat up. Sieve the sauce, season to taste and heat up. Serve it separately.

Turkey roulade with chestnuts

*1 turkey breast (c. 1 kg), 250 g tinned **chestnuts**, 100 g cooked ham cut into thin strips, 100 g butter, 2 eggs, 2 tbsps thick cream, 1 tbsp breadcrumbs, 1 tbsp each dried rosemary and sage, 1 bay leaf, 3 tbsps brandy, sugar, salt, pepper, 1 fresh rosemary sprig, 2 tbsps sunflower oil, ½ cup boiled water*

Rinse and dry the turkey breast, slit it open. Place on a board and gently pound with a mallet. Rub with the herbs and salt on both sides. Line with slices of ham.
STUFFING: Cream 75 g butter, adding egg yolks one at a time. Drain and dry the chestnuts, chop or grind finely. Combine with the breadcrumbs and butter. Add salt, pepper and sugar. Whisk the egg whites into stiff peaks, fold into the stuffing.
Spread the stuffing evenly on the prepared meat, sprinkle with 1 teaspoon brandy. Roll the meat up, tie with twine. Heat the oil in a heavy saucepan, brown the roulade on all sides. Sprinkle with the remaining brandy, put in the bay leaf and rosemary sprig. Cover and stew for one hour, from time to time basting with water and with pan juices. Towards the end adjust the seasoning. Serve hot or cold.

Stuffed turkey fillets

4 turkey breast fillets (c. 700 g), salt, pepper, 2 tbsps flour, 2 eggs, 4 tbsps shredded coconut, 4 tbsps sunflower oil

*STUFFING: 4 slices fresh or tinned pineapple, 1 tbsp **wheat germ oil**, 2 tbsps **soy sauce**, 1 tsp finely chopped ginger, ¼ tsp **curry powder**, 1 tbsp **sherry vinegar** or sherry*

STUFFING: Cut the pineapple slices into thin sticks. Heat the wheat germ oil in a frying pan. Fry the pineapple briskly, stirring all the time. Add ginger, curry and soy sauce. Stir and cook over a low heat for a short while. Pour in the vinegar or sherry, stir, reduce and leave to cool.
Rinse and dry the meat, pound gently with a mallet, sprinkle with salt and pepper. Spread the stuffing on each fillet. Roll up and secure with toothpicks. Dredge in flour, beaten egg and shredded coconut. Press the coating with your hand. Fry 3–4 minutes to each side in hot oil.

Piquant turkey thighs with soy

*600 g turkey thighs, 300 g cooked soy beans, 3 tbsps **soy sauce**, 8–10 cloves garlic, 1 chili pepper, 1–2 **star anise seeds**, 1 ½ tbsps sugar, 2 tbsps oil, 2 cups light stock, a pinch of cayenne pepper*

Chop the peeled garlic finely. Rinse the thighs, divide into 4 servings. Fry in hot oil. Add the cooked soy beans and garlic, stirring all the time fry for 2–3 minutes. Pour in the soy sauce and hot stock, add pepper, anise seeds and sugar. Stir and bring to a boil, then simmer over a low heat for 10 minutes until the liquid is reduced. Take out the anise seeds and pepper. Season with a pinch of cayenne. Serve with white bread and salads.

Turkey stew

*500 g turkey fillets, 5–6 dried **Chinese mushrooms**, 2 eggs, 2 tbsps potato flour, 2 chili peppers, 2 onions, 2 leeks (white parts only), 2 carrots, 4–5 celery sticks, 5–6 firm, fleshy tomatoes, salt, pepper, 4 tbsps peanut oil*

*MARINADE: 4 tbsps **rice wine**, 4 tbsps **soy sauce**, 1 tsp **five-spice powder***

Cover the rinsed mushrooms with lukewarm boiled water, leave aside for 2–3 hours. Rinse and dry the meat, cut into cubes.
MARINADE: Mix the wine with the soy sauce and five-spice powder.
Drain the mushrooms, cut into strips. Combine with the meat and cover with the marinade. Shake and leave aside for 15–20 minutes. Blanch and skin the tomatoes, cut in cubes.

Wash and finely slice the leeks. Wash the celery, remove stringy fibres, slice the stalks. Seed the peppers, chop finely. Julienne the peeled carrots. Slice the peeled onions. Heat half the oil in a saucepan. Put in the chili peppers, carrots, leaks, onions and celery. Briskly stir fry over a high heat, then turn the temperature down. Mix the eggs with the potato flour, add salt. Combine with the marinated meat and mushrooms. Heat the remaining oil in a frying pan, put in the meat and mushrooms mixture. Brown over a high heat. Together with the tomatoes combine with the vegetables. Stir and stew for a while. Serve with rice or white bread.

Curried turkey with almonds

600 g turkey breasts, juice of 1 lemon, 400 ml natural yogurt, 1 tbsp cream (12%), 2–3 cloves garlic, 2 tbsps each raisins and almond flakes, 1½ tsps **curry powder***, 1 tsp ground caraway, oil, 1–2 tbsps stock or boiled water*

Cut the turkey breasts into 3–4 cm cubes. Sprinkle with lemon juice, salt and curry powder. Mix and refrigerate for an hour. Blanch and drain the raisins. Heat 1–2 tablespoons oil in a frying pan, put in the peeled and chopped garlic and ground caraway, fry briskly. Add the meat cubes and brown for 4–5 minutes, then sprinkle with stock, stir, add the raisins and almond flakes. Pour in the yogurt, stir, cover and continue cooking for another 3–4 minutes. The dish needs plenty of sauce, therefore if necessary, add more yogurt or 2–3 tablespoons water. Serve with rice.

Turkey ragout

600 g turkey breasts, 1 tbsp lemon juice, 250 g fresh **shiitake mushrooms***, 4 shallots, 1 fresh tarragon sprig, salt, freshly ground pepper, 3 tbsps* **grape-seed oil***, 1 tbsp butter, 2 tbsps dry vermouth, ½ cup chicken or turkey stock (or stock from cube), 1 cup cream, 1 tbsp Dijon mustard, 3–4 tbsps finely chopped parsley*

Cut the rinsed and dried meat into thin slices, then into strips. Sprinkle with salt, pepper, lemon juice and I teaspoon oil. Shake and refrigerate for 15–20 minutes. Dice the peeled shallots. Clean the mushrooms and cut them into thick slices. Heat the oil in a heavy saucepan.

Put in the meat, briskly fry it over a high heat. Take out with a straining spoon. Turn down the heat, put the butter, shallots and mushrooms in the pan. Fry quickly, add the chopped tarragon leaves. Pour in the hot stock and vermouth. Reduce the liquid to make the sauce thick. Mix the cream with mustard. Put the meat into the sauce, pour over the cream (keep off the boil), add salt and pepper to taste. Before serving, sprinkle generously with chopped parsley.

Salads

Salad with roast beef

200 g roast beef, 3 small green bell peppers, 300 g firm, fleshy tomatoes, 3–4 scallions, 2 hard-boiled eggs, 3 tbsps finely chopped parsley

DRESSING: 3 tbsps **red vinegar***, 1 tsp sharp mustard, 3 tbsps* **corn germ oil***, ½ tsp each salt, freshly ground black pepper and paprika*

Mix thoroughly all dressing ingredients. Chill. Remove the stalks and seeds from the washed peppers, cut the flesh in thin strips. Blanch and skin the tomatoes, cut into large cubes, seed. Cut the roast beef into thin strips. Chop the scallions finely. Slice the shelled eggs. Combine all ingredients in a bowl. Pour the dressing over, shake the bowl. Sprinkle with chopped parsley.

Lentil salad with smoked turkey

1½ cups lentils, ¾ cup light chicken or vegetable stock, 100 g red onions, 200 g smoked turkey breast, 2 each small carrots and celery stalks, 1 tbsp chopped parsley, 1 tbsp chopped fresh thyme leaves

DRESSING: 1 tbsp mustard (preferably Dijon), 4 tbsps **red vinegar***, 2 tbsps olive oil, salt, pepper*

Chop the peeled onions finely. Rinse and drain the lentils. Put both in a saucepan, cover with the hot stock, add chopped thyme leaves. Bring to a boil, then cook over a low heat for 15 minutes, or when the lentils are soft but do not disintegrate. Drain the lentils, put in a large bowl. Combine all dressing ingredients. Pour the sauce over, shake the bowl. Peel the carrots, remove stringy fibres from the celery stalks. Rinse the carrots and celery, slice, combine with the lentils. Cover the bowl and refrigerate for 1–2 hours. Cut the turkey into fine slices, add to the lentils, mix. Before serving, adjust the seasoning if necessary and sprinkle chopped parsley on top.

Leek salad with bacon

3 leeks (white parts only), a pinch of sugar, 100 g streaky bacon

DRESSING: 3 tbsps **balsamic vinegar**, a pinch of each salt and cayenne pepper, 2 tbsps wheat germ oil, ½ tsp sharp mustard

Mix thoroughly all dressing ingredients. Wash the leeks thoroughly, cut into thin slices. Bring salted water to a boil, add sugar and blanch the leek for 1–2 minutes, then drain, rinse under cold water and drain again. Dice the bacon finely. Heat a heavy frying pan, put in the bacon, fry for crispy cracklings. Take out with a straining spoon, drain on a paper towel. Put the leeks into a bowl, pour the dressing over. Shake well and sprinkle with cracklings. Cover the bowl to keep the salad warm – it's how it's best.

Chickpea salad with chicken

2 tins chickpeas, 150 g cooked or roast chicken breasts, 1 small cucumber, 2–3 red chili peppers, 1–2 red onions, 1½ tbsps finely chopped mint and coriander leaves, 1 tsp **cumin** seeds, salt, freshly ground pepper

DRESSING: 3 tbsps **grape-seed oil**, 2 tbsps lemon juice, 1 tbsp **red vinegar**, 1 tsp honey, salt, pepper

Mix thoroughly all dressing ingredients, cover and refrigerate.

Drain the chickpeas. Finely chop the seeded peppers. Combine with the chickpeas in a bowl, sprinkle with salt and pepper. Cut the chicken meat into strips. Peel the cucumber, halve lengthwise, remove the seeds and cut the flesh in cubes. Dice the peeled onions. Toast the cumin seeds in a hot frying pan. Add the chicken and the remaining ingredients to the chickpeas. Pour the dressing over, shake the bowl. Sprinkle cumin, coriander and mint leaves on top.

Minty couscous salad

200 g couscous, ¾ cup light chicken stock (or stock from cube), ½ cup finely chopped **bamboo shoots**, 3 firm, fleshy tomatoes, 1 yellow bell pepper, 1 cucumber, 1 large red onion, ½ cup **pitted green olives**, lemon juice, 4 tbsps sunflower oil, 3 tbsps chopped fresh mint leaves, salt, pepper

Pour the couscous into a large bowl, cover with the hot stock (to ½ cm above the couscous). Mix with a fork and leave aside for 15 minutes.
Cut the peeled onion and cucumber into cubes. Wash and dry the bell pepper, remove the stalk and seeds, cut the flesh into thin strips. Rinse and drain the bamboo shoots. Blanch and skin the tomatoes, cut into cubes, seed. When the couscous grows in volume and gets cool, combine it with the remaining ingredients. Pour the oil over, sprinkle with lemon juice. Adjust the seasoning with salt, pepper and, if you like, a pinch of sugar. Shake the bowl gently. Sprinkle with chopped mint leaves, cover and refrigerate for 1–2 hours.

Oriental salad with crab sticks

300 g rice noodles, 14–16 crab sticks, 50 g smoked ham, 3 eggs, 1 fizzy mineral water, 1 tbsp **peanut oil**, 150 g cherry tomatoes, 12–15 cashew nuts, fresh coriander sprigs for garnishing

DRESSING: 2 tbsps **sherry vinegar** or sherry, 2 tbsps **soy sauce**, 1 tbsp **apple vinegar**, 1 tsp finely chopped fresh ginger, salt, freshly ground pepper, 2 tbsps ground coriander seeds

Mix all dressing ingredients in a bowl, cover and refrigerate.

Put the noodles into salted boiling water, cook for 5–6 minutes. Drain, rinse under cold water, drain again. Mix the eggs with mineral water. Heat the peanut oil in a frying pan, pour in the egg mixture and fry as an omelette. Gently transfer the omelette to a cutting board, leave to cool, then cut in cubes. Cut the crab sticks into smaller pieces, chop the ham, halve the cherry tomatoes. Cut the noodles into smaller pieces, put in a bowl, add the cashew nuts, tomatoes, crab sticks, omelette cubes and ham. Pour over the dressing, shake the bowl. Serve immediately.

Salad with anchovy dressing

8 hard-boiled eggs, 150 g pickled red peppers, 2–3 pickled cucumbers, 1 large apple, 1 tsp lemon juice, 2–3 red onions, 3 tbsps sweet corn (frozen or tinned)

*DRESSING: 1 cup mayonnaise, ½ cup natural yogurt, 3 tsps **anchovy paste**, 1 tsp tomato concentrate (30%), 1 tbsp chopped watercress, 1 tsp lemon juice, 1 tsp grated lemon rind, salt, pepper*

Mix all sauce ingredients in a bowl, cover and refrigerate.

Dice the shelled hard-boiled eggs. Cut the red peppers in strips. Dice the peeled and cored apple, sprinkle with lemon juice. Cut the peeled cucumbers into cubes. Halve the peeled onions, slice finely. Combine all salad ingredients, put in a bowl. Pour over the sauce, shake the bowl.

Salad of soy noodles

*250 g white beans, bay leaves, 1 cube vegetable stock, 250 g **soy noodles**, 4 cups water, ½ tsp salt, 250 g salami, 3–4 red onions, ½ cup **red vinegar**, 2 tsps each salt and paprika, 1 tsp ground pepper, ½ cup olive oil, 2 tbsps chopped parsley*

Rinse the beans, put in a saucepan, cover with lukewarm boiled water (c. 1 litre) and leave overnight. The following day cook the beans in the same water, with bay leaves and soup cube. Drain the cooked beans, remove the bay leaves.

Bring 4 cups water to a boil, put in the noodles, cook over a high heat for 6–8 minutes. Drain, rinse under cold water, drain again. Halve the peeled onions, slice finely. Cut the salami slices in thin strips.

Mix the vinegar with salt, paprika and pepper. Gradually pour in the olive oil and whisk all the time to get a smooth mixture. In a bowl, combine the onions with the salami, beans and noodles. Pour the dressing over, shake well and refrigerate. Before serving, shake the bowl again and garnish the salad with chopped parsley.

Chicken and asparagus salad

250–300 g chicken breast fillets, 1 tbsp butter, 1 tbsp lemon juice, 1 tsp sugar, 250 g green asparagus, salt, lettuce leaves, 2–3 cherry tomatoes and dill sprigs for garnishing

*MARINADE: ½ tsp honey, 1 tbsp lemon juice, ½ tsp grated lemon rind, 1 tbsp **sesame oil**, salt, pepper*

*DRESSING: 2 tbsps mayonnaise, 3 tbsps thick cream, 1 tsp sharp mustard, 1 tsp **worcester sauce**, 2 tbsp white vinegar*

MARINADE: In a bowl combine the honey with the lemon juice, lemon zest, salt, pepper and sesame oil.

Rinse and dry the fillets, cut in thin strips. Put in a bowl, cover with the marinade, mix, cover and leave for 2–3 hours. Then fry in melted butter and leave to cool. Bring salted water to a boil, add butter, sugar and lemon juice. Put in the cleaned asparagus and cook for 15 minutes. Drain, cut into smaller pieces, allow to cool. Mix all dressing ingredients. Combine the chicken strips with asparagus pieces in a bowl. Pour the dressing over, shake the bowl, then refrigerate. Serve on a bed of lettuce leaves, garnished with tomato halves and dill.

Chicken and cucumber salad

*¼ roast or boiled chicken, 1 small cucumber, 3 fresh chili peppers, ½ tsp brown sugar, 1 tbsp **Sichuan peppercorns**, 3 tbsps oil, ¼ tsp salt, dill sprigs*

Bone and skin the chicken, cut the meat into thin strips. Halve the cucumber lengthwise, remove the seeds, cut the flesh into matchsticks. Seed and finely chop the chili peppers. Toast Sichuan peppercorns in a little oil, then grind or pound in a mortar. Heat the remaining oil in a frying pan, put in the chili and briskly fry for 20–30 seconds. Add sugar, Sichuan pepper and salt. Stir, take off the heat, leave to cool. Combine the chicken meat with the cucumber (first squeeze out excess liquid) in a bowl. Cover with the oil from the frying pan. Refrigerate. Before serving, garnish with dill sprigs.

Fish and rice salad

750 g salmon fillets, 200 g long-grain rice, 2 cups vegetable stock (or stock from cube), 1 tbsp lemon juice, 1 tsp salt, 1 celeriac (c. 500 g), 400 g pineapple, 2 tbsps each chopped dill and chives

DRESSING: 2 egg yolks, 1 tbsp **soy sauce**, 1 tbsp mild mustard, 1 tbsp honey, ½ tsp black pepper, 1 tsp curry powder, 4 tbsps **safflower oil**, 1½ cups sour cream

DRESSING: Blend the egg yolks with the soy sauce, mustard, honey and curry powder. Whisking all the time, gradually add the oil. Combine the dressing with half the cream and refrigerate.
Scrub the celeriac, peel, julienne. Blanch in salted boiling water for 2–3 minutes. Drain, rinse under cold water, drain again. Sprinkle with 1 tablespoon lemon juice and a dash of salt. Pour the rinsed rice into a heavy saucepan, cover with the stock, bring to a boil, then simmer for 10 minutes. Place the fillets on top, cover and keep cooking over a low heat for another 10–15 minutes. Leave the rice to cool. Divide the fish into smaller pieces, remove bones if any. Combine the cold rice with the fish and celeriac in a bowl. Pour the dressing over, shake the bowl. Cover and refrigerate for 1–2 hours. Combine the remaining cream with chopped dill and chives. Cut the pineapple into small cubes. Add to the refrigerated salad together with the cream. Mix gently.

Salmon salad with quail eggs

20 quail eggs, 150 g smoked salmon, 3 tbsps **capers**

SAUCE: 1 cup cream (18%), 1 tsp grated horseradish, 2 tbsps watercress, 1 tbsp chopped dill, 1 tsp lemon juice, salt

Hard-boil the eggs (c. 3 minutes), rinse under cold water, shell and rinse again, halve them. Cut the fish in short, broad strips. Combine with the egg halves and capers, mix gently.
SAUCE: Whisk the cream with lemon juice, combine with the horseradish, watercress and dill, salt to taste. Pour over the salad, shake the bowl gently.

Mackerel salad

8 hard-boiled eggs, 3 tomatoes, 1 large red bell pepper, 1 cucumber, 2 boned smoked mackerels, 4 tbsps green peas (frozen or tinned), 10 **green olives stuffed with sweet pepper**

DRESSING: juice of 1 lemon, grated rind of ½ lemon, 2 cloves garlic, 3 tbsps olive oil, 1 tsp mustard, salt, pepper

Halve the shelled eggs lengthwise, then cut each half in 4 wedges. Blanch and skin the tomatoes, cut in wedges. Rinse the pepper, remove the stalk and seeds, cut the flesh into short strips. Peel the cucumber, cut in strips. Divide the mackerel into bite-size pieces. Halve the olives. Combine all ingredients in a bowl.
DRESSING: Mix the lemon juice with 3 tablespoons cold boiled water. Finely chop the peeled garlic. Blend the mustard gradually with oil and lemon juice. Add the garlic and lemon zest, salt and pepper to taste. Pour over the salad and shake the bowl.

Salad of sweet corn, rice and tuna

1 tin sweet corn, 1 tin tuna fish in brine, ¾ cup cooked rice, ½ cup pitted **green olives**, 1 small bell pepper, 1 small cooking apple, 1 tbsp lemon juice, 3 tbsps chopped chives, 1 tbsp chopped dill, 2–3 lettuce leaves

DRESSING: 2 tbsps lemon juice, 3 tbsps olive oil, 3 tbsps boiled water, salt, pepper, 1 tsp each honey and sharp mustard

Mix all ingredients of the dressing, refrigerate. Drain the tuna fish, crumble with a fork. Halve the olives. Remove the stalks and seeds from the bell pepper, rinse the flesh, cut in cubes. Rinse the apple, core it, cut in cubes, sprinkle with lemon juice. Combine the salad ingredients in a bowl. Pour the dressing over, shake the bowl. Refrigerate. Serve on a bed of lettuce leaves, sprinkled with chopped chives and dill.

Herring and leek salad

4 herring fillets, 3 leeks (c. 500 g, white parts only), 1 tbsp salt, ½ tsp sugar, 1 tsp vinegar, 6–8 cherry tomatoes and parsley sprigs for garnishing

*DRESSING: 1 cup cream, salt, sugar, freshly ground white pepper, 1 tbsp white vinegar, 3 tbsps **grape-seed oil***

DRESSING: Heat the cream lightly, season to taste. Add the vinegar and gradually pour in the oil, whisking continuously to obtain a smooth mixture. Leave aside to cool.
Bring salted water, with sugar and vinegar, to a boil. Wash the leeks thoroughly, slice them finely, put into the boiling water and cook for 2 minutes. Drain, rinse under very cold water and drain again. Wash and dry the fillets, cut them into small pieces, combine with the leek. Pour the dressing over, mix well, cover and refrigerate for 15 minutes. Before serving, garnish with tomato halves and parsley sprigs.

Creole fish salad

*250 g pikeperch fillets, ½ small celeriac, 1 tbsp lemon juice, 1–2 onions, ½ green bell pepper pod, 2 tbsps butter, 1 bay leaf, ¼ tsp salt, ¼ coffee spoon each cayenne pepper and powdered garlic, 1 lettuce, 6–8 firm, fleshy tomatoes, 1 tbsp **Worcester sauce**, ¼ cup dry white wine*

Rinse and dry the fillets, sprinkle with lemon juice and salt. Cut into strips and put in the fridge for 15 minutes. Scrub the celeriac, cook in salted boiling water for 2–3 minutes, take out. Rinse under cold water, peel, julienne and sprinkle with lemon juice. Chop the peeled onions finely. Seed the pepper, halve and cut into thin strips. Blanch and skin the tomatoes, cut into cubes (remove the seeds). Melt the butter in a heavy saucepan, soften the onion. Add the celeriac and green pepper. Stir and simmer over a low heat for 6–8 minutes. Turn up the heat, put in the tomatoes,

add the wine, Worcester sauce, bay leaf, salt, cayenne and powdered garlic. Bring to a boil, then stew for 10 minutes over a medium heat, stirring from time to time. Take out the bay leaf. Put in the fish strips. Stir gently and cook for 7 minutes. Line 4 individual bowls with shredded lettuce leaves, put a portion of the salad in each. Serve hot or cold.

Flemish herring salad

*300 g salted herring, 1 cup milk, 500 g small jacket potatoes, 2 large onions, 1 ½ tbsps **coconut oil**, 4 chicory heads, 3–4 tbsps vinegar, 5 tbsps **wheat germ oil**, a bunch each fresh tarragon and chervil*

Soak the herring, covered, in cold water for 3 hours, changing water three times. Skin and bone, put in a bowl, cover with milk and soak again for an hour. Chop the peeled onions finely.
Heat the coconut oil in a frying pan, fry the onions golden brown. Take out and drain on a paper towel. Clean the chicory, rinse and dry, cut into fairly wide strips. Chop the rinsed and dried tarragon and chervil finely (with a stainless knife).
Take out the herring, cut into even pieces. Peel the potatoes, cut in sticks. Combine the herring, potatoes, onion and chicory with vinegar and wheat germ oil. Season with salt and freshly ground pepper. Cover and refrigerate for an hour. Before serving, mix again and garnish with chopped greens.

Red bell pepper salad with mozzarella and basil

3 red bell peppers, 2 yellow bell peppers, 2 mozzarella balls, 4–5 basil sprigs for garnishing

*DRESSING: 4 tbsps **balsamic vinegar**, 2 tbsps olive oil, salt, freshly ground pepper*

Bake the washed peppers in the oven or over the gas fire. When the skin browns all over, wrap in foil and leave to cool, then skin the pods, cut lengthwise, remove the seed. Rinse and dry, cut in strips. Put in a bowl, sprinkle with 2 tablespoons vinegar. Cover and leave overnight in the fridge. Cut the mozzarella in thin slices. In a large serving dish arrange alternately mozzarella slices and strips of red and yellow peppers. Mix the remaining balsamic vinegar with oil, salt and pepper. Sprinkle the salad with the mixture, garnish with basil leaves.

Zucchini salad with ewes' cheese

300 g young zucchini, 1 tsp lemon juice,
*100 g pitted **black olives**, 100 g mid-dry ewes'*
cheese (feta), 50 g raisins, 1 tbsp dry white wine,
1–2 oregano sprigs, 2–3 leaves curly lettuce

DRESSING: 4 tbsps olive oil, ¼ tsp ground
*white mustard seeds, 2 tbsps **sherry vinegar**,*
2 tbsps semi-dry sherry, salt, pepper

Mix the dressing ingredients, refrigerate a bit. Rinse and dry the raisins, soak in wine for 5–8 minutes. Cut the cheese into cubes, slice the olives. Wash the zucchini, julienne, sprinkle with lemon juice. Combine with the raisins, olives and cheese in a bowl. Pour the dressing over, shake gently. Serve on a bed of lettuce leaves, sprinkled with oregano leaves.

Snap peas and carrot salad

200 g snap peas, 2–3 young carrots, 1 young kohlrabi,
1 cup mixed chopped leaves of basil, dill, coriander,
mint and parsley

*DRESSING: 1–2 shallots, 3 tbsps **white vinegar**, 1 tbsp*
*fairly sharp mustard, ½ cup **thistle oil**, salt, pepper*

DRESSING: Chop the peeled shallots finely. Combine with the vinegar, pepper, salt and mustard. Gradually add the oil, whisking all the time. Refrigerate for a while. Julienne the peeled carrots and kohlrabi, combine with the dressing, cover and refrigerate. Bring salted water to a boil, put in the rinsed snap peas and cook for 2–3 minutes. Drain, rinse under cold water, drain again. Add to the salad together with the chopped herbs, mix thoroughly. Leave aside for 15 minutes before you serve it.

Zucchini salad with ewes' cheese

Mozzarella salad

Mozzarella salad

4–5 firm, fleshy tomatoes, 300 g mozzarella, 1 tsp fresh oregano leaves and 2 tbsps basil leaves for garnishing

*DRESSING: 3 tbsps **poppy-seed oil**, 2–3 tbsps white vinegar, salt, pepper, a pinch of caster sugar (optional)*

DRESSING: Mix the vinegar with salt and pepper. Gradually add the oil, whisking vigorously all the time. Blanch and skin the tomatoes, skin and slice them. Slice mozzarella balls. In a large platter arrange alternately tomato and mozzarella slices. Sprinkle generously with the dressing, garnish with oregano and basil leaves.

Salad of French beans and leek

600 g young French beans, salt, 1 tsp butter, ½ tsp sugar, 1 tsp lemon juice, 1 small leek (only the white part), 2–3 savory sprigs

*DRESSING: 3 tbsps **hempseed oil**, 2 tbsps **herbal vinegar**, salt, pepper*

Mix thoroughly the dressing ingredients. Rinse the French beans, cut into 3 cm long pieces. Bring salted water to a boil, add the butter, lemon juice and sugar. Drop in the beans and cook for 10–12 minutes. Drain, rinse under cold water, drain again. Halve the leek lengthwise, wash thoroughly. Dry and slice finely. Combine with the French beans in a bowl, pour the dressing over. Cover and refrigerate for 20–30 minutes. Before serving, garnish with savory sprigs.

Apple and mushroom salad

2 large cooking apples, ½ tsp honey, 500 g button mushrooms (caps only), ¼ tsp pepper, 2 tbsps lemon juice, ½ cup chopped parsley

*DRESSING: 4 tbsps **hazelnut oil**, 1 tbsp **sherry vinegar**, 1 tbsp mineral water, 1 tsp finely chopped coriander leaves, ¼ tsp each white pepper and paprika, salt and sugar to taste*

Mix all dressing ingredients, refrigerate the mixture. Rinse and dry the mushrooms, slice them, sprinkle with pepper and half the lemon juice. Peel and core the apples, cut in sticks. Mix with the honey and the remaining lemon juice. Combine in a bowl with the mushrooms. Pour the dressing over, shake the bowl, refrigerate. Before serving, mix in the chopped parsley.

Watercress salad

400 g watercress shoots, 4 fine slices smoked bacon, 2 onions, 2 tbsps pumpkin seeds

*DRESSING: 3 tbsps **hemp oil**, 3 tbsps **white vinegar**, salt, pepper*

Mix all dressing ingredients, refrigerate the mixture. Chop the pumpkin seeds coarsely, toast in a hot frying pan. Dice the bacon, brown in a hot frying pan. Halve the peeled lemon, then slice it finely. Put the slices in a colander, scald with boiling water, rinse under cold water and drain well. Combine with the watercress shoots in a bowl. Pour the dressing over, put the crispy bacon on top. Shake the bowl, sprinkle the toasted pumpkin seeds.

Chicory salad with currants

400 g chicory heads, 50 g currants, 50 g hazelnuts, fresh mint leaves

*DRESSING: 2 egg yolks, 2 tbsps low-fat cream cheese, ½ tsp salt, ¼ tsp each sugar and freshly ground white pepper, 2 tbsps **apple vinegar**, 2 tbsps **thistle oil***

DRESSING: Blend the egg yolks with the cream cheese, salt, sugar, pepper and vinegar to obtain a smooth mixture. Refrigerate shortly.
Rinse the currants, soak them in warm water for 5–8 minutes, then drain thoroughly. Chop the hazelnuts coarsely. Hollow out the cones at the base of chicory heads, remove damaged leaves. Rinse and dry, then cut into thick slices. Combine in a bowl with the currants and hazelnuts. Pour the sauce over. Shake the bowl, sprinkle the salad on top with chopped mint leaves.

Californian salad

1 small iceberg lettuce, 4 firm, fleshy tomatoes,
1 cucumber, 1 red bell pepper, 1 green bell pepper,
100 g tinned sweet corn

DRESSING: ¾ cup thick cream, ¾ cup natural yogurt,
2 tbsps **sherry vinegar***, 1 tbsp tomato ketchup,*
salt, freshly ground white pepper, a pinch of sugar,
3 tbsps chopped dill

D*RESSING*: Mix the cream with the yogurt. Add the chopped dill, ketchup, vinegar, salt, pepper and sugar. Refrigerate.
Remove damaged leaves from the lettuce. Rinse the lettuce, drain thoroughly. Shred the leaves. Wash the tomatoes and cut into wedges. Rinse the cucumber (do not peel), slice. Remove the stalks and seeds from the peppers, rinse and dry the flesh, cut into strips. Drain the sweet corn. Combine all the ingredients in a bowl, shake well.

Italian artichoke salad

1 large tin of artichoke hearts in oil (c. 400 g),
1 cup pitted **black olives***, 1 lettuce, ¼ cup*
pine nuts*, 3 tbsps grated Parmesan*

DRESSING: 1 tbsp lemon juice, ¼ tsp grated lemon rind,
2–3 tbsps olive oil, salt, pepper, a pinch of caster sugar

M ix the dressing ingredients thoroughly.
Drain the artichoke hearts, cut in quarters. Halve the olives and add to the artichokes. Toast the pine nuts. Rinse and dry the lettuce leaves. Line a large serving dish with them, generously sprinkle with the dressing. Arrange the artichokes with olives on them. Sprinkle with Parmesan and pine nuts.

Vegetable salad with lentils

200 g cherry tomatoes, 1 large yellow bell
pepper, 3–4 scallions, 300 g brown lentils,
1–2 fresh thyme sprigs, 4–5 fresh basil sprigs

Italian artichoke salad

DRESSING: 3 tbsps **pumpkin seed oil**,
1 tsp mild mustard, 2 tbsps **white vinegar**,
salt, freshly ground pepper

Rinse the lentils, put into a saucepan, add a thyme sprig. Cover with water, bring to a boil, then cook over a low heat for 30 minutes. Drain the lentils, leave to cool. Mix all dressing ingredients, cover and refrigerate. Remove the stalks and seeds from the pepper, rinse and dry the flesh, cut into fine cubes. Halve the washed tomatoes (or quarter if larger). Chop finely the scallions together with the green parts. Combine all the ingredients in a bowl, cover with the dressing. Shake the bowl and refrigerate for 1–2 hours. Before serving, sprinkle generously with chopped basil leaves.

Spinach salad with oyster mushrooms

400 g fresh spinach leaves, 300 g oyster mushrooms, 3 tbsps butter, 3–4 leaves iceberg lettuce, 1 tbsp **walnut oil**, 100 g **pine nuts**

DRESSING: ¼ cup chicken stock from cube, 2–3 scallions (without the green parts), 1 large fleshy tomato, salt, pepper, 1 tbsp **sherry vinegar**, 4 tbsps **walnut oil**

Scald and skin the tomato. Cut into cubes (remove the seeds). Bring the stock to a boil, put in the tomatoes and chopped scallions. Cook 4–5 minutes, allow to cool. Sieve and mix thoroughly with the oil and vinegar. Add salt and pepper to taste. Refrigerate.
Toast the pine nuts in a hot frying pan for 1–2 minutes. Add 1 tablespoon oil, stir and take off the heat. Rinse the mushrooms, drain them and cut into thick strips. Melt the butter in a large frying pan. Stirring all the time fry the mushrooms for 3–4 minutes, then take off the heat. Cut off the stalks of spinach leaves. Rinse the spinach and lettuce leaves, dry, shred and combine with the mushrooms and sauce. Before serving, sprinkle with toasted pine nuts.

Young beetroot salad with caraway and horseradish

300 g beetroots, 3 tbsps chopped green caraway, 1 horseradish root, 1 tsp lemon juice

DRESSING: 3 tbsps **hazelnut oil**, 3 tbsps **red vinegar**, salt, sugar to taste

Mix the dressing ingredients. Scrub the beetroots. Bake them in the oven or cook in salted water. Leave to cool, then peel and slice finely. Scrub the horseradish, grate it into fine slivers. Sprinkle with the lemon juice and combine with the beetroots. Pour the dressing over, cover and refrigerate for 15 minutes. Before serving, mix in the green caraway.

Leek salad with apples and tomatoes

2 large leeks (c. 500 g, only the white parts), 2 cooking apples, 1 tsp lemon juice, 2 firm, fleshy tomatoes, 1–2 basil sprigs, salt, pepper, 1 tsp **balsamic vinegar**, 1 tbsp **walnut oil**, 1 tbsp **thistle** (**safflower**) **oil**

DRESSING: 300 g ripe tomatoes, 2 tbsps chopped basil leaves, salt, ½ tsp ground pepper, 1 tsp sugar, 4–6 tbsps **thistle oil**

DRESSING: Blanch and skin the tomatoes. Liquidize them with salt, pepper, sugar and basil. Blending all the time gradually pour in the oil to obtain a smooth mixture. Sieve it and refrigerate.
Blanch and skin the tomatoes, cut into cubes, remove the seeds. Sprinkle the tomatoes with safflower oil. Wash the leeks thoroughly, slice finely, sprinkle with walnut oil and balsamic vinegar. Cut the peeled and cored apples into sticks, sprinkle with lemon juice. Combine the leeks and apples in a bowl, refrigerate for 10 minutes. Pour ⅓ tomato sauce into a serving bowl, put in the salad, cover with the remaining sauce and garnish with basil leaves.

Tomato and French beans salad with capers

600 g fleshy tomatoes, 300 g French beans, 2 onions, a bunch of parsley, 3 cloves garlic, 60 g large **capers**, 20 **black olives**

DRESSING: ½ cup olive oil, 2 tbsps **red wine vinegar**, salt, freshly ground white pepper

Mix the olive oil with the vinegar, add salt and pepper to taste.

Blanch and skin the tomatoes. Cut into quarters and remove the seeds. Boil salted water, put in the beans and cook for 5–7 minutes. Drain, rinse under cold water, drain again. Dice finely the peeled onions.

Slice the peeled garlic, chop the parsley finely. In a bowl combine the tomatoes, beans, onion, parsley and garlic. Pour the dressing over, shake well. Cut the capers into slices, add to the salad. Mix thoroughly and garnish with sliced olives.

Lentil salad with herbal sauce

400 g green or brown lentils, 3–4 cloves garlic, 2 onions, 4 tbsps olive oil, 2 tbsps lemon juice, salt, 1 tsp ground coriander seeds, ½ tsp **ground cumin**, ¼ tsp each pepper and cayenne pepper, 1 tbsp each fresh coriander leaves and parsley, 2 tbsps chopped mint leaves

Rinse the lentils, put into salted boiling water and cook for 10 minutes. Drain and return to the saucepan. Add the peeled garlic, pour in enough boiled water to cover the lentils. Put a lid on and cook for 30 minutes, taking care that the lentils do not burn. Finely dice the peeled onions. Heat 2 tablespoons olive oil in a frying pan, soften the onions, add pepper, cumin, ground coriander and cayenne. Stirring continuously cook for 2–3 minutes, add salt. Drain the lentils. Combine with the onion, lemon juice and the remaining oil. Mix thoroughly, leave aside to cool, then cover and refrigerate for 1–2 hours. Before serving, put in the chopped coriander leaves, parsley and mint leaves.

Chinese cabbage salad with apples

4 sweetish cooking apples, 1 small Chinese cabbage, 2 green chili pods, 1 tbsp grated fresh ginger, ¾ tsp **turmeric**, 1 large red onion, 2 tbsps sunflower or **peanut oil**, juice of 2 limes or 1 lemon, salt, freshly ground pepper

Finely shred the rinsed and dried cabbage. Peel and core the apples, cut them in sticks, sprinkle with lemon juice and combine with the cabbage. Seed the chili pods, chop them finely. Peel and halve the onion, slice it finely. Heat oil in a frying pan, put in the onion, soften it for 2–3 minutes. Add chopped chili, turmeric and ginger. Keep frying for a while longer, stirring all the time. Take off the heat and leave to cool a bit. Combine with the cabbage, sprinkle with salt and pepper, and with lime (or lemon) juice. Mix, cover and refrigerate for 1–2 hours. Serve as a snack or as a side dish with fish and poultry.

Carrot salad with almonds

400 g carrots, 1 tbsp brewer's yeast, 3 tbsps almond flakes, salt, a pinch of caster sugar

DRESSING: 4–5 tbsps **poppy-seed oil**, 3 tbsps **rose vinegar**, 1 tbsp boiled water

Mix thoroughly the dressing ingredients. Toast the almond flakes in a frying pan. Grate coarsely the peeled and rinsed carrots. Sprinkle with sugar, salt and brewer's yeast. Pour the dressing over, mix well. Sprinkle with toasted almond flakes. Serve with roast or fried white meat or poultry.

Carrot salad with onion and garlic

500 g carrots, 2 red onions, 2–4 cloves garlic, 4 tbsps finely chopped parsley, juice of 1 lemon, 3–4 tbsps olive oil, ¾ tsp **ground cumin**, 1 tsp **turmeric**, salt, pepper

Halve the peeled onions, slice them. Chop the peeled garlic. Heat 2 tablespoosns oil in a frying pan. Put in the onions and garlic, add turmeric and cumin, briskly fry to soften. Take off the heat. Peel the carrots, slice them. Put in boiling salted water and cook 8–12 minutes. Drain, rinse under cold water, drain again. Put into a large bowl, combine with the onions. Sprinkle generously with lemon juice and oil. Shake the bowl, sprinkle the salad with chopped parsley, cover and refrigerate for 1–2 hours.

Carrot salad with soy sprouts

300 g carrots, 250 g soy sprouts, a bunch of chives, a walnut-size piece of ginger

DRESSING: 4 tbsps **soy sauce**, 3 tbsps vinegar, 3 tbsps soy oil, salt, pepper

Onion and olive salad

Chop the peeled ginger very finely. Mix the soy sauce with salt, pepper, lemon juice and ginger. Whisking all the time, gradually pour in the oil. Rinse and drain the soy sprouts. Peel and rinse the carrots, grate coarsely. Combine with the soy sprouts, sprinkle with the chopped chives, pour the dressing over and mix thoroughly.

Celeriac and carrot salad with almonds

125 g celeriac, 500 g carrots, 1 small leek (only the white part), 1 cooking apple, 1 tbsp lemon juice, lettuce leaves

DRESSING: 3 tbsps lemon juice, 1 tbsp **soy sauce**, 1 tbsp **sesame oil**, 2 tbsps finely chopped fresh mango, 1 tbsp orange juice, ¼ tsp grated orange rind, 2 tbsps mayonnaise, 1 tbsp cream, 1 tbsp liquid honey, 4–6 drops **Tabasco sauce** or a pinch of cayenne pepper, salt

Whisk all the dressing ingredients, then refrigerate. The dressing should be piquant with a sour-sweet overtone.
Peel the celeriac and carrots, rinse them, coarsely grate and immediately combine with the dressing. Peel and core the apple, cut in sticks, sprinkle with lemon juice. Wash the leek thoroughly, slice it. Combine the apple and leek with the dressed salad. Mix well. Serve on a bed of lettuce leaves.

Onion and olive salad

500 g red onions, 10 **green olives stuffed with peppers**, 10 **pitted black olives**, 2–3 lettuce leaves, parsley sprigs and 1 lime for garnishing

DRESSING: juice of 1 lemon, 1 tsp grated lemon rind, 2 tbsps white vinegar, 2 tbsps water, 3 tbsps olive oil, 1 tsp each dried thyme, tarragon and rosemary, salt

Scrub the lemon and lime, scald with boiling water. DRESSING: Combine the vinegar with 2 tablespoons water and herbs. Bring to a boil, cover and simmer for 3–4 minutes. Leave to cool, strain on a fine sieve. Add the lemon juice and zest to the vinegar. Whisking vigorously gradually pour in the oil.

Slice the peeled onions, divide into rings. Halve the olives, combine with the onions and dressing, refrigerate for 15 minutes. Cut the lime into wedges. Wash and drain the parsley. Serve the salad on a bed of lettuce leaves, garnished with lime wedges and parsley sprigs. This is an excellent accompaniment to fried and roast meat and fish.

Provençal salad

c. 300 g pickled **artichokes**, 600 g cherry tomatoes, 5 anchovy fillets, 10 pitted **black olives** and parsley sprigs for garnishing

DRESSING: 3 tbsps olive oil, 2 tbsps white vinegar, 3–4 cloves garlic, 2 tbsps chopped parsley, salt, pepper

DRESSING: Chop the peeled garlic, blend with salt, vinegar and pepper, gradually adding the oil to obtain a smooth mixture. Combine with the chopped parsley and refrigerate.
Rinse and quarter the tomatoes. Drain the artichokes and quarter them. Chop the anchovy fillets finely. Combine the tomatoes, artichokes and anchovies. Pour the dressing over, mix gently and chill a bit. Before serving, garnish with olives and parsley sprigs.

Artichoke salad

300 g artichokes in brine or oil (a small tin), ½ iceberg lettuce, 1 cup watercress, 4 shallots or small red onions, ½ cup almond flakes, salt, 1 tsp almond oil

DRESSING: ½ tsp each mustard and liquid honey, 3 tbsps **grape-seed oil**, 2 tbsps **red vinegar**, salt, freshly ground pepper

Mix thoroughly the dressing ingredients. Refrigerate. Put the almond flakes into a small bowl. Combine the almond oil with salt. Pour the mixture over the almonds, shake and leave for 15 minutes.
Rinse the lettuce and watercress, drain well. Shred the lettuce. Drain the artichokes, quarter them. Slice the peeled onions. In a large bowl combine the almond flakes with the artichokes, lettuce, onions and watercress. Before serving, pour the dressing over, shake gently.

Tomato salad with basil

*500 g firm, fleshy tomatoes, 2 hard-boiled eggs, ½ cup pitted **black olives**, 2–3 tbsps chopped basil leaves, 1 tbsp olive oil, 1 tbsp lemon juice, salt, pepper*

Blanch and skin the tomatoes. Slice them, arrange the slices on a platter. Chop the shelled eggs coarsely. Sprinkle them in the shape of a cross on top of the tomatoes. Sprinkle the whole with salt and pepper, and with basil. Slice the olives, put the slices on the tomatoes. Sprinkle with lemon juice and oil.

Broccoli salad with almonds

*600 g broccoli, 150 g button mushrooms (caps only), juice of 1 lemon, 100 g **green olives stuffed with almonds**, 10 basil leaves, 50 g almond flakes*

*DRESSING: 2 egg yolks, 1 tsp Dijon mustard, ½ tsp paprika, salt, sugar, freshly ground white pepper, freshly ground nutmeg, ¼ cup **grape-seed oil**, 2 tbsps white vinegar, 2 tbsps double cream with herbs, 2 tbsps milk*

DRESSING: Blend the egg yolks with the mustard and paprika, add salt, pepper, nutmeg and sugar. Keep blending while you gradually pour in the oil until you obtain a smooth mixture. Add the vinegar and cream, refrigerate for 15 minutes.
Wash the mushrooms, dry and slice them. Sprinkle with lemon juice and pepper. Mix and leave aside. Rinse the broccoli, divide into florets. Peel the broccoli stem, slice it and cook in boiling water for 2–3 minutes. Drain, rinse under cold water, drain again. Finely chop the basil leaves. Combine the broccoli, mushrooms, olives and basil with the dressing. Refrigerate for 10 minutes. Toast the almond flakes in a frying pan and sprinkle them on top of the salad before you serve it.

Artichoke salad with bell pepper and eggs

c. 300 g artichoke hearts in oil (1 tin), 1 green bell pepper, 4 leaves curly oakleaf lettuce, 4 hard-boiled eggs for garnishing

*DRESSING: 2 tbsps artichoke oil, 1 tbsp **hazelnut oil**, 2 tbsps white vinegar or lemon juice, 1 tsp each finely chopped fresh parsley, thyme and sage, 2 cloves garlic, salt, freshly ground white pepper*

DRESSING: Blend the peeled and chopped garlic with salt, pepper and vinegar. Whisking vigorously gradually pour in the artichoke oil and hazelnut oil. Refrigerate for 15 minutes.
Quarter the drained artichoke hearts. Seed and rinse the bell pepper, dry and cut in small cubes. Mix the chilled dressing with the chopped herbs. Combine the artichoke with pepper cubes. Pour the dressing over and mix gently. Quarter the shelled eggs. Line individual salad bowls with lettuce, put some salad in each. Garnish with egg quarters.

Artichoke salad with tomatoes

c. 400 g artichoke hearts (1 tin), 3 firm, fleshy tomatoes, 2 shallots, 1 tbsp each chopped chives and basil, 1 tsp chopped dill

*DRESSING: 4 tbsps **peanut oil**, 2 tbsps **red vinegar**, salt, freshly ground white pepper*

Drain and halve the artichoke hearts. Blanch and skin the tomatoes. Halve and seed them, dice the flesh. Finely slice the peeled shallots. Combine all ingredients in a bowl, sprinkle with salt, pepper and vinegar, coat with oil. Shake well, cover and refrigerate. Before serving, garnish with chopped herbs.

Asparagus salad with tuna sauce

800 g cooked white asparagus stalks, 5–6 hard-boiled quail eggs, 1 lemon, 1 ½ cups watercress

*SAUCE: 1 tin tuna in brine (150 g), 1 tbsp **Worcester sauce**, 4 tbsps **safflower (thistle) oil**, 2 tbsps lemon juice, ¼ tsp grated lemon rind, salt, pepper, a pinch of sugar*

SAUCE: Blend all ingredients with oil into a creamy sauce.
Cut the asparagus stalks into smaller pieces. Halve the shelled quail eggs. Peel and finely slice the lemon, remove

the pips. Dice half of the lemon slices. Combine the asparagus with 1 cup chopped watercress, egg halves and diced lemon. Fold in the sauce, sprinkle with the remaining watercress. Garnish with lemon slices.

Tunisian salad with cucumber

1 large cucumber, 1 cooking apple,
1 tsp lemon juice, 2 large firm, fleshy tomatoes,
½ coffee spoon ground **cumin**

DRESSING: 2 tbsps vinegar, 4 tbsps olive oil,
salt, 1 tsp **harissa**

Combine all dressing ingredients, whisk to obtain a smooth mixture. Refrigerate for 15 minutes. Blanch and skin the tomatoes, cut in larger cubes, remove the seeds. Peel and core the apple, cut into sticks, sprinkle with lemon juice. Peel the cucumber and cut into cubes. Combine with the apple and tomatoes. Pour the dressing over, mix and sprinkle with cumin. Refrigerate for 1 hour.

Spinach salad with oyster mushrooms and pine nuts

400 g fresh spinach leaves, 300 g oyster mushrooms,
3 tbsps butter, 3–4 leaves iceberg lettuce,
1 tbsp **walnut oil**, *10o g* **pine nuts**

SAUCE: ¼ cup chicken stock (or stock from cube),
2–3 scallions (without green part), 1 large fleshy tomato,
salt, pepper, 1 tbsp **sherry vinegar**, *4 tbsps* **walnut oil**

Blanch and skin the tomatoes, cut them into cubes, remove the seeds. Clean and chop the scallions. Bring the chicken stock to a boil, put in the tomatoes and scallions, cook 4–5 minutes, then leave to cool. Liquidize the tomatoes, sieve them, combine with the oil and vinegar. Add salt and pepper to taste and refrigerate for 20 minutes.
Roast the pine nuts in a hot frying pan for 1–2 minutes. Pour in 1 tablespoon oil, stir and take off the heat. Rinse and drain the mushrooms, cut them in thick strips. Melt the butter in a saucepan, put in the mushrooms and for 3–4 minutes stir fry over a high heat. Cut off the stalks from the spinach leaves. Rinse the spinach and lettuce leaves,

drain thoroughly, shred them. Combine with the sauce and mushrooms, sprinkled with pine nuts.

Chanterelle salad

500 g young chanterelles, 2 thyme sprigs,
6–8 fresh basil leaves, 1 tbsp **anchovy paste**,
1 clove garlic, juice of 1 lemon, ½ cup thick
mayonnaise, 3 tbsps chopped parsley

Clean and wash the mushrooms, drain well. Bring ½ litre salted water with thyme sprigs to a boil. Cook 5 minutes, then put in the chanterelles, cover and continue cooking over a medium heat for another 5 minutes. Drain them and leave to cool. Finely chop the basil leaves and peeled garlic, blend with the anchovy paste and lemon juice, then combine with the mayonnaise. In a large bowl mix the mushrooms with the sauce, cover and leave aside for 30 minutes. Before serving, sprinkle with chopped parsley. Serve with buttered toast.

Fish

Fish in vegetables

400 g white fish fillets (cod, panga), 1 tbsp lemon juice,
2–3 tbsps oil, 1 egg, 1–2 cloves garlic, 3 tbsps green peas
(fresh or frozen), 2–3 scallions, 300 g broccoli florets,
1 small red bell pepper, 200 g button mushrooms,
1 carrot, 2 tbsps water, 1 tbsp **soy sauce**, *½ tbsp grated*
fresh ginger, ¼ tsp **five-spice powder**, *salt, pepper*

Wash and dry the fish fillets, cut into bite-size pieces, sprinkle with lemon juice. Chop the peeled garlic and cleaned scallions finely. Remove the stalk and seeds from the pepper pod, rinse the flesh, dry and cut into strips. Slice the peeled carrot. Wash and dry the mushrooms, quarter them. Mix the egg with a pinch of salt and pepper.

Heat 1 tablespoon oil in a heavy frying pan. Fry the egg like an omelette, then take out, roll up and cut into strips. Pour the remaining oil into a wok, brush its sides with the fat. Put in the fish and garlic, stir fry over a high heat for 3–4 minutes. Take out the fish with a straining spoon and put the onion in. Soften it, add the broccoli florets, pepper strips, carrot slices, mushrooms and green peas. Stir fry for 2 minutes, put in the fish. Mix the soy sauce and ginger with water and five-spice powder. Pour into the wok, stir, add the omelette strips and cook for 1 minutes, stirring gently.

Serve with rice or noodles.

Marinated rockfish fillets

*800 g rockfish (flounder or sole) fillets, juice of 1 lime, 2 green bell peppers, 1 green chili pepper, 2 large onions, 2–3 carrots, ½ cup olive oil, 1 tbsp sugar (preferably brown), 1 tbsp ground **cardamom**, 1 tsp cayenne pepper, 1 tsp crumbled dried chili, 1 tsp black pepper coarsely ground, 2 bay leaves, salt, 1 cup boiled water, ¼ cup white vinegar*

Wash and dry the fillets, sprinkle with lime juice and salt. Cover and refrigerate for 20–30 minutes. Julienne the peeled carrots. Halve the peeled onions, slice them finely. Remove stalks and seeds from the green peppers and chili pepper, rinse and dry the flesh. Chop the chili pepper finely. Cut the bell peppers in thin strips.
Heat half the oil in a heavy saucepan. Soften the onions, put in the carrots and peppers. Stir fry briskly, then add sugar, cardamom, dried chili, pepper and cayenne. Stir well, put in the bay leaves, pour in water and vinegar. Cook uncovered to reduce the liquid.
Heat the remaining oil in a frying pan. Fry the fillets golden brown on both sides. Arrange the fried fish in a deep serving dish, cover with the vegetables and leave to cool. Cover the dish with foil and refrigerate for 2–3 hours.

Cod en papillote with mushrooms and sweet corn

*800 g fresh cod fillets, 2–3 tbsps dry white wine, 80 g fresh **ginger**, 8 button mushrooms, 1 leek (only the white part), 4–6 tbsps sweet corn (tinned or frozen), 1 tbsp lemon juice, 1 tbsp butter, salt, pepper*

Heat the oven to 180°C. Cut the fillets into 4 slices, dust with pepper and salt. Peel the ginger and slice diagonally. Wash and slice the mushrooms and leek. Place each fillet on a square of aluminium foil greased inside with butter. Put ginger slices on top. Cover with mushrooms, then slices of leek and finally 1 tablespoon sweet corn. Sprinkle with wine. Close each papillote, folding the edges together. Arrange them on a greased baking tin and cook for 15–20 minutes. Serve with potatoes, lettuce or tomatoes.

Cod with French beans

*600 g cod fillets, 4 largish onions, 250 g French beans, 1 tbsp plum jam, 3 tbsps lemon juice, 1 tsp each ground ginger and **turmeric**, ½ tsp chili powder, salt, 4 tbsps butter, 2 cups light fish stock*

Grate the peeled onions, blend with the ginger, chili and turmeric to obtain a smooth paste. Rinse and dry the fillets, cut into thick strips. Sprinkle sparsely with lemon juice and salt and refrigerate for 30 minutes. Rinse the French beans, top and tail them, cut into smaller pieces. Melt the butter in a shallow saucepan, put in the onion paste and stir fry for 2 minutes. Add the beans, stir and keep cooking for another 2 minutes. Pour in the hot stock, plum jam and the remaining lemon juice. Stir, cover and simmer over a low heat for 5 minutes. Put in the fish strips and cook for 20 minutes. Serve with rice and tomato salad.

Fried cod in caper sauce

*4 fresh cod fillets, 1 tbsp lemon juice, salt, freshly ground pepper, 2 tbsps flour, 3 tbsps olive oil, 4 tbsps butter, 4 tbsps **capers** (if in brine, first soak them), 2 tbsps dry white wine, a pinch of sugar, juice and grated rind of 1 large lemon, 1 small lemon, 3–4 tbsps finely chopped parsley*

Rinse and dry the fillets, sprinkle with lemon juice, salt and pepper, leave in the fridge for 10 minutes.
Heat a large, heavy frying pan, pour in 1 tablespoon oil, make sure the sides of the pan are sufficiently greased and

pour out the oil. Heat the remaining oil in the pan. Coat the fillets in flour and fry golden brown on both sides. Transfer them to an oven-proof dish and keep warm. Melt the butter in a small saucepan, add the drained capers and chopped parsley, briskly fry over a low heat. Put in the wine, lemon juice and zest, stir. Pour the sauce over the fish, garnish with lemon wedges and serve with boiled or baked potatoes and lettuce or chicory salad.

Halibut in fennel sauce

800 g halibut fillets, 1 tbsp flour, 1 tbsp olive oil for greasing, 1–2 basil sprigs for garnishing

*MARINADE: 2 tbsps olive oil, 1 tsp **balsamic vinegar**, salt, pepper*

*TOMATO SAUCE: 3 fleshy tomatoes, 1 tbsp olive oil, 1½ tbsps **balsamic vinegar**, salt, pepper*

*FENNEL SAUCE: 1–2 fennel bulbs, 3–4 small tomatoes, ½ cup pitted **black olives**, 1½ tbsps **capers**, 3 tbsps olive oil, 1 tbsp **balsamic vinegar**, 12–15 basil leaves, salt, pepper*

MARINADE: Mix the vinegar with salt and pepper. Whisking vigorously, gradually pour in the oil. Rinse and dry the fillets. Arrange in a deep dish. Pour the marinade over and refrigerate for 1–2 hours, turning over from time to time. Take out of the marinade, dry on a paper towel, dredge in flour on one side.
Heat the oven to 200°C. Line a baking tin with greaseproof paper and put in the oven for 10–15 minutes. Brush the paper with oil, arrange the fillets on it (uncoated side up) and return to the oven for 20 minutes.
FENNEL SAUCE: Blanch and skin the tomatoes, halve and seed them, dice the flesh. Clean the fennel bulbs, cut into small cubes. Chop the olives and basil leaves. In a bowl combine the tomatoes with the fennel, olives and leaves, add the capers, oil and vinegar, season with salt and pepper. Shake the bowl, cover with clingfilm and refrigerate the sauce for 2–3 hours.
TOMATO SAUCE: Blanch and skin the tomatoes, halve and seed them. Liquidize the flesh with the addition of oil and vinegar. Season with salt and pepper, heat up a little.

Pour the tomato sauce into a warm oven-proof dish. Arrange the fillets, cover them with the fennel sauce (or serve fennel sauce separately in a sauceboat). Garnish with basil leaves.

Thai fish en papillote

*600 g white fish fillets, 1 tbsp lemon juice, ½ tbsp chopped fresh ginger, 3 tbsps peanuts, 2 tbsps **coconut oil**, ½ tsp each **turmeric** and freshly ground black pepper, 1 tsp salt, ¾ cup thick coconut milk, 1 tbsp butter*

COCONUT-CORIANDER POWDER: 1 tbsp coriander seeds, 5 tbsps shredded coconut

PASTE: 4 shallots, 2–3 cloves garlic, 4 dried chili peppers, 5 cm piece lemon grass or grated skin of 1 lime

Soak the chili peppers in boiled water for 15 minutes. COCONUT-CORIANDER POWDER: In a hot frying pan toast the coriander seeds and shredded coconut until they begin smelling, but be careful not to burn them. Leave to cool, then pound in a mortar.
ONION PASTE: Seed the soaked chili peppers. Chop finely the peeled shallots, peeled garlic, lemon grass and chilis, then blend into a paste.
Toast the peanuts and chop them. Cut the fillets into 5x3 cm strips, sprinkle with lemon juice. Heat the coconut oil in a large, heavy frying pan. Put in the onion paste and fry briskly. Add turmeric, salt, pepper, coconut-coriander powder and peanuts. Stirring all the time fry for 1–2 minutes, then pour in the coconut milk and stir well.
Heat the oven to 160–180°C. Brush 4 square pieces of aluminium foil with butter. On each square place 1 tablespoon of the prepared thick sauce and 1–4 fish strips. Cover with the remaining sauce. Close the papillotes folding the edges together. Arrange them on a baking tin and cook in the oven for 10–15 minutes. Serve hot with rice or cold with white bread.

Fish with vegetables

400 g pollock or hake fillets, 1 each orange, green and yellow bell pepper, 4–5 firm, fleshy tomatoes, 1 large onion, 2–3 cloves garlic, 1 cup green peas (fresh or frozen), 15 pitted **black olives**, ½ cup vegetable stock, 4 tbsps olive oil, 3 tbsps lemon juice, 1 tbsp **Worcester sauce**, 2 tbsps flour, ½ tsp each dried thyme and basil, salt, pepper

Rinse and dry the fillets, cut in strips and sprinkle with lemon juice. Wash the peppers, remove stalks and seeds, cut the flesh into rings. Blanch and skin the tomatoes, cut in wedges. Halve the peeled onion, slice it. Chop the peeled garlic, blend it with salt. Heat 2 tablespoons oil in a frying pan. Dust the fish strips with flour and brown them. Heat the remaining oil in a saucepan. Soften the onion, add the peppers and tomatoes. Cover and cook over a low heat, adding the garlic and Worcester sauce. Towards the end put in the green peas and sliced olives. Add the stock, stir and put in the fried fish. Season with thyme, basil, pepper and salt and cook for another 15 minutes.

Flounder roulades with spinach cream cheese

6 flounder fillets, 1 tsp lemon juice, 300 g full-cream curd cheese, 300 g fresh spinach, 2 egg yolks, 3–5 cloves garlic, 3–5 drops **Tabasco**, a pinch of nutmeg, salt, pepper, 1 tbsp butter

Wash and dry the fillets, sprinkle with lemon juice and leave aside. Cut off the stalks from the spinach leaves. Rinse the leaves, blanch for 2–3 minutes in boiling salted water, drain, rinse under cold water, drain again. Chop the peeled garlic very finely.
Liquidize the cheese, spinach and egg yolks. Add the garlic and spices, mix thoroughly. Spread some mixture on each fillet, roll up, secure the end with a toothpick. Brush an oven-proof dish with butter. Put in the roulades and place in a preheated oven (200°C) for 15–20 minutes. Serve hot or cold with a piquant sauce.

Mediterranean baked fish

700 g thick fillets of turbot or sea bass (skinned), 3 medium-sized potatoes, 2 onions, 2 cloves garlic, 3 tomatoes, 2 tbsps olive oil, 2 tbsps butter, 1 bay leaf, 1 fresh thyme sprig, 2 tbsps orange juice, ¼ tsp grated orange rind, 1 glass dry white wine, ½ tsp **saffron filaments**, salt, freshly ground black pepper

Slice the peeled onions finely. Chop the peeled garlic. Blanch and skin the tomatoes, slice and seed them. Soak the saffron in 3–4 tablespoons boiling water. Heat oil in a frying pan. Put in the onions and stirring continuously fry over a low heat. When it is soft, add the garlic and keep frying a little longer. Scrub the potatoes, put in a saucepan, cover with salted boiling water and cook for 15 minutes. Drain them, allow to cool, skin and cut into thin slices. Heat the oven to 190°C. Brush an oven-proof dish with butter, line it with half the potato slices, cover with the fried onions, sprinkle with salt and pepper. Arrange fish fillets on top, together with crumbled laurel leaves and thyme leaves. Cover with tomato slices, followed by the layers of the remaining onions and potatoes. Sprinkle with salt and pepper.
Mix the soaked saffron with the wine, orange juice and orange zest. Pour the mixture over the top. Dot with butter and place uncovered in the preheated oven for 30–35 minutes.

Marinated flounder (or sole)

750 g fillets of flounder (or sole), 2 tbsps flour, salt, freshly ground pepper, ½ cup olive oil, 2–3 carrots, 2–3 celery stalks, 1 large onion, 2–3 bay leaves, 2 tbsps **pine nuts**, 2 tbsps raisins, 1 cup dry white wine, 1 cup white vinegar, parsley sprigs

Put the rinsed raisins in a small bowl, sprinkle with 1 tablespoon wine and leave aside for 15 minutes. Peel the carrots and onion, remove stringy fibres from the celery. Rinse the vegetables and slice finely. Rinse and dry the fillets, sprinkle with salt and pepper, dust with flour. Heat 3–4 tablespoons olive oil in a heavy frying pan. Briskly fry the fish golden brown on both sides. Take it out, drain on a paper towel. Heat the remaining oil in another frying pan. Put in the vegetables and stir fry for 20–30 seconds over a fairly high heat. Turn down the heat, add salt and laurel leaves and continue frying a little longer. Take out the vegetables with a straining spoon. Pour the wine and vinegar into the frying pan and reduce the liquid by half over a very high heat.
In a deep serving bowl or a large glass jar place alternately a layer of fish and a layer of vegetables, sprinkling each layer with raisins and pine nuts. Pour in the marinade, leave to cool, then put in the fridge for 2–3 days. Serve at room temperature, garnished with parsley.

Saffron fish with leeks

700 g white sea fish (panga for example), 2 young thin leeks, 2–3 tbsps butter, 1 tbsp **grape-seed oil**, 2 tbsps lemon juice, ¼ tsp grated lemon rind, ½ tsp powdered **saffron**, ½ cup cream, 1 glass dry wine (or vegetable stock), 1 tbsp flour, salt, pepper

Rinse and dry the fish, sprinkle with 1 tablespoon lemon juice and leave aside. Wash the leeks, slice finely. Sprinkle the fillets with salt and pepper, coat in flour. Heat the oil in a heavy frying pan, fry the fillets golden brown on both sides. Transfer them to a saucepan. Melt the remaining butter in a skillet, put in the leeks and stir fry to soften them, then pour in the wine or stock, add the saffron, stir and cook a little longer. Add the lemon zest and the remaining juice, pour in the cream, stir thoroughly and heat up. Put on top of the fish fillets and simmer together for a short while. Serve with pureed potatoes and tomato salad.

Trout stuffed with cucumber

4 cleaned trout (250–300 g each), salt, 1 tsp lemon juice

STUFFING: ½ cup peeled, seeded and chopped cucumber, ½ cup finely shredded carrot, 2 tbsps chopped onion, ½ tsp ground **cardamom**, 100 g butter, ½ cup chicken stock, 2 tbsps chopped parsley, 4 slices dried bread, salt, pepper

Heat the oven to 190°C. Rinse and dry the fish, rub with salt, sprinkle with lemon juice. Grease a baking tin with butter.
STUFFING: Melt 2 tablespoons butter in a small saucepan. Put in the chopped onion, soften it. Add the cucumber and carrot, dust with cardamom and stir fry for 4–6 minutes. Pour in the hot stock, bring to a boil, stir and leave to cool. Put in the chopped parsley, season with salt and pepper. Stuff the trout, arrange on the baking tin and coat with melted butter. Put in the preheated oven and cook for 20 minutes – after 10 minutes turn the fish over. Serve with rice, potato chips or white bread.

Broiled fish in mint sauce

4 fillets of silver carp, carp or trout

MARINADE: 1 ½ tbsp **garam masala**, 8–10 cloves garlic, 1 tbsp grated fresh ginger, 1 tbsp flour, 2 tbsps lemon juice, ½ tsp crumbled dry chili pepper, ½ cup natural yogurt, salt, pepper

MINT SAUCE: ½ cup chopped mint leaves, 1 tsp chopped coriander leaves, 2–3 cloves garlic, ½ tsp tomato concentrate, 1 tbsp lemon juice, 2–3 tbsps cream, salt

MARINADE: Press the peeled garlic. Blend it with the ginger, lemon juice, chili, garam masala, salt and pepper. Mix the yogurt with flour and combine it with the prepared paste.
Rinse and dry the fish. Spread some paste on each fillet, cover and refrigerate for 2–3 hours.
SAUCE: Press the garlic and blend it with the remaining ingredients. Cover and refrigerate for 45–50 minutes.
Grill the fillets 10 minutes to each side. Serve with the mint sauce.

Grilled salmon

700 g salmon (4 slices), 1 cup fresh mint leaves, 1 lime for garnishing

SAUCE: 6–8 cloves garlic, ½ tsp grated lemon rind, juice of 1 lemon, a pinch of cayenne pepper, ½ tsp **turmeric**, 6 tbsps olive oil, salt, pepper

Wash the lime, scald with boiling water, dry and slice finely.
SAUCE: Press the peeled garlic, blend with the lemon juice and zest, cayenne and turmeric, add salt and pepper. Whisking vigorously gradually pour in the oil.
Rinse and dry the fish, place in a shallow bowl. Spread some sauce on both sides of each slice, cover the bowl and leave aside for 20–30 minutes. Return the remaining sauce to the fridge.
Grill the salmon in the oven for 10 minutes. Then place the slices on a bed of mint leaves, garnish with lime slices.

Serve the chilled sauce in a sauceboat. Serve with rice or couscous and with tomato salad.

Salmon in piquant wasabi sauce

700 g salmon fillets, 1 tbsp lemon juice, 1 tbsp freshly ground pepper, salt, 2 tbsps olive oil

*SAUCE: 100 g butter, ½ cup **rice vinegar**, 2–3 tsps **wasabi paste**, 1–2 chopped scallions, 1 tsp finely chopped fresh ginger, 2 tbsps **soy sauce**, 3 tbsps thick cream*

Rinse and dry the fish, cut into 4 portions. Sprinkle with lemon juice, salt and coarsely ground pepper. Cover and refrigerate for 15 minutes.

Bring the vinegar to a boil in a small saucepan, put in the ginger, scallions and wasabi paste. Stirring all the time cook over a low heat to reduce to half the liquid. Add the cream, stir and again lightly reduce the sauce (it should be green and thick). Add the soy sauce, stir and keep warm.

Heat the oil in a heavy frying pan, fry the fillets 1–2 minutes to each side. Butter an oven-proof dish, put in the fillets. Heat the oven to 180°C. Gradually add small pieces of butter to the hot sauce and whisk vigorously. Pour the sauce over the fish and put into the preheated oven for 2–3 minutes. Serve with rice sprinkled with toasted sesame seeds and with green peas or lettuce.

Salmon in batter

*600 g salmon fillets, 400 g frozen puff pastry, 200 g fresh spinach leaves, 2 tbsps olive oil, 2–3 cloves garlic, 3–4 basil sprigs, 100 g mozzarella, 4 **sun-dried tomatoes** in brine, 1 egg*

*MARINADE: juice and grated rind of 1 lemon, 2 tbsps **sambal ulek** sauce, salt, a pinch of caster sugar*

Combine all marinade ingredients. Rinse and dry the fish, cut into 4 portions. Spread the prepared marinade on each piece and refrigerate for 15 minutes.

Chop the peeled garlic finely, crush with salt and basil leaves. Cut off the stalks from the spinach leaves. Rinse the spinach leaves, drain well. Heat the oil in a heavy frying pan, put in the spinach. Let it sweat a bit, add the garlic with basil, stir and fry for a while. Grease a baking tin with oil. Divide the puff pastry into four squares. Put some spinach on each square, place a salmon fillet. Cover with slices of mozzarella and pieces of drained sun-dried tomatoes. Seal the edges of each square. Brush with a mixed egg and bake in the oven (at 180–190°C) for 20–25minutes. Serve as a hot snack or the main course – with salads and basil or saffron sauce.

Baked fish

*Bream or pikeperch (1.2–1.3 kg), 1 tbsp coriander seeds, 4–5 cloves garlic, 1 tbsp **harissa** paste, 6 tbsps olive oil, 6 firm plum tomatoes, 1–2 red onions, 1 large lemon, 2–3 crumbled bay leaves, 1 tbsp each fresh thyme and rosemary leaves, salt, ground black pepper, mint and thyme leaves for garnishing*

*SAUCE: ⅓ cup **tahini** paste, lemon juice, 1–2 cloves garlic, 3 tbsps finely chopped fresh coriander leaves, ½ cup boiled water or fish stock*

Rinse and dry the cleaned fish, make several incisions on the sides.

Pound the coriander seeds in a mortar. Chop the peeled garlic. Blend the harissa paste with 3–4 tablespoons olive oil, garlic and the coriander seeds.

Spread the mixture inside and on the fish. Cut the scrubbed and scalded lemon into fine slices, remove the pips. Arrange the lemon slices on a plate, sprinkle with salt, pepper and the remaining oil. Peel and slice the onions. Blanch and skin the tomatoes, cut into slices.

Heat the oven to 200°C. Grease an oven-proof dish with oil, line with lemon, tomato and onion slices. Place the fish on top, sprinkle with chopped thyme and rosemary. Put into the hot oven and cook, uncovered, for 25–30 minutes (check if the fish is done pricking it with a fork in the thickest spot).

SAUCE: Into a small saucepan put the lemon juice, tahini, chopped garlic and coriander. Cover with water (or fish stock) and cook over a low heat, stirring continuously until the sauce is smooth. Serve in a sauceboat.

Cold sauces

Mexican sauce

*2 ripe avocados, 2–3 firm, fleshy tomatoes, 1–2 onions, 1½ tbsps finely chopped fresh coriander leaves, juice and grated rind of 1 lemon, 6–8 drops **Tabasco** sauce, ¼ tsp honey, salt, pepper*

Halve the avocados, remove the stones. Carefully scoop out the flesh, dice it, sprinkle with lemon juice. Blanch and skin the tomatoes, cut in thick cubes, remove the seeds. Chop the peeled onions. Liquidize the avocado flesh, ¾ tomato cubes and onions together with the honey, pepper, salt, lemon zest and Tabasco. Chop the remaining tomatoes very finely. Together with coriander, combine them with the sauce. Stir the sauce, cover and refrigerate for 3–4 hours. Serve with cold and smoked meats and pancakes, or as a dip with crudités.

Tuna and caper sauce

*2 tbsps small **capers**, 1 tin tuna fish in oil (c. 200 g), ¾ cup thick natural yogurt, juice and grated rind of 1 lemon, salt, pepper, a dash of cayenne pepper*

Drain the tuna. Blend it with the yogurt, cayenne, lemon juice and zest to obtain a smooth cream. Combine with the capers, correct the seasoning with salt and pepper. Refrigerate for half an hour. Serve with roast veal and fried or boiled fish.

Oriental sauce for frutti di mare and fish

*2 tbsps **wasabi paste**, 2 tbsps light stock, 2 tbsps pale **soy sauce***

Mix thoroughly all ingredients. Serve to grilled or fried fish, shrimps or boiled pork.

Tomato sauce with olives

*2 tbsps pitted **black olives**, 2 tbsps **green olives** stuffed with peppers, 1 onion, ½ cup ketchup, 4 tbsps olive oil, 1 tsp finely chopped parsley, 1 tsp lemon juice, 5–8 drops **Tabasco** sauce, ½ tsp sugar, salt, pepper*

Grate the peeled onion very finely. Chop the olives. Blend into a smooth sauce with the remaining ingredients, add the parsley and refrigerate. Before serving, pour into a sauceboat and garnish with olive slices. Serve with shashlyks, beefsteak and minced meat patties.

Home-made pesto 1

*2 cups fresh basil leaves (without stalks), ½ cup extra virgin olive oil, 3 tbsps **pine nuts**, 3–4 finely chopped peeled garlic cloves, ½ cup grated parmesan, 1 tbsp hot water, salt and pepper to taste*

Blend the basil leaves, oil, pine nuts and garlic into a smooth paste. Towards the end add the parmesan and water.

Home-made pesto 2

*100 g fresh basil leaves, 100 g grated parmesan (or pecorino), 4–5 cloves garlic, 50 g **pine nuts** (or walnuts or sunflower seeds or pumpkin seeds), ½ cup olive oil or **grape-seed oil***

Chop the peeled garlic and basil leaves. Liquidize together with the parmesan and chopped pine nuts, gradually adding oil. Season with pepper and salt. Put in a glass jar with a tightly fitting lid and store in the fridge.

Pesto with pumpkin seeds

*100 g pumpkin seeds, 3 cloves garlic, 2 cups basil leaves, 3 tbsps olive oil, 4 tbsps **pumpkin-seed oil**, 3 tbsps grated parmesan, salt, pepper*

Chop the peeled garlic and basil leaves. Heat a heavy frying pan, toast the pumpkin seeds 3–4 minutes, or until light brown. Blend the pumpkin seeds with the basil, garlic and parmesan, gradually adding oil, to obtain a smooth mixture. Season with pepper and salt to taste.

Rocket and watercress pesto

½ cup each rocket, basil and cress (or watercress) leaves, 1 clove garlic, ½ cup grated parmesan, 1–2 tbsps lemon juice, 3 tbsps pumpkin seeds, ½ cup olive oil, salt, freshly ground pepper

Chop the peeled garlic. Rinse the herbs, dry them. Toast the pumpkin seeds in a hot frying pan. Blend the garlic, herbs and pumpkin seeds, adding gradually olive oil to obtain a smooth mixture. Season with pepper and salt. Serve with pasta or steamed vegetables.

Spring pesto

60 g fresh coriander leaves, 10 leaves each mint, parsley and basil, 1 small japaleño pepper, 2–3 cloves garlic, 1 tbsp finely chopped fresh ginger, ½ tsp dried coriander, 4–5 tbsps **peanut oil**, 2–3 tbsps olive oil, 1½–2 tbsps lime juice, 60 g cashew nuts, salt, freshly ground pepper

Toast the nuts in a frying pan. Seed the japaleño pepper, chop the pod finely. Chop the peeled garlic. Blend the cashews with the dried coriander, garlic, japaleño and ginger. Add the coriander, mint and basil leaves. Blending all the time, gradually pour in the peanut and olive oils. Towards the end add the lime juice, salt and pepper and work into a smooth mixture. Serve mixed with pasta, garnished with basil, coriander and mint leave. It is also a good idea to put it into glass jars and store in the fridge.

Piquant sesame sauce

2 tbsps **tahini paste**, 2 tbsps **soy sauce**, 1 tbsp flavoured **rice vinegar**, 1 tbsp **sesame oil**, 1 tbsp **chili oil**, 1 ½ tsp sugar, 1 tsp salt, 1 tsp ground **Sichuan pepper**, 1 large, finely grated onion, 3–4 cloves garlic, chopped and crushed, ¼ tsp flavour enhancer (sodium glutamate)

Blend the tahini paste with the soy sauce, add sugar, salt, grated onion and garlic. Blending all the time gradually add the remaining ingredients. Makes an excellent accompaniment to boiled chicken or pork, or to fried shrimps and fish.

Sesame sauce with olives

½ cup each **tahini paste**, lemon juice and yogurt, ¼ to ½ cup boiled water, 2–3 cloves garlic, salt, 1 tbsp finely chopped green coriander, 1 hard-boiled egg, 1 tbsp pitted **black olives**, 1 coffee spoon **sesame oil**

Chop the peeled garlic finely, mix with salt. Whisk the tahini paste with the lemon juice, add the yogurt and garlic. Whisking vigorously, gradually add water until the sauce is like thick cream. Refrigerate for 20 minutes. Cut the shelled hard-boiled egg and olives into cubes, combine with the coriander. Add to the sauce, mix thoroughly, sprinkle with oil. Serve with white bread or as a dip with crudités or crackers.

Sesame sauce with caraway

4 tbsps **tahini paste**, 2–3 cloves garlic, ¼ tsp ground caraway, 2–3 tbsps lemon juice, 1–2 tbsps light stock or boiled water (optional), 1 tbsp chopped green mint or coriander leaves

Chop the peeled garlic finely, mix with salt and caraway. Add the lemon juice and tahini paste (and stock or boiled water if necessary). Mix thoroughly (the sauce should be like thick cream). Put in the chopped mint or coriander leaves. Best served with fried fish or meat.

Piquant yogurt sauce

75 g raisins, 3 tbsps boiled water, 3 tbsps dry white wine, 1 tsp potato flour, 1 small tbsp liquid honey, 1 tbsp lemon juice, ¼ tsp grated lemon rind, ¼ tsp marjoram, 1 tsp **Worcester sauce**, 2 cups yogurt, salt

Bring water to a boil in a saucepan, put in the rinsed raisins. Add the honey and a pinch of salt, bring to a boil again. Mix the wine with the potato flour. Gradually pour into the saucepan, stirring all the time. Simmer over a low heat until the mixture thickens, then take off the heat. Blend the yogurt with the lemon juice and zest, marjoram and Worcester sauce. Combine with the raisins, stir well and refrigerate for 30 minutes. Serve with roast and fried beef.

Hot sauces

Nutty horseradish sauce

½ cup chopped walnuts, 3 tbsps freshly grated horseradish, 1 tbsp mustard, 1½ tbsps **balsamic vinegar**, 1 tbsp honey, 3 tbsps butter, 1 tbsp flour, 1½ cups chicken stock (or stock from cube), 1 cup cream, salt and pepper to taste

Roast the walnuts in a frying pan, combine with the cream. Melt the butter in a saucepan, add the flour and mixing together prepare a white roux. Thin it down with some cool stock and stirring continuously cook until the mixture thickens. Add the mustard and grated horseradish, keep simmering. Add the vinegar and honey, stir and heat up. Pour in the cream. Heat up again, but keep off the boil. Season with pepper and salt. Serve with roast, fried and stewed meat or with egg dishes.

Oriental sauce

2 cups unsweetened coconut milk, 2 large onions, 4 cloves garlic, juice and grated rind of 1 lemon, 1 fresh chili pepper, 1 tbsp **anchovy paste** (or 1 small tin anchovies), salt, ½ tsp sugar, 2 tbsps sunflower or **grape-seed oil**

Finely chop the seeded chili pepper. Do the same with the peeled onions and garlic, combine with the lemon zest, sugar and anchovy paste (or finely chopped anchovies). Blend into a smooth mixture. Heat the oil in a saucepan, put in the onion mixture, stir fry for 2–3 minutes. Add the soy sauce, chili pepper, coconut milk and lemon juice. Stir and cook for 2–3 minutes. Recommended in particular with hard-boiled eggs.

Savoury sauce for beef

½ cup chopped walnuts, 4 shallots, 2–3 cloves garlic, 1 tbsp fresh grated ginger, 2 tbsps **soy oil**, 4 tbsps **soy sauce**, 1 tbsp **oyster sauce**, ½ cup boiled water or light beef stock, 1 tbsp **sesame oil**, 1 tbsp **chili sauce**, 3 tbsps corn or rice flour

Mix the corn (or rice) flour with water. Combine the soy sauce with the oyster sauce, chili sauce, sesame oil and water mixed with flour. Leave aside for 5–7 minutes. Finely chop the peeled onions and garlic. Heat 1 tablespoon soy oil in a wok (remember to brush the sides with oil), pour it out. Pour in the remaining soy oil, heat up. Put in the onions and garlic, fry a little. Add the grated ginger and walnuts and stirring continuously fry for 1–2 minutes. Stir thoroughly the prepared mixture of sauces, flour and water, pour into the wok and stirring all the time heat up until it thickens. Serve with fried rump steaks.

Spicy sauce for pork

4 each dried apricots and shallots, 4–5 pieces **sun-dried tomatoes** in oil, ¼ tsp each ground cinnamon and **star anise**, 2–3 cloves, 2 tbsps butter, 1 cup strong chicken or veal stock, 1 rosemary sprig, ¾ cup dry red wine, 1 tsp honey, salt, pepper

Wrap the cloves in a piece of gauze. Blanch the apricots with boiling water, drain them. Peel the shallots. Drain the sun-dried tomatoes. Melt the butter in a saucepan. Dice 3 apricots, shallots and tomatoes. Put in the saucepan together with the rosemary, cloves and cinnamon. Briskly fry, stirring all the time. Cover with the hot stock and bring to a boil. Pour in the wine and simmer over a low heat for 5–6 minutes. Take out the rosemary sprig and cloves. Liquidize the sauce. Cut the remaining apricot in strips. Return the sauce to the saucepan, add honey, salt and pepper to taste. Heat up and add the apricot. Serve with roast meat, pork in particular, and roast poultry.

Chestnut sauce with wine

1 small tin **chestnuts** (c. 250 g), 50 g button mushrooms (caps only), 1½ tbsps butter, 1 bay leaf, 1–2 thyme sprigs or ½ tsp dried thyme, 1 glass dry red wine, 1 tbsp brandy, salt, freshly ground pepper

Rinse and dry the mushrooms, cut them finely. Drain the chestnuts, liquidize with 4–5 tbsps brine. Melt the

Pork tenderloins in hoisin sauce

butter in a saucepan, put in the mushrooms and stir fry for 4–5 minutes. Add the pureed chestnuts, bay leaf and thyme. Pour in the wine and brandy. Stirring, cook over a low heat for 3–4 minutes. Take out the bay leaf and thyme sprig, season to taste and heat up. Recommended for pasta and noodles.

Carrot sauce with turmeric

*400 g carrots, 1 small zucchini, 1 tsp lemon juice, 1 large onion, 4 tbsps **grape-seed oil**, 1 walnut-size piece of ginger, 1 tbsp honey, 1 tsp **turmeric**, ½ tsp curry powder, ½ cup thick yogurt, 1 cup chicken stock, salt, pepper*

Scrape and rinse the carrots, peel the onion and ginger. Cut in cubes. Heat 2 tablespoons oil in a saucepan, put in the onion, soften a little. Add the carrots, ginger and honey. Stirring all the time, cook over a medium heat for 6–7 minutes. Sprinkle with turmeric, cover and simmer for 15 minutes.

Halve the washed zucchini, seed it. Grate the flesh, sprinkle with lemon juice. Heat the remaining oil in a frying pan, put in the zucchini and fry for 4–5 minutes. Sprinkle with salt, pepper and curry powder, stir and take off the heat. Liquidize the carrots, season to taste adding salt, honey and lemon juice if needed. Combine with the yogurt and fried zucchini. Serve with pasta.

Savoury sauce with green peppers

*1 cup double cream, ½ cup thick sour cream, ½ cup dry white wine, 1 cup chicken stock, 2 shallots, 2–3 cloves garlic, 1 tsp crushed pepper, 1 bay leaf, 1 tsp each **green peppers** in brine, pepper brine and potato flour, 1–2 tbsps cold boiled water, salt and sugar to taste, 25 g brandy (optional)*

Finely chop the peeled shallots and garlic. Put in a saucepan, add the bay leaf and crushed pepper. Cover with the hot stock and wine. Bring to a boil, then simmer over a low heat to reduce the liquid to ¾ cup. Strain the liquid. Drain the peppers, chop finely. Combine with the brine and double cream. Pour into the saucepan and bring to a boil. Mix the potato flour with water. Gradu-

ally add to the sauce, stirring all the time. Heat up until the sauce thickens. Season with salt and sugar to taste. Pour in the sour cream (and brandy), stir well and heat up, but keep off the boil. Serve with pork chops or fried and roast poultry.

Meat

Pork

Pork fried with chili pepper

*600 g fatty minced meat, 300 g fresh, medium sharp green chili peppers, 2 tbsps **rice wine** or dry sherry, 1 tsp **soy sauce**, 2 tbsps lard, 8–10 cloves garlic, 1 tbsp light soy sauce, 1 tbsp **sesame oil**, 1 tsp sugar, a pinch of salt*

Mix the meat with the wine, salt and soy sauce. Chop the peeled garlic. Cut the peppers lengthwise, remove the seeds, cut the flesh in strips. Heat the lard in a wok or a heavy frying pan and soften the garlic. Put in the meat and stirring vigorously fry over a high heat for 2 minutes. Add the peppers and keep frying for another 2 minutes. Add salt and sugar to taste and fry for a bit longer. Towards the end sprinkle with sesame oil. Serve with rice and Chinese cabbage salad.

Pork tenderloins in hoisin sauce

*300 g pork tenderloins, 200 g Chinese egg noodles, 150 g button mushrooms, 100 g snap peas, 3–4 scallions, 1 large red bell pepper, 3–4 cloves garlic, 2 tbsps sunflower oil, 1 tsp finely chopped fresh ginger, 4 tbsps **hoisin sauce**,*

Pork in chili sauce

1 tbsp **soy sauce**, 1 tbsp **sesame oil**, 2–3 tbsps
chopped chives, salt and pepper to taste

Rinse and dry the meat, cut into thin strips. Dice the scallions. Clean the snap peas, rinse and dry, halve the pods. Finely chop the peeled garlic. Rinse and dry the mushrooms. Remove the stalk and seeds from the bell pepper, cut the flesh in strips. Heat a wok or a heavy frying pan, pour in 1 tablespoon sunflower oil, carefully brush the sides with the oil, then pour it out. Pour in the remaining sunflower oil, briskly fry the garlic and ginger. Turn up the heat, put in the mushrooms and pepper strips, stir and fry over a high heat for 2 minutes. When they soften, put in the meat and brown a little. Add the snap peas and scallions and fry for another 2–3 minutes. Combine the soy sauce with the hoisin sauce. Gradually add the sesame oil, whisking vigorously until the mixture is foamy. Put the noodles into a bowl, cover with boiling water and leave aside for 5–7 minutes (or according to the package instructions). Drain them, put in a warm serving dish. Arrange the meat and vegetables around, pour the sauce over, sprinkle the top with chopped chives.

Pork in chili sauce

500 g loin or tenderloin of pork, 1 large onion,
1–2 carrots (c. 200 g), 1 young zucchini, 100 g tinned
bamboo shoots, 2 ½ cups cooked long-grain rice,
1 egg, 1 tbsp fizzy mineral water, 3 tbsps **sweet
chili sauce**, 2 tbsps sunflower oil, a dash of
Sichuan pepper, 1 tsp lemon juice, 1 tbsp each
chopped parsley and coriander leaves, salt

Rinse and dry the meat, cut in thin strips, sprinkle with Sichuan pepper and lemon juice, leave aside for 10 minutes. Rinse and drain the bamboo shoots, cut in strips. Julienne the peeled carrots and zucchini. Halve the peeled onion, then slice finely.
Heat ½ tablespoon sunflower oil in a large wok, brush the sides with the oil generously, then pour it out. Pour in the remaining oil, heat it up. Put in the meat and stirring continuously fry it over a fairly high heat for 5 minutes. Add the chili sauce, stir and keep cooking and stirring until the sauce thickens. Put in the onion, carrots, zucchini and bamboo shoots. Stir fry for another 2–3 minutes. Add the

rice and stirring all the time heat up. Mix the egg with the mineral water, pour the mixture into the wok. Stir fry until the egg sets. Serve immediately, sprinkled with chopped parsley and coriander.

Spare ribs in piquant sauce

1 kg lean spare ribs, ½ cup piquant ketchup, ¼ cup **soy sauce**, 2 tbsps **tahini paste**, 4 tbsps **sherry vinegar** or dry sherry, 2 tbsps vodka, 1 tsp potato flour, 1 tbsp finely chopped fresh ginger, 2–3 cloves garlic, 1 cup oil for deep frying

Mix the tahini paste, vinegar (or wine) and 4 table-spoons soy sauce. Rinse and dry the spare ribs, brush them generously with the mixture. Cover and refrigerate for 3–4 hours. Halve the peeled garlic cloves, brown in hot oil in a frying pan, then take out. Put in the spare ribs gradually, brown each batch on both sides. Take out and drain on a paper towel. Place in an oven-proof dish and keep warm. In the meantime mix the ketchup with the remaining soy sauce, ginger, vodka and potato flour. Pour the mixture into a small saucepan and simmer over a low heat, stirring all the time. Pour over the ribs and put the dish into a preheated oven for 8–10 minutes. Serve with rice or soy noodles and with salads.

Honey spare ribs

1½ kg spare ribs, 6–8 tbsps **soy sauce**, 4–5 tbsps sake or sherry, 2–3 tbsps liquid honey, 1 tbsp **sambal ulek paste**, 2–3 cloves garlic, fresh ginger, salt, pepper

MARINADE: Peel the garlic and ginger, chop finely. Mix with the honey, sake (or sherry), soy sauce, sambal ulek, ginger and garlic.
Rinse and dry the spare ribs, divide into portions. Put in a large bowl and pour the marinade over. Cover and refrigerate for 4–5 hours, turning the pieces over from time to time. Take out of the marinade, sprinkle with salt and pepper and grill or roast in the oven, basting with the marinade occasionally.

Pork in soy sauce

600 g lean pork off the bone, 3 hard-boiled eggs, 5–6 cloves garlic, ½ cup thick **soy sauce**,

1 cup water, 1 cinnamon stick, 1tbsp sugar, ½ tsp **five-spice powder**, 2 tbsps oil

Wash and dry the meat, knead well, cut in thin strips. Chop the peeled garlic. Heat the oil in a large, heavy frying pan, put in the garlic and fry over a low heat for 30 seconds. Turn the heat up, put in the meat and stir fry for 1–2 minutes. Turn the heat down, sprinkle the meat with sugar and cook for another minute. Add the cinnamon and five-spice powder, pour in the mixed boiled water and soy sauce. Simmer over a low heat until the meat is tender. Five minutes before you take the meat off the heat put in the quartered shelled eggs. Serve with rice or pasta and salads.

Marinated boiled pork slices

500 g lean pork ham, 1½ cup beef or chicken stock (or stock from cube), juice and grated rind of ½ lemon, salt

MARINADE: 15–17 **Sichuan peppercorns**, 2–3 **star anise seeds**, 1 tbsps finely chopped fresh ginger, ½ tsp salt

Rinse and dry the meat, rub with a pinch of salt and sprinkle with lemon juice. In a shallow saucepan bring the stock with lemon zest to a boil. Put in the meat, bring to a boil, then simmer over a low heat until the meat is tender. Leave to cool, then take out and cut into thin slices. Bring the stock again to a boil.
Put the chopped ginger in a large serving bowl, add the peppercorns and star anise. Pour in the hot stock, cover and leave for 5–7 minutes. Stir well and put the meat slices in. Leave the meat in the marinade for 30–40 minutes, then take out and drain. It will have a nice, delicate flavour.

VEAL

Veal medallions in ginger sauce

700 g fillet of veal, ¾ cup chicken or vegetable stock, ½ cup double cream, 1 tsp **ginger**, juice of 1 lemon, 3 carrots, 1 large leek, salt, white pepper, 1 tsp potato flour

Bring the stock to a boil, add ginger and lemon juice, leave aside to cool. Rinse and dry the meat, cut it in 4 slices. Put in a bowl, cover with the cool stock and refrigerate for 3–5 hours, turning the meat over from time to time.
Scrape, rinse and julienne the carrots. Wash the leek and slice it. Take out the meat, dry it. Bring the stock to a boil, put in the meat and cook over a low heat for 15 minutes. Take the meat out. Add the carrots and leek to the stock, cook over a fairly high heat for 5 minutes. Mix the potato flour with a little water, pour the mixture into the stock, cook stirring all the time until it thickens. Add the cream, season to taste, put in the meat and heat up. Serve with rice or noodles and salads.

Caucasian veal stew

700 g veal off the bone, 2–3 onions, 250 g frozen spinach, 2 tbsps lemon juice, ½ tsp grated lemon rind, a pinch of **saffron** (2–3 filaments), ¼ tsp ground coriander seeds, 1 cup chicken stock, 2 tbsps oil, 1 tbsp butter, 2–3 tbsps chopped fresh coriander (or parsley), salt, pepper

Rinse and dry the meat, cut into cubes. Put in a bowl, sprinkle with 1 teaspoon lemon juice, pepper, lemon zest and ground coriander. Mix, cover and leave aside for 15 minutes. Soak the saffron in 1 tablespoon boiling water. Dice the peeled onion. Heat the oil in a large heavy saucepan. Put in the meat and brown over a high heat for 3 minutes. Add the butter and onion and stirring all the time fry for another 3–4 minutes. Pour in the hot stock, add the saffron and a dash of salt, cover and simmer over a low heat for 25 minutes. Add the spinach and lemon juice, stir and keep cooking for 5–6 minutes. Season to

taste and mix in the chopped coriander (or parsley). Serve with rice or noodles.

Calves' kidneys with leek

2–3 calves' kidneys, 3 large leeks (only white parts), 2–3 large potatoes, 70 g lean bacon, 1 large fleshy tomato, 20 g fresh ginger, 1½ tbsps **soy sauce**, 1½ tbsps **oyster sauce**, 2 tbsps mild, sweetish mustard, ½ cup fresh basil leaves, ¼ cup **peanut oil**, ¼ cup veal or chicken stock (or stock from cube), 3 tbsps flour, 1 tbsp rice or potato flour, salt, freshly ground pepper

Halve the kidneys lengthwise, put in a bowl. Cover with cold water and leave aside for 20–30 minutes. Blanch and skin the tomatos, cut into cubes, remove the seeds. Peel and wash the potatoes, cut in cubes. Wash the leeks thoroughly, slice finely. Cut the peeled ginger in fine strips. Slice the bacon finely. Take the kidneys out of the water. Remove membranes, blood vessels and fat. Rinse and dry them, cut in thin slices. Sprinkle with salt and pepper, dredge in flour.
Heat 2 tablespoons oil in a wok, put in the kidney slices, stir fry over a fairly high heat for 2–3 minutes to make them crispy. Take them out with a straining spoon and keep warm. Pour out the oil from the wok. Pour fresh oil (reserve 1 tablespoon for later) into the wok. Put in the potatoes and fry golden brown. Add the leek and stirring all the time fry over a medium heat for 2–3 minutes. Take the potatoes and leeks out with a straining spoon. Empty the wok of the oil. Pour in the reserved tablespoon of oil, put in the ginger and briskly fry. Mix the rice (or potato) flour with the stock, pour into the oil with ginger and stirring heat up until the sauce thickens. Add the mustard, soy sauce and oyster sauce, bring to a boil. Put in the fried kidneys, potatoes, leeks, tomato and chopped basil, stir and heat up. Brown the bacon slices in a frying pan. Transfer the kidney fry to a serving dish, garnish with fried bacon.

Veal ragout with celery

600 g veal off the bone, 400 g celery, 1–2 cloves garlic, 2 cooking apples, 2 tbsps olive oil, 2 tbsps

Veal ragout with celery

butter, 1 tbsp flour, 1 tbsp **curry powder**, ½ cup stock, ¼ cup dry white wine, 1 cup thick cream, 1 tbsp each lemon juice and honey, salt and pepper

Rinse and dry the meat, cut into thin strips, sprinkle with salt and pepper. Remove stringy fibres from the celery sticks. Cut the celery into thick slices. Finely chop the peeled garlic. Heat the oil in a heavy saucepan, briskly brown the meat on all sides. Add the garlic, celery and butter. Stir fry for 2–3 minutes. Pour in the wine and stock, stir and cook together for 10 minutes. Peel and core the apples, cut them into sticks, sprinkle with lemon juice. Together with the honey and curry powder add them to the meat, season with salt and pepper. Stir and cook for 6–8 minutes. Mix the cream and flour, add to the sauce, stir and heat up (keeping off the boil) until the sauce thickens. Serve with rice.

BEEF

Shepherd's roulade

600 g beef off the bone (top flank or rump), 300 g spinach, 3 carrots, 4 hard-boiled eggs, 3 onions, 2 bay leaves, 2 cloves, 6 slices boiled ham, 1 tsp salt, ¼ tsp pepper, 1½ tsps marinated **green peppercorns**, 4 tbsps oil, 1 cup beef stock (or stock from cube), ½ cup dry red wine

Wash the spinach, drain thoroughly. Scrape and wash the carrots, julienne them. Shell and quarter the eggs. Cut the ham in strips. Peel the onions, slice two of them and stick the cloves in one. Slit the meat open lengthwise, lightly pound with a mallet, sprinkle with salt and pepper. Spread with spinach, carrots, egg quarters, onion slices and ham. Crush the green peppercorns lightly, sprinkle on top of the stuffing. Roll up the meat, secure with twine. Brown on all sides in hot oil. Transfer to a roasting tin, cover with the hot stock and wine, put in the onion stuffed with cloves. Place in a preheated oven (220°C) and roast for 70 minutes, turning the roulade over from time to time.

Leave to cool, then slice it. If you want to serve it hot, sieve the roasting juices and combine them with cream.

Beef with peppers

400 g fillet of beef, 1 small tin **bamboo shoots** (250 g), 3–4 scallions, 1–2 cloves garlic, 2 bell peppers, 4 tbsps soy oil, 1 tbsp ketchup, 1 tbsp **soy sauce**, ½ tsp each pepper and cayenne pepper, 1 cup chicken stock (or stock from cube), 2 tsps chopped coriander leaves

Rinse and dry the meat, cut in fine strips. Chop the scallions finely. Remove the stalks and seeds from the peppers, rinse the flesh and cut into strips. Crush the peeled garlic. Rinse the bamboo shoots, drain well, cut into fine pieces. Heat the oil in a wok or a heavy frying pan. Brown the meat for 1–2 minutes over a very high heat. Take out with a straining spoon, put in a warm bowl. In the same frying pan fry the scallions, peppers and bamboo shoots over a fairly high heat for 2–3 minutes, stirring continuously. Pour in the ketchup and soy sauce, season with pepper and salt. Stir and keep frying for 1–2 minutes. Add the meat and garlic, cover with the hot stock. Stir and heat up, stirring all the time, for 1–2 minutes. Before serving, garnish with chopped coriander.

Beef with tomatoes

500 g fillet of beef, 500 g firm, fleshy tomatoes, 1 small pod each red and green pepper, 2 onions, 2–3 cloves garlic, 1½ tsps chopped fresh ginger, 4 tbsps oil, 1 tsp **turmeric**, ½ tsp chili powder, salt, sugar

MARINADE: 3 tbsps **soy sauce**, ½ cup dry white wine, 2 tbsps oil, 1 tbsp honey, 1 tbsp corn flour, ½ cup boiled water

Mix all ingredients of the marinade. Rinse and dry the meat, cut into 2.5 cm long strips. Put in a bowl, cover with the marinade, mix well and refrigerate for 1–2 hours.
Remove the stalks and seeds from the peppers, cut the flesh into strips. Slice the peeled onions. Chop the peeled garlic finely. Blanch and skin the tomatoes, cut in cubes. Heat 2 tablespoons oil in a wok or a heavy frying pan. Fry

Devilled beefsteaks

the meat for 1 minute, then push it to the sides of the wok or take out with a straining spoon and keep warm. Pour the remaining oil into the wok. Fry the onions, garlic and ginger for 2 minutes. Add the peppers and tomatoes, turn down the heat and simmer for 10 minutes. Season with turmeric, chili, sugar and salt. Put in the meat, stir and heat up. Serve with rice and marinated cucumber or scallopini squash.

Devilled beefsteaks

800 g fillet of beef, ¼ cup **grape-seed oil**, *1 tbsp each red, black, green and white peppercorns, salt*

SAUCE: ¼ cup each **balsamic vinegar**, *beef stock and dry red wine, 2 tbsps butter, 1 tbsp flour, salt, ground pepper, a pinch of sugar*

Heat the oven to 200°C. Pound all peppercorns in a mortar. Rinse and dry the meat, remove membranes, cut into 4 steaks. Dredge with pepper. Heat the oil in a large, heavy frying pan. Brown the steaks on both sides. Transfer to an oven-proof dish, salt and place for 10 minutes in the preheated oven.
SAUCE: Mix the vinegar and wine, heat up, reduce a little. Melt the butter in a small saucepan, add the flour and mix to produce a white roux. Dilute it with cold stock and continue stirring until the sauce thickens. Add salt, pepper and sugar to taste. Pour in the vinegar with wine, stir. Coat the meat with the sauce. Serve with potato chips and lettuce.

Beef in tomato sauce

500 g fillet of beef, 4 tbsps olive oil, 3 tbsps each **soy sauce**, **sherry vinegar** *and tomato concentrate, 1 tsp ground ginger, 1–2 finely chopped garlic, 4–5 dried mushrooms, salt*

Soak the rinsed mushrooms in a little boiled water. Mix the soy sauce and vinegar with the garlic, ginger and 2 tablespoons oil. Rinse and dry the meat, cut into thin strips. Put in a bowl, cover with the prepared sauce, mix well and refrigerate for 3–4 hours. Cook the soaked mushrooms, leave to cool, then cut into strips. Reduce

the mushroom stock so that no more than ½ cup is left. Heat the remaining oil in a large, heavy frying pan. Put in the meat and fry over a high heat for 2 minutes, stirring all the time. Add the mushrooms and fry for another minute. Pour in the mushrooms stock mixed with the tomato concentrate, stir and heat up. Serve with pasta or rice.

Beef with bamboo shoots and vegetables

300 g fillet of beef, 1 each small green and red bell pepper, 1 fresh red chili pepper, 3–4 celery stalks, 1 small carrot, 100 g drained tinned **bamboo shoots**, *3 slices fresh ginger, 2–3 tbsps oil*

MARINADE: 2 tbsps light **soy sauce**, *2 tbsps* **sherry vinegar**, *1 tsp sugar, 1 ½ tsp corn flour*

SAUCE: ½ cup chicken stock (or stock from cube), 2 tbsps **hoisin sauce**, *1 tbsp dry sherry, 1 tsp rice or potato flour*

Rinse and dry the meat. Put in the freezer for 10 minutes. Combine all ingredients of the marinade. Take the meat out, cut into thin strips. Put in a bowl, cover with the marinade, mix well and leave aside for 30–40 minutes.
Prepare the sauce by mixing in a bowl the corn (or potato) flour with 2 tablespoons stock, hoisin sauce and sherry. Leave aside for a while.
Chop the ginger finely. Remove the stalks and seeds from the peppers, rinse the flesh and cut into strips. Scrape the carrot, remove stringy fibres from the celery stalks. Julienne the carrot, celery and bamboo shoots.
Heat the oil in a wok, put in the meat, fry over a high heat for 2–3 minutes, stirring all the time. Take out the browned meat with a straining spoon, put on a platter and keep warm. Turn down the heat, put in the chopped ginger and vegetables. Stir fry for 2 minutes to soften the vegetables. Then turn up the heat, pour in the prepared sauce, bring to a boil and cook for 30 minutes. Put in the meat and, stirring continuously heat up until the sauce thickens. Serve immediately with white bread, rice or soy noodles.

Oriental beef

Oriental beef

*500 g beef off the bone (top flank or rump), 2 young green zucchini, 2 young yellow zucchini, 150 g snap peas, 250 g button mushrooms, 1 red and 1 green bell pepper, 1 small Pekingese cabbage, 6–8 scallions, 2 tbsps **peanut oil** or sunflower oil, 1 tbsp potato flour, 1 tbsp water, salt*

*MARINADE: 1 tbsp **oyster sauce**, ¼ cup **soy sauce**, 2 tbsps finely chopped fresh ginger, 1 tbsp **sherry vinegar**, sherry or sake*

Combine the soy sauce with the vinegar or sherry (or sake), oyster sauce and chopped ginger. Wash and dry the meat, cut against the grain into long, thin strips. Put in a bowl, cover with the marinade and leave for 20–30 minutes. Remove the stalks and seeds from the peppers, rinse the flesh and cut into strips. Wash and dry the zucchini, cut into sticks. Shred the Pekingese cabbage finely. Dice the scallions (with leaves) into 3–4 cm pieces. Quarter the rinsed and drained mushrooms. Heat half the oil in a wok or a heavy frying pan, wash the sides with oil well. Brown the meat in batches, then take out with a straining spoon and place on a warm plate. When all the meat has been fried, pour in the remaining oil. Put in the snap peas, zucchini, mushrooms, peppers, cabbage and scallions. Fry over a high heat for 2–3 minutes, stirring all the time. Mix the potato flour with water, add to the vegetables, stir. Put in the fried meat and continue cooking over a high heat for 3 minutes. When the sauce thickens and the meat is very hot, take off the heat and serve immediately – with rice or with rice noodles.

Beef with sesame

*500 g beef off the bone (prime rib), 1 tsp lemon juice, 6–8 scallions, 1 large green bell pepper, 4–6 cloves garlic, 5 tbsps **soy sauce**, 2 tbsps **sesame seeds**, 2 tbsps **soy oil**, 2 tbsps **sherry vinegar** or dry sherry, 1 tsp **sesame oil***

Rinse and dry the meat, cut into thin strips, sprinkle with lemon juice. Finely chop the peeled garlic. Remove the stalks and seeds from the peppers, rinse the flesh and cut

into strips. Dice the washed scallions. Heat a frying pan, toast the sesame seeds for 1–2 minutes, or until they are nicely brown. Heat the soy oil in a wok or a heavy frying pan, put in the meat and brown it nicely. Add the peppers and garlic, stir fry for 2 minutes. Pour in the vinegar (or sherry) and soy sauce, add the scallions, stir and cook for another minutes. Sprinkle with sesame oil. Before serving sprinkle with sesame seeds. Serve with soy or rice noodles.

Stewed beef provençale

*1½ kg rump of beef, 250 g smoked streaky bacon, 250 g carrots, bouquet garni (bay leaf, 1–2 thyme sprigs, 3 parsley sprigs), 3–4 cloves garlic, 2 cups pitted **black olives**, 400 g diced tinned tomatoes*

MARINADE: ½ cup extra virgin olive oil, 1 onion, 4 shallots, 1 celery stalk, 1 carrot, ⅔ cup red wine, 6 peppercorns, 2 cloves garlic, 1 bay leaf, 1 thyme sprig, 2 parsley sprigs, salt

MARINADE: Peel and slice the onion, shallots and garlic. Remove stringy fibres from the celery stalk, slice it. Slice the scraped carrot. Heat the oil in a frying pan. Put in the vegetables and fry for 2 minutes. Pour in the wine, add the peppercorns, garlic, bay leaf, thyme and parsley sprigs, and salt. Cover and simmer over a low heat for 15–20 minutes. Then take off the heat and leave to cool.

Rinse the meat, put in a stoneware pot, pour in the marinade. Cover and refrigerate for 12–16 hours, turning the meat over once or twice.

Heat the oven to 160°C. Finely slice the bacon. Scrape and slice the carrots. Take the meat out of the marinade. Bard it with half the bacon slices. Line an oven-proof dish with the remaining bacon. Put the meat in, surround with the carrot slices, add the herbs and garlic. Pour the marinade over. Cover the dish with greaseproof paper or aluminium foil, put the lid on and place in the oven for 2 hours. Take out, put in the olives and tomatoes, cover again and return to the oven for another 30 minutes. Before serving, cut the meat into thin slices. Serve with fresh bread, potato chips or pasta and with flageolets.

Beef à la mode

Beef à la mode

*1½ kg rump of beef, 1 tbsp oil, 3 tbsps butter,
½ cup thick cream, ½ cup raisins, 1 slice dried
wholemeal bread*

*MARINADE: 2 cups dry red wine, ¾ cup **raspberry
vinegar**, 2 onions, 3 cloves garlic, 3–4 cloves,
2 bay leaves, 1 tsp thyme, ½ tsp rosemary, 1 tsp
juniper berries, 3 carrots, ½ celeriac, salt, pepper*

Cut the scraped carrots and peeled celeriac into smaller pieces. Chop the peeled garlic. Stick cloves into
washed onions. Put all herbs, spices and vegetables into a
saucepan, add the vinegar and wine. Bring to a boil, then
leave to cool.
Rinse and dry the meat. Knead with your hands well. Put
in a stoneware pot, pour the marinade over, cover and
refrigerate for 5–6 days – remember to turn the meat
over every day. Take the meat out of the marinade, dry it
and rub with salt.
Heat the oil in a large, heavy saucepan, add the butter and
melt it. Put in the meat and brown it nicely on all sides.
Strain the marinade. Add all the vegetables from the marinade to the meat and cook covered, basting with the marinade frequently. When the meat is almost done, take it out.
Liquidize the sauce, sieve it, return to the saucepan, put the
meat in and keep simmering. Rinse and blanch the raisins,
drain thoroughly. Grate the bread and together with the
raisins add to the sauce. Take the cooked meat out, cut into
slices. Add some cream to the sauce, heat up and put in
back the sliced meat. Serve with kasha, pasta or potatoes.

Piquant coconut beef

*600 g beef (top flank or rump), 6–8 scallions, 2 tbsps
grated fresh **ginger**, 2 red chili peppers, 1–3 cloves
garlic, 2 tsps grated lemon rind, 4 tbsps shredded
coconut, 3 tbsps oil, ½ cup water or vegetable stock,
1 cup coconut milk, 1 tsp sugar, ground black pepper*

Seed and finely chop the chili peppers. Dice the scallions.
Crush the peeled garlic. Heat a heavy frying pan, put
in the shredded coconut and toast golden brown over a
medium heat. Transfer to a plate and leave aside.

Beef meatballs with sesame seeds

Mix the scallions, ginger, chili, garlic, lemon juice and zest in a bowl. Leave aside for 15 minutes. Knead the rinsed and dried meat, cut into 2 cm cubes. Heat half the oil in a frying pan. Put in the meat cubes in batches, brown well on all sides. Take out with a straining spoon and transfer to a heavy saucepan. Add the remaining oil, heat up, put the prepared onion mixture and fry for 5 minutes. Put in the toasted shredded coconut and keep cooking for another minute, then combine with the meat. Pour water or stock into the frying pan, heat up, then combine with the meat. Add the coconut milk, sugar and pepper, stir and bring to a boil. Turn down the heat, cover and simmer for an hour, or until the meat is tender. Stir from time to time. Serve with rice. NB: The sauce should be fairly thick, but if too much liquid evaporates, you are advised to add a little coconut milk mixed with hot water.

Beef stew with green pepper

700 g beef off the bone (prime rib), 2 tbsps flour, 3 tbsps sunflower oil, 1 tbsp butter, 2 small onions, 1 large carrot, 1–2 celery stalks, 2 small parsnips, 1 tbsp marinated **green peppercorns***, 2 cups beef stock (or stock from cube), ½ tsp ground allspice, ½ cup cream*

Dice the peeled onions. Scrape the carrots and parsnips, rinse and slice. Remove stringy fibres from the celery stalks, slice them. Remove excess fat and stringy bits from the meat. Rinse and dry the meat, cut into cubes, dust with flour. In a large, heavy saucepan heat the oil. Brown the meat cubes in batches, take out with a straining spoon and transfer to a warm plate.
Put the butter into the saucepan, then the vegetables. Fry briskly, then put in the meat and green peppercorns, pour in the hot stock, add the allspice. Stir, bring to a boil. Cover and simmer over a low heat until the meat is tender. Take off the heat and combine with the cream. Best served with pasta and lettuce.

Beef meatballs with sesame seeds

600 g beef off the bone, 100 g fatty bacon or pork fat, 5–6 **shiitake mushrooms***, 100 g drained tinned* **bamboo shoots***, 1 cup finely chopped vegetables (white part of leek, 1 carrot, 1 celery stalk, 1–2 Pekingese*

cabbage leaves), 2 shallots, 1½ tbsps light **soy sauce***, 1½ tbsps* **sherry vinegar***, ½ tsp ground white pepper, salt, 1 tbsp corn or potato flour, oil for deep frying, 1 mixed egg, 1 tbsp* **sesame oil**

SAUCE: 3 tbsps **hoisin sauce***, 1½ tbsps light* **soy sauce***, 1 tbsp sugar, 2 tbsps* **white sesame seeds**

Dice the peeled shallots. Cover the shiitake mushrooms with lukewarm boiled water and leave aside for 15 minutes. Drain well and cut off the stems. Put the meat, bacon (or pork fat), mushrooms and bamboo shoots through a mincer. Combine with the chopped vegetables and shallots, season with salt, pepper, soy sauce and vinegar. Work into a smooth mixture, add the corn flour and again mix thoroughly. With moistened hands shape into walnut-size balls. Heat the oil in a shallow pan. Drop in the meatballs and cook until nicely brown. Take out with a straining spoon, drain excess fat on a paper towel.
Toast the sesame seeds in a hot frying pan. Pour in the sesame oil, soy sauce and hoisin sauce. Add sugar, stir and bring to a boil. Put in the meatballs. Shaking the frying pan over a high heat, coat the meatballs in the sauce and heat up. Serve with pasta or rice.

Beef slices with anchovy paste

700 g beef off the bone, 2 tbsps flour, salt, pepper, 3 tbsps clarified butter, ½ cup stock, ½ cup dry red wine, 4 tbsps **anchovy paste***, 1 cup thick cream*

Rinse and dry the meat, cut into 4 slices. Lightly pound with a mallet, sprinkle with pepper, dredge with flour and fry in butter. Transfer to a saucepan, cover with the stock and simmer for 8–10 minutes. Mix the anchovy paste with the wine (anchovies should be finely chopped). Pour into the meat, stir, cover and cook for 40 minutes. Towards the end, fold in the cream, shake the saucepan and continue cooking for 5 minutes. Serve with kasha, noodles or fried potatoes.

Ginger beefsteaks

600 g beef (prime rib), 1 tbsp oil, 1 tbsp butter, 1 tsp potato flour

MARINADE: ½ cup pineapple juice, ¼ cup **soy sauce**, 2 tbsps dry white wine, 1 tbsp finely chopped fresh ginger (or 1 tsp dry ginger), 1–2 cloves garlic (finely chopped), ¼ tsp ground mustard seeds

Mix the marinade ingredients.

Knead the rinsed and dried meat, cut into 4 slices. Lightly pound with a mallet, put in a deep dish, cover with the marinade and refrigerate for 4–6 hours. Turn the meat slices over from time to time. Take out of the marinade, fry in oil (adding butter towards the end) or grill. Bring the marinade to a boil, pour in 3 tablespoons water mixed with potato flour. Stir and heat up until the sauce thickens. Serve the sauce separately in a sauceboat.

Rib of beef in black sauce

800 g rib of beef, 1 ½ tbsps **fermented black bean paste**, ½ tsp salt, 3 tbsps dark **soy sauce**, 2 tbsps rice wine or dry sherry, 2–3 cloves garlic, 3 tbsps **peanut oil**, 1 tbsp **bamboo shoots** cut in fine strips, 2 tbsps finely chopped chives

Chop the peeled garlic and crush with salt. Rinse and dry the meat, divide into portions. Rub with salt with garlic and leave for 30–40 minutes. Mix the bean paste with the soy sauce and rice wine (or sherry). Briskly fry the ribs in oil until they are nicely brown. Pour in the prepared sauce and 1 cup water. Stir, cover and simmer until the meat is tender and the liquid is reduced by half. Before serving, coat the meat with the sauce, sprinkle with chopped chives and bamboo shoots. Serve with rice.

Lamb and mutton

Leg of lamb with savoury stuffing

1½ kg leg of mutton (off the bone), 4–6 cloves garlic, 1 lemon, 1 tbsp flour, 1 tbsp mild mustard, 1 tbsp each chopped parsley and fresh thyme, ½ tbsp chopped fresh rosemary, ½ tsp ground allspice, ½ tsp herbal salt, 1 tsp marinated **green peppercorns**, ¼ cup light stock or dry white wine, 1 tsp chopped fresh mint leaves, 1 tsp potato flour, 2 tbsps cold boiled water

Scrub the lemon, scald with boiling water, grate the rind. Peel off the white skin, slice and remove the pips. Remove the membranes and fat from the meat. Rinse and dry the meat, knead thoroughly. Cut the peeled garlic into sticks. Pound the peppercorns in a mortar. Combine the thyme, parsley and rosemary with the mustard, crushed pepper, lemon zest, allspice and salt. Blend to obtain a smooth paste.
Heat the oven to 180–190°C. Pierce the meat with a sharp-pointed knife in several places, fill the openings with the paste and a stick of garlic. Place the meat on grease-proof paper smeared with oil or on aluminium foil, brush with the remaining paste. Put lemon slices on top. Wrap up in the paper or foil and another piece of greaseproof paper. Place in a roasting tin and put in the preheated oven for 1 hour. Take it out, remove the paper and return to the oven to brown it (c. 30–40 minutes), basting with the stock or wine. Turn off the heat and leave the meat in the oven for another 10–15 minutes. Pour the roasting juices into a saucepan, combine with the potato flour mixed with water. Stirring all the time, hit up until the sauce thickens. Add the mint and season to taste. Cut the meat into slices. Serve with potato chips or baked potatoes, French beans or carrot salad. Serve the sauce separately in a sauceboat.

Lamb with bell peppers

*600 g lean lamb (off the bone), 1 each green, red and orange bell pepper, 1 large red onion, 5 tbsps **fermented black bean paste**, 1 tbsp **five-spice powder**, 4 tbsps sunflower oil, 1 egg yolk, 1 tbsp corn flour*

Rinse and dry the meat, cut into thin strips. Halve the peeled onion and slice it. Remove the stalks and seeds from the bell peppers, cut the flesh into strips. In a bowl mix the egg yolk with the corn flour and five-spice powder, then combine with the meat.

Heat 1 tablespoon oil in a wok, wash its sides with it, then pour out the oil. Heat the remaining oil, put in the meat and stir fry for 5–6 minutes to brown it. Add the onion and peppers, keep frying for another 5–6 minutes. Put in the bean paste, mix thoroughly and heat up. Serve with soy or rice noodles or with rice.

Lamb with vegetables

*600 g lean lamb (leg or saddle), 3–4 tbsps **pine nuts**, 1 tbsp each **peanut oil** and **sesame oil**, 300 g button mushrooms, 3 celery stalks, 3–4 scallions, 125 g green peas (fresh, tinned or frozen), 1 red bell pepper, 1 ½ cups bean sprouts*

*SAUCE: ½ cup beef stock (or stock from cube), 1 tbsp each potato flour, **sherry vinegar** or dry sherry and **soy sauce**, 1 tsp grated fresh ginger, 1 tbsp honey*

SAUCE: Mix all ingredients thoroughly, cover and leave aside for 15 minutes.

Slice the washed and dried mushrooms. Remove stringy fibres from the celery, cut the stalks into fine slices. Dice the scallions.
Remove membranes and fat from the meat. Rinse and dry it, cut against the grain into thin strips. Heat the peanut oil in a wok or a heavy frying pan, washing the sides with it. Stir fry the meat in batches to brown it. Take out browned strips of meat with a straining spoon, drain on a paper towel. Leave aside. Put the pine nuts into the frying pan, add the sesame oil, then the mushrooms, celery, green peas and scallions. Fry for 2 minutes over a high heat, stir-

ring all the time. Mix thoroughly the prepared sauce and pour into the frying pan. Put in the bean shoots and heat up until the sauce thickens. Put in the meat and heat up again. Serve immediately, with pasta or rice.

Mutton fillets

*700 g leg of mutton or lamb (off the bone), 70 g pork fat, 1 large onion, 2–3 cloves garlic, 1 cup dry red wine, 1 tsp potato flour, 3 tbsps oil, 1 tsp paprika, 3 tbsps chopped dill, 1 tsp chopped fresh tarragon leaves, ½ tsp **turmeric**, ½ coffee spoon ground ginger, salt, 1 cup meat or vegetable stock*

Rinse and dry the meat, remove membranes and fat. Cut the meat into 8 slices, pound each lightly with a mallet. Crush the peeled garlic, mix with salt. Rub the meat with the mixture and leave aside for 15–20 minutes. Heat the oil in a heavy frying pan, brown the meat slices on both sides, transfer them to a saucepan. Dice the pork fat, fry briskly in the same frying pan. Add the sliced peeled onion, brown lightly, then put into the saucepan. Cover the meat with the hot stock, put a lid on and simmer over a medium heat for 40 minutes. Take the lead off, reduce the sauce a little. Add the wine, turmeric, ginger and paprika, and salt to taste. Heat up. When the meat is tender, take it out, place on a warm serving dish and keep warm. Bring the sauce to a boil, add the tarragon and potato flour mixed with 1 tablespoon water. Stirring all the time, heat up until the sauce thickens. Pour the sauce over the meat, sprinkle with chopped dill on top. Serve with boiled potatoes or rice.

Oriental lamb stew

*600 g lamb or young, lean mutton (off the bone), 6–8 scallions, 2–3 cloves garlic, 1 Pekingese cabbage (c. 200 g), 1 tsp crushed **Sichuan pepper**, 2 tbsps dark **soy sauce**, 5 tbsps **oyster sauce**, 2 tbsps **peanut oil***

Rinse and dry the meat, cut into thin strips. Sprinkle with Sichuan pepper and mix thoroughly. Finely chop the peeled garlic. Dice the scallions. Rinse and dry the Pekingese cabbage, shred it into 1 ½ – 2 cm wide strips. Heat 1 tablespoon oil in a wok, wash its sides with it, then pour

Lamb stew with coriander

out the oil. Heat the remaining oil, put in the meat and stir fry for 5 minutes. When it browns nicely, put in the garlic and scallions, stir and add the soy sauce. Continue frying for 2–3 minutes. Put in the oyster sauce and shredded cabbage, stir fry for 2–3 minutes, or until the sauce begins to boil and the cabbage gets limp. Serve with noodles, rice or prawn crackers.

Lamb stew with coriander

*800 g leg of lamb (off the bone), 1 tbsp olive oil, 2–3 shallots or scallions (without leaves), 2–3 cloves garlic, 1 tbsp grated fresh ginger, 1 tbsp ground coriander seeds, 2 tbsps ground cumin, 1 tsp **turmeric**, ground black pepper, salt, 2 cups chicken stock, 4–5 tbsps finely chopped coriander leaves*

Peel and finely chop the onions and garlic. Clean the meat of membranes and excess fat, cut into bite-size cubes. Heat the oil in a heavy saucepan. Fry the meat in batches for 2 minutes over a medium heat until it nicely browns. Take out with a straining spoon and drain on a paper towel. Put the onions and garlic into the pan, fry for 2 minutes, then add all spices and continue frying for another 1–2 minutes. Return the fried meat to the pan, pour in the stock and half the coriander leaves, bring to a boil. Turn down the heat, cover and simmer for 45–55 minutes, or until the meat is tender. Add salt to taste, sprinkle with the remaining coriander leaves, mix well. Serve with rice and vegetables of the season.

Meatballs in tomato sauce

*600 g minced meat (pork or veal), 2 eggs, 70 g **pine nuts** or sunflower seeds, breadcrumbs, 2 small onions, 2 tsps dried thyme, 4 tbsps olive oil, salt, pepper*

*SAUCE: 1 tin skinned whole tomatoes (c. 300 g), 2 tbsps olive oil, salt, pepper, 2 tbsps chopped basil leaves, 2 finely diced **sun-dried tomatoes***

SAUCE: Heat the oil in a small heavy saucepan, put in the tomatoes and cook until they disintegrate. Season with pepper and salt, add the chopped basil and sun-dried tomatoes, stir. Keep it warm.

MEATBALLS: Brown the finely chopped peeled onion in a little oil. Toast the pine nuts (or sunflower seeds) in a hot frying pan. Combine the onion and the nuts with the meat, add the thyme and 1 egg. Season to taste and work into a smooth mixture. With moistened hands form 12 meatballs. Coat each meatball in mixed egg and dredge with breadcrumbs. Heat the remaining oil in a large, heavy frying pan. Fry the meatballs over a high heat for about 10 minutes. Serve with the prepared tomato sauce and rice.

Rabbit, Italian style

*1–1½ kg saddle of rabbit, 1 cup pitted **black olives**, 1 tin skinned whole tomatoes, 2–3 cloves garlic, 1–2 rosemary sprigs, 1 cup dry white wine (or light chicken stock + 1 tbsp lemon juice), ½ cup olive oil, salt, freshly ground pepper*

Finely chop the peeled garlic. Rinse and dry the rabbit. In a heavy saucepan brown it in hot oil on all sides. Sprinkle with garlic, salt and pepper, add rosemary and wine, cover and simmer for 20–25 minutes. Mash the tomatoes with a fork, put in the saucepan. Add the halved olives and stew until the meat is tender. Add salt and pepper if necessary.

Shrimps, prawns and crabs

Prawn cocktail

16 each white and green asparagus stalks (fresh or tinned), 1 tbsp sugar, 1 tbsp butter, 1 tbsp lemon juice, salt, 16 frozen king prawns, 16 cherry tomatoes, 3–4 cloves garlic, 2 tbsps **grape-seed oil**, sugar, salt, dill sprigs, 1 iceberg lettuce

SAUCE: ½ cup thick mayonnaise, 3 tbsps **balsamic vinegar**, a pinch of caster sugar

Clean the asparagus stalks, wash and dry them. Boil salted water with sugar, butter and lemon juice, put in the asparagus and cook for 10–15 minutes. Take out with a straining spoon, drain well. Cut off the tips and cut the stalks into 1 cm pieces. Heat the oil in a heavy frying pan. Put in the peeled and sliced garlic and the shrimps. Briskly fry over a high heat, then simmer a little longer and leave to cool. Halve the washed tomatoes. Cut the lettuce in strips.
SAUCE: Mix the mayonnaise with the balsamic vinegar and a pinch of sugar.
Combine the asparagus pieces with the tomatoes, pour the sauce over, mix and season to taste. In 4 bowls on a bed of lettuce strips place portions of asparagus and tomato mix, arrange the shrimps and asparagus tips on top, garnish with chopped dill.

Prawns in black bean sauce

500 g medium-size peeled prawns (frozen and boiled), 1 tbsp each **black bean sauce**, **oyster sauce** and dry sherry, ½ tsp ginger juice, 1 tsp sugar, 1–1½ tbsp boiled water, 1 tbsp oil

Put the frozen prawns in boiling water for 1–2 minutes, take out, rinse under cold water and dry. Peel a piece of fresh ginger, chop it finely, then put through a garlic press to produce juice. Mix the oyster sauce with the black bean sauce, ginger juice, sugar and sherry. Heat the oil in a heavy frying pan. Put in the prawns and fry for 1–2 minutes. Put in the prepared sauce and stirring all the time cook over a low heat for 1 minute. Add some water, stir and heat up for 2 minutes. Serve as a hot snack with white bread or rice and lettuce.

Fried shrimps in chili sauce

500–600 g frozen peeled shrimps, 3 egg whites, ¾ cup corn flour, oil for deep frying, 8–10 cloves garlic,

1 tbsp chopped fresh ginger, 1 tbsp **chili sauce**, 2 shallots, 2 tbsps **peanut oil**, 1 tsp **sesame oil**

SAUCE: 1 tbsp **light soy sauce**, a pinch of cayenne pepper, 1 tbsp sugar, ¼ cup dry sherry, ¼ cup chicken stock, salt, 1 tsp corn flour

Put the frozen shrimps in boiling water, cook for 1–2 minutes, take out, rinse under cold water and dry well.
SAUCE: Mix all ingredients of the sauce well.
Peel the shallots and garlic, chop finely. Heat the peanut oil in a frying pan. Put in the garlic, shallots and ginger and fry for 1–2 minutes. Add the chili sauce and the mixed ingredients of the sauce. Stirring all the time, cook 1–2 minutes, take off the heat but keep warm.
BATTER: Whisk the egg whites into stiff peaks. Combine with half the corn flour.
Heat the oil in a large frying pan. Dredge the shrimps in the remaining flour, then coat them in the batter and deep fry them in batches. Heat the oil again and return all shrimps to the frying pan for 30 seconds. Take them out with a straining spoon, drain on a paper towel. Arrange the shrimps in a warm serving dish. Pour the sesame oil into another frying pan, combine with the prepared sauce and heat up. Pour the sauce over the shrimps. Serve immediately.

Hot crab snack

2 tins crab meat (350 g), 250 g French beans, 3–4 scallions, 2–3 cloves garlic, ½ cup dry sherry, 1 tbsp soy oil, 2 tbsps **sesame oil**, 1 tbsp **soy sayce**, ½ tsp **chili sauce**, ½ tsp ground **Sichuan pepper**, grated rind of 1 lemon, juice of ½ lemon

Mix the sherry with the sesame oil, soy sauce, chili sauce and Sichuan pepper. Dice the onions, chop the peeled garlic finely. Bring salted water to a boil, put in the topped and tailed beans and cook for 8–10 minutes. Drain and keep warm. Heat the soy oil in a frying pan, put in the garlic and lemon zest, stir and fry for 20–30 seconds. Add the drained crab meat and continue frying for 1–2 minutes. Pour in the prepared sauce, stir, heat up and sprinkle with lemon juice. Arrange the hot crab meat in a warm platter, surround with the French beans and sprinkle with chopped scallions.

Fried shrimps in chili sauce

Cold buffet

Stuffed cucumbers

*6 short, firm cucumbers, 180 g honey, 120 g dehusked walnuts, 5 grains allspice (crushed in a mortar), a pinch of grated nutmeg, salt, pepper, 4–5 pieces **candied ginger**, 6 lettuce leaves*

Wash the cucumbers. Cut lengthwise in halves. Scoop out the flesh with a teaspoon, taking care not to damage the green skin. Chop the flesh finely, salt it, then drain in a sieve. Grind the walnuts, mix with the honey. Combine with the chopped cucumbers, season with allspice, nutmeg and pepper to taste. Liquidize the mixture. Fill the cucumber halves with it. Arrange the cucumbers on a bed of lettuce leaves, garnish with candied ginger.

Asparagus in sesame sauce

*500 g asparagus stalks, 1 tsp each lemon juice, sugar, honey and butter, 2–3 tbsps **sesame seeds**, 2–3 tbsps **soy sauce**, salt*

Boil salted water with sugar, butter and lemon juice. Put in the cleaned asparagus stalks and cook for 15 minutes. Take out the stalks, cut into 5–7 cm pieces, arrange in a serving dish. Toast the sesame seeds. In a small saucepan bring the soy sauce and honey to a boil, put in the sesame seeds, stir. Pour the sauce over the asparagus.

Admiral's chanterelles

*500 g chanterelles, 1 large onion, 2 tbsps butter, a bunch of dill, 200 g **soy noodles**, 5–6 leaves Pekingese cabbage*

*SAUCE: 2 tbsps **grape-seed oil**, 1 tbsp **rice vinegar**, 1 tsp white vinegar, salt, pepper*

Mix the sauce ingredients thoroughly. Refrigerate for 15 minutes.

Wash the mushrooms thoroughly, drain them, halve the larger ones. Chop the peeled onion and soften in butter. Put in the mushrooms, cover and stew for 30 minutes. Towards the end put in the chopped dill, salt and pepper to taste. Cook the noodles separately, strain, rinse under cold water, drain well. Combine the cool mushrooms and noodles, mix in the shredded cabbage leaves. Pour the sauce over, mix gently.

Piquant herring roulades

*8 herring fillets, 2 tbsps butter, 1 large onion, 1 each red and green bell pepper, 2 firm, fleshy tomatoes, 2 tbsps tomato paste, a pinch of sugar, 1 cup red wine, 3–4 drops **Tabasco sauce**, salt, pepper, 1 tsp paprika, ½ tsp **curry powder**, 2 tbsps each chopped parsley and chives, 2–3 lettuce leaves, 2–3 dill and parsley sprigs*

Rinse the fillets under running water, dry well. Halve the peeled onion, slice finely. Remove the stalks and seeds from the bell peppers, cut the flesh in strips. Blanch and skin the tomato, cut in cubes, remove the seeds.
In a frying pan soften the onion in butter, add the peppers and fry a little longer. Put in the tomato cubes, stir and fry for another 1–2 minutes. Mix the tomato paste with sugar, Tabasco and wine. Combine with the vegetables, stir and cook a little longer. Add the chopped dill and parsley, season with pepper, paprika, curry powder and salt, mix well. Take off the heat and leave to cool.
Roll up the herring fillets. Arrange them on a bed of lettuce leaves. Surround with the piquant vegetables, cover with foil and refrigerate for 2–3 hours. Before serving, garnish with dill and parsley sprigs.

Herring fillets with green peppercorns

300 g herring fillets, 1 small red bell pepper, 2–3 lettuce leaves, 5–6 dill sprigs

*SAUCE: 2–3 tbsps thick sour cream, ½ tsp lemon juice, ¼ tsp **Worcester sauce**, a pinch of each salt, caster sugar and white pepper, 1 tsp marinated green peppercorns*

SAUCE: In a bowl mix the cream with the lemon juice, Worcester sauce, salt, pepper and caster sugar. Add the drained green peppercorns, cover and refrigerate.
Rinse and dry the fillets, cut into wide strips. Seed and wash the bell pepper, chop finely and combine with the cream sauce. Line a serving dish with lettuce leaves, arrange the herring pieces on top, cover with the sauce. Garnish with dill sprigs.

Herring, Danish style

4 herrings, 2 cups milk, 8–10 hard-boiled quail eggs and 6–8 dill sprigs for garnishing

SAUCE: ½ cup thick mayonnaise, ½ cup thick sour cream, 1 tsp ketchup, 1 large onion, 3 tbsps **capers**, 1–2 pickled gherkins, a bunch of chives, 1 tsp **curry powder**, salt, pepper, sugar

SAUCE: Finely chop the peeled onion, half the dill and capers. Dice the gherkins. In a bowl mix the mayonnaise with the cream and curry powder. Combine with the onion, chopped dill and gherkins. Season with pepper, sugar and salt. Cover and refrigerate.
Soak the herrings in milk, then remove the skins and bones, wash and dry. Cut into bite-size pieces, arrange in a serving dish and cover with the sauce. Garnish with the shelled and halved quail eggs and dill sprigs.

Eggs in piquant sauce

8 hard-boiled eggs, 5–6 parsley sprigs and 2–3 pieces marinated red bell pepper for garnishing

SAUCE: 8 tbsps **ajvar paste**, 3 tbsps thick sour cream, 2 tbsps dry white wine, salt, pepper, a pinch of sugar to taste

Gently mix all ingredients of the sauce in a bowl. Cover and refrigerate for 20–30 minutes. Pour the sauce into a rather deep serving dish, arrange halves of the shelled eggs, garnish with strips of red pepper and with parsley sprigs.

Eggs, Chinese style

8 eggs, 1 tsp salt, 1 tbsp each light and dark **soy sauce**, 2 tbsps black tea leaves, 2 **anise stars**, a piece of cinnamon and a piece of dried orange peel, ½ tsp salt

Put the washed eggs into a saucepan, cover with water, add salt and cook over a low heat for 20 minutes. Take them out and put under running cold water. Crack the shells all over. Put the eggs in a saucepan, add the mixed light and dark soy sauce, tea leaves, anise seeds, cinnamon, orange peel and salt. Cover with 2 cups water, bring to a boil. Turn the heat down, put a lid on and simmer for 3 hours (adding more water when necessary). Leave aside for 36 hours. Before serving, remove the shells and quarter the eggs. Such eggs can be kept in the fridge for 4–5 days and preserve their flavour.

Brown eggs

4 hard-boiled eggs, 1 cup **soy sauce**, ½ tsp paprika, a pinch of sugar, 1 glass vodka

Bring the soy sauce with paprika and sugar to a boil. Put the shelled eggs in, add the vodka. Cover and cook for 10 minutes, then leave aside to cool. Serve coated with mayonnaise and sprinkled with chopped chives or use to garnish cold meat platters. Eggs prepared in this way are nicely brown in colour and have a sharp salty taste.

Marbled eggs

8 hard-boiled eggs in shells, 4 tbsps Chinese tea leaves, 4–5 tbsps **soy sauce**, 6 cloves, a piece of cinnamon, ½ tsp crushed dried chili pepper, 8 grains allspice, 15 peppercorns, 12 coriander seeds, 1 tsp salt, ½ tsp sugar, 1 glass vodka, 1–1½ cups water

In a shallow saucepan bring the water to a boil, add all the spices, soy sauce, tea leaves, salt, sugar and vodka. Crack the egg shells all over. Put the eggs in the saucepan and simmer over a low heat for 20 minutes, turning them over from time to time. Leave aside to cool, then remove the shells. Serve with various sauces or use to garnish cold meat platters.

Terrines and pastes

Chestnut terrine

1 tin chestnuts (c. 600 g), 100 g button mushrooms, 1 cup ground walnuts, 2 celery stalks, 1 small onion, 1–2 cloves garlic, 1 tbsp wholemeal flour, 1½ tbsps butter, 1 tsp paprika, 1–2 tbsps breadcrumbs, 2 tbsp **soy sauce**, *½ cup dry red wine, salt, freshly ground pepper*

Drain the chestnuts (reserve the brine). Put into salted boiling water and cook for 3–4 minutes. When tender, drain thoroughly, leave to cool, then chop finely or grind. Finely chop the peeled onion and garlic. Remove stringy fibres from the celery stalks, chop the stalks finely. Slice the cleaned mushrooms.

Melt the butter in a frying pan, put in the onion and garlic and stir fry for 2–3 minutes, or until light golden. Add the mushrooms, fry briskly over a high heat, then cover and simmer over a low heat for 7–8 minutes. Dust with the flour and paprika, stir. Pour in 4–5 tablespoons brine and the wine, bring to a boil, then stirring cook over a low heat for 4–5 minutes. When the mixture thickens, leave it to cool a little. Combine the chestnuts with the walnuts and celery. Fold in the mushroom mixture, add the soy sauce. Season with pepper and salt. Mix thoroughly, adding enough breadcrumbs to make the mixture thick and not too moist. Heat the oven to 190–200°C. Line a terrine mould with greaseproof paper, brush with oil or butter. Arrange the mixture in the mould, cover with aluminium foil and bake in the oven for 55–65 minutes. Serve hot or cold.

Terrine with redcurrants

250 g each pork, veal, streaky bacon and boned duck breast, 1 egg, 1 small glass brandy, 1 tbsp thick cream, 100 g redcurrants, 30 g **pistachios**, *1 tsp ground cinnamon, 2 crushed cloves, a pinch of grated nutmeg, salt, pepper, 1–2 sprigs of each fresh thyme and basil, 2 bay leafs, 1 tsp butter*

Heat the oven to 180–190°C. Rinse and stalk the currants. Rinse and dry the meat, cut in cubes, together with the pistachios put through a mincer with a fine-grade cutter, then through a blender to produce a smooth, soft mixture. Break in an egg, add the brandy, cream and spices (cinnamon, cloves, nutmeg, salt and pepper). Mix thoroughly, add the redcurrants and gently mix again. Grease a terrine mould with butter, put the mixture in. Even out the surface with a moistened knife, put the bay leaves and thyme and basil sprigs on top. Place the mould in a larger pan filled with water and put into the preheated oven. Bake for 60–70 minutes, then leave in the oven for another 15–20 minutes. Take out, put a plate of the right size on top, weigh it down to make the terrine more compact. Leave to cool. Serve with pickles and some savoury sauce.

Fish terrine

300 g pikeperch fillets (or any white sea fish soaked in milk, such as cod, hake or pollock), 2 egg whites, 300 g cream (36%), 60 g shelled **pistachios**, *3 tbsps chopped dill, 12 slices smoked salmon (200 g), ½ tsp chili powder, salt, pepper, 2 tbsps butter, cherry tomatoes and dill sprigs for garnishing*

Rinse the fillets, dry thoroughly, chop very finely. Whisk the egg whites a little. Finely chop the pistachios. In a bowl combine the fish with the egg whites, add salt, pepper and chili powder. Put the bowl in a larger pan filled with ice cubes and vigorously whisk or blend, slowly adding the cream, until the mixture is smooth and soft. Mix in the pistachios and dill. Heat the oven to 190°C. Brush an oven-proof dish with butter, line with the salmon slices, leaving the ends hanging over the side of the dish. Put in the forcemeat, fold up the ends of salmon slices. Place the dish in a baking tin filled with water, put in the preheated oven and bake for 30–35 minutes. Then turn off the oven and leave the terrine in for another 20 minutes. Take out, leave to cool, then gently transfer to a serving dish. Garnish with cherry tomatoes and dill sprigs.

Curd cheese with apples

250 g low-fat curd cheese, 2 cooking apples, 1 tbsp pickled **green peppercorns**, 1 large onion, 2 tbsps butter, 1cup dry white wine, juice of 1 lemon, salt, freshly ground black pepper, a pinch of sugar, 2 tbsps freshly grated horseradish, 2 tbsps finely chopped lemon balm, lemon balm leaves for garnishing

Finely chop the peeled onion. Grate the peeled apples, sprinkle with 1 tablespoon lemon juice. Melt the butter in a frying pan, soften the onion a little. Put in the apples and fry for 2–3 minutes. Add the green peppercorns and white wine, bring to a boil and take off the heat. Leave to cool, then combine with the curd cheese, grated horseradish, chopped lemon balm and the remaining lemon juice. Adjust the seasoning with salt, pepper and sugar, refrigerate for 15 minutes. Before serving, garnish with lemon balm leaves.

Curd cheese paste

300 g full-cream curd cheese, 1 clove garlic, ½ tsp freshly ground pepper, 2–3 **sun-dried tomatoes** in oil, 1 tsp chopped fresh oregano leaves, salt

Crush the peeled garlic and mix with salt. Drain the sun-dried tomatoes and chop finely. Combine with the garlic, cheese, oregano and pepper. Refrigerate.

Savoury Roquefort paste

250 g Roquefort cheese (or any other blue cheese), 150 g curd cheese, 10–15 marinated **green peppercorns**, 10–12 capers, 2 tbsps chopped parsley, ground green pepper

Blend the Roquefort with the curd cheese, add the chopped capers, marinated peppercorns and parsley. Season with ground green pepper. Serve with bread or use to stuff pancakes, mushrooms, artichokes or cucumbers.

Red bell pepper paste

3 red bell peppers, 1 small red onion, 2 tbsps olive oil, 1 tbsp chopped fresh basil leaves, 1–2 cloves garlic,

100 g mascarpone cheese, 2–3 **sun-dried tomatoes** in oil, 1 tbsps lemon juice, salt, freshly ground black pepper

Remove the stalks and seeds from the bell peppers, rinse and dry the flesh, quarter. Cut the peeled onion into thick slices. Heat the oven to 200°C. Put the peppers and onion on a baking sheet, sprinkle with olive oil and bake for 30 minutes, or until the peppers are soft. Leave to cool a little, then liquidize together with the sun-dried tomatoes and gradually adding the mascarpone, chopped peeled garlic, lemon juice and basil. Season with pepper and salt, transfer to a serving bowl and refrigerate.

Mackerel paste

1 large smoked mackerel (200–250 g), 1 tsp marinated **green pepper**, 1 small cucumber, 2 tbsps thick sour cream, 1 tbsp lemon juice, salt, dill sprigs for garnishing

Peel the cucumber, halve lengthwise, remove the seeds and chop the flesh finely. Sprinkle with salt, leave aside for a little, then drain of excess liquid. Drain the green pepper, chop finely.
Remove the skin and bones from the fish. Divide the flesh into small pieces. Blend with the cream and lemon juice until the mixture is smooth. Combine with the cucumber and chopped pepper, refrigerate for 20 minutes. Before serving, garnish with dill sprigs.

Pauper's caviar

2–3 young aubergines, 2–3 cloves garlic, ¼ cup **tahini paste**, salt, 3 tbsps lemon juice, ¼ tsp grated lemon rind, 2 tbsps olive oil, 1 tbsp **sesame seeds**

Rinse and dry the aubergines, prick them with a fork and bake in a preheated oven for about 50 minutes, or until their skin blackens. Leave to cool, then peel finely, halve lengthwise and remove the seeds. Blend the aubergines with the lemon juice, lemon zest and crushed peeled garlic mixed with salt. Blending all the time gradually add the oil and tahini paste. Put into a bowl, cover and refrigerate. Before serving, sprinkle with toasted sesame seeds.

Chickpea paste

*1 tin (300 g) chickpeas, 5 tbsps **tahini paste**, 4 tbsps **peanut oil**, 1 tbsp **sesame oil**, 2 tbsps **curry powder**, salt, pepper, 1 tbsp **sesame seeds**, parsley sprigs for garnishing*

Drain the chickpeas (reserve 1–2 tablespoons sauce). Blend them with the sesame paste, peanut oil, sesame oil and curry powder, add salt and pepper to taste. Transfer the smooth mixture to a serving bowl, cover and refrigerate for 2–3 hours. Before serving, sprinkle with toasted sesame seeds and garnish with parsley sprigs. Use as a bread spread or a dip for crudités, or serve it hot with rice. You may also use it as pancake filling.

Herbal paste

*1 bunch of each basil, thyme and sage, 3–4 cloves garlic, 10–12 pitted black olives, 1 tsp ground **cardamom**, 3 tbsps sunflower seeds, ¾ cup grated cheese, 1 cup olive oil, salt, pepper*

Rinse and dry the herbs, chop finely. Crush the peeled garlic. Blend the herbs, garlic, olives, sunflower seeds and cardamom, gradually adding the oil and grated cheese. Add salt and pepper to taste. Serve with meat or fish. If you add 3–5 tablespoons stock or wine, you may use it as a sauce with pasta, but remember not to heat it up or cook. In a tightly closed glass jar the paste will keep for 2 weeks in the fridge.

Preserves Pastes and sauces

Home-made tahini paste

*100 g **sesame seeds**, 1 tbsp olive oil, 1–2 tbsps **sesame oil***

Toast the sesame seeds lightly, then crush in a mortar or grind. Gradually adding the olive and sesame oils, blend into a smooth cream. Put in a glass jar, close tightly and store in the fridge.

This is an excellent condiment used in sauces, soups and stews. It goes well with steamed broccoli, Brussels sprouts and cauliflower and makes a tasty bread spread.

Home-made black bean paste

*60 g dried black beans, 2 cups vegetable stock (or stock from cube), 1 fresh chili pepper, 1½ tsps finely chopped fresh ginger, 1 tbsp **malt vinegar**, 1 tbsp **soy sauce**, 1 tbsp sugar*

Put the rinsed beans into a saucepan, cover with water and leave overnight. The following day drain, return to the saucepan, cover with boiled water and cook for 8–10 minutes, then drain again. Finely chop the seeded chili pepper, combine with the ginger and parboiled beans. Put into the saucepan, cover with the vegetable stock, add sugar, soy sauce and vinegar. Mix well, bring to a boil, then cook over a low heat for 40–45 minutes. Liquidize or sieve the beans, pour the paste into small glass jars, close tightly and store in the fridge. If you want it to keep longer, pasteurize for 15–20 minutes.

Home-made harissa

*50 g dried red chili peppers, 2–3 cloves garlic, 1 tsp caraway seeds, 1½ tsps **cumin**, 3 tbsps coriander seeds, 1 tsp dried mint leaves, salt, olive oil*

Seed the peppers, cover with a little boiled water and leave aside for half an hour. Drain and mince them. Peel and chop the garlic, crush it with salt. Blend all the ingredients with the addition of 5–6 tablespoons oil. Put in glass jars, close tightly and store in the fridge.

Home-made sambal ulek

250 g fresh red chili peppers, 1 tbsps each brown sugar and salt, 2 tbsps oil

Put the peppers in a hot frying pan, heat up over a medium heat, leave to cool. Seed the peppers, blend together with the salt, sugar and oil. If you want your sambal ulek to be really burning hot, do not seed the pepper pods.

Aubergine ajvar

2 kg young, fresh aubergines, 250 g yellow bell peppers, 100 g tomatoes, a bunch of parsley, a bunch of dill, 2 tbsps salt

Heat the oven to 200–220°C. Chop the parsley and dill very finely. Rinse the aubergines, peppers and tomatoes, put on a baking sheet and place in the oven. When they are ready, take them out, leave to cool, then skin and liquidize to produce a smooth paste. Add salt, pour into a heavy saucepan and bring to a boil. Turn down the heat and simmer, stirring frequently, until the paste is thick enough. Combine with the chopped parsley and dill, adjust the seasoning and pour into small glass jar. Close tightly and pasteurize for 15–20 minutes.

Home-made bell pepper ajvar

2 kg fleshy bell peppers (of different colours), 1 kg young aubergines, 1–2 bulbs garlic, salt, sugar, vinegar to taste, 3 tbsps sunflower oil

Rinse and dry the aubergines and peppers. Remove the stalks and seeds from the peppers. Place the aubergines and peppers on a baking sheet and put into a pre-heated oven. Bake them, leave to cool, then skin. Mush the vegetables with a fork or chop very finely. Heat the oil in a heavy saucepan, put in the vegetables and, stirring all the time, cook for 10 minutes. Chop the peeled garlic and crush with salt. Add to the vegetables, pour in the vinegar (c. 1 cup), add salt, sugar and pepper to taste. Stirring continuously, cook until the paste thickens. Put the paste into glass jars and pasteurize for 15–20 minutes.
It should be piquant, but not to vinegary. Depending on your preferences you may add more or less garlic, or enrich the paste with dried or fresh herbs.

Piquant ginger sauce

*40 g fresh ginger, 200 g sugar, 1 cup boiled water, 1 tsp **sambal ulek**, 2 tbsps **soy sauce**, 5 tbsps **red vinegar**, 1 tsp each freshly ground pepper, salt and rice or potato flour, 2 tbsps cold boiled water*

Chop or grate the peeled ginger very finely. Pour the sugar into a heavy hot saucepan and stirring all the time brown it. Still stirring, gradually add boiled water until the sugar melts. Add the ginger, salt, pepper and sambal ulek, soy sauce and vinegar. Mix thoroughly and simmer, uncovered, for 10 minutes. Mix the corn (or potato) flour with 2 tablespoons water. Pour the mixture into the boiling sauce. Stirring continuously, heat up until the sauce thickens. Pour the hot sauce into small glass jars. It will keep in the fridge for months. It goes well with cold meats and poultry.

Barbecue sauce

*2 large onions, 3–4 cloves garlic, 200 g (1 large tin) tomato concentrate, ½ cup dry white wine, ¼ cup white vinegar, 3 tbsps liquid honey (buckwheat or heather), 5 tbsps sunflower or soy oil, 1 tsp **Worcester sauce**, 3–5 drops **Tabasco sauce**, 1 tbsp mustard, ½ tsp each dried thyme, basil and savory, 1 bay leaf, celery salt and ground black pepper to taste* ix the tomato concentrate with wine. Finely chop the peeled onions and garlic. Heat the oil in a saucepan, soften the onions and garlic. Pour in the tomato concentrate with wine. Stirring, cook over a low heat for 6–8 minutes. Add the bay leaf, herbs, mustard, honey, Worcester sauce and Tabasco. Pour in the remaining wine, mix thoroughly and cook, uncovered, for 10 minutes, stirring frequently. Towards the end season with celery salt and pepper, and take out the bay leaf. Serve to fried and grilled meat. In a tightly closed glass jar it will keep for several days in the fridge.

Apricot and apple sauce

500 g dried apricots, 2 large cooking apples, 3 large onions, 125 g raisins, 2 cups **rose vinegar**, *250 g sugar, 1½ tsps salt, 1 tsp ground mustard seeds, 1 tsp finely chopped fresh ginger, ½ tsp ground allspice*

inse the apricots and cut in thin strips. Blanch and drain the raisins. Peel and core the apples, grate them coarsely. Put all the sauce ingredients into a saucepan, cover with the vinegar and bring to a boil, then cook over a low heat, stirring frequently, for 1 hour. Pour the hot sauce into glass jars, close tightly and pasteurize for 10–15 minutes. This way the sauce can keep for over a year. It is an excellent accompaniment to roast and fried meat, served hot or cold.

Miscellaneous

Pureed carrots and water chestnuts

500 g carrots, 1 small tin **water chestnuts**, *1 shallot or 1 brown onion, 2–3 eggs, 2–3 tbsps thick cream, 2 tbsps butter, ¾ cup milk, ¼ tsp grated nutmeg, salt, white pepper*

rate the scraped carrots. Drain the water chestnuts. Finely chop the peeled onions. Melt the butter in a saucepan, put in the carrots, add the milk, cover and cook over a low heat for 6–8 minutes, stirring occasionally. Slice 2 water chestnuts and leave aside. Dice the remaining chestnuts. Mix the eggs with the cream, add salt, pepper and nutmeg. Combine the carrots with the onion and diced chestnuts and liquidize, gradually adding the egg and cream mixture. Return to the saucepan, put in the sliced chestnuts, stir and heat up over a low heat. Serve with meat and poultry.

Hot snack of smoked mackerel

2 large smoked mackerels, 3–4 cloves garlic, 2–3 tbsps finely chopped scallions or young leek, 1 tsp chili pepper, a pinch of salt, 1 tbsp sunflower oil, 1 tsp **sesame oil**, *1 tbsp* **sesame seeds**

kin the fish, gently bone it. Finely chop the peeled garlic, mix with salt, chili pepper and chopped scallions (or leek). Toast the sesame seeds. In a large, heavy frying pan heat the sunflower oil, put in the fillets and fry over a medium heat on each side for 2–3 minutes, sprinkling them with the seasoned garlic. Turn down the heat, sprinkle the fish with sesame oil. Cook for 1 minute, sprinkle sesame seeds on top and keep frying for 1–2 minutes. Serve as a piquant snack with white bread, or with rice and daikon radish Korean style.

Pears in white wine

4 large, firm pears, 100 g sugar, 1 lemon, 4 green **cardamom seeds**, *1* **star anise seed**, *1 tbsp coloured peppercorns, 2 cups semi-dry white wine*

eel the pears finely (but do not core), put in a saucepan. Cover with wine and lemon juice, add sugar, peppercorns, cardamom and anise. Bring to a boil, then simmer for 20 minutes. Gently take out the pears, put in serving bowls. Cook the liquid over a medium heat for another 10 minutes. Strain it and pour over the fruit. Serve as a savoury dessert or a snack.

Piquant pudding

*400 g full-cream curd cheese, 200 g potatoes cooked in jackets, 2 tbsps butter, 150 g flour, 3 eggs, ½ cup milk, 2 tbsps each chopped parsley and dill, 1 tsp paprika, 1 tbsp mild **curry powder**, salt, pepper, butter and 3 tbsps breadcrumbs for the mould*

Put the peeled potatoes and cheese through a mincer. Separate the egg whites from the yolks. Cream the butter in a bowl, adding 1 egg yolk and 1 tablespoon potato and cheese mixture at a time, followed by flour, milk and chopped parsley and dill. Mix in salt, curry powder and paprika. Whisk the egg whites to stiff peaks and fold into the mixture. Butter a terrine mould, dust it with breadcrumbs. Put in the prepared mixture, close tightly with a lid. Put in a pot of boiling water (reaching to half the height of the mould). Cook covered for 45–50 minutes. When well done, the pudding is easy to transfer to a warm serving dish. Serve hot, with tomato, mushroom, chive or cream sauce.

Marinated mushrooms, Spanish style

*300 g button mushrooms (caps only), 1–2 shallots, 1–2 cloves garlic, 2 tbsps olive oil, 1 tbsp tomato paste (or pureed fresh tomatoes), ½ cup dry white wine, 2–3 cloves, a dash of **saffron** filaments, 1 tbsp hot water, salt, freshly ground black pepper, 1–2 tbsps chopped parsley*

Finely chop the peeled garlic and shallots. Cover the saffron with hot water and leave aside. Mix the tomato paste with the wine. In a heavy saucepan heat the oil, soften the shallots and garlic. Pour in the wine with the tomato paste, add the cloves and soaked saffron. Bring to a boil stirring continuously. Season to taste with pepper and salt, cover and simmer for 30–40 minutes (add some water if the sauce becomes too thick). Clean and dry the mushroom caps, put into the saucepan. Bring to a boil, then simmer for 4–6 minutes. Take off the heat and leave, covered, till it cools. Refrigerate overnight. Before serving, sprinkle with chopped parsley. Transferred to glass jars, such mushrooms will keep in the fridge for several days. They make an excellent savoury snack or can be added to salads.

Green salads

Spinach with sesame 1

*800 g spinach leaves, salt, 2–3 tbsps **soy sauce**, 1 glass brandy, 3 tbsps **sesame seeds**, a pinch of pepper*

Toast the sesame seeds. Mix the soy sauce with the brandy and a pinch of pepper. Cut off the stalks of spinach leaves. Wash and drain the leaves, put for 2–3 minutes in salted boiling water, then drain thoroughly and cut into wide strips. Put in a salad bowl, pour the dressing over. Shake the bowl. Sprinkle sesame seeds on top. Serve with meat or fish.

Spinach with sesame 2

*600 g young spinach leaves, 100 g **sesame seeds**, 1 tbsp each chopped parsley and chives*

*DRESSING: 5 tbsps olive oil, lemon juice, grated lemon rind, salt, pepper, ¼ tsp **curry powder***

Combine the dressing ingredients, refrigerate. Toast the sesame seeds. Cut off the stalks of spinach leaves. Wash and drain the leaves. Put in a salad bowl, sprinkle with chopped parsley and chives and with sesame seeds. Pour the sauce over and shake the bowl.

Lettuce with anchovy dressing

1 curly lettuce, 2 tbsps piquant grated ewes' cheese

*DRESSING: 2 tbsps **anchovy paste**, 1–2 cloves garlic, juice and grated rind of ½ lemon, 3 tbsps **grape-seed oil**, pepper*

DRESSING: Chop the peeled garlic finely, blend with the anchovy paste, lemon juice and zest, pepper and oil.
Rinse and drain the lettuce, shred larger leaves. Put in a bowl. Grate the cheese coarsely. Pour the dressing over the salad, sprinkle with the grated cheese. Serve with toasted bread.

Spinach with pine nuts

Spinach with pine nuts

500 g young spinach leaves, 1½ tbsps
pine nuts *(or pumpkin seeds)*

*DRESSING: 1–2 cloves garlic crushed with
salt, 1 tsp each honey and sharp mustard,
juice of ½ lemon, 2–3 tbsps oil*

Combine the dressing ingredients, refrigerate. Toast the pine nuts. Cut off the stalks of spinach leaves. Wash and drain the leaves, put for 2–3 minutes in salted boiling water, then drain thoroughly and cut into wide strips. Put in a salad bowl, pour the sauce over. Shake the bowl. Sprinkle sesame seeds on top. Serve with roast veal or poultry.

Lettuce with nasturtium leaves and flowers

*1 crisp lettuce (or curly, or oakleaf lettuce), 12–15 each
young nasturtium leaves and flowers, 5–6 dill sprigs*

DRESSING: 1 cucumber, 1 tsp Dijon mustard, 2 tbsps
sherry vinegar, *3 tbsps* **safflower oil**, *1–2 scallions,
1 tbsp chopped dill, salt, pepper and sugar to taste*

Finely chop the scallions (with leaves). Peel the cucumber, halve it. Julienne one half and chop the other finely, then liquidize with the mustard, vinegar and oil. Combine the liquidized cucumber with the scallions, dill and cucumber matchsticks. Season to taste with pepper, salt and sugar, mix thoroughly, refrigerate for 30 minutes. Put the rinsed and dried lettuce leaves in a salad bowl, pour the dressing over. Sprinkle with the nasturtium leaves cut in strips, garnish with nasturtium flowers and dill sprigs.

Red cabbage salad with oranges

800 g red cabbage, 4 oranges, 300 g tinned **chestnuts**,
*2 tbsps butter, 2 tbsps sugar, 100 g sultanas, 1 tbsp
dry red wine*

*DRESSING: ½ cup each orange juice and redcurrant
juice, 1–2 tbsps sugar, 2 tbsps* **red vinegar**,
*a pinch of ground cinnamon, salt, freshly
ground white pepper, 4 tbsps* **walnut oil**

DRESSING: Bring the orange and redcurrant juice with sugar to a boil. Keep simmering to reduce by half, then leave to cool. Whisk with the vinegar, spices and oil. Rinse and dry the cabbage, remove damaged leaves and the hard stalk. Quarter and shred finely. Put in a salad bowl, pour the dressing over, leave aside for 20 minutes. Rinse and drain the raisins, put into a small bowl, cover with the wine, leave aside for 15 minutes.

Peel the oranges, remove the white skin, divide the fruit into segments. Quarter half the orange segments, remove pips. Combine with the cabbage. Rinse and drain the chestnuts, quarter them. In a frying pan melt the butter with sugar, put in the chestnuts and fry over a medium heat for 5 minutes. Add the raisins and keep cooking for another 2 minutes, stirring all the time.

Divide the cabbage into 4 portions, surround each portion with orange segments, chestnuts and raisins. Serve as a snack or an exquisite side dish with roast poultry.

Piquant Chinese cabbage

*1 Chinese cabbage (500–600 g), 1 tbsp salt,
1 tbsp chopped fresh ginger, 2–3 tbsps* **peanut oil**,
¼ cup dark **Chinese vinegar**, *1 tbsp sugar,
1 tsp* **chili oil**

Rinse and dry the cabbage. Shred the leaves into fair-sized pieces. Place the leaves in layers in a large bowl, sprinkling each layer with salt. Cover with clingfilm and leave aside for 4–5 hours. Combine the cabbage with the chopped ginger. In a deep frying pan heat the peanut oil, add the sugar, chili oil and vinegar. Mix thoroughly and heat up. Pour the dressing over the cabbage, shake the bowl well, cover and leave aside for another 4 hours. Serve with roast and fried meat or fish. In a tightly closed dish such salad can keep in the fridge for a week.

Aubergines in anise sauce

Brussels sprouts with chestnuts

Vegetable dishes

Aubergines with sesame sauce

4 young, long aubergines, salt

*SAUCE: 2 tbsps **sesame paste**, 2 tbsps **sesame oil**, 3 tbsps light **soy sauce**, 2 tbsps white **rice vinegar**, 2 tbsps dry sherry, 1 tbsp **chili sauce**, 2 tbsps chopped coriander leaves, 3–4 cloves garlic, pepper, salt*

SAUCE: Chop the peeled garlic, crush with salt, add the chopped coriander leaves (or parsley), soy sauce, rice vinegar and chili sauce. Mix thoroughly, then blend with the sesame paste, sherry and pepper (if the sauce is too thick, add 1–2 tbsps lukewarm boiled water). Cover and refrigerate for several hours, preferably overnight.
Peel the aubergines, cut into thick slices, sprinkle with salt and leave aside for 15 minutes. Steam cook the slices for 15–20 minutes, then cut into thick strips. Put into a serving dish, coat with the sauce and serve immediately – as a snack or with meat or fish.

Aubergines in anise sauce

*700 g young aubergines, 1–2 large onions, 4–6 cloves garlic, 3 tbsps **peanut oil**, salt, ¼ cup light stock or hot water*

*SAUCE: ½ cup **soy sauce**, 3 tbsps honey, ½ cup raisins, 3 **star anise seeds***

Rinse and dry the aubergines, cut in slices. Chop the peeled onions and garlic. In a large frying pan heat the oil, soften the onions and garlic. Put in the aubergine slices and fry over a fairly high heat, until nicely golden brown on both sides. Sprinkle with some stock or water, cover and simmer for 5–8 minutes. Add a dash of salt. Rinse and drain the raisins. Pound the anise seeds in a mortar. In a

small saucepan heat the soy oil with the honey, add the anise and raisins. Cover and cook over a very low heat for 25–30 minutes. Arrange the fried aubergine slices in an oven-proof dish, pour the sauce over. Cover with foil and leave aside for 4–5 hours. Before serving, put into a hot oven to heat up. Serve as a hot snack or as a side dish with roast meat, fish or rice dishes.

Brussels sprouts with chestnuts

*800 g Brussels sprouts, 1 tbsp lemon juice, 800 g cooked or tinned **water chestnuts**, 2 ½ tbsps sugar, 1 tbsp butter, 1–2 tbsps Madeira wine, salt, freshly ground white pepper, grated nutmeg*

Rinse and clean the Brussels sprouts, remove damaged leaves. In a large saucepan bring water to a boil, add salt, 1 teaspoon sugar, lemon juice and 1 teaspoon butter. Put in the Brussels sprouts and cook 10 minutes, then drain. Rinse the chestnuts, drain and dry them. In a heavy saucepan melt the remaining sugar, put in the chestnuts, shake the pan to coat them in caramel. Add the remaining butter and the wine, put in the Brussels sprouts. Add salt, pepper and nutmeg to taste. Gently stir and continue cooking for 3–4 minutes.

Broccoli with olives

*350 g broccoli, ¼ cup chicken stock (or stock from cube), 1½ cups sliced **black olives**, 1–2 cloves garlic, 2 tbsps **sesame seeds**, 2 tbsps **soy oil**, 1 tbsp chopped orange rind, ½ tsp finely chopped fresh ginger, 1 tin (230 g) **water chestnuts**, 1 cup pea sprouts (fresh or tinned), 50 g marinated chili peppers*

Rinse the broccoli, divide into florets. Peel and slice the stalks. Drain and slice the water chestnuts. Peel and halve the garlic cloves. Seed and finely chop the peppers. Heat the oil in a heavy frying pan. Put in the sesame seeds and garlic halves, fry over a medium heat for 3 minutes. Add the orange rind and stirring all the time keep frying until the sesame seeds are nicely golden. Take out the garlic halves, add the ginger and stir. Put in the broccoli, olives, water chestnuts, pea sprouts and chili peppers. Stirring continuously keep frying over a medium heat for 7 minute,

Broccoli with olives

occasionally sprinkling with some hot stock. Serve with rice and soy or rice noodles.

Broccoli with Chinese cabbage

500 g broccoli, salt, 1 tsp sugar, 1 tsp lemon juice, 1 medium-sized Chinese cabbage, 1 large onion, 2–3 cloves garlic, 2 tbsps almond flakes, 3 tbsps sunflower oil, 4 tbsps black bean paste

Rinse the broccoli, divide into florets. Peel the stalks and cut into cubes. In a large saucepan bring water to a boil, add salt, sugar and lemon juice. Put in first the broccoli stalks and a minute later the florets. Cook 1–2 minutes. Take out with a straining spoon and drain well. Rinse and dry the Chinese cabbage, shred into strips. Halve and slice the peeled onion. Chop the peeled garlic finely. In a wok heat 1 tablespoon oil, wash the sides with it, then pour out. Pour in the remaining oil, heat it. Put in the onion and garlic and fry until light brown. Add the broccoli and almond flakes and, stirring all the time, fry for 2–3 minutes. Put in the shredded cabbage and fry for another 2–3 minutes. Add the black bean paste and stirring bring the whole to a boil. Serve immediately.

Stuffed zucchini

4 zucchini, 5 tbsps sunflower oil

STUFFING: 250 g mozzarella (2 or 4 balls), 1 tbsps small capers, 1 tbsp chopped fresh oregano leaves

SAUCE: 2–3 shallots, 2 each yellow and red bell peppers, 2–3 cloves garlic, 2 tbsps ajvar paste, 3 tbsps thick cream, salt, pepper, ½ tsp paprika

SAUCE: Finely chop the peeled shallots. Remove the stalks and seeds from the bell peppers, rinse the flesh, cut into thin strips. Crush the peeled garlic. In a heavy frying pan heat 2 tablespoons oil, put in the shallots and soften them. Add the pepper strips and stirring all the time cook for 2–3 minutes. Add the garlic and ajvar, stir and simmer over a low heat.
Rinse and dry the zucchini, halve lengthwise and gently scoop out some of the flesh. Put the scooped out halves

in slightly salty boiling water for 2 minutes. Take out, rinse under cold water and dry with a paper towel.
STUFFING: Cut the mozzarella into smaller pieces, put through a blender together with the capers and scooped out zucchini flesh. Combine with oregano, season with pepper and salt.
Fill the zucchini halves with the stuffing. Heat the oven to 200°C. Grease an oven-proof dish with oil, put in the zucchini halves, sprinkle with 2 tablespoons oil. Cover with aluminium foil and put in the oven for 20 minutes. Combine the fried bell peppers with the cream, add salt, pepper and paprika to taste, stir. Take the oven-proof dish out, remove the foil, surround the zucchini halves with the sauce and return to the oven. Continue baking uncovered for 5–6 minutes.

Oriental French beans with potatoes

2 tbsps each mustard seeds and caraway, 400 g French beans (topped and tailed), 150 g green peas, 150 g each potatoes and carrots (peeled and cut in cubes), 2 tsps turmeric, 1½ cups water or light chicken stock, ½ cup natural yogurt, 2 tbsps sesame oil, 1 tsp salt, 1 tsp ground coriander seeds

Heat a large, heavy frying pan, put in the caraway and mustard seeds, cover and fry over a fairly high heat. When the seeds begin to crack, add the French beans, peas, potatoes and carrots, as well as turmeric and water (or stock). Stir, cover and cook 15–20 minutes. Pour in the yogurt, add the oil, salt and coriander, stir. Return the lid and simmer over a medium heat for another 15–20 minutes. Serve as a hot snack with white bread or toast, or as a side dish with meat.

Oriental French beans

750 g French beans, 2 tbsps oil, 1 tsp finely chopped fresh ginger, 2–3 cloves garlic, 1 celery stalk, 250 g tinned water chestnuts, 1 small chili pepper, ½ cup chicken stock (or stock from cube)

Drain the water chestnuts, run under cold water, drain again and slice them. Remove stringy fibres from the

Oriental French beans with potatoes

celery, slice the stalk finely. Finely chop the peeled garlic. Seed the pepper and dice it. Top and tail the beans. Heat the oil in a heavy frying pan or wok. Put in the ginger and garlic and stir fry for 1 minute. Add the celery and chestnuts, fry for another 1–2 minutes until the celery softens. Take out the chestnuts and celery with a straining spoon, transfer to a warm plate. Put the French beans and chili pepper into the frying pan and stirring cook for 1 minute. Pour in the stock, bring to a boil. Turn down the heat, cover the pan and stew for 8–10 minutes, until the beans are softer. Combine with the celery and chestnuts, heat up for 1–2 minutes. Serve with rice or as a hot snack.

French beans in prawn sauce

*500 g French beans, 16 small shelled prawns (tinned or frozen), 12 shallots or 3 red onions, 4–5 fresh chili peppers, 1 tsp **prawn paste**, 8 macadamia nuts, 2 tbsps peanut oil (or any other vegetable oil), 2½–3 cups coconut milk (or 5–6 tbsps shredded coconut + 3 cups milk or cream), 1 tsp salt*

Peel the onions, seed the peppers. Finely chop the onions, nuts and peppers, then blend with the prawn paste into a smooth mixture. Rinse the French beans, top and tail them, cut into 5–6 cm pieces. In a heavy frying pan heat the oil, put in the nut and pepper mixture and, stirring, fry for 4–5 minutes. Add the French beans and gently stirring fry over a fairly high heat for a minute. Sprinkle with salt, cover with the coconut milk, turn down the heat and cook, uncovered, for 10–15 minutes. Towards the end put in the prawns, stir and continue cooking for another 2–3 minutes. Serve with white bread or rice.

Butter beans with raisins

*300 g butter beans, 4 cups boiled water, ½ cup oil, ¾ tsp each ground **star anise**, pepper and marjoram, ¼ tsp each **turmeric** and cayenne pepper, 1 cup raisins, ¼ cup white wine, 1 tbsp sugar, 2 tbsps lemon juice, 1½–2 cups water or light chicken stock (or stock from cube), salt*

Rinse the beans, cover with water and leave overnight to soak. The following day drain thoroughly. Cover the

rinsed raisins with the wine and leave aside for 15 minutes. In a large, heavy saucepan heat the oil, put in the mixed anise, marjoram and pepper, fry a little. Put in the beans, sprinkle with cayenne and turmeric, add the raisins with wine. Cover with hot water or stock, bring to a boil. Add sugar and lemon juice and cook over a low heat (uncovered). Replenish the liquid if too much of it evaporates too quickly. When the beans are done, add salt to taste and steam them – the dish should not contain any liquid. This original Indian dish is best served as a hot snack.

Snap peas with pesto

*150 g snap peas, 2 tbsps **pesto**, 10 **sun-dried tomatoes in oil**, 1 tin (250 g) mixed beans, salt, freshly ground pepper*

Put the snap peas in salted boiling water for 1–2 minutes, then drain, run under cold water and drain thoroughly again. Drain the tomatoes, cut in thin strips. Rinse the beans under running water, drain well. Mix the snap peas with the pesto, tomatoes and beans, season with black pepper.

Fried soy shoots

*400 g soy shoots, 3 tbsps **peanut oil**, 1 tbsp dark **sesame oil**, 2–3 cloves garlic, 3 shallots or 1 red onion, ½ tbsp chopped fresh ginger, 2 tbsps light **soy sauce**, salt*

Dice the peeled shallots and garlic. Rinse the soy shoots, remove brown parts. Heat the peanut oil in a large frying pan or wok, fry the garlic golden brown. Take it out and put the soy shoots and ginger in. Stir and fry 1–2 minutes over a fairly high heat. Add the shallots and soy sauce, stirring all the time cook for another 1–2 minutes. Towards the end add salt and sesame oil and mix thoroughly. The shoots should remain nicely crispy.

Baked Savoy cabbage

*1 Savoy cabbage, 1 tin (c. 500 g) **water chestnuts**, 100 g button mushrooms, 1 small leek (100–120 g, white part only), 1–2 cloves garlic, 2 tbsps butter, 1 tbsp lemon juice, 1 tbsp paprika, 1 egg, 1 tbsp chopped dill, salt, pepper*

Butter beans with raisins

STUFFING: Rinse the cabbage, blanch in salted boiling water for 3–4 minutes. Take out, drain, leave to cool. Separate 8–10 largest leaves, discard the hard ribs. Shred the remaining cabbage. Drain the chestnuts, chop finely. Wash the leek and mushrooms, slice them. Finely chop the peeled garlic. In a heavy frying pan, melt 1 ½ tablespoons butter, put in the leek, mushrooms, garlic and shredded cabbage. Stir fry over a low heat for 10 minutes. Add the chopped chestnuts, dill, lemon juice and paprika. Stir thoroughly and take off the heat. When the stuffing is cool, break in the egg, season with pepper and salt, mix thoroughly.

Brush an oven-proof dish with butter, line with cabbage leaves (reserve 2–3), so that they cover the sides of the dish. Spread the stuffing, cover with the remaining leaves. Put a smaller oven-proof dish on top to weigh the cabbage down. Put in a preheated oven and bake at 180–190°C for an hour. Serve as a snack or as the main course with boiled potatoes and with béchamel or tomato sauce.

Fried Chinese cabbage

1 Chinese cabbage (500 g), 1–2 large onions, 3 tbsps soy or **rice oil**, *¼ cup* **soy sauce**, *salt, 1 tsp* **Sichuan peppercorns** *and a dash of ground* **Sichuan pepper**

Rinse and drain the cabbage, separate the leaves. Cut the leaves in 2 cm wide strips, then each strip in triangles. Chop the peeled onions.

Heat a heavy frying pan or wok. Pour in the oil, briskly fry the Sichuan peppercorns, but do not burn them. Take the peppercorns out with a straining spoon. Soften the onions in the same oil. Put in the cabbage, stir, add the soy sauce and salt. Stirring continuously fry over a fairly high heat for 3–4 minutes (the oil must be very hot and the frying time short). Before serving, dust with ground Sichuan pepper.

Stewed Chinese cabbage

1 Chinese cabbage (500 g), 5–6 dried **shiitake mushrooms**, *1 fresh chili pepper, 4–5 scallions, 3–4 tbsps* **peanut oil**, *5 tbsps* **soy sauce**, *1 tbsp* **hoisin sauce**, *5 tbsps rice wine, ¾ cup vegetable stock (or stock from cube), 1 tsp sugar, salt, ½ tsp freshly ground pepper, 2–3 tbsps finely chopped parsley*

Cover the mushrooms with hot water and leave to soak for 30–45 minutes, then drain and cut into thin strips. Finely chop the seeded chili pepper. Rinse and dry the cabbage, separate the leaves. Cut the leaves in squares. Dice the scallions. In a heavy frying pan heat the oil, put in the cabbage and scallions and stir fry for 5–7 minutes. Add the mushrooms and chili, soy sauce, hoisin sauce, rice wine and hot vegetable stock. Stir, bring to a boil, then simmer over a low heat for 4–5 minutes, stirring all the time. Add salt, sugar and pepper to taste, stir. Before serving, sprinkle with chopped parsley.

Stewed cabbage with pine nuts 1

1 small white cabbage (c. 600 g), 4–5 scallions, 1 walnut-size piece of ginger, 75 g **pine nuts**, *1 large carrot, 2–3 cloves garlic, 4 tbsps* **chili sauce**, *3 tbsps soy oil, salt, pepper*

Rinse and dry the cabbage, shred it. Cut the peeled ginger in thin strips. Scrape and finely slice the carrot. Chop the peeled garlic finely. Heat 1 tablespoon oil in a large frying pan and fry the pine nuts golden brown, then take out with a straining spoon and leave aside. Pour the remaining oil into the frying pan, heat up. Put in the cabbage and carrot and stir fry for 10 minutes. Add the ginger and garlic, stir, sprinkle with water lightly and cook for 3–4 minutes. Mix the finely chopped scallions with the chili sauce, pour into the cabbage and stew for another 4–5 minutes, stirring all the time. Add salt and pepper to taste, sprinkle with the reserved pine nuts.

Stewed cabbage with pine nuts 2

1 small white cabbage (c. 600 g), 4–5 scallions, 2–3 cloves garlic, 1 carrot, 75 g **pine nuts**, *1 walnut-size piece of ginger, 3 tbsps soy oil, salt, pepper, ¼ tsp cayenne pepper, 1 tsp honey, ¼ cup stock, 2–3 tbsps dry white wine*

Rinse and dry the cabbage, shred it. Scrape and finely slice the carrot. Chop the peeled garlic and ginger finely. Heat the oil in a large frying pan, put in the cabbage and carrot and stir fry for 10 minutes. Add the ginger and garlic, sprinkle with some stock, stir and cook over a low

Stewed cabbage with pine nuts I

heat for 15 minutes. Toast the pine nuts golden brown, dice the scallions. Season the cabbage with pepper and cayenne, add salt and honey, sprinkle with wine and stir. Stew for a while longer, then add the toasted pine nuts and scallions and mix thoroughly.

Malaysian-style cabbage

*1 small white cabbage (600–700 g), 1½ tbsps **prawn paste**, 4 shallots, 1–2 cloves garlic, 1–2 chili peppers, 4–5 tbsps shredded coconut, 2 ½ cups milk, ½ cup cream (or 2 tbsps milk and ½ cup thick tinned coconut milk), 1½ – 2 tbsps **peanut oil**, ½ tsp salt*

COCONUT MILK (if tinned milk is not available): Cover 3 tablespoons shredded coconut with warm milk, leave aside for 30–40 minutes. Soak the remaining shredded coconut with warm cream and also leave aside for 30–40 minutes. Strain both, squeeze out the liquid from each separately. Rinse and dry the cabbage, shred it coarsely. Sliced the peeled garlic and shallots. Finely chop the seeded peppers. Heat the oil in a large frying pan or wok, briskly fry the onions and garlic for 2–3 minutes. Pour in the thin coconut milk, stirring all the time bring to a boil. Add the prawn paste and shredded cabbage. Stew uncovered, stirring occasionally, until the cabbage is tender. Add salt to taste. Pour in the thick coconut milk, stir and heat up.

Stuffed cucumbers

*1 kg cucumbers (of even size), 400 g minced pork, 2–3 scallions, 1 tbsp chopped fresh ginger, 1 tsp salt, ½ tsp flavour enhancer (sodium glutamate), 1 tsp sugar, ½ tsp ground **Sichuan pepper**, 1 tsp wheat flour, 1 egg white, 2 tbsps rice wine, 1 cup chicken stock, 1 tsp potato flour, 1 tbsp white **soy sauce**, 1 tbsp butter, 1 tbsp lard*

STUFFING: Chop the scallions, leave the green leaves aside to use in the sauce. Put the meat into a bowl, add the chopped onions, ginger and egg white, pour in the wine. Add salt, sugar, flavour enhancer, Sichuan pepper and wheat flour. Work into a smooth mixture.
Rinse and dry the cucumbers. Halve them lengthwise, scoop out the seeds. Heat the lard in a large frying pan,

put in the cucumber halves and fry for 1 minute. Take out with a straining spoon and leave to cool. Stuff with the forcemeat, arrange in an oven-proof dish. Sprinkle with melted butter, cover with aluminium foil. Put in a preheated oven and bake at 170–180°C for 20–25 minutes.
SAUCE: Bring the stock to a boil. Mix the potato flour with the soy sauce. Pour into the boiling stock, stir and heat up until the sauce thickens. Season with pepper and salt, mix in the chopped scallion leaves. Pour the sauce over the cucumbers. Serve with bread or rice.

Bell peppers with chestnuts

*1 each large green, red and yellow bell pepper, 1 tin (250 g) water chestnuts, 250 g leeks (white parts only), 2–3 cloves garlic, 3 tbsps light **soy sauce**, 1 tbsp **hoisin sauce**, 2 tbsps sunflower oil, 3 tbsps **peanut oil**, 2 tbsps toasted, coarsely chopped peanuts*

Rinse and dry the chestnuts, slice them. Remove the stalks and seeds from the bell peppers, rinse and dry the flesh, cut into strips. Wash the leeks thoroughly, slice them finely.
Heat the sunflower oil in a heavy frying pan, put in the leek and fry over a fairly high heat for 2–3 minutes, then take out with a straining spoon and drain on a paper towel. Chop the peeled garlic finely. Heat the peanut oil in a wok, put in the pepper strips and stir fry for 4–5 minutes. When they turn light brown, add the chestnuts and garlic, stir and fry for 1 minute. Pour in the soy sauce and hoisin sauce and fry for another 1–2 minutes, stirring all the time. Before serving, garnish with fried leek and toasted peanuts.

Fried lentils

*300 g lentils, 1 large onion, 125 g butter, 1 tsp **turmeric**, 1 tsp ground **cumin**, ½ tsp pepper, salt, 2–3 tbsps chopped dill*

Rinse the lentils, soak overnight in boiled water. The following day drain them. Finely chop the peeled onion. Melt half the butter in a shallow saucepan, briskly soften the onion. Put in the lentils, sprinkle with turmeric and stir fry for 2–3 minutes. Then cover and keep frying over a low heat, stirring occasionally so as they do not burn. When the lentils are half done, add the remaining butter, cumin and pepper. Stir and cook for a while longer. Add salt, stir and fry for 1–2 minutes. Before serving, sprinkle with chopped dill. Serve as a hot snack or as a side dish with meat.

Lentil balls with herbal sauce

*400 g yellow lentils, 3–4 tbsps flour, 3–4 chopped scallions, 2 seeded red chili peppers, 1½–2 tsps **garam masala**, 1 tsp each salt, ground caraway and chili powder, oil for deep frying*

SAUCE: 3–4 cups yogurt, 1½ tsps each chopped coriander and mint leaves, ½ tsp ground caraway, salt, 1 tsp lemon juice

SAUCE: Mix the sauce ingredients, refrigerate. Rinse the lentils, cover with boiled water and leave to soak for 4–6 hours. Drain, put through a mincer. Add the flour, chopped chili peppers, scallions, caraway, chili powder, salt and garam masala. Work into a smooth dough. With moistened hands shape into walnut-size balls, flatten a bit and fry in very hot oil (5–6 minutes for one batch). Drain thoroughly on a paper towel. Put in a large bowl, leave to cool, then coat with the sauce and refrigerate. Serve as a savoury snack.

Vegetable goulash

*500 g button mushrooms, 200 g green peas (fresh or tinned), 2 onions, 6–8 cloves garlic, 3–4 tbsps oil, 6–7 tbsps poppy-seed, 1 tsp ground **cardamom**, ¼ tsp each ground ginger and juniper berries, salt, pepper, 1 tbsp chopped green coriander leaves, ½ cup yogurt, ½ cup cream, ¼ cup light stock, 2 tbsps chopped almonds, 2 tbsps chopped parsley*

Rinse the mushrooms, slice. Put in a colander and blanch with boiling water. Run under cold water and drain. Finely chop the peeled garlic, combine with the ground ginger. Heat the oil in a heavy shallow saucepan, put in the cardamom and stirring fry for 1 minute. Add the finely chopped peeled onions, stir. Pour in the hot stock, heat up briskly. Mix the yogurt with the ground juniper berries, chopped coriander, ginger and garlic. Pour the mix-

ture into the saucepan and stirring continuously simmer over a low heat for 3–4 minutes. Blanch the green peas in lightly salted boiling water (or drain the tinned green peas). Put the green peas, mushrooms and poppy-seed into the saucepan. Cover and simmer for 5–8 minutes. Add the cream and chopped almonds, salt to taste, stir and heat up. Before serving, garnish with chopped parsley.

Garlicky potatoes

*8 large potatoes of even size, 4–6 cloves garlic, 1–2 tsps **Tabasco sauce**, 1 tsp salt, 4 tbsps **poppy-seed oil***

Heat the oven to 200–220°C. Chop the peeled garlic, crush it with salt, blend with the Tabasco sauce and oil. Peel and rinse the potatoes, slice them and dry on a paper towel. Put into a bowl, coat with the prepared sauce, then arrange on a baking tin and bake in the oven for 30–35 minutes. Half way through turn the slices over. Such potatoes make an excellent accompaniment to roast chicken and fried or grilled meat.

Saffron potatoes with zucchini

1 kg potatoes, 500 g zucchini, a dash of saffron filaments, ¾ cup full-fat milk, 2 tbsps extra virgin olive oil, 3–4 tbsps butter, salt, pepper

Pour the milk into a saucepan, add the powdered saffron. Bring to a boil, put a tight lid on and leave aside. Boil the peeled potatoes. Drain them, put into a saucepan and pour the saffron milk and oil over. Stir thoroughly and cook over a low heat for 5 minutes, stirring occasionally. Add 2 tablespoons butter, puree the potatoes and season to taste. Transfer the puree to a shallow oven-proof dish, cover tightly with aluminium foil and keep in a warm oven. Shortly before serving, grate the zucchini, blanch for a minute in boiling water, or until it turns bright green. Drain and combine with the remaining butter. Arrange the zucchini around the potatoes and serve with meat or with fried fish.

Potatoes, oriental style

1 kg potatoes boiled in jackets, 500 g fresh spinach, 1 onion, 3–4 cloves garlic, 1 tbsp chopped fresh ginger, 1 tsp each ground caraway,

Fried vegetables

mustard seeds and **turmeric**, ½ tsp ground fenugreek and chili powder, 2 tbsps oil, salt

Rinse and dry the spinach, shred the leaves. Cut the peeled potatoes into thick cubes, finely chop the peeled onion and garlic. Heat the oil in a large frying pan, briskly fry the onion, garlic and ginger. Add the remaining spices, salt to taste and stir fry for 2–3 minutes. Put in the potato cubes, stir well to coat them with oil and spices. Put the spinach leaves on top, cover and simmer over a low heat for 5–8 minutes. Such potatoes go particularly well with fish.

Fried vegetables

1 Chinese cabbage (c. 300 g), 200 g fresh spinach, 3–4 celery stalks, 1 leek (white part only), 200 g broccoli florets, 3–4 scallions, a walnut-size piece of fresh ginger, 1 tbsp **soy sauce**, 2 tbsps **oyster sauce**, 3 tbsps **walnut oil**, 1 tbsp **sesame oil**, lemon (or lime) juice, salt, freshly ground pepper, a pinch of sugar

Rinse and dry the cabbage, cut in broad strips. Remove stringy fibres from the celery, slice the stalks. Wash the leek thoroughly, cut in thick slices. Slice the peeled ginger finely. Blanch all the vegetables, including broccoli florets, for 1–2 minutes in boiling water, drain, rinse under cold water and drain well again. Remove the stalks from the spinach leaves. Wash the leaves, dry thoroughly, shred if too large. Cut the scallions into 3–4 cm pieces. Pour ½ tablespoon walnut oil into a hot heavy frying pan or wok, grease the sides with the oil, then pour it out. Heat the remaining walnut oil in the frying pan, put in the ginger and briskly fry. Add the scallions and the blanched vegetables, stir fry over a fairly high heat. Turn down the heat, pour in the soy sauce and oyster sauce, put in the spinach leaves, mix thoroughly (to coat all vegetables with oil). Add the lemon (or lime) juice, salt, pepper and sugar to taste. Sprinkle with sesame oil, stir and heat up for 1–2 minutes. Serve with rice or as a hot snack with white bread.

Stuffed mushrooms, Chinese style

24 large champignons, 3–4 scallions, 8–10 tinned **water chestnuts**, 250 g minced pork, 1 tbsp potato flour, 3 tbsps **soy sauce**, ½ tsp salt, a pinch of sugar, ¼

Garlicky potatoes

tsp finely chopped fresh ginger, 1 cup chicken stock (or stock from cube), 1 egg, oil for greasing a baking sheet

Cut off the stalks from the mushrooms, clean the caps with a paper towel. Blanch for 1–2 minutes in boiling water, drain, rinse with cold water and dry well. Rinse and dry the chestnuts.

STUFFING: Finely chop the onions, chestnuts and mushroom stalks. Combine with the meat, potato flour, 2 tablespoons soy sauce, salt, sugar and ginger.

Fill 12 mushroom caps with the forcemeat, cover with the remaining caps, press down. Grease a shallow oven-proof dish, arrange the mushrooms. Cover tightly with aluminium foil and for 25–30 minutes heat up over a medium heat on the hotplate. Transfer the mushrooms to a hot serving dish and keep warm. Add the hot stock to the sauce in the oven-proof dish, cook for 1–2 minutes, stirring all the time. Blend the egg with 1 tablespoon soy sauce, 1 tablespoon boiled water and finely chopped scallion leaves. Combine the mixture with the sauce, heat up stirring. Pour the sauce over the mushrooms and serve with rice or soy noodles.

Mushrooms in anchovy sauce

700 g button mushrooms, 1 large fleshy tomato, 2–3 shallots, 1 stalk **lemon grass** or 1 tsp grated lime rind, 2 tbsps **anchovy paste**, 4 tbsps butter, 3 tbsps olive oil, pepper, salt, 8 slices white bread, 1 tin anchovy fillets, 4 tbsps chopped parsley

Blanch and skin the tomato, cut in cubes, remove the seeds. Chop the lemon grass. Wash and dry the mushrooms. Finely slice the peeled shallots. Cream 3 tablespoons butter with the anchovy paste, refrigerate for 20 minutes. In a wok or a heavy frying pan heat 1 tablespoon oil, grease the sides with the oil, then pour it out. Heat the remaining oil in the frying pan, put in the mushrooms, shallots and lemon grass. Stir fry over a fairly high heat for 2–3 minutes. Add the tomatoes and 3 tablespoons chopped parsley. Turn down the heat and stirring continuously gradually add the anchovy butter. Season to taste. Blend the remaining butter with 1 tablespoon chopped parsley. Toast the bread. Spread each slice with parsley butter and put an anchovy fillet on top. Serve with the mushrooms.

Mushrooms in anchovy sauce

Index

Alphabetical list of dishes

A

Agrest marynowany	Marinated gooseberries	760
Agrest marynowany do sosów	Marinated gooseberries for sauce	760
Ajwar z bakłażanów	Aubergine ajvar	879
Andywja	Endive	608
Antrykot marynowany	Marinated entrecôte	402
Antrykot po prowansalsku	Entrecôte à la Provençale	402
Antrykot po włosku	Entrecôte, Italian style	402
Antrykot z grilla	Grilled entrecôte	402
Anyżki	Aniseed snaps	733
Anyżówka	Anisette	750
Arkas	Arkas	676
Aromatyczna kawa mrożona	Aromatic coffee	697
Aromatyczna zupa rybna	Spicy fish soup	115
Aromatyczny sos do wołowiny	Savoury sauce for beef	851
Aromatyczny sos z zielonym pieprzem	Savoury sauce with green peppers	853

B

Babka chlebowa	Bread baba	710
Babka kakaowa	Cocoa baba	709
Babka koronkowa	Lacy baba	707
Babka korzenna	Spicy baba	710
Babka migdałowa	Almond baba	709
Babka na białkach	White baba	709
Babka rodzynkowa	Raisin baba	707
Babka z gryczanej mąki	Buckwheat baba	710
Babka z szafranem	Saffron baba	707
Babka z tartego ciasta	Whisked baba	709
Babka ziemniaczana z gotowanym mięsem	Potato cake with cooked meat	237
Babka ziemniaczana z grzybami	Potato cake with mushrooms	237

Cietrzew w sosie pikantnym	Black grouse in spicy sauce	539
Comber jeleni na zimno	Venison saddle, served cold	522
Comber jeleni ze śmietaną	Venison saddle with cream	522
Comber z dzika w angielskim cieście	Saddle of wild boar in pastry	519
Cukinie faszerowane	Stuffed courgettes	612
Cukinie faszerowane pastą z jabłek i zielonego groszku	Courgettes stuffed with apple and green peas paste	613
Cukinie nadziewane grzybami	Courgettes stuffed with mushrooms	613
Cukinie nadziewane serem	Courgettes stuffed with Cheddar	613
Cukinie z orzechami	Courgettes with walnuts	612
Cukinie z ziołowo-migdałowym nadzieniem	Courgettes with herbs and almond stuffing	613
Cukiniowo-kalafiorowy krem	Cream of cauliflower and zucchini	794
Curry z indyka z migdałami	Curried turkey with almonds	827
Curry z kalafiora	Cauliflower curry	600
Curry z wątróbek z kurczaka	Chicken liver curry	819
Cygańska zupa z malin	Raspberry soup, Gypsy style	132
Cykoria w gorczycowym sosie	Endive in mustard seed dressing	609
Cykoria z nasionami lubczyku	Endive with oregano seeds	609
Cykoria zapiekana z sosem pomidorowym	Endive baked in tomato sauce	609
Cykoria zapiekana z szynką	Endive baked with ham	610
Cynaderki w winnym sosie	Kidneys in wine sauce	452
Cynaderki wołowe w sosie cebulowym	Ox kidneys in onion sauce	453
Cynaderki z jabłkami w śmietanowym sosie	Kidneys with apples in cream sauce	451
Cynamonowe gwiazdki	Cinnamon stars	733
Czekoladki oryginalne	Chocolate candies	759
Czereśnie po francusku	Cherry and raspberry soup	131
Czereśnie w porzeczkowej galaretce	Cherries in redcurrant jelly	771
Czernina po staropolsku	Old Polish black soup	103
Czerwona pokusa	Red temptation	589
Czerwona sałatka	Red salad	201
Czosnek konserwowy	Garlic in oil	771
Czosnek w winie	Garlic in wine	762
Czosnkowe ziemniaki	Garlicky potatoes	895
Czysta zupa grzybowa	Clear mushroom soup	117
Ćwikła	Ćwikła, or grated beets with horseradish	574

D

De volaille (kotlet z kury)	Chicken de volaille	464
Delikatna kostka z kaszy manny	Semolina cubes	807
Delikatne gołąbki pekińskie	Delicate gołąbki, Chinese style	591
Delikatny gulasz z dorsza	Delicate cod stew	325
Delikatny krem z zielonego groszku	Cream of peas	111
Dereniówka	Cornelian cherry vodka	750
Deser z razowego chleba	Brown bread dessert	687
Diabelski kawior	Devilled caviar	68
Dip ananasowy	Pineapple dip	52

Dip bakłażanowy	Aubergine dip	53
Dip bananowy	Banana dip	53
Dip chrzanowy	Horseradish dip	53
Dip chrzanowy różowy	Pink horseradish dip	53
Dip czosnkowy	Garlic dip	54
Dip czosnkowy z jajkami	Garlic dip with eggs	53
Dip jajeczny	Egg dip	54
Dip kminkowy	Caraway dip	54
Dip koktajlowy	Cocktail dip	54
Dip koperkowy	Dill dip	54
Dip łososiowy	Salmon dip	54
Dip marchewkowy	Carrot dip	54
Dip miętowy	Mint dip	56
Dip migdałowy	Almond dip	56
Dip ogórkowy	Cucumber dip	56
Dip orzechowy	Nut dip	56
Dip owocowy	Fruit dip	56
Dip pieczarkowy	Mushroom dip	57
Dip pikantny z rodzynkami	Savoury dip with raisins	57
Dip pomarańczowo-ziołowy	Orange and herb dip	57
Dip pomarańczowy	Orange dip	57
Dip pomidorowy	Tomato dip	57
Dip rzodkiewkowy	Radish dip	57
Dip serowo-bazyliowy	Cheese and basil dip	58
Dip szparagowy	Asparagus dip	58
Dip szynkowy	Ham dip	58
Dip z awokado	Avocado dip	52
Dip ziołowy	Herbal dip 58	
Domowa pasta z czarnej fasoli	Home–made black bean paste	878
Domowa rocotta	Home-made ricotta	204
Domowa tahini	Home–made tahini paste	878
Domowe pesto	Home–made pesto 849	
Domowy ajwar paprykowy	Homeñmade bell pepper ajvar	879
Domowy sambal oelek	Homeñmade sambal ulek	879
Domowy serek pieczarkowy	Home-made mushroom cheese spread	206
Domowy serek z kminkiem	Home-made caraway cheese spread	206
Dorsz gotowany z fasolką szparagową	Cod with French beans	844
Dorsz po białorusku	Cod, Belarus style	321
Dorsz po żydowsku	Cod, Jewish style	321
Dorsz w ostrym sosie	Cod in savoury sauce	322
Dorsz w sosie cytrynowym	Cod in lemony sauce	322
Dorsz w zielonym sosie	Cod in green sauce	325
Dorsz z folii z pieczarkami i kukurydzą	Cod en papillote with mushrooms and sweet corn	844
Dorsz zapiekany z pomidorami	Baked cod with tomatoes	321
Dorsz zapiekany z sosem grzybowym	Baked cod in mushroom sauce	321
Drobiowe żołądki po szanghajsku	Poultry gizzards	819

Farsz koweński	Kovno stuffing	154, 159
Farsz kresowy + małoruski	Ruthenian stuffing	154, 156
Farsz kujawski	Kuyavia stuffing	157
Farsz kurpiowski	Kurp stuffing	155
Farsz kurpiowski	Kurp stuffing	155
Farsz kurpiowski z soczewicą	Kurp stuffing with lentils	157
Farsz litewski	Lithuanian stuffing	154, 159
Farsz lwowski	Lvov stuffing	154, 156
Farsz lwowski z chrzanem	Lvov stuffing with horseradish	157
Farsz małopolski	Little Poland stuffing	155, 157
Farsz mazowiecki z makiem	Mazovian stuffing with poppy seed	160
Farsz mięsny do pyz	Meat stuffing for potato dumplings	144
Farsz myśliwski	Hunter's stuffing	159, 167
Farsz parówkowy do pyz	Frankfurter stuffing for potato dumplings	144
Farsz pasztetowy	Pâté stuffing	360
Farsz podolski	Podolyan stuffing	167
Farsz polski	Polish stuffing	155, 159
Farsz postny	Lent stuffing	155
Farsz poznański	Poznań stuffing	156
Farsz przemyski	Przemyśl stuffing	167
Farsz staropolski	Old Polish stuffing	154, 156
Farsz warszawski	Warsaw stuffing	158, 167
Farsz wileński	Vilnius stuffing	155
Farsz z grzybów suszonych	Stuffing from dried mushrooms	161
Farsz z kapusty	Cabbage stuffing	423
Farsz z kapusty do knedli	Cabbage stuffing for knedle	149
Farsz z kaszy	Kasha stuffing	360
Farsz z leśnych świeżych grzybów	Stuffing from fresh mushrooms	162
Farsz z orzechami	Hazelnut stuffing	160
Farsz z pieczarkami	Mushroom stuffing	155, 361, 423
Farsz z pieczarkami i soczewicą	Mushroom and lentil stuffing	156
Farsz z pokrzywą	Nettle stuffing	158
Farsz z rodzynkami	Stuffing with raisins	360
Farsz z ryb do knedli	Fish stuffing for knedle	149
Farsz z wątróbki	Liver stuffing	360, 481
Farsz zakonny	Monk's stuffing	154
Farsz ze szpinakiem	Spinach stuffing	158
Farsz ziemiański	Pike and horseradish stuffing	158
Farsz żydowski (kreplach)	Jewish stuffing (kreplach)	156
Farsze do nadziewania pomidorów	Stuffing for tomatoes	663
Fasola „Jaś" po myśliwsku	Giant white beans, hunter's style	573
Fasola "Jaś" z rodzynkami	Butter beans with raisins	890
Fasola „Jaś" w sosie owocowym	Giant white beans in fruit sauce	574
Fasola biała w sałacie	White beans in salad	571
Fasola szparagowa	French beans	571
Fasola zapiekana z grzybami	Baked beans with mushrooms	573

Frykadelki cielęce z ryżem	Veal fricadelles with rice	398
Frykadelki skandynawskie	Scandinavian fricadelles	422
Frykadelki z serem	Pork fricadelles with cheese	377
Frykas z kurczaka po polsku	Chicken fricassee, Polish style	468
Frykas z lina	Tench fricassee	310
Frykas z marynowanej wieprzowiny	Marinated pork fricassee	371
Frytki	Patisson chips	646

G

Galantyna z indyka	Turkey galantine	489
Galantyna z kaczki	Duck galantine	491
Galaretka ananasowa	Pineapple jelly	681
Galaretka domowa	Home-made aspic	63
Galaretka jeżynowa pikantna	Savoury blackberry jelly	759
Galaretka karmelowa	Caramel jelly	682
Galaretka morelowa	Apricot jelly	681
Galaretka owocowa	Fruit jelly	681
Galaretka z czarnych porzeczek	Blackcurrant jelly	759
Galaretka z kurczaka	Chicken in aspic	65
Galaretka z pigwy	Quince jelly	759
Galaretka z żołądków drobiowych	Chicken gizzards in aspic	471
Galaretka ze zsiadłego mleka	Soured milk jelly	681
Garus	Mixed fruit soup (garus)	133
Gąski po warszawsku	Firewood agarics, Warsaw style	764
Gąski w czosnkowym sosie	Firewood agarics in garlic sauce	557
Gęsia szyja nadziewana	Stuffed goose neck	476
Gęsia szyja po polsku	Goose neck, Polish style	476
Gęsie uda w ciemnym sosie	Goose thighs in dark sauce	476
Gęś nadziewana cielęciną	Goose stuffed with veal	474
Gęś nadziewana kaszą	Goose stuffed with kasha	475
Gęś nadziewana makaronem	Goose stuffed with pasta	821
Gęś pieczona z jabłkami i porami	Roast goose with apples and leeks	475
Gęś pieczona z ziołami	Roast goose with herbs	475
Gęś po polsku	Goose, Polish style	474
Gęś z jabłkami	Goose with apples	474
Gliwajn herbaciany	Brandy tea (Glühwein)	696
Głuszec na gorąco lub na zimno	Wood grouse served hot or cold	537
Głuszec pieczony ze śmietaną	Roast wood grouse in cream	536
Głuszec po staropolsku	Wood grouse, Old Polish style	536
Głuszec w jarzynach	Wood grouse in vegetables	536
Głuszec w sosie porzeczkowym	Wood grouse in redcurrant sauce	537
Głuszec w winie	Wood grouse in wine	537
Głuszec z oliwkami i kaparami	Wood grouse with olives and capers	536
Golonka peklowana	Pig's knuckles pickled in brine	371
Golonka w śliwkowym sosie	Pig's knuckles in prune sauce	372
Golonka z imbirem	Pig's knuckles with ginger	372

Grzane piwo ze śmietanką	Mulled beer with cream	693
Grzane wino	Mulled wine	693
Grzanki „diablotki"	Diablotins	244
Grzybek z parmezanem	Parmesan omelette cubes	243
Grzybowe kotlety	Mushroom cutlets	560
Grzybowy kawior	Mushroom caviar	68
Grzyby duszone	Stewed mushrooms	558
Grzyby duszone z orzechami	Stewed mushrooms with walnuts	558
Grzyby suszone smażone	Fried dried mushrooms	561
Gulasz bieszczadzki ze śliwkami	Carpathian goulash with prunes	370
Gulasz gdański z żurawinami	Gdańsk turkey goulash with cranberries	485
Gulasz góralski z kiszoną kapustą	Mutton goulash with sauerkraut	434
Gulasz hiszpański	Spanish goulash	443
Gulasz pikantny z soczewicy	Hot lentil goulash	633
Gulasz staropolski z grzybami	Old Polish goulash with cep mushrooms	370
Gulasz wołowy z porami	Beef goulash with leek	427
Gulasz wołowy z zielonym pieprzem	Beef stew with green pepper	867
Gulasz wołowy ze szparagami	Beef goulash with asparagus	427
Gulasz z boczniaków	Oyster mushroom goulash	559
Gulasz z cielęciny gdański	Veal goulash, Gdańsk style	390
Gulasz z cielęciny z szynką	Veal goulash with ham	391
Gulasz z fasolki szparagowej z kiełbasą	Yellow beans goulash with sausage	572
Gulasz z indyka	Turkey stew	826
Gulasz z królika	Rabbit goulash	437
Gulasz z serc wołowych	Goulash from beef hearts	443

H

Halibut w czerwonym winie	Halibut in red wine	325
Halibut w sosie pietruszkowym	Halibut in parsley sauce	325
Halibut z sosem z kopru włoskiego	Halibut in fennel sauce	845
Harissa domowa	Home–made harissa	879
Hiszpański gulasz z kurczaka	Spanish chicken stew	818

I

Imbirki	Ginger snaps	733
Imbirowe steki wołowe	Ginger beefsteaks	867
Imbirowe szaszłyki	Gingery pork shashliks	376
Imbirowy nektar	Ginger drink	696
Indycze żołądki faszerowane mięsem	Turkey gizzards stuffed with meat	490
Indyczka nadziewana oliwkami	Turkey hen stuffed with olives	482
Indyczka z farszem maronowo-wątróbkowym	Turkey stuffed with chestnuts and liver	824
Indyczka z nadzieniem ryżowym	Turkey hen with rice stuffing	482
Indyk pieczony nadziewany	Stuffed roast turkey	480
Indyk po staropolsku podwójnie nadziewany	Double stuffed turkey, Polish style	481

J

Jabłka duszone	Stewed apples	671
Jabłka nadziewane sałatką śledziową	Apples stuffed with herring salad	671
Jabłka w winnym sosie	Apples in wine sauce	685
Jabłka z kasztanami	Apples with chestnuts	685
Jabłka z nadzieniem z selera	Apples with celery stuffing	671
Jagły ze śliwkami	Millet kasha with prunes	216
Jagnię na dziko	Gamey lamb	428
Jagnię pieczone nadziewane	Stuffed milk lamb	428
Jagnięcina z papryką	Lamb with bell peppers	869
Jagnięcina z warzywami	Lamb with vegetables	869
Jagnięcy gulasz z porami	Lamb goulash with leek	434
Jajecznica białowieska	Białowieża eggs	188
Jajecznica kaszubska	Kashub eggs	188
Jajecznica kaszubska ze śledziem	Kashub eggs with herring	188
Jajecznica starego bacy	Old shepherd's eggs	188
Jajecznica z czosnkiem i octem	Scrambled eggs with garlic and vinegar	188
Jajecznica z orzechami	Scrambled eggs with walnuts	188
Jajecznica z serem	Scrambled eggs with cheese	189
Jajecznica ze szczypiorkiem	Scrambled eggs with chives	188
Jajeczniki czyli kołacze	Egg cakes, or kołacze	707
Jajka à la flaczki	Egg bake	199
Jajka brązowe	Brown eggs	875
Jajka dla łakomczuchów	Gourmet's eggs	181
Jajka Fedora	Fédora eggs	180
Jajka marmurkowe	Marbled eggs	875
Jajka na sposób chiński	Eggs, Chinese style	875
Jajka nadziewane rybą	Eggs stuffed with fish	184
Jajka panierowane	Breaded eggs	198
Jajka pieczone w winie	Eggs baked in wine	198
Jajka po polsku	Eggs, Polish style	187
Jajka po warszawsku	Eggs, Warsaw style	184
Jajka sadzone „Duchesse"	Eggs à la duchesse	189
Jajka sadzone à la orient	Oriental eggs	190
Jajka sadzone flamenco	Flamenco eggs	189
Jajka sadzone po rosyjsku	Eggs à la russe	191
Jajka sadzone po staropolsku	Fried eggs, Old Polish style	191
Jajka sadzone w bułce	Eggs in white bread	191
Jajka sadzone z papryką	Eggs with peppers	190
Jajka sadzone z piwem i serem	Eggs with beer and cheese	190
Jajka sadzone z serem	Fried eggs with cheese	191
Jajka sadzone ze szpinakiem	Eggs with spinach	191
Jajka smażone pikantne	Savoury fried eggs	198
Jajka smażone w cieście po cieszyńsku	Eggs in batter, Cieszyn style	198
Jajka śnieżne czyli polska zupa nic	Floating islands, or Polish sweet soup	678
Jajka w białym winie	Eggs in white wine	199

K

Kaczka z orzechowym nadzieniem	Duck with walnut stuffing	494
Kaczka z rożna	Spit–roasted duck	821
Kalafior w ziołowym sosie	Cauliflower in herbal dressing	600
Kalafiory au gratin	Cauliflower au gratin	599
Kalarepa na rumiano	Browned kohlrabi	627
Kalarepka duszona z rodzynkami	Kohlrabi stewed with raisins	628
Kalarepki faszerowane rakami	Kohlrabies stuffed with crayfish	628
Kalarepki nadziewane cielęciną	Kohlrabies stuffed with veal	628
Kalarepki nadziewane pieczarkami	Kohlrabies stuffed with mushrooms	628
Kalarepki po polski	Kohlrabies, Polish style	628
Kalarepki po włosku	Kohlrabies, Italian style	629
Kalmusówka (ajerówka)	Sweet flag vodka	751
Kanapkowa pasta z makreli	Mackerel paste	877
Kandyzowane łodyżki arcydzięgla	Candied angelica	759
Kanie panierowane	Breaded parasol mushrooms	556
Kapłon lub pularda na sposób bażanta	Capon or poulard à la pheasant	473
Kapusta biała domowa	Sauerkraut	768
Kapusta biała po hiszpańsku	White cabbage, Spanish style	584
Kapusta czerwona po śląsku	Sour red cabbage, Silesian style	768
Kapusta duszona w winie	Red cabbage stewed in wine	589
Kapusta duszona z imbirem	Red cabbage stewed with ginger	589
Kapusta duszona z jabłkami	Cabbage stewed with apples	586
Kapusta duszona z orzeszkami pinii	Stewed cabbage with pine nuts	892
Kapusta duszona ze śliwkami	Red cabbage stewed with prunes	589
Kapusta modra z winem	Red cabbage with wine	587
Kapusta pekińska duszona na czerwono	Stewed Chinese cabbage	892
Kapusta pekińska duszona z morelami	Stewed Chinese cabbage with apricots	594
Kapusta pekińska faszerowana	Stuffed Chinese cabbage	591
Kapusta pekińska kiszona	Chinese cabbage in brine	768
Kapusta pekińska z jabłkowo-orzechowym nadzieniem	Chinese cabbage with apple and walnut filling	591
Kapusta po malezyjsku	Malaysian-style cabbage	894
Kapusta po wiejsku	Cabbage, country style	585
Kapusta włoska duszona	Stewed savoy cabbage	594
Kapusta włoska duszona z orzechami laskowymi	Savoy cabbage stewed with hazelnuts	595
Kapusta włoska faszerowana	Stuffed savoy cabbage	594, 595
Kapusta zapiekana z rokpolem	Cabbage baked with blue cheese	585
Kapuśniak kresowy	Cabbage soup, Ruthenian style	121
Kapuśniak staropolski	Old Polish cabbage soup	121
Kapuśniak staropolski z czerwonej kapusty	Old Polish red cabbage soup	121
Kapuśniak wiosenny	Spring cabbage soup	120
Karasie duszone w kwasie buraczanym	Crucian carp in sour beet juice	314
Karasie po litewsku	Crucian carp, Lithuanian style	313
Karasie w śmietanie	Crucian carp in cream	313
Karasie z cebulą	Crucian carp with onion	314

Konfitury z owoców róży	Rose hip preserve	757
Konfitury z płatków róży	Rose-petal preserve	757
Konfitury z poziomek	Wild strawberry preserve	756
Konfitury z rajskich jabłuszek	Crab-apple preserve	758
Konfitury z zielonych pomidorów	Green tomato jam	757
Koniak podlaski	Podlasie brandy	751
Kopytka	Potato dumplings	145
Kopytka pikantne	Savoury potatoes	228
Kordiał czyli polewka głogowa	Hawthorn soup	105
Korniszony	Cocktail gherkins	766
Korzenne frykadelki	Spicy lamb fricadelles	433
Korzenny pasztet z grzybów	Spicy mushroom pâté	560
Korzenny sos do wieprzowiny	Spicy sauce for pork	851
Kostka z kaszki krakowskiej	Cubes of crushed buckwheat	807
Kostka z manny	Semolina cubes	243, 807
Kotleciki z kaszy manny	Semolina patties	807
Kotleciki z kaszy perłowej z serem	Pearl barley and cheese cutlets	217
Kotleciki z orzechami	Egg cutlets with walnuts	199
Kotleciki ziołowe	Pork fricadelles with herbs	377
Kotlety cielęce po litewsku	Veal cutlets, Lithuanian style	394
Kotlety cielęce po mediolańsku	Veal cutlets à la milanaise	394
Kotlety cielęce w sosie pomidorowym	Veal cutlets in tomato sauce	395
Kotlety cielęce ziołowe	Veal cutlets with herbs	394
Kotlety cygańskie	Gypsy cutlets	394
Kotlety jagnięce we francuskim cieście	Lamb cutlets in puff pastry	432
Kotlety jagnięce z oliwkami	Lamb chops with olives	432
Kotlety korzenne	Spicy pork chops	375
Kotlety schabowe po włosku	Pork chops, Italian style	373
Kotlety schabowe z kapustą	Pork chops with cabbage	373
Kotlety staropolskie z sarny	Roedeer cutlets, Old Polish style	526
Kotlety w pikantny sosie	Beef cutlets in savoury sauce	417
Kotlety z bobu	Broad beans cutlets	578
Kotlety z dzika z migdałami	Wild boar chops with almonds	520
Kotlety z indyka marynowane	Marinated turkey cutlets	484
Kotlety z indyka z migdałami	Turkey cutlets with almonds	484
Kotlety z jabłkami	Pork fillets with apples	375
Kotlety z jajek	Egg cutlets	199
Kotlety z kaszy gryczanej z grzybami	Buckwheat cutlets with mushrooms	213
Kotlety z kaszy gryczanej z serem	Buckwheat cutlets with cheese	213
Kotlety z miętą	Mutton cutlets with mint	432
Kotlety z suszonych grzybów	Cutlets from dried mushrooms	561
Kotlety z wołowego mózgu	Ox brain cutlets	451
Krążki karpia z chrzanem	Carp rings with horseradish	288
Krem biały ziemniaczany	White cream of potatoes	110
Krem chrzanowy z imbirem	Horseradish cream with ginger	622
Krem cytrynowy	Cream of lemon	106

Krem imbirowy	Ginger cream	684
Krem jarzynowy z ziołami	Cream of vegetables with herbs	113
Krem królewski z ryb	Royal cream of fish	110
Krem morelowy	Apricot cream	683
Krem orzechowy	Nut cream	684
Krem pomarańczowo-orzechowy	Orange and nut cream	683
Krem pomarańczowy	Orange cream	683
Krem przeoryszy i ciasteczka	Abbess's cream with cookies	682
Krem truskawkowy z pomarańczowym sokiem	Strawberry cream with orange juice	683
Krem truskawkowy z rumem	Strawberry cream with rum	682
Krem z brokułów	Cream of broccoli	106
Krem z buraków	Cream of beets	106
Krem z cukinii	Cream of zucchini	107
Krem z cykorii z imbirem	Cream of endive with ginger	113
Krem z dyni z sherry	Cream of pumpkin with sherry	113
Krem z gruszek	Cream of pears	112
Krem z kalafiora	Cream of cauliflower	108
Krem z orzechów włoskich	Cream of walnuts	111
Krem z pieczarek	Cream of mushrooms	110
Krem z ryb z chrzanem	Cream of fish with horseradish	110
Krem z salsefii lub skorzonery	Cream of salsify	112
Krem z selerów z serem	Cream of celeriac with cheese	107
Krem z selerów z szynką	Cream of celeriac with ham	107
Krem z suszonych śliwek	Prune cream	683
Krem z wina	Wine cream	684
Krem z ziemniaków i szczawiu	Cream of potatoes and sorrel	111
Krem ze szparagów	Cream of asparagus	112
Krem ze szparagów z koperkiem	Cream of asparagus with dill	113
Krem ze szpinaku	Cream of spinach	114, 794
Kreolska sałatka rybna	Creole fish salad	831
Krewetki w sosie z czarnej fasoli	Prawns in black bean sauce	872
Krokieciki z mózgu	Brain croquettes	450
Krokiety drobiowe	Chicken croquettes	174
Krokiety góralskie	Tatra croquettes	174
Krokiety jarzynowe	Vegetable croquettes	175
Krokiety staropolskie	Old Polish croquettes	174
Krokiety z gotowanej cielęciny	Veal croquettes with liver	399
Krokiety z jajek	Egg croquettes	175
Krokiety z orzechów	Walnut croquettes	249
Krokiety z tartej bułki	Breadcrumb croquettes	175
Krokiety z ziemniaków	Potato croquettes	174
Krokiety z żółtego sera	Cheese croquettes	175
Krokiety ziemniaczano-orzechowe	Potato and walnut croquettes	174
Królewska herbata	Royal tea	698
Królik duszony w śmietanie	Rabbit in cream	435
Królik duszony w winie	Rabbit in wine	435

Królik duszony ze śliwkami	Braised rabbit with prunes	434
Królik pieczony	Roast rabbit	435
Królik po włosku	Rabbit, Italian style	871
Królik w jarzynach	Rabbit in vegetables	434
Królik z pieczarkami i oliwkami	Rabbit with mushrooms and olives	435
Kruchalce wigilijne	Christmas Eve biscuits	732
Kruche ciasteczka	Savoury shortcrust cookies	244
Kruche ciasteczka	Shortcrust biscuits	735
Kruche ciasto	Shortcrust pastry – basic recipe	164
Krupnik chłopski	Peasants' krupnik	118
Krupnik czerwony ryżowy	Red rice krupnik	118
Krupnik kurpiowski	Kurp krupnik	745
Krupnik litewski	Lithuanian krupnik	745
Krupnik miodowy	Honey krupnik	745
Krupnik polski	Polish krupnik	745
Krupnik ryżowy	Rice krupnik	118
Krupnik z kaszy jęczmiennej	Barley krupnik	118
Krupnik z miętą	Krupnik with mint	119
Krupnik z pęcaku z grochem	Barley krupnik with peas	117
Krupnik z suszonymi śliwkami	Krupnik with prunes	119
Krupnik zielony ryżowy	Green rice krupnik	119
Kruszon brzoskwiniowo-morelowy	Peach and apricot bishop	695
Kruszon polski	Polish bishop	695
Kruszon pomarańczowy	Orange bishop	694
Kruszon staropolski	Old Polish bishop	695
Kruszon zwany bischof	Bishop	694
Kukurydza młoda z masłem	Sweetcorn cobs with butter	635
Kukurydza po meksykańsku	Sweetcorn, Mexican style	636
Kukurydza z warzywami	Corn with vegetables	637
Kukurydza zapiekana	Baked corns	637
Kulebiak z biało-zielonym farszem	Koulibiak with white and green filling	803
Kulebiak z farszem rybnym z sardelami	Koulibiak with fish and anchovy paste	803
Kulebiak z kapustą i grzybami	Koulebiac with cabbage and mushrooms	169
Kulebiak z kaszą jaglaną i sandaczem	Koulebiac with millet, mushrooms and pikeperch	169
Kulebiak z marchewką	Koulibiak with carrots	803
Kulebiak z rybą	Koulebiac with fish	168
Kulebiak z wołowiną	Koulibiak with beef	804
Kulebiak ze szpinakiem i jajkami na twardo	Koulebiac with spinach and hard-boiled eggs	168
Kuleczki serowe	Cheese balls	202
Kulki z soczewicy z ziołowym sosem	Lentil balls with herbal sauce	895
Kura nadziewana makaronem	Hen stuffed with noodles	472
Kura po myśliwsku	Stewing hen, hunter's style	473
Kura po żydowsku	Stuffed hen, Jewish style	473
Kurczak dla odchudzających się	Chicken for weight watchers	815
Kurczak duszony	Stewed chicken	463
Kurczak faszerowany	Stuffed chicken	815

Kurczak na biało	Chicken in white sauce	811
Kurczak nadziewany grzybami	Chicken stuffed with mushrooms	463
Kurczak nadziewany zielonym groszkiem	Chicken stuffed with green peas	463
Kurczak niedzielny	Sunday chicken	460
Kurczak pieczony z cytryną	Roast chicken with lemon	462
Kurczak pieczony z cząbrem	Roast chicken with savory	463
Kurczak po egipsku	Chicken à la égyptienne	812
Kurczak w maladze	Chicken in Malaga	460
Kurczak w orzechowym sosie	Chicken in nutty sauce	812
Kurczak w sosie kokosowym	Chicken in coconut sauce	811
Kurczak w sosie pesto	Chicken in pesto sauce	812
Kurczak z jarzynami	Chicken with vegetables	464
Kurczak z pistacjowym nadzieniem	Chicken with pistachio stuffing	811
Kurczę w śmietanie	Chicken in cream	463
Kurczęta po polsku	Chicken, Polish style	460
Kurczęta po polsku z szafranem	Chicken Polish style, with saffron	459
Kurki duszone	Chanterelle stew	556
Kurki duszone z pomidorami	Chanterelles in tomato sauce	557
Kurki po admiralsku	Admiralís chanterelles	874
Kurki w serowym sosie	Chanterelles in cheese sauce	556
Kurki w winie	Chanterelles in wine	764
Kuropatwy dla smakoszów	Partridges for gourmets	540
Kuropatwy duszone	Stewed partridges	542
Kuropatwy duszone w czerwonej kapuście	Partridges stewed in red cabbage	542
Kuropatwy duszone w kiszonej kapuście	Partridges stewed in sauerkraut	542
Kuropatwy duszone w sosie pomarańczowym	Partridges stewed in orange sauce	542
Kuropatwy nadziewane	Stuffed partridges	542
Kuropatwy nadziewane groszkiem	Partridges stuffed with green peas	543
Kuropatwy nadziewane wieprzowiną	Partridges stuffed with pork	543
Kuropatwy pieczone	Roast partridges	541
Kuropatwy pieczone z jałowcem	Roast partridges with juniper	541
Kuropatwy po myśliwsku	Partridges, hunter's style	540
Kuropatwy w jarzynach	Partridges with vegetables	541
Kuropatwy w sosie porzeczkowym	Partridges in redcurrant sauce	541
Kuropatwy w śmietanie	Partridges in cream	541
Kuropatwy w śniegu	Partridge in the snow	539
Kuropatwy w winie	Partridges in wine	540
Kuropatwy z jabłkami	Partridges with apples	540
Kuropatwy z papryką	Partridges with sweet peppers	540
Kurpiowska zupa grzybowa	Mushroom soup from the Kurp region	117
Kurpiowskie kiełbaski z opieniek	Kurp sausage from honey mushrooms	562
Kurpiowskie zrazy bite	Pounded Kurp zrazy	425
Kurze udka w cytrynowym auszpiku	Chicken in white sauce	811
Kurze udka z grilla	Grilled chicken legs	466
Kuskus z sosem paprykowym	Couscous with bell pepper sauce	808
Kutia	Koutia	722, 723

L

Lin w ostrym sosie	Tench in savoury sauce	311
Lin z grzybami duszony w winie	Tench and mushroom ragout in wine	310
Litewska zupa rybna	Lithuanian fish soup	115
Lukier biały	White icing	729
Lukier kawowy	Coffee icing	729
Lukier mleczny	Milk icing	728
Lukier pomarańczowy	Orange icing	729
Lukier ponczowy	Punch icing	729
Lukry bez gotowania	Uncooked icing I	728–729

Ł

Łatwa szarlotka	Easy apple tart	706
Łazanki z kapustą	Square noodles with cabbage	587
Łosoś dla smakoszy	Gourmet's salmon	297
Łosoś duszony w winie	Braised salmon in wine	297
Łosoś marynowany	Marinated salmon	296
Łosoś na dziko	Salmon, country style	300
Łosoś na kwaśno	Sour-flavoured salmon	298
Łosoś pieczony	Baked salmon	300
Łosoś w cebulowym sosie	Salmon in onion sauce	298
Łosoś w majonezie	Salmon in mayonnaise	296
Łosoś w ostrym sosie wasabi	Salmon in piquant wasabi sauce	848
Łosoś w sosie cytrynowym	Salmon in lemon juice	300
Łosoś w sosie szczawiowym	Salmon in sorrel sauce	297
Łosoś z grilla lub z rożna	Grilled or barbecued salmon	300
Łosoś z masłem	Salmon in butter	297
Łosoś z rusztu	Grilled salmon	847
Łosoś zapiekany po genewsku	Baked salmon, Geneva style	302
Łosoś zapiekany z krewetkami	Baked salmon with prawns	301
Łódeczki selerowe faszerowane serem	Celery boats stuffed with cheese	601
Łódeczki z cykorii	Endive boats	609
Łódzkie pecyny	Łódź potato dumplings	146
Łyska pieczona	Roast coot	547
Łyska po staropolsku	Coot, Old Polish style	547
Łyska w sosie żurawinowym	Coot in cranberry sauce	547
Łyska z sardelami	Coot with anchovies	547

M

Maciek z wątroby baraniej	Meatloaf from mutton liver	444
Maître d'hôtel	Maître d'hôtel	46
Majonez chrzanowy	Horseradish mayonnaise	622
Mak do łamańców	Poppyseed treat	723
Makagigi z makiem	Poppyseed sweetmeat	735
Makagigi z orzechów	Nutty sweetmeat	733
Makaron jajeczny z sosem ostrygowym	Chinese egg noodles with oyster sauce	800

Makaron kolorowy	Coloured macaroni	138
Makaron ryżowy smażony z wołowiną	Fried rice noodles with beef	799
Makaron ryżowy z sosem kokosowym	Rice noodles with coconut sauce	799
Makaron sojowy z warzywami	Soy noodles with vegetables	799
Makaron w sosie dyniowo-kaparowym	Pasta with pumpkin and caper sauce	799
Makaron z kaparami	Pasta with capers	798
Makaron z łososiem	Soy noodles with salmon	800
Makaron z łososiem w sosie serowym	Pasta with salmon in cheese sauce	301
Makaron z razowej mąki	Wholemeal macaroni	138
Makaron ziołowy	Macaroni with herbs	138
Makrela w sosie owocowym	Mackerel in fruity sauce	327
Makrela z kiszonym ogórkiem	Mackerel with soured cucumber	327
Małe liny gotowane w śmietanie	Small tench cooked in cream	312
Małopolski żur owsiany	Cracow oats zhur	102
Marchew na parze	Steamed carrots	596
Marchewka duszona z cebulą	Carrots stewed with onion	598
Marchewka duszona z estragonem	Stewed carrots with tarragon	597
Marchewka faszerowana	Stuffed carrots	598
Marchewka po litewsku	Carrots, Lithuanian style	598
Marchewka zapiekana	Baked carrots	598
Marynarski grog	Sailor's grog	693
Marynata do dzieczyzny pieczonej na ruszcie	Marinade for spit-roast game	505
Marynata do mięs czerwonych (wołowina, baranina)	Marinade for red meat (beef and mutton)	348
Marynata do pieczenia na dziko	Marinade for meat ą la game	348
Marynata do wszystkich rodzajów mięs	Marinade for all kinds of meat	348
Marynata winna	Wine marinade	348
Marynata z jarzynami	Marinade with vegetables	504
Marynata z macierzanką	Marinade with wild thyme	504
Marynata ziołowa	Herbal marinade	348
Marynaty do mięsa z dzika	Marinade for wild boar meat	504, 505
Marynowana wątróbka smażona	Fried marinated liver	447
Marynowane filety z karmazyna	Marinated rockfish fillets	844
Marynowane filety z kurczaka	Marinated chicken fillets	815
Marynowane pąki kwiatowe cykorii	Pickled wild succory buds	763
Marynowane piersi kaczki po chińsku	Marinated duck breasts, Chinese style	824
Marynowane plastry gotowanej wieprzowiny	Marinated boiled pork slices	856
Masa do piernika sułtańskiego	Filling for sultan's gingerbread	719
Masło anchois i Masło sardelowe	Anchovy butter	49
Masło bazyliowe	Basil butter	47
Masło borówkowe	Mountain cranberry butter	48
Masło chrzanowe	Horseradish butter	49
Masło cytrynowe	Lemon butter	48
Masło czosnkowe	Garlic butter	49
Masło estragonowe	Tarragon butter	47

Mózgi wołowe w zimnym sosie	Ox brains in cold sauce	448
Mózgi zapiekane z żółtym serem	Baked brains with cheese	450
Móżdżek cielęcy po francusku	Calf's brains, French style	449
Móżdżek cielęcy po młynarsku	Miller's brains	449
Móżdżek cielęcy po wiedeńsku	Calf's brains, Vienna style	449
Móżdżek cielęcy smażony	Calf's brains fried in butter	449
Mus krabowy z twarogiem	Crab mousse with curd cheese	59
Mus pomidorowy	Tomato mousse	62
Mus porzeczkowy	Blackcurrant mousse	679
Mus poziomkowy	Wild strawberry mousse	679
Mus serowy	Cheese mousse	59
Mus z brokułów	Broccoli mousse	59
Mus z jabłek	Apple mousse	679
Mus z łososia	Salmon mousse	60
Mus z łososia z krabami	Salmon and crab mousse	60
Mus z tuńczyka	Tuna mousse	62
Mus z wątróbek indyczych	Turkey liver mousse	63, 489
Mus z wędzonej makreli	Smoked mackerel mousse	62
Mus ze szczupaka	Pike mousse	62
Musztarda domowa	Home-made mustard	771

N

Nadzienie makowe	Rich poppy-seed filling	722
Nadzienie z całych kasztanów	Whole chestnut stuffing	480
Nadzienie z kasztanów (maronów)	Sweet chestnut stuffing	480
Nadzienie z mięsa z kasztanami	Chestnut and meat stuffing	480
Nadzienie z raków	Crayfish stuffing	481
Nadzienie z rodzynkami i migdałami	Stuffing with raisins and almonds	481
Nadzienie z suszonymi śliwkami i orzechami	Prune and nut stuffing	481
Nadzienie z szynki	Ham stuffing	481
Nadzienie z włoskich orzechów	Walnut stuffing	481
Nadziewane sznycle z kurczaka	Stuffed chicken schnitzels	203
Nadziewane szyjki z indyka w grzybowym sosie	Stuffed turkey necks in mushroom sauce	486
Nadziewany daikon	Stuffed daikon	656
Nadziewany kapłon lub pularda	Stuffed capon or poulard	473
Najprostsze łamańce z makiem	Shortcrust cookies and poppy seed	723
Najprostszy dip majonezowy	Simple mayonnaise dip	52
Najprostszy sos do sałaty	Simplest salad dressing	634
Naleśniki orzechowo-miodowe	Hazelnut and honey pancakes	173
Naleśniki pikantne – zielone	Green savoury pancakes	173
Nalewka Baśki	Barbara's vodka	752
Nalewka brzoskwiniowa	Peach brandy	750
Nalewka dereniowa staropolska	Old Polish cornelian cherry brandy	750
Nalewka herbaciana	Tea brandy	751
Nalewka jarzębinowa	Rowanberry vodka	751

P

Pasta śledziowa z boczkiem	Herring spread with bacon	76
Pasta śledziowa z chlebem	Herring spread with bread	76
Pasta śledziowa z jabłkami	Herring spread with apples	76
Pasta śledziowa z kolendrą	Herring spread with coriander	76
Pasta twarożkowa z gorczycą	Curd cheese paste with mustard seeds	67
Pasta twarożkowa z macierzanką i bazylią	Curd cheese spread with thyme and basil	68
Pasta witaminowa	Vitamin spread	72
Pasta wspaniała	Delicious spread	78
Pasta z arcydzięgla i mięty	Angelica and mint spread	67
Pasta z bakłażana	Aubergine spread	68
Pasta z białego sera	Curd cheese paste	877
Pasta z camemberta z migdałami	Camembert spread with almonds	74
Pasta z cebulą	Onion spread	73
Pasta z chrzanem	Horseradish spread	74
Pasta z ciecierzycy	Chickpea paste	878
Pasta z czerwonej fasoli	Red bean spread	70
Pasta z drobiowych wątróbek z serem	Chicken liver spread with cheese	77
Pasta z ementalera z rozmarynem	Emmental spread with rosemary	74
Pasta z fasolą	Bean spread	73
Pasta z fasolki szparagowej	String bean spread	70
Pasta z głuszca	Wood grouse terrine	538
Pasta z grochu z majerankiem	Pea spread with marjoram	68
Pasta z kaparami	Paste with capers	74
Pasta z kminkiem	Caraway spread	73
Pasta z łososiem	Salmon spread	72, 76
Pasta z morelami	Apricot spread	72
Pasta z orzechami	Walnut spread	74
Pasta z papryki	Pepper spread	70, 75
Pasta z pieczarek z jajkiem	Mushroom spread with egg	71
Pasta z pieczarek z sezamem	Mushroom spread with sesame seeds	71
Pasta z pieczonej papryki	Red bell pepper paste	877
Pasta z sardynkami	Sardine spread	73, 75
Pasta z selerem naciowym	Celery paste	72
Pasta z sera camembert	Camembert spread	74
Pasta z siemieniem lnianym	Linseed spread	72
Pasta z szałwią	Sage spread	78
Pasta z szynką	Ham spread	75, 78
Pasta z wątróbki po żydowsku	Chicken liver spread, Jewish style	77
Pasta z wątróbki z gorczycą	Liver spread with mustard	77
Pasta z wędzonego bekonu	Smoked bacon spread	78
Pasta z wędzonego kurczaka	Smoked chicken spread	77
Pasta z wędzonego pstrąga	Smoked trout spread	76
Pasta ze świeżych ziół	Herbal paste	878
Pasta zielona	Green spread	67
Pasta zielona z tuńczykiem	Green spread with tuna	75
Pasta ziołowa	Herbal paste	73, 878

Pasta ziołowa	Herbal spread	71
Pasternak	Parsnip	645
Pasternak glazurowany	Glazed parsnip	645
Pasternak panierowany	Breaded parsnip	646
Paszteciki maltańskie	Maltese patties	166
Paszteciki rybne	Fish patties	166
Paszteciki staropolskie	Old Polish patties	166
Pasztet cielęcy	Veal pâté	86
Pasztet domowy	Home-made meatloaf	87
Pasztet fasolowo-jabłkowy na zimno	Bean and apple pâté	80
Pasztet francuski z brokułów	Broccoli pâté	80
Pasztet francuski ze szpinaku	Spinach pâté, French style	82
Pasztet kaszubski ziemniaczany	Potato pâté, Kashub style	83
Pasztet litewski z wątroby wieprzowej	Pork liver pâté, Lithuanian style	85
Pasztet orzechowy	Nut pâté	79
Pasztet rybny	Fish terrine	876
Pasztet śląski z zająca	Hare pâté, Silesian style	86
Pasztet wiosenny z drobiu	Springtime chicken pâté	87
Pasztet z bażanta	Pheasant pâté	85, 535
Pasztet z jelenia	Roebuck pâté	526
Pasztet z kalafiora	Cauliflower pâté	83
Pasztet z karpia	Carp pâté	290
Pasztet z kasztanów	Chestnut terrine	876
Pasztet z królika	Rabbit pâté	437
Pasztet z kuropatw	Partridge pâté	543
Pasztet z leszcza	Bream pâté	84
Pasztet z łysek	Coot pâté	547
Pasztet z młodej marchewki	Carrot pâté	82
Pasztet z papryki	Bell pepper pâté	82
Pasztet z pieczarek	Mushroom pâté	79
Pasztet z pieczarek i migdałów	Mushroom and almond pâté	79
Pasztet z porów	Leek pâté	82
Pasztet z porzeczkami	Terrine with redcurrants	876
Pasztet z ryb we francuskim cieście	Fish pâté in puff pastry	316
Pasztet z sarnich podrobów	Pâté of venison offal	531
Pasztet z sarny na gorąco	Venison pâté served hot	532
Pasztet z suszonych borowików	Pâté from dried ceps	560
Pasztet z suszonych grzybów	Dried mushroom pâté	80
Pasztet z wątróbek drobiowych z tymiankiem	Chicken liver pâté with thyme	85
Pasztet z wątróbek drobiowych z wieprzowiną	Chicken liver and pork pâté	85
Pasztet z wątróbki cielęcej	Veal liver pâté	85
Pasztet z zająca	Hare pâté	513
Pasztet ze szpinaku z serem	Spinach and cheese pâté	83
Pasztet ze śledzi	Herring pâté	84

Pasztet ziemniaczany	Potato pâté	84
Patisony marynowane	Pickled scallopini squash	763
Patisony nadziewane kaszą	Patty pan squashes stuffed with kasha	647
Patisony po polsku	Patty pan squash, Polish style	646
Pączki Agaty – łatwe	Agatha's quick doughnuts	739
Pączki Krzyśka	Chris's doughnuts	738
Pączki lwowskie	Lvov doughnuts	737
Pączki Małgosi serowe	Margaret's cheese doughnuts	739
Pączki parzone	Scalded doughnuts	739
Pączki polskie	Polish doughnuts	737
Pączki warszawskie	Warsaw doughnuts	737
Pączki wileńskie	Vilnius doughnuts	739
Pączki z jabłek kurpiowskie	Kurp apple doughnuts	738
Pączki z konfiturą z wiśni Baśki	Doughnuts with cherry filling	738
Pączki z rodzynkami	Doughnuts with raisins	738
Pesto	Home–made pesto I	849
Pesto wiosenne	Spring pesto	850
Pesto z pestek dyni	Pesto with pumpkin seeds	849
Pędy chmielu w sezamowym sosie	Hop shoots in sesame sauce	620
Pędy chmielu w sosie ziołowym	Hop shoots in herbal sauce	620
Pieczarki faszerowane	Stuffed champignons	555
Pieczarki faszerowane mózgiem	Mushrooms stuffed with brains	450
Pieczarki faszerowane po chińsku	Stuffed mushrooms, Chinese style	897
Pieczarki marynowane po hiszpańsku	Marinated mushrooms, Spanish style	881
Pieczarki w sosie sardelowym	Mushrooms in anchovy sauce	899
Pieczarki z serem	Mushrooms with cheese	206
Pieczeń barania na sposób sarniny	Leg of mutton ą la venison	429
Pieczeń barania po myśliwsku	Hunter's leg of mutton	429
Pieczeń barania ziołowa	Leg of mutton with herbs	430
Pieczeń cielęca	Veal roast	380
Pieczeń cielęca à la sarna	Veal roast à la venison	380
Pieczeń cielęca à la Verdi	Roast veal à la Verdi	384
Pieczeń cielęca pikantna	Spicy veal roast	382
Pieczeń cielęca po angielsku	Veal roast à l'anglaise	384
Pieczeń cielęca po litewsku	Veal roast, Lithuanian style	382
Pieczeń cielęca z cytryną	Lemony veal roast	385
Pieczeń cielęca z czosnkiem	Garlicky veal roast	382
Pieczeń cielęca z estragonem	Roast veal with tarragon	385
Pieczeń cielęca z pieczarkami	Veal roast with mushrooms	382
Pieczeń cielęca z rożna	Spit-roasted veal	384
Pieczeń cielęca z suszonymi grzybami	Roast veal with dried mushrooms	385
Pieczeń cielęca z ziołami	Veal roast with herbs	382
Pieczeń jagnięca z migdałami	Roast lamb with almonds	428
Pieczeń szpikowana migdałami	Veal roast studded with almonds	384
Pieczeń św. Huberta	St Hubertus's roast	527
Pieczeń wieprzowa nadziewana	Stuffed pork roast	362

Pieczeń wieprzowa nadziewana warzywami	Pork stuffed with vegetables	362
Pieczeń wieprzowa nadziewana wątróbką	Pork roast stuffed with liver	362
Pieczeń wieprzowa po gospodarsku	Farmer's pork roast	361
Pieczeń wieprzowa z kminkiem	Pork roast with caraway	361
Pieczeń wieprzowa ze śliwkami	Pork roast with prunes	363
Pieczeń wołowa huzarska	Hussar's roast beef	408
Pieczeń wołowa marynowana	Beef à la mode	865
Pieczeń wołowa na dziko	Roast beef à la venison	408
Pieczeń wołowa staropolska	Braised joint of beef, Old Polish style	406
Pieczeń wołowa z miętą	Roast beef with mint	408
Pieczeń wołowa z rozmarynem	Roast beef with rosemary	410
Pieczeń wołowa z warzywami	Braised joint of beef with vegetables	408
Pieczeń z dzika po myśliwsku	Roast wild boar, hunter's style	516
Pieczeń z dzika w cieście	Roast wild boar in pastry	519
Pieczeń z dzika w sosie pikantnym	Roast wild boar in spicy sauce	516
Pieczeń z dzika w sosie z róży	Roast wild boar in rosehip sauce	517
Pieczeń z dzika z migdałami	Roast wild boar with almonds	517
Pieczeń z jelenia w sosie burgundzkim	Venison in bourguignonne sauce	522
Pieczeń z sarny	Roedeer roast	527
Pieczeń z sarny w dzikim sosie	Roedeer roast in wild sauce	527
Pieczeń z sarny zawijana	Rolled venison roast	527
Pieczeń z sarny ziołowa	Roast venison in herbs	528
Pieczeń z zająca z kminkiem	Roast hare with caraway seeds	509
Pieczona ryba	Baked fish	848
Pieczona włoska kapusta	Baked Savoy cabbage	890
Pieczone udka indycze z sosem myśliwskim	Roast turkey legs with hunter's sauce	485
Pieczone żeberka	Roast spare ribs	370
Pieprz turecki	Turkish pepper	650
Pierniczki całuski	Honey kisses	732
Pierniczki krakowskie	Cracow honey biscuits	732
Pierniczki miętowe warszawskie	Warsaw mint and honey biscuits	732
Piernik oblewany	Glazed gingerbread	720
Piernik staropolski	Old Polish gingerbread	719
Piernik sułtański	Sultan's gingerbread	719
Piernik tarty	Rum gingerbread	720
Piernik z makiem	Gingerbread with poppy seed	719
Pierniki klasztorne	Monastic gingerbread cookies	720
Pierogi leśne	Mushroom patties	165, 562
Pierogi poleskie smażone w głębokim tłuszczu	Deep-fried pierogi, Polish style	162
Pierogi ruskie	Russian pierogi	153
Piersi gęsi w ziołach	Goose breasts with herbs	476
Piersi kaczki marynowane	Marinated duck breasts	496
Piersi kaczki w sosie orzechowym	Duck breasts in hazelnut sauce	498
Piersi kaczki w sosie z gruszek	Duck breasts in pear sauce	496
Piersi kaczki z kapustą i porami	Duck breasts with cabbage and leeks	823
Piersi kaczki z orzeszkami	Duck breasts with peanuts	823

Piersi kurczaka po śródziemnomorsku	Chicken breasts, Mediterranean style	816
Pierś indycza nadziewana	Stuffed turkey breast	483
Pikantna jarzynka z pokrzywą	Spicy nettle	640
Pikantna kapusta pekińska	Piquant Chinese cabbage	883
Pikantna pasta z sera rokpol	Savoury Roquefort paste	877
Pikantna przystawka owocowa	Savoury fruit snack	667
Pikantna sałatka	Savoury cheese salad	73
Pikantna sałatka grzybowa	Savoury mushroom salad	554
Pikantna sałatka z zająca	Spicy hare salad	514
Pikantna surówka z gruszek	Savoury pear salad	668
Pikantna surówka z kapusty	Spicy red cabbage salad	588
Pikantna wołowina kokosowa	Piquant coconut beef	865
Pikantna zapiekanka z grzybami	Savoury mushroom bake	559
Pikantna zupa rybna	Piquant fish soup	116
Pikantna zupa z dyni	Savoury pumpkin soup	128
Pikantne ciasto z serem	Savoury cheese cake	202
Pikantne filety z kurczaka	Piquant chicken fillets	816
Pikantne grzanki z białego chleba	Savoury white bread croutons	243
Pikantne kurze skrzydełka	Piquant chicken wings	821
Pikantne maleństwa	Savoury titbits	771
Pikantne pstrągi	Savoury trout	307
Pikantne roladki z matiasów	Piquant herring roulades	874
Pikantne roladki z tołpygi	Savoury silver carp rolls	292
Pikantne udka z soją	Piquant turkey thighs with soy	826
Pikantny budyń	Piquant pudding	881
Pikantny bulion drobiowy	Savoury chicken broth	91
Pikantny gulasz z kurczaka	Piquant chicken goulash	818
Pikantny krem marchewkowy	Piquant cream of carrots	794
Pikantny krem orzechowo-migdałowy	Savoury cream of nuts and almonds	111
Pikantny krem z kasztanów	Piquant cream of chestnuts	793
Pikantny krem z zielonego groszku	Savoury cream of peas	111
Pikantny kurczak z jarzynami	Piquant chicken with vegetables	812
Pikantny mus jabłkowy	Spicy apple mousse	670
Pikantny sos imbirowy	Piquant ginger sauce	879
Pikantny sos jogurtowy	Piquant yogurt sauce	850
Pikantny sos sezamowy	Piquant sesame sauce	850
Pikle śląskie	Silesian pickles	766
Pikle wiejskie	Country-style pickles	765
Pikle z młodych pędów gorczycy	Pickled mustard sprigs	765
Pikle z rzepy	Pickled turnip	766
Pilaw z kaszy jaglanej	Millet pilaf	806
Pilaw z rybą wędzoną	Pilaf with smoked fish	221, 811
Pilaw z rybą wędzoną	Pilaf with smoked fish	811
Piwo z korzeniami	Beer with spices	692
Piwoszki	Cheese biscuits	733
Placek góralski	Tatra cheese pie	203

Przepiórki z pomarańczami	Quails with oranges	551
Przepiórki zapiekane z ziemniakami	Quails baked with potatoes	550
Przodek zajęczy w ostrym sosie	Fore part of hare in spicy sauce	509
Przodek zajęczy w sosie owocowym	Fore part of hare in fruit sauce	510
Przodek zajęczy ze śmietaną	Fore part of hare with cream	510
Przypkowska zupa cebulowa	Onion soup ą la Przypkowski	119
Przysmak serowy	Cheese relish	202
Pstrąg faszerowany w liściach kapusty	Stuffed trout in cabbage leaves	308
Pstrąg po holendersku	Trout, Dutch style	307
Pstrąg w kminkowym sosie	Trout in caraway sauce	310
Pstrągi marynowane	Marinated trout	308
Pstrągi nadziewane ogórkami	Trout stuffed with cucumber	847
Pstrągi po krakowsku	Trout, Cracow style	308
Pstrągi z szałwią	Trout with sage	308
Ptysie	Profiteroles	244
Pulpety z łoju	Suet balls	242
Pulpety z mózgu	Brains balls	242
Pulpety z resztek pieczeni cielęcej	Balls from roast veal trimmings	243
Pulpety z wątróbki	Liver balls	242
Pulpety ze szpiku	Bone marrow balls	242
Purée korzenne z cebuli	Spicy onion purée	246
Purée orientalne z selera	Oriental celeriac purée	248
Purée z bakłażanów z kolendrą	Aubergine purée with coriander	245
Purée z bakłażanów z sezamem	Aubergine purée with sesame seeds	245
Purée z białej fasoli	White bean purée	246
Purée z bobu	Broad bean purée	245
Purée z brukselki	Brussels sprouts purée	245
Purée z brukselki z migdałami	Brussels sprouts purée with almonds	245
Purée z cukinii i dyni słodko-kwaśne	Sweet and sour zucchini and pumpkin purée	246
Purée z czerwonej fasoli	Red bean purée	246
Purée z czerwonych buraków	Red beet purée	244
Purée z dyni	Pumpkin purée	246
Purée z jabłek	Apple purée	247
Purée z kapusty	Mashed cabbage	247
Purée z marchewki i kasztanów wodnych	Pureed carrots and water chestnuts	880
Purée z miętą	Potato purée with mint	228
Purée z papryki	Red pepper purée	247
Purée z pokrzywy z orzeszkami ziemnymi	Nettle purée with peanuts	247
Purée z rzepy	Mashed turnip	247
Purée z selera	Mashed celeriac	248
Purée z zielonego groszku	Mashed green peas	247
Pyzy tradycyjne	Traditional potato dumplings	144

R

Racuszki z kabaczka	Marrow pancakes	638
Racuszki z kaszy manny	Semolina drop scones	807

Racuszki z rodzynkami	Patties with raisins	207
Ragoût babuni	Granny's ragout	443
Ragoût cielęce z migdałami	Veal ragout with almonds	392
Ragoût cielęce z pieczarkami	Veal ragout with mushrooms	392
Ragoût cielęce z warzywami	Veal ragout with vegetables	391
Ragoût greckie	Greek ragout	819
Ragoût grzybowe z pomidorami	Mushroom ragout with tomatoes	558
Ragoût z cielęcych ozorków	Ragout from calves' tongues	439
Ragoût z cynaderek	Kidney ragout	454
Ragoût z kaczki z cukinią	Duck ragout with courgettes	498
Ragoût z królika	Rabbit ragout	437
Ragoût z kurczaka z dynią	Chicken ragout with pumpkin	470
Ragoût z kurczaka z rodzynkami	Chicken ragout with raisins	470
Ragoût z morszczuka	Hake ragout	328
Ragoût z podrobów wieprzowych	Pig's offal ragout	438
Ragoût z raków	Crayfish ragout	319
Ragoût z ryby z jabłkami	Fish ragout with apples	334
Ragoût z sarniej wątróbki	Ragout of roedeer liver	530
Ragoût z suszonymi śliwkami	Pork ragout with prunes	371
Ragoût z wołowiny z zielonymi szparagami	Beef ragout with green asparagus	427
Raki faszerowane	Stuffed crayfish	318
Raki po żmudzku	Crayfish, Samogitia style	318
Raki w śmietanie po polsku	Crayfish in cream, Polish style	318
Raki w winie	Crayfish in wine	318
Razowe grzanki do żuru lub grochówki	Brown bread croutons for white borsch or pea soup	243
Risotto drobiowe	Chicken risotto	220
Risotto grzybowe	Risotto with cep mushrooms	220
Risotto wegetariańskie	Vegetarian risotto	632
Risotto z papryką	Risotto with bell peppers	810
Risotto z pieczarkami	Mushroom risotto	221
Risotto z podrobów z porami	Risotto from giblets and leek	471
Risotto zielone	Green risotto	221
Rolada barania z szynką	Mutton roulade with ham	431
Rolada cielęca à la mode	Veal roulade à la mode	385
Rolada cielęca nadziewana jajkami	Veal roulade stuffed with eggs	386
Rolada cielęca nadziewana szynką i jajkami	Veal roulade stuffed with ham and eggs	386
Rolada cielęca staropolska	Veal roulade, Old Polish style	386
Rolada cielęca świąteczna	Gourmet's veal roulade	387
Rolada czosnkowo-ziołowa	Pork roulade with garlic and herbs	370
Rolada egzotyczna	Exotic roulade	806
Rolada kasztanowa	Turkey roulade with chestnuts	826
Rolada pasterska	Shepherd's roulade	859
Rolada wielkopolska	Great Poland roulade	413
Rolada wieprzowa po litewsku	Pork roulade, Lithuanian style	366
Rolada wołowa z serem	Beef roulade with cheese	410
Rolada z farszem mięsno-grzybowym	Pork roulade with meat and mushroom stuffing	366

Rolada z farszem orzechowo-grzybowym	Pork roulade with walnut and mushroom stuffing	368
Rolada z indyka z kaszą krakowską	Turkey roll with buckwheat grits	489
Rolada z kaczki	Duck roll	495
Rolada z kaczki z orzechami	Duck roll with hazelnuts	493
Rolada z ryby w galarecie	Fish roulade in aspic	334
Rolada z suszonymi śliwkami	Turkey roll with prunes	483
Roladki z indyka	Turkey roulades	824
Roladki z indyka w sosie musztardowym	Turkey mini rolls in mustard sauce	484
Roladki z kurczaka nadziewane porami	Chicken rolls stuffed with leeks	464
Rolmopsy	Rollmops	343
Rosół królewski	Royal broth	94
Rosół paryski	Broth à la parisienne	94
Rosół staropolski	Broth, Old Polish style	92
Rosół wołowy	Beef broth	94
Rosyjska sałatka z chrzanem	Russian salad with horseradish	622
Rosyjski koktajl z buraków	Russian beetroot cocktail	577
Rozbratel po galicyjsku	Beef cutlets, Galician style	417
Rozbratel po hambursku	Beef cutlets, Hamburg style	417
Rozbratel po wiedeńsku	Beef cutlets, Vienna style	419
Ruloniki z flądry ze szpinakowym twarożkiem	Flounder roulades with spinach cream cheese	846
Rumsztyk domowy	Rump steaks with horseradish	419
Rumsztyk flamandzki	Flemish rump steaks	420
Rumsztyk z estragonem	Rump steaks with tarragon	419
Ryba pieczona po śródziemnomorsku	Mediterranean baked fish	846
Ryba pieczona z kapustą	Fish baked with cabbage	333
Ryba po grecku	Fish, Greek style	316
Ryba po tajsku	Thai fish en papillote	845
Ryba w szafranie z porami	Saffron fish with leeks	847
Ryba w warzywach	Fish in vegetables	843
Ryba z grilla z sosem miętowym	Broiled fish in mint sauce	847
Ryba z warzywami	Fish with vegetables	845
Rybna rolada	Fish roulade	333
Rybne kotlety	Fish cutlets	335
Rydze kiszone	Saffron milk caps in brine	769
Rydze marynowane	Marinated saffron milk caps	764
Rydze po podlasku	Saffron milk caps, Podlasie style	556
Rydze solone	Salted saffron milk caps	769
Rydze w oliwie	Saffron milk caps in olive oil	769
Ryż cytrynowy	Lemony rice	222
Ryż czerwony	Red rice	222
Ryż imbirowy	Ginger rice	809
Ryż kokosowy	Coconut rice	809
Ryż korzenny	Spicy rice	809
Ryż migdałowy	Almond rice	222
Ryż morelowy	Apricot rice	809
Ryż pikantny	Piquant rice	808

Sałatka z buraków	Beet salad	575
Sałatka z buraków śledziowa	Beet and herring salad	576
Sałatka z buraków z czosnkiem	Beet salad with garlic	575
Sałatka z buraków z dymką	Beet salad with spring onions	575
Sałatka z buraków z jabłkiem i ananasem	Beet salad with apple and pineapple	575
Sałatka z buraków z orzechami	Beet salad with walnuts	575
Sałatka z cebuli i oliwek	Onion and olive salad	841
Sałatka z chmielu z czerwoną cebulą	Hop and red onion salad	620
Sałatka z ciecierzycy z kurczakiem	Chickpea salad with chicken	828
Sałatka z cukinii	Courgette salad	612
Sałatka z cukinii z owczym serem	Zucchini salad with ewes' cheese	832
Sałatka z cykorii z koryntkami	Chicory salad with currants	835
Sałatka z cykorii ze szpinakiem	Endive salad with spinach	609
Sałatka z czarną rzodkwią	Egg and Spanish radish salad	179
Sałatka z fasoli trójkolorowej	Three colour bean salad	572
Sałatka z fasolki z kozim serem	Bean salad with goat cheese	572
Sałatka z groszkiem i szynką	Green peas and ham salad	220
Sałatka z groszkiem, z papryką i jajkami	Green peas, sweet pepper and egg salad	647
Sałatka z groszkiem, z ziemniakami i kurczakiem	Green peas, potato and chicken salad	647
Sałatka z gruszek	Pear salad	668
Sałatka z indyka i młodych ziemniaków	Turkey salad with new potatoes	488
Sałatka z indyka z orzeszkami pinii	Turkey salad with pine nuts	487
Sałatka z indyka ze szparagami i owocami	Turkey salad with asparagus and fruit	488
Sałatka z jabłek i kapusty pekińskiej	Chinese cabbage salad with apples	839
Sałatka z jabłek i pieczarek	Apple and mushroom salad	835
Sałatka z jarmużu ze śmietaną	Kale salad with cream	626
Sałatka z kaczki i awokado	Duck salad with avocado	492
Sałatka z kalafiora	Cauliflower salad	599
Sałatka z kalarepki z rodzynkami	Kohlrabi salad with raisins	627
Sałatka z kapustą pekińską	Chinese cabbage salad	201
Sałatka z kapusty czerwono-biała	Red and white cabbage salad	588
Sałatka z kapusty włoskiej z nasionami pinii	Savoy cabbage salad with pine nuts	594
Sałatka z kapusty z jabłkami i chrzanem	Red cabbage salad with apples and horseradish	588
Sałatka z kapusty ze śmietaną	Red cabbage salad with cream	588
Sałatka z karczochów	Artichoke salad	841
Sałatka z kiełków rzeżuchy	Watercress salad	835
Sałatka z kukurydzy	Corn salad	637
Sałatka z kukurydzy z ryżem i tuńczykiem	Salad of sweet corn, rice and tuna	830
Sałatka z kukurydzy ze śliwkami	Corn salad with plums	636
Sałatka z kurczaka rzymska	Chicken salad, Roman style	459
Sałatka z kurczaka z marynowaną dynią	Chicken salad with marinated pumpkin	460
Sałatka z kurczaka z ogórkiem	Chicken and cucumber salad	829
Sałatka z kurczaka z ryżem	Chicken salad with rice	459
Sałatka z kurczaka ze szparagami	Chicken and asparagus salad	829
Sałatka z kurek	Chanterelle salad	843

Selerowa surówka z ogórkami	Celery salad with cucumber	607
Selerowa surówka z pomidorami	Celery and tomato salad	607
Selerowe frytki	Celeriac chips	249
Selery duszone w winie	Celeriac stewed in wine	606
Selery duszone ze śliwkami	Celeriac stewed with prunes	606
Selery faszerowane baleronem	Celeriac stuffed with cured pork shoulder	605
Selery faszerowane mięsem z drobiu	Celeriac stuffed with minced chicken	606
Selery naciowe zapiekane	Baked celery stalks	602
Selery nadziewane	Stuffed celeriac	602
Selery panierowane	Breaded celeriac	248
Selery po polsku	Celery, Polish style	608
Selery smażone	Fried celeriac	249
Selery w cieście piwnym	Celeriac in beer batter	604
Selery w occie	Marinated celeriac	601
Selery w sosie jajecznym	Celeriac in egg sauce	607
Selery z orzechami	Celeriac with hazelnuts	608
Selery zapiekane po polsku	Baked celeriac, Polish style	606
Ser gotowany w miodzie	Cheese in honey	207
Serca cielęce po gospodarsku	Calves' hearts, farmer's style	442
Serca w sosie pomidorowym	Beef hearts in tomato sauce	443
Sernik	Cheesecake	717
Sernik na kruchym cieście	Cherries, French style	760
Sernik wiedeński	Viennese cheesecake	718
Serowe ruloniki	Cheese rolls	203
Sezamowy sos z oliwkami	Sesame sauce with olives	850
Skromne nadzienie makowe	Modest poppyseed filling	722
Skrzydełka w orzechowej skorupce	Chicken wings in walnut shell	468
Skrzydełka z grilla	Grilled chicken wings	468
Skrzydełka z warzywami	Chicken wings with vegetables	466
Słodka zupa z kasztanów	Sweet chestnut soup	795
Słonka nadziewana	Stuffed woodcock	548
Słonka po mazursku	Woodcock, Mazurian style	548
Słonka po myśliwsku	Woodcock, hunter's style	548
Słonka po polsku	Woodcock, Polish style	548
Słonki (kwiczoły) w sosie cytrynowym	Woodcocks in lemon sauce	549
Smalac pikantny	Savoury lard spread	51
Smalec delikatny	Delicate lard spread	52
Smalec Haliny	Helen's lard spread	52
Smalec Krzysztofa	Christopher's lard spread	52
Smalec Urszuli	Ursula's lard spread	51
Smażona kapusta po pekińsku	Fried Chinese cabbage	892
Smażona soczewica	Fried lentils	894
Smażone kiełki sojowe	Fried soy shoots	890
Smażone krewetki w sosie chilli	Fried shrimps in chili sauce	872
Smażone warzywa	Fried vegetables	897
Smażony dorsz w kaparowym sosie	Fried cod in caper sauce	844

Soczewica	Lentils	632
Sok z pomidorów	Tomato juice	662
Sola po królewsku	Sole, royal style	332
Sola w pomarańczach	Sole with oranges	332
Sola z pieczarkami	Sole with mushrooms	333
Sos „Siedem ziół"	'Seven herbs' sauce	263
Sos „Capri"	'Capri' sauce	257
Sos „Vincent"	Vincent sauce	265
Sos agrestowy	Gooseberry sauce	267
Sos agrestowy pikantny	Savoury gooseberry chutney	769
Sos aksamitny	Velvet sauce	267
Sos andaluzyjski	Andalouse sauce	182
Sos andaluzyjski	Sauce à l'Andalouse	256
Sos angielski	English sauce	256
Sos anyżkowy	Aniseed sauce	277
Sos barbecue	Barbecue sauce	879
Sos bazyliowy	Basil sauce	183, 257
Sos beszamelowy – przepis podstawowy	Bechamel sauce	266
Sos beszamelowy pikantny	Savoury bechamel sauce	268
Sos biały – przepis podstawowy	White sauce (roux) – basic recipe	266
Sos biały kremowy – przepis podstawowy	White cream sauce – basic recipe	266
Sos brzoskwiniowy	Peach sauce	267, 277
Sos cebulowy	Onion sauce	257, 268
Sos chrzanowo-jabłkowy	Horseradish and apple sauce	257
Sos chrzanowy	Horseradish sauce	257, 268, 441
Sos chrzanowy z kaparami	Horseradish with capers	258
Sos chrzanowy z migdałami	Horseradish sauce with almonds	268, 622
Sos chrzanowy z morelami	Horseradish sauce with apricots	258
Sos chrzanowy z musztardą	Horseradish sauce with mustard	258
Sos chrzanowy z rodzynkami	Horseradish sauce with raisins	268
Sos chrzanowy zielony	Green horseradish sauce	258
Sos Cumberland	Cumberland sauce	258
Sos cytrynowy	Lemon sauce	269
Sos czekoladowy	Chocolate sauce	278
Sos czosnkowy	Garlic sauce	258, 259, 269
Sos diabelski	Devilled sauce	183, 259
Sos diabelski	Piquant sauce	269
Sos francuski do sałaty	French salad dressing	634
Sos głogowy	Hawthorn sauce	269
Sos gorczycowy	Mustard sauce	182, 259, 271
Sos góralski	Podhale sauce	259
Sos gruszkowy	Pear sauce	269, 670
Sos hiszpański	Spanish sauce	259
Sos holenderski	Sauce hollandaise	269
Sos holenderski pikantny (łatwy)	Piquant sauce hollandaise (a simple recipe)	270
Sos imbirowy	Ginger sauce	259

Surówka z ogórka z czosnkiem	Cucumber salad with garlic	616
Surówka z pasternaku	Parsnip salad	645
Surówka z porów	Leek salad	630
Surówka z rzepy z marchewką	Turnip salad with carrot	666
Surówka z rzeżuchą	Iceberg lettuce with watercress	634
Surówka ze szpinaku	Spinach with pine nuts	883
Surówka ze szpinaku z sezamem	Spinach with sesame	881
Suszone grzyby duszone	Stewed dried mushrooms	561
Syta moskiewska	Moscow honey drink	692
Syta władymirowska	Vladimir honey drink	692
Szafranowe ziemniaki z cukinią	Saffron potatoes with zucchini	895
Szafranowy kuskus	Saffron couscous	808
Szafranowy ryż z wątróbką	Saffron rice with chicken livers	810
Szary sos polski	Polish grey sauce	441
Szaszłyk barani z ziołami	Mutton shashliks with herbs	433
Szaszłyk z nerek baranich	Shashliks of sheep's kidneys	451
Szaszłyk ziołowy	Shish kebab with herbs	422
Szaszłyki z pieczarek	Champignon shashliks	562
Szaszłyki z sarny	Venison shashliks	528
Szaszłyki z wątróbki cielęcej	Calf's liver shashliks	448
Szczaw	Sorrel	658, 659
Szczaw na jarzynkę	Sorrel snack	659
Szczawiowa surówka wiosenna	Sorrel spring salad	659
Szczupak à la flamande	Pike à la flamande	302
Szczupak duszony z borowikami	Braised pike with mushrooms	307
Szczupak faszerowany pieczony	Stuffed baked pike	305
Szczupak lub sandacz po tatarsku	Pike or pikeperch, Tartar style	305
Szczupak na szaro	Pike in grey sauce	304
Szczupak po kujawsku	Pike, Kuyavian style	306
Szczupak po mazursku	Pike, Mazurian style	307
Szczupak po polsku	Pike, Polish style	306
Szczupak po staropolsku	Pike, Old Polish style	302
Szczupak po żydowsku	Pike, Jewish style	304
Szczupak prałatowski	Prelates' pike	305
Szczupak w sosie chrzanowym	Pike in horseradish sauce	305
Szczupak w żółtym sosie	Pike in yellow sauce	304
Szczupak z jajkami	Pike with eggs	302
Szczupak z kiszoną kapustą	Pike with sauerkraut	304
Szczupak z pietruszką	Pike with parsley	304
Szczupak z rożna ze śmietaną	Spit-grilled pike in cream	305
Sznucle z sarny z rozmarynem	Venison schnitzels with rosemary	529
Sznycle cielęce po szwajcarsku	Swiss veal schnitzels	397
Sznycle cielęce po wiedeńsku	Wiener schnitzels	396
Sznycle cielęce z anchois	Veal schnitzels with anchovy	397
Sznycle cielęce z wątróbką i pieczarkami	Veal schnitzels with liver and mushrooms	397
Sznycle serowe	Cheese schnitzels	203

Sznycle wieprzowe pikantne	Savoury pork schnitzels	376
Sznycle z głuszca	Wood grouse schnitzels	538
Szparagi	Asparagus	566
Szparagi w orzechowym sosie	Asparagus in hazelnut sauce	568
Szparagi w serowym sosie	Asparagus in cheese sauce	567
Szparagi w sosie awokado	Asparagus in avocado dressing	567
Szparagi z sezamowym sosem	Asparagus in sesame sauce	874
Szparagowy krem z łososiem	Cream of asparagus with salmon	112
Szparagowy tort	Asparagus gateau	568
Szpinak po rosyjsku	Spinach, Russian style	660
Szpinak z orzeszkami ziemnymi	Spinach with peanuts	661
Szpinak z sezamem 1	Spinach with sesame 1	881
Szpinak z sezamem 2	Spinach with sesame 2	881
Szpinakowa sałatka	Spinach salad	660
Szpinakowa zapiekanka	Baked spinach	661
Szpinakowa zapiekanka z szynką i serem	Baked spinach with ham and cheese	661
Szpinakowa zapiekanka z wołowiny	Spinach au gratin with beef	795
Szpinakowe ruloniki	Spinach rolls	660
Szpinakowy krem	Cream of spinach	794
Sztuczny sos żółwiowy	Mock turtle sauce	276
Sztufada korzenna	Spicy beef ą la mode	404
Sztufada na zimno	Cold beef ą la mode	406
Sztufada szpikowana	Larded beef ą la mode	404
Sztuka mięs po irlandzku	Beef, Irish style	400
Sztuka mięsa po litewsku	Boiled beef, Lithuanian style	403
Sztuka mięsa włoska z pieczeni baraniej	Roast mutton, Italian style	428
Szyjki gęsie po żydowsku	Goose necks, Jewish style	477
Szynka barania	Mutton ham	356
Szynka wieprzowa – marynowanie	Pork ham	356
Szynka z dzika	Wild boar ham	356
Szynka z warchlaka na gorąco	Ham of young boar, served hot	521

Ś

Śląskie „strzepate gałuszki"	Silesian potato dumplings	146
Śląskie knedle bułczane	Silesian bread-roll knedle	149
Śledzie à la Milanówek	Herring, Milanówek style	338
Śledzie faszerowane szpinakiem	Herring stuffed with spinach	343
Śledzie korzenne	Spicy herring	340
Śledzie marynowane w sosie musztardowym	Marinated herring in mustard sauce	343
Śledzie marynowane ze śmietaną, fasolą i jabłkiem	Marinated herring with cream, beans and apple	340
Śledzie pikantne w śmietanie	Savoury herring in cream	337
Śledzie po duńsku	Herring, Danish style	875
Śledzie po góralsku	Herring, Carpathian style	342
Śledzie po królewsku	Royal herring	337

Śledzie po węgiersku	Herring, Hungarian style	342
Śledzie po wileńsku	Herring, Lithuanian style	337
Śledzie w marynacie	Herring in marinade	342
Śledzie w oleju z musztardą	Herring in oil with mustard	340
Śledzie w sosie vinaigrette	Herring in vinaigrette	337
Śledzie w śmietanie	Herring in cream	337
Śledzie z suszonymi śliwkami	Herring with prunes	338
Śledzie zawijane	Rolled herring	342
Śledziowa sałatka kolorowa	Colourful herring salad	336
Śledziowa sałatka z czerwoną cebulą	Herring salad with red onion	335
Śledziowa sałatka z orzechami	Herring salad with nuts	335
Śledziowe jajka	Herring eggs	336
Śledziowe sznycle	Herring schnitzels	343
Śledziowe ślimaki	Herring snails	336
Śledziowy tatar	Herring tartare	342
Śledź imbirowy w orzechach	Ginger herring with nuts	336
Śledź w białym winie	Herring in white wine	340
Śledź w miodowym sosie	Herring in honey sauce	336
Śliwki faszerowane	Stuffed prunes	686
Śliwki faszerowane topionym serkiem	Plums stuffed with processed cheese	672
Śliwki kiszone	Plums in brine	768
Śliwki marnowane w czerwonym winie	Plums marinated in red wine	762
Śliwki nadziewane wątróbką	Prunes stuffed with turkey livers	672
Śliwki świąteczne	Christmas prunes	686
Śliwki świąteczne	Christmas prunes	686
Śliwki w marynacie	Marinated plums	761
Śliwki z nadzieniem orzechowym	Prunes stuffed with walnuts	672
Śliwowica cioci Zosi	Auntie's slivovitz	753
Śliwowica niesłodzona	Dry slivovitz	753
„Śniadanie kochanków"	Lovers' breakfast	199
Świąteczna sałatka z pokrzywą	Festive salad with nettle	640
Świąteczna zupa z węgorza (Kurpie)	Eel soup (Kurpie region)	115

T

Tajska zupa z kaczki z wodnymi kasztanami	Thai duck soup with water chestnuts	792
Tarninówka wuja Zdzisława	Uncle's sloe vodka	753
Tarta serowo-jogurtowa	Curd cheese and yogurt tart	802
Tarta z kapustą pekińską	Tart with a filling of Chinese cabbage	800
Tarta z kiszoną kapustą	Tart with a sauerkraut filling	801
Tarta z Ligurii	Ligurian tart	800
Tarta z tuńczykiem	Tart with tuna	801
Tarta z twarożkiem i serem feta	Tart with cream cheese and feta	802
Tarta ze szpinakiem i czerwoną soczewicą	Tart with spinach and lentils	801
Tołpyga ze szpinakiem	Silver carp with spinach	292
Tort chlebowy	Bread cake	724
Tort czekoladowy	Chocolate cake	725

Tort czekoladowy „comber"	Chocolate 'comber' cake	725
Tort czekoladowy Fedora (bez pieczenia)	Fedora chocolate cake (unbaked)	725
Tort czekoladowy polski	Polish chocolate cake	725
Tort czekoladowy Sachera	Sachertorte	725
Tort Grahama z orzechami	Graham's cake with walnuts	724
Tort kruchy	Shortcrust cake	727
Tort makowy	Poppyseed cake	726
Tort makowy na kruchym cieście	Shortcrust poppyseed cake	726
Tort migdałowy prababki	Granny's almond cake	724
Tort orzechowy czarny	Black walnut cake	727
Tort pomarańczowy	Orange cake	727
Tort przekładany konfiturami	Layered cake with fruit preserves	726
Tort serowy z pomidorowym sosem	Cheese bake with tomato sauce	805
Tort staroświecki	Traditional layered cake	723
Tort z gryczanej kaszy	Buckwheat cake	726
Tort z kremem z tuńczyka i serowym	Savoury tuna and cheese cake	805
Tort z małżami	Open tart with mussels	804
Tort z orzechów laskowych	Hazelnut cake	727
Tort z trzema kremami	Three-layered savoury cake	805
Tunezyjska sałatka z ogórkiem	Tunisian salad with cucumber	843
Twarożek z jabłkami	Curd cheese with apples	877
Twarożkowa zapiekanka z chmielem	Cottage cheese baked with hop	621

U

Udka kurczaka w sosie piri-piri	Chicken thighs in piri-piri sauce	818
Udka kurczaka z karczochami	Chicken thighs with artichokes	816
Udka w czosnkowym sosie	Chicken in pesto sauce	812
Udka z kurczaka na dziko	Chicken legs, hunter's style	466
Udka z kurczaka po diabelsku	Chicken legs, devil style	466
Udziec barani pieczony w folii	Leg of mutton in foil	430
Udziec barani z bazylią	Leg of mutton with basil	430
Udziec dziczy w soku wiśniowym	Wild boar haunch in sour cherry sauce	518
Udziec dziczy w ziołach	Wild boar haunch in herbs	518
Udziec jagnięcy z aromatycznym farszem	Leg of lamb with savoury stuffing	868
Udziec jeleni po myśliwsku	Venison haunch, hunter's style	522
Udziec jeleni w pikantnym sosie	Leg of roebuck in spicy sauce	523
Udziec jeleni z czosnkiem	Leg of roebuck with garlic	523
Uszy cielęce po sułtańsku	Calf's ears sultane	399

W

Warzywna zapiekanka	Vegetables au gratin	796
Warzywny mus w liściach szczawiu	Vegetable mousse on sorrel leaves	659
Warzywny pasztet z kabaczkami	Vegetable pâté with marrows	639
Wątroba wołowa pieczona	Roast beef liver	448
Wątróbka cielęca marynowana	Marinated veal liver	446

Wątróbka cielęca po lwowsku	Calf's liver, Lvov style	445
Wątróbka cielęca po sztrasbursku	Calf's liver strasbourgeoise	445
Wątróbka cielęca po żydowsku	Calf's liver, Jewish style	446
Wątróbka cielęca w winnym sosie	Calf's liver in wine sauce	446
Wątróbka cielęca w ziołowym sosie	Calf's liver in herbal sauce	444
Wątróbka cielęca z jabłkami	Calf's liver with apples	446
Wątróbka cielęca z pomidorami	Calf's liver with tomatoes	447
Wątróbka cielęca z rożna	Spit-roast veal liver	447
Wątróbka cielęca z szałwią	Calf's liver with sage	444
Wątróbka cielęca zapiekana z makaronem	Calf's liver baked with pasta	447
Wątróbka cielęca ze śmietaną	Calf's liver with cream	445
Wątróbka duszona	Braised pork liver	444
Wątróbka duszona w soku z granatów	Braised liver in pomegranate sauce	447
Wątróbka pikantna	Savoury pork liver	447
Wątróbka smażona po wiedeńsku	Calf's liver, Vienna style	445
Wątróbka w zielonym sosie	Calf's liver in green sauce	446
Wątróbka z bananami	Calf's liver with bananas	445
Wątróbki kacze z chińskimi grzybami	Duck (or turkey) livers with cloud ear mushrooms	824
Wątróbki z wiśniami	Chicken livers with sour cherries	470
Wędzony pstrąg w rzeżuchowym sosie	Smoked trout in watercress sauce	307
Węgorz duszony	Braised eel	315
Węgorz w galarecie	Eel in aspic	315
Węgorz w sosie pietruszkowym	Eel in parsley sauce	315
Węgorz zapiekany	Baked eel	315
Wiedeńskie wałeczki	Viennese biscuits	733
Wieprzowe filety na sposób chiński	Pork fillets, Chinese style	375
Wieprzowe ragoût z gruszkami	Pork ragout with pears	368
Wieprzowe steki w serowym sosie	Pork steaks in cheese sauce	378
Wieprzowina à la dzik	Pork à la wild boar	361
Wieprzowina smażona z ostrą papryką	Pork fried with chili pepper	853
Wieprzowina w cieście	Pork in puff pastry	362
Wieprzowina w sojowym sosie	Pork in soy sauce	856
Wieprzowina w sosie chilli	Pork in chili sauce	855
Wieprzowina zapiekana ze szczawiem	Pork and sorrel bake	368
Wigilijna kapusta z grochem	Christmas Eve sauerkraut with peas	587
Wigilijna zupa grzybowa	Christmas Eve mushroom soup	117
Wileńkie zacierki gryczane	Buckwheat hasty noodles, Lithuanian style	140
Winny sos z kasztanów	Chestnut sauce with wine	851
Wiosenny deser	Spring dessert	687
Wiśniak	Cherry liqueur	746
Wiśnie pikantne	Sour cherry relish	772
Wiśnie w marynacie	Marinated bitter cherries	762
Witaminowa surówka z chrzanem	Vitamin salad with horseradish	621
Włoska kapusta nadziewana mięsem	Savoy cabbage head stuffed with meat	595
Włoska sałatka z karczochami	Italian artichoke salad	836
Wołowe pulpety z sezamem	Beef meatballs with sesame seeds	867

Z

Zrazy z zająca wykwintne	Fancy fillets of hare	511
Zrazy z zająca zawijane	Rolled fillets of hare	510
Zrazy zawijane koronne	Royal rolled zrazy	423
Zrazy zawijane polskie	Polish rolled zrazy	423
Zrazy zawijane z kapustą	Rolled pork zrazy with sauerkraut	377
Zupa agrestowa	Gooseberry soup	133
Zupa cytrynowa	Lemony soup	127
Zupa fasolowa z suszonymi śliwkami	Bean soup with prunes	127
Zupa grzybowa z orzechami włoskimi	Mushroom soup with walnuts	791
Zupa koperkowa	Dill soup	127
Zupa migdałowa	Almond soup	126
Zupa ogórkowa	Cucumber soup	127
Zupa orzechowa	Walnut soup	126
Zupa pasterska	Shepherd's soup	127
Zupa rakowa	Crayfish bisque	318
Zupa ruska z pokrzywki	Ruthenian nettle soup	640
Zupa rybna z kurkumą	Fish soup with turmeric	792
Zupa rybna z rakami	Fish soup with crayfish	114
Zupa selerowa-jabłkowa	Celeriac and apple soup	127
Zupa z chmielu	Hop soup	126
Zupa z cukinii z sherry	Zucchini soup with sherry	793
Zupa z czerwonej papryki	Red pepper soup	128
Zupa z kaparów z pikantnymi pulpecikami	Caper soup with piquant meatballs	791
Zupa z karpia z rodzynkami	Carp soup with raisins	114
Zupa z kolorowej papryki z krewetkami	Bell pepper soup with shrimps	792
Zupa z leszcza	Bream soup	116
Zupa z lina	Tench soup	116
Zupa z mleczem karpia	Milt soup	116
Zupa z topionym serkiem	Soup with processed cheese	126
Zupa z zielonych szparagów z makaronem ryżowym	Green asparagus soup with rice noodles	791
Zupa ziołowa	Herbal soup	792
Zupa żółwiowa sztuczna	Mock turtle soup	125
Zupa-krem z czerwonej soczewicy	Cream of lentils	794
Zupa-krem z dyni	Cream of pumpkin	794
Zupa-krem z kurkami	Cream of chanterelles	793

Ż

Żeberka dzicze duszone	Stewed wild boar spareribs	519
Żeberka dzicze w sosie czereśniowym	Wild boar spareribs in cherry sauce	519
Żeberka sarnie w szarym sosie	Roedeer spareribs in grey sauce	531
Żeberka wołowe w czarnym sosie	Rib of beef in black sauce	868
Żeberka z pikantnym sosem	Spare ribs in piquant sauce	856
Żołądek wieprzowy duszony	Braised pig's stomach	455
Żołądek wieprzowy w jarzynach	Pig's stomach in vegetables	455
Żur na kiełbasie	Zhur with sausage	100